D1605504

1000 BEST-EVER RECIPES

1000 BEST-EVER RECIPES

Delicious recipes for every kind of meal and occasion,
with each dish described step-by-step in more than
1000 fabulous color photographs

EDITED BY
MARTHA DAY

JG PRESS

Notes

Bracketed terms are intended for
American readers.

For all recipes, quantities are given in both metric
and imperial measures and, where appropriate,
in standard cups and spoons. Follow one
set, but not a mixture, because they are
not interchangeable.

Standard spoon and cup measures are level.
1 tsp = 5ml, 1 tbsp = 15ml, 1 cup = 250ml/8fl oz.

Australian standard tablespoons are 20ml.
Australian readers should use 3 tsp in place of
1 tbsp for measuring small quantities of gelatine,
flour, salt etc.

American pints are 16fl oz/2 cups. American
readers should use 20fl oz/2 ½ cups in place
of 1 pint when measuring liquids.

Electric oven temperatures in this book are for
conventional ovens. When using a fan oven, the
temperature will probably need to be reduced by
about 10–20°C/20–40°F. Since ovens vary, you
should check with your manufacturer's instruction
book for guidance.

The nutritional analysis given for each recipe is
calculated per portion (i.e. serving or item), unless
otherwise stated. If the recipe gives a range, such
as Serves 4–6, then the nutritional analysis will be
for the smaller portion size, i.e. serves 6.

Medium (US large) eggs are used unless
otherwise stated.

Published by World Publications Group, Inc.
140 Laurel Street, East Bridgewater, MA 02333
www.wrldpub.net

Produced by Anness Publishing Ltd
Hermes House, 88–89 Blackfriars Road, London SE1 8HA
tel. 020 7401 2077; fax 020 7633 9499: www.annesspublishing.com

If you like the images in this book and would like to investigate using them for publishing,
promotions or advertising, please visit our website www.practicalpictures.com for more
information.

Publisher: Joanna Lorenz
Senior Managing Editors: Helen Sudell, Judith Simons and Conor Kilgallon
Editors: Lucy Doncaster, Simona Hill and Elizabeth Woodland
Design: SMI
Photographers: Karl Adamson, Edward Allwright, Steve Baxter, James Duncan,
Michelle Garrett, Amanda Heywood, Don Last, Patrick McLeavy, Michael Michaels
Additional photography: Sopexa UK
Recipes: Carla Capalbo, Maxine Clark, Frances Cleary, Carole Clements, Roz Denny,
Christine France, Sarah Gates, Shirley Gill, Rosamund Grant, Sue Maggs, Annie Nichols,
Jenny Stacey, Liz Trigg, Hilaire Walden, Laura Washburn, Steven Wheeler, Elizabeth Wolf-Cohen
Food for Photography: Joanne Craig, Wendy Lee, Jenny Shapter, Jane Stevenson,
Elizabeth Wolf-Cohen
Home Economists: Carla Capalbo, Jenny Shapter
Stylists: Madeleine Brehaut, Carla Capalbo, Michelle Garrett, Hilary Guy,
Amanda Heywood, Blake Minton, Kirsty Rawlings, Rebecca Sturrock, Fiona Tillett
Production Controller: Wendy Lawson

ETHICAL TRADING POLICY
At Anness Publishing we believe that business should be conducted in an ethical and
ecologically sustainable way, with respect for the environment and a proper regard to the
replacement of the natural resources we employ.
As a publisher, we use a lot of wood pulp to make high-quality paper for printing, and that
wood commonly comes from spruce trees. We are therefore currently growing more than
750,000 trees in three Scottish forest plantations: Berrymoss (130 hectares/320 acres), West
Touxhill (125 hectares/305 acres) and Deveron Forest (75 hectares/185 acres). The forests
we manage contain more than 3.5 times the number of trees employed each year in making
paper for the books we manufacture.
Because of this ongoing ecological investment program, you, as our customer, can have the
pleasure and reassurance of knowing that a tree is being cultivated on your behalf to
naturally replace the materials used to make the book you are holding.
Our forestry programme is run in accordance with the UK Woodland Assurance Scheme
(UKWAS) and will be certified by the internationally recognized Forest Stewardship Council
(FSC). The FSC is a non-government organization dedicated to promoting responsible
management of the world's forests. Certification ensures forests are managed in an
environmentally sustainable and socially responsible way. For further information about this
scheme, go to www.annesspublishing.com/trees

ISBN-10: 1-57215-510-8
ISBN-13: 978-1-57215-510-7

Printed and bound in Indonesia

Previously published in two separate volumes, 500 Cakes and Bakes and 500 Best-ever Recipes.

Contents

Introduction

There is something infinitely satisfying about creating a home-cooked meal or baking a delicious cake from scratch, and it will have the added benefits of tasting better, costing less and generally being healthier than a ready-made version. So, whether you are looking for a quick-and-easy midweek supper dish, an impressive dessert for a dinner party, or a cake for a special occasion, this book will provide the inspiration, guidance and all the information you need to ensure perfect results every time.

Drawn from across the globe, the recipes make good use of a wide variety of ingredients, ensuring that there is something for everyone. Choosing is made easy, with dishes grouped into chapters by type or occasion. They range from soups, appetizers, salads and vegetables, to pasta, rice, meat and fish main courses, as well as a mouthwatering selection of cakes, cookies, buns, bars and breads.

There is a fine selection of hearty soups, including Smoked Haddock and Potato Soup, New England Pumpkin Soup, or Scotch Broth. Or, for a lighter start to the meal why not indulge in Potted Shrimp, Stuffed Mushrooms or Minted Melon Salad. Sophisticated appetizers for a special occasion include Smoked Salmon and Dill Blinis, Chicken Liver Pâté with Marsala, or Pears and Stilton.

Fish and shellfish are increasingly popular in today's health-conscious society. Among the many mouthwatering recipes on offer are taste sensations such as Smoked Trout with Cucumber, Warm Salmon Salad, or Scallops with Ginger, as well as much-loved classics like Grilled Fresh Sardines, Fish and Chips, or Mixed Smoked Fish Kedgeree.

There are many occasions when a mouthwatering meat course will win the day. This volume will arm you with the confidence and conviction needed to present a perfect Roast Beef with Yorkshire Pudding or a melting Cottage Pie. Also included is a variety of more unusual dishes such as Duck with Chestnut Sauce, a simple yet impressive dinner party offering, and economical yet nutritious main courses that will appeal to adults and children alike, such as Sausage and Bean Ragoût.

The vegetable dishes in this book are creative concoctions that can be prepared at short notice for an accompaniment or for a well-balanced meal. Some are long-standing vegetarian favourites, such as Chickpea Stew; others are innovative versions of world-famous dishes, like Vegetables with Lentil Bolognese, which combines a colourful appearance with satisfying texture and harmonious flavours.

To finish, the moment that many have been waiting for: the dessert course. The choice of sweet dishes ranges from cool creations, such as fluffy mousses and super-smooth ices to the richest trifles, and dream desserts made from fruit, cream and chocolate. Comforting hot desserts include Orange Rice Pudding, Apple and Blackberry Nut Crumble, and Chocolate Amaretti Peaches, as well as a wide selection of pies and tarts.

If you wish to indulge in a mid-morning snack or afternoon tea, there is a wide range of irresistible recipes for home-baked foods, ranging from cookies, bars, brownies, muffins and scones to teabreads (quickbreads), breads, cakes and gateaux for every occasion, from Christmas and Easter to birthdays, christenings and weddings. Also included is a low-fat baking section for those of you who wish to enjoy a delicious, guilt-free treat.

This collection of recipes has been drawn together from the combined talents of some of the world's most respected cooks and food writers. With the help of this authoritative guide, you will be able to choose and create a wealth of tempting home-made dishes, as well as learning new skills and gaining the confidence to start experimenting and trying new foods.

Soups & Appetizers

What could be better than starting a meal with a warming, flavoursome soup or an elegant appetizer? Here you will find a wealth of dishes suitable for every occasion, ranging from simple family soups, such as Curried Parsnip Soup or White Bean Soup, to stunning pâtés, light bites and delicious dips, including Smoked Haddock Pâté, Bruschetta with Goat's Cheese, and Mexican Dip with Chips.

Tomato & Basil Soup

In the summer, when tomatoes are both plentiful and inexpensive, this is a lovely soup to make.

Serves 4
30ml/2 tbsp olive oil
I onion, chopped
2.5ml/½ tsp caster
    (superfine) sugar
I carrot, finely chopped
I potato, finely chopped
I garlic clove, crushed
675g/1½lb ripe tomatoes,
    coarsely chopped

5ml/1 tsp tomato purée (paste)
I bay leaf
I thyme sprig
I oregano sprig
4 fresh basil leaves, coarsely torn
300ml/½ pint/1¼ cups light
    chicken or vegetable stock
2–3 pieces sun-dried tomatoes in
    oil, drained
30ml/2 tbsp shredded fresh
    basil leaves
salt and ground black pepper

1 Heat the oil in a large pan over low heat. Add the onion, sprinkle with the sugar and cook gently for 5 minutes.

2 Add the chopped carrot and potato, stir well, then cover the pan with a tight-fitting lid and cook gently for a further 10 minutes, until the vegetables are beginning to soften but do not let them colour.

3 Stir in the garlic, tomatoes, tomato purée, bay leaf, thyme, oregano, torn basil leaves and stock and season to taste with salt and pepper. Cover the pan again with the lid and simmer gently for 25–30 minutes, or until the vegetables are tender.

4 Remove the pan from the heat and press the soup through a sieve (strainer) or food mill to extract all the skins and seeds. Taste the soup and season again with salt and pepper.

5 Return the soup to the rinsed-out pan and reheat gently, then ladle into four warmed soup bowls. Finely chop the sun-dried tomatoes and mix with a little of the oil from the jar. Add a spoonful to each serving, then sprinkle the shredded basil over the top and serve immediately.

Corn & Shellfish Chowder

"Chowder" comes from the French word *chaudron*, meaning a large pot in which the soup is cooked.

Serves 4
25g/1oz/2 tbsp butter
I small onion, chopped
350g/12oz can corn, drained
600ml/1 pint/2½ cups milk
2 spring onions (scallions),
    finely chopped

115g/4oz/1 cup peeled, cooked
    prawns (shrimp)
175g/6oz can white crab meat,
    drained and flaked
150ml/¼ pint/⅔ cup single
    (light) cream
pinch of cayenne pepper
salt and ground black pepper
4 whole prawns in the shell,
    to garnish

1 Melt the butter in a large, heavy pan over medium heat. Add the onion and cook, stirring occasionally, for 4–5 minutes, until softened.

2 Reserve 30ml/2 tbsp of the corn for the garnish and add the remainder to the pan, then pour in the milk. Bring the soup to the boil, then reduce the heat to low, cover the pan with a tight-fitting lid and simmer gently for 5 minutes.

3 Ladle the soup into a blender or food processor, in batches if necessary, and process until smooth.

4 Return the soup to the rinsed-out pan and stir in the spring onions, prawns, crab meat, cream and cayenne pepper. Reheat gently over low heat, stirring occasionally. Do not let the soup come to the boil.

5 Meanwhile, place the reserved corn kernels in a small frying pan without oil and dry-fry over a medium heat until golden and toasted.

6 When the soup is hot, season to taste with salt and pepper and ladle it into warmed soup bowls. Garnish each bowl with a sprinkling of the toasted corn kernels and a whole prawn and serve immediately.

Basil Energy 129kcal/538kJ; Protein 2.2g; Carbohydrate 13.4g, of which sugars 9.2g; Fat 7.8g, of which saturates 1.3g; Cholesterol 0mg; Calcium 26mg; Fibre 3g; Sodium 30mg.
Corn Energy 359kcal/1506kJ; Protein 22.2g; Carbohydrate 32.5g, of which sugars 17.3g; Fat 16.5g, of which saturates 9.7g; Cholesterol 130mg; Calcium 299mg; Fibre 1.5g; Sodium 646mg.

Spiced Parsnip Soup

This pale, creamy-textured soup is given a special touch with an aromatic mustard seed garnish.

Serves 4–6
40g/1¹/₂oz/3 tbsp butter
1 onion, chopped
675g/1¹/₂lb parsnips, diced
5ml/1 tsp ground coriander
2.5ml/¹/₂ tsp ground cumin
2.5ml/¹/₂ tsp ground turmeric
1.5ml/¹/₄ tsp chilli powder
1.2 litres/2 pints/5 cups chicken stock
150ml/¹/₄ pint/²/₃ cup single (light) cream
salt and ground black pepper
15ml/1 tbsp sunflower oil
10ml/2 tsp yellow mustard seeds and single cream, to garnish (optional)

1 Melt the butter in a large pan over medium heat. Add the onion and parsnips and cook gently, stirring occasionally, for about 3 minutes.

2 Stir in the spices and cook for 1 minute more. Add the stock, season to taste with salt and pepper and bring to the boil, then reduce the heat. Cover with a tight-fitting lid and simmer for about 45 minutes, until the parsnips are tender.

3 Cool slightly, then ladle the soup into a blender and process until smooth. Return the soup to the rinsed-out pan, add the cream, season and heat through gently over low heat.

4 Heat the oil in a small pan, add the yellow mustard seeds and cook briskly, stirring occasionally, until the mustard seeds start to pop and splutter. Remove the pan from the heat.

5 Ladle the soup into warmed soup bowls and pour a little of the hot spice mixture and a swirl of cream over each. Serve the soup immediately.

Variation
Crushed coriander seeds may be substituted for the mustard seeds in the garnish.

Pumpkin Soup

The flavour of this soup will develop and improve if it is made a day in advance.

Serves 4–6
900g/2lb pumpkin
45ml/3 tbsp olive oil
2 onions, chopped
2 celery sticks, chopped
450g/1lb tomatoes, chopped
1.5 litres/2¹/₂ pints/6¹/₄ cups vegetable stock
30ml/2 tbsp tomato purée (paste)
1 bouquet garni
2–3 rashers (strips) streaky (fatty) bacon, crisply fried and crumbled
30ml/2 tbsp chopped fresh flat leaf parsley
salt and ground black pepper

1 With a sharp knife cut the pumpkin into thin slices, discarding the skin and seeds.

2 Heat the olive oil in a large pan over medium heat. Add the onions and celery and cook, stirring occasionally, for about 5 minutes, until the vegetables are beginning to soften but do not let them colour

3 Add the pumpkin slices and tomatoes and cook, stirring occasionally, for a further 5 minutes.

4 Add the vegetable stock, tomato purée and bouquet garni to the pan and season with salt and pepper. Bring the soup to the boil, then reduce the heat to low, cover with a tight-fitting lid and simmer gently for 45 minutes.

5 Leave the soup to cool slightly, then remove and discard the bouquet garni. Ladle the soup into a food processor or blender, in batches if necessary, and process until smooth.

6 Press the soup through a sieve (strainer) and return it to the rinsed-out pan. Reheat gently, then taste and season again if necessary. Ladle the soup into warmed soup bowls. Sprinkle each serving with the crisp bacon and chopped parsley and serve immediately.

Parsnip Energy 187kcal/780kJ; Protein 3g; Carbohydrate 14.8g, of which sugars 7g; Fat 13.3g, of which saturates 7g; Cholesterol 28mg; Calcium 70mg; Fibre 5.2g; Sodium 59mg.
Pumpkin Energy 136kcal/565kJ; Protein 4.6g; Carbohydrate 7.2g, of which sugars 6.2g; Fat 10g, of which saturates 2.4g; Cholesterol 11mg; Calcium 58mg; Fibre 2.6g; Sodium 235mg.

Jerusalem Artichoke Soup

Topped with saffron cream, this unusual soup is wonderful to serve on a chilly winter's day.

Serves 4
50g/2oz/4 tbsp butter
1 onion, chopped
450g/1lb Jerusalem artichokes, peeled and cut into chunks
900ml/1½ pints/3¾ cups chicken stock
150ml/¼ pint/⅔ cup milk
150ml/¼ pint/⅔ cup double (heavy) cream
large pinch of saffron powder
salt and ground black pepper
chopped fresh chives, to garnish

1 Melt the butter in a large heavy pan over medium heat. Add the onion and cook, stirring occasionally, for 5–8 minutes, until softened but not browned.

2 Add the artichokes to the pan and stir until coated in the butter. Reduce the heat to low, cover the pan with a tight-fitting lid and cook gently for 10–15 minutes but do not let the artichokes brown. Pour in the stock and milk, then cover the pan again and simmer gently for about 15 minutes. Leave the soup to cool slightly, then ladle it into a food processor or blender, in batches if necessary, and process until smooth.

3 Strain the soup back into the rinsed-out pan. Add half the cream, season to taste with salt and pepper and reheat gently.

4 Lightly whip the remaining cream and saffron powder. Ladle the soup into warmed soup bowls and put a spoonful of saffron cream in the centre of each. Sprinkle with the chopped chives and serve immediately.

> **Cook's Tip**
> The flesh of Jerusalem artichokes discolours when it is exposed to the air. Fill a bowl with cold water and add about 30ml/ 2 tbsp lemon juice. As you peel the artichokes drop them into the acidulated water to prevent them from turning brown.

Broccoli & Stilton Soup

A really easy, but deliciously rich, soup – choose something simple for the main course, such as plainly cooked meat, poultry or fish.

Serves 4
350g/12oz/3 cups broccoli florets
25g/1oz/2 tbsp butter
1 onion, chopped
1 leek, white part only, chopped
1 small potato, diced
600ml/1 pint/2½ cups hot chicken stock
300ml/½ pint/1¼ cups milk
45ml/3 tbsp double (heavy) cream
115g/4oz Stilton cheese, rind removed, crumbled
salt and ground black pepper

1 Discard any tough stems from the broccoli florets. Set aside two small florets for the garnish.

2 Melt the butter in a large pan over medium heat. Add the onion and leek and cook, stirring occasionally, for 5–8 minutes, until softened but not coloured.

3 Add the broccoli and potato and pour in the stock. Cover the pan with a tight-fitting lid, reduce the heat to low and simmer for 15–20 minutes, until the vegetables are tender.

4 Leave the soup to cool slightly, then ladle it into a food processor or blender and process until smooth. Strain through a sieve (strainer) back into the rinsed-out pan.

5 Add the milk and cream, season to taste with salt and pepper and reheat gently. When the soup is hot stir in the cheese until it just melts, then remove the pan from the heat. Do not let it come to the boil.

6 Meanwhile, blanch the reserved broccoli florets in lightly salted, boiling water for 1–2 minutes, then drain and cut them vertically into thin slices.

7 Ladle the soup into warmed soup bowls and garnish each with the sliced broccoli florets and a generous grinding of black pepper. Serve immediately.

Artichoke Energy 310kcal/1277kJ; Protein 2.7g; Carbohydrate 4.7g, of which sugars 4.3g; Fat 31.3g, of which saturates 19.4g; Cholesterol 80mg; Calcium 116mg; Fibre 1.5g; Sodium 168mg.
Stilton Energy 312kcal/1296kJ; Protein 14.4g; Carbohydrate 11.3g, of which sugars 6.8g; Fat 23.3g, of which saturates 14.7g; Cholesterol 60mg; Calcium 251mg; Fibre 3.3g; Sodium 310mg.

Minestrone with Pesto

This hearty, Italian mixed vegetable soup is a great way to use up any leftover vegetables you may have.

Serves 4
30ml/2 tbsp olive oil
2 garlic cloves, crushed
1 onion, sliced
225g/8oz/2 cups diced
  lean bacon
2 small courgettes (zucchini),
  quartered and sliced
50g/2oz/1½ cups green
  beans, chopped
2 small carrots, diced
2 celery sticks, finely chopped

1 bouquet garni
50g/2oz/½ cup short-cut
  macaroni or other soup pasta
50g/2oz/½ cup frozen peas
200g/7oz can red kidney beans,
  drained and rinsed
50g/2oz/1 cup shredded
  green cabbage
4 tomatoes, peeled and seeded
salt and ground black pepper

For the toasts
8 slices French bread
15ml/1 tbsp ready-made
  pesto sauce
15ml/1 tbsp freshly grated
  Parmesan cheese

1 Heat the oil in a large pan over low heat. Add the garlic and onion and cook, stirring occasionally, for 5 minutes, until just softened but not coloured.

2 Add the bacon, courgettes, green beans, carrots and celery to the pan and stir-fry for a further 3 minutes.

3 Pour 1.2 litres/2 pints/5 cups water over the vegetables and add the bouquet garni. Cover the pan with a tight-fitting lid and simmer for 25 minutes.

4 Add the macaroni, peas and kidney beans and cook for a further 8 minutes. Then add the cabbage and tomatoes and cook for 5 minutes more, until all the vegetables and the pasta are tender.

5 To make the toasts, spread the bread slices with the pesto, sprinkle a little Parmesan over each one and gently brown under a hot grill (broiler). Remove and discard the bouquet garni from the soup, season to taste and serve with the toasts.

French Onion Soup

Onion soup comes in many different guises from light, smooth and creamy to this rich, dark brown version – the absolute classic recipe from France.

Serves 4
25g/1oz/2 tbsp butter
15ml/1 tbsp sunflower oil
3 large onions, thinly sliced
5ml/1 tsp soft dark brown sugar
15g/½ oz/1 tbsp plain (all-
  purpose) flour

2 x 300g/10oz cans condensed
  beef consommé
30ml/2 tbsp medium sherry
10ml/2 tsp Worcestershire sauce
8 slices French bread
15ml/1 tbsp French coarse-
  grained mustard
75g/3oz Gruyère cheese, grated
salt and ground black pepper
15ml/1 tbsp chopped fresh flat
  leaf parsley, to garnish

1 Heat the butter and oil in a large pan over low heat. Add the onions and brown sugar and cook gently, stirring occasionally, for at least 20 minutes, until the onions start to turn golden brown and caramelize. (Depending on the variety, you may need to cook them for longer.)

2 Stir in the flour and cook, stirring constantly, for a further 2 minutes. Pour in the consommé and stir in two cans of water, then add the sherry and Worcestershire sauce. Season with salt and pepper, cover the pan with a tight-fitting lid and simmer gently for a further 25–30 minutes.

3 Preheat the grill (broiler) and, just before you are ready to serve, toast the bread lightly on both sides. Spread one side of each slice with the mustard and top with the grated cheese. Grill (broil) the toasts until the cheese has melted and is bubbling and golden.

4 Ladle the soup into warmed soup bowls. Place two slices of toasted bread on top of each bowl of soup and sprinkle with chopped fresh parsley to garnish. Alternatively, place the toasted bread in the base of the bowls and ladle the soup over them, then garnish with the parsley. Serve immediately.

Minestrone Energy 570kcal/2396kJ; Protein 26.9g; Carbohydrate 72.8g, of which sugars 12.5g; Fat 21g, of which saturates 6g; Cholesterol 35mg; Calcium 247mg; Fibre 9g; Sodium 1635mg.
Onion Energy 415kcal/1745kJ; Protein 13g; Carbohydrate 61.6g, of which sugars 12.6g; Fat 14.1g, of which saturates 6.7g; Cholesterol 25mg; Calcium 240mg; Fibre 4.1g; Sodium 1022mg.

Curried Parsnip Soup

The spices in this soup impart a delicious, mild curry flavour redolent of the days of the British Raj.

Serves 4
25g/1oz/2 tbsp butter
1 garlic clove, crushed
1 onion, chopped
5ml/1 tsp ground cumin
5ml/1 tsp ground coriander
450g/1lb (about 4) parsnips, sliced
10ml/2 tsp medium curry paste
450ml/³⁄₄ pint/scant 2 cups chicken or vegetable stock
450ml/³⁄₄ pint/scant 2 cups milk
60ml/4 tbsp sour cream
good squeeze of lemon juice
salt and ground black pepper
60ml/4 tbsp natural (plain) yogurt and mango chutney, to serve
naan bread, cubed and toasted, and 15ml/1 tbsp toasted sesame seeds, to garnish

1 Heat the butter in a large pan over medium heat. Add the garlic and onion and cook, stirring occasionally, for 4–5 minutes, until lightly golden. Stir in the cumin and coriander and cook, stirring frequently, for a further 1–2 minutes.

2 Add the parsnips and stir until well coated with the butter, then stir in the curry paste, followed by the stock. Bring to the boil, then reduce the heat to low, cover the pan with a tight-fitting lid and simmer gently for 15 minutes, until the parsnips are tender.

3 Leave the soup to cool slightly, then ladle it into a blender or food processor, in batches if necessary, and process to a smooth purée.

4 Return the soup to the rinsed-out pan and stir in the milk. Heat gently for 2–3 minutes, then stir in 30ml/2 tbsp of the sour cream and lemon juice to taste. Season to taste with salt and pepper.

5 Ladle the soup into warmed bowls and top each serving with a spoonful of the remaining sour cream, the yogurt and the chutney. Garnish with cubes of toasted naan and toasted sesame seeds.

Red Pepper Soup with Lime

The beautiful rich red colour of this soup makes it a very attractive appetizer or light lunch.

Serves 4–6
5ml/1 tsp olive oil
4 fresh red (bell) peppers, seeded and chopped
1 large onion, chopped
1 garlic clove, crushed
1 small red chilli, sliced
45ml/3 tbsp tomato purée (paste)
juice and finely grated rind of 1 lime
900ml/1¹⁄₂ pints/3¹⁄₄ cups chicken stock
salt and ground black pepper
shreds of lime rind, to garnish

1 Heat the oil in a pan over low heat. Add the peppers and onion, cover with a tight-fitting lid and cook, shaking the pan occasionally, for about 5 minutes, until softened.

2 Stir in the garlic, then add the chilli and tomato purée. Stir in half the stock and bring to the boil. Cover the pan again and simmer for 10 minutes.

3 Leave to cool slightly, then ladle the soup into a food processor or blender, in batches if necessary, and process to a purée. Return it to the rinsed-out pan, stir in the remaining stock, the lime rind and juice and season to taste with salt and pepper.

4 Bring the soup back to the boil, then ladle it into warmed soup bowls. Sprinkle each bowl with a few shreds of lime rind and serve immediately.

Cook's Tip
Small, pointed chillies are usually hotter than the larger, blunt ones. If you prefer a milder flavour, halve the chilli lengthways and scrape out the seeds and surrounding membrane with the blade of the knife before slicing. Most of the heat of chilli is concentrated in this membrane. Wash your hands well after handling it and avoid touching your eyes.

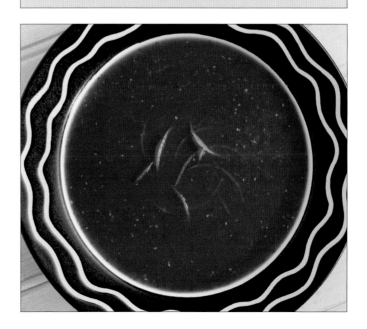

Parsnip Energy 207kcal/865kJ; Protein 6.5g; Carbohydrate 21.2g, of which sugars 13.2g; Fat 11.3g, of which saturates 6.6g; Cholesterol 29mg; Calcium 200mg; Fibre 5.4g; Sodium 104mg.
Red Pepper Energy 66kcal/274kJ; Protein 2.2g; Carbohydrate 12.5g, of which sugars 11g; Fat 1.1g, of which saturates 0.2g; Cholesterol 0mg; Calcium 25mg; Fibre 2.8g; Sodium 24mg.

Thai-style Corn Soup

This is a very quick and easy soup. If you are using frozen prawns, thaw them before adding to the soup.

Serves 4
2.5ml/½ tsp sesame or
   sunflower oil
2 spring onions (scallions),
   thinly sliced
1 garlic clove, crushed
600ml/1 pint/2½ cups chicken
   stock
425g/15oz can cream-style corn
225g/8oz/2 cups cooked, peeled
   prawns (shrimp)
5ml/1 tsp green chilli paste or
   chilli sauce (optional)
salt and ground black pepper
fresh coriander (cilantro) leaves,
   to garnish

1 Heat the oil in a large, heavy pan over medium heat. Add the spring onions and garlic and cook for about 1 minute, until softened but not browned.

2 Stir in the chicken stock, cream-style corn, prawns and chilli paste or sauce, if using. Bring the soup just to the boil, stirring occasionally, then remove the pan from the heat.

3 Season the soup to taste with salt and pepper, ladle it into warmed soup bowls, sprinkle with fresh coriander leaves to garnish and serve immediately.

Variations
• For a Chinese version of this soup add 5ml/1 tsp grated fresh root ginger to the pan with the spring onions (scallions) and garlic in step 1 and substitute finely shredded, cooked chicken for the prawns (shrimp) in step 2. Garnish the soup with rings of spring onion, using the green part only.
• For a more pungent version add 10ml/2 tsp grated galangal or fresh root ginger and 1 lemon grass stalk, cut into 2.5cm/1in lengths, to the pan with the spring onions and garlic in step 1. Remove and discard the pieces of lemon grass before ladling the soup into bowls. Serve with a sweet chilli sauce or a chilli relish handed separately.

Haddock & Broccoli Chowder

This hearty soup makes a meal in itself when served with crusty bread.

Serves 4
4 spring onions (scallions), sliced
450g/1lb new potatoes, diced
300ml/½ pint/1¼ cups fish stock
300ml/½ pint/1¼ cups milk
1 bay leaf
225g/8oz/2 cups broccoli
   florets, sliced
450g/1lb smoked haddock
   fillets, skinned
200g/7oz can corn, drained
ground black pepper
chopped spring onions, to garnish

1 Place the spring onions and potatoes in a pan and add the stock, milk and bay leaf. Bring to the boil, reduce the heat, cover and simmer for 10 minutes.

2 Add the broccoli. Cut the fish into bitesize chunks and add to the pan with the corn. Season with pepper, then cover again and simmer until the fish is cooked through.

3 Remove and discard the bay leaf, sprinkle the chopped spring onions over the soup and serve immediately.

Cock-a-leekie Soup

This healthy main course soup has a sweet touch.

Serves 4–6
1.5kg/3lb chicken
1 bouquet garni
4 leeks, thickly sliced
8–12 ready-to-eat prunes
salt and pepper

1 Simmer the chicken in a covered pan with 1.2 litres/2 pints/ 5 cups water and the bouquet garni for 40 minutes. Add the leeks and prunes and simmer for a further 20 minutes.

2 Discard the bouquet garni. Remove the chicken, discard the skin and bones and chop the flesh. Return the chicken to the pan and season to taste. Reheat the soup and serve.

Corn Soup Energy 177kcal/751kJ; Protein 13.1g; Carbohydrate 28.4g, of which sugars 10.4g; Fat 2g, of which saturates 0.3g; Cholesterol 110mg; Calcium 51mg; Fibre 1.6g; Sodium 394mg.
Haddock Energy 276kcal/1172kJ; Protein 30g; Carbohydrate 36g, of which sugars 10.7g; Fat 2.4g, of which saturates 0.6g; Cholesterol 43mg; Calcium 161mg; Fibre 3.5g; Sodium 1041mg.
Cock-a-leekie Energy 281kcal/1189kJ; Protein 24g; Carbohydrate 39.8g, of which sugars 38.4g; Fat 3.9g, of which saturates 0.9g; Cholesterol 92mg; Calcium 88mg; Fibre 10.1g; Sodium 94mg.

Green Pea & Mint Soup

This soup is equally delicious lightly chilled. Stir in the swirl of cream just before serving.

Serves 4
50g/2oz/4 tbsp butter
4 spring onions
 (scallions), chopped
450g/1lb/4 cups fresh or
 frozen peas

600ml/1 pint/2¹/₂ cups chicken or
 vegetable stock
2 large fresh mint sprigs
600ml/1 pint/2¹/₂ cups milk
pinch of sugar (optional)
salt and ground black pepper
single (light) cream and small
 fresh mint sprigs, to garnish
 (optional)

1 Heat the butter in a large pan over low heat. Add the spring onions and cook, stirring occasionally, for 3–5 minutes, until just softened but not coloured.

2 Stir the peas into the pan, add the stock and mint and bring to the boil. Cover and simmer very gently for about 30 minutes for fresh peas or 15 minutes if you are using frozen peas, until the peas are very tender.

3 Leave the soup to cook slightly, then ladle it into a food processor or blender, add the milk and process until smooth.

4 Return the soup to the rinsed-out pan and reheat gently. Season to taste with salt and pepper, adding a pinch of sugar if you like.

5 Ladle the soup into warmed bowls. Swirl a little cream into each, if using, then garnish with mint.

> **Cook's Tip**
> *Fresh peas are increasingly available during the summer months from grocers and supermarkets. The time and effort of podding them are well worthwhile, as they impart a unique flavour to this delicious, vibrant soup.*

Beetroot & Apricot Swirl

This soup is most attractive if you swirl together the two coloured purées, but mix them together if you prefer.

Serves 4
4 large cooked beetroot (beets),
 coarsely chopped

1 small onion, coarsely chopped
600ml/1 pint/2¹/₂ cups chicken
 stock
200g/7oz ready-to-eat
 dried apricots
250ml/8fl oz/1 cup orange juice
salt and ground black pepper

1 Place the beetroot and half of the onion in a pan with the stock. Bring to the boil, then reduce the heat, cover with a tight-fitting lid and simmer for about 10 minutes. Leave to cool slightly, then ladle the mixture into a food processor or blender, in batches if necessary, and process until smooth. Return to the rinsed-out pan and set aside.

2 Place the remaining onion in another pan with the apricots and orange juice, cover and simmer gently over low heat for about 15 minutes, until tender. Leave to cool slightly, then ladle the mixture into a food processor or blender and process until smooth. Return to the rinsed-out pan.

3 Gently reheat both purées. Season to taste with salt and pepper, then swirl the mixtures together in warmed individual soup bowls to create a marbled effect. Serve immediately.

> **Cook's Tip**
> *Beetroot (beets) are widely available ready cooked. To cook your own, first rinse them well under cold running water and trim the stalks to about 2.5cm/1in above the beetroot. Do not peel or cut off the long roots as this will cause the colour to bleed away. Place the beetroot in a pan, add enough water to cover and bring to the boil. Lower the heat, cover and simmer for about 1 hour, until tender. Drain, then peel the beetroot with your fingers when cool enough to handle.*

Green Pea Energy 242kcal/1012kJ; Protein 12.1g; Carbohydrate 18.3g, of which sugars 10.5g; Fat 13.9g, of which saturates 8.4g; Cholesterol 36mg; Calcium 226mg; Fibre 5.9g; Sodium 247mg.
Beetroot Swirl Energy 138kcal/587kJ; Protein 4g; Carbohydrate 31.4g, of which sugars 30.8g; Fat 0.5g, of which saturates 0g; Cholesterol 0mg; Calcium 63mg; Fibre 5.1g; Sodium 79mg.

Thai-style Chicken Soup

Like most Thai soups this one is quick and easy to prepare and may be served as a first course, a snack or a light lunch.

Serves 4
15ml/1 tbsp vegetable oil
1 garlic clove, finely chopped
2 x 175g/6oz boned chicken
    breast portions, skinned
    and chopped
2.5ml/¹/₂ tsp ground turmeric
1.5ml/¹/₄ tsp hot chilli powder
75ml/5 tbsp coconut cream
900ml/1¹/₂ pints/3³/₄ cups hot
    chicken stock

30ml/2 tbsp lemon or lime juice
30ml/2 tbsp crunchy
    peanut butter
50g/2oz thread egg noodles,
    broken into small pieces
15ml/1 tbsp finely chopped spring
    onions (scallions)
15ml/1 tbsp chopped fresh
    coriander (cilantro)
salt and ground black pepper
30ml/2 tbsp desiccated (dry
    unsweetened shredded)
    coconut and ¹/₂ red chilli,
    seeded and finely chopped,
    to garnish

1 Heat the oil in a large, heavy pan over medium heat. Add the garlic and stir-fry for 1 minute, until lightly golden. Add the chicken, turmeric and chilli powder and stir-fry for a further 3–4 minutes.

2 Mix together the coconut cream and chicken stock until thoroughly combined and pour into the pan. Add the lemon or lime juice, peanut butter and egg noodles and bring to the boil, stirring constantly. Lower the heat, cover and simmer gently for 15 minutes

3 Add the spring onions and coriander, season to taste with salt and pepper and cook for a further 5 minutes.

4 Meanwhile, heat a small frying pan, add the coconut and chilli and dry-fry, stirring constantly, for 2–3 minutes, until the coconut is lightly browned.

5 Ladle the soup into warmed soup bowls and sprinkle the coconut and chilli garnish over each. Serve immediately.

New England Pumpkin Soup

For a smooth-textured soup, process all the mixture in a food processor or blender.

Serves 4
25g/1oz/2 tbsp butter
1 onion, finely chopped
1 garlic clove, crushed
15g/¹/₂ oz/1 tbsp plain (all-
    purpose) flour
pinch of grated nutmeg
2.5ml/¹/₂ tsp ground cinnamon
350g/12oz pumpkin, seeded,
    peeled and diced

600ml/1 pint/2¹/₂ cups chicken
    stock
150ml/¹/₄ pint/²/₃ cup freshly
    squeezed orange juice
5ml/1 tsp brown sugar

For the croûtons
15ml/1 tbsp vegetable oil
2 slices multigrain bread,
    crusts removed
30ml/2 tbsp sunflower seeds
salt and ground black pepper

1 Melt the butter in a large pan over low heat. Add the onion and garlic and cook, stirring occasionally, for 4–5 minutes, until softened but not coloured.

2 Stir in the flour, nutmeg, cinnamon and pumpkin, then cover the pan and cook gently, stirring occasionally, for 6 minutes.

3 Add the chicken stock, orange juice and brown sugar. Cover the pan again, and bring to the boil, then simmer for 20 minutes until the pumpkin has softened.

4 Leave to cool slightly, then ladle half the mixture into a blender or food processor and process until smooth. Return the soup to the pan with the remaining chunky mixture. Season to taste and heat through, stirring constantly.

5 To make the croûtons, heat the oil in a frying pan, cut the bread into cubes and gently fry until just beginning to brown. Add the sunflower seeds and fry for 1–2 minutes. Drain the croûtons on kitchen paper. Serve the soup hot, garnished with a few of the croûtons sprinkled over the top and the remaining croûtons separately.

Thai Chicken Soup Energy 342kcal/1425kJ; Protein 25.7g; Carbohydrate 11.6g, of which sugars 2.4g; Fat 21.7g, of which saturates 13g; Cholesterol 65mg; Calcium 40mg; Fibre 1.4g; Sodium 111mg.
Pumpkin Soup Energy 189kcal/788kJ; Protein 4.1g; Carbohydrate 17.1g, of which sugars 6.4g; Fat 12.1g, of which saturates 4.1g; Cholesterol 13mg; Calcium 76mg; Fibre 2.2g; Sodium 109mg.

Split Pea & Courgette Soup

Rich and satisfying, this tasty and nutritious soup is ideal to serve on a chilly winter's day. Served with crusty bread it's perfect for lunch.

Serves 4

175g/6oz/1 cup yellow split peas
5ml/1 tsp sunflower oil
1 large onion, finely chopped
2 courgettes (zucchini), finely diced
900ml/1½ pints/3¾ cups chicken stock
2.5ml/½ tsp ground turmeric
salt and ground black pepper
warm crusty bread, to serve

1 Place the split peas in a bowl, cover with cold water and leave to soak for several hours or overnight. Drain, rinse in cold water and drain again.

2 Heat the oil in a pan over low heat. Add the onion, cover the pan with a tight-fitting lid and cook for about 8 minutes, until softened but not coloured.

3 Reserve a handful of diced courgettes and add the remainder to the pan. Increase the heat to medium and cook, stirring constantly, for 2–3 minutes.

4 Add the chicken stock and turmeric to the pan and bring to the boil. Reduce the heat to low, cover and simmer gently for 30–40 minutes, or until the split peas are tender. Season to taste with salt and pepper.

5 When the soup is almost ready, bring a large pan of water to the boil, add the reserved diced courgettes and cook for 1 minute, then drain and add to the soup before serving hot with warm crusty bread.

Cook's Tip
For a quicker alternative, use split red lentils for this soup. They do not require presoaking and cook very quickly. Adjust the amount of chicken stock used, if you need to.

Mediterranean Tomato Soup

Children will love this soup – especially if you use fancy pasta such as alphabet or animal shapes.

Serves 4

675g/1½lb ripe plum tomatoes
1 onion, quartered
1 celery stick
1 garlic clove
15ml/1 tbsp olive oil
450ml/¾ pint/scant 2 cups chicken stock
15ml/2 tbsp tomato purée (paste)
50g/2oz/½ cup small pasta shapes
salt and ground black pepper
fresh basil leaves, to garnish

1 Place the tomatoes, onion, celery and garlic in a pan with the olive oil. Cover with a tight-fitting lid and cook over low heat, shaking the pan occasionally, for 40–45 minutes, until the vegetables become very soft.

2 Leave to cool slightly, then spoon the vegetables into a food processor or blender and process until smooth. Press through a sieve (strainer) to remove the tomato seeds and skins, then return to the rinsed-out pan.

3 Stir in the stock and tomato purée and bring to the boil. Add the pasta and simmer gently for about 8 minutes, or until the pasta is tender. Season with salt and pepper to taste.

4 Ladle the soup into warmed soup bowls, sprinkle with basil leaves to garnish and serve immediately.

Cook's Tip
Plum tomatoes are best for this soup as they have a rich flavour and are less watery than some other varieties. They also have fewer seeds. However other types of tomato can be used, especially if they have been sun-ripened on the vine, which produces a delicious sweetness. Tomatoes that have ripened after picking are really not suitable but if you have to use them, add a good pinch of sugar at the beginning of step 3.

Split Pea Energy 182kcal/769kJ; Protein 12.2g; Carbohydrate 31.5g, of which sugars 6.1g; Fat 1.7g, of which saturates 0.2g; Cholesterol 0mg; Calcium 54mg; Fibre 3.7g; Sodium 19mg.
Tomato Energy 105kcal/444kJ; Protein 3.1g; Carbohydrate 16.3g, of which sugars 7.1g; Fat 3.5g, of which saturates 0.6g; Cholesterol 0mg; Calcium 23mg; Fibre 2.5g; Sodium 30mg.

White Bean Soup

Small white lima beans or pinto beans work well in this soup, or try butter beans for a change.

Serves 6
350g/12oz/1½ cups dried
   cannellini or other white beans
1 bay leaf
75ml/5 tbsp olive oil
1 onion, finely chopped
1 carrot, finely chopped
1 celery stick, finely chopped
3 tomatoes, peeled and
   finely chopped
2 garlic cloves, finely chopped
5ml/1 tsp fresh thyme leaves or
   2.5ml/½ tsp dried thyme
750ml/1¼ pints/3 cups boiling
   water
salt and ground black pepper
extra virgin olive oil, to serve

1 Pick over the beans carefully, discarding any stones or other particles. Place the beans in a large bowl, add cold water to cover and leave to soak overnight. Drain well.

2 Place the beans in a large pan, add water to cover, bring to the boil and cook for 20 minutes. Drain, return the beans to the pan, cover with cold water and bring to the boil again. Add the bay leaf and cook 1–2 hours, until the beans are tender. Drain again. Remove and discard the bay leaf.

3 Spoon about three-quarters of the beans into a food processor or blender and process to a purée. Alternatively, pass through a food mill, adding a little water if necessary.

4 Heat the oil in a large pan over medium heat. Add the onion and cook, stirring occasionally, for about 5 minutes, until softened but not coloured. Add the carrot and celery and cook, stirring occasionally, for a further 5 minutes.

5 Stir in the tomatoes, garlic and fresh or dried thyme. Cook, stirring frequently, for 6–8 minutes more.

6 Pour in the boiling water. Stir in the beans and the bean purée and season to taste with salt and pepper. Simmer for 10–15 minutes. Ladle into warmed soup bowls, drizzle with a little extra virgin olive oil and serve immediately.

Fish Soup

For extra flavour use some smoked fish in this soup and rub the bread with a garlic clove before toasting.

Serves 6
90ml/6 tbsp olive oil, plus extra
   to serve
1 onion, finely chopped
1 celery stick, chopped
1 carrot, chopped
60ml/4 tbsp chopped fresh flat
   leaf parsley
175ml/6fl oz/¾ cup dry
   white wine
3 tomatoes, peeled and chopped
2 garlic cloves, finely chopped
1.5 litres/2½ pints/6¼ cups
   boiling water
900g/2¼lb mixed fish fillets such
   as coley (pollock), rock salmon
   (huss), whiting, red mullet, red
   snapper or cod
salt and ground black pepper
12 slices French bread and
   50g/2oz Gruyère, to serve

1 Heat the oil in a large pan over low heat. Add the onion and cook, stirring occasionally, for about 5 minutes, until just softened but not coloured.

2 Stir in the celery and carrot and cook, stirring occasionally for a further 5 minutes. Add the parsley.

3 Pour in the wine, increase the heat to medium and cook until it has reduced by about half. Stir in the tomatoes and garlic and cook, stirring occasionally, for 3–4 minutes. Pour in the boiling water and bring back to the boil, then lower the heat and simmer for 15 minutes.

4 Add the fish fillets and simmer for 10–15 minutes, or until they are tender. Season to taste with salt and pepper.

5 Remove the fish from the soup with a slotted spoon. Discard the skin and any bones, then place the flesh in a food processor with the rest of the soup and process until smooth. Taste again for seasoning. If the soup is too thick, add a little more water.

6 To serve, heat the soup to simmering. Toast the rounds of bread and sprinkle with Gruyère. Place two in each soup plate before ladling the soup over them.

Bean Energy 249kcal/1050kJ; Protein 13.3g; Carbohydrate 28g, of which sugars 3.7g; Fat 10.2g, of which saturates 1.5g; Cholesterol 0mg; Calcium 66mg; Fibre 9.9g; Sodium 20mg.
Fish Energy 255kcal/1064kJ; Protein 28.1g; Carbohydrate 3.6g, of which sugars 3.3g; Fat 12.3g, of which saturates 1.8g; Cholesterol 69mg; Calcium 27mg; Fibre 1g; Sodium 102mg.

Barley & Vegetable Soup

This soup comes from the Alto Adige region in Italy's mountainous north. Not only tasty, it is thick, nourishing and warming.

Serves 6–8

225g/8oz/1 cup pearl barley
2 litres/3½ pints/8 cups beef
   stock or water, or a
   combination of both
45ml/3 tbsp olive oil
2 carrots, finely chopped
2 celery sticks, finely chopped
1 leek, thinly sliced
1 large potato, finely chopped
115g/4oz/½ cup diced ham
1 bay leaf
45ml/3 tbsp chopped
   fresh parsley
1 small fresh rosemary sprig
salt and ground black pepper
freshly grated Parmesan cheese,
   to serve

1 Pick over the barley and discard any stones or other particles. Wash the barley in cold water, then place it in a bowl, add cold water to cover and leave to soak for at least 3 hours.

2 Drain the barley and place it in a large pan with the stock or water. Bring to the boil, lower the heat and simmer for 1 hour. Skim off any scum.

3 Stir in the oil, carrots, celery, leek, potato and ham and add the bay leaf, parsley and rosemary. If necessary, add more water; the ingredients should be covered by at least 2.5cm/1in. Bring to the boil, then simmer for 1–1½ hours, or until the vegetables and barley are very tender.

4 Season to taste with salt and pepper. Ladle the soup into warmed soup bowls and serve immediately with grated Parmesan cheese for sprinkling.

> **Cook's Tip**
> *For extra flavour you could substitute a small ham bone for the diced ham. Shortly before serving remove the bone, cut off the meat and return it to the soup.*

Pasta & Dried Bean Soup

In Italy this soup is made with dried or fresh beans and served hot or at room temperature.

Serves 4–6

300g/11oz/1¼ cups dried
   borlotti or cannellini beans
400g/14oz can chopped plum
   tomatoes, with their juice
3 garlic cloves, crushed
2 bay leaves
90ml/6 tbsp olive oil, plus extra
   to serve
750ml/1¼ pints/3 cups water
10ml/2 tsp salt
200g/7oz/scant 2 cups ditalini or
   other small pasta
45ml/3 tbsp chopped fresh flat
   leaf parsley
ground black pepper
freshly grated Parmesan cheese,
   to serve

1 Place the beans in a bowl, add cold water to cover and leave to soak overnight. Drain the beans, rinse and drain well again.

2 Place the beans in a large pan and add water to cover. Bring to the boil and cook for 10 minutes. Drain, rinse and drain again, then return them to the pan. Add enough water to cover them by 2.5cm/1in. Stir in the tomatoes with their can juice, the garlic, bay leaves and olive oil and season with pepper. Bring to the boil, then lower the heat and simmer for 1½–2 hours, or until the beans are tender. Add more water during cooking if necessary to keep the beans covered.

3 Remove and discard the bay leaves. Pass about half of the bean mixture through a food mill or process to a purée in a food processor. Stir the purée into the pan with the remaining bean mixture. Add the measured water and bring the soup to the boil.

4 Add the salt and pasta. Stir, then cook until the pasta is just tender. Stir in the parsley.

5 Remove the pan from the heat and leave to stand for at least 10 minutes. Ladle the soup into warmed soup bowls and serve with extra olive oil for drizzling and grated Parmesan cheese for sprinkling.

Barley Energy 181kcal/762kJ; Protein 5.7g; Carbohydrate 29.4g, of which sugars 1.7g; Fat 5.3g, of which saturates 0.8g; Cholesterol 8mg; Calcium 27mg; Fibre 1g; Sodium 188mg.
Pasta Energy 360kcal/1518kJ; Protein 15.7g; Carbohydrate 49g, of which sugars 4.6g; Fat 12.6g, of which saturates 1.8g; Cholesterol 0mg; Calcium 78mg; Fibre 9.9g; Sodium 346mg.

Pasta & Chickpea Soup

The addition of a fresh rosemary sprig creates a typically Mediterranean flavour in this soup.

Serves 4–6
200g/7oz/generous 1 cup dried chickpeas
3 garlic cloves, peeled
1 bay leaf
90ml/6 tbsp olive oil
50g/2oz/¼ cup diced salt pork, pancetta or bacon
1 fresh rosemary sprig
600ml/1 pint/2½ cups water
150g/5oz/1¼ cups ditalini or other short hollow pasta
salt and ground black pepper
freshly grated Parmesan cheese, to serve (optional)

1 Place the chickpeas in a bowl, add cold water to cover and leave to soak overnight. Drain, rinse well and drain again.

2 Place the chickpeas in a large pan, add water to cover and bring to the boil. Cook for 15 minutes, then drain, rinse and drain again. Return the chickpeas to the pan. Add water to cover, one garlic clove, the bay leaf, half the olive oil and a pinch of pepper. Bring to the boil, then lower the heat and simmer for about 2 hours, until tender. Add more boiling water if necessary to keep the chickpeas covered.

3 Remove and discard the bay leaf. Pass about half the chickpeas through a food mill or process in a food processor with a little cooking liquid. Return the purée to the pan with the rest of the chickpeas and the remaining cooking water.

4 Heat the remaining olive oil in a frying pan. Add the pork, pancetta or bacon, rosemary and the remaining garlic cloves and cook gently, stirring frequently, until just golden. Remove and discard the rosemary and garlic.

5 Stir the meat with its flavoured oil into the chickpea mixture. Add the measured water and bring to the boil. Season to taste with salt and pepper. Stir in the pasta, and cook for about 10 minutes until it is just tender. Ladle the soup into warmed soup bowls and serve immediately with grated Parmesan cheese, if you like.

Pasta & Lentil Soup

Small brown lentils are usually used in this wholesome soup, but green lentils may be substituted.

Serves 4–6
225g/8oz/1 cup dried brown or green lentils
90ml/6 tbsp olive oil
50g/2oz/¼ cup finely diced ham or salt pork
1 onion, finely chopped
1 celery stick, finely chopped
1 carrot, finely chopped
2 litres/3½ pints/8 cups chicken stock or water
a few fresh marjoram leaves
a few fresh basil leaves
leaves from 1 fresh thyme sprig
175g/6oz/2½ cups ditalini or other small soup pasta
salt and ground black pepper
tiny fresh herb leaves, to garnish
crusty bread, to serve

1 Carefully check the lentils for small stones. Place them in a bowl, add cold water to cover and leave to soak for 2–3 hours. Drain, rinse and drain well again.

2 Heat the olive oil in a large, heavy pan over low heat, Add the ham or salt pork and cook, stirring occasionally, for 2–3 minutes.

3 Add the onion and cook gently, stirring occasionally, for about 5 minutes until softened but not coloured.

4 Stir in the celery and carrot and cook, stirring frequently, for a further 5 minutes. Add the lentils and stir to coat them evenly in the cooking fats.

5 Pour in the stock or water and add the sage and thyme. Increase the heat to medium and bring the soup to the boil. Lower the heat, cover the pan and simmer gently for about 1 hour, or until the lentils are tender. Season to taste with salt and pepper.

6 Stir in the pasta, increase the heat to medium and cook for about 10 minutes, until it is just tender. Remove the pan from the heat and leave to stand for a few minutes. Ladle the soup into warmed soup bowls and serve with crusty bread.

Pasta Energy 334kcal/1405kJ; Protein 14.2g; Carbohydrate 44.3g, of which sugars 3.2g; Fat 12.3g, of which saturates 1.8g; Cholesterol 5mg; Calcium 34mg; Fibre 3.1g; Sodium 120mg.
Chickpea Energy 309kcal/1297kJ; Protein 11.5g; Carbohydrate 35.1g, of which sugars 1.7g; Fat 14.6g, of which saturates 2.3g; Cholesterol 4mg; Calcium 60mg; Fibre 4.3g; Sodium 142mg.

Leek & Potato Soup

This classic combination is a perennial favourite with adults and children alike. It's a great winter warmer after a vigorous walk.

Serves 4
50g/2oz/4 tbsp butter
2 leeks, chopped

1 small onion, finely chopped
350g/12oz potatoes, chopped
900ml/1½ pints/3¾ cups
  chicken or vegetable stock
salt and ground black pepper
fresh parsley, finely chopped,
  to garnish
warm crusty bread and butter,
  to serve (optional)

1 Heat 25g/1oz/2 tbsp of the butter in a large pan over low heat. Add the leeks and onion and cook, stirring occasionally, for about 7 minutes, until softened but not coloured.

2 Add the chopped potatoes to the pan and cook, stirring occasionally, for 2–3 minutes. Add the chicken or vegetable stock and bring to the boil. Lower the heat, cover the pan with a tight-fitting lid and simmer gently for 30–35 minutes, until all the vegetables are very tender.

3 Season to taste with salt and pepper. Remove the pan from the heat and stir in the remaining butter in small pieces until completely melted. Ladle the soup into warmed soup bowls and serve immediately with warm crusty bread and butter, if you like.

Cook's Tips
• If you prefer a smoother textured soup, press the mixture through a sieve (strainer), using the base of a soup ladle, or pass it through a food mill. Never use a food processor or blender to purée potatoes as the starch in the vegetable will be broken down and will create an unpleasant gluey consistency.
• Carrots make a great addition to this soup, providing extra sweetness and bright colour. Simply add three or four sliced or diced carrots with the potatoes in step 2. You don't need to increase the quantity of stock.

Scotch Broth

Sustaining and warming, this traditional Scottish soup makes a delicious winter dish anywhere in the world.

Serves 6–8
900g/2lb lean neck (US shoulder)
  of lamb, cut into large even-
  size chunks
1.75 litres/3 pints/7½ cups water

1 large onion, chopped
50g/2oz/¼ cup pearl barley
1 bouquet garni
1 large carrot, chopped
1 turnip, chopped
3 leeks, chopped
½ small white cabbage, shredded
salt and ground black pepper
chopped fresh parsley,
  to garnish

1 Put the lamb and measured water into a large pan and bring to the boil over medium heat. Skim off the scum, then stir in the onion, barley and bouquet garni.

2 Bring the soup back to the boil, lower the heat, partly cover the pan and simmer gently for 1 hour.

3 Add the carrot, turnip, leeks and cabbage and season to taste with salt and pepper. Bring back to the boil, partly cover the pan again and simmer gently for about 35 minutes, until the vegetables are tender.

4 Remove and discard any surplus fat that has risen to the top of the soup, then ladle into warmed soup bowls, sprinkle with chopped parsley and serve immediately.

Cook's Tip
Lamb stock is too strongly flavoured for general use but ideal for making this soup. Put 1.3kg/3lb shoulder and/or breast bones of lamb into a large pan, add 2.75 litres/5 pints/11½ cups water and bring to the boil. Skim off the scum, then lower the heat and simmer for 45 minutes. Skim again and add 2 coarsely chopped carrots, 2 coarsely chopped onions, 1 bouquet garni, 1 bay leaf and 6 black peppercorns. Simmer for a further 2 hours, then strain and chill.

Leek & Potato Energy 182kcal/759kJ; Protein 3.4g; Carbohydrate 18.3g, of which sugars 4.3g; Fat 11.1g, of which saturates 6.7g; Cholesterol 27mg; Calcium 35mg; Fibre 3.3g; Sodium 88mg.
Scotch Broth Energy 267kcal/1118kJ; Protein 24.7g; Carbohydrate 12.9g, of which sugars 6.2g; Fat 13.3g, of which saturates 5.9g; Cholesterol 86mg; Calcium 58mg; Fibre 3.2g; Sodium 106mg.

SOUPS & APPETIZERS

Country Vegetable Soup

To ring the changes with this soup, vary the vegetables according to what you like and what vegetables are in season.

Serves 4
50g/2oz/4 tbsp butter
1 onion, chopped
2 leeks, sliced
2 celery sticks, sliced
2 carrots, sliced
2 small turnips, chopped
4 ripe tomatoes, peeled and chopped
1 litre/1¾ pints/4 cups chicken or vegetable stock
1 bouquet garni
115g/4oz/1 cup green beans, chopped
salt and ground black pepper
chopped fresh herbs such as tarragon, thyme, chives and parsley, to garnish

1 Melt the butter in a large, heavy pan over low heat. Add the onion and leeks and cook gently, stirring occasionally, for about 8 minutes, until softened but not coloured.

2 Add the celery, carrots and turnips and cook, stirring occasionally, for 3–4 minutes. Stir in the tomatoes and stock, add the bouquet garni and simmer the vegetables gently for about 20 minutes.

3 Add the beans to the soup and continue to cook until all the vegetables are tender. Season to taste with salt and pepper.

4 Ladle the soup into warmed soup bowls, garnish with chopped fresh herbs and serve immediately.

> **Cook's Tip**
> You can use the cooking water from a wide variety of vegetables and pulses as a flavoursome, easy and economical vegetable stock. Equally, vegetable peelings work well. Carrots, cauliflower, broccoli, green beans, leeks, lettuce, mushrooms, onions and potatoes are all good choices, but you should be light-handed with cabbage and members of the cabbage family, such as Brussels sprouts.

Split Pea & Bacon Soup

This soup is also called "London Particular", named after the notorious city fogs of the nineteenth century. The fogs, in turn, were named "pea-soupers".

Serves 4
15g/½ oz/1 tbsp butter
115g/4oz/⅔ cup chopped smoked lean back bacon
1 large onion, chopped
1 carrot, chopped
1 celery stick, chopped
75g/3oz/scant ½ cup split peas
1.2 litres/2 pints/5 cups chicken stock
2 rashers (strips) streaky (fatty) bacon
salt and ground black pepper
crispbreads, to serve
leaves from 1 sprig fresh thyme

1 Melt the butter in a pan over medium heat. Add the back bacon and cook until the fat runs. Stir in the onion, carrot and celery and cook for 2–3 minutes.

2 Add the split peas, followed by the stock. Bring to the boil, stirring occasionally, then lower the heat, cover with a tight-fitting lid and simmer for 45–60 minutes.

3 Meanwhile, preheat the oven to 180°C/350°F/Gas 4. Place the bread on a baking sheet and bake for about 20 minutes, until crisp and brown, then cut into dice.

4 When the soup is ready, season to taste with salt and pepper and ladle into warmed soup bowls.

5 Sprinkle each serving with the chopped bacon and thyme leaves and serve immediately with the crispbreads, or buttered, toasted bread.

> **Cook's Tip**
> For additional flavour you could spread the bread with herb or garlic butter before baking in the oven. Alternatively, you could sprinkle the bread slices with freshly grated Parmesan cheese and bake until it is golden and bubbling.

Vegetable Energy 160kcal/665kJ; Protein 3.6g; Carbohydrate 11.5g, of which sugars 10g; Fat 11.4g, of which saturates 6.8g; Cholesterol 27mg; Calcium 72mg; Fibre 5.4g; Sodium 106mg.
Pea & Bacon Energy 171kcal/710kJ; Protein 8.3g; Carbohydrate 9.9g, of which sugars 3.1g; Fat 11.2g, of which saturates 4.8g; Cholesterol 31mg; Calcium 31mg; Fibre 1.1g; Sodium 705mg.

Smoked Haddock & Potato Soup

This Scottish soup's traditional name is "cullen skink". A "cullen" is a town's port district and "skink" means stock or broth.

Serves 6

350g/12oz finnan haddock (smoked haddock)

1 onion, chopped
1 bouquet garni
900ml/1½ pints/3¾ cups water
500g/1¼lb potatoes, quartered
600ml/1 pint/2½ cups milk
40g/1½oz/3 tbsp butter
salt and ground black pepper
chopped fresh chives, to garnish
crusty bread, to serve (optional)

1 Put the haddock, onion, bouquet garni and measured water into a large pan and bring to the boil. Skim the scum from the surface, then cover the pan with a tight-fitting lid. Lower the heat and poach gently for 10–15 minutes, or until the haddock flakes easily.

2 Remove the poached fish from the pan using a fish slice or slotted spatula and remove the skin and bones. Flake the flesh and reserve. Return the skin and bones to the pan and simmer, uncovered, for 30 minutes.

3 Strain the fish stock and return to the rinsed-out pan, then add the potatoes and simmer for about 25 minutes, or until tender. Remove the potatoes from the pan using a slotted spoon. Add the milk to the pan and bring to the boil.

4 Meanwhile, mash the potatoes with the butter, then whisk into the milk in the pan until thick and creamy. Add the flaked fish to the pan and adjust the seasoning. Sprinkle with chopped chives, ladle into warmed soup bowls and serve immediately with crusty bread, if you like.

> **Cook's Tip**
> Try to find traditionally smoked fish, which is quite a pale colour, rather than chemically processed haddock, which has been dyed a bright yellow.

Mulligatawny Soup

Choose red split lentils for the best colour, although green or brown lentils could also be used.

Serves 4

50g/2oz/4 tbsp butter or 60ml/ 4 tbsp vegetable oil
2 large chicken pieces (about 350g/12oz each)
1 onion, chopped
1 carrot, chopped

1 small turnip, chopped
about 15ml/1 tbsp curry powder, to taste
4 cloves
6 black peppercorns, lightly crushed
50g/2oz/¼ cup lentils
900ml/1½ pints/3¾ cups chicken stock
40g/1½oz/¼ cup sultanas (golden raisins)
salt and ground black pepper

1 Heat the butter or oil in a large pan over medium-high heat. Add the chicken and cook, turning occasionally, for about 10 minutes, until golden brown all over. Using tongs, transfer the chicken to a plate.

2 Lower the heat, add the onion, carrot and turnip and cook, stirring occasionally, for about 10 minutes, until softened and lightly coloured. Stir in the curry powder, cloves and peppercorns and cook for 1–2 minutes, then add the lentils.

3 Pour the stock into the pan, bring to the boil, then add the sultanas. Return the chicken to the pan together with any juices from the plate. Lower the heat, cover and simmer gently for about 1¼ hours.

4 Remove the chicken from the pan and discard the skin and bones. Chop the flesh into bitesize chunks, return to the soup and reheat. Season to taste with salt and pepper. Ladle the soup into warmed soup plates and serve immediately.

> **Cook's Tip**
> Use a good quality curry powder, which will add subtle flavour as well as heat to this spicy soup.

Haddock Energy 205kcal/864kJ; Protein 16.1g; Carbohydrate 19g, of which sugars 6.4g; Fat 7.8g, of which saturates 4.7g; Cholesterol 41mg; Calcium 137mg; Fibre 1g; Sodium 132mg.
Mulligatawny Energy 513kcal/2136kJ; Protein 35.8g; Carbohydrate 17.3g, of which sugars 10.1g; Fat 33.9g, of which saturates 12.9g; Cholesterol 219mg; Calcium 42mg; Fibre 1.8g; Sodium 229mg.

Spinach, Bacon & Prawn Salad

Serve this hot salad with plenty of crusty bread to mop up the delicious juices.

Serves 4

105ml/7 tbsp olive oil
30ml/2 tbsp sherry vinegar
2 garlic cloves, finely chopped
5ml/1 tsp Dijon mustard
12 cooked king prawns (jumbo shrimp), in the shell
115g/4oz rindless streaky (fatty) bacon, cut into strips
115g/4oz/2 cups fresh young spinach leaves
½ head oak leaf lettuce, coarsely torn
salt and ground black pepper

1 To make the dressing, whisk together 90ml/6 tbsp of the olive oil with the vinegar, garlic and mustard in a small pan and season to taste with salt and pepper. Heat gently, whisking constantly, until slightly thickened, then remove from the heat and keep warm.

2 Carefully remove the heads and peel the prawns, leaving their tails intact. Cut along the back of each prawn and remove the dark vein. Set the prawns aside until needed.

3 Heat the remaining oil in a frying pan over medium heat. Add the bacon and cook, stirring occasionally, until golden and crisp. Add the prawns and stir-fry for a few minutes until warmed through.

4 Meanwhile, arrange the spinach leaves and lettuce leaves on four individual serving plates.

5 Spoon the bacon and prawns on to the leaves, then pour the hot dressing over them. Serve immediately.

Smoked Haddock Pâté

This easily prepared pâté is made with Arbroath Smokies, small haddock which have been salted and hot-smoked.

Serves 6

butter, for greasing
3 large Arbroath Smokies (about 225g/8oz each) or other smoked haddock
275g/10oz/1¼ cups medium-fat soft (farmer's) cheese
3 eggs, lightly beaten
30–45ml/2–3 tbsp lemon juice
ground black pepper
fresh chervil sprigs, to garnish
lemon wedges and lettuce leaves, to serve

1 Preheat the oven to 160°C/325°F/Gas 3. Generously grease six individual ramekins with butter.

2 Place the fish in an ovenproof dish and heat through in the oven for 10 minutes. Carefully remove and discard the skin and bones from the fish, then flake the flesh into a bowl.

3 Mash the fish with a fork and gradually work in the cheese, then the eggs. Add the lemon juice and season with black pepper to taste.

4 Divide the fish mixture among the six ramekins and place in a roasting pan. Pour hot water into the roasting pan to come about halfway up the sides of the dishes. Bake for 30 minutes, until just set.

5 Leave to cool for 2–3 minutes, then run a knife point around the edge of each dish and invert on to a warmed plate. Garnish with fresh chervil sprigs and serve immediately with the lemon wedges and lettuce.

Cook's Tip
Sherry vinegar lends its pungent, nutty flavour to this delicious salad. It is readily available in large supermarkets or delicatessens. However, ordinary red or white wine vinegar could be used instead if you like.

Variation
This pâté is also tasty made with hot-smoked trout fillets. You can then omit the initial cooking in step 2.

Pâté Energy 253kcal/1049kJ; Protein 17.9g; Carbohydrate 1.4g, of which sugars 1.4g; Fat 19.6g, of which saturates 6.6g; Cholesterol 151mg; Calcium 46mg; Fibre 0g; Sodium 527mg.
Salad Energy 320kcal/1325kJ; Protein 18.8g; Carbohydrate 0.9g, of which sugars 0.9g; Fat 26.8g, of which saturates 5.3g; Cholesterol 165mg; Calcium 117mg; Fibre 0.8g; Sodium 546mg.

Tomato & Mozzarella Salad

A quick, easy appetizer with a Mediterranean flavour.

Serves 4
450g/1lb large tomatoes, sliced
225g/8oz mozzarella cheese
1 red onion, chopped
10–12 black olives
60ml/4 tbsp olive oil

5ml/1 tsp red wine vinegar
2.5ml/½ tsp Dijon mustard
60ml/4 tbsp mixed chopped fresh
  herbs such as basil, parsley,
  oregano and chives
salt and ground black pepper
fresh basil, to garnish
  (optional)

1 Arrange the sliced tomatoes and mozzarella in circles on four plates. Sprinkle with the onion.

2 Whisk together the olive oil, vinegar, mustard, chopped herbs and seasoning. Pour over the salads.

3 Grind over plenty of black pepper and serve garnished with fresh herb sprigs, if you like.

Devilled Kidneys

This tangy dish makes an impressive appetizer.

Serves 4
10ml/2tsp Worcestershire sauce
15ml/1 tbsp English
  (hot) mustard
15ml/1 tbsp lemon juice

15ml/1 tbsp tomato
  purée (paste)
40g/1½oz/3 tbsp butter
1 shallot, chopped
8 prepared lamb's kidneys
salt and cayenne pepper
chopped fresh parsley, to
  garnish

1 Mix together the Worcestershire sauce, mustard, lemon juice and tomato purée in a bowl. Season with cayenne and salt.

2 Melt the butter in a frying pan and cook the shallot for 5 minutes. Stir in the kidneys and cook for 3 minutes on each side. Coat with the sauce and serve, sprinkled with parsley.

Asparagus with Tarragon Butter

Eating fresh asparagus with your fingers is correct but messy, so serve this dish with finger bowls.

Serves 4
500g/1¼lb fresh asparagus
115g/4oz/½ cup butter

30ml/2 tbsp chopped
  fresh tarragon
15ml/1 tbsp chopped fresh flat
  leaf parsley
grated rind of ½ lemon
15ml/1 tbsp lemon juice
salt and ground black pepper

1 Trim off the woody ends from the asparagus spears, then tie the spears into four equal bundles.

2 Pour water into a large frying pan to a depth of about 2.5cm/1in and bring to the boil. Add the bundles of asparagus, cover with a lid and cook for 6–8 minutes, until the asparagus is tender but still firm. Drain well and discard the strings.

3 Arrange the asparagus spears on four warmed serving plates. Make the tarragon butter by creaming together the remaining ingredients. Heat the flavoured butter gently until just melted, then pour it over the asparagus. Serve immediately.

Cook's Tip
Frugal – and clever – cooks waste nothing. Add the trimmed woody ends of the asparagus spears to the cooking water and reserve the water when you drain the spears. Discard the woody ends. Use the cooking water to flavour home-made soups, such as asparagus or green pea soup.

Variation
You can also serve the asparagus with parsley and orange butter. Use 45ml/3 tbsp finely chopped fresh flat leaf parsley instead of the tarragon, substitute 10ml/2 tsp orange rind for the lemon rind and use orange instead of lemon juice.

Salad Energy 301kcal/1250kJ; Protein 11.8g; Carbohydrate 6.2g, of which sugars 5.9g; Fat 25.7g, of which saturates 9.9g; Cholesterol 33mg; Calcium 219mg; Fibre 1.8g; Sodium 237mg.

Kidneys Energy 140kcal/584kJ; Protein 10.8g; Carbohydrate 2.3g, of which sugars 1.9g; Fat 9.9g, of which saturates 5.7g; Cholesterol 210mg; Calcium 24mg; Fibre 24g; Sodium 191mg.

Asparagus Energy 249kcal/1022kJ; Protein 4.1g; Carbohydrate 3g, of which sugars 2.8g; Fat 24.5g, of which saturates 15.1g; Cholesterol 61mg; Calcium 59mg; Fibre 2.6g; Sodium 179mg.

Egg & Tomato Salad with Crab

You could also adjust the quantities in this tasty salad to make a quick, light and healthy weekday meal.

Serves 4
1 round (butterhead) lettuce
2 x 200g/7oz cans crab
    meat, drained
4 hard-boiled eggs, sliced
16 cherry tomatoes, halved
½ green (bell) pepper, seeded
    and thinly sliced
6 pitted black olives, sliced

For the dressing
45ml/3 tbsp chilli sauce
250g/8fl oz/1 cup mayonnaise
10ml/2 tsp freshly squeezed
    lemon juice
½ green pepper, seeded and
    finely chopped
5ml/1 tsp prepared horseradish
5ml/1 tsp Worcestershire sauce

1 First make the dressing. Place all the ingredients in a bowl and mix well with a balloon whisk. Cover with clear film (plastic wrap) and set aside in a cool place until required.

2 Line four plates with the lettuce leaves. Divide the crab meat among them, mounding it up in the centre of each plate. Arrange the slices of egg around the outside with the tomato halves on top.

3 Spoon a little of the dressing over the crab meat. Arrange the green pepper slices on top and sprinkle with the olives. Serve immediately with the remaining dressing handed separately.

Variations
• Use freshly cooked or thawed frozen crab meat instead of canned.
• Substitute well-drained, canned tuna for the crab meat.
• Use peeled cooked prawns (shrimp) instead of crab meat, but try to avoid frozen ones as the texture can be woolly.
• Use 16 whole quail's eggs, boiled for 1½ minutes, then cooled and shelled, instead of sliced hard-boiled eggs.

Stuffed Mushrooms

These flavoursome mushrooms may also be served as an accompaniment to a main course.

Serves 4
25g/1oz/2 tbsp butter, plus extra
    for greasing and brushing
275g/10oz spinach,
    stalks removed

400g/14oz medium
    cap mushrooms
25g/1oz bacon, chopped
½ small onion, chopped
75g/5 tbsp double (heavy) cream
about 60ml/4 tbsp grated
    Cheddar cheese
30ml/2 tbsp fresh breadcrumbs
salt and ground black pepper
fresh parsley sprigs, to garnish

1 Preheat the oven to 190°C/375°F/Gas 5. Grease an ovenproof dish with butter. Wash but do not dry the spinach. Place it in a pan, cover and cook, stirring occasionally, for 4–5 minutes, until just wilted.

2 Place the spinach in a colander and squeeze out as much liquid as possible, then chop finely. Snap the stalks from the mushrooms and chop the stalks finely.

3 Melt the butter in a pan. Add the bacon, onion and mushroom stalks and cook for about 5 minutes. Stir in the spinach, cook for a few seconds, then remove the pan from the heat. Stir in the cream and season to taste with salt and pepper.

4 Brush the mushroom caps with melted butter, then place, gills uppermost, in a single layer in the prepared dish.

5 Divide the spinach mixture among the mushrooms. Mix together the cheese and breadcrumbs and sprinkle over the mushrooms, then bake for about 20 minutes until the mushrooms are tender. Serve warm, garnished with parsley.

Cook's Tip
Squeeze out all the excess water from the cooked spinach, otherwise the stuffing will be too soggy.

Salad Energy 608kcal/2515kJ; Protein 25.9g; Carbohydrate 4.8g, of which sugars 4.5g; Fat 54.2g, of which saturates 9g; Cholesterol 309mg; Calcium 171mg; Fibre 1.3g; Sodium 1018mg.
Mushrooms Energy 281kcal/1166kJ; Protein 9.9g; Carbohydrate 8.9g, of which sugars 2.7g; Fat 22.8g, of which saturates 13.5g; Cholesterol 58mg; Calcium 258mg; Fibre 2.9g; Sodium 388mg.

Pears & Stilton

Firm juicy pears and piquant cheese are a truly magical combination in this summer appetizer – a perfect start to an al fresco meal.

Serves 4
4 ripe pears
75g/3oz blue Stilton cheese
50g/2oz/3 tbsp curd
(farmer's) cheese

salt and ground black pepper
fresh watercress sprigs or mizuna,
to garnish

For the dressing
45ml/3 tbsp light olive oil
15ml/1 tbsp lemon juice
10ml/2 tsp toasted poppy seeds

1 First make the dressing. Place the olive oil, lemon juice and poppy seeds in a screw-topped jar and season with salt and pepper. Close the lid and shake well until combined.

2 Cut the pears in half lengthways, then scoop out the cores and cut away the calyx from the rounded end.

3 Beat together the Stilton, curd cheese and a little pepper. Divide this mixture among the cavities in the pears. Arrange the filled pear halves on individual plates.

4 Shake the dressing to mix it again, then spoon it over the pears. Serve garnished with watercress or mizuna.

> **Cook's Tip**
> The pears should be lightly chilled in the refrigerator before they are used in this dish.

> **Variation**
> Stilton is the classic British blue cheese used in this classic British dish but you could use blue Cheshire, Roquefort or Gorgonzola instead.

Potted Shrimp

Sometimes the simplest recipes are the best and this classic English appetizer has stood the test of time and remains very popular.

Serves 4
225g/8oz/2 cups shelled shrimp

225g/8oz/1 cup butter
pinch of ground mace
salt and cayenne pepper
fresh dill sprigs, to garnish
lemon wedges and thin slices
of brown bread and butter,
to serve

1 Chop a quarter of the shrimp. Melt half the butter over low heat, carefully skimming off any foam that rises to the surface.

2 Stir the chopped and whole shrimp and the mace into the pan, season to taste with salt and cayenne pepper and heat gently without boiling. Pour the shrimp and butter mixture into four individual pots or ramekins and set aside to cool.

3 Heat the remaining butter in a clean small pan, then carefully spoon the clear butter over the shrimp, leaving the sediment behind in the pan.

4 Leave until the butter is almost set, then place a dill sprig in the centre of each pot. Leave to set completely, then cover and chill in the refrigerator.

5 Remove the potted shrimps from the refrigerator about 30 minutes before serving to bring to room temperature. Serve with lemon wedges and thin slices of brown bread and butter.

> **Cook's Tip**
> This dish is traditionally prepared with the tiny European brown shrimp found off the east coast of England. They have a incomparably delicate flavour but are very boring to peel. You can substitute small prawns (US small to medium shrimp) if you like. In that case, chop between a third and half the shellfish in step 1.

Pears Energy 243kcal/1007kJ; Protein 7.2g; Carbohydrate 15.5g, of which sugars 15.5g; Fat 17.2g, of which saturates 6.4g; Cholesterol 21mg; Calcium 109mg; Fibre 3.5g; Sodium 208mg.
Shrimp Energy 461kcal/1901kJ; Protein 10.3g; Carbohydrate 0.4g, of which sugars 0.4g; Fat 46.6g, of which saturates 29.4g; Cholesterol 230mg; Calcium 55mg; Fibre 0g; Sodium 448mg.

Leek Terrine with Deli Meats

This attractive appetizer is surprisingly simple yet looks really spectacular. For best results it should be made a day ahead.

Serves 6
20–24 small young leeks
about 225g/8oz mixed sliced
  meats, such as prosciutto,
  coppa and pancetta

50g/2oz/½ cup walnuts, toasted
  and chopped
salt and ground black pepper

For the dressing
60ml/4 tbsp walnut oil
60ml/4 tbsp olive oil
30ml/2 tbsp white wine vinegar
5ml/1 tsp wholegrain mustard

1 Cut off the roots and most of the green part from the leeks. Wash them thoroughly under cold running water.

2 Bring a large pan of salted water to the boil. Add the leeks, bring the water back to the boil, then simmer for 6–8 minutes, until the leeks are just tender. Drain well.

3 Fill a 450g/1lb loaf tin (pan) with the leeks, placing them alternately head to tail and sprinkling each layer as you go with salt and pepper.

4 Put another loaf tin inside the first and gently press down on the leeks. Carefully invert both tins and let any water drain out. Place one or two weights on top of the tins and chill the terrine for at least 4 hours or overnight.

5 To make the dressing, whisk together the walnut and olive oils, vinegar and mustard in a small bowl. Season to taste.

6 Carefully turn out the terrine on to a board and cut into slices using a large, sharp knife. Lay the slices of leek terrine on serving plates and arrange the slices of meat beside them.

7 Spoon the dressing over the slices of terrine and sprinkle the chopped walnuts over the top. Serve immediately.

Garlic Prawns in Filo Tartlets

Tartlets made with crisp layers of filo pastry and filled with garlic prawns make a tempting, attractive and unusual appetizer.

Serves 4
For the tartlets
50g/2oz/4 tbsp butter, melted
2–3 large sheets filo pastry

For the filling
115g/4oz/½ cup butter
2–3 garlic cloves, crushed
1 fresh red chilli, seeded
  and chopped
350g/12oz/3 cups peeled,
  cooked prawns (shrimp)
30ml/2 tbsp chopped fresh
  parsley or chives
salt and ground black pepper

1 Preheat the oven to 200°C/400°F/Gas 6. Brush four individual 7.5cm/3in flan tins (pans) with melted butter.

2 Cut the filo pastry into twelve 10cm/4in squares and brush with the melted butter.

3 Place three squares of pastry inside each tin, overlapping them at slight angles and carefully frilling the edges and points while forming a good hollow in each centre. Bake the pastry for 10–15 minutes, until crisp and golden. Cool slightly and remove from the tins.

4 To make the filling, melt the butter in a large frying pan over medium-low heat. Add the garlic, chilli and prawns and cook, stirring frequently, for 1–2 minutes to warm through. Stir in the parsley or chives and season to taste with salt and pepper.

5 Using a spoon, divide the prawn filling among the tartlets and serve immediately.

Cook's Tips
• If using frozen filo pastry, leave it to thaw thoroughly first but keep it covered to prevent it from drying out.
• If using fresh filo pastry rather than frozen, wrap and freeze any leftover sheets for future use.

Terrine Energy 232kcal/962kJ; Protein 10.5g; Carbohydrate 3.3g, of which sugars 2.6g; Fat 19.7g, of which saturates 2.4g; Cholesterol 22mg; Calcium 37mg; Fibre 2.4g; Sodium 453mg.
Tartlets Energy 440kcal/1825kJ; Protein 17.6g; Carbohydrate 15g, of which sugars 0.7g; Fat 34.8g, of which saturates 21.6g; Cholesterol 259mg; Calcium 118mg; Fibre 1g; Sodium 419mg.

Celeriac Fritters with Mustard Dip

The contrast of the hot, crisp fritters and the cold mustard dip makes this a very tasty combination.

Serves 4
1 egg
115g/4oz/1 cup ground almonds
45ml/3 tbsp freshly grated
   Parmesan cheese
45ml/3 tbsp chopped fresh flat
   leaf parsley

1 celeriac (about 450g/1lb)
squeeze of lemon juice
oil, for deep-frying
salt and ground black pepper
sea salt flakes, for sprinkling

For the mustard dip
150ml/¼ pint/⅔ cup sour cream
15–30ml/1–2 tbsp wholegrain
   mustard

1 Beat the egg well and pour into a shallow dish. Mix together the almonds, grated Parmesan and parsley in a separate dish. Season to taste, then set aside.

2 Peel and cut the celeriac into strips about 1cm/½in wide and 5cm/2in long. Immediately drop the strips into a bowl of water with a little lemon juice added to prevent them from becoming discoloured.

3 Heat the oil in a deep-fat fryer to 180°C/350°F or until a cube of day-old bread browns in 30 seconds. Drain and then pat dry half the celeriac strips. Dip them into the beaten egg, then into the ground almond mixture, making sure that the pieces are coated completely and evenly.

4 Deep-fry the celeriac fritters, a few at a time, for about 2–3 minutes, until golden. Drain on kitchen paper and keep warm while you cook the remainder.

5 To make the mustard dip, mix together the sour cream, mustard and salt to taste. Spoon into a small serving bowl.

6 Heap the celeriac fritters on to warmed individual serving plates. Sprinkle with sea salt flakes and serve immediately with the mustard dip.

Smoked Salmon & Dill Blinis

Blinis, small pancakes of Russian origin, are so easy to make, yet they make a sophisticated dinner party appetizer and great canapés.

Serves 4
115g/4oz/1 cup buckwheat flour
115g/4oz/1 cup plain (all-
   purpose) flour
pinch of salt
15ml/1 tbsp easy-blend (rapid-
   rise) dried yeast

2 eggs
350ml/12fl oz/1½ cups warm
   milk
15ml/1 tbsp melted butter, plus
   extra for pan-frying
150ml/¼ pint/⅔ cup crème
   fraîche or sour cream
45ml/3 tbsp chopped fresh dill
225g/8oz smoked salmon,
   thinly sliced
fresh dill sprigs, to garnish

1 Mix together the buckwheat and plain flours in a large bowl with the salt. Sprinkle in the yeast and mix well. Separate one of the eggs. Whisk together the whole egg and the yolk, the warm milk and the melted butter.

2 Pour the egg mixture on to the flour mixture. Beat well to form a smooth batter. Cover with clear film (plastic wrap) and leave to rise in a warm place for 1–2 hours.

3 Whisk the remaining egg white in a large, grease-free bowl until stiff peaks form, then gently fold into the batter.

4 Preheat a heavy frying pan or griddle and brush with melted butter. Drop tablespoons of the batter on to the pan, spacing them well apart. Cook for about 40 seconds, until bubbles appear on the surface.

5 Flip over the blinis and cook for 30 seconds on the other side. Wrap in foil and keep warm in a low oven. Repeat with the remaining mixture, buttering the pan each time.

6 Combine the crème fraîche or sour cream and chopped dill. Top the blinis with slices of smoked salmon and and a spoonful of dill cream. Garnish with dill sprigs and serve immediately.

Blinis Energy 557kcal/2328kJ; Protein 26.3g; Carbohydrate 51.8g, of which sugars 5.5g; Fat 28.8g, of which saturates 16.3g; Cholesterol 178mg; Calcium 197mg; Fibre 1.5g; Sodium 1185mg.
Fritters Energy 434kcal/1796kJ; Protein 14g; Carbohydrate 4.6g, of which sugars 3.8g; Fat 40.2g, of which saturates 10g; Cholesterol 81mg; Calcium 297mg; Fibre 3.6g; Sodium 288mg.

Chicken Liver Pâté with Marsala

This is a really quick and simple pâté to make, yet it has a delicious – and quite sophisticated – flavour.

Serves 4

350g/12oz chicken livers, thawed
   if frozen

225g/8oz/1 cup butter
2 garlic cloves, crushed
15ml/1 tbsp Marsala
5ml/1 tsp chopped sage
salt and ground black pepper
8 fresh parsley leaves, to garnish
Melba toast, to serve

1 Pick over the chicken livers, then rinse and pat dry with kitchen paper. Melt 25g/1oz/2 tbsp of the butter in a frying pan over medium heat. Add the chicken livers and garlic and cook, stirring occasionally, for about 5 minutes, or until they are firm but still pink in their centres.

2 Transfer the livers to a food processor or blender using a slotted spoon. Add the Marsala and chopped sage.

3 Melt 150g/5oz/generous ½ cup of the remaining butter in the frying pan, stirring to loosen any sediment, then pour into the food processor or blender and process until smooth. Season well with salt and pepper.

4 Spoon the pâté into four individual pots and smooth the surface. Melt the remaining butter in a separate pan and pour it over the pâtés. Garnish with sage leaves and chill in the refrigerator until set. Serve with triangles of Melba toast.

Cook's Tip
To make Melba toast, first remove the crusts from medium-sliced white bread. Toast on both sides in a toaster or under the grill (broiler), until golden. Remove the toast and, using a sharp, serrated knife, cut horizontally through each slice to make two very thin slices. Cut each slice into quarters and toast the uncooked sides under the grill until golden and curling. Cool on a rack and store in an airtight container.

Salmon Rillettes

A variation on the classic French pork rillette, this appetizer is easier and less time consuming to make than the original.

Serves 6

350g/12oz salmon fillets
175g/6oz/¾ cup butter
1 leek, white part only,
   finely chopped

1 celery stick, finely chopped
1 bay leaf
150ml/¼ pint/⅔ cup dry
   white wine
115g/4oz smoked
   salmon trimmings
large pinch of ground mace
60ml/4 tbsp fromage frais
   (low-fat cream cheese)
salt and ground black pepper
salad leaves, to serve

1 Lightly season the salmon with salt and pepper. Melt 25g/1oz/2 tbsp of the butter in a frying pan over low heat. Add the celery and leek and cook, stirring occasionally, for about 5 minutes. Add the salmon and bay leaf and pour in the wine. Cover with a tight-fitting lid and cook for about 15 minutes, until the fish is tender. Set the salmon aside.

2 Strain the cooking liquid into another pan, bring to the boil and cook until reduced to 30ml/2 tbsp. Leave to cool.

3 Melt 50g/2oz/4 tbsp of the remaining butter in another pan and gently cook the smoked salmon until it turns pale pink. Leave to cool.

4 Remove the skin and any bones from the salmon fillets. Flake the flesh into a bowl and add the reduced cooking liquid. Beat in the remaining butter, the mace and fromage frais. Break up the smoked salmon trimmings and fold into the mixture with the pan juices. Taste and adjust the seasoning.

5 Spoon the salmon mixture into a dish or terrine and smooth the surface. Cover and chill in the refrigerator.

6 To serve the salmon rillettes, shape the mixture into oval quennelles using two dessert spoons and arrange on individual plates with the salad leaves.

Chicken Energy 507kcal/2090kJ; Protein 16g; Carbohydrate 1g, of which sugars 0.6g; Fat 48.3g, of which saturates 29.9g; Cholesterol 452mg; Calcium 18mg; Fibre 0.1g; Sodium 408mg.
Salmon Energy 373kcal/1542kJ; Protein 17.4g; Carbohydrate 1.2g, of which sugars 1g; Fat 31.4g, of which saturates 16.5g; Cholesterol 98mg; Calcium 33mg; Fibre 0.7g; Sodium 568mg.

Mexican Dip with Chips

This appetizer also makes a fabulous snack to serve with pre-dinner drinks.

Serves 4

2 avocados
juice of I lime
½ small onion, finely chopped
½ red chilli, seeded and
 finely chopped
3 tomatoes, peeled, seeded and
 finely diced
30ml/2 tbsp chopped fresh
 coriander (cilantro)

30ml/2 tbsp sour cream
salt and ground black pepper
15 ml/1 tbsp sour cream and
 a pinch of cayenne pepper,
 to garnish

For the chips

150g/5oz bag tortilla chips
30ml/2 tbsp finely grated mature
 (sharp) Cheddar cheese
1.5ml/¼ tsp chilli powder
10ml/2 tsp chopped fresh parsley

1 Halve and stone (pit) the avocados and scoop the flesh with a spoon, scraping the shells well. Place the flesh in a blender or food processor with the remaining dip ingredients, reserving the sour cream and cayenne pepper for the garnish. Process until fairly smooth. Transfer to a bowl, cover with clear film (plastic wrap) and chill in the refrigerator until required.

2 To make the chips, preheat the grill (broiler), then spread out the tortilla chips on a baking sheet. Mix the grated cheese with the chilli powder, sprinkle over the chips and grill (broil) for 1–2 minutes, until the cheese has melted.

3 Remove the avocado dip from the refrigerator, top with the sour cream and sprinkle with cayenne pepper. Serve the bowl on a plate surrounded by the tortilla chips, garnished with the chopped fresh parsley.

> **Cook's Tip**
> You can omit the fresh chilli and the chilli powder if you prefer the dip to have a milder flavour or you are planning to serve it to young children.

French Goat's Cheese Salad

The deep, tangy flavours of this salad would also make it satisfying enough for a light meal, if you wished.

Serves 4

200g/7oz bag prepared mixed
 salad leaves including some soft
 and bitter varieties
4 rashers (strips) rindless lean
 back bacon
16 thin slices French bread
115g/4oz/½ cup full-fat
 goat's cheese

For the dressing

60ml/4 tbsp olive oil
15ml/1 tbsp tarragon vinegar
10ml/2 tsp walnut oil
5ml/1 tsp Dijon mustard
5ml/1 tsp wholegrain mustard
salt and ground black pepper

1 Preheat the grill (broiler). Rinse and dry the salad leaves, then arrange them in four individual serving bowls. Set aside in a cool place but not the refrigerator.

2 To make the dressing, pout the olive oil, vinegar, walnut oil and both types of mustard in a screw-top jar. Close the lid and shake well until combined. Season and set aside until required.

3 Lay the bacon rashers flat on a board, then stretch them using the back of a knife. Cut each rasher into four pieces. Roll up each piece up and secure with a wooden cocktail stick (toothpick). Grill (broil) for about 2–3 minutes, until golden on one side of the rolls.

4 Meanwhile, slice the goat's cheese into eight and halve each slice. Top each slice of bread with a piece of goat's cheese and place under the grill. Turn over the bacon rolls and continue cooking with the goat's cheese toasts until the cheese is golden and bubbling and the bacon rolls are cooked through.

5 Arrange the bacon rolls and toasts on top of the prepared salad leaves. Shake the dressing well again to mix and spoon a little of it over each serving. Serve immediately.

Dip Energy 332kcal/1385kJ; Protein 6.6g; Carbohydrate 27.3g, of which sugars 4.2g; Fat 22.3g, of which saturates 6.2g; Cholesterol 12mg; Calcium 133mg; Fibre 4.9g; Sodium 390mg.
Salad Energy 498kcal/2087kJ; Protein 19.6g; Carbohydrate 48.9g, of which sugars 3.5g; Fat 26.3g, of which saturates 8.8g; Cholesterol 40mg; Calcium 230mg; Fibre 3.2g; Sodium 1152mg.

Chinese Garlic Mushrooms

High in protein and low in fat, marinated tofu makes an unusual stuffing for these baked mushroom caps.

Serves 4
8 large open mushrooms
3 spring onions (scallions), sliced
1 garlic clove, crushed
30ml/2 tbsp oyster sauce
5g/10oz packet marinated tofu, diced
200g/7oz can corn, drained
10ml/2 tsp sesame oil
salt and ground black pepper

1 Preheat the oven to 200°C/400°F/Gas 6. Finely chop the mushroom stalks and mix with the next three ingredients.

2 Stir in the diced marinated tofu and corn, season well, then spoon the filling into the mushroom caps.

3 Brush the edges of the mushrooms with the sesame oil. Place them in an ovenproof dish and bake for 12–15 minutes, until the mushrooms are just tender, then serve immediately.

Ricotta & Borlotti Bean Pâté

A lovely, light yet full-flavoured vegetarian pâté.

Serves 4
400g/14oz can borlotti beans, drained and rinsed
175g/6oz/¾ cup ricotta cheese
1 garlic clove
60ml/4 tbsp melted butter
juice of ½ lemon
30ml/2 tbsp chopped fresh parsley
15ml/1 tbsp chopped fresh thyme
salt and ground black pepper

1 Put the beans, ricotta, garlic, butter and lemon juice in a food processor or blender and process. Add the parsley and thyme, season with salt and pepper and process again.

2 Spoon into a serving dish or four lightly oiled and base-lined ramekins. Chill. Garnish with salad leaves and serve with warm crusty bread or toast.

Tomato & Cheese Tarts

These crisp little tartlets are easier to make than they look and are best eaten fresh from the oven.

Serves 4
2 sheets filo pastry
1 egg white
115g/4oz/½ cup low-fat soft (farmer's) cheese
handful of fresh basil leaves
3 small tomatoes, sliced
salt and ground black pepper

1 Preheat the oven to 200°C/400°F/Gas 5. Brush the sheets of filo pastry lightly with egg white and, using a sharp knife, cut into sixteen 10cm/4in squares.

2 Layer the squares in pairs in eight patty tins (muffin pans). Spoon the cheese into the pastry cases (pie shells). Season with salt and ground black pepper and top with basil leaves.

3 Arrange the tomato slices on the tartlets, season with salt and pepper and bake for 10–12 minutes, until golden. Serve warm or at room temperature.

Cook's Tip
Filo pastry can be made at home but the process is quite laborious and takes a long time. It is much easier to buy chilled or frozen ready-made dough. The sheets should be kept covered until you are working on them. Brushing with melted butter, oil or egg white before baking makes sure that the layers are crisp.

Variations
• Substitute crumbled goat's cheese or feta for the soft (farmer's) cheese or cut a goat's cheese log into eight slices.
• Use four red and four yellow cherry tomatoes, halved and in two-colour pairs, to decorate the tops of these tartlets.
• Sprinkle the tartlets with chopped fresh chives when they have been assembled.

Mushrooms Energy 86kcal/361kJ; Protein 7.9g; Carbohydrate 4g, of which sugars 3.2g; Fat 4.4g, of which saturates 0.6g; Cholesterol 0mg; Calcium 268mg; Fibre 2.2g; Sodium 701mg.
Pâté Energy 290kcal/1208kJ; Protein 11g; Carbohydrate 19.3g, of which sugars 5.1g; Fat 19.3g, of which saturates 11.9g; Cholesterol 50mg; Calcium 74mg; Fibre 6.2g; Sodium 481mg.
Tarts Energy 118kcal/497kJ; Protein 7.3g; Carbohydrate 17.9g, of which sugars 3.6g; Fat 2.8g, of which saturates 1.6g; Cholesterol 7mg; Calcium 65mg; Fibre 1.3g; Sodium 149mg.

Avocados with Tangy Topping

Lightly grilled with a tasty topping of red onions and cheese, this dish makes a delightful appetizer.

Serves 4
15ml/1 tbsp sunflower oil
1 small red onion, sliced
1 garlic clove, crushed

dash of Worcestershire sauce
2 ripe avocados, halved and
  stoned (pitted)
2 small tomatoes, sliced
15ml/1 tbsp chopped fresh basil,
  marjoram or parsley
50g/2oz Lancashire or mozzarella
  cheese, sliced
salt and ground black pepper

1 Heat the oil in a frying pan over low heat. Add the onion and garlic and cook, stirring occasionally, for about 5 minutes, until just softened. Shake in a little Worcestershire sauce.

2 Preheat the grill (broiler). Place the avocado halves on the grill (broiling) pan and spoon the onion mixture into the centres. Divide the tomato slices and fresh herbs among the four halves and top with the cheese.

3 Season well with salt and pepper and grill (broil) until the cheese melts and starts to brown.

Chilled Avocado Salad

This simple appetizer makes a delightful change from avocados with vinaigrette.

Serves 4
2 avocados
juice of 1 lemon

300ml/½ pint/1¼ cups Greek
  (US strained plain) yogurt
2 garlic cloves, crushed
2 orange (bell) pepper, seeded
  and diced
salt and ground black pepper

1 Peel, halve and stone (pit) the avocados. Dice the flesh and toss with the lemon juice. Mix together the yogurt and garlic, season and fold in the avocados. Place in a serving dish, sprinkle with the orange peppers and chill before serving.

Bruschetta with Goat's Cheese

Simple to prepare in advance, this tempting dish can be served as an appetizer or as part of a finger buffet.

Serves 4–6
For the tapenade
400g/14oz black olives, pitted
  and finely chopped
50g/2oz sun-dried tomatoes in oil,
  drained and chopped
30ml/2 tbsp capers, rinsed
  and chopped
15ml/1 tbsp green peppercorns,
  in brine, crushed

2 garlic cloves, crushed
45ml/3 tbsp chopped fresh basil
45–60ml/3–4 tbsp olive oil
salt and ground black pepper

For the bases
12 slices ciabatta or other
  crusty bread
olive oil, for brushing
2 garlic cloves, halved
115g/4oz/½ cup soft goat's
  cheese or other full-fat
  soft cheese
mixed fresh herb sprigs, to garnish

1 To make the tapenade, mix all the tapenade ingredients together and check the seasoning. It should not need too much. Leave to marinate overnight, if possible.

2 To make the bruschetta, toast both sides of the bread lightly until golden. Brush one side of each slice with with oil and then rub with the garlic cloves. Set aside until ready to serve.

3 Spread the bruschetta with the cheese, fluffing it up with a fork, and spoon the tapenade on top. Garnish with sprigs of mixed fresh herbs.

Cook's Tips
• Grill the bruschetta on a barbecue for a delicious smoky flavour if you are making this appetizer in the summer.
• Basil loses its characteristic flavour when dried – fresh basil is infinitely better. If the fresh herb is not available, you could substitute 15ml/1 tbsp good-quality pesto without sacrificing the flavour.

Avocados Energy 162kcal/668kJ; Protein 3.6g; Carbohydrate 2.9g, of which sugars 1.9g; Fat 15.1g, of which saturates 4.1g; Cholesterol 7mg; Calcium 56mg; Fibre 2.2g; Sodium 55mg.
Salad Energy 264kcal/1094kJ; Protein 7.7g; Carbohydrate 9.8g, of which sugars 7.3g; Fat 22.5g, of which saturates 7.1g; Cholesterol 0mg; Calcium 129mg; Fibre 4.3g; Sodium 62mg.
Bruschetta Energy 288kcal/1197kJ; Protein 8.1g; Carbohydrate 17.8g, of which sugars 1.5g; Fat 20.9g, of which saturates 5.8g; Cholesterol 18mg; Calcium 107mg; Fibre 2.8g; Sodium 1795mg.

Grilled Garlic Mussels

Use a combination of fresh herbs, such as oregano, basil and flat leaf parsley.

Serves 4
1.5kg/3–3½lb fresh mussels
120ml/4fl oz/½ cup dry
    white wine
50g/2oz/4 tbsp butter
2 shallots, finely chopped

2 garlic cloves, crushed
50g/2oz/½ cup dried
    white breadcrumbs
60ml/4 tbsp mixed chopped
    fresh herbs
30ml/2 tbsp freshly grated
    Parmesan cheese
salt and ground black pepper
chopped fresh parsley, to garnish

1 Scrub the mussels well under cold running water. Remove the "beards" and discard any mussels with damaged shells or that do not shut immediately when sharply tapped.

2 Place in a large, heavy pan with the wine. Cover with a tight-fitting lid and cook over high heat, shaking the pan occasionally for 5–8 minutes, until the mussels have opened.

3 Strain the mussels and reserve the cooking liquid. Discard any mussels that remain closed. Leave them to cool slightly, then remove and discard the top half of each shell.

4 Melt the butter in a pan over low heat. Add the shallots and cook, stirring occasionally, for 5 minutes, until softened. Add the garlic and cook for 1–2 minutes. Add the breadcrumbs and cook, stirring until lightly browned. Remove the pan from the heat and stir in the herbs. Moisten with a little of the reserved mussel liquid, then season to taste with salt and pepper.

5 Spoon the breadcrumb mixture over the mussels and arrange on baking sheets. Sprinkle with the grated Parmesan.

6 Cook the mussels under a hot grill (broiler), in batches, for about 2 minutes, until the topping is crisp and golden brown. Keep the cooked mussels warm in a low oven while grilling (broiling) the remainder. Garnish with chopped fresh parsley and serve immediately.

Nut Patties with Mango Relish

These spicy vegetarian patties can be made in advance, if you like, and reheated just before serving.

Serves 4–6
butter, for greasing
175g/6oz/1½ cups roasted
    and salted cashew nuts,
    finely chopped
175g/6oz/1½ cups walnuts,
    finely chopped
1 small onion, finely chopped
1 garlic clove, crushed
1 green chilli, seeded
    and chopped
5ml/1 tsp ground cumin
10ml/2 tsp ground coriander

2 carrots, coarsely grated
50g/2oz/1 cup fresh white
    breadcrumbs
30ml/2 tbsp chopped fresh
    coriander (cilantro)
15ml/1 tbsp lemon juice
1–2 eggs, lightly beaten
salt and ground black pepper
fresh coriander sprigs, to garnish

For the relish
1 large ripe mango, cut into
    small dice
1 small onion, cut into slivers
5ml/1 tsp grated fresh root ginger
pinch of salt
15ml/1 tbsp sesame oil
5ml/1 tsp black mustard seeds

1 Preheat the oven to 180°C/350°F/Gas 4. Lightly grease a baking sheet with butter.

2 Mix together the cashews, walnuts, onion, garlic, chilli, cumin, ground coriander, carrots, breadcrumbs and chopped coriander in a bowl and season with salt and pepper.

3 Sprinkle the lemon juice over the mixture and add enough of the beaten egg to bind it together. Using your hands, shape the mixture into twelve balls, then flatten slightly into round patties. Place them on the prepared baking sheet and bake for about 25 minutes, until golden brown.

4 To make the relish, mix together the mango, onion, fresh root ginger and salt. Heat the oil in a small frying pan, add the mustard seeds and cook for a few seconds until they pop and give off their aroma. Stir the seeds into the mango mixture and transfer the relish to a serving bowl. Serve with the nut patties, garnished with coriander sprigs.

Mussels Energy 289kcal/1211kJ; Protein 24g; Carbohydrate 10g, of which sugars 0.6g; Fat 15.2g, of which saturates 8.4g; Cholesterol 79mg; Calcium 333mg; Fibre 0.3g; Sodium 490mg.
Patties Energy 464kcal/1926kJ; Protein 12.8g; Carbohydrate 19.3g, of which sugars 8.4g; Fat 37.9g, of which saturates 5.2g; Cholesterol 32mg; Calcium 66mg; Fibre 3.5g; Sodium 167mg.

Dim Sum

A popular Chinese snack, these tiny dumplings are now fashionable in many specialist restaurants.

Serves 4
For the dough
150g/5oz/1¼ cups plain (all-purpose) flour
50ml/2fl oz/¼ cup boiling water
25ml/1½ tbsp cold water
7.5ml/½ tsp vegetable oil

For the filling
75g/3oz minced (ground) pork

45ml/3 tbsp chopped canned bamboo shoots
7.5ml/½ tsp light soy sauce, plus extra to serve
5ml/1 tsp dry sherry
5ml/1 tsp demerara (raw) sugar
2.5ml/½ tsp sesame oil
5ml/1 tsp cornflour (cornstarch)

To serve
mixed fresh lettuce leaves such as iceberg, frisée or Webbs
spring onion (scallion) curls
sliced red chilli
prawn (shrimp) crackers

1 To make the dough, sift the flour into a bowl. Stir in the boiling water, then the cold water together with the oil. Mix to form a ball and knead until smooth. Divide the mixture into sixteen equal pieces and shape into rounds.

2 For the filling, mix together the pork, bamboo shoots, soy sauce, sherry, sugar and oil. Then stir in the cornflour.

3 Place a little of the filling in the centre of each dim sum round. Carefully pinch the edges of the dough together to form little "purses".

4 Line a steamer with a damp dish towel. Place the dim sum in the steamer and steam for 5–10 minutes. Serve immediately on a bed of lettuce with soy sauce, spring onion curls, sliced red chilli and prawn crackers.

Variation
As an alternative filling, substitute cooked, peeled prawns (shrimp) for the pork.

Sesame Prawn Toasts

Serve about four of these delicious toasts per person with a soy sauce for dipping.

Serves 6
175g/6oz/1½ cups cooked, peeled prawns (shrimp)
2 spring onions (scallions), finely chopped
2.5cm/1in piece fresh root ginger, peeled and grated

2 garlic cloves, crushed
30ml/2 tbsp cornflour (cornstarch)
10ml/2 tsp soy sauce, plus extra for dipping
6 slices day-old bread from a small loaf, without crusts
40g/1½ oz sesame seeds
about 600ml/1 pint/2½ cups vegetable oil, for deep-frying

1 Place the prawns, spring onions, ginger and garlic cloves into a food processor fitted with a metal blade. Add the cornflour and soy sauce and process the mixture into a paste.

2 Spread the bread slices evenly with the paste and cut into triangles. Sprinkle with the sesame seeds, making sure they stick to the bread. Chill in the refrigerator for 30 minutes.

3 Heat the vegetable oil in a deep-fryer or large, heavy pan to 190°C/375°F or until a cube of day-old bread browns in 30 seconds. Using a slotted spoon, lower the toasts, in batches, into the oil, sesame-seed side down, and fry for 2–3 minutes, turning them over for the last minute. Remove with a slotted spoon and drain on absorbent kitchen paper. Keep the toasts warm while frying the remainder.

4 Place the toasts on individual dishes and serve immediately with little bowls of soy sauce for dipping.

Cook's Tip
Chinese soy sauce may be either light or dark. The former has a stronger flavour, while the latter is sweeter and is often used in cooking to give a richer colour to dishes. Light soy sauce is most usually used as a condiment and for dipping.

Dim Sum Energy 183kcal/773kJ; Protein 7.2g; Carbohydrate 31.5g, of which sugars 1.8g; Fat 3.8g, of which saturates 0.9g; Cholesterol 12mg; Calcium 55mg; Fibre 1.2g; Sodium 148mg.
Prawn Toasts Energy 207kcal/865kJ; Protein 8.7g; Carbohydrate 17.4g, of which sugars 1g; Fat 11.9g, of which saturates 1.5g; Cholesterol 57mg; Calcium 98mg; Fibre 1g; Sodium 427mg.

English Ploughman's Pâté

This is a contemporary interpretation of the traditional ploughman's lunch – bread, cheese and a variety of pickles.

Serves 4
50g/2oz/3 tbsp full-fat
    soft (farmer's) cheese
50g/2oz/½ cup grated Caerphilly
    or other crumbly white cheese
50g/2oz/½ cup grated Double
    Gloucester or other mellow,
    semi-hard cheese
4 pickled silverskin onions,
    drained and finely chopped
15ml/1 tbsp apricot chutney
30ml/2 tbsp butter, melted
30ml/2 tbsp chopped fresh chives
4 slices soft-grain bread
salt and ground black pepper
watercress or rocket (arugula) and
    cherry tomatoes, to serve

1 Mix together the soft cheese, grated cheeses, pickled onions, chutney and butter in a bowl and season lightly with salt and ground black pepper.

2 Spoon the mixture on to a sheet of greaseproof (waxed) paper and roll up into a cylinder, smoothing the mixture into a roll with your hands. Scrunch the ends of the paper together and twist them to seal. Place in the freezer for about 30 minutes, until the roll is just firm.

3 Spread the chives on a plate, then unwrap the chilled cheese pâté. Roll it in the chives until evenly coated. Wrap in clear film (plastic wrap) and chill for 10 minutes in the refrigerator.

4 Preheat the grill (broiler). Lightly toast the bread on both sides. Cut off the crusts and slice each piece in half horizontally to make two very thin slices. Cut each half into two triangles. Grill (broil) again, untoasted side up, until golden and curled at the edges.

5 Slice the pâté into rounds with a sharp knife and serve three or four rounds per person with the toast, watercress or rocket and cherry tomatoes.

Golden Cheese Puffs

Serve these deep-fried puffs – called *aigrettes* in France – with a fruity chutney and a green salad.

Makes 8
50g/2oz/½ cup plain (all-
    purpose) flour
15g/½oz/1 tbsp butter
1 egg
1 egg yolk
50g/2oz/½ cup finely grated
    mature (sharp) Cheddar cheese
15ml/1 tbsp freshly grated
    Parmesan cheese
2.5ml/½ tsp mustard powder
pinch of cayenne pepper
vegetable oil, for deep-frying
salt and ground black pepper
mango chutney and green salad,
    to serve

1 Sift the flour on to a square of greaseproof (waxed) paper and set aside. Place the butter and 150ml/⅔ pint/⅔ cup water in a pan and heat gently until the butter has melted.

2 Bring the liquid to the boil and tip in the flour all at once. Remove the pan from the heat and stir well with a wooden spoon until the mixture begins to leave the sides of the pan and forms a ball. Leave to cool slightly.

3 Beat the egg and egg yolk together in a bowl with a fork and then gradually add to the mixture in the pan, beating well after each addition.

4 Stir the Cheddar and Parmesan cheeses, mustard powder and cayenne pepper into the mixture and season to taste with salt and pepper.

5 Heat the vegetable oil in a deep-fryer or large, heavy pan to 190°C/375°F, or until a cube of day-old bread browns in 30 seconds. Drop four spoonfuls of the cheese mixture into the oil at a time and deep-fry for 2–3 minutes, until golden. Remove with a slotted spoon, drain on kitchen paper and keep hot in the oven while cooking the remaining mixture.

6 Serve two puffs per person with a spoonful of mango chutney and green salad.

Pâté Energy 288kcal/1200kJ; Protein 10.6g; Carbohydrate 18.7g, of which sugars 5.1g; Fat 19g, of which saturates 11.9g; Cholesterol 52mg; Calcium 267mg; Fibre 1.3g; Sodium 511mg.
Cheese Puffs Energy 162kcal/669kJ; Protein 3.5g; Carbohydrate 5.8g, of which sugars 0g; Fat 13.9g, of which saturates 4.1g; Cholesterol 61mg; Calcium 77mg; Fibre 0g; Sodium 90mg.

Kansas City Fritters

Crisp bacon and vegetable fritters are served with a spicy tomato salsa.

Makes 8
200g/7oz/1¾ cups canned corn, drained well
2 eggs, separated
75g/3oz/¾ cup plain (all-purpose) flour
75ml/5 tbsp milk
1 small courgette (zucchini), grated
2 rashers (strips) rindless lean back bacon, diced
2 spring onions (scallions), finely chopped

large pinch of cayenne pepper
45ml/3 tbsp sunflower oil
salt and ground black pepper
fresh coriander (cilantro) sprigs, to garnish

For the salsa
3 tomatoes, peeled, seeded and diced
½ small red (bell) pepper, seeded and diced
½ small onion, diced
15ml/1 tbsp lemon juice
15ml/1 tbsp chopped fresh coriander
dash of Tabasco sauce

1 To make the salsa, mix all the ingredients together in a bowl and season to taste with salt and pepper. Cover with clear film (plastic wrap) and chill until required.

2 Empty the corn into another bowl and mix in the egg yolks. Add the flour and blend in with a wooden spoon. When the mixture thickens, gradually blend in the milk.

3 Stir in the courgette, bacon, spring onions and cayenne pepper and season with salt and pepper. Whisk the egg whites in a grease-free bowl until stiff peaks form. Gently fold into the corn batter mixture.

4 Heat the oil in a large frying pan and place four spoonfuls of the mixture into it. Cook over a medium heat for 2–3 minutes on each side, until golden. Drain on kitchen paper and keep warm in the oven while cooking the remaining four fritters.

5 Serve two fritters each, garnished with coriander sprigs and a spoonful of the chilled tomato salsa.

Spinach & Cheese Dumplings

These tasty little dumplings are known as *gnocchi* in Italy, where they are extremely popular, especially in the northern regions.

Serves 4
butter, for greasing
40g/1½oz/½ cup freshly grated Parmesan cheese
175g/6oz cold mashed potato
75g/3oz/½ cup semolina
115g/4oz/1 cup frozen leaf spinach, thawed, squeezed out and chopped

115g/4oz/½ cup ricotta cheese
30ml/2 tbsp beaten egg
2.5ml/½ tsp salt
large pinch of grated nutmeg
pinch of ground black pepper
fresh basil sprigs, to garnish

For the butter sauce
75g/3oz/6 tbsp butter
5ml/1 tsp grated lemon rind
15ml/1 tbsp lemon juice
15ml/1 tbsp chopped fresh basil

1 Preheat the oven to 150°C/300°F/Gas 2. Lightly grease a flameproof dish with butter and place it in the oven to warm. Set aside 30ml/2 tbsp of the Parmesan cheese. Place the remainder in a bowl, add the potato, semolina, spinach, ricotta, beaten egg, salt, nutmeg and pepper and mix well.

2 Take walnut-size pieces of the mixture and roll each one back and forth along the prongs of a fork until ridged. Make 28 dumplings in this way. Preheat the grill (broiler).

3 Bring a large pan of water to the boil, reduce to a simmer and drop in the dumplings. As they cook they will rise to the surface; this takes about 2 minutes, then simmer for 1 minute more. Transfer the dumplings to the prepared dish.

4 Sprinkle the dumplings with the Parmesan cheese and grill under high heat for 2 minutes, or until lightly browned.

5 Meanwhile, heat the butter in a pan and stir in the lemon rind, lemon juice and basil. Season to taste with salt and pepper. Pour some of this butter over each portion and serve immediately, garnished with basil sprigs.

Fritters Energy 152kcal/636kJ; Protein 5.3g; Carbohydrate 17.2g, of which sugars 5.6g; Fat 7.4g, of which saturates 1.5g; Cholesterol 51mg; Calcium 42mg; Fibre 1.5g; Sodium 190mg.
Dumplings Energy 432kcal/1796kJ; Protein 18.2g; Carbohydrate 23.1g, of which sugars 2g; Fat 30.3g, of which saturates 18.2g; Cholesterol 126mg; Calcium 381mg; Fibre 1.4g; Sodium 465mg.

Tricolour Salad

This can be a simple appetizer if served on individual salad plates, or part of a light buffet meal laid out on a platter.

Serves 4–6
1 small red onion, thinly sliced
6 large full-flavoured tomatoes

extra virgin olive oil, to drizzle
50g/2oz rocket (arugula) or
 watercress, chopped
175g/6oz mozzarella cheese,
 thinly sliced
salt and ground black pepper
30ml/2 tbsp pine nuts, to
 garnish (optional)

1 Soak the onion slices in a bowl of cold water for about 30 minutes, then drain and pat dry with kitchen paper.

2 Cut a cross in the tops of the tomatoes, place in a heatproof bowl and pour boiling water over them. Leave for 1 minute, then drain and peel off the skins. Remove the cores and slice the flesh. Arrange half the sliced tomatoes on a large platter or divide them among small plates.

3 Drizzle liberally with olive oil, then layer with half the chopped rocket or watercress and half the soaked onion slices, seasoning well with salt and pepper. Add half the mozzarella, then drizzle with more olive oil and season again.

4 Repeat with the remaining tomato slices, salad leaves, onion slices, mozzarella and olive oil.

5 Season well to finish and complete with some olive oil and a good sprinkling of pine nuts, if using. Cover the salad with clear film (plastic wrap) and chill in the refrigerator for at least 2 hours before serving.

> **Cook's Tip**
> *When lightly salted, tomatoes make their own dressing with their natural juices. The sharpness of the rocket (arugula) or watercress offsets them wonderfully.*

Minted Melon Salad

Use two different varieties of melon in this salad, such as Charentais and Galia or Ogen.

Serves 4
2 ripe melons
fresh mint sprigs, to garnish

For the dressing
30ml/2 tbsp coarsely chopped
 fresh mint
5ml/1 tsp caster (superfine) sugar
30ml/2 tbsp raspberry vinegar
90ml/6 tbsp extra virgin olive oil
salt and ground black pepper

1 Halve the melons, then scoop out the seeds using a dessertspoon. Cut the melons into thin wedges using a large sharp knife and remove the skins.

2 Arrange the two different varieties of melon wedges alternately among four individual serving plates.

3 To make the dressing, whisk together the mint, sugar, vinegar and olive oil n a small bowl and season to taste with salt and pepper. Alternatively, put them in a screw-top jar, close the lid and shake well until combined.

4 Spoon the mint dressing over the melon wedges and garnish with mint sprigs. Chill in the refrigerator for about 15 minutes before serving.

> **Cook's Tip**
> *You can make raspberry vinegar yourself by steeping the fresh fruit in wine vinegar and then straining it. Steeping another batch of fruit in the same vinegar intensifies the flavour.*

> **Variation**
> *You could also try an orange-fleshed Cantaloupe with a pale green Ogen, or choose a small white-fleshed Honeydew for a different variation.*

Tricolour Energy 98kcal/408kJ; Protein 6.5g; Carbohydrate 4g, of which sugars 3.8g; Fat 6.3g, of which saturates 4.1g; Cholesterol 17mg; Calcium 129mg; Fibre 1.3g; Sodium 136mg.
Melon Energy 218kcal/904kJ; Protein 1.7g; Carbohydrate 15.7g, of which sugars 15.1g; Fat 16.8g, of which saturates 2.4g; Cholesterol 0mg; Calcium 59mg; Fibre 1g; Sodium 80mg.

Garlic Mushrooms

Serve these on toast for a quick, tasty appetizer or pop them into ramekins and serve with slices of warm crusty bread.

Serves 4
450g/1lb button (white) mushrooms, sliced if large
45ml/3 tbsp olive oil
45ml/3 tbsp stock or water
30ml/2 tbsp dry sherry (optional)
3 garlic cloves, crushed
115g/4oz/½ cup low-fat soft (farmer's) cheese
30ml/2 tbsp chopped fresh parsley
15ml/1 tbsp chopped fresh chives
salt and ground black pepper
toast or bread, to serve

1 Put the mushrooms into a large pan with the olive oil, stock or water and sherry, if using. Heat until the liquid is bubbling, then cover the pan with a tight-fitting lid and simmer gently for about 5 minutes.

2 Add the crushed garlic and stir well to mix. Cook for a further 2 minutes. Remove the mushrooms with a slotted spoon and set them aside. Cook the liquid until it reduces to about 30ml/2 tbsp. Remove the pan from the heat and stir in the soft cheese, parsley and chives.

3 Stir the mixture well until the cheese has completely melted, then return the mushrooms to the pan and stir so that they become coated with the cheese mixture. Season to taste with salt and pepper.

4 Pile the mushrooms on to thick slabs of hot toast and serve immediately. Alternatively, spoon them into four ramekins and serve accompanied by slices of crusty bread.

> **Cook's Tip**
> *Use a mixture of different types of mushrooms for this dish, if you like. Shiitake mushrooms, if you can find them, will give this appetizer a particularly rich flavour. Oyster mushrooms, on the other hand, offer an interesting texture.*

Vegetables with Tahini

This colourful appetizer is easily prepared in advance. For an *al fresco* meal, you could grill the vegetables on a barbecue.

Serves 4
2 red, green or yellow (bell) peppers, seeded and quartered
2 courgettes (zucchini), halved lengthways
2 small aubergines (eggplants), degorged and halved lengthways
1 fennel bulb, quartered
olive oil, for brushing
115g/4oz halloumi cheese, sliced
salt and ground black pepper
warm pitta or naan bread, to serve

For the tahini cream
225g/8oz tahini paste
1 garlic clove, crushed
30ml/2 tbsp olive oil
30ml/2 tbsp freshly squeezed lemon juice
120ml/4fl oz/½ cup cold water

1 Preheat the grill (broiler) or barbecue until hot. Brush the vegetables with the olive oil and cook until just browned, turning once. (If the peppers blacken and blister, don't worry. The skins can be peeled off when they are cool enough to handle.) Cook the vegetables until just softened.

2 Place all the vegetables in a shallow dish and season to taste with salt and pepper. Leave to cool slightly. They are best served warm rather than hot.

3 Meanwhile, brush the cheese slices with olive oil and grill (broil) these on both sides until they are just charred. Remove them from the grill (broiler) pan with a metal spatula.

4 To make the tahini cream, place all the ingredients, except the water, in a food processor or blender. Process for a few seconds to mix, then, with the motor still running, pour in the water and blend until smooth.

5 Place the vegetables and cheese slices on a platter and trickle over the tahini cream. Serve with plenty of warm pitta or naan bread while the cheese is still hot, as it will become rubbery as it cools down.

Mushrooms Energy 131kcal/542kJ; Protein 6.7g; Carbohydrate 1.8g, of which sugars 1.5g; Fat 11.3g, of which saturates 2.8g; Cholesterol 7mg; Calcium 65mg; Fibre 1.9g; Sodium 136mg.
Vegetables Energy 523kcal/2164kJ; Protein 19.1g; Carbohydrate 9.9g, of which sugars 9.1g; Fat 45.5g, of which saturates 9.7g; Cholesterol 17mg; Calcium 530mg; Fibre 9.1g; Sodium 136mg.

Fish & Shellfish

Delicate, succulent and delicious, fish and shellfish can be paired
with a wide range of other ingredients, such as lemons, fresh
herbs or flavoursome summer vegetables, to provide a
wholesome meal for every occasion. This chapter includes family
favourites, such as Fish and Chips or Tuna and Corn Fish Cakes,
as well as more sophisticated dishes, such as Scallops with
Ginger or Salmon with Herb Butter.

Herrings in Oatmeal with Mustard

In this delicious dish, crunchy-coated herrings are served with a piquant mustard sauce.

Serves 4
about 15ml/1 tbsp Dijon mustard
about 7.5ml/1½ tsp tarragon vinegar
175ml/6fl oz/¾ cup thick mayonnaise
4 herrings (about 225g/8oz each), gutted
1 lemon, halved
115g/4oz/1 cup medium oatmeal
salt and ground black pepper

1 Beat the mustard and vinegar to taste into the mayonnaise. Chill lightly in the refrigerator.

2 Place one fish at a time on a chopping board, cut-side down and opened out. Press gently all along the backbone with your thumbs. Turn the fish over and carefully lift away the backbone and discard.

3 Squeeze lemon juice over both sides of each fish, then season with salt and ground black pepper. Fold the fish in half, skin-side outwards.

4 Preheat the grill (broiler) until fairly hot. Place the oatmeal on a shallow plate, then coat each herring evenly in the oatmeal, pressing it on gently with your fingers.

5 Place the herrings on a grill (broiler) rack and grill (broil) the fish for about 3–4 minutes on each side, until the skin is golden brown and crisp and the flesh flakes easily. Serve hot with the mustard sauce, served separately.

> **Variation**
> For extra flavour coarsely chop 4 rashers (strips) of streaky (fatty) bacon and dry-fry in a heavy frying pan over low heat until golden and crisp. Drain on kitchen paper. Sprinkle the bacon over the cooked fish before serving.

Fish & Chips

The traditional British combination of battered fish and chips is served with lemon wedges.

Serves 4
115g/4oz/1 cup self-raising (self-rising) flour
150ml/¼ pint/⅔ cup water
675g/1½lb potatoes
675g/1½lb skinned cod fillet, cut into four
vegetable oil, for deep-frying
salt and ground black pepper
lemon wedges, to serve

1 Stir the flour and a pinch of salt together in a bowl, then form a well in the centre. Gradually pour into the water, whisking in the flour to make a smooth batter. Leave to stand for 30 minutes.

2 Cut the potatoes into strips about 1cm/½ in wide and 5cm/2in long. Place the potatoes in a colander, rinse in cold water, then drain and dry them well with kitchen paper.

3 Heat the oil in a deep-fat fryer or large heavy pan to 150°C/300°F, or until a cube of day-old bread browns in 50 seconds. Using the wire basket, lower the potatoes, in batches, into the oil and cook for 5–6 minutes, shaking the basket occasionally until the potatoes are soft but not browned. Remove the chips (French fries) from the oil and drain them thoroughly on kitchen paper.

4 Heat the oil in the fryer to 190°C/375°F, or until a cube of day-old bread browns in 30 seconds. Season the fish with salt and pepper. Stir the batter, then dip the pieces of fish in turn into it, allowing the excess to drain off.

5 Working in two batches if necessary, lower the fish into the oil and fry for 6–8 minutes, until crisp and brown. Drain the fish on kitchen paper and keep warm.

6 Add the chips, in batches, to the oil and cook them for 2–3 minutes, until golden and crisp. Keep hot until ready to serve, then sprinkle with salt and serve with the fish, accompanied by lemon wedges.

Herrings Energy 721kcal/2997kJ; Protein 35.3g; Carbohydrate 21.7g, of which sugars 0.6g; Fat 55.4g, of which saturates 10.6g; Cholesterol 109mg; Calcium 69mg; Fibre 2g; Sodium 476mg.
Fish & Chips Energy 820kcal/3429kJ; Protein 32.6g; Carbohydrate 71.2g, of which sugars 2.9g; Fat 40.5g, of which saturates 13g; Cholesterol 0mg; Calcium 132mg; Fibre 4.6g; Sodium 329mg.

Trout with Hazelnuts

The hazelnuts in this recipe make an interesting change from the almonds that are more often used.

Serves 4

50g/2oz/¹/₂ cup hazelnuts, chopped

65g/2¹/₂oz/5 tbsp butter
4 trout (about 275g/10oz each), gutted
30ml/2 tbsp lemon juice
salt and ground black pepper
lemon slices and fresh flat leaf parsley sprigs, to serve

1 Preheat the grill (broiler). Toast the nuts in a single layer, stirring frequently, until the skins split. Then transfer the nuts to a clean dish towel and rub to remove the skins. Leave the nuts to cool, then chop them coarsely.

2 Heat 50g/2oz/4 tbsp of the butter in a large frying pan. Season the trout inside and out with salt and pepper, then cook them, two at a time, for 12–15 minutes, turning once, until the trout are brown and the flesh flakes easily when tested with the point of a sharp kitchen knife.

3 Drain the cooked trout on kitchen paper, then transfer to a warm serving plate and keep warm while frying the remaining trout in the same way. (If your frying pan is large enough, you could, of course, cook the trout in one batch.)

4 Add the remaining butter to the frying pan and fry the hazelnuts until evenly browned. Stir the lemon juice into the pan and mix well, then quickly pour the buttery sauce over the trout and serve immediately, garnished with slices of lemon and flat leaf parsley sprigs.

> **Cook's Tip**
> *You can use a microwave to prepare the nuts instead of the grill (broiler). Spread them out in a shallow microwave dish and leave uncovered. Cook on full power until the skins split, then remove the skins using a dish towel as described above.*

Trout Wrapped in a Blanket

The "blanket" of bacon bastes the fish during cooking, keeping it moist and adding flavour at the same time.

Serves 4

butter, for greasing
juice of ¹/₂ lemon
4 trout (about 275g/10oz each), gutted

4 fresh thyme sprigs, plus extra to garnish
8 thin rashers (strips) rindless streaky (fatty) bacon
salt and ground black pepper
chopped fresh parsley, to garnish
lemon wedges, to serve
watercress and cherry tomato salad, to serve (optional)

1 Preheat the oven to 200°C/400°F/Gas 6. Lightly grease a shallow ovenproof dish with butter.

2 Squeeze lemon juice over the skin and inside the cavity of each fish, season all over with salt and ground black pepper, then put a thyme sprig in each cavity.

3 Stretch each bacon rasher using the back of a knife, then wrap two rashers around each fish. Place the fish in the prepared dish, with the loose ends of bacon tucked underneath to prevent them from unwinding.

4 Bake the trout for 15–20 minutes, until the flesh flakes easily when tested with the point of a sharp knife and the bacon is crisp and beginning to brown.

5 Transfer the fish to warmed individual plates and serve immediately garnished with chopped parsley and sprigs of thyme and accompanied by lemon wedges.

> **Variation**
> *Smoked streaky (fatty) bacon will impart a stronger flavour to the fish. If you like, use chopped fresh coriander (cilantro) in place of the parsley for the garnish.*

With Hazelnuts Energy 414kcal/1723kJ; Protein 38.7g; Carbohydrate 0.9g, of which sugars 0.6g; Fat 28.4g, of which saturates 10.7g; Cholesterol 187mg; Calcium 78mg; Fibre 0.8g; Sodium 237mg.
In a blanket Energy 316kcal/1323kJ; Protein 42.8g; Carbohydrate 0.1g, of which sugars 0.1g; Fat 16g, of which saturates 4.8g; Cholesterol 176mg; Calcium 64mg; Fibre 0.1g; Sodium 611mg.

Smoked Trout Salad

Horseradish goes just as well with smoked trout as it does with roast beef. It combines well with yogurt to make a lovely dressing.

Serves 4
1 oak leaf or other red lettuce, such as lollo rosso
225g/8oz small ripe tomatoes, cut into thin wedges
1/2 cucumber, peeled and thinly sliced
4 smoked trout fillets, about 200g/7oz each, skinned and coarsely flaked

For the dressing
pinch of English (hot) mustard powder
15–20ml/3–4 tsp white wine vinegar
30ml/2 tbsp light olive oil
100ml/3 1/2fl oz/scant 1/2 cup natural (plain) yogurt
about 30ml/2 tbsp grated fresh or bottled horseradish
pinch of caster (superfine) sugar

1 To make the dressing, mix together the mustard powder and vinegar in a bowl, then gradually whisk in the olive oil, yogurt, grated horseradish and sugar. Set aside in a cool place for about 30 minutes.

2 Place the lettuce leaves in a large bowl. Stir the dressing again, then pour half of it over the leaves and toss lightly using two spoons.

3 Arrange the lettuce on four individual plates with the tomatoes, cucumber and trout. Spoon the remaining dressing over the salads and serve immediately.

Cook's Tips
• *The addition of salt to the horseradish salad dressing should not be necessary because of the saltiness of the smoked trout fillets.*
• *Look for natural, uncoloured smoked trout fillets – they should be a delicate cream colour.*

Moroccan Fish Tagine

In Morocco *tagine* is the name of the large cooking pot used for this type of cooking, as well as the name of the dish.

Serves 4
2 garlic cloves, crushed
30ml/2 tbsp ground cumin
30ml/2 tbsp paprika
1 small fresh red chilli, seeded and finely chopped (optional)
30ml/2 tbsp tomato purée (paste)
60ml/4 tbsp lemon juice
4 whiting or cod steaks (about 175g/6oz each)
350g/12oz tomatoes, sliced
2 green (bell) peppers, seeded and thinly sliced
salt and ground black pepper
chopped fresh coriander (cilantro) or flat leaf parsley, to garnish

1 Mix together the garlic, cumin, paprika, chilli, if using, tomato purée and lemon juice in a bowl. Place the fish in a shallow dish and spread this mixture over it. Cover with clear film (plastic wrap) and chill in the refrigerator for about 30 minutes to let the flavours penetrate.

2 Preheat the oven to 200°C/400°F/Gas 6. Arrange half of the tomatoes and peppers in an ovenproof dish.

3 Cover with the fish, then arrange the remaining tomatoes and peppers on top. Cover the dish with foil and bake for about 45 minutes, until the fish is tender. Sprinkle with chopped coriander or parsley to serve.

Cook's Tips
• *Try different white fish in this dish, such as hoki, hake, ling or pollack.*
• *If you are preparing this dish for a dinner party, it can be assembled completely and stored in the refrigerator until you are ready to cook it.*
• *Green (bell) peppers have a pleasing sharpness that goes well with this dish, but if you want to add more colour, substitute a red or yellow pepper for one of the green ones.*

Trout Energy 303kcal/1268kJ; Protein 40.9g; Carbohydrate 4.4g, of which sugars 4.4g; Fat 13.7g, of which saturates 1g; Cholesterol 0mg; Calcium 81mg; Fibre 1g; Sodium 139mg.
Tagine Energy 174kcal/735kJ; Protein 33.7g; Carbohydrate 6.1g, of which sugars 5.9g; Fat 1.8g, of which saturates 0.4g; Cholesterol 81mg; Calcium 32mg; Fibre 2.5g; Sodium 135mg.

Prawn & Mint Salad

Using raw prawns makes all the difference to this salad, as the flavours marinate superbly into the prawns before cooking.

Serves 4
12 large raw prawns (shrimp)
15g/¹/₂ oz/1 tbsp unsalted
 (sweet) butter
15ml/1 tbsp Thai fish sauce
juice of 1 lime

45ml/3 tbsp thin coconut milk
2.5cm/1in piece of fresh root
 ginger, peeled and grated
5ml/1 tsp caster (superfine) sugar
1 garlic clove, crushed
2 fresh red chillies, seeded and
 finely chopped
30ml/2 tbsp fresh mint leaves
ground black pepper
225g/8oz light green lettuce
 leaves, such as round
 (butterhead), to serve

1 Pull off the heads from the prawns and peel them, leaving the tails intact. Make a small cut along the back of each prawn and remove the dark vein with the point of the knife.

2 Melt the butter in a large frying pan over medium heat. Add the prawns and cook, turning and tossing frequently, for about 3 minutes, until they turn pink.

3 Mix the Thai fish sauce, lime juice, coconut milk, ginger, sugar, garlic, chillies and pepper together in a large bowl.

4 Add the warm prawns to the sauce and toss well, then add the mint leaves and toss again.

5 Make a bed of green lettuce leaves on each of four individual plates and divide the prawns and sauce among them. Serve the salads immediately.

Cook's Tip
For a really tropical touch, garnish this flavoursome salad with some shavings of fresh coconut (made using a vegetable peeler) or with grated papaya. Use slightly unripe fruit and peel and remove the seeds before grating.

Mackerel with Tomatoes & Pesto

This rich and oily fish contrasts superbly with the slight sharpness of the tomato sauce. The aromatic pesto is excellent drizzled over the fish.

Serves 4
For the pesto sauce
50g/2oz/¹/₂ cup pine nuts
30ml/2 tbsp fresh basil leaves
2 garlic cloves, crushed

30ml/2 tbsp freshly grated
 Parmesan cheese
150ml/¹/₄ pint/²/₃ cup extra virgin
 olive oil

For the fish
4 fresh mackerel, gutted
30ml/2 tbsp olive oil
115g/4oz onion, coarsely chopped
450g/1lb tomatoes,
 coarsely chopped
salt and ground black pepper

1 To make the pesto sauce, place the pine nuts, basil and garlic cloves in a food processor fitted with a metal blade. Process until the mixture forms a coarse paste. Add the Parmesan cheese and, with the motor still running, gradually add the oil. Set aside in a cool place until required.

2 Preheat the grill (broiler) until very hot. Season the mackerel well with salt and pepper, place on the grill (broiler) rack and cook for 10 minutes on each side.

3 Meanwhile, heat the olive oil in a large, heavy pan over low heat. Add the onion and cook, stirring occasionally, for about 5 minutes, until softened but not coloured.

4 Stir in the tomatoes and cook, stirring occasionally, for 5–10 minutes, until just pulpy. Spoon the tomato mixture on to warmed serving plates, add the fish and top each one with a spoonful of pesto sauce. Serve immediately.

Cook's Tip
The pesto sauce can be made ahead and stored in the refrigerator until needed. Soften it again before using. For red pesto sauce, add some puréed sun-dried tomatoes after the oil.

Prawn Salad Energy 76kcal/319kJ; Protein 9.3g; Carbohydrate 1.5g, of which sugars 1.5g; Fat 3.7g, of which saturates 2.1g; Cholesterol 106mg; Calcium 59mg; Fibre 0.5g; Sodium 132mg.
Mackerel Energy 759kcal/3145kJ; Protein 39.3g; Carbohydrate 6.3g, of which sugars 5.6g; Fat 64.2g, of which saturates 11.6g; Cholesterol 100mg; Calcium 126mg; Fibre 1.8g; Sodium 194mg.

Mackerel with Mustard & Lemon

Mackerel must be really fresh to be enjoyed. Look for bright, firm-fleshed fish with iridescent scales and clear, unsunken eyes.

Serves 4
4 fresh mackerel (about
   275g/10oz each), gutted
175–225g/6–8oz/1¹/₂–2 cups
   spinach
salt and ground black pepper

For the mustard and lemon butter
115g/4oz/¹/₂ cup butter, melted
30ml/2 tbsp wholegrain mustard
grated rind of 1 lemon
30ml/2 tbsp lemon juice
45ml/3 tbsp chopped
   fresh parsley

1 To prepare each mackerel, use a sharp knife to cut off the head just behind the gills, then cut along the belly so that the fish can be opened out flat.

2 Place the fish on a chopping board, skin-side up, and press firmly all along the backbone to loosen it.

3 Turn the fish over and carefully pull the bone away from the flesh. Remove the tail and cut each fish in half lengthways. Rinse under cold running water and pat dry with kitchen paper. Score the skin three or four times, then season the fish all over with salt and pepper. Preheat the grill (broiler).

4 To make the mustard and lemon butter, mix together the melted butter, mustard, lemon rind and juice and parsley. Season with salt and pepper.

5 Place the mackerel on a grill (broiler) rack. Brush a little of the flavoured butter over the mackerel and grill (broil), basting occasionally, for 5 minutes on each side, until cooked through.

6 Arrange the spinach leaves in the centres of four large plates. Place the mackerel on top. Heat the remaining mustard and lemon butter in a small pan until sizzling and pour it over the mackerel. Serve immediately.

Whitebait with Herb Sandwiches

Whitebait are the tiny fry of sprats or herring and are always served whole. Cayenne pepper makes them spicy hot.

Serves 4
unsalted (sweet) butter,
   for spreading
6 slices multigrain bread
90ml/6 tbsp mixed chopped fresh
   herbs, such as parsley, chervil
   and chives
450g/1lb whitebait, thawed
   if frozen
65g/2¹/₂ oz/scant ³/₄ cup plain
   (all-purpose) flour
15ml/1 tbsp chopped
   fresh parsley
salt and cayenne pepper
groundnut (peanut) oil, for
   deep-frying
lemon slices, to garnish

1 Butter the bread slices. Sprinkle the herbs over three of the slices, then top with the remaining slices of bread. Remove the crusts and cut each sandwich into eight triangles. Place them on a plate, cover with clear film (plastic wrap) and set aside in a cool place.

2 Rinse the whitebait thoroughly under cold running water. Drain and then pat dry on kitchen paper.

3 Put the flour, chopped parsley, salt and cayenne pepper in a large plastic bag and shake to mix. Add the whitebait, a few at a time, and toss gently in the seasoned flour, until lightly coated. Heat the oil in a deep-fat fryer or large, heavy pan to 180°C/350°F, or until a cube of day-old bread browns in 30 seconds.

4 Lower the fish into the hot oil, in batches, and cook for 2–3 minutes, until golden and crisp. Lift out of the oil and drain well on kitchen paper. Keep warm in the oven until all the fish are cooked.

5 Sprinkle the whitebait with salt and more cayenne pepper, if you like, and garnish with the lemon slices. Serve immediately with the herb sandwiches.

Mackerel Energy 723kcal/2995kJ; Protein 44.7g; Carbohydrate 1.2g, of which sugars 1.1g; Fat 59.9g, of which saturates 22.5g; Cholesterol 181mg; Calcium 124mg; Fibre 1.4g; Sodium 369mg.
Whitebait Energy 776kcal/3222kJ; Protein 26.7g; Carbohydrate 27.7g, of which sugars 1.8g; Fat 62.9g, of which saturates 10.4g; Cholesterol 21mg; Calcium 1088mg; Fibre 2.3g; Sodium 569mg.

Sole Goujons with Lime Mayonnaise

This simple dish can be rustled up very quickly. It makes an excellent light lunch or supper.

Serves 4
675g/1 1/2lb sole fillets, skinned
2 eggs, beaten
115g/4oz/2 cups fresh
  white breadcrumbs
vegetable oil, for deep-frying
salt and ground black pepper
lime wedges, to serve

For the lime mayonnaise
200ml/7fl oz/scant 1 cup
  mayonnaise
1 small garlic clove, crushed
10ml/2 tsp capers, rinsed
  and chopped
10ml/2 tsp chopped gherkins
finely grated rind of 1/2 lime
10ml/2 tsp lime juice
15ml/1 tbsp chopped fresh
  coriander (cilantro)

1 To make the lime mayonnaise, mix together the mayonnaise, garlic, capers, gherkins, lime rind and juice and chopped coriander in a bowl. Season to taste with salt and pepper. Transfer to a serving bowl, cover with clear film (plastic wrap) and chill in the refrigerator until required.

2 Cut the sole fillets into finger-length strips. Dip them first into the beaten eggs and then into the breadcrumbs.

3 Heat the oil in a deep-fat fryer or large, heavy pan to 180°C/350°F, or until a cube of day-old bread browns in 30 seconds. Add the fish, in batches, and cook until golden and crisp. Remove from the oil and drain well on kitchen paper.

4 Pile the goujons on to warmed serving plates and serve with the lime wedges for squeezing over. Serve the lime mayonnaise separately.

> **Cook's Tip**
> Make sure you use good quality mayonnaise for the sauce, or – better still – make your own. But remember that pregnant women, the elderly and the very young should not eat raw egg.

Spicy Fish Rösti

Serve these delicious fish patties crisp and hot for lunch or supper with a mixed green salad.

Serves 4
350g/12oz large, firm
  waxy potatoes
350g/12oz salmon fillet, skinned
3–4 spring onions (scallions),
  finely chopped
5ml/1 tsp grated fresh root ginger
30ml/2 tbsp chopped fresh
  coriander (cilantro)
10ml/2 tsp lemon juice
30–45ml/2–3 tbsp sunflower oil
salt and cayenne pepper
lemon wedges, to serve
fresh coriander sprigs, to garnish

1 Bring a pan of water to the boil, add the potatoes with their skins on and cook for about 10 minutes. Drain and leave to cool for a few minutes.

2 Meanwhile, finely chop the salmon and place in a bowl. Stir in the spring onions, ginger, chopped coriander and lemon juice. Season to taste with salt and cayenne pepper.

3 When the potatoes are cool enough to handle, peel off the skins and grate the flesh coarsely. Gently stir the grated potato into the fish mixture. Form the mixture into 12 patties, pressing the mixture together but leaving the edges slightly uneven.

4 Heat the oil in a large frying pan over medium heat. Add the fish rösti, a few at a time, and cook for 3 minutes on each side, until golden brown and crisp. Remove from the pan and drain on kitchen paper. Keep warm while you cook the remaining rösti. Serve hot with lemon wedges for squeezing over and garnished with sprigs of fresh coriander.

> **Variation**
> You can also make these tasty patties with cod or coley (pollock) fillet or with a mixture of 225g/8oz white fish fillet and 115g/4 oz salmon fillet.

Sole Energy 978kcal/4047kJ; Protein 26.8g; Carbohydrate 25.2g, of which sugars 2.4g; Fat 86.3g, of which saturates 11.1g; Cholesterol 127mg; Calcium 87mg; Fibre 0.1g; Sodium 546mg.
Rösti Energy 208kcal/870kJ; Protein 17.7g; Carbohydrate 14.4g, of which sugars 1.4g; Fat 9.2g, of which saturates 1.2g; Cholesterol 40mg; Calcium 17mg; Fibre 1g; Sodium 63mg.

Mediterranean Fish Rolls

Sun-dried tomatoes, pine nuts and anchovies make a flavoursome stuffing for the fish.

Serves 4

75g/3oz/6 tbsp butter, plus extra
  for greasing
4 plaice or flounder fillets (about
  225g/8oz each), skinned
1 small onion, chopped
1 celery stick, finely chopped
115g/4oz/2 cups fresh
  white breadcrumbs
45ml/3 tbsp chopped
  fresh parsley
30ml/2 tbsp pine nuts, toasted
3–4 pieces sun-dried tomatoes in
  oil, drained and chopped
50g/2oz can anchovy fillets,
  drained and chopped
75ml/5 tbsp fish stock
ground black pepper

1 Preheat the oven to 180°C/350°F/Gas 4. Grease a shallow, ovenproof dish with butter. Using a sharp knife, cut the fish fillets in half lengthways to make eight smaller fillets.

2 Melt the butter in a heavy pan over low heat. Add the onion and celery, cover with a tight-fitting lid and cook, stirring occasionally, for about 15 minutes, until the vegetables are very soft but not coloured.

3 Mix together the breadcrumbs, parsley, pine nuts, sun-dried tomatoes and anchovies in a bowl. Stir in the softened vegetables with the buttery pan juices and season to taste with pepper.

4 Divide the stuffing into eight equal portions. Taking one portion at a time, form the stuffing into balls, then roll up each one inside a fish fillet. Secure each roll with a wooden cocktail stick (toothpick).

5 Place the rolled-up fillets in the prepared dish. Pour the fish stock over them and cover the dish with buttered foil. Bake for about 20 minutes, or until the fish flakes easily with the point of a sharp knife. Remove and discard the cocktail sticks, transfer the fish rolls to warmed plates, drizzle a little of the cooking juices over them and serve immediately.

Salmon with Watercress Sauce

Adding the watercress right at the end of cooking retains much of its flavour and colour.

Serves 4

300ml/½ pint/1¼ cups crème
  fraîche
30ml/2 tbsp chopped
  fresh tarragon
25g/1oz/2 tbsp butter
15ml/1 tbsp sunflower oil
4 salmon fillets, skinned
1 garlic clove, crushed
120ml/4fl oz/½ cup dry
  white wine
1 bunch of watercress or
  rocket (arugula)
salt and ground black pepper
mixed lettuce salad, to
  serve (optional)

1 Gently heat the crème fraîche in a small pan until just it is beginning to boil. Remove the pan from the heat and stir in half the tarragon. Leave the herb cream to infuse (steep) while cooking the fish.

2 Heat the butter and oil in a heavy frying pan over medium heat. Add the salmon fillets and cook for 3–5 minutes on each side. Remove them from the pan and keep warm.

3 Add the garlic to the pan and cook for 1 minute, then pour in the wine and leave it to bubble until it has reduced to about 15ml/1 tbsp.

4 Meanwhile, strip the leaves off the watercress stalks and chop them finely. Discard any damaged leaves. (Save the watercress stalks for soup, if you like.) If using rocket, trim the stems and chop the leaves finely.

5 Strain the herb cream into the frying pan and cook, stirring constantly, for a few minutes, until the sauce has thickened. Stir in the remaining tarragon and watercress or rocket, then cook for a few minutes, until the leaves have wilted but are still bright green. Season to taste with salt and pepper. Place the salmon fillets on warmed plates, spoon the sauce over them and serve immediately. The dish may be accompanied by a mixed lettuce salad if you like.

Fish Rolls Energy 528kcal/2213kJ; Protein 45.9g; Carbohydrate 24.6g, of which sugars 2.8g; Fat 28.1g, of which saturates 11g; Cholesterol 142mg; Calcium 189mg; Fibre 1.3g; Sodium 1100mg.
Salmon 743kcal/3078kJ; Protein 43.3g; Carbohydrate 2.2g, of which sugars 2g; Fat 60.3g, of which saturates 27.8g; Cholesterol 198mg; Calcium 153mg; Fibre 0.6g; Sodium 164mg.

Warm Salmon Salad

This light salad is perfect in summer. Serve it as soon as it is ready, or the salad leaves will lose their colour.

Serves 4
450g/1lb salmon fillet
30ml/2 tbsp sesame oil
grated rind of 1/2 orange
juice of 1 orange
5ml/1 tsp Dijon mustard
15ml/1 tbsp chopped
 fresh tarragon

45ml/3 tbsp groundnut
 (peanut) oil
115g/4oz fine green beans,
 trimmed
175g/6oz mixed salad leaves,
 such as young spinach leaves,
 radicchio and frisée
15ml/1 tbsp toasted sesame
 seeds
salt and ground black pepper

1 Skin the salmon fillet, if this has not already been done by your fish supplier, and cut the flesh into bitesize pieces with a sharp knife. Set aside.

2 To make the dressing, mix together the sesame oil, orange rind and juice, mustard and chopped tarragon in a bowl and season to taste with salt and ground black pepper. Set aside.

3 Heat the groundnut oil in a heavy frying pan over medium heat. Add the pieces of salmon and cook, stirring occasionally, for 3–4 minutes, or until lightly browned on the outside but still tender on the inside.

4 While the salmon is cooking, blanch the green beans in a pan of boiling salted water for 5–6 minutes, until tender but still slightly crisp.

5 Add the dressing to the salmon, toss together gently and cook for 30 seconds. Remove the pan from the heat.

6 Arrange the salad leaves on serving plates. Drain the beans and toss them over the leaves. Spoon the salmon and its cooking juices over the top, sprinkle with the toasted sesame seeds and serve immediately.

Red Mullet with Fennel

The delicately flavoured, almost sweet flesh of the fish is beautifully complemented by the aniseed-like taste of fennel.

Serves 4
3 small fennel bulbs
60ml/4 tbsp olive oil

2 small onions, sliced
2–4 fresh basil leaves
4 small or 2 large red mullet or
 snapper, gutted
grated rind of 1/2 lemon
150ml/1/4 pint/2/3 cup fish stock
50g/2oz/4 tbsp butter
juice of 1 lemon

1 Snip off the feathery fronds from the fennel bulbs, finely chop and reserve them for the garnish. Cut the fennel bulb into wedges, being careful to leave the layers attached at the root ends so that the pieces stay intact.

2 Heat the oil in a frying pan large enough to take the fish in a single layer. Add the wedges of fennel and the onions and cook over low heat, stirring occasionally, for 10–15 minutes, until softened and lightly browned.

3 Tuck a basil leaf inside the cavity of each fish, then place them on top of the vegetables. Sprinkle the lemon rind on top. Increase the heat to medium, pour in the stock and bring just to the boil. Lower the heat, cover with a tight-fitting lid and poach gently for 15–20 minutes, until the fish is tender.

4 Melt the butter in a small pan and, when it starts to sizzle and colour slightly, add the lemon juice. Pour the flavoured butter over the fish, sprinkle with the reserved fennel fronds and serve immediately.

Cook's Tip
Other fish with fine-flavoured flesh may also be cooked this way. These include sea bass, sea bream, porgy and goatfish. It's best to trim the fins of all types and it is essential with those that have sharp spines.

Salmon Energy 362kcal/1499kJ; Protein 24.3g; Carbohydrate 1.7g, of which sugars 1.4g; Fat 28.7g, of which saturates 5g; Cholesterol 56mg; Calcium 72mg; Fibre 1.3g; Sodium 53mg.
Red Mullet Energy 330kcal/1369kJ; Protein 20.7g; Carbohydrate 4.3g, of which sugars 3.6g; Fat 25.8g, of which saturates 8.1g; Cholesterol 27mg; Calcium 111mg; Fibre 3.4g; Sodium 190mg.

Sautéed Salmon with Cucumber

Cucumber is the classic accompaniment to salmon. Here it is served hot, but be careful not to overcook it.

Serves 4
450g/1lb salmon fillet
40g/1½oz/3 tbsp butter
2 spring onions (scallions), chopped
½ cucumber, seeded and cut into strips
60ml/4 tbsp dry white wine
120ml/4fl oz/½ cup crème fraîche
30ml/2 tbsp chopped fresh chives
2 tomatoes, peeled, seeded and diced
salt and ground black pepper

1 Skin the salmon fillet, if this has not already been done by your fish supplier. Using a very sharp knife cut the flesh into about 12 thin slices, then cut across into strips.

2 Melt the butter in a large frying pan over medium-low heat. Add the salmon and cook, stirring occasionally, for 1–2 minutes. Remove the salmon strips using a slotted spoon and set aside.

3 Add the spring onions to the pan and cook for 2 minutes. Stir in the cucumber and sauté for 1–2 minutes, until hot. Remove the cucumber and keep warm with the salmon.

4 Add the wine to the pan and let it bubble until well reduced. Stir in the cucumber, crème fraîche and half the chives and season to taste with salt and pepper. Return the salmon to the pan and warm through gently. Sprinkle the tomatoes and remaining chives over the top. Serve immediately.

> **Cook's Tip**
> *To skin a fish fillet, place it on a chopping board with the tail end towards you. Hold a sharp knife at an angle down towards the skin. Cut between the skin and the flesh, keeping the blade as close to the skin as possible. As the flesh is cut away, grasp the skin firmly with your other hand and continue cutting. A little salt sprinkled on your fingers makes this task less slippery.*

Tuna with Pan-fried Tomatoes

Meaty and filling tuna steaks are served here with juicy tomatoes and black olives.

Serves 2
2 tuna steaks (about 175g/6oz each)
90ml/6 tbsp olive oil
30ml/2 tbsp lemon juice
2 garlic cloves, chopped
5ml/1 tsp chopped fresh thyme
4 canned anchovy fillets, drained and chopped
225g/8oz plum tomatoes, halved
30ml/2 tbsp chopped fresh parsley
4–6 black olives, pitted and chopped
pinch of ground black pepper
crusty bread, to serve

1 Place the tuna steaks in a shallow, non-metallic dish. Mix 60ml/4 tbsp of the oil with the lemon juice, garlic, thyme, anchovies and black pepper in a jug (pitcher). Pour this mixture over the tuna, cover and leave to marinate for at least 1 hour.

2 Preheat the grill (broiler). Lift the tuna from the marinade and place on a grill (broiler) rack. Grill (broil) for 4 minutes on each side, or until the tuna feels firm to touch, basting with the marinade. Take care not to overcook.

3 Meanwhile, heat the remaining oil in a frying pan and cook the tomatoes for a maximum of 2 minutes on each side.

4 Divide the tomatoes equally between two serving plates and sprinkle the chopped parsley and olives over them. Top each with a tuna steak.

5 Add the remaining marinade to the pan juices and warm through. Pour over the tomatoes and tuna steaks and serve immediately with crusty bread for mopping up the juices.

> **Cook's Tip**
> *If you are unable to find fresh tuna steaks, you could replace them with salmon fillets, if you like – just grill (broil) them for one or two minutes more on each side.*

Tuna Energy 757kcal/3135kJ; Protein 32.8g; Carbohydrate 4.8g, of which sugars 4.5g; Fat 67.7g, of which saturates 18.8g; Cholesterol 130mg; Calcium 93mg; Fibre 2.4g; Sodium 1138mg.
Salmon Energy 412kcal/1709kJ; Protein 24.1g; Carbohydrate 3g, of which sugars 2.8g; Fat 32.8g, of which saturates 15.5g; Cholesterol 111mg; Calcium 54mg; Fibre 0.7g; Sodium 124mg.

Crunchy-topped Cod

It's easy to forget just how tasty and satisfying a simple, classic dish can be.

Serves 4

4 pieces cod fillet (about
    115g/4oz each), skinned
2 tomatoes, sliced

50g/2oz/1 cup fresh wholemeal
    (whole-wheat) breadcrumbs
30ml/2 tbsp chopped
    fresh parsley
finely grated rind and juice of
    ½ lemon
5ml/1 tsp sunflower oil
salt and ground black pepper

1 Preheat the oven to 200°C/400°F/Gas 6. Arrange the cod fillets in a wide, ovenproof dish.

2 Arrange the tomato slices on top. Mix together the breadcrumbs, fresh parsley, lemon rind and juice and the oil in a bowl. Season to taste with salt and pepper.

3 Spoon the crumb mixture evenly over the fish, then bake for 15–20 minutes. Serve immediately.

Cook's Tip
Over-fishing of cod – and some other members of the cod family – has reached a critical level in many parts of the world with the result that some stocks have been completely fished-out. Conservation initiatives are having some remedial effect, so it is strongly advised to check that the cod we are buying comes from a sustainable source. Otherwise, we may lose this useful fish with its lovely, white flaky flesh. Other members of the cod family that have not been so popular in recent decades are becoming increasingly available and some would make very acceptable substitutes in this dish. For example, coley, known as pollock in the United States, has a good flavour but is a rather unappealing greyish colour. However, the crunchy topping in this recipe overcomes this drawback. The various types of ling also have a good flavour and a firm texture and this is also true of another lesser known cousin of cod called pollack (not to be confused with pollock).

Fish Balls in Tomato Sauce

This quick meal is a good choice for young children, as there are no bones.

Serves 4

450g/1lb hoki or other white fish
    fillets, skinned
60ml/4 tbsp fresh wholemeal
    (whole-wheat) breadcrumbs

30ml/2 tbsp chopped chives or
    spring onion (scallion)
400g/14oz can chopped
    tomatoes
50g/2oz button (white)
    mushrooms, sliced
salt and ground black pepper

1 Cut the fish fillets into chunks; place in a food processor. Add the breadcrumbs, chives or spring onion. Season and process until the fish is chopped, but still with some texture. Divide the fish mixture into about 16 even-sized pieces, then mould them into balls with your hands.

2 Place the tomatoes and mushrooms in a pan; cook over medium heat until boiling. Add the fish balls, cover and simmer for about 10 minutes until cooked. Serve hot.

Tuna & Corn Fish Cakes

These economical tuna fish cakes are quick to make.

Serves 4

300g/11oz/1½ cups mashed
    potato
200g/7oz can tuna, drained

115g/4oz/½ cup canned
    corn, drained
30ml/2 tbsp chopped
    fresh parsley
50g/2oz/1 cup fresh
    breadcrumbs
salt and ground black pepper

1 Place the mashed potato in a bowl and stir in the tuna, corn and parsley. Season to taste and shape into eight patties.

2 Press the fish cakes into the breadcrumbs to coat them lightly, then place on a baking sheet. Grill (broil) under medium heat until crisp and golden, turning once. Serve immediately.

Cod Energy 160kcal/674kJ; Protein 24.7g; Carbohydrate 11.3g, of which sugars 1.9g; Fat 2g, of which saturates 0.3g; Cholesterol 58mg; Calcium 31mg; Fibre 0.8g; Sodium 175mg.
Fish Balls Energy 167kcal/709kJ; Protein 21.7g; Carbohydrate 14.8g, of which sugars 3.5g; Fat 2.8g, of which saturates 0.5g; Cholesterol 0mg; Calcium 44mg; Fibre 1.5g; Sodium 221mg.
Fish Cakes Energy 231kcal/976kJ; Protein 17.5g; Carbohydrate 29.8g, of which sugars 4.4g; Fat 5.5g, of which saturates 0.9g; Cholesterol 25mg; Calcium 53mg; Fibre 2.1g; Sodium 330mg.

Cod Creole

Inspired by the cuisine of the Caribbean, this lightly spiced fish dish is both colourful and delicious, as well as being quick and easy to prepare.

Serves 4

450g/1lb cod fillets
15ml/1 tbsp lime or lemon juice
10ml/2 tsp olive oil
1 onion, finely chopped
1 green (bell) pepper, seeded and sliced
2.5ml/½ tsp cayenne pepper
2.5ml/½ tsp garlic salt
425g/14oz can chopped tomatoes
boiled rice or potatoes, to serve

1 Skin the cod fillets if this has not already been done by your fish supplier, then cut the flesh into bitesize chunks and sprinkle with the lime or lemon juice.

2 Heat the oil in a large, non-stick frying pan over low heat. Add the onion and green pepper and cook, stirring occasionally, for about 5 minutes, until softened. Add the cayenne pepper and garlic salt.

3 Stir in the cod and the chopped tomatoes, increase the heat to medium and bring to the boil. Lower the heat, cover and simmer for about 5 minutes, or until the fish flakes easily. Transfer the fish and sauce to warmed plates and serve immediately with boiled rice or potatoes.

> **Cook's Tip**
> *This flavoursome dish is surprisingly light in calories and low in fat, so if you are worried about your waistline or conscientious about a healthy diet, this would be an excellent choice. In addition, (bell) peppers are a good source of vitamin C, while tomatoes are rich in the antioxidant lycopene, which is thought to lower the risk of some cancers. Processed and cooked tomatoes – in this case, canned tomatoes – are an even richer source because processing or cooking them makes it easier for the body to absorb lycopene.*

Salmon Pasta with Parsley Sauce

The parsley sauce is prepared and added at the last moment to the salmon mixture and does not have to be cooked separately.

Serves 4

450g/1lb salmon fillet
225g/8oz/2 cups pasta, such as penne
175g/6oz cherry tomatoes, halved
150ml/¼ pint/⅔ cup crème fraîche or sour cream
45ml/3 tbsp finely chopped fresh parsley
finely grated rind of ½ orange
salt and ground black pepper

1 Skin the salmon if this has not already been done by your fish supplier and cut the flesh into bitesize pieces. Spread out the pieces of fish on a heatproof plate and cover with foil.

2 Bring a large pan of salted water to the boil, add the pasta and bring back to the boil. Place the plate of salmon on top of the pan and cook for 10–12 minutes, until the pasta is just tender and the salmon is cooked.

3 Set the plate of salmon aside, then drain the pasta and return it to the pan. Add the tomatoes and salmon to the pasta and toss well.

4 Mix together the crème fraîche or sour cream, parsley and orange rind in a bowl and season with pepper to taste. Add the parsley sauce to the salmon and pasta, toss again and serve hot or leave to cool to room temperature.

> **Variations**
> *• Sea trout, also known as salmon trout, would also be beautifully complemented by the parsley sauce in this recipe. Other, perhaps less obvious substitutes could be gurnard (US sea robin) fillets.*
> *• You could also try using trout fillets and substitute grated lemon rind for the orange.*

Cod Energy 144kcal/607kJ; Protein 22.1g; Carbohydrate 7.9g, of which sugars 7.4g; Fat 2.9g, of which saturates 0.5g; Cholesterol 52mg; Calcium 26mg; Fibre 2.2g; Sodium 81mg.
Salmon Energy 469kcal/1971kJ; Protein 31.2g; Carbohydrate 45.4g, of which sugars 5g; Fat 19.3g, of which saturates 6.1g; Cholesterol 56mg; Calcium 100mg; Fibre 2.8g; Sodium 75mg.

Monkfish with Mexican Salsa

It is rare to see whole monkfish on sale generally, as only the tail is eaten. Apart from its delicious flavour and meaty texture, the tail has the advantage of having no pinbones.

Serves 4
675g/1½lb monkfish tail
45ml/3 tbsp olive oil
30ml/2 tbsp lime juice
1 garlic clove, crushed
15ml/1 tbsp chopped fresh
  coriander (cilantro)
salt and ground black pepper
fresh coriander sprigs and lime
  slices, to garnish

For the salsa
4 tomatoes, seeded, peeled
  and diced
1 avocado, stoned (pitted), peeled
  and diced
½ red onion, chopped
1 green chilli, seeded
  and chopped
30ml/2 tbsp chopped
  fresh coriander
30ml/2 tbsp olive oil
15ml/1 tbsp lime juice

1 To make the salsa, mix all the salsa ingredients and leave to stand at room temperature for about 40 minutes.

2 Prepare the monkfish. Using a sharp knife, remove the pinkish-grey membrane. Cut the fillets from either side of the backbone, then cut each fillet in half to give four steaks.

3 Mix together the oil, lime juice, garlic and coriander in a shallow non-metallic dish and season with salt and pepper. Turn the monkfish several times to coat with the marinade, then cover the dish and leave to marinate in a cool place or in the refrigerator, for 30 minutes. Preheat the grill (broiler).

4 Remove the monkfish from the marinade and grill (broil) for 10–12 minutes, turning once and brushing frequently with the marinade until cooked through.

5 Serve the monkfish garnished with coriander sprigs and lime slices and accompanied by the salsa.

Seafood Crêpes

The combination of fresh and smoked haddock imparts a wonderful flavour to the crêpe filling.

Serves 4–6
12 ready-made crêpes
melted butter, for brushing

For the filling
225g/8oz smoked haddock fillet
225g/8oz fresh haddock fillet

300ml/½ pint/1¼ cups milk
150ml/¼ pint/⅔ cup single
  (light) cream
40g/1½oz/3 tbsp butter
40g/1½oz/3 tbsp plain (all-
  purpose) flour
pinch of freshly grated nutmeg
2 hard-boiled eggs, shelled
  and chopped
salt and ground black pepper
sprinkling of Gruyère cheese and
  curly salad leaves, to serve

1 To make the filling, put the smoked and fresh haddock fillets in a large pan, add the milk and bring just to the boil. Lower the heat, cover and poach for 6–8 minutes, until just tender. Lift out the fish with a slotted spoon and, when cool enough to handle, remove the skin and bones. Reserve the milk. Pour the cream into a measuring jug (cup), then strain enough milk into the jug to make it up to 450ml/¾ pint/scant 2 cups.

2 Melt the butter in a pan over low heat. Stir in the flour and cook, stirring constantly, for 1 minute. Gradually add the milk mixture, stirring constantly to make a smooth sauce. Cook for 2–3 minutes. Season to taste with salt, pepper and nutmeg. Flake the haddock and fold into the sauce with the eggs. Remove the pan from the heat and leave to cool.

3 Preheat the oven to 180°C/350°F/Gas 4. Divide the filling among the crêpes. Fold the sides of each crêpe into the centre, then roll them up to enclose the filling completely. Brush four or six individual ovenproof dishes with melted butter and arrange two or three filled crêpes in each, or grease one large dish for all the crêpes. Brush the crêpes with melted butter and cook for 15 minutes.

4 Sprinkle over the Gruyère and cook for a further 5 minutes. Serve hot with a few curly salad leaves.

Monkfish Energy 320kcal/1335kJ; Protein 31g; Carbohydrate 4.9g, of which sugars 4.2g; Fat 19.6g, of which saturates 3.3g; Cholesterol 27mg; Calcium 36mg; Fibre 2.3g; Sodium 46mg.
Seafood Energy 567kcal/2373kJ; Protein 24.9g; Carbohydrate 47.8g, of which sugars 20.1g; Fat 32.1g, of which saturates 7.1g; Cholesterol 118mg; Calcium 188mg; Fibre 1.2g; Sodium 445mg.

Herbed Fish Croquettes

Deep-fry with clean oil every time as the fish will flavour the oil and taint any other foods later fried in it.

Serves 4
450g/1lb plaice or flounder fillets
300ml/½ pint/1¼ cups milk
450g/1lb cooked potatoes
1 fennel bulb, finely chopped
1 garlic clove, finely chopped
45ml/3 tbsp chopped
   fresh parsley
2 eggs
15g/½oz/1 tbsp unsalted
   (sweet) butter
225g/8oz/2 cups white
   breadcrumbs
30ml/2 tbsp sesame seeds
vegetable oil, for deep-frying
salt and ground black pepper

1 Put the fish fillets in a large pan, add the milk and bring just to the boil. Lower the heat, cover and poach gently for about 15 minutes, until the fish flakes easily with the tip of a knife. Remove the fillets with a slotted spoon and set aside until cool enough to handle. Reserve the milk.

2 Remove the skin and any bones from the fish and coarsely flake the flesh. Put the fish, potatoes, fennel, garlic, parsley, eggs and butter in a food processor fitted with a metal blade and process until thoroughly combined.

3 Add 30ml/2 tbsp of the reserved cooking milk, season to taste with salt and pepper and process briefly again.

4 Scrape the fish mixture into a bowl, cover with clear film (plastic wrap) and chill in the refrigerator for about 30 minutes.

5 Using your hands shape the fish mixture into 20 croquettes. Mix together the breadcrumbs and sesame seeds on a shallow plate. Roll the croquettes in the breadcrumb mixture to form a good coating.

6 Heat the oil in a large heavy pan to 180°C/350°F, or until a cube of day-old bread browns in 30 seconds. Deep-fry the croquettes, in batches, for about 4 minutes until golden brown. Drain well on kitchen paper and serve immediately.

Mixed Smoked Fish Kedgeree

An ideal breakfast dish on a cold weekend morning and a classic for brunch. Garnish with quartered hard-boiled eggs and season well.

Serves 6
450g/1lb mixed smoked fish
   such as smoked cod, smoked
   haddock and smoked mussels
   or oysters
300ml/½ pint/1¼ cups milk
175g/6oz/scant 1 cup long
   grain rice
1 slice of lemon
50g/2oz/4 tbsp butter
5ml/1 tsp medium-hot
   curry powder
2.5ml/½ tsp freshly
   grated nutmeg
15ml/1 tbsp chopped
   fresh parsley
salt and ground black pepper
2 hard-boiled eggs, to garnish

1 Put the fish, but not the shellfish, in a large pan, add the milk and bring just to the boil. Lower the heat, cover and poach for 10 minutes, or until it flakes easily with the tip of a knife.

2 Remove the fish with a slotted spoon and set aside until cool enough to handle. Discard the milk. Remove the skin and any bones from the fish and flake the flesh. Mix with the smoked shellfish in a bowl and set aside.

3 Bring a pan of salted water to the boil, add the rice and slice of lemon and boil for 10 minutes, or according to the instructions on the packet, until just tender. Drain well and discard the lemon.

4 Melt the butter in a large frying pan and add the rice and fish. Shake the pan to mix all the ingredients together.

5 Stir in the curry powder, nutmeg, parsley and seasoning. Serve immediately, garnished with quartered eggs.

Cook's Tip
When flaking the fish, keep the pieces fairly large to give the dish a chunky consistency.

Croquettes Energy 625kcal/2627kJ; Protein 35.9g; Carbohydrate 63.3g, of which sugars 4.3g; Fat 27.3g, of which saturates 5.8g; Cholesterol 246mg; Calcium 252mg; Fibre 4.6g; Sodium 681mg.
Kedgeree Energy 250kcal/1044kJ; Protein 17.7g; Carbohydrate 25.8g, of which sugars 2.5g; Fat 8.3g, of which saturates 5g; Cholesterol 55mg; Calcium 79mg; Fibre 0.1g; Sodium 950mg.

Spanish-style Hake

Hugely popular in Spain, hake is an unfairly neglected fish in many other countries.

Serves 4

30ml/2 tbsp olive oil
25g/1oz/2 tbsp butter
1 onion, chopped
3 garlic cloves, crushed
15g/¹⁄₂oz/1 tbsp plain (all-purpose) flour
2.5ml/¹⁄₂ tsp paprika
4 hake steaks (about 175g/6oz each)

250g/8oz fine green beans, cut into 2.5cm/1in lengths
350ml/12fl oz/1¹⁄₂ cups fresh fish stock
150ml/¹⁄₄ pint/²⁄₃ cup dry white wine
30ml/2 tbsp dry sherry
15–20 live mussels, scrubbed and debearded
45ml/3 tbsp chopped fresh parsley
salt and ground black pepper
crusty bread, to serve

1 Heat the oil and butter in a sauté or frying pan over low heat. Add the onion and cook, stirring occasionally, for about 5 minutes, until softened but not coloured. Add the garlic and cook for 1 minute more.

2 Mix together the flour and paprika, then lightly dust the hake with the mixture, shaking off any excess. Push the sautéed onion and garlic to one side of the pan.

3 Add the hake steaks to the pan and cook until golden on both sides. Stir in the beans, stock, wine and sherry and season to taste with salt and pepper. Bring to the boil and cook for about 2 minutes.

4 Discard any mussels with broken shells or that do not shut immediately when sharply tapped. Add the mussels and parsley to the pan, cover with a tight-fitting lid and cook for 5–8 minutes, until the mussels have opened. Discard any mussels that have remained closed.

5 Divide the hake, mussels and vegetables among warmed, shallow soup bowls and serve immediately with crusty bread to mop up the juices.

Fish Goujons

Any white fish fillets can be used to make these goujons – you could try a mixture of haddock and cod.

Serves 4

60ml/4 tbsp mayonnaise
30ml/2 tbsp natural (plain) yogurt
grated rind of ¹⁄₂ lemon
squeeze of lemon juice
15ml/1 tbsp chopped fresh parsley
15ml/1 tbsp capers, drained and chopped

2 sole fillets (about 175g/6oz each)
2 plaice or flounder fillets (about 175g/6oz each)
1 egg
115g/4oz/2 cups fresh white breadcrumbs
15ml/1 tbsp sesame seeds
pinch of paprika
vegetable oil, for deep-frying
salt and ground black pepper
watercress or mizuna, to garnish
4 lemon wedges, to serve

1 To make the lemon mayonnaise, mix the mayonnaise, yogurt, lemon rind and juice, parsley and capers in a bowl. Cover with clear film (plastic wrap) and chill until required.

2 Skin the fish fillets if this has not already been done by your fish supplier and cut them into thin strips with a sharp knife.

3 Lightly beat the egg in a shallow bowl with a fork. Mix together the breadcrumbs, sesame seeds and paprika in another shallow bowl and season with salt and pepper.

4 Dip the fish strips, one at a time, first into the beaten egg, then into the breadcrumb mixture and toss until coated evenly. Lay on a clean plate.

5 Heat about 2.5cm/1in of vegetable oil in a frying pan to 180°C/350°F, or until a cube of day-old bread browns in 30 seconds. Add the fish strips, in batches, and cook for 2–3 minutes, until lightly golden brown all over.

6 Remove with a slotted spoon, drain on kitchen paper and keep warm while frying the remainder. Garnish with watercress or mizuna. Serve with lemon wedges and lemon mayonnaise.

Hake Energy 338kcal/1409kJ; Protein 35.6g; Carbohydrate 6.9g, of which sugars 2.7g; Fat 15.2g, of which saturates 4.7g; Cholesterol 62mg; Calcium 68mg; Fibre 1.7g; Sodium 264mg.
Goujons Energy 482kcal/1997kJ; Protein 8.1g; Carbohydrate 24.5g, of which sugars 1.6g; Fat 39.7g, of which saturates 4.9g; Cholesterol 31mg; Calcium 126mg; Fibre 0.1g; Sodium 486mg.

Pan-fried Garlic Sardines

Lightly fry a sliced garlic clove to garnish the fish. This dish could also be made with sprats or fresh anchovies, if available.

4 garlic cloves
finely grated rind of 2 lemons
30ml/2 tbsp chopped
  fresh parsley
salt and ground black pepper

Serves 4
1.2kg/2¹/₂lb fresh sardines
30ml/2 tbsp olive oil

For the tomato bread
8 slices crusty bread, toasted
2 large ripe beefsteak tomatoes

1 First, scale the sardines. Hold each fish by the tail under cold running water and run your other hand all along the body from tail to head to scrape off the scales. Cut off the fish heads if you like. Slit open the belly of each fish, using a sharp knife, and remove the guts with your fingers. Rinse the body cavities well under cold running water and pat dry with kitchen paper.

2 Heat the olive oil in a heavy frying pan over medium-low heat. Add the garlic cloves and cook, stirring frequently, for 1–2 minutes, until softened.

3 Add the sardines to the pan and cook, turning once, for 4–5 minutes until light golden brown. Sprinkle the lemon rind and parsley over the fish and season to taste with salt and black pepper.

4 Cut the tomatoes in half and rub them on to the toast. Discard the skins. Serve the sardines with the tomato toast.

Cook's Tips
• *Scaling the sardines is, without question, a very messy and time-consuming business. However, the fish are so much nicer to eat when scaled that it is worth the effort. (Clear the discarded scales from the sink afterwards.)*
• *Make sure you use very ripe beefsteak tomatoes for this dish so they will rub on to the toast easily.*

Sea Bass en Papillote

Bring the unopened parcels to the table and let your guests uncover their own fish to release the delicious aroma of this dish.

Serves 4
4 small sea bass, scaled, gutted
  and with fins trimmed

130g/4¹/₂oz/generous
  ¹/₂ cup butter
450g/1lb spinach, coarse
  stalks removed
3 shallots, finely chopped
60ml/4 tbsp white wine
4 bay leaves
salt and ground black pepper

1 Preheat the oven to 180°C/350°F/Gas 4. Season both the inside and outside of the fish with salt and pepper.

2 Melt 50g/2oz/4 tbsp of the butter in a large, heavy pan over low heat. Add the spinach and cook gently, turning once or twice, until the spinach has broken down into a smooth purée. Remove from the heat and set aside to cool.

3 Melt another 50g/2oz/4 tbsp of the butter in a clean pan over low heat. Add the shallots and cook, stirring occasionally, for 5 minutes, until soft. Add to the spinach and leave to cool, then divide the spinach mixture among the cavities of the fish.

4 For each fish, fold a large sheet of greaseproof (waxed) paper in half, lay the fish on one half and cut around it to make a heart shape when opened out. The paper should be at least 5cm/2in larger all round than the fish. Remove the fish from the paper hearts.

5 Melt the remaining butter and brush a little on to the paper. Replace the fish and add 15ml/1 tbsp wine and a bay leaf to each parcel. Fold the other side of the paper over the fish and make small pleats to seal the two edges, starting at the curve of the heart. Brush the outsides with butter.

6 Transfer the parcels to a baking sheet and bake for 20–25 minutes, until the parcels are brown. Lift the parcels on to warmed plates with a metal spatula and serve immediately.

Sardines Energy 513kcal/2149kJ; Protein 47.4g; Carbohydrate 27.9g, of which sugars 4.5g; Fat 24.1g, of which saturates 5.8g; Cholesterol 0mg; Calcium 279mg; Fibre 2g; Sodium 504mg.
Sea Bass Energy 446kcal/1850kJ; Protein 35.2g; Carbohydrate 2.3g, of which sugars 2.1g; Fat 31.8g, of which saturates 17.7g; Cholesterol 201mg; Calcium 414mg; Fibre 2.4g; Sodium 469mg.

Scallops with Ginger

Scallops are at their best in winter. Rich and creamy, this dish is very simple to make and quite delicious.

Serves 4
8–12 shelled scallops
40g/1½oz/3 tbsp butter
2.5cm/1in piece fresh root ginger, finely chopped
1 bunch of spring onions (scallions), sliced diagonally
60ml/4 tbsp white vermouth
250ml/8fl oz/1 cup crème fraîche
salt and ground black pepper
chopped fresh parsley, to garnish

1 Remove the white muscle opposite the coral on each scallop if this has not already been done by your supplier. Separate the coral from the white part and cut the white part of the scallop in half horizontally. Reserve the corals.

2 Melt the butter in a frying pan over medium heat. Add the scallops, including the corals, and sauté for about 2 minutes until lightly browned. Take care not to overcook the scallops as this will toughen them.

3 Lift out the scallops with a slotted spoon and transfer to a warmed serving dish. Keep warm.

4 Add the ginger and spring onions to the pan and stir-fry for 2 minutes. Pour in the vermouth and leave to bubble until it has almost evaporated. Stir in the crème fraîche and cook for a few minutes until the sauce has thickened. Season to taste with salt and pepper.

5 Pour the sauce over the scallops, sprinkle with parsley and serve immediately.

Chilli Prawns

This delightful, spicy combination makes a lovely light main course for an informal supper.

Serves 3–4
45ml/3 tbsp olive oil
2 shallots, chopped
2 garlic cloves, chopped
1 fresh red chilli, chopped
450g/1lb ripe tomatoes, peeled, seeded and chopped
15ml/1 tbsp tomato purée (paste)
1 bay leaf
1 fresh thyme sprig
90ml/6 tbsp dry white wine
450g/1lb/4 cups cooked peeled large prawns (shrimp)
salt and ground black pepper
coarsely torn fresh basil leaves, to garnish

1 Heat the olive oil in a pan over low heat. Add the shallots, garlic and chilli and cook, stirring occasionally, for about 5 minutes, until the shallots have softened and the garlic starts to brown.

2 Increase the heat to medium, add the tomatoes, tomato purée, bay leaf, thyme sprig and wine and season to taste with salt and pepper. Bring to the boil, then lower the heat and simmer gently, stirring occasionally, for about 10 minutes, until the sauce has thickened. Remove and discard the bay leaf and thyme sprig.

3 Stir the prawns into the sauce and heat through for a few minutes. Taste and adjust the seasoning if necessary. Sprinkle the basil leaves over the top and serve immediately.

Cook's Tip
The orange-coloured coral of the scallop is the roe and this, with the round, white adductor muscle, this comprises the edible part. In Europe the coral is regarded as a delicacy, although in the United States it is usually discarded.

Cook's Tip
Avoid buying frozen cooked prawns (shrimp), if possible, as they often have a soggy texture and poor flavour, especially if they have been peeled before freezing. If freshly cooked prawns are not available, then consider using raw prawns and cook them in the sauce a little longer or pan-fry or boil them until they change colour before adding them in step 3.

Prawns Energy 202kcal/845kJ; Protein 21g; Carbohydrate 5.4g, of which sugars 5g; Fat 9.3g, of which saturates 1.4g; Cholesterol 219mg; Calcium 104mg; Fibre 1.5g; Sodium 234mg.
Scallops Energy 392kcal/1621kJ; Protein 13.6g; Carbohydrate 4.5g, of which sugars 2.5g; Fat 34.1g, of which saturates 22.4g; Cholesterol 115mg; Calcium 63mg; Fibre 0.4g; Sodium 168mg.

Cod with Spiced Red Lentils

This is a very tasty, filling and economical dish, with the added bonus of being a healthy option.

Serves 4

175g/6oz/³/₄ cup red lentils
1.25ml/¹/₄ tsp ground turmeric
600ml/1 pint/2¹/₂ cups fish stock
450g/1lb cod fillets
30ml/2 tbsp vegetable oil
7.5ml/1¹/₂ tsp cumin seeds
15ml/1 tbsp grated fresh
   root ginger
2.5ml/¹/₂ tsp cayenne pepper
15ml/1 tbsp lemon or lime juice
30ml/2 tbsp chopped fresh
   coriander (cilantro)
pinch of salt, to taste
fresh coriander leaves and lemon
   or lime wedges, to garnish

1 Put the lentils in a pan with the turmeric and fish stock. Bring to the boil, then lower the heat, cover with a tight-fitting lid and simmer for 20–25 minutes, until the lentils are just tender. Remove from the heat, season with salt and set aside.

2 Meanwhile, skin the cod fillets if this has not already been done by your supplier and cut the flesh into large chunks with a sharp knife. Place the pieces on a plate, cover with clear film (plastic wrap) and store in the refrigerator until required.

3 Heat the oil in a small, heavy frying pan over medium-low heat. Add the cumin seeds and cook, stirring occasionally, until they begin to pop and give off their aroma, then add the grated ginger and cayenne pepper. Stir-fry the spices for a few seconds more, then pour the mixture on to the lentils. Add the lemon or lime juice and the chopped coriander and stir them gently into the mixture.

4 Lay the pieces of cod on top of the lentils, cover the pan and then cook gently over low heat for 10–15 minutes, or until the fish is tender and cooked through.

5 Spoon the cod and lentil mixture on to warmed individual plates. Sprinkle the the whole coriander leaves over the top and garnish each serving with one or two lemon or lime wedges. Serve immediately.

Smoked Trout Pilaff

Smoked trout might seem a rather unusual partner for rice, but if you try it, you will find that this is a winning combination.

Serves 4

225g/8oz/1¹/₄ cups white
   basmati rice
40g/1¹/₂oz/3 tbsp butter
2 onions, sliced into rings
1 garlic clove, crushed
2 bay leaves
2 whole cloves
2 green cardamom pods
2 cinnamon sticks
5ml/1 tsp cumin seeds
4 smoked trout fillets, skinned
50g/2oz/¹/₂ cup slivered
   almonds, toasted
50g/2oz/generous ¹/₂ cup
   seedless raisins
30ml/2 tbsp chopped
   fresh parsley or
   coriander (cilantro)
mango chutney and poppadoms,
   to serve

1 Wash the rice thoroughly in several changes of water and, if there is time, leave to soak in cold water for 10–15 minutes. Drain well and set aside.

2 Melt the butter in a large pan over low heat. Add the onions and cook, stirring occasionally, for 10–20 minutes, until well browned.

3 Increase the heat, add the garlic, bay leaves, cloves, cardamom pods, cinnamon and cumin seeds and stir-fry for 1 minute.

4 Stir in the rice, then add 600ml/1 pint/2¹/₂ cups boiling water. Bring back to the boil, cover the pan with a tight-fitting lid, lower the heat and cook very gently for 20–25 minutes, until the water has been absorbed and the rice is tender.

5 Flake the smoked trout and add to the pan with the almonds and raisins. Fork through gently, then re-cover the pan and leave the smoked trout to warm in the rice for a few minutes.

6 Transfer the pilaff to warmed plates, sprinkle the parsley or coriander over the top and serve immediately with mango chutney and poppadoms.

Trout Energy 536kcal/2238kJ; Protein 27.8g; Carbohydrate 62.5g, of which sugars 14.9g; Fat 19.6g, of which saturates 5.8g; Cholesterol 21mg; Calcium 90mg; Fibre 2.8g; Sodium 130mg.
Cod Energy 279kcal/1174kJ; Protein 31g; Carbohydrate 24.6g, of which sugars 1.1g; Fat 6.9g, of which saturates 0.9g; Cholesterol 52mg; Calcium 33mg; Fibre 2.2g; Sodium 83mg.

Mediterranean Fish Stew

Use any combination of white fish you like in this tasty stew.

Serves 4

225g/8oz/2 cups cooked prawns (shrimp) in the shell
450g/1lb mixed white fish fillets, skinned and chopped (reserve skins for the stock)
45ml/3 tbsp olive oil
1 onion, chopped
1 leek, sliced
1 carrot, diced
1 garlic clove, chopped
2.5ml/½ tsp ground turmeric
150ml/¼ pint/⅔ cup dry white wine or (hard) cider
400g/14oz can chopped tomatoes
sprig of fresh parsley, thyme and fennel
1 bay leaf
small piece of orange rind
1 prepared squid, body cut into rings and tentacles chopped
12 fresh mussels, scrubbed
salt and ground black pepper
30–45ml/2–3 tbsp fresh Parmesan cheese shavings and fresh parsley, to garnish

For the rouille sauce
2 slices white bread, crusts removed
2 garlic cloves, crushed
½ fresh red chilli
15ml/1 tbsp tomato purée (paste)
45–60ml/3–4 tbsp olive oil

1 Remove the heads and peel the prawns, leaving the tails intact. Reserve the shells and devein the prawns. Make a stock by simmering the prawn shells and fish skins in 450ml/¾ pint/scant 2 cups water for 20 minutes. Strain and reserve.

2 Heat the oil in a large pan. Add the onion, leek, carrot and garlic and cook, stirring occasionally, for 6–7 minutes. Stir in the turmeric and add the wine, tomatoes, reserved stock, herbs and orange rind. Bring to the boil, cover and simmer for 20 minutes.

3 To make the rouille sauce, process all the sauce ingredients in a food processor or blender.

4 Add the fish and seafood to the pan and simmer for 5–6 minutes, until the mussels open. Remove the bay leaf and rind and season to taste. Serve with a spoonful of the rouille, garnished with Parmesan cheese and parsley.

Salmon with Herb Butter

Other fresh herbs could be used to flavour the butter – try mint, fennel, flat leaf parsley or oregano.

Serves 4

50g/2oz/4 tbsp butter, softened, plus extra for greasing
finely grated rind of ½ small lemon
15ml/1 tbsp lemon juice
15ml/1 tbsp chopped fresh dill
4 salmon steaks
2 lemon slices, halved
4 fresh dill sprigs
salt and ground black pepper

1 Place the butter, lemon rind, lemon juice and chopped dill in a small bowl, season with salt and pepper and mix together with a fork until thoroughly blended.

2 Spoon the butter on to a piece of greaseproof (waxed) paper and roll up, smoothing with your hands into a neat sausage shape. Twist the ends of the paper tightly, wrap in clear film (plastic wrap) and place in the freezer for about 20 minutes, until firm.

3 Meanwhile, preheat the oven to 190°C/375°F/Gas 5. Cut out four squares of foil each big enough to enclose a salmon steak and grease lightly with butter. Place a salmon steak in the centre of each square.

4 Remove the herb butter from the freezer, unwrap and slice into eight rounds. Place two rounds on top of each salmon steak, then place a halved lemon slice in the centre and a sprig of dill on top. Lift up the edges of the foil and crinkle them together until they are well sealed.

5 Lift the parcels on to a baking sheet and bake for about 20 minutes, until the fish is cooked through. (Loosen the top of one parcel to check, if necessary.)

6 Remove from the oven and transfer the unopened parcels to warmed plates with a fish slice or metal spatula. Open the parcels and slide the contents on to the plates with the cooking juices. Serve immediately.

Fish Stew Energy 505kcal/2112kJ; Protein 51.7g; Carbohydrate 15.8g, of which sugars 7.8g; Fat 23.8g, of which saturates 5.4g; Cholesterol 349mg; Calcium 252mg; Fibre 3.1g; Sodium 520mg.
Salmon Energy 364kcal/1511kJ; Protein 30.5g; Carbohydrate 0.2g, of which sugars 0.1g; Fat 26.8g, of which saturates 9.4g; Cholesterol 102mg; Calcium 39mg; Fibre 0.1g; Sodium 144mg.

Spanish Seafood Paella

Use monkfish instead of the cod, if you like, and add a red mullet or snapper cut into chunks.

Serves 4

60ml/4 tbsp olive oil
225g/8oz cod, skinned and cut into chunks
3 prepared baby squid, body cut into rings and tentacles chopped
1 onion, chopped
3 garlic cloves, finely chopped
1 red (bell) pepper, seeded and sliced
4 tomatoes, peeled and chopped
225g/8oz/1¼ cups Valencia or risotto rice
450ml/¾ pint/scant 2 cups fish stock
150ml/¼ pint/⅔ cup dry white wine
75g/3oz/¼ cup frozen peas
4–5 saffron threads, soaked in 30ml/2 tbsp hot water
115g/4oz/1 cup cooked peeled prawns (shrimp)
8 fresh mussels, scrubbed and debearded
salt and ground black pepper
15ml/1 tbsp chopped fresh parsley, to garnish
lemon wedges, to serve

1 Heat 30ml/2 tbsp of the olive oil in a heavy frying pan over medium heat. Add the cod and squid and stir-fry for 2 minutes. Transfer to a bowl.

2 Heat the remaining oil in the pan over low heat. Add the onion, garlic and red pepper and cook, stirring occasionally, for 6–7 minutes, until softened but not coloured.

3 Stir in the tomatoes and cook for a further 2 minutes, then add the rice, stirring to coat the grains with oil, and cook for 2–3 minutes more. Pour in the fish stock and wine and add the peas and saffron with its soaking water. Season to taste with salt and pepper.

4 Gently stir in the reserved cooked fish with all the juices, followed by the prawns. Push the mussels into the rice. Cover with a tight-fitting lid and cook over low heat for about 30 minutes, or until the stock has been absorbed. Remove from the heat, keep covered and leave to stand for 5 minutes. Sprinkle with parsley and serve with lemon wedges.

Spaghetti with Seafood Sauce

The tomato-based sauce in this dish is a traditional marinara, popular in Italy's coastal regions.

Serves 4

45ml/3 tbsp olive oil
1 onion, chopped
1 garlic clove, finely chopped
225g/8oz spaghetti
600ml/1 pint/2½ cups passata (bottled strained tomatoes)
15ml/1 tbsp tomato purée (paste)
5ml/1 tsp dried oregano
1 bay leaf
5ml/1 tsp sugar
225g/8 oz/2 cups cooked peeled prawns (shrimp)
175g/6oz cooked clam or cockle meat (rinsed well if canned or bottled)
15ml/1 tbsp lemon juice
45ml/3 tbsp chopped fresh parsley
25g/1oz/2 tbsp butter
salt and ground black pepper
4 cooked prawns, to garnish

1 Heat the olive oil in a large pan over low heat. Add the onion and garlic and cook, stirring occasionally, for 6–7 minutes, until softened but not coloured.

2 Meanwhile, cook the spaghetti in a large pan of boiling salted water for 10–12 minutes, or according to the instructions on the packet, until just tender.

3 Stir the passata, tomato purée, oregano, bay leaf and sugar into the onion mixture and season to taste with salt and pepper. Bring to the boil, then simmer for 2–3 minutes.

4 Add the prawns, clams or cockles, lemon juice and 30ml/ 2 tbsp of the parsley. Stir well, then cover and cook for a further 6–7 minutes.

5 Drain the spaghetti, return to the pan and add the butter. Using two large spoons, toss well to coat, then season with salt and pepper.

6 Divide the spaghetti among four warmed plates and top with the seafood sauce. Sprinkle with the remaining parsley, garnish with whole prawns and serve immediately.

Paella Energy 478kcal/1998kJ; Protein 29.8g; Carbohydrate 53.1g, of which sugars 6.9g; Fat 13.4g, of which saturates 2g; Cholesterol 198mg; Calcium 74mg; Fibre 2.1g; Sodium 181mg.
Spaghetti Energy 414kcal/1749kJ; Protein 28.3g; Carbohydrate 48.8g, of which sugars 7.8g; Fat 13.2g, of which saturates 3.5g; Cholesterol 198mg; Calcium 131mg; Fibre 2.9g; Sodium 1818mg.

Garlic Chilli Prawns

In Spain *gambas al ajillo* are traditionally cooked in small earthenware dishes, but a frying pan is just as suitable.

Serves 4
60ml/4 tbsp olive oil
2–3 garlic cloves, finely chopped
½ –1 fresh red chilli, seeded and chopped
16 cooked Mediterranean prawns (large shrimp)
15ml/1 tbsp chopped fresh parsley
salt and ground black pepper
lemon wedges and French bread, to serve

1 Heat the olive oil in a large frying pan over medium heat. Add the garlic and chilli and stir-fry for 1 minute, until the garlic begins to turn brown.

2 Add the prawns and stir-fry for 3–4 minutes, coating them well with the flavoured oil.

3 Add the parsley, remove from the heat and place four prawns in each of four warmed bowls. Spoon the flavoured oil over them. Serve with lemon wedges for squeezing and French bread to mop up the juices.

Tapas Prawns

These succulent prawns are simply irresistible as part of a *tapas* or *mezze*.

Serves 4
30ml/2 tbsp olive oil
4 garlic cloves, finely chopped
900g/2lb raw Mediteranean prawns (large shrimp), peeled
40g/1½oz/3 tbsp butter
15ml/1 tbsp orange juice
chopped fresh parsley, to garnish

1 Heat the oil in a frying pan. Add the garlic cloves and cook for 1–2 minutes. Add the prawns and cook, turning gently, for 2 minutes. Stir in the butter and orange juice and cook until the prawns have changed colour. Sprinkle with chopped parsley.

Deep-fried Spicy Whitebait

This is a delicious British dish – serve these tiny fish very hot and crisp.

Serves 4
450g/1lb whitebait
40g/1½oz/3 tbsp plain (all-purpose) flour
5ml/1 tsp paprika
pinch of cayenne pepper
12 fresh parsley sprigs
vegetable oil, for deep-frying
salt and ground black pepper
4 lemon wedges, to garnish

1 If using frozen whitebait, thaw in the bag, then drain off any water. Spread out the fish on kitchen paper and pat dry.

2 Place the flour, paprika and cayenne in a large plastic bag and add salt and pepper. Add the whitebait, in batches, and shake gently until all the fish are lightly coated with the flour mixture. Transfer to a plate.

3 Heat about 5cm/2in of oil in a pan or deep-fat fryer to 190°C/375°F, or until a cube of day-old bread browns in about 30 seconds.

4 Add the whitebait, in batches, and deep-fry in the hot oil for 2–3 minutes, until the coating is lightly golden and crisp. Remove from the pan with a slotted spoon, drain on kitchen paper and keep warm in the oven while frying the remainder.

5 When all the whitebait is cooked, drop the sprigs of parsley into the hot oil (don't worry if the oil spits slightly) and deep-fry for a few seconds until crisp. Drain on kitchen paper. Serve the whitebait immediately, garnished with the deep-fried parsley sprigs and lemon wedges.

Cook's Tip
There are two varieties of paprika, sweet and hot. Sweet paprika is quite mild, while hot paprika is spicier (but not as spicy as cayenne). Always check the label when buying.

Chilli Prawns Energy 157kcal/653kJ; Protein 13.3g; Carbohydrate 0.1g, of which sugars 0.1g; Fat 11.5g, of which saturates 1.7g; Cholesterol 146mg; Calcium 67mg; Fibre 0.2g; Sodium 144mg.
Tapas Prawns Energy 224kcal/928kJ; Protein 19.9g; Carbohydrate 1.4g, of which sugars 0.5g; Fat 15.3g, of which saturates 6.5g; Cholesterol 91mg; Calcium 127mg; Fibre 0.3g; Sodium 1434mg.
Whitebait Energy 591kcal/2446kJ; Protein 22g; Carbohydrate 6g, of which sugars 0.1g; Fat 53.5g, of which saturates 5g; Cholesterol 0mg; Calcium 968mg; Fibre 0.2g; Sodium 259mg.

Baked Fish Creole-style

Fish fillets cooked in a colourful pepper and tomato sauce are topped with a cheese crust.

Serves 4
15ml/1 tbsp sunflower oil
25g/1oz/2 tbsp butter, plus extra
    for greasing
1 onion, thinly sliced
1 garlic clove, chopped
1 red (bell) pepper, seeded, halved
    and sliced
1 green (bell) pepper, seeded,
    halved and sliced
400g/14oz can chopped
    tomatoes with basil
15ml/1 tbsp tomato
    purée (paste)
30ml/2 tbsp capers, drained
    and chopped
3–4 drops Tabasco sauce
4 tail end pieces cod or haddock
    fillets (about 175g/6oz
    each), skinned
6 basil leaves, shredded
45ml/3 tbsp fresh breadcrumbs
25g/1oz/¼ cup grated
    Cheddar cheese
10ml/2 tsp chopped fresh parsley
salt and ground black pepper
fresh basil sprigs, to garnish

1 Preheat the oven to 230°C/450°F/Gas 8. Heat the oil and half of the butter in a pan over low heat. Add the onion and cook, stirring occasionally, for about 6–7 minutes, until softened. Add the garlic, peppers, chopped tomatoes, tomato purée, capers and Tabasco and season to taste with salt and pepper. Cover and cook for 15 minutes, then uncover and simmer gently for 5 minutes to reduce slightly.

2 Grease an ovenproof dish, place the fish fillets in it, dot with the remaining butter and season lightly. Spoon the tomato and pepper sauce over the top and sprinkle with the shredded basil. Bake for about 10 minutes.

3 Meanwhile, mix together the breadcrumbs, cheese and parsley in a bowl. Remove the fish from the oven and sprinkle the cheese mixture over the top. Return to the oven and bake for about 10 minutes more. Let the fish stand for about a minute, then, using a fish slice or spatula, carefully transfer each topped fillet to warmed plates. Garnish with sprigs of fresh basil and serve immediately.

Tuna Fishcake Bites

An updated version of a traditional British tea-time dish, these delicious, little fishcakes would also make an elegant appetizer.

Serves 4
675g/1½lb potatoes
knob (pat) of butter
2 hard-boiled eggs, chopped
3 spring onions
    (scallions), chopped
grated rind of ½ lemon
5ml/1 tsp lemon juice
30ml/2 tbsp chopped
    fresh parsley
200g/7oz can tuna in oil, drained
10ml/2 tsp capers, drained
    and chopped
2 eggs, lightly beaten
115g/4oz/2 cups fresh
    white breadcrumbs
sunflower oil, for pan-frying
salt and ground black pepper
green salad, to serve

For the tartare sauce
60ml/4 tbsp mayonnaise
15ml/1 tbsp natural (plain) yogurt
15ml/1 tbsp finely
    chopped gherkins
15ml/1 tbsp capers, drained
    and chopped
15ml/1 tbsp chopped
    fresh parsley

1 Cook the potatoes in boiling salted water for 25–30 minutes, until tender. Drain and mash with the butter.

2 Mix the hard-boiled eggs, spring onions, lemon rind and juice, parsley, tuna, capers and 15ml/1 tbsp of the beaten eggs into the cooled potato. Season to taste, then cover and chill.

3 Mix all the sauce ingredients together. Chill in the refrigerator.

4 Roll the fishcake mixture into about 24 balls. Dip these into the remaining beaten eggs and then roll gently in the breadcrumbs until evenly coated. Transfer to a plate.

5 Heat 90ml/6 tbsp of the oil in a frying pan. Add the fish balls, in batches, and cook over medium heat, turning two or three times, for about 4 minutes, until browned all over. Drain on kitchen paper and keep warm in the oven while frying the remainder. Serve with the tartare sauce and a salad.

Baked Fish Energy 332kcal/1399kJ; Protein 38.1g; Carbohydrate 19.2g, of which sugars 10.2g; Fat 11.9g, of which saturates 5.4g; Cholesterol 82mg; Calcium 106mg; Fibre 3g; Sodium 308mg.
Fishcake Energy 567kcal/2380kJ; Protein 26.8g; Carbohydrate 54.5g, of which sugars 7.5g; Fat 28.4g, of which saturates 3.8g; Cholesterol 228mg; Calcium 111mg; Fibre 3g; Sodium 656mg.

Kashmir Coconut Fish Curry

The combination of spices in this dish give an interesting depth of flavour to the creamy curry sauce.

Serves 4

30ml/2 tbsp vegetable oil
2 onions, sliced
1 green (bell) pepper, seeded and sliced
1 garlic clove, crushed
1 dried chilli, seeded and chopped
5ml/1 tsp ground coriander
5ml/1 tsp ground cumin
2.5ml/¹/₂ tsp ground turmeric
2.5ml/¹/₂ tsp hot chilli powder
2.5ml/¹/₂ tsp garam masala

15g/¹/₂oz/1 tbsp plain (all-purpose) flour
300ml/¹/₂ pint/1¹/₄ cups coconut cream
675g/1¹/₂lb haddock fillet, skinned and chopped
4 tomatoes, peeled, seeded and chopped
15ml/1 tbsp lemon juice
30ml/2 tbsp ground almonds
30ml/2 tbsp double (heavy) cream
fresh coriander (cilantro) sprigs, to garnish
naan bread and boiled rice, to serve

1 Heat the oil in a large pan over low heat. Add the onions, green pepper and garlic and cook, stirring occasionally, for 6–7 minutes, until the onions and pepper have softened but not coloured.

2 Stir in the dried chilli, ground coriander, cumin, turmeric, chilli powder, garam masala and flour and cook, stirring constantly, for 1 minute more.

3 Mix the coconut cream with 300ml/¹/₂ pint/1¹/₄ cups boiling water and stir into the spicy vegetable mixture. Bring to the boil, cover with a tight-fitting lid and simmer gently for about 6 minutes.

4 Add the pieces of fish and the tomatoes, re-cover the pan and cook for 5–6 minutes, or until the fish has turned opaque and flakes easily with the tip of a knife. Uncover and gently stir in the lemon juice, ground almonds and cream and heat through for a few minutes. Season well, garnish with coriander and serve with naan bread and rice.

Mussels with Wine & Garlic

This famous French dish is traditionally known as *moules marinière*, and can be served as an appetizer or a main course.

Serves 4

1.75kg/4lb fresh mussels
15ml/1 tbsp olive oil
25g/1oz/2 tbsp butter

1 small onion or 2 shallots, finely chopped
2 garlic cloves, finely chopped
150ml/¹/₄ pint/²/₃ cup dry white wine
4 fresh parsley sprigs
ground black pepper
30ml/2 tbsp chopped fresh parsley, to garnish
French bread, to serve

1 Scrub the mussels under cold running water and pull off the beards. Discard any with broken shells or that do not shut immediately when sharply tapped.

2 Heat the oil and butter in a large pan over medium heat. Add the onion or shallots and garlic and cook, stirring occasionally, for 3–4 minutes.

3 Pour in the wine, add the parsley sprigs, stir well and bring to the boil. Add the mussels, cover with a tight-fitting lid and cook, shaking the pan occasionally, for 5–7 minutes, until the shells have opened. Discard any mussels that remain closed.

4 Transfer the mussels to warmed serving bowls with a slotted spoon. Strain the cooking juices through a fine strainer lined with muslin (cheesecloth) and spoon them over the shellfish. Sprinkle with the chopped parsley, season well with pepper and serve immediately with hot French bread.

Variation

This dish is served everywhere in France, but in the apple-growing region of Normandy it is made with (hard) cider rather than white wine. For a really rich dish, strain the cooking liquid into a pan, stir in 90ml/6 tbsp double (heavy) cream and cook for a few minutes before spooning over the mussels.

Curry Energy 496kcal/2068kJ; Protein 36.6g; Carbohydrate 18.9g, of which sugars 13.6g; Fat 31.1g, of which saturates 20.5g; Cholesterol 71mg; Calcium 75mg; Fibre 3.2g; Sodium 137mg.
Mussels Energy 224kcal/939kJ; Protein 20g; Carbohydrate 5.4g, of which sugars 1.1g; Fat 11g, of which saturates 4g; Cholesterol 83mg; Calcium 70mg; Fibre 0.2g; Sodium 460mg.

Thai Prawn Salad

This salad has the distinctive flavour of lemon grass, the bulbous grass used widely in South-east Asian cooking.

Serves 2
250g/9oz extra-large tiger prawns
(jumbo shrimp), thawed
if frozen
30ml/2 tbsp groundnut
(peanut) oil
15ml/1 tbsp Thai fish sauce
30ml/2 tbsp lime juice
7.5ml/1½ tsp soft light
brown sugar

1 small fresh red chilli,
finely chopped
1 spring onion (scallion),
finely chopped
1 small garlic clove, crushed
2.5cm/1in piece fresh lemon
grass, finely chopped
30ml/2 tbsp chopped fresh
coriander (cilantro)
45ml/3 tbsp dry white wine
8–12 Little Gem (Bibb) lettuce
leaves, to serve
fresh coriander sprigs,
to garnish

1 Remove the heads and peel the prawns. (Reserve the shells for making shellfish stock, if you like.) Make a shallow cut along the back of each prawn and remove the dark vein with the tip of the knife.

2 Heat the oil in a wok or heavy frying pan over medium heat. When it is very hot, add the prawns and stir-fry for 2–3 minutes, until they have changed colour. Be careful not to overcook them. Remove with a slotted spoon and drain on kitchen paper. Leave to cool.

3 Place the tiger prawns in a non-metallic bowl and add all the remaining ingredients except the lettuce and coriander sprigs. Stir thoroughly to combine and dissolve the sugar, cover with clear film (plastic wrap) and leave to marinate in the refrigerator for 2–3 hours, occasionally stirring and turning the prawns.

4 Arrange two or three of the lettuce leaves on each of four individual serving plates. Spoon the prawn salad and marinade on to the lettuce leaves. Garnish with fresh coriander sprigs and serve immediately.

Cajun Spiced Fish

Fillets of fish are coated with an aromatic blend of herbs and spices and pan-fried in butter.

Serves 4
5ml/1 tsp dried thyme
5ml/1 tsp dried oregano
5ml/1 tsp ground black pepper
1.25ml/¼ tsp cayenne pepper
10ml/2 tsp paprika

2.5ml/½ tsp garlic salt
4 tail end pieces of cod fillet
(about 175g/6oz each)
75g/3oz/6 tbsp butter
½ fresh red (bell) pepper, seeded
and sliced
½ green (bell) pepper, seeded
and sliced
fresh thyme sprigs, to garnish
grilled (broiled) tomatoes and
sweet potato purée, to serve

1 Place the dried thyme, oregano, black pepper, cayenne, paprika and garlic salt in a bowl and mix well. Dip the fish fillets in the spice mixture until lightly coated.

2 Heat 25g/1oz/2 tbsp of the butter in a large frying pan over medium-low heat. Add the red and green peppers and cook, stirring occasionally, for 4–5 minutes, until softened. Remove the peppers and keep warm.

3 Add the remaining butter to the pan and heat until it is sizzling. Add the cod fillets and cook over medium heat for 3–4 minutes on each side, until browned and cooked.

4 Transfer the fish to a warmed serving dish, surround with the peppers and garnish with thyme sprigs. Serve the spiced fish with some grilled tomatoes and sweet potato purée.

Cook's Tip
Cajun cooking is a rural tradition that originated in Louisiana over 200 years ago. It is an immensely flexible cuisine based on home-grown crops, locally caught fish and any game that could be hunted. It is often confused with Creole cuisine, which evolved in the same region but was created for the rich. Creole includes French, Spanish and African influences.

Thai Prawn Energy 130kcal/546kJ; Protein 22.4g; Carbohydrate 4.7g, of which sugars 4.6g; Fat 0.9g, of which saturates 0.2g; Cholesterol 244mg; Calcium 112mg; Fibre 0.3g; Sodium 240mg.
Cajun Fish Energy 295kcal/1228kJ; Protein 32.7g; Carbohydrate 3g, of which sugars 2.9g; Fat 16.9g, of which saturates 10g; Cholesterol 120mg; Calcium 31mg; Fibre 0.9g; Sodium 222mg.

Golden Fish Pie

This lovely light pie with a crumpled filo pastry topping makes a delicious lunch or supper dish.

Serves 4–6

675g/1½lb white fish fillets
300ml/½ pint/1¼ cups milk
½ onion, thinly sliced
1 bay leaf
6 black peppercorns
115g/4oz/1 cup cooked peeled prawns (shrimp)

115g/4oz/½ cup butter
50g/2oz/½ cup plain (all-purpose) flour
300ml/½ pint/1¼ cups single (light) cream
75g/3oz/¾ cup grated Gruyère cheese
1 bunch watercress, leaves only, chopped
5ml/1 tsp Dijon mustard
5 sheets filo pastry
salt and ground black pepper

1 Place the fish in a pan, pour in the milk and add the onion, bay leaf and peppercorns. Bring to the boil, lower the heat, cover with a lid and simmer for 10–12 minutes, until the fish is almost tender. Lift out the fish with a slotted spatula and place on a chopping board. Strain and reserve the cooking liquid.

2 Remove the skin and any bones from the fish, then coarsely flake the flesh and place in a shallow, ovenproof dish. Sprinkle the prawns over the fish.

3 Melt 50g/2oz/4 tbsp of the butter in a pan. Stir in the flour and cook, stirring constantly, for 1 minute. Stir in the reserved cooking liquid and cream. Bring to the boil, stirring, then simmer for 2–3 minutes, until thickened. Remove from the heat and stir in the Gruyère, watercress and mustard. Season with salt and pepper. Pour the mixture over the fish and leave to cool.

4 Preheat the oven to 190°C/375°F/Gas 5, then melt the remaining butter. Brush one sheet of filo pastry with a little melted butter, then crumple up loosely and place on top of the filling. Repeat with the remaining filo sheets and melted butter until they are all used up and the pie is completely covered. Bake for 25–30 minutes, until the pastry is golden and crisp. Serve immediately.

Special Fish Pie

This fish pie is colourful, healthy and best of all, it is very simple to make.

Serves 4

350g/12oz haddock fillet
30ml/2 tbsp cornflour (cornstarch)
115g/4oz/1 cup cooked peeled prawns (shrimp)
200g/7oz can corn, drained
75g/3oz/scant 1 cup frozen peas

150ml/¼ pint/⅔ cup skimmed milk
150ml/¼ pint/⅔ cup low-fat fromage frais (farmer's cheese)
75g/3oz/1½ cups fresh wholemeal (whole-wheat) breadcrumbs
40g/1½ oz/generous ¼ cup grated reduced-fat Cheddar cheese
salt and ground black pepper
fresh vegetables, to serve

1 Preheat the oven to 190°C/375°F/Gas 5. Skin the haddock fillet if this has not already been done by your fish supplier and cut the flesh into bitesize pieces. Toss the pieces of fish in the cornflour to coat evenly.

2 Place the fish, prawns, corn and peas in an ovenproof dish. Beat together the milk and fromage frais in a bowl and season with salt and pepper. Pour the mixture into the dish.

3 Mix together the breadcrumbs and grated cheese, then spoon evenly over the top, pressing down gently with the back of the spoon.

4 Bake for 25–30 minutes, or until the topping is golden brown. Serve hot with fresh vegetables.

> **Variations**
> • For a slightly more economical version of this dish, omit the prawns (shrimp) and increase the quantity of haddock fillet to 450g/1lb.
> • Substitute smoked haddock fillet for half the fresh fish.
> • Use frozen or drained canned broad (fava) beans instead of the peas.

Golden Fish Energy 344kcal/1442kJ; Protein 32g; Carbohydrate 17.5g, of which sugars 3.8g; Fat 16.4g, of which saturates 9g; Cholesterol 129mg; Calcium 239mg; Fibre 0.8g; Sodium 246mg.
Special Fish Energy 329kcal/1394kJ; Protein 34.1g; Carbohydrate 41.2g, of which sugars 10g; Fat 4.3g, of which saturates 1.7g; Cholesterol 94mg; Calcium 228mg; Fibre 2g; Sodium 490mg.

Smoked Trout with Cucumber

Smoked trout provides an easy and delicious first course or light meal. Serve at room temperature for the best flavour.

Serves 4

1 large cucumber
60ml/4 tbsp crème fraîche
    or Greek (US strained
    plain) yogurt
15ml/1 tbsp chopped
    fresh dill
4 smoked trout fillets
salt and ground black pepper
fresh dill sprigs, to garnish
crusty wholemeal (whole-wheat)
    bread, to serve

1 Peel the cucumber, cut in half lengthways and scoop out the seeds using a teaspoon. Cut the flesh into tiny dice.

2 Put the cucumber in a colander set over a plate and sprinkle with salt. Leave to drain for at least 1 hour to draw out the excess moisture.

3 Rinse the cucumber well, then pat dry on kitchen paper. Transfer the diced cucumber to a bowl and stir in the crème fraîche or yogurt, chopped dill and some freshly ground pepper. Chill the cucumber salad for about 30 minutes.

4 Arrange the trout fillets on individual plates. Spoon the cucumber and dill salad on one side and grind over a little black pepper. Garnish the dish with dill sprigs and serve immediately with crusty bread.

Cook's Tip
Trout is hot-smoked at a temperature of 75–100°C/ 167–212°F, which, in effect, cooks it at the same time. It, therefore, needs no further cooking. If you are planning to substitute another fish, make sure that it has also been hot-smoked, as, with the exception of salmon, most cold-smoked fish requires further cooking.

Fishcakes

Home-made fish cakes are an underrated food which bear little resemblance to the store-bought type.

Serves 4

450g/1lb mixed white and
    smoked fish fillets, such as
    haddock or cod, flaked
450g/1lb cooked, mashed
    potatoes
25g/1oz/2 tbsp butter, diced
45ml/3 tbsp chopped
    fresh parsley
1 egg, separated
1 egg, beaten
about 50g/2oz/1 cup fine white
    breadcrumbs made with day-
    old bread
salt and pepper
vegetable oil, for pan-frying

1 Place the fish in a large pan, season with salt and pepper and pour in water just to cover. Bring to the boil, then lower the heat, cover and simmer for about 15 minutes, until the flesh flakes easily with the tip of a knife. Remove the fish with a slotted spatula and leave until cool enough to handle. Discard the cooking liquid.

2 Remove and discard the skin and any bones from the fish and flake the flesh. Place the potatoes in a bowl and beat in the fish, butter, parsley and egg yolk. Season to taste with pepper.

3 Divide the fish mixture into eight equal portions, then, with floured hands, form each into a flat patty. Beat the remaining egg white with the whole egg. Dip each fish cake first into the beaten egg, then in breadcrumbs.

4 Heat the oil in a frying pan over a medium heat. Add the fish cakes and cook for 3–5 minutes on each side, until crisp and golden. Serve immediately.

Cook's Tip
Make smaller fishcakes to serve as an appetizer with a salad garnish. For a more luxurious version, make them with cooked fresh salmon or drained, canned red or pink salmon.

Trout Energy 146kcal/606kJ; Protein 15.2g; Carbohydrate 1.1g, of which sugars 1g; Fat 8.9g, of which saturates 4.1g; Cholesterol 17mg; Calcium 25mg; Fibre 0.3g; Sodium 47mg.
Fishcakes Energy 399kcal/1670kJ; Protein 27.5g; Carbohydrate 28.2g, of which sugars 2.1g; Fat 20.4g, of which saturates 5.6g; Cholesterol 160mg; Calcium 71mg; Fibre 2g; Sodium 252mg.

Stuffed Fish Rolls

Plaice or flounder fillets are a good choice for families because they are economical, easy to cook and free of bones.

Serves 4

1 courgette (zucchini), grated
2 carrots, grated
60ml/4 tbsp fresh wholemeal (whole-wheat) breadcrumbs
15ml/1 tbsp lime or lemon juice
4 plaice or flounder fillets
salt and ground black pepper
new potatoes, to serve

1 Preheat the oven to 200°C/400°F/Gas 6. Mix together the courgette and carrots in a bowl. Stir in the breadcrumbs and lime juice and season with salt and pepper.

2 Lay the fish fillets, skin-side up, on a board and divide the stuffing among them, spreading it evenly.

3 Roll up to enclose the stuffing and place in an ovenproof dish. Cover and bake for about 30 minutes, or until the fish flakes easily. Serve immediately with new potatoes.

Cook's Tip
Flat fish, such as plaice and flounder, have one light- and one dark-skinned side. Most people consider the darker skin to be unappetizing and many dislike any sort of skin. The skin is very easy to remove. Make a small cut between the skin and the flesh at the tail end of the fillet, then dip your fingers in salt to stop them from slipping, take a firm hold of the skin and simply pull it away from the flesh in one piece. Spread the filling on to the side where the skin was.

Variation
Substitute 115g/4oz/1 cup finely chopped cooked, peeled prawns or drained, canned crab meat for the carrots to create a more sophisticated version of this dish.

Mackerel Kebabs with Parsley

Oily fish, such as mackerel, are ideal for grilling as they cook quickly and need no extra oil.

Serves 4

450g/1lb mackerel fillets
finely grated rind and juice of 1 lemon
45ml/3 tbsp chopped fresh parsley
12 cherry tomatoes
8 pitted black olives
salt and ground black pepper
boiled rice or noodles and green salad, to serve

1 Cut the fish into 4cm/1½ in chunks and place in a non-metallic bowl with half the lemon rind and juice and half the parsley and season with salt and pepper. Cover the bowl with clear film (plastic wrap) and leave to marinate in a cool place for about 30 minutes.

2 Preheat the grill (broiler). Thread the chunks of fish on to eight long wooden or metal skewers, alternating them with the cherry tomatoes and olives. Grill (broil) the kebabs, turning occasionally, for 3–4 minutes, until the fish is cooked.

3 Mix the remaining lemon rind and juice with the remaining parsley in a small bowl, then season to taste with salt and pepper. Make a bed of plain boiled rice or noodles on each of four warmed serving plates and place two kebabs on each. Serve immediately with a green salad.

Cook's Tips
• If you are using wooden kebab skewers, it is a good idea to soak them in cold water for 30 minutes to prevent them from charring during cooking.
• These kebabs are also ideal for cooking on the barbecue. Serve with baked potatoes or crusty bread and salad.
• If you are going to marinate the fish for longer than 30 minutes, place it in the refrigerator. Otherwise, simply leave it in a cool place.

Fish Rolls Energy 139kcal/588kJ; Protein 15.5g; Carbohydrate 16.5g, of which sugars 5g; Fat 1.7g, of which saturates 0.3g; Cholesterol 32mg; Calcium 78mg; Fibre 2g; Sodium 217mg.
Mackerel Energy 265kcal/1100kJ; Protein 21.7g; Carbohydrate 1.5g, of which sugars 1.5g; Fat 19.1g, of which saturates 3.9g; Cholesterol 61mg; Calcium 44mg; Fibre 1.2g; Sodium 219mg.

Grilled Salmon Steaks with Fennel

Fennel grows wild all over the south of Italy where this dish originated. Its mild aniseed flavour goes well with fish.

Serves 4

juice of 1 lemon
45ml/3 tbsp chopped fresh
   fennel, or the green fronds from
   the top of a fennel bulb
5ml/1 tsp fennel seeds
45ml/3 tbsp olive oil
4 salmon steaks of the same
   thickness (about 700g/1½lb)
salt and ground black pepper
lemon wedges, to garnish

1 Combine the lemon juice, chopped fennel and fennel seeds with the olive oil in a non-metallic dish. Add the salmon steaks, turning them to coat them with the marinade. Sprinkle with salt and pepper. Cover with clear film (plastic wrap) and place in the refrigerator to marinate for about 2 hours.

2 Preheat the grill (broiler). Drain the fish and reserve the marinade. Place the salmon steaks in one layer on a grill (broiler) pan or shallow baking tray. Grill (broil) about 10cm/4in from the heat source for 3–4 minutes.

3 Turn the steaks over and spoon the remaining marinade over them. Grill for 3–4 minutes, or until the edges begin to brown. Serve immediately, garnished with lemon wedges.

Cook's Tips
• If you like, remove the skin from the salmon steaks before serving. Simply insert the prongs of a fork between the flesh and the skin at one end and roll the skin around the prongs in a fluid action.
• Take care not to overcook the salmon. Although it is an oily fish, the flesh dries out very easily when subjected to fierce heat. If you're going to cook on the barbecue, raise the grill rack well above the coals before starting.

Seafood Pilaff

This one-pan dish makes a satisfying meal. For a special occasion, use dry white wine instead of orange juice.

Serves 4

10ml/2 tsp olive oil
250g/9oz/1⅓ cups long
   grain rice
5ml/1 tsp ground turmeric
1 fresh red (bell) pepper, seeded
   and diced
1 small onion, finely chopped
2 courgettes (zucchini), sliced
150g/5oz button (white)
   mushrooms, halved
350ml/12fl oz/1½ cups fish or
   chicken stock
150ml/¼ pint/⅔ cup orange
   juice
350g/12oz white fish fillets
12 fresh mussels, scrubbed
   and debearded
salt and ground black pepper
grated rind of 1 orange, to garnish

1 Heat the oil in a large non-stick frying pan over low heat. Add the rice and turmeric and cook, stirring frequently, for about 1 minute.

2 Add the red pepper, onion, courgettes and mushrooms and cook, stirring constantly, for 1 minute more, then increase the heat to medium, stir in the stock and orange juice and bring to the boil.

3 Lower the heat and add the fish. Cover with a tight-fitting lid and simmer gently for about 15 minutes, until the rice is tender and the liquid has been absorbed.

4 Stir in the mussels, re-cover the pan and cook for about 5 minutes until the shells have opened. Discard any mussels that remain closed. Adjust the seasoning, sprinkle with orange rind and serve immediately.

Variation
You can use cooked, shelled mussels, available from the chiller cabinets in supermarkets, instead of live. Add them in step 4 and simply heat through before serving.

Salmon Energy 395kcal/1639kJ; Protein 35.8g; Carbohydrate 0.8g, of which sugars 0.8g; Fat 27.6g, of which saturates 4.5g; Cholesterol 88mg; Calcium 47mg; Fibre 1.1g; Sodium 84mg.
Pilaff Energy 394kcal/1663kJ; Protein 28.7g; Carbohydrate 59g, of which sugars 12.5g; Fat 6.3g, of which saturates 0.5g; Cholesterol 46mg; Calcium 620mg; Fibre 2.3g; Sodium 115mg.

Grilled Fresh Sardines

Fresh sardines are
flavoursome, firm-fleshed
and rather different in taste
and consistency from those
canned in oil.

Serves 4–6
*900kg/2lb fresh sardines, gutted
and with heads removed*

*olive oil, for brushing
45ml/3 tbsp chopped
fresh parsley
salt and ground black pepper
lemon or orange wedges,
to garnish*

1 Preheat the grill (broiler). Rinse the sardines under cold
running water. Pat dry with kitchen paper.

2 Brush the sardines lightly with olive oil and sprinkle
generously with salt and pepper. Place the sardines in one layer
in a grill (broiler) pan. Grill (broil) for about 3–4 minutes.

3 Turn, and cook for 3–4 minutes more, or until the skin begins
to brown. Serve immediately, sprinkled with parsley and
garnished with lemon wedges.

> **Cook's Tip**
> *Frozen sardines are now available in supermarkets and will
> keep well in the freezer for six weeks. Thaw them in the
> refrigerator overnight. Scrape off the scales with your hands,
> working from tail to head, then use a sharp pointed knife to slit
> the belly, remove the innards and cut the heads off. For a fuller
> flavour and to make them less likely to fall apart when you turn
> them, you might like to leave them whole, as they do in some
> Mediterranean countries.*

> **Variation**
> *Substitute parsley butter for the fresh parsley. Simply beat
> chopped fresh parsley and lemon juice to taste into butter.*

Red Mullet with Tomatoes

Red mullet is a popular fish
in Italy, and in this recipe
both its flavour and colour
are accentuated.

Serves 4
*4 red mullet or snapper (about
175–200g/6–7oz each)
450g/1lb tomatoes, peeled, or
400g/14oz can plum tomatoes*

*60ml/4 tbsp olive oil
60ml/4 tbsp finely chopped
fresh parsley
2 garlic cloves, finely chopped
120ml/4fl oz/½ cup dry
white wine
4 thin lemon slices, cut in half
salt and ground black pepper*

1 Scale and gut the fish or ask your fish supplier to do this for
you. Rinse well under cold running water and pat dry with
kitchen paper.

2 Finely chop the tomatoes. Heat the oil in a pan or flameproof
casserole large enough to hold the fish in one layer. Add the
parsley and garlic, and cook, stirring, for 1 minute. Stir in the
tomatoes and cook over medium heat, stirring occasionally, for
15–20 minutes. Season to taste with salt and pepper.

3 Add the fish to the tomato sauce and cook over medium to
high heat for 5 minutes. Add the wine and the lemon slices.
Bring the sauce back to the boil and cook for about 5 minutes
more. Turn the fish over and cook for a further 4–5 minutes,
until the fish flakes easily. Transfer the fish to a warmed serving
platter and keep warm until required.

4 Boil the sauce for 3–4 minutes to reduce it slightly, then
spoon it over the fish and serve immediately.

> **Cook's Tip**
> *The liver of red mullet is regarded as a delicacy so you can
> leave it intact when you gut the fish or ask your fish supplier to
> keep it for you. This does not apply if you are preparing this
> dish with red snapper.*

Sardines Energy 214kcal/893kJ; Protein 23.4g; Carbohydrate 0.2g, of which sugars 0.2g; Fat 13.2g, of which saturates 3.2g; Cholesterol 0mg; Calcium 131mg; Fibre 0.4g; Sodium 130mg.
Red Mullet Energy 256kcal/1067kJ; Protein 20.4g; Carbohydrate 4g, of which sugars 3.9g; Fat 15.7g, of which saturates 1.7g; Cholesterol 0mg; Calcium 105mg; Fibre 1.7g; Sodium 115mg.

Middle Eastern Sea Bream

Buy the smallest sea bream you can find to cook whole, allowing a serving of one fish for two people.

Serves 4

1.75kg/4lb sea bream or porgy or
   2 smaller sea bream or porgy
30ml/2 tbsp olive oil
75g/3oz/³/₄ cup pine nuts
1 large onion, finely chopped
450g/1lb ripe tomatoes,
   coarsely chopped
75g/3oz/¹/₂ cup raisins
2.5ml/¹/₂ tsp ground cinnamon
2.5ml/¹/₂ tsp mixed (apple
   pie) spice
45ml/3 tbsp chopped fresh mint
225g/8oz/generous 1 cup
   long grain rice
3 lemon slices
300ml/¹/₂ pint/1¹/₄ cups fish stock

1 Trim the fins, scale the fish, then gut or ask your fish supplier to do this for you. Rinse well under cold running water and pat dry with kitchen paper. Meanwhile, preheat the oven to 175°C/350°F/Gas 4.

2 Heat the oil in a large, heavy pan over medium-low heat. Add the pine nuts and stir-fry for 1 minute. Add the onions and continue to stir-fry until softened but not coloured.

3 Add the tomatoes and simmer for 10 minutes, then stir in the raisins, half the cinnamon, half the mixed spice and the mint.

4 Add the rice and lemon slices. Transfer to a large roasting pan and pour the fish stock over the top.

5 Place the fish on top and cut several slashes in the skin. Sprinkle over a little salt, the remaining mixed spice and the remaining cinnamon and bake for 30–35 minutes for large fish or 20–25 minutes for smaller fish.

> **Variation**
> If you like, use almonds instead of pine nuts. Use the same quantity of blanched almonds and split them in half before stir-frying.

Salmon with Spicy Pesto

This pesto uses sunflower seeds and chilli as its flavouring rather than the classic basil and pine nuts.

Serves 4

4 salmon steaks (about 225g/8oz
   each)
30ml/2 tbsp sunflower oil
finely grated rind and juice of 1 lime
pinch of salt

For the pesto
6 mild fresh red chillies, seeded
2 garlic cloves
30ml/2 tbsp pumpkin or
   sunflower seeds
freshly grated rind and juice of
   1 lime
75ml/5 tbsp olive oil
salt and ground black pepper

1 Insert a very sharp knife close to the top of the salmon's backbone. Working closely to the bone, cut your way to the end of the steak so one side of the steak has been released and one side is still attached. Repeat with the other side. Pull out any extra visible bones with a pair of tweezers.

2 Sprinkle a little salt on the surface and take hold of the end of the salmon, skin-side down. Insert a small sharp knife under the skin and, working away from you, cut off the skin, keeping as close to the skin as possible. Repeat with the three remaining pieces of fish.

3 Rub the sunflower oil into the boneless fish rounds and place in a non-metallic dish. Add the lime juice and rind, cover with clear film (plastic wrap) and place in the refrigerator to marinate for 2 hours.

4 To make the pesto, put the chillies, garlic, pumpkin or sunflower seeds, lime juice and rind in a food processor or blender and season with salt and pepper. Process until well mixed. With the motor running, gradually pour in the olive oil until the sauce has thickened and emulsified.

5 Preheat the grill (broiler). Drain the salmon from its marinade. Grill the fish steaks for about 5 minutes on each side and serve immediately with the spicy pesto.

Sea Bream Energy 562kcal/2348kJ; Protein 39.7g; Carbohydrate 46g, of which sugars 1.1g; Fat 24.1g, of which saturates 1.7g; Cholesterol 71mg; Calcium 89mg; Fibre 0.5g; Sodium 208mg.
Salmon Energy 653kcal/2719kJ; Protein 50.5g; Carbohydrate 1.4g, of which sugars 0.1g; Fat 49.6g, of which saturates 7.5g; Cholesterol 122mg; Calcium 60mg; Fibre 0.5g; Sodium 111mg.

Poultry & Game

Tender, tasty and infinitely adaptable, poultry and game play the
starring role in a wide range of roasts, pies, braises, bakes and
pan-fried dishes. Banish the blues with a winter warmer, such as
Chicken, Leek and Parsley Pie, Pot-roast Poussin, or Venison
with Cranberry Sauce. Or why not spice things up with
an exotic meal, such as Tandoori Chicken Kebabs,
or Creole Chicken Jambalaya?

Roast Chicken with Celeriac

Celeriac and brown breadcrumbs give the stuffing an unusual and delicious twist.

Serves 4
1.6kg/3½lb chicken
15g/½oz/1 tbsp butter

For the stuffing
450g/1lb celeriac, chopped
25g/1oz/2 tbsp butter
3 rashers (strips) bacon, chopped
1 onion, finely chopped
leaves from 1 fresh thyme
  sprig, chopped
leaves from 1 small fresh tarragon
  sprig, chopped
30ml/2 tbsp chopped
  fresh parsley
75g/3oz/1½ cups fresh
  brown breadcrumbs
dash of Worcestershire sauce
1 egg
salt and ground black pepper

1 To make the stuffing, cook the celeriac in a pan of boiling water until tender. Drain well and chop finely.

2 Melt the butter in a heavy pan over low heat. Add the bacon and onion and cook, stirring occasionally, for 5–7 minutes, until the onion is softened but not coloured.

3 Stir in the celeriac, thyme, tarragon and parsley and cook, stirring occasionally, for 2–3 minutes. Meanwhile, preheat the oven to 200°C/400°F/Gas 6

4 Remove the pan from the heat and stir in the fresh breadcrumbs, Worcestershire sauce and sufficient egg to bind the mixture. Season with salt and pepper. Use this mixture to stuff the neck end of the chicken. Season the chicken all over with salt and pepper and then rub the butter into the skin with your fingertips.

5 Place the chicken in a roasting pan and roast, basting occasionally with the cooking juices, for 1¼–1½ hours, until the juices run clear when the thickest part of the leg is pierced with the point of a sharp knife. Turn off the oven, prop the door open slightly and leave the chicken to rest for about 10 minutes before removing from the oven and carving.

Chicken with Lemon & Herbs

Chicken thighs tend to be overlooked when people are buying portions, yet the meat is full of flavour and two thighs will adequately serve one person.

Serves 2
50g/2oz/4 tbsp butter
2 spring onions, (scallions) white
  parts only, finely chopped
15ml/1 tbsp chopped
  fresh tarragon
15ml/1 tbsp chopped fresh fennel
juice of 1 lemon
4 chicken thighs
salt and ground black pepper
lemon slices and fresh herb
  sprigs, to garnish

1 Preheat the grill (broiler) to medium. Melt the butter in a small pan over low heat. Add the spring onions, tarragon, fennel and lemon juice and season with salt and pepper. Cook, stirring constantly, for 1 minute, then remove the pan from the heat.

2 Brush the chicken thighs generously with the herb mixture, then grill (broil), basting frequently with the herb mixture, for 10–12 minutes.

3 Turn the chicken over and baste again, then cook for a further 10–12 minutes, or until the chicken juices run clear when the thickest part of the thigh is pierced with the point of a knife.

4 Serve the chicken garnished with lemon slices and herb sprigs and accompanied by any remaining herb mixture.

Cook's Tip
Tarragon has a natural affinity with chicken. It is intensely aromatic with a hint of aniseed and so should be used sparingly. Make sure you buy French tarragon with its delicate leaves and fine flavour. Russian tarragon is virtually inedible. Fennel also has a strong aniseed flavour, so it too should be used with discretion.

Roast Chicken Energy 507kcal/2116kJ; Protein 43.6g; Carbohydrate 16.8g, of which sugars 2.4g; Fat 30g, of which saturates 11.6g; Cholesterol 233mg; Calcium 99mg; Fibre 1.9g; Sodium 692mg.
Lemon Chicken Energy 406kcal/1692kJ; Protein 42.1g; Carbohydrate 0.5g, of which sugars 0.4g; Fat 26.2g, of which saturates 14.7g; Cholesterol 263mg; Calcium 23mg; Fibre 0.3g; Sodium 333mg.

Chicken in Green Sauce

Slow, gentle cooking makes the chicken in this dish very succulent and tender.

Serves 4

25g/1oz/2 tbsp butter
15ml/1 tbsp olive oil
4 chicken portions (legs, breast portions or quarters)
1 small onion, finely chopped
150ml/¼ pint/⅔ cup medium-bodied dry white wine
150ml/¼ pint/⅔ cup chicken stock
leaves from 2 fresh thyme sprigs and 2 fresh tarragon sprigs
175g/6oz watercress, leaves removed, or baby spinach leaves, trimmed
150ml/¼ pint/⅔ cup double (heavy) cream
salt and ground black pepper
watercress leaves or mizuna, to garnish

1 Heat the butter and oil in a frying pan over medium heat. Add the chicken portions and cook, turning frequently, for 8–10 minutes, until browned all over. Transfer the chicken to a plate using a slotted spoon and keep warm in the oven.

2 Lower the heat, add the onion to the pan and cook, stirring occasionally, for 5–7 minutes, until softened but not coloured. Stir in the wine, increase the heat to medium and bring to the boil. Boil for 2–3 minutes, then add the stock and bring the mixture back to the boil.

3 Return the chicken to the pan, lower the heat, cover with a tight-fitting lid and simmer very gently for about 30 minutes, until the chicken juices run clear when the thickest part of the meat is pierced with the point of a knife. Transfer the chicken to a warm dish, cover and keep warm.

4 Boil the cooking juices hard until they are reduced to about 60ml/4 tbsp. Add the thyme, tarragon and watercress or spinach leaves and stir in the cream. Simmer over medium heat until slightly thickened.

5 Return the chicken to the pan, season to taste with salt and pepper and heat through for a few minutes. Transfer to warmed serving plates, garnish with watercress or mizuna and serve.

Spatchcocked Devilled Poussin

"Spatchcock" – also known as "butterflied" – refers to birds that have been split and skewered flat. This shortens the cooking time considerably.

Serves 4

15ml/1 tbsp English (hot) mustard powder
15ml/1 tbsp paprika
15ml/1 tbsp ground cumin
20ml/4 tsp tomato ketchup
15ml/1 tbsp lemon juice
65g/2½oz/5 tbsp butter, melted
4 poussins (about 450g/1lb each)
salt

1 Mix together the mustard, paprika, cumin, ketchup, lemon juice and a pinch of salt in a bowl until smooth, then gradually stir in the butter.

2 Using game shears or strong kitchen scissors, split each poussin along one side of the backbone, then cut down the other side of the backbone and remove it.

3 Open out a poussin, skin-side uppermost, then press down firmly with the heel of your hand. Pass a long skewer through one leg and out through the other to secure the bird open and flat. Repeat with the remaining birds.

4 Spread the mustard mixture evenly over the skin of the birds. Cover loosely and leave in a cool place for at least 2 hours to marinate. Preheat the grill (broiler).

5 Place the birds, skin-side uppermost, under the grill and cook for about 12 minutes. Turn the birds over, baste with any juices in the grill (broiler) pan, and cook for a further 7 minutes, until the juices run clear when the thickest part is pierced with the point of a knife. Serve immediately.

Cook's Tip
For an al fresco meal in the summer, these spatchcocked poussins may be cooked on a barbecue.

Chicken Energy 502kcal/2089kJ; Protein 44.5g; Carbohydrate 3.3g, of which sugars 3g; Fat 32.1g, of which saturates 17.3g; Cholesterol 227mg; Calcium 114mg; Fibre 0.9g; Sodium 215mg.
Poussin Energy 659kcal/2742kJ; Protein 50.2g; Carbohydrate 3g, of which sugars 2.9g; Fat 49.8g, of which saturates 18.4g; Cholesterol 296mg; Calcium 22mg; Fibre 0.1g; Sodium 442mg.

Stoved Chicken

"Stoved" is derived from the French *étouffer*, meaning to cook in a covered pot.

Serves 4

1kg/2lb potatoes, cut into
  5mm/¼in slices
2 large onions, thinly sliced
15ml/1 tbsp chopped fresh thyme
25g/1oz/2 tbsp butter
15ml/1 tbsp sunflower oil
2 large bacon rashers
  (strips), chopped
4 large chicken portions, halved
1 bay leaf
600ml/1 pint/2½ cups chicken
  stock
salt and ground black pepper

1 Preheat the oven to 150°C/300°F/Gas 2. Make a thick layer of half the potato slices in the base of a large, heavy, flameproof casserole, then cover with half the onion. Sprinkle with half the thyme and season with salt and pepper.

2 Heat the butter and oil in a large frying pan over medium heat. Add the bacon and chicken and cook, turning frequently, for 8–10 minutes, until the chicken is browned all over. Using a slotted spoon transfer the chicken and bacon to the casserole. Reserve the fat in the pan. Sprinkle the remaining thyme over the chicken and season with salt and pepper. Cover with the remaining onion, followed by a neat layer of overlapping potato slices. Season again with salt and pepper.

3 Pour the stock into the casserole, brush the potatoes with the reserved fat, then cover with a tight-fitting lid and cook in the oven for about 2 hours, until the chicken is tender.

4 Meanwhile, preheat the grill (broiler). Lift the casserole from the oven and remove the lid. Place under the grill and cook until the slices of potatoes are beginning to turn golden brown and crisp. Serve immediately.

> **Variation**
> *Instead of using large chicken portions, use thighs or drumsticks, or a mixture of the two.*

Chicken with Red Cabbage

Crushed juniper berries provide a distinctive flavour in this unusual casserole.

Serves 4

50g/2oz/¼ cup butter
4 large chicken portions, halved
1 onion, chopped
500g/1¼lb/5 cups finely
  shredded red cabbage
4 juniper berries, crushed
12 cooked chestnuts
120ml/4fl oz/½ cup full-bodied
  red wine
salt and ground black pepper

1 Melt the butter in a heavy, flameproof casserole over medium-low heat. Add the chicken pieces and cook, turning frequently, for 8–10 minutes, until lightly browned all over. Transfer the chicken to a plate using tongs.

2 Add the onion to the casserole and cook, stirring occasionally, for about 10 minutes, until softened and light golden brown. Stir the cabbage and juniper berries into the casserole, season with salt and pepper and cook over medium heat, stirring once or twice, for 6–7 minutes.

3 Stir the chestnuts into the casserole, then tuck the chicken pieces under the cabbage so that they are on the base of the casserole. Pour in the red wine.

4 Cover and cook gently for about 40 minutes, until the chicken juices run clear when the thickest part is pierced with the tip of a sharp knife and the cabbage is very tender. Taste and adjust the seasoning, if necessary, and serve immediately.

> **Cook's Tip**
> *Red cabbage needs to be braised gently to be sure that it will be tender. Cooking it in red wine is a traditional accompaniment to game, but it works extremely well with chicken. The red wine helps to maintain the spectacular colour and you could also use ruby port for a slightly richer flavour. Juniper berries add a delightful resinous aroma to the dish.*

Stoved Chicken Energy 524kcal/2206kJ; Protein 50.9g; Carbohydrate 48.2g, of which sugars 8.9g; Fat 15.5g, of which saturates 6g; Cholesterol 185mg; Calcium 53mg; Fibre 3.9g; Sodium 496mg.
With Red Cabbage Energy 405kcal/1697kJ; Protein 44.9g; Carbohydrate 18.6g, of which sugars 9.2g; Fat 14.9g, of which saturates 7.7g; Cholesterol 189mg; Calcium 94mg; Fibre 4.1g; Sodium 229mg.

Honey & Orange Glazed Chicken

This dish is popular in the United States and Australia and is ideal for an easy meal served with baked potatoes.

Serves 4
4 boneless chicken breast portions (about 175g/6oz each)
15ml/1 tbsp sunflower oil
4 spring onions (scallions), chopped
1 garlic clove, crushed
45ml/3 tbsp clear honey
60ml/4 tbsp fresh orange juice
1 orange, peeled and segmented
30ml/2 tbsp soy sauce
fresh lemon balm or flat leaf parsley, to garnish
baked potatoes and mixed salad, to serve

1 Preheat the oven to 190°C/375°F/Gas 5. Place the chicken portions, with skin still on, in a single layer in a shallow roasting pan and set aside.

2 Heat the sunflower oil in a small pan over low heat. Add the spring onions and garlic and cook, stirring occasionally, for about 2 minutes, until softened but not coloured.

3 Add the honey, orange juice, orange segments and soy sauce to the pan and cook, stirring constantly, until the honey has completely dissolved.

4 Pour the sauce over the chicken and bake, uncovered, for about 45 minutes, until the chicken is cooked, basting once or twice with the cooking juices. Check by piercing the thickest part with the point of a knife; the juices should run clear. Transfer the chicken to warmed individual plates, garnish with lemon balm or flat leaf parsley and serve immediately with baked potatoes and a salad.

> **Variation**
> *Create a slightly spicier version of this dish by substituting the same quantity of honey-flavoured mustard for the clear honey. Ensure the mustard has dissolved completely.*

Italian Chicken

Use chicken legs, breast portions or quarters in this colourful dish, and a different type of ribbon pasta if you like.

Serves 4
25g/1oz/1/4 cup plain (all-purpose) flour
4 chicken portions
30ml/2 tbsp olive oil
1 onion, chopped
2 garlic cloves, chopped
1 red (bell) pepper, seeded and chopped
400g/14oz can chopped tomatoes
30ml/2 tbsp red pesto sauce
4 sun-dried tomatoes in oil, drained and chopped
150ml/1/4 pint/2/3 cup chicken stock
5ml/1 tsp dried oregano
8 black olives, pitted
salt and ground black pepper
chopped fresh basil and whole basil leaves, to garnish
tagliatelle, to serve

1 Place the flour in a plastic bag and season with salt and pepper. Add the chicken portions and shake well until they are coated. Heat the oil in a flameproof casserole over medium heat. Add the chicken portions and cook, turning frequently, for 8–10 minutes, until browned all over. Remove with a slotted spoon and set aside.

2 Lower the heat, add the onion, garlic and red pepper and cook, stirring occasionally, for 5 minutes, until the onion is softened but not coloured.

3 Stir in the canned tomatoes, red pesto, sun-dried tomatoes, stock and oregano and bring to the boil.

4 Return the chicken portions to the casserole, season lightly with salt and pepper, cover with a tight-fitting lid and simmer gently for 30–35 minutes, until the chicken is cooked.

5 Add the black olives and simmer for a further 5 minutes. Transfer the chicken and vegetables to a warmed serving dish, sprinkle with the chopped basil and garnish with whole basil leaves. Serve immediately with hot tagliatelle.

Italian Chicken Energy 515kcal/2181kJ; Protein 51.6g; Carbohydrate 44.3g, of which sugars 39.1g; Fat 16g, of which saturates 3.5g; Cholesterol 162mg; Calcium 110mg; Fibre 12.7g; Sodium 345mg.
Glazed Chicken Energy 251kcal/1062kJ; Protein 42.4g; Carbohydrate 10.5g, of which sugars 10.5g; Fat 4.7g, of which saturates 0.9g; Cholesterol 123mg; Calcium 12mg; Fibre 0g; Sodium 642mg.

Creole Chicken Jambalaya

Clearly influenced by
Spanish paella, this New
Orleans speciality is
probably the best-known
dish of Creole cuisine.

Serves 4
1.2kg/2½lb fresh chicken
1½ onions
1 bay leaf
4 black peppercorns
30ml/2 tbsp vegetable oil
2 garlic cloves, chopped
1 green (bell) pepper, seeded
and chopped
1 celery stick, chopped

225g/8oz/1¼ cups long
grain rice
115g/4oz chorizo sausage, sliced
115g/4oz/1 cup chopped
cooked ham
400g/14oz can
chopped tomatoes
2.5ml/½ tsp hot chilli powder
2.5ml/½ tsp cumin seeds
2.5ml/½ tsp ground cumin
5ml/1 tsp dried thyme
115g/4oz/1 cup cooked peeled
prawns (shrimp)
dash of Tabasco sauce
salt and ground black pepper
chopped fresh parsley, to garnish

1 Place the chicken in a flameproof casserole and pour in
600ml/1 pint/2½ cups water. Add half an onion, the bay leaf and
peppercorns and bring to the boil. Lower the heat, cover and
simmer for 1½ hours. Then lift the chicken out of the pan.
Remove and discard the skin and bones and chop the meat.
Strain the stock and reserve.

2 Chop the remaining whole onion. Heat the oil in a large
frying pan over low heat. Add the onion, garlic, green pepper
and celery and cook, stirring occasionally, for 5 minutes. Stir in
the rice. Add the chorizo, ham and chicken and cook, stirring
frequently, for 2–3 minutes.

3 Pour in the tomatoes and 300ml/½ pint/1¼ cups of the
reserved stock and add the chilli, cumin and thyme. Bring to the
boil, cover and simmer gently for 20 minutes, or until the rice is
tender and the liquid absorbed.

4 Stir in the prawns and Tabasco. Cook for 5 minutes more,
then season to taste with salt and pepper. Serve immediately,
garnished with chopped fresh parsley.

Moroccan Chicken Couscous

The combination of sweet
and spicy flavours in the
sauce and couscous makes
this dish irresistible.

Serves 4
15g/½oz/1 tbsp butter
15ml/1 tbsp sunflower oil
4 chicken portions
2 onions, finely chopped
2 garlic cloves, crushed
2.5ml/½ tsp ground cinnamon
1.5ml/¼ tsp ground ginger
1.5ml/¼ tsp ground turmeric
30ml/2 tbsp orange juice
10ml/2 tsp clear honey
salt
fresh mint sprigs, to garnish

For the couscous
350g/12oz/2¼ cups couscous
5ml/1 tsp salt
10ml/2 tsp caster
(superfine) sugar
15ml/1 tbsp sunflower oil
2.5ml/½ tsp ground cinnamon
pinch of grated nutmeg
15ml/1 tbsp orange
blossom water
30ml/2 tbsp sultanas
(golden raisins)
50g/2oz/½ cup chopped
toasted almonds
45ml/3 tbsp chopped pistachios

1 Heat the butter and oil in a large pan over medium heat.
Add the chicken portions, skin-side down, and cook, turning
frequently, for 5–6 minutes, until golden. Turn them over. Add
the onions, garlic, spices, a pinch of salt, the orange juice and
300ml/½ pint/1¼ cups water. Cover and bring to the boil, then
lower the heat and simmer for about 30 minutes.

2 Mix the couscous with the salt and 350ml/12fl oz/1½ cups
water in a bowl. Leave for 5 minutes. Add the rest of the
ingredients for the couscous.

3 Line a steamer with baking parchment and spoon in the
couscous. Set the steamer over the pan of chicken and steam
for 10 minutes.

4 Remove the steamer and keep covered. Stir the honey into
the chicken liquid and boil rapidly for 3–4 minutes. Serve the
chicken on a bed of couscous with some sauce spooned over
it. Garnish with fresh mint and serve with the remaining sauce.

Jambalaya Energy 802kcal/3340kJ; Protein 50.4g; Carbohydrate 59g, of which sugars 10.5g; Fat 40.5g, of which saturates 11.3g; Cholesterol 250mg; Calcium 104mg; Fibre 2.9g; Sodium 785mg.
Chicken Couscous Energy 630kcal/2639kJ; Protein 51.4g; Carbohydrate 64.1g, of which sugars 16.5g; Fat 20.2g, of which saturates 4.2g; Cholesterol 170mg; Calcium 91mg; Fibre 2.5g; Sodium 169mg.

Rabbit with Mustard

Farmed rabbit is now becoming increasingly available in larger supermarkets, ready prepared and cut into serving portions.

Serves 4
15g/½oz/2 tbsp plain (all-purpose) flour
15ml/1 tbsp English (hot) mustard powder
4 large rabbit portions
25g/1oz/2 tbsp butter
30ml/2 tbsp sunflower oil
1 onion, finely chopped
150ml/¼ pint/⅔ cup beer
300ml/½ pint/1¼ cups chicken or veal stock
15ml/1 tbsp tarragon vinegar
25g/1oz/2 tbsp dark brown sugar
10–15ml/2–3 tsp prepared English mustard
salt and ground black pepper

To finish
50g/2oz/4 tbsp butter
30ml/2 tbsp sunflower oil
50g/2oz/1 cup fresh breadcrumbs
15ml/1 tbsp chopped fresh chives
15ml/1 tbsp chopped fresh tarragon

1 Preheat the oven to 160°C/325°F/Gas 3. Mix the flour and mustard powder together on a plate. Dip the rabbit portions in the flour mixture to coat. Reserve the excess flour.

2 Heat the butter and oil in a heavy, flameproof casserole over medium heat. Add the rabbit and cook, turning frequently, for 8–10 minutes, until browned all over. Transfer to a plate.

3 Lower the heat, add the onion to the pan and cook, stirring occasionally, for 5 minutes, until softened. Stir in any reserved flour mixture and cook, stirring, for 1 minute, then stir in the beer, stock and vinegar. Bring to the boil and add the sugar and black pepper. Simmer for 2 minutes. Return the rabbit and any juices that have collected to the casserole, cover with a tight-fitting lid and cook in the oven for 1 hour. Stir in the mustard and salt to taste, cover again and cook for a further 15 minutes.

4 To finish, heat together the butter and oil in a frying pan and fry the breadcrumbs, stirring frequently, until golden, then stir in the herbs. Transfer the rabbit to a warmed serving dish and sprinkle the breadcrumb mixture over the top.

Turkey Hot-pot

Turkey and sausages combine well with kidney beans and other vegetables in this hearty stew.

Serves 4
115g/4oz/scant ½ cup kidney beans, soaked overnight, drained and rinsed
40g/1½oz/3 tbsp butter
2 herb-flavoured pork sausages
450g/1lb turkey casserole meat
3 leeks, sliced
2 carrots, finely chopped
4 tomatoes, chopped
10–15ml/2–3 tsp tomato purée (paste)
1 bouquet garni
400ml/14fl oz/1½ cups chicken stock
salt and ground black pepper

1 Put the kidney beans in a pan, add water to cover and bring to the boil. Boil vigorously for 15 minutes, then drain and return to the pan. Add water to cover, bring to the boil, lower the heat and simmer for 40 minutes. Drain well and set aside.

2 Meanwhile, melt the butter in a flameproof casserole over medium-low heat. Add the sausages and cook, turning frequently, for 7–8 minutes, until browned all over and the fat runs. Remove from the casserole with tongs and drain well on kitchen paper

3 Stir the turkey into the casserole and cook, stirring occasionally, for about 5 minutes, until lightly browned all over, then transfer to a bowl using a slotted spoon.

4 Stir the leeks and carrot into the casserole and cook, stirring occasionally, for about 8 minutes, until lightly browned. Add the chopped tomatoes and tomato purée and simmer gently for about 5 minutes.

5 Chop the sausages and return to the casserole with the beans, turkey, bouquet garni and stock and season to taste with salt and pepper. Lower the heat, cover with a tight-fitting lid and simmer gently for about 1¼ hours, until the beans are tender and there is very little liquid. Spoon the stew on to warmed serving plates and serve immediately.

Rabbit Energy 531kcal/2209kJ; Protein 31.8g; Carbohydrate 21.3g, of which sugars 8.7g; Fat 35g, of which saturates 14.6g; Cholesterol 187mg; Calcium 48mg; Fibre 0.6g; Sodium 247mg.
Turkey Energy 474kcal/1994kJ; Protein 51.9g; Carbohydrate 27.9g, of which sugars 13.1g; Fat 18g, of which saturates 9g; Cholesterol 115mg; Calcium 116mg; Fibre 11.8g; Sodium 308mg.

Duck with Cumberland Sauce

A sophisticated dish: the sauce contains both port and brandy, making it very rich and quite delicious.

Serves 4

4 duck portions
grated rind and juice of 1 lemon
grated rind and juice of
  1 large orange
60ml/4 tbsp redcurrant jelly
60ml/4 tbsp port
pinch of ground mace or ginger
15ml/1 tbsp brandy
salt and ground black pepper
orange slices, to garnish

1 Preheat the oven to 190°C/375°F/Gas 5. Place a rack in a roasting pan. Prick the skin of the duck portions all over and sprinkle with salt and pepper. Place on the rack and roast for 45–50 minutes, until the skin is crisp and the juices run clear when the thickest part is pierced with the point of a knife.

2 Meanwhile, simmer the lemon and orange rinds and juices together in a small pan for 5 minutes.

3 Add the redcurrant jelly and stir until melted, then stir in the port. Bring to the boil and add the mace or ginger and salt and pepper, to taste.

4 Transfer the duck to a serving platter and keep warm. Pour the fat from the roasting pan, leaving the cooking juices. Place the pan over low heat and stir in the brandy. Cook, scraping the sediment from the base of the pan, and bring to the boil. Stir in the port mixture and serve with the duck, garnished with orange slices.

> **Cook's Tip**
> Duck is well known for being a fatty bird. Pricking the skin helps to release the fat during cooking. A clean darning needle is ideal for this. You can also use a fork, but try not to pierce the flesh. If the duck is then roasted on a rack over a roasting pan, the fat will collect beneath the duck preventing it from sitting in a lake of grease.

Coronation Chicken

Created in 1953 in honour of the coronation of HM Queen Elizabeth II, this cold chicken dish with a mild, curry-flavoured sauce is ideal for summer lunch parties and picnics.

Serves 8

1/2 lemon
2.25kg/5lb chicken
1 onion, quartered
1 carrot, quartered
1 large bouquet garni
8 black peppercorns, crushed
pinch of salt
fresh watercress or parsley sprigs,
  to garnish

For the sauce

1 small onion, chopped
15g/1/2oz/1 tbsp butter
15ml/1 tbsp curry paste
15ml/1 tbsp tomato
  purée (paste)
120ml/4fl oz/1/2 cup red wine
1 bay leaf
juice of 1/2 lemon, or to taste
10–15ml/2–3 tsp apricot jam
300ml/1/2 pint/1 1/4 cups
  mayonnaise
120ml/4fl oz/1/2 cup whipping
  cream, whipped
salt and ground black pepper

1 Put the lemon half in the chicken cavity, then place the chicken in a pan that it just fits. Add the onion, carrot, bouquet garni, peppercorns and salt.

2 Add sufficient water to come two-thirds of the way up the chicken and bring to the boil, then lower the heat, cover and simmer for about 1 1/2 hours, until the chicken juices run clear.

3 Transfer the chicken to a large bowl, pour the cooking liquid over it and leave to cool. When cool, transfer the chicken to a board. Remove the skin and bones and chop the flesh.

4 To make the sauce, cook the onion in the butter until soft. Add the curry paste, tomato purée, wine, bay leaf and lemon juice, then cook for 10 minutes. Add the jam; sieve and cool.

5 Beat the sauce mixture into the mayonnaise. Fold in the cream, season to taste with salt and pepper and add the lemon juice, then stir in with the chicken. Garnish and serve.

Duck Energy 277kcal/1162kJ; Protein 29.7g; Carbohydrate 12.2g, of which sugars 12.2g; Fat 9.8g, of which saturates 3g; Cholesterol 165mg; Calcium 21mg; Fibre 0g; Sodium 170mg.
Chicken Energy 480kcal/1994kJ; Protein 30.9g; Carbohydrate 2.8g, of which sugars 2.5g; Fat 37.3g, of which saturates 9.4g; Cholesterol 135mg; Calcium 22mg; Fibre 0.2g; Sodium 265mg.

Chinese Chicken with Cashew Nuts

The cashew nuts give this dish a delightful crunchy texture that contrasts well with the noodles.

Serves 4
4 skinless chicken breast fillets
  (about 175g/6oz each)
3 garlic cloves, crushed
60ml/4 tbsp soy sauce
30ml/2 tbsp cornflour
  (cornstarch)
225g/8oz/4 cups dried

egg noodles
45ml/3 tbsp groundnut (peanut)
  or sunflower oil
15ml/1 tbsp sesame oil
115g/4oz/1 cup roasted
  cashew nuts
6 spring onions (scallions), cut
  into 5cm/2in pieces and
  halved lengthways
spring onion curls and a little
  chopped fresh red chilli,
  to garnish

1 Slice the chicken into strips, place in a bowl and stir in the garlic, soy sauce and cornflour. Cover with clear film (plastic wrap) and chill in the refrigerator for about 30 minutes.

2 Meanwhile, bring a pan of water to the boil and add the egg noodles. Turn off the heat and leave to stand for 5 minutes. Drain well and reserve.

3 Heat the oils in a large frying pan or wok. Add the chilled chicken and marinade juices and stir-fry over high heat for 3–4 minutes, or until golden brown.

4 Add the cashew nuts and spring onions to the pan or wok and stir-fry for a further 2–3 minutes.

5 Add the drained noodles and stir-fry for 2 minutes more. Toss the noodles well and serve immediately, garnished with the spring onion curls and chopped chilli.

Cook's Tip
For a milder garnish, seed the red chilli before chopping or finely dice some red (bell) pepper instead.

Tandoori Chicken Kebabs

This popular dish originates from the Punjab, where it is traditionally cooked in clay ovens known as *tandoors*.

Serves 4
4 skinless chicken breast fillets
  (about 175g/6oz each)
15ml/1 tbsp lemon juice
45ml/3 tbsp tandoori paste
45ml/3 tbsp natural (plain) yogurt

1 garlic clove, crushed
30ml/2 tbsp chopped fresh
  coriander (cilantro)
1 small onion, cut into wedges
  and separated into layers
vegetable oil, for brushing
salt and ground black pepper
fresh coriander sprigs, to garnish
pilau rice and naan bread,
  to serve

1 Chop the chicken fillets into 2.5cm/1in dice and place in a bowl. Add the lemon juice, tandoori paste, yogurt, garlic and coriander and season with salt and pepper. Cover with clear film (plastic wrap) and leave to marinate in the refrigerator, stirring occasionally, for 2–3 hours.

2 Preheat the grill (broiler). Thread alternate pieces of marinated chicken and onion on to four skewers.

3 Brush the onions with a little oil, lay on a grill (broiler) rack and cook under high heat for 10–12 minutes, turning once. Transfer the skewers to warmed plates, garnish the kebabs with fresh coriander and serve immediately with pilau rice and warm naan bread.

Cook's Tip
For a special occasion or when cooking these kebabs on a barbecue, serve with a yogurt dip. Mix together 250ml/8fl oz/ 1 cup natural (plain) yogurt, 30ml/2 tbsp double (heavy) cream, 30ml/2 tbsp chopped fresh mint and ½ peeled, seeded and finely chopped cucumber in a bowl. Season to taste with salt and pepper. Cover with clear film (plastic wrap) and chill in the refrigerator until ready to serve. As an alternative to the mint you could use chopped fresh coriander (cilantro).

Tandoori Energy 222kcal/937kJ; Protein 42.8g; Carbohydrate 2g, of which sugars 1.7g; Fat 4.8g, of which saturates 0.9g; Cholesterol 123mg; Calcium 34mg; Fibre 0.2g; Sodium 115mg.
Chinese Energy 717kcal/3007kJ; Protein 55.5g; Carbohydrate 54.3g, of which sugars 4.2g; Fat 32.3g, of which saturates 6.1g; Cholesterol 139mg; Calcium 44mg; Fibre 2.8g; Sodium 1363mg.

Duck, Avocado & Berry Salad

Duck breasts are roasted with a honey and soy glaze until crisp, then served warm with fresh raspberries and avocado.

Serves 4
4 small or 2 large duck breast
    portions, halved if large
15ml/1 tbsp clear honey
15ml/1 tbsp dark soy sauce
mixed chopped fresh salad leaves
    such as lamb's lettuce, radicchio
    or frisée
2 avocados, stoned (pitted),
    peeled and cut into chunks
115g/4oz/1 cup raspberries
salt and ground black pepper

For the dressing
60ml/4 tbsp olive oil
15ml/1 tbsp raspberry vinegar
15ml/1 tbsp redcurrant jelly

1 Preheat the oven to 220°C/425°F/Gas 7. Prick the skin of each duck breast portion with a fork. Blend the honey and soy sauce together in a small bowl, then brush the mixture all over the skins of the duck.

2 Place the duck breast portions on a rack set over a roasting pan and season with salt and pepper. Roast for 15–20 minutes, until the skins are crisp and the meat cooked.

3 Meanwhile, to make the dressing, put the oil, vinegar and redcurrant jelly in a small bowl, season with salt and pepper and whisk well until evenly blended.

4 Slice the duck breast portions diagonally and arrange on four individual plates with the salad leaves, avocados and raspberries. Spoon the dressing over the top and serve immediately.

> **Cook's Tip**
> *Small avocados contain the most flavour and have a good texture. They should be ripe but not too soft, so avoid any with skins that are turning black.*

Chinese-style Chicken Salad

For a variation and to add more colour, add some cooked, peeled prawns to this lovely salad.

Serves 4
4 chicken breast fillets (about
    175g/6oz each)
60ml/4 tbsp dark soy sauce
pinch of Chinese five-spice powder
squeeze of lemon juice
1/2 cucumber, peeled and cut into
    thin batons
5ml/1 tsp salt
45ml/3 tbsp sunflower oil
30ml/2 tbsp sesame oil

15ml/1 tbsp sesame seeds
30ml/2 tbsp Chinese rice wine or
    dry sherry
2 carrots, cut into thin batons
8 spring onions
    (scallions), shredded
75g/3oz/1 cup beansprouts

For the sauce
60ml/4 tbsp crunchy
    peanut butter
10ml/2 tsp lemon juice
10ml/2 tsp sesame oil
1.5ml/1/4 tsp hot chilli powder
1 spring onion, finely chopped

1 Put the chicken into a pan and pour in water to cover. Add 15ml/1 tbsp of the soy sauce, the Chinese five-spice powder and lemon juice. Cover and bring to the boil, then lower the heat and simmer for 20 minutes. Drain the chicken and remove and discard the skin. Slice the flesh into thin strips.

2 Sprinkle the cucumber batons with salt, leave for 30 minutes, then rinse well and pat dry with kitchen paper.

3 Heat the oils in a small frying pan. Add the sesame seeds and cook for 30 seconds, then stir in the remaining soy sauce and the rice wine or sherry. Add the carrot batons and stir-fry for 2 minutes, then remove the pan from the heat.

4 Mix together the cucumber, spring onions, beansprouts, carrots, pan juices and chicken. Transfer to a shallow dish. Cover with clear film (plastic wrap) and chill in the refrigerator for 1 hour.

5 For the sauce, cream the first four ingredients together, then stir in the spring onion. Serve the chicken with the sauce.

Chicken Energy 452kcal/1886kJ; Protein 47g; Carbohydrate 4.1g, of which sugars 3g; Fat 27.2g, of which saturates 4.8g; Cholesterol 123mg; Calcium 53mg; Fibre 1.5g; Sodium 1720mg.
Duck Energy 345kcal/1438kJ; Protein 21.2g; Carbohydrate 8g, of which sugars 7.3g; Fat 27.2g, of which saturates 5g; Cholesterol 110mg; Calcium 26mg; Fibre 2.4g; Sodium 382mg.

Crumbed Turkey Steaks

The authentic Austrian dish, *wiener schnitzel,* uses veal escalopes, but turkey steaks make a tasty alternative.

Serves 4
4 turkey breast steaks (about 150g/5oz each)
40g/1½oz/⅓ cup plain (all-purpose) flour, seasoned
1 egg, lightly beaten
75g/3oz/1½ cups fresh white breadcrumbs
75ml/5 tbsp finely grated Parmesan cheese
25g/1oz/2 tbsp butter
45ml/3 tbsp sunflower oil
fresh parsley sprigs, to garnish
4 lemon wedges, to serve

1 Lay the turkey steaks between two sheets of clear film (plastic wrap). Beat each one with a rolling pin until flattened and even. Snip the edges of the steaks with kitchen scissors a few times to prevent them from curling during cooking.

2 Place the seasoned flour on one plate, the egg in a shallow bowl and the breadcrumbs and Parmesan mixed together on another plate.

3 Dip each side of the steaks into the flour and shake off any excess. Next, dip them into the egg and then gently press each side into the breadcrumbs and cheese until evenly coated.

4 Heat the butter and oil in a large frying pan over medium heat. Add the turkey steaks and cook for 2–3 minutes on each side, until golden. Transfer to warmed plates, garnish with fresh parsley sprigs and serve with lemon wedges.

Cook's Tip
The easiest way to make breadcrumbs is in a food processor. Tear the bread into 2.5cm/1in pieces and process in brief bursts with a metal blade. You can also use a blender in the same way, but work in small batches, emptying each one into a bowl before adding more bread. The traditional way is, of course, to use a grater, taking care not to damage your fingers.

Country Cider Hot-pot

Rabbit meat is now beginning to regain its popularity – it never lost it in some European countries – and, like all game, is a healthy, low-fat option.

Serves 4
25g/1oz/¼ cup plain (all-purpose) flour
4 boneless rabbit portions
25g/1oz/2 tbsp butter
15ml/1 tbsp vegetable oil
15 baby (pearl) onions
4 rashers (strips) streaky (fatty) bacon, chopped
10ml/2 tsp Dijon mustard
450ml/¾ pint/1¾ cups dry (hard) cider
3 carrots, chopped
2 parsnips, chopped
12 ready-to-eat prunes
1 fresh rosemary sprig
1 bay leaf
salt and ground black pepper
mashed potatoes, to serve (optional)

1 Preheat the oven to 160°C/325°F/Gas 3. Place the flour in a plastic bag, season with salt and pepper and shake to mix. Add the rabbit portions and shake until coated. Remove from the bag and set aside.

2 Heat the butter and oil in a flameproof casserole over medium-low heat. Add the onions and bacon and cook, stirring occasionally, for about 4 minutes, until the onions have softened. Remove with a slotted spoon and set aside.

3 Add the rabbit portions to the casserole and cook, turning frequently, for 8–10 minutes, until evenly browned all over. Spread a little of the mustard over the top of each portion.

4 Return the onions and bacon to the casserole, pour in the cider and add the carrots, parsnips, prunes, rosemary and bay leaf. Season generously with salt and pepper. Bring to the boil, then cover with a tight-fitting lid and transfer to the oven. Cook for about 1½ hours, until the meat is cooked through and the vegetables are tender.

5 Remove and discard the rosemary sprig and bay leaf and serve the rabbit hot with creamy mashed potatoes, if you like.

Turkey Energy 565kcal/2376kJ; Protein 64.9g; Carbohydrate 24.3g, of which sugars 0.7g; Fat 24g, of which saturates 9.4g; Cholesterol 191mg; Calcium 283mg; Fibre 0.8g; Sodium 538mg.
Hot-pot Energy 544kcal/2279kJ; Protein 41.1g; Carbohydrate 42.9g, of which sugars 32.2g; Fat 21g, of which saturates 8.2g; Cholesterol 136mg; Calcium 129mg; Fibre 8g; Sodium 488mg.

Turkey Pastitsio

A traditional Greek *pastitsio* is a rich, high-fat dish made with beef, but this lighter version is just as tasty.

Serves 4–6
450g/1lb lean minced (ground) turkey
1 large onion, finely chopped
60ml/4 tbsp tomato purée (paste)
250ml/8fl oz/1 cup red wine or chicken stock
5ml/1 tsp ground cinnamon

300g/11oz/3 cups macaroni
300ml/¹/₂ pint/1¹/₄ cups skimmed milk
25g/1oz/2 tbsp sunflower margarine
25g/1oz/¹/₄ cup plain (all-purpose) flour
5ml/1 tsp grated nutmeg
2 tomatoes, sliced
60ml/4 tbsp wholemeal (whole-wheat) breadcrumbs
salt and ground black pepper
green salad, to serve

1 Preheat the oven to 220°C/425°F/Gas 7. Fry the turkey and onion in a non-stick frying pan without adding any fat, stirring until the turkey is lightly browned.

2 Stir in the tomato purée, red wine or stock and cinnamon. Season with salt and pepper, then cover with a tight-fitting lid and simmer for 5 minutes.

3 Bring a pan of salted water to the boil, add the macaroni, bring back to the boil and cook for 8–10 minutes, until just tender. Drain well.

4 Spoon alternate layers of macaroni and the meat mixture into a wide ovenproof dish.

5 Place the milk, margarine and flour in a pan and whisk over medium heat until thickened and smooth. Add the nutmeg and season with salt and pepper to taste.

6 Pour the sauce evenly over the pasta and meat. Arrange the tomato slices on top and sprinkle lines of breadcrumbs over the surface. Bake for 30–35 minutes, or until golden brown and bubbling. Serve hot with a green salad.

Tuscan Chicken

A simple peasant casserole with all the flavours of Tuscan ingredients. The white wine can be replaced by chicken stock.

Serves 4
5ml/1 tsp olive oil
8 chicken thighs, skinned
1 onion, thinly sliced
2 red (bell) peppers, seeded and sliced
1 garlic clove, crushed

300ml/¹/₂ pint/1¹/₄ cups passata (bottled strained tomatoes)
150ml/¹/₄ pint/¹/₂ cup dry white wine
large fresh oregano sprig, or 5ml/1 tsp dried oregano
400g/14oz can cannellini beans, drained and rinsed
45ml/3 tbsp fresh breadcrumbs
salt and ground black pepper
fresh oregano or flat leaf parsley sprigs, to garnish

1 Heat the oil in a large, heavy pan over medium heat. Add the chicken and cook, turning frequently, for 8–10 minutes, until golden brown all over. Remove the chicken from the pan and keep hot.

2 Add the onion and red peppers to the pan, lower the heat and cook, stirring occasionally, for about 5 minutes, until softened but not coloured. Stir in the garlic.

3 Return the chicken to the pan and add the passata, wine and oregano. Season well with salt and pepper, bring to the boil, then cover the pan with a tight-fitting lid.

4 Lower the heat and simmer gently, stirring occasionally, for 30–35 minutes, or until the chicken is tender and the juices run clear when the thickest par is pierced with the point of a knife.

5 Preheat the grill (broiler). Stir in the cannellini beans and simmer for a further 5 minutes until heated through. Sprinkle with the breadcrumbs and cook under the grill for a few minutes, until golden brown.

6 Divide the chicken, beans and vegetables among warmed serving plates, garnish with herb sprigs and serve immediately.

Turkey Energy 406kcal/1716kJ; Protein 28.9g; Carbohydrate 56.8g, of which sugars 9.5g; Fat 5.5g, of which saturates 0.4g; Cholesterol 45mg; Calcium 117mg; Fibre 3.1g; Sodium 202mg.
Chicken Energy 379kcal/1599kJ; Protein 41.3g; Carbohydrate 35.8g, of which sugars 12.6g; Fat 6.2g, of which saturates 1.5g; Cholesterol 158mg; Calcium 118mg; Fibre 8.5g; Sodium 789mg.

Poussins with Grapes in Vermouth

This sauce could also be served with roast chicken, but poussins have the stronger flavour.

Serves 4

4 poussins (about 450g/1lb each)
50g/2oz/¼ cup butter, softened
2 shallots, chopped
60ml/4 tbsp chopped
   fresh parsley
225g/8oz/2 cups white grapes,
   preferably Muscatel, halved
   and seeded

150ml/¼ pint/⅔ cup white
   vermouth
5ml/1 tsp cornflour (cornstarch)
60ml/4 tbsp double
   (heavy) cream
30ml/2 tbsp pine
   nuts, toasted
salt and ground black pepper
watercress sprigs or mizuna,
   to garnish

1 Preheat the oven to 200°C/400°F/Gas 6. Spread the softened butter all over the poussins and put a hazelnut-sized piece in the cavity of each bird.

2 Mix together the shallots and parsley and place a quarter of the mixture inside each poussin. Put the poussins side by side in a large roasting pan and roast for 40–50 minutes, or until the juices run clear when the thickest part is pierced with the point of a sharp knife. Transfer the poussins to a warmed serving plate. Cover and keep warm.

3 Skim off most of the fat from the roasting pan, then add the grapes and vermouth. Place the pan over a low heat for a few minutes to warm and slightly soften the grapes. Lift the grapes out of the pan using a slotted spoon and place them around the poussins. Keep covered.

4 Stir the cornflour into the cream until smooth, then add to the pan juices. Cook gently, stirring constantly, for 3–4 minutes, until the sauce has thickened slightly. Season to taste with salt and pepper. Spoon the sauce around the poussins. Sprinkle with the toasted pine nuts and garnish with watercress sprigs or mizuna. Serve immediately.

Chicken Parcels with Herb Butter

These delightful individual filo pastry parcels contain a wonderfully moist and herb-flavoured filling.

Serves 4

4 skinless chicken breast fillets
   (about 175g/6oz each)
150g/5oz/generous ½ cup
   butter, softened, plus extra
   for greasing

90ml/6 tbsp mixed chopped fresh
   herbs, such as thyme, parsley,
   oregano and rosemary
5ml/1 tsp lemon juice
5 large sheets filo pastry, thawed
   if frozen
1 egg, beaten
30ml/2 tbsp freshly grated
   Parmesan cheese
salt and ground black pepper

1 Season the chicken fillets on both sides with salt and pepper. Melt 25g/1oz/2 tbsp of the butter in a frying pan over medium heat. Add the chicken and cook, turning once, for about 5 minutes, until lightly browned on both sides. Remove from the pan and leave to cool.

2 Preheat the oven to 190°C/375°F/Gas 5. Lightly grease a baking sheet with butter. Put the remaining measured butter, the herbs and lemon juice in a food processor or blender, season with salt and pepper and process until smooth. Melt half of this herb butter.

3 Take one sheet of filo pastry and brush with melted herb butter. Keep the other sheets covered with a damp dish towel. Fold the filo pastry sheet in half and brush again with butter. Place a chicken portion about 2.5cm/1in from the top end.

4 Dot the chicken with a quarter of the unmelted herb butter. Fold in the sides of the dough, then roll up to enclose the chicken completely. Place seam-side down on a lightly greased baking sheet. Repeat with the other chicken portions.

5 Brush the filo parcels with beaten egg. Cut the last sheet of filo into strips, then scrunch and arrange on top. Brush the parcels with the egg glaze, then sprinkle with Parmesan cheese. Bake for 35–50 minutes, until golden brown. Serve hot.

Poussins Energy 831kcal/3456kJ; Protein 52.1g; Carbohydrate 12.3g, of which sugars 11.1g; Fat 60.2g, of which saturates 21.8g; Cholesterol 308mg; Calcium 62mg; Fibre 1.2g; Sodium 270mg.
Chicken Energy 554kcal/2310kJ; Protein 42.5g; Carbohydrate 14.8g, of which sugars 0.5g; Fat 36.6g, of which saturates 22g; Cholesterol 240mg; Calcium 138mg; Fibre 0.6g; Sodium 417mg.

Pot-roast of Venison

The venison is marinated for 24 hours before preparation to give this rich dish an even fuller flavour.

Serves 4–5
1.75kg/4lb boned leg or shoulder of venison
75ml/5 tbsp sunflower oil
4 cloves
8 black peppercorns, lightly crushed
12 juniper berries, lightly crushed
250ml/8fl oz/1 cup full-bodied red wine
115g/4oz lightly smoked streaky (fatty) bacon, chopped
2 onions, finely chopped
2 carrots, chopped
150g/5oz large mushrooms, sliced
15g/½ oz/2 tbsp plain (all-purpose) flour
250ml/8fl oz/1 cup veal stock
30ml/2 tbsp redcurrant jelly
salt and ground black pepper

1 Put the venison in a bowl, add half the oil, the cloves, peppercorns, juniper berries and wine, cover with clear film (plastic wrap) and leave in a cold place or the refrigerator for 24 hours, turning the meat occasionally.

2 Preheat the oven to 160°C/325°F/Gas 3. Remove the venison from the bowl and pat dry. Reserve the marinade. Heat the remaining oil in a large shallow pan over medium heat. Add the venison and cook, turning once, for about 10 minutes, until evenly browned on both sides. Transfer to a plate.

3 Stir the bacon, onions, carrots and mushrooms into the pan and cook, stirring occasionally, for about 5 minutes. Stir in the flour and cook, stirring constantly, for 2 minutes, then remove the pan from the heat and gradually stir in the reserved marinade, stock and redcurrant jelly. Season with salt and pepper. Return the pan to the heat and bring to the boil, stirring constantly. Lower the heat and simmer for 2–3 minutes.

4 Transfer the venison and sauce to a casserole and cover with a tight-fitting lid. Cook in the oven, turning the the venison occasionally, for about 3 hours, until very tender. Remove the venison from the casserole and divide the sauce among warmed plates. Carve the venison and place on top. Serve.

Pheasant with Mushrooms

The wine and mushroom sauce in this recipe is given a lift by the inclusion of anchovy fillets.

Serves 4
1 pheasant, cut into portions
250ml/8fl oz/1 cup red wine
45ml/3 tbsp sunflower oil
60ml/4 tbsp Spanish sherry vinegar
1 large onion, chopped
2 rashers (strips) smoked bacon
350g/12oz chestnut (cremini) mushrooms, sliced
3 canned anchovy fillets, drained, soaked in water for 10 minutes and drained
350ml/12fl oz/1½ cups game, veal or chicken stock
1 bouquet garni
salt and ground black pepper

1 Place the pheasant portions in a dish. Add the wine, half the oil and half the vinegar, then sprinkle with half the onion. Season with salt and pepper. Cover the dish with clear film (plastic wrap) and leave in a cold place or the refrigerator, turning the pheasant portions occasionally, for 8–12 hours.

2 Preheat the oven to 160°C/325°F/Gas 3. Lift the pheasant portions from the dish and pat dry with kitchen paper. Reserve the marinade.

3 Heat the remaining oil in a flameproof casserole over medium heat. Add the pheasant portions and cook, turning frequently, for 8–10 minutes, until evenly browned all over. Transfer to a plate.

4 Cut the bacon into strips, then add to the casserole with the remaining onion. Cook over low heat, stirring occasionally, for 5 minutes, until the onion is softened but not coloured. Stir in the mushrooms and cook for about 3 minutes.

5 Stir in the anchovies and remaining vinegar and boil until reduced. Add the marinade, cook for 2 minutes, then add the stock and bouquet garni. Return the pheasant to the casserole, cover and bake for about 1½ hours. Transfer the pheasant to a serving dish. Boil the juices to reduce. Discard the bouquet garni, pour the juices over the pheasant and serve immediately.

Venison Energy 601kcal/2528kJ; Protein 83.1g; Carbohydrate 13g, of which sugars 9.6g; Fat 22.9g, of which saturates 5.9g; Cholesterol 187mg; Calcium 49mg; Fibre 1.9g; Sodium 566mg.
Pheasant Energy 457kcal/1910kJ; Protein 46.2g; Carbohydrate 6.4g, of which sugars 4.5g; Fat 23.1g, of which saturates 6.1g; Cholesterol 9mg; Calcium 102mg; Fibre 2g; Sodium 483mg.

Minty Yogurt Chicken

Marinated, grilled chicken thighs make a tasty light lunch or supper – and they are an economical buy, too.

Serves 4
8 chicken thigh portions

15ml/1 tbsp clear honey
30ml/2 tbsp lime juice
30ml/2 tbsp natural (plain) yogurt
60ml/4 tbsp chopped fresh mint
salt and ground black pepper
boiled new potatoes and tomato
salad, to serve (optional)

1 Skin the chicken thighs and slash the flesh at intervals with a sharp knife. Place them in a non-metal bowl. Mix together the honey, lime juice, yogurt and half the mint in another bowl and season with salt and pepper.

2 Spoon the marinade over the chicken, cover the bowl with clear film (plastic wrap) and leave to marinate in a cool place for 30 minutes.

3 Line a grill (broiler) pan with foil and preheat the grill (broiler). Remove the chicken from the marinade, place in the pan and cook, turning occasionally, for 15–20 minutes, until golden brown and the juices run clear when thickest part is pierced with point of a sharp knife.

4 Transfer the chicken thighs to warmed plates, sprinkle with the remaining mint and serve immediately with potatoes and tomato salad, if you like.

Cook's Tip
If you want to marinate the chicken for longer than 30 minutes, place the bowl in the refrigerator.

Variation
Substitute chicken drumsticks for the thighs and increase the cooking time by 5–10 minutes.

Mandarin Sesame Duck

The rind, juice and flesh of sweet mandarin oranges are used in this delightful dish.

Serves 4
4 duck leg or breast fillets
30ml/2 tbsp light soy sauce

45ml/3 tbsp clear honey
15ml/1 tbsp sesame seeds
4 mandarin oranges
5ml/1 tsp cornflour (cornstarch)
salt and ground black pepper

1 Preheat the oven to 180°C/350°F/Gas 4. Prick the duck skin all over. Slash the breast skin diagonally at intervals. Roast the duck for 1 hour. Mix 15ml/1 tbsp soy sauce with 30ml/2 tbsp honey and brush over the duck. Sprinkle with sesame seeds. Roast for a further 15 minutes.

2 Grate the rind from one mandarin and squeeze the juice from two. Place in a small pan and stir in the cornflour, remaining soy sauce and honey. Heat, stirring, until thickened and clear. Season with salt and pepper. Peel and slice the remaining mandarins. Serve the duck with the mandarin slices and sauce.

Sticky Ginger Chicken

For a fuller flavour, marinate the chicken drumsticks in the glaze for 30 minutes.

Serves 4
8 chicken drumsticks

30ml/2 tbsp lemon juice
25g/1oz light muscovado
   (brown) sugar
5ml/1 tsp grated fresh root ginger
10ml/2 tsp soy sauce
ground black pepper

1 Slash the chicken drumsticks about three times through the thickest part of the flesh. Mix all the remaining ingredients in a bowl, then toss the drumsticks in the glaze.

2 Cook them under a hot grill (broiler) or on a barbecue, turning occasionally and brushing with the glaze, until golden and the juices run clear when the thickest part is pierced.

Minty Yogurt Energy 179kcal/752kJ; Protein 31.8g; Carbohydrate 3.4g, of which sugars 3.4g; Fat 4.3g, of which saturates 1.3g; Cholesterol 158mg; Calcium 25mg; Fibre 0g; Sodium 142mg.
Mandarin Duck Energy 254kcal/1066kJ; Protein 31g; Carbohydrate 12g, of which sugars 10.9g; Fat 12g, of which saturates 2.3g; Cholesterol 165mg; Calcium 55mg; Fibre 0.5g; Sodium 704mg.
Sticky Ginger Energy 234kcal/980kJ; Protein 29.2g; Carbohydrate 6.5g, of which sugars 6.5g; Fat 10.3g, of which saturates 2.7g; Cholesterol 155mg; Calcium 20mg; Fibre 0g; Sodium 145mg.

Oat-crusted Chicken with Sage

Oats make an excellent, crunchy coating for savoury foods, and offer a good way to add extra fibre.

Serves 4
45ml/3 tbsp milk
10ml/2 tsp English (hot) mustard
40g/1½oz/½ cup rolled oats
45ml/3 tbsp chopped fresh sage leaves
8 chicken thighs or drumsticks, skinned
120ml/4fl oz/½ cup fromage frais (farmer's cheese)
5ml/1 tsp wholegrain mustard
salt and ground black pepper
fresh sage leaves, to garnish

1 Preheat the oven to 200°C/400°F/Gas 6. Mix together the milk and mustard in a small bowl.

2 Mix the oats with 30ml/2 tbsp of the chopped sage on a plate and season with salt and pepper. Brush the chicken with the milk mixture and press into the oats to coat evenly.

3 Place the chicken on a baking sheet and bake for about 40 minutes, or until the juices run clear when the thickest part is pierced with the point of a sharp knife.

4 Meanwhile, mix together the fromage frais, wholegrain mustard and remaining sage in a bowl and season to taste with salt and pepper. Transfer to a small serving dish.

5 Place the chicken on warmed serving plates and garnish with fresh sage leaves. Serve immediately with the dish of sauce.

Cook's Tips
• *If fresh sage is not available, choose another fresh herb, such as thyme, parsley or tarragon. Sage is one of those herbs that does not dry well, quickly becoming dusty and flavourless.*
• *These chicken thighs or drumsticks may be served hot or cold. They would be a good choice for a picnic. Pack the sauce separately in a plastic container or screw-top jar.*
• *If you find English (hot) mustard too spicy, substitute Dijon.*

Chicken in Creamy Orange Sauce

The brandy adds a rich flavour to the sauce, but omit it if you prefer and use orange juice alone.

Serves 4
8 chicken thighs or drumsticks, skinned
45ml/3 tbsp brandy
300ml/½ pint/1¼ cups fresh orange juice
3 spring onions (scallions), chopped
10ml/2 tsp cornflour (cornstarch)
90ml/6 tbsp fromage frais (farmer's cheese)
salt and ground black pepper
boiled rice or pasta and green salad, to serve (optional)

1 Cook the chicken pieces in a non-stick or heavy frying pan, without any added fat, over medium-low heat for 8–10 minutes, turning frequently until evenly browned all over.

2 Stir in the brandy, orange juice and spring onions and bring to the boil. Lower the heat, cover and simmer gently for about 15 minutes, or until the chicken is tender and the juices run clear when the thickest part is pierced with the point of a sharp knife.

3 Blend the cornflour with a little water in a small bowl, then mix into the fromage frais. Stir this into a small pan and cook over medium heat until boiling.

4 Season the sauce to taste with salt and pepper. Spoon the chicken and cooking juices on to warmed plates, pour the sauce over it and serve with plain boiled rice or pasta and green salad, if you like.

Cook's Tip
For an even healthier version of this dish, suitable for those who are watching their weight or cholesterol levels, use low-fat fromage frais (farmer's cheese) which is virtually fat-free. The sauce will still be beautifully creamy and rich tasting.

Oat-crusted Energy 238kcal/997kJ; Protein 32.2g; Carbohydrate 3g, of which sugars 3g; Fat 10.9g, of which saturates 3.1g; Cholesterol 157mg; Calcium 66mg; Fibre 0g; Sodium 163mg.
In Orange Sauce Energy 306kcal/1287kJ; Protein 43.7g; Carbohydrate 10.1g, of which sugars 7.7g; Fat 7.5g, of which saturates 2.9g; Cholesterol 212mg; Calcium 50mg; Fibre 0.2g; Sodium 198mg.

Normandy Roast Chicken

The chicken is turned over halfway through roasting so that it cooks evenly and stays wonderfully moist.

Serves 4
50g/2oz/¼ cup butter, softened
30ml/2 tbsp chopped
   fresh tarragon
1 small garlic clove, crushed
1.5kg/3–3½lb fresh chicken
5ml/1 tsp plain (all-purpose) flour
150ml/¼ pint/⅔ cup double
   (heavy) cream
squeeze of lemon juice
salt and ground black pepper
fresh tarragon and lemon slices,
   to garnish

1 Preheat the oven to 200°C/400°F/Gas 6. Mix together the butter, 15ml/1 tbsp of the chopped tarragon and the garlic in a bowl and season with salt and pepper. Spoon half the butter mixture into the cavity of the chicken.

2 Carefully lift the skin at the neck end of the bird from the breast flesh on each side, then gently push a little of the butter mixture into each pocket and smooth it down over the breasts with your fingers.

3 Season the bird and lay it, breast-side down, in a roasting pan. Roast for 45 minutes, then turn the chicken over and baste with the cooking juices. Cook for a further 45 minutes, until the juices run clear when the thickest part of the chicken is pierced with the point of a sharp knife.

4 When the chicken is cooked, lift it to drain out any juices from the cavity into the pan, then transfer the bird to a warmed platter, cover and keep warm.

5 Place the roasting pan over low heat and heat until sizzling. Stir in the flour and cook, stirring constantly, for 1 minute, then stir in the cream, the remaining tarragon, 150ml/¼ pint/⅔ cup water and the lemon juice. Season to taste with salt and pepper. Bring to the boil and cook, stirring constantly, for 2–3 minutes, until thickened. Carve the chicken into slices and place them on warmed plates. Garnish with tarragon and lemon slices and serve with the sauce handed separately.

Duck with Orange Sauce

This is a simple, yet more elegant-looking variation on the classic French whole duck.

Serves 4
4 duck breast portions
15ml/1 tbsp sunflower oil
2 oranges
150ml/¼ pint/⅔ cup fresh
   orange juice
15ml/1 tbsp port
30ml/2 tbsp Seville (Temple)
   orange marmalade
15g/½oz/1 tbsp butter
5ml/1 tsp cornflour (cornstarch)
salt and ground black pepper

1 Season the duck skin with salt and pepper. Heat the oil in a frying pan over a medium heat. Add the duck breast portions, skin-side down, cover and cook for 3–4 minutes, until just lightly browned. Turn the duck over, lower the heat slightly and cook, uncovered, for 5–6 minutes.

2 Peel the skin from the oranges and remove the white pith. Working over a bowl to catch any juice, slice either side of the membranes with a sharp knife to release the orange segments. Set the segments aside with the juice.

3 Remove the duck portions from the pan with a slotted spoon, drain on kitchen paper and keep warm in the oven while making the sauce.

4 Drain off the fat from the frying pan. Add the segmented oranges, all but 30ml/2 tbsp of the orange juice, the port and the orange marmalade. Bring to the boil and then reduce the heat slightly. Gradually whisk small knobs (pats) of the butter into the sauce, one piece at a time, and season to taste with salt and pepper.

5 Blend the cornflour with the reserved orange juice in a small bowl, pour into the pan and stir until the sauce has thickened slightly. Return the duck to the pan and cook over low heat for about 3 minutes. Remove the duck portions from the pan and cut into thick slices. Arrange them on warmed plates and spoon the sauce over them. Serve immediately.

Roast Chicken Energy 491kcal/2038kJ; Protein 37.6g; Carbohydrate 1.2g, of which sugars 1.1g; Fat 37.3g, of which saturates 17.8g; Cholesterol 210mg; Calcium 71mg; Fibre 0.5g; Sodium 228mg.
Duck Breasts Energy 307kcal/1289kJ; Protein 30.6g; Carbohydrate 16.5g, of which sugars 15.4g; Fat 15.7g, of which saturates 4.2g; Cholesterol 173mg; Calcium 60mg; Fibre 1.3g; Sodium 201mg.

Coq au Vin

Chicken is flamed in brandy, then braised in red wine with bacon, mushrooms and onions in this classic dish.

Serves 4

50g/2oz/¹/₂ cup plain
  (all-purpose) flour
1.5kg/3–3¹/₂lb chicken, cut into
  8 pieces
15ml/1 tbsp olive oil
65g/2¹/₂oz/5 tbsp butter
20 baby (pearl) onions

75g/3oz/¹/₂ cup diced streaky
  (fatty) bacon
about 20 button
  (white) mushrooms
30ml/2 tbsp brandy
1 bottle red Burgundy wine
bouquet garni
3 garlic cloves
5ml/1 tsp soft light brown sugar
salt and ground black pepper
15ml/1 tbsp chopped fresh
  parsley and croûtons, to garnish

1 Place 40g/1¹/₂oz/¹/₃ cup of the flour in a large plastic bag, season with salt and pepper and add the chicken pieces. Shake well to coat. Heat the oil and 50g/2oz/4 tbsp of the butter in a large flameproof casserole over low heat. Add the onions and bacon and cook, stirring occasionally, for about 10 minutes, until the onions have browned lightly. Add the mushrooms and cook for 2 minutes more. Remove with a slotted spoon and reserve.

2 Add the chicken pieces to the casserole, increase the heat to medium and cook, turning frequently, for about 5–6 minutes, until evenly browned all over. Add the brandy and, standing well back, ignite it with a match, then shake the casserole gently until the flames subside.

3 Add the wine, bouquet garni, garlic and sugar and season with salt and pepper. Bring to the boil, lower the heat, cover and simmer, stirring occasionally, for 1 hour. Add the onions, bacon and mushrooms, re-cover and cook for 30 minutes. Transfer the chicken, vegetables and bacon to a warmed dish.

4 Remove the bouquet garni and boil the liquid for 2 minutes. Cream the remaining butter and flour. Whisk in spoonfuls of the mixture to thicken the liquid. Pour the sauce over the chicken and serve garnished with parsley and croûtons.

Pot-roast Poussin

This dish is inspired by the French method of cooking these birds. Pot-roasting keeps them beautifully moist and succulent.

Serves 4

15ml/1 tbsp olive oil
1 onion, sliced
1 large garlic clove, sliced
50g/2oz/¹/₃ cup diced
  smoked bacon
2 poussins (about 450g/
  1lb each)
30ml/2 tbsp melted butter
2 baby celery hearts, each cut
  into 4 pieces

8 baby carrots
2 small courgettes (zucchini), cut
  into chunks
8 small new potatoes
600ml/1 pint/2¹/₂ cups chicken
  stock
150ml/¹/₄ pint/²/₃ cup dry
  white wine
1 bay leaf
2 fresh thyme sprigs
2 fresh rosemary sprigs
15ml/1 tbsp butter, softened
15g/¹/₂oz/2 tbsp plain (all-
  purpose) flour
salt and ground black pepper
fresh herbs, to garnish

1 Preheat the oven to 190°C/375°F/Gas 5. Heat the olive oil in a large flameproof casserole over low heat. Add the onions, garlic and bacon and cook, stirring occasionally, for 5–6 minutes, until the onions have softened. Brush the poussins with half the melted butter and season with salt and pepper. Add to the casserole with the vegetables. Pour in the stock and wine and add the herbs. Cover and bake for 20 minutes.

2 Remove the lid and brush the birds with the remaining melted butter. Bake for a further 25–30 minutes, until golden. Transfer the poussins to a warmed serving platter and cut each in half with poultry shears or scissors. Remove the vegetables with a slotted spoon and arrange them around the birds. Cover with foil and keep warm.

3 Remove the herbs from the casserole and discard. Mix the butter and flour to a paste. Bring the cooking liquid to the boil, then whisk in spoonfuls of paste until thickened. Season with salt and pepper and serve with the poussins and vegetables, garnished with herbs.

Poussin Energy 549kcal/2290kJ; Protein 30.8g; Carbohydrate 25.8g, of which sugars 7.5g; Fat 34g, of which saturates 12.4g; Cholesterol 163mg; Calcium 76mg; Fibre 3.5g; Sodium 372mg.
Coq au Vin Energy 630kcal/2618kJ; Protein 42.8g; Carbohydrate 19.3g, of which sugars 7.4g; Fat 41g, of which saturates 17.3g; Cholesterol 209mg; Calcium 67mg; Fibre 2.6g; Sodium 480mg.

Moroccan Spiced Roast Poussin

The poussins are stuffed with a fruity and aromatic rice mixture and glazed with spiced yogurt in this flavoursome dish. One bird is sufficient for two servings.

Serves 4
75g/3oz/1 cup cooked long
   grain rice
1 small onion, chopped
finely grated rind and juice of
   1 lemon
30ml/2 tbsp chopped fresh mint
45ml/3 tbsp chopped
   dried apricots
30ml/2 tbsp natural
   (plain) yogurt
10ml/2 tsp ground turmeric
10ml/2 tsp ground cumin
2 poussins (about 450g/1lb each)
salt and ground black pepper
lemon slices and fresh mint
   sprigs, to garnish

1 Preheat the oven to 200°C/400°F/Gas 6. Mix together the rice, onion, lemon rind, mint and apricots in a bowl. Stir in half the lemon juice, half the yogurt, half the turmeric and half the cumin and season with salt and pepper.

2 Stuff the poussins with the rice mixture at the neck end only, taking care not to overfill them. Reserve the spare stuffing to be served separately. Place the poussins side by side on a rack in a roasting pan.

3 Mix together the remaining lemon juice, yogurt, turmeric and cumin in a small bowl, then brush this all over the poussins. Cover them loosely with foil and cook in the oven for 30 minutes.

4 Remove the foil and roast for a further 15 minutes, or until the poussins are golden brown and the juices run clear, when the thickest part is pierced with the point of a sharp knife.

5 Transfer both the poussins to a chopping board and cut them in half with a sharp knife or poultry shears. Place half a bird on each of four warmed plates. Garnish with slices of lemon and fresh mint sprigs and serve immediately with the remaining rice and apricot mixture.

Chilli Chicken Couscous

Couscous is a very easy alternative to rice and makes a good base for all kinds of ingredients.

Serves 4
225g/8oz/2 cups couscous
1 litre/1¼ pints/4 cups boiling
   water
5ml/1 tsp olive oil
400g/14oz skinless boneless
   chicken, diced
1 yellow (bell) pepper, seeded
   and sliced
2 large courgettes (zucchini),
   thickly sliced
1 small green chilli, thinly sliced, or
   5ml/1 tsp chilli sauce
1 large tomato, diced
425g/15oz can chickpeas,
   drained and rinsed
salt and ground black pepper
fresh coriander (cilantro) or
   parsley sprigs, to garnish

1 Place the couscous in a large bowl and pour the boiling water over it. Cover and leave to stand for 30 minutes.

2 Heat the oil in a large, non-stick frying pan over medium heat. Add the chicken and stir-fry quickly to seal, then reduce the heat to low.

3 Stir in the yellow pepper, courgettes and chilli or chilli sauce and cook, stirring occasionally, for about 10 minutes, until the vegetables are softened.

4 Stir in the tomato and chickpeas, then add the couscous. Season to taste with salt and pepper and cook over medium heat, stirring constantly, until hot. Serve immediately garnished with sprigs of fresh coriander or parsley.

Cook's Tip
You can use dried chickpeas in this recipe. Soak them overnight in cold water, then drain, place in a pan and add water to cover. Bring to the boil, then cook for 2–2½ hours, until tender. Drain well and add to the pan in step 4. Some cooks like to add a pinch of bicarbonate of soda (baking soda) to the water when cooking chickpeas, but this is not essential.

Poussin Energy 354kcal/1478kJ; Protein 27g; Carbohydrate 20.3g, of which sugars 5g; Fat 18.4g, of which saturates 5g; Cholesterol 131mg; Calcium 25mg; Fibre 0.9g; Sodium 92mg.
Chicken Energy 394kcal/1661kJ; Protein 36.8g; Carbohydrate 50.9g, of which sugars 5.2g; Fat 6.1g, of which saturates 0.9g; Cholesterol 70mg; Calcium 86mg; Fibre 6g; Sodium 299mg.

Mediterranean Turkey Skewers

These skewers are easy to assemble, and can be cooked under a grill or on a charcoal barbecue.

Serves 4

90ml/6 tbsp olive oil
45ml/3 tbsp lemon juice
1 garlic clove, finely chopped
30ml/2 tbsp chopped fresh basil
2 courgettes (zucchini)
1 long thin aubergine (eggplant)
300g/11oz skinless boneless
    turkey, cut into 5cm/2in cubes
12–16 baby onions
1 red or yellow (bell) pepper,
    seeded and cut into 5cm/
    2in squares
salt and ground black pepper

1 Mix the olive oil with the lemon juice, garlic and basil in a small bowl. Season with salt and pepper.

2 Slice the courgettes and aubergine lengthways into strips 5mm/¼in thick. Cut the strips crossways about two-thirds of the way along their length. Discard the shorter lengths. Wrap half the turkey pieces with the courgette slices and the other half with the aubergine slices.

3 Prepare the skewers by alternating the turkey, onions and pepper pieces. (If you are using wooden skewers, soak them in water first. This will prevent them from charring during cooking.) Lay the prepared skewers on a platter and sprinkle with the flavoured oil. Cover with clear film (plastic wrap) and leave to marinate in a cool place for at least 30 minutes. Preheat the grill (broiler).

4 Grill (broil), turning occasionally, for 10 minutes, until the vegetables are tender and the turkey is cooked through. Transfer the skewers to warmed plates and serve immediately.

Variation
For extra colour, substitute red and yellow cherry tomatoes for the pickled onions or simply add one tomato to each end of each skewer.

Duck with Chestnut Sauce

Chestnuts play an important role in Italian cooking. This autumnal dish makes use of the sweet chestnuts that are freely gathered in the woods there.

Serves 4–5

1 fresh rosemary sprig
1 garlic clove, sliced
30ml/2 tbsp olive oil
4 duck breast fillets, trimmed of
    visible fat

For the sauce

450g/1lb/4 cups chestnuts
5ml/1 tsp olive oil
350ml/12fl oz/1½ cups milk
1 small onion, finely chopped
1 carrot, finely chopped
1 small bay leaf
30ml/2 tbsp cream, warmed
salt and ground black pepper

1 Pull the needles from the sprig of rosemary. Combine them with the garlic and oil in a shallow bowl. Pat the duck breast fillets dry with kitchen paper. Brush them with the marinade and leave to stand for at least 2 hours before cooking.

2 Preheat the oven to 180°C/350°F/Gas 4. Cut a cross in the flat side of each chestnut with a sharp knife. Place the chestnuts on a baking sheet with the oil and shake the sheet until they are coated. Bake for 20 minutes, then remove from the oven and peel when they are cool enough to handle.

3 Place the chestnuts in a heavy pan with the milk, onion, carrot and bay leaf. Cook over low heat for 10–15 minutes, until the chestnuts are tender, then season with salt and pepper. Discard the bay leaf. Press the mixture through a sieve (strainer).

4 Return the sauce to the pan. Heat gently while the duck breasts are cooking. Just before serving, stir in the cream. If the sauce is too thick, add a little more cream. Preheat the grill (broiler) or prepare a barbecue.

5 Cook the duck breasts until medium-rare, for 6–8 minutes. They should be pink inside. Slice into rounds and arrange on warmed plates. Serve with the heated sauce.

Turkey Energy 315kcal/1311kJ; Protein 22.7g; Carbohydrate 16.1g, of which sugars 12.9g; Fat 18.2g, of which saturates 2.8g; Cholesterol 43mg; Calcium 70mg; Fibre 4.9g; Sodium 46mg.
Duck Energy 366kcal/1535kJ; Protein 25.9g; Carbohydrate 35.2g, of which sugars 8.2g; Fat 16.4g, of which saturates 3.5g; Cholesterol 135mg; Calcium 68mg; Fibre 4.2g; Sodium 148mg.

Caribbean Chicken Kebabs

These kebabs have a rich, sunshine Caribbean flavour and the marinade keeps them moist without the need for oil.

Serves 4
500g/1¼lb skinless chicken
    breast fillets
finely grated rind of 1 lime
30ml/2 tbsp lime juice
15ml/1 tbsp rum or sherry
15g/½oz/1 tbsp light muscovado
    (brown) sugar
5ml/1 tsp ground cinnamon
2 mangoes, peeled, stoned (pitted)
    and diced
rice and salad, to serve

1 Cut the chicken into bitesize chunks and place in a non-metallic bowl with the lime rind and juice, rum or sherry, sugar and cinnamon. Toss well, cover with clear film (plastic wrap) and place in the refrigerator to marinate for 1 hour.

2 Preheat the grill (broiler). Drain the chicken, reserving the marinade. Thread the chicken on to four wooden skewers, alternating with the mango cubes.

3 Cook the skewers under the grill, turning occasionally and basting with the reserved marinade, for 8–10 minutes, until the chicken is tender and golden brown. Transfer to warmed plates and serve immediately with rice and salad.

Cook's Tips
• Mangoes have a large, flat, central stone (pit). The easiest way to prepare them is to cut the thickest possible lengthways slice from each side of the stone, then cut through the flesh in an even criss-cross pattern, leaving the skin intact. Turn the slice inside out so that the flesh stands up and cut it off the skin or scoop off the cubes with a spoon.
• Use a dark rum for the marinade to give a really rich and exotic flavour. However, if you don't like it – or the alternative of sherry – you can omit it. The kebabs will still taste delicious.
• Skinless boneless chicken thighs are a more economical alternative to breast portions.

Turkey Spirals

These little spirals may look difficult, but they're easy to make, and a very good way to pep up plain turkey.

Serves 4
4 thinly sliced turkey breast steaks
    (about 90g/3½oz each)
20ml/4 tsp tomato purée (paste)
15g/½oz/¼ cup large fresh
    basil leaves
1 garlic clove, crushed
15ml/1 tbsp skimmed milk
25g/1oz/2 tbsp wholemeal
    (whole-wheat) flour
salt and ground black pepper
passata (bottled strained
    tomatoes) or fresh tomato
    sauce, pasta and fresh basil,
    to serve

1 Preheat the grill (broiler). Place the turkey steaks on a board. Cover with clear film (plastic wrap) and flatten them slightly by beating gently with the side of a rolling pin.

2 Spread each turkey breast steak with tomato purée, then top with a few leaves of basil and a little crushed garlic. Season with salt and pepper.

3 Roll up firmly around the filling and secure with a wooden cocktail stick (toothpick). Brush with milk and sprinkle with flour to coat lightly.

4 Place the turkey rolls on a foil-lined grill (broiler) pan. Cook under a moderately hot grill, turning them occasionally, for 15–20 minutes, until thoroughly cooked.

5 Transfer the rolls to a chopping board and cut them into slices. Place the slices on warmed plates and serve with a spoonful or two of passata or fresh tomato sauce and pasta, sprinkled with fresh basil.

Variation
This recipe is also suitable for pork and veal escalopes (US scallops) and chicken breast portions.

Spirals Energy 164kcal/696kJ; Protein 32.7g; Carbohydrate 4.9g, of which sugars 1g; Fat 1.7g, of which saturates 0.6g; Cholesterol 67mg; Calcium 13mg; Fibre 0.7g; Sodium 95mg.
Kebabs Energy 195kcal/826kJ; Protein 30.6g; Carbohydrate 14.6g, of which sugars 14.3g; Fat 1.5g, of which saturates 0.5g; Cholesterol 88mg; Calcium 18mg; Fibre 2g; Sodium 77mg.

Chicken Stroganoff

This dish is based on the classic Russian dish (which is made with fillet of beef) and it is just as good.

Serves 4
4 skinless chicken breast fillets
45ml/3 tbsp olive oil

1 large onion, thinly sliced
225g/8oz mushrooms, sliced
300ml/½ pint/1¼ cups sour cream
salt and ground black pepper
15ml/1 tbsp chopped fresh parsley, to garnish

1 Divide the chicken into two natural fillets, place between two sheets of clear film (plastic wrap) and flatten each to a thickness of 5mm/¼in by beating lightly with the side of a rolling pin.

2 Remove the clear film and cut the meat into 2.5cm/1in strips diagonally across the fillets.

3 Heat 30ml/2 tbsp of the oil in a large frying pan over low heat. Add the onion and cook, stirring occasionally, for about 5 minutes, until softened but not coloured. Add the mushrooms and cook, stirring occasionally, for 5–8 minutes, until golden brown. Remove the onion and mushrooms and keep warm.

4 Increase the heat to medium and add the remaining oil to the pan. Add the chicken, in small batches, and cook, stirring frequently, for 3–4 minutes, until lightly coloured. Keep each batch warm while cooking the next.

5 Return all the chicken, onion and mushrooms to the pan and season with salt and pepper. Stir in the sour cream and bring to the boil. Sprinkle with fresh parsley and serve immediately.

> **Variation**
> Substitute smetana for the sour cream but do not let it boil as it will curdle. It is widely used in Russian cooking and is a good, low-fat substitute for cream.

Autumn Pheasant

Pheasant is worth buying as it is low in fat, full of flavour and never dry when cooked in this way.

Serves 4
1 oven-ready pheasant
2 small onions, quartered

3 celery sticks, thickly sliced
2 red eating apples, thickly sliced
120ml/4fl oz/½ cup stock
15ml/1 tbsp clear honey
30ml/2 tbsp Worcestershire sauce
pinch of freshly grated nutmeg
30ml/2 tbsp toasted hazelnuts
salt and ground black pepper

1 Preheat the oven to 180°C/350°F/Gas 4. Cook the pheasant without additional fat in a non-stick frying pan over medium-low heat, turning occasionally, for 8–10 minutes, until golden brown all over. Remove from the pan and keep hot.

2 Add the onions and celery to the pan, lower the heat and cook, stirring occasionally, for 8–10 minutes, until lightly browned. Spoon the vegetables into a casserole and place the pheasant on top. Tuck the apple slices around it.

3 Pour in the stock and add the honey and Worcestershire sauce. Sprinkle with nutmeg, season with salt and pepper, cover with a tight-fitting lid and bake for 1¼–1½ hours, or until tender. Sprinkle with the hazelnuts and serve immediately.

> **Cook's Tips**
> • Pheasant should be hung by the neck to develop its distinctive flavour for 7–14 days, depending on the degree of gaminess you like. After hanging, it must be plucked, cleaned and trussed.
> • If you are buying the bird ready-prepared, it will almost certainly have already been hung. Make sure that all the tendons have been removed from the legs.
> • This recipe provides an excellent method of cooking older cock birds, which tend to be rather tough and dry if they are just roasted. It is also a good choice for frozen birds as freezing has an adverse effect on their texture.

Pheasant Energy 311kcal/1300kJ; Protein 30.6g; Carbohydrate 8.9g, of which sugars 8.4g; Fat 17.3g, of which saturates 4.6g; Cholesterol 230mg; Calcium 66mg; Fibre 1.4g; Sodium 169mg.
Stroganoff Energy 421kcal/1758kJ; Protein 40.7g; Carbohydrate 9.8g, of which sugars 7.4g; Fat 24.7g, of which saturates 10.8g; Cholesterol 146mg; Calcium 103mg; Fibre 2g; Sodium 118mg.

Chicken Tikka

The red food colourings give this dish its traditional bright colour. Serve with lemon wedges and a crisp mixed salad.

Serves 4

1.75kg/3½lb chicken
mixed fresh salad leaves such as
    frisée, oakleaf lettuce or
    radicchio, and lemon wedges
    to serve

For the marinade

150ml/¼ pint/⅔ cup natural
    (plain) yogurt
5ml/1 tsp ground paprika
10ml/2 tsp grated fresh
    root ginger
1 garlic clove, crushed
10ml/2 tsp garam masala
2.5ml/½ tsp salt
red food colouring (optional)
juice of 1 lemon

1 Cut the chicken into eight even-size pieces, using a sharp knife or cleaver.

2 Mix all the marinade ingredients in a large dish, add the chicken pieces and turn to coat. Cover with clear film (plastic wrap) and leave in the refrigerator for 4 hours or overnight to allow the flavours to penetrate the flesh.

3 Preheat the oven to 200°C/400°F/Gas 6. Remove the chicken pieces from the marinade and arrange them in a single layer in a large ovenproof dish. Reserve the marinade. Bake the chicken, basting occasionally with the marinade, for 30–40 minutes, or until tender.

4 Arrange on a bed of salad leaves on individual plates, top with the chicken and serve immediately with lemon wedges. Alternatively, leave the chicken to cool, then serve cold on a bed of salad leaves.

Cook's Tip

This dish would also make an excellent appetizer. Cut the chicken into smaller pieces and reduce the cooking time slightly, then serve with lemon wedges and a simple salad garnish.

Simple Chicken Curry

Curry powder can be bought in three different strengths – mild, medium and hot. Use whichever type you prefer.

Serves 4

8 chicken legs, each piece
    including thigh and drumstick
30ml/2 tbsp groundnut
    (peanut) oil
1 onion, thinly sliced

1 garlic clove, crushed
15ml/1 tbsp medium
    curry powder
25g/1oz/¼ cup plain (all-
    purpose) flour
450ml/¾ pint/scant 2 cups
    chicken stock
1 beefsteak tomato
15ml/1 tbsp mango chutney
15ml/1 tbsp lemon juice
salt and ground black pepper
boiled rice, to serve

1 Cut the chicken legs in half. Heat the oil in a large flameproof casserole over medium heat. Add the chicken pieces and cook, turning frequently, for 8–10 minutes, until evenly browned on both sides. Remove the chicken from the casserole and keep warm.

2 Add the onion and garlic to the casserole, lower the heat and cook, stirring occasionally, for about 5 minutes, until the onion is softened but not coloured. Stir in the curry powder and cook, stirring constantly, for a further 2 minutes.

3 Stir in the flour and cook, stirring constantly, for 1 minute, then gradually blend in the chicken stock, stirring well. Season with salt and pepper.

4 Bring to the boil, return the chicken pieces to the casserole, cover and simmer for 20–30 minutes, until tender.

5 Skin the beefsteak tomato by blanching in boiling water for about 15 seconds, then running it under cold water to loosen the skin. Peel and cut into small dice.

6 Add to the chicken with the mango chutney and lemon juice. Heat through gently and adjust the seasoning to taste. Serve with boiled rice and Indian accompaniments.

Tikka Energy 416kcal/1730kJ; Protein 46g; Carbohydrate 2.1g, of which sugars 0.2g; Fat 24.8g, of which saturates 8.5g; Cholesterol 203mg; Calcium 21mg; Fibre 0.5g; Sodium 173mg.
Curry Energy 571kcal/2392kJ; Protein 38.9g; Carbohydrate 78.9g, of which sugars 4g; Fat 10.8g, of which saturates 2g; Cholesterol 158mg; Calcium 43mg; Fibre 0.8g; Sodium 180mg.

Chicken Biryani

A biryani – from the Urdu – is a dish mixed with rice which resembles a risotto. It provides a one-pan meal.

Serves 4

275g/10oz/1½ cups basmati rice, rinsed and drained
2.5ml/½ tsp salt
5 cardamom pods
2–3 cloves
1 cinnamon stick
45ml/3 tbsp vegetable oil
3 onions, sliced
675g/1½lb skinless boneless chicken, diced
1.5ml/¼ tsp ground cloves
5 cardamom pods, seeds removed and ground
1.5ml/¼ tsp hot chilli powder
5ml/1 tsp ground cumin
5ml/1 tsp ground coriander
2.5ml/½ tsp ground black pepper
3 garlic cloves, finely chopped
5ml/1 tsp finely chopped fresh root ginger
juice of 1 lemon
4 tomatoes, sliced
30ml/2 tbsp chopped fresh coriander (cilantro)
150ml/¼ pint/⅔ cup natural (plain) yogurt
2.5ml/½ tsp saffron threads soaked in 10ml/2 tsp hot milk
45ml/3 tbsp toasted flaked (sliced) almonds and fresh coriander sprigs, to garnish
natural yogurt, to serve

1 Preheat the oven to 190°C/375°F/Gas 5. Bring a large pan of salted water to the boil and add the rice, salt, cardamom pods, cloves and cinnamon stick. Bring back to the boil and cook for 2 minutes. Drain, leaving the whole spices in the rice.

2 Heat the oil in a frying pan over low heat. Add the onions and cook, stirring occasionally, for about 10 minutes, until lightly browned. Add the chicken, ground spices, garlic, ginger and lemon juice and stir-fry for 5 minutes.

3 Transfer to a casserole and top with the tomatoes. Add the coriander, yogurt and rice in layers. Drizzle over the saffron and milk, then 150ml/¼ pint/⅔ cup water.

4 Cover and bake for 1 hour. Transfer to a warmed serving platter and remove the whole spices. Garnish with toasted almonds and coriander and serve with yogurt.

Spatchcock of Poussin

Also called spring chicken, poussins are between four and six weeks old and weigh 350–600g/12oz–1¼ lb. The very young, smallest birds make an attractive serving for one person.

Serves 4

4 poussins
15ml/1 tbsp mixed chopped fresh herbs, such as rosemary and parsley, plus extra to garnish
15ml/1 tbsp lemon juice
50g/2oz/¼ cup butter, melted
salt and ground black pepper
lemon slices, to garnish
boiled new potatoes and salad, to serve (optional)

1 Remove any trussing strings from the birds and, using a pair of kitchen scissors, cut down on either side of the backbone. Lay the poussins flat, skin-side up, and flatten with the help of a rolling pin or mallet, or use the heel of your hand.

2 Thread the legs and wings on to skewers to keep the poussins flat while they are cooking.

3 Brush both sides with melted butter and season with salt and pepper. Sprinkle with lemon juice and herbs.

4 Preheat the grill (broiler) and cook, skin-side uppermost, for 6 minutes, until golden brown. Turn over, brush with more melted butter and grill (broil) for a further 6–8 minutes, until the juices run clear when the thickest part is pierced with the point of a sharp knife.

5 Transfer the poussins to serving plates and remove the skewers. Garnish with chopped herbs and lemon slices and serve immediately with boiled new potatoes and salad.

Variation
Squab, another very tender, young bird that provides an adequate single portion, is also ideal for this method of preparation and simple cooking.

Biryani Energy 628kcal/2623kJ; Protein 41.5g; Carbohydrate 71.4g, of which sugars 13.4g; Fat 19.7g, of which saturates 2.9g; Cholesterol 642mg; Calcium 163mg; Fibre 3.6g; Sodium 174mg.
Poussin Energy 621kcal/2582kJ; Protein 50.1g; Carbohydrate 0.3g, of which sugars 0.3g; Fat 46.7g, of which saturates 16.4g; Cholesterol 288mg; Calcium 21mg; Fibre 0g; Sodium 256mg.

Chicken, Leek & Parsley Pie

A filling pie with a two-cheese sauce, this dish is ideal for serving on a cold winter's day.

Serves 4–6

3 skinless chicken breast fillets
1 carrot, thickly sliced
1 small onion, quartered
6 black peppercorns
1 bouquet garni
450g/1lb shortcrust pastry dough, thawed if frozen
50g/2oz/¼ cup butter
2 leeks, thinly sliced

50g/2oz/¼ cup grated
    Cheddar cheese
25g/1oz/⅓ cup freshly grated
    Parmesan cheese
45ml/3 tbsp chopped
    fresh parsley
30ml/2 tbsp wholegrain mustard
5ml/1 tsp cornflour (cornstarch)
300ml/½ pint/1¼ cups double
    (heavy) cream
beaten egg, to glaze
salt and ground black pepper
mixed green salad leaves, to serve

1 Put the chicken, carrot, onion, peppercorns and bouquet garni in a shallow pan, add water and bring just to the boil. Lower the heat and poach gently, for 20–30 minutes, until tender. Leave to cool in the liquid, then drain and cut into strips.

2 Preheat the oven to 200°C/400°F/Gas 6. Divide the dough into two pieces, one slightly larger than the other. Use the larger piece to line an 18 x 28cm/7 x 11in baking tin (pan). Prick the base, bake for 15 minutes, then leave to cool.

3 Melt the butter in a frying pan over low heat. Add the leeks and cook, stirring occasionally, for 5–8 minutes, until soft. Stir in the cheeses and parsley.

4 Spread half the leek mixture over the pastry base, cover with the chicken strips, then top with the remaining leek mixture. Mix together the mustard, cornflour and cream in a bowl. Season with salt and pepper and pour into the pie.

5 Moisten the pastry base edges. Use the remaining pastry to cover the pie. Brush with beaten egg and bake for 30–40 minutes, until golden and crisp. Serve with salad.

Hampshire Farmhouse Flan

This English flan will satisfy even the heartiest appetite.

Serves 4

225g/8oz/2 cups wholemeal
    (whole-wheat) flour
50g/2oz/¼ cup butter, cubed
50g/2oz/¼ cup white cooking fat
5ml/1 tsp caraway seeds
5ml/1 tbsp vegetable oil
1 onion, chopped
1 garlic clove, crushed
225g/8oz/2 cups chopped
    cooked chicken

75g/3oz watercress or baby
    spinach leaves, chopped
grated rind of ½ lemon
2 eggs, lightly beaten
175ml/6fl oz/¾ cup double
    (heavy) cream
45ml/3 tbsp natural (plain) yogurt
large pinch of grated nutmeg
45ml/3 tbsp grated
    Caerphilly cheese
beaten egg, to glaze
salt and ground black pepper

1 Put the flour into a bowl with a pinch of salt. Add the butter and cooking fat and rub in with your fingertips until the mixture resembles breadcrumbs.

2 Stir in the caraway seeds and 45ml/3 tbsp iced water and mix to a firm dough. Knead until smooth, then use to line an 18 x 28cm/7 x 11in loose-based flan tin (pan). Reserve the dough trimmings. Prick the base and chill for 20 minutes. Heat a baking sheet in the oven at 200°C/400°F/Gas 6.

3 Heat the oil in a frying pan over low heat. Add the onion and garlic and cook, stirring occasionally, for 5 minutes, until softened. Leave to cool. Meanwhile, line the pastry case (pie shell) with greaseproof (waxed) paper and baking beans. Bake for 10 minutes, remove the paper and beans and bake for a further 5 minutes.

4 Mix the onion mixture, chicken, watercress or spinach and lemon rind; spoon into the pastry case. Beat the eggs, cream, yogurt, nutmeg, cheese and seasoning; pour over the chicken mixture. Cut the pastry trimmings into 1cm/½in strips. Brush with egg, then twist and lay in a lattice over the flan. Press on the ends. Bake for 35 minutes, until golden.

Chicken Energy 620kcal/2584kJ; Protein 28.2g; Carbohydrate 39.4g, of which sugars 3.2g; Fat 39.7g, of which saturates 24.1g; Cholesterol 151mg; Calcium 237mg; Fibre 3.3g; Sodium 218mg.
Flan Energy 773kcal/3216kJ; Protein 28.2g; Carbohydrate 38g, of which sugars 2.9g; Fat 57.4g, of which saturates 30.2g; Cholesterol 244mg; Calcium 181mg; Fibre 5.6g; Sodium 247mg.

Chicken & Ham Pie

This is a rich pie flavoured with fresh herbs and lightly spiced with mace – ideal for taking on a picnic.

Serves 8
400g/14oz shortcrust pastry dough, thawed if frozen
800g/1¾lb chicken breast portions
350g/12oz uncooked gammon (smoked or cured ham)
60ml/4 tbsp double (heavy) cream
6 spring onions (scallions), finely chopped
15ml/1 tbsp chopped fresh tarragon
10ml/2 tsp chopped fresh thyme
grated rind and juice of ½ large lemon
5ml/1 tsp ground mace
beaten egg or milk, to glaze
salt and ground black pepper

1 Preheat the oven to 190°C/375°F/Gas 5. Roll out one-third of the pastry dough and use it to line a 20cm/8in pie tin (pan), 5cm/2in deep. Place on a baking sheet.

2 Mince (grind) 115g/4oz of the chicken with the gammon, then mix with the cream, spring onions, herbs, lemon rind and 15ml/1 tbsp of the lemon juice in a bowl. Season lightly with salt and pepper. Cut the remaining chicken into 1cm/½in pieces and mix with the remaining lemon juice and the mace in another bowl and season with salt and pepper.

3 Make a layer of one-third of the gammon mixture in the pastry base, cover with half the chopped chicken, then add another layer of one-third of the gammon. Add all the remaining chicken followed by the remaining gammon.

4 Dampen the edges of the pastry base and roll out the remaining pastry to make a lid for the pie. Use the trimmings to make a lattice decoration. Make a small hole in the centre of the pie, then brush the top with beaten egg or milk.

5 Bake the pie for 20 minutes. Lower the oven temperature to 160°C/325°F/Gas 3 and bake for a further 1–1¼ hours, until the pastry is golden brown. Transfer the pie to a wire rack and leave to cool before serving.

Chicken Charter Pie

A light pie with a fresh taste; it is versatile enough to use for light meals or informal dinners.

Serves 4
50g/2oz/¼ cup butter
4 chicken legs
1 onion, finely chopped
150ml/¼ pint/⅔ cup milk
150ml/¼ pint/⅔ cup sour cream
4 spring onions (scallions), cut into quarters
20g/¾oz/⅓ cup fresh parsley leaves, finely chopped
225g/8oz puff pastry dough, thawed if frozen
120ml/4fl oz/½ cup double (heavy) cream
2 eggs, beaten, plus extra for glazing
salt and ground black pepper

1 Melt the butter in a frying pan over medium heat. Add the chicken legs and cook, turning frequently, for 8–10 minutes, until evenly browned all over. Transfer to a plate.

2 Add the onion to the pan, lower the heat and cook, stirring occasionally, for 5 minutes, until softened but not coloured. Stir the milk, sour cream, spring onions and parsley into the pan, season with salt and pepper and bring to the boil, then simmer for 2 minutes.

3 Return the chicken to the pan with any juices, cover and cook gently for 30 minutes. Transfer the chicken mixture to a 1.2 litre/2 pint/5 cup pie dish. Leave to cool.

4 Preheat the oven to 220°C/425°F/Gas 7. Place a narrow strip of pastry on the edge of the pie dish. Moisten the strip, then cover the dish with the pastry. Press the edges together. Make a hole in the centre of the pastry and insert a small funnel of foil. Brush the pastry with beaten egg to glaze, then bake for 15–20 minutes.

5 Lower the oven temperature to 180°C/350°F/Gas 4. Mix the cream and eggs, then pour into the pie through the funnel. Shake the pie to distribute the cream, then return to the oven for 5–10 minutes. Leave the pie in a warm place for about 5–10 minutes before serving, or cool completely.

Charter Pie Energy 713kcal/2967kJ; Protein 37.8g; Carbohydrate 25g, of which sugars 4.9g; Fat 52.6g, of which saturates 22.8g; Cholesterol 250mg; Calcium 154mg; Fibre 0.4g; Sodium 426mg.
Chicken & Ham Pie Energy 431kcal/1803kJ; Protein 34.8g; Carbohydrate 23.8g, of which sugars 0.8g; Fat 22.5g, of which saturates 8.3g; Cholesterol 98mg; Calcium 57mg; Fibre 1.1g; Sodium 647mg.

Venison with Cranberry Sauce

Venison steaks are now readily available. Lean and low in fat, they make a healthy and delicious choice for a special occasion.

Serves 4

1 orange
1 lemon
75g/3oz/¾ cup fresh or frozen unthawed cranberries
5ml/1 tsp grated fresh root ginger
1 fresh thyme sprig, plus extra to garnish
5ml/1 tsp Dijon mustard
60ml/4 tbsp redcurrant jelly
150ml/¼ pint/⅔ cup port
30ml/2 tbsp sunflower oil
4 venison steaks
2 shallots, finely chopped
salt and ground black pepper
fresh thyme sprigs, to garnish
mashed potatoes and steamed broccoli, to serve

1 Pare the rind from half the orange and half the lemon using a vegetable peeler, then cut into very fine strips. Blanch the strips in a small pan of boiling water for 5 minutes, until tender. Drain the strips and refresh under cold water.

2 Squeeze the juice from the orange and lemon and pour into a small pan. Add the cranberries, ginger, thyme sprig, mustard, redcurrant jelly and port. Cook over medium-low heat, stirring frequently, until the jelly has melted. Bring to the boil, stirring constantly, cover and lower the heat. Simmer gently for 15 minutes, until the cranberries are just tender.

3 Heat the oil in a large, heavy frying pan over a high heat. Add the venison steaks and cook for 2–3 minutes. Turn them over and add the shallots. Cook on the other side for 2–3 minutes, or until done to your taste. Just before the end of cooking, pour in the sauce and add the strips of orange and lemon rind. Leave the sauce to bubble for a few seconds to thicken slightly, then remove and discard the thyme sprig. Taste and adjust the seasoning, if necessary.

4 Transfer the venison steaks to warmed plates and spoon the sauce over them. Garnish with thyme sprigs and serve immediately accompanied by creamy mashed potatoes and steamed broccoli.

Turkey & Mangetout Stir-fry

Have all the ingredients prepared before you start cooking this dish, as it will be ready in minutes.

Serves 4

30ml/2 tbsp sesame oil
90ml/6 tbsp lemon juice
1 garlic clove, crushed
1cm/½in piece fresh root ginger, peeled and grated
5ml/1 tsp clear honey
450g/1lb turkey fillets, cut into strips
115g/4oz/1 cup mangetouts (snow peas), trimmed
30ml/2 tbsp groundnut (peanut) oil
50g/2oz/½ cup cashew nuts
6 spring onions (scallions), cut into strips
225g/8oz can water chestnuts, drained and thinly sliced
pinch of salt
saffron rice, to serve

1 Mix together the sesame oil, lemon juice, garlic, ginger and honey in a shallow non-metallic dish. Add the turkey and mix well. Cover and leave to marinate for 3–4 hours.

2 Blanch the mangetouts in boiling salted water for about 1 minute. Drain and refresh under cold running water.

3 Drain the turkey strips and reserve the marinade. Heat the groundnut oil in a wok or large frying pan, add the cashews and stir-fry for 1–2 minutes, until golden brown. Remove the nuts from the pan using a slotted spoon and set aside.

4 Add the turkey and stir-fry for 3–4 minutes, until golden brown. Add the spring onions, mangetouts, water chestnuts and reserved marinade. Cook for a few minutes, until the turkey is tender and the sauce is bubbling and hot. Stir in the cashew nuts and serve immediately with saffron rice.

Cook's Tip
This dish could be served on a bed of medium-width egg noodles for a quick meal.

Venison Energy 259kcal/1092kJ; Protein 33.7g; Carbohydrate 14.1g, of which sugars 13.5g; Fat 8.9g, of which saturates 1.9g; Cholesterol 75mg; Calcium 16mg; Fibre 0.7g; Sodium 91mg.
Turkey Energy 369kcal/1546kJ; Protein 43.6g; Carbohydrate 5.3g, of which sugars 3.4g; Fat 19.5g, of which saturates 3.8g; Cholesterol 83mg; Calcium 52mg; Fibre 1.9g; Sodium 173mg.

Farmhouse Venison Pie

A simple and satisfying pie; the venison is cooked in a rich gravy, topped with potato and parsnip mash.

Serves 4

45ml/3 tbsp sunflower oil
1 onion, chopped
1 garlic clove, crushed
3 rashers (strips) rindless streaky (fatty) bacon, chopped
675g/1½lb minced (ground) venison
115g/4oz button (white) mushrooms, chopped
25g/1oz/¼ cup plain (all-purpose) flour
450ml/¾ pint/scant 2 cups beef stock
150ml/¼ pint/⅔ cup port
2 bay leaves
5ml/1 tsp chopped fresh thyme
5ml/1 tsp Dijon mustard
15ml/1 tbsp redcurrant jelly
675g/1½lb potatoes
450g/1lb parsnips
1 egg yolk
50g/2oz/¼ cup butter
pinch of freshly grated nutmeg
45ml/3 tbsp chopped fresh parsley
salt and ground black pepper
green vegetables, to serve (optional)

1 Heat the oil in a large frying pan over low heat. Add the onion, garlic and bacon and cook, stirring occasionally, for about 5 minutes, until the onion is softened. Add the venison and mushrooms and cook for a few minutes, stirring, until browned.

2 Stir in the flour and cook for 1–2 minutes, then add the stock, port, herbs, mustard and redcurrant jelly. Season with salt and pepper. Bring to the boil, cover with a tight-fitting lid and simmer for 30–40 minutes, until tender. Spoon into a large pie dish or four individual ovenproof dishes.

3 While the venison and mushroom mixture is cooking, preheat the oven to 200°C/400°F/Gas 6. Cut the potatoes and parsnips into large chunks. Cook together in salted boiling water for 20 minutes, or until tender. Drain and mash, then beat in the egg yolk, butter, nutmeg, parsley and seasoning.

4 Spread the potato and parsnip mixture over the meat and bake for 30–40 minutes, until hot and golden brown. Serve immediately with green vegetables, if you like.

Normandy Pheasant

Calvados, cider, apples and cream – the produce of Normandy – make this a rich and flavoursome dish.

Serves 4

2 oven-ready pheasants
15ml/1 tbsp olive oil
25g/1oz/2 tbsp butter
60ml/4 tbsp Calvados or applejack
450ml/¾ pint/scant 2 cups dry (hard) cider
1 bouquet garni
3 eating apples
150ml/¼ pint/⅔ cup double (heavy) cream
salt and ground black pepper
fresh thyme sprigs, to garnish

1 Preheat the oven to 160°C/325°F/Gas 3. Cut both pheasants into four pieces. Discard the backbones and knuckles.

2 Heat the oil and butter in a large flameproof casserole. Working in two batches, add the pheasant pieces to the casserole and brown them over a high heat. Return all the pheasant pieces to the casserole.

3 Standing well back, pour over the Calvados or applejack and ignite it with a match. Shake the casserole and when the flames have subsided, pour in the cider, then add the bouquet garni and season to taste with salt and pepper. Bring to the boil, cover with a tight-fitting lid and simmer for about 50 minutes.

4 Peel, core and thickly slice the apples. Tuck the apple slices around the pheasant. Cover and cook for 5–10 minutes, or until the pheasant is tender. Transfer the pheasant and apples to a warmed serving plate. Keep warm.

5 Remove and discard the bouquet garni, then boil the sauce rapidly to reduce by half to a syrupy consistency. Stir in the cream and simmer for a further 2–3 minutes, until thickened. Taste the sauce and adjust the seasoning, if necessary. Spoon the sauce over the pheasant pieces and serve immediately, garnished with fresh thyme sprigs.

Venison Energy 723kcal/3033kJ; Protein 48.5g; Carbohydrate 59.6g, of which sugars 20.4g; Fat 30.3g, of which saturates 11.2g; Cholesterol 174mg; Calcium 128mg; Fibre 9g; Sodium 447mg.
Pheasant Energy 805kcal/3347kJ; Protein 58.8g; Carbohydrate 8.1g, of which sugars 8.1g; Fat 52.9g, of which saturates 24.6g; Cholesterol 525mg; Calcium 91mg; Fibre 0.8g; Sodium 191mg.

Meat

Stewed, roasted, grilled or fried, meat plays an integral role in many main dishes. Sustaining and versatile, beef, pork and lamb can be combined with vegetables as part of a one-pot meal, or simply cooked on their own and served with an accompaniment. In this chapter you will find recipes from around the world, including Irish Stew, Hungarian Beef Goulash, Indian Curried Lamb Samosas, or Greek Lamb Pie.

Roast Beef with Yorkshire Pudding

This classic British dish is often served at Sunday lunch, accompanied by potatoes, mustard and horseradish sauce.

Serves 6
1.75kg/4lb rib of beef
30–60ml/2–4 tbsp vegetable oil
300ml/½ pint/1¼ cups vegetable or veal stock, wine or water

salt and ground black pepper

For the puddings
50g/2oz/½ cup plain (all-purpose) flour
1 egg, beaten
150ml/¼ pint/⅔ cup water mixed with milk
vegetable oil, for cooking

1 Weigh the beef and calculate the cooking time. Allow 15 minutes per 450g/1lb plus 15 minutes for rare meat, 20 minutes plus 20 minutes for medium, and 25–30 minutes plus 25 minutes for well-done.

2 Preheat the oven to 220°C/425°F/Gas 7. Heat the oil in a roasting pan. Place the meat on a rack, fat-side uppermost, then put the rack in the roasting pan. Baste the beef with the oil and cook for the required time, basting occasionally.

3 To make the Yorkshire puddings, stir the flour, salt and pepper together in a bowl and form a well in the centre. Pour the egg into the well, then slowly pour in the milk mixture, stirring in the flour to give a smooth batter. Leave to stand for 30 minutes.

4 A few minutes before the meat is ready, spoon a little oil in each of 12 patty tins (muffin pans) and place in the oven until very hot. Remove the meat, season, then cover loosely with foil and keep warm. Quickly divide the batter among the patty tins, then bake for 15–20 minutes, until well risen and brown.

5 Spoon off the fat from the roasting pan. Add the stock, wine or water and bring to the boil, stirring constantly. Cook for a few minutes, stirring. Season to taste with salt and pepper, then serve with the beef and Yorkshire puddings.

Beef Olives

So-called because of their shape, these beef rolls contain a delicious filling made with bacon, parsley and mushrooms.

Serves 4
25g/1oz/2 tbsp butter
2 rashers (strips) bacon, finely chopped
115g/4oz mushrooms, chopped
15ml/1 tbsp chopped fresh parsley
grated rind and juice of 1 lemon
115g/4oz/2 cups fresh white breadcrumbs
675g/1½lb topside (pot roast) of beef, cut into 8 thin slices
40g/1½oz/⅓ cup plain (all-purpose) flour
45ml/3 tbsp vegetable oil
2 onions, sliced
450ml/¾ pint/scant 2 cups brown veal stock
salt and ground black pepper

1 Preheat the oven to 160°C/325°F/Gas 3. Melt the butter in a pan over medium heat. Add the bacon and mushrooms and cook, stirring occasionally for 3 minutes. Mix them with the chopped parsley, lemon rind and juice and breadcrumbs in a bowl and season with salt and pepper.

2 Spread an equal quantity of the breadcrumb mixture evenly over the beef slices, leaving a narrow border clear around the edges. Roll up the slices and tie securely with fine string, then dip the beef rolls in the flour to coat lightly, shaking off any excess flour.

3 Heat the oil in a frying pan over medium heat. Add the beef rolls and cook, turning frequently, for 3–4 minutes, until evenly browned all over. Remove the rolls from the pan and keep warm. Add the onions and cook, stirring occasionally, for about 8 minutes, until browned. Stir in the remaining flour and cook until lightly browned. Pour in the stock, stirring constantly, bring to the boil, stirring, and simmer for 2–3 minutes.

4 Transfer the rolls to a casserole, pour the sauce over the top, then cover with a tight-fitting lid and cook in the oven for 2 hours. Lift out the "olives" using a slotted spoon and remove the string. Return them to the sauce and serve hot.

Roast Beef Energy 590kcal/2461kJ; Protein 68.5g; Carbohydrate 7.1g, of which sugars 0.7g; Fat 32g, of which saturates 11.9g; Cholesterol 202mg; Calcium 46mg; Fibre 0.3g; Sodium 204mg
Beef Olive Energy 519kcal/2181kJ; Protein 46.9g; Carbohydrate 38.1g, of which sugars 6.6g; Fat 21g, of which saturates 6.9g; Cholesterol 104mg; Calcium 90mg; Fibre 2.7g; Sodium 584mg.

Beef in Guinness

Guinness gives this stew a deep, rich flavour. Use Beamish or another stout if you prefer.

Serves 6
900g/2lb braising steak, cut into 4cm/1½in dice
plain (all-purpose) flour, for coating
45ml/3 tbsp vegetable oil
I large onion, sliced
I carrot, thinly sliced
2 celery sticks, thinly sliced
10ml/2 tsp sugar
5ml/1 tsp English (hot) mustard powder
15ml/1 tbsp tomato purée (paste)
2.5 x 7.5cm/1 x 3in strip orange rind
I bouquet garni
600ml/1 pint/2½ cups Guinness
salt and ground black pepper

I Toss the beef in flour to coat, shaking off any excess. Heat 30ml/2 tbsp of the oil in a large shallow pan over medium heat. Add the beef, in batches, and cook, stirring frequently, for 8–10 minutes, until lightly browned. Transfer to a bowl.

2 Add the remaining oil to the pan and lower the heat. Add the onion and cook, stirring occasionally, for about 8 minutes, until lightly browned. Add the carrot and celery and cook, stirring occasionally, for a further 5 minutes.

3 Stir in the sugar, mustard, tomato purée, orange rind and Guinness, season with salt and pepper, add the bouquet garni and bring to the boil.

4 Return the meat and any juices in the bowl to the pan. Add water, if necessary, so that the meat is covered. Cover the pan with a tight-fitting lid and simmer over low heat for 2–2½ hours, until the meat is very tender.

Cook's Tip
Like most stews, this can be prepared up to 2 days ahead and stored in the refrigerator, once cooled. The flavours and richness will intensify during this time.

Cottage Pie

This traditional dish is a favourite with adults and children alike.

Serves 4
30ml/2 tbsp vegetable oil
I onion, finely chopped
I carrot, finely chopped
115g/4oz chopped mushrooms
500g/1¼lb lean minced (ground) braising steak
300ml/½ pint/1¼ cups brown veal stock or water
15g/½oz/2 tbsp plain (all-purpose) flour
I bay leaf
10–15ml/2–3 tsp Worcestershire sauce
15ml/1 tbsp tomato purée (paste)
675g/1½lb potatoes, boiled
25g/1oz/2 tbsp butter
45ml/3 tbsp hot milk
15ml/1 tbsp chopped fresh tarragon
salt and ground black pepper

I Heat the oil in a pan over low heat. Add the onion, carrot and mushrooms and cook, stirring occasionally, for about 10 minutes, until the onion is softened and lightly browned. Stir the beef into the pan and cook, stirring to break up the lumps, for about 8 minutes, until lightly browned.

2 Blend a few spoonfuls of the stock or water with the flour, then stir into the pan. Stir in the remaining stock or water and bring to a simmer, stirring constantly.

3 Add the bay leaf, Worcestershire sauce and tomato purée, then cover with a tight-fitting lid and cook very gently for I hour, stirring occasionally. Uncover towards the end of cooking to allow any excess liquid to evaporate, if necessary.

4 Preheat the oven to 190°C/375°F/Gas 5. Gently heat the potatoes for a couple of minutes, then mash with the butter, milk and seasoning.

5 Add the tarragon to the meat mixture and season to taste with salt and pepper, then pour into a pie dish. Cover the meat with an even layer of mashed potatoes and mark the top of the pie with the prongs of a fork. Bake for about 25 minutes, until golden brown. Serve immediately.

Beef Energy 367kcal/1529kJ; Protein 35.3g; Carbohydrate 6.9g, of which sugars 5.7g; Fat 19.6g, of which saturates 6.4g; Cholesterol 87mg; Calcium 32mg; Fibre 1.2g; Sodium 119mg.
Cottage Pie Energy 281kcal/1179kJ; Protein 7.2g; Carbohydrate 34.6g, of which sugars 6.2g; Fat 13.7g, of which saturates 5.1g; Cholesterol 22mg; Calcium 50mg; Fibre 2.9g; Sodium 132mg.

Irish Stew

This wholesome and filling stew is given a slight piquancy by the inclusion of a little anchovy sauce.

Serves 4

4 rashers (strips) smoked streaky (fatty) bacon
2 celery sticks, chopped
2 large onions, sliced
8 middle neck (US shoulder) lamb chops (about 1kg/2¼lb total weight)
1kg/2¼lb potatoes, sliced
300ml/½ pint/1¼ cups brown veal stock
7.5ml/1½ tsp Worcestershire sauce
5ml/1 tsp anchovy sauce
salt and ground black pepper
fresh parsley, to garnish

1 Preheat the oven to 160°C/325°F/Gas 3. Dice the bacon and then cook in a heavy frying pan, without any added fat, over medium-low heat for 3–5 minutes, until the fat runs. Add the celery and one-third of the onions and cook, stirring occasionally, for about 10 minutes, until softened and browned.

2 Layer the lamb chops, potatoes, vegetable and bacon mixture and remaining onions in a heavy, flameproof casserole, seasoning each layer with salt and pepper as you go. Finish with a layer of potatoes.

3 Pour the veal stock, Worcestershire sauce and anchovy sauce into the bacon and vegetable cooking juices in the pan. Bring to the boil, stirring constantly. Pour the mixture into the casserole, adding water, if necessary, so that the liquid comes halfway up the sides of the casserole.

4 Cover the casserole with a tight-fitting lid, then cook in the oven for 3 hours, until the meat and vegetables are very tender. Return to the oven for longer if necessary. Serve immediately, sprinkled with chopped fresh parsley. Alternatively, leave to cool, then chill in the refrigerator overnight. Spoon off any fat that has solidified on the surface of the stew and reheat thoroughly in the oven or on the stove before serving.

Oatmeal & Herb Rack of Lamb

Ask the butcher to remove the chine bone that runs along the eye of the meat – this will make carving easier.

Serves 6

2 best end necks (cross rib) of lamb (about 900kg/2lb each)
finely grated rind of 1 lemon
60ml/4 tbsp medium oatmeal
50g/2oz/1 cup fresh white breadcrumbs
60ml/4 tbsp chopped fresh parsley
25g/1oz/2 tbsp butter, melted
30ml/2 tbsp clear honey
salt and ground black pepper
fresh herb sprigs, to garnish
roasted baby vegetables and gravy, to serve

1 Preheat the oven to 200°C/400°F/Gas 6. Using a small sharp knife, cut through the skin and meat of both pieces of lamb about 2.5cm/1in from the tips of the bones. Pull off the fatty meat to expose the bones, then scrape around each bone tip until completely clean.

2 Trim all the skin and most of the fat from the meat, then lightly score the remaining fat with a sharp knife. Repeat with the second rack.

3 Mix together the lemon rind, oatmeal, breadcrumbs and parsley in a bowl. Season with salt and pepper and stir in the melted butter until thoroughly combined.

4 Brush the fatty side of each rack of lamb with honey, then press the oatmeal mixture evenly over the surface with your fingers until well coated.

5 Place the racks in a roasting pan with the oatmeal sides uppermost. Roast for 40–50 minutes, depending on whether you like rare or medium lamb. Cover loosely with foil if browning too much.

6 To serve, slice each rack into three and place two chops on each of six warmed plates. Garnish with fresh herb sprigs and serve immediately with roasted baby vegetables and gravy made with the pan juices.

Stew Energy 823kcal/3453kJ; Protein 80g; Carbohydrate 50.3g, of which sugars 10.4g; Fat 34.9g, of which saturates 14.8g; Cholesterol 266mg; Calcium 137mg; Fibre 4.4g; Sodium 540mg.
Lamb Energy 719kcal/2979kJ; Protein 40g; Carbohydrate 15g, of which sugars 1.4g; Fat 55.9g, of which saturates 27.1g; Cholesterol 171mg; Calcium 59mg; Fibre 1.2g; Sodium 227mg.

Beef Wellington

This English dish is so-named because of a supposed resemblance in shape and colour to the Duke of Wellington's boot.

Serves 8
1.4kg/3lb fillet (tenderloin) of beef
15g/¹/₂oz/1 tbsp butter
30ml/2 tbsp vegetable oil
¹/₂ small onion, finely chopped
175g/6oz mushrooms, chopped
175g/6oz liver pâté
freshly squeezed lemon juice
a few drops of Worcestershire sauce
400g/14oz puff pastry dough,
  thawed if frozen
beaten egg, to glaze
salt and ground black pepper
fresh flat leaf parsley, to garnish

1 Preheat the oven to 220°C/425°F/Gas 7. Season the beef with pepper, then tie it at intervals with string.

2 Heat the butter and oil in a roasting pan over high heat. Add the beef and cook, turning frequently, for 8–10 minutes, until evenly browned all over. Transfer the roasting pan to the oven and cook for 20 minutes. Remove the beef from the oven, transfer to a plate and leave to cool. Remove and discard the string.

3 Meanwhile, scrape the cooking juices into a pan, add the onion and mushrooms and cook over low heat, stirring occasionally, for about 5 minutes, until the onion is softened but not coloured. Leave to cool, then mix with the pâté. Add the lemon juice and Worcestershire sauce. Preheat the oven again to 220°C/425°F/Gas 7.

4 Roll out the pastry dough to a large rectangle 5mm/¹/₄in thick. Spread the pâté mixture on the beef, then place it in the centre of the dough. Dampen the edges of the dough, then fold it over the beef to make a neat parcel, tucking in the ends tidily. Press firmly to seal.

5 Place the pastry parcel on a baking sheet with the join underneath and brush with beaten egg. Bake in the oven for 25–45 minutes, depending how well done you like the beef. Serve in generous slices, garnished with parsley.

Butterflied Cumin & Garlic Lamb

Ground cumin and garlic give the lamb a wonderful Middle-Eastern flavour.

Serves 6
1.75kg/4lb leg of lamb
60ml/4 tbsp extra virgin olive oil
30ml/2 tbsp ground cumin
4–6 garlic cloves, crushed
salt and ground black pepper
toasted almond and raisin rice,
  to serve
fresh coriander (cilantro) sprigs
  and lemon wedges, to garnish

1 To butterfly the lamb, cut away the meat from the bone using a small sharp knife. Remove any excess fat and the thin, parchment-like membrane. Flatten the meat with a rolling pin to an even thickness, then prick the fleshy side of the lamb well with the tip of a knife. Place the lamb in a large, shallow dish.

2 Mix together the olive oil, cumin and garlic in a bowl and season with pepper. Spoon the mixture all over the lamb, then rub it well into the crevices. Cover the dish with clear film (plastic wrap) and place the lamb in the refrigerator to marinate overnight.

3 Preheat the oven to 200°C/400°F/Gas 6. Spread the lamb, skin side down, on a rack in a roasting pan. Season with salt and roast for 45–60 minutes, until crusty brown on the outside but still pink in the centre.

4 Remove the lamb from the roasting pan and place on a board. Cover with foil and leave it to rest for about 10 minutes. Cut into diagonal slices, place on warmed plates and serve immediately with the toasted almond and raisin rice. Garnish with fresh coriander sprigs and lemon wedges.

Cook's Tip
The lamb may be cooked on the barbecue rather than roasted in the oven. Thread it on to two long skewers and grill over hot coals for 20–25 minutes on each side, until it is cooked to your liking.

Beef Energy 511kcal/2131kJ; Protein 41.7g; Carbohydrate 19.3g, of which sugars 1.2g; Fat 30.6g, of which saturates 7.2g; Cholesterol 128mg; Calcium 41mg; Fibre 0.4g; Sodium 320mg.
Lamb Energy 505kcal/2106kJ; Protein 59.8g; Carbohydrate 0g, of which sugars 0g; Fat 29.5g, of which saturates 12.8g; Cholesterol 225mg; Calcium 23mg; Fibre 0g; Sodium 128mg.

Lamb with Mint Sauce

In this flavoursome dish, the classic British combination of lamb and mint is given an original twist.

Serves 4
8 lamb noisettes, 2–2.5cm/
    ³⁄₄–1 in thick
30ml/2 tbsp vegetable oil
45ml/3 tbsp medium-bodied dry
    white wine, or vegetable or
    veal stock

salt and ground black pepper
fresh mint sprigs, to garnish

For the sauce
30ml/2 tbsp boiling water
5–10ml/1–2 tsp sugar
leaves from a small bunch of
    fresh mint, finely chopped
about 30ml/2 tbsp white
    wine vinegar

1 To make the sauce, stir the water and sugar together in a heatproof bowl, then add the mint and vinegar to taste. Season with salt and pepper. Leave to stand for 30 minutes.

2 Season the lamb with pepper. Heat the oil in a large, heavy frying pan. Add the lamb, in batches if necessary so that the pan is not crowded, and cook for about 3 minutes on each side for meat that is pink in the middle.

3 Transfer the lamb to a warmed plate and season with salt, then cover and keep warm.

4 Stir the wine or stock into the cooking juices, scraping up the sediment from the base of the pan, and bring to the boil. Leave to bubble for a couple of minutes, then pour over the lamb. Garnish the lamb noisettes with small sprigs of mint and serve hot with the mint sauce.

Cook's Tip
In the past, cooks used more sugar to counteract the sharpness of the vinegar in the mint sauce. Add more to taste, if you like. It was also common to sprinkle the mint leaves with 5ml/1 tsp sugar before chopping them finely.

Somerset Pork with Apples

A creamy cider sauce accompanies tender pieces of pork and sliced apples to make a rich supper dish.

Serves 4
25g/1oz/2 tbsp butter
500g/1¼lb pork loin, cut into
    bitesize pieces
12 baby (pearl) onions, peeled
10ml/2 tsp grated lemon rind

300ml/½ pint/1¼ cups dry
    (hard) cider
150ml/¼ pint/²⁄₃ cup veal stock
2 crisp eating apples such as
    Granny Smith, cored and sliced
45ml/3 tbsp chopped
    fresh parsley
100ml/3½fl oz/scant ½ cup
    whipping cream
salt and ground black pepper

1 Melt the butter in a large sauté or frying pan over medium heat. Add the pork, in batches, and cook, stirring frequently, for about 8 minutes, until browned all over. Transfer the pork to a bowl with a slotted spoon.

2 Add the onions to the pan and lower the heat. Cook, stirring occasionally, for 8–10 minutes, until lightly browned.

3 Stir in the lemon rind, cider and stock, bring to the boil and cook for about 3 minutes. Return all the pork to the pan, cover and simmer gently for about 25 minutes, until tender.

4 Add the apples to the pan and cook for a further 5 minutes. Using a slotted spoon, transfer the pork, onions and apples to a warmed serving dish, cover and keep warm.

5 Stir the parsley and cream into the pan and leave to bubble to thicken the sauce slightly. Season with salt and pepper, then pour over the pork and serve immediately.

Cook's Tip
Veal stock is mellow in flavour and does not overpower other ingredients. The mainstay of restaurant kitchens, it's used less frequently at home. Chicken stock is a satisfactory alternative.

Lamb Energy 332kcal/1384kJ; Protein 29.6g; Carbohydrate 1.6g, of which sugars 1.4g; Fat 22.3g, of which saturates 8.5g; Cholesterol 114mg; Calcium 22mg; Fibre 0g; Sodium 130mg.
Pork Energy 375kcal/1563kJ; Protein 28.7g; Carbohydrate 15g, of which sugars 12.7g; Fat 20.5g, of which saturates 11.3g; Cholesterol 118mg; Calcium 58mg; Fibre 2.2g; Sodium 141mg.

Pork with Plums

Plums poached in apple juice are used here to make a delightfully fruity sauce for pork chops.

Serves 4

450g/1lb ripe plums, halved and stoned (pitted)
300ml/½ pint/1¼ cups apple juice
40g/1½oz/3 tbsp butter
15ml/1 tbsp oil
4 pork chops (about 200g/7oz each)
1 onion, finely chopped
pinch of freshly ground mace
salt and ground black pepper
fresh sage leaves, to garnish

1 Put the plums and the apple juice in a pan and bring just to the boil. Lower the heat and simmer until tender. Strain off and reserve the juice. Place half the plums and a little of the juice in a food processor or blender and process to a purée.

2 Meanwhile, heat the butter and oil in a large frying pan over medium heat. Add the chops and cook for about 4 minutes on each side until evenly browned. Transfer them to a plate.

3 Add the onion to the frying pan and lower the heat. Cook, stirring occasionally, for about 5 minutes, until it is softened but not coloured.

4 Return the chops to the pan. Pour over the plum purée and all the reserved apple juice. Simmer, uncovered, for 10–15 minutes, until the chops are cooked through.

5 Add the remaining plums to the pan, then add the mace and season to taste with salt and pepper. Warm the sauce through over medium heat and serve garnished with fresh sage leaves.

> **Cook's Tip**
> When buying plums, look for firm fruit with a little "give" but avoid any that are squashy. Use within one or two days of purchase because they over-ripen very rapidly.

Lancashire Hot-pot

Browning the lamb and kidneys, plus the extra vegetables and herbs, adds flavour to the traditional basic ingredients.

Serves 4

45ml/3 tbsp vegetable oil
8 medium neck (US shoulder) lamb chops (about 900g/2lb total weight)
175g/6oz lamb's kidneys, cored and cut into large pieces
900g/2lb potatoes, thinly sliced
3 carrots, thickly sliced
450g/1lb leeks, sliced
3 celery sticks, sliced
15ml/1 tbsp chopped fresh thyme
30ml/2 tbsp chopped fresh parsley
small fresh rosemary sprig
600ml/1 pint/2½ cups veal or chicken stock
salt and ground black pepper

1 Preheat the oven to 170°C/325°F/Gas 3. Heat the oil in a frying pan over medium heat. Add the chops, in batches if necessary, and cook for 2–3 minutes on each side, until evenly browned. Transfer to a plate.

2 Add the kidneys to the pan, in batches if necessary, and cook for 1–2 minutes on each side, until evenly browned. Transfer to the plate with the chops. Reserve the fat in the pan.

3 Make alternate layers of lamb chops, kidneys, three-quarters of the potatoes and the carrots, leeks and celery. Sprinkle the herbs over each layer as you go and season each layer with salt and pepper. Tuck the rosemary sprig down the side.

4 Arrange the remaining potato slices on top to cover the meat and vegetables completely. Pour over the veal or chicken stock, brush the potato topping with the reserved fat from the frying pan, then cover the casserole with a tight-fitting lid and bake for 2½ hours.

5 Increase the oven temperature to 220°C/425°F/Gas 7. Uncover the casserole and cook for a further 30 minutes, until the potato topping is golden brown. Serve immediately straight from the casserole.

Pork Energy 620kcal/2595kJ; Protein 65.4g; Carbohydrate 17.4g, of which sugars 17.4g; Fat 32.6g, of which saturates 13.1g; Cholesterol 241mg; Calcium 40mg; Fibre 1.8g; Sodium 232mg.
Hot-Pot Energy 810kcal/3400kJ; Protein 76.7g; Carbohydrate 43.7g, of which sugars 9.3g; Fat 37.8g, of which saturates 13.2g; Cholesterol 363mg; Calcium 140mg; Fibre 6.2g; Sodium 285mg.

Pork Loin with Celery

Have a change from a plain Sunday roast and try this whole loin of pork in an unusual celery and cream sauce instead.

Serves 4
15ml/1 tbsp vegetable oil
50g/2oz/1/4 cup butter
1kg/2 1/4lb boned, rolled loin
  of pork, rind removed
  and trimmed
1 onion, chopped
1 bouquet garni

3 fresh dill sprigs
150ml/1/4 pint/2/3 cup dry
  white wine
150ml/1/4 pint/2/3 cup water
sticks from 1 celery head, cut into
  2.5cm/1in lengths
25g/1oz/1/4 cup plain (all-
  purpose) flour
150ml/1/4 pint/2/3 cup double
  (heavy) cream
squeeze of lemon juice
salt and ground black pepper
chopped fresh dill, to garnish

1 Heat the oil and half the butter in a heavy flameproof casserole just large enough to hold the pork and celery. Add the pork and cook, turning frequently, for 8–10 minutes, until evenly browned. Transfer the pork to a plate.

2 Add the onion to the casserole, lower the heat and cook, stirring occasionally, for 5 minutes, until softened but not coloured. Add the bouquet garni and dill sprigs, place the pork on top and add any juices from the plate. Pour in the wine and water, season to taste, cover and simmer gently for 30 minutes.

3 Turn the pork, arrange the celery around it, cover again and cook for 40 minutes, until the pork and celery are tender. Transfer the pork and celery to a serving plate, cover and keep warm. Discard the bouquet garni and dill.

4 Cream the remaining butter with the flour, then whisk into the cooking liquid while it is barely simmering. Cook for 2–3 minutes, stirring occasionally. Stir the cream into the casserole, bring to the boil and add a squeeze of lemon juice.

5 Slice the pork, spoon a little sauce over the slices and garnish with dill. Serve with the remaining sauce handed separately.

Spiced Lamb with Apricots

Inspired by Middle Eastern cooking, this fruity, spicy casserole is simple to make yet looks impressive.

Serves 4
115g/4oz ready-to-eat
  dried apricots
50g/2oz/scant 1/2 cup seedless
  raisins
2.5ml/1/2 tsp saffron threads
150ml/1/4 pint/2/3 cup orange
  juice
15ml/1 tbsp red wine vinegar
30–45ml/2–3 tbsp olive oil
1.5kg/3–3 1/2 lb leg of lamb, boned
  and diced

1 onion, chopped
2 garlic cloves, crushed
10ml/2 tsp ground cumin
1.25ml/1/4 tsp ground cloves
15ml/1 tbsp ground coriander
25g/1oz/1/4 cup plain (all-
  purpose) flour
600ml/1 pint/2 1/2 cups lamb or
  chicken stock
45ml/3 tbsp chopped fresh
  coriander (cilantro)
salt and ground black pepper
saffron rice mixed with toasted
  almonds and chopped fresh
  coriander, to serve

1 Mix together the dried apricots, raisins, saffron, orange juice and vinegar in a bowl. Cover with clear film (plastic wrap) and leave to soak for 2–3 hours.

2 Preheat the oven to 160°C/325°F/Gas 3. Heat 30ml/2 tbsp oil in a large flameproof casserole over medium heat. Add the lamb, in batches, and cook, stirring frequently, for 5–8 minutes, until evenly browned. Remove and set aside.

3 Add a little more oil to the casserole, if necessary, and lower the heat. Add the onion and garlic and cook, stirring occasionally, for 5 minutes, until softened but not coloured.

4 Stir in the spices and flour and cook for 1–2 minutes more. Return the meat to the casserole. Stir in the stock, fresh coriander and the soaked fruit with its liquid. Season to taste with salt and pepper, then bring to the boil. Cover the casserole with a tight-fitting lid and simmer for 1 1/2 hours (adding extra stock if necessary), or until the lamb is tender. Serve with saffron rice mixed with toasted almonds and fresh coriander.

Pork Energy 669kcal/2783kJ; Protein 55.6g; Carbohydrate 8.1g, of which sugars 3g; Fat 43.5g, of which saturates 22.9g; Cholesterol 236mg; Calcium 105mg; Fibre 1.8g; Sodium 336mg.
Lamb Energy 765kcal/3192kJ; Protein 58.5g; Carbohydrate 27.5g, of which sugars 23.4g; Fat 47.5g, of which saturates 14.7g; Cholesterol 218mg; Calcium 53mg; Fibre 2.5g; Sodium 181mg.

Ruby Bacon Chops

This dish can be prepared with minimal effort, yet still looks impressive.

Serves 4
1 ruby grapefruit

4 lean bacon loin chops
45ml/3 tbsp redcurrant jelly
ground black pepper
fresh vegetables, to serve

1 Cut off all the peel and pith from the grapefruit with a sharp knife. Cut out the segments, catching the juice in a bowl.

2 Fry the bacon chops in a non-stick frying pan without fat, turning them once, until golden. Add the reserved grapefruit juice and redcurrant jelly to the pan and stir until the jelly has melted. Add the grapefruit segments, season with pepper and serve hot with fresh vegetables.

Beef Strips with Orange & Ginger

Stir-frying is a good way of cooking with the minimum of fat, so it's one of the quickest as well as one of the healthiest ways to cook.

Serves 4
450g/1lb rump (round) steak, cut into strips

grated rind and juice of
  1 orange
15ml/1 tbsp soy sauce
1 tbsp cornflour (cornstarch)
2.5cm/1in fresh root ginger,
  finely chopped
10ml/2 tsp sesame oil
1 carrot, cut into small strips
2 spring onions, (scallions), sliced

1 Place the beef strips in a bowl and sprinkle with the orange rind and juice. Leave to marinate for 30 minutes. Drain the liquid and reserve, then mix the meat with the soy sauce, cornflour and ginger.

2 Heat the oil in a wok and stir-fry the beef for 1 minute. Add the carrot and stir-fry for 2–3 minutes. Stir in the spring onions and the reserved liquid, then boil, stirring, until thickened. Serve.

Beef & Mushroom Burgers

It's worth making your own burgers to cut down on fat and for the added flavour – in this recipe the meat is extended with mushrooms for extra fibre.

Serves 4
1 small onion, coarsely chopped
150g/5oz/2 cups small
  cup mushrooms
450g/1lb lean minced
  (ground) beef

50g/2oz/1 cup fresh
  white breadcrumbs
5ml/1 tsp dried mixed herbs
15ml/1 tbsp tomato
  purée (paste)
plain (all-purpose) flour,
  for shaping
salt and ground black pepper

To serve
tomato or barbecue relish
salad
burger buns or pitta bread

1 Put the onion and mushrooms in a food processor and process until finely chopped. Add the beef, breadcrumbs, herbs and tomato purée and season with salt and pepper. Process until the mixture binds together but still has some texture.

2 Scrape the mixture into a bowl and divide into 8–10 pieces. Flour your hands and shape the pieces into patties. Place on a baking sheet or large plate, cover with clear film (plastic wrap) and chill in the refrigerator for 30 minutes.

3 Cook the burgers in a non-stick frying pan, without any added fat, or under a preheated grill (broiler), turning once, for 12–15 minutes, until evenly cooked. Serve immediately with relish and salad, in burger buns or pitta bread.

Cook's Tip
Home-made burgers have a looser texture than the store-bought variety. It is useful to chill them before cooking as this helps the burgers to firm up, so they are less likely to disintegrate when turned during cooking. If you are grilling (broiling) them, don't transfer them from the baking sheet to the grill (broiler) pan.

Bacon Energy 328kcal/1379kJ; Protein 47.7g; Carbohydrate 10.5g, of which sugars 10.5g; Fat 10.9g, of which saturates 3.5g; Cholesterol 129mg; Calcium 20mg; Fibre 0.5g; Sodium 92mg.
Beef Strips Energy 212kcal/885kJ; Protein 25.7g; Carbohydrate 3.8g, of which sugars 0.3g; Fat 10.5g, of which saturates 4.3g; Cholesterol 65mg; Calcium 7mg; Fibre 0g; Sodium 341mg.
Burgers Energy 266kcal/1115kJ; Protein 27.6g; Carbohydrate 14.3g, of which sugars 3.7g; Fat 11.3g, of which saturates 4.8g; Cholesterol 63mg; Calcium 44mg; Fibre 1.5g; Sodium 209mg.

Steak, Kidney & Mushroom Pie

If you prefer, you can omit the kidneys from this pie and substitute more braising steak in their place.

Serves 4
30ml/2 tbsp sunflower oil
1 onion, chopped
115g/4oz bacon, finely chopped
500g/1¼ lb braising steak, diced
25g/1oz/¼ cup plain (all-
  purpose) flour
115g/4oz lamb's kidneys
large bouquet garni
400ml/14fl oz/1¾ cups beef
  stock
115g/4oz button
  (white) mushrooms
225g/8oz puff pastry dough,
  thawed if frozen
beaten egg, to glaze
salt and ground black pepper

1 Preheat the oven to 160°C/325°F/Gas 3. Heat the oil in a heavy pan over low heat. Add the onion and bacon and cook, stirring occasionally, for about 8 minutes, until lightly browned.

2 Toss the steak in the flour. Stir the meat into the pan, in batches, and cook, stirring frequently, until evenly browned. Toss the kidneys in flour, add to the pan with the bouquet garni and cook briefly, stirring occasionally, until browned.

3 Transfer the meat and onions to a casserole, pour in the stock, cover with a tight-fitting lid and cook in the oven for 2 hours. Remove the casserole from the oven, stir in the mushrooms, season with salt and pepper and leave to cool.

4 Preheat the oven to 220°C/425°F/Gas 7. Roll out the pastry to 2cm/¾in larger than the top of a 1.2 litre/2 pint/5 cup pie dish. Cut off a pastry strip and fit it around the dampened rim of the dish. Brush the pastry strip with water.

5 Tip the meat mixture into the dish. Lay the pastry over the dish, press the edges together to seal, then knock them up with the back of a knife. Make a small slit in the pastry, brush with beaten egg and bake for 20 minutes. Lower the oven temperature to 180°C/350°F/Gas 4 and bake for a further 20 minutes, until the pastry is risen, golden and crisp.

Lamb Pie with Mustard Thatch

This makes a pleasant change from a classic shepherd's pie – and it is a healthier option, as well.

Serve 4
750g/1½lb potatoes, diced
30ml/2 tbsp skimmed milk
15ml/1 tbsp wholegrain or
  French mustard
450g/1lb lean minced
  (ground) lamb
1 onion, chopped
2 celery sticks, sliced
2 carrots, diced
150ml/¼ pint/⅔ cup beef stock
60ml/4 tbsp rolled oats
15ml/1 tbsp Worcestershire sauce
30ml/2 tbsp chopped fresh
  rosemary or 10ml/2 tsp
  dried rosemary
salt and ground black pepper
fresh vegetables, to serve

1 Cook the potatoes in boiling lightly salted water for about 20 minutes, until tender. Drain well and mash until smooth, then stir in the milk and mustard. Meanwhile, preheat the oven to 200°C/400°F/Gas 6.

2 Break up the lamb with a fork and cook without any additional fat in a non-stick pan until lightly browned. Add the onion, celery and carrots to the pan and cook for 2–3 minutes, stirring constantly.

3 Stir in the stock and rolled oats. Bring to the boil, then add the Worcestershire sauce and rosemary and season to taste with salt and pepper.

4 Turn the meat mixture into a 1.75 litre/3 pint/7½ cup ovenproof dish and spread the potato topping evenly over the top, swirling with the edge of a knife. Bake for 30–35 minutes, or until golden. Serve hot with fresh vegetables.

> **Variation**
> Substitute low-fat natural (plain) yogurt for the milk and 30ml/
> 2 tbsp chopped fresh mint for the mustard for a herb-flavoured
> thatch that is still a healthy option.

Steak Energy 597kcal/2488kJ; Protein 42.5g; Carbohydrate 27g, of which sugars 1.7g; Fat 36.7g, of which saturates 7.5g; Cholesterol 178mg; Calcium 57mg; Fibre 0.7g; Sodium 742mg.
Lamb Energy 382kcal/1605kJ; Protein 25.9g; Carbohydrate 35.1g, of which sugars 6.8g; Fat 16.4g, of which saturates 7.6g; Cholesterol 89mg; Calcium 78mg; Fibre 2.9g; Sodium 169mg.

Sausage & Bean Ragoût

This is an economical and nutritious main course that children will love. Serve with warm garlic and herb bread, if you like.

Serves 4

350g/12oz/2 cups dried flageolet or cannellini beans, soaked overnight in cold water
45ml/3 tbsp olive oil
1 onion, finely chopped
2 garlic cloves, crushed
450g/1lb good-quality chunky sausages, skinned and thickly sliced
15ml/1 tbsp tomato purée (paste)
400g/14oz can chopped tomatoes
30ml/2 tbsp chopped fresh parsley
15ml/1 tbsp chopped fresh thyme
salt and ground black pepper
chopped fresh thyme and parsley, to garnish

1 Drain and rinse the soaked beans and place them in a pan with enough water to cover. Bring to the boil, cover the pan with a tight-fitting lid and simmer for about 1 hour, or until tender. Drain the beans and set aside.

2 Heat the oil in a frying pan over medium-low heat. Add the onion, garlic and sausages and cook, stirring and turning occasionally, until golden.

3 Stir in the tomato purée, tomatoes, chopped parsley and thyme. Season with salt and pepper, then bring to the boil.

4 Add the beans, lower the heat, cover with a lid and cook gently, stirring occasionally, for about 15 minutes, until the sausage slices are cooked through. Divide the ragoût among warmed plates, garnish with chopped fresh thyme and parsley and serve immediately.

Cook's Tip
For a spicier version, add some skinned, thinly sliced chorizo or kabanos sausage along with the cooked beans for the last 15 minutes of cooking.

Peppered Steaks with Madeira

This is a really easy dish for special occasions. Mixed peppercorns have an excellent flavour, although black pepper will do.

Serves 4

15ml/1 tbsp mixed dried peppercorns (green, pink and black)
4 fillet (beef tenderloin) or sirloin steaks (about 175g/6oz each)
15ml/1 tbsp olive oil, plus extra oil for pan-frying
1 garlic clove, crushed
60ml/4 tbsp Madeira
90ml/6 tbsp beef stock
150ml/¼ pint/⅔ cup double (heavy) cream
salt

1 Finely crush the peppercorns using a spice grinder, coffee grinder or mortar and pestle, then press them evenly on to both sides of the steaks.

2 Place the steaks in a shallow non-metallic dish, then add the olive oil, garlic and Madeira. Cover the dish with clear film (plastic wrap) and leave to marinate in a cold place or the refrigerator for at least 4–6 hours, or preferably overnight for a more intense flavour.

3 Remove the steaks from the dish, reserving the marinade. Brush a little olive oil over a large heavy frying pan and heat until it is hot.

4 Add the steaks to the pan and cook over high heat, according to taste. Allow about 3 minutes' cooking time per side for a medium steak or 2 minutes per side for rare. Remove the steaks from the frying pan and keep them warm.

5 Add the reserved marinade and the beef stock to the pan and bring to the boil, then leave the sauce to bubble gently until it is well reduced.

6 Add the double cream to the pan, season with salt to taste, and stir until the sauce has thickened slightly. Place the peppered steaks on warmed plates and serve immediately with the sauce handed separately.

Ragoût Energy 745kcal/3114kJ; Protein 32.3g; Carbohydrate 54.1g, of which sugars 8.2g; Fat 45.9g, of which saturates 15.2g; Cholesterol 53mg; Calcium 146mg; Fibre 15.6g; Sodium 889mg.
Steaks Energy 471kcal/1956kJ; Protein 41.8g; Carbohydrate 2.5g, of which sugars 2.5g; Fat 30.8g, of which saturates 16.4g; Cholesterol 141mg; Calcium 28mg; Fibre 0g; Sodium 131mg.

Pork with Mozzarella & Sage

Here is a variation of the famous dish *saltimbocca alla romana* – the mozzarella cheese adds a delicious creamy flavour.

Serves 2–3
225g/8oz pork fillet (tenderloin)
1 garlic clove, crushed
75g/3oz mozzarella cheese, cut into 6 slices
6 slices prosciutto
6 large sage leaves
25g/1oz/2 tbsp butter
salt and ground black pepper
potato wedges roasted in olive oil and green beans, to serve

1 Trim any excess fat from the pork, then cut the meat crossways into six pieces about 2.5cm/1in thick.

2 Stand each piece of pork on its end and flatten by beating with the side of a rolling pin. Rub each piece with garlic, place on a plate, cover with clear film (plastic wrap) and set aside for 30 minutes in a cool place.

3 Place a slice of mozzarella on top of each piece of pork and season with salt and pepper. Lay a slice of prosciutto on top of each, crinkling it a little to fit. Press a sage leaf on to each and secure with a wooden cocktail stick (toothpick).

4 Melt the butter in a large, heavy frying pan. Add the pieces of pork and cook for about 2 minutes on each side, until the mozzarella begins to melt. Remove and discard the cocktail sticks, divide the pork among warmed serving plates and serve immediately with roasted potatoes and green beans.

Cook's Tips
• *The original saltimbocca, which means "jump in the mouth", was made with veal escalopes (US scallops) and there is no reason why you should not also use these for this variation.*
• *Try to find traditional mozzarella made with buffalo rather than cow's milk, as it has a better flavour and more delicate texture when melted.*

Five-spice Lamb

This aromatic lamb casserole is a perfect dish to serve at an informal lunch or supper party.

Serves 4
30–45ml/2–3 tbsp vegetable oil
1.5kg/3–3½lb leg of lamb, boned and diced
1 onion, chopped
10ml/2 tsp grated fresh root ginger
1 garlic clove, crushed
5ml/1 tsp Chinese five-spice powder
30ml/2 tbsp hoisin sauce
15ml/1 tbsp soy sauce
300ml/½ pint/1¼ cups passata (bottled strained tomatoes)
250ml/8fl oz/1 cup lamb or chicken stock
1 red (bell) pepper, seeded and diced
1 yellow (bell) pepper, seeded and diced
30ml/2 tbsp chopped fresh coriander (cilantro)
15ml/1 tbsp sesame seeds, toasted
salt and ground black pepper
boiled rice, to serve

1 Preheat the oven to 160°C/325°F/Gas 3. Heat 30ml/2 tbsp of the oil in a large, flameproof casserole. Add the lamb, in batches, and cook over high heat, stirring frequently, until evenly browned. Remove to a plate and set aside.

2 Add the onion, ginger and garlic to the casserole with a little more of the oil, if necessary. Lower the heat and cook, stirring occasionally, for 5 minutes, until softened but not coloured.

3 Return the lamb to the casserole. Stir in the five-spice powder, hoisin sauce, soy sauce, passata and stock and season to taste with salt and pepper. Bring to the boil, then cover with a tight-fitting lid and cook in the oven for about 1¼ hours.

4 Remove the casserole from the oven and stir in the red and yellow peppers. Cover the casserole again and return to the oven for a further 15 minutes, or until the lamb is very tender.

5 Sprinkle with the chopped fresh coriander and toasted sesame seeds. Spoon on to warmed, individual plates and serve immediately accompanied by rice, if you like.

Pork Energy 245kcal/1018kJ; Protein 25.3g; Carbohydrate 0.3g, of which sugars 0.3g; Fat 15.8g, of which saturates 9.1g; Cholesterol 94mg; Calcium 99mg; Fibre 0g; Sodium 502mg.
Lamb Energy 453kcal/1892kJ; Protein 39.2g; Carbohydrate 9.4g, of which sugars 8.7g; Fat 29.1g, of which saturates 10.9g; Cholesterol 143mg; Calcium 59mg; Fibre 2.4g; Sodium 606mg.

Rich Beef Casserole

Use a full-bodied red wine such as a Burgundy to create the flavoursome sauce in this casserole.

Serves 4–6
900g/2lb braising steak steak, cut into cubes
2 onions, coarsely chopped
1 bouquet garni
6 black peppercorns
15ml/1 tbsp red wine vinegar
1 bottle red wine
45–60ml/3–4 tbsp olive oil
3 celery sticks, thickly sliced
50g/2oz/½ cup plain (all-purpose) flour
300ml/½ pint/1¼ cups beef stock
30ml/2 tbsp tomato purée (paste)
2 garlic cloves, crushed
175g/6oz chestnut (cremini) mushrooms, halved
400g/14oz can artichoke hearts, drained and halved
chopped fresh rosemary, to garnish

1 Put the meat, onions, bouquet garni, peppercorns, vinegar and wine in a bowl. Cover with clear film (plastic wrap) and leave to marinate in the refrigerator overnight.

2 The next day, preheat the oven to 160°C/325°F/Gas 3. Drain the meat, reserving the marinade, and pat dry. Heat the oil in a large flameproof casserole. Add the meat and onions, in batches, and cook, stirring frequently, until the meat is evenly browned, adding a little more oil if necessary. Remove and set aside. Add the celery to the casserole and cook, stirring frequently, until browned, then remove and set aside.

3 Sprinkle the flour into the casserole and cook, stirring constantly, for 1 minute. Gradually add the reserved marinade and the stock, and bring to the boil, stirring constantly. Return the meat, onions and celery to the casserole, then stir in the tomato purée and garlic.

4 Cover the casserole with a tight-fitting lid and cook in the oven for about 2¼ hours. Stir in the mushrooms and artichokes, cover again and cook for a further 15 minutes, until the meat is tender. Garnish with rosemary and serve hot with creamy mashed potatoes, if you like.

Roast Pork with Sage & Onion

Pork roasted with a sage and onion stuffing makes a perfect Sunday lunch dish.

Serves 6–8
1.3–1.6kg/3–3½lb boneless loin of pork
60ml/4 tbsp fine, dry breadcrumbs
10ml/2 tsp chopped fresh sage
25ml/1½ tbsp plain (all-purpose) flour
300ml/½ pint/1¼ cups cider
150ml/¼ pint/⅔ cup hot water
5–10ml/1–2 tsp redcurrant jelly
salt and ground black pepper

For the stuffing
25g/1oz/2 tbsp butter
50g/2oz bacon, finely chopped
2 large onions, finely chopped
75g/3oz/1½ cups fresh white breadcrumbs
30ml/2 tbsp chopped fresh sage
5ml/1 tsp chopped fresh thyme
10ml/2 tsp grated lemon rind
1 small egg, beaten

1 Preheat the oven to 220°C/425°F/Gas 7. To make the stuffing, melt the butter in a heavy pan and fry the bacon until it begins to brown. Add the onions and cook gently until softened, but do not allow to brown. Mix with the breadcrumbs, sage, thyme, lemon rind and egg, then season well with salt and pepper.

2 Cut the rind off the joint of pork in one piece and score it well. Place the pork fat-side down and season. Add a layer of stuffing, then roll up and tie neatly. Lay the rind over the pork and rub in 5ml/1 tsp salt. Roast for 2–2½ hours, basting occasionally. Reduce the temperature to 190°C/375°F/Gas 5 after 20 minutes. Shape the remaining stuffing into balls and add to the roasting pan for the last 30 minutes.

3 Remove the rind from the pork. Increase the temperature to 220°C/425°F/Gas 7 and roast the rind for a further 20–25 minutes, until crisp. Mix the breadcrumbs and sage and press them into the pork fat. Cook the pork for 10 minutes, then cover and set aside in a warm place for 15–20 minutes.

4 Remove all but 30–45ml/2–3 tbsp of the fat from the pan. Place over medium heat, stir in the flour, the cider and water. Cook for 10 minutes. Strain the gravy into a clean pan, add the jelly and cook for 5 minutes. Serve with the pork and crackling.

Beef Energy 457kcal/1905kJ; Protein 36.8g; Carbohydrate 12.2g, of which sugars 4.7g; Fat 20g, of which saturates 6.5g; Cholesterol 87mg; Calcium 77mg; Fibre 2.3g; Sodium 169mg.
Pork Energy 446Kcal/1874kJ; Protein 52.8g; Carbohydrate 26.4g, of which sugars 5.1g; Fat 15.1g, of which saturates 6g; Cholesterol 185mg; Calcium 76mg; Fibre 1.7g; Sodium 479mg.

Beef Casserole & Dumplings

A traditional English recipe, this delicious casserole is topped with light herbed dumplings for a filling meal.

Serves 4
15ml/1 tbsp oil
450g/1lb minced (ground) beef
16 button (pearl) onions
2 carrots, thickly sliced
2 celery sticks, thickly sliced
25g/1oz/¼ cup plain (all-purpose) flour
600ml/1 pint/2½ cups beef stock
salt and ground black pepper
broccoli florets, to serve (optional)

For the dumplings
115g/4oz/1 cup shredded vegetable suet
50g/2oz/½ cup self-raising (self-rising) flour
15ml/1 tbsp chopped fresh parsley

1 Preheat the oven to 180°C/350°F/Gas 4. Heat the oil in a flameproof casserole over medium heat. Add the beef and cook, stirring frequently to break up the meat, for 5 minutes, until brown and sealed.

2 Add the onions and cook, stirring occasionally, for 5 minutes, until softened but not coloured.

3 Stir in the carrots, celery and flour and cook, stirring constantly, for 1 minute.

4 Gradually stir in the beef stock, season to taste with salt and pepper and bring to the boil. Cover with a tight-fitting lid and cook in the oven for 1¼ hours.

5 For the dumplings, mix together the suet, flour and parsley in a bowl. Stir in sufficient cold water to form a smooth dough and knead lightly.

6 Roll the dumpling mixture into eight equal-size balls between the palms of your hands and place them around the top of the casserole. Return the casserole, uncovered, to the oven for a further 20 minutes, until the dumplings are cooked. Serve with broccoli florets, if you like.

Stilton Burgers

This tasty recipe contains a delicious surprise: encased in the crunchy burger is lightly melted Stilton cheese.

Serves 4
450g/1lb minced (ground) beef
1 onion, finely chopped
1 celery stick, chopped
5ml/1 tsp mixed dried herbs
5ml/1 tsp mustard
50g/2oz/½ cup crumbled Stilton cheese
4 burger buns
salt and ground black pepper
burger buns, salad and mustard pickle, to serve

1 Preheat the grill (broiler). Place the minced beef in a bowl with the chopped onion and celery. Mix together, then season with salt and pepper.

2 Stir in the herbs and mustard, bringing all the ingredients together to form a firm mixture.

3 Divide the mixture into eight equal portions and roll them into balls between the palms of your hands. Place four on a chopping board and flatten each one slightly into a round.

4 Divide the crumbled cheese between the four rounds, placing a portion in the centre of each. Flatten the remaining balls into rounds and place on top, covering the cheese. Gently mould the mixture together, encasing the crumbled cheese completely, and shape into four burgers.

5 Grill (broil) under medium heat, turning once, for 10 minutes, or until cooked through. Split the burger buns and place a burger inside each. Serve with burger buns, a freshly made salad and some mustard pickle.

Cook's Tip
These burgers could be made with minced (ground) lamb or pork for a change, but make sure that they are thoroughly cooked and not pink inside.

Casserole Energy 619kcal/2567kJ; Protein 25.3g; Carbohydrate 25.5g, of which sugars 6.9g; Fat 46.8g, of which saturates 21.2g; Cholesterol 68mg; Calcium 68mg; Fibre 2.7g; Sodium 117mg.
Burgers Energy 519kcal/2177kJ; Protein 32.2g; Carbohydrate 42.8g, of which sugars 2.8g; Fat 25.5g, of which saturates 10.8g; Cholesterol 76mg; Calcium 156mg; Fibre 1.6g; Sodium 632mg.

Indian Curried Lamb Samosas

Authentic samosa pastry is difficult to make but these samosas work equally well using puff pastry.

Serves 4

15ml/1 tbsp vegetable oil
1 garlic clove, crushed
175g/6oz minced (ground) lamb
4 spring onions (scallions), finely chopped
10ml/2 tsp medium-hot curry paste
4 ready-to-eat dried apricots, chopped
1 small potato, diced
10ml/2 tsp apricot chutney
30ml/2 tbsp frozen peas
squeeze of lemon juice
15ml/1 tbsp chopped fresh coriander (cilantro)
225g/8oz puff pastry dough, thawed if frozen
beaten egg, to glaze
5ml/1 tsp cumin seeds
salt and ground black pepper
45ml/3 tbsp natural (plain) yogurt with chopped fresh mint, to serve
fresh mint sprigs, to garnish

1 Preheat the oven to 220°C/425°F/Gas 7 and dampen a large non-stick baking sheet. Heat the oil in a pan over medium heat and cook the garlic for 30 seconds, then add the lamb. Cook, stirring frequently, for about 5 minutes, until the meat is well browned.

2 Stir in the spring onions, curry paste, apricots and potato, and cook for 2–3 minutes. Then add the chutney, peas and 60ml/4 tbsp water. Cover and simmer for 10 minutes, stirring occasionally. Stir in the lemon juice and coriander, season to taste with salt and pepper, remove and leave to cool.

3 Roll out the pastry and cut into four 15cm/6in squares. Place a quarter of the curry mixture in the centre of each square and brush the edges with beaten egg. Fold over to make a triangle and seal the edges. Knock up the edges with the back of a knife and make a small slit in the top of each.

4 Brush each samosa with beaten egg and sprinkle with the cumin seeds. Place on the damp baking sheet and bake for about 20 minutes. Serve garnished with mint sprigs and with the minty yogurt handed separately.

Breton Pork & Bean Casserole

This is a traditional French dish, called *cassoulet*. There are many variations in the different regions of France.

Serves 4

30ml/2 tbsp olive oil
1 onion, chopped
2 garlic cloves, chopped
450g/1lb pork shoulder, diced
350g/12oz lean lamb (preferably leg), diced
225g/8oz coarse pork and garlic sausage, cut into chunks
400g/14oz can chopped tomatoes
30ml/2 tbsp red wine
15ml/1 tbsp tomato purée (paste)
1 bouquet garni
400g/14oz can cannellini beans, drained and rinsed
50g/2oz/1 cup fresh brown breadcrumbs
salt and ground black pepper
green salad and French bread, to serve

1 Preheat the oven to 160°C/325°F/Gas 3. Heat the oil in a large flameproof casserole over low heat. Add the onion and garlic and cook, stirring occasionally, for about 5 minutes, until softened but not coloured. Remove with a slotted spoon and set aside on a plate.

2 Add the pork, lamb and sausage chunks to the casserole, increase the heat to high and cook, stirring frequently, for about 8 minutes, until evenly browned. Return the onion and garlic to the casserole.

3 Stir in the chopped tomatoes, wine and tomato purée and add 300ml/½ pint/1¼ cups water. Season to taste with salt and pepper and add the bouquet garni. Cover with a tight-fitting lid and bring to the boil, then transfer the casserole to the oven and cook for 1½ hours.

4 Remove and discard the bouquet garni. Stir in the cannellini beans and sprinkle the breadcrumbs over the top. Return the casserole to the oven and cook, uncovered, for a further 30 minutes, until the meat is tender and the topping is golden brown. Serve immediately with a green salad and French bread to mop up the juices.

Samosas Energy 392kcal/1642kJ; Protein 13.7g; Carbohydrate 36.8g, of which sugars 12.4g; Fat 22.7g, of which saturates 3.2g; Cholesterol 34mg; Calcium 66mg; Fibre 2.3g; Sodium 212mg.
Casserole Energy 724kcal/3030kJ; Protein 56.6g; Carbohydrate 37.7g, of which sugars 9.2g; Fat 39g, of which saturates 14g; Cholesterol 164mg; Calcium 138mg; Fibre 8.1g; Sodium 1086mg.

Pan-fried Mediterranean Lamb

The warm, summery flavours of the Mediterranean are combined for a simple weekday meal.

Serves 4

8 lean lamb cutlets
(US rib chops)
1 onion, thinly sliced
2 red (bell) peppers, seeded
and sliced
400g/14oz can plum tomatoes
1 garlic clove, crushed
45ml/3 tbsp chopped fresh basil
30ml/2 tbsp chopped pitted
black olives
salt and ground black pepper
pasta, to serve (optional)

1 Trim any excess fat from the lamb, then cook in a non-stick frying pan, without any added fat, turning frequently, for 4–5 minutes, until golden brown all over.

2 Add the onion and red peppers to the pan. Cook, stirring, for a few minutes to soften, then add the plum tomatoes, garlic and fresh basil leaves.

3 Cover and simmer for 20 minutes, or until the lamb is tender. Stir in the olives, season to taste with salt and pepper and serve hot, with pasta if you like.

> **Cook's Tip**
> Lamb cutlets (US rib chops) are much thinner than chops taken from the loin and it is necessary to cut off the fat before cooking. However, they are less expensive than chops and the meat has a very sweet flavour.

> **Variations**
> • The red (bell) peppers give this dish a slightly sweet taste. If you prefer, use green peppers for a more savoury stew.
> • Substitute sliced green olives stuffed with pimiento for the chopped black ones.

Greek Lamb Pie

Ready-made filo pastry is so easy to use and gives a most professional look to this lamb and spinach pie.

Serves 4

sunflower oil, for brushing
450g/1lb minced (ground) lamb
1 onion, sliced
1 garlic clove, crushed
400g/14oz can plum tomatoes
30ml/2 tbsp chopped fresh mint
5ml/1 tsp freshly grated nutmeg
350g/12oz young spinach leaves
275g/10oz filo pastry, thawed if
frozen
5ml/1 tsp sesame seeds
salt and ground black pepper
green salad or vegetables,
to serve (optional)

1 Preheat the oven to 200°C/400°F/Gas 6. Lightly oil a 22cm/8½in round springform tin (pan).

2 Cook the lamb and onion, without any added fat, in a non-stick pan over medium heat, stirring frequently, for about 5 minutes, until the meat is golden brown.

3 Stir in the garlic, tomatoes with their can juices, mint and nutmeg and season with salt and pepper. Bring to the boil, stirring occasionally. Lower the heat and simmer gently, stirring occasionally, until most of the liquid has evaporated. Remove the pan from the heat and leave to cool.

4 Wash the spinach and remove any tough stalks, then cook in a large pan with only the water clinging to the leaves for about 2 minutes, until just wilted. Drain well, squeezing out as much liquid as possible.

5 Lightly brush each sheet of filo pastry with oil and lay in overlapping layers in the prepared tin, leaving enough pastry overhanging the sides to wrap over the top.

6 Spoon in the meat mixture and spinach, then wrap the pastry over to enclose, scrunching it slightly. Lightly brush the top of the pie with oil, sprinkle with sesame seeds and bake for about 25–30 minutes, or until golden and crisp. Serve hot, with a green salad or vegetables.

Pan-Fried Energy 637kcal/2634kJ; Protein 23.9g; Carbohydrate 9.9g, of which sugars 9.3g; Fat 56g, of which saturates 27.3g; Cholesterol 117mg; Calcium 33mg; Fibre 2.8g; Sodium 272mg.
Lamb Pie Energy 446kcal/1872kJ; Protein 29.2g; Carbohydrate 39.7g, of which sugars 5.9g; Fat 20g, of which saturates 7.7g; Cholesterol 87mg; Calcium 248mg; Fibre 4.5g; Sodium 211mg.

Corned Beef & Egg Hash

This classic American hash is a perennially popular brunch dish and should be served with chilli sauce for an authentic touch.

Serves 4

30ml/2 tbsp vegetable oil
25g/1oz/2 tbsp butter
1 onion, finely chopped
1 small green (bell) pepper, seeded and diced
2 large boiled potatoes, diced
350g/12oz can corned beef, diced
1.5ml/¼ tsp freshly grated nutmeg
1.5ml/¼ tsp paprika
4 eggs
salt and ground black pepper
chopped fresh parsley, to garnish
chilli sauce, to serve

1 Heat the oil and butter in a large frying pan. Add the onion and cook, stirring occasionally, for 5–6 minutes until softened.

2 Mix together the green pepper, potatoes, corned beef, nutmeg and paprika in a bowl. Season with salt and pepper. Add to the pan and toss gently. Press down lightly and cook over a medium heat for 3–4 minutes, until a golden brown crust has formed on the underside.

3 Stir the mixture to distribute the crust, then repeat the process twice, until the mixture is well browned.

4 Make four wells in the hash and crack an egg into each one. Cover and cook gently for 4–5 minutes, until the egg whites are just set.

5 Sprinkle with chopped parsley and cut the hash into quarters. Serve immediately with chilli sauce.

> **Cook's Tip**
> *Put the can of corned beef in the refrigerator for 30 minutes before using. It will firm up and you will be able to cut it into cubes more easily than if it is used at room temperature.*

Cheese Pasta Bolognese

If you like lasagne, you will love this dish. It is especially popular with children too.

Serves 4

30ml/2 tbsp olive oil
1 onion, chopped
1 garlic clove, crushed
1 carrot, diced
2 celery sticks, chopped
2 rashers (strips) streaky (fatty) bacon, finely chopped
5 button (white) mushrooms, chopped
450g/1lb lean minced (ground) beef
120ml/4fl oz/½ cup red wine
15ml/1 tbsp tomato purée (paste)
200g/7oz can chopped tomatoes
fresh thyme sprig
225g/8oz/2 cups dried penne pasta
300ml/½ pint/1¼ cups milk
25g/1oz/2 tbsp butter
25g/1oz/¼ cup plain (all-purpose) flour
150g/5oz/ mozzarella cheese, diced
60ml/4 tbsp freshly grated Parmesan cheese
salt and ground black pepper
fresh basil sprigs, to garnish

1 Heat the oil in a pan over low heat. Add the onion, garlic, carrot and celery and cook, stirring occasionally, for 5 minutes, until softened. Add the bacon and cook for 3–4 minutes. Add the mushrooms and cook for 2 minutes. Add the beef and cook, stirring frequently, for 5–6 minutes, until well browned.

2 Add the wine, tomato purée, 45ml/3 tbsp water, the tomatoes and thyme sprig. Bring to the boil, cover, and simmer gently for 30 minutes.

3 Preheat the oven to 200°C/400°F/Gas 6. Cook the pasta. Meanwhile, place the milk, butter and flour in a pan and heat gently, whisking until thickened. Stir in the mozzarella and half the Parmesan. Season with salt and pepper.

4 Drain the pasta and stir into the cheese sauce. Uncover the Bolognese sauce and boil rapidly for 2 minutes. Spoon the sauce into an ovenproof dish, top with the pasta mixture and sprinkle with the remaining Parmesan. Bake for 25 minutes, or until golden. Garnish with basil and serve hot.

Pasta Energy 806kcal/3369kJ; Protein 46.1g; Carbohydrate 54.6g, of which sugars 9.6g; Fat 44.1g, of which saturates 21.1g; Cholesterol 122mg; Calcium 461mg; Fibre 3.3g; Sodium 503mg.
Hash Energy 403kcal/1683kJ; Protein 30.4g; Carbohydrate 13g, of which sugars 5.1g; Fat 26.1g, of which saturates 10.5g; Cholesterol 277mg; Calcium 64mg; Fibre 1.4g; Sodium 868mg.

Bacon & Sausage Sauerkraut

Juniper berries and crushed coriander seeds flavour this traditional dish from Alsace.

Serves 4
30ml/2 tbsp vegetable oil
1 large onion, thinly sliced
1 garlic clove, crushed
450g/1lb bottled sauerkraut, rinsed and drained
1 eating apple, cored and chopped
5 juniper berries
5 coriander seeds, crushed
450g/1lb piece of lightly smoked bacon loin roast
225g/8oz whole smoked pork sausage, pricked
175ml/6fl oz/³/₄ cup unsweetened apple juice
150ml/¹/₄ pint/²/₃ cup chicken stock
1 bay leaf
8 small salad potatoes

1 Preheat the oven to 180°C/350°F/Gas 4. Heat the oil in a flameproof casserole over medium heat. Add the onion and garlic and cook, stirring occasionally, for 3–4 minutes, until softened but not coloured. Stir in the sauerkraut, apple, juniper berries and coriander seeds.

2 Lay the piece of bacon loin and the sausage on top of the sauerkraut, pour in the apple juice and stock, and add the bay leaf. Cover and bake in the oven for about 1 hour.

3 Remove from the oven and put the potatoes in the casserole. Add a little more stock if necessary, cover and bake for a further 30 minutes, or until the potatoes are tender.

4 Just before serving, lift out the bacon and sausages on to a board and slice. Spoon the sauerkraut on to a warmed platter, top with the meat and surround with the potatoes.

> **Cook's Tip**
> *Sauerkraut is finely sliced, salted and fermented white cabbage. It is available in bottles and cans and, as it is pasteurized, it does not require the very long cooking times traditionally associated with this speciality.*

Best-ever American Burgers

These meaty quarter-pounders are far superior in both taste and texture to any burgers you can buy ready-made.

Makes 4 burgers
15ml/1 tbsp vegetable oil
1 small onion, chopped
450g/1lb minced (ground) beef
1 large garlic clove, crushed
5ml/1 tsp ground cumin
10ml/2 tsp ground coriander
30ml/2 tbsp tomato purée (paste) or ketchup
5ml/1 tsp wholegrain mustard
dash of Worcestershire sauce
30ml/2 tbsp mixed chopped fresh herbs, such as parsley, thyme and oregano or marjoram
15ml/1 tbsp lightly beaten egg
salt and ground black pepper
plain (all-purpose) flour, for shaping
vegetable oil, for frying (optional)
burger buns, mixed salad, chips (French fries) and relish, to serve

1 Heat the oil in a frying pan, Add the onion and cook, stirring occasionally, for 5 minutes, until softened. Remove from the pan, drain on kitchen paper and leave to cool.

2 Mix together the beef, garlic, spices, tomato purée or ketchup, mustard, Worcestershire sauce, herbs, beaten egg and seasoning in a bowl. Stir in the cooled onions.

3 Sprinkle a board with flour and shape the mixture into four burgers with floured hands and a spatula. Cover and chill in the refrigerator for 15 minutes.

4 Heat a little oil in a pan and fry the burgers over medium heat for about 5 minutes each side, depending on how rare you like them. Alternatively, cook under a medium grill (broiler) for the same time. Serve with buns, salad, chips and relish.

> **Cook's Tip**
> *If you prefer, make eight smaller burgers to serve in buns, with melted cheese and tomato slices.*

Burger Energy 298kcal/1237kJ; Protein 23.5g; Carbohydrate 2.3g, of which sugars 1.9g; Fat 21.7g, of which saturates 8.3g; Cholesterol 91mg; Calcium 20mg; Fibre 0.4g; Sodium 117mg.
Sauerkraut Energy 562kcal/2347kJ; Protein 42.6g; Carbohydrate 31.8g, of which sugars 14.4g; Fat 30.2g, of which saturates 10g; Cholesterol 49mg; Calcium 118mg; Fibre 5.1g; Sodium 2352mg.

Ginger Pork with Black Bean Sauce

Preserved black beans provide a unique flavour in this dish. Look for them in specialist Chinese grocers.

Serves 4

350g/12oz pork fillet (tenderloin)
1 garlic clove, crushed
15ml/1 tbsp grated fresh
   root ginger
90ml/6 tbsp chicken stock
30ml/2 tbsp dry sherry
15ml/1 tbsp light soy sauce
5ml/1 tsp sugar
10ml/2 tsp cornflour (cornstarch)
45ml/3 tbsp groundnut
   (peanut) oil
2 yellow (bell) peppers, seeded
   and cut into strips
2 red (bell) peppers, seeded and
   cut into strips
1 bunch of spring onions
   (scallions), sliced diagonally
45ml/3 tbsp preserved black
   beans, coarsely chopped
fresh coriander (cilantro) sprigs,
   to garnish

1 Cut the pork into thin slices across the grain of the meat. Put the slices into a dish and mix them with the garlic and ginger. Cover with clear film (plastic wrap) and leave to marinate at room temperature for 15 minutes.

2 Blend together the stock, sherry, soy sauce, sugar and cornflour in a small bowl, then set the sauce mixture aside.

3 Heat the oil in a wok or large frying pan. Add the pork slices and stir-fry for 2–3 minutes. Add the yellow and red peppers and spring onions and stir-fry for a further 2 minutes.

4 Add the beans and sauce mixture and cook, stirring constantly, until thick. Serve immediately, garnished with the fresh coriander sprigs.

> **Cook's Tip**
> *If you cannot find preserved black beans, use the same amount of black bean sauce instead.*

Golden Pork & Apricot Casserole

The rich golden colour and warm spicy flavour of this simple casserole make it ideal for a chilly winter's day.

Serves 4

4 lean pork loin chops
1 onion, thinly sliced
2 yellow (bell) peppers, seeded
   and sliced
10ml/2 tsp medium curry powder
15g/½ oz/2 tbsp plain (all-
   purpose) flour
250ml/8fl oz/1 cup chicken stock
115g/4oz ready-to-eat
   dried apricots
30ml/2 tbsp wholegrain mustard
salt and ground black pepper
boiled rice or new potatoes, to
   serve (optional)

1 Trim the excess fat from the pork. Cook the chops, without any additional fat, in a large heavy or non-stick pan over medium heat for about 6 minutes, until lightly browned.

2 Lower the heat, add the onion and yellow peppers to the pan and cook, stirring frequently, for about 5 minutes, until softened but not coloured.

3 Stir in the curry powder and the flour and cook, stirring constantly, for 1 minute.

4 Gradually stir in the stock, then add the apricots and mustard and bring to the boil over medium heat. Cover with a tight-fitting lid, lower the heat and simmer gently for 25–30 minutes, until the chops are cooked through and tender. Season to taste with salt and pepper and serve immediately, with boiled rice or new potatoes, if you like.

> **Variations**
> • *This recipe also works well with chicken breast portions – with or without the skin – instead of pork chops. However, you will need to heat 15ml/1 tbsp sunflower oil in the pan for the initial browning in step 1.*
> • *Substitute the same quantity of ready-to-eat prunes for the apricots and use red (bell) peppers instead of yellow.*

Ginger Pork Energy 302kcal/1263kJ; Protein 23.8g; Carbohydrate 22.1g, of which sugars 13.4g; Fat 12.8g, of which saturates 3.1g; Cholesterol 55mg; Calcium 41mg; Fibre 4 1g; Sodium 341mg.
Golden Pork Energy 281kcal/1181kJ; Protein 34.9g; Carbohydrate 20.9g, of which sugars 16.7g; Fat 6.9g, of which saturates 2.2g; Cholesterol 95mg; Calcium 64mg; Fibre 4.1g; Sodium 124mg.

Sukiyaki-style Beef

This dish incorporates all the traditional Japanese elements – meat, vegetables, noodles and tofu.

Serves 4

450g/1lb thick rump (round) steak
200g/7oz/3½ cups Japanese rice noodles
15ml/1 tbsp shredded suet
200g/7oz firm tofu, cut into dice

8 shiitake mushrooms, trimmed
2 leeks, sliced into 2.5cm/ 1in lengths
90g/3½ oz/scant 1 cup baby spinach, to serve

For the stock
15g/½oz/1 tbsp caster (superfine) sugar
90ml/6 tbsp rice wine
45ml/3 tbsp dark soy sauce
120ml/4fl oz/½ cup water

1 If there is time, chill the steak in the freezer for 30 minutes to make it easier to slice thinly. Cut the steak into thin even-size slices with a very sharp knife.

2 Blanch the rice noodles in a large pan of boiling water for 2 minutes, then drain well.

3 Mix together all the ingredients for the stock in a bowl, stirring until the sugar has dissolved. Set aside.

4 Heat a wok, then add the suet. When the suet has melted, add the steak and stir-fry for 2–3 minutes, until it is cooked but still pink in colour.

5 Pour the stock over the beef and add the tofu, mushrooms and leeks. Cook, stirring occasionally, for 4 minutes, until the leeks are tender. Divide the different ingredients equally among individual plates, spoon the stock over them and serve immediately with a few baby spinach leaves each.

> **Cook's Tip**
> *Add a touch of authenticity and serve this complete meal with chopsticks and a porcelain spoon to collect the stock juices.*

Stir-fried Pork with Mustard

Fry the apple for this dish very carefully, because it will disintegrate if it is overcooked.

Serves 4

500g/1¼lb pork fillet (tenderloin)
1 tart eating apple, such as Granny Smith
40g/1½oz/3 tbsp unsalted (sweet) butter
15g/½oz/1 tbsp caster (superfine) sugar

1 small onion, finely chopped
30ml/2 tbsp Calvados or brandy
15ml/1 tbsp Meaux or coarse grain mustard
15ml/¼ pint/⅔ cup double (heavy) cream
30ml/2 tbsp chopped fresh parsley
salt and ground black pepper
fresh flat leaf parsley sprigs, to garnish

1 Cut the pork fillet into thin even size slices with a sharp knife. Peel and core the apple, then cut it into thick slices.

2 Heat a wok, then add half the butter. When the butter is hot, add the apple slices, sprinkle the sugar over them and stir-fry for 2–3 minutes. Remove the apple from the wok and set aside. Wipe out the wok with kitchen paper.

3 Reheat the wok, then add the remaining butter and stir fry the pork fillet and onion together for 2–3 minutes, until the pork is golden and the onion has begun to soften.

4 Stir in the Calvados or brandy, bring to the boil and cook until it has reduced by about half. Stir in the mustard.

5 Add the cream and simmer gently for about 1 minute, then stir in the parsley. Transfer to warmed plates, divide the apple among them and serve garnished with sprigs of flat leaf parsley.

> **Cook's Tip**
> *If you haven't got a wok, use a large frying pan, preferably with deep, sloping sides.*

Beef Energy 489kcal/2044kJ; Protein 34.7g; Carbohydrate 49g, of which sugars 6.9g; Fat 16.7g, of which saturates 6.5g; Cholesterol 68mg; Calcium 328mg; Fibre 2.4g; Sodium 916mg.
Pork Energy 278kcal/1162kJ; Protein 27.5g; Carbohydrate 7.8g, of which sugars 7.4g; Fat 15.4g, of which saturates 8.2g; Cholesterol 105mg; Calcium 42mg; Fibre 1.2g; Sodium 154mg.

Hungarian Beef Goulash

Spicy beef stew served with caraway flavoured dumplings will satisfy even the hungriest Hungarian.

Serves 4
30ml/2 tbsp vegetable oil
1 kg/2lb braising steak, diced
2 onions, chopped
1 garlic clove, crushed
15g/½oz/2 tbsp plain (all-purpose) flour
10ml/2 tsp paprika
5ml/1 tsp caraway seeds
400g/14oz can chopped tomatoes

300ml/½ pint/1¼ cups beef stock
1 large carrot, chopped
1 red (bell) pepper, seeded and chopped
salt and ground black pepper
sour cream, to serve
pinch of paprika, to garnish

For the dumplings
115g/4oz/1 cup self-raising (self-rising) flour
40g/2oz/½ cup shredded suet
15ml/1 tbsp chopped fresh parsley
2.5ml/½ tsp caraway seeds

1 Heat the oil in a flameproof casserole over high heat. Add the meat and cook, stirring frequently, for 5 minutes, until evenly browned. Remove with a slotted spoon.

2 Lower the heat, add the onions and garlic and cook, stirring occasionally, for about 5 minutes, until softened but not coloured. Stir in the flour, paprika and caraway seeds and cook, stirring constantly, for 2 minutes.

3 Return the meat to the casserole and stir in the tomatoes and stock. Bring to the boil, cover and simmer for 2 hours.

4 To make the dumplings, sift the flour and seasoning into a bowl, add the suet, parsley, caraway seeds and 45–60ml/3–4 tbsp water and mix to a soft dough. Divide into eight pieces and roll into balls. Cover and set aside.

5 After 2 hours, stir the carrot and red pepper into the goulash, and season. Drop the dumplings into the casserole, cover and simmer for a further 25 minutes. Serve in bowls topped with a spoonful of sour cream sprinkled with paprika.

Pork Satay with Peanut Sauce

These delightful little satay sticks from Thailand make a good light meal or a drinks party snack.

Makes 8
½ small onion, chopped
2 garlic cloves, crushed
30ml/2 tbsp lemon juice
15ml/1 tbsp soy sauce
5ml/1 tsp ground coriander
2.5ml/½ tsp ground cumin
5ml/1 tsp ground turmeric
30ml/2 tbsp vegetable oil
450g/1lb pork fillet (tenderloin)
salt and ground black pepper
fresh coriander (cilantro) sprigs, to garnish
boiled rice, to serve

For the sauce
150ml/¼ pint/⅔ cup coconut cream
60ml/4 tbsp crunchy peanut butter
15ml/1 tbsp lemon juice
2.5ml/½ tsp ground cumin
2.5ml/½ tsp ground coriander
5ml/1 tsp soft brown sugar
15ml/1 tbsp soy sauce
1–2 dried red chillies, seeded and chopped
15ml/1 tbsp chopped fresh coriander

For the salad
½ small cucumber, peeled and diced
15ml/1 tbsp white wine vinegar
15ml/1 tbsp chopped fresh coriander

1 Put the onion, garlic, lemon juice, soy sauce, ground coriander, cumin, turmeric and oil in a food processor and process until smooth. Cut the pork into strips, mix with the spice marinade in a bowl, cover with clear film (plastic wrap) and chill.

2 Preheat the grill (broiler). Thread two or three pork pieces on to each of eight soaked wooden skewers and grill (broil) for 2–3 minutes on each side, basting with the marinade.

3 To make the sauce, put all the ingredients into a pan, bring to the boil, stirring constantly, and simmer for 5 minutes.

4 Mix together all the salad ingredients. Arrange the satay sticks on a platter, garnish with coriander sprigs and season. Serve immediately with the sauce and boiled rice.

Goulash Energy 751kcal/3136kJ; Protein 62.1g; Carbohydrate 41.2g, of which sugars 13.2g; Fat 38.9g, of which saturates 15.4g; Cholesterol 153mg; Calcium 159mg; Fibre 4.6g; Sodium 282mg.
Satay Energy 189kcal/784kJ; Protein 14.5g; Carbohydrate 2.9g, of which sugars 2.2g; Fat 13.3g, of which saturates 5.8g; Cholesterol 35mg; Calcium 25mg; Fibre 0.9g; Sodium 70mg.

Stir-fried Pork with Lychees

No extra oil or fat is needed to cook this dish, as the pork produces enough on its own.

Serves 4
450g/1lb fatty pork, such as belly pork, with the skin on or off
30ml/2 tbsp hoisin sauce
4 spring onions (scallions), sliced diagonally
175g/6oz lychees, peeled, stoned (pitted) and cut into slivers
salt and ground black pepper
fresh lychees and parsley sprigs, to garnish

1 Cut the pork into bitesize pieces and place in a dish. Pour the hoisin sauce over it and toss to coat. Cover with clear film (plastic wrap) and leave to marinate in a cool place for at least 30 minutes.

2 Heat a wok, then add the pork and stir-fry for 5 minutes, until crisp and golden. Add the spring onions and stir-fry for a further 2 minutes.

3 Sprinkle the lychee slivers over the pork, and season well with salt and pepper. Transfer to warmed plates, garnish with lychees and parsley sprigs and serve immediately.

Cook's Tip
Lychees have a very pretty pink skin which cracks easily when the fruit is pressed between finger and thumb, making them easy to peel. The fruit is a soft, fleshy berry and contains a long, shiny, brown seed. This is inedible and must be removed. The sweet flesh is pearly white and fragrant, similar in texture to a grape. When buying lychees, avoid any that are turning brown, as they will be over-ripe. Equally, avoid under-ripe lychees with green or beige skins. Look for fruit with as much red or pink in the skins as possible. Fresh lychees are delicate and should be used as soon after purchase as possible, but can be stored in the refrigerator for up to a week. If you cannot buy the fresh fruit, you could use drained canned lychees, but they do not have the same fragrance or flavour.

Sizzling Beef with Celeriac Straw

The crisp celeriac batons look like fine pieces of straw when cooked and have a mild celery-like flavour.

Serves 4
450g/1lb celeriac
150ml/¼ pint/⅔ cup vegetable oil
1 red (bell) pepper
6 spring onions (scallions)
450g/1lb rump (round) steak
60ml/4 tbsp beef stock
30ml/2 tbsp sherry vinegar
10ml/2 tsp Worcestershire sauce
10ml/2 tsp tomato purée (paste)
salt and ground black pepper

1 Peel the celeriac and then cut it into fine batons, using a cleaver if you have one or a large sharp knife.

2 Heat a wok, then add two-thirds of the oil. When the oil is hot, add the celeriac batons, in batches, and stir-fry until golden brown and crisp. Drain well on kitchen paper. Discard the oil.

3 Seed the red pepper and cut it and the spring onions into 2.5cm/1in lengths, cutting diagonally. Cut the steak into strips, across the grain of the meat.

4 Heat the wok again, then add the remaining oil. When the oil is hot, add the red pepper and spring onions and stir-fry for 2–3 minutes.

5 Add the steak strips and stir-fry for a further 3–4 minutes, until well browned. Add the stock, vinegar, Worcestershire sauce and tomato purée. Season well with salt and pepper and serve with the celeriac "straw".

Cook's Tip
The Chinese use a large cleaver for preparing most vegetables. With a little practice, you will discover that it is the ideal kitchen utensil for cutting fine vegetable batons and chopping thin strips of meat.

Pork Energy 465kcal/1926kJ; Protein 17.9g; Carbohydrate 8.7g, of which sugars 8.6g; Fat 40.1g, of which saturates 14.8g; Cholesterol 81mg; Calcium 17mg; Fibre 0.5g; Sodium 206mg.
Beef Energy 318kcal/1324kJ; Protein 26.2g; Carbohydrate 5g, of which sugars 4.8g; Fat 21.6g, of which saturates 3.9g; Cholesterol 66mg; Calcium 66mg; Fibre 2.2g; Sodium 174mg.

Turkish Lamb & Apricot Stew

Couscous flavoured with almonds and parsley accompanies this rich and delicious stew of lamb, apricots and chickpeas.

Serves 4

1 large aubergine
  (eggplant), diced
30ml/2 tbsp sunflower oil
1 onion, chopped
1 garlic clove, crushed
5ml/1 tsp ground cinnamon
3 cloves
450g/1lb boned leg of lamb, diced
400g/14oz can
  chopped tomatoes

115g/4oz ready-to-eat
  dried apricots
115g/4oz/1 cup canned
  chickpeas, drained and rinsed
5ml/1 tsp clear honey
salt and ground black pepper

To serve

400g/14oz/2 cups couscous,
  prepared
30ml/2 tbsp olive oil
30ml/2 tbsp chopped almonds,
  fried in a little oil
30ml/2 tbsp chopped
  fresh parsley

1 Place the diced aubergine in a colander, sprinkle with salt and leave for about 30 minutes. Heat the oil in a large flameproof casserole. Add the onion and garlic and cook, stirring occasionally, for about 5 minutes, until softened.

2 Stir in the cinnamon and cloves and cook, stirring constantly, for 1 minute. Add the lamb and cook, stirring frequently, for 5–6 minutes, until evenly browned.

3 Rinse, drain and pat dry the aubergine with kitchen paper, add to the casserole and cook, stirring constantly, for 3 minutes. Add the tomatoes, 300ml/½ pint/1¼ cups water and the apricots, and season to taste with salt and pepper. Bring to the boil, then lower the heat, cover with a tight-fitting lid and simmer gently for about 45 minutes.

4 Stir the chickpeas and honey into the stew and cook for a final 15–20 minutes, or until the lamb is tender. Serve the dish accompanied by couscous with the olive oil, fried almonds and chopped parsley stirred into it.

Curried Lamb & Lentils

This colourful curry is packed with protein and low in fat, so it makes a tasty yet healthy meal.

Serves 4

8 lean boned lamb leg steaks
  (about 500g/1¼lb
  total weight)
1 onion, chopped
2 carrots, diced

1 celery stick, chopped
15ml/1 tbsp hot curry paste
30ml/2 tbsp tomato
  purée (paste)
475ml/16fl oz/2 cups chicken or
  veal stock
175g/6oz/1 cup green lentils
salt and ground black pepper
fresh coriander (cilantro) leaves,
  to garnish
boiled rice, to serve

1 Cook the lamb steaks in a large, non-stick frying pan, without any added fat, for 2–3 minutes on each side, until browned.

2 Add the onion, carrots and celery and cook, stirring occasionally, for 2 minutes, then stir in the curry paste, tomato purée, stock and lentils.

3 Bring to the boil, lower the heat, cover with a tight-fitting lid and simmer gently for 30 minutes, until tender. Add some extra stock, if necessary.

4 Season to taste with salt and pepper. Spoon the curry on to warmed plates and serve immediately, garnished with coriander and accompanied by rice.

Cook's Tip

Lentils are one of the few pulses (legumes) that do not require prolonged soaking in cold water before cooking. However, just like dried beans and peas, they should not be seasoned with salt until after cooking or their skins will become unpleasantly tough. Both green and brown lentils keep their shape well, as do the rather more expensive small Puy lentils. Red and yellow lentils are not suitable for this recipe as they tend to disintegrate during cooking.

Turkish Lamb Energy 462kcal/1931kJ; Protein 28.5g; Carbohydrate 23.2g, of which sugars 17.6g; Fat 29.1g, of which saturates 7.8g; Cholesterol 86mg; Calcium 77mg; Fibre 5.8g; Sodium 114mg.
Curried Lamb Energy 381kcal/1600kJ; Protein 35.5g; Carbohydrate 28.4g, of which sugars 4.3g; Fat 14.7g, of which saturates 6.6g; Cholesterol 95mg; Calcium 47mg; Fibre 3.2g; Sodium 144mg.

Middle-Eastern Lamb Kebabs

Skewered, grilled meats are
a staple of Middle Eastern
cooking. Here, marinated
lamb is grilled with a
colourful mix of vegetables.

Makes 4
450g/1lb boned leg of lamb, diced
75ml/5 tbsp olive oil
15ml/1 tbsp chopped fresh
  oregano or thyme, or
  10ml/2 tsp dried oregano
15ml/1 tbsp chopped
  fresh parsley
juice of 1/2 lemon
1/2 small aubergine (eggplant),
  thickly sliced and quartered
4 baby (pearl) onions, halved
2 tomatoes, quartered
4 fresh bay leaves
salt and ground black pepper
pitta bread and natural (plain)
  yogurt, to serve

1 Place the lamb in a non-metallic bowl. Mix together the olive oil, oregano or thyme, parsley and lemon juice in a jug (pitcher) and season with salt and pepper. Pour over the lamb and mix well. Cover with clear film (plastic wrap) and leave to marinate in the refrigerator for about 1 hour.

2 Preheat the grill (broiler). Thread the marinated lamb, aubergine, onions, tomatoes and bay leaves alternately on to four large skewers. (If using wooden skewers, soak them first.) Reserve the marinade.

3 Place the kebabs on a grill (broiler) rack and brush the vegetables liberally with the reserved marinade. Cook the kebabs under medium heat for 8–10 minutes on each side, basting once or twice with the juices that have collected in the bottom of the pan. Serve the kebabs immediately, accompanied by hot pitta bread and yogurt.

Cook's Tips
• For a more piquant marinade, add one or two peeled and crushed garlic cloves.
• These kebabs can also be cooked for the same length of time on a barbecue.

Mexican Spiced Roast Leg of Lamb

Make sure you push the
garlic slices deeply into the
meat or they will burn and
develop a bitter flavour.

Serves 4
1 small leg or half leg of lamb
  (about 1.25kg/2 1/2lb)
15ml/1 tbsp dried oregano
5ml/1 tsp ground cumin
5ml/1 tsp hot chilli powder
2 garlic cloves
45ml/3 tbsp olive oil
30ml/2 tbsp red wine vinegar
300ml/1/2 pint/1 1/4 cups chicken
  or veal stock
salt and ground black pepper
fresh oregano sprigs, to garnish

1 Preheat the oven to 220°C/425°F/Gas 7. Place the leg of lamb on a large chopping board.

2 Place the oregano, cumin and chilli powder in a bowl. Crush one of the garlic cloves and add it to the bowl. Pour in half the olive oil and mix well to form a paste.

3 Using a sharp knife, make a criss-cross pattern of fairly deep slits going through the skin and just into the meat of the leg of lamb. Press the spice paste into the slits with the back of a round-bladed knife. Peel and thinly slice the remaining garlic clove, then cut each slice in half. Push the pieces of garlic deeply into the slits made in the meat.

4 Place the lamb in a roasting pan. Mix together the vinegar and remaining oil in a bowl and pour over the meat. Season with salt and pepper.

5 Roast the lamb for about 15 minutes, then lower the oven temperature to 180°C/350°F/Gas 4 and roast for a further 1 1/4 hours (or a little longer if you like your meat well done).

6 Transfer the lamb to a carving board, cover with foil and leave to stand. Place the roasting pan over medium heat, pour in the stock and bring to the boil, scraping up the sediment from the base of the pan. Cook, stirring constantly, for 2–3 minutes, until slightly thickened. Carve the lamb and serve, garnished with oregano sprigs and accompanied by the gravy.

Kebabs Energy 339kcal/1409kJ; Protein 22.6g; Carbohydrate 2.7g, of which sugars 2.4g; Fat 26.5g, of which saturates 7.9g; Cholesterol 86mg; Calcium 16mg; Fibre 0.7g; Sodium 102mg.
Roast Leg Energy 733kcal/3073kJ; Protein 94.8g; Carbohydrate 4.1g, of which sugars 0.4g; Fat 37.8g, of which saturates 13.1g; Cholesterol 313mg; Calcium 27mg; Fibre 1g; Sodium 198mg.

Spiced Lamb Bake

A delicious shepherd's pie from South Africa. The recipe was originally poached from the Afrikaners' Malay slaves.

Serves 4

15ml/1 tbsp vegetable oil
1 onion, chopped
675g/1½lb minced (ground) lamb
30ml/2 tbsp medium curry paste
30ml/2 tbsp mango chutney
30ml/2 tbsp freshly squeezed lemon juice
60ml/4 tbsp chopped, blanched almonds
30ml/2 tbsp sultanas (golden raisins)
200ml/7fl oz/scant 1 cup coconut cream
2 eggs
2 bay leaves
salt and ground black pepper
broccoli florets, to serve (optional)

1 Preheat the oven to 180°C/350°F/Gas 4. Heat the oil in a large, heavy frying pan over low heat. Add the onion and cook, stirring occasionally, for 5–6 minutes, until softened but not coloured.

2 Add the minced lamb, increase the heat to medium and cook, stirring frequently to break up the lumps, for 6–8 minutes, until evenly browned.

3 Stir in the curry paste, mango chutney, lemon juice, almonds and sultanas, season well with salt and pepper and cook, stirring occasionally, for about 5 minutes.

4 Transfer the mixture to an ovenproof dish and cook in the oven, uncovered, for 10 minutes.

5 Meanwhile, beat the coconut cream with the eggs in a bowl and season with salt and pepper.

6 Remove the dish from the oven and pour the coconut custard over the meat mixture. Lay the bay leaves on the top and return the dish to the oven for 30–35 minutes, or until the top is set and golden. Spoon the bake on to warmed plates and serve immediately with cooked broccoli if you like.

Boeuf Bourguignon

This French classic is named after the region it comes from, Burgundy, where the local red wine is used to flavour it.

Serves 4

30ml/2 tbsp olive oil
225g/8oz piece streaky (fatty) bacon, diced
12 baby (pearl) onions
900g/2lb braising steak, cut into 5cm/2in cubes
1 large onion, thickly sliced
15g/½oz/2 tbsp plain (all-purpose) flour
about 450ml/¾ pint/scant 2 cups red Burgundy wine
1 bouquet garni
1 garlic clove
225g/8oz button (white) mushrooms, halved
salt and ground black pepper
chopped fresh parsley, to garnish

1 Heat the oil in a flameproof casserole over low heat. Add the bacon and baby onions and cook, stirring occasionally, for 7–8 minutes, until the onions are evenly browned and the bacon fat has become translucent. Remove with a slotted spoon and set aside on a plate.

2 Add the beef to the casserole, increase the heat to medium and cook, stirring frequently, until evenly browned all over. Add the sliced onion and cook, stirring occasionally for a further 4–5 minutes.

3 Sprinkle in the flour and cook, stirring constantly, for 1 minute. Gradually stir in the wine, add the bouquet garni and garlic and season with salt and pepper. Bring to the boil, then lower the heat, cover with a tight-fitting lid and simmer gently for about 2 hours.

4 Stir in the baby onions and bacon and add a little extra wine, if necessary. Add the mushrooms. Replace the lid of the casserole and cook for a further 30 minutes, or until the meat is very tender. Remove and discard the bouquet garni and garlic. Taste and adjust the seasoning, if necessary, then ladle the stew on to warmed plates, garnish with chopped fresh parsley and serve immediately.

Boeuf Energy 749kcal/3117kJ; Protein 63.3g; Carbohydrate 15.2g, of which sugars 8.8g; Fat 40.3g, of which saturates 14g; Cholesterol 167mg; Calcium 69mg; Fibre 2.8g; Sodium 868mg.
Lamb Energy 657kcal/2732kJ; Protein 40.1g; Carbohydrate 12.5g, of which sugars 11.7g; Fat 50.1g, of which saturates 23.4g; Cholesterol 225mg; Calcium 94mg; Fibre 1.6g; Sodium 243mg.

Greek Pasta Bake

Another excellent main meal (called *pastitsio* in Greece), this recipe is both economical and filling.

Serves 4
15ml/1 tbsp olive oil
450g/1lb minced (ground) lamb
1 onion, chopped
2 garlic cloves, crushed
30ml/2 tbsp tomato purée (paste)
25g/1oz/¼ cup plain (all-purpose) flour
300ml/½ pint/1¼ cups lamb or chicken stock
2 large tomatoes
115g/4oz cup pasta shapes
450g/1lb tub Greek (US strained plain) yogurt
2 eggs, lightly beaten
salt and ground black pepper
green salad, to serve

1 Preheat the oven to 190°C/375°F/Gas 5. Heat the oil in a large pan over medium heat. Add the lamb and cook, stirring frequently, for 5 minutes. Add the onion and garlic and cook, stirring occasionally, or a further 5 minutes.

2 Stir in the tomato purée and flour. Cook, stirring constantly, for 1 minute, then gradually stir in the stock and season to taste with salt and pepper. Bring to the boil, then lower the heat and simmer for 20 minutes.

3 Slice the tomatoes, spoon the meat mixture into an ovenproof dish and arrange the tomatoes on top.

4 Bring a pan of salted water to the boil and cook the pasta shapes for 8–10 minutes until just tender. Drain well.

5 Mix together the pasta, yogurt and eggs in a bowl. Spoon the mixture on top of the tomatoes and bake for 1 hour. Serve immediately with a crisp green salad.

Cook's Tip
Choose open pasta shapes for this dish rather than tubes, so the sauce coats the pasta all over. Try shells, spirals or bows.

Bacon Koftas

These easy koftas are good for barbecues and summer grills, served with lots of fresh salad.

Serves 4
225g/8oz lean smoked back bacon, coarsely chopped
75g/3oz/1½ cups fresh wholemeal (whole-wheat) breadcrumbs
2 spring onions (scallions), chopped
15ml/1 tbsp chopped fresh parsley
finely grated rind of 1 lemon
1 egg white
pinch of paprika
ground black pepper
lemon rind and fresh parsley leaves, to garnish
rice, to serve (optional)

1 Preheat the grill (broiler). Place the bacon in a food processor with the breadcrumbs, spring onions, parsley, grated lemon rind and egg white and season with pepper. Process the mixture until it is finely chopped and is beginning to bind together. Alternatively, use a mincer (meat grinder).

2 Scrape the bacon mixture into a bowl and divide into eight even-size pieces. Shape the pieces into long ovals around eight soaked wooden or bamboo skewers.

3 Sprinkle the koftas with paprika and cook under a hot grill, turning occasionally, for 8–10 minutes, until evenly browned all over and cooked through. Alternatively, cook them on a barbecue in the same way. Garnish with lemon rind and parsley leaves, then serve hot with cooked rice, if you like.

Cook's Tips
• *This is a good way to spread a little meat a long way as each portion requires only 50g/2oz bacon. Use good quality bacon, preferably dry cured, for this recipe.*
• *Bacon is a very useful stand-by, as it will keep for up to 3 weeks if stored in the coolest part of the refrigerator. If you buy pre-packed bacon, take note of the "use by" date printed on the packaging.*

Pasta Energy 555kcal/2321kJ; Protein 36.9g; Carbohydrate 33g, of which sugars 7.5g; Fat 32.8g, of which saturates 14.1g; Cholesterol 182mg; Calcium 230mg; Fibre 2.2g; Sodium 219mg.
Koftas Energy 194kcal/813kJ; Protein 13g; Carbohydrate 14.7g, of which sugars 0.6g; Fat 9.7g, of which saturates 3.5g; Cholesterol 30mg; Calcium 30mg; Fibre 0.5g; Sodium 1040mg.

Peking Beef & Pepper Stir-fry

Once the steak has marinated, this colourful dish can be prepared in just a few minutes.

Serves 4

350g/12oz rump (round) or
  sirloin steak, sliced into strips
30ml/2 tbsp soy sauce
30ml/2 tbsp medium sherry
15ml/1 tbsp cornflour
  (cornstarch)
5ml/1 tsp brown sugar
15ml/1 tbsp sunflower oil
15ml/1 tbsp sesame oil
1 garlic clove, finely chopped
15ml/1 tbsp grated fresh
  root ginger
1 red (bell) pepper, seeded
  and sliced
1 yellow (bell) pepper, seeded
  and sliced
115g/4oz/1 cup sugar snap peas
4 spring onions (scallions), cut into
  5cm/2in pieces
30ml/2 tbsp oyster sauce
hot noodles, to serve

1 Mix together the steak strips, soy sauce, sherry, cornflour and brown sugar in a bowl. Cover with clear film (plastic wrap) and leave in a cool place to marinate for 30 minutes.

2 Heat a wok or large frying pan and add the sunflower and sesame oils. When the oils are hot add the garlic and ginger and stir-fry for about 30 seconds.

3 Add the red and yellow peppers, sugar snap peas and spring onions and stir-fry over high heat for 3 minutes.

4 Add the steak with the marinade juices to the wok or frying pan and stir-fry for a further 3–4 minutes.

5 Finally, pour in the oyster sauce and 60ml/4 tbsp water and cook, stirring constantly, until the sauce has thickened slightly. Serve immediately with hot noodles.

> **Cook's Tip**
> *Although it is made from oysters, plus other ingredients, oyster sauce will not impart a fishy flavour to the meat.*

Texan Barbecued Ribs

This barbecue or oven-roast dish of pork spare ribs cooked in a sweet and sour sauce is a favourite in the United States.

Serves 4

1.5kg/3lb (about 16) lean pork
  spare ribs
1 onion, finely chopped
1 large garlic clove, crushed
120ml/4fl oz/½ cup tomato
  purée (paste)
30ml/2 tbsp orange juice
30ml/2 tbsp red wine vinegar
5ml/1 tsp mustard
10ml/2 tsp clear honey
25g/1oz/2 tbsp soft light
  brown sugar
dash of Worcestershire sauce
30ml/2 tbsp vegetable oil
salt and ground black pepper
chopped fresh parsley, to garnish

1 Preheat the oven to 200°C/400°F/Gas 6. Place the pork spare ribs in a single layer in a large, shallow roasting pan and bake for 20 minutes.

2 Meanwhile, mix together the onion, garlic, tomato purée, orange juice, wine vinegar, mustard, clear honey, brown sugar, Worcestershire sauce and oil in a pan and season with salt and pepper. Bring to the boil, then lower the heat and simmer for about 5 minutes.

3 Remove the ribs from the oven and reduce the oven temperature to 180°C/350°F/Gas 4. Spoon half the sauce over the ribs, covering them well and bake for 20 minutes. Turn them over, baste with the remaining sauce and cook for 25 minutes.

4 Sprinkle the spare ribs with parsley before serving and allow three or four ribs per person.

> **Cook's Tip**
> *Use American mustard for an authentic flavour. It is sweet and mild with a very soft consistency. Otherwise, Dijon mustard, which is sharper and hotter, would work well.*

Stir-Fry Energy 225kcal/940kJ; Protein 22.7g; Carbohydrate 11.9g, of which sugars 8.9g; Fat 9.9g, of which saturates 2.4g; Cholesterol 52mg; Calcium 23mg; Fibre 3g; Sodium 713mg.
Ribs Energy 664kcal/2761kJ; Protein 56.5g; Carbohydrate 14.6g, of which sugars 14.2g; Fat 42.4g, of which saturates 13.8g; Cholesterol 199mg; Calcium 41mg; Fibre 1.1g; Sodium 258mg.

Skewers of Lamb with Mint

For a more substantial meal, you could serve these skewers on a bed of flavoured rice or couscous.

Serves 4
300ml/½ pint/1¼ cups Greek (US strained plain) yogurt
½ garlic clove, crushed
generous pinch of saffron powder
30ml/2 tbsp chopped fresh mint
30ml/2 tbsp clear honey
45ml/3 tbsp olive oil
3 lamb neck (US shoulder) fillets (about 675g/1½ lb total)
1 aubergine (eggplant), cut into 2.5cm/1in cubes
2 small red onions, quartered
salt and ground black pepper
small fresh mint leaves, to garnish
mixed salad and hot pitta bread, to serve

1 Mix together the yogurt, garlic, saffron, mint, honey and oil in a shallow dish and season with pepper.

2 Trim the lamb and cut into 2.5cm/1in cubes. Add to the marinade and stir until well coated. Cover with clear film (plastic wrap) and leave to marinate in the refrigerator for at least 4 hours or preferably overnight.

3 Blanch the diced aubergine in a pan of salted boiling water for 1–2 minutes. Drain well and pat dry on kitchen paper.

4 Preheat the grill (broiler). Drain the lamb and reserve the marinade. Thread the lamb, aubergine and onion pieces alternately on to skewers. (If you are using wooden skewers, soak them in water for 30 minutes first to prevent them from charring during cooking.)

5 Grill (broil) for 10–12 minutes, turning and basting occasionally with the reserved marinade, until the lamb and vegetables are tender. Alternatively, cook the kebabs on the barbecue for the same length of time.

6 Transfer the skewers to plates and serve immediately, garnished with mint leaves and accompanied by a mixed salad and hot pitta bread.

Beef Stew with Red Wine

A slow-cooked casserole of tender beef in a red wine and tomato sauce, with black olives and red pepper.

Serves 6
75ml/5 tbsp olive oil
1.2kg/2½lb braising steak, cut into 3cm/1½in cubes
1 onion, very thinly sliced
2 carrots, chopped
45ml/3 tbsp finely chopped fresh parsley
1 garlic clove, chopped
1 bay leaf
a few fresh thyme sprigs
pinch of freshly ground nutmeg
250ml/8fl oz/1 cup red wine
400g/14oz can plum tomatoes, chopped, with their juice
120ml/4fl oz/½ cup beef or chicken stock
about 15 black olives, pitted and halved
salt and ground black pepper
1 large red (bell) pepper, seeded and cut into strips

1 Preheat the oven to 180°C/350°F/Gas 4. Heat 45ml/3 tbsp of the oil in a large heavy flameproof casserole over medium heat. Add the meat, in batches, and cook, stirring frequently, until evenly browned all over. Remove to a side plate as the meat is browned and set aside until needed.

2 Add the remaining oil, the onion and carrots to the casserole and lower the heat. Cook, stirring occasionally, for about 5 minutes, until the onion has softened but not coloured. Add the parsley and garlic and cook, stirring occasionally, for a further 3–4 minutes.

3 Return the meat to the casserole, increase the heat and stir well to mix the vegetables with the meat. Stir in the bay leaf, thyme and nutmeg. Add the wine, bring to the boil and cook, stirring constantly, for 4–5 minutes. Stir in the tomatoes, stock and olives and mix well. Season to taste with salt and pepper. Cover the casserole with a tight-fitting lid and transfer to the oven. Bake for 1½ hours.

4 Remove the casserole from the oven. Stir in the strips of pepper. Return the casserole to the oven and cook, uncovered, for 30 minutes more, or until the beef is tender.

Lamb Energy 526kcal/2194kJ; Protein 39.7g; Carbohydrate 15.4g, of which sugars 13.4g; Fat 35.4g, of which saturates 14g; Cholesterol 128mg; Calcium 155mg; Fibre 3.1g; Sodium 204mg.
Beef Energy 464kcal/1929kJ; Protein 42.7g; Carbohydrate 4.5g, of which sugars 4.1g; Fat 27.5g, of which saturates 8.3g; Cholesterol 106mg; Calcium 44mg; Fibre 1.8g; Sodium 321mg.

Vegetarian Dishes

With such a wide range of vegetables now on offer throughout the year, there is no end of recipes when it comes to cooking for vegetarians. In this chapter you will find sustaining dishes such as Chilli Beans with Basmati Rice, Multi-mushroom Stroganoff, and Chunky Vegetable Paella. Or why not try something a bit lighter, such as Tomato Omelette Envelopes, Green Lentil and Cabbage Salad, or Spinach and Potato Galette?

Cheese Bubble & Squeak

This London breakfast dish was originally made on Mondays with leftover vegetables from the previous Sunday's lunch.

Serves 4
about 450g/1lb/3 cups mashed potatoes
about 225g/8oz/4 cups shredded cooked cabbage or kale
1 egg, lightly beaten
115g/4oz/1 cup grated Cheddar cheese
pinch of freshly grated nutmeg
salt and ground black pepper
plain (all-purpose) flour, for coating
vegetable oil, for frying

1 Mix together the mashed potatoes, cabbage or kale, egg, cheese and nutmeg in a bowl and season with salt and pepper. Divide the mixture into eight pieces and shape into patties.

2 Place the patties on a large plate, cover with clear film (plastic wrap) and chill in the refrigerator for 1 hour or or more, if possible, as this helps firm up the mixture.

3 Gently toss the patties in the flour to coat lightly. Heat about 1cm/½in oil in a frying pan until it is quite hot.

4 Carefully slide the patties into the oil and cook for about 3 minutes on each side, until golden and crisp. Remove with a slotted spatula, drain on kitchen paper and serve hot and crisp.

Soufflé Omelette

This delectable fluffy omelette is light and delicate enough to melt in the mouth.

Serves 1
2 eggs, separated
30ml/2 tbsp cold water
15ml/1 tbsp chopped fresh coriander (cilantro)
7.5ml/1½ tsp olive oil
30ml/2 tbsp mango chutney
25g/1oz/¼ cup grated Jarlsberg cheese
salt and ground black pepper

1 Beat the egg yolks together with the cold water and coriander in a bowl and season with salt and pepper.

2 Whisk the egg whites in another grease-free bowl until stiff peaks form, then gently fold them into the egg yolk mixture with a rubber spatula.

3 Heat the oil in a frying pan, pour in the egg mixture and reduce the heat. Do not stir. Cook until the omelette becomes puffy and golden brown on the underside (carefully lift one edge with a spatula to check).

4 Spoon the chutney over the omelette and sprinkle with the Jarlsberg. Fold over and slide on to a warmed plate. Serve immediately. (If you like, place the pan under a hot grill/broiler to set the top before adding the chutney and cheese.)

Variation
For traditional bubble and squeak, heat 30ml/2 tbsp vegetable oil in a frying pan. Add 1 finely chopped onion and cook over low heat, stirring occasionally, for about 5 minutes, until softened but not coloured. Using a slotted spoon, transfer the onion to a bowl and mix with the other ingredients in step 1, omitting the cheese and using finely chopped cooked cabbage or Brussels sprouts. Use the same frying pan, with additional oil, for cooking the patties in step 4.

Cook's Tip
If there is any trace of grease – and that includes any yolk – egg whites will not foam when whisked. It's best to use a glass, china or metal bowl. Plastic is easily scratched and then traces of grease are almost impossible to remove. The perfect choice is a copper bowl as the egg whites react with the metal to create a full and stable foam. However, do not leave the whisked whites to stand in a copper bowl, as they will turn grey. Whatever the material, the bowl should be a generous size to allow plenty of room for whisking.

Omelette Energy 377kcal/1570kJ; Protein 19g; Carbohydrate 14.9g, of which sugars 14.8g; Fat 27g, of which saturates 9.2g; Cholesterol 405mg; Calcium 249mg; Fibre 0.3g; Sodium 648mg.
Bubble & Squeak Energy 281kcal/1175kJ; Protein 11.6g; Carbohydrate 21g, of which sugars 4.3g; Fat 16.7g, of which saturates 7.4g; Cholesterol 75mg; Calcium 254mg; Fibre 2.3g; Sodium 242mg.

VEGETARIAN DISHES

Aubergine & Red Pepper Pâté

This simple pâté of baked aubergine, pink peppercorns and red peppers has more than a hint of garlic.

Serves 4

3 aubergines (eggplants)

2 large red (bell) peppers
5 garlic cloves, unpeeled
7.5ml/1½ tsp pink peppercorns
    in brine, drained and crushed
30ml/2 tbsp chopped fresh
    coriander (cilantro)
mixed salad leaves, to serve

1 Preheat the oven to 200°C/400°F/Gas 6. Arrange the whole aubergines, peppers and garlic cloves on a baking sheet and bake for 10 minutes. Transfer the garlic cloves to a chopping board. Turn over the aubergines and peppers and return them to the oven for a further 20 minutes.

2 Meanwhile, peel the garlic cloves and place them in a blender or food processor.

3 When the peppers are blistered and charred, use tongs to transfer them to a plastic bag, tie the top and leave to cool. Return the aubergines to the oven for a further 10 minutes.

4 Remove the aubergines from the oven. Split them in half and scoop the flesh into a sieve (strainer) placed over a bowl. Press the flesh with a spoon to remove the bitter juices.

5 Add the aubergine flesh to the garlic and process until smooth. Place in a large mixing bowl.

6 Peel and seed the red peppers and chop the flesh. Stir it into the aubergine mixture. Mix in the pink peppercorns and chopped fresh coriander and serve immediately on a bed of mixed salad leaves.

Cook's Tip
Serve the pâté with Melba toast, oatcakes, fingers of olive focaccia or mini pitta breads.

Red Pepper Watercress Parcels

The peppery watercress flavour contrasts delightfully with sweet red pepper in these crisp filo parcels.

Makes 8

3 red (bell) peppers
175g/6oz watercress or
    rocket (arugula)

225g/8oz 1 cup ricotta cheese
50g/2oz/½ cup toasted,
    chopped almonds
8 sheets filo pastry, thawed
    if frozen
30ml/2 tbsp olive oil
salt and ground black pepper

1 Preheat the oven to 190°C/375°F/Gas 5 and preheat the grill (broiler). Place the red peppers on a baking sheet and grill (broil), turning occasionally with tongs, until blistered and charred. Use tongs to transfer to a plastic bag, tie the top and leave to cool.

2 When the peppers are cool enough to handle, peel and seed them. Pat dry with kitchen paper.

3 Place the peppers and watercress or rocket in a food processor and pulse until coarsely chopped. Spoon the mixture into a bowl. Stir in the ricotta and almonds and season to taste with salt and pepper.

4 Working with one sheet of filo pastry at a time and keeping the others covered, cut out two 18cm/7in and two 5cm/2in squares from each sheet. Brush one large square with a little olive oil and place a second large square at an angle of 45 degrees to form a star shape.

5 Place one of the smaller squares in the centre of the star shape, brush lightly with olive oil and top with the second small square.

6 Top with one-eighth of the red pepper mixture. Bring the edges together to form a purse shape and twist to seal. Place on a lightly greased baking sheet and cook for 25–30 minutes, until golden. Serve immediately.

Pâté Energy 51kcal/213kJ; Protein 2.2g; Carbohydrate 8.9g, of which sugars 8.4g; Fat 1g, of which saturates 0.2g; Cholesterol 0mg; Calcium 22mg; Fibre 4.4g; Sodium 7mg.
Parcels Energy 163kcal/677kJ; Protein 5.9g; Carbohydrate 10.9g, of which sugars 5.7g; Fat 10.9g, of which saturates 3.4g; Cholesterol 12mg; Calcium 67mg; Fibre 2.1g; Sodium 15mg.

Nutty Cheese Balls

An extremely quick and simple recipe. Try making smaller portions to serve as canapés at a drinks party.

Serves 4
225g/8oz/1 cup low-fat soft (farmer's) cheese
50g/2oz/1/2 cup Dolcelatte or Gorgonzola cheese
15ml/1 tbsp finely chopped onion
15ml/1 tbsp finely chopped celery
15ml/1 tbsp finely chopped fresh parsley
15ml/1 tbsp finely chopped gherkin
5ml/1 tsp brandy or port (optional)
pinch of paprika
50g/2oz/1/2 cup walnuts, coarsely chopped
90ml/6 tbsp chopped fresh chives
salt and ground black pepper

To serve
crusty bread
mixed salad leaves
sliced radishes

1 Put the soft cheese and Dolcelatte or Gorgonzola in a bowl and beat with a spoon until combined and quite smooth.

2 Add the onion, celery, parsley, gherkin, brandy or port, if using, paprika and walnuts, season with salt and pepper and stir well to combine.

3 Divide the mixture into 12 pieces and roll each piece into a ball between the palms of your hands.

4 Roll each ball gently in the chopped chives and place on a plate. Cover with clear film (plastic wrap) or foil, and chill in the refrigerator for about 1 hour. Serve with crusty bread, mixed salad leaves and sliced radishes.

> **Variation**
> For an alternative look, mix the chives with the rest of the ingredients in step 2 but omit the walnuts. Instead, chop the walnuts very finely and use to coat the cheese balls in step 4. For a larger number of guests make one batch of each type and serve a mixture of the two.

Fried Tomatoes with Polenta Crust

This recipe works well with green tomatoes freshly picked from the garden or greenhouse.

Serves 4
4 large firm under-ripe tomatoes
115g/4oz/scant 1 cup polenta or coarse cornmeal
5ml/1 tsp dried oregano or marjoram
2.5ml/1/2 tsp garlic powder
1 egg
plain (all-purpose) flour, for dredging
vegetable oil, for deep-frying
salt and ground black pepper
salad, to serve

1 Cut the tomatoes into thick slices. Mix the polenta or cornmeal with the oregano or marjoram and garlic powder in a shallow bowl.

2 Lightly beat the egg in another shallow bowl and season with salt and pepper. Put the flour in a third shallow bowl. Dip the tomato slices first into the flour, then into the egg and finally into the polenta or cornmeal mixture.

3 Fill a shallow frying pan one-third full of vegetable oil and heat steadily until quite hot.

4 Slip the tomato slices into the oil carefully, a few at a time, and fry on each side until crisp. Remove with a slotted spoon and drain well on kitchen paper. Repeat with the remaining tomatoes, reheating the oil in between each batch. Serve immediately with salad.

> **Variations**
> • This is also a tasty way to cook mushrooms. Coat 450g/1lb whole button (white) mushrooms with flour, seasoned egg and the polenta mixture and deep-fry until crisp.
> • Substitute goat's cheese or mozzarella for the tomatoes. Cut 225–275g/8–10oz cheese into fairly thick slices, then coat and cook as in the recipe. Bocconcini, bitesize balls of mozzarella, would be perfect for this treatment.

Cheese Balls Energy 213kcal/883kJ; Protein 13.4g; Carbohydrate 4g, of which sugars 3.5g; Fat 16.9g, of which saturates 6g; Cholesterol 23mg; Calcium 170mg; Fibre 1.4g; Sodium 409mg.
Tomatoes Energy 215kcal/897kJ; Protein 5g; Carbohydrate 24.1g, of which sugars 3.1g; Fat 10.9g, of which saturates 1.5g; Cholesterol 48mg; Calcium 15mg; Fibre 1.6g; Sodium 27mg.

Bean Purée with Grilled Vegetables

The slightly bitter radicchio and chicory make a wonderful marriage with the creamy citrus bean purée.

Serves 4
400g/14oz can cannellini beans
45ml/3 tbsp low-fat fromage
   blanc (farmer's cheese)
finely grated rind and juice of
   1 large orange
15ml/1 tbsp finely chopped
   fresh rosemary
4 heads of chicory
   (Belgian endive)
2 radicchio
15ml/1 tbsp walnut oil

1 Preheat the grill (broiler). Drain the beans, rinse, and drain again. Put the beans, cheese, half the orange rind, the orange juice and rosemary in a food processor or blender and process until combined. Set aside.

2 Cut the heads of chicory in half lengthways. Cut each radicchio into eight wedges.

3 Spread out the chicory and radicchio on a baking sheet and brush with walnut oil. Grill (broil) for 2–3 minutes. Serve the leaves with the bean purée, sprinkled with the remaining orange rind.

Variations
• For a Middle Eastern flavour, substitute 30ml/2 tbsp tahini, also known as sesame seed paste, for the orange juice and omit the orange rind. Add 4 chopped spring onions (scallions) to the mixture in the food processor or blender and substitute chopped fresh mint for the rosemary. If the mixture seems too thick, add 15ml/1 tbsp olive oil. Garnish with fresh mint sprigs.
• For a North African flavour, substitute canned broad (fava) beans for the cannellini beans, 1½ lemons for the orange and 5ml/1 tsp ground cumin for the rosemary.
• For a Tex-Mex treat, substitute canned red kidney beans for the cannellini beans, 2 limes for the orange and 2–3 seeded and finely chopped fresh red chillies for the rosemary.

Broccoli & Chestnut Terrine

Served hot or cold, this versatile terrine is just as suitable for a dinner party as for a picnic.

Serves 4–6
450g/1lb/4 cups broccoli florets
225g/8oz/2 cups cooked
   chestnuts, coarsely chopped
50g/2oz/1 cup fresh wholemeal
   (whole-wheat) breadcrumbs
60ml/4 tbsp low-fat natural
   (plain) yogurt
30ml/2 tbsp finely grated
   Parmesan cheese
pinch of freshly grated nutmeg
2 eggs, lightly beaten
salt and ground black pepper
boiled new potatoes and mixed
   salad leaves, to serve

1 Preheat the oven to 180°C/350°F/Gas 4. Base-line a 900g/2lb non-stick loaf tin (pan) with baking parchment.

2 Blanch or steam the broccoli for 3–4 minutes, until just tender. Drain well. Reserve a quarter of the smallest florets and chop the rest finely.

3 Mix together the chestnuts, breadcrumbs, yogurt, Parmesan and nutmeg and season to taste with salt and pepper. Fold in the chopped broccoli, reserved florets and the beaten eggs.

4 Spoon the broccoli mixture into the prepared tin. Place in a roasting pan and pour in boiling water to come about halfway up the sides of the loaf tin. Bake for 20–25 minutes.

5 Remove the terrine from the oven and invert on to a warmed plate or tray. Cut into even slices and serve immediately with new potatoes and salad leaves. Alternatively, leave the terrine in the loaf tin to cool completely, then turn out and serve cold.

Cook's Tip
If you do not have a non-stick loaf tin (pan), grease it lightly with olive or sunflower oil after base-lining.

Purée Energy 148kcal/623kJ; Protein 8.2g; Carbohydrate 19.6g, of which sugars 5.3g; Fat 4.6g, of which saturates 1.1g, Cholesterol 1mg; Calcium 105mg; Fibre 6.9g; Sodium 396mg.
Terrine Energy 169kcal/711kJ; Protein 9.4g; Carbohydrate 22g, of which sugars 4.5g; Fat 5.4g, of which saturates 1.9g; Cholesterol 69mg; Calcium 152mg; Fibre 3.7g; Sodium 157mg.

Asparagus Rolls with Herb Sauce

For a taste sensation, try tender asparagus spears wrapped in crisp filo pastry served with a rich, buttery herb sauce.

Serves 2
50g/2oz/¼ cup butter, plus extra for greasing
5 sheets filo pastry
10 asparagus spears
salad, to garnish (optional)

For the sauce
2 shallots, finely chopped
1 bay leaf
150ml/¼ pint/⅔ cup dry white wine
175g/6oz/¾ cup butter, softened
15ml/1 tbsp chopped fresh herbs, such as parsley, basil and thyme
salt and ground black pepper
chopped fresh chives, to garnish

1 Preheat the oven to 200°C/400°F/Gas 6. Grease a baking sheet. Melt the ¼ cup butter. Cut the filo pastry sheets in half. Brush a half sheet with melted butter. Fold one corner of the sheet down to the bottom edge to give a wedge shape.

2 Trim the asparagus, then lay a spear on top at the longest pastry edge and roll up towards the shortest edge. Make nine more rolls in the same way.

3 Lay the rolls on the prepared baking sheet. Brush with the remaining melted butter. Bake in the preheated oven for about 8 minutes, until golden.

4 Meanwhile, put the shallots, bay leaf and wine into a pan. Cover with a tight-fitting lid and cook over high heat until the wine is reduced to 45–60ml/3–4 tbsp.

5 Strain the wine mixture into a bowl. Whisk in the ¾ cup butter, a little at a time, until the sauce is smooth and glossy.

6 Stir in the herbs and season to taste with salt and pepper. Return to the pan and keep the sauce warm. Serve the asparagus rolls on warmed individual plates with a salad garnish, if you like. Sprinkle the butter sauce with a few chopped chives and hand around separately.

Baked Squash with Parmesan

Spaghetti squash is an unusual vegetable – when baked, the flesh separates into long strands.

Serves 2
1 spaghetti squash
115g/4oz/½ cup butter
45ml/3 tbsp mixed chopped fresh herbs such as parsley, chives and oregano
1 garlic clove, crushed
1 shallot, chopped
5ml/1 tsp lemon juice
50g/2oz/⅔ cup freshly grated Parmesan cheese
salt and ground black pepper

1 Preheat the oven to 180°C/350°F/Gas 4. Cut the squash in half lengthways. Place the halves, cut-sides down, in a roasting pan. Pour a little water around them, then bake for about 40 minutes, until tender.

2 Meanwhile, put the butter, herbs, garlic, shallot and lemon juice in a food processor or blender and process until thoroughly blended and creamy in consistency. Season to taste with salt and pepper.

3 When the squash is tender, scrape out and discard any seeds, then cut a thin slice from the base of each half, so that they will sit level. Place the squash halves on warmed serving plates.

4 Using a fork, pull out a few of the spaghetti-like strands in the centre of each. Add a spoonful of herb butter, then sprinkle with a little of the grated Parmesan. Serve the remaining herb butter and Parmesan separately, adding them as you pull out more strands.

> **Cook's Tip**
> Spaghetti squash is also good served with simple garlic butter. If you don't want to bother making a herb butter of any sort, serve with a dish of ready-made pesto.

Squash Energy 597kcal/2467kJ; Protein 13g; Carbohydrate 10.4g, of which sugars 8g; Fat 56.2g, of which saturates 35.5g; Cholesterol 148mg; Calcium 420mg; Fibre 3.9g; Sodium 622mg.
Asparagus Energy 986kcal/4066kJ; Protein 5.1g; Carbohydrate 20.7g, of which sugars 4.6g; Fat 93.4g, of which saturates 58.7g; Cholesterol 240mg; Calcium 121mg; Fibre 3g; Sodium 694mg.

Multi-mushroom Stroganoff

A pan-fry of sliced mushrooms swirled with sour cream makes a delicious accompaniment to pasta or rice.

Serves 3–4

45ml/3 tbsp olive oil

450g/1lb fresh mixed wild and cultivated mushrooms such as ceps, shiitakes or oysters, sliced

3 spring onions (scallions), sliced

2 garlic cloves, crushed

30ml/2 tbsp dry sherry or vermouth

300ml/½ pint/1¼ cups sour cream or crème fraîche

15ml/1 tbsp chopped fresh marjoram or thyme leaves

chopped fresh parsley, to garnish

rice, pasta or potatoes, to serve

1 Heat the oil in a large frying pan over low heat. Add the mushrooms and cook, stirring occasionally, for about 5 minutes, until they are softened and just cooked.

2 Add the spring onions, garlic and sherry or vermouth and cook for 1 minute more. Season well with salt and pepper.

3 Stir in the sour cream or crème fraîche and heat to just below boiling point. Stir in the marjoram or thyme, then sprinkle over the parsley. Serve with rice, pasta or boiled new potatoes.

Cook's Tips
• To create the most interesting flavour in this dish, use at least three different varieties of mushroom, preferably incorporating some woodland or wild mushrooms.
• It is important not to let the mixture boil after adding the cream. Like single (light) cream, sour cream and crème fraîche have a tendency to curdle when heated even though they both contain slightly more butterfat (single cream 19 per cent, sour cream 20 per cent, crème fraîche 15–40 per cent). Curdling is also much more likely to occur if the other ingredients in the pan include something acidic, such as lemon juice or, as in this case, sherry or vermouth.

Ratatouille with Cheese Croûtons

Crunchy croûtons and creamy Camembert cheese provide a tasty topping on hot, bought or home-made ratatouille.

Serves 2

3 thick slices white bread

225g/8oz firm Camembert cheese

60ml/4 tbsp olive oil

1 garlic clove, chopped

400g/14oz can ratatouille

fresh parsley sprigs, to garnish

1 Trim the crusts from the bread slices and discard. Cut the bread into 2.5cm/1in squares. Cut the Camembert cheese into 2.5cm/1in cubes.

2 Heat 45ml/3 tbsp of the oil in a frying pan. Add the bread cubes and cook over a high heat, stirring constantly, for about 5 minutes, until golden all over. Reduce the heat, add the garlic and cook for 1 minute more. Remove the croûtons with a slotted spoon and drain on kitchen paper.

3 Put the ratatouille in a pan and place over medium heat, stirring occasionally, until hot.

4 Heat the remaining oil in the frying pan. Add the cheese cubes and sear over high heat for 1 minute. Divide the hot ratatouille between two serving bowls, spoon the croûtons and cheese on top, garnish with parsley and serve immediately.

Cook's Tip
To make your own ratatouille, heat 45ml/3 tbsp olive oil in a heavy pan and add the following vegetables sequentially: 3 sliced aubergines (eggplants), 1 seeded green (bell) pepper, cut into strips, 3 peeled and chopped tomatoes, 1 sliced onion, 2 chopped garlic cloves and 3 sliced courgettes (zucchini). Add a bouquet garni, season with salt and pepper, cover and cook over very low heat for 30 minutes. Add 30ml/2 tbsp olive oil, cover and simmer for a further 30–40 minutes.

Stroganoff Energy 253kcal/1044kJ; Protein 4.4g; Carbohydrate 3.6g, of which sugars 3.4g; Fat 23.8g, of which saturates 10.7g; Cholesterol 45mg; Calcium 80mg; Fibre 1.4g; Sodium 38mg.
Ratatouille Energy 829kcal/3442kJ; Protein 28.5g; Carbohydrate 26.2g, of which sugars 8.2g; Fat 66.2g, of which saturates 25.2g; Cholesterol 105mg; Calcium 374mg; Fibre 2.6g; Sodium 861mg.

Tofu & Crunchy Vegetables

High protein tofu is nicest if it is marinated lightly before it is cooked.

Serves 4

2 x 225g/8oz packets
   smoked tofu, diced
45ml/3 tbsp soy sauce
30ml/2 tbsp dry sherry
   or vermouth
15ml/1 tbsp sesame oil
45ml/3 tbsp groundnut (peanut)
   or sunflower oil

2 leeks, thinly sliced
2 carrots, cut into batons
1 large courgette (zucchini),
   thinly sliced
115g/4oz baby corn, halved
115g/4oz button (white) or
   shiitake mushrooms, sliced
15ml/1 tbsp sesame seeds
cooked noodles dressed with
   sesame oil, to serve (optional)

1 Place the tofu in a shallow dish. Mix together the soy sauce, sherry or vermouth and sesame oil and pour over the tofu. Cover with clear film (plastic wrap) and leave to marinate in a cool place for at least 30 minutes. Drain the tofu cubes and reserve the marinade.

2 Heat a wok or large, heavy frying pan and add the groundnut oil. When the oil is hot, add the tofu cubes and stir-fry until browned all over. Remove the tofu from the pan.

3 Add the leeks, carrots, courgette and baby corn to the pan and stir-fry for about 2 minutes. Add the mushrooms and cook for 1 minute more.

4 Return the tofu to the pan and pour in the reserved marinade. Heat, stirring gently, until bubbling, then sprinkle with the sesame seeds. Serve immediately with hot cooked noodles dressed with a little sesame oil, if you like.

Cook's Tip
The actual cooking of this dish takes just a few minutes, so have all the ingredients prepared before you start.

Sprouting Beans & Pak Choi

Stir-frying is a great way to cook vegetables as they retain their colour, texture and most of their nutrients.

Serves 4

45ml/3 tbsp groundnut
   (peanut) oil
3 spring onions (scallions), sliced
2 garlic cloves, cut into slivers
2.5cm/1in piece fresh root ginger,
   cut into slivers
1 carrot, cut into thick batons
150g/5oz/scant 1 cup sprouting
   beans (lentils, mung beans,
   chickpeas)

200g/7oz pak choi (bok
   choy), shredded
50g/2oz/½ cup unsalted cashew
   nuts or halved almonds

For the sauce

45ml/3 tbsp light soy sauce
30ml/2 tbsp dry sherry
15ml/1 tbsp sesame oil
150ml/¼ pint/⅔ cup cold water
5ml/1 tsp cornflour (cornstarch)
5ml/1 tsp clear honey
salt and ground black pepper

1 Heat a large wok and add the oil. When the oil is hot add the spring onions, garlic, ginger and carrot and stir-fry over medium heat for 2 minutes.

2 Add the sprouting beans and stir-fry for a further 2 minutes. Add the pak choi and cashew nuts or almonds and stir-fry until the leaves are just wilting.

3 Mix all the sauce ingredients together in a jug (pitcher) and pour into the wok, stirring constantly.

3 When all the vegetables are coated in a thin glossy sauce season with salt and pepper. Serve immediately.

Variation
You can use a variety of other Chinese greens besides pak choi (bok choy). Try Chinese leaves (Chinese cabbage), Chinese flowering cabbage, Chinese spinach, also known as callalo, or Chinese water spinach.

Tofu Energy 251kcal/1040kJ; Protein 12.6g; Carbohydrate 7.2g, of which sugars 5.8g; Fat 18.3g, of which saturates 2.4g; Cholesterol 0mg; Calcium 578mg; Fibre 3.8g; Sodium 877mg.
Pak Choi Energy 230kcal/954kJ; Protein 5g; Carbohydrate 11.3g, of which sugars 7.6g; Fat 17.7g, of which saturates 3.3g; Cholesterol 0mg; Calcium 46mg; Fibre 2.4g; Sodium 848mg.

Curried Eggs

Hard-boiled eggs are served on a mild creamy sauce with just a hint of curry.

Serves 2

4 eggs
15ml/1 tbsp sunflower oil
1 small onion, chopped
2.5cm/1in piece of fresh root
   ginger, grated
2.5ml/½ tsp ground cumin
2.5ml/½ tsp garam masala

22.5ml/1½ tbsp tomato
   purée (paste)
10ml/2 tsp tandoori paste
10ml/2 tsp freshly squeezed
   lemon juice
50ml/2fl oz/¼ cup single
   (light) cream
15ml/1 tbsp finely chopped fresh
   coriander (cilantro)
salt and ground black pepper
fresh coriander sprigs, to garnish

1 Put the eggs in a pan of water. Bring to the boil, lower the heat and simmer for 10 minutes.

2 Meanwhile, heat the oil in a frying pan over medium heat. Add the onion and cook, stirring occasionally, for 2–3 minutes. Add the ginger and cook, stirring constantly, for 1 minute more.

3 Stir in the ground cumin, garam masala, tomato purée, tandoori paste, lemon juice and cream. Cook for 1–2 minutes more, but do not allow the mixture to boil. Stir in the chopped coriander and season to taste with salt and pepper.

4 Drain the eggs, remove the shells and cut each egg in half. Spoon the sauce into a serving bowl, top with the eggs and garnish with fresh coriander. Serve immediately.

Tomato Omelette Envelopes

These delicious chive omelettes are folded and filled with tomato and melting Camembert cheese.

Serves 2

1 small onion
4 tomatoes
30ml/2 tbsp vegetable oil

4 eggs
30ml/2 tbsp chopped fresh chives
115g/4oz Camembert cheese,
   rinded and diced
salt and ground black pepper
lettuce leaves and Granary
   (whole-wheat) bread, to
   serve (optional)

1 Cut the onion in half and cut each half into thin wedges. Cut the tomatoes into wedges of similar size.

2 Heat 15ml/1 tbsp of the oil in a frying pan. Add the onion and cook over medium heat for 2 minutes. Increase the heat, add the tomatoes and cook for a further 2 minutes, then remove the pan from the heat.

3 Beat the eggs with the chives in a bowl and season with salt and pepper. Heat the remaining oil in an omelette pan. Add half the egg mixture and tilt the pan to spread thinly. Cook for 1 minute. Flip the omelette over and cook for 1 minute more. Remove from the pan and keep hot. Make a second omelette with the remaining egg mixture.

4 Return the tomato mixture to high heat. Add the cheese and toss the mixture over the heat for 1 minute.

5 Divide the mixture between the omelettes and fold them over. Serve immediately with crisp lettuce leaves and chunks of Granary bread, if you like.

> ## Cook's Tip
> *It is recommended that you store eggs in the refrigerator for health reasons. Do not wash them, but equally do not use dirty eggs. Store eggs pointed ends downwards, and remove from the refrigerator about 30 minutes before you want to cook them to allow them to come to room temperature. This will help prevent them from cracking.*

> ## Variation
> *Add 2–3 sliced mushrooms to the tomato-onion filling. For a mushroom omelette, substitute 6–8 button (white) mushrooms for the tomato. They will need a slightly longer cooking time.*

Omelette Energy 488kcal/2027kJ; Protein 26g; Carbohydrate 8.6g, of which sugars 7.9g; Fat 38.2g, of which saturates 15.1g; Cholesterol 434mg; Calcium 226mg; Fibre 2.4g; Sodium 479mg.
Curried Eggs Energy 310kcal/1286kJ; Protein 14.6g; Carbohydrate 2.7g, of which sugars 2.6g; Fat 27.2g, of which saturates 7.5g; Cholesterol 394mg; Calcium 133mg; Fibre 1.6g; Sodium 180mg.

Potatoes with Blue Cheese

So often served as a mere accompaniment, potatoes also make a satisfying main dish, as here.

Serves 4
450g/1lb small new potatoes
small head of celery, sliced
small red onion, thinly sliced

115g/4oz blue cheese, mashed
150ml/¼ pint/⅔ cup single (light) cream
90g/3½ oz/scant 1 cup walnut pieces
30ml/2 tbsp chopped fresh parsley
salt and ground black pepper

1 Put the potatoes in a pan, add water to cover and bring to the boil. Cook for about 15 minutes, adding the sliced celery and onion to the pan for the last 5 minutes or so.

2 Drain the vegetables well and put them into a warmed, shallow serving dish, making sure that they are evenly distributed. Keep warm.

3 Put the cheese and cream in a small pan and melt over low heat, stirring frequently. Do not allow the mixture to boil, but heat it until it scalds.

4 Season the sauce to taste with salt and pepper, bearing in mind that the cheese will already be quite salty. Pour it over the vegetables and sprinkle the walnuts and chopped parsley over the top. Serve immediately.

Cook's Tip
Choose any blue cheese you like, such as Stilton, Danish blue, Blue Vinney or blue Brie.

Variation
Substitute a thinly sliced fennel bulb for the celery if you like its distinctive aniseed-like flavour.

Greek Spinach & Cheese Pies

These individual spinach, feta and Parmesan cheese pies are easy to make using ready-made filo pastry.

Makes 4
15ml/1 tbsp olive oil
1 small onion, finely chopped
275g/10oz/2½ cups spinach, stalks removed

50g/2oz/4 tbsp butter, melted
4 sheets filo pastry
1 egg
large pinch of freshly grated nutmeg
75g/3oz/¾ cup crumbled feta cheese
15ml/1 tbsp freshly grated Parmesan cheese
salt and ground black pepper

1 Preheat the oven to 190°C/375°F/Gas 5. Heat the oil in a large pan over low heat. Add the onion and cook, stirring occasionally, for 5–6 minutes, until softened. Add the spinach leaves and cook, stirring, until the spinach has wilted and most of the liquid has evaporated. Remove from the heat and leave to cool completely.

2 Brush four 10cm/4in diameter loose-based tartlet tins (muffin pans) with melted butter. Cut two sheets of filo into eight 14cm/4½in squares each.

3 Brush four squares at a time with melted butter. Line the first tartlet tin with one square, gently easing it into the base and up the sides. Leave the edges overhanging. Lay the remaining squares on top of the first, turning them so the corners form a star shape. Repeat for the remaining tins.

4 Beat the egg with the nutmeg and seasoning, then stir in the cheeses and spinach. Divide the mixture among the tins and smooth level. Fold the overhanging pastry over the filling.

5 Cut the third pastry sheet into eight 10cm/4in rounds. Brush with butter and place two on top of each tartlet. Press around the edges to seal. Brush the last pastry sheet with butter and cut into strips. Gently twist each strip and lay them on top of the tartlets. Bake for 30–35 minutes, until golden brown. Serve the pies hot or cold.

Potatoes Energy 419kcal/1744kJ; Protein 13.3g; Carbohydrate 22g, of which sugars 4.8g; Fat 31.6g, of which saturates 11.4g; Cholesterol 42mg; Calcium 261mg; Fibre 3.6g; Sodium 439mg.
Cheese Pies Energy 287kcal/1191kJ; Protein 9.9g; Carbohydrate 17.2g, of which sugars 2.5g; Fat 20.3g, of which saturates 10.7g; Cholesterol 91mg; Calcium 269mg; Fibre 2.2g; Sodium 502mg.

Chilli Beans with Basmati Rice

Red kidney beans, chopped tomatoes and hot chilli make a great combination in this colourful dish.

Serves 4
350g/12oz/2 cups basmati rice
30ml/2 tbsp olive oil
1 large onion, chopped
1 garlic clove, crushed
15ml/12 tbsp hot chilli powder
15g/½oz/2 tbsp plain (all-purpose) flour
15ml/1 tbsp tomato purée (paste)
400g/14oz can chopped tomatoes
400g/14oz can red kidney beans, drained
150ml/¼ pint/⅔ cup hot vegetable stock
salt and ground black pepper
chopped fresh parsley, to garnish

1 Wash the rice several times under cold running water. Drain well. Bring a large pan of water to the boil. Add the rice and cook for 10–12 minutes, until tender. Meanwhile, heat the oil in a frying pan over low heat. Add the onion and garlic and cook, stirring occasionally, for about 2 minutes.

2 Stir the chilli powder and flour into the onion and garlic mixture and cook, stirring frequently, for 2 minutes more.

3 Stir in the tomato purée and chopped tomatoes. Rinse and drain the kidney beans well and add to the pan with the hot vegetable stock. Cover and simmer gently, stirring occasionally, for 12 minutes.

4 Season the chilli sauce to taste with salt and pepper. Drain the rice and serve immediately with the chilli beans, garnished with a little chopped fresh parsley.

Cook's Tip
You can also serve the chilli beans with pasta, such as penne or conchiglie, or with hot pitta bread. They also make a really scrumptious filling for baked potatoes.

Lentil Stir-fry

Mushrooms, artichoke hearts, sugar snap peas and green lentils make a satisfying stir-fry supper.

Serves 2–3
115g/4oz/1 cup sugar snap peas
25g/1oz/2 tbsp butter
1 small onion, chopped
115g/4oz cup brown cap (cremini) mushrooms, sliced
400g/14oz can artichoke hearts, drained and halved
400g/14oz can green lentils, drained and rinsed
60ml/4 tbsp single (light) cream
25g/1oz/¼ cup flaked (sliced) almonds, toasted
salt and ground black pepper
French bread, to serve

1 Bring a pan of salted water to the boil, add the sugar snap peas and cook for about 4 minutes, until just tender. Drain, refresh under cold running water, then drain again. Pat the peas dry with kitchen paper and set aside.

2 Melt the butter in a frying pan. Add the onion and cook over medium heat, stirring occasionally, for 2–3 minutes.

3 Add the mushrooms to the pan. Stir until well combined, then cook for 2–3 minutes, until just tender.

4 Add the artichoke hearts, sugar snap peas and lentils to the pan and cook, stirring constantly, for 2 minutes.

5 Stir in the cream and almonds and cook for 1 minute, but do not allow the mixture to come to the boil. Season to taste with salt and pepper. Spoon the stir-fry on to warmed plates and serve immediately with chunks of French bread.

Cook's Tip
Use dried green lentils if you prefer. Cook them in a pan of boiling water for 30–45 minutes first (without adding any salt), then drain well and add them to the stir-fry with the artichokes and sugar snap peas.

Chilli Beans Energy 523kcal/2194kJ; Protein 15.5g; Carbohydrate 100.1g, of which sugars 11.5g; Fat 7.1g, of which saturates 1g; Cholesterol 0mg; Calcium 120mg; Fibre 8.5g; Sodium 410mg.
Lentil Energy 345kcal/1443kJ; Protein 18.4g; Carbohydrate 30.9g, of which sugars 4.7g; Fat 17.3g, of which saturates 7.4g; Cholesterol 29mg; Calcium 139mg; Fibre 9.7g; Sodium 144mg.

Arabian Spinach

Stir-fry spinach with onions and spices, then mix in a can of chickpeas and you have a quick, delicious main meal.

Serves 4
30ml/2 tbsp olive or sunflower oil
1 onion, sliced
2 garlic cloves, crushed
5ml/1 tsp cumin seeds
400g/14oz/3½ cups spinach, washed and shredded
425g/15oz can chickpeas, drained and rinsed
knob (pat) of butter
salt and ground black pepper

1 Heat the oil in a large frying pan or wok over low heat. Add the onion and cook, stirring occasionally, for about 5 minutes, until softened but not coloured. Add the garlic and cumin seeds and cook, stirring constantly, for another minute.

2 Add the spinach, in batches, stirring until the leaves begin to wilt. Fresh spinach leaves collapse down dramatically on cooking and they will all fit into the pan.

3 Stir in the chickpeas and butter and season to taste with salt and pepper. Reheat until just bubbling, then serve immediately. Drain off any pan juices, if you like, but this dish is rather good served with a little sauce.

Cook's Tip
Always use spinach within a day of purchase as it does not keep well and quickly becomes slimy. Store it in a cool place and wash thoroughly and spin dry before cooking.

Variations
• You can use other canned pulses (legumes) besides chickpeas for this dish. Ful medames, for example, would be a good choice, as their nutty flavour goes particularly well with cumin.
• For a more substantial dish, top with hot, quartered hard-boiled eggs.

Courgettes en Papillote

An impressive dinner party side dish, these puffed paper parcels should be broken open at the table.

Serves 4
2 courgettes (zucchini)
1 leek
225g/8oz young asparagus, trimmed
4 fresh tarragon sprigs
4 garlic cloves, unpeeled
1 egg, beaten
salt and ground black pepper

1 Preheat the oven to 200°C/400°F/Gas 6. Using a vegetable peeler, slice the courgettes lengthways into thin strips.

2 Cut the leek into very fine julienne strips and cut the asparagus evenly into 5cm/2in lengths.

3 Cut out four sheets of greaseproof (waxed) paper measuring about 30 x 38cm/12 x 15in and fold in half. Draw a large curve to make a heart shape when unfolded. Cut along the inside of the line and open out.

4 Divide the courgettes, leek and asparagus evenly among each paper heart, positioning the filling on one side of the fold line, and topping each with a sprig of fresh tarragon and an unpeeled garlic clove. Season to taste with salt and pepper.

5 Brush the edges lightly with the beaten egg and fold over. Pleat the edges together so that each parcel is completely sealed. Lay the parcels on a baking sheet and bake for about 10 minutes. Serve immediately.

Variation
Experiment with other combinations of vegetables and herbs such as sugar snap peas or mangetouts (snow peas) and mint; baby carrots and rosemary; fine green beans or baby broad (fava) beans and savory; asparagus and basil – the possibilities are almost endless. Always include a member of the onion family, preferably one with a mild flavour.

Spinach Energy 201kcal/841kJ; Protein 11.4g; Carbohydrate 21g, of which sugars 3.4g; Fat 8.4g, of which saturates 1g; Cholesterol 0mg; Calcium 220mg; Fibre 6.6g; Sodium 146mg.
Courgettes Energy 60kcal/249kJ; Protein 5.7g; Carbohydrate 4.2g, of which sugars 3.7g; Fat 2.4g, of which saturates 0.6g; Cholesterol 48mg; Calcium 58mg; Fibre 2.8g; Sodium 20mg.

Green Lentil & Cabbage Salad

This warm crunchy salad makes a satisfying meal if served with crusty French bread or wholemeal rolls.

Serves 4–6
225g/8oz/1 cup Puy lentils
1.3 litres/2¼ pints/6 cups cold
   water
3 garlic cloves
1 bay leaf
1 small onion, peeled and studded
   with 2 cloves
15ml/1 tbsp olive oil
1 red onion, thinly sliced
15ml/1 tbsp fresh thyme leaves
350g/12oz/3 cups finely
   shredded cabbage
finely grated rind and juice of
   1 lemon
15ml/1 tbsp raspberry vinegar
salt and ground black pepper

1 Rinse the lentils in cold water and place in a large pan with the water, 1 peeled garlic clove, bay leaf and clove-studded onion. Bring to the boil and cook for about 10 minutes. Reduce the heat, cover the pan with a tight-fitting lid and simmer gently for 15–20 minutes. Drain well. Remove and discard the onion, garlic and bay leaf.

2 Heat the oil in a large pan over low heat. Add the red onion, 2 crushed garlic cloves and thyme and cook, stirring occasionally, for 5 minutes, until the onion has softened.

3 Add the shredded cabbage and cook, stirring occasionally, for 3–5 minutes, until just cooked but still crunchy.

4 Stir in the cooked lentils, grated lemon rind and juice and the raspberry vinegar. Season with salt and pepper to taste and serve immediately.

> **Variation**
> *This recipe works equally well with other types of cabbage. Choose whatever is in season: white cabbage or Savoy, or try fresh spring greens (collards) instead.*

Tomato & Basil Tart

You could make individual tartlets instead of one large tart if you prefer, but reduce the baking time slightly.

Serves 6–8
175g/6oz/1½ cups plain (all-
   purpose) flour
2.5ml/½ tsp salt
115g/4oz/½ cup butter or
   margarine, chilled
45–75ml/3–5 tbsp water
salt and ground black pepper

For the filling
30ml/2 tbsp extra virgin olive oil
175g/6oz mozzarella cheese,
   thinly sliced
12 fresh basil leaves
   6 coarsely torn
4–5 tomatoes, cut into
   5mm/¼in slices
60ml/4 tbsp freshly grated
   Parmesan cheese

1 Sift the flour and salt into a bowl, then rub in the butter until the mixture resembles breadcrumbs. Add 45ml/3 tbsp water and combine with a fork until the dough holds together. Mix in more water if necessary. Gather the dough into a ball, wrap in baking parchment and chill in the refrigerator for 40 minutes. Preheat the oven to 190°C/375°F/Gas 5.

2 Roll out the dough to a thickness of 5mm/¼in and use to line a 28cm/11in fluted loose-based flan tin (pan). Prick the base all over and chill in the refrigerator for 20 minutes.

3 Line the pastry case (pie shell) with a sheet of baking parchment and fill with dried beans. Place the flan tin on a baking sheet and bake blind for 15 minutes. Remove from the oven but leave the oven switched on.

4 Remove the beans and paper. Brush the pastry case with oil. Line with the mozzarella. Sprinkle the torn basil over the top.

5 Arrange the tomato slices over the cheese. Dot with the whole basil leaves. Season with salt and pepper, and sprinkle with Parmesan and oil. Bake for 35 minutes. If the cheese exudes a lot of liquid during baking, tilt the tin and spoon it off to keep the crust crisp. Serve hot or at room temperature.

Salad Energy 151kcal/638kJ; Protein 10.2g; Carbohydrate 22.8g, of which sugars 4.4g; Fat 2.7g, of which saturates 0.3g; Cholesterol 0mg; Calcium 60mg; Fibre 4.9g; Sodium 9mg.
Tart Energy 307kcal/1279kJ; Protein 9.6g; Carbohydrate 19g, of which sugars 2.4g; Fat 21.9g, of which saturates 12.5g; Cholesterol 51mg; Calcium 207mg; Fibre 1.3g; Sodium 262mg.

Spinach & Potato Galette

Creamy layers of potato, spinach and fresh herbs make a warming and filling supper dish.

Serves 6
900g/2lb large potatoes
450g/1lb/4 cups spinach
400g/14oz/1¾ cups low-fat cream cheese
15ml/1 tbsp wholegrain mustard
2 eggs
50g/2oz mixed chopped fresh herbs, such as chives, parsley, chervil or sorrel
salt and ground black pepper

1 Preheat the oven to 180°C/350°F/Gas 4. Base-line a deep 23cm/9in round cake tin (pan) with baking parchment.

2 Place the potatoes in a large pan and add cold water to cover. Bring to the boil, cover and cook for 10 minutes. Drain well and leave to cool slightly before slicing thinly.

3 Wash the spinach and place in another large pan with only the water that is clinging to the leaves. Cover and cook, stirring once, until the spinach has just wilted. Drain well in a sieve (strainer) and squeeze out the excess moisture with the back of a spoon. Chop the spinach finely.

4 Beat together the cream cheese, mustard and eggs in a bowl, then stir in the chopped spinach and fresh herbs.

5 Place a layer of the sliced potatoes in the lined tin, arranging them in concentric circles. Top with a spoonful of the cream cheese mixture and spread out. Continue layering, seasoning with salt and pepper as you go, until all the potatoes and the cream cheese mixture are used up.

6 Cover the tin with a piece of foil, scrunched around the edge, and place in a roasting pan.

7 Pour boiling water into the roasting pan to come about halfway up the sides and cook the galette in the oven for 45–50 minutes. Turn out on to a plate and serve immediately or leave to cool completely and serve cold.

Cowboy Hot-pot

A great dish to serve as a children's main meal, which adults will enjoy too – if they are allowed to join the posse.

Serves 4–6
45ml/3 tbsp sunflower oil
1 onion, sliced
1 red (bell) pepper, seeded and sliced
1 sweet potato or 2 carrots, chopped
115g/4oz/scant ½ cup chopped green beans
400g/14oz can baked beans
200g/7oz can corn
15ml/1 tbsp tomato purée (paste)
5ml/1 tsp barbecue spice seasoning
115g/4oz cheese (preferably smoked), diced
450g/1lb potatoes, thinly sliced
25g/1oz/2 tbsp butter, melted
salt and ground black pepper

1 Preheat the oven to 190°C/375°F/Gas 5. Heat the oil in a frying pan over low heat. Add the onion, red pepper and sweet potato or carrots and cook, stirring occasionally, for about 5 minutes, until softened but not coloured.

2 Increase the heat to medium and stir in the green beans, baked beans, corn (and liquid), tomato purée and barbecue spice seasoning. Bring to the boil, then lower the heat and simmer for 5 minutes.

3 Transfer the vegetable mixture to an ovenproof dish and stir in the diced cheese.

4 Cover the vegetable and cheese mixture with the potato slices, brush generously with the melted butter and season with salt and pepper. Bake the hot-pot for 30–40 minutes, until golden brown on top and the potato is cooked. Serve immediately straight from the dish.

Cook's Tip
Use any vegetable mixture you like in this versatile hot-pot, depending on what you have to hand.

Galette Energy 239kcal/1004kJ; Protein 16.9g; Carbohydrate 27.9g, of which sugars 5.6g; Fat 8.4g, of which saturates 4.2g; Cholesterol 79mg; Calcium 240mg; Fibre 3.5g; Sodium 440mg.
Hot-pot Energy 351kcal/1470kJ; Protein 12g; Carbohydrate 40.1g, of which sugars 11.1g; Fat 16.6g, of which saturates 7.3g; Cholesterol 27mg; Calcium 199mg; Fibre 5.7g; Sodium 503mg.

Quorn with Ginger, Chilli & Leeks

Quorn easily absorbs different flavours and retains a good firm texture, making it ideal for stir-frying.

Serves 4

225g/8oz packet Quorn, diced
45ml/3 tbsp dark soy sauce
30ml/2 tbsp dry sherry
   or vermouth
10ml/2 tsp clear honey
150ml/¼ pint/⅔ cup vegetable
   stock
10ml/2 tsp cornflour (cornstarch)
45ml/3 tbsp sunflower or
   groundnut (peanut) oil
3 leeks, thinly sliced
1 red chilli, seeded and sliced
2.5cm/1in piece fresh root
   ginger, shredded
salt and ground black pepper
rice or egg noodles, to serve

1 Toss the Quorn in the soy sauce and sherry or vermouth in a bowl until well coated. Leave to marinate for 30 minutes.

2 Drain the Quorn and reserve the marinade in a jug (pitcher). Mix the marinade with the honey, vegetable stock and cornflour to make a paste.

3 Heat the oil in a wok or large frying pan and, when hot, add the Quorn and stir-fry until it is crisp on the outside. Remove the Quorn and set aside.

4 Reheat the oil. Add the leeks, chilli and ginger and stir-fry for about 2 minutes, until they are just soft. Season to taste with salt and pepper.

5 Return the Quorn to the pan, together with the marinade mixture, and stir well until the liquid is thick and glossy. Serve immediately with rice or egg noodles.

Cook's Tip
Quorn is a versatile, mycoprotein food, now available in most supermarkets. If you cannot find it, you could use tofu instead.

Chinese Potatoes with Chilli Beans

This Chinese-inspired dish is made particularly appealing by its tasty sauce.

Serves 4

4 potatoes, cut into thick chunks
30ml/2 tbsp sunflower or
   groundnut (peanut) oil
3 spring onions (scallions), sliced
1 large chilli, seeded and sliced
2 garlic cloves, crushed
400g/14oz can red kidney
   beans, drained
30ml/2 tbsp dark soy sauce
15ml/1 tbsp sesame oil
salt and ground black pepper
15ml/1 tbsp sesame seeds,
   to sprinkle
chopped fresh coriander (cilantro)
   or parsley, to garnish

1 Put the potatoes in a pan, add cold water to cover and bring to the boil. Cover and cook for about 15 minutes, until they are just tender but still firm. Take care not to overcook them. Drain well and set aside.

2 Heat the oil in a wok or large, heavy frying pan. Add the spring onions and chilli and stir-fry over a medium heat for about 1 minute, then add the garlic and stir-fry for a few seconds longer.

3 Rinse and drain the kidney beans, then add them to the pan with the potatoes, stirring well. Finally, stir in the soy sauce and sesame oil.

4 Season to taste with salt and pepper and cook the vegetables until they are well heated through. Sprinkle with the sesame seeds and serve immediately, garnished with the chopped fresh coriander or parsley.

Cook's Tip
Coriander (cilantro) is also known as Chinese parsley and Greek parsley and it does resemble flat leaf parsley in appearance. However, the flavour is quite different. It is intensely aromatic, almost spicy, and goes especially well with chillies. It is one of those herbs that you either love or loathe.

Quorn Energy 158kcal/657kJ; Protein 8.6g; Carbohydrate 5.1g, of which sugars 3.8g; Fat 10.6g, of which saturates 1.4g; Cholesterol 0mg; Calcium 27mg; Fibre 4.9g; Sodium 939mg.
Potatoes Energy 272kcal/1141kJ; Protein 9.7g; Carbohydrate 34.8g, of which sugars 5.7g; Fat 11.4g, of which saturates 1.6g; Cholesterol 0mg; Calcium 107mg; Fibre 7.6g; Sodium 936mg.

Corn & Bean Tamale Pie

This hearty dish has a cheese-flavoured polenta topping which covers corn and kidney beans in a rich hot sauce. It is substantial enough for meat-eaters.

Serves 4

2 corn on the cob
30ml/2 tbsp vegetable oil
1 onion, chopped
2 garlic cloves, crushed
1 red (bell) pepper, seeded
  and chopped
2 green chillies, seeded
  and chopped
10ml/2 tbsp ground cumin
450g/1lb ripe tomatoes, peeled,
  seeded and chopped

15ml/1 tbsp tomato purée
  (paste)
425g/15oz can red kidney beans,
  drained and rinsed
15ml/1 tbsp chopped
  fresh oregano
oregano leaves, to garnish

For the topping

115g/4oz/scant 1 cup polenta
15g/½oz/2 tbsp plain (all-
  purpose) flour
2.5ml/½ tsp salt
10ml/2 tsp baking powder
1 egg, lightly beaten
120ml/4fl oz/½ cup milk
15g/½oz/1 tbsp butter, melted
50g/2oz/½ cup grated smoked
  Cheddar cheese

1 Preheat the oven to 220°C/425°F/Gas 7. Husk the corn on the cob, then par-boil for 8 minutes. Drain well, leave to cool slightly, then remove the kernels with a sharp knife.

2 Heat the oil in a large pan. Add the onion, garlic and red pepper and cook over low heat, stirring occasionally, for about 5 minutes, until softened. Add the chillies and cumin and cook, stirring constantly, for 1 minute. Stir in the tomatoes, tomato purée, beans, corn kernels and oregano. Season with salt and pepper. Simmer, uncovered, for 10 minutes.

3 To make the topping, mix the polenta, flour, salt, baking powder, egg, milk and butter to form a thick batter.

4 Transfer the bean mixture to an ovenproof dish, spoon the polenta mixture over and spread evenly. Bake for 30 minutes. Remove from the oven, sprinkle the cheese over the top, then bake for a further 5–10 minutes, until golden.

Pepper & Potato Tortilla

A traditional Spanish dish, tortilla is best eaten cold in chunky wedges and makes an ideal picnic food.

Serves 4

2 potatoes
45ml/3 tbsp olive oil
1 large onion, thinly sliced
2 garlic cloves, crushed

1 green (bell) pepper, seeded and
  thinly sliced
1 red (bell) pepper, seeded and
  thinly sliced
6 eggs, beaten
115g/4oz/1 cup grated
  mature (sharp) Cheddar or
  Mahón cheese
salt and ground black pepper

1 Do not peel the potatoes, but scrub them well under cold running water. Par-boil them for about 10 minutes, then drain and, when they are cool enough to handle, slice them thickly. Preheat the grill (broiler).

2 Heat the oil in a large non-stick or well seasoned frying pan. Add the onion, garlic and green and red peppers and cook over medium heat, stirring occasionally, for about 5 minutes, until softened but not coloured.

3 Add the potatoes, lower the heat and cook, stirring occasionally, until the potatoes are completely cooked and the vegetables are soft. Add a little extra olive oil if the pan seems too dry.

4 Pour in half the beaten eggs, then sprinkle over half the grated cheese. Add the rest of the eggs. Season with salt and pepper and sprinkle with the remaining cheese.

5 Continue to cook over low heat, without stirring, half covering the pan with a lid to help set the eggs.

6 When the mixture is firm, place the pan under the hot grill for a few seconds to seal the top lightly. Leave the tortilla in the pan to cool. This helps it firm up further and makes it easier to turn out. Cut into generous wedges or squares and serve at room temperature.

Pie Energy 513kcal/2154kJ; Protein 19.5g; Carbohydrate 71.1g, of which sugars 19.8g; Fat 17.6g, of which saturates 6.4g; Cholesterol 69mg; Calcium 233mg; Fibre 10.2g; Sodium 758mg.
Tortilla Energy 321kcal/1333kJ; Protein 13.1g; Carbohydrate 19.6g, of which sugars 10.2g; Fat 21.1g, of which saturates 8.3g; Cholesterol 123mg; Calcium 256mg; Fibre 3g; Sodium 254mg.

Chickpea Stew

This hearty chickpea and vegetable stew is delicious served with garlic-flavoured mashed potato.

Serves 4
30ml/2 tbsp olive oil
1 small onion, finely chopped
225g/8oz carrots, halved
   lengthways and thinly
   sliced
2.5ml/½ tsp ground cumin
5ml/1 tsp ground coriander

25g/1oz/¼ cup plain (all-
   purpose) flour
225g/8oz courgettes
   (zucchini), sliced
200g/7oz can corn, drained
400g/14oz can chickpeas,
   drained and rinsed
30ml/2 tbsp tomato
   purée (paste)
200ml/7fl oz/scant 1 cup hot
   vegetable stock
salt and ground black pepper
mashed potato, to serve

1 Heat the olive oil in a frying pan. Add the onion and carrots and cook over medium heat, stirring occasionally, for about 5 minutes, until the onion has softened but not coloured.

2 Add the ground cumin, coriander and flour and cook, stirring constantly, for 1 minute more.

3 Cut the courgette slices in half and add to the pan with the corn, chickpeas, tomato purée and vegetable stock. Stir well. Cook for 10 minutes, stirring frequently.

4 Season the stew to taste with salt and pepper. Spoon on to warmed plates and serve immediately with mashed potato.

Cook's Tip
To make garlic mash, add 4–6 finely chopped or crushed garlic cloves to the potatoes about 15 minutes after they began boiling. Reserve 30–45ml/2–3 tbsp of the cooking liquid when you drain the potatoes. Heat a little milk with the reserved liquid, add a little butter and remove the pan from the heat. Add the potatoes and garlic and mash well with a potato masher. Beat with a wooden spoon and season with salt and pepper.

Potato & Broccoli Stir-fry

This wonderful stir-fry combines potato, broccoli and red pepper with just a hint of fresh ginger.

Serves 2
450g/1lb potatoes
45ml/3 tbsp groundnut
   (peanut) oil

50g/2oz/4 tbsp butter
1 small onion, chopped
1 red (bell) pepper, seeded
   and chopped
225g/8oz broccoli, broken
   into florets
2.5cm/1in piece of fresh root
   ginger, grated
salt and ground black pepper

1 Peel the potatoes and cut them into 1cm/½in dice. Heat the oil in a large frying pan. Add the potatoes and cook over a high heat, stirring and tossing frequently, for about 8 minutes, until browned and just tender.

2 Drain off the oil from the pan. Add the butter to the potatoes in the pan. As soon as it melts, add the onion and red pepper and stir-fry for 2 minutes.

3 Add the broccoli florets and ginger to the pan. Stir-fry for a further 2–3 minutes, taking care not to break up the potatoes. Season to taste with salt and pepper and serve immediately.

Cook's Tip
Always use a vegetable peeler with a swivel blade for peeling potatoes. As most of the nutrients are directly beneath the skin, it is important to peel them as thinly as possible.

Variations
• *Substitute 1 finely chopped celery stick and 1 thinly sliced carrot for the red (bell) pepper.*
• *For a milder tasting dish, omit the ginger, replace the broccoli with peeled, seeded and diced tomatoes and flavour with torn fresh basil leaves.*

Stew Energy 288kcal/1211kJ; Protein 11.2g; Carbohydrate 42g, of which sugars 12.3g; Fat 9.5g, of which saturates 1.3g; Cholesterol 0mg; Calcium 88mg; Fibre 7.3g; Sodium 388mg.
Stir-fry Energy 2442kcal/10069kJ; Protein 10.2g; Carbohydrate 46.4g, of which sugars 11.8g; Fat 247.4g, of which saturates 55.9g; Cholesterol 53mg; Calcium 96mg; Fibre 7g; Sodium 190mg.

Vegetables with Lentil Bolognese

Instead of the more traditional cheese sauce, it makes a pleasant change to top lightly steamed vegetables with a delicious lentil sauce.

Serves 6
1 small cauliflower broken
   into florets
225g/8oz/2 cups broccoli florets
2 leeks, thickly sliced
225g/8oz Brussels sprouts, halved
   if large

For the lentil Bolognese
sauce
45ml/3 tbsp olive oil

1 onion, chopped
2 garlic cloves, crushed
2 carrots, coarsely grated
2 celery sticks, chopped
115g/4oz/1/2 cup red lentils
400g/14oz can
   chopped tomatoes
30ml/2 tbsp tomato
   purée (paste)
450ml/3/4 pint/2 cups vegetable
   stock
15ml/1 tbsp fresh marjoram,
   chopped, or 5ml/1 tsp
   dried marjoram
salt and ground black pepper

1 First make the lentil Bolognese sauce. Heat the oil in a large pan over low heat. Add the onion, garlic, carrots and celery and cook, stirring occasionally, for about 5 minutes, until softened but not coloured.

2 Increase the heat to medium and add the lentils, tomatoes, tomato purée, stock and marjoram. Bring the mixture to the boil, then lower the heat, partially cover the pan with a lid and simmer gently for 20–30 minutes, until the sauce is thick and soft. Season to taste with salt and pepper

3 Meanwhile, place the cauliflower, broccoli, leeks and Brussels sprouts in a steamer set over a pan of boiling water, cover and cook for 8–10 minutes, until all the vegetables are just tender but still have a little crunch.

4 Drain the vegetables and place in a warmed, shallow serving dish. Spoon the lentil Bolognese sauce on top, stir lightly to mix and serve immediately.

Black Bean & Vegetable Stir-fry

This colourful and very flavoursome vegetable mixture is coated in a classic Chinese sauce.

Serves 4
8 spring onions (scallions)
225g/8oz button
   (white) mushrooms
1 red (bell) pepper

1 green (bell) pepper
2 large carrots
60ml/4 tbsp sesame oil
2 garlic cloves, crushed
60ml/4 tbsp black bean sauce
90ml/6 tbsp warm water
225g/8oz/scant 3 cups
   beansprouts
salt and ground black pepper

1 Thinly slice the spring onions and button mushrooms. Set aside in separate bowls.

2 Cut both the peppers in half, remove and discard the seeds and slice the flesh into thin strips.

3 Cut the carrots in half. Cut each half into thin strips lengthways. Stack the slices and cut through them to make very fine strips.

4 Heat the oil in a large wok or frying pan until very hot. Add the spring onions and garlic and stir-fry for 30 seconds.

5 Add the mushrooms, peppers and carrots. Stir-fry over high heat for a further 5–6 minutes, until just beginning to soften.

6 Mix the black bean sauce with the water. Add to the wok or frying pan and cook for a further 3–4 minutes. Stir in the beansprouts and stir-fry for a final 1 minute, until all the vegetables are coated in the sauce. Season to taste with salt and pepper. Serve immediately.

> **Cook's Tip**
> *Black bean sauce is available in jars and cans. Once opened it should be stored in the refrigerator.*

Bolognese Energy 195kcal/817kJ; Protein 11.8g; Carbohydrate 20.5g, of which sugars 8.8g; Fat 7.8g, of which saturates 1.3g; Cholesterol 0mg; Calcium 83mg; Fibre 7.2g; Sodium 46mg.
Stir-fry Energy 196kcal/817kJ; Protein 6.5g; Carbohydrate 16.1g, of which sugars 9.4g; Fat 12.2g, of which saturates 1.9g; Cholesterol 0mg; Calcium 45mg; Fibre 4.6g; Sodium 19mg.

Tomato & Okra Stew

Okra is an unusual and delicious vegetable. It releases a sticky sap when cooked, which helps to thicken the stew.

Serves 4

15ml/1 tbsp olive oil
1 onion, chopped
400g/14oz can pimientos, drained
2 x 400g/14oz cans
   chopped tomatoes
275g/10oz okra
30ml/2 tbsp chopped
   fresh parsley
salt and ground black pepper

1 Heat the oil in a pan over medium heat. Add the onion and cook, stirring occasionally, for 2–3 minutes, until it is just beginning to soften.

2 Coarsely chop the pimientos and add to the onion. Add the tomatoes with their can juices and mix well.

3 Cut the tops off the okra and cut into halves or quarters if large. Add them to the pan. Season to taste with plenty of salt and pepper.

4 Bring the vegetable stew to the boil, then lower the heat, cover the pan with a tight-fitting lid and simmer gently for about 12 minutes, until all the vegetables are tender and the sauce has thickened. Stir in the chopped parsley, transfer to a warmed serving dish and serve immediately.

Cook's Tip

Okra, also known as bhindi, gumbo and ladies' fingers, is now available all year round. Do not buy pods any longer than 7.5–10cm/3–4in as larger ones tend to be fibrous. Look for clean, dark green pods – a brown tinge indicates staleness. They should feel firm and slightly springy when squeezed and should snap easily, not bend. Store them in the salad drawer of the refrigerator where they will keep for a few days. When preparing, if the ridges look tough or damaged, scrape them with a sharp knife.

Chunky Vegetable Paella

This Spanish rice dish is now enjoyed the world over. This version includes aubergine and chickpeas.

Serves 6

large pinch of saffron threads
1 aubergine (eggplant), cut into
   thick chunks
90ml/6 tbsp olive oil
1 large onion, thickly sliced
3 garlic cloves, crushed
1 yellow (bell) pepper, seeded
   and sliced
1 red (bell) pepper, seeded
   and sliced
10ml/2 tsp paprika
225g/8oz/1¼ cups Valencia or
   risotto rice
600ml/1 pint/2½ cups vegetable
   stock
450g/1lb fresh tomatoes, peeled
   and chopped
115g/4oz mushrooms, sliced
115g/4oz/scant ½ cup cut
   green beans
400g/14oz can chickpeas

1 Place the saffron in a small bowl, add 45ml/3 tbsp hot water and set aside to steep.

2 Place the aubergine chunks in a colander, sprinkle with salt and leave to drain for 30 minutes. Rinse thoroughly under cold running water and pat dry with kitchen paper.

3 Heat the oil in a large paella or frying pan over low heat. Add the onion, garlic, yellow and red peppers and aubergine and cook, stirring occasionally, for about 5 minutes, until the onion has softened but not coloured. Sprinkle in the paprika and stir well.

4 Increase the heat to medium and mix in the rice, then pour in the vegetable stock and add the tomatoes. Stir in the saffron with its soaking water. Season well with salt and pepper. Bring the mixture to the boil, then lower the heat and simmer gently for about 15 minutes, uncovered, shaking the pan frequently and stirring occasionally.

5 Stir in the mushrooms, green beans and chickpeas with their can juices. Simmer gently for a further 10 minutes, then serve hot, direct from the pan.

Stew Energy 122kcal/515kJ; Protein 4.8g; Carbohydrate 16.7g, of which sugars 15.6g; Fat 4.6g, of which saturates 0.9g; Cholesterol 0mg; Calcium 152mg; Fibre 7g; Sodium 97mg.
Paella Energy 385kcal/1610kJ; Protein 11g; Carbohydrate 54.5g, of which sugars 12g; Fat 14.2g, of which saturates 2g; Cholesterol 0mg; Calcium 79mg; Fibre 7.7g; Sodium 160mg.

Onion & Gruyère Tart

The secret of this tart is to cook the onions very slowly until they almost caramelize.

Serves 4
175g/6oz/1½ cups plain (all-purpose) flour
pinch of salt
75g/3oz/6 tbsp butter, diced
1 egg yolk

For the filling
50g/2oz/4 tbsp butter

450g/1lb onions, thinly sliced
15–30ml/1–2 tbsp wholegrain mustard
2 eggs, plus 1 egg yolk
300ml/½ pint/1 cup double (heavy) cream
75g/3oz/¾ cup grated Gruyère cheese
pinch of freshly grated nutmeg
salt and ground black pepper

1 To make the pastry, sift the flour and salt into a bowl. Add the butter and rub it into the flour with your fingertips until the mixture resembles fine breadcrumbs. Add the egg yolk and 15ml/1 tbsp cold water and mix to a firm dough. Chill in the refrigerator for 30 minutes.

2 Preheat the oven to 200°C/400°F/Gas 6. Knead the dough, then roll it out on a lightly floured work surface and use to line a 23cm/9in loose-based flan tin (pan). Prick the base all over with a fork, line the pastry case (pie shell) with baking parchment and fill with baking beans.

3 Bake the pastry case blind for 15 minutes. Remove the paper and beans and bake for a further 10–15 minutes, until the pastry case is crisp. Meanwhile, melt the butter in a pan, add the onions, cover with a tight-fitting lid and cook over low heat, stirring occasionally, for 20 minutes, until golden.

4 Reduce the oven temperature to 180°C/350°F/Gas 4. Spread the pastry case with mustard and top with the onions. Mix together the eggs, egg yolk, cream, cheese and nutmeg and season with salt and pepper. Pour over the onions. Bake for 30–35 minutes, until golden. Remove the tart from the oven and leave to cool slightly. Serve warm.

Potato & Spinach Gratin

Pine nuts add a satisfying crunch to this gratin of wafer-thin potato slices and spinach in a wonderfully creamy cheese sauce.

Serves 2
450g/1lb potatoes
1 garlic clove, crushed
3 spring onions (scallions), thinly sliced

150ml/¼ pint/⅔ cup single (light) cream
250ml/8fl oz/1 cup milk
225g/8oz frozen chopped spinach, thawed
115g/4oz/1 cup grated mature (sharp) Cheddar cheese
25g/1oz/¼ cup pine nuts
salt and ground black pepper
lettuce and tomato salad, to serve

1 Peel the potatoes and cut them carefully into wafer-thin slices. This is most easily done with a mandoline or the slicing attachment of a food processor. Spread the slices out in a large, heavy, non-stick frying pan.

2 Sprinkle the crushed garlic and sliced spring onions evenly over the potatoes.

3 Mix together the cream and milk in a jug (pitcher) and pour the mixture over the potatoes. Place the pan over low heat, cover with a tight-fitting lid and cook for 8 minutes, or until the potatoes are tender.

4 Drain the spinach thoroughly, then, using both hands, squeeze it as dry as possible. Add the spinach to the potatoes, mixing lightly. Cover the pan with a tight-fitting lid and cook for 2 minutes more.

5 Season to taste with salt and pepper, then spoon the mixture into a gratin dish. Preheat the grill (broiler).

6 Sprinkle the grated cheese and pine nuts evenly over the potato and spinach mixture. Lightly toast under the grill for 2–3 minutes, until the cheese has melted and the topping is golden brown. Serve the gratin immediately with a lettuce and tomato salad.

Tart Energy 904kcal/3746kJ; Protein 15g; Carbohydrate 36.7g, of which sugars 3g; Fat 78.2g, of which saturates 47g; Cholesterol 384mg; Calcium 272mg; Fibre 1.6g; Sodium 383mg.
Gratin Energy 527kcal/2212kJ; Protein 28.1g; Carbohydrate 45.3g, of which sugars 11.7g; Fat 27.3g, of which saturates 11.6g; Cholesterol 79mg; Calcium 413mg; Fibre 5.1g; Sodium 183mg.

Pasta, Pizza & Grains

Simple kitchen staples such as rice, couscous, bulgur wheat and

pasta are ideal ingredients for creating hearty, sustaining meals.

This chapter includes family-friendly pasta dishes, such as

Macaroni Cheese with Mushrooms, or Tuna Lasagne; impressive

rice dishes, such as Champagne Risotto

or Creole Jambalaya; and a wide range of pizzas, including

Pepperoni Pizza and Quattro Formaggi.

Pasta with Spring Vegetables

Pasta tossed with broccoli, leeks, asparagus and fennel makes an attractive dish, bursting with fresh flavours.

Serves 4
115g/4oz/1 cup broccoli florets
115g/4oz baby leeks
225g/8oz asparagus
1 small fennel bulb
115g/4oz/1 cup fresh or frozen peas
40g/1½ oz/3 tbsp butter
1 shallot, chopped
45ml/3 tbsp mixed chopped fresh herbs, such as parsley, thyme and sage
300ml/½ pint/1¼ cups double (heavy) cream
350g/12oz/3 cups dried penne pasta
salt and ground black pepper
freshly grated Parmesan cheese, to serve

1 Divide the broccoli florets into tiny sprigs. Cut the leeks and asparagus diagonally into 5cm/2in lengths. Trim the fennel bulb and remove any tough outer leaves. Cut into wedges, leaving the layers attached at the root ends so the pieces stay intact.

2 Cook each vegetable separately in boiling salted water until just tender – use the same water for each vegetable. Drain well and keep warm.

3 Melt the butter in a separate pan, add the chopped shallot and cook, stirring occasionally, until softened but not browned. Stir in the herbs and cream and cook for a few minutes, until slightly thickened.

4 Meanwhile, bring a large pan of lightly salted water to the boil and cook the penne for 10 minutes or until al dente. Drain well and add to the cream sauce with all the vegetables. Toss gently to combine and season to taste with plenty of pepper. Serve immediately, with plenty of grated Parmesan cheese.

Cook's Tip
If you are not keen on the aniseed taste of fennel, you can use a small onion instead. Prepare in the same way.

Pasta Carbonara

This classic Roman dish is traditionally made with spaghetti, but is equally good with fresh egg tagliatelle.

Serves 4
350–450g/12oz–1lb fresh tagliatelle pasta
15ml/1 tbsp olive oil
225g/8oz piece of ham or bacon, cut into 2.5cm/1in sticks
115g/4oz button mushrooms, sliced (optional)
4 eggs, lightly beaten
75ml/5 tbsp single (light) cream
30ml/2 tbsp finely grated Parmesan cheese
salt and ground black pepper

1 Bring a large pan of lightly salted water to the boil, add a little oil and cook the tagliatelle for 6–8 minutes or until al dente.

2 Meanwhile, heat the oil in a frying pan and cook the ham for 3–4 minutes, then add the mushrooms, if using and fry for a further 3–4 minutes. Turn off the heat and set the pan aside. Lightly beat the eggs and cream together in a bowl and season well with salt and pepper.

3 When the pasta is cooked, drain it well and return to the pan. Add the ham, mushrooms and any pan juices and stir well into the pasta.

4 Pour in the egg and cream mixture, together with half the grated Parmesan cheese. Stir well – as you do this the eggs will cook in the heat of the pasta. Pile the pasta on to warmed serving plates, sprinkle with the remaining Parmesan cheese. Serve immediately.

Cook's Tip
For an authentic Italian flavour, use slices of pancetta. Made from pork belly, it is cured in salt and spices to give it a delicious taste. Pancetta is sold at Italian delicatessens and is now increasingly available from larger supermarkets.

Vegetables Energy 767kcal/3196kJ; Protein 16.5g; Carbohydrate 64g, of which sugars 7.8g; Fat 51.3g, of which saturates 30.6g; Cholesterol 124mg; Calcium 138mg; Fibre 7.8g; Sodium 93mg.
Carbonara Energy 535kcal/2257kJ; Protein 31.7g; Carbohydrate 66g, of which sugars 4g; Fat 18.1g, of which saturates 6.6g; Cholesterol 241mg; Calcium 165mg; Fibre 3.2g; Sodium 838mg.

Spinach & Hazelnut Lasagne

Hazelnuts add a delicious crunchy texture to the spinach layer of this wholesome lasagne.

Serves 4
900g/2lb/8 cups fresh spinach
300ml/½ pint/1¼ cups vegetable
 stock
1 onion, finely chopped
1 garlic clove, crushed

75g/3oz/¾ cup hazelnuts
30ml/2 tbsp chopped fresh basil
6 sheets no pre-cook lasagne
400g/14oz can chopped
 tomatoes
250ml/8fl oz/1 cup mascarpone
 or fromage frais
salt and ground black pepper
flaked hazelnuts and chopped
 fresh parsley

1 Preheat the oven to 200°C/400°F/Gas 6. Wash the spinach and place in a pan with just the water that clings to the leaves. Cook over high heat for 2 minutes until wilted. Drain well.

2 Heat 30ml/2 tbsp of the stock in a pan and simmer the onion and garlic until soft. Stir in the spinach, hazelnuts and chopped fresh basil.

3 Arrange a layer of the spinach mixture in a large rectangular ovenproof dish. Top with a layer of lasagne, then a layer of chopped tomatoes, seasoning with salt and pepper as you work. Continue in this way, finishing with a layer of pasta.

4 Pour in the remaining stock, then spread the mascarpone or fromage frais over the top. Bake for 45 minutes. Serve hot, sprinkled with hazelnuts and chopped parsley.

> **Cook's Tip**
> If you're short of time, use frozen spinach instead of fresh – you will need 450g/1lb.

Tagliatelle with Hazelnut Pesto

Hazelnuts are used instead of pine nuts in this pesto sauce, providing a healthier, lower-fat option.

Serves 4
2 garlic cloves, crushed
25g/1oz fresh basil leaves

25g/1oz/¼ cup chopped
 hazelnuts
200g/7oz/scant 1 cup soft cheese
225g/8oz tagliatelle
ground black pepper

1 Place the garlic, basil, hazelnuts and cheese in a food processor or blender and process to a thick paste.

2 Bring a large pan of lightly salted water to the boil and cook the tagliatelle until *al dente*. Drain well.

3 Spoon the sauce into the hot pasta, tossing until melted. Sprinkle with pepper and serve immediately.

Spaghetti with Tuna Sauce

Tuna is combined with tomatoes, garlic and chilli to make a great piquant sauce for pasta.

Serves 4
225g/8oz dried spaghetti or
 450g/1lb fresh spaghetti

400g/14oz can chopped
 tomatoes
1 garlic clove
425g/15oz canned tuna
4 black olives
2.5ml/½ tsp chilli sauce
 (optional)
salt and ground black pepper

1 Bring a large pan of lightly salted water to the boil and cook the spaghetti until *al dente*. Drain well and keep hot.

2 Place the chopped tomatoes in a pan with the garlic and simmer for 2–3 minutes. Add the tuna, olives and chilli sauce, if using, and heat well. Toss with the spaghetti and heat through. Season to taste with salt and pepper and serve immediately.

Lasagne Energy 442kcal/1853kJ; Protein 19.6g; Carbohydrate 48.8g, of which sugars 12.3g; Fat 19.9g, of which saturates 4.8g; Cholesterol 5mg; Calcium 501mg; Fibre 8.6g; Sodium 350mg.
Tagliatelle Energy 392kcal/1642kJ; Protein 12.1g; Carbohydrate 42.2g, of which sugars 2.3g; Fat 20.6g, of which saturates 10.1g; Cholesterol 45mg; Calcium 90mg; Fibre 2.4g; Sodium 169mg.
Spaghetti Energy 413kcal/1748kJ; Protein 36.3g; Carbohydrate 44.8g, of which sugars 5g; Fat 11.2g, of which saturates 1.9g; Cholesterol 53mg; Calcium 36mg; Fibre 2.7g; Sodium 386mg.

Penne with Broccoli & Chilli

Simple to make, yet filled with tasty flavours, this dish is ideal for an easy midweek meal. Try using other pasta shapes, such as fusilli spirals.

Serves 4
350g/12oz/3 cups penne pasta
450g/1lb/4 cups small broccoli
   florets
30ml/2 tbsp stock
1 garlic clove, crushed
1 small red chilli, finely sliced, or
   2.5ml/½ tsp chilli sauce
60ml/4 tbsp natural (plain)
   low-fat yogurt
30ml/2 tbsp toasted pine nuts or
   cashew nuts
salt and ground black pepper

1 Bring a large pan of lightly salted water to the boil, add the pasta and return to the boil. Place the broccoli in a steamer basket over the top. Cover and cook for 8–10 minutes, until both are just tender. Drain.

2 Heat the stock in a pan and add the crushed garlic and chilli or chilli sauce. Stir over a low heat for 2–3 minutes.

3 Stir in the broccoli, pasta and yogurt. Season to taste with salt and pepper, then sprinkle with nuts and serve immediately.

Cook's Tips
• *For the best results, it is important that the broccoli is very fresh – it should be bright green and firm, not limp. Cut the florets into bite-size pieces, removing any woody stem.*
• *To toast pine nuts for sprinkling on top, heat a dry heavy frying pan, add the pine nuts and toss quickly over medium heat until they turn pale golden. Do not allow them to brown, otherwise they will taste bitter.*

Variation
For a milder sauce you could omit the chilli. Instead, add some diced ham with the garlic to give extra flavour and texture.

Linguine with Pesto Sauce

Pesto, the famous Italian basil sauce, originates in Liguria, where the sea breezes are said to give the local basil a particularly fine flavour. Pesto is traditionally made with a pestle and mortar, but it is easier to make in a food processor or blender.

Serves 5–6
65g/2½ oz fresh basil leaves
3–4 garlic cloves, peeled
45ml/3 tbsp pine nuts
75ml/5 tbsp extra virgin
   olive oil
50g/2oz/scant ¾ cup freshly
   grated Parmesan cheese
60ml/4 tbsp freshly grated
   Pecorino cheese
salt and ground black pepper
500g/1¼ lb linguine pasta

1 Place the basil leaves, garlic cloves, pine nuts, 2.5ml/½ tsp salt and olive oil in a food processor or blender and process until smooth. Transfer to a bowl.

2 Stir in the Parmesan and Pecorino cheeses and stir to combine thoroughly. Season to taste with salt and pepper.

3 Bring a large pan of lightly salted water the boil and cook the linguine until it is *al dente*. Just before draining the pasta, take out about 60ml/4 tbsp of the cooking water and stir it into the pesto sauce.

4 Drain the pasta and toss with the sauce. Serve at once, with extra cheese if wished.

Cook's Tip
• *Pecorino cheese is not as widely available as Parmesan. If you cannot find it, use all Parmesan instead. For the best flavour, buy a piece of Parmesan and grate it yourself.*
• *Pesto sauce is handy to have as a standby in the freezer. It's a good idea to freeze the pesto in an ice cube tray so that you can use as little or as much as you like. Freeze at the end of step 1, before adding the cheese.*

Penne Energy 397kcal/1678kJ; Protein 17.3g; Carbohydrate 68.3g, of which sugars 6g; Fat 7.9g, of which saturates 0.8g; Cholesterol 0mg; Calcium 114mg; Fibre 5.6g; Sodium 24mg.
Linguine Energy 476kcal/2000kJ; Protein 17.6g; Carbohydrate 56.1g, of which sugars 2.9g; Fat 21.7g, of which saturates 5.6g; Cholesterol 18mg; Calcium 258mg; Fibre 2.6g; Sodium 217mg.

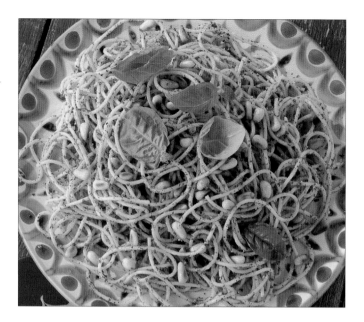

Tagliatelle with Saffron Mussels

Mussels bathed in a delicate saffron and cream sauce are served with tagliatelle for a simple, yet sophisticated, lunch or supper dish.

Serves 4
1.8kg/4–4¹/₂lb live mussels in the shell
150ml/¹/₄ pint/²/₃ cup dry white wine

2 shallots, finely chopped
350g/12oz dried tagliatelle
25g/1oz/2 tbsp butter
2 garlic cloves, crushed
250ml/8fl oz/1 cup double (heavy) cream
large pinch of saffron threads
1 egg yolk
salt and ground black pepper
30ml/2 tbsp chopped fresh parsley, to garnish

1 Scrub the mussels well under cold running water. Remove the "beards" and discard any mussels that are open.

2 Place the mussels in a large pan with the white wine and chopped shallots. Cover with a tight-fitting lid and cook over high heat for 5–8 minutes, shaking the pan occasionally, until the mussels have opened.

3 Drain the mussels, reserving the cooking liquid. Discard any mussels that remain closed. Shell all but a few of the mussels and keep warm. Bring the reserved cooking liquid to the boil, then reduce by half. Strain into a jug (cup).

4 Bring a large pan of lightly salted water to the boil and cook the tagliatelle for 10 minutes or until *al dente*.

5 Meanwhile, melt the butter in a frying pan and fry the garlic for 1 minute. Pour in the reduced mussel liquid, cream and saffron threads. Heat gently until the sauce thickens slightly.

6 Remove the pan from the heat and stir in the egg yolk and shelled mussels. Season to taste with salt and pepper.

7 Drain the tagliatelle and transfer to warmed serving bowls. Spoon the sauce over and sprinkle with chopped parsley. Garnish with the mussels in shells and serve immediately.

Spaghetti with Herb Sauce

Fresh herbs make a wonderful aromatic sauce – the heat from the pasta releases their flavour to delicious effect. Serve with chunks of warm ciabatta.

Serves 4
50g/2oz chopped mixed fresh herbs such as parsley, basil and thyme

2 garlic cloves, crushed
60ml/4 tbsp pine nuts, toasted
150ml/¹/₄ pint/²/₃ cup olive oil
350g/12oz dried spaghetti
60ml/4 tbsp freshly grated Parmesan cheese
salt and ground black pepper
fresh basil leaves, to garnish

1 Put the herbs, garlic and half the pine nuts into a food processor or blender. With the machine running slowly, add the oil and process to form a thick purée.

2 Bring a large pan of lightly salted water to the boil and cook the spaghetti until *al dente*. Drain thoroughly.

3 Transfer the herb purée to a large warm bowl, then add the spaghetti and Parmesan. Toss well to coat the pasta with the sauce. Season with salt and pepper.

4 Sprinkle the remaining pine nuts and the basil leaves over the pasta and serve immediately.

Cook's Tip
When cooking long strands of pasta like spaghetti, drop one end of the pasta into the boiling water and, as it softens, push it down gently until it bends in the middle and is completely immersed. Refer to the packet instructions for cooking times as these can vary from type to type. As a general rule, dried pasta needs 8–10 minutes. Do not be tempted to overcook pasta; it should be cooked until al dente, that is, until is it is tender but still firm to the bite. Always test pasta for doneness just before you think it should be ready, to avoid overcooking.

Spaghetti Energy 699kcal/2924kJ; Protein 18.9g; Carbohydrate 65.8g, of which sugars 3.8g; Fat 41.9g, of which saturates 7.5g; Cholesterol 15mg; Calcium 229mg; Fibre 3.5g; Sodium 171mg.
Tagliatelle Energy 803kcal/3366kJ; Protein 34.8g; Carbohydrate 67.6g, of which sugars 5.3g; Fat 43.1g, of which saturates 21.7g; Cholesterol 152mg; Calcium 339mg; Fibre 3.3g; Sodium 335mg.

Pasta Rapido with Parsley Pesto

This fresh, lively sauce will stir the appetite and pep up any pasta supper. Made with parsley and almonds, it makes a tasty change from the more familiar basil and pine nut pesto.

Serves 4–6
450g/1lb/4 cups dried pasta
75g/3oz/¾ cup whole almonds
50g/2oz/½ cup flaked (sliced)
   almonds toasted
25g/1oz/⅓ cup freshly grated
   Parmesan cheese
pinch of salt

For the sauce
40g/1½oz fresh flat leaf parsley
2 garlic cloves, crushed
45ml/3 tbsp olive oil
45ml/3 tbsp lemon juice
5ml/1 tsp sugar
250ml/8fl oz/1 cup boiling water

1 Bring a large pan of lightly salted water to the boil and cook the pasta until *al dente*.

2 Meanwhile, toast the whole and flaked almonds separately under a medium grill (broiler) until golden brown. Set the flaked almonds aside.

3 To make the sauce, chop the parsley finely in a food processor. Add the whole almonds and reduce to a fine consistency. Add the garlic, olive oil, lemon juice, sugar and water. Process to make a sauce.

4 Drain the pasta and transfer to a warmed serving bowl. Add half of the sauce and toss to combine well. (Keep the rest of the sauce for another dish.) Top with freshly grated Parmesan cheese and the reserved flaked almonds, and serve.

> **Cook's Tip**
> *The unused parsley pesto sauce will keep in a screw-top jar in the refrigerator for up to ten days. Serve it with any type of cooked pasta or try using the sauce as a topping for lightly cooked broccoli or grilled chicken thighs.*

Macaroni Cheese with Mushrooms

An old favourite is given a new twist with the addition of mushrooms and a light sprinkling of pine nuts. It is finished off under the grill to give a glorious golden top.

Serves 4
450g/1lb/4 cups quick-cooking
   dried elbow macaroni
45ml/3 tbsp olive oil
225g/8oz button (white)
   mushrooms, sliced
2 fresh thyme sprigs
50g/2oz/4 tbsp plain
   (all-purpose) flour
1 vegetable stock cube
600ml/1 pint/2½ cups milk
2.5ml/½ tsp celery salt
5ml/1 tsp Dijon mustard
175g/6oz/1½ cups grated
   Cheddar cheese
25g/1oz/⅓ cup freshly grated
   Parmesan cheese
25g/1oz/¼ cup pine nuts
salt and ground black pepper

1 Bring a large pan of lightly salted water to the boil and cook the macaroni until *al dente*.

2 Meanwhile, heat the oil in a heavy pan, add the mushrooms and thyme, cover and cook over gentle heat for 2–3 minutes. Stir in the flour and remove from the heat. Add the stock cube and stir continuously until evenly blended. Stir in the milk a little at a time, stirring after each addition.

3 Add the celery salt, mustard and Cheddar cheese and season to taste with salt and pepper. Stir to combine well, then simmer for about 1–2 minutes, stirring continuously, until the sauce has thickened.

4 Preheat the grill (broiler) to medium. Drain the macaroni well, toss into the sauce and turn into four individual dishes or one large flameproof gratin dish. Scatter with grated Parmesan cheese and pine nuts, then grill (broil) until brown and bubbly.

> **Variation**
> *Add 115g/4oz crisply fried bacon pieces and a handful of fresh spinach to the sauce just before adding the macaroni.*

Pasta Energy 688kcal/2894kJ; Protein 23.1g; Carbohydrate 87.3g, of which sugars 6.4g; Fat 29.9g, of which saturates 4.1g; Cholesterol 6mg; Calcium 199mg; Fibre 6.2g; Sodium 79mg.
Macaroni Energy 831kcal/3497kJ; Protein 35.2g; Carbohydrate 100.7g, of which sugars 11.4g; Fat 33.9g, of which saturates 14.2g; Cholesterol 58mg; Calcium 628mg; Fibre 4.4g; Sodium 456mg.

Pasta with Roasted Pepper Sauce

A touch of chilli powder gives this delicious pepper and tomato sauce a slight kick. Serve with a rocket salad for a tasty supper.

Serves 4
2 red (bell) peppers
2 yellow (bell) peppers
45ml/3 tbsp olive oil
1 onion, sliced
2 garlic cloves, crushed
2.5ml/½ tsp mild chilli powder
400g/14oz can chopped plum
  tomatoes
450g/1lb/4 cups dried pasta
  shells or spirals
salt and ground black pepper
freshly grated Parmesan cheese,
  to serve

1 Preheat the oven to 200°C/400°F/Gas 6. Place the peppers on a baking sheet and bake for about 20 minutes, or until they are beginning to char and blister. Alternatively, grill (broil) the peppers, turning them from time to time.

2 Rub the skins off the peppers under cold water, or place the charred peppers in a bowl, cover with kitchen paper and leave to cool for 10 minutes, then peel off the skins. Halve the skinned peppers, remove the seeds and roughly chop the flesh.

3 Heat the oil in a pan and cook the onion and garlic gently for 5 minutes, until soft and golden.

4 Stir in the chilli powder, cook for 2 minutes, then add the tomatoes and peppers. Bring to the boil and simmer for about 10–15 minutes, until slightly thickened and reduced. Season with salt and pepper to taste.

5 Bring a large pan of lightly salted water to the boil and cook the pasta until *al dente*. Drain well and toss with the sauce. Serve piping hot with lots of freshly grated Parmesan cheese.

> **Variation**
> *Add other vegetables such as French beans or courgettes (zucchini) or even chickpeas to make the dish more substantial.*

Stir-fried Vegetables with Pasta

This is a colourful oriental-style dish, easily prepared using pasta instead of Chinese noodles.

Serves 4
1 carrot
175g/6oz small courgettes
  (zucchini)
175g/6oz runner or other green
  beans
175g/6oz baby corn on the cob
450g/1lb dried ribbon pasta such
  as tagliatelle
pinch of salt
30ml/2 tbsp corn oil, plus extra
  for tossing the pasta
1cm/½ in piece fresh root ginger,
  peeled and finely chopped
2 garlic cloves, finely chopped
90ml/6 tbsp yellow bean sauce
6 spring onions (scallions), sliced
  into 2.5cm/1in lengths
30ml/2 tbsp dry sherry
5ml/1 tsp sesame seeds

1 Slice the carrot and courgettes diagonally into chunks. Slice the beans diagonally, then cut the baby corn on the cob diagonally in half.

2 Bring a large pan of lightly salted water to the boil and cook the pasta until *al dente*. Drain, then rinse under hot water. Toss in a little oil.

3 Heat 30ml/2 tbsp oil in a wok or frying pan until smoking and add the ginger and garlic. Stir-fry for 30 seconds, then add the carrots, courgettes and beans.

4 Stir-fry for 3–4 minutes then stir in the yellow bean sauce. Stir-fry for 2 minutes, add the spring onions, sherry and pasta and stir-fry for a further 1 minute until piping hot. Sprinkle with sesame seeds and serve immediately.

> **Variation**
> *You can vary the vegetables as you wish. Try strips of red (bell) pepper, sugar snap peas, button mushrooms and beansprouts. Make sure the wok is very hot before adding the vegetables.*

Pasta Energy 537kcal/2273kJ; Protein 16.1g; Carbohydrate 98.9g, of which sugars 18.3g; Fat 11.3g, of which saturates 1.7g; Cholesterol 0mg; Calcium 53mg; Fibre 7.3g; Sodium 20mg.
Stir-fried Vegetables Energy 560kcal/2370kJ; Protein 21.6g; Carbohydrate 100g, of which sugars 8g; Fat 9.1g, of which saturates 1.3g; Cholesterol 0mg; Calcium 86mg; Fibre 7.5g; Sodium 513mg.

Tagliatelle with Gorgonzola Sauce

Gorgonzola, the Italian creamy blue cheese, is used to create a mouthwatering sauce for pasta. Serve with a mixed green salad as a foil to the richness of the dish.

Serves 4

25g/1oz/2 tbsp butter, plus extra
  for tossing the pasta
225g/8oz Gorgonzola cheese
150ml/¼ pint/⅔ cup double
  (heavy) or whipping cream
30ml/2 tbsp dry vermouth
5ml/1 tsp cornflour (cornstarch)
30ml/1 tbsp chopped fresh sage
450g/1lb dried tagliatelle
salt and ground black pepper
sage leaves, to garnish (optional)

1 Melt the butter in a heavy pan (it needs to be thick-based to prevent the cheese from burning). Stir in 175g/6oz/1½ cups crumbled Gorgonzola cheese and stir over very gentle heat for 2–3 minutes, until the cheese has melted.

2 Pour in the cream, vermouth and cornflour, whisking well to amalgamate. Stir in the chopped sage, then season to taste with salt and pepper. Cook, whisking all the time, until the sauce boils and thickens. Set aside.

3 Bring a large pan of lightly salted water to the boil and cook the tagliatelle until al dente. Drain well and toss with a little butter to coat evenly.

4 Reheat the sauce gently, whisking well. Divide the pasta among four serving bowls, top with the sauce and sprinkle over the remaining cheese. Garnish with sage leaves, if using, then serve immediately.

> **Cook's Tip**
> If you do not have vermouth, you can use a good quality dry sherry in its place very successfully. The Gorgonzola can be substituted by another well-flavoured, creamy blue cheese such as Danish Blue or Pipo Crème.

Rigatoni with Garlic Crumbs

A spicy treat: pasta tubes coated in a chilli-flavoured tomato sauce, topped with crunchy garlicky crumbs.

Serves 4–6

45ml/3 tbsp olive oil
2 shallots, chopped
8 streaky (fatty) bacon rashers
  (strips), chopped
10ml/2 tsp crushed dried chillies
400g/14oz can chopped
  tomatoes with herbs
6 slices white bread, crusts
  removed
115g/4oz/½ cup butter
2 garlic cloves, chopped
450g/1lb/4 cups dried rigatoni
salt and ground black pepper
fresh herbs sprigs, to garnish

1 Heat the oil in a pan and fry the shallots and bacon gently for 6–8 minutes until golden. Add the dried chillies and chopped tomatoes, half-cover with a lid and simmer for about 20 minutes, stirring occasionally.

2 Meanwhile, place the bread in a blender or food processor and process to fine crumbs. Heat the butter in a frying pan and stir-fry the garlic and breadcrumbs until golden and crisp. (Be careful not to let the crumbs catch and burn.)

3 Bring a large pan of lightly salted water to the boil and cook the rigatoni until al dente. Drain well.

4 Toss the pasta with the tomato sauce and divide among four bowls. Sprinkle with the crumbs and garnish with herbs.

> **Cook's Tip**
> To keep the breadcrumbs crisp and dry after frying, drain them on kitchen paper and place in a low oven until ready to use.

> **Variation**
> To make this dish suitable for vegetarians, leave out the bacon, or replace it with sliced mushrooms.

Tagliatelle Energy 746kcal/3131kJ; Protein 26.1g; Carbohydrate 86g, of which sugars 5.2g; Fat 34.7g, of which saturates 24.2g; Cholesterol 58mg; Calcium 334mg; Fibre 3.3g; Sodium 750mg.
Rigatoni Energy 645kcal/2708kJ; Protein 18.4g; Carbohydrate 75g, of which sugars 6.1g; Fat 32.3g, of which saturates 14.1g; Cholesterol 65mg; Calcium 68mg; Fibre 3.5g; Sodium 771mg.

Pasta with Tomatoes & Basil

This pretty-coloured pasta dish relies for its success on the slightly peppery taste of the basil. It is deliciously fresh tasting. Serve it with warm rustic bread and a glass of dry white wine for a lunch dish.

Serves 4
450g/1lb/4 cups dried penne
450g/1lb ripe cherry tomatoes
25g/1oz fresh basil
45ml/3 tbsp olive oil
salt and ground black pepper
Parmesan cheese shavings,
   to serve (optional)

1 Bring a large pan of lightly salted water to the boil and cook the pasta until *al dente*.

2 Meanwhile, halve the tomatoes. Wash and dry the basil.

3 Heat the oil in a large pan and gently cook the tomatoes for barely 1 minute. The tomatoes should only just be heated through and not be allowed to disintegrate.

4 Drain the pasta and add to the pan, then add the basil. Carefully stir to mix and heat through. Season to taste with salt and pepper. Serve hot, with plenty of shaved Parmesan cheese, if you like.

Cook's Tip
Basil has a distinctive peppery taste that is useful for adding character to all sorts of salad dishes. It is usually available in supermarkets. Alternatively, why not grow your own: it is very easy to grow in the garden or even in a window-box, and this will ensure that you have a plentiful supply to hand.

Variations
• *Add a crushed garlic clove to the pan with the tomatoes, or just add a dash of balsamic vinegar for added flavour.*
• *You could replace the basil with rocket (arugula), if you like.*

Pasta Spirals with Pepperoni

A warming supper dish, this tangy pepperoni and tomato sauce could be served on any type of pasta.

Serves 4
1 red (bell) pepper
1 green (bell) pepper
30ml/2 tbsp olive oil, plus extra
   for tossing the pasta
1 onion, chopped
800g/1¾ lb canned chopped
   tomatoes
30ml/2 tbsp tomato purée
   (paste)
10ml/2 tsp paprika
175g/6oz pepperoni or chorizo
45ml/3 tbsp chopped fresh
   parsley
450g/1lb/4 cups dried long pasta
   spirals
salt and ground black pepper

1 Cut the peppers in half, then remove the seeds and cores. Cut the flesh into dice.

2 Heat the oil in a pan, add the onion and cook for about 2 minutes, until beginning to colour. Stir in the peppers, tomatoes, tomato purée and paprika, then bring to the boil and simmer uncovered for 15–20 minutes, until the sauce is reduced and thickened.

3 Slice the sausage and stir into the sauce with about half the chopped parsley. Season to taste with salt and pepper and continue to simmer until the sausage is cooked through.

4 While the sauce is simmering, cook the pasta in plenty of lightly salted boiling water until *al dente*. Drain well.

5 Toss the pasta with the remaining parsley mixed with a little extra olive oil. Divide the pasta among warmed bowls and top with the sauce. Serve immediately.

Cook's Tip
All types of sausage are suitable to include in this dish. If using fresh, raw sausages, cook them first, then cut up and add to the sauce, or cook thoroughly with the onion in step 2.

Tomatoes & Rocket Energy 483kcal/2044kJ; Protein 14.8g; Carbohydrate 87.2g, of which sugars 7.5g; Fat 10.8g, of which saturates 1.5g; Cholesterol 0mg; Calcium 68mg; Fibre 4.8g; Sodium 40mg.
Pasta Spirals Energy 610kcal/2579kJ; Protein 22.5g; Carbohydrate 100.4g, of which sugars 17.9g; Fat 16g, of which saturates 3.6g; Cholesterol 50mg; Calcium 87mg; Fibre 8g; Sodium 402mg.

Pasta Bows with Smoked Salmon

For a quick dish with a touch of luxury, this recipe is hard to beat – a divine combination of creamy smoked salmon sauce and pretty pasta shapes.

Serves 4
6 spring onions (scallions), sliced
50g/2oz/¼ cup butter
90ml/6 tbsp dry white wine or
   vermouth
450ml/¾ pint/scant 2 cups
   double (heavy) cream
a pinch of freshly grated nutmeg
225g/8oz smoked salmon
30ml/2 tbsp chopped fresh dill or
   15ml/1 tbsp dried dill
freshly squeezed lemon juice
450g/1lb/4 cups dried farfalle
salt and ground black pepper

1 Slice the spring onions finely. Melt the butter in a pan and fry the spring onions for about 1 minute until they begin to soften.

2 Add the wine or vermouth and boil hard to reduce to about 30ml/2 tbsp. Stir in the cream and add salt, pepper and nutmeg to taste. Bring to the boil and simmer for about 2–3 minutes, until slightly thickened.

3 Cut the smoked salmon into 2.5cm/1in squares and stir into the sauce with the dill. Taste and add a little lemon juice. Keep the sauce warm.

4 Bring a large pan of lightly salted water to the boil and cook the pasta until *al dente*. Drain well and toss with the sauce.

Cook's Tip
Smoked salmon trimmings are perfectly adequate for this dish.

Variation
This dish could also be prepared with canned salmon, broken into bitesize pieces, if you prefer.

Pasta with Tuna & Capers

A piquant sauce of tuna, capers, anchovies and fresh basil combines brilliantly with pasta, creating an easy dish full of punchy flavours.

Serves 4
400g/14oz can tuna in oil
30ml/2 tbsp olive oil
2 garlic cloves, crushed
800g/1¾ lb canned chopped
   tomatoes
6 canned anchovy fillets, drained
30ml/2 tbsp capers in vinegar,
   drained
30ml/2 tbsp chopped fresh basil
450g/1lb/4 cups dried garganelle,
   penne or rigatoni
salt and ground black pepper
fresh basil sprigs, to garnish

1 Drain the oil from the tuna into a pan, add the olive oil and heat gently until it stops spitting.

2 Add the garlic and fry until golden. Stir in the tomatoes and simmer for 25 minutes until thickened.

3 Flake the tuna and cut the anchovies in half. Stir into the sauce with the capers and chopped basil. Season to taste with salt and pepper.

4 Bring a large pan of lightly salted water to the boil and cook the pasta until *al dente*. Drain well and toss with the sauce. Garnish with fresh basil sprigs and serve immediately.

Cook's Tip
Tubular pasta is particularly good with this sauce as the tasty bits get trapped in the tube cavities. Other hollow shapes, such as conchiglie (shells) and lumache (snails), will also work well.

Variation
This piquant sauce could be made without the addition of tomatoes – just heat the oil, add the other ingredients and heat through gently before tossing with the pasta.

Tuna & Capers Energy 666kcal/2817kJ; Protein 43.1g; Carbohydrate 89.6g, of which sugars 9.9g; Fat 17.6g, of which saturates 2.8g; Cholesterol 53mg; Calcium 68mg; Fibre 5.3g; Sodium 488mg.
Pasta Bows Energy 1144kcal/4770kJ; Protein 30g; Carbohydrate 86.5g, of which sugars 6.8g; Fat 75.3g, of which saturates 44.8g; Cholesterol 201mg; Calcium 104mg; Fibre 3.5g; Sodium 1165mg.

Pasta with Prawns & Feta Cheese

Pasta tubes tossed with fresh prawns and sharp-tasting feta cheese is a winning combination. Serve with a mixed salad for an impressive light meal.

Serves 4
450g/1lb/4 cups medium raw prawns (shrimp)

6 spring onions (scallions)
50g/2oz/4 tbsp butter
225g/8oz feta cheese
small bunch fresh chives
450g/1lb/4 cups dried penne, garganelle or rigatoni
salt and ground black pepper

1 Remove the heads from the prawns by twisting and pulling off. Peel the prawns and discard the shells. With a sharp knife, remove the black intestinal vein running down the back of larger prawns and discard. Chop the spring onions.

2 Melt the butter in a frying pan and cook the prawns until they turn pink, then add the spring onions and cook gently for a further 1 minute.

3 Cut the feta cheese into 1cm/½in dice. Stir the cheese into the prawn mixture and season to taste with pepper.

4 Cut the chives into 2.5cm/1in lengths and stir half into the prawn mixture.

5 Bring a large pan of lightly salted water to the boil and cook the pasta until *al dente*. Drain well, pile into a warmed serving dish and top with the sauce. Scatter with the remaining chives and serve immediately.

Cook's Tips
• *Substitute goat's cheese for the feta cheese if you like; prepare the dish in the same way.*
• *If raw prawns are unavailable, use cooked prawns but cook the spring onions first, then add the prawns to heat through.*

Tagliatelle with Prosciutto & Parmesan

Consisting of a few prime Italian ingredients, this pasta dish is simplicity itself to make yet tastes wonderful. Serve with a tomato salad and chunks of ciabatta.

Serves 4
115g/4oz prosciutto
450g/1lb tagliatelle
75g/3oz/6 tbsp butter
50g/2oz/½ cup grated Parmesan cheese
salt and ground black pepper
a few fresh sage leaves, to garnish

1 Cut the prosciutto into strips of the same width as the tagliatelle. Bring a large pan of lightly salted water to the boil and cook the tagliatelle until *al dente*.

2 Meanwhile, melt the butter gently in a pan, stir in the prosciutto strips and heat through over very gently heat, being careful not to let them colour.

3 Drain the tagliatelle well and pile into a warm serving dish. Sprinkle all the Parmesan cheese over the top.

4 Pour the buttery prosciutto over the top of the tagliatelle and Parmesan. Season well with pepper and garnish with the sage leaves.

Cook's Tips
• *Buy Parmesan cheese in a block and grate it yourself. The flavour is far superior to that of ready-grated Parmesan cheese.*
• *Prosciutto, the Italian cured ham, is available from Italian delicatessens and supermarkets. The famous Parma ham is a superior type, coming from the Parma region of Italy.*
• *Both fresh and dried tagliatelle are good with this sauce. For a change, use green spinach-flavoured tagliatelle, or try a mix of green and white ribbons – bundles of these are called* paglia e fieno, *which means "straw and hay" in Italian.*

Prawns & Feta Energy 707kcal/2980kJ; Protein 42.5g; Carbohydrate 84.7g, of which sugars 5.1g; Fat 24.4g, of which saturates 14.6g; Cholesterol 285mg; Calcium 328mg; Fibre 3.5g; Sodium 1104mg.
Tagliatelle Energy 612kcal/2576kJ; Protein 23.8g; Carbohydrate 83.8g, of which sugars 4.1g; Fat 22.5g, of which saturates 12.9g; Cholesterol 69mg; Calcium 184mg; Fibre 3.3g; Sodium 598mg.

Cannelloni al Forno

This recipe provides a lighter, healthier alternative to the usual beef-filled, béchamel-coated version.

Serves 4–6

450g/1lb boned chicken breast, skinned and cooked
225g/8oz mushrooms
2 garlic cloves, crushed
30ml/2 tbsp chopped fresh parsley
15ml/1 tbsp chopped fresh tarragon
1 egg, beaten
squeeze of lemon juice
12–18 cannelloni tubes
butter, for greasing
1 jar passata (bottled strained tomatoes)
50g/2oz/scant ¾ cup freshly grated Parmesan cheese
salt and ground black pepper
fresh parsley sprigs, to garnish

1 Preheat the oven to 200°C/400°F/Gas 6. Place the chicken in a food processor and blend until finely minced. Transfer to a bowl and set aside.

2 Place the mushrooms, garlic, parsley and tarragon in the food processor and blend until finely minced. Beat the mushroom mixture into the chicken with the egg, and season with salt and pepper and lemon juice to taste.

3 Bring a large pan of lightly salted water to the boil and cook the cannelloni until *al dente*. Drain well on a clean dish towel.

4 Place the filling in a piping bag fitted with a large plain nozzle. Use this to fill each tube of cannelloni.

5 Lay the filled cannelloni tightly together in a single layer in a buttered shallow ovenproof dish. Spoon over the passata and sprinkle with Parmesan cheese. Bake in the oven for 30 minutes or until brown and bubbling. Garnish with sprigs of parsley.

> **Cook's Tip**
> *Passata is sieved (strained) ripe tomatoes and is a convenient store-cupboard item. It is available from larger supermarkets.*

Fettuccine all'Alfredo

A classic from Rome, this dish is simply pasta tossed with cream, butter and freshly grated Parmesan cheese. It makes a great supper dish, served with a crisp green salad to cut through the richness.

Serves 4

25g/1oz/2 tbsp butter
150ml/¼ pint/⅔ cup double (heavy) cream, plus 60ml/4 tbsp extra
450g/1lb dried fettuccine
50g/2oz/scant ¾ cup freshly grated Parmesan cheese, plus extra to serve
pinch of freshly grated nutmeg
salt and ground black pepper

1 Place the butter and 150ml/¼ pint/⅔ cup cream in a heavy pan. Bring to the boil, then simmer for 1 minute until the mixture has slightly thickened.

2 Bring a large pan of lightly salted water to the boil and cook the fettuccine until it is *al dente* – it should still be a little firm to the bite.

3 Drain the pasta very thoroughly and return to the pan with the cream sauce.

4 Place the pan on the heat and turn the pasta in the sauce to coat it evenly.

5 Add the remaining cream, the Parmesan cheese, salt and pepper to taste and a little grated nutmeg. Toss until well coated and heated through. Serve immediately with some extra grated Parmesan cheese sprinkled on top.

> **Variations**
> *For a little extra colour, fresh or frozen peas make an attractive addition to the sauce. You could also try stirring in thin strips of ham if you are not catering for vegetarians. The fettuccine ribbons can be replaced by spaghetti very successfully.*

Cannelloni Energy 375kcal/1589kJ; Protein 31.8g; Carbohydrate 51.8g, of which sugars 4.5g; Fat 6g, of which saturates 2.4g; Cholesterol 93mg; Calcium 151mg; Fibre 3.2g; Sodium 308mg.
Fettuccine Energy 674kcal/2830kJ; Protein 19.1g; Carbohydrate 84g, of which sugars 4.4g; Fat 31.4g, of which saturates 18.6g; Cholesterol 77mg; Calcium 198mg; Fibre 3.3g; Sodium 186mg.

Broccoli & Ricotta Cannelloni

Delicious vegetable-filled cannelloni baked in tomato.

Serves 4
60ml/4 tbsp olive oil, plus extra
 for brushing
12 dried cannelloni tubes
450g/1lb/4 cups broccoli florets
75g/3oz/1½ cups fresh
 breadcrumbs
150ml/¼ pint/⅔ cup milk
225g/8oz/1 cup ricotta cheese
pinch of freshly grated nutmeg

90ml/6 tbsp grated Parmesan
30ml/2 tbsp pine nuts
salt and ground black pepper

For the tomato sauce
30ml/2 tbsp olive oil
1 onion, finely chopped
1 garlic clove, crushed
2 x 400g/14oz cans chopped
 Italian plum tomatoes
15ml/1 tbsp tomato purée (paste)
4 black olives, pitted and chopped
5ml/1 tsp dried thyme

1 Preheat the oven to 190°C/375°F/Gas 5 and lightly grease an ovenproof dish with olive oil. Bring a large pan of water to the boil, add a little olive oil and simmer the cannelloni tubes, uncovered, for about 6–7 minutes, or until nearly cooked.

2 Meanwhile, steam or boil the broccoli for 10 minutes, until tender. Drain the pasta, rinse under cold water and reserve. Drain the broccoli and leave to cool, then place in a blender or food processor and process until smooth. Set aside.

3 Place the breadcrumbs in a bowl, add the milk and oil and stir until softened. Add the ricotta, broccoli purée, nutmeg, 60ml/4 tbsp of the Parmesan cheese and seasoning; set aside.

4 To make the sauce, heat the oil in a frying pan, add the onion and garlic and fry for 5–6 minutes, until softened but not brown. Stir in the tomatoes, tomato purée, black olives, thyme and seasoning. Boil rapidly for 2–3 minutes, then pour into the dish.

5 Spoon the cheese mixture into a piping bag fitted with a 1cm/½in nozzle. Standing each cannelloni tube upright on a board, pipe the filling into each tube. Lay in rows in the tomato sauce. Brush the tops with oil and sprinkle with the remaining Parmesan and pine nuts. Bake for 25–30 minutes until golden.

Cannelloni with Mixed Vegetables

This version of the classic beef-filled cannelloni introduces a variety of vegetables topped with cheese sauce.

Serves 4
8 dried cannelloni tubes
115g/4oz spinach
tomatoes and green salad,
 to serve (optional)

For the filling
15ml/1 tbsp oil
175g/6oz/¾ cup minced
 (ground) beef

2 garlic cloves, crushed
25g/1oz/¼ cup plain
 (all-purpose) flour
120ml/4fl oz/½ cup beef stock
1 small carrot, finely chopped
1 small yellow courgette
 (zucchini), chopped
salt and ground black pepper

For the sauce
25g/1oz/2 tbsp butter
25g/1oz/¼ cup plain
 (all-purpose) flour
250ml/8fl oz/1 cup milk
50g/2oz/⅔ cup freshly grated
 Parmesan cheese

1 Preheat the oven to 180°C/350°F/Gas 4. To make the filling, heat the oil in a large pan. Add the minced beef and garlic, and cook for 5 minutes, stirring frequently.

2 Add the flour and cook for a further 1 minute. Slowly stir in the stock and bring to the boil, stirring. Add the carrot and courgette and season with salt and pepper to taste. Cook over medium heat for 10 minutes.

3 Carefully spoon the beef mixture into the cannelloni tubes and arrange in an ovenproof dish.

4 Blanch the spinach in boiling water for 3 minutes. Drain well and place on top of the cannelloni tubes in the dish.

5 To make the sauce, melt the butter in a pan. Add the flour and cook for 1 minute. Stir in the milk and cook, stirring, until smooth and thick. Add the grated cheese and season well.

6 Pour the sauce over the cannelloni and spinach and bake for 30 minutes. Serve with tomatoes and a green salad, if liked.

Mixed Energy 491kcal/2062kJ; Protein 24.7g; Carbohydrate 52.6g, of which sugars 7.5g; Fat 21.7g, of which saturates 10.2g; Cholesterol 56mg; Calcium 326mg; Fibre 3.1g; Sodium 283mg.
Broccoli Energy 733kcal/3074kJ; Protein 31.8g; Carbohydrate 74.3g, of which sugars 15.3g; Fat 36.3g, of which saturates 13.1g; Cholesterol 48mg; Calcium 440mg; Fibre 7.6g; Sodium 555mg.

Smoked Trout Cannelloni

The smoked trout filling gives this cannelloni dish a deliciously different taste.

Serves 4–6

1 large onion, finely chopped
1 garlic clove, crushed
60ml/4 tbsp vegetable stock
2 x 400g/14oz cans chopped
   Italian plum tomatoes
2.5ml/½ tsp dried mixed herbs
1 smoked trout, about
   400g/14oz, or 225g/8oz fillets
75g/3oz/¾ cup frozen
   peas, thawed

75g/3oz/1½ cups fresh
   breadcrumbs
16 cannelloni tubes
salt and ground black pepper
25ml/1½ tbsp freshly grated
   Parmesan cheese

For the cheese sauce

25g/1oz/2 tbsp butter
25g/1oz/¼ cup plain
   (all-purpose) flour
350ml/12fl oz/1½ cups
   skimmed milk
freshly grated nutmeg

1 Simmer the onion, garlic and stock in a large covered pan for 3 minutes. Uncover and continue to cook, stirring the mixture occasionally, until the stock has reduced entirely.

2 Stir the tomatoes and herbs into the onion mixture. Simmer, uncovered, for a further 10 minutes, until very thick.

3 Meanwhile, skin the smoked trout. Carefully flake the flesh and discard the bones. Mix the fish together with the tomato mixture, peas, breadcrumbs, salt and ground black pepper.

4 Preheat the oven to 190°C/375°F/Gas 5. Spoon the filling into the cannelloni tubes and arrange them side by side in a lightly greased ovenproof dish.

5 To make the sauce, melt the butter in a pan, add the flour and cook for 2–3 minutes, whisking constantly. Pour in the milk and bring to the boil, whisking, until the sauce thickens. Simmer for 2–3 minutes, stirring. Season with salt, pepper and nutmeg.

6 Pour the sauce over the cannelloni and sprinkle with the Parmesan. Bake in the oven for 35–40 minutes, until golden.

Tuna Lasagne

Two popular Italian ingredients, tuna and pasta, combine to make a tasty lasagne that is sure to be a big hit with all the family.

Serves 6

12–16 fresh or dried
   lasagne sheets
15g/½oz butter
1 small onion, finely chopped
1 garlic clove, finely chopped
115g/4oz mushrooms,
   thinly sliced
60ml/4 tbsp dry white
   wine (optional)

600ml/1 pint/2½ cups cheese
   sauce (see Smoked
   Trout Cannelloni)
150ml/¼ pint/⅔ cup whipping
   cream
45ml/3 tbsp fresh
   parsley, chopped
2 x 200g/7oz cans tuna, drained
2 canned pimientos, cut into strips
65g/2½oz/generous ½ cup
   frozen peas, thawed
115g/4oz mozzarella
   cheese, grated
30ml/2 tbsp freshly grated
   Parmesan cheese
salt and ground black pepper

1 For fresh lasagne, cook in a pan of salted boiling water until *al dente*. For dried, soak in a bowl of hot water for 3–5 minutes. Place the lasagne in a colander and rinse with cold water. Lay on a dish towel to drain.

2 Preheat the oven to 180°C/350°F/Gas 4. Melt the butter in a pan and cook the onion until soft.

3 Add the garlic and mushrooms to the pan and cook until soft, stirring occasionally. Pour in the wine, if using. Boil for 1 minute, then stir in the white sauce, cream and parsley. Season.

4 Spoon a thin layer of sauce over the base of a 30 x 23cm/ 12 x 9in baking dish. Cover with a layer of lasagne sheets.

5 Flake the tuna. Scatter half the tuna, pimiento strips, peas and mozzarella over the lasagne. Spoon one-third of the remaining sauce over the top and cover with another layer of lasagne.

6 Repeat the layers, ending with pasta and sauce. Sprinkle with the Parmesan. Bake for 30–40 minutes, or until lightly browned.

Trout Energy 410kcal/1735kJ; Protein 23.4g; Carbohydrate 62.3g, of which sugars 12g; Fat 9.3g, of which saturates 2.1g; Cholesterol 21mg; Calcium 186mg; Fibre 4.5g; Sodium 919mg.
Tuna Energy 653kcal/2744kJ; Protein 36.3g; Carbohydrate 69.1g, of which sugars 9.1g; Fat 27.7g, of which saturates 14g; Cholesterol 88mg; Calcium 313mg; Fibre 3.2g; Sodium 754mg.

Baked Tortellini with Three Cheeses

In this gloriously rich dish, stuffed pasta shapes are smothered in cheese and baked until meltingly tender. Bay leaves and basil add a delicate herbal touch to the finished dish. For the best balance of flavours, choose tortellini with a meat or vegetable filling.

Serves 4–6
450g/1lb fresh tortellini
2 eggs
350g/12oz/1½ cups ricotta or curd (farmer's) cheese
25g/1oz/2 tbsp butter
25g/1oz fresh basil leaves
115g/4oz smoked mozzarella cheese
60ml/4 tbsp freshly grated Parmesan cheese
salt and ground black pepper

1 Preheat the oven to 190°C/375°F/Gas 5. Bring a pan of lightly salted water to the boil, add the tortellini and cook until *al dente*. Drain well.

2 Beat the eggs with the ricotta or curd cheese and season well with salt and pepper.

3 Use the butter to grease an ovenproof dish. Spoon in half the tortellini, pour half the cheese mixture over and cover with half the basil leaves.

4 Cover with the mozzarella and remaining basil. Top with the rest of the tortellini and spread the remaining ricotta or curd cheese mixture over.

5 Sprinkle evenly with the Parmesan cheese. Bake in the oven for 35–45 minutes, or until golden brown and bubbling.

> **Cook's Tip**
> If smoked mozzarella cheese is not available, try using a smoked German cheese or even grated smoked Cheddar as an alternative. Grated mature Cheddar cheese can also be used instead of some of the grated Parmesan.

Lasagne with Three Cheeses

This rich lasagne was invented in the United States by Italian immigrants who made use of the abundant ingredients available to them.

Serves 6–8
25g/1oz/2 tbsp butter
15ml/1 tbsp olive oil
225–250g/8–9oz/2–2¼ cups button mushrooms, quartered
30ml/2 tbsp chopped fresh flat leaf parsley
1 quantity Classic Bolognese Sauce (see page 10)

250–350ml/8–12fl oz/1–1½ cups hot beef stock
9–12 fresh lasagne sheets, pre-cooked if necessary
450g/1lb/2 cups ricotta cheese
1 large (US extra large) egg
3 x 130g/4½oz packets mozzarella cheese, drained and thinly sliced
115g/4oz/1¼ cups freshly grated Parmesan cheese
salt and ground black pepper

1 Preheat the oven to 190°C/375°F/Gas 5. Melt the butter in the oil in a frying pan. Add the mushrooms, with salt and pepper to taste, and toss over medium to high heat for 5–8 minutes, until the mushrooms are tender and quite dry. Remove the pan from the heat and stir in the parsley.

2 Heat the Bolognese Sauce and stir in enough hot beef stock to make the sauce quite runny. Stir in the mushroom and parsley mixture, then spread about a quarter of this sauce over the bottom of a baking dish. Cover with 3–4 sheets of lasagne.

3 Beat together the ricotta and egg in a bowl, with salt and pepper to taste, then spread about a third of the mixture over the lasagne sheets. Cover with a third of the mozzarella slices, then sprinkle with about a quarter of the grated Parmesan.

4 Repeat these layers twice, using half the remaining meat sauce each time, and finishing with the remaining Parmesan.

5 Bake the lasagne for 30–40 minutes, or until the cheese topping is golden brown and bubbling. Allow to stand for about 10 minutes before serving.

Tortellini Energy 484kcal/2034kJ; Protein 27.3g; Carbohydrate 57.7g, of which sugars 4.5g; Fat 18.5g, of which saturates 10.6g; Cholesterol 107mg; Calcium 286mg; Fibre 2.2g; Sodium 491mg.
Lasagne Energy 533kcal/2226kJ; Protein 32.5g; Carbohydrate 29.7g, of which sugars 3.1g; Fat 32.4g, of which saturates 18.7g; Cholesterol 121mg; Calcium 370mg; Fibre 1.4g; Sodium 402mg.

Shellfish Lasagne

This is a luxury lasagne with a superb flavour.

Serves 4–6

4–6 fresh scallops, shelled
450g/1lb raw large peeled
  prawns (shrimp)
1 garlic clove, crushed
75g/3oz/6 tbsp butter
50g/2oz/1/2 cup plain (all-
  purpose) flour
600ml/1 pint/2 1/2 cups hot milk
100ml/3 1/2fl oz/scant 1/2 cup
  double (heavy) cream

100ml/3 1/2fl oz/scant 1/2 cup dry
  white wine
2 sachets saffron powder
good pinch of cayenne pepper
130g/4 1/2oz Fontina cheese,
  thinly sliced
75g/3oz/1 cup freshly grated
  Parmesan cheese
6–8 fresh lasagne sheets, pre-
  cooked if necessary
salt and ground black pepper

1 Preheat the oven to 190°C/375°F/Gas 5. Cut the scallops, their corals and the prawns into bite-size pieces and spread in a dish. Sprinkle with the garlic and salt and pepper to taste. Melt a third of the butter in a medium pan, add the scallops, corals and prawns and toss over medium heat for 1–2 minutes, or just until the prawns turn pink. Remove with a slotted spoon.

2 Add the remaining butter to the pan and melt over low heat. Sprinkle in the flour and cook, stirring, for 1–2 minutes, then increase the heat to medium and add the hot milk a little at a time, whisking vigorously after each addition. Bring to the boil and cook, stirring, until the sauce is smooth and very thick. Whisk in the cream, wine, saffron powder, cayenne and salt and pepper to taste, then remove the sauce from the heat.

3 Spread about a third of the sauce in a baking dish. Arrange half the Fontina slices over the sauce and sprinkle with about a third of the grated Parmesan. Scatter about half the shellfish evenly on top, then cover with half the lasagne sheets. Repeat the layers, then cover with the remaining sauce and Parmesan.

4 Bake the lasagne for 30–40 minutes, or until golden brown and bubbling. Allow to stand for 10 minutes before serving.

Cannelloni with Tuna

Children love this pasta dish. Fontina cheese has a sweet, nutty flavour and very good melting qualities. Look for it in large supermarkets and Italian delicatessens.

Serves 4–6

50g/2oz/1/4 cup butter
50g/2oz/1/2 cup plain (all-
  purpose) flour

about 900ml/1 1/2 pints/3 3/4 cups
  hot milk
2 x 200g/7oz cans tuna, drained
115g/4oz/1 cup grated Fontina
  cheese
1.5ml/1/4 tsp grated nutmeg
12 no pre-cook cannelloni tubes
50g/2oz/2/3 cup freshly grated
  Parmesan cheese
salt and ground black pepper
fresh herbs, to garnish

1 Melt the butter in a heavy pan, add the flour and stir over low heat for 1–2 minutes. Remove the pan from the heat and gradually add 350 ml/12 fl oz/1 1/2 cups of the milk, beating vigorously after each addition. Return the pan to the heat and whisk for 1–2 minutes, until the sauce is very thick and smooth. Remove from the heat.

2 Mix the drained tuna with about 120 ml/4 fl oz/1/2 cup of the warm white sauce in a bowl. Add salt and black pepper to taste. Preheat the oven to 180°C/350°F/Gas 4.

3 Gradually whisk the remaining milk into the rest of the sauce, return to the heat and simmer, whisking, until thickened. Add the grated Fontina and nutmeg, and season with salt and pepper to taste. Simmer for a few minutes, stirring frequently. Pour one-third of the sauce into a baking dish.

4 Fill the cannelloni tubes with the tuna mixture, pushing it in with the handle of a teaspoon. Place the cannelloni in a single layer in the dish. Thin the remaining sauce with a little more milk if necessary, then pour it over the cannelloni.

5 Sprinkle the sauce with freshly grated Parmesan cheese and bake for 30 minutes, or until the top is golden. Serve immediately, garnished with herbs.

Tuna Energy 502kcal/2110kJ; Protein 32.2g; Carbohydrate 44.3g, of which sugars 2.6g; Fat 22.7g, of which saturates 11.4g; Cholesterol 76mg; Calcium 293mg; Fibre 1.7g; Sodium 467mg.
Shellfish Energy 638kcal/2670kJ; Protein 43.8g; Carbohydrate 38.1g, of which sugars 6.4g; Fat 34g, of which saturates 20.8g; Cholesterol 259mg; Calcium 536mg; Fibre 1.2g; Sodium 650mg.

Onion & Gorgonzola Pizzas

These small pizzas are good for snacks or party food.

Serves 4
1 quantity Basic Pizza Dough (see below)
30ml/2 tbsp garlic oil

2 small red onions
150g/5oz Gorgonzola cheese, rind removed and diced
2 garlic cloves, cut into strips lengthways
10ml/2 tsp chopped fresh sage
pinch of black pepper

1 Preheat the oven to 220°C/425°F/Gas 7. Divide the dough into eight pieces and roll out to small ovals about 5mm/¼in thick. Place well apart on two greased baking sheets and prick with a fork. Brush well with 15ml/1 tbsp of the garlic oil.

2 Halve, then slice the onions into thin wedges. Scatter over the pizza bases. Sprinkle with the cheese, then the garlic and sage. Drizzle the remaining oil on top and grind over plenty of pepper. Bake for 10–15 minutes until crisp and golden.

Basic Pizza Dough

Making your own pizza base is easy – and it tastes great.

Makes one 25–30cm/ 10–12in round pizza base
175g/6oz/1½ cups strong white flour

1.25ml/¼ tsp salt
5ml/1 tsp easy-blend (rapid-rise) dried yeast
120–150ml/4–5fl oz/½–¾ cup lukewarm water
15ml/1 tbsp olive oil

1 Sift the flour and salt into a large mixing bowl and stir in the yeast. Make a well in the centre and pour in the water and oil. Mix to a soft dough. Knead the dough on a lightly floured board for 10 minutes until smooth and elastic.

2 Place in a greased bowl, cover with clear film (plastic wrap) and leave to double in size for about 1 hour. Turn out on to a floured surface; knead gently for 2–3 minutes. Use as required.

Feta & Roasted Garlic Pizzettes

These pizzettes are for garlic lovers. Mash down the cloves as you eat them – they should be meltingly soft and sweet-tasting.

Serves 4
1 garlic bulb, unpeeled
45ml/3 tbsp olive oil
1 red (bell) pepper, seeded and quartered

1 yellow (bell) pepper, seeded and quartered
2 plum tomatoes
1 quantity Basic Pizza Dough (see below left)
175g/6oz/1½ cups crumbled feta cheese
pinch of black pepper
15–30ml/1–2 tbsp chopped fresh oregano, to garnish

1 Preheat the oven to 220°C/425°F/Gas 7. Break the garlic into cloves, discarding the outer papery layers. Toss in 15ml/1 tbsp of the olive oil.

2 Place the peppers skin-side up on a baking sheet and grill (broil), turning them until the skins are evenly charred. Place in a covered bowl for 10 minutes, then peel off the skins. Cut the flesh into strips.

3 Make a slash in the skin of each tomato, then put them in a bowl and pour over boiling water. Leave for 30 seconds, then plunge into cold water. Peel, seed and roughly chop the flesh.

4 Divide the pizza dough into four pieces and roll out each one on a lightly floured surface to an equal-sized circle of about 13cm/5in diameter. Place the dough circles well apart on two greased baking sheets, then push up the dough edges to form a thin rim around the dough circles.

5 Brush the dough circles with half the remaining oil and scatter over the chopped tomatoes. Top with the peppers, crumbled feta cheese and garlic cloves. Drizzle over the remaining oil and season to taste with pepper.

6 Bake in the oven for 15–20 minutes until crisp and golden. Garnish with chopped oregano and serve immediately.

Mussel & Leek Pizzas

Serve these lovely little seafood pizzas with a crisp green salad for a light lunch.

Serves 4
450g/1lb live mussels in the shell
120ml/4fl oz/1/2 cup dry white wine
1 quantity Basic Pizza Dough (see page 158)
15ml/1 tbsp olive oil
50g/2oz Gruyère cheese
50g/2oz mozzarella cheese
2 small leeks, thinly sliced
salt and ground black pepper

1 Preheat the oven to 220°C/425°F/Gas 7. Place the mussels in a bowl of cold water to soak, then scrub well. Remove the beards, and discard any mussels that are open.

2 Place the mussels in a pan. Pour over the dry white wine, cover with a tight-fitting lid and cook over high heat, shaking the pan occasionally, for 5–10 minutes until the mussels open.

3 Drain off the cooking liquid. Remove the mussels from their shells, discarding any that remain closed. Leave to cool.

4 Divide the dough into four pieces and roll out each one on a lightly floured surface to a 13cm/5in circle. Place well apart on two greased baking sheets, then push up the dough edges to form a thin rim around the dough circles.

5 Brush the pizza bases with the oil. Grate the cheeses and sprinkle half evenly over the bases. Arrange the leeks over the cheese. Bake for 10 minutes, then remove from the oven.

6 Arrange the mussels on top. Season with salt and pepper and sprinkle over the remaining cheese. Bake for a further 5–10 minutes until crisp and golden. Serve immediately.

Cook's Tip
Frozen or canned mussels can also be used but will give a different flavour and texture to these pizzettes.

Wild Mushroom Pizzas

With their delicate earthy flavour, wild mushrooms make a delicious topping for these little pizzas. Serve as an unusual starter or for a stylish light meal.

Serves 4
45ml/3 tbsp olive oil
350g/12oz fresh mixed wild mushrooms, washed and sliced
2 shallots, chopped
2 garlic cloves, finely chopped
30ml/2 tbsp chopped fresh mixed thyme and flat leaf parsley
1 quantity Basic Pizza Dough (see page 158)
40g/1½ oz/generous ¼ cup grated Gruyère cheese
30ml/2 tbsp freshly grated Parmesan cheese
salt and ground black pepper

1 Preheat the oven to 220°C/425°F/Gas 7. Heat 30ml/2 tbsp of the oil in a frying pan and fry the mushrooms, shallots and garlic over medium heat, stirring occasionally, until all the juices have evaporated.

2 Stir in half the herbs and season with salt and pepper then set aside to cool.

3 Divide the dough into four pieces and roll out each one on a lightly floured surface to a 13cm/5in circle. Place well apart on two greased baking sheets, then push up the dough edges to form a thin rim around the dough circles.

4 Brush the pizza bases with the remaining oil and spoon the wild mushrooms on top. Mix together the Gruyère and Parmesan, then sprinkle over the mushroom mixture.

5 Bake the pizza for 15–20 minutes until crisp and golden. Remove from the oven and scatter over the remaining herbs.

Cook's Tip
Fresh wild mushrooms add a distinctive flavour to the topping, but if they are unavailable, a mixture of cultivated mushrooms, such as shiitake, oyster and chestnut, would do just as well.

Mussel & Leek Energy 343kcal/1441kJ; Protein 16.3g; Carbohydrate 35.6g, of which sugars 2g; Fat 13.6g, of which saturates 5.5g; Cholesterol 33mg; Calcium 280mg; Fibre 2.5g; Sodium 214mg.
Mushroom Energy 340kcal/1425kJ; Protein 11.4g; Carbohydrate 35.6g, of which sugars 1.7g; Fat 17.8g, of which saturates 5.5g; Cholesterol 17mg; Calcium 234mg; Fibre 2.5g; Sodium 160mg.

Ham, Pepper & Mozzarella Pizzas

Succulent roasted peppers, salty proscuitto and creamy mozzarella make a delicious topping for these pizzas.

Serves 2

1 red (bell) pepper
1 yellow (bell) pepper
4 thick slices ciabatta bread
4 slices proscuitto, cut into thick strips
75g/3oz mozzarella cheese
ground black pepper
tiny fresh basil leaves, to garnish

1 Place the peppers skin-side up on a baking sheet and grill (broil), turning them until the skins are evenly charred. Place in a bowl, cover with a cloth and leave for 10 minutes. Peel the skins from the peppers and remove the seeds and cores. Cut the flesh into thick strips.

2 Lightly toast the slices of ciabatta bread on both sides until they are golden.

3 Arrange the strips of pepper on the toasted bread with the strips of proscuitto.

4 Thinly slice the mozzarella and arrange on top. Grind over plenty of pepper. Place under a hot grill (broiler) for 2–3 minutes until the cheese is bubbling.

5 Garnish each pizza with basil leaves and serve immediately.

> **Cook's Tip**
> For added flavour, cut a garlic clove in half and rub the cut side over the toasted bread before adding the topping.

> **Variation**
> Try using pieces of sun-dried tomato in oil instead of the peppers and use Emmenthal cheese instead of mozzarella.

Fruity French Bread Pizza

Using a base of French bread, these pizzas are quick and easy to make. Perfect for all the family.

Serves 4

2 small baguettes
1 jar ready-made tomato sauce or pizza topping
75g/3oz sliced cooked ham
4 rings canned pineapple, drained and chopped
½ small green (bell) pepper, seeded and cut into thin strips
75g/3oz mature Cheddar cheese
salt and ground black pepper

1 Preheat the oven to 200°C/400°F/Gas 6. Cut the baguettes in half lengthways and toast the outsides under a grill (broiler) until crisp and golden.

2 Spread the tomato sauce or pizza topping over the toasted baguette halves.

3 Cut the ham into strips and arrange on the baguettes with the pineapple and pepper. Season with salt and pepper.

4 Grate the Cheddar and sprinkle over the top of the pineapple and pepper. Bake in the oven for 15–20 minutes until crisp and golden. Serve immediately.

> **Cook's Tip**
> These pizzas may be grilled (broiled) instead of baked in the oven. Cook them for the same length of time under a medium grill (broiler) but check that they do not burn.

> **Variation**
> If you have time, make your own tomato sauce. Soften a sliced garlic clove and small onion in olive oil. Add a handful of herbs and 400g/14oz can tomatoes with 15ml/1 tbsp sun-dried tomato paste and a splash of wine. Simmer for 30 minutes.

Ham, Pepper Energy 466kcal/1965kJ; Protein 26.3g; Carbohydrate 63.6g, of which sugars 14.2g; Fat 13.6g, of which saturates 6.4g; Cholesterol 45mg; Calcium 274mg; Fibre 5.1g; Sodium 1173mg.
French Bread Energy 420kcal/1779kJ; Protein 18.3g; Carbohydrate 67.4g, of which sugars 13g; Fat 10.1g, of which saturates 5.1g; Cholesterol 31mg; Calcium 281mg; Fibre 4g; Sodium 1056mg.

Marinara Pizza

The combination of garlic, good quality olive oil and oregano gives this pizza an unmistakably Italian flavour.

Serves 2–3

1 quantity Basic Pizza Dough
  (see page 158)

675g/1½ lb ripe plum tomatoes
60ml/4 tbsp extra virgin olive oil
4 garlic cloves, cut into slivers
15ml/1 tbsp chopped fresh
  oregano
salt and ground black pepper

1 Roll out the pizza dough to a 25–30cm/10–12in circle and place on a greased baking sheet. Push up the edge of the dough to form a thin rim around the dough circle.

2 Make a slash in the skin of each tomato, then put them all in a heatproof bowl and pour over boiling water. Leave for 30 seconds, then plunge the tomatoes into cold water. Peel and seed, then roughly chop the flesh.

3 Preheat the oven to 220°C/425°F/Gas 7. Heat 30ml/2 tbsp of the oil in a pan. Add the tomatoes and cook, stirring frequently, for about 5 minutes until soft.

4 Place the tomatoes in a metal sieve (strainer) and leave them to drain for about 5 minutes. Transfer the tomatoes to a food processor or blender and purée until smooth.

5 Brush the pizza base with half the remaining oil. Spoon over the tomatoes and sprinkle with garlic and oregano. Drizzle over the remaining oil and season to taste.

6 Bake for 15–20 minutes until crisp. Serve immediately.

> **Cook's Tip**
> Ready-made pizza bases are handy if you are short of time. They are available from most supermarkets and come in a range of sizes. It is useful to keep a few in the freezer.

Quattro Formaggi

Rich and cheesy, these individual pizzas are quick to make, and the aroma of melting cheese is irresistible.

Serves 4

1 quantity Basic Pizza Dough
  (see page 158)
15ml/1 tbsp garlic oil
½ small red onion, very thinly
  sliced

50g/2oz Dolcelatte cheese
50g/2oz mozzarella cheese
50g/2oz/½ cup grated Gruyère
  cheese
30ml/2 tbsp freshly grated
  Parmesan cheese
15ml/1 tbsp chopped fresh thyme
ground black pepper

1 Preheat the oven to 220°C/425°F/Gas 7. Divide the dough into four pieces and roll out each one on a lightly floured surface into a 13cm/5in circle. Place well apart on two greased baking sheets, then push up the dough edges to make a thin rim. Brush with garlic oil and top with the red onion.

2 Cut the Dolcelatte and mozzarella cheeses into dice and arrange over the bases. Mix together the Gruyère, Parmesan and thyme and sprinkle over the pizzas.

3 Grind plenty of pepper over the pizzas. Bake for 15–20 minutes until the base is crisp and golden and the cheeses are bubbling. Serve immediately.

> **Cook's Tip**
> To make garlic oil, put 3–4 peeled garlic cloves in a jar and pour in 120ml/4fl oz/½ cup olive oil. Cover tightly and store in the refrigerator for up to 1 month.

> **Variation**
> Any variety of cheese that melts readily can be used, but a mixture of soft and hard cheeses gives the best result.

Marinara Energy 415kcal/1742kJ; Protein 8.1g; Carbohydrate 54.5g, of which sugars 8.1g; Fat 19.8g, of which saturates 3g; Cholesterol 0mg; Calcium 100mg; Fibre 4.6g; Sodium 23mg.
Formaggi Energy 397kcal/1661kJ; Protein 14.6g; Carbohydrate 39.7g, of which sugars 3.9g; Fat 20.8g, of which saturates 9.3g; Cholesterol 37mg; Calcium 283mg; Fibre 2.3g; Sodium 405mg.

Rocket & Tomato Pizza

Peppery rocket leaves and aromatic basil add colour and flavour to this pizza.

Serves 2

10ml/2 tsp olive oil, plus extra
    for oiling and drizzling
1 garlic clove, crushed
150g/5oz/1 cup canned chopped
    tomatoes
2.5ml/½ tsp sugar
30ml/2 tbsp torn basil leaves
2 tomatoes, seeded and chopped

150g/5oz/⅔ cup mozzarella
    cheese, sliced
20g/¾oz/1 cup rocket leaves
rock salt and ground black pepper

For the pizza base

225g/8oz/2 cups strong white
    bread flour, sifted
5ml/1 tsp salt
2.5ml/½ tsp easy-blend
    (rapid-rise) dried yeast
15ml/1 tbsp olive oil
150ml/¼ pint/⅔ cup warm water

1 To make the pizza base, place the flour, salt and yeast in a bowl. Make a well in the centre and add the oil and warm water. Mix to form a soft dough.

2 Turn out the dough on to a lightly floured work surface and knead for 5 minutes. Cover with the upturned bowl and leave to rest for about 5 minutes, then knead for a further 5 minutes until the dough is smooth and elastic. Place in a lightly oiled bowl and cover with clear film (plastic wrap). Leave in a warm place for about 45 minutes until doubled in size.

3 Preheat the oven to 220°C/425°F/Gas 7. To make the topping, heat the oil in a frying pan and fry the garlic for 1 minute. Add the tomatoes and sugar and cook for 5–7 minutes until reduced and thickened. Stir in the basil and season to taste with salt and pepper. Set aside.

4 Knead the risen dough lightly, then roll out to form a rough 30cm/12in round. Place on a lightly oiled baking sheet and push up the edges of the dough to form a shallow, even rim. Spoon the tomato mixture over the pizza base, then top with the fresh tomatoes and mozzarella. Adjust the seasoning and drizzle with a little olive oil. Bake for 10–12 minutes until crisp and golden. Arrange the rocket over the pizza just before serving.

Four Seasons Pizza

The topping on this pizza is divided into four quarters, one for each "season", creating a colourful effect.

Serves 4

450g/1lb peeled plum tomatoes,
    weighed whole (or canned
    without their juice)
75ml/5 tbsp olive oil
115g/4oz mushrooms, thinly
    sliced
1 garlic clove, finely chopped

1 quantity Basic Pizza Dough
    (see page 158)
350g/12oz/scant 2½ cups diced
    mozzarella cheese
4 thin slices of ham, cut into
    5cm/2in squares
32 black olives, pitted and halved
8 artichoke hearts, preserved in
    oil, drained and cut in half
5ml/1 tsp oregano leaves, fresh or
    dried
salt and ground black pepper

1 Preheat the oven to 240°C/475°F/Gas 9 for at least 20 minutes before baking the pizza. Strain the tomatoes through the medium holes of a food mill placed over a bowl, scraping in all the pulp.

2 Heat 30ml/2 tbsp of the oil in a pan and lightly sauté the mushrooms. Stir in the garlic and set aside.

3 Roll out the pizza dough to a 25–30cm/10–12in circle and place on a greased baking sheet. Push up the edge of the dough to form a thin rim around the dough circle.

4 Spread the puréed tomatoes on the prepared pizza dough, up to the rim. Sprinkle evenly with the mozzarella cheese. Spread the mushrooms over one quarter of the pizza.

5 Arrange the ham on one quarter and the olives on another quarter. Arrange the artichoke hearts on the remaining quarter.

6 Sprinkle the whole of the pizza with oregano and season with salt and pepper. Sprinkle over the remaining olive oil. Immediately place the pizza in the oven and bake for about 15–20 minutes, or until the crust is golden brown and the topping is bubbling.

Rocket Energy 735Kcal/3087kJ; Protein 26.1g; Carbohydrate 93g, of which sugars 7.3g; Fat 31.3g, of which saturates 12.7g; Cholesterol 44mg; Calcium 459mg; Fibre 5.5g; Sodium 330mg.
Four Seasons Energy 586kcal/2442kJ; Protein 24.3g; Carbohydrate 37.9g, of which sugars 4.5g; Fat 38.5g, of which saturates 15.2g; Cholesterol 58mg; Calcium 410mg; Fibre 3.7g; Sodium 1080mg.

Fiorentina Pizza

Fresh spinach is the star ingredient of this pizza. A grating of nutmeg heightens its flavour.

Serves 2–3

1 quantity Basic Pizza Dough
   (see page 158)
175g/6oz/1½ cups fresh spinach
45ml/3 tbsp olive oil
1 small red onion, thinly sliced
1 jar ready-made tomato sauce or pizza topping
pinch of freshly grated nutmeg
150g/5oz mozzarella cheese
1 egg
25g/1oz/¼ cup grated Gruyère cheese

1 Preheat the oven to 220°C/425°F/Gas 7. Roll out the pizza dough to a 25–30cm/10–12in circle and place on a greased baking sheet. Push up the edge of the dough to form a thin rim.

2 Remove the stalks from the spinach and wash the leaves in plenty of cold water. Drain well and pat dry with kitchen paper.

3 Heat 15ml/1 tbsp of the oil in a large frying pan and fry the onion until softened. Add the spinach and continue to fry until just wilted. Drain off any excess liquid.

4 Brush the pizza base with half the remaining oil. Spread over the tomato sauce or pizza topping, then top with the spinach mixture. Grate over some nutmeg.

5 Thinly slice the mozzarella cheese and arrange over the spinach. Drizzle over the remaining oil. Bake for 10 minutes, then remove from the oven.

6 Make a small well in the centre of the pizza and drop the egg into the hole. Sprinkle over the Gruyère and return to the oven for a further 5–10 minutes until crisp and golden.

> **Cook's Tip**
> The egg adds the finishing touch to this spinach pizza. Try not to overcook it, as it is best when the yolk is still slightly soft.

Chilli Beef Pizza

Minced beef and red kidney beans combined with oregano, cumin and chillies turn this pizza into a Mexican extravaganza.

Serves 4

1 quantity Basic Pizza Dough
   (see page 158)
30ml/2 tbsp olive oil
1 red onion, finely chopped
1 garlic clove, crushed
½ red (bell) pepper, seeded and finely chopped
175g/6oz/¾ cup lean minced (ground) beef
2.5ml/½ tsp ground cumin
2 fresh red chillies, seeded and chopped
115g/4oz/scant ½ cup (drained weight) canned red kidney beans, rinsed
1 jar ready-made tomato sauce or pizza topping
15ml/1 tbsp chopped fresh oregano
50g/2oz/½ cup grated mozzarella cheese
75g/3oz/¾ cup grated oak-smoked Cheddar cheese
salt and ground black pepper

1 Preheat the oven to 220°C/425°F/Gas 7. Roll out the pizza dough to a 25–30cm/10–12in circle and place on a greased baking sheet. Push up the edge of the dough to form a thin rim.

2 Heat 15ml/1 tbsp of the oil in a frying pan and gently fry the onion, garlic and pepper until soft. Increase the heat, add the beef and brown well, stirring constantly.

3 Add the cumin and chillies and continue to cook, stirring, for about 5 minutes. Add the kidney beans and season with salt and pepper. Remove from the heat.

4 Spread the tomato sauce over the pizza base. Spoon the beef mixture over the top, then sprinkle with the oregano.

5 Arrange over the mozzarella and Cheddar cheeses on top, then sprinkle with the remaining olive oil. Immediately place the pizza in the oven and bake for about 15–20 minutes, or until the crust is golden brown and the topping is bubbling.

Fiorentina Energy 515kcal/2150kJ; Protein 20.9g; Carbohydrate 40.8g, of which sugars 5.2g; Fat 30.8g, of which saturates 11.4g; Cholesterol 104mg; Calcium 415mg; Fibre 3.2g; Sodium 634mg.
Chilli Beef Energy 494kcal/2067kJ; Protein 22.7g; Carbohydrate 43.9g, of which sugars 5g; Fat 26.1g, of which saturates 10.6g; Cholesterol 54mg; Calcium 280mg; Fibre 4.1g; Sodium 411mg.

Tuna, Anchovy & Caper Pizza

Packed with Italian flavours, this substantial pizza is great for an informal gathering.

Serves 2–3

115g/4oz/1 cup self- raising (self-rising) flour
115g/4oz/1 cup self-raising wholemeal (self-rising whole-wheat) flour
pinch of salt
50g/2oz/¼ cup butter, diced
about 150ml/¼ pint/⅔ cup milk

For the topping

30ml/2 tbsp olive oil
1 jar ready-made tomato sauce or pizza topping
1 small red onion
200g/7oz can tuna, drained
15ml/1 tbsp capers
12 black olives, pitted
45ml/3 tbsp freshly grated Parmesan cheese
50g/2oz can anchovy fillets, drained and halved lengthways
ground black pepper

1 Place the flours and salt in a bowl and rub in the butter until the mixture resembles fine breadcrumbs. Add the milk and mix to a soft dough with a wooden spoon. Knead on a lightly floured surface until smooth.

2 Preheat the oven to 220°C/425°F/Gas 7. Roll out the dough on a lightly floured surface to a 25cm/10in circle. Place on a greased baking sheet and brush with 15ml/1 tbsp of the oil. Spread the tomato sauce or pizza topping evenly over the dough, leaving the edge uncovered.

3 Cut the onion into thin wedges and arrange on top. Roughly flake the tuna with a fork and scatter over the onion. Sprinkle over the capers, black olives and Parmesan cheese.

4 Place the anchovy fillets over the top of the pizza in a criss-cross pattern. Drizzle over the remaining oil, then grind over plenty of pepper. Bake for 15–20 minutes until crisp and golden. Serve immediately.

> **Variation**
> If you have time, make your own herb-flavoured tomato sauce.

Salmon & Avocado Pizza

Smoked and fresh salmon make a delicious and luxurious pizza topping when mixed with avocado.

Serves 3–4

150g/5oz salmon fillet
120ml/4fl oz/½ cup dry white wine
1 quantity Basic Pizza Dough (see page 158)
15ml/1 tbsp olive oil
400g/14oz can chopped tomatoes, drained well
115g/4oz/scant 1 cup grated mozzarella
1 small avocado
10ml/2 tsp lemon juice
30ml/2 tbsp crème fraîche
75g/3oz smoked salmon, cut into strips
15ml/1 tbsp capers
30ml/2 tbsp snipped fresh chives, to garnish
ground black pepper

1 Place the salmon fillet in a frying pan, pour over the wine and season with pepper. Bring slowly to the boil over gentle heat, remove from the heat, cover with a tight-fitting lid and leave to cool. (The fish will cook in the cooling liquid.) Skin and flake the salmon into small pieces, removing any bones.

2 Preheat the oven to 220°C/425°F/Gas 7. Roll out the pizza dough to a 25–30cm/10–12in circle and place on a greased baking sheet. Push up the edge of the dough to form a thin rim.

3 Brush the pizza base with the oil and spread the drained tomatoes over the top. Sprinkle half the mozzarella. Bake for 10 minutes, then remove from the oven.

4 Meanwhile, halve, stone and peel the avocado. Cut the flesh into small dice and toss in the lemon juice.

5 Dot teaspoonfuls of the crème fraîche over the pizza base. Arrange the fresh and smoked salmon, avocado, capers and remaining mozzarella on top. Season to taste with pepper.

6 Bake for 5–10 minutes until crisp and golden. Sprinkle over the chives and serve immediately.

Tuna Energy 713kcal/2985kJ; Protein 37.8g; Carbohydrate 58.5g, of which sugars 3.8g; Fat 38.1g, of which saturates 15g; Cholesterol 97mg; Calcium 328mg; Fibre 5.7g; Sodium 1518mg.
Salmon Energy 451kcal/1884kJ; Protein 22g; Carbohydrate 31g, of which sugars 5.3g; Fat 25.3g, of which saturates 8.6g; Cholesterol 53mg; Calcium 193mg; Fibre 3.3g; Sodium 282mg.

Mushroom & Pancetta Pizzas

Try to use a mix of wild and cultivated mushrooms to give these individual pizzas lots of earthy flavour.

Serves 4

1 quantity Basic Pizza Dough
  (see page 158)
60ml/4 tbsp olive oil
2 garlic cloves, crushed

225g/8oz fresh mixed ceps
  and chestnut mushrooms,
  roughly chopped
75g/3oz pancetta, roughly
  chopped
15ml/1 tbsp chopped fresh
  oregano
45ml/3 tbsp freshly grated
  Parmesan cheese
salt and ground black pepper

1 Preheat the oven to 220°C/425°F/Gas 7. Divide the dough into four pieces and roll out each one on a lightly floured surface to a 13cm/5in circle. Place well apart on two greased baking sheets.

2 Heat 30ml/2 tbsp of the olive oil in a frying pan and fry the garlic and mushrooms gently until the mushrooms are tender and the juices have evaporated. Season to taste with salt and pepper, then cool.

3 Brush the pizza bases with 15ml/1 tbsp oil, then spoon over the mushrooms. Scatter over the pancetta and oregano.

4 Sprinkle the toppings with grated Parmesan cheese and drizzle over the remaining oil. Bake for 10–15 minutes, until crisp. Serve immediately.

Cook's Tip
• Pancetta is available in larger supermarkets and Italian delicatessens. If you have difficulty finding it, use chopped slices of streaky (fatty) bacon in its place.
• If fresh ceps are not available, you can add extra flavour to cultivated mushrooms by adding some dried porcini mushrooms, which are sold in larger supermarkets. Soak them in hot water for 20 minutes until soft before adding to the pan in step 2.

Pepperoni Pizza

This classic pizza is sure to go down well with family and friends alike. Who can resist a slice of home-made pizza, topped with a luscious combination of tangy pepperoni, sweet pepper and lashings of cheese?

Serves 4
For the sauce
30ml/2 tbsp olive oil
1 onion, finely chopped
1 garlic clove, crushed
400g/14oz can chopped
  tomatoes with herbs
15ml/1 tbsp tomato
  purée (paste)

For the pizza base
275g/10oz/2½ cups plain
  (all-purpose) flour
2.5ml/½ tsp salt
5ml/1 tsp easy-blend (rapid-rise)
  dried yeast
30ml/2 tbsp olive oil

For the topping
½ each red, yellow and green
  (bell) pepper, sliced into rings
150g/5oz mozzarella cheese,
  sliced
75g/3oz pepperoni sausage,
  thinly sliced
8 black olives, pitted
3 sun-dried tomatoes, chopped
2.5ml/½ tsp dried oregano
olive oil, for drizzling

1 To make the sauce, heat the oil and fry the onions and garlic until softened. Add the tomatoes and tomato purée, then boil rapidly for 5 minutes until reduced slightly. Leave to cool.

2 To make the pizza base, sift the flour and salt into a bowl. Sprinkle over the yeast and make a well in the centre. Pour in 175ml/6fl oz/¾ cup warm water and the olive oil. Mix to a soft dough. Knead the dough on a lightly floured surface for about 5–10 minutes until smooth. Roll out to a 25cm/10in round, press up the edges slightly and place on a greased baking sheet.

3 Spread over the tomato sauce and top with the peppers, mozzarella, pepperoni, olives and sun-dried tomatoes. Sprinkle over the oregano and drizzle with olive oil.

4 Cover loosely and leave in a warm place for 30 minutes. Meanwhile, preheat the oven to 220°C/425°F/ Gas 7. Bake for 25–30 minutes, then serve.

Mushroom Energy 344kcal/1435kJ; Protein 12g; Carbohydrate 27g, of which sugars 1.7g; Fat 21.6g, of which saturates 5.5g; Cholesterol 23mg; Calcium 180mg; Fibre 1.6g; Sodium 488mg.
Pepperoni Energy 521kcal/2184kJ; Protein 17.5g; Carbohydrate 62.4g, of which sugars 8.6g; Fat 24g, of which saturates 8.2g; Cholesterol 43mg; Calcium 256mg; Fibre 4.7g; Sodium 484mg.

Crab & Parmesan Calzonelli

These calzonelli – purses of pizza dough filled with a luxurious creamy crab filling – make attractive and impressive party food.

Makes 10–12
I quantity Basic Pizza Dough (see page 158)
115g/4oz mixed prepared crab meat, defrosted if frozen
15ml/1 tbsp double (heavy) cream
30ml/2 tbsp freshly grated Parmesan cheese
30ml/2 tbsp chopped fresh parsley
I garlic clove, crushed
salt and ground black pepper
fresh parsley sprigs, to garnish

I Preheat the oven to 200°C/400°F/Gas 6. Roll out the pizza dough on a lightly floured surface to 3mm/⅛in thick. Using a 7.5cm/3in plain round pastry cutter, stamp out ten to twelve circles of dough.

2 In a bowl, mix the crab meat with the cream, Parmesan cheese, parsley and garlic. Season to taste with salt and pepper.

3 Spoon a little of the filling on to one half of each circle. Dampen the edges of the dough with water and fold over to enclose the filling.

4 Seal the edges by pressing with a fork. Place well apart on two greased baking sheets. Bake for 10–15 minutes until golden. Garnish with parsley sprigs.

> **Cook's Tip**
> *Make sure that the pizza dough is rolled out thinly and evenly.*

> **Variation**
> *If you prefer, use prawns (shrimp) instead of crab meat. If buying frozen prawns, make sure they are fully defrosted first.*

Farmhouse Pizza

This is the ultimate party pizza. Served cut into fingers, it is ideal for a large and hungry gathering.

Serves 8
90ml/6 tbsp olive oil
225g/8oz button (white) mushrooms, sliced
2 quantities Basic Pizza Dough (see page 158)
I jar ready-made tomato sauce or pizza topping
300g/10oz mozzarella cheese, thinly sliced
115g/4oz wafer-thin smoked ham slices
6 bottled artichoke hearts in oil, drained and sliced
50g/2oz can anchovy fillets, drained and halved lengthways
10 black olives, pitted and halved
30ml/2 tbsp chopped fresh oregano
15ml/3 tbsp freshly grated Parmesan cheese
ground black pepper

I Preheat the oven to 220°C/425°F/Gas 7. In a large frying pan, heat 30ml/2 tbsp of the oil. Gently fry the mushrooms for 5 minutes until all the juices have evaporated. Remove from the heat and leave to cool.

2 Roll out the dough on a lightly floured surface to make a 30 x 25cm/12 x 10in rectangle. Transfer to a greased baking sheet, then push up the dough edges to form a thin rim. Brush with 30ml/2 tbsp of the oil.

3 Spread the tomato sauce or pizza topping over the dough, then arrange the sliced mozzarella over the sauce.

4 Scrunch up the ham and arrange on top with the artichoke hearts, mushrooms and anchovies.

5 Dot with the black olives, then sprinkle over the chopped oregano and grated Parmesan. Drizzle over the remaining oil and season to taste with pepper.

6 Bake for about 25 minutes until the pizza crust is crisp and golden. Serve immediately.

Farmhouse Energy 412kcal/1725kJ; Protein 17.2g; Carbohydrate 36.4g, of which sugars 2g; Fat 23g, of which saturates 8g; Cholesterol 38mg; Calcium 259mg; Fibre 2.4g; Sodium 822mg.
Calzonelli Energy 84kcal/354kJ; Protein 4.2g; Carbohydrate 11.4g, of which sugars 0.3g; Fat 2.7g, of which saturates 1.1g; Cholesterol 11mg; Calcium 68mg; Fibre 0.6g; Sodium 82mg.

Ham & Mozzarella Calzone

A calzone is a kind of "inside-out" pizza – the dough is on the outside and the filling on the inside. This is particuarly good food for eating *al fresco*.

Serves 2

1 quantity Basic Pizza Dough
    (see page 158)
115g/4oz/¹/₂ cup ricotta cheese
30ml/2 tbsp freshly grated
    Parmesan cheese
1 egg yolk
30ml/2 tbsp chopped fresh basil
75g/3oz cooked ham, finely
    chopped
75g/3oz mozzarella cheese, cut
    into small dice
olive oil, for brushing
salt and ground black pepper

1 Preheat the oven to 220°C/425°F/Gas 7. Divide the dough in half and roll out each piece on a lightly floured surface to an 18cm/7in circle.

2 In a bowl, mix together the ricotta and Parmesan cheeses, then stir in the egg yolk and basil. Season with salt and pepper.

3 Spread the mixture over half of each circle, leaving a 2.5cm/1in border, then arrange the ham and mozzarella on top.

4 Dampen the edges with water, then fold over the dough to enclose the filling.

5 Press the edges firmly together to seal. Place on two greased baking sheets. Brush with oil and make a small hole in the top of each to allow the steam to escape.

6 Bake for 15–20 minutes until golden. Serve immediately.

> **Cook's Tips**
> • *For a vegetarian version, replace the ham with fried mushrooms or chopped cooked spinach.*
> • *For a decorative finishing touch, seal the edges of the uncooked dough circles by pressing with a fork.*

Aubergine & Shallot Calzone

Aubergines, shallots and sun-dried tomatoes make an unusual filling for calzone.

Serves 2

4 baby aubergines (eggplants)
45ml/3 tbsp olive oil
3 shallots, chopped
1 garlic clove, chopped
6 pieces sun-dried tomatoes in oil,
    drained and chopped
1.5ml/¹/₄ tsp dried red chilli flakes
10ml/2 tsp chopped fresh thyme
1 quantity Basic Pizza Dough
    (see page 158)
75g/3oz/generous ¹/₂ cup diced
    mozzarella cheese
salt and ground black pepper
15–30ml/1–2 tbsp freshly grated
    Parmesan cheese, to serve

1 Preheat the oven to 220°C/425°F/Gas 7. Trim the baby aubergines, then cut into small dice.

2 Heat 30ml/2 tbsp oil in a heavy frying pan. Add the shallots and fry over low heat, stirring occasionally, for 5 minutes until softened by not browned.

3 Add the aubergines, garlic, sun-dried tomatoes, red chilli flakes and thyme to the shallots and season with salt and pepper. Cook for 4–5 minutes, stirring frequently, until the aubergine is beginning to soften.

4 Divide the dough in half and roll out each piece on a lightly floured surface to an 18cm/7in circle. Spread the aubergine mixture over half of each circle, leaving a 2.5cm/1in border, then arrange the mozzarella on top.

5 Dampen the edges with water, then fold the dough over to enclose the filling. Press the edges firmly together to seal. Place on two greased baking sheets.

6 Brush with half the remaining oil and make a small hole in the top of each to allow the steam to escape. Bake for about 15–20 minutes until golden. Remove from the oven and brush with the remaining oil. Sprinkle over the Parmesan and serve the calzone immediately.

Mozzarella Energy 686kcal/2877kJ; Protein 34.8g; Carbohydrate 70.2g, of which sugars 3.5g; Fat 31.5g, of which saturates 15.6g; Cholesterol 183mg; Calcium 453mg; Fibre 2.7g; Sodium 769mg.
Aubergine Energy 672kcal/2814kJ; Protein 20.5g; Carbohydrate 75.6g, of which sugars 7.8g; Fat 34.1g, of which saturates 10.3g; Cholesterol 29mg; Calcium 378mg; Fibre 7.4g; Sodium 240mg.

Root Vegetable Couscous

Harissa is a very fiery Tunisian chilli sauce which is now available ready-made from larger supermarkets.

Serves 4
350g/12oz/2¼ cups couscous
45ml/3 tbsp olive oil
4 baby onions, halved
675g/1½lb fresh mixed root vegetables such as carrots, swede (ratabega), turnip, celeriac and sweet potatoes, cubed
2 garlic cloves, crushed
pinch of saffron threads
2.5ml/½ tsp each ground cinnamon and ginger
2.5ml/½ tsp ground turmeric
5ml/1 tsp each ground cumin and coriander

15ml/1 tbsp tomato purée (paste)
450ml/¾ pint/scant 2 cups hot vegetable stock
1 small fennel bulb, quartered
115g/4oz/1 cup cooked or canned chickpeas
50g/2oz/½ cup seedless raisins
30ml/2 tbsp chopped fresh coriander (cilantro)
30ml/2 tbsp chopped fresh flat leaf parsley
salt and ground black pepper

For the spiced sauce
15ml/1 tbsp olive oil
15ml/1 tbsp lemon juice
15ml/1 tbsp chopped fresh coriander (cilantro)
2.5–5ml/½–1 tsp harissa

1 Put the couscous in a bowl, cover with hot water, then drain. Heat the oil in a frying pan and gently fry the onions for 3 minutes. Add the root vegetables and fry for 5 minutes. Add the garlic and spices and cook for 1 minute, stirring.

2 Transfer the vegetable mixture to a large deep pan. Stir in the tomato purée, stock, fennel, chickpeas, raisins, chopped coriander and flat leaf parsley. Bring to the boil. Put the couscous into a muslin-lined steamer and place this over the vegetable mixture. Cover and simmer for 20 minutes, or until the vegetables are tender.

3 To make the sauce, put 250ml/8fl oz/1 cup of the vegetable liquid in a bowl and mix with all of the sauce ingredients.

4 Spoon the couscous on to a plate and pile the vegetables on top. Serve at once, handing round the sauce separately.

Risotto with Mushrooms

The addition of wild mushrooms gives a lovely woody flavour to this dish.

Serves 4
25g/1oz dried wild mushrooms, preferably porcini
350ml/12fl oz/1½ cups warm water
900ml/1½ pints/3¾ cups meat or chicken stock
175g/6oz fresh cultivated mushrooms

juice of ½ lemon
75g/3oz/6 tbsp butter
30ml/2 tbsp finely chopped fresh parsley
30ml/2 tbsp olive oil
1 small onion, finely chopped
275g/10oz/1½ cups arborio risotto rice
120ml/4fl oz/½ cup dry white wine
45ml/3 tbsp freshly grated Parmesan cheese
salt and ground black pepper

1 Place the dried mushrooms in a small bowl with the warm water. Leave to soak for at least 40 minutes. Remove the mushrooms and rinse, then filter the soaking water through a sieve (strainer) lined with kitchen paper into a pan. Add the stock and leave to simmer until needed.

2 Slice the fresh mushrooms. Toss with the lemon juice. Melt a third of the butter in a large frying pan. Stir in the mushrooms and cook until they begin to brown. Stir in the parsley, cook for 30 seconds more, then transfer to a side dish.

3 Heat another third of the butter with the olive oil in the mushroom pan and cook the onion until golden. Add the rice and stir for 1–2 minutes. Add all the mushrooms. Pour in the wine and cook until it has evaporated.

4 Add a ladleful of the hot stock and stir gently until it has been absorbed. Continue adding a ladleful of stock at a time, until all the stock has been absorbed and the rice is tender and creamy.

5 Remove the risotto pan from the heat. Stir in the remaining butter and the Parmesan. Grind in a little pepper, and taste again for salt; adjust if necessary. Allow the risotto to rest for 3–4 minutes before serving.

Couscous Energy 444kcal/1855kJ; Protein 9.5g; Carbohydrate 75.1g, of which sugars 24.2g; Fat 13.5g, of which saturates 1.8g; Cholesterol 0mg; Calcium 115mg, Fibre 7.5g; Sodium 131mg.
Risotto Energy 518kcal/2150kJ; Protein 10.6g; Carbohydrate 56.5g, of which sugars 1.2g; Fat 25.2g, of which saturates 12.9g; Cholesterol 51mg; Calcium 161mg; Fibre 0.7g; Sodium 240mg.

Tomato Risotto

This pretty risotto makes a lovely summery meal, served with a chilled white wine.

Serves 4
675g/1½ lb firm ripe tomatoes
50g/2oz/¼ cup butter
1 onion, finely chopped
1.2 litres/2 pints/5 cups vegetable stock
275g/10oz/1½ cups arborio rice
400g/14oz can cannellini beans, drained
50g/2oz/½ cup finely grated Parmesan cheese
salt and ground black pepper
10–12 fresh basil leaves, shredded and freshly grated Parmesan cheese, to serve

1 Halve the tomatoes and scoop out the seeds into a sieve (strainer) placed over a bowl. Press the seeds with a spoon to extract all the juice. Set the juuice aside.

2 Grill (broil) the tomatoes skin-side up until evenly charred and blistered. Rub off the skins and dice the flesh.

3 Melt the butter in a large frying pan and cook the onion for 5 minutes until beginning to soften. Add the tomatoes and the reserved juice. Season with salt and pepper, then cook, stirring occasionally, for about 10 minutes. Meanwhile, bring the vegetable stock to the boil in another pan.

4 Add the rice to the tomatoes and stir to coat, then add a ladleful of the stock and stir gently until it has been absorbed. Continue adding a ladleful of stock at a time, until all the stock has been absorbed and the rice is tender and creamy.

5 Stir in the cannellini beans and grated Parmesan and heat through for a few minutes. Just before serving the risotto, sprinkle each portion with shredded basil leaves and Parmesan.

> **Cook's Tip**
> If possible, use plum tomatoes in this dish, as they have a fresh, vibrant flavour and meaty texture.

Grilled Polenta with Peppers

Golden slices of herby polenta taste delicious topped with yellow and red pepper strips, heightened with balsamic vinegar.

Serves 4
2 red (bell) peppers
2 yellow (bell) peppers
115g/4oz/scant 1 cup polenta
25g/1oz/2 tbsp butter
15–30ml/1–2 tbsp mixed chopped herbs such as parsley, thyme and sage
melted butter, for brushing
60ml/4 tbsp olive oil
1–2 garlic cloves, cut into slivers
15ml/1 tbsp balsamic vinegar
salt and ground black pepper
fresh herb sprigs, to garnish

1 Preheat the oven to 200°C/400°F/Gas 6. Place the peppers on a baking sheet and bake for about 20 minutes or until they are beginning to char and blister.

2 Put the charred peppers in a bowl, cover and leave to cool for 10 minutes, then peel off the skins. Remove the seeds and cores, then cut the flesh into strips. Set aside.

3 Bring 600ml/1 pint/2½ cups salted water to the boil in a heavy pan. Trickle in the polenta, beating continuously, then cook gently for 15–20 minutes, stirring occasionally, until the mixture is no longer grainy and comes away from the sides of the pan.

4 Remove the pan from the heat and beat in the butter, chopped herbs and plenty of pepper. Pour the polenta into a pudding bowl, smooth the surface and leave until cold and firm.

5 Turn out the polenta on to a board and cut into thick slices. Brush the polenta slices with melted butter and grill (broil) each side for about 4–5 minutes, until golden brown.

6 Meanwhile, heat the olive oil in a frying pan, add the garlic and peppers and stir-fry for 1–2 minutes. Stir in the balsamic vinegar and season with salt and pepper.

7 Spoon the pepper mixture over the polenta slices and garnish with fresh herb sprigs. Serve immediately.

Risotto Energy 531kcal/2220kJ; Protein 18.4g; Carbohydrate 79.2g, of which sugars 9.8g; Fat 15.9g, of which saturates 9.4g; Cholesterol 39mg; Calcium 252mg; Fibre 8.1g; Sodium 618mg.
Polenta Energy 309kcal/1280kJ; Protein 4.6g; Carbohydrate 32.5g, of which sugars 10.7g; Fat 17.8g, of which saturates 5g; Cholesterol 13mg; Calcium 16mg; Fibre 3.5g; Sodium 45mg.

Two Cheese Risotto

This undeniably rich and creamy risotto is just the thing to serve on cold winter evenings when everyone needs warming up.

Serves 3–4

1 litre/1¾ pints/4 cups vegetable
  or chicken stock
7.5ml/1½ tsp olive oil
50g/2oz/¼ cup butter
1 onion, finely chopped

1 garlic clove, crushed
275g/10oz/1½ cups risotto rice,
  preferably Vialone Nano
175ml/6fl oz/¾ cup dry
  white wine
75g/3oz/¾ cup Fontina
  cheese, cubed
50g/2oz/⅔ cup freshly grated
  Parmesan cheese, plus extra,
  to serve
salt and ground
  black pepper

1 Heat the stock in a pan and leave to simmer until needed.

2 Heat the olive oil with half the butter in a pan and gently fry the onion and garlic for 5–6 minutes, until soft. Add the rice and cook, stirring all the time, until the grains are coated in fat and have become slightly translucent around the edges.

3 Pour in the white wine. Cook, stirring, until it has been absorbed, then add a ladleful of hot stock. Cook, stirring, until the stock has been absorbed. Gradually add the remaining stock, a little at a time, allowing the rice to absorb the liquid before adding more, and stirring constantly.

4 When the rice is half cooked, stir in the Fontina cheese, and continue cooking and adding stock gradually. Keep stirring.

5 When the risotto is creamy and the grains are tender but still *al dente*, stir in the remaining butter and the Parmesan. Season with salt and pepper, then remove the pan from the heat. Cover and leave to stand for 3–4 minutes before serving.

> **Variation**
> *Stir in a handful of chopped fresh herbs with the Parmesan.*

Brown Rice Risotto with Mushrooms

A classic risotto of mixed mushrooms, herbs and fresh Parmesan cheese, but made using brown long-grain rice. Serve with a mixed leaf salad tossed in a balsamic dressing for a stylish lunch.

Serves 4

15g/½oz/2 tbsp dried
  porcini mushrooms
150ml/¼ pint/⅔ cup warm
  water
15ml/1 tbsp olive oil
4 shallots, finely chopped

2 garlic cloves, crushed
250g/9oz/1⅓ cups brown
  long-grain rice
900ml/1½ pints/3¾ cups well-
  flavoured vegetable stock
450g/1lb/6 cups mixed
  mushrooms, such as closed cup,
  chestnut and field mushrooms,
  sliced if large
30–45ml/2–3 tbsp chopped
  fresh flat leaf parsley
50g/2oz/⅔ cup freshly grated
  Parmesan cheese
salt and ground
  black pepper

1 Put the dried porcini in a bowl and pour over the warm water. Leave the mushrooms to soak for 20 minutes, then lift out with a slotted spoon. Filter the soaking water through a layer of kitchen paper in a sieve (strainer) and reserve. Roughly chop the porcini.

2 Heat the oil in a large pan, add the shallots and garlic and cook gently for 5 minutes, stirring. Add the brown rice to the shallot mixture and stir to coat the grains in oil.

3 Stir the vegetable stock and the porcini soaking liquid into the rice mixture in the pan. Bring to the boil, lower the heat and simmer, uncovered, for about 20 minutes, or until most of the liquid has been absorbed, stirring frequently.

4 Add all the mushrooms, stir well and cook the risotto for a further 10–15 minutes, until the liquid has been absorbed.

5 Season with salt and pepper to taste, stir in the chopped parsley and grated Parmesan and serve immediately.

Champagne Risotto

This may seem rather extravagant, but it makes a really beautifully flavoured risotto, perfect for that special anniversary dinner.

Serves 3–4

750ml/1¼ pints/3 cups light
  vegetable or chicken stock
25g/1oz/2 tbsp butter
2 shallots, finely chopped
275g/10oz/1½ cups risotto rice,
  preferably Carnaroli

½ bottle or 300ml/½ pint/
  1¼ cups champagne
150ml/¼ pint/⅔ cup double
  (heavy) cream
40g/1½oz/½ cup freshly
  grated Parmesan cheese
10ml/2 tsp very finely chopped
  fresh chervil
salt and ground black pepper
black truffle shavings,
  to garnish (optional)

1 Heat the stock in a pan and leave to simmer until needed.

2 Melt the butter in a pan and fry the shallots for 2–3 minutes until softened. Add the rice and cook, stirring all the time, until the grains are evenly coated in butter and are beginning to look translucent around the edges.

3 Pour in about two-thirds of the champagne and cook over a high heat so that the liquid bubbles fiercely. Cook, stirring constantly, until all the liquid has been absorbed, then begin to add the hot stock.

4 Add the stock, a ladleful at a time, making sure that each addition has been completely absorbed before adding the next. The risotto should gradually become creamy and velvety and all the stock should be absorbed.

5 When the rice is tender but still *al dente*, stir in the remaining champagne and the double cream and grated Parmesan. Taste for seasoning.

6 Remove from the heat, cover and leave to stand for a few minutes. Stir in the chervil and serve topped with a few truffle shavings, if you like.

Fried Rice Balls Stuffed with Mozzarella

These deep-fried balls of risotto are stuffed with mozzarella cheese. They are very popular snacks in Italy, which is hardly surprising as they are quite delicious.

Serves 4

1 quantity Two Cheese Risotto
3 eggs
115g/4oz/⅔ cup diced
  mozzarella cheese
oil, for deep-frying
breadcrumbs and flour, to coat
dressed frisée lettuce and cherry
  tomatoes, to serve

1 Put the risotto in a bowl and allow it to cool completely. Beat two of the eggs together, then stir them into the cold risotto until well mixed.

2 Use your hands to form the rice mixture into balls the size of a large egg. If the mixture is too moist to hold its shape well, stir in a few tablespoons of breadcrumbs. Poke a hole into the centre of each ball with your finger, then fill it with a few small cubes of mozzarella, and close the hole over again with the rice mixture.

3 Heat the oil for deep-frying until a small piece of bread sizzles as soon as it is dropped in.

4 Spread some flour on a plate. Beat the remaining egg in a shallow bowl. Sprinkle another plate with breadcrumbs. Roll the balls in the flour, then in the egg, and finally in the breadcrumbs.

5 Fry them a few at a time in the hot oil, until golden and crisp. Drain on kitchen paper while the remaining balls are being fried. Serve hot, with a salad of frisée lettuce and tomatoes.

> **Cook's Tip**
> *This is the perfect way to use leftover risotto.*

Champagne Energy 468kcal/1941kJ; Protein 8g; Carbohydrate 48.3g, of which sugars 4.2g; Fat 23.1g, of which saturates 14.3g; Cholesterol 60mg; Calcium 130mg; Fibre 0.2g; Sodium 128mg.
Rice Balls Energy 505kcal/2111kJ; Protein 15g; Carbohydrate 44.8g, of which sugars 1.1g; Fat 30.9g, of which saturates 8.5g; Cholesterol 160mg; Calcium 168mg; Fibre 0.7g; Sodium 1095mg.

Pesto Risotto

If you buy the pesto – and there are some excellent varieties available nowadays from Italian delicatessens – this is just about as easy as a risotto gets.

Serves 3–4
1 litre/1¾ pints/4 cups vegetable stock
30ml/2 tbsp olive oil
2 shallots, finely chopped
1 garlic clove, crushed
275g/10oz/1½ cups risotto rice
175ml/6fl oz/¾ cup dry white wine
45ml/3 tbsp pesto sauce
25g/1oz/⅓ cup freshly grated Parmesan cheese, plus extra, to serve (optional)
salt and ground black pepper

1 Heat the stock in a pan and leave to simmer until needed.

2 Heat the olive oil in a pan and fry the shallots and garlic for 4–5 minutes, until the shallots are soft but not browned.

3 Add the rice and cook over medium heat, stirring all the time, until the grains of rice are coated in oil and the outer part of the grain is translucent and the inner part opaque.

4 Pour in the wine. Cook, stirring, until all of it has been absorbed, then add a ladleful of the hot stock. Cook, stirring, until the stock has been absorbed. Gradually add the remaining stock, a little at a time, allowing the rice to absorb the liquid before adding more, and stirring constantly.

5 After about 20 minutes, when all the stock has been absorbed and the rice is creamy and tender but *al dente*, stir in the pesto and Parmesan. Taste and add salt and pepper to taste, then cover and leave to stand for 3–4 minutes. Spoon into a bowl and serve, with extra Parmesan, if you like.

> **Variation**
> *Green basil pesto sauce is used for this recipe, but red pesto, made with red peppers, can also be used.*

Pumpkin & Apple Risotto

Pumpkin and other winter squash appear in many classic Italian recipes. If pumpkins are out of season, butternut or onion squash work well as a substitute.

Serves 3–4
225g/8oz butternut squash or pumpkin flesh, peeled and seeded
1 cooking apple
25g/1oz/2 tbsp butter
900ml–1 litre/1½–1¾ pints/3¾–4 cups vegetable stock
25ml/1½ tbsp olive oil
1 onion, finely chopped
1 garlic clove, crushed
275g/10oz/1½ cups risotto rice, such as Vialone Nano
175ml/6fl oz/¾ cup fruity white wine
75g/3oz/1 cup freshly grated Parmesan cheese
salt and ground black pepper

1 Cut the squash into small pieces. Peel, core and roughly chop the apple. Place in a pan and pour in 120ml/4fl oz/½ cup water. Bring to the boil, then simmer for 15–20 minutes, until the squash is very tender. Drain, return the squash mixture to the pan and add half the butter. Mash the mixture roughly with a fork to break up any large pieces, but leave the mixture chunky.

2 Heat the stock in a pan and leave to simmer until needed.

3 Heat the oil and remaining butter in a pan and fry the onion and garlic until the onion is soft. Add the rice and cook, stirring constantly, over medium heat for 2 minutes, until the rice is coated in oil and the grains are slightly translucent.

4 Add the wine and stir into the rice. When all the liquid has been absorbed, begin to add the stock a ladleful at a time, making sure each addition has been absorbed before adding the next. This should take about 20 minutes.

5 When roughly two ladlefuls of stock are left, add the squash and apple mixture together with another addition of stock. Continue to cook, stirring well and adding the rest of the stock, until the risotto is very creamy. Stir in the Parmesan, season to taste and serve immediately.

Pesto Energy 421kcal/1751kJ; Protein 9.3g; Carbohydrate 56.5g, of which sugars 1.3g; Fat 14.1g, of which saturates 3.2g; Cholesterol 9mg; Calcium 126mg; Fibre 0.3g; Sodium 98mg.
Pumpkin Energy 439kcal/1831kJ; Protein 13.2g; Carbohydrate 59.1g, of which sugars 3.6g; Fat 13.3g, of which saturates 7.1g; Cholesterol 32mg; Calcium 261mg; Fibre 1.1g; Sodium 215mg.

Roasted Pepper Risotto

The smoky flavour of the red (bell) peppers gives this risotto a divinely earthy taste.

Serves 3–4
1 red (bell) pepper
1 yellow (bell) pepper
1 litre/1¾ pints/4 cups vegetable stock
15ml/1 tbsp olive oil
25g/1oz/2 tbsp butter
1 onion, chopped
2 garlic cloves, crushed
275g/10oz/1½ cups risotto rice
50g/2oz/⅔ cup freshly grated Parmesan cheese
salt and ground black pepper
freshly grated Parmesan cheese, to serve (optional)

1 Preheat the grill (broiler) to high. Cut the peppers in half, remove the seeds and cores and arrange, cut-side down, on a baking sheet. Place under the grill for 5–6 minutes, until the skin is charred. Put the peppers in a plastic bag, tie the ends and leave for 4–5 minutes.

2 Peel the peppers when they are cool enough to handle and the steam has loosened the skin. Cut into thin strips. Bring the stock to the boil in a pan and leave to simmer until required.

3 Heat the oil and butter in a pan and fry the onion and garlic for 4–5 minutes over low heat, until the onion begins to soften. Add the peppers and cook the mixture for a further 3–4 minutes, stirring occasionally.

4 Stir in the rice. Cook over medium heat for 3–4 minutes, stirring all the time, until the rice is evenly coated in oil and the outer part of each grain has become translucent.

5 Add a ladleful of stock. Cook, stirring, until all the liquid has been absorbed. Continue to add the stock, a ladleful at a time, making sure that each quantity has been absorbed before adding the next.

6 When the rice is tender but is still *al dente*, stir in the Parmesan and season to taste. Cover and leave to stand for 3–4 minutes, then serve, with extra Parmesan, if using.

Jerusalem Artichoke Risotto

This is a simple and warming risotto, which benefits from the delicious and distinctive flavour of Jerusalem artichokes.

Serves 3–4
400g/14oz Jerusalem artichokes
40g/1½oz/3 tbsp butter
1 litre/1¾ pints/4 cups vegetable stock
15ml/1 tbsp olive oil
1 onion, finely chopped
1 garlic clove, crushed
275g/10oz/1½ cups risotto rice
120ml/4fl oz/½ cup fruity white wine
10ml/2 tsp fresh thyme, finely chopped
40g/1½oz/½ cup freshly grated Parmesan cheese, plus extra, to serve
salt and ground black pepper
fresh thyme sprigs, to garnish

1 Peel the artichokes, cut them into pieces and immediately add them to a pan of lightly salted water. Simmer them until tender, then drain and mash with 15g/½oz/1 tbsp of the butter. Add a little more salt, if needed.

2 Boil the stock in a pan and leave to simmer until required.

3 Heat the oil and the remaining butter in a pan and fry the onion and garlic for 5–6 minutes, until soft. Add the rice and cook over a medium heat for about 2 minutes, until the grains are translucent around the edges.

4 Pour in the wine, stir until it has been absorbed, then start adding the simmering stock, a ladleful at a time, making sure each quantity has been absorbed before adding the next.

5 When you have just one ladleful of stock to add, stir in the mashed artichokes and the chopped thyme. Season with salt and pepper. Continue cooking until the risotto is creamy and the artichokes are hot.

6 Stir in the Parmesan cheese. Remove from the heat, cover the pan and leave the risotto to stand for a few minutes. Spoon into a warmed serving dish, garnish with fresh thyme and serve with Parmesan.

Pepper Energy 362kcal/1509kJ; Protein 11.1g; Carbohydrate 61.7g, of which sugars 6.2g; Fat 7.6g, of which saturates 3.1g; Cholesterol 13mg; Calcium 174mg; Fibre 1.6g; Sodium 140mg.
Artichoke Energy 418kcal/1741kJ; Protein 9.6g; Carbohydrate 56g, of which sugars 1.2g; Fat 14.8g, of which saturates 7.7g; Cholesterol 31mg; Calcium 179mg; Fibre 1.1g; Sodium 231mg.

Okra Fried Rice

This spicy rich dish gains its creamy consistency from the natural juices of the sliced okra.

Serves 3–4
30ml/2 tbsp vegetable oil
15g/½ oz/1 tbsp butter or
  margarine
1 garlic clove, crushed
½ red onion, finely chopped
115g/4oz okra, topped and tailed
30ml/2 tbsp diced green and red
  (bell) peppers
2.5ml/½ tsp dried thyme
2 green chillies, finely chopped
2.5ml/½ tsp five-spice powder
1 vegetable stock cube
30ml/2 tbsp soy sauce
15ml/1 tbsp chopped fresh
  coriander (cilantro)
225g/8oz/2½ cups cooked rice
salt and ground black pepper
fresh coriander sprigs, to garnish

1 Heat the oil and butter or margarine in a frying pan or wok and cook the garlic and onion over medium heat for 5 minutes until softened.

2 Thinly slice the okra, add to the pan or wok and sauté gently for 6–7 minutes.

3 Add the green and red peppers, thyme, chillies and five-spice powder. Cook gently for 3 minutes, then crumble in the vegetable stock cube.

4 Add the soy sauce, coriander and rice and heat through, stirring well. Season to taste with salt and pepper. Serve hot, garnished with coriander sprigs.

Cook's Tips
• *Okra is a five-sided green pod with a tapering end. When buying okra, choose small firm pods that are brightly coloured. Avoid any that are bendy and browning at the edges or tips.*
• *When preparing chillies, wear rubber gloves if possible, as chillies contain a substance that burns sensitive skin. Wash the knife, board and your hands (if not protected) after preparation. Never rub your eyes or touch your lips after handling chillies.*

Asparagus & Cheese Risotto

It's important to use arborio rice for this Italian dish in order to achieve the creamy texture that is characteristic of an authentic risotto.

Serves 4
1.5ml/¼ tsp saffron threads
750ml/1¼ pints/3 cups hot
  chicken stock
25g/1oz/2 tbsp butter
30ml/2 tbsp olive oil
1 large onion, finely chopped
2 garlic cloves, finely chopped
225g/8oz/1¼ cups arborio
  risotto rice
300ml/½ pint/1¼ cups dry white
  wine
225g/8oz asparagus tips, cooked
75g/3oz/1 cup freshly grated
  Parmesan cheese
salt and ground black pepper
fresh Parmesan cheese shavings,
  to garnish
ciabatta bread rolls and green
  salad, to serve

1 Sprinkle the saffron over the stock and leave to infuse for 5 minutes. Heat the butter and oil in a frying pan and fry the onion and garlic for about 6 minutes until softened.

2 Add the rice and stir-fry for 1–2 minutes to coat the grains with the butter and oil. Pour on 300ml/½ pint/1¼ cups of the stock and saffron. Cook gently, stirring frequently, until the liquid is absorbed. Repeat with another 300ml/½ pint/1¼ cups stock. When that is absorbed, add the wine and continue to cook, stirring, until the rice has a creamy consistency.

3 Add the asparagus and remaining stock, and stir until the liquid is absorbed and the rice is tender. Stir in the Parmesan cheese and season to taste with salt and pepper.

4 Spoon the risotto on to warmed plates and garnish with the Parmesan cheese shavings. Serve immediately with hot ciabatta rolls and a mixed green salad.

Cook's Tip
If preferred, you can use whole asparagus spears, cut into 5cm/2in lengths, but the stems should not be too thick.

Indian Pilau Rice

Basmati rice is simply flavoured with aromatic spices and seeds to create a delightfully fragrant dish.

Serves 4

225g/8oz/1¼ cups basmati rice, rinsed well
30ml/2 tbsp vegetable oil
1 small onion, finely chopped
1 garlic clove, crushed
5ml/1 tsp fennel seeds
15ml/1 tbsp sesame seeds
2.5ml/½ tsp ground turmeric
5ml/1 tsp ground cumin
1.5ml/¼ tsp salt
2 whole cloves
4 green cardamom pods, lightly crushed
5 black peppercorns
450ml/¾ pint/scant 2 cups chicken stock
15ml/1 tbsp ground almonds
fresh coriander (cilantro) sprigs, to garnish

1 Soak the rice in water for 30 minutes. Heat the oil in a pan, and fry the onions and garlic gently for 5–6 minutes, until soft.

2 Stir in the fennel and sesame seeds, the turmeric, cumin, salt, cloves, cardamom pods and peppercorns and cook for about 1 minute. Drain the rice well, add to the pan and stir-fry for a further 3 minutes.

3 Pour on the chicken stock. Bring to the boil, then cover with a tight-fitting lid, reduce the heat to very low and simmer gently for 20 minutes, without removing the lid, until all the liquid has been absorbed.

4 Remove from the heat and leave to stand for 2–3 minutes. Fluff up the rice with a fork and stir in the ground almonds. Garnish with coriander sprigs and serve immediately.

Cook's Tips
• *Basmati rice is the most popular choice for Indian dishes, but you could use long grain rice instead.*
• *Green cardamoms are more suitable for this dish than the black variety as they are more delicate in flavour and texture.*

Louisiana Rice

Minced pork and chicken livers with mixed vegetables make a tasty dish that is a meal in itself.

Serves 4

60ml/4 tbsp vegetable oil
1 small aubergine (eggplant), diced
225g/8oz minced (ground) pork
1 green (bell) pepper, seeded and chopped
2 celery sticks, chopped
1 onion, chopped
1 garlic clove, crushed
5ml/1 tsp cayenne pepper
5ml/1 tsp paprika
5ml/1 tsp ground black pepper
2.5ml/½ tsp salt
5ml/1 tsp dried thyme
2.5ml/½ tsp dried oregano
475ml/16fl oz/2 cups chicken stock
225g/8oz chicken livers, minced (ground)
150g/5oz/¾ cup long grain rice
1 bay leaf
45ml/3 tbsp chopped fresh parsley
celery leaves, to garnish

1 Heat the oil in a frying pan until really hot, then stir-fry the aubergine for about 5 minutes. Add the pork and cook for about 6–8 minutes, until browned, using a wooden spoon to break up any lumps.

2 Add the green pepper, celery, onion, garlic, cayenne pepper, paprika, black pepper, salt, thyme and oregano. Cover and cook over high heat for 5 6 minutes, stirring frequently from the bottom to scrape up and distribute the crispy bits of pork.

3 Pour on the chicken stock and stir, scraping the bottom of the pan clean. Readuce the heat to medium, cover the pan and cook for 6 minutes. Stir in the chicken livers, cook for a further 2 minutes, then stir in the rice and add the bay leaf.

4 Reduce the heat, cover and simmer for about 6–7 minutes more. Turn off the heat and leave to stand for a further 10–15 minutes until the rice is tender.

5 Remove the bay leaf and stir in the chopped parsley. Serve the rice hot, garnished with the celery leaves.

Louisiana Rice Energy 406kcal/1690kJ; Protein 24.7g; Carbohydrate 35.2g, of which sugars 4.7g; Fat 18.4g, of which saturates 3.8g; Cholesterol 251mg; Calcium 34mg; Fibre 2.1g; Sodium 92mg.
Pilau Rice Energy 302kcal/1258kJ; Protein 5.8g; Carbohydrate 46.4g, of which sugars 1g; Fat 10.1g, of which saturates 1.1g; Cholesterol 0mg; Calcium 49mg; Fibre 0.8g; Sodium 2mg.

Chinese Special Fried Rice

This staple of Chinese cuisine consists of a mixture of chicken, shrimps and vegetables with fried rice.

Serves 4

200g/7oz/1 cup long grain white rice
45ml/3 tbsp groundnut (peanut) oil
1 garlic clove, crushed
4 spring onions (scallions), finely chopped
115g/4oz/1 cup diced cooked chicken
115g/4oz/1 cup peeled, cooked shrimps
50g/2oz/½ cup frozen peas
1 egg, beaten with a pinch of salt
50g/2oz/1 cup finely shredded lettuce
30ml/2 tbsp light soy sauce
pinch of caster (superfine) sugar
salt and ground black pepper
15ml/1 tbsp chopped, roasted cashew nuts, to garnish

1 Rinse the rice in two to three changes of warm water to wash away some of the starch. Drain well.

2 Put the rice in a pan and add 15ml/1 tbsp of the oil and 350ml/12fl oz/1½ cups water. Cover and bring to the boil, stir once, then cover and simmer for 12–15 minutes, until nearly all the water has been absorbed. Turn off the heat, cover and leave to stand for 10 minutes. Fluff up with a fork and leave to cool.

3 Heat the remaining oil in a wok or frying pan and stir-fry the garlic and spring onions for 30 seconds.

4 Add the chicken, shrimps and peas and stir-fry for about 1–2 minutes, then add the cooked rice and stir-fry for a further 2 minutes. Pour in the egg and stir-fry until just set. Stir in the lettuce, soy sauce, sugar and salt and pepper to taste.

5 Transfer to a warmed serving bowl, sprinkle with the chopped cashew nuts and serve immediately.

Cook's Tip
When using a wok, preheat it before adding the oil. Swirl the oil around the sides and heat it up before adding the ingredients.

Lemony Bulgur Wheat Salad

This Middle-Eastern salad, called *tabbouleh,* is delicious as an accompaniment to grilled meats or fish, or on its own as a light snack.

Serves 4

2 tomatoes, peeled and chopped
225g/8oz/1½ cups bulgur wheat
4 spring onions (scallions), finely chopped
75ml/5 tbsp chopped fresh mint
75ml/5 tbsp chopped fresh parsley
15ml/1 tbsp chopped fresh coriander (cilantro)
juice of 1 lemon
75ml/5 tbsp olive oil
salt and ground black pepper
fresh mint sprigs, to garnish

1 Make a slash in the skin of each tomato, then put them all in a heatproof bowl and pour over boiling water. Leave for 30 seconds, then plunge the tomatoes into cold water. Peel and seed, then roughly chop the flesh. Set aside.

2 Place the bulgur wheat in a bowl, pour on enough boiling water to cover and leave to soak for 20 minutes.

3 Line a colander with a clean dish towel. Turn the soaked bulgur wheat into the centre, let it drain, then gather up the sides of the dish towel and squeeze out any remaining liquid. Turn the bulgur wheat into a large bowl.

4 Add the spring onions, mint, parsley, coriander and tomatoes. Mix well, then pour over the lemon juice and olive oil. Season generously with salt and pepper, then toss so that all the ingredients are combined.

5 Chill in the refrigerator for a couple of hours before serving, garnished with mint.

Variation
Add some pitted, halved black olives to the salad just before serving for extra tangy flavour.

Fried Rice Energy 343kcal/1434kJ; Protein 20.2g; Carbohydrate 40.5g, of which sugars 4.2g; Fat 11.2g, of which saturates 1.6g; Cholesterol 124mg; Calcium 91mg; Fibre 2.4g; Sodium 632mg.
Wheat Salad Energy 194kcal/811kJ; Protein 4.3g; Carbohydrate 31.2g, of which sugars 2.3g; Fat 6.5g, of which saturates 0.9g; Cholesterol 0mg; Calcium 56mg; Fibre 1.6g; Sodium 12mg.

Tanzanian Vegetable Rice

This light, fluffy dish of steamed rice flavoured with colourful vegetables makes a versatile accompaniment.

Serves 4–6
350g/12oz/2 cups basmati rice
45ml/3 tbsp vegetable oil

1 onion, chopped
750ml/1¼ pints/3 cups vegetable
   stock or water
2 garlic cloves, crushed
115g/4oz/1 cup sweetcorn
½ fresh red or green (bell)
   pepper, chopped
1 large carrot, grated

1 Rinse the rice in a sieve (strainer) under cold water, then leave to drain for about 15 minutes.

2 Heat the oil in a large pan, add the onion and fry for a few minutes over medium heat until just softened.

3 Add the rice and stir-fry for about 10 minutes, taking care to stir continuously so that the rice does not stick to the bottom of the pan.

4 Add the stock or water and the garlic and stir well. Bring to the boil and cook over high heat for 5 minutes, then reduce the heat, cover with a tight-fitting lid and leave the rice to cook for 20 minutes.

5 Scatter the corn over the rice, then spread the pepper on top and lastly sprinkle over the grated carrot.

6 Cover tightly and continue to steam over low heat until the rice is cooked. Gently fork through the rice to fluff up and serve immediately.

> **Variation**
> Vary the vegetables according to what you have to hand. Sliced courgettes (zucchini) or small broccoli florets would work well, while frozen peas make an easy, colourful addition. Defrost them before adding to the rice.

Rice with Seeds & Spices

A change from plain boiled rice, this spicy dish makes a colourful accompaniment to curries.

Serves 4
5ml/1 tsp sunflower oil
2.5ml/½ tsp ground turmeric
6 green cardamom pods, lightly
   crushed
5ml/1 tsp coriander seeds, lightly
   crushed

1 garlic clove, crushed
200g/7oz/1 cup basmati rice
400ml/14fl oz/1⅔ cups stock
120ml/4fl oz/½ cup natural
   (plain) yogurt
15ml/1 tbsp toasted sunflower
   seeds
15ml/1 tbsp toasted sesame
   seeds
salt and ground black pepper
fresh coriander (cilantro) leaves, to
   garnish

1 Heat the oil in a non-stick frying pan and fry the spices and garlic for about 1 minute, stirring constantly.

2 Add the rice and stock and stir to mix. Bring to the boil, then cover and simmer for 15 minutes or until just tender.

3 Stir in the yogurt and the toasted sunflower and sesame seeds. Season with salt and pepper to taste and serve immediately, garnished with coriander leaves.

> **Cook's Tips**
> • If you have time, soak the rice for 30 minutes in cold water before cooking.
> • Although basmati rice gives the best texture and flavour, you could substitute ordinary long grain rice if you prefer.

> **Variation**
> You can always add some unsalted nuts to the dish, to give interesting texture. Shelled pistachios would be a good choice, as they add extra colour, but peanuts, almonds and cashews will all taste just as delicious.

Tanzanian Energy 449kcal/1877kJ; Protein 8.1g; Carbohydrate 83g, of which sugars 7.7g; Fat 9.3g, of which saturates 1.1g; Cholesterol 0mg; Calcium 30mg; Fibre 1.8g; Sodium 85mg.
Seeds & Spices Energy 248kcal/1035kJ; Protein 6.6g; Carbohydrate 42.2g, of which sugars 2.3g; Fat 5.7g, of which saturates 0.9g; Cholesterol 0mg; Calcium 117mg; Fibre 0.6g; Sodium 27mg.

Lemon & Herb Risotto Cake

This unusual rice dish can be served as a light main course with salad, or as a satisfying side dish.

Serves 4

1 small leek, thinly sliced
600ml/1 pint/2½ cups chicken or
   vegetable stock
225g/8oz/1¼ cups risotto rice

finely grated rind of 1 lemon
30ml/2 tbsp chopped fresh chives
30ml/2 tbsp chopped
   fresh parsley
75g/3oz/generous ½ cup grated
   mozzarella cheese
salt and ground black pepper
fresh parsley and lemon wedges,
   to garnish

1 Preheat the oven to 200°C/400°F/Gas 6. Lightly oil a 22cm/8½in round loose-bottomed cake tin (pan).

2 Put the sliced leek in a large pan with 45ml/3 tbsp of the stock. Cook over medium heat, stirring occasionally, for about 5 minutes until softened. Add the rice and the remaining stock.

3 Bring to the boil. Lower the heat, cover the pan with a tight-fitting lid and simmer gently, stirring occasionally, for about 20 minutes, or until all the liquid has been absorbed.

4 Stir in the lemon rind, chives, chopped parsley and grated mozzarella cheese and season with salt and pepper to taste. Spoon into the tin, cover with foil and bake for 30–35 minutes or until lightly browned.

5 Carefully turn out the risotto cake and cut into slices. Serve immediately, garnished with parsley and lemon wedges.

Cook's Tips
• *This risotto cake is equally delicious served cold, so it makes ideal picnic food. Chill until needed, then pack layered with kitchen foil or baking parchment.*
• *If you cannot obtain risotto rice, use short grain rice – the type normally used for puddings – instead.*

Bulgur & Lentil Pilaff

Many of the ingredients for this tasty, aromatic dish can be found in a well-stocked store cupboard.

Serves 4

5ml/1 tsp olive oil
1 large onion, thinly sliced
2 garlic cloves, crushed
5ml/1 tsp ground coriander
5ml/1 tsp ground cumin

5ml/1 tsp ground turmeric
2.5ml/½ tsp ground allspice
225g/8oz/1¼ cups bulgur wheat
about 750ml/1¼ pints/3 cups
   vegetable stock or water
115g/4oz/1½ cups sliced button
   (white) mushrooms
115g/4oz/½ cup green lentils
cayenne pepper
salt and ground black pepper
fresh parsley sprigs, to garnish

1 Heat the oil in a non-stick pan and fry the onion, garlic, ground coriander, cumin, turmeric and allspice and fry over low heat, stirring constantly, for 1 minute.

2 Stir in the bulgur wheat and cook, stirring constantly, for about 2 minutes, until lightly browned. Add the stock or water, mushrooms and lentils.

3 Bring to the boil, cover, then simmer over very low heat for 25–30 minutes, until the bulgur wheat and lentils are tender and all the liquid has been absorbed. Add more stock or water during cooking, if necessary.

4 Season well with salt, black pepper and cayenne pepper. Transfer to a warmed serving dish and serve immediately, garnished with parsley sprigs.

Cook's Tips
• *Bulgur wheat is very easy to cook and can be used in almost any way you would normally use rice – hot or cold. Some of the finer grades need hardly any cooking, so check the packet instructions for cooking times.*
• *Green lentils can be cooked without presoaking. They cook quite quickly and keep their shape.*

Risotto Energy 260kcal/1086kJ; Protein 8.4g; Carbohydrate 46g, of which sugars 0.9g; Fat 4.4g, of which saturates 2.6g; Cholesterol 11mg; Calcium 110mg; Fibre 1.2g; Sodium 79mg.
Pilaff Energy 242kcal/1016kJ; Protein 11.3g; Carbohydrate 47g, of which sugars 3.2g; Fat 2.1g, of which saturates 0.2g; Cholesterol 0mg; Calcium 45mg; Fibre 3.6g; Sodium 7mg.

Creole Jambalaya

A fusion of exciting flavours, this colourful dish of chicken thighs, vegetables and rice is very enticing. Serve this nourishing dish surrounded by fresh frisée salad leaves.

Serves 6

4 chicken thighs, boned, skinned and diced
about 300ml/½ pint/1¼ cups chicken stock
1 large green (bell) pepper, seeded and sliced
3 celery sticks, sliced
4 spring onions (scallions), sliced
400g/14oz can tomatoes
5ml/1 tsp ground cumin
5ml/1 tsp ground allspice
2.5ml/½ tsp cayenne pepper
5ml/1 tsp dried thyme
300g/10oz/1½ cups long grain rice
200g/7oz/scant 2 cups peeled, cooked prawns (shrimp)
salt and ground black pepper

1 Fry the chicken in a non-stick pan without fat, turning occasionally, until golden brown.

2 Add 15ml/1 tbsp stock to the pan with the sliced green pepper, celery stick and spring onions. Cook for a few minutes, stirring occasionally, until softened, then stir in the tomatoes, cumin, allspice, cayenne pepper and thyme.

3 Stir in the rice and the remaining stock. Bring to the boil, then reduce the heat, cover tightly and simmer for about 20 minutes, stirring occasionally, until the rice is tender. Add more stock during cooking, if necessary.

4 Stir the peeled prawns into the rice, then return to low heat to warm through the prawns. Season to taste with salt and pepper and serve immediately.

> ### Variation
> Traditionally, Jambalayas are made with ham, so try adding 115g/4oz diced cooked ham with the vegetables.

Minted Couscous Castles

These pretty little timbales are perfect for serving as part of a summer lunch. They are virtually fat-free, so you can happily indulge yourself without feeling remotely guilty.

Serves 6

225g/8oz/1¼ cups couscous
475ml/16fl oz/2 cups boiling vegetable stock
15ml/1 tbsp lemon juice
2 tomatoes, diced
30ml/2 tbsp chopped fresh mint
oil, for brushing
salt and ground black pepper
fresh mint sprigs, to garnish

1 Place the couscous in a bowl and pour over the boiling stock. Cover the bowl and leave to stand for 30 minutes, until all the stock has been absorbed and the grains are tender.

2 Stir in the lemon juice with the tomatoes and chopped mint. Adjust the seasoning with salt and pepper.

3 Brush the insides of four cups or individual moulds lightly with oil. Spoon in the couscous mixture and pack down firmly. Chill for several hours.

4 Invert the castles on to a platter and serve cold, garnished with mint. Alternatively, cover and heat gently in a low oven, then turn out and serve hot.

> ### Cook's Tip
> You will need the "instant" type of couscous for this dish, which is now widely available from most supermarkets. However, this type of quick couscous is not always immediately distinguishable from traditional couscous, which requires steaming first, so always check the instructions on the packet before buying. Only Moroccan couscous is produced in this "instant" form. The grains of traditional couscous can vary in size depending on the country of origin; the grains of Moroccan couscous are small, whereas Lebanese couscous is about the size of chickpeas.

Castles Energy 94kcal/396kJ; Protein 2.7g; Carbohydrate 20.7g, of which sugars 1g; Fat 0.5g, of which saturates 0g; Cholesterol 0mg; Calcium 27mg; Fibre 0.3g; Sodium 4mg.
Jambalaya Energy 290kcal/1214kJ; Protein 24g; Carbohydrate 42.1g, of which sugars 2.1g; Fat 2.5g, of which saturates 0.6g; Cholesterol 135mg; Calcium 52mg; Fibre 0.7g; Sodium 134mg.

Red Fried Rice

In this delicious version of egg fried rice, the vibrant colours of red onion, red pepper and cherry tomatoes add lots of eye appeal. An ideal dish for a quick supper.

Serves 2

115g/4oz/³/4 cup basmati rice

30ml/2 tbsp groundnut (peanut) oil

1 small red onion, chopped

1 red (bell) pepper, seeded and chopped

225g/8oz cherry tomatoes, halved

2 eggs, beaten

salt and ground black pepper

1 Rinse the rice several times under cold running water. Drain well. Bring a large pan of water to the boil, add the rice and cook for 10–12 minutes.

2 Meanwhile, heat the oil in a wok until very hot and stir-fry the onion and red pepper for 2–3 minutes. Add the cherry tomatoes and stir-fry for a further 2 minutes.

3 Pour in the beaten eggs all at once. Cook for 30 seconds without stirring, then stir to break up the eggs as they set.

4 Drain the cooked rice thoroughly, add to the wok and toss it over the heat with the vegetable and egg mixture for 3 minutes. Season the fried rice with salt and pepper to taste.

Cook's Tips
• Basmati rice is good for this dish as its slightly crunchy texture complements the softness of the egg.
• It is possible to stir-fry in a frying pan, if you don't have a wok. However, the heat will be less evenly distributed and it is harder to toss the ingredients.

Variation
Add diced cooked ham or chicken with dashes of soy sauce.

Fruity Brown Rice

An oriental-style dressing gives this colourful rice salad extra piquancy.

Serves 4

115g/4oz/²/3 cup brown rice

1 small red (bell) pepper, seeded and diced

200g/7oz can sweetcorn kernels, drained

45ml/3 tbsp sultanas (golden raisins)

225g/8oz can pineapple pieces in fruit juice

15ml/1 tbsp light soy sauce

15ml/1 tbsp sunflower oil

15ml/1 tbsp hazelnut oil

1 garlic clove, crushed

5ml/1 tsp finely chopped fresh root ginger

salt and ground black pepper

4 spring onions (scallions), diagonally sliced, to garnish

1 Bring a large pan of lightly salted water to the boil and cook the brown rice for about 30 minutes, or until it is just tender. Drain thoroughly, rinse under cold water and drain again. Set aside to cool.

2 Turn the rice into a large serving bowl and add the red pepper, sweetcorn and sultanas. Drain the pineapple pieces, reserving the juice, then add to the rice mixture and toss lightly.

3 Pour the reserved pineapple juice into a clean screw-top jar. Add the soy sauce, sunflower and hazelnut oils, garlic and chopped root ginger. Season to taste with salt and pepper. Close the jar tightly and shake vigorously to combine.

4 Pour the dressing over the salad and toss well. Scatter the spring onions over the top and serve.

Cook's Tip
• Hazelnut oil gives a distinctive flavour to any salad dressing. Like olive oil, it contains mainly mono-unsaturated fats.
• Brown rice is often mistakenly called wholegrain. In fact, the outer husk is completely inedible and is removed from all rice, but the bran layer is left intact on brown rice.

Red Rice Energy 437kcal/1821kJ; Protein 12.6g; Carbohydrate 57.4g, of which sugars 10.5g; Fat 17.6g, of which saturates 3.1g; Cholesterol 190mg; Calcium 62mg; Fibre 3g; Sodium 85mg.
Fruity Rice Energy 189kcal/797kJ; Protein 3g; Carbohydrate 35.5g, of which sugars 14.4g; Fat 4.8g, of which saturates 0.6g; Cholesterol 0mg; Calcium 18mg; Fibre 1.9g; Sodium 272mg.

Nut Pilaff with Omelette Rolls

This pilaff fuses together a wonderful mixture of textures – soft fluffy rice with crunchy nuts and omelette rolls.

Serves 2
175g/6oz/1 cup basmati rice
15ml/1 tbsp sunflower oil
1 small onion, chopped
1 red (bell) pepper, finely diced
350ml/12fl oz/1½ cups hot vegetable stock
2 eggs
25g/1oz/¼ cup salted peanuts
15ml/1 tbsp soy sauce
salt and ground black pepper
fresh parsley sprigs, to garnish

1 Rinse the rice several times under cold running water. Drain thoroughly and set aside.

2 Heat half the oil in a large frying pan and fry the onion and red pepper for 2–3 minutes, then stir in the rice and stock. Bring to the boil, lower the heat slightly and simmer for 10 minutes until the rice is tender.

3 Meanwhile, beat the eggs lightly and season to taste with salt and pepper. Heat the remaining oil in a second large frying pan. Pour in the eggs and tilt the pan to cover the base thinly. Cook the omelette for 1 minute, then flip it over and cook the other side for 1 minute.

4 Slide the omelette on to a clean board and roll it up tightly. Cut the omelette roll into eight slices.

5 Stir the peanuts and the soy sauce into the pilaff and add black pepper to taste. Turn the pilaff into a serving dish, then carefully arrange the omelette rolls on top and garnish with the parsley. Serve immediately.

> **Variation**
> *To ring the changes, try salted cashew nuts or toasted flaked almonds instead of the peanuts.*

Aubergine Pilaff

This hearty dish is made with bulgur wheat and aubergine, flavoured with fresh mint. It is a perfect choice for a midweek supper as it can be prepared within 15 minutes.

Serves 2
2 aubergines (eggplants)
60–90ml/4–6 tbsp sunflower oil
1 small onion, finely chopped
175g/6oz/1 cup bulgur wheat
450ml/¾ pint/scant 2 cups vegetable stock
30ml/2 tbsp pine nuts, toasted
15ml/1 tbsp chopped fresh mint
salt and ground black pepper

For the garnish
lime wedges
lemon wedges
fresh mint sprigs

1 Trim the ends from the aubergines, then slice them lengthways. Cut each slice into neat sticks and then into 1cm/½in dice.

2 Heat 60ml/4 tbsp of the oil in a large heavy frying pan, add the onion and fry over medium heat for 1 minute. Add the the diced aubergine. Increase the heat to high and cook, stirring frequently, for about 4 minutes until just tender. Add the remaining oil if needed.

4 Stir in the bulgur wheat, mixing well, then pour in the vegetable stock. Bring to the boil, then lower the heat and simmer for 10 minutes or until all the liquid has evaporated. Season to taste with salt and pepper.

5 Stir in the pine nuts and mint, then spoon the pilaff on to individual plates. Garnish each portion with lime and lemon wedges. Sprinkle with torn mint leaves for extra colour and serve immediately.

> **Variation**
> *Use courgettes (zucchini) instead of aubergine, or for something completely different, substitute pumpkin or acorn squash.*

Nut Energy 550kcal/2292kJ; Protein 17.4g; Carbohydrate 80g, of which sugars 8.4g; Fat 17.7g, of which saturates 3.4g; Cholesterol 190mg; Calcium 69mg; Fibre 2.6g; Sodium 609mg.
Aubergine Energy 542kcal/2248kJ; Protein 9.6g; Carbohydrate 52.2g, of which sugars 5.3g; Fat 34g, of which saturates 3.5g; Cholesterol 0mg; Calcium 83mg; Fibre 3.7g; Sodium 7mg.

Vegetables & Salads

Fresh, appetizing vegetables are packed with vitamins and minerals and can be used to create a variety of tempting dishes. Select from hearty, warming recipes, such as Tex-Mex Baked Potatoes with Chilli, or Winter Vegetable Hot-pot; simple accompaniments, such as Parsnips with Almonds, or Vegetable Ribbons; or light, fresh salads, such as Fresh Tuna Salad Niçoise, or Classic Greek Salad.

Ratatouille

Bursting with Mediterranean flavours, this tasty dish may be served hot or cold, as a tasty starter, side dish or vegetarian main course.

Serves 4

2 large aubergines (eggplants), roughly chopped
150ml/¼ pint/⅔ cup olive oil
2 onions, sliced
2 garlic cloves, chopped
4 courgettes (zucchini), roughly chopped
1 large red (bell) pepper, seeded and roughly chopped
2 large yellow (bell) peppers, seeded and roughly chopped
1 fresh rosemary sprig
1 fresh thyme sprig
5ml/1 tsp coriander seeds, crushed
3 plum tomatoes, peeled, seeded and chopped
8 basil leaves, roughly torn
salt and ground black pepper
fresh parsley or basil sprigs, to garnish

1 Place the aubergines in a colander, sprinkle with salt and place a plate with a weight on top. Leave for 30 minutes to extract the bitter juices.

2 Heat the olive oil in a large pan and gently fry the onions for about 6–7 minutes until just softened. Add the garlic and cook for a further 2 minutes, stirring frequently.

3 Rinse the aubergines under cold running water, then drain and pat dry with kitchen paper. Add the aubergines to the pan of onions, together with the courgettes and peppers. Increase the heat and sauté for a few minutes until just turning brown.

4 Add the rosemary, thyme and coriander seeds, then cover the pan and cook gently for about 30 minutes.

5 Add the tomatoes and season to taste with salt and pepper. Cook gently for a further 10 minutes, until the vegetables are soft but not too mushy.

6 Remove the sprigs of herbs. Stir in the torn basil leaves and adjust the seasoning. Leave to cool slightly and serve warm or cold, garnished with sprigs of parsley or basil.

Lemony Carrots

The carrots are cooked until just tender in a lemony stock which is then thickened to make a light tangy sauce.

Serves 4

450g/1lb carrots, thinly sliced
bouquet garni
15ml/1 tbsp freshly squeezed lemon juice
pinch of freshly grated nutmeg
20g/¾ oz/1½ tbsp butter
15ml/½ oz/1 tbsp plain (all-purpose) flour
salt and ground black pepper

1 Bring 600ml/1 pint/2½ cups water to the boil in a large pan, then add the carrots, bouquet garni and lemon juice. Add a pinch of nutmeg and season to taste with salt and pepper.

2 Bring back to the boil, then lower the heat slightly and simmer until the carrots are tender. Remove the carrots using a slotted spoon, then keep warm.

3 Boil the cooking liquid hard until it has reduced to about 300ml/½ pint/1¼ cups. Discard the bouquet garni.

4 Mash 15g/½oz/1 tbsp of the butter and all of the flour together, then gradually whisk into the simmering reduced cooking liquid, whisking well after each addition. Continue to simmer for about 3 minutes, stirring frequently, until the sauce has thickened.

5 Return the carrots to the pan, heat through in the sauce, then remove from the heat. Stir in the remaining butter and serve immediately.

Cook's Tip
A bouquet garni is a small bunch of herbs, usually bay leaves, parsley and thyme, tied together with string or in a muslin bag. If you make your own, you can add different herbs to suit a dish. Dried bouquet garnis are sold in supermarkets.

Carrots Energy 89kcal/372kJ; Protein 1.1g; Carbohydrate 11.8g, of which sugars 8.4g; Fat 4.5g, of which saturates 2.7g; Cholesterol 11mg; Calcium 34mg; Fibre 2.8g; Sodium 59mg.
Ratatouille Energy 349kcal/1442kJ; Protein 6.4g; Carbohydrate 21.6g, of which sugars 19.1g; Fat 26.9g, of which saturates 4g; Cholesterol 0mg; Calcium 82mg; Fibre 7.3g; Sodium 18mg.

Fried Spring Greens

Nutrient-rich leafy vegetables make a healthy side dish.

Serves 4

15ml/1 tbsp olive oil
75g/3oz rindless smoked streaky (fatty) bacon, chopped
1 large onion, thinly sliced
2 garlic cloves, finely chopped
900g/2lb spring greens (collards), shredded
salt and ground black pepper

1 Heat the oil in a frying pan and fry the bacon for 2 minutes. Add the onion and garlic and fry for 3 minutes until softened.

2 Reduce the heat, add the spring greens and season with salt and pepper. Cook, covered, over gentle heat for about 15 minutes until the greens are tender. Serve immediately.

Parsnips with Almonds

Parsnips are sweetly spiced to bring out their flavour.

Serves 4

450g/1lb small parsnips
35g/1¼ oz/scant 3 tbsp butter
25g/1oz/¼ cup flaked (sliced) almonds
15g/½ oz/1 tbsp soft light brown sugar
pinch of ground mixed spice
15ml/1 tbsp lemon juice
salt and ground black pepper
chopped fresh chervil or parsley, to garnish

1 Cook the parsnips in boiling salted water until almost tender. Drain well. When the parsnips are cool enough to handle, cut each in half across its width, then quarter lengthways.

2 Melt the butter in a pan. Gently cook the parsnips and almonds, stirring and turning until they are lightly flecked with brown.

3 Mix together the sugar and spice, sprinkle over the parsnips and stir to mix. Trickle over the lemon juice. Season to taste with salt and pepper and heat for 1 minute. Garnish with herbs.

Turnips with Orange

Turnips coated in a delicious orange-flavoured buttery sauce make a wonderful alternative to the more usual potato side dish.

Serves 4

50g/2oz/¼ cup butter
15ml/1 tbsp vegetable oil
1 small shallot, finely chopped
450g/1lb small turnips, peeled and quartered
300ml/½ pint/1¼ cups freshly squeezed orange juice
salt and ground black pepper
roughly torn fresh flat leaf parsley, to garnish

1 Heat the butter and oil in a pan and cook the shallot gently, stirring occasionally, until softened but not coloured.

2 Add the turnips to the shallot and cook over medium heat, shaking the pan frequently, until the turnips start to absorb the butter and oil.

3 Pour the orange juice on to the turnips, turn to coat well, then simmer gently for about 30 minutes, until the turnips are tender and the orange juice is reduced to a buttery sauce. Season with salt and pepper, if required, then garnish with parsley and serve immediately.

Cook's Tips
• Sprinkle toasted nuts, such as flaked (sliced) almonds or chopped walnuts, over the turnips to add a contrast in textures.
• Use tender, young turnips, available in early summer. They have creamy coloured flesh and skins tinged with purple or green.

Variation
Use a mixture of parsnips and carrots; cut into large chunks and add 10ml/2 tsp soft light brown sugar with the orange juice to bring out the sweetness of the vegetables.

Spring Greens Energy 156kcal/644kJ; Protein 9.9g; Carbohydrate 8.2g, of which sugars 6.9g; Fat 9.5g, of which saturates 2.2g; Cholesterol 12mg; Calcium 478mg; Fibre 7.9g; Sodium 282mg.
Parsnips Energy 190kcal/794kJ; Protein 3.4g; Carbohydrate 18.5g, of which sugars 10.7g; Fat 11.9g, of which saturates 5.1g; Cholesterol 19mg; Calcium 65mg; Fibre 5.7g; Sodium 66mg.
Turnips Energy 176kcal/732kJ; Protein 1.7g; Carbohydrate 13.2g, of which sugars 12.6g; Fat 13.5g, of which saturates 6.9g; Cholesterol 27mg; Calcium 68mg; Fibre 3g; Sodium 101mg.

Red Cabbage with Pears & Nuts

A sweet and sour, spicy red cabbage dish, with the added juiciness of pears and extra crunch of walnuts.

Serves 6
15ml/1 tbsp walnut oil
1 onion, sliced
2 whole star anise
5ml/1 tsp ground cinnamon
pinch of ground cloves

450g/1lb red cabbage, finely
   shredded
25g/1oz/2 tbsp soft dark
   brown sugar
45ml/3 tbsp red wine vinegar
300ml/½ pint/1¼ cups red wine
150ml/¼ pint/⅔ cup port
2 pears, cut into 1cm/½in cubes
115g/4oz/⅔ cup raisins
115g/4oz/1 cup walnut halves
salt and ground black pepper

1 Heat the oil in a large heavy pan. Add the sliced onion and cook over low heat, stirring occasionally, for about 5 minutes until softened.

2 Add the star anise, cinnamon, cloves and cabbage and cook for about 3 minutes more.

3 Stir in the sugar, vinegar, red wine and port. Cover the pan and simmer gently for 10 minutes, stirring occasionally.

4 Stir in the cubed pears and raisins and cook without replacing the lid for a further 10 minutes, or until the cabbage is tender. Season to taste with salt and pepper. Mix in the walnut halves and serve immediately.

Cook's Tip
The vinegar and wine help to preserve the beautiful colour of the cabbage as well as adding to the flavour.

Variation
Omit the star anise and cinnamon and add 15ml/1tbsp juniper berries with the ground cloves.

Swiss Soufflé Potatoes

A fabulous combination of rich and satisfying ingredients – cheese, eggs, cream, butter and potatoes. This is the perfect dish for cold-weather entertaining.

Serves 4
4 baking potatoes, about
   900g/2lb total weight
115g/4oz/1 cup grated
   Gruyère cheese
115g/4oz/½ cup herb butter
60ml/4 tbsp double (heavy)
   cream
2 eggs, separated
salt and ground black pepper
snipped fresh chives, to garnish

1 Preheat the oven to 220°C/425°F/Gas 7. Scrub the potatoes, then prick them all over with a fork. Bake for 1–1½ hours until tender. Remove them from the oven and reduce the temperature to 180°C/350°F/Gas 4.

2 Cut each potato in half and scoop out the flesh into a bowl. Place the potato shells on a baking sheet and return them to the oven to crisp up while you are making the filling.

3 Mash the potato flesh, then add the Gruyère cheese, herb butter, cream and egg yolks. Beat well until smooth, then season to taste with salt and pepper.

4 Whisk the egg whites until stiff peaks form, then carefully fold into the potato mixture. Pile the mixture into the potato shells and bake for 20–25 minutes until risen and golden brown.

5 Transfer the potatoes to a warmed serving dish, garnish with chives and serve immediately.

Cook's Tip
To make the herb butter, mix 45ml/3 tbsp finely chopped fresh parsley and 10ml/2 tsp finely chopped fresh dill with 115g/4oz/½ cup softened butter. Season with a little salt.

Red Cabbage Energy 202kcal/847kJ; Protein 1.8g; Carbohydrate 30.1g, of which sugars 29.8g; Fat 2.1g, of which saturates 0.2g; Cholesterol 0mg; Calcium 60mg; Fibre 3.2g; Sodium 23mg.
Potatoes Energy 585kcal/2431kJ; Protein 14.3g; Carbohydrate 32.7g, of which sugars 3.1g; Fat 44.5g, of which saturates 27.2g; Cholesterol 205mg; Calcium 251mg; Fibre 2g; Sodium 443mg.

Cauliflower with Three Cheeses

The mingled flavours of three cheeses give a new twist to cauliflower cheese. Serve with roasted cherry tomatoes and chunks of hot olive bread for an elegant meat-free meal.

Serves 4
4 baby cauliflowers
250ml/8fl oz/1 cup single
  (light) cream
75g/3oz dolcelatte cheese, diced
75g/3oz mozzarella cheese, diced
45ml/3 tbsp freshly grated
  Parmesan cheese
pinch of freshly grated nutmeg
ground black pepper
toasted breadcrumbs, to garnish

1 Cook the cauliflowers in a large pan of boiling salted water for 8–10 minutes until just tender.

2 Meanwhile, put the cream in a small pan with the cheeses. Heat gently until the cheeses have melted, stirring occasionally. Season to taste with nutmeg and pepper.

3 When the cauliflowers are cooked, drain them thoroughly and place one on each of four warmed plates.

4 Carefully spoon a little of the cheese sauce over each cauliflower and sprinkle each with a few of the toasted breadcrumbs. Serve immediately.

> **Cook's Tips**
> • For a more economical dish or if baby cauliflowers are not available, use one large cauliflower instead. Cut it into quarters with a large sharp knife and remove the central core.
> • The luxurious sauce is very simple to make as it does not use a butter and flour base like a conventional cheese sauce. To make the sauce slightly less rich, replace the cream with milk.
> • To make the toasted breadcrumbs, use bread that is a couple of days old and turn into crumbs in a food processor. Toast until golden, shaking often. You could also use chopped nuts instead.

Thai Vegetables with Noodles

This dish makes a delicious vegetarian supper on its own, or it could be served as an accompaniment.

Serves 4
225g/8oz/4 cups egg noodles
15ml/1 tbsp sesame oil
45ml/3 tbsp groundnut (peanut) oil
2 garlic cloves, thinly sliced
2.5cm/1in piece fresh root ginger,
  finely chopped
2 fresh red chillies, seeded and
  sliced
115g/4oz/1 cup broccoli florets
115g/4oz baby corn on the cob
175g/6oz shiitake or oyster
  mushrooms, sliced
1 bunch spring onions (scallions),
  sliced
115g/4oz pak choi (bok choy) or
  Chinese leaves (Chinese
  cabbage), shredded
115g/4oz/generous 1 cup
  beansprouts
15–30ml/1–2 tbsp dark soy
  sauce
salt and ground black pepper

1 Bring a pan of salted water to the boil and cook the egg noodles according to the instructions on the packet. Drain well and toss in the sesame oil. Set aside.

2 Heat the groundnut oil in a wok or large frying pan and stir-fry the garlic and ginger for 1 minute. Add the chillies, broccoli, baby corn on the cob and mushrooms and stir-fry for a further 2 minutes.

3 Add the spring onions, shredded pak choi or Chinese leaves and beansprouts and stir-fry for another 2 minutes. Toss in the drained noodles, adding soy sauce and pepper to taste.

4 Continue to cook over high heat, stirring, for a further 2–3 minutes, until the ingredients are well mixed and warmed through. Serve immediately.

> **Variation**
> This is a very versatile dish – you can vary the vegetables as you wish. Try replacing the broccoli with asparagus tips or use mangetouts (snow peas) instead of the Chinese leaves.

Thai Vegetables Energy 364kcal/1528kJ; Protein 12g; Carbohydrate 44.3g, of which sugars 4g; Fat 16.7g, of which saturates 3.4g; Cholesterol 17mg; Calcium 102mg; Fibre 4.7g; Sodium 744mg.
Cauliflower Energy 318kcal/1318kJ; Protein 17.4g; Carbohydrate 4.4g, of which sugars 3.9g; Fat 25.8g, of which saturates 16.3g; Cholesterol 71mg; Calcium 371mg; Fibre 1.8g; Sodium 453mg.

Potato Gnocchi with Hazelnut Sauce

These delicate Italian potato dumplings are dressed with a wonderful, creamy-tasting hazelnut sauce.

Serves 4
675g/1½ lb large potatoes
115g/4oz/1 cup plain (all-purpose) flour, plus extra for dusting

For the hazelnut sauce
115g/4oz/½ cup hazelnuts, roasted
1 garlic clove, roughly chopped
½ tsp grated lemon rind
½ tsp lemon juice
30ml/2 tbsp sunflower oil
150g/5oz/¾ cup low-fat fromage frais
salt and ground black pepper

1 To make the sauce, put just over half of the hazelnuts in a blender or food processor with the garlic, grated lemon rind and juice. Process until coarsely chopped. With the motor running, gradually add the oil until the mixture is smooth. Spoon into a heatproof bowl and mix in the fromage frais. Season to taste with salt and pepper.

2 Put the potatoes in a pan of cold water. Bring to the boil and cook for 20–25 minutes. Drain well. When cool enough to handle, peel them and pass through a food mill into a bowl.

3 Add the flour a little at a time, until the mixture is smooth and slightly sticky. Add salt to taste. Roll out the mixture on to a floured board to form a sausage 1cm/½in in diameter. Cut into 2cm/¾in lengths. Roll one piece at at time on a floured fork to make the characteristic ridges. Flip on to a floured plate or tray.

4 Cook a batch of gnocchi in a large pan of boiling water for 3–4 minutes. Lift out with a slotted spoon and keep hot while cooking the rest of the gnocchi in the same way.

5 To heat the sauce, place the bowl over a pan of simmering water and heat gently, being careful not to let it curdle. Pour the sauce over the gnocchi. Roughly chop the remaining hazelnuts, scatter them over the top and serve immediately.

Winter Vegetable Hot-pot

Made with a variety of root vegetables, this one-pot dish is richly flavoured, and substantial enough to make a vegetarian main course.

Serves 4
2 onions, sliced
4 carrots, sliced
1 small swede, sliced
2 parsnips, sliced
3 small turnips, sliced
½ celeriac, cut into matchsticks
2 leeks, thinly sliced
30ml/2 tbsp mixed chopped fresh herbs, such as parsley and thyme
1 garlic clove, chopped
1 bay leaf, crumbled
300ml/½ pint/1¼ cups vegetable stock
15g/½ oz/1 tbsp plain (all-purpose) flour
675g/1½ lb red-skinned potatoes, scrubbed and thinly sliced
50g/2oz/¼ cup butter
salt and ground black pepper

1 Preheat the oven to 190°C/375°F/Gas 5. Arrange all the vegetables, except the potatoes, in layers in a large casserole with a tight-fitting lid, seasoning them lightly with salt and pepper and sprinkling them with chopped fresh herbs, garlic and crumbled bay leaf as you go.

2 Blend the vegetable stock into the flour and pour over the vegetables. Arrange the potatoes in overlapping layers on top. Dot with butter and cover tightly.

3 Cook in the oven for 1¼ hours, or until the vegetables are tender. Remove the lid from the casserole and cook for a further 15–20 minutes until the top layer of potatoes is golden and crisp at the edges. Serve immediately.

Cook's Tips
• *Make sure the root vegetables are cut into even-size slices so they cook uniformly.*
• *For cheesy toasts to serve with the hot-pot, toast slices of French bread on one side. Turn over and sprinkle the other side with grated Gruyère cheese, then grill (broil) until golden.*

Gnocchi Energy 495kcal/2071kJ; Protein 11.9g; Carbohydrate 52.9g, of which sugars 5.3g; Fat 27.6g, of which saturates 4.3g; Cholesterol 3mg; Calcium 132mg; Fibre 4.5g; Sodium 35mg.
Hot-Pot Energy 367kcal/1542kJ; Protein 8.5g; Carbohydrate 58.2g, of which sugars 24.5g; Fat 12.8g, of which saturates 7g; Cholesterol 27mg; Calcium 203mg; Fibre 13.1g; Sodium 178mg.

Vegetable Ribbons

This elegant vegetable side dish looks very impressive.

Serves 4
3 carrots
3 courgettes (zucchini)
120ml/4fl oz/½ cup chicken stock
30ml/2 tbsp freshly chopped parsley
salt and ground black pepper

1 Using a vegetable peeler or sharp knife, cut the carrots and courgettes into thin ribbons.

2 Bring the chicken stock to the boil in a pan and add the carrots. Return the stock to the boil, then add the courgettes. Boil rapidly for 2–3 minutes, or until the vegetable ribbons are just tender. Stir in the chopped parsley, season lightly with salt and ground black pepper and serve immediately.

Runner Beans with Tomatoes

Try to use tender young beans for this dish. If you use older ones, you will need to remove the "strings" down the sides before cooking.

Serves 4
675g/1½ lb/2 cups sliced runner (green) beans
40g/1½oz/3 tbsp butter
4 ripe tomatoes, peeled and chopped
salt and ground black pepper
chopped fresh tarragon, to garnish

1 Bring a pan of water to the boil, add the beans, return to the boil and cook for 3 minutes. Drain well.

2 Heat the butter in a pan, add the tomatoes and beans and season with salt and pepper. Cover the pan with a tight-fitting lid and simmer gently for about 10–15 minutes until tender.

3 Turn the beans and tomatoes into a warm serving dish, garnish with tarragon and serve immediately.

Rosemary Roasties

Theses potatoes are roasted with their skins on, giving them far more flavour than traditional roast potatoes. They are the ideal accompaniment to roast lamb.

Serves 4
1kg/2lb small red potatoes
30ml/2 tbsp olive oil
30ml/2 tbsp fresh rosemary leaves
pinch of paprika
salt

1 Leave the potatoes whole with the skins on, or if large, cut in half. Place the potatoes in a large pan of cold water and bring to the boil, then drain immediately.

2 Meanwhile, preheat the oven to 240°C/475°F/Gas 9.

3 Return the potatoes to the pan and drizzle the oil over them. Shake the pan to coat the potatoes evenly in the oil.

4 Transfer the potatoes to a roasting pan. Sprinkle with the rosemary, paprika and salt, then roast in the oven for 30 minutes, until the potatoes are golden brown and crisp; turn them once during cooking so that they brown evenly.

5 Remove the roasties from the oven, drain on kitchen paper and serve immediately.

Cook's Tip
The potatoes can be cut into smaller wedges, in which case the boiling stage can be omitted. Serve wedges with mayonnaise as an alternative to chips, or offer as canapés with drinks.

Variation
Add about 10 unpeeled garlic cloves to the roasting pan with the potatoes, adding a little extra oil and tossing well to coat. Roast the garlic with the potatoes; they will develop a sweet taste.

Ribbons Energy 42kcal/175kJ; Protein 2g; Carbohydrate 7.4g, of which sugars 6.9g; Fat 0.7g, of which saturates 0.2g; Cholesterol 0mg; Calcium 39mg; Fibre 2.5g; Sodium 183mg.
Runner Beans Energy 129kcal/536kJ; Protein 3.5g; Carbohydrate 8.6g, of which sugars 7.9g; Fat 9.2g, of which saturates 5.5g; Cholesterol 21mg; Calcium 65mg; Fibre 4.4g; Sodium 70mg.
Roasties Energy 189kcal/801kJ; Protein 4.3g; Carbohydrate 40.3g, of which sugars 3.3g; Fat 2.3g, of which saturates 0.4g; Cholesterol 0mg; Calcium 15mg; Fibre 2.5g; Sodium 28mg.

Courgette & Tomato Bake

In this tasty French dish, the vegetables are baked with bacon, rice and cheese.

Serves 4

45ml/3 tbsp olive oil
1 onion, chopped
1 garlic clove, crushed
3 rashers (strips) lean bacon, chopped
4 courgettes (zucchini), grated
2 tomatoes, peeled, seeded and chopped
115g/4oz/scant ¾ cup cooked long grain rice
10ml/2 tsp chopped fresh thyme
15ml/1 tbsp chopped fresh parsley
60ml/4 tbsp grated Parmesan cheese
2 eggs, lightly beaten
15ml/1 tbsp fromage frais or mascarpone
salt and ground black pepper

1 Preheat the oven to 180°C/350°F/Gas 4. Grease a shallow ovenproof dish with a little olive oil.

2 Heat the oil in a frying pan and fry the onion and garlic for 5 minutes until softened.

3 Add the bacon and fry for 2 minutes, then stir in the courgettes and fry for a further 8 minutes, stirring from time to time and allowing some of the liquid to evaporate. Remove the pan from the heat.

4 Add the tomatoes, cooked rice, herbs, 30ml/2 tbsp of the Parmesan cheese, the eggs and fromage frais or mascarpone, then season to taste with salt and pepper. Mix together well.

5 Spoon the mixture into the dish and sprinkle over the remaining Parmesan. Bake for 45 minutes until set and golden.

Cook's Tip
For a dinner party, divide the mixture among four lightly greased individual gratin dishes and bake at the same temperature for about 25 minutes until set and golden.

Spanish Green Beans with Ham

Spanish raw-cured Serrano ham is now increasingly available in supermarkets, but if you have difficulty finding it, you can use Parma ham or bacon instead.

Serves 4

450g/1lb green beans
45ml/3 tbsp olive oil
1 onion, thinly sliced
2 garlic cloves, finely chopped
75g/3oz Serrano ham, chopped
salt and ground black pepper

1 Top and tail the beans, then cook them in boiling salted water for about 5–6 minutes until they are just tender.

2 Meanwhile, heat the oil in a pan, add the onion and fry for 5 minutes until softened and translucent. Add the garlic and ham and cook for a further 1–2 minutes.

3 Drain the beans, then add them to the pan and cook, stirring occasionally, for 2–3 minutes. Season well with salt and pepper.

Tomato & Aubergine Gratin

This tasty Mediterranean dish is perfect with plainly cooked meat or poultry.

Serves 6

2 aubergines (eggplants), thinly sliced
45ml/3 tbsp olive oil
400g/14oz ripe tomatoes, sliced
40g/1½oz/½ cup freshly grated Parmesan cheese
salt and ground black pepper

1 Preheat the grill (broiler). Arrange the aubergines on a foil-lined grill rack. Brush with olive oil and grill (broil) for 15–20 minutes until golden, turning once and brushing with more oil.

2 Preheat the oven to 200°C/400°F/Gas 6. Toss the aubergine and tomato slices together with salt and pepper and put in a shallow ovenproof dish. Sprinkle with the cheese. Bake for 20 minutes, until the vegetables are hot and the top is golden.

Courgette Energy 302kcal/1255kJ; Protein 16.4g; Carbohydrate 14.6g, of which sugars 5.2g; Fat 20.2g, of which saturates 6.5g; Cholesterol 120mg; Calcium 249mg; Fibre 2.1g; Sodium 495mg.
Spanish Beans Energy 127kcal/523kJ; Protein 5.8g; Carbohydrate 5g, of which sugars 3.6g; Fat 9.5g, of which saturates 1.5g; Cholesterol 11mg; Calcium 46mg; Fibre 2.7g; Sodium 226mg.
Gratin Energy 101kcal/420kJ; Protein 3.7g; Carbohydrate 3.5g, of which sugars 3.4g; Fat 8.1g, of which saturates 2.3g; Cholesterol 7mg; Calcium 91mg; Fibre 2g; Sodium 80mg.

Sweet Potatoes with Bacon

This sweet potato dish is often served for Thanksgiving in North America to celebrate the settlers' first harvest.

Serves 4
2 large sweet potatoes (about 450g/1lb each), washed
50g/2oz/½ cup soft light brown sugar
30ml/2 tbsp lemon juice
40g/1½ oz/3 tbsp butter, plus extra for greasing
4 rashers (strips) smoked streaky (fatty) bacon, cut into thin strips
salt and ground black pepper
sprig of flat leaf parsley, to garnish

1 Preheat the oven to 190°C/375°F/Gas 5 and lightly butter a shallow ovenproof dish. Cut the unpeeled sweet potatoes crossways into four and place the pieces in a pan of boiling water. Cover with a tight-fitting lid and cook for about 25 minutes until just tender.

2 Drain the potatoes and, when cool enough to handle, peel and slice quite thickly. Place in a single layer in the prepared dish, arranging so that each slice overlaps one another.

3 Sprinkle over the sugar and lemon juice and dot with butter. Top with the bacon and season with salt and pepper.

4 Bake, uncovered, for 35–40 minutes, basting once or twice, until the potatoes are tender.

5 Preheat the grill (broiler) to high. Grill (broil) the potatoes for about 2–3 minutes, until they are browned and the bacon crispy. Garnish with parsley and serve immediately.

Cook's Tip
Sweet potatoes are now widely available in supermarkets. The orange-fleshed variety not only looks attractive but tastes delicious, particularly when the sweetness is enhanced, as here.

Potatoes Baked with Tomatoes

This dish from the south of Italy is utterly delicious, yet simplicity itself to make – mouthwatering layers of vegetables and cheese, baked until meltingly tender.

Serves 6
2 large red or yellow onions, thinly sliced
900g/2¼ lb potatoes, thinly sliced
450g/1lb fresh tomatoes, or canned, with their juice, sliced
90ml/6 tbsp olive oil
115g/4oz/1 cup freshly grated Parmesan or mature Cheddar cheese
few sprigs of fresh basil
salt and ground black pepper

1 Preheat the oven to 180°C/350°F/Gas 4. Brush a large baking dish generously with oil.

2 Arrange a layer of onions in the dish, followed by layers of potatoes and tomatoes. Pour on a little of the oil and sprinkle with cheese. Season with salt and pepper.

3 Repeat until the vegetables are used up, ending with an overlapping layer of potatoes and tomatoes. Tear the basil leaves into pieces, then add them here and there among the vegetables. Sprinkle the top with cheese and a little oil.

4 Pour on 50ml/2fl oz/¼ cup water. Bake for 1 hour, or until tender. If the top begins to brown too much, place a sheet of foil on top of the dish during cooking.

Cook's Tip
When ripe, flavourful tomatoes are available, use these instead of the canned variety; the resulting dish will be delicious and have a more authentic Italian flavour.

Variation
Add chopped, fried smoked bacon to the layer of onions.

Sweet Potatoes Energy 291kcal/1220kJ; Protein 5.4g; Carbohydrate 37.1g, of which sugars 19.5g; Fat 14.5g, of which saturates 7.4g; Cholesterol 38mg; Calcium 37mg; Fibre 2.7g; Sodium 421mg.
Potatoes Energy 309kcal/1290kJ; Protein 9.8g; Carbohydrate 31.7g, of which sugars 8g; Fat 16.7g, of which saturates 4.9g; Cholesterol 15mg; Calcium 211mg; Fibre 3.2g; Sodium 189mg.

Stuffed Onions

Roasted onions, filled with a ham and cheese stuffing, make a winning lunch dish. If you use small onions, they also made a tasty side dish.

Serves 6
6 large onions
75g/3oz/scant ½ cup ham, cut into small dice
1 egg

50g/2oz/½ cup dried breadcrumbs
45ml/3 tbsp finely chopped fresh parsley
1 garlic clove, chopped
pinch of freshly grated nutmeg
75g/3oz/¾ cup freshly grated cheese such as Parmesan or mature Cheddar
90ml/6 tbsp olive oil
salt and ground black pepper

1 Peel the onions without cutting through the bases. Cook them in a large pan of boiling water for about 20 minutes. Drain, then refresh in plenty of cold water.

2 Using a small sharp knife, cut around and scoop out each central section. Remove about half the inside (save it for soup). Lightly sprinkle the empty cavities with salt and leave the onions to drain upside down.

3 Preheat the oven to 200°C/400°F/Gas 6. Beat the ham into the egg in a small bowl. Stir in the breadcrumbs, parsley, garlic, nutmeg and all but 45ml/3 tbsp of the grated cheese. Add 45ml/3 tbsp of the oil, then season with salt and pepper.

4 Pat the insides of the onions dry with kitchen paper. Using a small spoon, fill them with the stuffing. Arrange the onions in a single layer in an oiled baking dish.

5 Sprinkle the tops with the remaining cheese and then with oil. Bake for 45 minutes, or until the onions are tender and golden on top. Serve immediately.

> **Cook's Tip**
> *These are particularly good with a home-made tomato sauce.*

Aubergine Baked with Cheeses

The key to this speciality of southern Italy is a good home-made tomato sauce.

Serves 4–6
900g/2lb aubergines (eggplants), thinly sliced
flour, for coating
olive oil, for frying and greasing
40g/1½ oz/½ cup freshly grated Parmesan cheese

400g/14oz mozzarella cheese, sliced very thinly
salt and ground black pepper

For the tomato sauce
60ml/4 tbsp olive oil
1 onion, very finely chopped
1 garlic clove, chopped
450g/1lb fresh tomatoes, or canned, chopped, with the juice
few fresh basil or parsley sprigs

1 Layer the aubergine slices in a colander, sprinkling each layer with a little salt. Leave to drain for about 20 minutes, then rinse under cold running water and pat dry with kitchen paper.

2 To make the tomato sauce, cook the onion in the oil until translucent. Stir in the garlic and the tomatoes (if using fresh tomatoes, add 45ml/3 tbsp water). Season to taste with salt and pepper, then add the basil or parsley. Simmer gently for 30 minutes, stirring occasionally. Purée in a food mill, if you wish.

3 Pat the aubergine slices dry, then coat them lightly in flour. Heat a little oil in a large non-stick frying pan. Add a single layer of aubergines, cover and cook over low to medium heat until softened. Turn and cook on the other side. Remove from the pan with a slotted spoon and repeat with the remaining slices.

4 Preheat the oven to 180°C/350°F/Gas 4. Grease a wide shallow baking dish. Spread a little tomato sauce in the base. Cover with a layer of aubergine. Sprinkle with a few teaspoons of Parmesan, season to taste with salt and pepper, and cover with a layer of mozzarella. Spoon on some tomato sauce.

5 Repeat until all the ingredients are used up, ending with a covering of the tomato sauce and a sprinkling of Parmesan. Sprinkle with a little olive oil, and bake for about 45 minutes until golden and bubbling.

Aubergine Energy 345kcal/1433kJ; Protein 17.2g; Carbohydrate 7.7g, of which sugars 5.9g; Fat 27.6g, of which saturates 12.3g; Cholesterol 45mg; Calcium 347mg; Fibre 3.9g; Sodium 346mg.
Stuffed Onions Energy 140kcal/584kJ; Protein 8.7g; Carbohydrate 13.4g, of which sugars 5.2g; Fat 5.9g, of which saturates 3.1g; Cholesterol 51mg; Calcium 145mg; Fibre 1.7g; Sodium 320mg.

Mushrooms with Chipotle Chillies

Chipotle chillies are *jalapeños* that have been smoke-dried. They are the perfect foil for the mushrooms in this simple warm salad. Serve with lots of warm bread to soak up the tasty juices.

Serves 6

2 chipotle chillies
450g/1lb/6 cups button (white) mushrooms
60ml/4 tbsp vegetable oil
1 onion, finely chopped
2 garlic cloves, chopped
fresh coriander (cilantro), to garnish

1 Soak the dried chillies in a bowl of hot water for about 10 minutes. Drain, then trim and remove the seeds. Chop finely.

2 Cut the mushrooms in half, if large. Heat the oil in a large frying pan. Add the onion, garlic, chillies and mushrooms and stir to coat in the oil. Fry for 6–8 minutes until the onion has softened. Transfer to a warmed dish. Chop some of the coriander, leaving some whole leaves, and use to garnish.

Baked Fennel with Parmesan

The delicate aniseed flavour of fennel is delicious with the sharpness of Parmesan cheese. Try serving with pasta dishes and risottos.

Serves 4–6

900g/2lb fennel bulbs, washed and cut in half
50g/2oz/¼ cup butter
40g/1½ oz/½ cup freshly grated Parmesan cheese

1 Cook the fennel bulbs in a large pan of boiling water until softened but not mushy. Drain well. Preheat the oven to 200°C/400°F/Gas 6.

2 Cut the fennel bulbs lengthways into four or six pieces. Place them in a buttered baking dish. Dot with butter, then sprinkle with the grated Parmesan. Bake in the oven for about 20 minutes until the cheese is golden brown. Serve immediately.

Courgettes with Sun-dried Tomatoes

Sun-dried tomatoes have a concentrated sweet flavour that goes particularly well with courgettes.

Serves 6

10 sun-dried tomatoes, dry or preserved in oil and drained
175ml/6fl oz/¾ cup warm water

75ml/5 tbsp olive oil
1 large onion, finely sliced
2 garlic cloves, finely chopped
900g/2lb courgettes (zucchini), cut into thin strips
salt and ground black pepper

1 Slice the sun-dried tomatoes into thin strips. Place in a bowl with the warm water. Allow to stand for 20 minutes.

2 Heat the oil in a large frying pan or pan, add the onion and cook over low to medium heat, stirring, until it has softened and turned translucent.

3 Stir in the garlic and the courgettes. Cook for about a further 5 minutes, continuing to stir the mixture.

4 Stir in the tomatoes and their soaking liquid. Season to taste with salt and pepper. Increase the heat slightly and cook until the courgettes are just tender. Serve hot or cold.

Cook's Tip
Sprinkle with grated Parmesan just before serving, if you wish.

Variation
For courgettes in rich tomato sauce, cook the courgettes up to the end of step 3, then add one 400g/14oz can drained chopped tomatoes and 4 peeled and chopped fresh tomatoes. Stir in 5ml/1 tsp vegetable bouillon powder and 30ml/2tbsp tomato purée (paste). Simmer for 10–15 minutes, until the sauce has thickened. Season with salt and pepper and serve.

Mushrooms Energy 83kcal/341kJ; Protein 2g; Carbohydrate 1.2g, of which sugars 0.8g; Fat 7.8g, of which saturates 0.9g; Cholesterol 0mg; Calcium 12mg; Fibre 1g; Sodium 5mg.
Baked Fennel Energy 96kcal/397kJ; Protein 3g; Carbohydrate 0.7g, of which sugars 0.6g; Fat 9.1g, of which saturates 5.7g; Cholesterol 24mg; Calcium 90mg; Fibre 0.8g; Sodium 127mg.
Courgettes Energy 141kcal/580kJ; Protein 3.2g; Carbohydrate 5.9g, of which sugars 4.9g; Fat 11.7g, of which saturates 1.7g; Cholesterol 0mg; Calcium 47mg; Fibre 2g; Sodium 4mg.

Broccoli Cauliflower Gratin

Broccoli and cauliflower look and taste good when served together, and this dish is much lighter than a classic cauliflower cheese.

Serves 4

1 small cauliflower (weighing about 250g/9oz)
1 head broccoli (weighing about 250g/9oz)
120ml/4fl oz/½ cup natural (plain) low-fat yogurt
75g/3oz/¼ cup grated reduced-fat Cheddar cheese
5ml/1 tsp wholegrain mustard
30ml/2 tbsp wholemeal (whole-wheat) breadcrumbs
salt and ground black pepper

1 Break the cauliflower and broccoli into florets and cook in lightly salted boiling water for 8–10 minutes, until just tender. Drain well and arrange in a flameproof dish.

2 Preheat the grill (broiler) to medium hot. Mix together in a bowl the yogurt, grated cheese and mustard. Season the mixture to taste with pepper and spoon over the cauliflower and broccoli florets.

3 Sprinkle the breadcrumbs over the top of the dish and place under the grill until golden brown. Serve immediately.

Cook's Tip

When preparing the cauliflower and broccoli, discard the tougher parts of the stalks, then break the florets into even-size pieces so they will cook evenly.

Variations

Chopped nuts make a good alternative to breadcrumbs in this light dish; almonds, hazelnuts or walnuts would all be suitable. Alternatively, add chopped ham to the dish before topping with the sauce, but this will increase the saturated fat content.

Tex-Mex Baked Potatoes with Chilli

A great way to spice up baked potatoes – top them with a chilli bean sauce then serve with sour cream.

Serves 4

2 large potatoes
15ml/1 tbsp oil, plus extra for rubbing
1 garlic clove, crushed
1 small onion, chopped
½ small red (bell) pepper, seeded and chopped
225g/8oz/1 cup lean minced (ground) beef
½ small fresh red chilli, seeded and chopped
5ml/1 tsp ground cumin
pinch of cayenne pepper
200g/7oz can chopped tomatoes
30ml/2 tbsp tomato purée (paste)
2.5ml/½ tsp dried oregano
2.5ml/½ tsp dried marjoram
200g/7oz can red kidney beans, drained and rinsed
15ml/1 tbsp chopped fresh coriander (cilantro)
60ml/4 tbsp sour cream
salt and ground black pepper
chopped fresh parsley, to garnish

1 Preheat the oven to 220°C/425°F/Gas 7. Rub the potatoes with a little oil and pierce with a skewer. Bake them on the top shelf for about 1 hour until cooked through.

2 Meanwhile, heat the oil in a pan and fry the garlic, onion and pepper gently for 4–5 minutes, until softened.

3 Add the beef and cook over medium heat, stirring, until browned all over. Stir in the chilli, cumin, cayenne pepper, tomatoes, tomato purée, oregano and marjoram, then add 60ml/4 tbsp water.

4 Cover the pan with a tight-fitting lid and simmer for about 25 minutes, stirring occasionally.

5 Remove the lid, stir in the kidney beans and cook for 5 minutes. Turn off the heat and stir in the chopped fresh coriander. Season to taste with salt and pepper and set aside.

6 Cut the baked potatoes in half and place them in serving bowls. Top with the chilli mixture and a dollop of soured cream, then garnish with chopped fresh parsley. Serve immediately.

Gratin Energy 137kcal/573kJ; Protein 13.5g; Carbohydrate 11.1g, of which sugars 5g; Fat 4.5g, of which saturates 2.3g; Cholesterol 8mg; Calcium 273mg; Fibre 2.9g; Sodium 218mg.
Tex-Mex Energy 327kcal/1369kJ; Protein 17.7g; Carbohydrate 30.6g, of which sugars 8.2g; Fat 15.7g, of which saturates 6.4g; Cholesterol 43mg; Calcium 71mg; Fibre 5.2g; Sodium 277mg.

Spanish Chilli Potatoes

The Spanish name for this dish, *patatas bravas*, means fierce, hot potatoes. Reduce the amount of chilli if you find it too fiery.

Serves 4
900g/2lb new or salad potatoes
60ml/4 tbsp olive oil
1 onion, finely chopped
2 garlic cloves, crushed

15ml/1 tbsp tomato purée (paste)
200g/7oz can chopped tomatoes
15ml/1 tbsp red wine vinegar
2–3 small dried red chillies, seeded and chopped finely, or 5–10ml/1–2 tsp hot chilli powder
5ml/1 tsp paprika
salt and ground black pepper
fresh flat leaf parsley sprig, to garnish

1 Cook the potatoes in their skins in boiling water for 10–12 minutes, or until just tender. Drain them well and leave to cool, then cut in half and set aside.

2 Heat the oil in a large pan and fry the onion and garlic for 5–6 minutes until just softened. Stir in the tomato purée, tomatoes, vinegar, chilli and paprika and simmer for about 5 minutes.

3 Add the potatoes and mix into the sauce mixture to coat. Cover with a tight-fitting lid and simmer gently for about 8–10 minutes, or until the potatoes are tender.

4 Season well with salt and pepper, then transfer to a warmed serving dish. Serve, garnished with a sprig of flat leaf parsley.

> **Cook's Tip**
> *Dried chillies will last for years, but they lose their savour over time, so buy only small quantities as you need them.*

Bombay Spiced Potatoes

A delicately aromatic mixture of whole and ground spices are used to flavour the potatoes in this classic Indian dish.

Serves 4
4 large potatoes (Maris Piper or King Edward), diced
60ml/4 tbsp sunflower oil
1 garlic clove, finely chopped

10ml/2 tsp brown mustard seeds
5ml/1 tsp black onion seeds (optional)
5ml/1 tsp ground turmeric
5ml/1 tsp ground cumin
5ml/1 tsp ground coriander
5ml/1 tsp fennel seeds
generous squeeze of lemon juice
salt and ground black pepper
chopped fresh coriander (cilantro) and lemon wedges, to garnish

1 Bring a pan of salted water to the boil, add the potatoes and simmer for about 4 minutes until just tender. Drain well.

2 Heat the oil in a large frying pan and add the garlic along with all the whole and ground spices. Stir-fry gently for 1–2 minutes until the mustard seeds start to pop.

3 Add the potatoes and stir-fry over medium heat for about 5 minutes, or until they are heated through and well coated with the spicy oil.

4 Season well with salt and pepper, then sprinkle over the lemon juice. Garnish with coriander and lemon wedges.

> **Cook's Tip**
> *Keep an eye open for black onion seeds – kalonji – in Indian or Pakistani food stores.*

> **Variation**
> *For spiced potatoes and spinach, blanch about 450g/1lb fresh young spinach in boiling water for 2 minutes, then drain and squeeze dry. Add with the potatoes in step 3.*

> **Variation**
> *Stir in a few spoonfuls of sour cream at the end of step 3.*

Bombay Spiced Energy 260kcal/1091kJ; Protein 4.8g; Carbohydrate 35.2g, of which sugars 2.8g; Fat 12.1g, of which saturates 1.5g; Cholesterol 0mg; Calcium 39mg; Fibre 3.4g; Sodium 40mg.
Spanish Chilli Energy 273kcal/1148kJ; Protein 4.6g; Carbohydrate 39.5g, of which sugars 5.9g; Fat 11.9g, of which saturates 1.9g; Cholesterol 0mg; Calcium 22mg; Fibre 3.1g; Sodium 39mg.

Spicy Jacket Potatoes

These lightly spiced potatoes make a glorious snack, light lunch or accompaniment to a meal.

Serves 2–4
2 large baking potatoes
5ml/1 tsp sunflower oil
1 small onion, chopped

2.5cm/1in piece fresh root ginger, grated
5ml/1 tsp ground cumin
5ml/1 tsp ground coriander
2.5ml/½ tsp ground turmeric
generous pinch of garlic salt
natural (plain) yogurt and fresh coriander (cilantro) sprigs, to serve

1 Preheat the oven to 220°C/425°F/Gas 7. Scrub the potatoes, then prick them all over with a fork. Bake for 1–1½ hours until tender. Remove them from the oven and reduce the temperature to 180°C/350°F/Gas 4.

2 Cut each potato in half and scoop out the flesh into a bowl. Place the potato shells on a baking sheet and return them to the oven to crisp up while you are making the filling.

3 Heat the oil in a non-stick frying pan, add the onion and fry for a few minutes until softened. Stir in the ginger, cumin, coriander and turmeric.

4 Stir over gentle heat for about 2 minutes, then add the potato flesh and garlic salt to taste. Mix well. Continue to cook the potato mixture gently for a further 2 minutes, stirring occasionally.

5 Remove the potato shells from the oven. Carefully spoon the potato mixture back into the shells and top each with a spoonful of natural yogurt and a sprig or two of fresh coriander. Serve immediately.

> **Cook's Tip**
> For the best results, choose a floury variety of potato, such as King Edward or Maris Piper.

Florets Polonaise

Steamed vegetables make a delicious and extremely healthy accompaniment.

Serves 6
500g/1¼lb cauliflower and broccoli

finely grated rind of ½ lemon
1 large garlic clove, crushed
25g/1oz/1½ cup wholegrain breadcrumbs, lightly baked or grilled (broiled) until crisp
2 eggs, hard-boiled and shelled
salt and ground black pepper

1 Trim the cauliflower and broccoli and break into florets, then place in a steamer over a pan of boiling water and steam for about 12 minutes. (If you prefer, boil the vegetables in salted water for 5–7 minutes, until just tender.) Drain the vegetables well and transfer to a warmed serving dish.

2 Meanwhile, make the topping. In a bowl, combine the lemon rind with the garlic and breadcrumbs. Finely chop the eggs and stir into the breadcrumb mixture. Season with salt and black pepper to taste, then sprinkle over the cooked vegetables.

Two Beans Provençal

This would make a tasty side dish for any main course.

Serves 4
5ml/1 tsp olive oil
1 small onion, finely chopped
1 garlic clove, crushed

225g/8oz/scant 1 cup green beans
225g/8oz/scant 1 cup runner (green) beans
2 tomatoes, peeled and chopped
salt and ground black pepper

1 Heat the oil in a heavy or non-stick frying pan, add the onion and sauté over medium heat until softened but not browned.

2 Add the garlic, both beans and the tomatoes. Season well with salt and pepper, then cover tightly. Cook over fairly low heat, shaking the pan from time to time, for about 30 minutes, or until the beans are tender. Serve immediately.

Spicy Potatoes Energy 85kcal/361kJ; Protein 2g; Carbohydrate 17.6g, of which sugars 2.2g; Fat 1.2g, of which saturates 0.2g; Cholesterol 0mg; Calcium 18mg; Fibre 1.5g; Sodium 17mg.
Two Beans Energy 47kcal/195kJ; Protein 2.5g; Carbohydrate 6.3g, of which sugars 5.3g; Fat 1.4g, of which saturates 0.3g; Cholesterol 0mg; Calcium 46mg; Fibre 3.1g; Sodium 5mg.

Chinese Crispy Seaweed

In northern China, a special kind of seaweed is used for this dish, but spring greens make a very successful alternative. Serve as part of a Chinese spread.

Serves 4
225g/8oz spring greens (collards)
groundnut (peanut) or sunflower
    oil, for deep-frying
1.5ml/¼ tsp salt
10ml/2 tsp soft light brown sugar
30–45ml/2–3 tbsp toasted,
    flaked (sliced) almonds

1 Cut out and discard any tough stalks from the spring greens. Place about six leaves on top of each other, then roll them up into a tight roll.

2 Using a sharp knife, slice across into thin shreds. Lay on a tray and leave to dry for about 2 hours.

3 Heat about 5–7.5cm/2–3in of oil in a wok or pan to 190°C/375°F. Carefully place a handful of the leaves into the oil – it will bubble and spit for the first 10 seconds and then die down. Deep-fry for about 45 seconds, or until a slightly darker green: do not let the leaves burn.

4 Remove with a slotted spoon, drain on kitchen paper and transfer to a serving dish. Keep warm in the oven while frying the remainder.

5 When you have fried all the shredded leaves, sprinkle with the salt and sugar and toss lightly. Garnish with the toasted almonds and serve immediately.

Cook's Tips
• Make sure that your deep frying pan is deep enough to allow the oil to bubble up during cooking. The pan should be less than half full.
• The sugar gives the "seaweed" its characteristic sweet flavour; add to taste.

Leek & Parsnip Purée

This vegetable purée makes a delectable accompaniment to roasted meat or chicken.

Serves 4
2 large leeks, sliced
3 parsnips, sliced
knob (pat) of butter

45ml/3 tbsp top of the milk or
    single (light) cream
30ml/2 tbsp fromage frais or
    cream cheese
generous squeeze of lemon juice
salt and ground black pepper
large pinch of freshly grated
    nutmeg, to garnish

1 Steam or boil the leeks and parsnips together for about 15 minutes until tender. Drain well, then place in a food processor or blender.

2 Add the remaining ingredients and process until really smooth, then season with salt and pepper to taste. Transfer to a warmed bowl and garnish with a sprinkling of nutmeg.

Mexican-style Green Peas

This is a great way to make the most of fresh peas.

Serves 4
15ml/1 tbsp olive oil
2 garlic cloves, halved
1 onion, halved and thinly sliced

2 tomatoes, peeled, seeded and
    chopped into dice
400g/14oz/scant 3 cups shelled
    fresh peas
salt and ground black pepper
fresh chives, to garnish

1 Heat the oil in a pan and cook the garlic until golden. Scoop it out with a slotted spoon and discard. Add the onion to the pan and fry until translucent. Add the tomatoes and peas.

2 Pour 30ml/2 tbsp water into the pan and stir to mix. Lower the heat and cover the pan tightly. Cook for about 10 minutes, until the peas are cooked. Season with plenty of salt and pepper, then transfer the mixture to a heated dish. Garnish with fresh chives and serve immediately.

Crispy Seaweed Energy 171kcal/707kJ; Protein 3.3g; Carbohydrate 4.4g, of which sugars 3.9g; Fat 15.7g, of which saturates 1.7g; Cholesterol 0mg; Calcium 137mg; Fibre 2.5g; Sodium 13mg.
Leek Purée Energy 98kcal/413kJ; Protein 3.9g; Carbohydrate 13.3g, of which sugars 7.5g; Fat 3.6g, of which saturates 1.7g; Cholesterol 6mg; Calcium 75mg; Fibre 5.7g; Sodium 32mg.
Mexican Peas Energy 130kcal/541kJ; Protein 7.8g; Carbohydrate 15.6g, of which sugars 6.3g; Fat 4.6g, of which saturates 0.8g; Cholesterol 0mg; Calcium 32mg; Fibre 5.9g; Sodium 11mg.

Middle-Eastern Vegetable Stew

This spiced dish of mixed vegetables can be served as a side dish or as a vegetarian main course.

Serves 4–6
45ml/3 tbsp vegetable or chicken stock
1 green (bell) pepper, seeded and sliced
2 courgettes (zucchini), sliced
2 carrots, sliced

2 celery sticks, sliced
2 potatoes, diced
400g/14oz can chopped tomatoes
5ml/1 tsp chilli powder
30ml/2 tbsp chopped fresh mint
15ml/1 tbsp ground cumin
400g/14oz can chickpeas, drained
salt and ground black pepper
fresh mint sprigs, to garnish

1 Heat the vegetable or chicken stock in a large flameproof casserole until boiling, then add the sliced pepper, courgettes, carrots and celery. Stir over high heat for 2–3 minutes, until the vegetables are just beginning to soften.

2 Add the potatoes, tomatoes, chilli powder, mint and cumin. Add the chickpeas and bring to the boil.

3 Reduce the heat, cover the casserole with a tight-fitting lid and simmer for 30 minutes, or until all the vegetables are tender. Season to taste with salt and pepper and serve hot, garnished with mint leaves.

Cook's Tip
As a vegetarian main course, this dish is delicious with a couscous accompaniment. Soak 275g/10oz/1⅔ cups couscous in boiling vegetable stock for 10 minutes. Fluff up with a fork, then add about 15 pitted black olives, 2 small courgettes (zucchini) cut into strips and some toasted flaked (sliced) almonds. Whisk together 60ml/4 tbsp olive oil, 15ml/1 tbsp lemon juice and 15ml/1 tbsp each chopped coriander (cilantro) and parsley. Whisk in a pinch of cumin, cayenne pepper and salt. Pour the dressing over the salad and toss to mix.

Summer Vegetable Braise

Tender young vegetables are ideal for quick cooking in a minimum of liquid.

salt and ground black pepper
chopped fresh parsley and snipped fresh chives, to garnish

Serves 4
175g/6oz baby carrots
175g/6oz/1½ cups sugar snap peas or mangetouts (snow peas)
115g/4oz baby corn
90ml/6 tbsp vegetable stock
10ml/2 tsp lime juice

1 Place the baby carrots, peas and baby corn in a large heavy pan with the vegetable stock and lime juice. Bring to the boil.

2 Cover the pan and reduce the heat, then simmer for about 6–8 minutes, shaking the pan occasionally, until the vegetables are just tender.

3 Season the vegetables to taste with salt and pepper, then stir in the chopped fresh parsley and snipped chives. Cook the vegetables for a few seconds more, stirring them once or twice until the herbs are well mixed, then serve.

Cook's Tip
This dish would be excellent for anyone on a low-fat diet.

Variations
• *Mix and match the summer vegetables as you wish: asparagus and young broad beans would make good additions.*
• *You can cook a winter version of this dish using seasonal root vegetables. Cut the peeled vegetables into even-size chunks and cook for slightly longer.*

Vegetable Stew Energy 149kcal/630kJ; Protein 7.8g; Carbohydrate 24.9g, of which sugars 6.8g; Fat 2.7g, of which saturates 0.4g; Cholesterol 0mg; Calcium 66mg; Fibre 5.7g; Sodium 172mg.
Summer Braise Energy 36kcal/151kJ; Protein 2.7g; Carbohydrate 5.9g, of which sugars 5.1g; Fat 0.3g, of which saturates 0.1g; Cholesterol 0mg; Calcium 33mg; Fibre 2.5g; Sodium 340mg.

Straw Potato Cake

This potato cake is so-named in France because of its resemblance to a woven straw doormat. But, of course, it tastes mouthwateringly good.

Serves 4
450g/1lb baking potatoes
22.5ml/1½ tbsp melted butter
15ml/1 tbsp vegetable oil
salt and ground black pepper

1 Peel the baking potatoes and grate them coarsely, then immediately toss them with the melted butter and season well with salt and pepper.

2 Heat the oil in a large frying pan. Add the potato mixture and press down to form an even layer that covers the base of the pan. Cook over medium heat for 7–10 minutes until the underside is well browned.

3 Loosen the potato cake by shaking the pan or running a thin palette knife under it.

4 To turn it over, invert a large baking sheet over the frying pan and, holding it tightly against the pan, turn them both over together. Lift off the frying pan, return it to the heat and add a little more oil if it looks dry. Slide the potato cake into the frying pan and continue cooking until it is crisp and browned on the second side. Serve immediately.

> **Cook's Tip**
> Make several small potato cakes instead of one large one, if you prefer. Simply adjust the cooking time.

> **Variation**
> Replace some of the potato with grated carrot or parsnip, or add some grated cheese and a pinch of freshly grated nutmeg to the raw potato and butter mix.

Sautéed Wild Mushrooms

This is a quick dish to prepare and makes an ideal side dish for all kinds of grilled and roast meats.

Serves 6
900g/2lb fresh mixed wild and cultivated mushrooms such as morels, porcini, chanterelles, oyster or shiitake

30ml/2 tbsp olive oil
25g/1oz/2 tbsp unsalted (sweet) butter
2 garlic cloves, chopped
3 or 4 shallots, finely chopped
45–60ml/3–4 tbsp chopped fresh parsley, or a mixture of different chopped fresh herbs
salt and ground black pepper

1 Wash and carefully dry the mushrooms. Trim the stems and cut the mushrooms into quarters, or slice if they are very large.

2 Heat the oil in a large frying pan over medium-hot heat. Add the butter and swirl to melt, then stir in the mushrooms and cook for 4–5 minutes until beginning to brown.

3 Add the garlic and shallots to the pan and cook for a further 4–5 minutes until the mushrooms are tender and any liquid given off has evaporated. Season to taste with salt and pepper and stir in the parsley or mixed herbs and serve hot.

> **Cook's Tip**
> Use as many different varieties of cultivated and wild mushrooms as you can find for a maximum taste.

> **Variation**
> For marinated mushrooms, fry 1 small chopped onion and 1 garlic clove in 30ml/2 tbsp olive oil. Stir in 15ml/1 tbsp tomato purée (paste) and 50ml/2fl oz/¼ cup dry white wine and a pinch of saffron threads. Season, cover and simmer gently for 45 minutes. Add 225g/8oz mushrooms, cover and cook for 5 minutes. Cool, still covered, then chill before serving.

Potato Cake Energy 145kcal/609kJ; Protein 2g; Carbohydrate 18.2g, of which sugars 1.5g; Fat 7.7g, of which saturates 3.4g; Cholesterol 12mg; Calcium 8mg; Fibre 1.1g; Sodium 47mg.
Wild Mushrooms Energy 92kcal/381kJ; Protein 3.2g; Carbohydrate 2.2g, of which sugars 1.4g; Fat 8g, of which saturates 2.9g; Cholesterol 9mg; Calcium 29mg; Fibre 2.3g; Sodium 36mg.
Celeriac (opposite) Energy 41kcal/171kJ; Protein 1g; Carbohydrate 1.7g, of which sugars 1.7g; Fat 3.5g, of which saturates 2g; Cholesterol 8mg; Calcium 78mg; Fibre 2.1g; Sodium 135mg.

Cannellini Bean Purée

This easy dish is wonderful with warm pitta bread.

Serves 4

400g/14oz can cannellini beans, rinsed and drained
45ml/3tbsp fromage frais or cream cheese
grated rind and juice of 1 large orange
15ml/1 tbsp finely chopped fresh rosemary
4 heads chicory (Belgian endive), halved lengthways
2 radicchio, cut into 8 wedges
15ml/1 tbsp walnut oil

1 Purée the drained beans in a blender or food processor with the fromage frais, orange rind and juice and the rosemary.

2 Lay the chicory and radicchio on a baking tray and brush with the walnut oil. Grill (broil) for 2–3 minutes until beginning to brown. Serve immediately with the purée.

Celeriac Purée

Many chefs add potato to celeriac purée, but this recipe highlights the pure flavour of the vegetable.

Serves 4

1 large celeriac (about 800g/1¾ lb), peeled
15g/½ oz/1 tbsp butter
pinch of grated nutmeg
salt and ground black pepper

1 Cut the celeriac into large dice, put in a pan with enough cold water to cover and add a little salt. Bring to the boil over medium-hot heat and cook gently for about 10–15 minutes until tender.

2 Drain the celeriac, reserving a little of the cooking liquid, and place in a food processor fitted with a metal blade or a blender. Process until smooth, adding a little of the cooking liquid if the purée needs thinning.

3 Stir in the butter and season to taste with salt, pepper and nutmeg. Reheat, if necessary, before serving.

Creamy Spinach Purée

Crème fraîche or béchamel sauce usually gives this dish its creamy richness. Here is a quick light alternative.

Serves 4

675g/1½lb/6 cups leaf spinach, stems removed
115g/4oz/½ cup full or medium-fat soft cheese
milk (if required)
pinch of freshly grated nutmeg
salt and ground black pepper

1 Rinse the spinach, shake lightly and place in a deep frying pan or wok. Cook over medium heat for about 3–4 minutes until wilted. Drain in a colander, pressing with the back of a spoon. The spinach does not need to be completely dry.

2 Process the spinach and soft cheese in a food processor or blender to form a purée, then transfer to a bowl. If the purée is too thick, add a little milk. Season to taste with salt, pepper and nutmeg. Transfer to a heavy pan and reheat gently to serve.

Hummus

This popular dish is widely available in supermarkets, but nothing compares to the home-made variety. It is very easy to make.

Serves 4–6

175g/6oz/1 cup cooked chickpeas
120ml/4fl oz/½ cup tahini paste
3 garlic cloves
juice of 2 lemons
45–60ml/3–4 tbsp water
salt and ground black pepper

1 Place the chickpeas, tahini paste, garlic, lemon juice, seasoning and a little of the water in a blender or food processor. Process until smooth, adding a little more water, if necessary. Chill before serving.

Hummus Energy 303kcal/1282kJ; Protein 18.5g; Carbohydrate 44.7g, of which sugars 5.2g; Fat 6.9g, of which saturates 1.2g; Cholesterol 0mg; Calcium 88mg; Fibre 7.2g; Sodium 16mg.
Cannellini Energy 143kcal/602kJ; Protein 8.2g; Carbohydrate 20.5g, of which sugars 6.3g; Fat 3.6g, of which saturates 0.4g; Cholesterol 0mg; Calcium 96mg; Fibre 6.7g; Sodium 397mg.
Spinach Energy 94kcal/388kJ; Protein 7.4g; Carbohydrate 3.6g, of which sugars 3.4g; Fat 5.5g, of which saturates 2.8g; Cholesterol 12mg; Calcium 287mg; Fibre 3.6g; Sodium 236mg.

Frankfurter Salad

A last-minute salad you can throw together using store-cupboard ingredients.

Serves 4
675g/1½ lb new potatoes
2 eggs

350g/12oz frankfurters
1 round (butterhead) lettuce, leaves separated
225g/8oz young spinach
30–45ml/2–3 tbsp oil and vinegar dressing
salt and ground black pepper

1 Boil the new potatoes in lightly salted water for 20 minutes. Drain, cover and keep warm.

2 Hard-boil the eggs for 12 minutes, then shell and quarter. Score the skins of the frankfurters cork-screw fashion, cover with boiling water and simmer for 5 minutes. Drain; keep warm.

3 Distribute the lettuce and spinach leaves among 4 plates, moisten the potatoes and frankfurters with dressing and arrange over the salad. Top with the eggs. Season with salt and pepper.

New Potato & Chive Salad

The secret is to add the dressing while the potatoes are still hot so that they absorb all the flavours.

Serves 4–6
675g/1½ lb new potatoes
45ml/3 tbsp olive oil

15ml/1 tbsp white wine vinegar
4ml/¾ tsp Dijon mustard
4 spring onions (scallions), finely chopped
175ml/6fl oz/¾ cup good quality mayonnaise
45ml/3 tbsp snipped fresh chives
salt and ground black pepper

1 Cook the potatoes, unpeeled, in boiling salted water until tender. Meanwhile, whisk together the oil, vinegar and mustard.

2 Drain the potatoes well, then immediately toss lightly with the vinegar mixture and spring onions and leave to cool. Stir in the mayonnaise and chives, season to taste and chill.

Watercress Potato Salad Bowl

New potatoes tossed with watercress, tomatoes and pumpkin seeds make a colourful, nutritious salad.

Serves 4
450g/1lb small new potatoes, unpeeled

1 bunch watercress
200g/7oz cherry tomatoes, halved
30ml/2 tbsp pumpkin seeds
45ml/3 tbsp low-fat fromage frais or natural (plain) yogurt
15ml/1 tbsp cider vinegar
5ml/1 tsp soft light brown sugar
salt and paprika

1 Cook the potatoes in lightly salted boiling water until just tender, then drain and leave to cool.

2 Toss together the potatoes, watercress, tomatoes and pumpkin seeds. Whisk together the fromage frais, vinegar, sugar, salt and paprika and, just before serving, toss with the salad.

Mixed Leafy Salad

This flavourful salad makes an ideal side dish for serving with meat and fish.

Serves 4
15g/1oz/½ cup mixed fresh herbs, such as chervil, tarragon (use sparingly), dill, basil, marjoram (use sparingly), flat leaf parsley, mint, sorrel, fennel and coriander (cilantro)

350g/12oz mixed salad leaves, such as rocket (arugula), radicchio, chicory (Belgian endive), watercress, frisée, baby spinach and oakleaf lettuce

For the dressing
50ml/2fl oz/¼ cup extra virgin olive oil
15ml/1 tbsp cider vinegar
salt and ground black pepper

1 Wash the herbs and salad leaves, then dry in a salad spinner, or use two clean, dry dish towels to pat them dry.

2 To make the dressing, blend together the olive oil and vinegar in a small bowl and season with salt and pepper to taste. Place all the leaves in a salad bowl. Toss with the dressing and serve.

Frankfurter Energy 472kcal/1969kJ; Protein 20g; Carbohydrate 30.9g, of which sugars 5g; Fat 29.3g, of which saturates 9.7g; Cholesterol 162mg; Calcium 146mg; Fibre 3.5g; Sodium 998mg.
Chive Salad Energy 334kcal/1385kJ; Protein 2.6g; Carbohydrate 19g, of which sugars 2.2g; Fat 28g, of which saturates 4.2g; Cholesterol 22mg; Calcium 27mg; Fibre 1.6g; Sodium 147mg.
Watercress Energy 152kcal/644kJ; Protein 6.1g; Carbohydrate 23.1g, of which sugars 5.2g; Fat 4.6g, of which saturates 0.7g; Cholesterol 0mg; Calcium 114mg; Fibre 2.8g; Sodium 45mg.

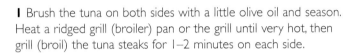

Fresh Tuna Salad Niçoise

Fresh tuna transforms this classic colourful salad from the south of France into something really special.

Serves 4
4 tuna steaks, about 150g/5oz each
30ml/2 tbsp olive oil
225g/8oz fine French beans, trimmed
1 small cos lettuce or 2 Little Gem lettuces
4 new potatoes, boiled
4 ripe tomatoes, or 12 cherry tomatoes
2 red peppers, seeded and cut into thin strips
4 hard-boiled eggs, sliced
8 drained anchovy fillets in oil, halved lengthways
16 large black olives
salt and ground black pepper
12 fresh basil leaves, to garnish

For the dressing
15ml/1 tbsp red wine vinegar
90ml/6 tbsp olive oil
1 fat garlic clove, crushed

1 Brush the tuna on both sides with a little olive oil and season. Heat a ridged grill (broiler) pan or the grill until very hot, then grill (broil) the tuna steaks for 1–2 minutes on each side.

2 Cook the beans in a pan of lightly salted boiling water for 4–5 minutes or until crisp-tender. Drain, refresh under cold water and drain again.

3 Separate the lettuce leaves and wash and dry them. Arrange them on four individual serving plates. Slice the potatoes and tomatoes, if large (leave cherry tomatoes whole) and divide them among the plates. Arrange the fine French beans and red pepper strips over them.

4 Shell the hard-boiled eggs, then cut them into thick slices. Place two half eggs on each plate with an anchovy fillet draped over. Arrange four olives on to each plate.

5 To make the dressing, whisk together the vinegar, olive oil and garlic and season to taste. Drizzle over the salads, arrange the tuna steaks on top, sprinkle over the basil and serve.

Caesar Salad

A famous combination of crisp lettuce, crunchy croûtons and Parmesan cheese in an egg dressing.

Serves 4
1 large cos or romaine lettuce
4 thick slices white or granary bread, without crusts
45ml/3 tbsp olive oil
1 garlic clove, crushed
75ml/5 tbsp freshly grated Parmesan cheese

For the dressing
1 egg
1 garlic clove, chopped
30ml/2 tbsp lemon juice
dash of Worcestershire sauce
3 anchovy fillets, chopped
120ml/4fl oz/½ cup olive oil
salt and ground black pepper

1 Preheat the oven to 220°C/425°F/Gas 7. Separate, rinse and dry the lettuce leaves. Tear the outer leaves roughly and chop the heart. Arrange the lettuce in a large salad bowl.

2 Dice the bread and mix with the olive oil and garlic in a separate bowl until the bread has soaked up the oil. Lay the bread dice on a baking sheet and place in the oven for about 6–8 minutes until golden. Remove and leave to cool.

3 To make the dressing, break the egg into the bowl of a food processor or blender and add the garlic, lemon juice, Worcestershire sauce and one of the anchovy fillets. Process until smooth.

4 With the motor running, pour in the olive oil in a thin stream until the dressing has the consistency of thin cream. Season to taste with salt and pepper, if needed.

5 Pour the dressing over the salad leaves and toss well, then toss in the garlic croûtons, Parmesan cheese and finally the remaining anchovies and serve immediately.

Cook's Tip
Keep an eye on the croûtons in the oven; don't let them burn.

Leafy Salad (opposite) Energy 92kcal/380kJ; Protein 0.8g; Carbohydrate 1.6g, of which sugars 1.6g; Fat 9.2g, of which saturates 1.4g; Cholesterol 0mg; Calcium 32mg; Fibre 1g; Sodium 4mg.
Niçoise Energy 578kcal/2408kJ; Protein 46.4g; Carbohydrate 15g, of which sugars 10.6g; Fat 37.5g, of which saturates 7.1g; Cholesterol 235mg; Calcium 127mg; Fibre 4.7g; Sodium 585mg.
Caesar Energy 420kcal/1740kJ; Protein 12.2g; Carbohydrate 13.6g, of which sugars 1.9g; Fat 35.6g, of which saturates 8.2g; Cholesterol 68mg; Calcium 288mg; Fibre 1.1g; Sodium 443mg.

Grilled Pepper Salad

This tangy salad hails from southern Italy where all the ingredients thrive in the Mediterranean sun. Serve as a colourful side salad for a cold spread, or as a fresh-tasting starter, topped with a sprinkling of basil.

Serves 6

4 large (bell) peppers, red or
   yellow or a combination of both

30ml/2 tbsp capers in salt,
   vinegar or brine, rinsed
18–20 black or green olives

For the dressing
90ml/6 tbsp extra virgin olive oil
2 garlic cloves, chopped
30ml/2 tbsp balsamic or wine
   vinegar
salt and ground black pepper

1 Place the whole peppers under a hot grill (broiler) and grill (broil), turning occasionally, until they are beginning to char and blister on all sides.

2 Put the charred peppers in a bowl, cover with kitchen paper and leave to cool for 10 minutes, then peel off the skins. Remove the seeds and cores, then cut the flesh into quarters.

3 Cut the peppers into strips and arrange them in a serving dish. Distribute the capers and olives evenly over them.

4 To make the dressing, mix the oil and garlic together in a small bowl, crushing the garlic with a spoon to release as much flavour as possible. Mix in the vinegar and season to taste with salt and pepper.

5 Pour the dressing over the salad, mix well and allow to stand for at least 30 minutes before serving.

Cook's Tip
Charring the peppers under the grill helps to bring out their delicious sweet flavour. It also lifts the skin from the pepper flesh, making peeling easy.

Tuna & Bean Salad

This popular salad makes a good light meal, and can be very quickly assembled from store-cupboard ingredients.

Serves 4–6

2 x 400g/14oz cans cannellini or
   borlotti beans
2 x 200g/7oz cans tuna fish,
   drained

60ml/4 tbsp extra virgin olive oil
30ml/2 tbsp lemon juice
15ml/1 tbsp chopped fresh
   parsley
3 spring onions (scallions), thinly
   sliced
salt and ground black pepper
fresh parsley sprigs, to garnish
   (optional)

1 Pour the beans into a large sieve (strainer) and rinse under cold running water. Drain well. Place in a serving dish.

2 Break the tuna into fairly large flakes with a fork and arrange over the beans.

3 Make the dressing by combining the oil with the lemon juice in a small bowl. Season with salt and pepper, and stir in the parsley. Mix well. Pour the dressing over the beans and tuna.

4 Sprinkle the sliced spring onions over the salad and toss well. Garnish with parsley, if using, and serve immediately.

Cook's Tip
If you prefer a milder onion flavour, gently sauté the spring onions in a little oil until softened, before adding to the salad.

Variation
For a vegetarian version, roast, peel and dice 2 red (bell) peppers, saving any juices. Fry 1 large crushed garlic clove in 30ml/2 tbsp olive oil until soft, then add a handful of chopped parsley, the pepper and juices, plus 15ml/1 tbsp balsamic vinegar. Pour over the beans, toss together, season and serve.

Bean Salad Energy 294kcal/1235kJ; Protein 27.4g; Carbohydrate 23.9g, of which sugars 4.9g; Fat 10.5g, of which saturates 1.7g; Cholesterol 33mg; Calcium 105mg; Fibre 8.4g; Sodium 714mg.
Pepper Salad Energy 148kcal/612kJ; Protein 1.5g; Carbohydrate 8g, of which sugars 7.2g; Fat 12.4g, of which saturates 1.8g; Cholesterol 0mg; Calcium 15mg; Fibre 2.3g; Sodium 192mg.

Warm Chicken Liver & Tomato Salad

Warm salads are especially welcome during the autumn months when the evenings are growing shorter and cooler. Serve with French bread for mopping up the delicious juices.

Serves 4

225g/8oz/4 cups young spinach, stems removed
1 frisée lettuce

105ml/7 tbsp groundnut (peanut) or sunflower oil
175g/6oz rindless bacon, cut into strips
3 slices day-old bread, without crusts, cut into short fingers
450g/1lb chicken livers
115g/4oz cherry tomatoes
salt and ground black pepper

1 Wash the spinach and the frisée lettuce leaves, then dry thoroughly in a salad spinner Place in a salad bowl.

2 Heat 60ml/4 tbsp of the oil in a large frying pan and cook the bacon for 3–4 minutes until crisp and brown. Remove the bacon with a slotted spoon and leave to drain on a piece of kitchen paper.

3 To make the croûtons, fry the bread in the bacon-flavoured oil, tossing until crisp and golden. Drain on kitchen paper.

4 Heat the remaining 45ml/3 tbsp of oil in the frying pan and fry the chicken livers briskly for 2–3 minutes. Transfer the livers and pan juices to the salad leaves in the bowl, add the fried bacon, croûtons and cherry tomatoes. Season with salt and pepper, toss gently and serve.

> **Cook's Tip**
> *Although fresh chicken livers are preferable, frozen ones could be used in this salad. It is important to make sure they are completely thawed before cooking.*

Maryland Salad

A harmonious blend of sweet and savoury flavours, this salad makes a stunning main-course salad.

Serves 4

4 free-range chicken breast fillets
olive oil, for brushing
225g/8oz rindless unsmoked bacon
4 corn on the cob
40g/1½oz/3 tbsp butter, softened
4 ripe bananas, peeled and halved
4 firm tomatoes, halved

4 escarole or round (butterhead) lettuces
1 bunch watercress, weighing about 115g/4oz
salt and ground black pepper

For the dressing
75ml/5 tbsp groundnut (peanut) oil
15ml/1 tbsp white wine vinegar
5ml/1 tsp maple syrup
10ml/2 tsp mild mustard

1 Season the chicken fillets with salt and pepper, brush with oil and barbecue or grill (broil) for 15 minutes, turning once, until cooked through. Keep warm.

2 Barbecue or grill the bacon for 8–10 minutes or until crisp. Keep warm.

3 Bring a large pan of salted water to the boil. Trim and husk the corn on the cob, then add to the boiling water and cook for 20 minutes. Brush with butter and brown over the barbecue or under the grill.

4 Barbecue or grill the bananas and tomatoes for 6–8 minutes, brushing with butter, if you wish.

5 To make the dressing, combine the oil, vinegar, maple syrup and mustard with 15ml/1 tbsp water in a screw-top jar and shake well. Put the lettuce leaves in a bowl with the watercress, then toss with the dressing.

6 Divide the salad leaves among four large plates. Slice the chicken and arrange over the leaves with the bacon, banana, corn and tomatoes. Serve immediately.

Chicken Liver Energy 441kcal/1834kJ; Protein 31g; Carbohydrate 11.7g, of which sugars 3.5g; Fat 30.3g, of which saturates 6g; Cholesterol 451mg; Calcium 149mg; Fibre 2.4g; Sodium 934mg.
Maryland Energy 613kcal/2562kJ; Protein 48.9g; Carbohydrate 29.3g, of which sugars 26.8g; Fat 34.1g, of which saturates 12.2g; Cholesterol 156mg; Calcium 102mg; Fibre 3.3g; Sodium 1193mg.

Leeks with Mustard Dressing

Leeks are turned into an unusual and truly delicious salad when married with a mustardy dressing.

Serves 4
8 slim leeks, each about
    13cm/5in long
5–10/1–2 tsp Dijon mustard
10ml/2 tsp white wine vinegar
1 hard-boiled egg, halved
    lengthways
75ml/5 tbsp light olive oil
10ml/2 tsp chopped
    fresh parsley
salt and ground
    black pepper

1 Place the leeks in a steamer over a pan of boiling water and cook until they are just tender.

2 Meanwhile, stir together the mustard and vinegar in a bowl. Scoop the egg yolk into the bowl and, using a fork, mash thoroughly into the vinegar mixture.

3 Gradually work in the oil to make a smooth sauce, then season to taste with salt and pepper.

4 Lift the leeks out of the steamer and place on several layers of kitchen paper, then cover the leeks with several more layers of kitchen paper and dry.

5 Transfer the leeks to a serving dish while still warm, spoon the dressing over them and allow to cool. Finely chop the egg white using a large sharp knife, then mix with the chopped fresh parsley and scatter over the leeks. Chill before serving.

Cook's Tips
• Pencil-slim baby leeks are increasingly available nowadays, and are beautifully tender. Use three or four of these smaller leeks per serving.
• It is important that the leeks are thoroughly dried before placing in the serving dish, and they should still be warm when the dressing is added so that they absorb all the flavours.

Lettuce, Cucumber & Herb Salad

For a really quick salad, look out for pre-packed bags of mixed baby lettuce leaves in the supermarket.

Serves 4
1/2 cucumber
mixed lettuce leaves
1 bunch watercress, weighing
    about 115g/4oz
1 chicory (Belgian endive)
    head, sliced
45ml/3 tbsp mixed chopped fresh
    herbs such as parsley, thyme,
    tarragon, chives and chervil

For the dressing
15ml/1 tbsp white wine vinegar
5ml/1 tsp Dijon mustard
75ml/5 tbsp olive oil
salt and ground black pepper

1 Peel the cucumber, if you wish, then cut it in half lengthways and scoop out the seeds. Thinly slice the flesh. Tear the lettuce leaves into bite-size pieces.

2 Toss the cucumber, lettuce, watercress, chicory and herbs together in a large salad bowl, or arrange them in the bowl in layers, if you prefer.

3 To make the dressing, mix the vinegar and mustard together, then whisk in the oil and season with salt and pepper.

4 Stir the dressing and pour over the salad. Toss lightly to coat the salad vegetables and leaves and serve immediately.

Cook's Tip
Do not dress the salad until just before serving, otherwise the lettuce leaves will wilt.

Variation
To turn the salad into a light lunch dish, toss in some crisply fried bacon pieces and toasted pine nuts.

Leeks Energy 162kcal/670kJ; Protein 3.1g; Carbohydrate 2.5g, of which sugars 1.9g; Fat 15.7g, of which saturates 2.4g; Cholesterol 48mg; Calcium 48mg; Fibre 2.2g; Sodium 23mg.
Lettuce Energy 149kcal/612kJ; Protein 2.1g; Carbohydrate 2.7g, of which sugars 2.1g; Fat 14.6g, of which saturates 2.2g; Cholesterol 0mg; Calcium 100mg; Fibre 2g; Sodium 21mg.

Goat's Cheese Salad

The robust flavours of the goat's cheese and buckwheat combine especially well with figs and walnuts in this salad.

Serves 4

175g/6oz/1 cup couscous
30ml/2 tbsp toasted buckwheat
1 hard-boiled egg
4 ripe figs
30ml/2 tbsp chopped fresh parsley
60ml/4 tbsp olive oil, preferably Sicilian
45ml/3 tbsp walnut oil
115g/4oz rocket (arugula)
1/2 frisée lettuce, separated into leaves
175g/6oz crumbly white goat's cheese
50g/2oz/1/2 cup broken walnuts, toasted

1 Place the couscous and buckwheat in a bowl, cover with boiling water and leave to soak for 15 minutes. Place in a sieve (strainer), if necessary, to drain off any remaining water, then spread out on a metal tray and allow to cool.

2 Shell the hard-boiled egg and pass it through a fine grater. Trim the figs and almost cut each into four, leaving the pieces joined at the base.

3 Toss together the egg, parsley and couscous in a bowl. Mix together the two oils and use half to moisten the couscous and buckwheat mixture.

4 Put the lettuce leaves in a bowl and dress with the remaining oil, then divide among four large plates.

5 Pile the couscous into the centre of the leaves, crumble on the goat's cheese, scatter with toasted walnuts, and add the trimmed figs. Serve immediately.

> **Cook's Tip**
> Serve this strongly flavoured salad with a gutsy red wine from the Rhône or South of France.

Sweet Potato & Carrot Salad

A medley of colours, this warm salad not only looks great but has a fabulous sweet-and-sour flavour.

Serves 4

1 sweet potato
2 carrots, cut into thick diagonal slices
3 tomatoes
8–10 iceberg lettuce leaves
75g/3oz/1/2 cup canned chickpeas, drained

For the dressing

15ml/1 tbsp clear honey
90ml/6 tbsp natural (plain) yogurt
2.5ml/1/2 tsp salt
5ml/1 tsp ground black pepper

For the garnish

15ml/1 tbsp walnuts
15ml/1 tbsp sultanas (golden raisins)
1 small onion, cut into rings

1 Peel the sweet potato and cut roughly into cubes. Boil it until it is soft but not mushy, then drain and set aside.

2 Boil the carrots for just a few minutes, making sure that they remain crunchy. Drain the carrots and mix with the sweet potato in a large bowl.

3 Slice the tops off the tomatoes, then scoop out the seeds with a spoon and discard. Roughly chop the flesh. Slice the lettuce into strips across the leaves.

4 Line a salad bowl with the shredded lettuce leaves. Mix the chickpeas and tomatoes with the sweet potato and carrots, then place in the centre of the lettuce.

5 To make the dressing, put the honey and yogurt in a bowl with salt and pepper to taste, then mix well, using a fork. Garnish the salad with the walnuts, sultanas and onion rings. Pour the dressing over the top just before serving.

> **Variation**
> Use baby new potatoes instead of the sweet potato cubes.

Goat's Cheese Energy 595kcal/2469kJ; Protein 18g; Carbohydrate 38.7g, of which sugars 12.3g; Fat 41.8g, of which saturates 11.3g; Cholesterol 88mg; Calcium 243mg; Fibre 3.3g; Sodium 381mg.
Sweet Potato Energy 158kcal/669kJ; Protein 4.8g; Carbohydrate 27.7g, of which sugars 16.6g; Fat 4g, of which saturates 0.6g; Cholesterol 0mg; Calcium 94mg; Fibre 4.4g; Sodium 101mg.

Wild Rice with Grilled Vegetables

A colourful array of summer vegetables, served on wild and white rice tossed in a garlicky dressing, provides a lovely main-course salad.

Serves 4

225g/8oz/1¼ cups wild and long grain rice mixture
1 large aubergine (eggplant), thickly sliced
1 red, 1 yellow and 1 green (bell) pepper, seeded and cut into quarters
2 red onions, sliced
225g/8oz brown cap or shiitake mushrooms
2 small courgettes (zucchini), cut in half lengthways
olive oil, for brushing
30ml/2 tbsp chopped fresh thyme

For the dressing

90ml/6 tbsp extra virgin olive oil
30ml/2 tbsp balsamic vinegar
2 garlic cloves, crushed
salt and ground black pepper

1 Put the rice mixture in a pan of cold salted water. Bring to the boil, reduce the heat, cover with a tight-fitting lid and cook gently for 30–40 minutes or according to the packet instructions, until all the grains are tender.

2 To make the dressing, mix together the olive oil, vinegar, garlic and salt and pepper to taste in a small bowl or screw-top jar until well blended. Set aside while you cook the vegetables.

3 Arrange the vegetables on a grill (broiler) rack. Brush with olive oil and grill (broil) for 8–10 minutes, until tender and well browned, turning them occasionally and brushing again with oil.

4 Drain the rice and toss in half the dressing. Turn into a serving dish and arrange the grilled vegetables on top. Pour over the remaining dressing and sprinkle over the fresh thyme.

> **Cook's Tip**
> *Wild rice is not a rice at all, but is actually a type of wild grass. It has a wonderfully nutty flavour and also adds attractive texture when mixed with long grain rice.*

Baby Leaf Salad with Croûtons

Crispy croûtons, made from Italian ciabatta bread, give a lovely crunch to this mixed leaf and avocado salad.

Serves 4

15ml/1 tbsp olive oil
1 garlic clove, crushed
15ml/1 tbsp freshly grated Parmesan cheese
15ml/1 tbsp chopped fresh parsley
4 slices ciabatta bread, crusts removed, cut into small dice
1 large bunch watercress
1 large handful of rocket (arugula)
1 bag mixed baby salad leaves, including oakleaf and cos lettuce
1 ripe avocado

For the dressing

45ml/3 tbsp olive oil
15ml/1 tbsp walnut oil
juice of ½ lemon
2.5ml/½ tsp Dijon mustard
salt and ground black pepper

1 Preheat the oven to 190°C/375°F/Gas 5. Put the oil, garlic, Parmesan, parsley and bread in a bowl and toss to coat well. Spread out the diced bread on a baking sheet and bake for about 8 minutes until crisp. Leave to cool.

2 Remove any coarse or discoloured stalks or leaves from the watercress and place in a serving bowl with the rocket and baby salad leaves.

3 Halve the avocado and remove the stone (pit). Peel and cut into chunks, then add it to the salad bowl.

4 To make the dressing, mix together the oils, lemon juice, mustard and salt and pepper to taste in a small bowl or screw-top jar until evenly blended. Pour over the salad and toss well. Sprinkle over the croûtons and serve at once.

> **Cook's Tip**
> *Walnut oil adds a lovely nutty flavour to the dressing, but if you do not have any, just use olive oil only and add 15ml/1 tbsp balsamic vinegar instead of the lemon juice, if you prefer.*

Baby Leaf Energy 334kcal/1397kJ; Protein 9.7g; Carbohydrate 26.9g, of which sugars 2.1g; Fat 21.6g, of which saturates 4g; Cholesterol 4mg; Calcium 238mg; Fibre 3.2g; Sodium 348mg.
Wild Rice Energy 438kcal/1824kJ; Protein 8.6g; Carbohydrate 60.3g, of which sugars 13.6g; Fat 18.1g, of which saturates 2.7g; Cholesterol 0mg; Calcium 56mg; Fibre 5.1g; Sodium 12mg.

Fresh Spinach & Avocado Salad

Young, tender spinach leaves make a change from lettuce. They are delicious served with avocado, cherry tomatoes and radishes in an unusual tofu sauce.

Serves 4–6
1 large avocado
juice of 1 lime
225g/8oz/4 cups baby spinach leaves
115g/4oz cherry tomatoes
4 spring onions (scallions), sliced
1/2 cucumber
50g/2oz radishes, sliced

For the dressing
115g/4oz soft silken tofu
45ml/3 tbsp milk
10ml/2 tsp mustard
2.5ml/1/2 tsp white wine vinegar
cayenne pepper
salt and ground black pepper
radish roses and fresh herb sprigs, to garnish

1 Cut the avocado in half, remove the stone and strip off the skin. Cut the flesh into slices. Transfer to a plate, drizzle over the lime juice and set aside.

2 Rinse and thoroughly dry the baby spinach leaves. Put them in a mixing bowl.

3 Cut the larger cherry tomatoes in half and add all the tomatoes to the mixing bowl with the spring onions. Cut the cucumber into even-size chunks and add to the bowl with the sliced radishes.

4 To make the dressing, put the silken tofu, milk, mustard, wine vinegar and a pinch of cayenne in a food processor or blender. Add salt and pepper to taste, then process for 30 seconds until the dressing is smooth.

5 Scrape the dressing into a bowl and add a little extra milk if you like a thinner consistency. Sprinkle with a little extra cayenne, garnish with radish roses and herb sprigs.

6 Arrange the avocado slices with the spinach salad on a serving dish and serve immediately, with the tofu dressing handed round separately.

Russian Salad

This hearty salad became fashionable in the hotel dining rooms of Europe in the 1920s and 1930s.

Serves 4
115g/4oz large button (white) mushrooms
120ml/4fl oz/1/2 cup mayonnaise
15ml/1 tbsp lemon juice
350g/12oz peeled, cooked prawns (shrimp)
1 large dill pickle, finely chopped, or 30ml/2 tbsp capers
115g/4oz broad (fava) beans
115g/4oz small new potatoes, scrubbed or scraped
115g/4oz young carrots, trimmed and peeled
115g/4oz baby sweetcorn
115g/4oz baby turnips, trimmed
15ml/1 tbsp olive oil, preferably French or Italian
4 hard-boiled eggs, shelled
salt and ground black pepper
25g/1oz canned anchovy fillets, cut into fine strips, to garnish
paprika, to garnish

1 Slice the mushrooms thinly, then cut into matchsticks. Combine the mayonnaise and lemon juice. Fold the mayonnaise into the mushrooms and prawns, add the dill pickle or capers, then season to taste with salt and pepper.

2 Bring a large pan of salted water to the boil, add the broad beans and cook for 3 minutes. Drain and cool under running water, then pinch the beans between thumb and forefinger to release them from their tough skins.

3 Boil the potatoes for 20 minutes and the remaining vegetables for 6 minutes. Drain and cool under running water.

4 Toss the vegetables with the olive oil and divide among four shallow bowls. Spoon on the dressed prawns and place a hard-boiled egg in the centre. Garnish the egg with strips of anchovy and sprinkle with paprika. Serve immediately.

Cook's Tip
It's worth the effort of removing the broad bean skins, as the bright green beans beneath are exceptionally tender.

Russian Energy 455kcal/1890kJ; Protein 28.1g; Carbohydrate 12.8g, of which sugars 5g; Fat 32.8g, of which saturates 5.7g; Cholesterol 387mg; Calcium 162mg; Fibre 4.3g; Sodium 963mg.
Spinach Energy 71kcal/293kJ; Protein 2.8g; Carbohydrate 2g, of which sugars 1.6g; Fat 5.7g, of which saturates 1.2g; Cholesterol 0mg; Calcium 135mg; Fibre 1.7g; Sodium 46mg.

Pear & Roquefort Salad

The partnership of blue cheese with sweet fruit and crunchy nuts is magical.

Serves 4
50g/2oz/½ cup hazelnuts
3 ripe pears
lemon juice
about 175g/6oz mixed fresh
   salad leaves

175g/6oz Roquefort cheese

For the dressing
30ml/2 tbsp hazelnut oil
45ml/3 tbsp olive oil
15ml/1 tbsp cider vinegar
5ml/1 tsp Dijon mustard
salt and ground black pepper

1 Toast the hazelnuts in a dry frying pan over low heat for about 2 minutes until golden, tossing frequently to prevent them from burning. Chop the nuts and set aside.

2 To make the dressing, mix together the oils, vinegar and mustard in a bowl or place in a screw-top jar and shake to combine. Season to taste with salt and pepper.

3 Peel, core and slice the pears, then toss them in the lemon juice to prevent them from discolouring.

4 Divide the salad leaves among four serving plates, then place the pears on top. Crumble the cheese and scatter over the salad along with the toasted hazelnuts. Spoon over the dressing and serve immediately.

Cook's Tip
Choose ripe but firm Comice or Williams' pears for this salad. Toss the pears, cheese and nuts with the leaves, if you prefer.

Variation
Replace the hazelnuts with walnuts, and use watercress instead of mixed salad – the peppery leaves go well with the pears.

Mediterranean Mixed Pepper Salad

This Italian-style salad is great to serve as part of a cold lunch spread, with salamis, hams and chunks of warm ciabatta bread.

Serves 4
2 red (bell) peppers, halved and seeded

2 yellow (bell) peppers, halved and seeded
150ml/¼ pint/⅔ cup olive oil
1 onion, thinly sliced
2 garlic cloves, crushed
generous squeeze of lemon juice
chopped fresh parsley, to garnish

1 Place the peppers, skin-side up, under a hot grill (broiler) and grill (broil) until beginning to char and blister. Put the pepper pieces in a bowl, cover with kitchen paper and leave to cool for 10 minutes,

2 Meanwhile, heat 30ml/2 tbsp of the olive oil in a frying pan and fry the onion for about 5–6 minutes over medium heat, stirring occasionally, until softened and translucent. Remove from the heat and reserve.

3 Remove the peppers from the bowl, then peel off and discard the skins. Slice each pepper half into fairly thin strips.

4 Place the peppers, cooked onion and any oil from the pan into a bowl. Add the crushed garlic and pour in the remaining olive oil. Add a generous squeeze of lemon juice and season to taste with salt and pepper. Mix well, cover and marinate for 2–3 hours, stirring the mixture once or twice.

5 Just before serving, garnish the pepper salad with chopped fresh parsley.

Variation
Add 4 peeled and halved tomatoes to the pepper and onion mixture. Use a red onion and finish off with a sprinkling of black olive halves and torn basil leaves.

Pear Energy 381kcal/1579kJ; Protein 11.4g; Carbohydrate 12.8g, of which sugars 12.5g; Fat 31.9g, of which saturates 10.3g; Cholesterol 33mg; Calcium 256mg; Fibre 3.7g; Sodium 539mg.
Mixed Pepper Energy 299kcal/1233kJ; Protein 2.9g; Carbohydrate 14.4g, of which sugars 11.7g; Fat 25.8g, of which saturates 3.8g; Cholesterol 0mg; Calcium 20mg; Fibre 3.5g; Sodium 8mg.

Californian Salad

Full of vitality and vitamins, this is a lovely light and healthy salad for sunny summer days.

Serves 4

1 small crisp lettuce, torn into pieces
225g/8oz/4 cups young spinach leaves
2 carrots, coarsely grated
115g/4oz cherry tomatoes, halved
2 celery sticks, thinly sliced

75g/3oz/1/2 cup raisins
50g/2oz/1/2 cup blanched almonds or unsalted cashew nuts, halved
30ml/2 tbsp sunflower seeds
30ml/2 tbsp sesame seeds, lightly toasted

For the dressing

45ml/3 tbsp extra virgin olive oil
30ml/2 tbsp cider vinegar
10ml/2 tsp clear honey
juice of 1 small orange
salt and ground black pepper

1 Put the lettuce, spinach, carrots, tomatoes and celery in a large bowl. Add the raisins, almonds and the sunflower and sesame seeds.

2 Put all the dressing ingredients in a screw-top jar and shake well to combine, then pour over the salad.

3 Toss the salad thoroughly and divide among four small salad bowls. Season with salt and pepper and serve immediately.

Cook's Tips

• *For tomato and mozzarella toasts to serve with the salad, cut French bread diagonally into slices, then toast lightly on both sides. Spread some sun-dried tomato paste on one side of each slice. Cut some mozzarella into small pieces and arrange over the tomato paste. Put on baking sheets, sprinkle with chopped herbs and black pepper to taste and drizzle with olive oil. Bake in a hot oven for 5 minutes or until the mozzarella has melted. Leave to settle for a few minutes before serving.*
• *If the tomatoes are hard and tasteless, try roasting them in the oven with a little olive oil, then add to the salad.*

Scandinavian Cucumber & Dill

This refreshing salad is good with hot and spicy food.

Serves 4

2 cucumbers
30ml/2 tbsp snipped fresh chives

30ml/2 tbsp chopped fresh dill
150ml/1/4 pint/2/3 cup sour cream or fromage frais
salt and ground black pepper

1 Slice the cucumbers as thinly as possible, preferably in a food processor or with a slicer. Place the slices in layers in a colander (strainer), sprinkling each layer evenly, but not too heavily, with salt. Set over a plate to catch the juices.

2 Leave the cucumber to drain for up to 2 hours, then lay out the slices on a clean dish towel and pat them dry. Mix the cucumber with the herbs, cream or fromage frais and plenty of pepper. Serve immediately.

Spinach & Roast Garlic Salad

This salad makes the most of the health-giving qualities of spinach and garlic.

Serves 4

12 garlic cloves, unpeeled
60ml/4 tbsp extra virgin olive oil

450g/1lb/8 cups baby spinach leaves
50g/2oz/1/2 cup pine nuts, lightly toasted
juice of 1/2 lemon
salt and ground black pepper

1 Preheat the oven to 190°C/375°F/Gas 5. Place the unpeeled garlic cloves in a small roasting pan, drizzle over 30ml/2 tbsp of the olive oil and toss to coat. Bake for about 15 minutes until slightly charred.

2 Place the garlic cloves, still in their skins, in a salad bowl. Add the spinach, pine nuts, lemon juice and remaining olive oil. Toss well and season with salt and pepper. Serve immediately, gently squeezing the softened garlic purée out of the skins to eat.

Californian Energy 319kcal/1327kJ; Protein 7.9g; Carbohydrate 23.5g, of which sugars 21.7g; Fat 22.1g, of which saturates 2.6g; Cholesterol 0mg; Calcium 205mg; Fibre 5g; Sodium 114mg.
Scandinavian Energy 88kcal/361kJ; Protein 1.9g; Carbohydrate 2.8g, of which sugars 2.7g; Fat 7.7g, of which saturates 4.7g; Cholesterol 23mg; Calcium 69mg; Fibre 1g; Sodium 21mg.
Spinach Energy 222kcal/915kJ; Protein 5.1g; Carbohydrate 4g, of which sugars 3.5g; Fat 20.7g, of which saturates 2.3g; Cholesterol 0mg; Calcium 238mg; Fibre 4.1g; Sodium 23mg.

Chicory, Fruit & Nut Salad

Mildly bitter chicory is wonderful with sweet fruit, and is delicious when complemented by a creamy curry sauce.

Serves 4

45ml/3 tbsp mayonnaise
15ml/1 tbsp Greek-style (US strained, plain) yogurt
15ml/1 tbsp mild curry paste
90ml/6 tbsp single (light) cream
½ iceberg lettuce
2 heads chicory (Belgian endive)
50g/2oz/1 cup flaked coconut
50g/2oz/½ cup cashew nuts
2 red eating apples
75g/3oz/½ cup currants

1 Mix together the mayonnaise, Greek-style yogurt, curry paste and single cream in a small bowl. Cover and chill until required.

2 Tear the iceberg lettuce into even-size pieces and put into a salad bowl.

3 Cut the root end off each head of chicory and discard. Slice the chicory, or separate the leaves, and add to the salad bowl. Preheat the grill (broiler).

4 Spread out the coconut flakes on a baking sheet. Grill (broil) for 1 minute until golden. Turn into a bowl and set aside. Toast the cashew nuts for 2 minutes until golden.

5 Quarter the apples and cut out the cores. Slice the apple quarters and add to the lettuce with the toasted coconut, cashew nuts and currants.

6 Stir up the chilled dressing and pour over the salad. Toss lightly together and serve immediately.

> **Cook's Tip**
> *Choose a sweet, well-flavoured variety of red apple for this salad, such as Royal Gala. Leave on the skins to provide added colour and texture.*

Spicy Corn Salad

This simple and colourful, sweet-flavoured salad is served warm with a delicious, spicy dressing.

Serves 4

30ml/2 tbsp vegetable oil
450g/1lb drained canned corn, or frozen corn, thawed
1 green (bell) pepper, seeded and diced
1 small red chilli, seeded and finely diced
4 spring onions (scallions), sliced
45ml/3 tbsp chopped fresh parsley
225g/8oz cherry tomatoes, halved
salt and ground black pepper

For the dressing

2.5ml/½ tsp sugar
30ml/2 tbsp white wine vinegar
2.5ml/½ tsp Dijon mustard
15ml/1 tbsp chopped fresh basil
15ml/1 tbsp mayonnaise
1.5ml/¼ tsp chilli sauce

1 Heat the oil in a frying pan. Add the corn, green pepper, chilli and spring onions. Cook over medium heat for about 5 minutes, until softened, stirring frequently.

2 Transfer the vegetables to a salad bowl. Stir in the parsley and the cherry tomatoes.

3 To make the dressing, combine all the ingredients in a small bowl and whisk together.

4 Pour the dressing over the corn mixture. Season with salt and pepper to taste. Toss well to combine, then serve immediately, while the salad is still warm.

> **Cook's Tip**
> *Don't touch your eyes with your hands while preparing the chilli.*

> **Variation**
> *If serving the salad to children, you can make the flavour milder by omitting the fresh chilli and the chilli sauce.*

Chicory Energy 323kcal/1347kJ; Protein 5.7g; Carbohydrate 22.5g, of which sugars 19.8g; Fat 24.1g, of which saturates 8.7g; Cholesterol 21mg; Calcium 105mg; Fibre 4g; Sodium 122mg.
Corn Energy 245kcal/1032kJ; Protein 4.7g; Carbohydrate 35.9g, of which sugars 16.6g; Fat 10.2g, of which saturates 1.4g; Cholesterol 3mg; Calcium 39mg; Fibre 3.6g; Sodium 338mg.

Tomato & Bread Salad

This salad is a traditional peasant dish from Tuscany and was created to use up bread that was several days old. The success of the dish depends on the quality of the tomatoes – they must be ripe and well flavoured. Serve with a green salad for a good contrast in colour and texture.

Serves 4
400g/14oz stale white or brown
   bread or rolls
4 large tomatoes
1 large red onion, or 6 spring
   onions (scallions)
a few fresh basil leaves, to garnish

For the dressing
60ml/4 tbsp extra virgin olive oil
30ml/2 tbsp white wine vinegar
salt and ground black pepper

1 Cut the bread or rolls into thick slices. Place in a shallow bowl and add enough cold water to soak the bread. Leave for at least 30 minutes.

2 Cut the tomatoes into chunks and place in a serving bowl. Finely slice the onion or spring onions and add them to the tomatoes. Squeeze as much water out of the bread as possible. Add the bread to the vegetables.

3 To make the dressing, whisk the olive oil with the vinegar, then season with salt and pepper.

4 Pour the dressing over the salad and mix well. Decorate with the basil leaves. Allow to stand in a cool place for a least 2 hours before serving.

Cook's Tip
Tomatoes left to ripen on the vine will have the best flavour so try to buy "vine-ripened" varieties. If you can only find unripened tomatoes, you can help them along by putting them in a paper bag with a ripe tomato or leaving them in a fruit bowl with a banana; the gases the ripe fruits give off will ripen them, but, unfortunately, this process cannot improve the flavour.

Fennel & Orange Salad

This light and refreshing salad originated in Sicily, following the old custom of serving fennel at the end of a meal, to help digestion. The delicate aniseed flavour of the fennel marries well with sweet oranges.

Serves 4
2 large fennel bulbs (about
   675g/1½ lb total)
2 sweet oranges
2 spring onions (scallions),
   to garnish

For the dressing
60ml/4 tbsp extra virgin olive oil
30ml/2 tbsp fresh lemon juice
salt and ground black pepper

1 Wash the fennel bulbs and remove any brown or stringy outer leaves. Slice the bulbs and stems into thin pieces. Place in a shallow serving bowl.

2 Peel the oranges with a sharp knife, cutting away the white pith. Slice thinly. Cut each slice into thirds. Arrange over the fennel, adding any juice from the oranges.

3 To make the dressing, mix the oil and lemon juice together. Season with salt and pepper. Pour the dressing over the salad and mix well.

4 Slice the white and green sections of the spring onions thinly. Sprinkle over the salad and serve immediately.

Cook's Tips
• *For a delicate orange rind garnish to enhance the flavour of the salad, use a vegetable peeler to cut thin strips of rind from the unpeeled oranges, leaving the pith behind. Then cut the pieces into thin matchstick strips and cook in a small pan of boiling water for 2–3 minutes. Drain and dry on kitchen paper, then sprinkle on top of the salad before serving.*
• *When buying fennel, choose firm round bulbs. The outer layers should be crisp and white, with the texture of green celery.*

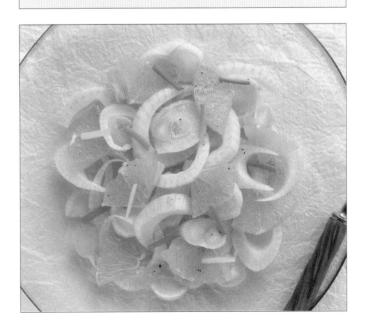

Tomato Energy 369kcal/1557kJ; Protein 9.7g; Carbohydrate 56.4g, of which sugars 8.5g; Fat 13.3g, of which saturates 1.7g; Cholesterol 0mg; Calcium 130mg; Fibre 3.2g; Sodium 531mg.
Fennel Energy 148kcal/614kJ; Protein 2.5g; Carbohydrate 9.6g, of which sugars 9.4g; Fat 11.4g, of which saturates 1.6g; Cholesterol 0mg; Calcium 78mg; Fibre 5.4g; Sodium 23mg.

Parmesan & Poached Egg Salad

Soft poached eggs, hot croûtons and cool crisp salad leaves make a lively and unusual combination.

Serves 2

½ small loaf white bread
75ml/5 tbsp extra virgin olive oil
2 eggs
115g/4oz mixed salad leaves
2 garlic cloves, crushed
10ml/½ tbsp white wine vinegar
30ml/2 tbsp freshly shaved
    Parmesan cheese
ground black pepper

1 Remove the crust from the bread and discard it. Cut the bread into 2.5cm/1in cubes.

2 Heat 30ml/2 tbsp of the oil in a large frying pan. Add the bread cubes and cook for about 5 minutes, tossing the cubes occasionally, until they are crisp and golden brown all over.

3 Bring a pan of water to the boil. Break the eggs into separate cups, then carefully slide into the water. Gently poach the eggs for about 4 minutes until they are lightly cooked.

4 Meanwhile, divide the salad leaves between two plates. Remove the croûtons from the pan and arrange over the leaves. Wipe the frying pan clean with kitchen paper.

5 Heat the remaining oil in the frying pan and cook the garlic and vinegar over high heat for about 1 minute. Pour the warm dressing over the salad leaves and croûtons. Place a poached egg on each salad. Scatter with shavings of Parmesan cheese and a little freshly ground black pepper.

> **Cook's Tip**
> *Add a dash of vinegar to the water before poaching the eggs. This helps to keep the whites together. To ensure that a poached egg has a good shape, swirl the water with a spoon before sliding in the egg.*

Classic Greek Salad

Anyone who has spent a holiday in Greece will have eaten a version of this salad – the Greek equivalent to a mixed salad.

Serves 4

1 cos lettuce
½ cucumber, halved lengthways
4 tomatoes
8 spring onions (scallions)
75g/3oz Greek black olives
115g/4oz feta cheese
90ml/6 tbsp white wine vinegar
150ml/¼ pint/⅔ cup extra virgin
    olive oil
salt and ground black pepper
rustic bread, to serve (optional)

1 Tear the lettuce leaves into pieces and place them in a large serving bowl. Slice the cucumber and add to the bowl.

2 Cut the tomatoes into wedges and put them into the bowl.

3 Slice the spring onions. Add them to the bowl along with the olives and toss well.

4 Cut the feta cheese into dice and add to the salad.

5 Put the vinegar and olive oil into a small bowl and season to taste with salt and pepper. Whisk well. Pour the dressing over the salad and toss to combine. Serve at once with extra olives and chunks of bread, if you wish.

> **Cook's Tips**
> *• This salad can be assembled in advance, but should only be dressed just before serving. Keep the dressing at room temperature as chilling deadens its flavours.*
> *• The success of this salad relies on using the freshest of ingredients and a good olive oil.*

> **Variation**
> *The lettuce can be left out for a salad with a bit more bite.*

Poached Egg Energy 632kcal/2641kJ; Protein 21g; Carbohydrate 50.3g, of which sugars 3.6g; Fat 40.1g, of which saturates 8.6g; Cholesterol 205mg; Calcium 335mg; Fibre 2g; Sodium 755mg.
Greek Salad Energy 347kcal/1433kJ; Protein 6.3g; Carbohydrate 5.4g, of which sugars 5.3g; Fat 33.5g, of which saturates 8g; Cholesterol 20mg; Calcium 148mg; Fibre 2.5g; Sodium 849mg.

Avocado, Tomato & Mozzarella

This popular, attractive salad is made from ingredients representing the colours of the Italian flag – a sunny, cheerful dish! The addition of pasta turns it into a main course for a light lunch.

Serves 4
175g/6oz/1½ cups farfalle
6 ripe red tomatoes
225g/8oz mozzarella cheese
1 large ripe avocado
30ml/2 tbsp chopped fresh basil
30ml/2 tbsp pine nuts, toasted
fresh basil sprig, to garnish

For the dressing
90ml/6 tbsp olive oil
30ml/2 tbsp wine vinegar
5ml/1 tsp balsamic vinegar
 (optional)
5ml/1 tsp wholegrain mustard
pinch of sugar
salt and ground black pepper

1 Bring a large pan of lightly salted water to the boil and cook the pasta bows until *al dente*.

2 Slice the tomatoes and mozzarella cheese into thin rounds. Halve the avocado, remove the stone (pit) and peel off the skin. Slice the flesh lengthways.

3 Place the dressing ingredients in a small bowl and whisk together to combine.

4 Arrange the tomato, mozzarella and avocado slices in overlapping slices around the edge of a flat serving plate.

5 Toss the pasta with half of the dressing and the chopped basil. Pile into the centre of the plate. Pour over the remaining dressing, scatter over the pine nuts and garnish with basil.

Cook's Tip
The pale green flesh of the avocado quickly discolours once it is cut. Prepare it at the last minute and place immediately in dressing. If you must prepare it ahead, squeeze lemon juice over the cut side and cover with clear film (plastic wrap).

Pear & Pecan Nut Salad

Toasted pecan nuts have a special affinity with crisp white pears. Their robust flavours combine well with a rich Blue Cheese and Chive dressing to make this a salad to remember.

Serves 4
75g/3oz/½ cup shelled pecan
 nuts, roughly chopped
3 crisp pears
175g/6oz/3 cups young spinach,
 stems removed
1 escarole or round (butterhead)
 lettuce
1 radicchio
salt and ground black pepper
crusty bread, to serve

1 Toast the pecan nuts under a medium grill (broiler) to bring out their flavour.

2 Cut the pears into quarters and remove the cores, but leave the skins intact. Cut into even slices.

3 Place the spinach, lettuce and radicchio leaves in a large bowl. Add the sliced pears and toasted pecans, then pour over the dressing and toss well.

4 Divide the salad among four plates and season with salt and pepper. Serve the salad with warm crusty bread.

Cook's Tip
• The pecan nuts will burn very quickly under the grill, so keep constant watch over them and remove them as soon as they change colour.
• To make 350ml/12 fl oz/1½ cups of Blue Cheese and Chive Dressing: remove the rind from 75g/3 oz blue cheese (Stilton, Bleu d'Auvergne or Gorgonzola) and combine with a third of 150ml/¼ pint/⅔ cup natural (plain) yogurt. Then add the remaining yogurt, 45ml/3 tbsp of olive oil and 30ml/1 tbsp lemon juice. and mix well. Stir in 15ml/1 tbsp chopped chives and season to taste with ground black pepper.

Cold Desserts

Cold desserts are the perfect way to finish a meal, whether it is a family affair or a special occasion. Here, you will find a range of recipes suitable for every taste, whatever the weather. Indulge your senses with Chocolate Chestnut Roulade, Summer Pudding, or Creamy Mango Cheesecake. Or why not try your hand at making a delectable home-made iced dessert, such as Rippled Chocolate Ice Cream?

Cranachan

Crunchy toasted oatmeal
and soft raspberries
combine to give this
Scottish dessert a lovely
texture, while whisky adds a
touch of punchy taste.

Serves 4

60ml/4 tbsp clear honey
45ml/3 tbsp whisky
50g/2oz/¾ cup medium
    oatmeal
300ml/½ pint/1¼ cups double
    (heavy) cream
350g/12oz/2 cups raspberries

1 Put the honey in a small pan with the whisky. Heat gently to warm the honey in the whisky, then leave to cool.

2 Preheat the grill (broiler). Spread the oatmeal in a very shallow layer in the grill pan and toast, stirring occasionally, until browned. Leave to cool.

3 Whip the cream in a large bowl until soft peaks form, then gently stir in the oatmeal and the honey and whisky mixture until well combined.

4 Reserve a few raspberries for decoration, then layer the remainder with the oat mixture in four stemmed glasses. Cover and chill for 2 hours.

5 About 30 minutes before serving, remove the glasses from the refrigerator to bring to room temperature. Decorate with the reserved raspberries.

> **Cook's Tip**
> For finger biscuits to serve with the dessert, cream 150g/5oz/
> 10 tbsp butter with 75g/3oz/6 tbsp caster (superfine) sugar
> until light and fluffy, then beat in an egg, a few drops of almond
> extract and 225g/8oz/2 cups plain (all-purpose) flour. Spoon
> into a piping (pastry) bag, fitted with a plain nozzle, and pipe
> 7.5cm/3in fingers on to baking sheets lined with baking
> parchment. Bake at 230°C/450°F/Gas 8 for 5 minutes. Cool.

Old English Trifle

This old-fashioned dessert never fails to please. If you are making it for children, replace the sherry and brandy with orange juice.

Serves 6

75g/3oz day-old sponge (pound)
    cake, broken into bitesize pieces
8 ratafia biscuits (almond
    macaroons), broken into halves
100ml/3½fl oz/⅓ cup medium
    sherry
30ml/2 tbsp brandy
350g/12oz/3 cups prepared fruit
    such as raspberries, peaches or
    strawberries

300ml/½ pint/1¼ cups double
    (heavy) cream
40g/1½oz/scant ½ cup toasted
    flaked (sliced) almonds, to
    decorate
strawberries, to decorate

For the custard

4 egg yolks
25g/1oz/2 tbsp caster
    (superfine) sugar
450ml/¾ pint/scant 2 cups single
    (light) or whipping cream
a few drops of vanilla extract

1 Put the sponge cake and ratafias in a glass serving dish, then sprinkle over the sherry and brandy and leave until they have been absorbed.

2 To make the custard, whisk the egg yolks and caster sugar together. Bring the cream to the boil in a heavy pan, then pour on to the egg yolk mixture, stirring constantly.

3 Return the mixture to the pan and heat very gently, stirring all the time with a wooden spoon, until the custard thickens enough to coat the back of the spoon; do not allow to boil. Stir in the vanilla extract. Leave to cool, stirring occasionally.

4 Put the fruit in an even layer over the sponge cake and ratafias in the serving dish, then strain the custard over the fruit and leave to set.

5 Lightly whip the cream, then spread it evenly over the custard. Chill the trifle well. Decorate with flaked almonds and strawberries just before serving.

Cherry Syllabub

This recipe follows the style of the earliest syllabubs from the sixteenth and seventeenth centuries, producing a frothy creamy layer over a liquid one. It's easy to make and delicious.

Serves 4
225g/8oz/2 cups ripe dark cherries, stoned (pitted) and chopped

30ml/2 tbsp Kirsch
2 egg whites
30ml/2 tbsp lemon juice
150ml/¼ pint/⅔ cup sweet white wine
75g/3oz/generous ¼ cup caster (superfine) sugar
300ml/½ pint/1¼ cups double (heavy) cream

1 Divide the chopped cherries among six tall dessert glasses and sprinkle over the Kirsch.

2 Whisk the egg whites in a clean, grease-free bowl until stiff peaks form. Gently fold in the lemon juice, wine and sugar.

3 In a separate bowl (but using the same whisk), lightly beat the cream, then fold into the egg white mixture.

4 Spoon the cream mixture over the cherries, then chill overnight. Serve straight from the refrigerator.

Cook's Tip
Be careful not to overbeat the egg whites otherwise they will separate, which will spoil the consistency of the dessert. Whip the cream until it just forms soft peaks.

Variation
To ring the changes, try using crushed fresh raspberries or chopped ripe peaches instead of the cherries. Ratafia biscuits (almond macaroons) are the perfect accompaniment.

Damask Cream

It is important not to move this elegant dessert while it is setting, or it will separate.

Serves 4
600ml/1 pint/2½ cups milk
40g/1½ oz/3 tbsp caster (superfine) sugar

several drops of triple-strength rose water
10ml/2 tsp rennet
60ml/4 tbsp double (heavy) cream
sugared rose petals, to decorate (optional)

1 Gently heat the milk and 25g/1oz/2 tbsp of the sugar, stirring, until the sugar has melted and the temperature of the mixture feels neither hot nor cold. Stir rose water to taste into the milk, then remove the pan from the heat and stir in the rennet.

2 Pour the milk into a serving dish and leave undisturbed for 2–3 hours, until set. Stir the remaining sugar into the cream, then carefully spoon over the junket. Decorate with sugared rose petals, if you wish.

Mandarins in Orange-flower Syrup

Mandarins, tangerines, clementines, mineolas: any of these citrus fruits are suitable to use in this refreshing recipe.

Serves 4
11 mandarins
15ml/1 tbsp icing (confectioners') sugar
10ml/2 tsp orange-flower water

1 Pare some rind from one mandarin and cut it into fine shreds for decoration. Squeeze the juice from two mandarins and reserve it. Peel eight further mandarins, removing the white pith. Arrange the whole fruit in a wide dish.

2 Mix the reserved juice with the icing sugar and orange-flower water and pour over the fruit. Cover and chill. Blanch the rind in boiling water for 30 seconds. Drain, cool and sprinkle over the mandarins, with pistachio nuts if you wish.

Syllabub Energy 531kcal/2201kJ; Protein 3.3g; Carbohydrate 29.6g, of which sugars 29.6g; Fat 40.3g, of which saturates 25.1g; Cholesterol 103mg; Calcium 60mg; Fibre 0.5g; Sodium 54mg.
Damask Energy 183kcal/767kJ; Protein 5.4g; Carbohydrate 17.8g, of which sugars 17.8g; Fat 10.6g, of which saturates 6.6g; Cholesterol 29mg; Calcium 193mg; Fibre 0g; Sodium 69mg.
Mandarins Energy 61kcal/261kJ; Protein 1.2g; Carbohydrate 14.8g, of which sugars 14.8g; Fat 0.1g, of which saturates 0g; Cholesterol 0mg; Calcium 41mg; Fibre 1.5g; Sodium 5mg.

Chocolate Blancmange

An old-fashioned dessert that deserves a revival! Serve with thin cream for a touch of luxury.

Serves 4

60ml/4 tbsp cornflour (cornstarch)
600ml/1 pint/2½ cups milk
40g/1½ oz/3 tbsp caster (superfine) sugar
50–115g/2–4oz plain (semi-sweet) chocolate, chopped
vanilla extract, to taste
white and plain (semisweet) chocolate curls, to decorate

1 Rinse a 750ml/1¼ pint/3 cup fluted mould with cold water and leave it upside down to drain. Blend the cornflour to a smooth paste with a little of the milk.

2 Bring the remaining milk to the boil, preferably in a non-stick pan, then pour on to the blended mixture, stirring constantly.

3 Pour all the milk back into the pan and bring slowly to the boil over low heat, stirring constantly until the mixture boils and thickens. Remove the pan from the heat, then add the sugar, chopped chocolate and a few drops of vanilla extract. Stir until the chocolate has melted.

4 Pour the chocolate mixture into the mould and leave in a cool place for several hours to set.

5 To unmould the blancmange, place a large serving plate on top, then, holding the plate and mould firmly together, invert them. Give both plate and mould a gentle but firm shake to loosen the blancmange, then lift off the mould. Scatter white and plain chocolate curls over the top of the blancmange to decorate, and serve at once.

> **Cook's Tip**
> For a special dinner party, flavour the chocolate mixture with crème de menthe or orange-flavoured liqueur instead of vanilla, and set the blancmange in individual moulds.

Yogurt Ring with Tropical Fruit

An impressive, light and colourful dessert with a truly tropical flavour, combining a magical mix of exotic fruits.

Serves 6

175ml/6fl oz/¾ cup tropical fruit juice
15ml/1 tbsp powdered gelatine
3 egg whites
150ml/¼ pint/⅔ cup low-fat natural (plain) yogurt
finely grated rind of 1 lime

For the filling
1 mango
2 kiwi fruit
10–12 physalis (Cape gooseberries), plus extra to decorate
juice of 1 lime

1 Pour the tropical fruit juice into a small pan and sprinkle the powdered gelatine over the surface. Heat gently until the gelatine has dissolved.

2 Whisk the egg whites in a clean, grease-free bowl until they hold soft peaks. Continue whisking hard, gradually adding the yogurt and lime rind.

3 Continue whisking hard and pour in the hot gelatine mixture in a steady stream, until evenly mixed.

4 Quickly pour the mixture into a 1.5 litre/2½ pint/6¼ cup ring mould. Chill the mould until the mixture has set. The mixture will separate into two layers.

5 To make the filling, halve, stone (pit), peel and dice the mango. Peel and slice the kiwi fruit. Remove the husks from the physalis and cut the fruit in half. Toss all the fruits together in a bowl and stir in the lime juice.

6 Run a knife around the edge of the ring to loosen the mixture. Dip the mould quickly into hot water, then place a serving plate on top. Holding the plate and mould firmly together, invert them, then lift off the mould. Spoon all the prepared fruit into the centre of the ring, decorate with extra physalis and serve immediately.

Blancmange Energy 225kcal/954kJ; Protein 5.9g; Carbohydrate 39.2g, of which sugars 25.3g; Fat 6.2g, of which saturates 3.7g; Cholesterol 10mg; Calcium 192mg; Fibre 0.3g; Sodium 74mg.
Yogurt Ring Energy 63kcal/267kJ; Protein 5.4g; Carbohydrate 10.1g, of which sugars 10g; Fat 0.4g, of which saturates 0.2g; Cholesterol 0mg; Calcium 59mg; Fibre 1.1g; Sodium 55mg.

Peach Melba

The original dish created for the opera singer Dame Nellie Melba had peaches and ice cream served in grand style upon an ice swan.

Serves 4
*300g/11oz/scant 2 cups
   fresh raspberries*
squeeze of lemon juice
*icing (confectioners') sugar,
   to taste*
*2 large ripe peaches or
   425g/15oz can sliced peaches*
8 scoops vanilla ice cream

1 Press the raspberries through a non-metallic sieve (strainer) to form a purée.

2 Add a little lemon juice to the raspberry purée and sweeten to taste with icing sugar.

3 If using fresh peaches, cover them with boiling water for 4–5 seconds, then slip off the skins. Halve the peaches along the indented line, then slice neatly. If using canned peaches, place them in a strainer and drain them well.

4 Place two scoops of ice cream in each of 4 individual glass dishes, top with peach slices, then pour over the raspberry purée. Serve immediately.

Cook's Tip
For homemade vanilla ice cream, put 300ml/½ pint/1¼ cups milk in a heavy pan, with a split vanilla pod (bean). Bring to the boil, then remove from the heat and leave for 15 minutes. Remove the pod and scrape the seeds into the milk. Whisk 4 egg yolks with 75g/3oz/6 tbsp caster (superfine) sugar and 5ml/1 tsp cornflour (cornstarch) until thick and foamy. Gradually whisk in the hot milk. Return to the pan and cook, stirring, until thick. Cool. Whip 300ml/½ pint/1¼ cups double (heavy) cream until thick; fold into the custard. Pour into a freezer container. Freeze for 6 hours or until firm, beating twice during this time.

Summer Pudding

Unbelievably simple to make and totally delicious, this is a real warm weather classic. It's also a productive way of using up leftover bread.

Serves 4
*about 8 thin slices white bread,
   at least one day old*
*800g/1¾lb mixed
   summer fruits*
about 30ml/2 tbsp sugar

1 Remove the crusts from the bread. Cut a round from one slice of bread to fit in the base of a 1.2 litre/2 pint/5 cup round, deep bowl and place in position. Cut strips of bread about 5cm/2in wide and use to line the sides of the bowl, overlapping the strips as you work.

2 Place the fruit, sugar and 30ml/2 tbsp water in a large heavy pan and heat gently, shaking the pan occasionally, until the fruit juices begin to run.

3 Reserve about 45ml/3 tbsp fruit juice, then spoon the fruit and remaining juice into the prepared bowl, taking care not to dislodge the bread lining.

4 Cut the remaining bread to fit entirely over the fruit. Stand the bowl on a plate and cover with a saucer or small plate that will just fit inside the top of the bowl. Place a heavy weight on top. Chill the pudding and the reserved fruit juice overnight.

5 Run a knife carefully around the inside of the bowl rim, then invert the pudding on to a cold serving plate. Pour over the reserved juice, making sure that all the bread is completely covered, and serve.

Cook's Tips
• *Use a good mix of summer fruits for this pudding – red and blackcurrants, raspberries, strawberries and loganberries.*
• *Summer pudding freezes well so make an extra one to enjoy during the winter.*

Peach Melba Energy 256kcal/1078kJ; Protein 6.1g; Carbohydrate 32.9g, of which sugars 31.6g; Fat 10.6g, of which saturates 7.4g; Cholesterol 29mg; Calcium 144mg; Fibre 3g; Sodium 75mg.
Pudding Energy 206kcal/872kJ; Protein 6.2g; Carbohydrate 45.2g, of which sugars 19.9g; Fat 1.2g, of which saturates 0g; Cholesterol 0mg; Calcium 95mg; Fibre 3g; Sodium 293mg.

Raspberries with Fruit Purée

Three colourful fruit purées, swirled together, make a kaleidoscopic garnish for a nest of raspberries.

Serves 4–6

200g/7oz/1¼ cups raspberries
120ml/4fl oz/½ cup red wine
icing (confectioners') sugar,
  for dusting

For the decoration

1 large mango, peeled
  and chopped
400g/14oz kiwi fruit, peeled
  and chopped
200g/7oz/1¼ cups raspberries
icing (confectioners') sugar,
  to taste
hazelnut cookies,
  to serve

1 Place the raspberries in a bowl with the red wine and allow to macerate for about 2 hours.

2 To make the decoration, purée the mango in a food processor, adding water if necessary. Press through a sieve (strainer) into a bowl. Purée the kiwi fruit in the same way, then make a third purée from the remaining raspberries. Sweeten the purées with sifted icing sugar, if necessary.

3 Spoon each purée on to a serving plate, separating the kiwi and mango with the raspberry purée as if creating a four-wedged pie. Gently tap the plate on the work surface to settle the purées against each other.

4 Using a skewer, draw a spiral outwards from the centre of the plate to the rim. Drain the macerated raspberries, pile them in the centre, and dust them heavily with icing sugar.

Cook's Tip
For hazelnut bites, cream 115g/4oz/½ cup butter with 75g/3oz/⅔ cup icing (confectioners') sugar until light and fluffy. Beat in 115g/4oz/1 cup flour, 75g/3oz/¾ cup ground hazelnuts and 1 egg yolk. Shape into small balls and place on lined baking sheets. Press a hazelnut into the centre of each. Bake at 180°C/350°F/Gas 4 for 10 minutes and allow to cool.

Apricot & Orange Jelly

This refreshing jelly is the perfect way to round off a summer. Decorate with slivers of fresh apricot or blanched orange rind shreds, if you prefer.

Serves 4

350g/12oz well-flavoured fresh
  ripe apricots, stoned (pitted)
50–75g/2–3oz/about ⅓ cup
  sugar
about 300ml/½ pint/1¼ cups
  freshly squeezed orange juice
15ml/1 tbsp powdered gelatine
single (light) cream, to serve
finely chopped candied orange
  peel, to decorate

1 Heat the apricots, sugar and 120ml/4fl oz/½ cup of the orange juice, stirring until the sugar has dissolved. Simmer gently until the apricots are tender.

2 Press the apricot mixture through a nylon sieve (strainer) into a small measuring jug (cup).

3 Pour 45ml/3 tbsp of the orange juice into a small heatproof bowl, sprinkle over the gelatine and leave for about 5 minutes, until spongy.

4 Place the bowl over a pan of hot water and heat until the gelatine has dissolved. Slowly pour into the apricot mixture, stirring, constantly. Make up to 600ml/1 pint/2½ cups with the remaining orange juice.

5 Pour the apricot mixture into four individual dishes and chill in the refrigerator until set.

6 Just before serving, pour a thin layer of cream over the surface of the jellies and decorate with candied orange peel.

Variation
You could also make this light dessert with nectarines or peaches instead of the apricots.

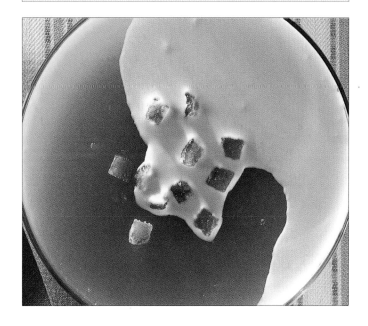

Fruit Purée Energy 69kcal/294kJ; Protein 1.7g; Carbohydrate 11.9g, of which sugars 11.7g; Fat 0.5g, of which saturates 0.1g; Cholesterol 0mg; Calcium 34mg; Fibre 3.3g; Sodium 6mg.
Orange Jelly Energy 116kcal/496kJ; Protein 4.4g; Carbohydrate 26g, of which sugars 26g; Fat 0.2g, of which saturates 0g; Cholesterol 0mg; Calcium 27mg; Fibre 1.6g; Sodium 10mg.

Summer Berry Medley with Red Sauce

Make the most of seasonal fruits in this refreshing, easy-to-make dessert.

Serves 4–6
450–675g/1–1½ lb/4½ cups
  fresh mixed soft summer fruits
  such as strawberries,
  raspberries, blueberries,
  redcurrants and blackcurrants
vanilla ice cream or crème
  fraîche, to serve

For the sauce
175g/6oz/1½ cups redcurrants,
  stripped from their stalks
175g/6oz/1 cup raspberries
50g/2oz/¼ cup caster
  (superfine) sugar
30–45ml/2–3 tbsp crème
  de framboise

1 To make the sauce, place the redcurrants in a bowl with the raspberries, caster sugar and crème de framboise. Cover and leave to macerate for 1–2 hours.

2 Put the macerated fruit, together with its juices, in a pan and cook over a low heat for 5–6 minutes, stirring occasionally, until the fruit is just tender.

3 Pour the fruit into a blender or food processor and process until smooth. Press through a nylon sieve (strainer) to remove any pips (seeds). Leave to cool, then chill.

4 Divide the mixed soft fruit among four individual dishes and pour over the sauce. Serve immediately with vanilla ice cream or crème fraîche.

Cook's Tips
• The red sauce is also good swirled into mascarpone or plain yogurt. Try it as a topping for peaches or bananas and cream.
• Crème de framboise is raspberry-flavoured liqueur. You could use Kirsch or an orange-flavoured liqueur instead.

Gooseberry & Elderflower Cream

Fresh-tasting gooseberries and fragrant elderflowers give this dessert an attractive flavour. For the best presentation, serve the cream in individual dishes, prettily decorated with sprigs of mint.

Serves 4
500g/1¼ lb/4¼ cups
  gooseberries
300ml/½ pint/1¼ cups double
  (heavy) cream
about 115g/4oz/1 cup sifted icing
  (confectioners') sugar, to taste
30ml/2 tbsp elderflower cordial
fresh mint sprigs, to decorate
amaretti, to serve

1 Place the gooseberries in a heavy pan, cover and cook over low heat, shaking the pan occasionally, until the gooseberries are tender. Turn the gooseberries into a bowl, crush them, then leave to cool completely.

2 Whip the cream until soft peaks form, then fold in half of the crushed gooseberries. Sweeten with icing sugar and add elderflower cordial to taste. Sweeten the remaining gooseberries with icing sugar.

3 Layer the cream mixture and the crushed gooseberries in four dessert dishes or tall glasses, then cover and chill. Decorate the dessert with the fresh mint sprigs and serve with amaretti.

Cook's Tips
• If you prefer, the cooked gooseberries can be puréed and sieved (strained) instead of crushed.
• When elderflowers are in season, instead of using the cordial, cook two or three elderflower heads with the gooseberries.

Variation
The elderflower cordial can be replaced by orange flower water to produce a delicately fragrant dessert.

Berry Medley Energy 85kcal/361kJ; Protein 1.3g; Carbohydrate 16.5g, of which sugars 16.5g; Fat 0.2g, of which saturates 0g; Cholesterol 0mg; Calcium 41mg; Fibre 2.6g; Sodium 7mg.
Gooseberry Energy 509kcal/2115kJ; Protein 2.7g; Carbohydrate 35.1g, of which sugars 35.1g; Fat 40.8g, of which saturates 25.1g; Cholesterol 103mg; Calcium 87mg; Fibre 3g; Sodium 21mg.

Clementines in Cinnamon Caramel

The combination of sweet yet sharp clementines and caramel sauce, flavoured with a hint of spice, is divine. Serve with thick yogurt or crème fraîche to make a delicious dessert for family and friends.

Serves 4–6
8–12 clementines
225g/8oz/generous 1 cup sugar
300ml/½ pint/1¼ cups warm water
2 cinnamon sticks
30ml/2 tbsp orange-flavoured liqueur
25g/1oz/¼ cup shelled pistachio nuts

1 Using a vegetable peeler, pare the rind from two clementines, and cut it into fine strips. Set aside.

2 Peel the clementines, removing all the pith but keeping them intact. Put the fruits in a serving bowl.

3 Gently heat the sugar in a pan until it melts and turns a rich golden brown. Immediately turn off the heat.

4 Cover your hand with a dish towel and pour in the warm water (the mixture will bubble violently). Bring slowly to the boil, stirring until the caramel has dissolved. Add the shredded rind and whole cinnamon sticks, then simmer for 5 minutes. Stir in the orange-flavoured liqueur.

5 Leave the syrup to cool for about 10 minutes, then pour over the clementines. Cover the bowl and chill for several hours or overnight.

6 Blanch the pistachios in boiling water. Drain, cool and remove the dark outer skins. Scatter over the clementines and serve.

Variation
Use oranges instead of clementines: using a sharp knife, remove the rind and pith, cutting downwards, then slice horizontally.

Pasta Timbales with Apricot Sauce

This unusual dessert is made like a rice pudding, but uses tiny pasta shapes instead of the rice. It looks very attractive.

Serves 4
100g/4oz/1 cup orzo or other small soup pasta
75g/3oz/⅓ cup caster (superfine) sugar
pinch of salt
25g/1oz/2 tbsp butter
1 vanilla pod (bean), split
750ml/1¼ pints/3 cups milk
300ml/½ pint/1¼ cups ready-made custard
45ml/3 tbsp Kirsch
15ml/1 tbsp powdered gelatine
oil, for greasing
400g/14oz can apricots in juice
lemon juice to taste
fresh flowers, to decorate (optional)

1 Place the pasta, sugar, pinch of salt, butter, vanilla pod and milk into a heavy pan and bring to the boil. Turn down the heat and simmer for 25 minutes until the pasta is tender and most of the liquid is absorbed. Stir frequently to prevent it from sticking.

2 Remove the vanilla pod and transfer the pasta to a bowl to cool. Stir in the custard and add 30ml/2 tbsp of the kirsch.

3 Sprinkle the gelatine over 45ml/2 tbsp water in a small bowl set in a pan of barely simmering water. Allow to become spongy and heat gently to dissolve. Stir into the pasta.

4 Lightly oil 4 timbale moulds and spoon in the pasta. Chill for 2 hours until set.

5 Meanwhile, purée the apricots in a food processor or blender, then pass through a sieve (strainer) and add lemon juice and Kirsch to taste. Dilute with a little water if too thick.

6 Run a knife around the edge of each timbale to loosen the mixture. To turn out, place an individual plate on the top of each mould, then holding the plate and mould firmly together, invert them. Serve with apricot sauce and decorated with fresh flowers if you wish.

Timbales Energy 425kcal/1797kJ; Protein 12g; Carbohydrate 67.6g, of which sugars 47.3g; Fat 10.2g, of which saturates 5.3g; Cholesterol 26mg; Calcium 332mg; Fibre 1.7g; Sodium 156mg.
Clementines Energy 215kcal/912kJ; Protein 1.7g; Carbohydrate 46.8g, of which sugars 46.7g; Fat 2.4g, of which saturates 0.3g; Cholesterol 0mg; Calcium 50mg; Fibre 1.3g; Sodium 28mg.

Blackberry Brown Sugar Meringue

A rich dessert which is elegant enough to be served at an autumnal dinner party.

Serves 6

For the meringue
175g/6oz/¾ cup soft light brown sugar
3 egg whites
5ml/1 tsp distilled malt vinegar
2.5ml/½ tsp vanilla extract

For the filling
350–450g/12oz–1lb/3–4 cups blackberries
30ml/2 tbsp crème de cassis
300ml/½ pint/1¼ cups double (heavy) cream
15ml/1 tbsp icing (confectioners') sugar, sifted
small blackberry leaves, to decorate (optional)

1 Preheat the oven to 160°C/325°F/Gas 3. Draw a 20cm/8in circle on a sheet of non-stick baking parchment, turn over and place on a baking sheet. Spread the brown sugar out on a baking sheet, dry in the oven for 8–10 minutes, then sieve (sift).

2 Whisk the egg whites in a clean, grease-free bowl until stiff. Add half the dried brown sugar, 15g/½oz/1 tbsp at a time, whisking well after each addition. Add the vinegar and vanilla extract, then fold in the remaining sugar.

3 Spoon the meringue on to the drawn circle on the paper, making a hollow in the centre. Bake for 45 minutes, then turn off the oven and leave the meringue in the oven with the door slightly open, until cold. Meanwhile, place the blackberries in a bowl, sprinkle over the crème de cassis and leave to macerate for 30 minutes.

4 When the meringue is cold, carefully peel off the baking parchment and transfer to a serving plate. Lightly whip the cream with the icing sugar and spoon into the centre. Top with the blackberries and decorate with blackberry leaves, if you like.

> **Variation**
> *Fill with a mix of raspberries, strawberries and red currants.*

Australian Hazelnut Pavlova

A hazelnut meringue base is topped with orange cream, nectarines and raspberries in this famous dessert.

Serves 4–6
3 egg whites
175g/6oz/1 cup caster (superfine) sugar
5ml/1 tsp cornflour (cornstarch)
5ml/1 tsp white wine vinegar
40g/1½ oz/generous ¼ cup chopped roasted hazelnuts
250ml/8fl oz/1 cup double (heavy) cream
15ml/1 tbsp orange juice
30ml/2 tbsp natural (plain) thick and creamy yogurt
2 ripe nectarines, stoned (pitted) and sliced
225g/8oz/2 cups raspberries, halved
15–30ml/1–2 tbsp redcurrant jelly, warmed

1 Preheat the oven to 140°C/275°F/Gas 1. Lightly grease a baking sheet. Draw a 20cm/8in circle on a sheet of baking parchment. Place pencil-side down on the baking sheet.

2 Place the egg whites in a clean, grease-free bowl and whisk until stiff peaks form. Whisk in the caster sugar 15g/½oz/1 tbsp at a time, whisking well after each addition.

3 Add the cornflour, vinegar and hazelnuts and fold in carefully with a large metal spoon.

4 Spoon the meringue on to the marked circle and spread out to the edges, making a dip in the centre. Bake for about 1¼–1½ hours, until crisp. Cool completely; transfer to a serving platter.

5 Whip the double cream and orange juice until the mixture is just thick, stir in the yogurt and spoon on to the meringue. Top with the prepared fruit and drizzle over the warmed redcurrant jelly. Serve immediately.

> **Variation**
> *For extra colour, add a couple of peeled and sliced kiwi fruit.*

Meringue Energy 404kcal/1684kJ; Protein 2.9g; Carbohydrate 36.9g, of which sugars 36.9g; Fat 27g, of which saturates 16.7g; Cholesterol 69mg; Calcium 66mg; Fibre 1.8g; Sodium 45mg.
Pavlova Energy 427kcal/1783kJ; Protein 5g; Carbohydrate 44.1g, of which sugars 43.2g; Fat 26.9g, of which saturates 14.3g; Cholesterol 57mg; Calcium 71mg; Fibre 2.2g; Sodium 50mg.

Apricot Mousse

Dried apricots are used to flavour this delightful, light and airy dessert. Serve in dainty stemmed glass dishes for a pretty effect.

Serves 4

300g/10oz ready-to-eat dried apricots
300ml/½ pint/1¼ cups fresh orange juice
200g/7oz/¾ cup low-fat Greek (US strained plain) yogurt
2 egg whites
fresh mint sprigs, to decorate

1 Place the apricots in a pan with the orange juice and heat gently until boiling. Cover the pan and gently simmer the apricots for 3 minutes.

2 Cool slightly, then place in a food processor or blender and process until smooth. Stir in the Greek yogurt.

3 Whisk the egg whites in a clean, grease-free bowl until stiff enough to hold soft peaks, then fold gently into the puréed apricot mixture.

4 Spoon the mousse into four stemmed glasses or one large serving dish. Chill in the refrigerator before serving, decorated with sprigs of fresh mint.

Cook's Tips
• This fluffy dessert can be made with any dried fruits instead of apricots – try dried peaches, prunes or apples.
• When folding in whisked egg whites, always use a large metal spoon, and employ a light cutting action.

Variation
To make a speedier, fool-type dessert, omit the egg whites and simply swirl together the apricot mixture and the yogurt.

Apple Foam with Blackberries

A light-as-air dessert, with lots of contrast in colour, flavour and texture, this is the perfect dish for people wanting to cut down on their fat intake.

Serves 4

225g/8oz/2 cups blackberries
150ml/¼ pint/⅔ cup apple juice
5ml/1 tsp powdered gelatine
15ml/1 tbsp clear honey
2 egg whites

1 Place the blackberries in a pan with 60ml/4 tbsp of the apple juice and heat gently until the fruit is soft. Remove from the heat, cool, then chill in the refrigerator.

2 Sprinkle the gelatine over the remaining apple juice in a small pan and stir over gentle heat until dissolved. Stir in the honey.

3 Whisk the egg whites in a clean, grease-free bowl until stiff peaks form. Continue whisking hard and gradually pour in the hot gelatine mixture until well mixed.

4 Quickly spoon the foam into rough mounds on individual plates. Chill. To serve, spoon the blackberries and juice around the foam rounds.

Cook's Tips
• Make sure you dissolve the gelatine over very low heat. It must not boil, otherwise it will lose its setting ability.
• Use a balloon, rotary or electric whisk to whisk the egg whites, or use an electric whisk. The bowl must be completely clean, otherwise, if there is any grease in the bowl, the egg whites will not achieve optimum volume. Do not overbeat the egg whites, as this makes them dry and they will not fold in evenly.

Variation
Any seasonal soft fruit can be used to accompany the apple foam if blackberries are not available.

Mousse Energy 180kcal/768kJ; Protein 8.7g; Carbohydrate 37.4g, of which sugars 37.4g; Fat 0.6g, of which saturates 0.1g; Cholesterol 1mg; Calcium 107mg; Fibre 4.8g; Sodium 65mg.
Apple Foam Energy 49kcal/209kJ; Protein 3.1g; Carbohydrate 9.5g, of which sugars 9.5g; Fat 0.2g, of which saturates 0g; Cholesterol 0mg; Calcium 27mg; Fibre 1.8g; Sodium 33mg.

Raspberry Passion Fruit Swirls

If passion fruit is not available, this simple dessert can be made with raspberries alone.

Serves 4
300g/11oz/generous 2½ cups raspberries

2 passion fruit
350ml/12fl oz/1½ cups Greek (US strained plain) yogurt
25g/1oz/2 tbsp caster (superfine) sugar
raspberries and sprigs of fresh mint, to decorate

1 Mash the raspberries in a small bowl with a fork until the juice runs. Scoop out the passion fruit pulp into a separate bowl, add the yogurt and sugar and mix well.

2 Spoon alternate spoonfuls of the raspberry pulp and the yogurt mixture into stemmed glasses or one large serving dish, stirring lightly to create a swirled effect.

3 Decorate the desserts with whole raspberries and sprigs of fresh mint. Serve chilled.

Frudités with Honey Dip

A colourful and tasty variation on the popular savoury crudités, this dessert is great fun for impromptu entertaining. Use any combination of fresh fruit you wish.

Serves 4
225g/8oz/1 cup Greek (US strained plain) yogurt
45ml/3 tbsp clear honey
selection of fruits such as apples, grapes, strawberries, peaches and cherries, for dipping

1 Place the yogurt in a dish, beat until smooth, then stir in the honey, leaving a marbled effect.

2 Cut a selection of fruits into wedges or bitesize pieces or leave whole, depending on your choice. Arrange on a platter with the bowl of dip in the centre. Chill before serving.

Crème Caramel

This creamy, caramel-flavoured custard from France is popular worldwide.

Serves 4–6
115g/4oz/generous ½ cup granulated (white) sugar
300ml/½ pint/1¼ cups milk

300ml/½ pint/1¼ cups single (light) cream
6 eggs
75g/3oz/generous ¼ cup caster (superfine) sugar
2.5ml/½ tsp vanilla extract

1 Preheat the oven to 150°C/300°F/Gas 2 and half-fill a large roasting pan with water.

2 Place the granulated sugar in a pan with 60ml/4 tbsp water and heat gently, swirling the pan occasionally, until the sugar has dissolved. Increase the heat and boil for a good caramel colour. Immediately pour the caramel into an ovenproof soufflé dish. Place in the roasting pan and set aside.

3 To make the egg custard, heat the milk and cream together in a pan until almost boiling. Meanwhile, beat the eggs, caster sugar and vanilla extract together in a mixing bowl using a large balloon whisk.

4 Whisk the hot milk into the eggs and sugar, then strain the liquid through a sieve (strainer) into the soufflé dish, on top of the cooled caramel base.

5 Transfer the tin to the centre of the oven and bake for about 1½–2 hours (topping up the water level after 1 hour), or until the custard has set in the centre. Lift the dish carefully out of the water and leave to cool, then cover and chill overnight.

6 Run a knife around the edge of the chilled custard, then place an inverted plate (large enough to hold the caramel sauce that will flow out as well) on top of the dish. Holding the dish and plate together, turn upside down. Give both plate and dish a gentle but firm shake to loosen the crème caramel, then lift off the mould. Serve immediately.

Swirls Energy 97kcal/414kJ; Protein 8g; Carbohydrate 16.4g, of which sugars 16.4g; Fat 0.4g, of which saturates 0.2g; Cholesterol 1mg; Calcium 99mg; Fibre 2.1g; Sodium 33mg.
Frudités Energy 97kcal/407kJ; Protein 3.7g; Carbohydrate 9.7g, of which sugars 9.7g; Fat 5.7g, of which saturates 2.9g; Cholesterol 0mg; Calcium 85mg; Fibre 0g; Sodium 41mg.
Caramel Energy 318kcal/1335kJ; Protein 9.8g; Carbohydrate 36.6g, of which sugars 36.6g; Fat 16g, of which saturates 8.2g; Cholesterol 221mg; Calcium 150mg; Fibre 0g; Sodium 108mg.

Strawberries in Spiced Grape Jelly

Strawberries set in a fruity jelly delicately flavoured with cinnamon makes this the ideal dessert to serve after a filling main course.

Serves 4
450ml/³/₄ pint/scant 2 cups red grape juice
1 cinnamon stick
1 small orange
15ml/1 tbsp powdered gelatine
225g/8oz/2 cups strawberries, chopped, plus extra to decorate

1 Place the grape juice in a pan with the cinnamon stick. Thinly pare the rind from the orange. Add most of it to the pan, but shred some pieces and set them aside for the decoration.

2 Place the pan over very low heat heat for 10 minutes, then remove the cinnamon stick and orange rind.

3 Squeeze the juice from the orange into a bowl and sprinkle over the powdered gelatine. Stir into the grape juice until the gelatine has completely dissolved. Allow to cool until just starting to set.

4 Stir in the strawberries, then quickly turn the mixture into a 1 litre/1³/₄ pint/4 cup mould or serving dish. Chill until set.

5 To serve, dip the mould quickly into hot water and turn the jelly out on to a serving plate. Decorate with whole strawberries and the reserved shreds of orange rind.

Cook's Tip
Do not wash the strawberries until just before you hull them. Dip them quickly in water, then pat dry on kitchen paper.

Variation
Use a different flavoured fruit juice, such as cranberry juice.

Plum & Port Sorbet

This sophisticated sorbet is deliciously refreshing.

Serves 4
900g/2lb ripe red plums, stoned (pitted) and halved

75g/3oz/6 tbsp caster (superfine) sugar
45ml/3 tbsp ruby port or red wine
crisp sweet cookies, to serve

1 Place the plums in a pan with the sugar and 45ml/3 tbsp water. Stir over low heat until the sugar has melted. Cover and simmer gently for about 5 minutes until the fruit is soft.

2 Turn into a food processor or blender and purée until smooth, then stir in the port or red wine. Cool completely, then turn into a plastic freezer container and freeze until the sorbet is firm around the edges. Process until smooth. Spoon back into the freezer container and freeze until solid.

3 Allow to soften slightly at room temperature for about 15–20 minutes before serving in scoops, with sweet cookies.

Quick Apricot Blender Whip

This is one of the quickest desserts you could make and also one of the prettiest. Decorate with lightly toasted slivered almonds if you like.

Serves 4
400g/14oz can apricot halves
15ml/1 tbsp Grand Marnier or brandy
175ml/6fl oz/³/₄ cup Greek (US plain strained) yogurt

1 Drain the juice from the apricot halves and place the fruit in a blender or food processor with the Grand Marnier or brandy. Process until smooth.

2 Spoon the fruit purée and the yogurt in alternate spoonfuls into four tall glasses, swirling them together slightly to give a marbled effect. Serve immediately.

Grape Jelly Energy 80kcal/338kJ; Protein 4g; Carbohydrate 16.6g, of which sugars 16.6g; Fat 0.2g, of which saturates 0g; Cholesterol 0mg; Calcium 31mg; Fibre 0.6g; Sodium 11mg.
Sorbet Energy 173kcal/738kJ; Protein 1.5g; Carbohydrate 40.8g, of which sugars 40.8g; Fat 0.2g, of which saturates 0g; Cholesterol 0mg; Calcium 40mg; Fibre 3.6g; Sodium 6mg.
Apricot Whip Energy 117kcal/491kJ; Protein 5.4g; Carbohydrate 11.9g, of which sugars 11.7g; Fat 4.9g, of which saturates 0.6g; Cholesterol 1mg; Calcium 140mg; Fibre 2.3g; Sodium 50mg.

Blackberry & Apple Romanoff

The unbeatable combination of blackberries and apples gives this rich iced dessert delicious flavour. Surprisingly easy to make, the dish offers a stunning finale to a meal.

Serves 6–8
350g/12oz sharp eating apples, peeled, cored and chopped
40g/1½ oz/3 tbsp caster (superfine) sugar
250ml/8fl oz/1 cup whipping cream
5ml/1 tsp grated lemon rind
90ml/6 tbsp Greek (US strained plain) yogurt
50g/2oz (about 4–6) crisp meringues, roughly crumbled
225g/8oz/2 cups blackberries (fresh or frozen)
whipped cream, a few blackberries and fresh mint leaves, to decorate

1 Line a 900ml–1.2 litre/1½–2 pint/4–5 cup round, deep freezerproof bowl with clear film (plastic wrap). Toss the chopped apples into a pan with 1oz/2 tbsp sugar and cook for 2–3 minutes until softened. Mash with a fork and leave to cool.

2 Whip the cream and fold in the lemon rind, yogurt, the remaining sugar, the mashed apples and the meringues.

3 Gently stir in the blackberries, then turn the mixture into the prepared bowl and freeze for 1–3 hours.

4 Loosen the edges with a knife, then turn out on to a plate and remove the clear film. Decorate with whirls of whipped cream, blackberries and mint leaves.

> **Cook's Tip**
> *If you would prefer a more fruity decoration, try serving with a blackberry sauce. Put 225g/8oz blackberries in a pan with a little sugar and cook over low heat for about 5 minutes until just soft. Press half through a sieve (strainer), then mix the purée with the rest of the berries. Cool. Add a splash of crème de cassis liqueur, if you wish. Spoon a little over the dessert and serve the rest as an accompanying sauce.*

Tangerine Trifle

An unusual variation on a traditional trifle – of course, you can add a little alcohol if you wish.

Serves 4
5 trifle sponges, halved lengthways
30ml/2 tbsp apricot jam
15–20 ratafia biscuits (almond macaroons)
142g/4¾oz packet tangerine jelly (gelatine)
300g/11oz can mandarin oranges, drained, reserving juice
600ml/1 pint/2½ cups ready-made custard
whipped cream and shreds of orange rind, to decorate
caster (superfine) sugar, for sprinkling

1 Spread the halved sponge cakes with apricot jam and arrange in the base of a deep serving bowl or glass dish. Sprinkle the ratafias over the top.

2 Break up the jelly into a heatproof measuring jug (cup), add the juice from the canned mandarins and dissolve in a pan of hot water or in the microwave. Stir until the liquid is clear.

3 Make up to 600ml/1 pint/2½ cups with ice-cold water, stir well and leave to cool for up to 30 minutes. Scatter the mandarin oranges over the cake and ratafias.

4 Pour the jelly over the mandarin oranges, cake and ratafias and chill for 1 hour or more.

5 When the jelly has set, pour the custard over the top and chill again in the refrigerator.

6 When ready to serve, pipe the whipped cream over the custard. Wash the orange rind shreds, sprinkle them with caster sugar and use to decorate the trifle.

> **Cook's Tip**
> *For an even better flavour, why not make your own custard?*

Trifle Energy 566kcal/2392kJ; Protein 12.9g; Carbohydrate 106.7g, of which sugars 74.2g; Fat 11g, of which saturates 3.2g; Cholesterol 116mg; Calcium 244mg; Fibre 1.4g; Sodium 240mg.
Romanoff Energy 198kcal/825kJ; Protein 2.1g; Carbohydrate 17.6g, of which sugars 17.6g; Fat 13.8g, of which saturates 8.5g; Cholesterol 33mg; Calcium 52mg; Fibre 1.6g; Sodium 25mg.

Tofu Berry Brulée

If you feel that classic brulée is too rich for you, then this lighter variation is a must. Made from tofu, it is low in fat yet tastes great. Use any soft fruits that are in season.

Serves 4
225g/8oz/2 cups red berry fruits
    such as strawberries,
    raspberries and redcurrants
300g/11oz packet silken tofu
45ml/3 tbsp icing (confectioners')
    sugar
65g/2½ oz/¼ cup demerara
    (raw) sugar

1 Halve or quarter any large strawberries, but leave the smaller ones whole. Mix with the other chosen berries.

2 Place the tofu and icing sugar in a food processor or blender and process until smooth.

3 Stir in the fruits and spoon into a flameproof dish with a 900ml/1½ pint/3¾ cup capacity. Sprinkle the top with enough demerara sugar to cover evenly.

4 Place under a very hot grill (broiler) until the sugar melts and caramelizes. Chill well before serving.

Cook's Tips
• Choose silken tofu rather than firm tofu as it gives a smoother texture in this type of dish. Firm tofu is better for cooking in chunks.
• Tofu is make from soya beans and is a popular vegetarian ingredient as it is a good source of protein. It is bland in taste, but absorbs other flavours well.

Variation
For a more indulgent version, replace the tofu with double (heavy) cream and add a few drops of vanilla extract.

Peach & Ginger Pashka

A low-fat version of the Russian Easter favourite – a glorious cheese dessert flavoured with peaches and preserved stem ginger.

Serves 4
350g/12oz/1½ cups low-fat
    cottage cheese
2 peaches or nectarines, peeled
90g/3½oz/scant ½ cup low-fat
    natural (plain) yogurt

2 pieces preserved stem ginger in
    syrup, drained and chopped,
    plus 30ml/2 tbsp syrup from
    the jar
2.5ml/½ tsp vanilla extract

To decorate
1 peach or nectarine, peeled and
    sliced
10ml/2 tsp slivered almonds,
    toasted

1 Drain the cottage cheese and rub it through a fine sieve (strainer) into a bowl. Remove the stones (pits) from the peaches or nectarines and roughly chop.

2 Mix together the chopped peaches or nectarines in a large bowl with the low-fat cottage cheese, yogurt, preserved stem ginger and syrup and vanilla extract.

3 Line a new, clean flower pot or a strainer with a piece of clean, fine cloth, such as muslin (cheesecloth).

4 Add the cheese mixture and wrap over the cloth to cover. Place a saucer on top and weigh down. Stand over a bowl in a cool place and leave to drain overnight.

5 To serve, unwrap the cloth and turn the pashka out on to a serving plate. Decorate the pashka with peach or nectarine slices and toasted almonds.

Cook's Tip
Rather than making one large pashka, line 4 to 6 cups or ramekins with a clean cloth or muslin and divide the mixture evenly among them.

Brulée Energy 178kcal/754kJ; Protein 6.7g; Carbohydrate 32.7g, of which sugars 32.4g; Fat 3.2g, of which saturates 0.4g; Cholesterol 0mg; Calcium 406mg; Fibre 0.6g; Sodium 8mg.
Pashka Energy 79kcal/334kJ; Protein 9.3g; Carbohydrate 8.6g, of which sugars 8.6g; Fat 1.1g, of which saturates 0.7g; Cholesterol 3mg; Calcium 116mg; Fibre 0.8g; Sodium 197mg.

Mango Ice Cream

Canned mangoes are used to make a deliciously rich and creamy ice cream, with a delicate oriental flavour.

Serves 4–6
2 x 425g/15oz cans sliced
  mango, drained
50g/2oz/¼ cup caster
  (superfine) sugar
30ml/2 tbsp lime juice
45ml/3 tbsp hot water
15ml/1 tbsp powdered gelatine
350ml/12fl oz/1½ cups double
  (heavy) cream, lightly whipped
fresh mint sprigs, to decorate

1 Reserve four slices of mango for decoration and chop the remainder. Place the chopped mango pieces in a bowl with the caster sugar and lime juice.

2 Put the hot water in a small heatproof bowl and sprinkle over the gelatine. Place the bowl over a pan of gently simmering water and stir until the gelatine has dissolved. Pour on to the mango mixture and mix well.

3 Add the lightly whipped cream and fold into the mango mixture. Pour the mixture into a plastic freezer container and freeze until half frozen.

4 Place the half-frozen ice cream in a food processor or blender and process until smooth. Spoon back into the container and return to the freezer to freeze completely.

5 Remove from the freezer 10 minutes before serving and place in the refrigerator. Serve scoops of ice cream decorated with pieces of the reserved sliced mango and fresh mint sprigs.

Cook's Tip
• *Transferring the ice cream to the refrigerator for a short time before serving allows it to soften slightly, making scooping easier and helping the flavour to be more pronounced.*
• *Use a metal scoop to serve the ice cream, dipping the scoop briefly in warm water between servings. Or simply slice, if easier.*

Brown Bread Ice Cream

This delicious textured ice cream is irresistible served with a blackcurrant sauce.

Serves 6
50g/2oz/½ cup roasted and
  chopped hazelnuts, ground
75g/3oz/1½ cups wholemeal
  (whole-wheat) breadcrumbs
50g/2oz/¼ cup demerara
  (raw) sugar
3 egg whites
115g/4oz/generous ⅔ cup caster
  (superfine) sugar
300ml/½ pint/1¼ cups double
  (heavy) cream
a few drops of vanilla extract

For the sauce
225g/8oz/2 cups blackcurrants
75g/3oz/generous ⅓ cup caster
  (superfine) sugar
15ml/1 tbsp crème de cassis
fresh mint sprigs, to decorate

1 Combine the hazelnuts and breadcrumbs on a baking sheet, then sprinkle over the demerara sugar. Place under a medium grill (broiler) and cook until crisp and browned.

2 Whisk the egg whites in a clean, grease-free bowl until stiff, then gradually whisk in the caster sugar until thick and glossy. Whip the cream until soft peaks form and fold into the meringue with the breadcrumb mixture and vanilla extract.

3 Spoon the mixture into a 1.2 litre/2 pint/5 cup loaf tin (pan). Smooth the top level, then cover and freeze until firm.

4 To make the sauce, put the blackcurrants in a small bowl with the sugar. Toss gently to mix and leave for about 30 minutes. Purée the blackcurrants in a food processor or blender, then press through a nylon sieve (strainer) until smooth. Add the crème de cassis and chill.

5 To serve, arrange a slice of ice cream on a plate, spoon over a little sauce and decorate with fresh mint sprigs.

Cook's Tip
Crème de cassis is the famous French blackcurrant liqueur.

Brown Bread Energy 526kcal/2198kJ; Protein 5.4g; Carbohydrate 55.3g, of which sugars 45.8g; Fat 32.4g, of which saturates 17.1g; Cholesterol 69mg; Calcium 97mg; Fibre 2.2g; Sodium 141mg.
Mango Energy 409kcal/1701kJ; Protein 1.4g; Carbohydrate 32.4g, of which sugars 32.3g; Fat 31.3g, of which saturates 19.5g; Cholesterol 80mg; Calcium 44mg; Fibre 0.9g; Sodium 17mg.

Berry Frozen Yogurt

A super-easy iced dessert, using frozen summer fruits.

Serves 6
350g/12oz/3 cups frozen
  summer fruits

200l/7fl oz/scant 1 cup Greek
  (US strained plain) yogurt
25g/1oz/¼ cup icing
  (confectioners') sugar

1 Put all the ingredients into a food processor and process until combined but still quite chunky. Spoon into six 150ml/¼ pint/⅔ cup ramekin dishes. Cover with cling film (plastic wrap) and freeze for 2 hours until firm.

2 To turn out, dip briefly in hot water and invert on to individual plates, tapping the bases of the dishes to release the desserts.

Rippled Chocolate Ice Cream

Rich, smooth and packed with chocolate, this heavenly ice cream is a real treat.

Serves 4
60ml/4 tbsp chocolate and
  hazelnut spread

450ml/¾ pint/scant 2 cups
  double (heavy) cream
15ml/1 tbsp icing (confectioners')
  sugar
50g/2oz plain (semisweet)
  chocolate, chopped
chocolate curls, to decorate

1 Mix together the chocolate and hazelnut spread and 75ml/5 tbsp of the double cream in a bowl.

2 Place the remaining cream in another bowl, sift in the icing sugar and beat until softly whipped. Lightly fold in the chocolate and hazelnut mixture with the chopped chocolate until the mixture is rippled. Transfer to a plastic freezer container and freeze for 3–4 hours, until firm.

3 Remove from the freezer about 10 minutes before serving. Serve in scoops, topped with a few chocolate curls.

Frozen Lemon Soufflé with Blackberry Sauce

This tangy iced dessert is complemented wonderfully by the richly coloured blackberry sauce.

Serves 6
grated rind of 1 lemon and juice
  of 2 lemons
15ml/1 tbsp powdered gelatine
5 eggs, separated
150g/5oz/1¼ cups caster
  (superfine) sugar

a few drops of vanilla extract
400ml/14fl oz/1⅔ cups whipping
  cream

For the sauce
175g/6oz/1½ cups blackberries
  (fresh or frozen)
25–40g/1–1½oz/2–3 tbsp caster
  (superfine) sugar
a few fresh blackberries and
  blackberry leaves, to decorate

1 Place the lemon juice in a small pan and heat through. Sprinkle on the gelatine and leave to dissolve, or gently heat further until clear. Allow to cool.

2 Put the lemon rind, egg yolks, sugar and vanilla extract into a large bowl and whisk until the mixture is very thick, pale and really creamy.

3 Whisk the egg whites in a clean, grease-free bowl until almost stiff. Whip the cream until stiff.

4 Stir the gelatine mixture into the yolk mixture, then fold in the whipped cream and lastly the egg whites. When lightly but thoroughly blended, turn into a 1.5 litre/2½ pint/6¼ cup soufflé dish and freeze for about 2 hours.

5 To make the sauce, place the blackberries in a pan with the sugar and cook for 4–6 minutes until the juices begin to run and all the sugar has dissolved. Pass through a nylon sieve (strainer) to remove the seeds, then chill until ready to serve.

6 When the soufflé is almost frozen, scoop or spoon out on to individual plates and serve with the blackberry sauce.

Yogurt Energy 71kcal/295kJ; Protein 2.6g; Carbohydrate 8.5g, of which sugars 8.5g; Fat 3.5g, of which saturates 1.7g; Cholesterol 0mg; Calcium 62mg; Fibre 0.7g; Sodium 28mg.
Chocolate Energy 719kcal/2971kJ; Protein 3.4g; Carbohydrate 22.9g, of which sugars 22.6g; Fat 68.9g, of which saturates 41.2g; Cholesterol 155mg; Calcium 81mg; Fibre 0.4g; Sodium 33mg.
Soufflé Energy 438kcal/1821kJ; Protein 7g; Carbohydrate 33.8g, of which sugars 33.8g; Fat 31.6g, of which saturates 18.1g; Cholesterol 229mg; Calcium 90mg; Fibre 0.9g; Sodium 77mg.

Fruited Rice Ring

This unusual chilled rice pudding ring is topped with a tasty mix of dried fruits that have been simmered until meltingly soft. The delicious combination of the fruits and rice makes this a truly healthy dish.

Serves 4
65g/2½ oz/¼ cup short grain pudding rice
900ml/1½ pints/3¾ cups semi-skimmed (low-fat) milk
1 cinnamon stick
175g/6oz mixed dried fruit
175ml/6fl oz/¾ cup orange juice
40g/1½oz/3 tbsp caster (superfine) sugar
finely grated rind of 1 small orange

1 Place the rice, milk and cinnamon stick in a large pan and bring to the boil. Cover and simmer, stirring occasionally, for about 1½ hours, until all the liquid has been absorbed.

2 Meanwhile, place the dried fruit and orange juice in a pan and bring to the boil. Cover and simmer very gently for about 1 hour, until tender and all the liquid has been absorbed.

3 Remove the cinnamon stick from the rice and discard. Stir in the caster sugar and orange rind.

4 Carefully spoon the cooked fruit into the base of a lightly oiled 1.5 litre/2½ pint/6¼ cup ring mould. Spoon the rice over the fruit, smoothing it down firmly. Chill.

5 Run a knife around the edge of the mould and turn out the rice carefully on to a serving plate.

Cook's Tip
Rather than using a ring mould and turning out the dish, you may prefer to serve the dessert straight from individual small dishes. In this case, spoon the cooked rice into 6 dishes, then top with the cooked fruit. Chill well before serving.

Apple & Hazelnut Shortcake

This is a variation on the classic strawberry shortcake and is equally delicious.

Serves 8–10
3 sharp eating apples
5ml/1 tsp lemon juice
15–25g/½–1oz/1–2 tbsp caster (superfine) sugar
15ml/1 tbsp chopped fresh mint, or 5ml/1 tsp dried mint
250ml/8fl oz/1 cup whipping cream
a few drops of vanilla extract
a few fresh mint leaves and whole hazelnuts, to decorate

For the hazelnut shortcake
150g/5oz/1¼ cups plain wholemeal (whole-wheat) flour
50g/2oz/½ cup ground hazelnuts
50g/2oz/½ cup icing (confectioners') sugar, sifted
150g/5oz/generous 1 cup unsalted butter

1 To make the hazelnut shortcake, process the flour, ground hazelnuts and icing sugar with the butter in a food processor in short bursts, until they come together. Bring the dough together, adding a very little iced water if needed. Knead briefly, wrap and chill for 30 minutes.

2 Preheat the oven to 160°C/325°F/Gas 3. Cut the dough in half and roll out each half to an 18cm/7in round. Place on baking parchment on baking sheets. Bake for 40 minutes, or until crisp. Allow to cool.

3 Peel, core and chop the apples into a pan with the lemon juice. Add sugar to taste, then cook for 2–3 minutes, until just soft. Mash the apple gently with the mint and leave to cool.

4 Whip the cream with the vanilla extract. Place one shortbread base on a serving plate. Spread half the apple and half the cream on top.

5 Place the second shortcake on top, then spread over the remaining apple and cream, swirling the top layer of cream gently. Decorate the top with mint leaves and a few whole hazelnuts, then serve at once.

Rice Ring Energy 334kcal/1418kJ; Protein 10.1g; Carbohydrate 67.6g, of which sugars 54.7g; Fat 4.1g, of which saturates 2.4g; Cholesterol 13mg; Calcium 315mg; Fibre 1g; Sodium 123mg.
Shortcake Energy 333kcal/1386kJ; Protein 3.3g; Carbohydrate 23.1g, of which sugars 13.8g; Fat 25.9g, of which saturates 14.4g; Cholesterol 58mg; Calcium 36mg; Fibre 2.2g; Sodium 99mg.

Apricot & Almond Jalousie

Jalousie means "shutter", and the slatted pastry topping of this pie looks exactly like French window shutters. The dish not only looks attractive, but tastes wonderful, too.

Serves 4

225g/8oz ready-made puff pastry
a little beaten egg
90ml/6 tbsp apricot conserve
25g/1oz/2 tbsp caster (superfine) sugar
30ml/2 tbsp flaked almonds
cream, to serve

1 Preheat the oven to 220°C/425°F/Gas 7. Roll out the pastry on a lightly floured surface and cut into a square measuring 30cm/12in. Cut in half to make two rectangles.

2 Place one piece of pastry on a wetted baking sheet and brush all round the edges with beaten egg. Spread the apricot conserve over the unbrushed part of the rectangle.

3 Fold the remaining rectangle in half lengthways and cut about eight diagonal slits from the centre fold to within about 1cm/½in from the edge all the way along.

4 Unfold the cut pastry and lay it on top of the pastry on the baking sheet. Press the pastry edges together well to seal and knock them up with the back of a knife.

5 Brush the slashed pastry with water and sprinkle over the caster sugar and flaked almonds.

6 Bake in the oven for 25–30 minutes, until well risen and golden brown. Remove the jalousie from the oven and leave to cool. Serve sliced, accompanied by cream.

Cook's Tip

Make smaller individual jalousies and serve them with morning coffee, if you like. Use other flavours of fruit conserve to ring the changes – a summer berry conserve would be delicious.

Chocolate Eclairs

These choux pastry éclairs are filled with a luscious vanilla-flavoured cream.

115g/4oz plain (semisweet) chocolate
25g/1oz/2 tbsp butter

Serves 12

300ml/½ pint/1¼ cups double (heavy) cream
10ml/2 tsp icing (confectioners') sugar, sifted
1.5ml/¼ tsp vanilla extract

For the pastry

65g/2½oz/9 tbsp plain (all-purpose) flour
pinch of salt
50g/2oz/¼ cup butter, diced
2 eggs, lightly beaten

1 Preheat the oven to 200°C/400°F/Gas 6. Grease a large baking sheet and line with baking parchment.

2 To make the pastry, sift the flour and salt on to a small sheet of baking parchment. Very gently heat the butter and 150ml/¼ pint/⅔ cup water in a pan until the butter has melted. Bring to a rolling boil, then remove from the heat and immediately tip in all the flour. Beat vigorously to mix well. Return the pan to a low heat. Beat the mixture until it leaves the sides of the pan and forms a ball. Set aside and allow to cool for 2–3 minutes.

3 Beat in the eggs, a little at a time, to form a smooth, shiny paste. Spoon into a piping (pastry) bag fitted with a 2.5cm/1in plain nozzle. Pipe 10cm/4in lengths on to the baking sheet.

4 Bake for 25–30 minutes, or until the pastries are well risen and golden brown. Make a neat slit along the side of each to release the steam. Lower the temperature to 180°C/350°F/Gas 4 and bake for a further 5 minutes. Cool on a wire rack.

5 To make the filling, whip the cream with the icing sugar and vanilla until it just holds its shape. Pipe into the éclairs.

6 Place the chocolate and 30ml/2 tbsp water in a small bowl set over a pan of hot water. Melt, stirring, then remove from the heat and gradually stir in the butter. Use the chocolate mixture to coat the éclairs. Place on a wire rack and leave to set.

Jalousie Energy 339kcal/1423kJ; Protein 4.9g; Carbohydrate 43.5g, of which sugars 23.2g; Fat 18g, of which saturates 0.3g; Cholesterol 0mg; Calcium 56mg; Fibre 0.6g; Sodium 186mg.
Eclairs Energy 253Kcal/1046kJ; Protein 2.7g; Carbohydrate 10.8g, of which sugars 6.5g; Fat 22.4g, of which saturates 13.5g; Cholesterol 86mg; Calcium 30mg; Fibre 0.4g; Sodium 58mg.

Chilled Chocolate Slice

This is a very rich family pudding, but it is also designed to use up the occasional leftover.

Serves 6–8
115g/4oz/½ cup butter, melted
225g/8oz ginger nut biscuits (gingersnaps), finely crushed
50g/2oz stale sponge cake crumbs

60–75ml/4–5 tbsp orange juice
115g/4oz stoned (pitted) dates
25g/1oz/¼ cup finely chopped nuts
175g/6oz dark (bittersweet) chocolate
300ml/½ pint/1¼ cups whipping cream
grated chocolate and icing (confectioners') sugar, to decorate

1 Mix together the butter and ginger nut biscuit crumbs, then pack around the sides and base of an 18cm/7in loose-based flan tin (pan). Chill while making the filling.

2 Put the cake crumbs into a large bowl with the orange juice and leave to soak. Warm the dates thoroughly, then mash and blend into the cake crumbs along with the nuts.

3 Melt the chocolate with 45–60ml/3–4 tbsp of the cream. Softly whip the rest of the cream, then fold in the melted chocolate mixture.

4 Stir the cream and chocolate mixture into the crumbs and mix well. Pour into the prepared tin, mark into portions with a sharp knife and leave to set.

5 Scatter the grated chocolate over the top and dust with icing sugar. Serve cut into wedges.

> **Cook's Tip**
> This dessert is delicious served with slices of fresh fruit, such as peaches, mango or pineapple. Alternatively, offer plums or nectarines poached in a little wine and sugar, or try orange segments in a syrup made from sugar, water and orange juice.

Pecan Cake

This delicious cake is an example of the French influence on Mexican cooking. Serve with a few redcurrants for a splash of uplifting colour.

Serves 8–10
115g/4oz/1 cup pecan nuts
115g/4oz/½ cup butter, softened
115g/4oz/½ cup soft light brown sugar
5ml/1 tsp vanilla extract

4 large eggs, separated
75g/3oz/⅔ cup plain (all-purpose) flour
pinch of salt
12 whole pecan nuts, to decorate
whipped cream or crème fraîche, to serve

For drizzling
50g/2oz/¼ cup butter
120ml/4fl oz/scant ½ cup clear honey

1 Preheat the oven to 180°C/350°F/Gas 4. Grease a 20cm/8in round cake tin (pan). Toast the nuts in a dry frying pan for 5 minutes, shaking frequently. Grind finely and place in a bowl.

2 Cream the butter with the sugar in a mixing bowl, then beat in the vanilla extract and egg yolks.

3 Add the flour to the ground nuts and mix well. Whisk the egg whites with the salt in a clean, grease-free bowl until soft peaks form. Fold the whites into the butter mixture, then gently fold in the flour and nut mixture.

4 Spoon the mixture into the cake tin and bake for 30 minutes or until a skewer inserted in the centre comes out clean.

5 Cool the cake in the tin for 5 minutes, then remove the sides of the tin. Stand the cake on a wire rack until cold.

6 Remove the cake from the base of the tin if necessary, then return it to the rack and arrange the pecans on top. Transfer to a plate. Melt the butter for drizzling in a small pan, add the honey and bring to the boil, stirring. Lower the heat and simmer for 3 minutes, then pour over the cake. Serve with whipped cream or crème fraîche.

Pecan Cake Energy 428Kcal/1785kJ; Protein 6.2g; Carbohydrate 34.7g, of which sugars 27.4g; Fat 30.5g, of which saturates 12.5g; Cholesterol 158mg; Calcium 51mg; Fibre 1g; Sodium 170mg.
Chocolate Slice Energy 545kcal/2269kJ; Protein 4.8g; Carbohydrate 45.8g, of which sugars 32g; Fat 39.3g, of which saturates 22.6g; Cholesterol 85mg; Calcium 80mg; Fibre 1.4g; Sodium 198mg.

Iced Chocolate & Nut Gâteau

Autumn hazelnuts add crunchiness to this popular iced dinner-party dessert.

Serves 6–8

75g/3oz/¾ cup shelled hazelnuts
about 32 sponge (lady fingers) fingers
150ml/¼ pint/⅔ cup cold strong black coffee
30ml/2 tbsp Cognac or other brandy
450ml/¾ pint/scant 2 cups double (heavy) cream
75g/3oz/⅔ cup icing (confectioners') sugar, sifted
150g/5oz plain (semisweet) chocolate
icing (confectioners') sugar and unsweetened cocoa powder, for dusting

1 Preheat the oven to 200°C/400°F/Gas 6. Spread out the hazelnuts on a baking sheet and toast them in the oven for 5 minutes until golden. Transfer the nuts to a clean dish towel and rub off the skins. Cool, then chop finely.

2 Line a 1.2 litre/2 pint/5 cup loaf tin (pan) with clear film (plastic wrap) and cut the sponge fingers to fit the base and sides. Reserve the remaining fingers.

3 Mix the coffee with the Cognac or other brandy in a shallow dish. Dip the sponge fingers briefly into the coffee mixture and return to the tin, sugary side down.

4 Whip the cream with the icing sugar until it holds soft peaks. Roughly chop 75g/3oz of the chocolate, and fold into the cream with the hazelnuts.

5 Melt the remaining chocolate in a heatproof bowl set over a pan of barely simmering water. Cool, then fold into the cream mixture. Spoon into the tin.

6 Moisten the remaining sponge fingers in the coffee mixture and lay over the filling. Wrap and freeze until firm.

7 Remove the gâteau from the freezer 30 minutes before serving. Turn out and dust with icing sugar and cocoa powder.

Chocolate Chestnut Roulade

Don't worry if this moist sponge cracks as you roll it up – this is the sign of a good roulade.

Serves 8

175g/6oz plain (semisweet) chocolate
30ml/2 tbsp strong black coffee
5 eggs, separated
175g/6oz/scant 1 cup caster (superfine) sugar
250ml/8fl oz/1 cup double (heavy) cream
225g/8oz unsweetened chestnut purée
45–60ml/3–4 tbsp icing (confectioners') sugar, plus extra for dusting
single (light) cream, to serve

1 Preheat the oven to 180°C/350°F/Gas 4, then line and oil a 33 x 23cm/13 x 9in Swiss roll tin (jell roll pan); use non-stick baking parchment. Melt the chocolate in a bowl over gently simmering water, then stir in the coffee. Leave to cool slightly.

2 Whisk the egg yolks and caster sugar together until thick and light, then stir in the cooled chocolate mixture. Whisk the egg whites in another clean bowl until stiff. Stir a spoonful into the chocolate mixture to lighten it, then gently fold in the rest.

3 Pour the mixture into the prepared tin and spread level. Bake for 20 minutes. Remove from the oven, cover with a dish towel and leave to cool in the tin for several hours.

4 Whip the double cream until soft peaks begin to form. Mix together the chestnut purée and icing sugar, then fold into the whipped cream.

5 Dust a sheet of greaseproof (waxed) paper with icing sugar. Turn out the roulade on to this paper and peel off the lining paper. Trim the sides. Gently spread the chestnut cream evenly over the roulade to within 2.5cm/1in of the edges. Using the greaseproof paper to help you, carefully roll up the roulade as tightly and evenly as possible.

6 Chill the roulade for about 2 hours, then dust liberally with icing sugar. Serve cut into thick slices with cream poured over.

Iced Chocolate Energy 631kcal/2628kJ; Protein 8.2g; Carbohydrate 49.7g, of which sugars 38.3g; Fat 44.9g, of which saturates 23.3g; Cholesterol 192mg; Calcium 90mg; Fibre 1.5g; Sodium 57mg.
Roulade Energy 469kcal/1961kJ; Protein 6.2g; Carbohydrate 53.5g, of which sugars 44.9g; Fat 27.1g, of which saturates 15.2g; Cholesterol 163mg; Calcium 68mg; Fibre 1.7g; Sodium 57mg.

Baked American Cheesecake

The lemon-flavoured cream cheese provides a subtle filling for this classic dessert.

Makes 9 squares
175g/6oz/1½ cups crushed digestive biscuits (graham crackers)
40g/1½ oz/3 tbsp butter, melted, plus extra for greasing

For the topping
450g/1lb/2½ cups curd (farmer's) cheese or full-fat soft (cream) cheese

115g/4oz/generous ½ cup caster (superfine) sugar
3 eggs
finely grated rind of 1 lemon
15ml/1 tbsp lemon juice
2.5ml/½ tsp vanilla extract
15ml/1 tbsp cornflour (cornstarch)
30ml/2 tbsp sour cream
150ml/¼ pint/⅔ cup sour cream and 1.5ml/¼ tsp ground cinnamon, to decorate

1 Preheat the oven to 170°C/325°F/Gas 3. Lightly grease an 18cm/7in square loose-based cake tin (pan), then line the base with baking parchment.

2 Place the crushed biscuits and butter in a bowl and mix well. Turn into the base of the prepared cake tin and press down firmly with a potato masher.

3 To make the topping, place the curd or soft cheese in a mixing bowl, add the sugar and beat well until smooth. Add the eggs one at a time, beating well after each addition.

4 Stir in the lemon rind and juice, the vanilla extract, cornflour and 30ml/2 tbsp sour cream. Beat until the mixture is smooth. Pour the mixture on to the biscuit base and level the surface.

5 Bake for 1¼ hours, or until the cheesecake has set in the centre. Turn off the oven but leave the cheesecake inside until completely cold.

6 Remove the cheesecake from the tin, top with the sour cream and swirl with the back of a spoon. Sprinkle with cinnamon and serve cut into squares.

Frozen Strawberry Mousse Cake

Children love this cake because it is pink and pretty, and it is just like an ice cream treat.

Serves 4–6
425g/15oz can strawberries in syrup
15ml/1 tbsp powdered gelatine

6 trifle sponges
45ml/3 tbsp strawberry conserve
200ml/7fl oz/scant 1 cup crème fraîche
200ml/7fl oz/scant 1 cup whipped cream, to decorate

1 Strain the syrup from the strawberries into a large heatproof jug (cup). Sprinkle over the gelatine and stir well. Stand the jug in a pan of hot water and stir until the gelatine has dissolved.

2 Leave to cool, then chill in the refrigerator for just under 1 hour, until beginning to set. Meanwhile, cut the sponge cake in half lengthways, then spread the cut surfaces evenly with the strawberry conserve.

3 Slowly whisk the crème fraîche into the strawberry jelly, then whisk in the canned strawberries. Line a deep 20cm/8in loose-based cake tin (pan) with non-stick baking parchment.

4 Pour half the strawberry mousse mixture into the tin, arrange the sponge cakes over the surface and then spoon over the remaining mousse mixture, pushing down any sponge cakes which rise up.

5 Freeze for 1–2 hours until firm. Unmould the cake and carefully remove the lining paper. Transfer to a serving plate. Decorate with whirls of cream, a few strawberry leaves and a fresh strawberry, if you have them.

Cook's Tip
For a glamorous finishing touch, spoon the whipped cream into a piping (pastry) bag fitted with a star nozzle and pipe swirls.

Cheesecake Energy 311kcal/1302kJ; Protein 11.4g; Carbohydrate 30.8g, of which sugars 18.5g; Fat 17.4g, of which saturates 9.7g; Cholesterol 105mg; Calcium 112mg; Fibre 0.4g; Sodium 396mg.
Mousse Cake Energy 419kcal/1746kJ; Protein 5.1g; Carbohydrate 36.5g, of which sugars 29.1g; Fat 29.1g, of which saturates 18.1g; Cholesterol 148mg; Calcium 73mg; Fibre 0.8g; Sodium 54mg.

Creamy Mango Cheesecake

This low-fat cheesecake is as creamy as any other, but makes a healthier dessert option – so there's no need to hold back!

Serves 4
115g/4oz/1¼ cups rolled oats
40g/1½ oz/3 tbsp sunflower margarine
30ml/2 tbsp clear honey

1 large ripe mango
300g/10oz/1¼ cups low-fat soft cheese
150ml/¼ pint/⅔ cup low-fat natural (plain) yogurt
finely grated rind of 1 small lime
45ml/3 tbsp apple juice
20ml/4 tsp powdered gelatine
fresh mango and lime slices, to decorate

1 Preheat the oven to 200°C/400°F/Gas 6. Place the rolled oats in a mixing bowl and add the margarine and honey. Mix well together, then press into the base of a 20cm/8in loose-bottomed cake tin (pan).

2 Bake the oat base for 12–15 minutes, then remove the tin from the oven and leave to cool.

3 Peel, stone (pit) and roughly chop the mango. Place in a food processor or blender with the cheese, yogurt and lime rind and process until smooth.

4 Put the apple juice in a small pan and place over heat until boiling. Remove from the heat, sprinkle the gelatine over the apple juice, then stir until dissolved. Stir into the mango and cheese mixture.

5 Pour into the tin and chill until set. Remove from the tin and decorate with mango and lime slices.

Cook's Tip
For a richer, no-cook base, process 150g/5oz/1½ cups digestive biscuits (graham crackers) to form crumbs. Melt 40g/1½oz/ 3 tbsp butter, stir in the crumbs, then press into the tin and chill.

Lemon Cheesecake

A lovely light cream cheese filling is presented on an elegant brandy snap base.

Serves 8
½ x 142g/4¾oz packet lemon jelly (gelatine)
45–60ml/3–4 tbsp boiling water
50g/1lb/2 cups low-fat cream cheese

10ml/2 tsp grated lemon rind
75–115g/3–4oz/about ½ cup caster (superfine) sugar
a few drops of vanilla extract
150ml/¼ pint/⅔ cup Greek (US strained plain) yogurt
8 brandy snaps
a few fresh mint leaves and icing sugar, to decorate

1 Dissolve the jelly in the boiling water in a heatproof measuring jug (cup) and, when clear, add enough cold water to make up to 150ml/¼ pint/⅔ cup. Chill until the jelly begins to thicken. Meanwhile, line a 450g/1lb loaf tin (pan) with clear film (plastic wrap).

2 Cream the cheese with the lemon rind, sugar and vanilla and beat until light and smooth. Then fold in the thickening lemon jelly and the yogurt. Spoon into the prepared tin and chill until set. Preheat the oven to 160°C/325°F/Gas 3.

3 Place two or three brandy snaps at a time on a baking sheet. Place in the oven for no more than 1 minute, until soft enough to unroll and flatten out completely. Leave on a cold plate or tray to harden again. Repeat with the remaining brandy snaps.

4 To serve, turn the cheesecake out on to a board with the help of the clear film. Cut into eight slices and place one slice on each brandy snap base. Decorate with mint leaves and dust with icing sugar before serving.

Variation
Use a packet of orange jelly instead of lemon and use grated orange rind instead of the lemon. Omit the vanilla extract and decorate with pared orange rind shreds in place of mint.

Mango Energy 373kcal/1567kJ; Protein 21.2g; Carbohydrate 38.6g, of which sugars 17.6g; Fat 17.1g, of which saturates 4.1g; Cholesterol 19mg; Calcium 180mg; Fibre 2.9g; Sodium 451mg.
Lemon Energy 237kcal/1000kJ; Protein 10.9g; Carbohydrate 36.3g, of which sugars 33.9g; Fat 7.2g, of which saturates 3g; Cholesterol 14mg; Calcium 119mg; Fibre 0.1g; Sodium 299mg.

Hot Desserts

The ultimate comfort food on a cold day, hot desserts lift the

spirits and provide the best possible finale to any type of meal.

Choose from family favourites, such as Sticky Toffee Pudding,

Bread and Butter Pudding, and Baked Rice Pudding, as well

as fruit-based desserts, such as Plum and Walnut Crumble,

Warm Autumn Compôte, or Thai-fried Bananas.

Kentish Cherry Batter Pudding

Kent, known as the "Garden of England", is particularly well known for cherries and the dishes made from them. This method of baking the fruit in batter is an absolute winner.

Serves 4
45ml/3 tbsp Kirsch (optional)
450g/1lb dark cherries, pitted
50g/2oz/½ cup plain
   (all-purpose) flour
50g/2oz/¼ cup caster
   (superfine) sugar
2 eggs, separated
300ml/½ pint/1¼ cups milk
75g/3oz/6 tbsp butter, melted
caster (superfine) sugar,
   for sprinkling

1 Sprinkle the Kirsch, if using, over the cherries in a small bowl and leave them to soak for about 30 minutes.

2 Mix the flour and sugar together, then slowly stir in the egg yolks and milk to make a smooth batter. Stir in half the butter and set aside for 30 minutes.

3 Preheat the oven to 220°C/425°F/Gas 7, then pour the remaining butter into a 600ml/1 pint/2½ cup baking dish and put in the oven to heat.

4 Whisk the egg whites until stiff peaks form, then fold into the batter with the cherries and Kirsch, if using. Pour into the dish and bake for 15 minutes.

5 Reduce the oven temperature to 180°C/350°F/Gas 4 and bake for 20 minutes, or until golden and set in the centre. Serve sprinkled with sugar.

Baked Stuffed Apples

When apples are plentiful, this traditional pudding is a popular and easy choice. The delectable filling of dried apricots, honey and ground almonds gives a new twist to an old favourite.

Serves 4
75g/3oz/scant 1 cup ground
   almonds
25g/1oz/2 tbsp butter, softened
5ml/1 tsp clear honey
1 egg yolk
50g/2oz dried apricots, chopped
4 cooking apples, preferably
   Bramleys

1 Preheat the oven to 200°C/400°F/Gas 6. Beat together the almonds, butter, honey, egg yolk and apricots.

2 Stamp out the cores from the cooking apples using a large apple corer, then score a line with the point of a sharp knife around the circumference of each apple.

3 Lightly grease a shallow baking dish, then arrange the cooking apples in the dish.

4 Using a small spoon, divide the apricot mixture among the cavities in the apples, then bake in the oven for 45–60 minutes, until the apples are fluffy.

Cook's Tip
Scoring the apples around the middle helps to prevent them from bursting during cooking.

Variations
To ring the changes, replace the dried apricots with seedless raisins or sultanas (golden raisins). Alternatively, fill the cored apples with chopped dates, mixed with finely chopped walnuts and little soft light brown sugar, then top each with a knob (pat) of butter and bake as above.

Cook's Tip
It is worth the effort of pitting the cherries as it makes the dish easier to eat. Use a cherry stoner (pitter) or slit each fruit with the point of a small sharp knife and prise out the stones (pits).

Baked Apples Energy 237kcal/989kJ; Protein 5.5g; Carbohydrate 16.3g, of which sugars 15.8g; Fat 17.2g, of which saturates 4.5g; Cholesterol 64mg; Calcium 65mg; Fibre 3.8g; Sodium 47mg.
Pudding Energy 357kcal/1493kJ; Protein 8g; Carbohydrate 39.4g, of which sugars 29.8g; Fat 19.8g, of which saturates 11.4g; Cholesterol 140mg; Calcium 147mg; Fibre 1.4g; Sodium 183mg.

Sticky Toffee Pudding

Filling, warming and packed with calories, this delightfully gooey steamed pudding is still a firm favourite.

Serves 6

115g/4oz/1 cup toasted walnuts, chopped
175g/6oz/¾ cup butter, plus extra for greasing
175g/6oz/1 cup soft brown sugar
60ml/4 tbsp double (heavy) cream
30ml/2 tbsp lemon juice
2 eggs, beaten
115g/4oz/1 cup self-raising (self-rising) flour

1 Grease a 900ml/1½ pint/3¾ cup heatproof deep bowl and add half the chopped nuts.

2 Heat 50g/2oz/¼ cup of the butter with 50g/2oz/¼ cup of the sugar, the cream and 15ml/1 tbsp of the lemon juice in a small pan, stirring until smooth. Pour half into the greased bowl, then swirl to coat it a little way up the sides. Reserve the rest of the sauce for serving.

3 Beat the remaining butter and sugar until light and fluffy, then gradually beat in the eggs. Fold in the flour and the remaining nuts and lemon juice and spoon into the bowl.

4 Cover the bowl with greaseproof (waxed) paper with a pleat folded in the centre, then tie securely with string.

5 Place the bowl in a pan with enough water to come halfway up the sides of the bowl. Cover with a lid and bring to the boil. Keep the water boiling gently and steam the pudding for 1¼ hours, topping up the water as required, until the pudding is completely set in the centre. Alternatively, steam the pudding in a steamer.

6 Just before serving, gently warm the reserved sauce. To serve, run a knife around the edge of the pudding to loosen it, then turn out on to a warm plate. Pour the warm sauce over the pudding and serve immediately.

Easy Chocolate & Orange Soufflé

The base of this delicious soufflé is a simple semolina mixture, rather than the thick white sauce of most sweet soufflés. The finished dish looks most impressive.

Serve 4

butter, for greasing
600ml/1 pint/2½ cups milk
50g/2oz/scant ½ cup semolina
50g/2oz/¼ cup soft light brown sugar
grated rind of 1 orange
90ml/6 tbsp fresh orange juice
3 eggs, separated
65g/2½oz plain (semisweet) chocolate, grated
icing (confectioners') sugar, for sprinkling
pouring (half-and-half) cream, to serve (optional)

1 Preheat the oven to 200°C/400°F/Gas 6. Butter a shallow 1.75 litre/3 pint/7½ cup ovenproof dish.

2 Pour the milk into a heavy pan, sprinkle over the semolina and brown sugar, then heat, stirring the mixture constantly, until boiling and thickened.

3 Remove the pan from the heat; beat in the orange rind and juice, egg yolks and all but 15ml/1 tbsp of the chocolate.

4 Whisk the egg whites until stiff but not dry, then lightly fold one-third into the semolina mixture. Fold in the remaining egg white in two batches.

5 Spoon the mixture into the dish and bake for about 30 minutes until just set in the centre and risen.

6 Sprinkle the top with the remaining chocolate and icing sugar, then serve immediately with pouring cream, if you wish.

> **Variation**
> For a sophisticated touch, replace 15ml/1 tbsp of the orange juice with the same amount of orange-flavoured liqueur, such as Cointreau or Grand Marnier.

Toffee Energy 603kcal/2510kJ; Protein 7.2g; Carbohydrate 46.4g, of which sugars 31.6g; Fat 44.6g, of which saturates 20.2g; Cholesterol 139mg; Calcium 80mg; Fibre 1.3g; Sodium 206mg.
Chocolate Energy 308kcal/1300kJ; Protein 12.1g; Carbohydrate 42.1g, of which sugars 32.3g; Fat 11.5g, of which saturates 5.5g; Cholesterol 153mg; Calcium 218mg; Fibre 0.7g; Sodium 123mg.

Plum & Walnut Crumble

Walnuts add a lovely crunch to the fruit layer in this rich and warming crumble. Serve with dollops of whipped cream for a tasty dessert.

Serves 4–6

75g/3oz/³⁄₄ cup walnut pieces
900g/2lb plums
175g/6oz/1 cup demerara (raw) sugar
75g/3oz/6 tbsp butter or hard margarine, cut into dice
175g/6oz/1¹⁄₂ cups plain (all-purpose) flour

1 Preheat the oven to 180°C/350°F/Gas 4. Spread the nuts on a baking sheet and place in the oven for 8–10 minutes until evenly coloured.

2 Butter a 1.2 litre/2 pint/5 cup baking dish. Halve and stone (pit) the plums, then put them into the dish and stir in the nuts and half of the demerara sugar.

3 Rub the butter or margarine into the flour until the mixture resembles coarse crumbs. Stir in the remaining sugar and continue to rub in until fine crumbs are formed.

4 Cover the fruit with the crumb mixture and press it down lightly. Bake the pudding for about 45 minutes, until the top is golden brown and the fruit tender.

Cook's Tip

For speed, use a food processor to rub the butter into the flour.

Variations
• *To make an oat and cinnamon crumble, substitute rolled oats for half the flour in the crumble mixture and add 2.5–5ml/ ¹⁄₂ –1 tsp ground cinnamon, to taste.*
• *Try replacing the walnuts with hazelnuts or almonds.*

Baked Rice Pudding

Ready-made rice pudding simply cannot compare with this creamy home-made version, especially if you like the golden skin.

Serves 4

50g/2oz/¹⁄₄ cup short grain pudding rice
25g/1oz/2 tbsp soft light brown sugar
50g/2oz/¹⁄₄ cup butter, plus extra for greasing
900ml/1¹⁄₂ pints/3³⁄₄ cups milk
small strip of lemon rind
pinch of freshly grated nutmeg
fresh mint sprigs, to decorate
raspberries, to serve

1 Preheat the oven to 150°C/300°F/Gas 2, then butter a 1.2 litre/2 pint/5 cup shallow baking dish.

2 Put the rice, sugar and butter into the prepared dish, then stir in the milk and lemon rind. Sprinkle a little nutmeg over the surface of the mixture.

3 Bake the rice pudding in the oven for about 2¹⁄₂ hours, stirring after 30 minutes and another couple of times during the next 2 hours until the rice is tender and the pudding has a thick and creamy consistency.

4 If you like skin on top, leave the rice pudding undisturbed for the final 30 minutes of cooking (otherwise, stir it again). Serve the rice pudding immediately, decorated with fresh mint sprigs and raspberries.

Variations
• *Use 1.5ml/¹⁄₄ tsp ground cinnamon or mixed spice instead of the grated nutmeg for a change of flavour.*
• *Baked rice pudding is even more delicious with fruit. Add some sultanas (golden raisins), raisins or chopped ready-to-eat dried apricots to the pudding, or serve it alongside sliced fresh peaches or nectarines, or whole fresh strawberries.*

Crumble Energy 325kcal/1361kJ; Protein 4.1g; Carbohydrate 36.5g, of which sugars 26.9g; Fat 19.2g, of which saturates 7.2g; Cholesterol 27mg; Calcium 58mg; Fibre 3.2g; Sodium 81mg.
Pudding Energy 266kcal/1114kJ; Protein 8.7g; Carbohydrate 27.2g, of which sugars 17.2g; Fat 14.2g, of which saturates 8.9g; Cholesterol 40mg; Calcium 278mg; Fibre 0g; Sodium 173mg.

Floating Islands in Plum Sauce

This unusual dessert is simpler to make than it looks, and is quite delicious. It also has the added bonus of being low in fat.

Serves 4
450g/1lb red plums
300ml/½ pint/1¼ cups apple juice
2 egg whites
30ml/2 tbsp concentrated apple juice syrup
pinch of freshly grated nutmeg (optional)

1 Halve the plums and remove the stones (pits). Place them in a wide pan with the apple juice.

2 Bring to the boil, then cover with a tight-fitting lid and leave to simmer gently until the plums are tender.

3 Meanwhile, place the egg whites in a grease-free, dry bowl and whisk until stiff peaks form.

4 Gradually whisk in the apple juice syrup, whisking until the meringue holds fairly firm peaks.

5 To make the "islands", use a tablespoon to scoop the meringue mixture carefully into the gently simmering plum sauce. (You may need to cook them in two batches.)

6 Cover again and allow to simmer gently for 2–3 minutes, until the meringues are just set. Serve immediately, sprinkled with a little freshly grated nutmeg.

Cook's Tip
• A bottle of concentrated apple juice is a useful store-cupboard sweetener, but if you don't have any, just use a little honey instead.
• This is useful for entertaining as the plum sauce can be made in advance and reheated just before you cook the meringues.

Souffléed Rice Pudding

The fluffy egg whites in this unusually light rice pudding make the portions seem much more substantial, without adding lots of extra unwanted fat.

Serves 4
65g/2½ oz/⅓ cup short grain pudding rice
45ml/3 tbsp clear honey
750ml/1¼ pints/3 cups semi-skimmed milk
1 vanilla pod (bean) or 2.5ml/ ½ tsp vanilla extract
2 egg whites
5ml/1 tsp finely grated nutmeg

1 Place the pudding rice, clear honey and the milk in a heavy or non-stick pan and bring to the boil. Add the vanilla pod, if using.

2 Lower the heat and cover with a tight-fitting lid. Leave to simmer gently for about 1–1¼ hours, stirring occasionally to prevent sticking, until most of the liquid has been absorbed.

3 Remove the vanilla pod from the pan, or if using vanilla extract, add this to the rice mixture now. Set aside so that the mixture cools slightly. Preheat the oven to 220°C/425°F/Gas 7.

4 Place the egg whites in a clean dry bowl and whisk until stiff peaks form.

5 Using a metal spoon or spatula, fold the egg whites evenly into the rice mixture and turn into a 1 litre/1¾ pint/4 cup ovenproof dish.

6 Sprinkle with grated nutmeg and bake for 15–20 minutes, until the pudding is well risen and golden brown.

Cook's Tip
You can use skimmed milk instead of semi-skimmed if you like, but take care when it is simmering as, with so little fat, it tends to boil over very easily.

Islands Energy 94kcal/406kJ; Protein 2.2g; Carbohydrate 22.5g, of which sugars 22.5g; Fat 0.2g, of which saturates 0g; Cholesterol 0mg; Calcium 22mg; Fibre 1.8g; Sodium 38mg.
Pudding Energy 183kcal/773kJ; Protein 9.1g; Carbohydrate 30.4g, of which sugars 17.4g; Fat 3.3g, of which saturates 2g; Cholesterol 11mg; Calcium 230mg; Fibre 0g; Sodium 112mg.

Eve's Pudding

The apples beneath the topping are the reason for this pudding's name.

Serves 4–6

115g/4oz/½ cup butter, softened
115g/4oz/generous ½ cup caster (superfine) sugar
2 eggs, beaten
grated rind and juice of 1 lemon
90g/3½ oz/scant 1 cup self-raising (self-rising) flour
40g/1½ oz/generous ¼ cup ground almonds
115g/4oz/½ cup soft brown sugar
500–675g/1½ lb cooking apples, cored and thinly sliced
25g/1oz/¼ cup flaked (sliced) almonds
ready-made fresh custard or single (light) cream, to serve

1 Beat together the butter and caster sugar in a large mixing bowl until the mixture is very light and fluffy.

2 Gradually beat the eggs into the butter mixture, beating well after each addition, then fold in the lemon rind, flour and ground almonds.

3 Mix the brown sugar with the apples and lemon juice in a bowl, then turn into an ovenproof dish. Spoon the topping mixture on top of the apples, levelling the surface, then sprinkle with the flaked almonds.

4 Bake for 40–45 minutes, until golden. Serve immediately with fresh custard or cream.

> **Variations**
> • To ring the changes, replace half the apples with fresh blackberries. Halved apricots and sliced peaches can also be used instead of the apples.
> • To vary the topping, leave out the ground and flaked almonds and use demerara (raw) sugar instead of the caster sugar, then serve sprinkled with icing (confectioners') sugar.

Cabinet Pudding

Rich custard is baked with dried fruit and sponge cake to make a delightful old-fashioned dessert that is sure to cause a stir.

Serves 4

25g/1oz/2½ tbsp raisins, chopped
30ml/2 tbsp brandy (optional)
25g/1oz glacé (candied) cherries, halved
25g/1oz angelica, chopped
2 trifle sponge (pound) cakes
50g/2oz ratafias (almond macaroons)
2 eggs
2 egg yolks
25g/1oz/2 tbsp sugar
450ml/¾ pint/1¾ cups single (light) cream or milk
few drops of vanilla extract

1 Soak the raisins in the brandy, if using, for several hours.

2 Butter a 750ml/1¼ pint/3 cup charlotte mould and arrange some of the cherries and angelica in the base.

3 Dice the sponge cakes and crush the ratafias. Mix with the remaining cherries and angelica, raisins and brandy, if using, and spoon into the mould.

4 Lightly whisk together the eggs, egg yolks and sugar. Bring the cream or milk just to the boil, then stir into the egg mixture with the vanilla extract.

5 Strain the egg mixture into the mould, then set aside for 15–30 minutes. Preheat the oven to 160°C/325°F/Gas 3.

6 Place the mould in a roasting pan. Cover with baking parchment and pour boiling water into the roasting pan. Bake for 1 hour, or until set. Leave for 2–3 minutes, then loosen the edge with a knife and turn out on to a warmed plate.

> **Cook's Tip**
> If you do not have a traditional charlotte mould, you can use a deep round cake tin (pan) instead.

Cabinet Energy 424kcal/1769kJ; Protein 10.5g; Carbohydrate 31.3g, of which sugars 23.1g; Fat 29.5g, of which saturates 16.2g; Cholesterol 286mg; Calcium 160mg; Fibre 0.5g; Sodium 128mg.
Eve's Energy 697kcal/2926kJ; Protein 9.5g; Carbohydrate 90g, of which sugars 72.4g; Fat 35.9g, of which saturates 16.5g; Cholesterol 156mg; Calcium 126mg; Fibre 3.9g; Sodium 218mg.

Strawberry & Apple Crumble

A high-fibre, low-fat version of the classic apple crumble that will appeal to both children and adults alike.

2.5ml/½ tsp ground cinnamon
30ml/2 tbsp orange juice
natural (plain) yogurt, to
   serve (optional)

Serves 4
450g/1lb cooking apples
150g/5oz/1¼ cups strawberries,
   hulled
30ml/2 tbsp caster
   (superfine) sugar

For the crumble
45ml/3 tbsp plain wholemeal
   (whole-wheat) flour
50g/2oz/⅔ cup rolled oats
30ml/2 tbsp low-fat spread

1 Preheat the oven to 180°C/350°F/Gas 4. Peel, core and cut the apples into approximately 5mm/¼in size slices. Halve the strawberries.

2 Toss together the apples, strawberries, sugar, cinnamon and orange juice. Transfer the mixture to a 1.2 litre/2 pint/5 cup ovenproof dish.

3 To make the crumble, combine the flour and oats in a bowl and mix in the low-fat spread with a fork.

4 Sprinkle the crumble evenly over the fruit. Bake for 40–45 minutes, until golden brown and bubbling. Serve warm, with yogurt, if you like.

Cook's Tip
Use cooking apples rather than eating ones, as their soft cooked texture combines well with the crunchy topping.

Variation
Blackberries, raspberries or redcurrants can be used instead of the strawberries very successfully.

Castle Puddings with Custard Sauce

These attractive sponge puddings make a lovely finale to a dinner party.

2 eggs, beaten
few drops of vanilla extract
130g/4½ oz/generous 1 cup self-raising (self-rising) flour
mint sprigs, to decorate

Serves 4
about 45ml/3 tbsp blackcurrant,
   strawberry or raspberry jam
115g/4oz/½ cup butter, softened,
   plus extra for greasing
115g/4oz/generous ½ cup caster
   (superfine) sugar

For the custard sauce
4 eggs
15–25g/½–1oz/1–2 tbsp sugar
450ml/¾ pint/scant 2 cups milk
few drops of vanilla extract

1 Preheat the oven to 180°C/350°F/Gas 4. Butter eight dariole moulds. Put about 10ml/2 tsp of your chosen jam in the base of each mould.

2 Beat the butter and sugar together until light and fluffy, then gradually beat in the eggs, beating well after each addition, and add the vanilla extract towards the end. Lightly fold in the flour, then divide the mixture among the moulds. Bake the puddings for about 20 minutes until well risen and a light golden colour.

3 To make the custard, whisk the eggs and sugar together. Bring the milk to the boil in a heavy, preferably non-stick, pan, then slowly pour on to the egg mixture, stirring constantly.

4 Return the milk mixture to the pan and heat very gently, stirring, until it thickens enough to coat the back of a spoon; do not allow to boil. Cover the pan and remove from the heat.

5 Remove the moulds from the oven. Leave to stand for a few minutes, then turn the puddings out on to warmed individual plates. Decorate with mint and serve with the custard.

Cook's Tip
If you do not have dariole moulds, use ramekin dishes instead.

Crumble Energy 200kcal/846kJ; Protein 3.8g; Carbohydrate 38.7g, of which sugars 21g; Fat 4.4g, of which saturates 0.9g; Cholesterol 0mg; Calcium 41mg; Fibre 3.4g; Sodium 59mg.
Puddings Energy 644kcal/2701kJ; Protein 16.7g; Carbohydrate 72.5g, of which sugars 47.7g; Fat 34.3g, of which saturates 18.6g; Cholesterol 353mg; Calcium 247mg; Fibre 1g; Sodium 334mg.

Bread & Butter Pudding

An unusual version of a classic recipe, this pudding is made with French bread and mixed dried fruit. As a finishing touch, it is served with a whisky-flavoured cream

Serves 4–6

4 ready-to-eat dried apricots, finely chopped
15ml/1 tbsp raisins
30ml/2 tbsp sultanas (golden raisins)
15ml/1 tbsp chopped mixed (candied) peel
1 French loaf (about 200g/7oz), thinly sliced
50g/2oz/¼ cup butter, melted, plus extra for greasing

450ml/¾ pint/scant 2 cups milk
150ml/¼ pint/⅔ cup double (heavy) cream
115g/4oz/½ cup caster (superfine) sugar
3 eggs
2.5ml/½ tsp vanilla extract
30ml/2 tbsp whisky

For the cream
150ml/¼ pint/⅔ cup double (heavy) cream
30ml/2 tbsp Greek-style (US strained, plain) yogurt
15–30ml/1–2 tbsp whisky
15g/½oz/1 tbsp caster (superfine) sugar

1 Preheat the oven to 180°C/350°F/Gas 4. Butter a deep 1.5 litre/2½ pint/6¼ cup ovenproof dish. Mix together the dried fruits. Brush the bread on both sides with butter.

2 Fill the dish with alternate layers of bread and dried fruit, starting with fruit and finishing with bread. Heat the milk and cream in a pan until just boiling. Whisk together the sugar, eggs and vanilla extract.

3 Whisk the milk mixture into the eggs, then strain into the dish. Sprinkle the whisky over the top. Press the bread down, cover with foil and leave to stand for 20 minutes.

4 Place the foil-covered dish in a roasting pan, half filled with water, and bake for 1 hour, or until the custard is just set. Remove the foil and cook for 10 minutes more until golden.

5 Just before serving, heat all the cream ingredients in a small pan, stirring. Serve with the hot pudding.

Chocolate Amaretti Peaches

This dessert is quick and easy to prepare, yet sophisticated enough to serve at the most elegant dinner party.

Serves 4
115g/4oz amaretti, crushed
50g/2oz plain (semisweet) chocolate, chopped

grated rind of ½ orange
15ml/1 tbsp clear honey
1.5ml/¼ tsp ground cinnamon
1 egg white, lightly beaten
4 firm ripe peaches
butter, for greasing
150ml/¼ pint/⅔ cup white wine
15g/½ oz/1 tbsp caster (superfine) sugar
whipped cream, to serve

1 Preheat the oven to 190°C/375°F/Gas 5. Mix together the crushed amaretti, chocolate, orange rind, honey and cinnamon in a bowl. Add the beaten egg white and mix to bind the mixture together.

2 Halve and stone (pit) the peaches and fill the cavities with the chocolate mixture, mounding it up slightly.

3 Arrange the stuffed peaches in a lightly buttered shallow ovenproof dish which will just hold the fruit comfortably. Pour the wine into a measuring jug and stir in the sugar.

4 Pour the wine mixture around the peaches. Bake for 30–40 minutes, until the peaches are tender. Serve with a little of the cooking juices spooned over and the whipped cream.

Cook's Tip
Italian amaretti are crisp little cookies, flavoured with bitter almonds. They are now available from supermarkets.

Variation
This dessert can also be prepared using fresh nectarines or apricots instead of peaches. Use 2 apricots per person.

Pudding Energy 622kcal/2597kJ; Protein 10.5g; Carbohydrate 55.6g, of which sugars 37.8g; Fat 39g, of which saturates 23g; Cholesterol 186mg; Calcium 203mg; Fibre 1.6g; Sodium 350mg.
Peaches Energy 275kcal/1163kJ; Protein 4g; Carbohydrate 45.3g, of which sugars 32.7g; Fat 7.4g, of which saturates 3.8g; Cholesterol 1mg; Calcium 55mg; Fibre 2.2g; Sodium 114mg.

Warm Autumn Compôte

This is a simple yet sophisticated dessert featuring succulent ripe autumnal fruits. Serve with vanilla-flavoured cream and thin, crisp cookies.

Serves 4
75g/3oz/generous ¼ cup caster (superfine) sugar
1 bottle red wine
1 vanilla pod (bean), split
1 strip pared lemon rind
4 pears
2 purple figs, quartered
225g/8oz/2 cups raspberries
lemon juice, to taste

1 Put the caster sugar and red wine in a large pan and heat gently until the sugar has completely dissolved. Add the vanilla pod and lemon rind and bring to the boil. Reduce the heat and simmer for 5 minutes.

2 Peel and halve the pears, then scoop out the cores, using a melon baller or teaspoon. Add the pears to the syrup and poach for about 15 minutes, turning them several times so they colour evenly.

3 Add the quartered figs and poach for a further 5 minutes, until the fruits are tender.

4 Transfer the poached pears and figs to a serving bowl using a slotted spoon, then scatter over the raspberries.

5 Return the syrup to the heat and boil rapidly to reduce slightly and concentrate the flavour. Add a little lemon juice to taste. Strain the syrup over the fruits and serve warm.

Cook's Tip
Serve with vanilla cream: using 300ml/½ pint/1¼ cups double (heavy) cream, place half in a pan with a vanilla pod (bean). Bring almost to the boil, then cool for 30 minutes. Remove the pod, mix with the remaining cream and add sugar to taste.

Apple Soufflé Omelette

Apples sautéed until they are slightly caramelized make a delicious autumn filling for this sweet, light-as-air omelette.

Serves 2
4 eggs, separated
30ml/2 tbsp single (light) cream
15g/½oz/1 tbsp caster (superfine) sugar

15g/½ oz/1 tbsp butter
sifted icing (confectioners') sugar, for dredging

For the filling
1 eating apple, peeled, cored and sliced
25g/1oz/2 tbsp butter
25g/1oz/2 tbsp soft light brown sugar
45ml/3 tbsp single (light) cream

1 To make the filling, sauté the apple slices in the butter and sugar until just tender. Stir in the cream and keep warm, while making the omelette.

2 Place the egg yolks in a bowl with the cream and sugar and beat well. Whisk the egg whites until stiff peaks form, then fold into the yolk mixture.

3 Melt the butter in a large heavy frying pan, then pour in the soufflé mixture and spread evenly. Cook for 1 minute until golden underneath, then place under a hot grill (broiler) to brown the top.

4 Slide the omelette on to a plate, spoon the apple mixture on to one side, then fold over. Dredge the icing sugar over thickly, then quickly mark in a criss-cross pattern with a hot metal skewer. Serve immediately.

Cook's Tips
• *When cooking the top, remove the omelette as soon as it is browned. Do not overcook at this stage otherwise the light texture of the omelette will be damaged.*
• *You can replace the apples with fresh raspberries or strawberries when they are in season.*

Compôte Energy 318kcal/1342kJ; Protein 2g; Carbohydrate 47.9g, of which sugars 47.9g; Fat 0.5g, of which saturates 0.1g; Cholesterol 0mg; Calcium 84mg; Fibre 6.6g; Sodium 28mg.
Omelette Energy 459kcal/1910kJ; Protein 14.1g; Carbohydrate 24.9g, of which sugars 24.9g; Fat 34.8g, of which saturates 18.1g; Cholesterol 444mg; Calcium 106mg; Fibre 0.6g; Sodium 274mg.

Warm Lemon & Syrup Cake

This simple cake is made special by the lemony syrup which is poured over it when baked.

Serves 8
3 eggs
175g/6oz/3/4 cup butter, softened
175g/6oz/scant 1 cup caster
  (superfine) sugar
175g/6oz/1 1/2 cups self-raising
  (self-rising) flour
50g/2oz/1/2 cup ground almonds

1.5ml/1/4 tsp freshly grated
  nutmeg
50g/2oz candied lemon peel,
  finely chopped
grated rind of 1 lemon
30ml/2 tbsp freshly squeezed
  lemon juice
poached pears, to serve

For the syrup
175g/6oz/scant 1 cup caster
  (superfine) sugar
juice of 3 lemons

1 Preheat the oven to 180°C/350°F/Gas 4. Lightly grease and base-line a deep round 20cm/8in cake tin (pan).

2 Place all the cake ingredients in a large bowl and beat well for 2–3 minutes until light and fluffy.

3 Turn the mixture into the prepared tin, spread level and bake for 1 hour, or until golden and firm to the touch.

4 To make the syrup, put the caster sugar, lemon juice and 75ml/5 tbsp water in a pan. Place over low heat and stir until the sugar has completely dissolved, then boil, without stirring, for 1–2 minutes.

5 Turn out the cake on to a plate with a rim. Prick the surface of the cake all over with a fork, then pour over the hot syrup. Leave to soak for about 30 minutes. Serve the cake warm with thin wedges of poached pears.

> **Cook's Tip**
> To speed up the preparation, mix the ingredients together in a food processor, but take care not to overbeat.

Papaya & Pineapple Crumble

Fruit crumbles are always popular with children and adults, but you can ring the changes with this great exotic variation.

Serves 4–6
175g/6oz/1 1/2 cups plain
  (all-purpose) flour
75g/3oz/6 tbsp butter, diced
75g/3oz/generous 1/4 cup caster
  (superfine) sugar
75g/3oz/1/2 cup mixed
  chopped nuts

For the filling
1 medium-ripe pineapple
1 large ripe papaya
15g/1/2 oz/1 tbsp caster
  (superfine) sugar
5ml/1 tsp mixed (apple pie) spice
grated rind of 1 lime
natural (plain) yogurt, to serve

1 Preheat the oven to 180°C/350°F/Gas 4. To make the topping, sift the flour into a bowl and rub in the butter until the mixture resembles breadcrumbs. Stir in the caster sugar and mixed chopped nuts.

2 To make the filling, peel the pineapple, remove the eyes, then cut in half. Cut away the core and cut the flesh into bitesize chunks. Halve the papaya and scoop out the seeds using a spoon. Peel, then cut the flesh into similar size pieces.

3 Put the pineapple and papaya chunks into a large ovenproof dish. Sprinkle over the sugar, mixed spice and lime rind and toss gently to mix.

4 Spoon the crumble topping over the fruit and spread out evenly with a fork, but don't press it down. Bake in the oven for 45–50 minutes, until golden brown. Serve the crumble hot or warm with natural yogurt.

> **Variation**
> If unavailable, the papaya can be replaced with fresh mango.

Syrup Cake Energy 488kcal/2047kJ; Protein 6g; Carbohydrate 66.5g, of which sugars 50.1g; Fat 23.9g, of which saturates 12.3g; Cholesterol 118mg; Calcium 138mg; Fibre 1.4g; Sodium 259mg.
Crumble Energy 403kcal/1690kJ; Protein 5.5g; Carbohydrate 54.8g, of which sugars 32.5g; Fat 19.5g, of which saturates 7.3g; Cholesterol 27mg; Calcium 96mg; Fibre 4g; Sodium 84mg.

Zabaglione

A much-loved simple Italian dessert traditionally made with Marsala, an Italian fortified wine.

Serves 4
4 egg yolks
50g/2oz/¼ cup (superfine) sugar
60ml/4 tbsp Marsala
amaretti, to serve

1 Half fill a medium pan with water and bring to a simmer.

2 Place the egg yolks and caster sugar in a large heatproof bowl and whisk with an electric whisk until the mixture turns pale yellow and thick.

3 Gradually add the Marsala, about 15ml/1 tbsp at a time, whisking well after each addition (at this stage the mixture will be quite runny).

4 Place the bowl over the pan of gently simmering water and continue to whisk for at least 5–7 minutes, until the mixture becomes thick and mousse-like; when the beaters are lifted they should leave a thick trail on the surface of the mixture. (If you don't beat the mixture for long enough, the zabaglione will be too runny and will probably separate.)

5 Pour into four warmed stemmed glasses and serve immediately with the amaretti for dipping.

> ### Cook's Tip
> *If you don't have any Marsala, substitute Madeira, a medium-sweet sherry or a dessert wine.*

> ### Variation
> *For chocolate zabaglione, whisk in 20ml/4 tsp unsweetened cocoa powder with the Marsala at step 3.*

Thai-fried Bananas

In this very easy dessert, bananas are simply fried in butter, sugar and lime juice.

Serves 4
40g/1½ oz/3 tbsp unsalted (sweet) butter
4 large slightly under-ripe bananas
15ml/1 tbsp desiccated (dry unsweetened shredded) coconut
50g/2oz/¼ cup soft light brown sugar
60ml/4 tbsp lime juice
2 lime slices, to decorate
thick and creamy natural (plain) yogurt, to serve

1 Heat the butter in a large frying pan or wok and fry the bananas for 1–2 minutes on each side until golden. Meanwhile, dry-fry the coconut in a small frying pan until golden; reserve.

2 Sprinkle the sugar into the pan with the bananas, add the lime juice and cook, stirring, until dissolved. Sprinkle the coconut over the bananas, decorate with lime and serve with yogurt.

Hot Spiced Bananas

Bananas baked in a rum and fruit syrup are perfect for impromptu entertaining.

Serves 6
6 ripe bananas
butter, for greasing
200g/7oz/1 cup light muscovado (brown) sugar
250ml/8fl oz/1 cup unsweetened pineapple juice
120ml/4fl oz/½ cup dark rum
2 cinnamon sticks
12 whole cloves

1 Preheat the oven to 180°C/350°F/Gas 4. Cut the bananas, at a slant, into 2.5cm/1in pieces. Arrange in a greased baking dish.

2 Mix the sugar and pineapple juice in a pan. Heat gently until the sugar has dissolved, stirring occasionally. Add the rum, cinnamon sticks and cloves. Bring to the boil, then remove from the heat. Pour over the bananas and bake for 25–30 minutes until the bananas are hot and tender.

Zabaglione Energy 134kcal/561kJ; Protein 3g; Carbohydrate 14.9g, of which sugars 14.9g; Fat 5.5g, of which saturates 1.6g; Cholesterol 202mg; Calcium 31mg; Fibre 0g; Sodium 10mg.
Thai-fried Energy 241kcal/1013kJ; Protein 1.5g; Carbohydrate 36.6g, of which sugars 34.3g; Fat 10.9g, of which saturates 7.3g; Cholesterol 21mg; Calcium 15mg; Fibre 1.6g; Sodium 64mg.
Hot Spiced Energy 288kcal/1221kJ; Protein 1.5g; Carbohydrate 62.4g, of which sugars 60.1g; Fat 0.3g, of which saturates 0.1g; Cholesterol 0mg; Calcium 27mg; Fibre 1.1g; Sodium 6mg.

Crêpes Suzette

This dish is a classic of French cuisine and still enjoys worldwide popularity.

Makes 8
115g/4oz/1 cup plain (all-purpose) flour
pinch of salt
1 egg
1 egg yolk
300ml/½ pint/1¼ cups semi-skimmed milk
15g/½ oz/1 tbsp butter, melted, plus extra, for shallow frying

For the sauce
2 large oranges
50g/2oz/¼ cup butter
50g/2oz/¼ cup soft light brown sugar
15ml/1 tbsp Grand Marnier
15ml/1 tbsp brandy

1 Sift the flour and salt into a bowl and make a well in the centre. Crack the egg and extra yolk into the well. Stir the eggs to incorporate all the flour. When the mixture thickens, gradually pour in the milk, beating well after each addition, until a smooth batter is formed. Stir in the butter, transfer to a jug, cover and chill for 30 minutes.

2 Heat a shallow frying pan, add a little butter and melt until sizzling. Pour in a little batter, tilting the pan to cover the base. Cook over medium heat for 1–2 minutes until lightly browned underneath, then flip and cook for a further minute. Make eight crêpes and stack them on a plate.

3 Pare the rind from one of the oranges and reserve about 5ml/1 tsp. Squeeze the juice from both oranges.

4 To make the sauce, melt the butter in a large frying pan and heat the sugar with the orange rind and juice until dissolved and gently bubbling. Fold each crêpe into quarters. Add to the pan one at a time, coat in the sauce and fold in half again. Move to the side of the pan to make room for the others.

5 Pour on the Grand Marnier and brandy and cook gently for 2–3 minutes, until the sauce has slightly caramelized. Sprinkle with the reserved orange rind and serve immediately.

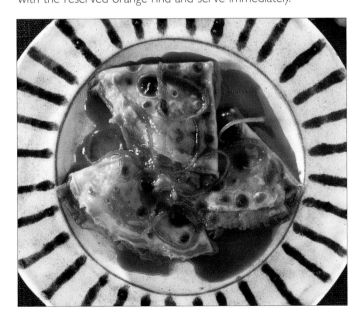

Bananas with Dark Rum & Raisins

A classic way of serving bananas, the rum is set alight just before serving. This gives the fruit a wonderful flavour, making an irresistible dish.

Serves 4
40g/1½ oz/scant ¼ cup seedless raisins
75ml/5 tbsp dark rum
50g/2oz/4 tbsp unsalted (sweet) butter
50g/2oz/¼ cup soft light brown sugar
4 bananas, halved lengthways
1.5ml/¼ tsp grated nutmeg
1.5ml/¼ tsp ground cinnamon
30ml/2 tbsp slivered almonds, toasted
chilled cream or vanilla ice cream, to serve (optional)

1 Put the raisins in a bowl with the rum. Leave them to soak for about 30 minutes to plump up.

2 Melt the butter in a frying pan, add the sugar and stir until completely dissolved. Add the bananas and cook for a few minutes until tender.

3 Sprinkle the spices over the bananas, then pour over the soaked raisins and rum. Carefully set alight using a long taper and stir gently to mix.

4 Scatter over the slivered almonds and serve immediately with chilled cream or vanilla ice cream, if you wish.

> **Cook's Tips**
> • Chose almost-ripe bananas with evenly coloured skins, either all yellow or just green at the tips. Over-ripe bananas will not hold their shape as well when cooked.
> • Setting light to the rum – known as flambéeing – dispels most of the alcohol content, but gives the bananas an intense flavour. Stand well back when you set the rum alight and shake the pan gently until the flames subside.

Crêpes Energy 195kcal/818kJ; Protein 4.4g; Carbohydrate 23.8g, of which sugars 12.8g; Fat 8.9g, of which saturates 5.1g; Cholesterol 69mg; Calcium 100mg; Fibre 1.3g; Sodium 79mg.
Bananas Energy 352kcal/1474kJ; Protein 3.1g; Carbohydrate 43.8g, of which sugars 41.3g; Fat 14.8g, of which saturates 7g; Cholesterol 27mg; Calcium 38mg; Fibre 1.9g; Sodium 85mg.

Apple & Blackberry Nut Crumble

This much-loved dish of apples and blackberries is topped with a golden, sweet crumble. The addition of nuts gives an extra-delicious crunchy texture.

Serves 4
900g/2lb (about 4 medium) cooking apples, peeled, cored and sliced
115g/4oz/1/2 cup butter, diced, plus extra for greasing
115g/4oz/1/2 cup soft light brown sugar
175g/6oz/1 1/2 cups blackberries
75g/3oz/3/4 cup wholemeal (whole-wheat) flour
75g/3oz/3/4 cup plain (all-purpose) flour
2.5ml/1/2 tsp ground cinnamon
45ml/3 tbsp chopped mixed nuts, toasted
custard, cream or ice cream, to serve

1 Preheat the oven to 180°C/350°F/Gas 4. Lightly butter a 1.2 litre/2 pint/5 cup ovenproof dish.

2 Place the apples in a pan with 25g/1oz/2 tbsp of the butter, 25g/1oz/2 tbsp of the sugar and 15ml/1 tbsp water. Cover with a tight-fitting lid and cook gently for about 10 minutes, until the apples are just tender but still holding their shape.

3 Remove from the heat and gently stir in the blackberries. Spoon the mixture into the ovenproof dish and set aside while you make the topping.

4 To make the crumble topping, sift the flours and cinnamon into a bowl, tipping in any of the bran left in the sieve (strainer). Add the remaining 75g/3oz/6 tbsp butter and rub into the flour with your fingertips until the mixture resembles fine breadcrumbs. Alternatively, you can use a food processor to do this stage for you.

5 Stir in the remaining sugar and the nuts and mix well. Sprinkle the crumble topping over the fruit.

6 Bake the crumble for 35–40 minutes until the top is golden brown. Serve immediately with custard, cream or ice cream.

Orange Rice Pudding

In Spain, Greece, Italy and Morocco creamy rice puddings are a favourite dish, especially when sweetened with honey. This version is enhanced with a fresh orange flavour.

Serves 4
50g/2oz/1/4 cup short grain pudding rice
600ml/1 pint/2 1/2 cups milk
30–45ml/2–3 tbsp clear honey, to taste
finely grated rind of 1/2 small orange
150ml/1/4 pint/2/3 cup double (heavy) cream
15ml/1 tbsp chopped pistachios, toasted and thin strips of orange rind, to garnish

1 Mix the rice with the milk, honey and orange rind in a pan and bring to the boil, then reduce the heat, cover the pan with a tight-fitting lid and simmer very gently for about 1 1/4 hours, stirring regularly.

2 Remove the lid and continue cooking and stirring for about 15–20 minutes, until the rice is creamy.

3 Pour in the cream and simmer for 5–8 minutes longer. Serve the rice sprinkled with the chopped toasted pistachios and orange rind in individual warmed bowls.

Cook's Tip
Make sure you use short grain rice for this recipe; the small chalky grains absorb liquid well, producing a creamy texture.

Variation
For a more fragrant version, omit the grated orange rind and stir in 15ml/1 tbsp orange flower water, 15ml/1 tbsp ground almonds and 5ml/1 tsp almond extract at step 3, along with the cream. Serve sprinkled with chopped dates and pistachios.

Pudding Energy 355kcal/1477kJ; Protein 7.4g; Carbohydrate 26.6g, of which sugars 16.5g; Fat 24.8g, of which saturates 14.4g; Cholesterol 60mg; Calcium 206mg; Fibre 0.2g; Sodium 94mg.
Crumble Energy 573kcal/2398kJ; Protein 6.8g; Carbohydrate 68.3g, of which sugars 42.3g; Fat 32.2g, of which saturates 15.7g; Cholesterol 61mg; Calcium 86mg; Fibre 5.6g; Sodium 181mg.

Blackberry Charlotte

The perfect sweet warmer for cold days, serve this delicious charlotte with whipped cream or some home-made custard.

Serves 4
65g/2 1/2oz/5 tbsp unsalted (sweet) butter
175g/6oz/3 cups fresh
 white breadcrumbs

50g/2oz/4 tbsp soft brown sugar
60ml/4 tbsp golden
 (light corn) syrup
finely grated rind and juice
 of 2 lemons
50g/2oz walnut halves
450g/1lb blackberries
450g/1lb cooking apples, peeled,
 cored and finely sliced

1 Preheat the oven to 180°C/350°F/ Gas 4. Grease a 450ml/ ¾ pint/2 cup dish with 15g/½oz/1 tbsp of the butter.

2 Melt the remaining butter over a low heat in a large pan, then add the breadcrumbs. Sauté them over a medium heat for 5–7 minutes, until the crumbs are a little crisp and golden. Leave to cool slightly.

3 Place the sugar, syrup, lemon rind and juice in a large pan and gently warm them. Add the crumbs.

4 Process the walnuts until they are finely ground. Add to the crumb mixture and stir to combine.

5 Arrange a thin layer of blackberries on the dish. Top the blackberries with a thin layer of crumbs. Add a thin layer of apple, topping it with another thin layer of crumbs.

6 Repeat the process with another layer of blackberries, followed by a layer of crumbs. Continue in this way until you have used up all the ingredients, finishing with a layer of crumbs.

7 The mixture should be piled well above the top edge of the dish, because it shrinks during cooking. Place in the preheated oven and bake for 30 minutes, until the crumbs are golden and the fruit is soft.

Banana, Maple & Lime Crêpes

Crêpes are a treat any day of the week, and they can be made in advance and stored in the freezer for convenience.

Serves 4
115g/4oz/1 cup plain
 (all-purpose) flour
1 egg white

250ml/8fl oz/1 cup skimmed milk
sunflower oil, for frying

For the filling
4 bananas, sliced
45ml/3 tbsp maple or golden
 (light corn) syrup
30ml/2 tbsp freshly squeezed
 lime juice
strips of lime rind, to decorate

1 Beat together the flour, egg white, milk and 50ml/2f oz/¼ cup water until the mixture is smooth and bubbly. Chill in the refrigerator until ready to use.

2 Heat a small amount of oil in a non-stick frying pan and pour in enough batter just to coat the base. Swirl it around the pan to coat evenly.

3 Cook until golden, then toss or turn and cook the other side. Place on a plate, cover with foil and keep hot while making the remaining pancakes.

4 To make the filling, place the bananas, syrup and lime juice in a pan and simmer gently for 1 minute. Spoon into the pancakes and fold into quarters. Sprinkle with shreds of lime rind to decorate. Serve immediately.

> **Cook's Tip**
> To freeze the crêpes, interleaf them with baking parchment and seal in a plastic bag. They should be used within 3 months.

> **Variation**
> Use strawberries instead of bananas, and orange in place of lime.

Charlotte Energy 546Kcal/2294kJ; Protein 8.5g; Carbohydrate 81g, of which sugars 48.2g; Fat 23.1g, of which saturates 9.2g; Cholesterol 35mg; Calcium 133mg; Fibre 6.7g; Sodium 498mg.
Crêpes Energy 299kcal/1263kJ; Protein 6.8g; Carbohydrate 57.2g, of which sugars 33g; Fat 6.4g, of which saturates 0.9g; Cholesterol 2mg; Calcium 125mg; Fibre 2g; Sodium 75mg.

Spiced Pears in Cider

A cider sauce, delicately flavoured with cinnamon and lemon, transforms pears into an elegant dessert.

Serves 4
4 medium-firm pears
250ml/8fl oz/1 cup dry cider

thinly pared strip of lemon rind
1 cinnamon stick
25g/1oz/2 tbsp light muscovado (brown) sugar
5ml/1 tsp arrowroot
blanched shreds of lemon rind, to decorate

1 Peel the pears thinly, leaving them whole with the stalks on. Place in a pan with the cider, lemon rind and cinnamon. Cover and simmer gently, turning the pears occasionally, for 15–20 minutes, or until tender.

2 Lift out the pears with a slotted spoon. Boil the syrup, uncovered, to reduce by about half. Remove the lemon rind and cinnamon stick, then stir in the sugar.

3 Mix the arrowroot with 15ml/1 tbsp cold water in a small bowl until smooth, then stir into the syrup. Bring to the boil and stir over medium heat until thickened and clear.

4 Pour the sauce over the pears and sprinkle with lemon rind shreds. Leave to cool slightly, before serving.

Cook's Tips
• Any variety of pear can be used for cooking, but choose a firm variety such as Conference for this recipe.
• Using whole pears looks impressive but if you prefer they can be halved and cored before cooking. This will shorten the cooking time slightly.

Variation
The cider can be substituted with red wine for pink-tinted pears.

Fruity Bread Pudding

A delicious old-fashioned family favourite with a lighter, healthier touch for today. The perfect way to round off a family meal.

Serves 4
75g/3oz/2/3 cup mixed dried fruit
150ml/1/4 pint/2/3 cup apple juice

115g/4oz stale brown or white bread, diced
5ml/1 tsp mixed (apple pie) spice
1 large banana, sliced
150ml/1/4 pint/2/3 cup skimmed milk
15g/1/2 oz/1 tbsp demerara (raw) sugar
natural (plain) yogurt, to serve

1 Preheat the oven to 200°C/400°F/Gas 6. Place the mixed dried fruit in a small pan with the apple juice and bring to the boil over medium heat.

2 Remove the pan from the heat and stir in the diced bread, mixed spice and banana. Spoon the mixture into a shallow 1.2 litre/2 pint/5 cup ovenproof dish, then pour over the milk.

3 Sprinkle with demerara sugar and bake for about 25–30 minutes, until the pudding is firm and golden brown. Serve immediately with natural yogurt.

Cook's Tips
• Different types of bread will absorb varying amounts of liquid, so you may need to reduce the amount of milk used to allow for this.
• This is a good way to use up stale, leftover bread. Any type of bread is suitable, but wholemeal (whole-wheat) gives a healthier slant to the dish. Remove the crusts before cutting into dice.

Variation
You can experiment as much as you like with the dried fruit. A mix of raisins, sultanas (golden raisins) and chopped ready-to-eat apricots or dates works well.

Pears Energy 107kcal/454kJ; Protein 0.5g; Carbohydrate 23.2g, of which sugars 23.2g; Fat 0.2g, of which saturates 0g; Cholesterol 0mg; Calcium 25mg; Fibre 3.3g; Sodium 9mg.
Pudding Energy 178kcal/759kJ; Protein 4.4g; Carbohydrate 40.9g, of which sugars 27g; Fat 0.8g, of which saturates 0.1g; Cholesterol 1mg; Calcium 97mg; Fibre 1.1g; Sodium 176mg.

Apple Couscous Pudding

Couscous makes a delicious and healthy family pudding.

Serves 4
600ml/1 pint/2½ cups apple juice
115g/4oz/⅔ cup couscous
40g/1½ oz/scant ¼ cup sultanas (golden raisins)
2.5ml/½ tsp mixed spice
1 large cooking apple, peeled, cored and sliced
25g/1oz/2 tbsp light brown sugar

1 Preheat the oven to 200°C/400°F/Gas 6. Place the apple juice, couscous, sultanas and spice in a pan and bring to the boil, stirring. Cover. Simmer for 10–12 minutes to absorb the liquid.

2 Spoon half the mixture into a 1.2 litre/1 pint/5 cup ovenproof dish and top with half the apple slices. Top with the remaining couscous. Arrange the remaining apple slices overlapping on the top and sprinkle with the sugar. Bake for 25–30 minutes, or until the apples are golden brown. Serve immediately.

Crunchy Gooseberry Crumble

Gooseberries make the perfect filling for this extra special crumble.

Serves 4
500g/1¼ lb/4¼ cups gooseberries
50g/2oz/¼ cup caster (superfine) sugar
75g/3oz/1 cup rolled oats
75g/3oz/1 cup wholemeal (whole-wheat) flour
60ml/4 tbsp sunflower oil
50g/2oz/¼ cup demerara (raw) sugar
30ml/2 tbsp chopped walnuts
natural (plain) yogurt, to serve

1 Preheat the oven to 200°C/400°F/Gas 6. Place the gooseberries in a pan with the caster sugar. Cover the pan and cook over low heat for 10 minutes, until the gooseberries are just tender. Transfer to an ovenproof dish.

2 To make the crumble, place the oats, flour and oil in a bowl and stir with a fork until evenly mixed. Stir in the demerara sugar and walnuts, then spread evenly over the gooseberries. Bake for 25–30 minutes, or until golden. Serve with yogurt.

Gingerbread Upside-down Pudding

A proper pudding goes down well on a cold winter's day. This one is quite quick to make and looks very impressive.

Serves 4–6
sunflower oil, for brushing
15g/½ oz/1 tbsp light soft brown sugar
4 peaches, halved and stoned (pitted), or canned peach halves, drained
8 walnut halves

For the base
130g/4½ oz/1 cup wholemeal (whole-wheat) flour
2.5ml/½ tsp bicarbonate of soda (baking soda)
7.5ml/1½ tsp ground ginger
5ml/1 tsp ground cinnamon
115g/4oz/½ cup muscovado (molasses) sugar
1 egg
120ml/4fl oz/½ cup skimmed milk
50ml/2fl oz/¼ cup sunflower oil

1 Preheat the oven to 180°C/350°F/Gas 4. Brush the base and sides of a 23cm/9in round springform cake tin (pan) with oil. Sprinkle the soft brown sugar evenly over the base.

2 Arrange the peaches, cut-side down, in the tin with a walnut half in each.

3 To make the base, sift together the flour, bicarbonate of soda, ginger and cinnamon, then stir in the sugar. Beat together the egg, milk and oil, then mix into the dry ingredients until smooth.

4 Pour the mixture evenly over the peaches and bake for 35–40 minutes, until firm to the touch. Turn out on to a serving plate. Serve hot with yogurt or custard, if you like.

> **Cook's Tips**
> • To turn out the pudding successfully, run the point of a sharp knife round the edge of the pudding, then place a serving plate upside-down on top. Holding the plate and tin together firmly, invert. Release the sides and remove the tin.
> • The soft brown sugar caramelizes during baking, creating a delightfully sticky topping.

Couscous Energy 180kcal/767kJ; Protein 2.2g; Carbohydrate 44.6g, of which sugars 29.8g; Fat 0.5g, of which saturates 0g; Cholesterol 0mg; Calcium 26mg; Fibre 0.5g; Sodium 6mg.
Crumble Energy 591kcal/2496kJ; Protein 18.1g; Carbohydrate 84.5g, of which sugars 60.7g; Fat 22.8g, of which saturates 2.1g; Cholesterol 0mg; Calcium 352mg; Fibre 30.3g; Sodium 27mg.
Gingerbread Energy 274kcal/1155kJ; Protein 6.6g; Carbohydrate 42.7g, of which sugars 29.3g; Fat 9.8g, of which saturates 1.1g; Cholesterol 32mg; Calcium 62mg; Fibre 3.3g; Sodium 24mg.

Pies & Tarts

Whether you are looking for an impressive tart for an elegant dinner party or a simple pie for a family meal, there is a recipe here to suit every taste and occasion. Choose from fruity favourites, such as Lemon Meringue Pie, Pear and Hazelnut Flan, or Raspberry Tart, or for the chocolate-lover there are a range of delectable desserts, including Black Bottom Pie, Chocolate Nut Tart or Truffle Filo Tarts.

Peach Leaf Pie

Pastry leaves top this most attractive spiced summer pie.

Serves 8
1.2kg/2½lb ripe peaches
juice of 1 lemon
90g/3½oz/½ cup caster
 (superfine) sugar
45ml/3 tbsp cornflour (cornstarch)
1.5ml/¼ tsp freshly grated nutmeg
2.5ml/½ tsp ground cinnamon
1 egg beaten with 15ml/1 tbsp
 water, to glaze

25g/1oz/2 tbsp cold
 butter, diced

For the pastry
275g/10oz/2½ cups plain
 (all-purpose) flour
4ml/¾ tsp salt
115g/4oz/½ cup cold
 butter, diced
60g/2¼oz/4½ tbsp cold
 white cooking fat or
 lard, diced
75–90ml/5–6 tbsp iced water

1 To make the pastry, sift the flour and salt into a bowl. Rub in the butter and fat using your fingertips or a pastry cutter until the mixture resembles breadcrumbs. Stir in just enough water to bind the dough. Gather into two balls, one slightly larger than the other. Wrap and chill for at least 20 minutes. Place a baking sheet in the oven and preheat to 220°C/425°F/Gas 7.

2 Drop the peaches into boiling water for 20 seconds, then transfer to a bowl of cold water. When cool, peel off the skins. Slice the flesh and combine with the lemon juice, sugar, cornflour and spices. Set aside.

3 Roll out the larger dough ball to 3mm/⅛in thick. Use to line a 23cm/9in pie plate. Chill. Roll out the remaining dough to 5mm/¼in thick. Cut out leaves 7.5cm/3in long. Mark veins. With the scraps, roll a few balls.

4 Brush the pastry base with egg glaze. Add the peaches and dot with the butter. Starting from the outside edge, cover the peaches with a ring of leaves. Place a second, staggered ring above. Continue until covered. Place the balls in the centre.

5 Brush with glaze. Bake for 10 minutes. Lower the heat to 180°C/350°F/Gas 4 and bake for 35–40 minutes more.

Walnut & Pear Lattice Pie

For the lattice top, either weave strips of pastry or use a special pastry cutter to create a lattice effect.

Serves 6–8
450g/1lb shortcrust pastry,
 thawed if frozen
450g/1lb pears, peeled, cored
 and thinly sliced
50g/2oz/¼ cup caster
 (superfine) sugar

25g/1oz/¼ cup plain
 (all-purpose) flour
2.5ml/½ tsp grated lemon rind
25g/1oz/generous ¼ cup raisins
 or sultanas (golden raisins)
25g/1oz/4 tbsp chopped walnuts
2.5ml/½ tsp ground cinnamon
50g/2oz/½ cup icing
 (confectioners') sugar
15ml/1 tbsp lemon juice
about 10ml/2 tsp cold water

1 Preheat the oven to 190°C/375°F/Gas 5. Roll out half of the pastry and use it to line a 23cm/9in tin that is about 5cm/2in deep.

2 Combine the pears, caster sugar, flour and lemon rind. Toss to coat the fruit. Mix in the raisins, nuts and cinnamon. Put the filling into the pastry case and spread it evenly.

3 Roll out the remaining pastry and use to make a lattice top. Bake the pie for 55 minutes, or until the pastry is golden brown on top.

4 Combine the icing sugar, lemon juice and water in a bowl and stir until smooth. Remove the pie from the oven. Drizzle the glaze evenly over the top, on the pastry and filling. Leave the pie to cool in its tin on a wire rack.

Variation
Try this tasty pie with apples instead of pears or combine fresh peaches or apricots with almonds instead of using pears and walnuts. To skin the peaches or apricots, drop them into boiling water for 20 seconds and then remove them and plunge them into cold water. Peel away the skins.

Peach Pie Energy 424kcal/1778kJ; Protein 4.8g; Carbohydrate 54.2g, of which sugars 22.8g; Fat 22.4g, of which saturates 12.2g; Cholesterol 44mg; Calcium 68mg; Fibre 3.1g; Sodium 112mg.
Pear Pie Energy 366kcal/1536kJ; Protein 4.3g; Carbohydrate 49.7g, of which sugars 21.5g; Fat 18.1g, of which saturates 5.1g; Cholesterol 8mg; Calcium 70mg; Fibre 2.6g; Sodium 228mg.

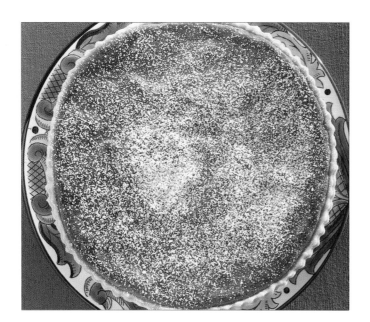

Bakewell Tart

This classic tart, with its crisp pastry base and delicious almond sponge filling, is always popular.

Serves 4
225g/8oz ready-made puff pastry
30ml/2 tbsp raspberry or
   apricot jam

2 eggs
2 egg yolks
115g/4oz/½ cup caster
   (superfine) sugar
115g/4oz/½ cup butter, melted
50g/2oz/⅔ cup ground almonds
few drops of almond extract
sifted icing (confectioners') sugar,
   for dredging

1 Preheat the oven to 200°C/400°F/Gas 6. Roll out the pastry on a lightly floured surface and use it to line an 18cm/7in pie plate or fluted loose-based flan tin (pan). Spread the jam over the base of the pastry case (pie shell).

2 Whisk the eggs, egg yolks and sugar together in a large bowl until thick and pale.

3 Gently stir the butter, ground almonds and almond extract into the egg mixture.

4 Pour the mixture into the pastry case and bake for about 30 minutes until the filling is just set and browned. Dredge with icing sugar before eating hot, warm or cold.

Cook's Tips
• *Since the pastry case isn't baked blind first, place a baking sheet in the oven while it preheats, then place the pie dish or flan tin on the hot sheet. This will ensure that the base of the pastry case cooks through.*
• *Fresh, ready-made puff pastry is sold in the chilled section of supermarkets. Rich and buttery, puff pastry takes time and patience to make, as the method involves a drawn-out folding and rolling process. The ready-made version is more practical.*
• *Although the pastry base technically makes this a tart, the original recipe refers to it as a pudding.*

Yorkshire Curd Tart

The distinguishing characteristic of this old-fashioned tart is the allspice, or "clove pepper" as it was once known locally. The tart is quite delicious, without tasting too sweet.

Serves 8
225g/8oz/2 cups plain
   (all-purpose) flour
115g/4oz/½ cup butter, diced
1 egg yolk
15–30ml/1–2 tbsp chilled water

For the filling
large pinch of allspice
*90g/3½ oz/scant ½ cup soft
   light brown sugar*
3 eggs, beaten
grated rind and juice of 1 lemon
40g/1½ oz/3 tbsp butter, melted
450g/1lb/2 cups curd cheese
*75g/3oz/½ cup raisins or
   sultanas (golden raisins)*
*single (thin) cream, to serve
   (optional)*

1 To make the pastry, place the flour in a mixing bowl. Add the butter and rub it into the flour with your fingertips until the mixture resembles breadcrumbs. Stir the egg yolk into the flour mixture with just enough of the water to bind to a dough.

2 Turn the dough on to a lightly floured surface, knead lightly and briefly, then form into a ball. Roll out the pastry thinly and use to line a 20cm/8in fluted loose-based flan tin (pan). Chill for 15 minutes in the refrigerator.

3 Meanwhile, preheat the oven to 190°C/375°F/Gas 5. To make the filling, mix the allspice with the sugar, then stir in the eggs, lemon rind and juice, melted butter, curd cheese and raisins.

4 Pour the filling into the pastry case (pie shell), then bake for about 40 minutes until the pastry is cooked and the filling is lightly set and golden. Serve warm, with cream, if you wish.

Cook's Tip
Although it is not traditional, mixed (apple pie) spice would make a good substitute for the ground allspice.

Bakewell Energy 701kcal/2922kJ; Protein 10.8g; Carbohydrate 57.1g, of which sugars 36.7g; Fat 50g, of which saturates 17.1g; Cholesterol 260mg; Calcium 110mg; Fibre 0.9g; Sodium 395mg.
Curd Tart Energy 480kcal/2005kJ; Protein 16.2g; Carbohydrate 48.2g, of which sugars 23.7g; Fat 27g, of which saturates 15.8g; Cholesterol 173mg; Calcium 153mg; Fibre 1.2g; Sodium 451mg.

Mississippi Pecan Pie

This fabulous dessert started life in the United States but has become an international favourite.

Serves 4–6
115g/4oz/1 cup plain
  (all-purpose) flour
50g/2oz/¼ cup butter, diced
25g/1oz/2 tbsp caster
  (superfine) sugar
1 egg yolk

For the filling
175g/6oz/5 tbsp golden
  (light corn) syrup
50g/2oz/¼ cup dark muscovado
  (molasses) sugar
50g/2oz/¼ cup butter
3 eggs, lightly beaten
2.5ml/½ tsp vanilla extract
150g/5oz/1¼ cups pecan nuts
cream or ice cream, to serve

1 Place the flour in a bowl. Rub the butter into the flour with your fingertips until the mixture resembles breadcrumbs. (Alternatively use a food processor.) Stir in the sugar, egg yolk and about 30ml/2 tbsp cold water. Mix to a dough and knead on a lightly floured surface until smooth.

2 Roll out the pastry and use to line a 20cm/8in fluted loose-based flan tin (pan). Prick the base, then line with baking parchment and fill with baking beans. Chill for 30 minutes. Meanwhile, preheat the oven to 200°C/400°F/Gas 6.

3 Bake the pastry case blind for 10 minutes. Remove the paper and beans and continue to bake for 5 more minutes. Reduce the oven temperature to 180°C/350°F/Gas 4.

4 To make the filling, heat the syrup, sugar and butter in a pan until the sugar dissolves. Remove from the heat and cool slightly. Whisk in the eggs and vanilla extract and stir in the nuts. Pour into the pastry case (pie shell) and bake for 35–40 minutes, until the filling is set. Serve with cream or ice cream.

Variation
Use maple syrup instead of golden syrup.

Upside-down Apple Tart

Cox's Pippin apples are perfect to use in this tart because they hold their shape so well.

Serves 4
50g/2oz/¼ cup butter, softened
40g/1½ oz/3 tbsp caster
  (superfine) sugar
1 egg
115g/4oz/1 cup plain
  (all-purpose) flour

pinch of salt
whipped cream, to serve

For the apple layer
75g/3oz/6 tbsp butter, softened,
  plus extra for greasing
75g/3oz/scant ½ cup soft light
  brown sugar
10 eating apples, peeled, cored
  and thickly sliced

1 To make the pastry, beat together the butter and sugar until pale and creamy. Beat in the egg, then sift in the flour and salt and mix to a soft dough. Knead, wrap in cling film (plastic wrap) and chill for 1 hour.

2 For the apple layer, grease a 23cm/9in cake tin (pan), then add 50g/2oz/¼ cup of the butter. Place over low heat to melt the butter. Remove from the heat and sprinkle over 50g/2oz/¼ cup of the sugar. Arrange the apple slices on top, sprinkle with the remaining sugar and dot with the remaining butter.

3 Preheat the oven to 230°C/450°F/Gas 8. Place the cake tin on the hob again over low to medium heat for about 15 minutes, until a light golden caramel forms on the base.

4 Roll out the pastry on a lightly floured surface to around the same size as the tin and lay it on top of the apples. Tuck the pastry edges down around the sides of the apples.

5 Bake for about 20–25 minutes until the pastry is golden. Remove from the oven and leave to stand for 5 minutes.

6 Place an upturned plate on top of the tin and, holding the two together with a dish towel, turn the apple tart out on to the plate. Serve while still warm with whipped cream.

Pie Energy 373kcal/1563kJ; Protein 5.7g; Carbohydrate 51.1g, of which sugars 36.5g; Fat 17.6g, of which saturates 9.8g; Cholesterol 164mg; Calcium 59mg; Fibre 0.6g; Sodium 218mg.
Tart Energy 550kcal/2310kJ; Protein 5.4g; Carbohydrate 74.8g, of which sugars 52.9g; Fat 27.7g, of which saturates 16.7g; Cholesterol 114mg; Calcium 78mg; Fibre 4.9g; Sodium 215mg.

American Spiced Pumpkin Pie

This spicy sweet pie is traditionally served at Thanksgiving in the United States and Canada, when pumpkins are plentiful.

Serves 4–6
175g/6oz/1½ cups plain (all-purpose) flour
pinch of salt
75g/3oz/6 tbsp unsalted butter
15g/½ oz/1 tbsp caster (superfine) sugar

For the filling
450g/1lb peeled fresh pumpkin, diced, or 400g/14oz canned pumpkin, drained
115g/4oz/1 cup soft light brown sugar
1.5ml/¼ tsp salt
1.5ml/¼ tsp allspice
2.5ml/½ tsp ground cinnamon
2.5ml/½ tsp ground ginger
2 eggs, lightly beaten
120ml/4fl oz/½ cup double (heavy) cream
whipped cream, to serve

1 To make the pastry, place the flour in a bowl with a pinch of salt. Rub in the butter with your fingertips until the mixture resembles breadcrumbs. Add the sugar and 30–45ml/2–3 tbsp water, then mix to a soft dough. Knead briefly, flatten into a round, wrap in cling film (plastic wrap) and chill for 1 hour.

2 Preheat the oven to 200°C/400°F/Gas 6 with a baking sheet inside the oven. If using fresh pumpkin, steam for 15 minutes, then cool. Process in a food processor or blender to form a smooth purée.

3 Line a deep pie tin (pan) with the pastry. Prick the base. Cut out leaf shapes from the excess pastry and mark veins with the back of a knife. Brush the edges with water and stick on the leaves to overlap around the pastry edge. Chill.

4 Mix together the pumpkin purée, sugar, salt, spices, eggs and cream and pour into the pastry case (pie shell).

5 Place on the preheated baking sheet and bake for 15 minutes. Then reduce the temperature to 180°C/350°F/Gas 4 and cook for a further 30 minutes, or until the filling is set and the pastry golden. Serve warm with whipped cream.

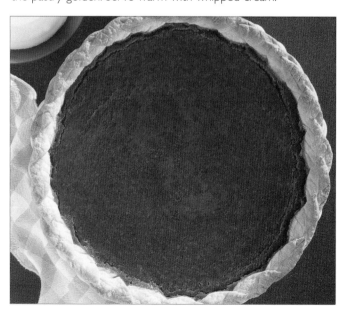

Pear & Blueberry Pie

Pears combine brilliantly with blueberries to create a lovely fruit pie that is just as delicious served cold as it is warm.

Serves 4
225g/8oz/2 cups plain (all-purpose) flour
pinch of salt
50g/2oz/¼ cup lard (shortening), diced
50g/2oz/¼ cup butter, diced
675g/1½ lb/4½ cups blueberries
25g/1oz/2 tbsp caster (superfine) sugar, plus extra for sprinkling
15ml/1 tbsp arrowroot
2 ripe but firm pears, peeled, cored and sliced
2.5ml/½ tsp ground cinnamon
grated rind of ½ lemon
beaten egg, to glaze
crème fraîche, to serve (optional)

1 Sift the flour and salt into a bowl. Rub in the fats with your fingertips until the mixture resembles fine breadcrumbs. Mix to a dough with 45ml/3 tbsp cold water. Chill for 30 minutes.

2 Place 225g/8oz/2 cups of the blueberries in a pan with the sugar. Cover with a lid and cook gently until the blueberries have softened. Press through a nylon sieve (strainer). Return the puréed blueberries to the pan.

3 Blend the arrowroot with 30ml/2 tbsp cold water and add to the blueberries in the pan. Bring to the boil, stirring until thickened. Allow to cool slightly.

4 Preheat the oven to 190°C/375°F/Gas 5 with a baking sheet inside the oven. Roll out just over half the pastry on a lightly floured surface and use to line a 20cm/8in shallow pie dish.

5 Mix together the remaining blueberries, the pears, ground cinnamon and lemon rind and spoon into the dish. Pour over the blueberry purée.

6 Use the remaining pastry to cover the pie. Make a slit in the centre. Brush with egg and sprinkle with caster sugar. Bake on the baking sheet for 40–45 minutes, until golden. Serve warm, with crème fraîche, if you wish.

Pumpkin Energy 411kcal/1721kJ; Protein 5.9g; Carbohydrate 47.4g, of which sugars 24.8g; Fat 23.4g, of which saturates 13.8g; Cholesterol 117mg; Calcium 96mg; Fibre 1.7g; Sodium 106mg.
Blueberry Energy 493kcal/2063kJ; Protein 7.1g; Carbohydrate 66.4g, of which sugars 23.6g; Fat 23.8g, of which saturates 11.7g; Cholesterol 38mg; Calcium 162mg; Fibre 8.6g; Sodium 84mg.

Blueberry Pie

Serve this tangy blueberry pie with crème fraîche, double (heavy) cream or vanilla ice cream.

Serves 6–8

450g/1lb shortcrust pastry, thawed if frozen
500g/1¼lb/5 cups blueberries
165g/5½oz/generous ¾ cup caster (superfine) sugar
45ml/3 tbsp plain (all-purpose) flour
5ml/1 tsp grated orange rind
1.5ml/¼ tsp freshly grated nutmeg
30ml/2 tbsp orange juice
5ml/1 tsp lemon juice

1 Preheat the oven to 190°C/375°F/Gas 5. On a lightly floured surface, roll out half of the pastry and use it to line a 23cm/9in pie dish that is 5cm/2in deep.

2 Combine the blueberries, 150g/5oz/¾ cup of the sugar, the flour, orange rind and nutmeg. Toss the mixture gently to coat all the fruit.

3 Pour the blueberry mixture into the pastry case and spread evenly. Sprinkle over the citrus juices.

4 Roll out the remaining pastry and use to cover the pie. Cut out small decorative shapes from the top. Use to decorate the pastry, and finish the edge.

5 Brush the top with water and sprinkle with the remaining caster sugar. Bake for 45 minutes, or until the pastry is golden brown. Serve warm or at room temperature.

> **Cook's Tip**
> To twist the edge of a double-crust pie hold the edges of the pie between your thumb and index finger and twist the edges together at 1cm/½in intervals. Alternatively, make a scalloped pattern by holding the finger of one hand against the top edge of the pie and squeezing the pastry with the thumb and forefinger of your other hand on the outside edge of the pie.

Lemon Meringue Pie

Crisp on top and soft beneath, here is a classic dish whose popularity never seems to wane.

Serves 8

225g/8oz shortcrust pastry, thawed if frozen
grated rind and juice of 1 large lemon
250ml/8fl oz/1 cup plus 15ml/ 1 tbsp cold water
115g/4oz/generous ½ cup caster (superfine) sugar plus 90ml/ 6 tbsp extra
25g/1oz/2 tbsp butter
45ml/3 tbsp cornflour (cornstarch)
3 eggs, separated
a pinch of salt
a pinch of cream of tartar

1 Line a 23cm/9in pie dish with the pastry, folding under a 1cm/½in overhang to give a firm edge. Crimp the edge and chill for 20 minutes.

2 Preheat the oven to 200°C/400°F/Gas 6. Prick the pastry case base, line with baking parchment and fill with baking beans. Bake for 12 minutes.

3 Remove the paper and beans and bake until golden, 6–8 minutes more.

4 In a pan, combine the lemon rind and juice with 250ml/8fl oz/ 1 cup of the water, 115g/4oz/generous ½ cup of the sugar, and the butter. Bring to the boil.

5 Meanwhile, dissolve the cornflour in the remaining water. Add the egg yolks. Beat into the lemon mixture, return to the boil and whisk until thick, about 5 minutes. Cover the surface with baking parchment and leave to cool.

6 For the meringue, beat the egg whites, using an electric hand whisk, with the salt and cream of tartar until stiffly peaking. Add the remaining sugar a spoonful at a time and beat until glossy.

7 Spoon the lemon mixture into the pastry case. Spoon the meringue on top, sealing it with the pastry rim. Bake until golden, 12–15 minutes.

Blueberry Energy 371kcal/1559kJ; Protein 4.4g; Carbohydrate 55.8g, of which sugars 25.7g; Fat 16g, of which saturates 4.9g; Cholesterol 8mg; Calcium 93mg; Fibre 3.2g; Sodium 228mg.
Lemon Energy 254kcal/1067kJ; Protein 4.1g; Carbohydrate 33.4g, of which sugars 15.3g; Fat 12.6g, of which saturates 4.7g; Cholesterol 82mg; Calcium 44mg; Fibre 0.5g; Sodium 162mg.

Open Apple Pie

An open pie like this looks attractive and uses less pastry than a double-crust pie. If using eating apples for this pie, make sure they are firm-fleshed rather than soft.

Serves 8
1.3–1.6kg/3–3½lb tart eating
   or cooking apples
45g/1¾oz/scant ¼ cup caster
   (superfine) sugar
10ml/2 tsp ground cinnamon
grated rind and juice of 1 lemon

25g/1oz/2 tbsp butter, diced
30–45ml/2–3 tbsp honey,
   to glaze

For the pastry
275g/10oz/2½ cups plain
   (all-purpose) flour
2.5ml/½ tsp salt
115g/4oz/½ cup cold
   butter, diced
60g/2¼oz/4½ tbsp white
   cooking fat or
   lard, diced
75–90ml/5–6 tbsp iced water

1 To make the pastry, sift the flour and salt into a bowl. Add the butter and fat and rub in using your fingertips or a pastry cutter until the mixture resembles coarse breadcrumbs.

2 Stir in just enough water to bind the dough. Gather the dough into a ball, wrap in clear film (plastic wrap) and chill for at least 20 minutes.

3 Preheat the oven to 200°C/400°F/Gas 6. Place a baking sheet in the oven.

4 Peel, core and slice the apples thinly. Combine with the sugar, cinnamon, lemon rind and juice.

5 Roll out the pastry to a 30cm/12in circle. Use to line a 23cm/9in pie dish, leaving an overhanging edge. Fill with the apples. Fold in the edges and crimp loosely. Dot the apples with diced butter.

6 Bake on the hot baking sheet until the pastry is golden and the apples are tender, about 45 minutes.

7 Melt the honey in a pan and brush over the apples to glaze. Serve warm or at room temperature.

Apple & Orange Pie

A tasty variation of an old favourite, this easy-to-make two-fruit pie will be a big hit. Make sure you choose really juicy oranges or even blood oranges for succulent results. It's delicious served with lashings of cream.

Serves 4
400g/14oz ready-made shortcrust
   (unsweetened) pastry
3 oranges, peeled
900g/2lb cooking apples, cored
   and thickly sliced
25g/1oz/2 tbsp demerara (raw)
   sugar
beaten egg, to glaze
caster (superfine) sugar,
   for sprinkling

1 Roll out the pastry on a lightly floured surface to about 2cm/¾in larger than the top of a 1.2 litre/2 pint/5 cup pie dish. Cut off a narrow strip around the edge of the pastry and fit on the rim of the pie dish.

2 Preheat the oven to 190°C/375°F/Gas 5. Hold one orange at a time over a bowl to catch the juice, and cut down between the membranes to remove the segments.

3 Mix the orange segments and juice, the apples and sugar in the pie dish. Place a pie funnel in the centre of the dish.

4 Dampen the pastry strip. Cover the dish with the rolled out pastry and press the edges to the pastry strip. Brush the top with beaten egg, then bake for 35–40 minutes, until lightly browned. Sprinkle with caster sugar before serving.

Cook's Tip
If you have time, make your own shortcrust pastry. Sift 225g/8oz/2 cups plain (all-purpose) flour and a pinch of salt into a bowl. Add 115g/4oz/½ cup diced butter and rub in with your fingertips until the mixture resembles breadcrumbs. Mix to a dough with about 45ml/3 tbsp cold water, then wrap and chill for 30 minutes before rolling out as above.

Open Pie Energy 418kcal/1755kJ; Protein 4g; Carbohydrate 53.7g, of which sugars 27.5g; Fat 22.5g, of which saturates 12.2g; Cholesterol 44mg; Calcium 62mg; Fibre 4.1g; Sodium 112mg.
Orange Pie Energy 610kcal/2566kJ; Protein 8.1g; Carbohydrate 86.1g, of which sugars 40.2g; Fat 28.5g, of which saturates 8.8g; Cholesterol 14mg; Calcium 168mg; Fibre 8.1g; Sodium 413mg.

Festive Apple Pie

Warming spices transform this pie into a special dish.

Serves 8

900g/2lb cooking apples
15g/½oz/2 tbsp plain
  (all-purpose) flour
115g/4oz/generous ½ cup caster
  (superfine) sugar
25ml/1½ tbsp fresh lemon juice
2.5ml/½ tsp ground cinnamon
2.5ml/½ tsp mixed (apple
  pie) spice
1.5ml/¼ tsp ground ginger
1.5ml/¼ tsp freshly grated nutmeg
1.5ml/¼ tsp salt
50g/2oz/¼ cup butter, diced

For the pastry

275g/10oz/2½ cups plain
  (all-purpose) flour
5ml/1 tsp salt
75g/3oz/6 tbsp cold
  butter, diced
50g/2oz/4 tbsp cold white cooking
  fat or lard, diced
50–120ml/2–4fl oz/¼–½ cup iced
  water

1 To make the pastry, sift the flour and salt into a bowl. Add the butter and fat, and rub it in until the mixture resembles coarse breadcrumbs.

2 Stir in just enough water to bind the pastry. Form into two balls, wrap in clear film (plastic wrap) and chill in the refrigerator for 20 minutes.

3 Roll out one ball on a lightly floured surface, and use it to line a 23cm/9in pie dish. Preheat a baking sheet in the oven at 220°C/425°F/Gas 7.

4 Peel, core and slice the apples. Toss with the flour, sugar, lemon juice, cinnamon, mixed spice, ginger and nutmeg, and the salt. Spoon into the pastry case and dot with butter.

5 Roll out the remaining pastry ball. Place on top of the pie and trim to leave a 2cm/¾in overhang. Fold this under the pastry base and press to seal. Crimp the edge. Form the scraps into leaf shapes and balls. Arrange on the pie and cut steam vents.

6 Bake on the baking sheet for 10 minutes. Reduce the heat to 180°C/350°F/Gas 4 and bake for 40 minutes, or until golden.

Rhubarb & Cherry Pie

The unusual partnership of rhubarb and cherries works well in this fruity pie. Serve it warm, with a scoop of clotted cream or vanilla ice cream.

Serves 8

450g/1lb rhubarb, cut into
  2.5cm/1in pieces
450g/1lb canned pitted tart red
  or black cherries, drained
275g/10oz/scant 1½ cups caster
  (superfine) sugar
45ml/3 tbsp quick-cooking tapioca
milk, for glazing

For the pastry

275g/10oz/2½ cups plain
  (all-purpose) flour
5ml/1 tsp salt
75g/3oz/6 tbsp cold
  butter, diced
50g/2oz/4 tbsp cold white cooking
  fat or lard, diced
50–120ml/2–4fl oz/¼–½ cup
  iced water

1 To make the pastry, sift the flour and salt into a bowl. Add the butter and fat and rub in until the mixture resembles breadcrumbs.

2 Stir in enough water to bind. Form into two balls, wrap in clear film (plastic wrap) and chill for 20 minutes.

3 Preheat a baking sheet in the oven at 200°C/400°F/Gas 6. Roll out one pastry ball and use to line a 23cm/9in pie dish, leaving a 1cm/½in overhang.

4 Mix together the rhubarb pieces, black cherries, caster sugar and tapioca, and spoon into the pastry case.

5 Roll out the remaining pastry ball, cut out four leaf shapes using a leaf cutter or a sharp knife, and use to cover the pie, leaving a 2cm/¾in overhang. Fold this overhang under the pastry base and flute to create an attractive edge.

6 Roll small balls from the scraps, mark veins in the leaves and use to decorate the pie.

7 Glaze the top and bake on the baking sheet until golden, 40–50 minutes. Serve with clotted cream.

Apple Energy 392kcal/1644kJ; Protein 3.9g; Carbohydrate 53.3g, of which sugars 25.7g; Fat 19.6g, of which saturates 10.7g; Cholesterol 39mg; Calcium 66mg; Fibre 2.9g; Sodium 836mg.
Rhubarb Energy 442kcal/1868kJ; Protein 4.3g; Carbohydrate 78.9g, of which sugars 47.4g; Fat 14.4g, of which saturates 7.5g; Cholesterol 26mg; Calcium 129mg; Fibre 2.2g; Sodium 312mg.

De Luxe Mincemeat Tart

Fruity home-made mincemeat is the perfect partner to crumbly, nutty pastry in this rich and festive pie.

Serves 8
225g/8oz/2 cups plain
  (all-purpose) flour
10ml/2 tsp ground cinnamon
50g/2oz/½ cup finely
  ground walnuts
115g/4oz/½ cup butter
50g/2oz/¼ cup caster (superfine)
  sugar, plus extra
  for dusting
1 egg
2 drops vanilla extract
15ml/1 tbsp cold water

For the mincemeat
2 eating apples, peeled, cored
  and grated
225g/8oz/generous 1½ cups raisins
115g/4oz/½ cup ready-to-eat
  dried apricots, chopped
115g/4oz/⅔ cup ready-to-eat
  dried figs or prunes, chopped
225g/8oz/2 cups green grapes,
  halved and seeded
50g/2oz/½ cup chopped almonds
finely grated rind of 1 lemon
30ml/2 tbsp lemon juice
30ml/2 tbsp brandy or port
1.5ml/¼ tsp mixed (apple
  pie) spice
115g/4oz/½ cup soft light
  brown sugar
25g/1oz/2 tbsp butter, melted

1 Process the flour, cinnamon, nuts and butter in a food processor or blender to make fine crumbs. Turn into a bowl and stir in the sugar. Beat the egg with the vanilla extract and water, and stir into the dry ingredients. Form a soft dough, knead until smooth, then wrap and chill for 30 minutes.

2 Mix the mincemeat ingredients together. Use two-thirds of the pastry to line a 23cm/9in, loose-based flan tin (tart pan). Trim and fill with the mincemeat.

3 Roll out the remaining pastry and cut into 1cm/½in strips. Arrange the strips in a lattice over the top of the pastry, wet the joins and press them together. Chill for 30 minutes.

4 Preheat a baking sheet in the oven at 190°C/375°F/Gas 5. Brush the pastry with water and dust with caster sugar. Bake the tart on the baking sheet for 30–40 minutes. Cool in the tin on a wire rack for 15 minutes, then remove the tin.

Crunchy Apple & Almond Flan

Don't put sugar with the apples as this produces too much liquid. The sweetness is in the pastry and topping.

Serves 8
75g/3oz/6 tbsp butter
175g/6oz/1½ cups plain
  (all-purpose) flour
25g/1oz/¼ cup ground almonds
25g/1oz/2 tbsp caster
  (superfine) sugar
1 egg yolk
15ml/1 tbsp cold water

1.5ml/¼ tsp almond extract
675g/1½lb cooking apples
25g/1oz/2 tbsp raisins

For the topping
115g/4oz/1 cup plain
  (all-purpose) flour
1.5ml/¼ tsp mixed (apple
  pie) spice
50g/2oz/¼ cup butter, cut into
  small cubes
50g/2oz/4¼ cup demerara
  (raw) sugar
50g/2oz/½ cup flaked (sliced) almonds

1 To make the pastry, rub the butter into the flour using your fingertips or a pastry cutter until it resembles breadcrumbs. Stir in the almonds and sugar.

2 Whisk the egg yolk, water and almond extract together and mix into the dry ingredients to form a soft dough. Knead until smooth, wrap, and leave to rest for 20 minutes.

3 To make the topping, sift the flour and spice into a bowl and rub in the butter. Stir in the sugar and almonds.

4 Roll out the pastry and use to line a 23cm/9in loose-based flan tin (tart pan). Trim the top and chill for 15 minutes.

5 Preheat a baking sheet in the oven at 190°C/375°F/Gas 5. Peel, core and slice the apples thinly. Arrange over the pastry in overlapping, concentric circles, doming the centre. Sprinkle with the raisins.

6 Cover with the topping mixture, pressing it on lightly. Bake on the hot baking sheet for 25–30 minutes, or until the top is golden brown and the apples are tender (test them with a fine skewer). Leave the flan to cool in the tin for 10 minutes before serving.

Mincemeat Energy 434kcal/1822kJ; Protein 4.8g; Carbohydrate 63.6g, of which sugars 42.1g; Fat 19.6g, of which saturates 8.1g; Cholesterol 57mg; Calcium 74mg; Fibre 1.8g; Sodium 108mg.
Flan Energy 358kcal/1499kJ; Protein 6.2g; Carbohydrate 42.5g, of which sugars 14.6g; Fat 19.3g, of which saturates 8.8g; Cholesterol 59mg; Calcium 86mg; Fibre 3.2g; Sodium 102mg.

Treacle Tart

Although called Treacle Tart, this old favourite is always made with syrup. It is straightforward to make – even this version with a simple lattice topping.

Serves 4–6
175ml/6fl oz/³/₄ cup golden
   (light corn) syrup
75g/3oz/1¹/₂ cups fresh
   white breadcrumbs
grated rind of 1 lemon
30ml/2 tbsp fresh lemon juice

For the pastry
175g/6oz/1¹/₂ cups plain
   (all-purpose) flour
2.5ml/¹/₂ tsp salt
75g/3oz/6 tbsp cold
   butter, diced
40g/1¹/₂oz/3 tbsp cold
   margarine, diced
45–60ml/3–4 tbsp iced water

1 To make the pastry, sift together the flour and salt, add the fats and rub in until the mixture resembles coarse breadcrumbs. Stir in enough water to bind.

2 Form into a ball, wrap in clear film (plastic wrap) and chill for 20 minutes.

3 Roll out the pastry and use to line a 20cm/8in pie dish. Chill for 20 minutes. Reserve the pastry trimmings.

4 Preheat a baking sheet in the oven at 200°C/400°F/Gas 6.

5 In a pan, warm the golden syrup until thin and runny. Stir in the breadcrumbs and lemon rind. Leave for 10 minutes, then stir in the lemon juice. Spread into the pastry case.

6 Roll out the pastry trimmings and cut into 12 thin strips. Lay six strips on the filling, then lay the other six at an angle over them to form a simple lattice.

7 Bake on the baking sheet for 10 minutes. Lower the heat to 190°C/375°F/Gas 5. Bake until golden, about 15 minutes more. Serve warm or cold.

Almond Syrup Tart

Almonds and a rich pastry make a treacle tart with a difference.

Serves 6
75g/3oz/1¹/₂ cups fresh
   white breadcrumbs
225g/8oz/scant 1 cup golden
   (light corn) syrup

finely grated rind of ¹/₂ lemon
10ml/2 tsp lemon juice
225g/8oz rich shortcrust pastry
25g/1oz/¹/₄ cup flaked
   (sliced) almonds
milk, to glaze (optional)
cream, custard or ice cream,
   to serve

1 Preheat the oven to 200°C/400°F/Gas 6. Line a 23cm/9in flan tin (tart pan) with the rich shortcrust pastry. Line the pastry with baking parchment and fill with baking beans.

2 Bake for 15 minutes and then remove the beans and paper and cook for 10 minutes more.

3 Combine the breadcrumbs with the golden syrup and the lemon rind and juice.

4 Spoon into the pastry case and spread out evenly. Sprinkle the flaked almonds evenly over the top.

5 Brush the pastry with milk to glaze, if you like. Bake for 25–30 minutes, or until the pastry and filling are golden brown.

6 Transfer to a wire rack to cool. Serve warm or cold, with cream, custard or ice cream.

> **Rich Shortcrust Pastry**
> *Sift 150g/5oz/1¹/₄ cups plain (all-purpose) flour with a pinch of salt into a bowl. Add 75g/3oz/6 tbsp unsalted (sweet) butter or margarine cut into pieces, and rub in with your fingertips or a pastry cutter. Stir in 1 egg yolk, 7.5ml/1¹/₂ tsp caster (superfine) sugar and 15ml/1 tbsp water. Gather the dough together, wrap in clear film (plastic wrap) and chill for 30 minutes.*

Treacle Energy 373kcal/1567kJ; Protein 4.4g; Carbohydrate 55.5g, of which sugars 24g; Fat 16.3g, of which saturates 7.7g; Cholesterol 27mg; Calcium 64mg; Fibre 1.2g; Sodium 304mg.
Almond Energy 407kcal/1712kJ; Protein 5.3g; Carbohydrate 63g, of which sugars 30.6g; Fat 16.6g, of which saturates 4.6g; Cholesterol 7mg; Calcium 75mg; Fibre 1.5g; Sodium 397mg.

Black Bottom Pie

Chocolate and rum make a winning combination over a crunchy ginger base.

Serves 8

10ml/2 tsp powdered gelatine
45ml/3 tbsp cold water
2 eggs, separated
150g/5oz/³/₄ cup caster (superfine) sugar
15g/¹/₂oz/2 tbsp cornflour (cornstarch)
2.5ml/¹/₂ tsp salt
475ml/16fl oz/2 cups milk
50g/2oz plain (semisweet) chocolate, finely chopped
30ml/2 tbsp rum
1.5ml/¹/₄ tsp cream of tartar
chocolate curls, to decorate

For the crust

175g/6oz/2 cups ginger nut cookies (gingersnaps), crushed
65g/2¹/₂oz/5 tbsp butter, melted

1 Preheat the oven to 180°C/350°F/Gas 4. Mix the crushed ginger nut cookies and melted butter. Press evenly over the base and side of a 23cm/9in pie plate. Bake for 6 minutes. Sprinkle the gelatine over the water and leave to soften.

2 Beat the egg yolks in a large bowl and set aside. In a pan, combine half the sugar, the cornflour and salt. Gradually stir in the milk. Boil for 1 minute, stirring constantly.

3 Whisk the hot milk mixture into the yolks, pour back into the pan and return to the boil, whisking. Cook for 1 minute, still whisking. Remove from the heat.

4 Pour 225g/8oz of the custard mixture into a bowl. Add the chopped chocolate and stir until melted. Stir in half the rum and pour into the pie crust. Whisk the softened gelatine into the plain custard until dissolved, then stir in the remaining rum. Set the pan in cold water to reach room temperature.

5 Beat the egg whites and cream of tartar until they form stiff peaks. Add the remaining sugar gradually, beating thoroughly after each addition. Fold the cooled custard into the egg whites, then spoon over the chocolate mixture in the pie crust. Chill the pie until it is set, about 2 hours. Decorate with chocolate curls and serve immediately.

Pumpkin Pie

A North American classic, this pie is traditionally served at Thanksgiving.

Serves 8

40g/1¹/₂oz/scant ¹/₃ cup pecan nuts, chopped
250g/9oz puréed pumpkin
475ml/16fl oz/2 cups single (light) cream
130g/4¹/₂oz/³/₄ cup soft light brown sugar
1.5ml/¹/₄ tsp salt
5ml/1 tsp ground cinnamon
2.5ml/¹/₂ tsp ground ginger
1.5ml/¹/₄ tsp ground cloves
1.5ml/¹/₄ tsp freshly grated nutmeg
2 eggs

For the pastry

165g/5¹/₂oz/1¹/₃ cups plain (all-purpose) flour
2.5ml/¹/₂ tsp salt
115g/4oz/²/₃ cup lard or white cooking fat
30–45ml/2–3 tbsp iced water

1 Preheat the oven to 220°C/425°F/Gas 7. To make the pastry, sift the flour and salt into a mixing bowl. Rub in the fat until the mixture resembles coarse breadcrumbs. Sprinkle in enough water to bind, then form the mixture into a ball. Wrap in clear film (plastic wrap) and chill in the refrigerator for 20 minutes.

2 Roll out the pastry to a 5mm/¹/₄in thickness. Use to line a 23cm/9in pie plate. Trim and flute the edge. Sprinkle the chopped pecan nuts over the base of the case.

3 Beat together the pumpkin, cream, sugar, salt, spices and eggs. Pour the pumpkin mixture into the pastry case. Bake for 10 minutes, then reduce the heat to 180°C/350°F/Gas 4 and continue baking until the filling is set, about 45 minutes. Leave the pie to cool in the plate, set on a wire rack.

Cook's Tip

For perfect pastry every time, handle the pastry as little and as lightly as you can. There is no need to knead it, just gather it up into a ball before rolling it out. Chill it, and try to keep the working surface cool (a marble slab is ideal) when rolling out the pastry.

Black Energy 248kcal/1040kJ; Protein 5.2g; Carbohydrate 25.8g, of which sugars 14.6g; Fat 13.7g, of which saturates 7.6g; Cholesterol 69mg; Calcium 111mg; Fibre 0.5g; Sodium 166mg.
Pumpkin Energy 434kcal/1809kJ; Protein 6.2g; Carbohydrate 35.3g, of which sugars 19.4g; Fat 30.8g, of which saturates 13.8g; Cholesterol 94mg; Calcium 108mg; Fibre 1.2g; Sodium 60mg.

Chocolate Nut Tart

This is a sophisticated tart – strictly for grown-ups!

Serves 6 – 8

225g/8oz sweet shortcrust pastry, thawed if frozen
200g/7oz/1¾ cups dry amaretti
90g/3½oz/generous ½ cup blanched almonds
50g/2oz/⅓ cup blanched hazelnuts
45ml/3 tbsp caster (superfine) sugar
200g/7oz plain (semisweet) cooking chocolate
45ml/3 tbsp milk
50g/2oz/¼ cup butter
45ml/3 tbsp amaretto liqueur or brandy
30ml/2 tbsp single (light) cream

1 Grease a shallow loose-based 25cm/10in flan tin (tart pan). Roll out the pastry on a lightly floured surface, and use it to line the tin. Trim the edge, prick the base with a fork and chill for 30 minutes.

2 Grind the amaretti in a blender or food processor. Tip into a mixing bowl.

3 Set eight whole almonds aside and place the rest in the food processor or blender with the hazelnuts and sugar. Grind to a medium texture. Add the nuts to the amaretti, and mix well to combine thoroughly.

4 Preheat the oven to 190°C/375°F/Gas 5. Slowly melt the chocolate with the milk and butter in the top of a double boiler or in a heatproof bowl over a pan of simmering water. Once the chocolate has melted, stir until smooth.

5 Pour the chocolate mixture into the dry ingredients, and mix well. Add the liqueur or brandy and the cream.

6 Spread the filling evenly in the pastry case. Bake for 35 minutes, or until the crust is golden brown and the filling has puffed up and is beginning to darken.

7 Allow to cool to room temperature. Split the reserved almonds in half and use to decorate the tart.

Pecan Nut Tartlets

These delightful individual tartlets make an elegant dinner-party dessert.

Serves 6

425g/15oz shortcrust pastry, thawed if frozen
175g/6oz/1 cup pecan nut halves
3 eggs, beaten
25g/1oz/2 tbsp butter, melted
275g/10oz/¾ cup golden (light corn) syrup
2.5ml/½ tsp vanilla extract
115g/4oz/generous ½ cup caster (superfine) sugar
15ml/1 tbsp plain (all-purpose) flour

1 Preheat the oven to 180°C/350°F/Gas 4. Roll out the pastry and use to line six 10cm/4in tartlet tins (pans). Divide the pecan nut halves between the pastry cases.

2 Combine the eggs with the butter, and add the golden syrup and vanilla extract. Sift over the caster sugar and flour, and blend well. Fill the pastry cases with the mixture and leave until the nuts rise to the surface.

3 Bake for 35–40 minutes, or until a skewer inserted into the centre comes out clean. Cool in the tins for 15 minutes, then turn out on to a wire rack to cool completely.

Basic Shortcrust Pastry

Mix together 225g/8oz/1 cups flour, a pinch of salt and 115g/4oz/½ cup butter. Using your fingertips or a pastry cutter, rub the butter into the flour until the mixture resembles fine breadcrumbs. Mix in the water and gather together to form a firm dough. Wrap the dough in clear film (plastic wrap) and chill for 30 minutes. Use this recipe when 350g/12oz pastry is required – enough to line a 23cm/9in flan tin (tart pan). For 425g/15oz pastry you will need 275g/10oz flour to 150g/5oz butter.
• If you use half butter and half white vegetable fat (shortening) you will have a lighter and less rich crust.
• For Sweet Shortcrust Pastry, add 50g/2oz/¼ cup sugar to the flour.

Chocolate Energy 644kcal/2685kJ; Protein 9.6g; Carbohydrate 56.4g, of which sugars 32g; Fat 42.4g, of which saturates 13.4g; Cholesterol 21mg; Calcium 122mg; Fibre 3g; Sodium 241mg.
Pecan Energy 828kcal/3463kJ; Protein 10.6g; Carbohydrate 95g, of which sugars 58.2g; Fat 47.8g, of which saturates 11.2g; Cholesterol 115mg; Calcium 118mg; Fibre 2.9g; Sodium 486mg.

Pear & Hazelnut Flan

A delicious flan for Sunday lunch. Grind the hazelnuts yourself if you prefer, or use ground almonds instead.

Serves 6 – 8
115g/4oz/1 cup plain
  (all-purpose) flour
115g/4oz/1 cup plain wholemeal
  (whole-wheat) flour
115g/4oz/1/2 cup sunflower
  margarine
45ml/3 tbsp cold water

For the filling
50g/2oz/1/2 cup self-raising
  (self-rising) flour
115g/4oz/1 cup ground hazelnuts
5ml/1 tsp vanilla extract
50g/2oz/1/4 cup caster
  (superfine) sugar
50g/2oz/1/4 cup butter, softened
2 eggs, beaten
400g/14oz can pears in
  natural juice
45ml/3 tbsp raspberry jam
few chopped hazelnuts, to decorate

1 For the pastry, stir the flours together, then rub in the margarine using your fingertips or a pastry cutter until the mixture resembles fine breadcrumbs. Mix to a firm dough with the water.

2 Roll out the dough and use to line a 23–25cm/9–10in flan tin (tart pan), pressing it up the sides after trimming, so that the pastry sits a little above the tin. Prick the base with a fork, line with baking parchment and fill with baking beans. Chill for 30 minutes.

3 Preheat the oven to 200°C/400°F/Gas 6. Place the flan tin on a baking sheet and bake blind for 20 minutes. Remove the paper and beans after 15 minutes.

4 To make the filling beat together the flour, hazelnuts, vanilla extract, sugar and eggs. If the misture is too thick, stir in some of the juice from the canned pears.

5 Reduce the oven temperature to 180°C/350°F/Gas 4. Spread the jam on the pastry case and spoon over the filling.

6 Drain the pears and arrange them, cut side down, in the filling. Sprinkle over the nuts for decoration. Bake for 30 minutes, or until risen, firm and golden brown.

Latticed Peaches

When fresh peaches are out of season, make this elegant dessert using canned peach halves instead .

Serves 6
115g/4oz/1 cup plain
  (all-purpose) flour
45ml/3 tbsp butter or
  sunflower margarine
45ml/3 tbsp natural (plain) yogurt
30ml/2 tbsp orange juice
milk, to glaze

For the filling
3 ripe peaches
45ml/3 tbsp ground almonds
30ml/2 tbsp natural
  (plain) yogurt
finely grated rind of
  1 small orange
1.5ml/1/4 tsp almond extract

For the sauce
1 ripe peach
45ml/3 tbsp orange juice

1 Lightly grease a baking sheet. Sift the flour into a bowl and rub in the butter or margarine. Stir in the yogurt and orange juice to make a firm dough. Roll out half the pastry thinly and stamp out six rounds with a 7.5cm/3in cookie cutter. Place on the baking sheet.

2 Drop the peaches into boiling water for 20 seconds. Remove and plunge into cold water. Remove the skins, halve and remove the stones (pits). Mix together the almonds, yogurt, orange rind and almond extract. Spoon into the hollows of each peach half and place, cut side down, on the pastry rounds.

3 Roll out the remaining pastry thinly and cut into thin strips. Arrange the strips over the peaches to form a lattice, brushing with milk to secure firmly. Trim the ends. Chill for 30 minutes.

4 Preheat the oven to 200°C/400°F/Gas 6. Brush with milk and bake for 15–18 minutes, or until golden brown.

5 To make the sauce, skin the peach as before and halve it to remove the stone. Place the flesh in a food processor or blender, with the orange juice, and purée until the mixture is smooth. Serve the peaches hot, with the peach sauce spooned around them.

Flan Energy 389kcal/1626kJ; Protein 7.6g; Carbohydrate 40.9g, of which sugars 16g; Fat 22.8g, of which saturates 3.5g; Cholesterol 49mg; Calcium 69mg; Fibre 3.6g; Sodium 138mg.
Peaches Energy 196kcal/822kJ; Protein 4.7g; Carbohydrate 21.6g, of which sugars 6.8g; Fat 10.8g, of which saturates 4.3g; Cholesterol 16mg; Calcium 75mg; Fibre 1.9g; Sodium 59mg.

Surprise Fruit Tarts

Strawberry cream with a dash of liqueur makes a beautiful filling. These delicious and simple little tarts are the perfect summer treat.

Serves 6
4 large or 8 small sheets filo
   pastry, thawed if frozen
65g/2½ oz/5 tbsp butter or
   margarine, melted
250ml/8fl oz/1 cup
   whipping cream
45ml/3 tbsp strawberry jam

15ml/1 tbsp Cointreau or other
   orange-flavoured liqueur
115g/4oz/1 cup seedless black
   grapes, halved
115g/4oz/1 cup seedless white
   grapes, halved
150g/5oz fresh pineapple,
   cubed, or drained canned
   pineapple chunks
115g/4oz/⅔ cup raspberries
30ml/2 tbsp icing
   (confectioners') sugar
6 sprigs fresh mint,
   to decorate

1 Preheat the oven to 180°C/350°F/Gas 4. Grease six cups of a bun tray. Stack the filo sheets and cut with a sharp knife or scissors into 24 pieces, each 12cm/4½in square.

2 Lay four squares of pastry in each of the six greased cups, rotating them slightly to make star-shaped baskets.

3 Press the pastry firmly into the cups. Brush the pastry baskets lightly with butter or margarine.

4 Bake until the pastry is crisp and golden, about 5–7 minutes. Cool on a wire rack.

5 In a bowl, lightly whip the cream until soft peaks form. Gently fold the strawberry jam and Cointreau into the cream.

6 Just before serving, spoon a little of the cream mixture into each pastry basket. Top with the halved grapes, pineapple and raspberries.

7 Sprinkle with icing sugar; decorate each basket with a small sprig of mint and serve immediately.

Truffle Filo Tarts

The dainty filo pastry cups can be prepared a day ahead and then stored in an airtight container until they are needed.

Makes 24 cups
3–6 sheets filo pastry
   (depending on size),
   thawed if frozen
45g/1½oz/3 tbsp unsalted
   (sweet) butter, melted

sugar, for sprinkling
lemon rind, to decorate

For the truffle mixture
250ml/8fl oz/1 cup double
   (heavy) cream
225g/8oz plain (semisweet)
   or dark (bittersweet)
   chocolate, chopped
50g/2oz/¼ cup unsalted
   (sweet) butter, diced
30ml/2 tbsp brandy

1 To make the truffle mixture, in a pan over medium heat bring the double cream to the boil. Remove from the heat and add the chocolate, stirring until melted. Beat in the butter and add the brandy. Strain into a bowl and chill for 1 hour.

2 Preheat the oven to 200°C/400°F/Gas 6. Grease a bun tray with 24 cups, each 4cm/1½in. Cut each filo sheet into 6cm/2½in squares. Cover with a damp dish towel. Keeping the other filo sheets covered, place one square on a work surface. Brush lightly with melted butter, turn over and brush the other side. Sprinkle with a pinch of sugar.

3 Butter another square and place it over the first at an angle. Sprinkle with sugar. Butter a third square and place over the first two, unevenly, so that the corners form an uneven edge. Press the layered square into the tray. Continue to fill the tray.

4 Bake the filo cups for 4–6 minutes, or until golden. Cool for 10 minutes on a wire rack in the tray. Remove from the tray and cool completely.

5 Stir the chocolate mixture, which should be just thick enough to pipe. Spoon the mixture into a piping (pastry) bag fitted with a medium star nozzle and pipe a swirl into each cup. Decorate with lemon rind.

Fruit Energy 359kcal/1496kJ; Protein 3g; Carbohydrate 28.6g, of which sugars 15.9g; Fat 26.1g, of which saturates 16.2g; Cholesterol 67mg; Calcium 65mg; Fibre 1.6g; Sodium 81mg.
Truffle Energy 149kcal/621kJ; Protein 1.2g; Carbohydrate 10.2g, of which sugars 6.1g; Fat 11.5g, of which saturates 7.1g; Cholesterol 23mg; Calcium 16mg; Fibre 0.4g; Sodium 27mg.

Apple Strudel

Ready-made filo pastry makes a good substitute for paper-thin strudel pastry in this classic Austrian dish.

Serves 10–12
75g/3oz/generous ½ cup raisins
30ml/2 tbsp brandy
5 eating apples
3 large cooking apples
90g/3½oz/scant ½ cup soft dark brown sugar
5ml/1 tsp ground cinnamon
grated rind and juice of 1 lemon
25g/1oz/scant ½ cup dry breadcrumbs
50g/2oz/½ cup chopped pecan nuts or walnuts
12 sheets filo pastry, thawed if frozen
175g/6oz/¾ cup butter, melted
icing (confectioners') sugar, for dusting

1 Soak the raisins in the brandy for 15 minutes.

2 Peel, core and thinly slice the apples. Combine with the dark brown sugar, cinnamon, lemon rind and juice, half the breadcrumbs, and pecan nuts or walnuts.

3 Preheat the oven to 190°C/375°F/Gas 5. Grease two baking sheets. Unfold the filo pastry and cover with a damp dish towel. One by one, butter and stack the sheets to make two six-sheet piles.

4 Sprinkle half the reserved breadcrumbs over the last sheet and spoon half the apple mixture along the bottom edge. Roll up from this edge, Swiss roll (jelly roll) style. Place on a baking sheet, seam side down, and fold the ends under to seal. Repeat to make a second strudel. Brush both with butter.

5 Bake in the oven for 45 minutes, cool slightly, then dust with icing sugar.

> ### Cook's Tip
> *Filo pastry is delicate and needs to be kept covered with a damp dish towel when out of the packet and waiting to be used. Otherwise, it will dry out and crack before you are able to use it.*

Cherry Strudel

A refreshing variation on traditional apple strudel. Serve with whipped cream, if you like.

Serves 8
65g/2½oz/1¼ cups fresh breadcrumbs
175g/6oz/¾ cup butter, melted
200g/7oz/1 cup caster (superfine) sugar
15ml/1 tbsp ground cinnamon
5ml/1 tsp grated lemon rind
450g/1lb/2 cups sour cherries, pitted
8 sheets filo pastry
icing (confectioners') sugar, for dusting

1 In a frying pan, fry the breadcrumbs in 65g/2½oz/5 tbsp of the butter until golden. Set aside.

2 In a large mixing bowl, toss together the sugar, cinnamon and lemon rind. Stir in the cherries.

3 Preheat the oven to 190°C/375°F/Gas 5, and grease a baking sheet.

4 Unfold the filo sheets. Keep the unused sheets covered with a damp dish towel. Lift off one sheet and place on a piece of baking parchment. Brush the pastry with butter. Sprinkle an eighth of the breadcrumbs over the surface.

5 Lay a second sheet of filo pastry on top, brush with butter and sprinkle with breadcrumbs. Continue until you have used up all the pastry.

6 Spoon the cherry mixture along the bottom edge of the strip. Starting at the cherry-filled end, roll up the dough Swiss roll (jelly roll) style.

7 Use the paper to flip the strudel on to the baking sheet, seam-side down. Carefully fold under the ends to seal. Brush the top with melted butter.

8 Bake the strudel for 45 minutes. Cool slightly, then dust with a fine layer of icing sugar.

Apple Energy 231kcal/966kJ; Protein 2.3g; Carbohydrate 21.3g, of which sugars 8.6g; Fat 15.2g, of which saturates 7.9g; Cholesterol 31mg; Calcium 33mg; Fibre 1.5g; Sodium 109mg.
Cherry Energy 370kcal/1553kJ; Protein 3.2g; Carbohydrate 51.2g, of which sugars 33.2g; Fat 18.4g, of which saturates 11.4g; Cholesterol 47mg; Calcium 57mg; Fibre 1.2g; Sodium 197mg.

Strawberry Tart

This tart is best assembled just before serving, but you can bake the pastry case and make the filling ahead.

Serves 6
350g/12oz rough-puff or puff pastry, thawed if frozen
225g/8oz/1 cup cream cheese
grated rind of ½ orange
30ml/2 tbsp orange liqueur or orange juice
45–60ml/3–4 tbsp icing (confectioners') sugar, plus extra for dusting (optional)
450g/1lb/4 cups ripe strawberries, hulled

1 Preheat the oven to 200°C/400°F/Gas 6. Roll out the pastry to about a 3mm/⅛in thickness and use to line a 28 × 10cm/11 × 4in rectangular flan tin (tart pan). Trim the edges, then chill for 30 minutes.

2 Prick the base of the pastry all over with a fork. Line with foil, fill with baking beans and bake for 15 minutes. Remove the foil and beans and bake for a further 10 minutes, or until the pastry is browned. Gently press down on the pastry base to deflate, then leave to cool on a wire rack.

3 Beat together the cheese, orange rind, liqueur or orange juice and icing sugar to taste. Spread the cheese filling in the pastry case. Halve the strawberries and arrange them on top of the filling. Dust with icing sugar, if you like.

> **Rough-puff Pastry**
> Cut 175g/6oz/¾ cup butter into small pieces. Sift 8oz/225g/2 cups plain (all-purpose) flour into a bowl and add the butter, 5ml/1 tsp salt, 5ml/1 tsp lemon juice and 150ml/¼ pint/⅔ cup iced water. Mix together with a knife. Turn on to a work surface and gather it together. Roll into a rectangle. Fold up the bottom third to the centre, fold the top third to meet it and then turn the pasty a quarter turn. Repeat the rolling and folding. Wrap and chill for 20 minutes (or pop into the freezer for 5 minutes). Roll, fold and chill twice more.

Alsatian Plum Tart

Fruit and custard tarts, similar to a fruit flan, are typical in Alsace. Sometimes they have a yeast dough base instead of pastry. You can use other seasonal fruits in this tart, or a mixture of fruit, if you like.

Serves 6 – 8
450g/1lb ripe plums, halved and stoned (pitted)
30ml/2 tbsp Kirsch or plum brandy
350g/12oz shortcrust or sweet shortcrust pastry, thawed if frozen
30ml/2 tbsp seedless raspberry jam

For the custard filling
2 eggs
25g/1oz/4 tbsp icing (confectioners') sugar
175ml/6fl oz/¾ cup double (heavy) cream
grated rind of ½ lemon
1.5ml/¼ tsp vanilla extract

1 Preheat the oven to 200°C/400°F/Gas 6. Mix the plums with the Kirsch or brandy and set aside for about 30 minutes.

2 Roll out the pastry thinly and use to line a 23cm/9in flan tin (tart pan). Prick the base of the pastry case all over with a fork, and line with foil. Add a layer of baking beans and bake for 15 minutes, or until slightly dry and set. Remove the foil and the baking beans.

3 Brush the base of the pastry case with a thin layer of jam, then bake for a further 5 minutes.

4 Remove the pastry case from the oven and transfer to a wire rack. Reduce the oven temperature to 180°C/350°F/Gas 4.

5 To make the custard filling, beat the eggs and sugar until well combined, then beat in the cream, lemon rind, vanilla extract and any juice from the plums.

6 Arrange the plums, cut side down, in the pastry case and pour over the custard mixture. Bake for about 30–35 minutes, or until a knife inserted into the centre comes out clean. Serve the tart warm or at room temperature.

Strawberry Energy 434kcal/1805kJ; Protein 5.2g; Carbohydrate 34.4g, of which sugars 13.5g; Fat 32.2g, of which saturates 11.1g; Cholesterol 36mg; Calcium 87mg; Fibre 0.8g; Sodium 299mg.
Plum Energy 375kcal/1563kJ; Protein 4.8g; Carbohydrate 31.7g, of which sugars 11.6g; Fat 25.5g, of which saturates 11.5g; Cholesterol 84mg; Calcium 65mg; Fibre 1.7g; Sodium 200mg.

Almond Mincemeat Tartlets

A lemony iced sponge
topping encloses mincemeat
in a rich almond pastry.

Makes 36
275g/10oz/2½ cups plain
 (all-purpose) flour
75g/3oz/¾ cup icing
 (confectioners') sugar
5ml/1 tsp ground cinnamon
175g/6oz/¾ cup butter
50g/2oz/½ cup ground almonds
1 egg yolk
45ml/3 tbsp milk
450g/1lb mincemeat
15ml/1 tbsp brandy or rum

For the lemon filling
115g/4oz/½ cup butter
 or margarine
115g/4oz/generous ½ cup caster
 (superfine) sugar
175g/6oz/1½ cups self-raising
 (self-rising) flour
2 large (US extra large) eggs
finely grated rind of
 1 large lemon

For the lemon icing
115g/4oz/1 cup icing
 (confectioners') sugar
15ml/1 tbsp lemon juice

1 Sift the flour, sugar and cinnamon into a bowl and rub in the
butter using your fingertips or a pastry cutter until it resembles
breadcrumbs. Add the ground almonds and bind with the egg
yolk and milk to a soft, pliable dough. Knead until smooth, wrap
in clear film (plastic wrap) and chill for 30 minutes.

2 Preheat the oven to 190°C/375°F/Gas 5. On a lightly floured
surface, roll out the pastry and cut out 36 fluted rounds with a
pastry cutter. Mix the mincemeat with the brandy or rum and
put a small teaspoonful in the base of each pastry case. Chill.

3 To make the lemon sponge filling, whisk the butter or
margarine, sugar, flour, eggs and lemon rind together until smooth.
Spoon on top of the mincemeat, dividing it evenly, and level the
tops. Bake for 20–30 minutes, or until golden brown and springy
to the touch. Remove and leave to cool on a wire rack.

4 To make the lemon icing, sift the icing sugar and mix with the
lemon juice to a smooth coating consistency. Spoon into a
piping bag and drizzle a zigzag pattern over each tart. (If you're
short of time, simply dust the tartlets with icing sugar.)

Mince Pies with Orange Pastry

Home-made mince pies are
so much nicer than shop-
bought, especially with this
flavoursome pastry.

Makes 18
225g/8oz/2 cups plain
 (all-purpose) flour
30g/1½oz/⅓ cup icing
 (confectioners') sugar

10ml/2 tsp ground cinnamon
150g/5oz/generous 1 cup cold
 butter, diced
grated rind of 1 orange
about 60ml/4 tbsp iced water
225g/8oz/1½ cups mincemeat
1 egg, beaten, to glaze
icing (confectioners') sugar,
 for dusting

1 Sift together the flour, icing sugar and cinnamon. Rub in the
butter until it resembles fine breadcrumbs. Stir in the grated
orange rind.

2 Mix to a firm dough with the water. Knead lightly, then roll
out to a 5mm/¼in thickness. Using a 6cm/2½in round cookie
cutter, stamp out 18 circles, then stamp out 18 smaller
5cm/2in circles.

3 Line two bun trays with the larger circles. Place a small
spoonful of mincemeat into each pastry case and top with the
smaller pastry circles, pressing the edges to seal.

4 Glaze the tops with egg glaze and leave to rest in the refrigerator
for 30 minutes. Preheat the oven to 200°C/400°F/Gas 6.

5 Bake for 15–20 minutes, or until golden brown. Remove to
cool on wire racks. Serve just warm, dusted with icing sugar.

> **Cook's Tip**
> *This sweet and spicy pastry works for all kinds of sweet pies
> and tarts. This quantity will line a 23cm/9in flan tin (tart pan)
> as well as leaving enough for a lattice or cut-out pastry shapes
> to decorate the top. It is particularly suitable for autumn fruit
> pies made with apples, plums or pears.*

Tartlets Energy 177kcal/746kJ; Protein 1.8g; Carbohydrate 26.4g, of which sugars 16.9g; Fat 7.8g, of which saturates 4.4g; Cholesterol 34mg; Calcium 32mg; Fibre 0.6g; Sodium 57mg.
Pies Energy 145kcal/610kJ; Protein 1.3g; Carbohydrate 19.3g, of which sugars 9.7g; Fat 7.6g, of which saturates 4.4g; Cholesterol 18mg; Calcium 24mg; Fibre 0.6g; Sodium 53mg.

Candied Fruit Pie

Use good-quality candied fruits for the best flavour. Try half digestive (graham crackers) and half ginger nut cookies (gingersnaps) for the crust, if you prefer.

Serves 10
15ml/1 tbsp rum
50g/2oz/¼ cup mixed glacé (candied) fruit, chopped
475ml/16fl oz/2 cups milk
20ml/4 tsp powdered gelatine
90g/3½oz/½ cup caster (superfine) sugar
2.5ml/½ tsp salt
3 eggs, separated
250ml/8fl oz/1 cup whipping cream, whipped
chocolate curls, to decorate

For the crust
175g/6oz/2 cups crushed digestive cookies (graham crackers)
75g/3oz/5 tbsp butter, melted
15ml/1 tbsp caster (superfine) sugar

1 To make the crust mix the digestive cookies, butter and sugar. Press evenly over the base and sides of a 23cm/9in pie plate. Chill.

2 Stir together the rum and glacé fruit. Set aside. Pour 120ml/4fl oz/½ cup of the milk into a small bowl. Sprinkle over the gelatine and leave for 5 minutes to soften.

3 In the top of a double boiler or in a heatproof bowl over a pan of simmering water, combine 50g/2oz/4 tbsp of the sugar, the remaining milk and the salt. Stir in the gelatine mixture. Cook, stirring, until the gelatine dissolves. Whisk in the egg yolks and cook, stirring, until thick enough to coat the back of the spoon. Pour the custard over the glacé fruit mixture, set in a bowl of iced water.

4 Beat the egg whites until they form soft peaks. Add the remaining sugar and beat just to blend. Fold a large dollop of the egg whites into the cooled gelatine mixture. Pour into the remaining egg whites and fold together. Fold in the cream.

5 Pour into the pie crust and chill until firm. Decorate with chocolate curls.

Chocolate Chiffon Pie

As the name suggests, this is a wonderfully smooth and light-textured pie.

Serves 8
200g/7oz plain (semisweet) chocolate, chopped
250ml/8fl oz/1 cup milk
15ml/1 tbsp powdered gelatine
90g/3½oz/1 cup caster (superfine) sugar
2 large (US extra large) eggs, separated
5ml/1 tsp vanilla extract
1.5ml/¼ tsp salt
350ml/12fl oz/1½ cups whipping cream, whipped
whipped cream and chocolate curls, to decorate

For the crust
200g/7oz/2⅓ cups crushed digestive cookies (graham crackers)
75g/3oz/6 tbsp butter, melted

1 Place a baking sheet in the oven and preheat the oven to 180°C/350°F/Gas 4. To make the crust, mix the cookies and butter together and press over the base and sides of a 23cm/9in pie plate. Bake for 8 minutes.

2 Grate the chocolate and set aside. Place the milk in the top of a double boiler or in a heatproof bowl over a pan of simmering water. Sprinkle over the gelatine and leave for 5 minutes to soften.

3 In the top of a double boiler or in a heatproof bowl as before, put 40g/1½oz/scant ¼ cup sugar, the chocolate and egg yolks. Stir until dissolved. Add the vanilla extract. Transfer the pan or bowl to a bowl of ice and stir until the mixture reaches room temperature. Remove from the ice.

4 Beat the egg whites and salt until they form soft peaks. Add the remaining sugar and beat just to blend. Fold a dollop of the egg whites into the chocolate mixture, then pour back into the whites and fold in carefully.

5 Fold in the cream and pour into the pie crust. Freeze until just set, about 5 minutes, then chill for 3–4 hours. Decorate with whipped cream and chocolate curls.

Fruit Energy 334kcal/1392kJ; Protein 5.2g; Carbohydrate 29.3g, of which sugars 19.6g; Fat 22.3g, of which saturates 12.8g; Cholesterol 109mg; Calcium 106mg; Fibre 0.4g; Sodium 200mg.
Chocolate Energy 557kcal/2323kJ; Protein 6.4g; Carbohydrate 47.5g, of which sugars 33.5g; Fat 39.3g, of which saturates 23.1g; Cholesterol 127mg; Calcium 109mg; Fibre 1.2g; Sodium 251mg.

Chocolate Pear Tart

Chocolate and pears have a natural affinity, well used in this luxurious pudding that makes an attractive dinner-party dessert.

Serves 8
115g/4oz plain (semisweet) chocolate, grated
3 large firm, ripe pears
1 egg
1 egg yolk
120ml/4fl oz/½ cup single (light) cream

2.5ml/½ tsp vanilla extract
45ml/3 tbsp caster (superfine) sugar

For the pastry
150g/5oz/1¼ cups plain (all-purpose) flour
1.5ml/¼ tsp salt
30ml/2 tbsp caster (superfine) sugar
115g/4oz/½ cup cold unsalted (sweet) butter, diced
1 egg yolk
15ml/1 tbsp lemon juice

1 To make the pastry, sift the flour and salt into a bowl. Add the sugar and butter. Rub in using your fingertips or a pastry cutter until the mixture resembles coarse breadcrumbs.

2 Stir in the egg yolk and lemon juice. Form a ball, wrap in clear film (plastic wrap), and chill for 20 minutes.

3 Preheat the oven to 200°C/400°F/Gas 6. Roll out the pastry and use to line a 25cm/10in flan (tart) dish.

4 Sprinkle the pastry case with the grated chocolate.

5 Peel, halve and core the pears. Cut in thin slices crossways, then fan out slightly. Transfer the pears to the tart using a metal spatula and arrange like spokes of a wheel.

6 Whisk together the egg and egg yolk, cream and vanilla extract. Ladle over the pears and sprinkle with sugar.

7 Bake on a baking sheet for 10 minutes. Reduce the heat to 180°C/350°F/Gas 4 and cook until the custard is set and the pears begin to caramelize, about 20 minutes more. Serve while still warm.

Pear & Apple Crumble Tart

This pie combines the old favourites of fruit pies and crumbles in one delicious treat. You could use just one fruit in this pie if you prefer.

Serves 8
3 firm pears
4 cooking apples
175g/6oz/scant 1 cup caster (superfine) sugar
30ml/2 tbsp cornflour (cornstarch)
1.5ml/¼ tsp salt
grated rind of 1 lemon
30ml/2 tbsp fresh lemon juice

75g/3oz/generous ½ cup raisins
75g/3oz/⅔ cup plain (all-purpose) flour
5ml/1 tsp ground cinnamon
75g/3oz/6 tbsp cold butter, diced

For the pastry
150g/5oz/1¼ cups plain (all-purpose) flour
2.5ml/½ tsp salt
65g/2½oz/5 tbsp cold white vegetable fat (shortening), diced
30ml/2 tbsp iced water

1 To make the pastry, sift the flour and salt into a bowl. Add the fat and rub in using your fingertips until the mixture resembles breadcrumbs. Stir in enough water to bind.

2 Wrap in clear film (plastic wrap) and chill for 30 minutes. Form into a ball, roll out, and use to line a 23cm/9in pie dish, leaving a 1cm/½in overhang. Fold this under for double thickness. Flute the edge, then chill.

3 Preheat a baking sheet in the oven at 230°C/450°F/Gas 8. Peel, core and slice the fruit. Quickly combine in a bowl with one-third of the sugar, the cornflour, salt, lemon rind and juice, and the raisins.

4 For the crumble topping, combine the remaining sugar, flour, cinnamon and butter in a bowl. Rub in until the mixture resembles coarse breadcrumbs. Spoon the filling into the pastry case. Sprinkle the crumbs over the top.

5 Bake on the baking sheet for 10 minutes, then reduce the heat to 180°C/350°F/Gas 4. Cover the pie loosely with foil and bake for a further 35–40 minutes.

Chocolate Energy 357kcal/1493kJ; Protein 4.8g; Carbohydrate 39.5g, of which sugars 25.1g; Fat 21.1g, of which saturates 12.4g; Cholesterol 114mg; Calcium 68mg; Fibre 2.2g; Sodium 106mg.
Crumble Energy 390kcal/1639kJ; Protein 3.3g; Carbohydrate 61.3g, of which sugars 39.9g; Fat 16.3g, of which saturates 8.2g; Cholesterol 28mg; Calcium 65mg; Fibre 3.1g; Sodium 190mg.

Chocolate Lemon Tart

The unusual chocolate pastry is simple to make and complements the tangy lemon filling superbly in this rich tart, generously topped with chocolate curls.

Serves 8–10

245g/8³/₄oz/1¹/₄ cups caster (superfine) sugar
6 eggs
grated rind of 2 lemons
160ml/5¹/₂fl oz/generous ²/₃ cup fresh lemon juice
160ml/5¹/₂fl oz/generous ²/₃ cup whipping cream
chocolate curls, to decorate

For the pastry

180g/6¹/₄oz/generous 1¹/₂ cups plain (all-purpose) flour
30ml/2 tbsp unsweetened cocoa powder
25g/1oz/¹/₄ cup icing (confectioners') sugar
2.5ml/¹/₂ tsp salt
115g/4oz/¹/₂ cup cold butter, diced
15ml/1 tbsp water

1 Grease a 25cm/10in flan tin (tart pan). To make the pastry, sift the flour, cocoa powder, icing sugar and salt into a bowl. Set aside.

2 Melt the butter or margarine and water in a large pan over a low heat.

3 Pour over the flour mixture and stir until the dough is smooth.

4 Press the dough evenly over the base and sides of the flan tin. Chill while preparing the filling.

5 Place a baking sheet on the top shelf of the oven and preheat to 190°C/375°F/Gas 5.

6 Whisk the sugar and eggs until the sugar is dissolved. Add the lemon rind and juice, and mix well. Add the cream.

7 Pour the filling into the pastry case and bake on the hot baking sheet until the filling is set, about 20–25 minutes.

8 Leave the tart on a wire rack to cool completely, then decorate with chocolate curls.

Kiwi Ricotta Cheese Tart

This rich tart makes an elegant dinner-party dessert.

Serves 8

75g/3oz/¹/₂ cup blanched almonds, ground
130g/4¹/₂oz/scant ³/₄ cup caster (superfine) sugar
900g/2lb/4 cups ricotta cheese
250ml/8fl oz/1 cup whipping cream
1 egg and 3 egg yolks
15ml/1 tbsp plain (all-purpose) flour
pinch of salt
30ml/2 tbsp rum
grated rind of 1 lemon
30ml/2 tbsp lemon juice
30ml/2 tbsp honey
5 kiwi fruit

For the pastry

150g/5oz/1¹/₄ cups plain (all-purpose) flour
15ml/1 tbsp caster (superfine) sugar
2.5ml/¹/₂ tsp salt
2.5ml/¹/₂ tsp baking powder
75g/3oz/6 tbsp butter
1 egg yolk
45–60ml/3–4 tbsp whipping cream

1 Mix the flour, sugar, salt and baking powder in a bowl. Add the butter and rub in. Mix in the egg yolk and mix to bind the pastry. Wrap in clear film (plastic wrap) and chill for 30 minutes.

2 Preheat the oven to 220°C/425°F/Gas 7. On a lightly floured surface, roll out the dough to a 3mm/¹/₈in thickness. Use to line a 23cm/9in springform cake tin (pan). Prick the pastry all over with a fork. Line with baking parchment and fill with dried beans. Bake for 10 minutes. Remove the paper and beans and bake for another 6–8 minutes. Reduce the oven temperature to 180°C/350°F/Gas 4.

3 Mix the almonds with 15ml/1 tbsp of the sugar. Beat the ricotta until creamy then add the cream, egg, yolks, remaining sugar, flour, salt, rum, lemon rind and 30ml/2 tbsp lemon juice. Mix well, add the almonds and mix in. Pour into the pastry case and bake for 1 hour, until golden. Cool and chill.

4 Mix the honey and remaining lemon juice. Halve the kiwi fruit lengthways then slice. Arrange over the tart and brush with the honey glaze.

Chocolate Energy 368kcal/1540kJ; Protein 6.5g; Carbohydrate 43.1g, of which sugars 29g; Fat 20.1g, of which saturates 11.4g; Cholesterol 155mg; Calcium 72mg; Fibre 0.9g; Sodium 245mg.
Kiwi Energy 688kcal/2865kJ; Protein 17.8g; Carbohydrate 47g, of which sugars 30.9g; Fat 48g, of which saturates 25.9g; Cholesterol 231mg; Calcium 109mg; Fibre 2.1g; Sodium 84mg.

Lime Tart

Fresh limes make a tasty filling for a tart, but you can use lemons instead of limes, with yellow food colouring, if you prefer.

Serves 8
3 large egg yolks
400g/14oz can sweetened condensed milk
15ml/1 tbsp grated lime rind
120ml/4fl oz/1/2 cup fresh lime juice
green food colouring (optional)
120ml/4fl oz/1/2 cup whipping cream

For the base
115g/4oz/11/3 cups crushed digestive cookies (graham crackers)
65g/21/2oz/5 tbsp butter or margarine, melted

1 Preheat the oven to 180°C/350°F/Gas 4. To make the base, place the crushed cookies in a bowl and add the butter or margarine. Mix well to combine.

2 Press the mixture evenly over the base and sides of a 23cm/9in pie dish. Bake for 8 minutes, then cool.

3 Beat the egg yolks until thick. Beat in the condensed milk, lime rind and juice and green food colouring, if using. Pour into the pastry case and chill until set, about 4 hours.

4 To serve, whip the cream. Pipe a line of cream around the edge of the tart and then pipe a lattice pattern over the top, or spoon dollops around the edge if you only have enough time to make a quick topping.

Cook's Tip
Crushed cookies make a useful base for all kinds of tarts. You can put the cookies into a food processor and pulse it to make them into crumbs, or put them into a large plastic bag and use a rolling pin to roll over the bag. Make the crumbs as fine or as coarse as you like. There is no need to cook the base if you want to use it for an uncooked cold filling; the case can just be chilled.

Fruit Tartlets

Glazed fresh fruit on cream and nestled in an individual tart just screams warm summer days. You could make one large fruit tart for an elegant dessert, if you like.

Makes 8
175ml/6fl oz/3/4 cup redcurrant jelly
15ml/1 tbsp fresh lemon juice
175ml/6fl oz/3/4 cup whipping cream
675g/11/2lb fresh fruit, such as strawberries, raspberries, kiwi fruit, peaches, grapes or currants, peeled and sliced as necessary

For the pastry
150g/5oz/10 tbsp cold butter, diced
65g/21/2oz/generous 1/4 cup soft dark brown sugar
45ml/3 tbsp unsweetened cocoa powder
200g/7oz/13/4 cups plain (all-purpose) flour
1 egg white

1 To make the pastry, melt the butter, brown sugar and cocoa in a large pan over a low heat. Remove from the heat and sift over the flour. Stir, then add enough egg white to bind the dough. Form into a ball, wrap in clear film (plastic wrap), and chill for 30 minutes.

2 Grease eight 8cm/3in tartlet tins (pans). Roll out the pastry between two sheets of baking parchment. Stamp out eight 10cm/4in rounds with a fluted cookie cutter.

3 Line the tartlet tins with the chilled pastry and prick the bases with a fork. Chill for a further 15 minutes. Preheat the oven to 180°C/350°F/Gas 4.

4 Bake the pastry cases until firm, about 20–25 minutes. Cool, then turn out of the tins.

5 Melt the redcurrant jelly with the lemon juice, and brush over the tartlet bases. Whip the cream and spread thinly in the tartlet cases. Arrange the fresh fruit on top. Brush with the jelly glaze and serve when the glaze has set.

Lime Energy 373kcal/1558kJ; Protein 6.6g; Carbohydrate 38.1g, of which sugars 30.2g; Fat 22.6g, of which saturates 13g; Cholesterol 133mg; Calcium 178mg; Fibre 0.3g; Sodium 215mg.
Fruit Energy 437kcal/1828kJ; Protein 5.2g; Carbohydrate 49.5g, of which sugars 29.8g; Fat 25.6g, of which saturates 15.9g; Cholesterol 63mg; Calcium 80mg; Fibre 2.4g; Sodium 196mg.

Creamy Banana Pie

Do not prepare the topping for this pie too soon before serving or the banana slices will discolour.

Serves 6
200g/7oz/2¼ cups finely crushed ginger cookies
65g/2½oz/5 tbsp butter or margarine, melted
2.5ml/ ½ tsp freshly grated nutmeg or ground cinnamon
175g/6oz/1 ripe banana, mashed

350g/12oz/1½ cups cream cheese, at room temperature
50ml/generous 3 tbsp thick natural (plain) yogurt or sour cream
45ml/3 tbsp dark rum or 5ml/1 tsp vanilla extract

For the topping
250ml/8fl oz/1 cup whipping cream
3–4 bananas

1 Preheat the oven to 190°C/375°F/Gas 5. For the crust, combine the crushed cookies, butter or margarine and grated nutmeg or ground cinnamon. Mix together thoroughly with a wooden spoon.

2 Press the cookie mixture into a 23cm/9in pie dish, building up thick sides with a neat edge. Bake the crust for 5 minutes, then leave to cool.

3 Beat the mashed bananas with the cream cheese. Fold in the yogurt or sour cream and rum or vanilla extract. Spread the filling in the cookie case. Chill for at least 4 hours or preferably overnight.

4 To make the topping, whip the cream until soft peaks form. Spread over the pie filling. Slice the bananas and arrange on top in a decorative pattern. Serve immediately.

> **Variation**
> As banana slices will discolour very quickly, for the decorative top you could use thinly sliced strawberries instead. They will complement the banana cream filling perfectly.

Red Berry Sponge Tart

When soft berry fruits are in season, serve this delicious tart warm, with scoops of vanilla ice cream.

Serves 4
450g/1lb/4 cups soft berry fruits, such as raspberries, blackberries, blackcurrants, redcurrants, strawberries and blueberries

2 eggs
50g/2oz/¼ cup caster (superfine) sugar, plus extra to taste (optional)
15ml/1 tbsp plain (all-purpose) flour
75g/3oz/¾ cup ground almonds
vanilla ice cream, to serve

1 Preheat the oven to 190°C/375°F/Gas 5. Grease and line a 23cm/9in pie plate with baking parchment.

2 Sprinkle the fruit in the base of the plate with a little sugar if the fruits are tart.

3 Beat the eggs and sugar together for 3–4 minutes, or until they leave a thick trail across the surface.

4 Combine the flour and almonds in a bowl, then carefully fold into the egg mixture with a metal spatula, retaining as much air as possible.

5 Spread the sponge mixture evenly on top of the fruit base, bake in the preheated oven for 15 minutes, then turn out on to a serving plate and serve warm.

> **Variation**
> For a more substantial tart, line the pie plate, or use a flan tin (tart pan), with 350g/12oz shortcrust pastry. Line the pastry with baking parchment and fill with baking beans. Bake the crust for 15 minutes and then remove the paper and beans and bake for 10 minutes more. Add the fruit as step 1 and continue with the recipe.

Banana Energy 753kcal/3128kJ; Protein 6.2g; Carbohydrate 50.4g, of which sugars 33.8g; Fat 58.1g, of which saturates 35.6g; Cholesterol 122mg; Calcium 148mg; Fibre 1.5g; Sodium 369mg.
Sponge Tart Energy 195kcal/816kJ; Protein 6.7g; Carbohydrate 19.2g, of which sugars 16.5g; Fat 10.7g, of which saturates 1.3g; Cholesterol 76mg; Calcium 71mg; Fibre 2.2g; Sodium 36mg.

Chocolate Cheesecake Tart

You can use all digestive cookies (graham crackers) for the base of this tart, if you prefer.

Serves 8
350g/12oz/1½ cups cream cheese
60ml/4 tbsp whipping cream
225g/8oz/generous 1 cup caster (superfine) sugar
50g/2oz/½ cup unsweetened cocoa powder

2.5ml/½ tsp ground cinnamon
3 eggs
whipped cream and chocolate curls, to decorate

For the base
75g/3oz/1 cup crushed digestive cookies (graham crackers)
40g/1½oz/scant 1 cup crushed amaretti
75g/3oz/6 tbsp butter, melted

1 Preheat a baking sheet in the oven at 180°C/350°F/Gas 4.

2 To make the base, mix the crushed cookies and melted butter in a bowl.

3 Press the mixture over the base and sides of a 23cm/9in pie dish. Bake for 8 minutes. Leave to cool, but keep the oven on.

4 Beat the cream cheese and cream together until smooth. Beat in the sugar, cocoa and cinnamon until blended.

5 Add the eggs, one at a time, beating just enough to blend.

6 Pour into the cookie base and bake on the baking sheet for 25–30 minutes. The filling will sink down as it cools.

7 Decorate the top of the tart with whipped cream and chocolate curls.

Chocolate Curls
For short chocolate curls, run a vegetable peeler against the long side of a bar of chocolate. To make long curls, see p251.

Frozen Strawberry Tart

When it's a hot summer's day and you want a cooling dessert, but don't fancy ice cream, what could be better than this frozen tart?

Serves 8
225g/8oz/1 cup cream cheese
250ml/8fl oz/1 cup sour cream
500g/1¼lb/5 cups strawberries

For the base
65g/2½oz/5 tbsp butter
115g/4oz/1⅓ cups digestive cookies (graham crackers)
15ml/1 tbsp caster (superfine) sugar

1 To make the base, melt the butter in a large pan. Crush the cookies with a rolling pin, then add to the melted butter. Stir in the sugar and combine thoroughly.

2 Press the mixture over the base and sides of a 23cm/9in pie dish. Freeze until firm.

3 Blend together the cream cheese and sour cream in a large bowl. Reserve 90ml/6 tbsp of the strawberries on one side, and add the remainder to the cream cheese mixture.

4 Scrape the filling into the cookie base and freeze until it is firm, about 6–8 hours.

5 To serve, allow the tart to thaw a little in the refrigerator for 20 minutes and then spoon some of the reserved strawberries on top.

Cook's Tips
• *Raspberries will work equally well instead of strawberries for this tart.*
• *This is an ideal tart to make in advance, as it will be stored in the freezer. If you do this you will need to buy a few extra strawberries to decorate the top when you are ready to serve it.*

Chocolate Energy 514kcal/2139kJ; Protein 6.1g; Carbohydrate 40.8g, of which sugars 32.7g; Fat 37.5g, of which saturates 22.3g; Cholesterol 145mg; Calcium 98mg; Fibre 1g; Sodium 350mg.
Strawberry Energy 339kcal/1404kJ; Protein 3.2g; Carbohydrate 16.8g, of which sugars 8.9g; Fat 29.2g, of which saturates 17.8g; Cholesterol 69mg; Calcium 82mg; Fibre 1g; Sodium 237mg.

Tarte Tatin

A special *tarte tatin* tin is ideal, but an ovenproof frying pan can be used quite successfully.

Serves 8–10
225g/8oz puff or shortcrust pastry, thawed if frozen
10–12 large eating apples
30ml/2 tbsp lemon juice
115g/4oz/½ cup cold butter, diced
115g/4oz/generous ½ cup caster (superfine) sugar
2.5ml/½ tsp ground cinnamon
crème fraîche or whipped cream, to serve

1 On a lightly floured surface, roll out the pastry to a 28cm/11in round less than 5mm/¼in thick. Transfer to a lightly floured baking sheet and chill. Peel, halve and core the apples, and sprinkle with lemon juice.

2 In a 25cm/10in *tarte tatin* tin (pan) or a small frying pan that can go into the oven, cook the butter, sugar and cinnamon until the butter has melted and the sugar has dissolved. Cook for 6–8 minutes, or until the mixture is a medium caramel colour. Remove from the heat and arrange the apple halves, standing on their edges, in the tin.

3 Return the tin to the heat and simmer for 20–25 minutes, or until the apples are tender and coloured. Remove from the heat and cool slightly.

4 Preheat the oven to 230°C/450°F/Gas 8. Place the pastry over the apples and tuck the edges inside the tin around the apples. Pierce the pastry in two or three places, then bake for 25–30 minutes, or until the pastry is golden and the filling is bubbling. Cool in the tin for 10–15 minutes.

5 To serve, run a sharp knife around the edge of the tin to loosen the pastry. Cover with a serving plate and carefully invert the tin and plate together. It is best to do this over a sink in case any caramel drips. Lift off the tin and loosen any apples that stick with a metal spatula. Serve the tart warm with crème fraîche or whipped cream.

Rich Chocolate Pie

A delicious rich and creamy pie generously decorated with chocolate curls.

Serves 8
75g/3oz plain (semisweet) chocolate
50g/2oz/¼ cup butter or margarine
45ml/3 tbsp golden (light corn) syrup
3 eggs, beaten
150g/5oz/¾ cup caster (superfine) sugar
5ml/1 tsp vanilla extract
115g/4oz milk chocolate
475ml/16fl oz/2 cups whipping cream

For the pastry
165g/5½oz/1⅓ cups plain (all-purpose) flour
2.5ml/½ tsp salt
115g/4oz/⅔ cup lard or white cooking fat (shortening), diced
30–45ml/2–3 tbsp iced water

1 Preheat the oven to 220°C/425°F/Gas 7. To make the pastry, sift the flour and salt into a bowl. Rub in the fat until the mixture resembles coarse breadcrumbs. Add water until the pastry forms a ball.

2 Roll out the pastry and use to line a 20–23cm/8–9in flan tin (tart pan). Flute the edge. Prick the base and sides of the pastry case with a fork. Bake until lightly browned, about 10–15 minutes. Cool in the tin on a wire rack.

3 Reduce the oven temperature to 180°C/350°F/Gas 4. In the top of a double boiler or in a heatproof bowl over a pan of simmering water, melt the plain chocolate, the butter or margarine, and the golden syrup. Remove from the heat and stir in the eggs, sugar and vanilla extract. Pour the chocolate mixture into the pastry case. Bake until the filling is set, about 35–40 minutes. Cool in the tin on a wire rack.

4 For the decoration, use the heat of your hands to soften the milk chocolate slightly. Use a swivel-headed vegetable peeler to shave off short, wide curls. Chill until needed.

5 Before serving, lightly whip the cream until soft peaks form. Spread the cream over the surface of the chocolate filling. Decorate with the milk chocolate curls.

Tart Energy 236kcal/986kJ; Protein 1.6g; Carbohydrate 25.8g, of which sugars 17.7g; Fat 15g, of which saturates 6g; Cholesterol 25mg; Calcium 24mg; Fibre 1g; Sodium 141mg.
Pie Energy 712kcal/2962kJ; Protein 7.2g; Carbohydrate 55.8g, of which sugars 40g; Fat 52.7g, of which saturates 28.9g; Cholesterol 164mg; Calcium 121mg; Fibre 1g; Sodium 109mg.

Red Berry Tart with Lemon Cream

This jewel-like flan filled with summer fruits is best filled just before serving so that the pastry remains mouth-wateringly crisp.

Serves 6–8
200g/7oz/scant 1 cup cream
   cheese, softened
45ml/3 tbsp lemon curd
grated rind and juice of 1 lemon
icing (confectioners') sugar,
   to taste (optional)
225g/8oz/2 cups mixed red
   berry fruits
45ml/3 tbsp redcurrant jelly

For the pastry
150g/5oz/1¼ cups plain
   (all-purpose) flour
25g/1oz/¼ cup cornflour
   (cornstarch)
30g/1½oz/scant ⅓ cup icing
   (confectioners') sugar
90g/3½oz/7 tbsp cold
   butter, diced
5ml/1 tsp vanilla extract
2 egg yolks, beaten

1 To make the pastry, sift the flour, cornflour and sugar together. Rub in the butter until the mixture resembles breadcrumbs.

2 Beat the vanilla extract into the egg yolks, then stir into the flour mixture to make a firm dough. Add cold water if the dough is too dry.

3 Roll out the pastry and use it to line a 23cm/9in round flan tin (tart pan). Trim the edges. Prick the base with a fork and leave to rest in the refrigerator for 30 minutes.

4 Preheat the oven to 200°C/400°F/Gas 6. Line the flan with baking parchment and fill with baking beans. Place on a baking sheet and bake for 20 minutes, removing the paper and beans after 15 minutes. Leave to cool, then remove the pastry case from the flan tin.

5 Cream the cheese, lemon curd, and lemon rind and juice, adding icing sugar if you wish. Spread the mixture into the base of the flan. Top with the mixed red berry fruits. Warm the redcurrant jelly and trickle over the fruits just before serving.

Peach and Almond Tart

The delicate flavour of almond goes beautifully with ripe summer peaches.

Serves 8–10
115g/4oz/⅔ cup blanched almonds
15g/½oz/2 tbsp plain
   (all-purpose) flour
90g/3½oz/7 tbsp unsalted
   (sweet) butter
115g/4oz/1 cup, plus 30ml/2 tbsp
   caster (superfine) sugar
1 egg, plus 1 egg yolk

1.5ml/¼ tsp vanilla extract, or
   10ml/2 tsp rum
4 large ripe peaches, peeled

For the pastry
185g/6½oz/generous 1½ cups
   plain (all-purpose) flour
2.5ml/½ tsp salt
90g/3½oz/scant ¼ cup cold
   unsalted (sweet) butter, diced
1 egg yolk
10–45ml/2–3 tbsp iced water

1 To make the pastry, sift the flour and salt into a bowl. Rub in the butter until the mixture resembles coarse breadcrumbs.

2 Stir in the egg yolk and enough water to bind the pastry. Gather into a ball, wrap and chill for 20 minutes. Preheat a baking sheet in the centre of a 200°C/400°F/Gas 6 oven.

3 Roll out the pastry 3mm/⅛in thick. Transfer to a 25cm/10in pie dish. Trim the edge, prick the base and chill.

4 Grind the almonds with the flour. With an electric mixer, cream the butter and 115g/4oz/scant ¾ cup of the sugar until light and fluffy. Gradually beat in the egg and yolk. Stir in the almonds and vanilla or rum. Spread in the pastry case.

5 Halve the peaches and remove the stones (pits). Cut the fruit crossways in thin slices and fan out. Transfer to the tart, placing the fruit on top of the almond cream and arranging like the spokes of a wheel.

6 Bake until the pastry browns, about 10–15 minutes. Lower the heat to 180°C/350°F/Gas 4 and bake until the almond cream sets, about 15 minutes more. 10 minutes before the end of the cooking time, sprinkle with the remaining sugar.

Red Berry Energy 253kcal/1059kJ; Protein 3.6g; Carbohydrate 30.5g, of which sugars 12g; Fat 13.8g, of which saturates 7.9g; Cholesterol 75mg; Calcium 65mg; Fibre 0.9g; Sodium 87mg.
Peach Energy 376kcal/1569kJ; Protein 6.3g; Carbohydrate 33.4g, of which sugars 17.5g; Fat 24.8g, of which saturates 11.4g; Cholesterol 102mg; Calcium 78mg; Fibre 2.4g; Sodium 134mg.

Pear & Almond Cream Tart

Fanned pears, glazed with brandy, rest on a light almond filling. This tart is equally successful made with other orchard fruits such as nectarines, peaches, apricots or apples.

Serves 6
350g/12oz shortcrust or sweet
    shortcrust pastry, thawed
    if frozen
3 firm pears
lemon juice
15ml/1 tbsp peach brandy or
    cold water
60ml/4 tbsp peach jam, sieved

For the filling
90g/3½oz/generous ½ cup
    blanched whole almonds
50g/2oz/¼ cup caster
    (superfine) sugar
65g/2½oz/5 tbsp butter
1 egg, plus 1 egg white
a few drops of almond extract

1 Roll out the pastry and use to line a 23cm/9in flan tin. Chill in the refrigerator while you make the filling.

2 For the filling, put the almonds and sugar in a food processor or blender and pulse until finely ground but not pasty. Add the butter and process until creamy, then add the egg, egg white and almond extract, and mix well.

3 Preheat a baking sheet in the oven at 190°C/375°F/Gas 5.

4 Peel the pears, halve them, remove the cores and rub with lemon juice. Put the pear halves, cut side down, on a board and slice thinly crossways, keeping the slices together.

5 Pour the filling into the pastry case. Slide a metal spatula under one pear half and press the top to fan out the slices. Transfer to the tart, placing the fruit on the filling like the spokes of a wheel.

6 Bake the tart on the baking sheet for 50–55 minutes, or until the filling is set and well browned. Cool on a wire rack.

7 Heat the brandy or water with the jam. Brush over the top of the hot tart to glaze. Serve at room temperature.

Lemon Tart

This tart, a classic of France, has a refreshing tangy flavour.

Serves 8–10
350g/12oz shortcrust or sweet
    shortcrust pastry, thawed
    if frozen
grated rind of 2 or 3 lemons
150ml/¼ pint/⅔ cup freshly
    squeezed lemon juice
90g/3½oz/½ cup caster
    (superfine) sugar
60ml/4 tbsp crème fraîche or
    double (heavy) cream
4 eggs, plus 3 egg yolks
icing (confectioners') sugar,
    for dusting

1 Preheat a baking sheet in the oven to 190°C/375°F/Gas 5.

2 Roll out the pastry and use to line a 23cm/9in flan tin (tart pan). Prick the base with a fork, line with foil and fill with baking beans.

3 Bake for 15 minutes, or until the edges are dry. Remove the foil and beans, and bake for a further 5–7 minutes, or until golden.

4 Beat together the lemon rind, juice and caster sugar, then gradually add the crème fraîche or double cream, beating after each addition until well blended.

5 Beat in the eggs, one at a time, then beat in the egg yolks.

6 Pour the filling into the baked pastry case. Return it to the oven and bake for about 15–20 minutes, or until the filling is set. If the pastry begins to brown too much, cover the edges with foil.

7 Leave the tart to cool, and dust lightly with icing sugar before serving.

> **Variation**
> *This tart would also taste great made with oranges.*

Pear Energy 544kcal/2271kJ; Protein 8.4g; Carbohydrate 51.5g, of which sugars 24.4g; Fat 34.7g, of which saturates 11.7g; Cholesterol 63mg; Calcium 106mg; Fibre 3.9g; Sodium 330mg.
Lemon Energy 268kcal/1122kJ; Protein 5.6g; Carbohydrate 27g, of which sugars 10.9g; Fat 16.1g, of which saturates 5.8g; Cholesterol 148mg; Calcium 57mg; Fibre 0.7g; Sodium 173mg.

Maple Walnut Tart

Makes sure you use 100 per cent pure maple syrup in this decadent tart for the truly authentic flavour.

Serves 8
3 eggs
1.5ml/¼ tsp salt
50g/2oz/¼ cup caster (superfine) sugar
50g/2oz/¼ cup butter, melted
250ml/8fl oz/1 cup pure maple syrup
115g/4oz/1 cup chopped walnuts
whipped cream, to decorate

For the pastry
65g/2½oz/9 tbsp plain (all-purpose) flour
65g/2½oz/9 tbsp wholemeal (whole-wheat) flour
1.5ml/¼ tsp salt
50g/2oz/4 tbsp cold butter, diced
40g/1½oz/3 tbsp cold white cooking fat (shortening) or lard, diced
1 egg yolk

1 To make the pastry, mix the plain and wholemeal flours and salt in a bowl. Add the butter and white cooking fat and rub in until the mixture resembles coarse breadcrumbs.

2 Stir in the egg yolk and 30–45ml/2–3 tbsp iced water to bind. Form into a ball, wrap in clear film (plastic wrap) and chill for 20 minutes. Preheat a baking sheet in the oven to 220°C/425°F/Gas 7.

3 Roll out the pastry and use to line a 23cm/9in pie dish. Use the trimmings to stamp out small heart shapes. Arrange on the pastry case rim with a little water.

4 Prick the pastry base with a fork, line with baking parchment and fill with baking beans. Bake for 10 minutes. Remove the paper and beans and bake until golden, about 3–6 minutes more.

5 Whisk together the eggs, salt and sugar. Stir in the butter and maple syrup. Set the pastry case on a baking sheet. Pour in the filling, then sprinkle with the walnuts.

6 Bake until just set, about 35 minutes. Cool on a wire rack. Decorate with piped whipped cream.

Pecan Tart

Serve this tart warm, accompanied by ice cream or whipped cream, if you wish.

Serves 8
3 eggs
pinch of salt
200g/7oz/scant 1 cup soft dark brown sugar
120ml/4fl oz/½ cup golden (light corn) syrup
30ml/2 tbsp fresh lemon juice
75g/3oz/6 tbsp butter, melted
150g/5oz/1¼ cups chopped pecan nuts
50g/2oz/⅓ cup pecan nut halves

For the pastry
175g/6oz/1½ cups plain (all-purpose) flour
15ml/1 tbsp caster (superfine) ugar
5ml/1 tsp baking powder
2.5ml/½ tsp salt
75g/3oz/6 tbsp cold unsalted (sweet) butter, diced
1 egg yolk
45–60ml/3–4 tbsp whipping cream

1 To make the pastry, sift together the flour, caster sugar, baking powder and salt in a bowl. Add the butter and rub in using your fingertips or a pastry cutter until the mixture resembles coarse breadcrumbs.

2 Blend the egg yolk and whipping cream, and stir into the flour mixture.

3 Form the pastry into a ball, then roll out and use to line a 23cm/9in pie dish. Trim and flute the edge neatly and chill for 20 minutes.

4 Preheat a baking sheet in the oven at 200°C/400°F/Gas 6. Lightly whisk the eggs and salt. Mix in the sugar, syrup, lemon juice and butter. Stir in the chopped pecan nuts.

5 Pour into the pastry case and arrange the pecan nut halves in concentric circles on top.

6 Bake on the baking sheet for 10 minutes. Reduce the heat to 160°C/325°F/Gas 3 and bake for 25 minutes more.

Maple Energy 442kcal/1846kJ; Protein 6.8g; Carbohydrate 43.3g, of which sugars 32g; Fat 28.1g, of which saturates 10.2g; Cholesterol 128mg; Calcium 52mg; Fibre 1.5g; Sodium 190mg.
Pecan Energy 587kcal/2449kJ; Protein 7.5g; Carbohydrate 56.7g, of which sugars 39.6g; Fat 38.3g, of which saturates 13.4g; Cholesterol 142mg; Calcium 82mg; Fibre 1.9g; Sodium 185mg.

Velvety Mocha Tart

A creamy smooth filling tops a dark light-textured base in this wondrous dessert decorated with cream and chocolate-coated coffee beans.

Serves 8

10ml/2 tsp instant espresso coffee
30ml/2 tbsp hot water
175g/6oz plain (semisweet) chocolate
25g/1oz bitter cooking chocolate

350ml/12fl oz/1½ cups whipping cream, slightly warmed
120ml/4fl oz/½ cup whipped cream, to decorate
chocolate-coated coffee beans, to decorate

For the base

150g/5oz/2½ cups crushed chocolate wafers
30ml/2 tbsp caster (superfine) sugar
65g/2½oz/5 tbsp butter, melted

1 To make the base, combine the crushed chocolate wafers with the sugar and butter in a bowl.

2 Press the mixture over the base and sides of a 23cm/9in pie dish. Chill.

3 Dissolve the coffee in the water. Set aside to cool.

4 Melt the plain and bitter chocolates in the top of a double boiler or in a heatproof bowl over a pan of simmering water.

5 Once the chocolate has melted, remove from the double boiler and set the base of the pan in cold water to cool.

6 Whip the cream until light and fluffy. Add the coffee and whip until the cream just holds its shape.

7 When the chocolate is at room temperature, fold it gently into the cream.

8 Pour into the cookie base and chill until firm. Decorate with piped whipped cream and chocolate-coated coffee beans just before serving.

Coconut Cream Tart

Toasted coconut tops this creamy, unusual tart.

Serves 8

150g/5oz/generous 1½ cups desiccated (dry unsweetened shredded) coconut
150g/5oz/¾ cup caster (superfine) sugar
25g/1oz/¼ cup cornflour (cornstarch)
1.5ml/¼ tsp salt
600ml/1 pint/2½ cups milk
50ml/2fl oz whipping cream

2 egg yolks
25g/1oz/2 tbsp unsalted (sweet) butter
10ml/2 tsp vanilla extract

For the pastry

150g/5oz/1¼ cups plain (all-purpose) flour
1.5ml/¼ tsp salt
45g/1½oz/3 tbsp cold butter, diced
25g/1oz/3 tbsp cold vegetable fat (shortening) or lard
30–45ml/2–3 tbsp iced water

1 To make the pastry, sift the flour and salt into a bowl, add the fats and rub in until the mixture resembles coarse breadcrumbs. With a fork, stir in just enough water to bind the pastry. Gather into a ball, wrap in clear film (plastic wrap) and chill for 20 minutes. Preheat the oven to 220°C/425°F/Gas 7.

2 Roll out the pastry 3mm/⅛in thick. Line a 23cm/9in pie dish. Trim and flute the edges, prick the base, line with baking parchment and fill with baking beans. Bake for 10–12 minutes. Remove the paper and beans, reduce the heat to 180°C/350°F/Gas 4 and bake until brown, 10–15 minutes.

3 Spread 50g/2oz/⅔ cup of the coconut on a baking sheet and toast in the oven until golden, 6–8 minutes. Put the sugar, cornflour and salt in a pan. In a bowl, whisk the milk, cream and egg yolks. Add the egg mixture to the pan.

4 Cook over a low heat, stirring, until the mixture comes to the boil. Boil for 1 minute, then remove from the heat. Add the butter, vanilla extract and remaining coconut.

5 Pour into the pre-baked pastry case. When cool, sprinkle toasted coconut in a ring in the centre.

Mocha Energy 507kcal/2103kJ; Protein 3.6g; Carbohydrate 30.3g, of which sugars 27g; Fat 42.1g, of which saturates 26.2g; Cholesterol 83mg; Calcium 71mg; Fibre 0.8g; Sodium 83mg.
Coconut Energy 400kcal/1671kJ; Protein 6.2g; Carbohydrate 39.6g, of which sugars 23.4g; Fat 25.2g, of which saturates 17g; Cholesterol 78mg; Calcium 140mg; Fibre 2.9g; Sodium 101mg.

Orange Tart

If you like oranges, this is the dessert for you!

Serves 8

200g/7oz/1 cup caster (superfine) sugar
250ml/8fl oz/1 cup fresh orange juice, strained
2 large navel oranges
165g/5½oz/scant 1 cup whole blanched almonds
50g/2oz/¼ cup butter
1 egg

15ml/1 tbsp plain (all-purpose) flour
45ml/3 tbsp apricot jam

For the pastry

210g/7½oz/scant 2 cups plain (all-purpose) flour
2.5ml/½ tsp salt
50g/2oz/¼ cup cold butter, diced
40g/1½oz/3 tbsp cold margarine, diced
45–60ml/3–4 tbsp iced water

1 To make the pastry, sift the flour and salt into a bowl. Add the butter and margarine, and rub in using your fingertips or a pastry cutter until the mixture resembles coarse breadcrumbs. Stir in just enough water to bind the dough. Wrap and chill for 20 minutes.

2 Roll out the pastry to a 5mm/¼ in thickness. Use to line a 20cm/8in tart tin. Trim and chill until needed.

3 In a pan, combine 165g/5½oz/¾ cup of the sugar and the orange juice and boil until thick and syrupy. Cut the unpeeled oranges into 5mm/¼in slices. Add to the syrup. Simmer gently for 10 minutes. Put on a wire rack to dry. When cool, cut in half. Reserve the syrup. Place a baking sheet in the oven and heat to 200°C/400°F/Gas 6.

4 Grind the almonds finely in a blender or food processor. Cream the butter and remaining sugar until light and fluffy. Beat in the egg and 30ml/2 tbsp of the orange syrup. Stir in the almonds and flour.

5 Melt the jam over a low heat, then brush over the pastry case. Pour in the almond mixture. Bake on the baking sheet until set, about 20 minutes, then cool. Arrange overlapping orange slices on top. Boil the remaining syrup until thick and brush over the top to glaze.

Raspberry Tart

A luscious tart of rich custard beneath juicy fresh raspberries.

Serves 8

4 egg yolks
65g/2½oz/generous ¼ cup caster (superfine) sugar
45ml/3 tbsp plain (all-purpose) flour
300ml/½ pint/1¼ cups milk
1.5ml/¼ tsp salt
2.5ml/½ tsp vanilla extract
450g/1lb/2⅔ cups fresh raspberries

75ml/5 tbsp redcurrant jelly
15ml/1 tbsp orange juice

For the pastry

185g/6½oz/1⅔ cups plain (all-purpose) flour
2.5ml/½ tsp baking powder
1.5ml/¼ tsp salt
15ml/1 tbsp sugar
grated rind of ½ orange
75g/3oz/6 tbsp cold butter, diced
1 egg yolk
45–60ml/3–4 tbsp whipping cream

1 To make the pastry, sift the flour, baking powder and salt into a bowl. Stir in the sugar and orange rind. Add the butter and rub in using your fingertips or a pastry cutter until the mixture resembles breadcrumbs. Stir in the egg yolk and cream to bind. Form into a ball, wrap in clear film (plastic wrap) and chill.

2 For the filling, beat the egg yolks and sugar until thick and creamy. Gradually stir in the flour. Bring the milk and salt just to the boil, then remove from the heat. Whisk into the egg yolk mixture, return to the pan and continue whisking over a medium-high heat until just bubbling. Cook for 3 minutes to thicken. Transfer to a bowl. Stir in the vanilla extract, then cover with baking parchment.

3 Preheat the oven to 200°C/400°F/Gas 6. Roll out the pastry and use to line a 25cm/10in pie dish. Prick the base with a fork, line with baking parchment and fill with baking beans. Bake for 15 minutes. Remove the paper and beans, and bake until golden, about 6–8 minutes more. Leave to cool.

4 Spread an even layer of the custard filling in the pastry case and arrange the raspberries on top. Melt the redcurrant jelly and orange juice in a pan and brush over the top to glaze.

Orange Energy 500kcal/2093kJ; Protein 8.6g; Carbohydrate 59.4g, of which sugars 37.4g; Fat 27g, of which saturates 7.7g; Cholesterol 50mg; Calcium 130mg; Fibre 3.1g; Sodium 137mg.
Raspberry Energy 323kcal/1359kJ; Protein 6.9g; Carbohydrate 44g, of which sugars 22.1g; Fat 14.6g, of which saturates 7.8g; Cholesterol 154mg; Calcium 126mg; Fibre 2.3g; Sodium 86mg.

Plum Pie

When the new season's plums are in the shops, treat someone special with this lightly spiced plum pie.

Serves 8
900g/2lb red or purple plums
grated rind of 1 lemon
15ml/1 tbsp fresh lemon juice
115–175g/4–6oz/generous ¹/₂–
　scant 1 cup caster
　(superfine) sugar
45ml/3 tbsp quick-cooking
　tapioca

1.5ml/¹/₄ tsp salt
2.5ml/¹/₂ tsp ground cinnamon
1.5ml/¹/₄ tsp freshly grated nutmeg

For the pastry
275g/10oz/2¹/₂ cups plain
　(all-purpose) flour
5ml/1 tsp salt
75g/3oz/6 tbsp cold butter, diced
50g/2oz/4 tbsp cold white cooking
　fat (shortening) or lard, diced
50–120ml/2–4fl oz/¹/₄–¹/₂ cup
　iced water
milk, for glazing

1 To make the pastry, sift the flour and salt into a bowl. Add the butter and fat and rub in with your fingertips or a pastry cutter until the mixture resembles coarse breadcrumbs.

2 Stir in just enough water to bind the pastry. Form into two balls, wrap in clear film (plastic wrap) and chill for 20 minutes.

3 Preheat a baking sheet in the oven at 220°C/425°F/Gas 7. Roll out a pastry ball and use to line a 23cm/9in pie dish.

4 Halve and stone (pit) the plums, and chop roughly. Mix the lemon rind and juice, the chopped plums, caster sugar, tapioca and salt together in a bowl and mix in the spices, then transfer to the pastry-lined pie dish.

5 Roll out the remaining pastry, place on a baking sheet lined with baking parchment, and stamp out four hearts. Transfer the pastry lid to the pie using the paper.

6 Trim the pastry to leave a 2cm/³/₄in overhang. Fold this under the pastry base and pinch to seal. Arrange the hearts on top. Brush with milk and bake for 15 minutes. Reduce the heat to 180°C/350°F/Gas 4 and bake for a further 30–35 minutes.

Lattice Berry Pie

Choose any berries you like for this handsome pie.

Serves 8
450g/1lb/about 4 cups berries,
　such as bilberries, blueberries
　and blackcurrants
115g/4oz/generous ¹/₂ cup caster
　(superfine) sugar
45ml/3 tbsp cornflour (cornstarch)
30ml/2 tbsp fresh lemon juice
25g/1oz/2 tbsp butter, diced

For the pastry
275g/10oz/2¹/₂ cups plain
　(all-purpose) flour
4ml/³/₄ tsp salt
115g/4oz/¹/₂ cup cold
　butter, diced
40g/1¹/₂oz/3 tbsp cold white
　cooking fat (shortening)
　or lard, diced
75–90ml/5–6 tbsp iced water
1 egg, beaten with 15ml/1 tbsp
　water, for glazing

1 To make the pastry, sift the flour and salt into a bowl. Add the butter and fat and rub in with your fingertips or a pastry cutter until the mixture resembles coarse breadcrumbs. Stir in just enough water to bind. Form into two balls, wrap in clear film (plastic wrap) and chill for 20 minutes.

2 Roll out one ball and use to line a 23cm/9in pie dish, leaving a 1cm/¹/₂in overhang. Brush the base with egg.

3 Mix the berries with the caster sugar, cornflour and lemon juice, reserving a few berries for decoration. Spoon this filling into the pastry case and dot with the butter. Brush egg around the pastry rim.

4 Preheat the oven to 220°C/425°F/Gas 7. Roll out the remaining pastry on a baking sheet lined with baking parchment. With a serrated pastry wheel, make 24 thin strips. Use the scraps to cut out leaf shapes, and mark veins.

5 Weave the strips in a close lattice and transfer to the pie. Seal the edges and trim. Arrange the leaves around the rim. Brush with egg and bake for 10 minutes.

6 Reduce the heat to 180°C/350°F/Gas 4 and bake the pie for a further 40–45 minutes. Decorate with the reserved berries.

Berry Energy 384kcal/1607kJ; Protein 3.9g; Carbohydrate 50.4g, of which sugars 19g; Fat 19.9g, of which saturates 11.2g; Cholesterol 42mg; Calcium 69mg; Fibre 1.7g; Sodium 114mg.
Plum Energy 360kcal/1516kJ; Protein 4.1g; Carbohydrate 57g, of which sugars 25.5g; Fat 14.5g, of which saturates 7.5g; Cholesterol 26mg; Calcium 73mg; Fibre 2.9g; Sodium 61mg.

Cakes & Gateaux

With so many mouthwatering recipes on offer, you may
find that you are spoilt for choice in this chapter. Tantalizing
tea-time treats include Spice Cake with Ginger Frosting,
Tangy Lemon Cake and One-stage Chocolate Sponge.
There are also plenty of sophisticated gateaux, including
St Clement's Cake, Coffee, Peach and Almond Daquoise,
or Black Forest Gateau.

Banana Ginger Parkin

The combination of banana and ginger give a new slant to the traditional recipe for this delicious cake.

Makes 16–20 squares
200g/7oz/1¾ cups plain (all-purpose) flour
10ml/2 tsp bicarbonate of soda (baking soda)
10ml/2 tsp ground ginger
150g/5oz/1¼ cups medium oatmeal
50g/2oz/¼ cup muscovado sugar (molasses)
75g/3oz/6 tbsp sunflower margarine
150g/5oz/3 tbsp golden (light corn) syrup
1 egg, beaten
3 ripe bananas, mashed
75g/3oz/¾ cup icing (confectioners') sugar
preserved stem ginger, to decorate (optional)

1 Preheat the oven to 160°C/325°F/Gas 3. Grease and line an 18 x 28cm/7 x 11in cake tin (pan).

2 Sift together the flour, bicarbonate of soda and ginger in a bowl, then stir in the oatmeal.

3 Melt the sugar, margarine and syrup in a pan over a low heat, then stir into the flour mixture.

4 Beat the egg and mashed bananas into the flour mixture until thoroughly combined. Spoon the mixture into the prepared tin and bake for about 1 hour, or until firm to the touch.

5 Leave the cake to cool in the tin for 5 minutes, then turn it out on to a wire rack and allow it to cool completely.

6 If you want to keep the cake for a few months, wrap it in foil and put it in an air-tight container without cutting it. If you want to eat it immediately, cut it into squares.

7 Make the icing when you want to serve the cake: sift the icing sugar into a bowl and stir in just enough water to make a smooth, runny icing. Drizzle the icing over each square of cake in a zigzag pattern and top with a piece of stem ginger, if you like.

Gooseberry Cake

This cake is delicious served warm with whipped cream.

Makes one 18cm/7in square cake
115g/4oz/½ cup butter
165g/5½oz/1⅓ cups self-raising (self-rising) flour
5ml/1 tsp baking powder
2 eggs, beaten
115g/4oz/generous ½ cup caster (superfine) sugar
5–10ml/1–2 tsp rose water
pinch of freshly grated nutmeg
115g/4oz jar gooseberries in syrup, drained, juice reserved
caster (superfine) sugar, to decorate
whipped cream, to serve

1 Preheat the oven to 180°C/350°F/Gas 4. Grease an 18cm/7in square cake tin (pan) and line the base and sides with baking parchment. Grease the paper.

2 Gently melt the butter in a pan, then transfer to a large bowl and allow to cool.

3 Sift together the flour and baking powder and add to the butter in the bowl.

4 Beat in the eggs, one at a time, the sugar, rose water and grated nutmeg, until you have a smooth batter.

5 Mix in 15–30ml/1–2 tbsp of the reserved gooseberry juice from the jar, then pour half of the batter mixture into the prepared tin. Sprinkle over the gooseberries and pour over the remaining batter mixture.

6 Bake for about 45 minutes, or until a skewer inserted into the centre of the cake comes out clean.

7 Leave in the tin for 5 minutes, then turn out on a wire rack, peel off the lining paper and allow to cool for a further 5 minutes.

8 Dredge with caster sugar and serve immediately with whipped cream, or leave the cake to cool completely before decorating.

Parkin Energy 157kcal/662kJ; Protein 2.4g; Carbohydrate 29.2g, of which sugars 15.8g; Fat 4.2g, of which saturates 0.7g; Cholesterol 10mg; Calcium 25mg; Fibre 1g; Sodium 57mg.
Gooseberry Energy 2080kcal/8719kJ; Protein 30.1g; Carbohydrate 263.9g, of which sugars 138.2g; Fat 108.1g, of which saturates 63.3g; Cholesterol 626mg; Calcium 392mg; Fibre 7.3g; Sodium 857mg.

Crunchy-topped Sponge Loaf

This light sponge makes a perfect tea-time treat.

Makes one 450g/1lb loaf
200g/7oz/scant 1 cup butter, softened
finely grated rind of 1 lemon
150g/5oz/5 tbsp caster (superfine) sugar
3 eggs
75g/3oz/²⁄₃ cup plain (all-purpose) flour, sifted

150g/5oz/1¼ cups self-raising (self-rising) flour, sifted

For the topping
45ml/3 tbsp clear honey
115g/4oz/²⁄₃ cup mixed (candied) peel
50g/2oz/½ cup flaked (sliced) almonds

1 Preheat the oven to 180°C/350°F/Gas 4. Grease and line a 450g/1lb loaf tin (pan) with baking parchment.

2 Beat together the butter, lemon rind and sugar until light and fluffy. Blend in the eggs, one at a time.

3 Sift together the flours, then stir into the egg mixture. Fill the loaf tin with the batter. Bake for 45 minutes, or until a skewer inserted into the centre comes out clean. Leave to cool in the tin for 5 minutes.

4 Turn the loaf out on to a wire rack, peel off the lining paper and leave to cool completely.

5 To make the topping, melt the honey with the mixed peel and almonds. Remove from the heat, stir briefly, then spread over the top of the loaf. Cool before serving.

Cook's Tip
This recipe uses chopped mixed (candied) peel for the topping. To make it extra-special it is worth buying some good quality peel from a delicatessen, as the flavour is far superior. The peel comes in large pieces, so chop it into smaller chunks.

Irish Whiskey Cake

Other whiskies could be used in this cake.

Makes one 23 x 13cm/ 9 x 5in cake
175g/6oz/1½ cups chopped walnuts
75g/3oz/generous ½ cup raisins, chopped
75g/3oz/scant ½ cup currants
115g/4oz/1 cup plain (all-purpose) flour

5ml/1 tsp baking powder
1.5ml/¼ tsp salt
115g/4oz/½ cup butter
225g/8oz/generous 1 cup caster (superfine) sugar
3 eggs, separated, at room temperature
5ml/1 tsp freshly grated nutmeg
2.5ml/½ tsp ground cinnamon
75ml/5 tbsp Irish whiskey
icing (confectioners') sugar, for dusting

1 Preheat the oven to 160°C/325°F/Gas 3. Grease a 23 x 13cm/9 x 5in loaf tin (pan) and line the base.

2 Mix the walnuts, raisins and currants with 30ml/2 tbsp of the flour and set aside. Sift together the remaining flour, baking powder and salt into a bowl.

3 In another bowl, cream the butter and sugar together until light and fluffy. Beat in the egg yolks.

4 Mix the nutmeg, cinnamon and whiskey in a small bowl. Fold into the butter mixture, alternating with the flour mixture.

5 Beat the egg whites until stiff. Fold into the whiskey mixture until just blended. Fold into the walnut mixture. Fill the loaf tin and bake for about 1 hour. Cool in the tin.

7 Meanwhile, make a template with which you can create a pattern on top of the cake. Fold a long strip of paper into a concertina and draw two diagonal lines from the bottom to the top. Cut along the lines and open out the strip. Cut it in half to give you two strips and lay these on top of the cake. Once the cake has cooled completely, position the templates and dust with icing sugar. Remove the template and serve in slices.

Loaf Energy 3768kcal/15772kJ; Protein 52.9g; Carbohydrate 438.6g, of which sugars 265.8g; Fat 212.9g, of which saturates 111.5g; Cholesterol 997mg; Calcium 788mg; Fibre 16.2g; Sodium 1772mg.
Cake Energy 4152kcal/17355kJ; Protein 60.4g; Carbohydrate 433.8g, of which sugars 344.9g; Fat 233.2g, of which saturates 74.6g; Cholesterol 816mg; Calcium 655mg; Fibre 12.6g; Sodium 992mg.

Autumn Dessert Cake

Greengages, plums or semi-dried prunes are delicious in this recipe. Serve with cream or ice cream.

Serves 6–8
115g/4oz/¹/₂ cup butter, softened
150g/5oz/³/₄ cup caster
   (superfine) sugar
3 eggs, beaten
75g/3oz/³/₄ cup ground hazelnuts
150g/5oz/1¹/₄ cups chopped
   pecan nuts

50g/2oz/¹/₂ cup plain
   (all-purpose) flour
5ml/1 tsp baking powder
2.5ml/¹/₂ tsp salt
675g/1¹/₂lb/3 cups plums,
   greengages or
   semi-dried prunes
60ml/4 tbsp lime marmalade
15ml/1 tbsp lime juice
30ml/2 tbsp blanched almonds,
   chopped, to decorate

1 Stone (pit) the plums, greengages or prunes and set aside until they are needed.

2 Preheat the oven to 180°C/350°F/Gas 4. Grease a 23cm/9in round, fluted flan tin (tart pan).

3 Beat the softened butter and caster sugar until light and fluffy. Gradually beat in the eggs, alternating with the ground hazelnuts. Do not overbeat.

4 Stir in the pecan nuts, then sift and fold in the flour, baking powder and salt. Spoon into the tart tin.

5 Bake for 45 minutes, or until a skewer inserted into the centre comes out clean.

6 Arrange the fruit on the base. Return to the oven and bake for 10–15 minutes, or until the fruit has softened. Transfer to a wire rack to cool, then turn out.

7 Warm the marmalade and lime juice gently. Brush over the fruit, then sprinkle with the almonds.

8 Allow to set, then chill before serving.

Apple Crumble Cake

In the autumn use windfall apples. Served warm with thick cream or custard, this cake doubles as a dessert.

Serves 8–10
75g/3oz/²/₃ cup self-raising
   (self-rising) flour
¹/₂ tsp ground cinnamon
40g/1¹/₂oz/3 tbsp butter
25g/1oz/2 tbsp caster
   (superfine) sugar

For the base
50g/2oz/¹/₄ cup butter, softened
75g/3oz/6 tbsp caster
   (superfine) sugar

1 egg, beaten
115g/4oz/1 cup self-raising
   (self-rising) flour, sifted
2 cooking apples, peeled, cored
   and sliced
50g/2oz/¹/₃ cup sultanas
   (golden raisins)

To decorate
1 red dessert apple, cored,
   thinly sliced and tossed in
   lemon juice
25g/1oz/2 tbsp caster (superfine)
   sugar, sifted
pinch of ground cinnamon

1 Preheat the oven to 180°C/350°F/Gas 4. Grease a deep 18cm/7in springform tin (pan), line the base with baking parchment and grease the paper.

2 To make the topping, sift the flour and cinnamon into a mixing bowl. Rub the butter into the flour using your fingertips or a pastry cutter until it resembles breadcrumbs, then stir in the sugar. Set aside.

3 To make the base, put the butter, sugar, egg and flour into a bowl and beat for 1–2 minutes, or until smooth. Spoon into the prepared tin.

4 Mix together the apple slices and sultanas, and spread them evenly over the top. Sprinkle with the topping.

5 Bake for about 1 hour. Cool in the tin for 10 minutes before turning out on to a wire rack and peeling off the lining paper. Serve warm or cool, decorated with slices of red dessert apple and sprinkled with caster sugar and cinnamon.

Autumn Energy 481kcal/2007kJ; Protein 7.1g; Carbohydrate 39g, of which sugars 33.7g; Fat 34.2g, of which saturates 9.7g; Cholesterol 102mg; Calcium 74mg; Fibre 3.2g; Sodium 122mg.
Apple Energy 211kcal/890kJ; Protein 2.7g; Carbohydrate 33.7g, of which sugars 19.3g; Fat 8.3g, of which saturates 4.9g; Cholesterol 38mg; Calcium 42mg; Fibre 1.1g; Sodium 64mg.

Rich Fruit Cake

Sweet sherry adds to the fruit and spices in this cake.

**Makes one 23 x 8cm/
9 x 3in cake**
150g/5oz/generous ¹/₂ cup currants
170g/6oz/generous 1 cup raisins
50g/2oz/¹/₂ cup sultanas
   (golden raisins)
50g/2oz/¹/₄ cup glacé (candied)
   cherries, halved
45ml/3 tbsp sweet sherry
175g/6oz/³/₄ cup butter
200g/7oz/scant 1 cup soft dark
   brown sugar
2 eggs, at room temperature
200g/7oz/1³/₄ cups plain
   (all-purpose) flour
10ml/2 tsp baking powder
10ml/2 tsp each ground ginger,
   allspice, and cinnamon
15ml/1 tbsp golden (light
   corn) syrup
15ml/1 tbsp milk
55g/2oz/¹/₃ cup cut mixed
   (candied) peel
115g/4oz/1 cup chopped walnuts

For the decoration
120ml/4fl oz/scant ¹/₂ cup
   orange marmalade
crystallized citrus fruit slices
glacé (candied) cherries

1 A day in advance, combine the dried fruit and cherries in a bowl. Stir in the sherry, cover and soak overnight.

2 Preheat the oven to 150°C/300°F/Gas 2. Line and grease a 23 x 7.5cm/9 x 3in springform tin (pan) with baking parchment. Place a tray of hot water in the bottom of the oven.

3 Cream the butter and sugar. Beat in the eggs, one at a time. Sift the flour, baking powder and spices together three times. Fold into the butter mixture in three batches. Fold in the syrup, milk, dried fruit and liquid, mixed peel and walnuts.

4 Spoon into the prepared tin, spreading the mixture out so that there is a slight depression in the centre. Bake for about 2½–3 hours. Cover with foil when the top is golden to prevent over-browning. Cool in the tin on a rack. To decorate, melt the marmalade over a low heat, then brush over the top of the cake. Decorate the cake with the crystallized citrus fruit slices and glacé cherries.

Light Fruit Cake

Dried fruit soaked in wine and rum gives this fruit cake an exquisite flavour. For the best taste, wrap it in foil and store it for a week before cutting.

**Makes two 23 x 13cm/
9 x 5in cakes**
225g/8oz/1 cup prunes
225g/8oz/1¹/₃ cups dates
225g/8oz/1 cup currants
225g/8oz/generous 1¹/₄ cups
   sultanas (golden raisins)
250ml/8fl oz/1 cup dry
   white wine
250ml/8fl oz/1 cup rum
350g/12oz/3 cups plain
   (all-purpose) flour
10ml/2 tsp baking powder
5ml/1 tsp ground cinnamon
2.5ml/¹/₂ tsp freshly grated nutmeg
225g/8oz/1 cup butter,
   at room temperature
225g/8oz/generous 1 cup caster
   (superfine) sugar
4 eggs, lightly beaten
5ml/1 tsp vanilla extract

1 Stone (pit) the prunes and dates and chop finely. Place in a bowl with the currants and sultanas. Stir in the wine and rum and leave, covered, for 2 days. Stir occasionally.

2 Preheat the oven to 150°C/300°F/Gas 2 with a tray of hot water in the bottom. Line two 23 x 13cm/9 x 5in loaf tins (pans) with baking parchment and grease the paper.

3 Sift together the dry ingredients. Cream the butter and sugar together until light and fluffy. Gradually add the eggs and vanilla extract. Fold in the flour mixture in three batches, and finally fold in the dried fruit mixture and its liquid.

4 Divide the mixture between the prepared tins and bake until a skewer inserted into the centre comes out clean, about 1½ hours. Leave to stand for 20 minutes, then unmould the cake on to a wire rack to cool completely.

> **Variation**
> *You can use a combination of any dried fruit, such as apricots, figs and cranberries in place of the prunes and/or dates.*

Light Energy 3456kcal/14545kJ; Protein 42.5g; Carbohydrate 524.1g, of which sugars 390.7g; Fat 107.4g, of which saturates 62.2g; Cholesterol 620mg; Calcium 659mg; Fibre 20.7g; Sodium 900mg.
Rich Energy 4509kcal/18916kJ; Protein 28.3g; Carbohydrate 629.3g, of which sugars 628.5g; Fat 220.7g, of which saturates 95.2g; Cholesterol 363mg; Calcium 642mg; Fibre 14.6g; Sodium 1480mg.

Light Jewelled Fruit Cake

If you want to cover this cake with marzipan and icing, omit the almond decoration.

Makes one 20cm/8in round or 18cm/7in square cake
115g/4oz/½ cup currants
115g/4oz/⅔ cup sultanas (golden raisins)
225g/8oz/1 cup mixed glacé (candied) cherries, quartered
50g/2oz/⅓ cup mixed (candied) peel, finely chopped
30ml/2 tbsp rum, brandy or sherry
225g/8oz/1 cup butter
225g/8oz/generous 1 cup caster (superfine) sugar
finely grated rind of 1 orange
grated rind of 1 lemon
4 eggs
50g/2oz/½ cup chopped almonds
50g/2oz/5 tbsp ground almonds
225g/8oz/2 cups plain (all-purpose) flour

For the decoration
50g/2oz/⅓ cup whole blanched almonds (optional)
15ml/1 tbsp apricot jam

1 A day in advance, soak the currants, sultanas, glacé cherries and mixed peel in the rum, brandy or sherry, cover and leave to soak overnight.

2 Grease and line a 20cm/8in round cake tin (pan) or an 18cm/7in square cake tin with a double thickness of baking parchment. Preheat the oven to 160°C/325°F/Gas 3. Beat the butter, sugar, and orange and lemon rinds together until light and fluffy. Beat in the eggs, one at a time.

3 Mix in the chopped almonds, ground almonds, soaked fruits (with the liquid) and the flour. Spoon into the cake tin and level the top. Bake for 30 minutes.

4 To decorate, arrange the almonds, if using, on top of the cake (do not press them into the cake or they will sink during cooking). Return the cake to the oven and cook for 1½–2 hours, or until the centre is firm to the touch. Let the cake cool in the tin for 30 minutes, then turn it out in its paper on to a wire rack. When cold, wrap foil over the paper and store in a cool place. To finish, warm the jam, then sieve it and use to glaze the cake.

Creole Christmas Cake

Makes one 23cm/9in cake
450g/1lb/3 cups raisins
225g/8oz/1 cup currants
115g/4oz/¾ cup sultanas (golden raisins)
115g/4oz/½ cup ready-to-eat prunes, chopped
115g/4oz/⅔ cup candied orange peel, chopped
115g/4oz/1 cup chopped walnuts
60ml/4 tbsp dark brown sugar
5ml/1 tsp vanilla extract
5ml/1 tsp ground cinnamon
1.5ml/¼ tsp each nutmeg and ground cloves
5ml/1 tsp salt

60ml/4 tbsp each rum, brandy and whisky

For the second stage
225g/8oz/2 cups plain (all-purpose) flour
5ml/1 tsp baking powder
225g/8oz/1 cup demerara (raw) sugar
225g/8oz/1 cup butter
4 eggs, beaten

For the topping
225g/8oz/scant ¾ cup apricot jam, sieved
pecan halves and crystallized kumquat slices, to decorate

1 Put the fruit, nuts, sugar, spices, salt and alcohol into a pan, mix well and heat gently. Simmer over low heat for 15 minutes. Remove from the heat and cool. Transfer to a lidded jar and leave in the refrigerator for 7 days, stirring at least once a day.

2 Preheat the oven to 140°C/275°F/Gas 1. Line a 23cm/9in round cake tin (pan) with a double thickness of baking parchment and grease it well. Beat the flour, baking powder, sugar and butter together until smooth, then gradually beat in the eggs until the mixture is well blended and smooth.

3 Fold in the fruit mixture from the jar and stir well to mix. Spoon the mixture into the prepared tin, level the surface and bake in the centre of the oven for 3 hours. Cover with foil and continue baking for 1 hour, or until the cake feels springy. Cool on a wire rack then remove from the tin. Wrap in foil until needed. The cake will keep well for 1 year.

4 To decorate, heat the jam with 30ml/2 tbsp water, and brush half over the cake. Arrange the nuts and fruit over the cake and brush with the remaining apricot glaze.

Creole Energy 8205kcal/34536kJ; Protein 87.7g; Carbohydrate 1285g, of which sugars 1112.7g; Fat 293.5g, of which saturates 130.3g; Cholesterol 1241mg; Calcium 1430mg; Fibre 38.6g; Sodium 2437mg.
Jewelled Energy 5298kcal/22248kJ; Protein 66g; Carbohydrate 751.5g, of which sugars 578.7g; Fat 239.3g, of which saturates 126.1g; Cholesterol 1241mg; Calcium 1080mg; Fibre 19.6g; Sodium 1909mg.

Iced Angel Cake

Served with fromage frais or low-fat yogurt and fresh raspberries, this makes a light dessert.

Serves 10

40g/1½oz/scant ½ cup cornflour (cornstarch)

40g/1½oz/scant ½ cup plain (all-purpose) flour

8 egg whites

225g/8oz/generous 1 cup caster (superfine) sugar, plus extra for sprinkling

5ml/1 tsp vanilla extract

icing (confectioners') sugar, for dusting

1 Preheat the oven to 180°C/350°F/Gas 4. Sift both flours into a bowl.

2 Whisk the egg whites in a large grease-free bowl until very stiff, then gradually add the sugar and vanilla extract, a spoonful of sugar at a time, whisking until the mixture is thick and glossy.

3 Fold in the flour mixture with a large metal spoon. Spoon into an ungreased 25cm/10in angel cake tin, smooth the surface and bake for 40–45 minutes.

4 Sprinkle a piece of baking parchment with caster sugar and set an egg cup in the centre. Invert the cake tin over the paper, balancing the cake on the egg cup. When cold, the cake will drop out of the tin. Transfer it to a plate and serve.

Variation

Make a lemon icing by mixing 175g/6oz/1½ cups icing (confectioners') sugar with 15–30ml/1–2 tbsp lemon juice. Drizzle over the cake and decorate with physalis.

Cook's Tip

You can also bake this cake in a 20cm/8in cake tin (pan); it will probably take a little longer to cook. When it is well-risen and springy to the touch it is done.

Spice Cake with Ginger Frosting

Preserved stem ginger makes the frosting for this cake particularly delicious.

Makes one 20cm/8in round cake

300ml/10fl oz/1¼ cups milk

30ml/2 tbsp golden (light corn) syrup

10ml/2 tsp vanilla extract

75g/3oz/¾ cup chopped walnuts

175g/6oz/¾ cup butter, at room temperature

285g/10½oz/1½ cups caster (superfine) sugar

1 whole egg, plus 3 egg yolks

275g/10oz/2½ cups plain (all-purpose) flour

15ml/1 tbsp baking powder

5ml/1 tsp freshly grated nutmeg

5ml/1 tsp ground cinnamon

2.5ml/½ tsp ground cloves

1.5ml/¼ tsp ground ginger

1.5ml/¼ tsp mixed (apple pie) spice

preserved stem ginger pieces, to decorate

For the frosting

175g/6oz/¾ cup cream cheese

25g/1oz/2 tbsp unsalted (sweet) butter

200g/7oz/1¾ cups icing (confectioners') sugar

30ml/2 tbsp finely chopped preserved stem ginger

30ml/2 tbsp syrup from stem ginger

1 Preheat the oven to 180°C/350°F/Gas 4. Line and grease three 20cm/8in shallow round cake tins (pans) with baking parchment. In a bowl, combine the milk, golden syrup, vanilla extract and chopped walnuts.

2 Cream the butter and caster sugar until light and fluffy. Beat in the egg and egg yolks.

3 Add the milk and syrup mixture, and stir well. Sift together the flour, baking powder and spices three times. Add to the butter mixture in four batches, folding in carefully.

4 Divide the mixture between the tins. Bake for 25 minutes. Leave in the tins for 5 minutes, then cool on a wire rack.

5 For the frosting, combine the cream cheese with the butter, icing sugar, stem ginger and ginger syrup, beating with a wooden spoon until smooth. Spread the frosting between the layers and over the top. Decorate with pieces of stem ginger.

Angel Energy 1788kcal/7618kJ; Protein 42.6g; Carbohydrate 426.4g, of which sugars 299.8g; Fat 1.9g, of which saturates 0.3g; Cholesterol 0mg; Calcium 354mg; Fibre 4.1g; Sodium 645mg.g.
Spice Energy 5257kcal/21970kJ; Protein 45.4g; Carbohydrate 572g, of which sugars 571.5g; Fat 326g, of which saturates 169.8g; Cholesterol 1405mg; Calcium 1003mg; Fibre 2.6g; Sodium 2159mg.

Lemon Coconut Layer Cake

Makes one 20cm/8in round cake

175g/6oz/1½ cups plain (all-purpose) flour, sifted with 1.5ml/¼ tsp salt
7 eggs
350g/12oz/1¾ cups caster (superfine) sugar
15ml/1 tbsp grated orange rind
grated rind of 1½ lemons
juice of 1 lemon
65g/2½oz/scant 1 cup desiccated (dry unsweetened shredded) coconut

15ml/1 tbsp cornflour (cornstarch)
120ml/4fl oz/½ cup water
40g/1½oz/3 tbsp butter

For the icing
75g/3oz/6 tbsp unsalted (sweet) butter
175g/6oz/1½ cups icing (confectioners') sugar
grated rind of 1½ lemons
30ml/2 tbsp lemon juice
200g/7oz/2½ cups desiccated (dry unsweetened shredded) coconut

1 Preheat the oven to 180°C/350°F/Gas 4. Line and grease three 20cm/8in shallow round cake tins (pans) with baking parchment.

2 Place six of the eggs in a bowl set over a pan of hot water and beat until frothy. Beat in 225g/8oz/generous 1 cup sugar until the mixture doubles in volume. Remove from the heat. Fold in the orange rind, half the lemon rind, 15ml/1 tbsp of the lemon juice and the coconut. Sift over the flour mixture and gently fold in.

3 Divide between the cake tins. Bake for 20–25 minutes. Leave in the tins for 5 minutes, then cool on a wire rack.

4 Blend the cornflour with a little cold water to dissolve. Whisk in the remaining egg until blended. In a pan, mix the remaining lemon rind and juice, water, remaining sugar and butter. Bring to the boil. Whisk in the cornflour, return to the boil and whisk until thick. Remove, cover with clear film (plastic wrap) until cool.

5 Cream the butter and icing sugar. Stir in the lemon rind and enough lemon juice to obtain a spreadable consistency. Sandwich the cake layers with the lemon custard. Spread the icing over the top and sides. Cover with the coconut.

Lemon Yogurt Ring

The glaze gives this dessert a refreshing finishing touch.

Serves 12
225g/8oz/1 cup butter, at room temperature
285g/10½oz/1½ cups caster (superfine) sugar
4 eggs, separated
10ml/2 tsp grated lemon rind
90ml/6 tbsp lemon juice
250ml/8fl oz/1 cup natural (plain) yogurt

275g/10oz/2½ cups plain (all-purpose) flour
10ml/2 tsp baking powder
5ml/1 tsp bicarbonate of soda (baking soda)
2.5ml/½ tsp salt

For the glaze
115g/4oz/1 cup icing (confectioners') sugar
30ml/2 tbsp lemon juice
45–60ml/3–4 tbsp natural (plain) yogurt

1 Preheat the oven to 180°C/350°F/Gas 4. Grease a 3-litre/5¼-pint/13¼-cup *bundt* or fluted tube tin and dust lightly with flour.

2 Cream the butter and caster sugar in a large bowl until light and fluffy. Add the egg yolks, one at a time, beating well after each addition. Add the lemon rind, juice and yogurt, and stir gently to incorporate.

3 Sift together the flour, baking powder and bicarbonate of soda. In another bowl, beat the egg whites and salt until they hold stiff peaks.

4 Fold the dry ingredients into the butter mixture, then fold in a spoonful of egg whites to lighten the mixture. Fold in the remaining egg whites.

5 Pour into the tin and bake until a skewer inserted in the centre comes out clean, about 50 minutes. Leave in the tin for 15 minutes, then turn out and cool on a wire rack.

6 To make the glaze, sift the icing sugar into a bowl. Stir in the lemon juice and just enough yogurt to make a smooth glaze. Set the cooled cake on the wire rack over a sheet of baking parchment. Pour over the glaze and allow to set.

Cake Energy 5225kcal/21906kJ; Protein 74.3g; Carbohydrate 659.5g, of which sugars 517.6g; Fat 274g, of which saturates 173.1g; Cholesterol 1927mg; Calcium 760mg; Fibre 20.4g; Sodium 1793mg.
Ring Energy 387kcal/1626kJ; Protein 5.8g; Carbohydrate 54.6g, of which sugars 37.1g; Fat 17.8g, of which saturates 10.5g; Cholesterol 104mg; Calcium 109mg; Fibre 0.7g; Sodium 160mg.

Carrot Cake with Geranium Cheese

The scented cheese topping makes this carrot cake special.

**Makes one 23 x 12cm/
9 x 5in cake**
115g/4oz/1 cup self-raising
  (self-rising) flour
5ml/1 tsp bicarbonate of soda
  (baking soda)
2.5ml/½ tsp ground cinnamon
2.5ml/½ tsp ground cloves
200g/7oz/scant 1 cup soft
  brown sugar
225g/8oz/generous 1½ cups
  grated carrot
150g/5oz/scant 1 cup sultanas
  (golden raisins)

150g/5oz/½ cup finely chopped
  preserved stem ginger
150g/5oz/scant 1 cup pecan nuts
150ml/¼ pint/⅔ cup sunflower oil
2 eggs, lightly beaten

For the topping
2 or 3 lemon-scented
  geranium leaves
225g/8oz/2 cups icing
  (confectioners') sugar
60g/2¼oz/generous 4 tbsp cream
  cheese
30g/1¼oz/generous 2 tbsp
  softened butter
5ml/1 tsp grated lemon rind

1 For the topping, put the geranium leaves, torn into small pieces, in a small bowl and mix with the icing sugar. Leave in a warm place overnight for the sugar to take up the scent.

2 For the cake, sift the flour, bicarbonate of soda and spices together. Add the sugar, grated carrots, sultanas, stem ginger and pecan nuts. Stir well, then add the oil and beaten eggs. Mix with an electric mixer for 5 minutes.

3 Preheat the oven to 180°C/350°F/Gas 4. Then grease a 23 x 13cm/9 x 5in loaf tin (pan), line the base with baking parchment, and grease the paper. Pour the mixture into the tin and bake for about 1 hour. Remove the cake from the oven, leave to stand for a few minutes, and then cool on a wire rack.

4 Meanwhile, make the cream cheese topping. Remove the pieces of geranium leaf from the icing sugar and discard. Place the cream cheese, butter and lemon rind in a bowl. Using an electric mixer, gradually add the icing sugar, beating well until smooth. Spread over the top of the cooled cake.

Carrot & Courgette Cake

This unusual sponge has a delicious creamy topping.

**Makes one 18cm/7in square
cake**
1 carrot
1 courgette (zucchini)
3 eggs, separated
115g/4oz/1 cup soft light
  brown sugar
30ml/2 tbsp ground almonds
finely grated rind of 1 orange

150g/5oz/1¼ cups self-raising
  (self-rising) wholemeal
  (whole-wheat) flour
5ml/1 tsp ground cinnamon
5ml/1 tsp icing (confectioners')
  sugar, for dusting
fondant carrots and courgettes
  (zucchini), to decorate

For the topping
175g/6oz/¾ cup low-fat soft cheese
5ml/1 tsp clear honey

1 Preheat the oven to 180°C/350°F/Gas 4. Line an 18cm/7in square tin (pan) with baking parchment. Coarsely grate the carrot and courgette.

2 Put the egg yolks, sugar, ground almonds and orange rind into a bowl and whisk until very thick and light. Sift together the flour and cinnamon, and fold into the mixture together with the grated vegetables. Add any bran left in the sieve.

3 Whisk the egg whites until stiff and carefully fold them in, a little at a time. Spoon into the tin. Bake in the oven for 1 hour, covering the top with foil after 40 minutes. Leave to cool in the tin for 5 minutes, then turn out on to a wire rack and remove the lining paper.

4 To make the topping, beat together the cheese and honey, and spread over the cake. Dust with icing sugar and decorate with fondant carrots and courgettes.

Cook's Tip
To make fondant carrots and courgettes, roll tinted sugarpaste into the shapes and paint details using a fine paintbrush. Use thin lengths of green sugarpaste to make the carrot tops.

Carrot Energy 5413kcal/22706kJ; Protein 47.4g; Carbohydrate 740.3g, of which sugars 649.3g; Fat 272.2g, of which saturates 57.6g; Cholesterol 502mg; Calcium 789mg; Fibre 21.4g; Sodium 624mg.
Courgette Energy 1455kcal/6145kJ; Protein 68.5g; Carbohydrate 237.8g, of which sugars 144.5g; Fat 35g, of which saturates 14.5g; Cholesterol 613mg; Calcium 476mg; Fibre 17.1g; Sodium 1010mg.

Banana Coconut Cake

Slightly over-ripe bananas are best for this perfect coffee-morning cake topped with honey and coconut.

Makes one 18cm/7in square cake
115g/4oz/½ cup butter, softened
115g/4oz/generous ½ cup caster (superfine) sugar
2 eggs
115g/4oz/1 cup self-raising (self-rising) flour
50g/2oz/½ cup plain (all-purpose) flour
5ml/1 tsp bicarbonate of soda (baking soda)
120ml/4fl oz/½ cup milk
2 large bananas, peeled and mashed
75g/3oz/1 cup desiccated (dry unsweetened shredded) coconut, toasted

For the topping
25g/1oz/2 tbsp butter
30ml/2 tbsp clear honey
115g/4oz/2 cups shredded coconut

1 Preheat the oven to 190°C/375°F/Gas 5. Grease a deep 18cm/7in square cake tin (pan), line with baking parchment and grease the paper.

2 Beat the butter and sugar until smooth and creamy. Beat in the eggs, one at a time. Sift together the flours and bicarbonate of soda, sift half into the butter mixture and stir to mix.

3 Combine the milk and mashed banana, and beat half into the egg mixture. Stir in the remaining flour and banana mixtures and the toasted coconut. Transfer the batter to the cake tin and smooth the surface.

4 Bake for 1 hour, or until a skewer inserted into the centre of the cake comes out clean. Leave in the tin for 5 minutes, then turn out on to a wire rack, peel off the paper and leave to cool completely.

5 To make the topping, gently melt the butter and honey in a small pan. Stir in the shredded coconut and cook, stirring, for 5 minutes or until lightly browned. Remove from the heat and allow to cool slightly. Spoon the topping over the cake and allow to cool.

St Clement's Cake

A tangy orange-and-lemon cake makes a spectacular centrepiece when decorated with fruits, silver dragées and fresh flowers.

Makes one 23cm/9in ring cake
175g/6oz/¾ cup butter
75g/3oz/scant ⅓ cup soft light brown sugar
3 eggs, separated
grated rind and juice of 1 orange and 1 lemon
150g/5oz/1¼ cups self-raising (self-rising) flour
75g/3oz/6 tbsp caster (superfine) sugar
15g/½oz/1 tbsp ground almonds
350ml/12fl oz/1½ cups double (heavy) cream
15ml/1 tbsp Grand Marnier
16 crystallized orange and lemon slices, silver dragées, sugared almonds and fresh flowers, to decorate

1 Preheat the oven to 180°C/350°F/Gas 4. Grease and flour a 900ml/1½ pint/3¾ cup ring mould.

2 Cream half the butter and all of the brown sugar until pale and light. Beat in the egg yolks, orange rind and juice and fold in 75g/3oz/⅔ cup flour.

3 Cream the remaining butter and the caster sugar in another bowl. Stir in the lemon rind and juice and fold in the remaining flour and the ground almonds. Whisk the egg whites until they form stiff peaks, and fold into the batter.

4 Spoon the two mixtures alternately into the prepared tin. Using a skewer or small spoon, swirl through the mixture to create a marbled effect. Bake for 45–50 minutes, or until risen, and a skewer inserted in the cake comes out clean. Cool in the tin for 10 minutes then transfer to a wire rack to cool.

5 Whip the cream and Grand Marnier together until lightly thickened. Spread over the cake and swirl a pattern over the icing with a metal spatula. Decorate the ring with the crystallized fruits, dragées and sugared almonds to resemble a jewelled crown. Arrange a few fresh flowers with their stems wrapped in foil in the centre.

Banana Energy 3291kcal/13744kJ; Protein 43g; Carbohydrate 332.2g, of which sugars 201.8g; Fat 208.5g, of which saturates 144.6g; Cholesterol 686mg; Calcium 560mg; Fibre 24.4g; Sodium 1092mg.
St Clements Energy 4486kcal/18629kJ; Protein 43.4g; Carbohydrate 281.3g, of which sugars 166.6g; Fat 358.8g, of which saturates 213.6g; Cholesterol 1424mg; Calcium 614mg; Fibre 5.8g; Sodium 1363mg.

Apple Cake

A deliciously moist cake with a silky icing.

Makes one ring cake

675g/1½lb apples, peeled, cored and quartered
500g/1¼lb/generous 4½ cups caster (superfine) sugar
15ml/1 tbsp water
350g/12oz/3 cups plain (all-purpose) flour
9ml/1¾ tsp bicarbonate of soda (baking soda)
5ml/1 tsp ground cinnamon
5ml/1 tsp ground cloves
175g/6oz/generous 1 cup raisins
150g/5oz/1¼ cups chopped walnuts
225g/8oz/1 cup butter or margarine, at room temperature
5ml/1 tsp vanilla extract

For the icing

115g/4oz/1 cup icing (confectioners') sugar
1.5ml/¼ tsp vanilla extract
30–45ml/2–3 tbsp milk

1 Put the apples, 50g/2oz/¼ cup of the sugar and the water in a pan and bring to the boil. Simmer for 25 minutes, stirring occasionally to break up any lumps. Leave to cool. Preheat the oven to 160°C/325°F/Gas 3. Thoroughly butter and flour a 1.75-litre/3-pint/7½-cup tube tin (pan).

2 Sift the flour, bicarbonate of soda and spices into a bowl. Remove 30ml/2 tbsp of the mixture to another bowl and toss with the raisins and 115g/4oz/1 cup of the walnuts.

3 Cream the butter or margarine and remaining sugar together until light and fluffy. Fold in the apple mixture gently. Fold the flour mixture into the apple mixture. Stir in the vanilla extract and the raisin and walnut mixture. Pour into the tube tin. Bake until a skewer inserted in the centre comes out clean, about 1½ hours. Cool completely in the tin on a wire rack, then unmould on to the rack.

4 To make the icing, put the sugar in a bowl and stir in the vanilla extract and 15ml/1 tbsp milk. Add more milk until the icing is smooth and has a thick pouring consistency. Transfer the cake to a serving plate and drizzle the icing over the top. Sprinkle with the remaining nuts. Allow the icing to set.

Chocolate Amaretto Marquise

This light-as-air marquise is perfect for a special occasion, served with amaretto cream.

Makes one cake

15ml/1 tbsp sunflower oil
75g/3oz/7–8 amaretti, crushed
25g/1oz/2 tbsp unblanched almonds, toasted and finely chopped
450g/1lb plain (semisweet) chocolate, broken into pieces
75ml/5 tbsp amaretto liqueur
75ml/5 tbsp golden (light corn) syrup
475ml/16fl oz/2 cups double (heavy) cream
cocoa powder, to dust

For the amaretto cream

350ml/12fl oz/1½ cups whipping or double (heavy) cream
30–45ml/2–3 tbsp amaretto liqueur

1 Lightly oil a 23cm/9in heart-shaped or springform cake tin (pan). Line the base with baking parchment and oil the paper. In a small bowl, combine the crushed amaretti and the toasted and chopped almonds. Sprinkle evenly over the base of the tin.

2 Place the chocolate, amaretto liqueur and golden syrup in a pan over very low heat. Stir frequently until the chocolate is melted and the mixture is smooth. Allow to cool for 6–8 minutes, or until the mixture feels just warm.

3 Beat the cream until it just begins to hold its shape. Stir a large spoonful into the chocolate mixture, then quickly add the remaining cream and gently fold into the chocolate mixture. Pour into the prepared tin and tap the tin gently on the work surface to release any large air bubbles. Cover the tin with clear film (plastic wrap) and leave in the refrigerator overnight.

4 To unmould, run a thin-bladed sharp knife under hot water and dry carefully. Run the knife around the edge of the tin to loosen, place a serving plate over the tin, then invert to unmould. Carefully peel off the paper then dust with cocoa. To make the amaretto cream, whip the cream and liqueur together and serve separately.

Apple Energy 7049kcal/29657kJ; Protein 66.1g; Carbohydrate 1103.7g, of which sugars 835.9g; Fat 294.1g, of which saturates 126.6g; Cholesterol 482mg; Calcium 1141mg; Fibre 30.4g; Sodium 1553mg.
Chocolate Energy 7040kcal/29238kJ; Protein 46.4g; Carbohydrate 448.7g, of which sugars 411.5g; Fat 548.8g, of which saturates 324.4g; Cholesterol 1025mg; Calcium 742mg; Fibre 14.2g; Sodium 674mg.

Tangy Lemon Cake

The lemon syrup forms a crusty topping when it has completely cooled. Leave the cake in the tin until ready to serve.

Makes one 900g/2lb loaf
175g/6oz/³⁄₄ cup butter
175g/6oz/scant 1 cup caster (superfine) sugar

3 eggs, beaten
175g/6oz/1¹⁄₂ cups self-raising (self-rising) flour
grated rind of 1 orange
grated rind of 1 lemon

For the syrup
115g/4oz/generous ¹⁄₂ cup caster (superfine) sugar
juice of 2 lemons

1 Preheat the oven to 180°C/350°F/Gas 4. Grease a 900g/2lb loaf tin (pan).

2 Beat the butter and sugar together until light and fluffy, then gradually beat in the eggs.

3 Fold in the flour and the orange and lemon rinds.

4 Turn the cake mixture into the prepared cake tin and bake for 1¹⁄₄–1¹⁄₂ hours, or until set in the centre, risen and golden.

5 Remove the cake from the oven, but leave it in the tin rather than turning out on to a wire rack.

6 To make the syrup, gently heat the sugar in a small pan with the lemon juice until the sugar has completely dissolved, then boil for 15 seconds.

7 Pour the syrup over the hot cake in the tin and leave to cool completely.

> **Cook's Tip**
> You can use a skewer to pierce holes over the cake's surface so that the syrup will drizzle through and soak into the cake. There will still be a crusty, sugary top, but the cake itself will be moist.

Pineapple & Apricot Cake

This is not a long-keeping cake, but it does freeze, well wrapped in baking parchment and then foil.

Makes one 18cm/7in square or 20cm/8in round cake
175g/6oz/³⁄₄ cup unsalted (sweet) butter
150g/5oz/generous ³⁄₄ cup caster (superfine) sugar
3 eggs, beaten
few drops vanilla extract

225g/8oz/2 cups plain all-purpose) flour
1.5ml/¹⁄₄ tsp salt
7.5ml/1¹⁄₂ tsp baking powder
225g/8oz/1 cup ready-to-eat dried apricots, chopped
115g/4oz/¹⁄₂ cup each chopped crystallized ginger and crystallized pineapple
grated rind and juice of ¹⁄₂ orange
grated rind and juice of ¹⁄₂ lemon
a little milk

1 Preheat the oven to 180°C/350°F/Gas 4. Double line an 18cm/7in square or 20cm/8in round cake tin (pan).

2 Cream the butter and sugar together until light and fluffy.

3 Gradually beat in the eggs with the vanilla extract, beating well after each addition.

4 Sift together the flour, salt and baking powder. Add a little of the flour with the last of the egg, then fold in the remainder.

5 Gently fold in the apricots, ginger and pineapple and the orange and lemon rinds, then add sufficient fruit juice and milk to give the batter a fairly soft dropping consistency.

6 Spoon the batter into the prepared cake tin and smooth the top with a wet spoon.

7 Bake for 20 minutes, then reduce the oven temperature to 160°C/325°F/Gas 3 and bake for a further 1¹⁄₂–2 hours, or until a skewer inserted into the centre comes out clean.

8 Leave the cake to cool completely in the tin. Wrap in fresh paper before storing in an airtight tin.

Lemon Energy 2849kcal/11927kJ; Protein 36.3g; Carbohydrate 331.9g, of which sugars 201.9g; Fat 162.6g, of which saturates 96.2g; Cholesterol 944mg; Calcium 830mg; Fibre 5.4g; Sodium 1912mg.
Pineapple Energy 3400kcal/14276kJ; Protein 52.3g; Carbohydrate 455.1g, of which sugars 283.7g; Fat 165.6g, of which saturates 96.3g; Cholesterol 944mg; Calcium 748mg; Fibre 25.9g; Sodium 1326mg.

Sour Cream Crumble Cake

The consistency of this cake, with its two layers of crumble, is sublime.

Makes one 23cm/9in square cake
115g/4oz/½ cup butter, at room temperature
130g/4½oz/scant ¾ cup caster (superfine) sugar
3 eggs
210g/7½oz/scant 2 cups plain (all-purpose) flour

5ml/1 tsp bicarbonate of soda (baking soda)
5ml/1 tsp baking powder
250ml/8fl oz/1 cup sour cream

For the topping
225g/8oz/1 cup soft dark brown sugar
10ml/2 tsp ground cinnamon
115g/4oz/1 cup finely chopped walnuts
50g/2oz/¼ cup cold butter, diced

1 Preheat the oven to 180°C/350°F/Gas 4. Line the base of a 23cm/9in square cake tin (pan) with baking parchment and grease the paper and sides.

2 To make the topping, place the brown sugar, cinnamon and walnuts in a bowl. Mix, then add the butter and rub in using your fingertips or a pastry cutter until the mixture resembles breadcrumbs.

3 To make the cake, cream the butter until soft. Add the sugar and beat until light and fluffy. Add the eggs, one at a time, beating well after each addition.

4 In another bowl, sift the flour, bicarbonate of soda and baking powder together three times. Fold the dry ingredients into the butter mixture in three batches, alternating with the sour cream. Fold until blended after each addition.

5 Pour half of the batter into the prepared tin and sprinkle over half of the topping. Pour the remaining batter on top and sprinkle over the remaining topping.

6 Bake until browned, 60–70 minutes. Leave in the tin for 5 minutes, then turn out on a wire rack to cool completely.

Plum Crumble Cake

This cake can also be made with the same quantity of apricots or cherries.

Serves 8–10
675g/1½lb red plums
150g/5oz/10 tbsp butter or margarine, at room temperature
150g/5oz/¾ cup caster (superfine) sugar
4 eggs, at room temperature
7.5ml/1½ tsp vanilla extract

150g/5oz/1¼ cups plain (all-purpose) flour
5ml/1 tsp baking powder

For the topping
115g/4oz/1 cup plain (all-purpose) flour
130g/4½oz/generous 1 cup soft light brown sugar
7.5ml/1½ tsp ground cinnamon
75g/3oz/6 tbsp butter, diced

1 Halve and stone (pit) the plums and set them aside.

2 Preheat the oven to 180°C/350°F/Gas 4. Using baking parchment, line a 25 x 5cm/10 x 2in tin (pan) and grease the paper.

3 To make the topping, combine the flour, light brown sugar and cinnamon in a bowl. Add the butter and rub in well using your fingertips or a pastry cutter until it resembles coarse breadcrumbs.

4 Cream the butter or margarine and sugar until light and fluffy. Beat in the eggs, one at a time. Stir in the vanilla. Sift the flour and baking powder into a bowl then fold into the creamed mixture in three batches.

5 Pour the batter into the prepared tin. Arrange the plums on top and sprinkle with the topping.

6 Bake until a skewer inserted in the centre comes out clean, about 45 minutes. Cool in the tin.

7 To serve, run a knife around the inside edge of the cake and invert on to a plate. Invert again on to a serving plate so that the topping is uppermost.

Sour Cream Energy 4867kcal/20353kJ; Protein 65.4g; Carbohydrate 548.4g, of which sugars 387.6g; Fat 283.5g, of which saturates 128.7g; Cholesterol 1073mg; Calcium 938mg; Fibre 10.5g; Sodium 1348mg.
Plum Energy 426kcal/1787kJ; Protein 5.7g; Carbohydrate 57g, of which sugars 36.8g; Fat 21.1g, of which saturates 12.4g; Cholesterol 124mg; Calcium 77mg; Fibre 1.9g; Sodium 168mg.

Pineapple Upside-down Cake

Canned pineapple rings make this a useful and unusual cake to make with a few ingredients that you might already have in the cupboard.

Makes one 25cm/10in round cake
115g/4oz/½ cup butter
200g/7oz/scant 1 cup soft dark brown sugar
450g/1lb canned pineapple slices, drained
4 eggs, separated
grated rind of 1 lemon
pinch of salt
115g/4oz/generous ½ cup caster (superfine) sugar
75g/3oz/⅔ cup plain (all-purpose) flour
5ml/1 tsp baking powder

1 Preheat the oven to 180°C/350°F/Gas 4. Melt the butter in a 25cm/10in ovenproof cast-iron frying pan. Then reserve 15ml/1 tbsp butter. Add the brown sugar to the pan and stir to blend. Place the pineapple slices on top in one layer. Set aside.

2 Whisk together the egg yolks, reserved butter and lemon rind until well blended. Set aside.

3 Beat the egg whites and salt until they form stiff peaks. Gradually fold in the caster sugar, then the egg yolk mixture.

4 Sift the flour and baking powder together. Carefully fold into the egg mixture in three batches.

5 Pour the mixture over the pineapple. Bake until a skewer inserted in the centre comes out clean, about 30 minutes.

6 While still hot, invert on to a serving plate. Serve hot or cold.

> **Variation**
> For an apricot cake, replace the pineapple slices with 225g/8oz/1¾ cups dried ready-to-eat apricots.

Upside-down Pear & Ginger Cake

This light spicy sponge, topped with glossy baked fruit and ginger, makes an excellent pudding.

Serves 6–8
900g/2lb can pear halves, drained
120ml/8 tbsp finely chopped preserved stem ginger
120ml/8 tbsp ginger syrup from the jar
175g/6oz/1½ cups self-raising (self-rising) flour
2.5ml/½ tsp baking powder
5ml/1 tsp ground ginger
175g/6oz/¾ cup soft light brown sugar
175g/6oz/¾ cup butter, softened
3 eggs, lightly beaten

1 Preheat the oven to 180°C/350°F/Gas 4. Base-line and grease a deep 20cm/8in round cake tin (pan).

2 Fill the hollow in each pear with half the chopped preserved stem ginger. Arrange, flat sides down, in the base of the cake tin, then spoon over half the ginger syrup.

3 Sift together the flour, baking powder and ground ginger. Stir in the sugar and butter, add the eggs and beat until creamy, about 1–2 minutes.

4 Spoon the mixture into the cake tin. Bake in the oven for 50 minutes, or until a skewer inserted in the centre of the cake comes out clean. Leave the cake in the tin for 5 minutes. Turn out on to a wire rack, peel off the lining paper and leave to cool completely.

5 Add the reserved ginger to the pear halves and drizzle over the remaining syrup.

> **Cook's Tip**
> Canned pears are ideal for this cake, but you can also core, peel and halve fresh pears, and then poach them until tender in a little white wine to cover with 50g/2oz/½ cup sugar added.

Pineapple Energy 2858kcal/12025kJ; Protein 35.7g; Carbohydrate 443g, of which sugars 385.9g; Fat 117.7g, of which saturates 66.3g; Cholesterol 1006mg; Calcium 443mg; Fibre 4.6g; Sodium 1003mg.
Pear Energy 433kcal/1818kJ; Protein 5g; Carbohydrate 61.4g, of which sugars 44.7g; Fat 20.4g, of which saturates 12g; Cholesterol 118mg; Calcium 66mg; Fibre 2.3g; Sodium 205mg.

Cranberry & Apple Ring

Tangy cranberries add an unusual flavour to this moist cake, which is best eaten very fresh.

Makes one ring cake
225g/8oz/2 cups self-raising
  (self-rising) flour
5ml/1 tsp ground cinnamon

75g/3oz/scant ¹/₂ cup light
  muscovado (brown) sugar
1 eating apple, cored and diced
75g/3oz/³/₄ cup fresh or
  frozen cranberries
60ml/4 tbsp sunflower oil
150ml/¹/₄ pint/²/₃ cup apple juice
cranberry jelly and apple slices,
  to decorate

1 Preheat the oven to 180°C/350°F/Gas 4. Lightly grease a 1-litre/1³/₄-pint/4-cup ring tin (pan) with oil.

2 Sift together the flour and ground cinnamon in a large bowl, then stir in the light muscovado sugar.

3 Toss together the diced apple and cranberries in a small bowl.

4 Stir the apple mixture into the dry ingredients, then add the oil and apple juice and beat together until everything is thoroughly combined.

5 Spoon the cake mixture into the prepared ring tin and bake for 35–40 minutes, or until the cake is firm to the touch.

6 Leave the cake in the tin for 5 minutes, then turn out on to a wire rack and leave to cool completely.

7 To serve, arrange apple slices over the cake and drizzle warmed cranberry jelly over the top.

Cook's Tip
This moist, tangy ring would be an ideal alternative to Christmas cake for those who do not like such dense, rich cakes. It would also be a good way of using up any left-over cranberries or cranberry jelly.

Greek Honey & Lemon Cake

A wonderfully moist and tangy cake, you could ice it if you wished.

Makes one 19cm/7¹/₂in square cake
40g/1¹/₂oz/3 tbsp sunflower
  margarine
60ml/4 tbsp clear honey
finely grated rind and juice of
  1 lemon

150ml/¹/₄ pint/²/₃ cup milk
150g/5oz/1¹/₄ cups plain
  (all-purpose) flour
7.5ml/1¹/₂ tsp baking powder
2.5ml/¹/₂ tsp freshly
  grated nutmeg
50g/2oz/¹/₃ cup semolina
2 egg whites
10ml/2 tsp sesame seeds

1 Preheat the oven to 200°C/400°F/Gas 6. Lightly oil and base-line a 19cm/7¹/₂in square deep cake tin (pan).

2 Place the margarine and 45ml/3 tbsp of the honey in a pan and heat gently until melted.

3 Reserve 15ml/1 tbsp lemon juice, then stir in the rest with the lemon rind and milk.

4 Sift together the flour, baking powder and nutmeg, then beat in with the semolina. Whisk the egg whites until they form soft peaks, then fold evenly into the mixture.

5 Spoon into the cake tin and sprinkle with sesame seeds. Bake for 25–30 minutes, or until golden brown. Mix the reserved honey and lemon juice, and drizzle over the cake while warm. Cool in the tin, then cut into fingers to serve.

Cook's Tip
Baking powder is a useful raising agent for making cakes and is used with plain (all-purpose) flour. When mixed with a liquid it forms a gas that causes the cake to rise. It also acts further when the cake is baked. Always check the use-by date on the packet and replace as necessary for successful baking.

Cranberry Energy 1565kcal/6610kJ; Protein 22.1g; Carbohydrate 280.7g, of which sugars 109.2g; Fat 47.2g, of which saturates 5.7g; Cholesterol 0mg; Calcium 371mg; Fibre 9.2g; Sodium 17mg.
Honey Energy 1307kcal/5510kJ; Protein 32.4g; Carbohydrate 208.7g, of which sugars 55.6g; Fat 43.8g, of which saturates 9.2g; Cholesterol 12mg; Calcium 474mg; Fibre 6.5g; Sodium 525mg.

Pear & Cardamom Spice Cake

Fresh pears and cardamoms – a classic combination – are used together in this moist fruit and nut cake.

Makes one 20cm/8in round cake

115g/4oz/½ cup butter
115g/4oz/generous ½ cup caster (superfine) sugar
2 eggs, lightly beaten
225g/8oz/2 cups plain (all-purpose) flour
15ml/1 tbsp baking powder
30ml/2 tbsp milk
crushed seeds from 2 cardamom pods
50g/2oz/½ cup walnuts, finely chopped
15ml/1 tbsp poppy seeds
500g/1¼lb dessert pears, peeled, cored and thinly sliced
3 walnut halves, to decorate
clear honey, to glaze

1 Preheat the oven to 180°C/350°F/Gas 4. Grease and baseline a 20cm/8in round, loose-based cake tin (pan).

2 Cream the butter and sugar in a large bowl until pale and light. Gradually beat in the eggs.

3 Sift over the flour and baking powder, and fold in gently with the milk.

4 Stir in the cardamom seeds, chopped nuts and poppy seeds. Reserve one-third of the pear slices, and chop the remainder. Fold into the creamed mixture.

5 Transfer to the cake tin. Smooth the surface, making a small dip in the centre. Place the walnut halves in the centre of the cake and fan the reserved pear slices around the walnuts, covering the cake mixture.

6 Bake for 1¼–1½ hours, or until a skewer inserted into the centre comes out clean.

7 Remove the cake from the oven and brush with the honey. Leave in the tin for 20 minutes, then transfer to a wire rack to cool completely before serving.

Spiced Honey Nut Cake

A combination of ground pistachio nuts and breadcrumbs replaces flour in this recipe, resulting in a light, moist sponge cake.

Makes one 20cm/8in square cake

115g/4oz/generous ½ cup caster (superfine) sugar
4 eggs, separated
grated rind and juice of 1 lemon
130g/4½oz/generous 1 cup ground pistachio nuts
50g/2oz/scant 1 cup dried breadcrumbs

For the glaze

1 lemon
90ml/6 tbsp clear honey
1 cinnamon stick
15ml/1 tbsp brandy

1 Preheat the oven to 180°C/350°F/Gas 4. Grease and baseline a 20cm/8in square cake tin (pan).

2 Beat the sugar, egg yolks, lemon rind and juice together in a large bowl until pale and creamy. Fold in 115g/4oz/1 cup of the ground pistachio nuts and the breadcrumbs.

3 Whisk the egg whites until stiff peaks form and fold into the creamed mixture.

4 Transfer to the cake tin and bake for 15 minutes, or until risen and springy to the touch. Cool in the tin for 10 minutes, then transfer to a wire rack.

5 To make the glaze pare thin pieces of lemon rind and then cut them into very thin strips using a sharp knife.

6 Squeeze the lemon juice into a small pan and add the honey and cinnamon stick. Bring the mixture to the boil, add the shredded rind, and simmer fast for 1 minute. Cool slightly and stir in the brandy.

7 Place the cake on a serving plate, prick all over with a skewer so that the syrupy glaze will drain into the cake, and pour over the cooled syrup, lemon shreds and cinnamon stick. Sprinkle over the reserved pistachio nuts.

Pear Energy 2781kcal/11648kJ; Protein 44.8g; Carbohydrate 348.8g, of which sugars 177g; Fat 143.8g, of which saturates 66.6g; Cholesterol 628mg; Calcium 592mg; Fibre 19.7g; Sodium 882mg.
Honey Energy 1965kcal/8248kJ; Protein 55g; Carbohydrate 238.3g, of which sugars 197.6g; Fat 95.2g, of which saturates 15.8g; Cholesterol 761mg; Calcium 387mg; Fibre 9g; Sodium 1366mg.

American Carrot Cake

This light and spicy carrot cake has the traditional topping.

Makes one 20cm/8in round cake
250ml/8fl oz/1 cup corn oil
175g/6oz/scant 1 cup caster (superfine) sugar
3 eggs
175g/6oz/1 1/2 cups plain (all-purpose) flour
7.5ml/1 1/2 tsp baking powder
7.5ml/1 1/2 tsp bicarbonate of soda (baking soda)
1.5ml/1/4 tsp salt
7.5ml/1 1/2 tsp ground cinnamon

a good pinch of freshly grated nutmeg
1.5ml/1/4 tsp ground ginger
115g/4oz/1 cup chopped walnuts
225g/8oz/generous 1 1/2 cups finely grated carrots
5ml/1 tsp vanilla extract
30ml/2 tbsp sour cream
8 tiny marzipan carrots, to decorate

For the frosting
175g/6oz/3/4 cup full-fat soft cheese
25g/1oz/2 tbsp butter, softened
225g/8oz/2 cups icing (confectioners') sugar, sifted

1 Preheat the oven to 180°C/350°F/Gas 4. Grease and line two 20cm/8in loose-based round cake tins (pans).

2 Put the corn oil and sugar into a bowl and beat well. Add the eggs, one at a time, and beat thoroughly. Sift the flour, baking powder, bicarbonate of soda, salt, cinnamon, nutmeg and ginger into the bowl and beat well.

3 Fold in the chopped walnuts and grated carrots, and stir in the vanilla extract and sour cream.

4 Divide the mixture between the prepared cake tins and bake in the centre of the oven for about 65 minutes, or until a skewer inserted into the centre of the cakes comes out clean. Leave to cool in the tins on a wire rack. Meanwhile, beat all the frosting ingredients together until smooth.

5 Sandwich the cakes together with a little frosting. Spread the remaining frosting over the top and sides of the cake. Just before serving, decorate with the marzipan carrots.

Passion Cake

This cake is associated with Passion Sunday. The carrot and banana give it a rich, moist texture.

Makes one 20cm/8in round cake
200g/7oz/1 3/4 cups self-raising (self-rising) flour
10ml/2 tsp baking powder
5ml/1 tsp cinnamon
2.5ml/1/2 tsp freshly grated nutmeg
150g/5oz/10 tbsp butter, softened, or sunflower margarine
150g/5oz/generous 1 cup soft light brown sugar
grated rind of 1 lemon

2 eggs, beaten
2 carrots, coarsely grated
1 ripe banana, mashed
115g/4oz/3/4 cup raisins
50g/2oz/1/2 cup chopped walnuts or pecan nuts
30ml/2 tbsp milk
6–8 walnuts, halved, to decorate
coffee crystal sugar, to decorate

For the frosting
200g/7oz/scant 1 cup cream cheese, softened
30g/1 1/2oz/scant 1/3 cup icing (confectioners') sugar
juice of 1 lemon
grated rind of 1 orange

1 Line and grease a deep 20cm/8in round cake tin (pan). Preheat the oven to 180°C/350°F/Gas 4. Sift the flour, baking powder and spices into a bowl.

2 In another bowl, cream the butter or margarine and sugar with the lemon rind until it is light and fluffy, then beat in the eggs. Fold in the flour mixture, then the carrots, banana, raisins, chopped nuts and milk.

3 Spoon the mixture into the prepared cake tin, level the top and bake for about 1 hour, or until risen and the top is springy to the touch. Turn the tin upside down and allow the cake to cool in the tin for 30 minutes. Then turn out on to a wire rack and leave to cool completely. When cold, split the cake in half.

4 To make the frosting, cream the cheese with the icing sugar, lemon juice and orange rind, then sandwich the two halves of the cake together with half of the frosting. Spread the rest of the frosting on top and decorate with walnut halves and sugar.

Carrot Energy 5897kcal/24604kJ; Protein 61.9g; Carbohydrate 576.8g, of which sugars 441.6g; Fat 387.8g, of which saturates 106.3g; Cholesterol 808mg; Calcium 911mg; Fibre 14.9g; Sodium 992mg.
Passion Energy 4318kcal/18033kJ; Protein 50.9g; Carbohydrate 456.2g, of which sugars 300.8g; Fat 267.4g, of which saturates 144.1g; Cholesterol 890mg; Calcium 798mg; Fibre 14.7g; Sodium 1777mg.

Caribbean Fruit & Rum Cake

Definitely a festive treat, this spicy cake contains both rum and sherry.

Makes one 25cm/10in round cake

450g/1lb/2 cups currants
450g/1lb/3¼ cups raisins
225g/8oz/1 cup prunes, pitted
115g/4oz/¾ cup mixed (candied) peel
400g/14oz/1¾ cups soft dark brown sugar
5ml/1 tsp mixed (apple pie) spice
90ml/6 tbsp rum, plus more if needed
300ml/½ pint/1¼ cups sherry, plus more if needed
450g/1lb/4 cups self-raising (self-rising) flour
450g/1lb/2 cups butter, softened
10 eggs, beaten
5ml/1 tsp vanilla extract

1 Finely chop the currants, raisins, prunes and peel in a food processor. Combine them in a bowl with 115g/4oz/generous ½ cup of the sugar, the mixed spice, rum and sherry.

2 Put in a large screwtop jar or in a bowl with a lid, and leave for 2 weeks. Stir daily and add more rum or sherry if you wish.

3 Preheat the oven to 160°C/325°F/Gas 3. Grease and then line a 25cm/10in round cake tin (pan) with a double layer of baking parchment.

4 Sift the flour into a bowl, and set aside. Cream together the butter and remaining sugar, and beat in the eggs until the mixture is smooth and creamy. Add a spoonful of flour halfway through adding the eggs, to stop the mixture curdling.

5 Add the fruit mixture, then gradually stir in the remaining flour and vanilla extract. Mix well, adding more sherry if the mixture is too stiff; it should just fall off the back of the spoon.

6 Spoon the mixture into the prepared tin, cover loosely with foil and bake for about 2½ hours, or until the cake is firm and springy. Leave to cool in the tin overnight.

Thai Rice Cake

This unusual celebration gateau is made from fragrant Thai rice, covered with a tangy cream icing and topped with fresh fruits.

Makes one 25cm/10in round cake

225g/8oz/1¼ cups Thai fragrant rice
1 litre/1¾ pints/4 cups milk
115g/4oz/½ cup caster (superfine) sugar
6 cardamom pods, crushed open
2 bay leaves
300ml/½ pint/1¼ cups whipping cream
6 eggs, separated

For the topping
300ml/½ pint/1¼ cups double (heavy) cream
200g/7oz/scant 1 cup quark
5ml/1 tsp vanilla extract
grated rind of 1 lemon
30g/1½oz/scant ¼ cup caster (superfine) sugar
soft berry fruits and sliced star fruit (carambola) or kiwi fruit, to decorate

1 Grease and line a deep 25cm/10in round cake tin (pan). Boil the rice in unsalted water for 3 minutes, then drain.

2 Return the rice to the pan with the milk, sugar, cardamom pods and bay leaves. Bring to the boil, then simmer for 20 minutes, stirring occasionally.

3 Allow to cool, then remove the bay leaves and any cardamom husks. Turn into a bowl. Beat in the cream and then the egg yolks. Preheat the oven to 180°C/350°F/Gas 4.

4 Whisk the egg whites until they form soft peaks and fold into the rice mixture. Spoon into the cake tin and bake for 45–50 minutes, or until risen and golden brown. The centre should be slightly wobbly – it will firm up as it cools.

5 Chill overnight in the tin. Turn out on to a large serving plate. Whip the double cream until stiff, then mix in the quark, vanilla extract, lemon rind and sugar.

6 Cover the top and sides of the cake with the cream. Decorate with soft berry fruits and sliced star fruit or kiwi fruit.

Fruit Energy 10550kcal/44342kJ; Protein 135.9g; Carbohydrate 1536g, of which sugars 1193.1g; Fat 436.8g, of which saturates 250.8g Cholesterol 2862mg; Calcium 2081mg; Fibre 49.8g Sodium 4174mg.
Rice Energy 5009kcal/20846kJ; Protein 115.1g; Carbohydrate 400.5g, of which sugars 220.5g; Fat 333.6g, of which saturates 196.1g; Cholesterol 1929mg; Calcium 2066mg; Fibre 0g; Sodium 1074mg.

Luxurious Chocolate Cake

This attractive and delicious chocolate cake contains no flour and has a light mousse-like texture.

Makes one 20cm/8in round cake

9 x 25g/1oz squares plain (semisweet) chocolate

175g/6oz/³⁄₄ cup butter, softened
130g/3¹⁄₂oz/²⁄₃ cup caster (superfine) sugar
225g/8oz/2 cups ground almonds
4 eggs, separated
4 x 25g/1oz squares white chocolate, melted, to decorate

1 Preheat the oven to 180°C/350°F/Gas 4. Grease and base-line a 20cm/8in springform cake tin (pan).

2 Melt the chocolate in a heatproof bowl over a pan of simmering water. Beat 115g/4oz/¹⁄₂ cup butter and all the sugar until light and fluffy in a large bowl. Add two-thirds of the plain chocolate, the almonds and egg yolks, and beat well.

3 Whisk the egg whites in another clean, dry bowl until stiff peaks form. Fold them into the chocolate mixture, then transfer to the tin and smooth the surface. Bake for 50–55 minutes, or until a skewer inserted into the centre comes out clean.

4 Cool in the tin for 5 minutes, then remove from the tin and transfer to a wire rack. Remove the lining paper and cool completely.

5 Place the remaining butter and remaining melted chocolate in a pan. Heat very gently, stirring constantly, until melted. Place a large sheet of baking parchment under the wire rack to catch any drips. Pour the chocolate topping over the cake, allowing the topping to coat the top and sides. Leave to set for at least 1 hour.

6 To decorate, fill a paper piping (icing) bag with the melted white chocolate and snip the end. Drizzle the white chocolate around the edges. Use any remaining chocolate to pipe leaves on to baking parchment or greaseproof (waxed) paper. Allow to set then place on top of the cake.

One-stage Chocolate Sponge

For family teas, quick and easy favourites like this chocolate cake are invaluable.

Makes one 18cm/7in round cake

175g/6oz/³⁄₄ cup soft margarine, at room temperature
115g/4oz/generous ¹⁄₂ cup caster (superfine) sugar
50g/2oz/4 tbsp golden (light corn) syrup

175g/6oz/1¹⁄₂ cups self-raising (self-rising) flour, sifted
45ml/3 tbsp unsweetened cocoa powder, sifted
2.5ml/¹⁄₂ tsp salt
3 eggs, beaten
a little milk, as required
150ml/¹⁄₄ pint/²⁄₃ cup whipping cream
15–30ml/1–2 tbsp fine shred marmalade
icing (confectioners') sugar, for dusting

1 Preheat the oven to 180°C/350°F/Gas 4. Lightly grease or line two 18cm/7in shallow round cake tins (pans).

2 Place the margarine, sugar, syrup, flour, cocoa powder, salt and eggs in a large bowl, and cream together until well blended using a wooden spoon or electric whisk. If the mixture seems a little thick, stir in 15–30ml/1–2 tbsp milk, until you have a soft dropping consistency.

3 Spoon the mixture into the prepared tins and bake for about 30 minutes, changing shelves if necessary after 15 minutes, until the tops are just firm and the cakes are springy to the touch.

4 Leave the cakes to cool for 5 minutes, then remove from the tins and leave to cool completely on a wire rack.

5 Whip the cream and fold in the marmalade, then use to sandwich the two cakes together. Sprinkle the top with sifted icing sugar.

> **Cook's Tip**
> *You could also use butter at room temperature cut into small pieces for this one-stage sponge mixture.*

Luxurious Energy 5162kcal/21484kJ; Protein 93.4g; Carbohydrate 353.6g, of which sugars 345.5g; Fat 385.5g, of which saturates 163.5g; Cholesterol 1148mg; Calcium 1099mg; Fibre 22.3g; Sodium 1503mg.
One-stage Energy 3476kcal/14495kJ; Protein 47.3g; Carbohydrate 315.7g, of which sugars 177.1g; Fat 234g, of which saturates 78.4g; Cholesterol 732mg; Calcium 556mg; Fibre 10.9g; Sodium 2022mg.

Mocha Victoria Sponge

A light coffee- and cocoa-flavoured sponge with a rich buttercream topping.

Makes one 18cm/7in round cake
175g/6oz/¾ cup butter
175g/6oz/generous ¾ cup caster (superfine) sugar
3 eggs
175g/6oz/1½ cups self-raising (self-rising) flour, sifted
15ml/1 tbsp strong black coffee
15ml/1 tbsp unsweetened cocoa powder mixed with 15–30ml/1–2 tbsp boiling water

For the coffee buttercream
150g/5oz/10 tbsp butter
15ml/1 tbsp coffee extract or 10ml/2 tsp instant coffee powder dissolved in 15–30ml/1–2 tbsp warm milk
275g/10oz/2½ cups icing (confectioners') sugar

1 Preheat the oven to 180°C/350°F/Gas 4. Grease and base-line two 18cm/7in shallow round cake tins (pans). Cream the butter and sugar in a large bowl until light and fluffy. Add the eggs, one at a time, beating well after each addition. Fold in the flour.

2 Divide the mixture between two bowls. Fold the coffee into one and the cocoa mixture into the other.

3 Place alternate spoonfuls of each mixture side by side in the cake tins. Bake for 25–30 minutes. Turn out on to a wire rack to cool.

4 For the buttercream, beat the butter until soft. Gradually beat in the remaining ingredients until smooth.

5 Sandwich the cakes, bases together, with a third of the buttercream. Cover the top and side with the remainder.

Cook's Tip
When mixing eggs into creamed sugar and butter, whisk only briefly, and if the mixture begins to curdle add a spoonful of the flour before you add any more of the eggs.

One-stage Victoria Sandwich

This recipe can be used as the base for other cakes.

Makes one 18cm/7in round cake
175g/6oz/1½ cups self-raising (self-rising) flour
a pinch of salt
175g/6oz/¾ cup butter, softened
175g/6oz/scant 1 cup caster (superfine) sugar
3 eggs
300ml/½ pint/1¼ cups double (heavy) cream
60–90ml/4–6 tbsp raspberry jam
caster (superfine) sugar or icing (confectioners') sugar

1 Preheat the oven to 180°C/350°F/Gas 4. Grease two 18cm/7in shallow round cake tins (pans), line the bases with baking parchment and grease the paper.

2 Put the flour, salt, butter, caster sugar and eggs into a large bowl. Whisk the ingredients together until smooth and creamy.

3 Divide the mixture between the prepared cake tins and smooth the surfaces. Bake for 25–30 minutes, or until a skewer inserted into the centre of the cakes comes out clean.

4 Turn out on to a wire rack, peel off the lining paper and leave to cool. Whip the cream until soft peaks form.

5 Place one of the cakes on a serving plate and spread with the cream and the raspberry jam. Place the other cake on top. Dredge the top of the cake with icing sugar.

Variation
Sponge Cake with Strawberries and Cream is delicious on a summer's day. Whip 300ml/½ pint/1¼ cups double (heavy) cream with 5ml/1 tsp icing (confectioners') sugar until stiff. Wash and hull 450g/1lb/4 cups strawberries, then cut them in half. Spread one of the cakes with half of the cream and sprinkle over half of the strawberries. Place the other cake on top, spread with the remaining cream and arrange the remaining strawberries.

One-stage Energy 2965kcal/12419kJ; Protein 37.5g; Carbohydrate 361.3g, of which sugars 227.9g; Fat 162.8g, of which saturates 96.2g; Cholesterol 944mg; Calcium 462mg; Fibre 5.4g; Sodium 1304mg.
Mocha Energy 4668kcal/19505kJ; Protein 42.2g; Carbohydrate 506.1g, of which sugars 371g; Fat 289.6g, of which saturates 176.4g; Cholesterol 1265mg; Calcium 612mg; Fibre 7.2g; Sodium 2355mg.

Cherry Batter Cake

This colourful tray bake looks pretty cut into neat squares or fingers. Its unusual topping makes it especially tasty.

Makes one 33 x 23cm/ 13 x 9in cake
225g/8oz/2 cups self-raising (self-rising) flour
5ml/1 tsp baking powder
75g/3oz/6 tbsp butter, softened
150g/5oz/scant 1 cup soft light brown sugar
1 egg, lightly beaten

150ml/¼ pint/⅔ cup milk
icing (confectioners') sugar, for dusting
whipped cream, to serve (optional)

For the topping
675g/1½lb jar black cherries or blackcurrants, drained
175g/6oz/¾ cup soft light brown sugar
50g/2oz/½ cup self-raising (self-rising) flour
50g/2oz/¼ cup butter, melted

1 Preheat the oven to 190°C/375°F/Gas 5. Grease and line a 33 x 23cm/13 x 9in Swiss roll tin (jelly roll pan) with baking parchment, and grease the paper.

2 To make the base, sift the flour and baking powder into a large bowl. Add the butter, sugar, egg and milk.

3 Beat until the mixture becomes smooth, then turn into the prepared tin and smooth the surface.

4 To make the topping, sprinkle the drained cherries or blackcurrants evenly over the batter mixture.

5 Mix together the brown sugar, flour and melted butter, and spoon evenly over the fruit.

6 Bake for 40 minutes, or until the top is golden brown and the centre is firm to the touch.

7 Leave to cool for 15 minutes in the tin, then turn out and leave on a wire rack to cool completely. Dust with icing sugar. Serve with whipped cream, if you like.

Lemon & Apricot Cake

This cake is soaked in a tangy lemon syrup after baking to keep it really moist.

Makes one 23 x 13cm/ 9 x 5in loaf
175g/6oz/¾ cup butter, softened
175g/6oz/1½ cups self-raising (self-rising) flour
2.5ml/½ tsp baking powder
175g/6oz/generous ¾ cup caster (superfine) sugar
3 eggs, lightly beaten
finely grated rind of 1 lemon

175g/6oz/1½ cups ready-to-eat dried apricots, finely chopped
75g/3oz/¾ cup ground almonds
40g/1½oz/6 tbsp pistachio nuts, chopped
50g/2oz/½ cup flaked (sliced) almonds
15g/½oz/2 tbsp whole pistachio nuts

For the syrup
45ml/3 tbsp caster (superfine) sugar
freshly squeezed juice of 1 lemon

1 Preheat the oven to 180°C/350°F/Gas 4. Grease and line a 23 x 13cm/9 x 5in loaf tin (pan) with baking parchment and grease the paper.

2 Place the butter in a large bowl. Sift over the flour and baking powder, then add the sugar, eggs and lemon rind.

3 Using an electric whisk or a wooden spoon, beat for 1–2 minutes, or until smooth and glossy, then stir in the apricots, ground almonds and chopped pistachio nuts.

4 Spoon the mixture into the loaf tin and smooth the surface. Sprinkle with the flaked almonds and the whole pistachio nuts.

5 Bake for 1¼ hours, or until a skewer inserted into the centre of the cake comes out clean. Check the cake after 45 minutes and cover with a piece of foil when the top is nicely browned. Leave the cake to cool in the tin.

6 To make the lemon syrup, gently dissolve the sugar in the lemon juice in a small pan over a low heat. Spoon the syrup over the cake. When the cake is completely cooled, turn it carefully out of the tin and peel off the lining paper.

Lemon Energy 4358kcal/18221kJ; Protein 80.6g; Carbohydrate 443.9g, of which sugars 305.8g; Fat 264g, of which saturates 105.8g; Cholesterol 944mg; Calcium 967mg; Fibre 29.1g; Sodium 1622mg.
Cherry Energy 3770kcal/15932kJ; Protein 43g; Carbohydrate 686g, of which sugars 476.4g; Fat 114.4g, of which saturates 68.8g; Cholesterol 466mg; Calcium 890mg; Fibre 12.6g; Sodium 974mg.

Fruit Salad Cake

You can use any combination of dried fruits in this rich, dark fruit cake.

Makes one 18cm/7in round cake
175g/6oz/1 cup roughly chopped mixed dried fruit, such as apples, apricots, prunes and peaches
250ml/8fl oz/1 cup hot tea
225g/8oz/2 cups self-raising (self-rising) wholemeal (whole-wheat) flour
5ml/1 tsp freshly grated nutmeg
50g/2oz/¼ cup muscovado (molasses) sugar
45ml/3 tbsp sunflower oil
45ml/3 tbsp skimmed milk
demerara (raw) sugar, for sprinkling

1 Soak the dried fruits in the tea for several hours or overnight. Drain and reserve the liquid.

2 Preheat the oven to 180°C/350°F/Gas 4. Grease an 18cm/7in round cake tin (pan) and line the base with baking parchment.

3 Sift the flour into a bowl with the nutmeg. Stir in the muscovado sugar, and the dried fruit and tea. Add the oil and milk, and mix well.

4 Spoon the mixture into the prepared cake tin and sprinkle with demerara sugar.

5 Bake for 50–55 minutes, or until firm. Turn out on to a wire rack to cool.

Cook's Tips
• *For successful baking always level the mixture in the cake tin (pan) before baking.*
• *Test that the cake is cooked before the stated cooking time as oven temperatures can vary and it might take less time. Fan-assisted ovens usually cook foods more quickly.*
• *Check that the oven shelf is level, as an uneven surface will cause the cake to cook lopsidedly.*

Fairy Cakes with Blueberries

This luxurious treatment of fairy cakes means they will be as popular with adults as with children.

Makes 8–10
115g/4oz/½ cup soft margarine
115g/4oz/½ cup caster (superfine) sugar
5ml/1 tsp grated lemon rind
a pinch of salt
2 eggs, beaten
115g/4oz/1 cup self-raising (self-rising) flour, sifted
120ml/4fl oz/½ cup whipping cream
75–115g/3–4oz/¾–1 cup blueberries
icing (confectioners') sugar, for dusting

1 Preheat the oven to 190°C/375°F/Gas 5. Cream the margarine, sugar, lemon rind and salt in a large bowl until pale and fluffy.

2 Gradually beat in the eggs, then fold in the flour.

3 Spoon the mixture into eight to ten paper cases on baking sheets and bake for 15–20 minutes, or until just golden.

4 Leave the cakes to cool, then scoop out a circle of sponge from the top of each using the point of a small sharp knife, and set them aside.

5 Whip the cream and place a spoonful in each cake, plus a couple of blueberries. Replace the lids at an angle and sift over some icing sugar.

Variation
These fairy cakes are perfect for making into Angel Cakes with butter icing. Slice the domed top from the cake and cut in two. Make some butter icing and flavour it as you like (orange or chocolate are particular favourites with children). Spread some butter icing on the top of each cake and position the cut tops with the cut sides outwards to look like wings.

Fruit Salad Energy 1482kcal/6266kJ; Protein 37.4g; Carbohydrate 261.9g, of which sugars 122.8g; Fat 39.1g, of which saturates 4.7g; Cholesterol 2mg; Calcium 295mg; Fibre 31.3g; Sodium 54mg.
Fairy Cakes Energy 231kcal/962kJ; Protein 2.7g; Carbohydrate 21.5g, of which sugars 13g; Fat 15.5g, of which saturates 3.4g; Cholesterol 51mg; Calcium 63mg; Fibre 0.6g; Sodium 151mg.

Jewel Cake

This pretty cake is excellent served as a teatime treat.

**Makes one 23 x 13cm/
9 x 5in cake**

115g/4oz/½ cup mixed glacé
   (candied) cherries, halved,
   washed and dried
50g/2oz/4 tbsp preserved stem
   ginger in syrup, chopped,
   washed and dried
50g/2oz/⅓ cup chopped mixed
   (candied) peel
115g/4oz/1 cup self-raising
   (self-rising) flour
75g/3oz/⅔ cup plain
   (all-purpose) flour

25g/1oz/¼ cup cornflour
   (cornstarch)
175g/6oz/¾ cup butter
175g/6oz/scant 1 cup caster
   (superfine) sugar
3 eggs
grated rind of 1 orange

To decorate
175g/6oz/1½ cups icing
   (confectioners') sugar, sifted
30–45ml/2–3 tbsp freshly
   squeezed orange juice
50g/2oz/¼ cup mixed glacé
   (candied) cherries, chopped
25g/1oz/2½ tbsp mixed
   (candied) peel, chopped

1 Preheat the oven to 180°C/350°F/Gas 4. Grease and line a 23 x 13cm/9 x 5in loaf tin (pan) and grease the paper.

2 Place the glacé cherries, stem ginger and mixed peel in a plastic bag with 25g/1oz/¼ cup of the self-raising flour and shake to coat evenly. Sift together the remaining flours and cornflour.

3 In a large bowl, beat together the butter and sugar until light and fluffy. Beat in the eggs, one at a time. Fold in the sifted flours with the orange rind, then stir in the dried fruit.

4 Transfer the mixture to the cake tin and bake for 1¼ hours, or until a skewer inserted into the centre comes out clean. Leave in the tin for 5 minutes, then cool on a wire rack.

5 For the decoration, mix the icing sugar with the orange juice until smooth. Drizzle the icing over the cake.

6 Mix together the glacé cherries and mixed peel, then use to decorate the cake. Allow the icing to set before serving.

Iced Paradise Cake

Serve this rich and creamy delight chilled.

**Makes one 23 x 13cm/
9 x 5in cake**

3 eggs
75g/3oz/scant ½ cup caster
   (superfine) sugar
65g/12½oz/9 tbsp plain
   (all-purpose) flour, sifted
15g/½oz/2 tbsp cornflour
   (cornstarch), sifted
90ml/6 tbsp dark rum
250g/9oz/1½ cups plain
   (semisweet) chocolate chips

30ml/2 tbsp golden (light
   corn) syrup
30ml/2 tbsp water
400ml/14fl oz/1⅔ cups double
   (heavy) cream, whipped
115g/4oz/generous 1 cup
   desiccated (dry unsweetened
   shredded) coconut, toasted
25g/1oz/2 tbsp unsalted
   (sweet) butter
30ml/2 tbsp single (light) cream
50g/2oz/⅓ cup white chocolate
   chips, melted
coconut curls, to decorate
cocoa powder, for dusting

1 Preheat the oven to 200°C/400°F/Gas 6. Grease and flour two baking sheets. Line a 23 x 13cm/9 x 5in loaf tin (pan) with clear film (plastic wrap).

2 Whisk the eggs and sugar together in a heatproof bowl. Place over a pan of simmering water and whisk until pale and thick. Whisk off the heat until cool. Fold in the flour and cornflour. Pipe 30 7.5cm/3in sponge fingers on to the baking sheets. Bake for 8–10 minutes. Cool slightly, then transfer to a wire rack.

3 Line the base and sides of the loaf tin with sponge fingers. Brush with rum. Melt 75g/3oz/½ cup chocolate chips, the syrup, water and 30ml/2 tbsp rum in a bowl over simmering water.

4 Stir the chocolate mixture and coconut into the cream. Pour into the tin and top with the remaining fingers. Brush with the remaining rum. Cover with clear film and freeze until firm.

5 Melt the remaining chocolate with the butter and single cream as before, then cool slightly. Turn the cake out on to a wire rack. Coat with the icing. Chill. Drizzle with white chocolate zigzags. Chill. Sprinkle with coconut curls and dust with cocoa powder.

Jewel Energy 4369kcal/18404kJ; Protein 41.5g; Carbohydrate 726.1g, of which sugars 560.5g; Fat 164.9g, of which saturates 96.5g; Cholesterol 982mg; Calcium 1042mg; Fibre 11.5g; Sodium 2007mg.
Paradise Energy 5502kcal/22864kJ; Protein 62.6g; Carbohydrate 349.1g, of which sugars 226.4g; Fat 416.4g, of which saturates 267.8g; Cholesterol 1204mg; Calcium 760mg; Fibre 26.4g; Sodium 653mg.

Pound Cake with Red Fruit

This orange-scented cake is good for tea, or served as a dessert with cream.

Makes one 20 x 10cm/ 8 x 4in cake
450g/1lb/4 cups fresh raspberries, strawberries or pitted cherries, or a combination of any of these
175g/6oz/generous ¾ cup caster (superfine) sugar, plus 15–30ml/ 1–2 tbsp, plus extra for sprinkling
15ml/1 tbsp lemon juice
175g/6oz/1½ cups plain (all-purpose) flour
10ml/2 tsp baking powder
pinch of salt
175g/6oz/¾ cup unsalted (sweet) butter, softened
3 eggs
grated rind of 1 orange
15ml/1 tbsp orange juice

1 Reserve a few whole fruits for decorating. In a blender or food processor, process the fruit until smooth. Add 15–30ml/1–2 tbsp sugar and the lemon juice, and process again. Strain the sauce and chill.

2 Grease the base and sides of a 20 x 10cm/8 x 4in loaf tin (pan) and line the base with baking parchment. Grease the paper. Sprinkle with sugar and tip out any excess. Preheat the oven to 180°C/350°F/Gas 4.

3 Sift together the flour, baking powder and a pinch of salt. In another bowl, beat the butter until creamy. Add the sugar and beat until light and fluffy. Add the eggs, one at a time, beating well after each addition.

4 Beat in the orange rind and juice. Gently fold the flour mixture into the butter mixture in three batches, then spoon the mixture into the loaf tin and tap gently to release any air bubbles.

5 Bake for 35–40 minutes, or until the top is golden and it is springy to the touch. Leave the cake in its tin on a wire rack for 10 minutes, then remove the cake from the tin and cool for 30 minutes. Remove the paper and serve slices of cake with a little of the fruit sauce, decorated with the reserved fruit.

Madeleines

These little tea cakes, baked in a special tin with shell-shaped cups, are best eaten on the day they are made.

Makes 12
165g/5½oz/generous 1¼ cups plain (all-purpose) flour
5ml/1 tsp baking powder
2 eggs
75g/3oz/¾ cup icing (confectioners') sugar, plus extra for dusting
grated rind of 1 lemon or orange
15ml/1 tbsp lemon or orange juice
75g/3oz/6 tbsp unsalted (sweet) butter, melted and slightly cooled

1 Preheat the oven to 190°C/375°F/Gas 5. Generously grease a 12-cup madeleine tin (pan). Sift together the flour and the baking powder.

2 Beat the eggs and icing sugar in a large bowl until the mixture is thick and creamy and leaves ribbon trails. Gently fold in the lemon or orange rind and juice.

3 Beginning with the flour mixture, alternately fold in the flour and melted butter in four batches. Leave to stand for 10 minutes, then spoon into the tin. Tap gently to release any air bubbles.

4 Bake for 12–15 minutes, rotating the tin halfway through cooking. The cake is cooked when a skewer inserted in the centre comes out clean.

5 Turn out on to a wire rack to cool completely and dust with icing sugar before serving.

> **Cook's Tip**
> *These cakes look sweet baked in the traditional Madeleine tins (pans), but cooking equipment suppliers now stock all kinds of novelty cake tins, such as flowers, stars and hearts that would be suitable for using with this recipe. You could even drizzle some orange-flavoured glacé icing over the tops.*

Pound Cake Energy 2927kcal/12264kJ; Protein 43.5g; Carbohydrate 341.9g, of which sugars 208.6g; Fat 164.1g, of which saturates 96.6g; Cholesterol 944mg; Calcium 569mg; Fibre 16.7g; Sodium 1301mg.
Madeleines Energy 130kcal/547kJ; Protein 2.4g; Carbohydrate 17.3g, of which sugars 6.8g; Fat 6.2g, of which saturates 3.5g; Cholesterol 45mg; Calcium 28mg; Fibre 0.4g; Sodium 50mg.

Chocolate Orange Battenburg Cake

A tasty variation on the traditional pink-and-white Battenburg cake. Use good quality marzipan for the best flavour.

Makes one 18cm/7in long rectangular cake
115g/4oz/½ cup soft margarine
115g/4oz/½ cup caster (superfine) sugar

2 eggs, beaten
a few drops of vanilla extract
15g/½oz/1 tbsp ground almonds
115g/4oz/1 cup self-raising (self-rising) flour, sifted
grated rind and juice of ½ orange
15g/½oz/2 tbsp unsweetened cocoa powder, sifted
30–45ml/2–3 tbsp milk
1 jar chocolate and nut spread
225g/8oz white marzipan

1 Preheat the oven to 180°C/350°F/Gas 4. Grease and line an 18cm/7in square cake tin (pan) with baking parchment. Put a double piece of foil across the middle of the tin, to divide it into two equal oblongs.

2 Cream the margarine and sugar. Beat in the eggs, vanilla extract and almonds. Divide the mixture evenly into two halves.

3 Fold half of the flour into one half, with the orange rind and enough juice to give a soft dropping consistency. Fold the rest of the flour and the cocoa powder into the other half, with enough milk to give a soft dropping consistency. Fill the tin with the two mixes and level the top.

4 Bake for 15 minutes, reduce the heat to 160°C/325°F/Gas 3 and cook for 20–30 minutes, or until the top is just firm. Leave to cool in the tin for a few minutes. Turn out on to a board, cut each cake into two strips and trim evenly. Leave to cool.

5 Using the chocolate and nut spread, sandwich the cakes together, Battenburg-style.

6 Roll out the marzipan on a board lightly dusted with cornflour to a rectangle 18cm/7in wide and long enough to wrap around the cake. Wrap the paste around the cake, putting the join underneath. Press to seal.

Best-ever Chocolate Sandwich

A three-layered cake is ideal for a birthday party.

Makes one 20cm/8in round cake
115g/4oz/1 cup plain (all-purpose) flour
50g/2oz/½ cup unsweetened cocoa powder
5ml/1 tsp baking powder
6 eggs
225g/8oz/generous 1 cup caster (superfine) sugar

10ml/2 tsp vanilla extract
115g/4oz/½ cup unsalted (sweet) butter, melted

For the icing
225g/8oz plain (semisweet) chocolate, chopped
75g/3oz/6 tbsp unsalted (sweet) butter
3 eggs, separated
250ml/8fl oz/1 cup whipping cream
45ml/3 tbsp caster (superfine) sugar

1 Preheat the oven to 180°C/350°F/Gas 4. Line three 20cm/8in round shallow cake tins (pans) with baking parchment, grease the paper and dust with flour. Sift the flour, cocoa powder, baking powder and a pinch of salt together three times.

2 Place the eggs and sugar in the top of a double boiler. Beat until doubled in volume. Add the vanilla extract. Fold in the flour mixture in three batches, then the melted butter. Transfer the mixture into the tins. Bake until the cakes pull away from the tin sides, about 25 minutes. Transfer to a wire rack.

3 To make the icing, melt the chocolate in the top of a double boiler. Off the heat, stir in the butter and egg yolks. Return to the heat and stir until thick. Whip the cream until firm.

4 In another bowl, beat the egg whites until stiff peaks form. Add the sugar and beat until glossy. Fold the cream, then the egg whites, into the chocolate mixture. Chill the cake for 20 minutes, then sandwich together and cover with icing.

Variation
Try coffee butter icing (see p510) instead of chocolate icing.

Battenburg Energy 3916kcal/16370kJ; Protein 52.8g; Carbohydrate 426.6g, of which sugars 334g; Fat 234.1g, of which saturates 41.6g; Cholesterol 389mg; Calcium 830mg; Fibre 9.3g; Sodium 1403mg.
Sandwich Energy 5787kcal/24151kJ; Protein 95g; Carbohydrate 528g, of which sugars 432.6g; Fat 382.2g, of which saturates 220.4g; Cholesterol 2393mg; Calcium 879mg; Fibre 15.2g; Sodium 2352mg.

Marbled Chocolate & Peanut Cake

A deliciously rich treat for a special tea.

Serves 12–14

115g/4oz unsweetened chocolate, chopped
225g/8oz/1 cup unsalted (sweet) butter, softened
225g/8oz/1 cup peanut butter
200g/7oz/1 cup caster (superfine) sugar
225g/8oz/1 cup soft light brown sugar
5 eggs
275g/10oz/2½ cups plain (all-purpose) flour
10ml/2 tsp baking powder
2.5ml/½ tsp salt
125ml/4fl oz/½ cup milk
50g/2oz/⅓ cup chocolate chips

For the chocolate–peanut butter glaze
25g/1oz/2 tbsp butter, diced
25g/1oz/2 tbsp smooth peanut butter
45ml/3 tbsp golden (light corn) syrup
5ml/1 tsp vanilla extract
175g/6oz plain (semisweet) chocolate, broken into pieces

1 Preheat the oven to 180°C/350°F/Gas 4. Grease and flour a 3-litre/5¼-pint/13¼-cup tube tin (pan) or ring mould. Melt the chocolate in a double boiler or in a heatproof bowl over a pan of simmering water.

2 Beat the butter, peanut butter and sugars until light and creamy. Add the eggs, one at a time, beating well after each addition. Sift together the flour, baking powder and salt. Add to the butter mixture alternately with the milk.

3 Pour half the batter into another bowl. Stir the melted chocolate into one half and stir the chocolate chips into the other half. Drop alternate large spoonfuls of the two batters into the tin or mould. Using a knife, pull through the batters to create a swirled marbled effect; do not let the knife touch the side or base of the tin. Bake for 50–60 minutes, or until the top springs back when touched. Cool in the tin on a wire rack for 10 minutes. Then unmould on to the wire rack.

4 Combine the glaze ingredients and 15ml/1 tbsp water in a small pan. Melt over a low heat, stirring. Cool slightly, then drizzle over the cake, allowing it to run down the sides.

Chocolate Layer Cake

The surprise ingredient – beetroot – makes a beautifully moist cake.

Makes one 23cm/9in cake

unsweetened cocoa powder, for dusting
225g/8oz can cooked whole beetroot, drained and juice reserved
115g/4oz/½ cup unsalted (sweet) butter, softened
550g/1lb 6oz/2¾ cups soft light brown sugar
3 eggs
15ml/1 tbsp vanilla extract
75g/3oz unsweetened chocolate, melted
285g/10oz/2½ cups plain (all-purpose) flour
10ml/2 tsp baking powder
2.5ml/½ tsp salt
120ml/4fl oz/½ cup buttermilk
chocolate curls, to decorate (optional)

For the frosting
4750ml/16fl oz/2 cups double (heavy) cream
500g/1¼lb plain (semisweet) chocolate, chopped
15ml/1 tbsp vanilla extract

1 Preheat the oven to 180°C/350°F/Gas 4. Grease two 23cm/9in cake tins (pans) and dust with cocoa powder. Grate the beetroot and add it to its juice. Beat the butter, brown sugar, eggs and vanilla until pale and fluffy. Beat in the chocolate.

2 Sift together the flour, baking powder and salt. With the mixer on low speed and beginning and ending with flour mixture, alternately beat in flour and buttermilk. Add the beetroot and juice and beat for 1 minute. Transfer to the tins.

3 Bake for 30–35 minutes. Cool in the tin for 10 minutes, then unmould and transfer to wire rack to cool.

4 To make the frosting, heat the cream in a pan until it just begins to boil, stirring occasionally to prevent scorching. Remove from the heat and stir in the chocolate, until melted and smooth. Stir in the vanilla extract. Strain into a bowl and chill, stirring every 10 minutes, for 1 hour.

5 Sandwich and cover the cake with the frosting, and top with chocolate curls, if you like. Allow to set for 20–30 minutes, then chill before serving.

Layer Energy 9521kcal/39888kJ; Protein 94.2g; Carbohydrate 1196.3g, of which sugars 972.4g; Fat 518.1g, of which saturates 312.1g; Cholesterol 1472mg; Calcium 1419mg; Fibre 27.5g; Sodium 1382mg.
Marbled Energy 450kcal/1876kJ; Protein 7.9g; Carbohydrate 34.4g, of which sugars 33.1g; Fat 32.3g, of which saturates 16g; Cholesterol 108mg; Calcium 46mg; Fibre 1.5g; Sodium 210mg.

Chocolate Fairy Cakes

Make these delightful butter-iced fairy cakes to serve for a children's party.

Makes 24

115g/4oz good quality plain
   (semi-sweet) chocolate, cut
   into small pieces
15ml/1 tbsp water
300g/10oz/2½ cups plain
   (all-purpose) flour
5ml/1 tsp baking powder

2.5ml/½ tsp bicarbonate of soda
   (baking soda)
a pinch of salt
300g/11oz/generous 1½ cups
   caster (superfine) sugar
175g/6oz/¾ cup butter or
   margarine, at room temperature
150ml/¼ pint/⅔ cup milk
5ml/1 tsp vanilla extract
3 eggs
1 recipe quantity butter icing,
   flavoured to taste, see p248

1 Preheat the oven to 180°C/350°F/Gas 4. Grease and flour 24 deep bun cups, about 6.5cm/2¾in in diameter, or use paper cases in the tins (pans).

2 Put the chocolate and water in a bowl set over a pan of almost simmering water. Heat until melted and smooth, stirring. Remove from the heat and leave to cool.

3 Sift the flour, baking powder, bicarbonate of soda, salt and sugar into a large bowl. Add the chocolate mixture, butter or margarine, milk and vanilla extract.

4 With an electric mixer on medium-low speed, beat until smoothly blended. Increase the speed to high and beat for 2 minutes. Add the eggs and beat for 2 more minutes.

5 Divide the mixture evenly among the prepared bun tins and bake for 20–25 minutes, or until a skewer inserted into the centre of a cake comes out clean.

6 Cool in the tins for 10 minutes, then turn out to cool completely on a wire rack.

7 Ice the top of each cake with butter icing, swirling it into a peak in the centre.

Chocolate Mint-filled Cupcakes

For extra mint flavour, chop eight thin mint cream-filled after-dinner mints and fold into the cake batter.

Makes 12

225g/8oz/2 cups plain
   (all-purpose) flour
5ml/1 tsp bicarbonate of soda
   (baking soda)
a pinch of salt
50g/2oz/½ cup unsweetened
   cocoa powder
150g/5oz/10 tbsp unsalted
   (sweet) butter, softened
300g/11oz/generous 1½ cups
   caster (superfine) sugar

3 eggs
5ml/1 tsp peppermint extract
250ml/8fl oz/1 cup milk

For the filling
300ml/½ pint/1¼ cups double
   (heavy) or whipping cream
5ml/1 tsp peppermint extract

For the glaze
175g/6oz plain
   (semisweet) chocolate
115g/4oz/½ cup unsalted
   (sweet) butter
5ml/1 tsp peppermint extract

1 Preheat the oven to 180°C/350°F/Gas 4. Line a 12-cup bun tray with paper cases. Sift together the dry ingredients.

2 In another bowl, beat the butter and sugar until light and creamy. Add the eggs, one at a time, beating well after each addition; beat in the peppermint. On low speed, beat in the flour mixture alternately with the milk, until just blended. Spoon into the paper cases.

3 Bake for 12–15 minutes. Transfer to a wire rack to cool. When cool, remove the paper cases.

4 To make the filling, whip the cream and peppermint extract until stiff. Spoon into a piping (icing) bag fitted with a small plain nozzle. Pipe 15ml/1 tbsp into each cake through the base.

5 To make the glaze, melt the chocolate and butter in a heatproof bowl over a pan of simmering water, stirring until smooth. Remove from the heat and stir in the peppermint extract. Cool, then spread on top of each cake.

Fairy Cakes Energy 228kcal/957kJ; Protein 2.5g; Carbohydrate 30.6g, of which sugars 21g; Fat 11.5g, of which saturates 3.3g; Cholesterol 33mg; Calcium 40mg; Fibre 0.5g; Sodium 95mg.
Cupcakes Energy 535kcal/2234kJ; Protein 6.3g; Carbohydrate 52g, of which sugars 37.1g; Fat 35.1g, of which saturates 21.4g; Cholesterol 123mg; Calcium 100mg; Fibre 1.4g; Sodium 209mg.

Rich Chocolate Nut Cake

Use walnuts or pecan nuts for the cake sides if you prefer.

Makes one 23cm/9in round cake
225g/8oz/1 cup butter
225g/8oz plain (semisweet) chocolate
115g/4oz/1 cup unsweetened cocoa powder
350g/12oz/1¾ cups caster (superfine) sugar

6 eggs
85ml/3fl oz/5½ tbsp brandy
225g/8oz/2 cups finely chopped hazelnuts

For the glaze
50g/2oz/¼ cup butter
150g/5oz cooking chocolate
30ml/2 tbsp milk
5ml/1 tsp vanilla extract

1 Preheat the oven to 180°C/350°F/Gas 4. Line a 23 × 5cm/ 9 × 2in round tin (pan) with baking parchment and grease the paper.

2 Melt the butter and chocolate in the top of a double boiler. Leave to cool.

3 Sift the cocoa powder into a bowl. Add the sugar and eggs, and stir until just combined. Pour in the chocolate mixture and brandy.

4 Fold in three-quarters of the hazelnuts, then pour the mixture into the prepared cake tin.

5 Set the tin in a roasting pan and pour 2.5cm/1in hot water into the outer pan. Bake until the cake is firm to the touch, about 45 minutes. Leave for 15 minutes, then unmould on to a wire rack. When cool, wrap in baking parchment and chill for at least 6 hours.

6 To make the glaze, melt the butter and chocolate with the milk and vanilla extract as before.

7 Place the cake on a wire rack over a plate. Drizzle the glaze over, letting it drip down the sides. Cover the cake sides with the remaining nuts. Transfer to a serving plate when set.

Multi-layer Chocolate Cake

For a change, sandwich the cake layers with softened vanilla ice cream. Freeze before serving.

Makes one 20cm/8in round cake
115g/4oz plain (semisweet) chocolate
175g/6oz/¾ cup butter
450g/1lb/2¼ cups caster (superfine) sugar
3 eggs

5ml/1 tsp vanilla extract
175g/6oz/1½ cups plain (all-purpose) flour
5ml/1 tsp baking powder
115g/4oz/1 cup chopped walnuts

For the filling and topping
350ml/12fl oz/1½ cups whipping cream
225g/8oz plain (semisweet) chocolate
15ml/1 tbsp vegetable oil

1 Preheat the oven to 180°C/350°F/Gas 4. Line two 20cm/8in shallow round cake tins (pans) with baking parchment and grease the paper.

2 Melt the chocolate and butter in the top of a double boiler or in a heatproof bowl over a pan of simmering water. Transfer to a bowl and stir in the sugar. Add the eggs and vanilla and mix.

3 Sift over the flour and baking powder. Stir in the chopped walnuts.

4 Pour the mixture into the prepared cake tins. Bake until a skewer inserted into the centre comes out clean, about 30 minutes. Leave to stand for 10 minutes, then unmould on to a wire rack to cool completely.

5 To make the filling and topping, whip the cream until firm. Slice the cakes in half horizontally. Sandwich them together with the cream and cover the cake with the remainder. Chill.

6 To make the chocolate curls, melt the chocolate and oil as before. Stir to combine well. Spread on to a non-porous surface. Just before it sets, hold the blade of a knife at an angle to the chocolate and scrape across the surface to make curls. Use to decorate the cake and add tiny curls made with the tip of a rounded knife as well, if you like.

Rich Energy 7802kcal/32523kJ; Protein 113.7g; Carbohydrate 633.7g, of which sugars 612.6g; Fat 532.7g, of which saturates 241.2g; Cholesterol 1752mg; Calcium 1030mg; Fibre 37.9g; Sodium 3249mg.
Multi-layer Energy 7850kcal/32796kJ; Protein 79.4g; Carbohydrate 836.4g, of which sugars 699.2g; Fat 488.8g, of which saturates 249.3g; Cholesterol 1332mg; Calcium 1024mg; Fibre 17.9g; Sodium 1419mg.

Chocolate Frosted Layer Cake

The contrast between the frosting and the sponge creates a dramatic effect when the cake is cut.

Makes one 20cm/8in round cake
225g/8oz/1 cup butter or margarine, at room temperature
300g/11oz/scant 1½ cups caster (superfine) sugar
4 eggs, separated
10ml/2 tsp vanilla extract
385g/13½oz/3⅓ cups plain (all-purpose) flour
10ml/2 tsp baking powder
1.5ml/¼ tsp salt
250ml/8fl oz/1 cup milk

For the frosting
150g/5oz plain (semisweet) chocolate
120ml/4fl oz/½ cup sour cream
1.5ml/¼ tsp salt

1 Preheat the oven to 180°C/350°F/Gas 4. Line two 20cm/8in round cake tins (pans) with baking parchment and grease the paper. Dust the tins with flour. Tap to remove any excess.

2 Cream the butter or margarine until soft. Gradually add the sugar and beat until light and fluffy. Beat the egg yolks, then add to the butter mixture with the vanilla extract.

3 Sift the flour with the baking powder three times. Set aside. Beat the egg whites with the salt until they form stiff peaks.

4 Fold the dry ingredients into the butter mixture in three batches, alternating with the milk. Add a dollop of the egg white to the batter and fold in to lighten the mixture. Fold in the remainder until just blended.

5 Spoon into the cake tins and bake until the cakes pull away from the sides, about 30 minutes. Leave in the tins for 5 minutes, then turn out on to a wire rack to cool completely.

6 To make the frosting, melt the chocolate in the top of a double boiler or in a heatproof bowl over a pan of simmering water. When cool, stir in the sour cream and salt. Sandwich the layers with frosting, then spread on the top and side.

Devil's Food Cake with Orange

Chocolate and orange always taste great together.

Makes one 23cm/9in round cake
50g/2oz/½ cup unsweetened cocoa powder
175ml/6fl oz/¾ cup boiling water
175g/6oz/¾ cup butter, at room temperature
350g/12oz/2 cups soft dark brown sugar
3 eggs
275g/10oz/2½ cups plain (all-purpose) flour
7.5ml/1½ tsp bicarbonate of soda (baking soda)
1.5ml/¼ tsp baking powder
120ml/4fl oz/½ cup sour cream
blanched orange rind shreds, to decorate

For the frosting
300g/11oz/scant 1½ cups caster (superfine) sugar
2 egg whites
60ml/4 tbsp orange juice concentrate
15ml/1 tbsp lemon juice
grated rind of 1 orange

1 Preheat the oven to 180°C/350°F/Gas 4. Line two 23cm/9in cake tins (pans) with baking parchment and grease the paper. In a bowl, mix the cocoa powder and water until smooth.

2 Cream the butter and sugar until light and fluffy. Add the eggs, one at a time, beating well after each addition. When the cocoa mixture is lukewarm, add to the butter mixture. Sift together the flour, bicarbonate of soda and baking powder twice. Fold into the cocoa mixture in three batches, alternating with the sour cream. Pour into the tins and bake until the cakes pull away from the sides, 30–35 minutes. Leave to cool in the tins for 15 minutes, then turn out on to a wire rack to cool completely.

3 To make the frosting, place all the ingredients in the top of a double boiler or in a heatproof bowl over a pan of simmering water. With an electric mixer, beat until the mixture holds soft peaks. Continue beating off the heat until thick enough to spread.

4 Sandwich the cake layers with frosting, then spread over the top and side. Decorate with orange rind shreds.

Layer Energy 5530kcal/23187kJ; Protein 83.4g; Carbohydrate 709.9g, of which sugars 415.2g; Fat 282.3g, of which saturates 167g; Cholesterol 1337mg; Calcium 1306mg; Fibre 15.7g; Sodium 1838mg.
Devil's Food Energy 5459kcal/23002kJ; Protein 68.3g; Carbohydrate 906.2g, of which sugars 690.9g; Fat 199g, of which saturates 117.8g; Cholesterol 1016mg; Calcium 1038mg; Fibre 14.8g; Sodium 1983mg.

Almond Cake

Serve this wonderfully nutty cake with a cup of coffee, or, for a treat, with a glass of almond liqueur.

Makes one 23cm/9in round cake

225g/8oz/1⅓ cups blanched, toasted whole almonds
75g/3oz/¾ cup icing (confectioners') sugar
3 eggs
25g/1oz/2 tbsp butter, melted
2.5ml/½ tsp almond extract
25g/1oz/4 tbsp plain (all-purpose) flour
3 egg whites
15ml/1 tbsp caster (superfine) sugar
toasted whole almonds, to decorate

1 Preheat the oven to 160°C/325°F/Gas 3. Line a 23cm/9in round cake tin (pan) with baking parchment and grease the paper.

2 Coarsely chop the almonds and grind them with half the icing sugar in a blender or food processor. Transfer to a mixing bowl.

3 Beat in the whole eggs and remaining icing sugar with an electric whisk until the mixture forms ribbon trails when the whisk is lifted out of the batter. Mix in the butter and almond extract. Sift over the flour and fold in.

4 Beat the egg whites until they peak softly. Add the caster sugar and beat until stiff and glossy. Fold into the almond mixture in four batches.

5 Spoon the mixture into the cake tin and bake until golden brown, 15–20 minutes. Leave to cool in the tin for 10 minutes and then turn out on a wire rack to cool completely. Decorate the cake with toasted almonds.

> **Cook's Tip**
> *Always use pure extracts as flavourings in your baking. Extracts are 100 per cent pure and natural, and their flavour is far superior to that of essences and other flavourings.*

French Chocolate Cake

This is typical of a French home-made cake – dense, dark and delicious. Serve with cream or a fruit coulis.

Makes one 24cm/9½in round cake

150g/5oz/¾ cup caster (superfine) sugar
275g/10oz plain (semisweet) chocolate, chopped
175g/6oz/¾ cup unsalted (sweet) butter, cut into pieces
10ml/2 tsp vanilla extract
5 eggs, separated
40g/1½oz/¼ cup plain (all-purpose) flour, sifted
a pinch of salt
icing (confectioners') sugar, for dusting

1 Preheat the oven to 160°C/325°F/Gas 3. Butter a 24cm/9½in springform tin (pan), sprinkle with sugar and tap out the excess.

2 Set aside 45ml/3 tbsp of the caster sugar. Place the chopped chocolate, butter and remaining sugar in a heavy pan and cook gently over a low heat until melted, stirring occasionally.

3 Remove the pan from the heat, stir in the vanilla extract and leave to cool slightly.

4 Beat the egg yolks, one at a time, into the chocolate mixture, then stir in the flour.

5 Beat the egg whites with the salt until soft peaks form. Sprinkle over the reserved sugar and beat until stiff and glossy. Beat one-third of the whites into the chocolate mixture to lighten it, then fold in the rest.

6 Pour the mixture into the tin and tap it gently to release any air bubbles.

7 Bake the cake for 35–45 minutes, or until well risen and the top springs back when touched lightly. Transfer to a wire rack, remove the sides of the tin and leave the cake to cool. Remove the tin base, dust the cake with icing sugar and transfer to a serving plate.

Chocolate Energy 3799kcal/15862kJ; Protein 50.6g; Carbohydrate 363.5g, of which sugars 330.6g; Fat 249.1g, of which saturates 145.2g; Cholesterol 1341mg; Calcium 400mg; Fibre 8.1g; Sodium 1437mg.
Almond Energy 2258kcal/9407kJ; Protein 77.8g; Carbohydrate 129.2g, of which sugars 104g; Fat 163.1g, of which saturates 27.7g; Cholesterol 624mg; Calcium 718mg; Fibre 17.4g; Sodium 582mg.

Caramel Layer Cake

Just the ticket for all those with a sweet tooth.

Makes one 20cm/8in round cake
275g/10oz/2½ cups plain
    (all-purpose) flour
7.5ml/1½ tsp baking powder
175g/6oz/¾ cup butter,
    at room temperature
165g/5½oz/generous ¾ cup
    caster (superfine) sugar
4 eggs, beaten

5ml/1 tsp vanilla extract
120ml/4fl oz/½ cup milk
whipped cream, to decorate
caramel threads, to decorate
    (optional)

For the frosting
285g/10½oz/1⅓ cups soft dark
    brown sugar
250ml/8fl oz/1 cup milk
25g/1oz/2 tbsp unsalted
    (sweet) butter
45–75ml/3–5 tbsp whipping cream

1 Preheat the oven to 180°C/350°F/Gas 4. Line two 20cm/8in cake tins (pans) with baking parchment and grease the paper. Sift the flour and baking powder together three times.

2 Cream the butter and caster sugar until light and fluffy. Slowly mix in the beaten eggs. Add the vanilla extract. Fold in the flour mixture, alternating with the milk. Divide the batter between the cake tins and spread evenly. Bake until the cakes pull away from the sides of the tin, about 30 minutes. Cool in the tins for 5 minutes, then turn out and cool on a wire rack.

3 To make the frosting, bring the brown sugar and milk to the boil, cover and cook for 2 minutes. Uncover and continue to boil, without stirring, until the mixture reaches 119°C/238°F (soft ball stage) on a sugar thermometer.

4 Remove the pan from the heat and add the butter, but do not stir it in. Leave to cool until lukewarm, then beat until smooth. Stir in enough cream to obtain a spreadable consistency.

5 Sandwich the cake together with one-third of the frosting and then cover the top and side. Decorate with whipped cream, and caramel threads if you like.

Marbled Spice Cake

You could bake this cake in a 20cm/8in round tin (pan) if you do not have a kugelhopf.

Makes one ring cake
75g/3oz/6 tbsp butter, softened
115g/4oz/generous ½ cup caster
    (superfine) sugar
2 eggs, lightly beaten
a few drops of vanilla extract

130g/4½oz/generous 1 cup plain
    (all-purpose) flour
7.5ml/1½ tsp baking powder
45ml/3 tbsp milk
45ml/3 tbsp black treacle (molasses)
5ml/1 tsp mixed (apple pie) spice
2.5ml/½ tsp ground ginger
175g/6oz/1½ cups icing
    (confectioners') sugar, sifted,
    to decorate

1 Preheat the oven to 180°C/350°F/Gas 4. Grease and flour a 900g/2lb kugelhopf or ring mould.

2 Cream together the butter and sugar until light and fluffy. Beat in the eggs and vanilla extract.

3 Sift together the flour and baking powder, then fold into the butter mixture, alternating with the milk.

4 Add the treacle and spices to one-third of the mixture. Drop alternating spoonfuls of the two mixtures into the tin. Run a knife through them to give a marbled effect.

5 Bake for 50 minutes, or until a skewer inserted into the centre comes out clean. Leave in the tin for 10 minutes, then turn out on to a wire rack to cool.

6 To decorate, make a smooth icing with the icing sugar and some warm water. Drizzle over the cake and leave to set.

> **Cook's Tip**
> Cakes baked in ring moulds take a little less time to cook than those baked in a round tin (pan) because the tube in the centre allows the air to circulate. So adjust the time accordingly if you use a round tin instead.

Caramel Energy 5236kcal/21969kJ; Protein 66.1g; Carbohydrate 701.3g, of which sugars 491.8g; Fat 260.9g, of which saturates 155.2g; Cholesterol 1375mg; Calcium 1169mg; Fibre 8.5g; Sodium 1676mg.
Spice Energy 2427kcal/10247kJ; Protein 28.7g; Carbohydrate 436.9g, of which sugars 337.6g; Fat 75.2g, of which saturates 42.9g; Cholesterol 543mg; Calcium 708mg; Fibre 4g; Sodium 716mg.

Raspberry Meringue Gateau

A rich hazelnut meringue filled with cream and raspberries makes a delicious combination of textures and tastes.

Serves 8
4 egg whites
225g/8oz/generous 1 cup caster (superfine) sugar
a few drops of vanilla extract
5ml/1 tsp malt vinegar
115g/4oz/1⅔ cup toasted chopped hazelnuts, ground

300ml/½ pint/1¼ cups double (heavy) cream
350g/12oz/2 cups raspberries
icing (confectioners') sugar, for dusting
raspberries and mint sprigs, to decorate

For the sauce
225g/8oz/1⅓ cups raspberries
45ml/3 tbsp icing (confectioners') sugar
15ml/1 tbsp orange liqueur

1 Preheat the oven to 180°C/350°F/Gas 4. Grease two 20cm/8in shallow round cake tins (pans) and line the bases with baking parchment.

2 Whisk the egg whites in a large bowl until they hold stiff peaks, then gradually whisk in the caster sugar a tablespoon at a time, whisking well after each addition.

3 Continue whisking the meringue mixture for a minute or two until very stiff, then fold in the vanilla extract, malt vinegar and the ground hazelnuts. Divide the meringue mixture between the prepared tins and spread level. Bake for 50–60 minutes, or until crisp. Remove the meringues from the tins and leave to cool on a wire rack.

4 Meanwhile, make the sauce. Purée the raspberries with the icing sugar and orange liqueur in a blender or food processor, then press the purée through a nylon sieve to remove any pips. Chill the sauce until ready to serve.

5 Whip the cream until just thickened then fold in the raspberries. Sandwich the meringue rounds with the raspberry cream. Dust with icing sugar, and then decorate with fruit and mint. Serve the meringue with the sauce.

Strawberry Mint Sponge

This combination of summer fruit, fresh mint and ice cream will prove popular with everyone.

Makes one 20cm/8in round cake
6–10 fresh mint leaves, plus extra to decorate
175g/6oz/scant 1 cup caster (superfine) sugar

175g/6oz/¾ cup butter
175g/6oz/1½ cups self-raising (self-rising) flour
3 eggs
1.2 litres/2 pints/5 cups strawberry ice cream, softened
600ml/1 pint/2½ cups double (heavy) cream
30ml/2 tbsp mint liqueur
350g/12oz/3 cups fresh strawberries

1 Tear the fresh mint leaves into pieces, mix with the sugar, and leave overnight. Remove the leaves from the sugar the next day.

2 Preheat the oven to 190°C/375°F/Gas 5. Grease and line a 20cm/8in deep springform tin (pan).

3 Cream the butter and mint-flavoured sugar, add the flour, and then the eggs. Pour the mixture into the prepared tin.

4 Bake for 20–25 minutes, or until a skewer inserted in the centre comes out clean. Turn out on to a wire rack to cool completely. When cool, split into two layers.

5 Wash the cake tin and line with clear film (plastic wrap). Put the cake base back in the tin. Spread evenly with the softened ice cream, then cover with the top half of the cake. Freeze for 3–4 hours.

6 Whip the cream with the mint liqueur. Turn the cake out on to a serving plate and quickly spread a layer of whipped cream all over it, leaving a rough finish. Freeze until 10 minutes before serving.

7 Decorate the cake with the strawberries and place fresh mint leaves around it.

Raspberry Energy 445kcal/1860kJ; Protein 6.1g; Carbohydrate 40.5g, of which sugars 40.3g; Fat 29.5g, of which saturates 13.3g; Cholesterol 51mg; Calcium 76mg; Fibre 2.7g; Sodium 61mg.
Strawberry Energy 7965kcal/33162kJ; Protein 86.7g; Carbohydrate 636.8g, of which sugars 480.7g; Fat 574.1g, of which saturates 340.9g; Cholesterol 1839mg; Calcium 2245mg; Fibre 9.3g; Sodium 2305mg.

Chestnut Cake

This rich, moist cake can be made up to a week in advance and kept, undecorated and wrapped, in an airtight tin.

Serves 8–10

150g/5oz/1¼ cups plain (all-purpose) flour
a pinch of salt
225g/8oz/1 cup butter, softened
150g/5oz/¾ cup caster (superfine) sugar
425g/15oz can chestnut purée
9 eggs, separated
105ml/7 tbsp dark rum
300ml/½ pint/1¼ cups double (heavy) cream
115g/4oz/1 cup icing (confectioners') sugar
marrons glacés and icing sugar, to decorate

1 Preheat the oven to 180°C/350°F/Gas 4. Grease and line a 20cm/8in springform tin (pan).

2 Sift the flour and salt and set aside. Beat the butter and sugar together until light and fluffy. Fold in two-thirds of the chestnut purée, with the egg yolks. Fold in the flour and salt.

3 Whisk the egg whites in a clean, dry bowl until stiff peaks form. Beat a little of the egg whites into the chestnut and butter mixture, until evenly blended, then fold in the remainder. Transfer the cake mixture to the tin and smooth the surface. Bake in the centre of the oven for about 1¼ hours, or until a skewer comes out clean. Leave in the tin and place on a wire rack.

4 Using a skewer, pierce holes over the cake. Sprinkle with 60ml/4 tbsp rum, then leave to cool. Remove the cake from the tin, peel off the lining paper and cut horizontally into two layers. Place the base layer on a serving plate. Whisk the cream with the remaining rum, icing sugar and chestnut purée until smooth.

5 To assemble, spread two-thirds of the chestnut cream mixture over the bottom layer and place the other layer on top. Spread some chestnut cream over the top and side of the cake. Using a piping (icing) bag and a large star nozzle, pipe the remainder of the chestnut cream in large swirls around the edge of the cake. Decorate with chopped marrons glacés and icing sugar.

Marbled Ring Cake

Glaze this cake with runny glacé icing if you prefer.

Makes one 25cm/10in ring cake

115g/4oz plain (semisweet) chocolate
350g/12oz/3 cups plain (all-purpose) flour
5ml/1 tsp baking powder
450g/1lb/2 cups butter, at room temperature
725g/1lb 10oz/3¾ cups caster (superfine) sugar
15ml/1 tbsp vanilla extract
10 eggs, at room temperature
icing (confectioners') sugar, for dusting

1 Preheat the oven to 180°C/350°F/Gas 4. Line a 25 x 10cm/10 x 4in ring mould with baking parchment and grease the paper. Dust with flour. Melt the chocolate in the top of a double boiler or in a heatproof bowl over a pan of simmering water, stirring occasionally. Set aside.

2 Sift together the flour and baking powder. In another bowl, cream the butter, sugar and vanilla extract until light and fluffy. Add the eggs, two at a time, then gradually blend in the flour mixture.

3 Spoon half the mixture into the ring mould. Stir the melted chocolate into the remaining mixture, then spoon into the tin. With a metal spatula, swirl the mixtures to create a marbled effect.

4 Bake until a skewer inserted in the centre comes out clean, about 1¾ hours. Cover with foil halfway through baking. Leave to cool in the tin for 15 minutes, then unmould and transfer to a wire rack to cool completely. To serve, dust with icing sugar.

> **Cook's Tip**
> With marbling cake mixtures, less is definitely more! Three or four wide swirling movements are all you will need to create the effect. If you over-swirl the batter the definition of the marbling will become lost.

Chestnut Energy 588kcal/2448kJ; Protein 8.6g; Carbohydrate 43.5g, of which sugars 19.5g; Fat 40.9g, of which saturates 23.4g; Cholesterol 260mg; Calcium 93mg; Fibre 2.2g; Sodium 212mg.
Ring Energy 8720kcal/36545kJ; Protein 107.5g; Carbohydrate 1105.3g, of which sugars 837.6g; Fat 462.1g, of which saturates 269.9g; Cholesterol 2869mg; Calcium 1278mg; Fibre 13.7g; Sodium 3488mg.

Chocolate & Nut Gateau

Hazelnuts give an interesting crunchy texture to this delicious iced dessert.

Serves 6–8
75g/3oz/½ cup shelled hazelnuts
about 32 sponge fingers
150ml/¼ pint/⅔ cup cold strong black coffee
30ml/2 tbsp brandy
450ml/¾ pint/scant 2 cups double (heavy) cream
75g/3oz/¾ cup icing (confectioners') sugar, sifted
150g/5oz plain (semisweet) chocolate
icing sugar and unsweetened cocoa powder, for dusting

1 Preheat the oven to 200°C/400°F/Gas 6. Spread out the hazelnuts on a baking sheet and toast them in the oven for 5 minutes until golden.

2 Transfer the nuts to a clean dish towel and rub off the skins while still warm. Cool the nuts and then finely chop them.

3 Line a 1.2 litre/2 pint/5 cup loaf tin (pan) with clear film (plastic wrap) and cut enough sponge fingers to fit the base and sides. Reserve the remaining fingers.

4 Mix the coffee and brandy in a shallow dish. Dip the sponge fingers briefly into the coffee mixture and return to the tin, sugary side down.

5 Whip the cream with the icing sugar until it forms soft peaks. Roughly chop 75g/3oz of the chocolate, and fold into the cream with the hazelnuts.

6 Melt the remaining chocolate in a double boiler or a heatproof bowl over a pan of barely simmering water. Cool, then fold into the cream mixture. Spoon into the tin.

7 Moisten the remaining cookies in the coffee mixture and lay over the filling. Wrap and freeze until firm.

8 Remove from the freezer 30 minutes before serving. Turn out on to a serving plate and dust with icing sugar and cocoa.

Chocolate & Orange Angel Cake

This light-as-air sponge with its fluffy icing is the answer to a cake-lover's prayer.

Makes one 20cm/8in ring cake
25g/1oz/¼ cup plain (all-purpose) flour
15g/½oz/2 tbsp unsweetened cocoa powder
15g/½oz/2 tbsp cornflour (cornstarch)
a pinch of salt
5 egg whites
2.5ml/½ tsp cream of tartar
115g/4oz/generous ½ cup caster (superfine) sugar
blanched and shredded rind of 1 orange, to decorate

For the icing
200g/7oz/1 cup caster (superfine) sugar
1 egg white

1 Preheat the oven to 180°C/350°F/Gas 4. Sift the flour, cocoa powder, cornflour and salt together three times.

2 Beat the egg whites in a large bowl until foamy. Add the cream of tartar, then whisk until soft peaks form.

3 Add the caster sugar to the egg whites a spoonful at a time, whisking after each addition. Sift a third of the flour and cocoa mixture over the meringue and gently fold in. Repeat twice more.

4 Spoon the mixture into a non-stick 20cm/8in ring mould and level the top. Bake for 35 minutes, or until springy when lightly pressed. Turn upside-down on to a wire rack and leave to cool in the tin. Carefully ease out of the tin.

5 To make the icing, put the sugar in a pan with 75ml/5 tbsp cold water. Stir over a low heat until dissolved. Boil until the syrup reaches soft ball stage (119°C/238°F on a sugar thermometer). Remove from the heat.

6 Whisk the egg white until stiff. Add the syrup in a thin stream, whisking all the time, until the mixture is very thick and fluffy.

7 Spread the icing over the top and sides of the cooled cake. Sprinkle the orange rind over the top of the cake and serve.

Gateau Energy 481kcal/1993kJ; Protein 3.2g; Carbohydrate 23.2g, of which sugars 22.9g; Fat 41.4g, of which saturates 22.4g; Cholesterol 78mg; Calcium 52mg; Fibre 1.1g; Sodium 15mg.
Angel Cake Energy 1495kcal/6373kJ; Protein 24.1g; Carbohydrate 364.1g, of which sugars 329.6g; Fat 3.7g, of which saturates 2g; Cholesterol 0mg; Calcium 233mg; Fibre 2.6g; Sodium 535mg.

Chocolate Date Cake

A stunning cake that tastes wonderful. Rich and gooey – it's a chocoholic's delight!

Serves 8
4 egg whites
115g/4oz/generous ½ cup caster (superfine) sugar
200g/7oz plain (semisweet) chocolate
175g/6oz/1 cup Medjool dates, stoned (pitted) and chopped

175g/6oz/1½ cups chopped walnuts or pecan nuts
5ml/1 tsp vanilla extract

For the frosting
200g/7oz/scant 1 cup fromage frais or ricotta cheese
200g/7oz/scant 1 cup mascarpone
a few drops of vanilla extract
icing (confectioners') sugar, to taste

1 Preheat the oven to 180°C/350°F/Gas 4. Grease and base-line a 20cm/8in springform tin (pan).

2 To make the frosting, mix together the fromage frais or ricotta and mascarpone, add a few drops of vanilla extract and icing sugar to taste, then set aside.

3 Whisk the egg whites until they form stiff peaks. Whisk in 30ml/2 tbsp of the caster sugar until the meringue is thick and glossy, then fold in the remainder.

4 Chop 175g/6oz of the chocolate. Carefully fold into the meringue with the dates, nuts and 5ml/1 tsp of the vanilla extract. Pour into the prepared tin, spread level and bake for about 45 minutes, or until risen around the edges.

5 Allow to cool in the tin for about 10 minutes, then unmould, peel off the lining paper and leave to cool completely. Swirl the frosting over the top of the cake.

6 Melt the remaining chocolate in a double boiler or in a heatproof bowl over a pan of simmering water. Spoon into a small paper piping (icing) bag and drizzle the chocolate over the cake. Chill before serving.

Chocolate Potato Cake

Mashed potato makes this cake moist and delicious.

Makes a 23cm/9in cake
oil, for greasing
200g/7oz/1 cup sugar
250g/9oz/generous 1 cup butter
4 eggs, separated
275g/10oz/dark (bittersweet) chocolate

75g/3oz/¾ cup mashed potato
225g/8oz/2 cups self-raising (self-rising) flour
5ml/1 tsp cinnamon
45ml/3 tbsp milk

To garnish
white and dark (bittersweet) chocolate shavings

1 Preheat the oven to 180°C/350°F/Gas 4. Grease and line a 23cm/9in round cake tin with baking parchment. In a bowl, cream together the sugar and 225g/8oz/1 cup of the butter until light, then beat the egg yolks into the creamed mixture one at a time until it is smooth and creamy.

2 Finely chop or grate 175g/6oz of the chocolate and stir it into the creamed mixture with the ground almonds. Pass the mashed potato through a sieve (strainer) or ricer and stir it into the creamed chocolate mixture. Sift together the flour and cinnamon and fold into the mixture with the milk. Whisk the egg whites until they hold stiff but not dry peaks, and fold into the cake mixture.

3 Spoon into the prepared tin and smooth over the top, but make a slight hollow in the middle to help keep the surface of the cake level during cooking. Bake in the oven for 1¼ hours until a toothpick inserted in the centre comes out clean. Allow the cake to cool slightly in the tin, then turn out and cool on a wire rack.

4 Meanwhile break up the remaining chocolate into a heatproof bowl and stand it over a pan of hot water. Add the remaining butter and stir well until the chocolate has melted. Peel off the lining paper and trim the top of the cake so that it is level. Smooth over the chocolate icing and allow to set. Decorate with chocolate shavings.

Chocolate Energy 441kcal/1841kJ; Protein 10.2g; Carbohydrate 40.3g, of which sugars 39.9g; Fat 27.6g, of which saturates 9.1g; Cholesterol 14mg; Calcium 70mg; Fibre 1.8g; Sodium 45mg.
Potato Energy 5749Kcal/24034kJ; Protein 87.1g; Carbohydrate 590.9g, of which sugars 391.8g; Fat 354.8g, of which saturates 188.1g; Cholesterol 1465mg; Calcium 1408mg; Fibre 21.5g; Sodium 2731mg.

Strawberry Shortcake Gateau

A light cookie-textured sponge forms the base of this summertime dessert.

Makes one 20cm/8in round cake

225g/8oz/2 cups fresh
  strawberries, hulled
30ml/2 tbsp ruby port
225g/8oz/2 cups self-raising
  (self-rising) flour
10ml/2 tsp baking powder
75g/3oz/6 tbsp unsalted (sweet)
  butter, diced
40g/1½oz/3 tbsp caster
  (superfine) sugar
1 egg, lightly beaten
15–30ml/1–2 tbsp milk
melted butter, for brushing
250ml/8fl oz/1 cup double
  (heavy) cream
icing (confectioners') sugar,
  for dusting

1 Preheat the oven to 220°C/425°F/Gas 7. Grease and base-line two 20cm/8in shallow, round, loose-based cake tins (pans).

2 Reserve 5 strawberries, slice the remainder and marinate in the port for about 1–2 hours. Strain, reserving the port.

3 Sift the flour and baking powder into a bowl. Rub in the butter until the mixture resembles fine breadcrumbs and stir in the sugar. Work in the egg and 15ml/1 tbsp of the milk to form a soft dough, adding more milk if needed.

4 Knead briefly on a lightly floured surface and divide into two pieces. Roll out each piece, mark one into eight wedges, and transfer both to the prepared cake tins. Brush with a little melted butter and bake for 15 minutes. Cool in the tins for 10 minutes, then transfer to a wire rack to cool completely.

5 Cut the marked cake into wedges. Reserving a little cream for decoration, whip the remainder until it holds its shape, and fold in the reserved port and marinated strawberry slices. Spread over the round cake. Place the wedges on top tilting them at a slight angle, and dust with icing sugar.

6 Whip the remaining cream and use to pipe swirls on each wedge. Halve the reserved strawberries and decorate the cake.

Almond & Raspberry Roll

A light and airy sponge cake is rolled up with a fresh cream and raspberry filling for a decadent tea-time treat.

Makes one 23cm/9in long roll

3 eggs
75g/3oz/6 tbsp caster
  (superfine) sugar
50g/2oz/½ cup plain
  (all-purpose) flour
30ml/2 tbsp ground almonds
caster (superfine) sugar,
  for dusting
250ml/8fl oz/1 cup double
  (heavy) cream
225g/8oz/1⅓ cups fresh raspberries
16 flaked almonds, toasted,
  to decorate

1 Preheat the oven to 200°C/400°F/Gas 6. Grease a 33 x 23cm/13 x 9in Swiss roll tin (jelly roll pan) and line with baking parchment. Grease the paper.

2 Whisk the eggs and sugar in a heatproof bowl until blended. Place the bowl over a pan of simmering water and whisk until thick and pale.

3 Whisk off the heat until cool. Sift over the flour and almonds, and fold in gently.

4 Transfer to the prepared tin and bake for 10–12 minutes, until risen and springy to the touch.

5 Invert the cake in its tin on to baking parchment dusted with caster sugar. Leave to cool, then remove the tin and lining paper.

6 Reserve a little cream, then whip the remainder until it holds its shape. Fold in all but 8 raspberries and spread the mixture over the cooled cake, leaving a narrow border. Roll the cake up and sprinkle with caster sugar.

7 Whip the reserved cream until it just holds its shape, and spoon or pipe a line along the top of the roll in the centre. Decorate the cream with the reserved raspberries and toasted flaked almonds.

Strawberry Energy 2911kcal/12118kJ; Protein 34.4g; Carbohydrate 239.1g, of which sugars 67.7g; Fat 204.9g, of which saturates 124.7g; Cholesterol 694mg; Calcium 556mg; Fibre 9.4g; Sodium 610mg.
Almond Energy 2166kcal/9012kJ; Protein 37.3g; Carbohydrate 133.9g, of which sugars 95g; Fat 169g, of which saturates 89.8g; Cholesterol 914mg; Calcium 446mg; Fibre 9.4g; Sodium 282mg.

Orange & Walnut Swiss Roll

This unusual cake is tasty enough to serve alone, but you could also pour over some single (light) cream.

Makes one 23cm/9in long roll
4 eggs, separated
115g/4oz/generous ½ cup caster (superfine) sugar
115g/4oz/1 cup very finely chopped walnuts
a pinch of cream of tartar

a pinch of salt
icing (confectioners') sugar, for dusting

For the filling
300ml/½ pint/1¼ cups whipping cream
15ml/1 tbsp caster (superfine) sugar
grated rind of 1 orange
15ml/1 tbsp orange-flavoured liqueur

1 Preheat the oven to 180°C/350°F/Gas 4. Line a 30 × 23cm/ 12 × 9in Swiss roll tin (jelly roll pan) with baking parchment and grease the paper.

2 Beat the egg yolks and sugar until thick. Stir in the walnuts. In another bowl beat the egg whites with the cream of tartar and salt until stiffly peaking. Fold into the walnut mixture.

3 Pour the mixture into the prepared tin and level the top. Bake for 15 minutes. Invert the cake on to baking parchment dusted with icing sugar. Peel off the lining paper. Roll up the cake with the sugared paper. Leave to cool.

4 For the filling, whip the cream until softly peaking. Fold in the caster sugar, orange rind and liqueur.

5 Unroll the cake. Spread with the filling, then re-roll. Chill. To serve, dust with icing sugar.

> **Cook's Tip**
> Rolling up the Swiss roll (jelly roll) while still warm ensures that it will re-roll around its cream filling when it is cold without cracking.

Chocolate Roll

Fresh cream in a chocolate roll is always popular.

Makes one 33cm/13in long roll
225g/8oz plain (semisweet) chocolate
45ml/3 tbsp water
30ml/2 tbsp rum, brandy or strong coffee

7 eggs, separated
175g/6oz/scant 1 cup caster (superfine) sugar
1.5ml/¼ tsp salt
icing (confectioners') sugar, for dusting
350ml/12fl oz/1½ cups whipping cream

1 Preheat the oven to 180°C/350°F/Gas 4. Line and grease a 38 × 33cm/15 × 13in Swiss roll tin (jelly roll pan) with baking parchment. Combine the chocolate, water and rum or other flavouring in the top of a double boiler or in a heatproof bowl over a pan of simmering water. Heat until melted. Set aside.

2 With an electric mixer, beat the egg yolks and sugar until thick. Stir in the melted chocolate. In another bowl, beat the egg whites and salt until they hold stiff peaks. Fold a large dollop of egg whites into the yolk mixture to lighten it, then carefully fold in the rest of the egg whites.

3 Pour the mixture into the tin and smooth evenly with a metal spatula. Bake for 15 minutes. Remove from the oven, cover with baking parchment and a damp cloth. Leave to stand for 1–2 hours. With an electric mixer, whip the cream until stiff. Set aside.

4 Run a knife along the inside edge of the tin to loosen the cake, then invert the cake on to a sheet of baking parchment that has been dusted with icing sugar.

5 Whip the cream until it holds its shape. Peel off the lining paper. Spread with an even layer of whipped cream, then roll up the cake using the sugared paper. Chill for several hours. Before serving, dust with an even layer of icing sugar.

Orange Energy 2788kcal/11573kJ; Protein 48.6g; Carbohydrate 151.4g, of which sugars 150.6g; Fat 221.9g, of which saturates 88.3g; Cholesterol 1076mg; Calcium 465mg; Fibre 4g; Sodium 372mg.
Chocolate Energy 3732kcal/15572kJ; Protein 62.9g; Carbohydrate 330g, of which sugars 327.9g; Fat 242.9g, of which saturates 137g; Cholesterol 1713mg; Calcium 567mg; Fibre 5.6g; Sodium 601mg.

Apricot Brandy-snap Roulade

A magnificent combination of soft and crisp textures, this cake looks impressive and is easy to prepare.

Makes one 33cm/13in long roll

4 eggs, separated
7.5ml/1½ tsp fresh orange juice
115g/4oz/generous ½ cup caster (superfine) sugar
175g/6oz/1½ cups ground almonds
4 brandy snaps, crushed, to decorate

For the filling
150g/5oz canned apricots, drained
300ml/½ pint/1¼ cups double (heavy) cream
25g/1oz/¼ cup icing (confectioners') sugar

1 Preheat the oven to 190°C/375°F/Gas 5. Base-line and grease a 33 x 23cm/13 x 9in Swiss roll tin (jelly roll pan).

2 Beat together the egg yolks, orange juice and sugar until thick and pale, about 10 minutes. Fold in the ground almonds.

3 Whisk the egg whites until they hold stiff peaks. Fold into the almond mixture, then transfer to the Swiss roll tin and smooth the surface.

4 Bake for 20 minutes, or until a skewer inserted into the centre comes out clean. Leave to cool in the tin, covered with a just-damp dish towel.

5 To make the filling, process the apricots in a blender or food processor until smooth. Whip the cream and icing sugar until it holds soft peaks. Fold in the apricot purée.

6 Spread the crushed brandy snaps over a sheet of baking parchment. Spread one-third of the cream mixture over the cake, then carefully invert it on to the brandy snaps. Peel off the lining paper.

7 Use the remaining cream mixture to cover the whole cake, then roll up the roulade from a short end, being careful not to disturb the brandy snap coating. Transfer the roulade to a serving dish.

Apricot & Orange Roulade

This sophisticated dessert is very good served with a spoonful of thick yogurt or crème fraîche.

Makes one 33cm/13in long roll

4 egg whites
115g/4oz/generous ½ cup golden caster (superfine) sugar
50g/2oz/½ cup plain (all-purpose) flour
finely grated rind of 1 orange
45ml/3 tbsp orange juice

For the filling
115g/4oz/½ cup ready-to-eat dried apricots
150ml/¼ pint/⅔ cup orange juice

For the decoration
10ml/2 tsp icing (confectioners') sugar
shredded orange rind

1 Preheat the oven to 200°C/400°F/Gas 6. Base-line and grease a 33 x 23cm/13 x 9in Swiss roll tin (jelly roll pan).

2 Place the egg whites in a large bowl and whisk until they hold soft peaks. Gradually add the sugar, whisking well between each addition, until all of the sugar has been incorporated.

3 Fold in the flour, orange rind and juice. Spoon the mixture into the prepared tin and spread it evenly.

4 Bake the cake for 15–18 minutes, or until the sponge is firm and light golden in colour. Turn out on to a sheet of baking parchment and roll it up loosely from one short side. Leave to cool completely.

5 Roughly chop the apricots and place them in a pan with the orange juice. Cover and leave to simmer until most of the liquid has been absorbed. Purée the apricots in a food processor or blender until smooth.

6 Unroll the roulade and spread with the apricot mixture. Roll up. To decorate, arrange strips of paper diagonally across the roll, sprinkle lightly with icing sugar and then remove the paper. Sprinkle the top with orange rind.

Brandy-snap Energy 3674kcal/15272kJ; Protein 69.4g; Carbohydrate 208.1g, of which sugars 193.9g; Fat 291.3g, of which saturates 114.1g; Cholesterol 1172mg; Calcium 809mg; Fibre 14.7g; Sodium 511mg.
Orange Energy 1145kcal/4878kJ; Protein 29.1g; Carbohydrate 270.4g, of which sugars 232.3g; Fat 1.5g, of which saturates 0.1g; Cholesterol 0mg; Calcium 271mg; Fibre 9g; Sodium 427mg.

Classic Cheesecake

Dust the top of the cheesecake with icing (confectioners') sugar to decorate, if you wish.

Serves 8

50g/2oz/²⁄₃ cup crushed digestive
  cookies (graham crackers)

900g/2lb/4 cups cream cheese,
  at room temperature
245g/8³⁄₄oz/
  generous 1¼ cups sugar
grated rind of 1 lemon
45ml/3 tbsp lemon juice
5ml/1 tsp vanilla extract
4 eggs

1 Preheat the oven to 160°C/325°F/Gas 3. Grease a 20cm/8in springform tin (pan).

2 Place on a 30cm/12in circle of foil. Press it up the sides to seal tightly. Press the crushed cookies into the base of the tin.

3 Beat the cream cheese until smooth. Add the sugar, lemon rind and juice. Add the vanilla extract, and beat until blended. Beat in the eggs, one at a time.

4 Pour into the prepared tin. Set the tin in a larger baking tray and place in the oven. Pour enough hot water into the outer tray to come 2.5cm/1in up the side of the tin.

5 Bake until the top is golden brown, about 1½ hours. Cool in the tin.

6 Run a knife around the edge to loosen, then remove the rim of the tin. Chill for at least 4 hours before serving.

Cook's Tips
• *For a perfect cheesecake bring all the ingredients to room temperature first.*
• *Use a springform tin (pan) if possible.*
• *Don't open the oven door during baking.*
• *Cool slowly away from draughts.*
• *Chill the cake before removing the base of the pan.*

Chocolate Cheesecake

Substitute digestive cookies (graham crackers) for the base for a change.

Serves 10–12

275g/10oz plain
  (semisweet) chocolate
1.1kg/2½lb/5 cups cream
  cheese, at room temperature
200g/7oz/1 cup caster
  (superfine) sugar

10ml/2 tsp vanilla extract
4 eggs
15ml/1 tbsp unsweetened
  cocoa powder
175ml/6fl oz/³⁄₄ cup sour cream

For the base

200g/7oz/2⅓ cups crushed
  chocolate cookies
75g/3oz/6 tbsp butter, melted
2.5ml/½ tsp ground cinnamon

1 Preheat the oven to 180°C/350°F/Gas 4. Grease the base and sides of a 23 × 7.5cm/9 × 3in springform tin (pan).

2 For the base, thoroughly mix the crushed cookies with the butter and cinnamon in a large bowl. Press the mixture into the base of the prepared tin.

3 Melt the chocolate in the top of a double boiler or in a heatproof bowl over a pan of simmering water. Set aside to cool slightly.

4 Beat the cream cheese until smooth. Add the sugar and vanilla extract and beat until blended. Beat in the eggs one at a time. mixing well after each addition.

5 Stir the cocoa powder into the sour cream. Add to the cream cheese mixture. Stir in the melted chocolate.

6 Pour the cream cheese mixture over the crust. Bake for 1 hour. Cool in the tin, then remove the rim. Chill before serving.

Variation
For a sweeter, less intense flavour, use milk chocolate instead of plain (semisweet) chocolate.

Classic Energy 680kcal/2823kJ; Protein 7.2g; Carbohydrate 36.3g, of which sugars 32.9g; Fat 57.5g, of which saturates 34.8g; Cholesterol 205mg; Calcium 147mg; Fibre 0.1g; Sodium 412mg.
Chocolate Energy 772kcal/3204kJ; Protein 8g; Carbohydrate 43.8g, of which sugars 37.1g; Fat 64.1g, of which saturates 38.9g; Cholesterol 182mg; Calcium 146mg; Fibre 1.1g; Sodium 431mg.

Marbled Cheesecake

A cheesecake with a difference: marbled chocolate and vanilla.

Serves 10
900g/2lb/4 cups cream cheese, at room temperature
200g/7oz/1 cup caster (superfine) sugar

4 eggs
5ml/1 tsp vanilla extract
50g/2oz/½ cup unsweetened cocoa powder, dissolved in 75ml/5 tbsp hot water
65g/2½oz/1 cup crushed digestive cookies (graham crackers)

1 Preheat the oven to 180°C/350°F/Gas 4. Grease and base-line a 20 x 7.5cm/8 x 3in cake tin (pan).

2 With an electric mixer, beat the cheese until smooth and creamy. Add the sugar and beat to incorporate. Beat in the eggs, one at a time. Do not overmix.

3 Divide the mixture between two bowls. Stir the vanilla extract into one, then add the chocolate mixture to the other.

4 Pour a cupful of the vanilla mixture into the centre of the tin to make an even layer. Slowly pour over a cupful of chocolate mixture in the centre. Repeat, alternating cupfuls of the batter in a circular pattern until both are used up.

5 Set the tin in a larger baking tray and pour in hot water to come 4cm/1½in up the sides of the cake tin. Bake until the top of the cake is golden, about 1½ hours. It will rise during baking but will sink later. Leave to cool in the tin on a rack.

6 To turn out, run a knife around the inside edge. Place a flat plate, bottom-side up, over the tin and invert on to the plate.

7 Sprinkle the crushed cookies evenly over the base, gently place another plate over them, and invert again.

8 Cover and chill for at least 3 hours, or overnight. To serve, cut slices with a sharp knife dipped in hot water.

Baked Cheesecake with Fresh Fruits

Vary the fruit decoration to suit the season for this rich, creamy dessert.

Serves 12
175g/6oz/2 cups crushed digestive cookies (graham crackers)
50g/2oz/¼ cup unsalted (sweet) butter, melted
450g/1lb/2 cups curd (farmer's) cheese
150ml/¼ pint/⅔ cup sour cream

115g/4oz/generous ½ cup caster (superfine) sugar
3 eggs, separated
grated rind of 1 lemon
30ml/2 tbsp Marsala
2.5ml/½ tsp almond extract
50g/2oz/½ cup ground almonds
50g/2oz/⅓ cup sultanas (golden raisins)
450g/1lb prepared mixed fruits, such as figs, cherries, peaches and strawberries, to decorate

1 Preheat the oven to 180°C/350°F/Gas 4. Grease and line the sides of a 25cm/10in round springform tin (pan) with baking parchment. Combine the cookies and butter, and press into the base of the tin. Chill for 20 minutes.

2 For the cake mixture, beat together the cheese, cream, sugar, egg yolks, lemon rind, Marsala and almond extract until smooth and creamy.

3 Whisk the egg whites until stiff and fold into the cheese mixture with the almonds and sultanas until evenly combined. Pour over the cookie base and bake for 45 minutes, until risen and just set in the centre.

4 Leave in the tin until completely cold. Carefully remove the tin and peel away the lining paper.

5 Chill the cheesecake for at least 1 hour before decorating with the prepared fruits, just before serving.

Cook's Tip
Don't add the fruit topping in advance or it will make the cake soggy.

Marbled Energy 552kcal/2287kJ; Protein 6.8g; Carbohydrate 26.3g, of which sugars 21.9g; Fat 47.5g, of which saturates 28.6g; Cholesterol 164mg; Calcium 123mg; Fibre 0.8g; Sodium 389mg.
Baked Energy 296kcal/1238kJ; Protein 7.6g; Carbohydrate 27.1g, of which sugars 19g; Fat 18g, of which saturates 9g; Cholesterol 83mg; Calcium 56mg; Fibre 1.1g; Sodium 139mg.

Tofu Berry "Cheesecake"

Strictly speaking, this summery "cheesecake" is not a cheesecake at all, as it's based on tofu – but who would guess?

200g/7oz/scant 1 cup natural (plain) yogurt
15ml/1 tbsp/1 sachet powdered gelatine
60ml/4 tbsp apple juice

Serves 6
50g/2oz/¼ cup margarine
30ml/2 tbsp apple juice
115g/4oz/5¾ cups bran flakes

For the filling
275g/10oz/1½ cups silken tofu or low-fat soft cheese

For the topping
175g/6oz/1½ cups mixed summer soft fruits, such as strawberries, raspberries, redcurrants, blackberries
30ml/2 tbsp redcurrant jelly
30ml/2 tbsp hot water

1 Place the margarine and apple juice in a pan and heat gently until melted. Crush the cereal and stir it into the pan. Spoon into a 23cm/9in round flan tin (tart pan) and press down firmly. Leave to set.

2 For the filling, place the tofu or low-fat soft cheese and yogurt in a food processor or blender and process until smooth. Dissolve the gelatine in the apple juice and stir into the tofu mixture.

3 Spread the tofu mixture over the chilled base, smoothing it evenly. Chill until set.

4 Remove the flan tin and place the "cheesecake" on a serving plate. Arrange the soft fruits over the top. Melt the redcurrant jelly with the hot water. Leave it to cool, and then spoon it over the fruit to serve.

Cook's Tip
For a vegetarian version use vegetarian gelatine.

Baked Blackberry Cheesecake

The first scented blackberries of the season make this cheesecake truly scrumptious. Serve with a dollop of cream if you like.

Serves 6
175g/6oz/¾ cup cottage cheese
150g/5oz/scant ¾ cup natural (plain) yogurt

15ml/1 tbsp plain (all-purpose) wholemeal (whole-wheat) flour
25g/1oz/2 tbsp golden caster (superfine) sugar
1 egg
1 egg white
finely grated rind and juice of ½ lemon
200g/7oz/scant 2 cups fresh or frozen and thawed blackberries

1 Preheat the oven to 180°C/350°F/Gas 4. Lightly grease and base-line an 18cm/7in shallow round cake tin (pan) with baking parchment.

2 Place the cottage cheese in a food processor or blender and process until smooth. Place in a bowl, then add the yogurt, flour, sugar, egg and egg white, and mix. Add the lemon rind, juice and blackberries, reserving a few.

3 Transfer the mixture to the prepared tin and bake for 30–35 minutes, or until just set. Turn off the oven and leave the cake in it for a further 30 minutes.

4 Run a knife around the edge of the cheesecake and turn it out. Remove the lining paper and place the cheesecake on a warm serving plate.

5 Decorate the cheesecake with the reserved blackberries and serve warm.

Cook's Tip
Wild blackberries are the best for this cheesecake, but if you are unable to gather any, use cultivated or frozen ones instead.

Tofu Energy 204kcal/854kJ; Protein 7.7g; Carbohydrate 23.2g, of which sugars 13.8g; Fat 9.5g, of which saturates 0.5g; Cholesterol 0mg; Calcium 311mg; Fibre 2.8g; Sodium 253mg.
Blackberry Energy 88kcal/368kJ; Protein 7g; Carbohydrate 9.9g, of which sugars 7.8g; Fat 2.4g, of which saturates 1.1g; Cholesterol 37mg; Calcium 108mg; Fibre 1.1g; Sodium 142mg.

Coffee, Peach & Almond Daquoise

Makes one 23cm/9in gateau

5 eggs, separated
425g/15oz/generous 2 cups caster
 (superfine) sugar
15ml/1 tbsp cornflour
 (cornstarch)
175g/6oz/1½ cups ground
 almonds, toasted
135ml/4½fl oz/
 generous ½ cup milk
275g/10oz/1¼ cups unsalted

(sweet) butter, diced
45–60ml/3–4 tbsp coffee extract
2 x 400g/14oz cans peach halves
 in juice, drained
65g/2½oz/generous ½ cup flaked
 (sliced) almonds, toasted
icing (confectioners') sugar,
 for dusting
a few fresh mint leaves,
 to decorate

1 Preheat the oven to 150°C/300°F/Gas 2. Draw three 23cm/9in circles on to baking parchment and invert on to baking sheets.

2 Whisk the egg whites until stiff. Gradually whisk in 275g/10oz/scant 1½ cups of the sugar until thick and glossy. Fold in the cornflour and almonds. Using a 1cm/½in plain icing nozzle, pipe the meringue to cover the circles drawn on the paper. Bake for 2 hours. Turn on to wire racks to cool.

3 For the pastry cream, beat together the egg yolks and remaining sugar until thick and pale. Heat the milk in a small pan to boiling point and beat into the egg mixture. Return to the pan and heat until the mixture coats the back of a spoon. Strain into a large bowl and beat until lukewarm. Gradually beat in the butter until glossy. Beat in the coffee extract.

4 Trim the meringues and crush the trimmings. Reserve 3 peach halves, chop the rest. Divide the pastry cream between two bowls, and fold the peaches into one bowl with the crushed meringue. Use to sandwich the meringues together and place on a serving plate.

5 Ice the cake with the plain pastry cream. Cover the top with flaked almonds and dust generously with icing sugar. Thinly slice the reserved peaches and use to decorate the cake edge. Add some mint leaves.

Mocha Brazil Layer Torte

**Makes one 20cm/8in
round cake**

3 egg whites
115g/4oz/generous ½ cup caster
 (superfine) sugar
15ml/1 tbsp coffee extract
75g/3oz/¾ cup brazil nuts,
 toasted and finely ground
20cm/8in chocolate sponge cake

For the icing

175g/6oz/1 cup plain (semisweet)
 chocolate chips
30ml/2 tbsp coffee extract
30ml/2 tbsp water
600ml/1 pint/2½ cups double
 (heavy) cream, whipped

For the decoration

12 chocolate triangles
12 chocolate-coated coffee beans

1 Preheat the oven to 150°C/300°F/Gas 2. Draw two 20cm/8in circles on baking parchment and place on a baking sheet. Grease, base-line and flour a 20cm/8in round springform tin (pan).

2 Whisk the egg whites until stiff. Whisk in the sugar until glossy. Fold in the coffee extract and nuts. Using a 1cm/½in plain nozzle, pipe to cover circles drawn on the paper.

3 Bake the meringues for 2 hours, then remove from the oven and leave to cool. Increase the oven temperature to 180°C/350°F/Gas 4.

4 To make the icing, melt the chocolate chips, coffee extract and water in a bowl over a pan of simmering water. Remove from the heat and fold in the whipped cream.

5 Cut the cake into three equal layers. Trim the meringue discs to the same size and assemble the cake with a layer of sponge, a little icing and a meringue disc, ending with sponge.

6 Reserve a little of the remaining icing; use the rest to cover the cake completely, forming a swirling pattern over the top.

7 Using the reserved icing, and a piping (icing) bag with a star nozzle, pipe 24 small rosettes on top of the cake. Top alternately with the coffee beans and the chocolate triangles.

Daquoise Energy 5984kcal/24978kJ; Protein 95.1g; Carbohydrate 560.1g, of which sugars 539.8g; Fat 390.1g, of which saturates 163.1g; Cholesterol 1546mg; Calcium 1190mg; Fibre 24.2g; Sodium 2237mg.
Torte Energy 6236kcal/25900kJ; Protein 60.3g; Carbohydrate 395g, of which sugars 327.8g; Fat 501.5g, of which saturates 242g; Cholesterol 833mg; Calcium 770mg; Fibre 7.6g; Sodium 1624mg.

Fresh Fruit Genoese

This Italian classic can be made with any selection of seasonal fruits.

Serves 8–10

For the sponge
175g/6oz/1½ cups plain (all-purpose) flour
a pinch of salt
4 eggs
115g/4oz/generous ½ cup caster (superfine) sugar

90ml/6 tbsp orange-flavoured liqueur

For the filling and topping
60ml/4 tbsp vanilla sugar
600ml/1 pint/2½ cups double (heavy) cream
450g/1lb mixed fresh fruits
150g/5oz/1¼ cups chopped pistachio nuts
60ml/4 tbsp apricot jam, warmed and sieved

1 Preheat the oven to 180°C/350°F/Gas 4. Grease and line the base of a 20cm/8in springform cake tin (pan) with baking parchment.

2 Sift the flour and salt together three times, then set aside. Using an electric mixer, beat the eggs and sugar together for 10 minutes until thick and pale.

3 Fold the flour mixture gently into the egg and sugar mixture. Transfer the cake mixture to the prepared tin and bake for 30–35 minutes. Leave the cake in the tin for about 5 minutes, and then transfer to a wire rack, remove the paper and cool completely.

4 Cut the cake horizontally into two layers, and place one layer on a plate. Sprinkle both layers with liqueur.

5 To make the filling and topping, add the vanilla sugar to the cream and whisk until the cream holds soft peaks. Spread two-thirds of the cream over the cake base layer and top with half the fruit.

6 Top with the second layer and spread the top and sides with the remaining cream. Press the nuts around the sides, arrange the remaining fruit on top. Brush the fruit with the warmed apricot jam.

Fruit Gateau with Heartsease

This strawberry gateau would be lovely to serve as a dessert at a summer lunch party in the garden.

Makes one ring cake
90g/3½oz/scant ½ cup soft margarine
90g/3½oz/½ cup caster (superfine) sugar
10ml/2 tsp clear honey
150g/5oz/1¼ cups self-raising (self-rising) flour

2.5ml/½ tsp baking powder
30ml/2 tbsp milk
2 eggs
15ml/1 tbsp rose water
15ml/1 tbsp Cointreau

To decorate
16 heartsease pansy flowers
1 egg white, lightly beaten
caster (superfine) sugar
icing (confectioners') sugar
450g/1lb/4 cups strawberries
strawberry leaves

1 Preheat the oven to 190°C/375°F/Gas 5. Grease and lightly flour a ring mould. Put the soft margarine, sugar, honey, flour, baking powder, milk and eggs into a mixing bowl and beat well for 1 minute. Add the rose water and the Cointreau, and mix well.

2 Pour the mixture into the mould and bake for 40 minutes. Allow to stand for a few minutes, and then turn out on to a serving plate.

3 Crystallize the heartsease pansies by painting them with the lightly beaten egg white and sprinkling with caster sugar. Leave to dry thoroughly.

4 Sift icing sugar over the cake. Fill the centre of the ring with strawberries – if they will not all fit, place some around the edge. Decorate with the crystallized heartsease flowers and some strawberry leaves.

> **Cook's Tip**
> Rose water is distilled from rose petals and water, and it is not only useful for cakes but can also be added to ice creams and sorbets, jams, jellies, milk puddings and fruit salads.

Genoese Energy 815kcal/3411kJ; Protein 8.5g; Carbohydrate 99.6g, of which sugars 85.9g; Fat 43g, of which saturates 21.8g; Cholesterol 158mg; Calcium 128mg; Fibre 2g; Sodium 132mg.
Gateau Energy 1586kcal/6630kJ; Protein 25.4g; Carbohydrate 180.3g, of which sugars 142.2g; Fat 86.1g, of which saturates 3.5g; Cholesterol 382mg; Calcium 294mg; Fibre 6.5g; Sodium 969mg.

Nut & Apple Gateau

Pecan nuts and apples give this gateau a beautiful texture and flavour.

Makes one 23cm/9in round cake

115g/4oz/⅔ cup pecan nuts or walnuts, toasted
50g/2oz/½ cup plain (all-purpose) flour
10ml/2 tsp baking powder
1.5ml/¼ tsp salt
2 large cooking apples
3 eggs
225g/8oz/generous 1 cup caster (superfine) sugar
5ml/1 tsp vanilla extract
175ml/6fl oz/¾ cup whipping cream

1 Preheat the oven to 160°C/325°F/Gas 3. Line two 23cm/9in cake tins (pans) with baking parchment and grease the paper.

2 Finely chop the nuts. Reserve 25ml/1½ tbsp and place the remainder in a mixing bowl. Sift over the flour, baking powder and salt, and stir well.

3 Peel and core the apples. Cut into 3mm/⅛in dice, then stir into the flour mixture. Beat the eggs until frothy. Gradually add the sugar and vanilla extract, and beat until ribbon trails form when you lift the whisk out of the mixture, about 8 minutes. Fold in the flour mixture.

4 Pour the mixture into the prepared cake tins and bake until a skewer inserted into the centre comes out clean, about 35 minutes. Leave to stand in the tin for 10 minutes, then turn out on to a wire rack to cool.

5 Whip the cream until firm. Use half for the filling. Using a large star nozzle, pipe rosettes on the top and then sprinkle over the reserved nuts to finish.

> **Cook's Tip**
> Toast the nuts on a foil-covered grill (broiling) pan under a hot grill (broiler) or in the oven until golden brown.

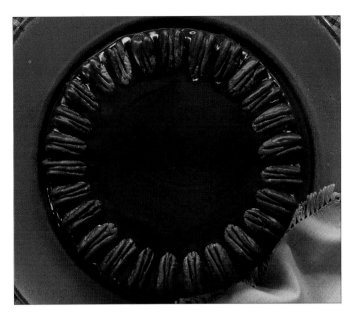

Chocolate Pecan Nut Torte

This torte uses finely ground nuts instead of flour. Toast and cool the nuts before grinding finely in a processor.

Makes one 20cm/8in round cake

200g/7oz plain (semisweet) chocolate, chopped
150g/5oz/10 tbsp unsalted (sweet) butter, diced
4 eggs
100g/3½oz/½ cup caster (superfine) sugar
10ml/2 tsp vanilla extract
115g/4oz/1 cup ground pecan nuts
10ml/2 tsp ground cinnamon
24 toasted pecan nut halves, to decorate (optional)

For the chocolate glaze
115g/4oz plain (semisweet) chocolate, chopped
60g/2oz/¼ cup unsalted (sweet) butter, cut into pieces
30ml/2 tbsp honey
a pinch of ground cinnamon

1 Preheat the oven to 180°C/350°F/Gas 4. Grease a 20cm/8in springform tin (pan), line with baking parchment, then grease the paper. Wrap the tin with foil.

2 Melt the chocolate and butter in a double boiler or in a heatproof bowl over a pan of simmering water, stirring until smooth. Set aside. Beat the eggs, sugar and vanilla extract until frothy. Stir in the melted chocolate and butter, ground nuts and cinnamon.

3 Pour into the tin. Place in a large roasting pan and pour boiling water into the roasting pan, to come 2cm/¾in up the side of the springform tin. Bake for 25–30 minutes, or until the edge of the cake is set, but the centre soft. Remove the foil and set on a wire rack.

4 To make the glaze, melt the chocolate, butter, honey and cinnamon as before, stirring until smooth. Remove from the heat. Dip the toasted pecan halves halfway into the glaze and place on baking parchment to set. Remove the cake from its tin and invert on to a wire rack. Remove the paper. Pour the glaze over the cake, tilting the rack to spread it. Use a metal spatula to smooth the sides. Arrange the nuts on top.

Gateau Energy 2807kcal/11741kJ; Protein 39.3g; Carbohydrate 303.2g, of which sugars 263.3g; Fat 168.6g, of which saturates 55.5g Cholesterol 755mg Calcium 454mg Fibre 10.2g Sodium 274mg.
Torte Energy 4744kcal/19729kJ; Protein 53.2g; Carbohydrate 335.4g, of which sugars 330.8g; Fat 363.6g, of which saturates 175.2g; Cholesterol 1228mg; Calcium 380mg; Fibre 13.3g; Sodium 1582mg.

Coconut Lime Gateau

Fresh lime and coconut give this gateau a fabulous flavour.

Makes one 23cm/9in round cake

225g/8oz/2 cups plain (all-purpose) flour
12.5ml/2½ tsp baking powder
1.5ml/¼ tsp salt
225g/8oz/1 cup butter, at room temperature
225g/8oz/generous 1 cup caster (superfine) sugar
grated rind of 2 limes
4 eggs
60ml/4 tbsp fresh lime juice
75g/3oz/1 cup desiccated (dry unsweetened shredded) coconut

For the frosting

450g/1lb/generous 2 cups granulated sugar
60ml/4 tbsp water
a pinch of cream of tartar
1 egg white, whisked until stiff

1 Preheat the oven to 180°C/350°F/Gas 4. Grease and base-line two 23cm/9in shallow round cake tins (pans). Sift together the flour, baking powder and salt.

2 Beat the butter until soft. Add the sugar and lime rind, and beat until pale and fluffy. Beat in the eggs, one at a time.

3 Gradually fold in the dry ingredients, alternating with the lime juice, then stir in two-thirds of the coconut.

4 Divide the mixture between the cake tins, level the tops and bake for 30–35 minutes. Cool in the tins on a wire rack for 10 minutes, then turn out and peel off the lining paper.

5 Bake the remaining coconut on a baking sheet until golden brown, stirring occasionally.

6 To make the frosting, heat the sugar, water and cream of tartar until dissolved, stirring. Boil to reach 120°C/250°F on a sugar thermometer. Remove from the heat and, when the bubbles subside, whisk in the egg white until thick.

7 Sandwich and cover the cake with the frosting. Sprinkle over the toasted coconut. Leave to set before serving.

Exotic Celebration Gateau

Use any tropical fruits you can find to make a spectacular display of colours and tastes for this cream-covered confection.

Makes one 20cm/8in ring gateau

175g/6oz/¾ cup butter, softened
175g/6oz/scant 1 cup caster (superfine) sugar
3 eggs, beaten
250g/9oz/2¼ cups self-raising (self-rising) flour
30–45ml/2–3 tbsp milk
90–120ml/6–8 tbsp light rum

For the decoration

400ml/14fl oz/1⅔ cups double (heavy) cream
25g/1oz/¼ cup icing (confectioners') sugar, sifted
450g/1lb mixed fresh exotic and soft fruits, such as figs, redcurrants, star fruit (carambola) and kiwi fruit
90ml/6 tbsp apricot jam, warmed and sieved
30ml/2 tbsp warm water
icing (confectioners') sugar

1 Preheat the oven to 190°C/375°F/Gas 5. Grease and flour a deep 20cm/8in ring mould.

2 Beat together the butter and sugar until light and fluffy. Gradually beat in the eggs, then fold in the sifted flour and the milk.

3 Spoon the mixture into the ring mould. Level the top. Bake the cake for 45 minutes, or until a skewer inserted into the centre comes out clean. Turn out on to a wire rack and leave to cool completely.

4 Place the cake on a serving plate. Make holes randomly over the cake with a skewer. Drizzle over the rum and allow it to soak in.

5 To decorate, beat together the cream and icing sugar until the mixture holds soft peaks. Spread all over the cake. Arrange the fruits in the hollow centre of the cake. Mix the apricot jam and warm water together, then brush over the fruit. Sift over some icing sugar to finish.

Coconut Energy 5859kcal/24634kJ; Protein 58g; Carbohydrate 886.4g, of which sugars 714.9g; Fat 256.6g, of which saturates 163.9g; Cholesterol 1241mg; Calcium 846mg; Fibre 17.3g; Sodium 1773mg.
Exotic Energy 5783kcal/24084kJ; Protein 57.2g; Carbohydrate 481.4g, of which sugars 289.6g; Fat 394.7g, of which saturates 238.5g; Cholesterol 1528mg; Calcium 933mg; Fibre 16.3g; Sodium 1428mg.

Chocolate & Fresh Cherry Gateau

Make this sophisticated cake for a special occasion.

Makes one 20cm/8in round cake
115g/4oz/½ cup butter
150g/5oz/¾ cup caster (superfine) sugar
3 eggs, lightly beaten
175g/6oz/1 cup plain (semisweet) chocolate chips, melted
60ml/4 tbsp Kirsch
150g/5oz/1¼ cups self-raising (self-rising) flour
5ml/1 tsp ground cinnamon
2.5ml/½ tsp ground cloves
350g/12oz fresh cherries, pitted and halved

45ml/3 tbsp morello cherry jam, warmed
5ml/1 tsp lemon juice

For the frosting
115g/4oz/⅔ cup plain chocolate chips
50g/2oz/¼ cup unsalted (sweet) butter
60ml/4 tbsp double (heavy) cream

To decorate
18 fresh cherries dipped in 75g/3oz/½ cup white chocolate chips, melted, and a few rose leaves, washed and dried

1 Preheat the oven to 160°C/325°F/Gas 3. Grease, base-line and flour a 20cm/8in round springform tin (pan).

2 Cream the butter and 115g/4oz/½ cup of the sugar until pale. Beat in the eggs. Stir in the chocolate and half the Kirsch. Fold in the flour and spices. Transfer to the tin and bake for 55–60 minutes. Cool for 10 minutes, then transfer to a wire rack.

3 For the filling, bring the cherries, the remaining kirsch and sugar to the boil, cover, and simmer for 10 minutes. Uncover for a further 10 minutes until syrupy. Leave to cool.

4 Halve the cake horizontally. Cut a 1cm/½in deep circle from the middle of the base, leaving a 1cm/½in edge. Crumble this cake into the filling mixture and fill the cut-away depression.

5 Sieve the jam and lemon juice. Brush all over the cake. For the frosting, melt all the ingredients. Cool, pour over the cake. Decorate with chocolate-dipped cherries and leaves.

Coffee Almond Flower Gateau

This delicious cake can be made quite quickly. Ring the changes by using a coffee-flavoured sponge.

Makes one 20cm/8in round cake

475g/1lb 2oz/2¼ cups coffee-flavour butter icing
2 x 20cm/8in round sponge cakes with chopped nuts
75g/3oz plain (semisweet) chocolate
20 blanched almonds
4 chocolate-coated coffee beans

1 Reserve 60ml/4 tbsp of the butter icing for piping and use the rest to sandwich the sponge cakes together and cover the top and side of the cake. Smooth the top with a metal spatula and serrate the side with a scraper to give a ridged effect.

2 Melt the chocolate in a double boiler or in a heatproof bowl over a pan of simmering water. Remove the pan from the heat.

3 Dip half of each almond in the chocolate at a slight angle. Leave to dry on baking parchment. Leave the bowl of chocolate over the pan of hot water so it does not set. .

4 Arrange the almonds on top of the cake to represent flowers. Place a chocolate-coated coffee bean for the flower centres. Spoon the remaining melted chocolate into a baking parchment piping (icing) bag. Cut a small piece off the end in a straight line. Pipe the chocolate in wavy lines over the top of the cake and in small beads around the top edge.

5 Transfer the cake to a serving plate. Place the reserved butter icing in a fresh piping bag fitted with a fine writing nozzle. Pipe beads of icing all around the bottom of the cake, then top with small beads of chocolate.

Cook's Tip
Either the quick mix sponge or the Genoese sponge cake recipes would be suitable for this cake.

Chocolate Energy 5172kcal/21630kJ; Protein 60.1g; Carbohydrate 587.6g, of which sugars 470.7g; Fat 287.9g, of which saturates 171.5g; Cholesterol 1022mg; Calcium 781mg; Fibre 16.6g; Sodium 1337mg.
Coffee Energy 5901kcal/24633kJ; Protein 58.9g; Carbohydrate 605.1g, of which sugars 491.7g; Fat 377.2g, of which saturates 150.2g; Cholesterol 990mg; Calcium 792mg; Fibre 13.8g; Sodium 2877mg.

Vegan Chocolate Gateau

Containing no dairy or other animal produce, this gateau is a rare treat for vegans and tastes really delicious.

Makes one 20cm/8in gateau
275g/10oz/2¹/2 cups self-raising (self-rising) wholemeal (whole-wheat) flour
50g/2oz/¹/2 cup unsweetened cocoa powder
15ml/1 tbsp baking powder
250g/9oz/1¹/4 cups caster (superfine) sugar
a few drops of vanilla extract

135ml/9 tbsp sunflower oil
350ml/12fl oz/1¹/2 cups water
sifted unsweetened cocoa powder and 25g/1oz/¹/4 cup chopped nuts, to decorate

For the chocolate fudge
50g/2oz/¹/4 cup soya margarine
45ml/3 tbsp water
250g/9oz/2¹/4 cups icing (confectioners') sugar
30ml/2 tbsp unsweetened cocoa powder

1 Preheat the oven to 160°C/325°F/Gas 3. Grease and line a deep 20cm/8in round cake tin (pan) with baking parchment, and grease the paper.

2 Sift the flour, cocoa and baking powder into a large mixing bowl. Add the sugar and vanilla extract, then gradually beat in the oil and water to make a smooth batter. Pour the mixture into the cake tin and smooth the surface.

3 Bake for 45 minutes. Leave in the tin for 5 minutes, then turn out on to a wire rack to cool completely. Cut the cake in half.

4 To make the chocolate fudge, gently melt the margarine with the water. Remove from the heat, add the icing sugar and cocoa powder, and beat until smooth and shiny. Allow to cool until firm enough to spread and pipe.

5 Place a layer of cake on a serving plate and spread over two-thirds of the chocolate fudge. Top with the other layer of cake. Fill a piping (icing) bag with the remaining chocolate fudge. Using a large star nozzle, pipe chocolate fudge stars over the top of the cake. Sprinkle with cocoa powder and chopped nuts.

Black Forest Gateau

A perfect gateau for a special tea party, or for serving as a sumptuous dinner-party dessert.

Makes one 20cm/8in gateau
5 eggs
175g/6oz/scant 1 cup caster (superfine) sugar
50g/2oz/¹/2 cup plain (all-purpose) flour
50g/2oz/¹/2 cup unsweetened cocoa powder
75g/3oz/6 tbsp butter, melted

For the filling
75–90ml/5–6 tbsp Kirsch
600ml/1 pint/2¹/2 cups double (heavy) cream
425g/15oz can black cherries, drained, pitted and chopped

To decorate
chocolate curls
15–20 fresh cherries, preferably with stems
icing (confectioners') sugar

1 Preheat the oven to 180°C/350°F/Gas 4. Base-line and grease two deep 20cm/8in round cake tins (pans).

2 Beat together the eggs and sugar for 10 minutes, or until thick and pale. Sift over the flour and cocoa powder, and fold in gently. Trickle in the melted butter and fold in gently.

3 Transfer the mixture to the cake tins. Bake for 30 minutes, or until springy to the touch.

4 Leave in the tins for 5 minutes, then turn out on to a wire rack, peel off the lining paper and leave to cool. Cut each cake in half horizontally and sprinkle with the Kirsch.

5 Whip the cream until softly peaking. Combine two-thirds of the cream with the chopped cherries. Place a layer of cake on a serving plate and spread with one-third of the filling. Repeat twice, and top with a layer of cake. Use the reserved cream to cover the top and side of the gateau.

6 Decorate the side of the gateau with chocolate curls, and place more in the centre of the top of the cake. Arrange fresh cherries around the edge and finally dredge the top with icing sugar.

Vegan Energy 4418kcal/18619kJ; Protein 46.9g; Carbohydrate 746.7g, of which sugars 527.8g; Fat 158.8g, of which saturates 21.8g; Cholesterol 0mg; Calcium 780mg; Fibre 19.1g; Sodium 1200mg.
Black Forest Energy 5386kcal/22373kJ; Protein 58.3g; Carbohydrate 316.8g, of which sugars 272.9g; Fat 423.1g, of which saturates 253.7g; Cholesterol 1934mg; Calcium 742mg; Fibre 10.1g; Sodium 1458mg.

Walnut Coffee Gateau

Serves 8–10

150g/5oz/scant 1 cup walnuts
150g/5oz/³⁄₄ cup caster
  (superfine) sugar
5 eggs, separated
50g/2oz/scant 1 cup dry breadcrumbs
15ml/1 tbsp unsweetened
  cocoa powder
15ml/1 tbsp instant coffee
30ml/2 tbsp rum or lemon juice

1.5ml/¼ tsp salt
90ml/6 tbsp redcurrant
  jelly, warmed
chopped walnuts, for decorating

For the frosting
225g/8oz plain (semisweet)
  chocolate
750ml/1¼ pint/3 cups
  whipping cream

1 To make the frosting, combine the chocolate and cream in the top of a double boiler until the chocolate melts. Cool, then cover and chill overnight, or until the mixture is firm.

2 Preheat the oven to 180°C/350°F/Gas 4. Line and grease a 23 × 5cm/9 × 2in cake tin (pan). Grind the nuts with 45ml/3 tbsp of the sugar in a food processor, blender or coffee grinder.

3 With an electric mixer, beat the egg yolks and remaining sugar until thick and pale. Fold in the walnuts. Stir in the breadcrumbs, cocoa, coffee and rum or lemon juice.

4 In another bowl, beat the egg whites with the salt until they hold stiff peaks. Fold carefully into the walnut mixture. Pour the meringue batter into the prepared tin and bake until the top of the cake springs back when touched, about 45 minutes. Allow the cake to stand for 5 minutes, then turn out and cool, before slicing the cake in half horizontally.

5 With an electric mixer, beat the chocolate frosting mixture on low speed until it becomes lighter, about 30 seconds. Brush some of the redcurrant jelly over the cut cake layer. Spread with some of the chocolate frosting, then sandwich with the remaining cake layer. Brush the top of the cake with some more jelly, then cover the side and top with the remaining frosting. Make a starburst pattern with a knife and sprinkle chopped walnuts around the edge.

Sachertorte

A rich cake, ideal for a self-confessed chocoholic.

**Makes one 23cm/9in
round cake**
115g/4oz plain
  (semisweet) chocolate
90g/3oz/6 tbsp unsalted (sweet)
  butter, at room temperature
50g/2oz/¼ cup caster
  (superfine) sugar
4 eggs, separated, plus 1
  egg white
1.5ml/¼ tsp salt

65g/2½oz/9 tbsp plain
  (all-purpose) flour, sifted

For the topping
75ml/5 tbsp apricot jam
250ml/8fl oz/1 cup plus
  15ml/1 tbsp water
15g/½ oz/1 tbsp unsalted
  (sweet) butter
175g/6oz plain chocolate
75g/3oz/scant ½ cup caster
  (superfine) sugar
ready-made chocolate
  decorating icing

1 Preheat the oven to 160°C/325°F/Gas 3. Line and grease a 23cm/9in cake tin (pan). Melt the chocolate in a heatproof bowl over a pan of simmering water and set aside.

2 Cream the butter and sugar until light and fluffy. Stir in the chocolate, then beat in the egg yolks, one at a time.

3 Beat the egg whites with the salt until stiff. Fold a dollop of whites into the chocolate mixture to lighten it. Fold in the remaining whites in three batches, alternating with the sifted flour. Pour into the tin and bake until a skewer comes out clean, about 45 minutes. Turn out on to a wire rack.

4 To make the topping, melt the jam with 15ml/1 tbsp of the water, then strain for a smooth consistency. For the frosting, melt the butter and chocolate as before. In a heavy pan, dissolve the sugar in the remaining water, then boil until it reaches 107°C/225°F (thread stage) on a sugar thermometer. Plunge the base of the pan into cold water for 1 minute. Stir into the chocolate. Cool for a few minutes.

5 Brush the jam over the cake, then spread the frosting over the top and sides. Leave overnight. Decorate with chocolate icing.

Gateau Energy 651kcal/2707kJ; Protein 9.5g; Carbohydrate 43.5g, of which sugars 38.5g; Fat 50.1g, of which saturates 24.9g; Cholesterol 175mg; Calcium 101mg; Fibre 1.8g; Sodium 149mg.
Sachertorte Energy 3484kcal/14593kJ; Protein 50g; Carbohydrate 417.9g, of which sugars 365.7g; Fat 190.6g, of which saturates 109.8g; Cholesterol 1002mg; Calcium 395mg; Fibre 9.3g; Sodium 1038mg.

Special Occasion Cakes

From Christmas, New Year and Easter to weddings, christenings
and birthdays, cakes are the best way to celebrate a special
occasion. With expert advice and step-by-step instructions,
these recipes will enable you to create the perfect cake
for every event, whether you choose the Russian Easter cake
Kulich, a Greek New Year Cake, or pick one of the many
other kinds of celebration cakes.

Dundee Cake

This is the perfect recipe for a festive occasion when a lighter fruit cake is required.

Makes one 20cm/8in round cake
175g/6oz/³⁄4 cup butter
175g/6oz/³⁄4 cup soft light brown sugar
3 eggs
225g/8oz/2 cups plain (all-purpose) flour
10ml/2 tsp baking powder
5ml/1 tsp ground cinnamon
2.5ml/¹⁄2 tsp ground cloves
1.5ml/¹⁄4 tsp freshly grated nutmeg
225g/8oz/generous 1¹⁄2 cups sultanas (golden raisins)
175g/6oz/generous 1 cup raisins
175g/6oz/³⁄4 cup glacé (candied) cherries, halved
115g/4oz/³⁄4 cup chopped mixed (candied) peel
50g/2oz/¹⁄2 cup chopped blanched almonds
grated rind of 1 lemon
30ml/2 tbsp brandy
115g/4oz/1 cup whole blanched almonds, to decorate

1 Preheat the oven to 160°C/325°F/Gas 3. Grease a 20cm/8in round deep cake tin (pan) and line with baking parchment.

2 Cream the butter and sugar until pale and light. Add the eggs, one at a time, beating well after each addition.

3 Sift together the flour, baking powder and spices. Put the nutmeg, sultanas, raisins, glacé cherries, mixed peel, almonds, lemon rind and brandy into a bowl.

4 Fold the flour mixture into the egg mixture alternately with the fruit mixture until evenly combined. Transfer to the cake tin. Smooth the surface, then make a small dip in the centre so that the cake will not rise to a point.

5 Decorate the top of the cake by pressing the blanched almonds in decreasing circles over the entire surface. Bake for 2–2¹⁄4 hours, or until a skewer inserted in the centre of the cake comes out clean.

6 Leave to cool in the tin for 30 minutes then transfer the cake to a wire rack to cool completely.

Kulich

This rich Russian yeast cake is traditionally made at Eastertime.

Makes two cakes
15ml/1 tbsp active dried yeast
90ml/6 tbsp lukewarm milk
75g/3oz/6 tbsp caster (superfine) sugar
500g/1¹⁄4 lb/5 cups plain (all-purpose) flour
a pinch of saffron threads
30ml/2 tbsp dark rum
2.5ml/¹⁄2 tsp ground cardamom seeds
2.5ml/¹⁄2 tsp ground cumin
50g/2oz/¹⁄4 cup unsalted (sweet) butter
2 eggs plus 2 egg yolks
¹⁄2 vanilla pod (bean), finely chopped
25g/1oz/2 tbsp each crystallized ginger, mixed (candied) peel, almonds and currants, chopped

For the decoration
75g/3oz/³⁄4 cup icing (confectioners') sugar, sifted
7.5–10ml/1¹⁄2–2 tsp warm water
a drop of almond extract
2 candles
blanched almonds
mixed (candied) peel

1 Blend together the yeast, milk, 25g/1oz/¹⁄4 cup sugar and 50g/2oz/¹⁄2 cup flour. Leave in a warm place for 15 minutes, or until frothy. Soak the saffron in the rum for 15 minutes.

2 Sift together the remaining flour and spices and rub in the butter. Stir in the rest of the sugar. Add the yeast mixture, saffron liquid and remaining ingredients. Knead the dough until smooth. Put in an oiled bowl, cover with clear film (plastic wrap) and leave until doubled in size.

3 Preheat the oven to 190°C/375°F/Gas 5. Grease, line and flour two 500g/1¹⁄4lb coffee tins or 15cm/6in clay flowerpots.

4 Knock back (punch down) the dough and form into two rounds. Press into the tins or pots, cover and leave to rise for 30 minutes. Bake for 35 minutes for the pots or 50 minutes for the tins. Remove from the tins or pots and cool.

5 To decorate, mix together the icing sugar, water and almond extract. Pour over the cakes. Decorate with the candles, nuts and peel.

Dundee Cake Energy 5855kcal/24598kJ; Protein 87.4g; Carbohydrate 831.7g, of which sugars 655.8g; Fat 258.1g, of which saturates 103.6g; Cholesterol 944mg; Calcium 1393mg; Fibre 34.3g; Sodium 1828mg.
Kulich Energy 1521kcal/6432kJ; Protein 33.3g; Carbohydrate 282.3g, of which sugars 91.8g; Fat 33g, of which saturates 16.4g; Cholesterol 347mg; Calcium 505mg; Fibre 8.4g; Sodium 293mg.

Yule Log

This rich seasonal treat could provide an economical alternative to a traditional iced fruit cake.

Makes one 28cm/11in roll

4 eggs, separated
150g/5oz/¾ cup caster
   (superfine) sugar
5ml/1 tsp vanilla extract

a pinch of cream of tartar
115g/4oz/1 cup plain
   (all-purpose) flour, sifted
250ml/8fl oz/1 cup
   whipping cream
300g/11oz plain (semisweet)
   chocolate, chopped
30ml/2 tbsp rum or Cognac
icing (confectioners') sugar,
   for dusting

1 Preheat the oven to 190°C/375°F/Gas 5. Grease, line and flour a 40 × 28cm/16 × 11in Swiss roll tin (jelly roll pan).

2 Whisk the egg yolks with all but 25g/1oz/¼ cup of the sugar until pale and thick. Add the vanilla extract.

3 Whisk the egg whites with the cream of tartar until they form soft peaks. Add the reserved sugar and continue whisking until the mixture is stiff and glossy.

4 Fold half the flour into the yolk mixture. Add a quarter of the egg whites and fold in to lighten the mixture. Fold in the remaining flour, then the remaining egg whites.

5 Spread the mixture in the tin. Bake for 15 minutes. Turn on to paper sprinkled with caster sugar. Roll up and leave to cool.

6 Put the cream into a small pan and bring it to the boil. Put the chocolate in a bowl and add the cream. Stir until the chocolate has melted, then beat until it is fluffy and has thickened to a spreading consistency. Mix one-third of the chocolate cream with the rum or Cognac.

7 Unroll the cake and spread with the rum mixture. Re-roll and cut off about a quarter, at an angle. Arrange to form a branch. Spread the chocolate cream over the cake. Mark with a fork, add Christmas decorations and dust with icing sugar.

Chocolate Chestnut Roulade

A traditional version of Bûche de Nöel, the delicious French Christmas gateau.

Makes one 33cm/13in long roll

225g/8oz plain
   (semisweet) chocolate
50g/2oz white chocolate
4 eggs, separated
115g/4oz/generous ½ cup caster
   (superfine) sugar

For the chestnut filling

150ml/¼ pint/⅔ cup double
   (heavy) cream
225g/8oz can chestnut purée
50–65g/2–2½oz/ 4–5 tbsp icing
   (confectioners') sugar, plus
   extra for dusting
15–30ml/1–2 tbsp brandy

1 Preheat the oven to 180°C/350°F/Gas 4. Line and grease a 23 × 33cm/9 × 13in Swiss roll tin (jelly roll pan).

2 For the chocolate curls, melt 50g/2oz of the plain and all of the white chocolate in separate bowls set over pans of simmering water. When melted, spread on a non-porous surface and leave to set. Hold a long sharp knife at a 45-degree angle to the chocolate and push it along the chocolate, using a sawing motion. Put the curls on baking parchment.

3 Melt the remaining plain chocolate. Beat the egg yolks and caster (superfine) sugar until thick and pale. Stir in the chocolate.

4 Whisk the egg whites until they form stiff peaks, then fold into the chocolate mixture. Turn into the prepared tin and bake for 15–20 minutes. Cool, covered with a just-damp dish towel, on a wire rack.

5 Sprinkle a sheet of baking parchment with caster (superfine) sugar. Turn the roulade out on to it. Peel off the lining paper and trim the edges of the roulade. Cover with the dish towel.

6 To make the filling, whip the cream until softly peaking. Beat together the chestnut purée, icing sugar and brandy until smooth, then fold in the cream. Spread over the roulade and roll it up. Top with chocolate curls and dust with icing sugar.

Log Energy 3826kcal/16020kJ; Protein 56.6g; Carbohydrate 443.4g, of which sugars 353g; Fat 208.4g, of which saturates 119.9g; Cholesterol 1042mg; Calcium 599mg; Fibre 11.1g; Sodium 373mg.
Roulade Energy 3496kcal/14645kJ; Protein 48g; Carbohydrate 424.1g, of which sugars 355.5g; Fat 187.3g, of which saturates 104.4g; Cholesterol 980mg; Calcium 585mg; Fibre 14.9g; Sodium 416mg.

Chocolate Christmas Cups

These fabulous little confections would be perfect to serve during the Christmas festivities. You will need about 70–80 foil or paper sweet cases to make and serve them.

Makes about 35 cups
275g/10oz plain (semisweet) chocolate, broken into pieces
175g/6oz cooked, cold Christmas pudding
75ml/2½fl oz/⅓ cup brandy or whisky
chocolate leaves and a few crystallized cranberries, to decorate

1 Place the chocolate in a double boiler or in a bowl over a pan of hot water. Heat gently until the chocolate is melted, stirring until the chocolate is smooth.

2 Using a pastry brush, brush or coat the base and sides of about 35 paper or foil sweet cases. Allow to set, then repeat, reheating the melted chocolate if necessary, and apply a second coat. Leave to cool and set completely, 4–5 hours or overnight. Reserve the remaining chocolate.

3 Crumble the Christmas pudding in a small bowl, sprinkle with the brandy or whisky and allow to stand for 30–40 minutes, until the spirit is absorbed.

4 Spoon a little of the pudding mixture into each cup, smoothing the top. Reheat the remaining chocolate and spoon over the top of each cup to cover the surface of each cup to the edge. Leave to set.

5 When completely set, peel off the cases and place in clean foil cases. Decorate with chocolate leaves and crystallized cranberries.

> **Cook's Tip**
> To crystallize cranberries for decoration, beat an egg white until frothy. Dip each berry in egg white then in sugar. Leave to dry.

Eggless Christmas Cake

This simple cake contains a wealth of fruit and nuts to give it that traditional Christmas flavour. It is decorated with large pieces of glacé (candied) fruits.

Makes one 18cm/7in square cake
75g/3oz/½ cup sultanas (golden raisins)
75g/3oz/scant ½ cup raisins
75g/3oz/scant ½ cup currants
75g/3oz/scant ½ cup glacé (candied) cherries, halved
50g/2oz/⅓ cup mixed (candied) peel

250ml/8fl oz/1 cup apple juice
25g/1oz/2 tbsp toasted hazelnuts
30ml/2 tbsp pumpkin seeds
2 pieces preserved stem ginger in syrup, chopped
finely grated rind of 1 lemon
120ml/4fl oz/½ cup milk
50ml/2fl oz/¼ cup sunflower oil
225g/8oz/2 cups self-raising (self-rising) wholemeal (whole-wheat) flour
10ml/2 tsp mixed (apple pie) spice
45ml/3 tbsp brandy or dark rum
apricot jam, for brushing
glacé (candied) fruits, to decorate

1 Soak the sultanas, raisins, currants, cherries and mixed peel in the apple juice overnight.

2 Preheat the oven to 150°C/300°F/Gas 2. Grease and line an 18cm/7in square cake tin (pan).

3 Transfer the soaked fruit to a large bowl. Add the hazelnuts, pumpkin seeds, ginger and lemon rind to the fruit.

4 Stir in the milk and oil. Sift the flour and spice into another bowl, then add to the fruit mixture with the brandy or rum. Combine thoroughly.

5 Spoon the mixture into the prepared cake tin and bake for about 1½ hours, or until the cake is golden brown and firm to the touch.

6 Turn out and cool on a wire rack. Warm the apricot jam and sieve it. Brush over the cake to glaze it and decorate with glacé fruits.

Flourless Fruit Cake

This makes the perfect base for a birthday cake for anyone who needs to avoid eating flour.

Makes one 25cm/10in round cake
450g/1lb/1⅓ cups mincemeat
350g/12oz/2 cups dried mixed fruit
115g/4oz/½ cup ready-to eat dried apricots, chopped
115g/4oz/⅔ cup ready-to-eat dried figs, chopped
115g/4oz/½ cup glacé (candied) cherries, halved
115g/4oz/1 cup walnut pieces
225g/8oz/8–10 cups cornflakes, crushed
4 eggs, lightly beaten
410g/14½oz can evaporated milk
5ml/1 tsp mixed (apple pie) spice
5ml/1 tsp baking powder
mixed glacé (candied) fruits, chopped, to decorate (optional)

1 Preheat the oven to 150°C/300°F/Gas 2.

2 Grease a 25cm/10in round cake tin (pan), line the base and sides with a double thickness of baking parchment and grease the paper.

3 Put the mincemeat, dried mixed fruit, figs and glacé cherries into a large bowl. Beat together until well combined.

4 Add the walnut pieces and cornflakes. Stir in the eggs, evaporated milk, mixed spice and baking powder.

5 Turn into the cake tin and smooth the surface.

6 Bake for about 1¾ hours, or until a skewer inserted in the centre of the cake comes out clean.

7 Allow the cake to cool in the tin for 10 minutes, then turn out on to a wire rack, peel off the lining paper and leave to cool completely.

8 Once the cake has cooled, decorate with the chopped glacé fruits, if you like.

Glazed Christmas Ring

Whole brazil nuts decorate this fabulous fruit-packed cake.

Makes one 25cm/10in ring cake
225g/8oz/generous 1⅓ cups sultanas (golden raisins)
175g/6oz/¾ cup raisins
175g/6oz/generous 1 cup currants
175g/6oz/1 cup dried figs, chopped
90ml/6 tbsp whisky
45ml/3 tbsp orange juice
225g/8oz/1 cup butter
225g/8oz/1cup dark soft brown sugar
5 eggs
250g/9oz/2¼ cups plain (all-purpose) flour
15ml/1 tbsp baking powder
15ml/1 tbsp mixed (apple pie) spice
115g/4oz/½ cup glacé (candied) cherries, chopped
115g/4oz/1 cup chopped brazil nuts
50g/2oz/⅓ cup chopped mixed (candied) peel
50g/2oz/½ cup ground almonds
grated rind and juice 1 orange
30ml/2 tbsp thick-cut orange marmalade

To decorate
150ml/¼ pint/⅔ cup thick-cut orange marmalade
15ml/1 tbsp orange juice
175g/6oz/¾ cup glacé (candied) cherries
115g/4oz/⅔ cup dried figs, halved
75g/3oz/½ cup whole brazil nuts

1 Put the dried fruits in a bowl, pour over 60ml/4 tbsp of the whisky and all the orange juice, and marinate overnight.

2 Preheat the oven to 160°C/325°F/Gas 3. Grease and line a 25cm/10in ring mould. Cream the butter and sugar. Beat in the eggs. Sift together the flour, baking powder and mixed spice. Fold into the egg mixture, alternating with the remaining ingredients, except the whisky. Transfer to the tin.

3 Bake for 1 hour, then reduce the oven temperature to 150°C/300°F/Gas 2 and bake for a further 1¾–2 hours.

4 Prick the cake all over and pour over the reserved whisky. Cool in the tin for 30 minutes, then transfer to a wire rack. Boil the marmalade and orange juice for 3 minutes. Stir in the fruit and nuts. Cool, then spoon over the cake and leave to set.

Cake Energy 5252kcal/22194kJ; Protein 111.3g; Carbohydrate 939.6g, of which sugars 755.7g; Fat 142.5g, of which saturates 23.3g; Cholesterol 848mg; Calcium 2125mg; Fibre 35.8g; Sodium 3371mg.
Ring Energy 9132kcal/38385kJ; Protein 120.5g; Carbohydrate 1340.7g, of which sugars 1147.5g; Fat 380.9g, of which saturates 158.8g; Cholesterol 1431mg; Calcium 2500mg; Fibre 58.7g; Sodium 2368mg.

Noel Cake

If you like a traditional royal-iced Christmas cake, this is a simple design using only one icing and easy-to-pipe decorations.

Makes one 20cm/8in round cake

20cm/8in round rich fruit cake
30ml/2 tbsp apricot jam, warmed and sieved
750g/1lb 10oz marzipan
900g/2lb/6 cups royal icing
green and red food colouring

Materials/equipment

23cm/9in round silver cake board
3 baking parchment piping (icing) bags
44 large gold dragées
fine writing nozzles
2 very fine writing nozzles
2.5m/2½ yd gold ribbon, 2cm/¾in wide
2.5m/2½ yd red ribbon, 5mm/¼in wide

1 Brush the fruit cake with apricot jam, cover with the marzipan and place on the cake board.

2 Using a metal spatula flat-ice the top of the cake with two layers of royal icing and leave to dry. Ice the sides of the cake and then peak the royal icing using the metal spatula, leaving a space around the centre for the ribbon. Leave to dry. Reserve the remaining royal icing.

3 Pipe tiny beads of icing around the top edge of the cake and place a gold dragée on alternate beads.

4 Using the fine writing nozzle, write "NOEL" across the cake and pipe holly leaves, stems and berries around the top.

5 Secure the ribbons around the side of the cake. Tie a red bow and attach to the front of the cake. Use the remaining ribbon for the board. Leave to dry overnight.

6 Tint 30ml/2 tbsp of the royal icing bright green and 15ml/1 tbsp bright red. Using a very fine writing nozzle, over-pipe "NOEL" in red, then the edging beads and berries. Overpipe the holly in green with the other very fine nozzle. Leave to dry.

Christmas Tree Cake

No piping is involved in this bright and colourful cake, making it an easy choice.

Makes one 20cm/8in round cake

45ml/3 tbsp apricot jam
20cm/8in round rich fruit cake

900g/2lb marzipan
green, red, yellow and purple food colouring
225g/8oz/1½ cups royal icing
edible silver balls

Materials/equipment

25cm/10in round cake board

1 Warm, then sieve the apricot jam and brush the cake with it. Colour 675g/1½lb/4½ cups of the marzipan green. Use to cover the cake. Leave to dry overnight.

2 Secure the cake to the cake board with a thin layer of royal icing. Spread the icing halfway up the cake side. Press the flat side of a metal spatula into the icing, then pull away sharply to form peaks.

3 Make three different-size Christmas tree templates. Tint half the remaining marzipan a deeper green than marzipan used for the cake. Using the templates, cut out three tree shapes and arrange them on the cake.

4 Divide the remaining marzipan into three and then colour red, yellow and purple. Use a little of each marzipan to make five 9cm/3in rolls. Loop them alternately around the top edge of the cake. Make small red balls and press on to the loop ends.

5 Use the remaining marzipan to make the tree decorations. Arrange on the trees, securing with water, if necessary. Finish the cake by adding silver balls to the Christmas trees.

Cook's Tip
A rich fruit cake suitable for a Christmas cake improves with storage so remember to make yours at least 3 weeks before you begin decorating and icing.

Noel Energy 10111kcal/42759kJ; Protein 100.9g; Carbohydrate 1948.7g, of which sugars 1780.7g; Fat 218.3g, of which saturates 43.7g; Cholesterol 692mg; Calcium 1949mg; Fibre 36.8g; Sodium 2514mg.
Tree Energy 9354kcal/39507kJ; Protein 107.1g; Carbohydrate 1694.8g, of which sugars 1526.8g; Fat 237.3g, of which saturates 45.3g; Cholesterol 692mg; Calcium 1863mg; Fibre 39.6g; Sodium 2535mg.

Christmas Stocking Cake

A bright and happy cake that is sure to delight children at Christmas time. The stocking, packed with toys, is simple to make.

Makes one 20cm/8in square cake
20cm/8in square rich fruit cake
45ml/3 tbsp apricot jam, warmed and sieved
900g/2lb marzipan
1.2kg/2½lb/7½ cups sugarpaste icing
15ml/1 tbsp royal icing
red and green food colouring

Materials/equipment
25cm/10in square silver cake board
1.5m/1½ yd red ribbon, 2cm/¾in wide
1m/1yd green ribbon, 2cm/¾in wide

1 Brush the cake with the apricot jam and place on the cake board. Cover with marzipan.

2 Set aside 225g/8oz/1½ cups of the sugarpaste icing. Cover the cake with the remainder. Leave to dry.

3 Secure the red ribbon around the board and the green ribbon around the cake with royal icing.

4 Divide the sugarpaste in half and roll out one half. Using a template, cut out two sugarpaste stockings, one 5mm/¼in larger all round. Put the smaller one on top of the larger one.

5 Divide the other half of the sugarpaste into two and tint one red and the other green. Roll out and cut each colour into seven 1cm/½in strips. Alternate the strips on top of the stocking. Roll lightly to fuse and press the edges together. Leave to dry.

6 Shape the remaining white sugarpaste into four parcels. Trim each with red and green sugarpaste ribbons. Use the remaining red and green sugarpaste to make thin strips to decorate the cake sides. Secure in place with royal icing and stick small sugarpaste balls to cover the joins. Arrange the stocking and parcels on the cake top.

Marbled Cracker Cake

Here is a Christmas cake that is decorated in a most untraditional way! Sugarpaste is easy to make yourself but if you are in a hurry you can buy it.

Makes one 20cm/8in round cake
20cm/8in round rich fruit cake
45ml/3 tbsp apricot jam, warmed and sieved
675g/1½lb marzipan
750g/1¾ lb/5¼ cups sugarpaste icing
red and green food colouring
edible gold balls

Materials /equipment
wooden cocktail sticks (toothpicks)
25cm/10in round cake board
red, green and gold thin gift-wrapping ribbon
3 red and 3 green ribbon bows

1 Brush the cake with the jam. Roll out the marzipan and use to cover the cake. Leave to dry overnight.

2 Form a roll with 500g/1¼lb/3¾ cups of the sugarpaste icing. With a cocktail stick, dab a few drops of red colouring on to the icing. Repeat with the green. Knead lightly.

3 Roll out the icing until it has marbled. Brush the marzipan with water and cover with the icing. Position the cake on the cake board.

4 Colour half of the remaining sugarpaste icing red and the remainder green. Use half of each colour to make five crackers, about 6cm/2½ in long. Decorate each with a gold ball. Leave to dry on baking parchment.

5 Roll out the remaining red and green icings, and cut into 1cm/½ in wide strips. Cut into 12 red and 12 green diamonds. Attach them alternately around the top and base of the cake with water.

6 Cut the ribbons into 10cm/4in lengths. Arrange them with the crackers on top of the cake. Attach the bows with softened sugarpaste icing, positioning them between the diamonds at the top cake edge.

Stocking Energy 11915kcal/50432kJ; Protein 110.5g; Carbohydrate 2373.9g, of which sugars 2205.9g; Fat 237.3g, of which saturates 45.3g; Cholesterol 692mg; Calcium 2208mg; Fibre 39.6g; Sodium 2566mg.
Cracker Energy 9858kcal/41695kJ; Protein 97g; Carbohydrate 1908.3g, of which sugars 1740.3g; Fat 208.7g, of which saturates 43g; Cholesterol 692mg; Calcium 1901mg; Fibre 35.3g; Sodium 2503mg.

Greek New Year Cake

A "good luck", foil-wrapped gold coin is traditionally baked into this cake.

Makes one 23cm/9in square cake
275g/10oz/2½ cups plain (all-purpose) flour
10ml/2 tsp baking powder
50g/2oz/½ cup ground almonds

225g/8oz/1 cup butter, softened
175g/6oz/generous ¾ cup caster (superfine) sugar, plus extra for sprinkling
4 eggs
150ml/¼ pint/⅔ cup fresh orange juice
50g/2oz/⅓ cup blanched almonds
15g/½ oz/1 tbsp sesame seeds

1 Preheat the oven to 180°C/350°F/Gas 4. Grease a 23cm/9in square cake tin (pan), line with baking parchment and grease the paper.

2 Sift together the flour and baking powder and stir in the ground almonds.

3 Cream the butter and sugar until light and fluffy. Beat in the eggs, one at a time. Fold in the flour mixture, alternating with the orange juice.

4 Spoon the mixture into the prepared cake tin. Arrange the blanched almonds on top, then sprinkle over the sesame seeds. Bake for 50 minutes, or until a skewer inserted in the centre comes out clean.

5 Leave in the tin for 5 minutes, then turn out on to a wire rack and peel off the lining paper. Sprinkle with caster sugar before serving.

Cook's Tip
Be careful not to overbeat the mixture if you are using an electric whisk, as this will cause the cooked cake to sag in the middle. Scrape the mixture from the sides of the bowl as you mix so that all the ingredients are well incorporated.

Starry New Year Cake

Makes one 23cm/9in round cake
23cm/9in round Madeira cake
675g/1½lb/3 cups butter icing
750g/1lb 10oz/5½ cups sugarpaste icing
grape violet and mulberry food colouring
gold, lilac shimmer and primrose sparkle powdered food colouring

Materials/equipment
fine paintbrush
star-shaped cutter
florist's wire, cut into short lengths
28cm/11in round cake board
purple ribbon with gold stars

1 Cut the cake into three layers. Sandwich together with three-quarters of the butter icing. Spread the rest thinly over the top and side of the cake.

2 Tint 500g/1¼lb/3¾ cups of the sugarpaste icing purple with the grape violet and mulberry food colouring. Roll out and use to cover the cake. Leave to dry overnight.

3 Place the cake on a sheet of baking parchment. Water down some gold and lilac food colouring. Use a paintbrush to flick each colour in turn over the cake. Leave to dry.

4 For the stars, divide the remaining sugarpaste icing into three pieces. Tint one portion purple with the grape violet food colouring, one with the lilac shimmer and one with the primrose sparkle.

5 Roll out each colour to 3mm/⅛in thick. Cut out ten stars in each colour and highlight the stars by flicking on the watered-down gold and lilac colours.

6 While the icing is soft, push the florist's wire through the middle of 15 of the stars. Leave to dry overnight. Put the cake on the board.

7 Arrange the stars on top of the cake. Secure the unwired ones with water. Secure the ribbon around the base.

Greek Energy 4261kcal/17800kJ; Protein 74.9g; Carbohydrate 418g, of which sugars 205.7g; Fat 266.7g, of which saturates 128.4g; Cholesterol 1241mg; Calcium 887mg; Fibre 16.1g; Sodium 1691mg.
Starry Energy 6452kcal/27052kJ; Protein 46.7g; Carbohydrate 886.7g, of which sugars 711.5g; Fat 326.3g, of which saturates 197.7g; Cholesterol 533mg; Calcium 593mg; Fibre 7.2g; Sodium 4579mg.

Simnel Cake

This is a traditional marzipan and fruit cake to celebrate Easter, but it is delicious at any time of the year.

Makes one 20cm/8in round cake

225g/8oz/1 cup butter, softened
225g/8oz/generous 1 cup caster (superfine) sugar
4 eggs, beaten
500g/1¼lb/3⅓ cups mixed dried fruit
115g/4oz/½ cup glacé (candied) cherries
45ml/3 tbsp sherry (optional)
275g/10oz/2½ cups plain (all-purpose) flour
15ml/1 tbsp mixed (apple pie) spice
5ml/1 tsp baking powder
675g/1½lb yellow marzipan
1 egg yolk, beaten
ribbons, sugared eggs and sugarpaste animals, to decorate

1 Preheat the oven to 160°C/325°F/Gas 3. Grease a deep 20cm/8in round cake tin (pan), line with a double thickness of baking parchment and grease the paper.

2 Beat together the butter and sugar until light and fluffy. Gradually beat in the eggs. Stir in the dried fruit, glacé cherries and sherry, if using. Sift over the flour, mixed spice and baking powder, then fold in.

3 Roll out half the marzipan to a 20cm/8in round. Spoon half of the cake mixture into the cake tin and place the round of marzipan on top. Add the other half of the cake mixture and smooth the surface.

4 Bake for 2½ hours, or until golden and springy to the touch. Leave in the tin for 15 minutes, then turn out on to a wire rack, peel off the lining paper and leave to cool.

5 Roll out the reserved marzipan to fit the cake. Brush the cake top with egg yolk and place the marzipan on top. Flute the edges and make a pattern on top with a fork. Brush with more egg yolk. Put the cake on a baking sheet and grill (broil) for 5 minutes to brown the top lightly. Cool before decorating with sugared eggs and little animals made with sugarpaste.

Easter Sponge Cake

This light lemon quick-mix sponge cake is decorated with lemon butter icing and cut-out marzipan flowers.

Makes one 20cm/8in round cake

3-egg quantity lemon-flavour quick-mix sponge cake
675g/1½lb/3 cups lemon-flavour butter icing
50g/2oz/½ cup flaked (sliced) almonds, toasted

To decorate
50g/2oz home-made or commercial white marzipan
green, orange and yellow food colouring

1 Preheat the oven to 160°C/325°F/Gas 3. Bake the cakes in two lined and greased 20cm/8in shallow round cake tins (pans) for 35–40 minutes, or until they are golden brown and spring back when lightly pressed in the centre.

2 Loosen the edges of the cakes with a metal spatula, turn out, remove the lining paper and cool on a wire rack.

3 Sandwich the cakes together with one-quarter of the butter icing. Spread the side of the cake evenly with one-third of the remaining butter icing.

4 Press the almonds on to the sides to cover evenly. Spread the top of the cake evenly with half the remaining icing.

5 Finish with a metal spatula dipped in hot water, spreading backwards and forwards to give an even lined effect.

6 Place the remaining icing into a nylon piping (icing) bag fitted with a medium-size gateau nozzle, and pipe a scroll edging.

7 Using the marzipan and food colouring, make six cut-out daffodils, and then ten green and eight orange cut-out marzipan flowers.

8 Arrange the flowers on the cake and leave the icing to set.

Simnel Energy 8108kcal/34162kJ; Protein 104g; Carbohydrate 1323.3g, of which sugars 1113.8g; Fat 303.9g, of which saturates 132.5g; Cholesterol 1442mg; Calcium 1557mg; Fibre 33.4g; Sodium 2080mg.
Easter Energy 4115kcal/17189kJ; Protein 38.6g; Carbohydrate 453g, of which sugars 330.6g; Fat 251.2g, of which saturates 0.5g; Cholesterol 0mg; Calcium 409mg; Fibre 5.8g; Sodium 2890mg.

Easter Egg Nest Cake

Celebrate Easter with this colourfully adorned, fresh-tasting lemon sponge cake. The marzipan nests are easy to make and could be made with sugarpaste if you prefer.

350g/12oz/1½ cups lemon-flavour butter icing
225g/8oz marzipan
pink, green and purple food colouring
small foil-wrapped chocolate eggs

Makes one 20cm/8in ring cake

20cm/8in lemon sponge ring cake

Materials/equipment
25cm/10in cake board

1 Cut the cake in half horizontally and sandwich together with one-third of the butter icing. Place on the cake board.

2 Use the remaining icing to cover the cake. Smooth the top and swirl the side with a metal spatula.

3 For the marzipan braids, divide the marzipan into three and tint the pieces pink, green and purple.

4 Cut each portion in half. Using half of each colour, roll thin sausages long enough to go around the base of the cake. Pinch the ends together, then twist the strands into a rope. Pinch the other ends to seal.

5 Place the coloured marzipan rope on the cake board around the base of the cake.

6 For the nests, take the remaining portions of coloured marzipan and divide each into five pieces. Roll each piece into a 16cm/6¼in rope.

7 Take a rope of each colour and pinch the ends together. Twist the strands to form a multicoloured rope and pinch the other ends to secure. Form into a circle. Repeat to make five nests.

8 Space the nests evenly on the cake. Place small chocolate eggs in the nests.

Mother's Day Bouquet

A piped bouquet of flowers can bring as much pleasure as a fresh one for a Mother's Day treat.

2 x 18cm/7in round sponge cakes
green, blue, yellow and pink food colouring

Makes one 18cm/7in round cake

675g/1½lb/3 cups butter icing

Materials/equipment
serrated scraper
medium writing and petal nozzles
5 baking parchment piping bags

1 Reserve one-third of the butter icing for decorating. Sandwich together the two sponges with one-third of the remaining butter icing and place on a serving plate.

2 Cover the top and side with the remaining butter icing, smoothing the top with a metal spatula and serrating the side using a scraper.

3 Divide the reserved butter icing into four bowls. Tint the portions green, blue, yellow and pink.

4 Decorate the top of the cake first. Use medium writing nozzles for the blue and green icing and medium petal nozzles for the yellow and pink. Pipe on the vase and flowers.

5 For the side decoration, spoon the remaining yellow icing into a fresh piping bag fitted with a medium writing nozzle. Pipe the stems, then the flowers and flower centres.

6 Finish by piping green beads at the top and base edges of the cake.

Cook's Tips
• Use paste colours rather than liquid colours when colouring icing. They are available from sugarcraft suppliers and there is a wide range of shades available.
• If piping your own flowers seems a little too advanced, you can use sugar flowers instead.

Nest Energy 5187kcal/21670kJ; Protein 51.1g; Carbohydrate 571.9g, of which sugars 439.9g; Fat 315.1g, of which saturates 115.3g; Cholesterol 991mg; Calcium 643mg; Fibre 9.7g; Sodium 2916mg.
Mother's Day Energy 7340kcal/30671kJ; Protein 65.7g; Carbohydrate 838.7g, of which sugars 618.7g; Fat 436.4g, of which saturates 162.2g; Cholesterol 1545mg; Calcium 885mg; Fibre 9g; Sodium 4490mg.

Mother's Day Basket

Any Mum would be thrilled to receive this delightful cake.

Makes one 15cm/6in cake

175g/6oz/1½ cups self-raising (self-rising) flour, sifted
175g/6oz/scant 1 cup caster (superfine) sugar
175g/6oz/¾ cup soft margarine
3 eggs
900g/2lb/4 cups orange-flavour butter icing

Materials/equipment

thin 15cm/6in round silver cake board
baking parchment piping (icing) bag
basketweave nozzle
foil
1m/1yd mauve ribbon, 1cm/½in wide
fresh flowers
50cm/20in spotted mauve ribbon, 3mm/⅛in wide

1 Preheat the oven to 160°C/325°F/Gas 3. Lightly grease and base-line a 15cm/6in brioche mould.

2 Place the self-raising flour, sugar, margarine and eggs in a bowl, mix together then beat for 1–2 minutes, or until smooth.

3 Transfer to the prepared mould and bake for about 1¼ hours, or until risen and golden. Leave to cool in the tin for 15 minutes and then remove from the tin and leave to cool completely.

4 Place the cooled cake upside-down on the cake board. Cover the sides with one-third of the butter icing. Using a basketweave nozzle, pipe the sides with a basketweave pattern.

5 Carefully invert the cake on to the board and spread the top with butter icing. Pipe a shell edging with the basketweave nozzle. Pipe the basketweave pattern over the cake top, starting at the edge. Leave to set.

6 Fold a strip of foil several layers thick. Wrap the plain ribbon around the strip and bend up the ends to secure the ribbon. Form the foil into a handle and press into the icing.

7 Finish by tying a posy of fresh flowers with the spotted ribbon and making a mixed ribbon bow for the handle.

Basket Cake

This is a perfect cake for a retirement gathering or other special occasion.

Makes one basket-shaped cake

20cm/8in round Madeira cake
225g/8oz pastillage
450g/1lb/2 cups coloured butter icing
chocolates or sweets (candies)

and ribbon for decoration

Materials/equipment

2 baking parchment piping (icing) bags, fitted with a plain nozzle and a basketweave nozzle

1 Cut a template from card to the same size as the top of the cake, fold it in half and cut along the fold. Roll out the pastillage fairly thinly and cut out two pieces for the lid, using the cardboard templates as a guide. Leave to dry thoroughly in a warm, dry place.

2 Coat the top of the cake with butter icing. Fill both piping bags with butter icing and pipe a plain vertical line on the side of the cake, and another about 2.5cm/1in inside the top of the cake. Pipe short lengths of basketweave across each line.

3 Pipe another plain line along the ends of the basketweave strips. Pipe the next row of basketweave strips in the spaces left between the existing strips and over the new plain line. Continue until the side of the cake and the area on the top is completely covered.

4 Brush the underside of the pastillage lid with powder food colour, then pipe a basketweave on top of the lid.

5 Divide the top of the cake in half and pipe a line of basketweave along this central line. Use two or three pieces of pastillage to support each lid half in an open position on the cake.

6 Fill the area under each lid half with chocolates or sweets, and decorate with ribbon.

Mother's Day Energy 8096kcal/33735kJ; Protein 41.4g; Carbohydrate 741.6g, of which sugars 608.3g; Fat 572.7g, of which saturates 265.4g; Cholesterol 1637mg; Calcium 732mg; Fibre 5.4g; Sodium 4680mg.
Basket Energy 5292kcal/22160kJ; Protein 45.4g; Carbohydrate 677.4g, of which sugars 502.2g; Fat 285.2g, of which saturates 171.6g; Cholesterol 426mg; Calcium 478mg; Fibre 7.2g; Sodium 4264mg.

Valentine's Heart Cake

Cut-out hearts make a simple but effective decoration for a special cake. This cake could also be used to celebrate a special birthday or anniversary.

Makes one 20cm/8in square cake
20cm/8in square light fruit cake
45ml/3 tbsp apricot jam, warmed and sieved
900g/2lb marzipan
1.3kg/3lb/9 cups royal icing
115g/4oz/¾ cup sugarpaste icing
red food colouring

Materials/equipment
25cm/10in square cake board
5cm/2in heart-shaped cutter
2.5cm/1in heart-shaped cutter
4 baking parchment piping (icing) bags
1 very fine writing nozzle,
    1 fine writing nozzle and
    1 medium star nozzle

1 Brush the cake with the apricot jam. Roll out the marzipan and use to cover the cake. Leave to dry overnight.

2 Secure the cake on the cake board with a little royal icing. Flat-ice the cake with three or four layers of smooth icing using a metal spatula or smoother. Set aside some royal icing in an airtight container for piping.

3 Tint the sugarpaste icing red. Roll it out and cut 12 hearts with the larger cutter. Stamp out the middles with the smaller cutter. Cut four more small hearts. Dry on baking parchment.

4 Using the very fine writing nozzle, pipe wavy lines in royal icing around the four small hearts. Leave to dry.

5 Using a fresh piping bag and the star nozzle, pipe swirls around the top and base of the cake.

6 Colour 15ml/1 tbsp of the remaining royal icing red and pipe red dots on top of each white swirl with the very fine nozzle.

7 Secure the ribbon in place. Using the fine writing nozzle, pipe beads down each corner, avoiding the ribbon. Decorate the cake with the hearts, using royal icing to secure them.

Valentine's Box of Chocolates Cake

This cake would also make a wonderful surprise for Mother's Day.

Makes one 20cm/8in heart-shaped cake
20cm/8in heart-shaped chocolate sponge cake
275g/10oz marzipan
120ml/8 tbsp apricot jam, warmed and sieved
900g/2lb/6 cups sugarpaste icing
red food colouring
225g/8oz/about 16–20 hand-made chocolates

Materials/equipment
23cm/9in square piece of stiff card
23cm/9in square cake board
piece of string
small heart-shaped cutter
length of ribbon
small paper sweet (candy) cases

1 Place the cake on the card, draw around it and cut out the heart shape. It will be used to support the box lid. Cut through the cake horizontally just below the dome. Place the top section on the card and the base on the cake board.

2 Use the string to measure around the outside of the base. Roll the marzipan into a long sausage to the measured length. Place on the cake around the outside edge.

3 Brush both sections of the cake with apricot jam. Tint the sugarpaste icing red and cut off one-third. Cut another 50g/2oz/8 tbsp portion from the larger piece. Set aside. Use the large piece to cover the base section of cake. Use your hand to smooth the sugarpaste around the curves.

4 Stand the lid on a raised surface. Use the reserved one-third of sugarpaste icing to cover the lid. Roll out the remaining piece of icing and stamp out small hearts with the cutter. Stick them around the edge of the lid with water. Tie the ribbon in a bow and secure on top of the lid with some diluted sugarpaste.

5 Place the chocolates in the paper cases and arrange in the cake base. Position the lid slightly off-centre, to reveal the chocolates. Remove the ribbon before serving.

Heart Energy 13123kcal/55505kJ; Protein 129.4g; Carbohydrate 2553.1g, of which sugars 2331.1g; Fat 336.3g, of which saturates 112.6g; Cholesterol 0mg; Calcium 2029mg; Fibre 17.1g; Sodium 4011mg.
Chocolates Energy 9848kcal/41510kJ; Protein 103.8g; Carbohydrate 1647.4g, of which sugars 1428.4g; Fat 361.9g, of which saturates 40.6g; Cholesterol 14mg; Calcium 1389mg; Fibre 10.9g; Sodium 4466mg.

Double Heart Engagement Cake

For a celebratory engagement party, these sumptuous cakes make the perfect centrepiece.

Makes two 20cm/8in heart-shaped cakes
350g/12oz plain
　(semisweet) chocolate
2 x 20cm/8in heart-shaped
　chocolate sponge cakes

675g/1½lb/3 cups coffee-flavour
　butter icing
icing (confectioners') sugar,
　for dusting
fresh raspberries, to decorate

Materials/equipment
2 x 23cm/9in heart-shaped
　cake boards

1 Melt the chocolate in a double boiler or in a heatproof bowl over a pan of simmering water. Pour the chocolate on to a smooth, non-porous surface and spread it out with a metal spatula. Leave to cool until just set, but not hard.

2 To make the chocolate curls, hold a large sharp knife at a 45-degree angle to the chocolate and push it along the chocolate in short sawing movements. Leave to set on baking parchment.

3 Cut each cake in half horizontally. Use one-third of the butter icing to sandwich the cakes together. Use the remaining icing to coat the tops and sides of the cakes.

4 Place the cakes on the cake boards. Generously cover the tops and sides of the cakes with the chocolate curls, pressing them gently into the butter icing.

5 Sift a little icing sugar over the top of each cake and decorate with raspberries. Chill until ready to serve.

> **Variation**
> *If you are making this cake when fresh raspberries are not available, try glacé-icing-coated physalis, crystallized fruits or tiny chocolate flowers instead.*

Heart-shaped Cake

Sugarpaste is a super icing for covering a cake neatly.

Makes one 20cm/8in heart-shaped cake
20cm/8in heart-shaped light
　fruit cake
30ml/2 tbsp apricot jam warmed
　and sieved
900g/2lb marzipan
900g/2lb/6 cups sugarpaste icing
red food colouring
225g/8oz/1½ cups
　royal icing

Materials/equipment
25cm/10in silver heart-shaped
　cake board
large and medium heart-shaped
　plunger cutters
1m/1yd red ribbon, 2.5cm/1in wide
1m/1yd looped red ribbon,
　1cm/½ in wide
50cm/20in red ribbon,
　5mm/¼in wide
baking parchment piping
　(pastry) bag
small star nozzle
fresh red rosebud

1 Brush the cake with apricot jam, place on the cake board and cover with marzipan.

2 Cover the cake and board with sugarpaste icing. Use your hand to remove any joins. Leave to dry overnight.

3 Tint the sugarpaste icing red. Cut out 18 large and 21 medium hearts. Leave to dry on baking parchment.

4 Secure the wide ribbon around the cake board. Secure a band of the looped ribbon around the side of the cake with a bead of icing.

5 Tie a bow with long tails and attach to the side of the cake with a bead of icing.

6 Using the star nozzle, pipe a row of royal icing stars around the base of the cake and attach a medium heart to every third star. Pipe stars around the cake top, and arrange large red hearts on each one.

7 Tie a bow on to the rosebud stem and place on the cake top just before serving.

Double Heart Energy 4694kcal/19625kJ; Protein 47.3g Carbohydrate 520.7g, of which sugars 410.6g; Fat 283.8g, of which saturates 94.5g Cholesterol 277mg; Calcium 535mg; Fibre 4.4g Sodium 2927mg.
Heart-shaped Energy 10835kcal/45851kJ; Protein 103.4g Carbohydrate 2148.6g, of which sugars 2000.6g Fat 262.3g, of which saturates 78.2g Cholesterol 0mg; Calcium 1675mg Fibre 17.1g Sodium 2743mg.

Cloth-of-roses Cake

This lovely cake simply says "congratulations". It is a very pretty cake that is bound to impress your guests.

Makes one 20cm/8in round cake
20cm/8in round light fruit cake
45ml/3 tbsp apricot jam, warmed and sieved
675g/1½lb marzipan
900g/2lb/6 cups sugarpaste icing
yellow, orange and green food colouring
115g/4oz/¾ cup royal icing

Materials/equipment
25cm/10in cake board
5.5cm/2¼in plain cutter
petal cutter
thin yellow ribbon

1 Brush the cake with apricot jam. Cover with marzipan and leave to dry overnight.

2 Cut off 675g/1½lb/4½ cups of the sugarpaste icing and divide in half. Colour pale yellow and pale orange.

3 Make a baking parchment template for the orange icing by drawing a 25cm/10in circle round the cake board then, using the plain cutter, draw scallops around the outside of the circle.

4 Cover the side of the cake with yellow sugarpaste icing. Place the cake on the board. Using the template, cut out the orange sugarpaste icing. Place on the cake and bend the scallops slightly. Leave to dry overnight.

5 For the roses and leaves, cut off three-quarters of the remaining sugarpaste icing and divide into four. Tint pale yellow, deep yellow, orange, and marbled yellow and orange.

6 Make 18 roses by making a small cone of sugarpaste and then flattening five small balls of paste and attaching them to the cone. Arrange the petals. Tint the remaining icing green.

7 Cut out 24 leaves with a petal cutter. Dry on baking parchment. Secure the leaves and roses with royal icing. Decorate the cake with the ribbon.

Rose Blossom Wedding Cake

Serves 80
23cm/9in square rich fruit cake
15cm/6in square rich fruit cake
75ml/5 tbsp apricot jam, warmed and sieved
1.6kg/3½lb marzipan
1.6kg/3½lb/10½ cups royal icing, to coat
675g/1½lb/4½ cups royal icing, to pipe
pink and green food colouring

Materials/equipment
28cm/11in square cake board
20cm/8in square cake board
very fine writing and small star nozzles
baking parchment piping (icing) bags
thin pink ribbon
8 pink bows
3 or 4 cake pillars
12 miniature roses
a few fern sprigs

1 Brush the cakes with the jam and cover with marzipan. Leave to dry overnight, then secure to their boards with icing. Flat-ice with four layers, drying each layer overnight, then for several days.

2 Use the very fine writing nozzle to pipe double triangles in white icing on baking parchment. You will need at least 40 pieces. Tint some icing pale pink and some pale green. Using very fine writing nozzles, pipe pink dots on the corners of the top triangles and green on the corners of the lower triangles.

3 Use a pin to mark out the triangles on the tops and sides of each cake. Using a very fine writing nozzle, pipe double white lines over the pin marks, then pipe cornelli inside all the triangles. With a small star nozzle, pipe white shells around the top and base edges of each cake, between the triangles.

4 Using the very fine writing nozzles, pipe pink and green dots on the cake corners. Secure the sugar pieces to the cakes and boards with icing. Attach the ribbons and bows. Assemble the cake on the pillars and decorate with roses and fern sprigs.

Cook's Tip
Cornelli work is a series of continuous 'm' shapes piped horizontally across an area in separate horizontal lines.

Cloth-of-Roses Energy 8469kcal/35840kJ; Protein 80.3g; Carbohydrate 1682.1g, of which sugars 1563.6g; Fat 204.1g, of which saturates 62.1g; Cholesterol 0mg; Calcium 1302mg; Fibre 12.8g; Sodium 2190mg.
Rose Blossom Energy 253kcal/1071kJ; Protein 2.5g; Carbohydrate 48.8g, of which sugars 44.6g; Fat 5.5g, of which saturates 1.1g; Cholesterol 17mg; Calcium 49mg; Fibre 0.9g; Sodium 63mg.

Basketweave Wedding Cake

Flavour the buttercream to your preference.

Serves 150
25cm/10in, 20cm/8in and
15cm/6in square
Madeira cakes
2.75kg/6lb/12 cups butter icing

Materials/equipment
30cm/12in square silver
cake board
20cm/8in and 15cm/6in thin
silver cake board
smooth scraper
12 small greaseproof piping
(icing) bags
medium writing and
basketweave nozzles
1.5m/1½yd pale lilac ribbon,
2.5cm/1in wide
2.5m/2½yd deep lilac ribbon,
5mm/¼in wide
30 fresh lilac-coloured freesias

1 Level the cake tops, then invert the cakes on to the boards and cover with butter icing. Use a smooth scraper on the sides and a metal spatula to smooth the top. Leave to set for 1 hour.

2 Pipe a line of icing with the medium writing nozzle on to the corner of the large cake, from the base to the top.

3 Using the basketweave nozzle, pipe a basketweave pattern. Pipe all around the side of the cake and neaten the top edge with a shell border, using the basketweave nozzle. Repeat for the second cake.

4 To decorate the top of the small cake, start at the edge with a straight plain line, then pipe across with the basketweave nozzle, spacing the lines equally apart.

5 When the top is complete, work the design around the sides, making sure the top and side designs align. Leave the cakes overnight to set.

6 Fit the wide and narrow lilac ribbons around the board. Use the remaining narrow ribbon to tie eight small bows with long tails. Trim off the flower stems.

7 Assemble the cakes. Decorate with the bows and flowers.

Chocolate-iced Anniversary Cake

This attractive cake is special enough to celebrate any wedding anniversary. The unusual glossy chocolate icing looks delicious contrasted with the exotic fruits.

Makes one 20cm/8in round cake
20cm/8in round Madeira cake
475g/1lb 2oz/2¼ cups chocolate-
flavour butter icing

For the chocolate icing
175g/6oz plain chocolate
150ml/¼ pint/⅔ cup single
(light) cream
2.5ml/½ tsp instant coffee powder

To decorate
chocolate buttons, quartered
selection of fresh fruits, such as
kiwi fruit, nectarines, peaches,
apricots and physalis, peeled
and sliced as necessary

Materials/equipment
medium star nozzle
baking parchment piping
(icing) bag
gold ribbon, about 5mm/¼ in wide
florist's wire

1 Cut the cake horizontally into three and sandwich together with three-quarters of the butter icing. Place on a wire rack over a baking sheet.

2 To make the satin chocolate icing, put all the ingredients in a pan and melt over a very low heat until smooth. Immediately pour over the cake to coat completely. Use a metal spatula, if necessary. Allow to set.

3 Transfer the cake to a serving plate. Using a medium star nozzle, pipe butter icing scrolls around the top edge. Decorate with chocolate button pieces and fruit.

4 Make seven ribbon decorations. For each one, make two small loops from ribbon and secure the ends with a twist of florist's wire.

5 Cut the wire to the length you want and use to position the decoration in the fruit. Remove before serving.

Wedding Energy 180kcal/754kJ; Protein 1.5g; Carbohydrate 26.1g, of which sugars 20.2g; Fat 8.4g, of which saturates 5g; Cholesterol 11mg; Calcium 17mg; Fibre 0.2g; Sodium 134mg.
Anniversary Energy 6708kcal/28073kJ; Protein 73g; Carbohydrate 800.4g, of which sugars 615g; Fat 379.1g, of which saturates 228.8g; Cholesterol 519mg; Calcium 767mg; Fibre 20.6g; Sodium 5031mg.

Silver Wedding Cake

This pretty cake is perfect for this special occasion.

Makes one 25cm/10in round cake

25cm/10in round rich or light fruit cake
60ml/4 tbsp apricot jam, warmed and sieved
1.2kg/2½lb marzipan
1.5kg/3lb/9 cups royal icing

For the petal paste
10ml/2 tsp powdered gelatine
75ml/5 tbsp cold water
10ml/2 tsp liquid glucose
10ml/2 tsp white vegetable fat
450g/1lb/4 cups icing (confectioners') sugar, sifted

5ml/1 tsp gum tragacanth, sifted
1 egg white

Materials/equipment
30cm/12in round silver cake board
1.5m/1½ yd white ribbon, 2.5cm/1in wide
2m/2yd silver ribbon, 2.5cm/1in wide
club cocktail cutter
tiny round cutter
baking parchment piping (icing) bag
very fine writing nozzle
50 large silver dragées
1.5m/1½yd silver ribbon, 5mm/¼in wide
7 silver leaves
"25" silver cake decoration

1 Brush the cake with apricot jam and cover with marzipan. Place on the board. Flat-ice the top and side of the cake with three or four layers of royal icing. Leave to dry overnight, then ice the board. Reserve the remaining royal icing. Secure the wider ribbons around the board and cake with icing.

2 For the petal paste, melt the first four ingredients in a pan set over a bowl of hot water. Mix the sugar, gum tragacanth, egg white and gelatine mixture to a paste and knead until smooth. Leave for 2 hours, then re-knead. Make 65 cut-outs using the two cutters. Leave to dry overnight.

3 Arrange 25 cut-outs around the top of the cake and secure with icing beads piped with a very fine writing nozzle. Repeat at the base. Pipe icing beads between and press a silver dragée in each. Leave to dry. Thread the thin ribbon through the cutouts. Arrange seven cut-outs and seven dragées in the centre. Position the leaves and the number "25".

Golden Wedding Heart Cake

You can buy specialist cake-decorating equipment from sugarcraft suppliers to help you achieve these professional effects.

Makes one 23cm/9in round cake

60ml/4 tbsp apricot jam
23cm/9in round rich fruit cake
900g/2lb marzipan
900g/2lb/6 cups sugarpaste icing
cream food colouring
115g/4oz/¾ cup royal icing

Materials/equipment
28cm/11in round cake board
crimping tool
pins
small heart-shaped plunger tool
7.5cm/3in plain cutter
dual large and small blossom cutter
stamens
frill cutter
wooden cocktail stick (toothpick)
foil-wrapped chocolate hearts

1 Warm, then sieve the apricot jam and brush over the cake. Cover with marzipan and leave to dry overnight.

2 Tint 675g/1½lb/4½ cups of the sugarpaste icing very pale cream and cover the cake. Put on the board. Crimp the top edge using the crimping tool. With pins, mark eight equidistant points around the top edge. Crimp slanting lines to the base. Emboss the base edge with the heart-shaped plunger. Use the plain cutter to emboss a circle on top.

3 Divide the remaining sugarpaste icing in two and tint one cream and the other pale cream. Using half of each colour, make flowers with the blossom cutter. Make pinholes in the large flowers. Leave to dry then secure the stamens in the holes with royal icing.

4 Make eight frills with the remainder of the sugarpaste icing using the frill cutter, and a cocktail stick to trim and fill the edges. Attach the frills with water next to the crimped lines on the cake side. Crimp the edges of the deeper coloured frills.

5 Secure the flowers on the top and side of the cake with royal icing. Place the chocolate hearts in the centre.

Silver Energy 14213kcal/60177kJ; Protein 129.1g; Carbohydrate 2876.9g, of which sugars 2706.8g; Fat 322.6g, of which saturates 91.6g; Cholesterol 0mg; Calcium 2178mg; Fibre 22.8g; Sodium 3210mg.
Golden Energy 9846kcal/41683kJ; Protein 90.6g; Carbohydrate 1980.3g, of which sugars 1868.3g; Fat 196.3g, of which saturates 33.3g; Cholesterol 461mg; Calcium 1762mg; Fibre 32.1g; Sodium 1789mg.

Marzipan Bell Cake

This cake can be easily adapted to make a christening cake if you leave out the holly decorations.

Makes one 18cm/7in round cake
18cm/7in round rich or light fruit cake
30ml/2 tbsp apricot jam, warmed and sieved
900g/2lb marzipan
green, yellow and red food colouring

Materials/equipment
20cm/8in round silver cake board
crimping tool
bell and holly leaf cutter
1m/1yd red ribbon, 2cm/³⁄₄in wide
1m/1yd green ribbon, 5mm/¹⁄₄in wide
25cm/10in red ribbon, 5mm/¹⁄₄ in wide

1 Brush the cake with apricot jam and place on the cake board.

2 Tint two-thirds of the marzipan pale green. Use to cover the cake. Crimp the top edge of the cake with a crimping tool to make a scalloped pattern.

3 Tint a small piece of remaining marzipan bright yellow, another bright red and the rest bright green. Make two yellow bells using the bell cutter and clappers by rolling out a small ball of marzipan.

4 Cut out 11 green holly leaves and mark the veins with the back of a knife.

5 Make two green bell ropes, 16 red holly berries and two bell-rope ends. Leave all the decorations to dry.

6 Secure the wide red and fine green ribbons around the side of the cake with a pin. Tie a double bow from red and green fine ribbon and attach to the side with a pin.

7 Arrange the bells, clappers, bell ropes, holly leaves and berries on top of the cake and secure with apricot jam.

Christening Sampler

Be creative for this delightful Christening sampler.

Serves 30
20cm/8in square rich fruit cake
45ml/3 tbsp apricot jam, warmed and sieved
450g/1lb marzipan
675g/1¹⁄₂lb/4¹⁄₂ cups sugarpaste icing

brown, yellow, orange, purple, cream, blue, green and pink food colouring

Materials/equipment
25cm/10in square cake board
fine paintbrush
small heart-shaped cutter

1 Brush the cake with apricot jam. Roll out the marzipan, cover the cake and leave to dry overnight. Roll out 150g/5oz/1 cup of the sugarpaste icing to fit the cake top. Brush the top with water and cover with the icing.

2 Colour 300g/10oz/2 cups of the icing brown and roll out four pieces measuring the length and about 1cm/¹⁄₂ in wider than the cake sides. Brush the cake sides with water and cover with the brown paste, folding over the extra width at the top and cutting the corners at an angle to make the picture frame.

3 Place on a cake board. With a fine paintbrush, paint over the sides with watered-down brown food colouring to represent wood grain.

4 Take the remaining icing and colour small amounts yellow, orange, brown, purple and cream and two shades of blue, green and pink. Leave a little white. Use these colours to shape the ducks, teddy bear, bulrushes, water, branch and leaves. Cut out a pink heart and make the baby's initial from white icing.

5 Mix the white and pink icings together for the apple blossom flowers. Make the shapes for the border. Attach the decorations to the cake with a little water.

6 Use the leftover colours to make "threads". Arrange in loops around the base of the cake on the board.

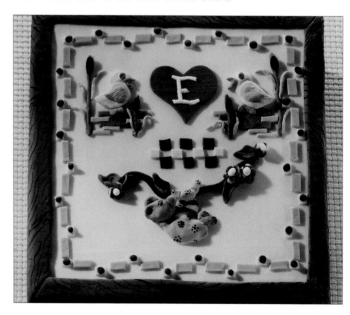

Bell Energy 6323kcal/26653kJ; Protein 86g; Carbohydrate 1053g, of which sugars 942g; Fat 225.3g, of which saturates 60.9g; Cholesterol 0mg; Calcium 1046mg; Fibre 17.1g; Sodium 2059mg.
Christening Energy 299kcal/1267kJ; Protein 2.8g; Carbohydrate 58.5g, of which sugars 52.9g; Fat 6g, of which saturates 1.4g; Cholesterol 23mg; Calcium 58mg; Fibre 1g; Sodium 82mg.

Teddy Bear Christening Cake

To personalize the cake, make a simple plaque for the top and pipe on the name of the new baby.

Makes one 20cm/8in square cake

20cm/8in square light fruit cake
45ml/3 tbsp apricot jam, warmed and sieved
900g/2lb marzipan
800g/1¾lb/5¼ cups sugarpaste icing
cornflour (cornstarch), for dipping
peach, yellow, blue and brown food colouring
115g/4oz/¾ cup royal icing

Materials/equipment

25cm/10in square cake board
crimping tool
fine paintbrush
wooden cocktail stick (toothpick)
peach ribbon
small blue ribbon bow

1 Brush the cake with the apricot jam. Roll out the marzipan and use to cover the cake. Leave to dry overnight.

2 Colour 500g/1¼lb/3¾ cups of the sugarpaste icing peach, then roll it out. Brush the marzipan with water and cover the cake with the sugarpaste.

3 Place the cake on the board. Using a crimping tool dipped in cornflour, crimp the top and base edges of the cake.

4 Divide the remaining sugarpaste into three. Leave one-third white and tint one-third yellow. Divide the last third in two, tint one half peach and the other blue.

5 Make flowers from the peach and blue sugarpaste. Leave to dry. Reserve the blue trimmings. Make a yellow teddy bear and paint on its features with brown food colouring. Give it a blue button. Leave to dry. Make a blue blanket and frill the white edge with a cocktail stick. Secure the frill to the blanket with water.

6 Decorate the cake with the ribbon, place the bear on top under its blanket, securing with royal icing. Secure the flowers and the bear's bow-tie in the same way.

Daisy Christening Cake

A ring of daisies sets off this pretty pink christening cake.

Makes one 20cm/8in round cake

20cm/8in round rich fruit cake
45ml/3 tbsp apricot jam, warmed and sieved
675g/1½lb marzipan
900g/2lb/6 cups royal icing
pink and yellow food colouring
115g/4oz/¾ cup sugarpaste icing

Materials/equipment

25cm/10in round cake board
fine paintbrush
5cm/2in fluted cutter
wooden cocktail stick (toothpick)
2 baking parchment piping (icing) bags
small star nozzle
pink and white ribbon

1 Brush the cake with the apricot jam. Roll out the marzipan and use to cover the cake. Leave to dry overnight.

2 Use a little royal icing to secure the cake to the board. Tint three-quarters of the royal icing pink. Flat-ice the cake with three or four layers, using white for the top and pink for the side. Allow each layer to dry overnight before applying the next. Set aside a little of both icings in airtight containers.

3 Make 28 daisies. For each daisy, shape a small piece of sugarpaste icing to look like a golf tee. Snip the edges and curl them slightly. Dry on baking parchment. Trim the stems and paint the edges pink and the centres yellow.

4 To make the plaque, roll out the remaining sugarpaste icing and cut out a circle with the fluted cutter. Roll a cocktail stick around the edge until it frills. Dry on baking parchment, then paint the name and the edges with pink food colouring.

5 Pipe twisted ropes (see p253) around the top and base of the cake with the reserved white royal icing. Then pipe a row of stars around the top of the cake with the star nozzle.

6 Stick the plaque in the centre with royal icing. Stick on the daisies and decorate with the ribbons.

Teddy Bear Energy 9344kcal/39534kJ; Protein 92.3g; Carbohydrate 1834.2g, of which sugars 1715.8g; Fat 232.7g, of which saturates 64.4g; Cholesterol 0mg; Calcium 1450mg; Fibre 17.1g; Sodium 2235mg.
Daisy Energy 10646kcal/45057kJ; Protein 98g; Carbohydrate 2117.3g, of which sugars 1949.3g; Fat 208.7g, of which saturates 43g; Cholesterol 692mg; Calcium 2007mg; Fibre 35.3g; Sodium 2515mg.

Birthday Parcel

Use any combination of colours you fancy for the icing.

blue, orange and green food colouring
icing (confectioners') sugar, for dusting

Serves 10
15cm/6in square Madeira cake
275g/10oz/1⅓ cup orange-flavour butter icing
45ml/3 tbsp apricot jam, warmed and sieved
450g/1lb/3 cups sugarpaste icing

Materials/equipment
15–18cm/7–8in square cake board
small triangular and round cocktail cutters

1 Cut the cake in half horizontally and sandwich together with the butter icing. Brush the cake with apricot jam. Colour three-quarters of the sugarpaste icing blue. Divide the remaining sugarpaste icing in half and colour one half orange and the other half green. Wrap the orange and green sugarpaste separately in clear film (plastic wrap) and set aside. Roll out the blue icing on a work surface lightly dusted with icing sugar and use it to cover the cake. Position on the cake board.

2 While the sugarpaste covering is still soft, use the cocktail cutters to cut out triangles and circles from the blue icing, lifting out the shapes to expose the cake.

3 Roll out the orange and green icings and cut out circles and triangles to fill the exposed holes in the blue icing. Roll out the trimmings and cut three orange strips, 2cm/¾in wide and long enough to go over the corner of the cake, and 3 very thin green strips the same length as the orange ones. Place the strips next to each other to make three striped ribbons, and secure the pieces together with a little water.

4 Place one striped ribbon over one corner of the cake, securing with a little water. Place a second strip over the opposite corner. Cut the remaining ribbon in half. Bend each half to make loops and attach both to one corner of the cake with water to form a loose bow.

Chocolate Fruit Birthday Cake

The modelled marzipan fruits on this moist chocolate Madeira cake make an eye-catching decoration.

red, yellow, orange, green and purple food colouring
whole cloves
angelica strips

Makes one 18cm/7in square cake
18cm/7in square deep chocolate Madeira cake
45ml/3 tbsp apricot jam, warmed and sieved
450g/1lb marzipan
450g/1lb/2 cups chocolate fudge icing

Materials/equipment
20cm/8in square silver cake board
medium gateau nozzle
nylon piping (icing) bag
75cm/2½ft yellow ribbon, 1cm/½in wide

1 Level the cake top and invert. Brush over the top and sides of the cake with apricot jam.

2 Use two-thirds of the marzipan to cover the cake. Reserve the trimmings.

3 Place the cake on a wire rack over a tray and pour three-quarters of the chocolate fudge icing over the top, spreading it evenly over the top and sides with a metal spatula.

4 Leave for 10 minutes, then place on the cake board.

5 Using the reserved icing and a medium gateau nozzle, pipe large stars around the top edge and base of the cake. Leave to set.

6 Colour small quantities of the reserved marzipan for the fruits and use it to model bananas, peaches, pears, cherries and grapes. Use the angelica strips and cloves to make stalks for those fruits which require them.

7 Secure the ribbon around the sides of the cake. Decorate the top with the marzipan fruits.

Eighteenth Birthday Cake

A really striking cake for an eighteenth birthday. Change the shape if you don't have the diamond-shaped tin. If you don't have an "18" template you can easily make one out of paper, using a computer or photocopier to enlarge the number.

1.2kg/2½lb marzipan
1.6kg/3½lb/10½ cups sugarpaste
black food colouring
30ml/2 tbsp royal icing

Materials/equipment
38 x 23cm/15 x 9in diamond-
    shaped cake board
"18" template
small baking parchment piping
    (icing) bag
fine writing nozzle
2m/2yd white ribbon,
    2.5cm/1in wide
2m/2yd black ribbon,
    3mm/⅛in wide

Serves 80
33.5 x 20cm/13 x 8in diamond-
    shaped deep rich or light
    fruit cake
45ml/3 tbsp apricot jam, warmed
    and sieved

1 Make the cake using quantities for a 23cm/9in round cake. Brush the top and sides with apricot jam and cover in marzipan.

2 Place on the cake board. Cover the cake using 1.2kg/2½lb/7½ cups sugarpaste icing. Knead the trimmings into the remaining sugarpaste and tint black.

3 Use two-thirds of the black sugarpaste to cover the board.

4 Use a quarter of the remaining sugarpaste to cut out a number "18" using a template.

5 Use the remainder to cut out a variety of bow ties, wine glasses and music notes. Leave to dry on baking parchment.

6 Tint the royal icing black. Using the fine writing nozzle, attach the cut-outs to the cake top and sides.

7 Tie four small bows with the black ribbon. Secure with royal icing to the top corners. Position and secure black ribbon around the cake base and white ribbon around the board.

Flickering Candle Birthday Cake

Flickering stripy candles are ready to blow out on this birthday cake for all ages.

pink, yellow, purple and jade
    food colouring
edible silver balls

Makes one 20cm/8in square cake
20cm/8in square Madeira cake
350g/12oz/1½ cups butter icing
45ml/3 tbsp apricot jam, warmed
    and sieved
800g/1¾lb/5¼ cups
    sugarpaste icing

Materials/equipment
23cm/9in square cake board
small round cutter
pink and purple food
    colouring pens
5mm/¼ in-wide jade-
    coloured ribbon

1 Cut the cake into three layers. Sandwich the layers together with the butter icing and brush the cake with the apricot jam.

2 Roll out 500g/1¼lb/3¾ cups of the sugarpaste icing and use to cover the cake. Position on the cake board.

3 Divide the remaining sugarpaste into four pieces and tint them pink, yellow, pale purple and jade.

4 Make the candles from jade and the flames from yellow icing. Press a silver ball into their bases. Position the candles and flames on the cake with a little water. Mould strips in yellow and purple icing to go around the candles. Secure with water.

5 Cut small wavy pieces from the pink and purple icing for smoke, and arrange them, using water, above the candles.

6 Cut out yellow circles with the cutter for the side decorations. Mould small pink balls and press a silver ball into their centres. Attach using water.

7 Using food colouring pens, draw wavy lines and dots coming from the purple and pink wavy icings. Decorate the sides of the cake board with the ribbon, securing at the back with a little softened sugarpaste.

Eighteenth Energy 169kcal/713kJ; Protein 1.5g; Carbohydrate 34g, of which sugars 31.9g; Fat 3.3g, of which saturates 0.6g; Cholesterol 9mg; Calcium 31mg; Fibre 0.5g; Sodium 33mg.
Candle Energy 6841kcal/28896kJ; Protein 45.4g; Carbohydrate 1305.7g of which sugars 1141.4g; Fat 195.4g, of which saturates 115.3g; Cholesterol 213mg; Calcium 762mg; Fibre 6.8g; Sodium 3517mg.

Jazzy Chocolate Gateau

This cake is made with Father's Day in mind, although you can make it for anyone who loves chocolate.

175g/6oz fudge frosting
115g/4oz/1 cup glacé icing
5ml/1 tsp weak coffee
8 tbsp chocolate nut spread

Serves 12–15
2 x quantity chocolate-flavour
    quick-mix sponge cake mix
75g/3oz plain
    (semisweet) chocolate
75g/3oz white chocolate

Materials/equipment
2 x 20cm/8in round cake tins
baking parchment piping
    (icing) bag
fine writing nozzle

1 Preheat the oven to 160°C/325°F/Gas 3. Grease two 20cm/8in cake tins (pans), line the bases with baking parchment and grease the paper. Divide the cake mixture evenly between the tins and smooth the surfaces.

2 Bake in the centre of the oven for about 20–30 minutes, or until firm to the touch. Turn out on to a wire rack, peel off the lining paper and leave to cool.

3 Melt the chocolates in two separate bowls over pans of simmering water, pour on to baking parchment and spread evenly. As it begins to set, place another sheet of baking paper on top and turn the chocolate "sandwich" over. When set, peel off the paper and turn the chocolate sheets over. Cut out haphazard triangular shapes of chocolate and set aside.

4 Sandwich the two cakes together using the fudge frosting. Place the cake on a stand or plate. Colour the glacé icing using the weak coffee and add enough water to form a spreading consistency. Spread the icing on top of the cake almost to the edges. Cover the side of the cake with chocolate nut spread.

5 Press the chocolate pieces around the side of the cake and, using a piping bag fitted with the fine nozzle, decorate the top of the cake with "jazzy" lines over the glacé icing.

Flower Birthday Cake

A simple birthday cake decorated with piped yellow and white flowers and ribbons will be received with delight whatever the recipient's age.

Materials/equipment
23cm/9in round silver cake board
petal nozzle, very fine and fine
    writing nozzles, and medium
    star nozzle
baking parchment piping
    (icing) bags
1m/1yd white ribbon,
    2cm/¾in wide
2m/2yd coral ribbon,
    1cm/½in wide
25cm/10in coral ribbon,
    5mm/¼in wide

Makes one 18cm/7in round cake
18cm/7in round light fruit cake
30ml/2 tbsp apricot jam, warmed
    and sieved
675g/1½lb marzipan
1.2kg/2½lb/7½ cups royal icing
yellow and orange food colouring

1 Brush the cake with apricot jam and cover with marzipan. Place on the board.

2 Flat-ice the top and side of the cake with three layers of royal icing smoothed using a metal spatula.

3 Leave the icing to dry, then ice the board. Reserve the remaining royal icing.

4 Tint one-third of the reserved royal icing yellow and 15ml/1 tbsp of it orange.

5 Using the petal nozzle for the petals and the very fine writing nozzle for the centres, make four white narcissi with yellow centres and nine yellow narcissi with orange centres.

6 Use the star nozzle to pipe shell edgings to the cake top and base. Pipe "Happy Birthday" using the fine writing nozzle. Overlay in orange using the very fine writing nozzle.

7 Secure the ribbons around the board and cake side. Finish with a coral bow.

Cake Energy 8600kcal/36442kJ; Protein 71.2g; Carbohydrate 1792.2g, of which sugars 1702.6g; Fat 151.3g, of which saturates 26.2g; Cholesterol 369mg; Calcium 1505mg; Fibre 24.8g; Sodium 1432mg.
Gateau Energy 444kcal/1862kJ; Protein 6g; Carbohydrate 58g, of which sugars 43.5g; Fat 22.5g, of which saturates 2.6g; Cholesterol 2mg; Calcium 84mg; Fibre 0.2g; Sodium 304mg.

Petal Retirement Cake

A sugar gift card is a delightful touch for this cake.

Makes one 20cm/8in petal-shaped cake
20cm/8in petal-shaped deep light fruit cake
45ml/3 tbsp apricot jam, warmed and sieved
900g/2lb marzipan
mulberry and pink food colouring
900g/2lb/6 cups sugarpaste icing
275g/10oz petal paste
15ml/1 tbsp royal icing

Materials/equipment
23cm/9in petal-shaped silver cake board
foam sponge
large and small blossom plunger cutters
very fine writing nozzle
2m/2yd white ribbon, 2cm/³⁄₄in wide
2m/2yd fuchsia ribbon, 1cm/¹⁄₂in wide
2m/2yd fuchsia ribbon, 3mm/¹⁄₈in wide
baking parchment piping (icing) bag
pink food colouring pen
fresh flowers

1 Brush the cake with jam and put on the board. Cover with marzipan. Knead mulberry colouring into the sugarpaste icing. Use to cover the cake and board. Dry overnight.

2 Tint the petal paste with pink colouring. Roll and cut out a 5 × 2.5cm/2 × 1in rectangle. Fold in half and make holes in the top edges of the fold for the ribbon. Dry over a foam sponge to make the card. Cut out 30 large and four small plunger blossom flowers. Leave to dry.

3 Using the royal icing and the very fine writing nozzle, secure the white and narrow fuchsia ribbons around the board and the medium ribbon around the cake base. Tie six small bows from the narrow ribbon for the base.

4 Attach the large flowers to the side of the cake with icing. Secure the small flowers to the board. Draw a design and write a message inside the card with the pen. Thread ribbon through the holes and tie a bow. Place the card on the cake top with the fresh flowers.

Pansy Retirement Cake

You can use other edible flowers such as nasturtiums, roses or tiny primroses for this cake, if you prefer.

Makes one 20cm/8in round cake
20cm/8in round light fruit cake
45ml/3 tbsp apricot jam, warmed and sieved
675g/1¹⁄₂lb marzipan
1.2kg/2¹⁄₂lb/7¹⁄₂ cups royal icing
orange food colouring
about 7 sugar-frosted pansies (orange and purple)

Materials/equipment
25cm/10in round cake board
2 baking parchment piping (icing) bags
medium star and very fine writing nozzles
2cm/³⁄₄in wide purple ribbon
3mm/¹⁄₈in wide dark purple ribbon

1 Brush the cake with the apricot jam. Roll out the marzipan and use to cover the cake. Leave to dry overnight.

2 Secure the cake to the cake board with a little royal icing. Tint a quarter of the royal icing pale orange. Flat-ice the cake with three layers of smooth icing using a metal spatula.

3 Use the orange icing for the top and the white for the side. Set aside a little of both icings in airtight containers for decoration.

4 Spoon the reserved white royal icing into a baking parchment piping bag fitted with a medium star nozzle. Pipe a row of scrolls around the cake top. Pipe a second row directly underneath the first row in the reverse direction. Pipe another row of scrolls around the base of the cake.

5 Spoon the reserved orange icing into a fresh piping bag fitted with a very fine writing nozzle. Pipe around the outline of the top of each scroll. Pipe a row of single orange dots below the lower row of reverse scrolls at the top and a double row of dots above the base row of scrolls.

6 Arrange the sugar-frosted pansies on top of the cake. Decorate the side with the ribbons.

Petal Energy 10015kcal/42406kJ; Protein 93.6g; Carbohydrate 2022.2g, of which sugars 1910.2g; Fat 196.3g, of which saturates 33.3g; Cholesterol 461mg; Calcium 1789mg; Fibre 32.1g; Sodium 1849mg.
Pansy Energy 8982kcal/38056kJ; Protein 75.1g; Carbohydrate 1862.4g, of which sugars 1761.6g; Fat 159.5g, of which saturates 28.6g; Cholesterol 415mg; Calcium 1586mg; Fibre 26.3g; Sodium 1591mg.

Hallowe'en Pumpkin Patch Cake

Celebrate Hallowe'en with this autumn-coloured cake, colourfully decorated with sugarpaste pumpkins.

Makes one 20cm/8in round cake
175g/6oz/generous 1 cup sugarpaste icing
brown and orange food colouring
2 x 20cm/8in round chocolate sponge cakes
675g/1½lb/3 cups orange-flavour butter icing

chocolate chips
angelica

Materials/equipment
wooden cocktail stick (toothpick)
fine paintbrush
23cm/9in round cake board
serrated scraper
thick writing nozzle
baking parchment piping (icing) bag

1 For the pumpkins, tint a very small piece of the sugarpaste icing brown, and the rest orange.

2 Shape some balls of the orange icing the size of walnuts and some a bit smaller.

3 Make ridges with a cocktail stick. Make stems from the brown icing and secure with water. Paint highlights on the pumpkins in orange. Leave to dry on baking parchment.

4 Cut both cakes in half horizontally. Use one-quarter of the butter icing to sandwich the cakes together.

5 Place the cake on the board. Use two-thirds of the remaining icing to cover the cake. Texture the icing using a serrated scraper.

6 Using a thick writing nozzle, pipe a twisted rope pattern around the top and base edges of the cake with the remaining butter icing. Decorate with chocolate chips.

7 Cut the angelica into diamond shapes and arrange on the cake with the pumpkins.

Fudge-frosted Starry Roll

Whether it's for a birthday or another occasion, this sumptuous-looking cake is sure to please.

Makes one 23cm/9in long roll
23 x 33cm/9 x 13in sponge roll
175g/6oz/¾ cup chocolate butter icing
50g/2oz white chocolate
50g/2oz plain (semisweet) chocolate

For the fudge frosting
75g/3oz plain (semisweet) chocolate, broken into pieces
350g/12oz/3 cups icing (confectioners') sugar, sifted
75g/3oz/6 tbsp butter or margarine
65ml/4½ tbsp milk or single (light) cream
7.5ml/1½ tsp vanilla extract

Materials/equipment
small star cutter
several baking parchment piping (icing) bags
big star nozzle

1 Unroll the sponge roll and spread with the butter icing. Re-roll and set aside.

2 For the decorations, melt the white chocolate in a bowl set over a pan of simmering water and spread on to a non-porous surface. Leave to firm up slightly, then cut out stars with the star cutter. Leave to set on baking parchment. To make lace curls, melt the plain chocolate as before and then cool slightly. Cover a rolling pin with baking parchment. Pipe zigzags on the paper and leave on the rolling pin until cool.

3 To make the frosting, stir all the ingredients over a low heat until melted. Remove from the heat and beat frequently until cool and thick. Cover the cake with two-thirds of the frosting, swirling with a metal spatula.

4 With a big star nozzle, use the remaining frosting to pipe diagonal lines on to the cake.

5 Position the lace curls and stars. Transfer the cake to a serving plate and decorate with more stars.

Hallowe'en Energy 6909kcal/28947kJ; Protein 62.7g; Carbohydrate 874.6g, of which sugars 701g; Fat 375.6g, of which saturates 104.2g; Cholesterol 426mg; Calcium 875mg; Fibre 0g; Sodium 4679mg.
Starry Roll Energy 5460kcal/23020kJ; Protein 60.6g; Carbohydrate 916.8g, of which sugars 837.4g; Fat 198g, of which saturates 70.5g; Cholesterol 150mg; Calcium 1066mg; Fibre 13.2g; Sodium 2139mg.

Lucky Horseshoe Cake

This horseshoe-shaped cake, is made from a round cake and the shape is then cut out using a template.

Makes one 25cm/10in horseshoe cake

25cm/10in rich fruit cake
60ml/4 tbsp apricot jam, warmed and sieved
800g/1¾lb marzipan
1kg/2¼lb/6¾ cups sugarpaste icing

peach and blue food colouring
edible silver balls
115g/4oz/¾ cup royal icing

Materials/equipment

30cm/12in round cake board
crimping tool
pale blue ribbon, 3mm/⅛in wide
craft (utility) knife
modelling tool
large and small blossom cutters

1 Make a horseshoe template and use to shape the cake. Brush the cake with the apricot jam. Roll out 350g/12oz/2¼ cups of the marzipan to a 25cm/10in circle. Using the template, cut out the shape and place on the cake.

2 Measure the inside and outside of the cake. Cover with the remaining marzipan. Place the cake on the board and leave overnight. Tint 800g/1¾lb/5¼ cups of the sugarpaste icing peach. Cover the cake as before. Crimp the top edge.

3 Draw and measure the ribbon insertion on the template. Cut 13 pieces of ribbon fractionally longer than each slit. Make the slits through the template with a scalpel. Insert the ribbon with a modelling tool. Leave to dry overnight.

4 Make a tiny horseshoe template. Tint half the remaining sugarpaste icing pale blue. Using the template, cut out nine blue shapes. Mark each horseshoe with a sharp knife.

5 Cut out 12 large and 15 small flowers with the blossom cutters. Press a silver ball into the centres of the larger blossoms. Leave to dry. Repeat with the white icing. Decorate the cake and board with the ribbon, horseshoes and blossoms, securing with royal icing.

Bluebird Bon-voyage Cake

This delightful cake is a special way to see someone off on an exciting journey.

Makes one 20cm/8in round cake

450g/1lb/3 cups royal icing
blue food colouring
800g/1¾lb/5¼ cups sugarpaste icing
20cm/8in round Madeira cake

350g/12oz/1½ cups butter icing
45ml/3 tbsp apricot jam, warmed and sieved
edible silver balls

Materials/equipment

very fine writing nozzle
baking parchment piping (icing) bags
25cm/10in round cake board
thin pale blue ribbon

1 Soften two-thirds of the royal icing by adding a few drops of water. Make the rest stiffer by adding a little icing (confectioners') sugar. Tint the softer icing bright blue. Cover and leave overnight.

2 Draw two different-size bird templates on a piece of paper. Lay a sheet of baking parchment over the templates and trace the outline of the birds using the stiffer royal icing and a very fine writing nozzle. Fill in the run-outs with the stiffer icing. Repeat until you have four large and five small birds. Leave to dry for at least 2 days.

3 Tint two-thirds of the sugarpaste icing blue. Form all the sugarpaste into small rolls and place them alternately together on a work surface. Form into a round and knead to marble.

4 Cut the cake horizontally into three and sandwich together with the butter icing. Place the cake on the board, flush with an edge, and brush with apricot jam. Roll out the marbled icing and use to cover the cake and board.

5 Using the very fine writing nozzle and the stiffer royal icing, pipe a wavy line around the edge of the board. Position the balls evenly in the icing. Secure the birds to the cake with royal icing. Pipe beads of white icing for eyes and stick on a ball. Drape the ribbon between the beaks, securing with icing.

Horseshoe Energy 8428kcal/35700kJ; Protein 73.6g; Carbohydrate 1733g, of which sugars 1654.6g; Fat 159g, of which saturates 25g; Cholesterol 323mg; Calcium 1459mg; Fibre 25.7g; Sodium 1304mg.
Bluebird Energy 8614kcal/36357kJ; Protein 44.8g; Carbohydrate 1600g, of which sugars 1446.7g; Fat 270.1g, of which saturates 163.2g; Cholesterol 426mg; Calcium 923mg; Fibre 6.3g; Sodium 3952mg.

Box of Chocolates Cake

This sophisticated cake is perfect for an adult's birthday and will delight chocolate lovers.

Makes one 15cm/6in square cake

15cm/6in square
  sponge cake
50g/2oz/4 tbsp butter icing
30ml/2 tbsp apricot jam, warmed
  and sieved

350g/12oz marzipan
350g/12oz/2¼ cups
  sugarpaste icing
red food colouring
wrapped chocolates

Materials/equipment

20cm/8in square cake board
small paper sweet
  (candy) cases
1.35m/1½yd x 4cm/1½in-wide
  gold and red ribbon

1 Split the cake in half and sandwich together with butter icing. Cut a shallow square from the top of the cake, leaving a 1cm/¼in border around the edge.

2 Place on the cake board and brush with apricot jam. Cover with a layer of marzipan.

3 Roll out the sugarpaste icing and cut an 18cm/7in square. Ease it into the hollow dip and trim. Tint the remaining sugarpaste icing red and use to cover the sides.

4 Put the chocolates into paper cases and arrange in the box. Tie the ribbon around the sides with a big bow.

Cook's Tip

If you often make cakes using sugarpaste it is worth investing in a smoother. This is a flat plastic tool with a handle, and it is useful for achieving a professional finish. Use the smoother to smooth the sugarpaste over the top of the cake, using your hand to finish rounded edges. Then push the smoother down the sides of the cake and press the edge along the base where the sugarpaste meets the board. This will give a neat edge for you to cut away with a knife.

Strawberry Cake

Use a heart-shaped mould or cut a round cake to shape using a template for this cake.

Makes one 900g/2lb cake

650g/1lb 7oz/scant 4½ cups
  marzipan
green, red and yellow
  food colouring

30ml/2 tbsp apricot jam, warmed
  and sieved
900g/2lb heart-shaped sponge cake
caster (superfine) sugar,
  for dusting

Materials/equipment

30cm/12in round
  cake board
icing smoother

1 Tint 175g/6oz/generous 1 cup of the marzipan green. Brush the cake board with apricot jam, roll out the green marzipan and use to cover the board. Trim the edges. Use an icing smoother to flatten and smooth the marzipan.

2 Brush the remaining apricot jam over the top and sides of the cake. Position the cake on the cake board. Tint 275g/10oz/ scant 2 cups of the remaining marzipan red. Roll it out to 5mm/¼in thick and use to cover the cake, smoothing down the sides. Trim the edges. Use the handle of a teaspoon to indent the "strawberry" evenly and lightly all over.

3 For the stalk, tint 175g/6oz/generous 1 cup of the marzipan bright green. Cut it in half and roll out one portion into a 10 x 15cm/4 x 6in rectangle. Cut "V" shapes out of the rectangle, leaving a 2.5cm/1in border across the top, to form the calyx. Position on the cake, curling the "V" shapes to make them look realistic.

4 Roll the rest of the green marzipan into a sausage shape 13cm/5in long. Bend it slightly, then position it on the board to form the stalk.

5 For the strawberry pips, tint the remaining marzipan yellow. Pull off tiny pieces and roll them into tear-shaped pips. Place them in the indentations all over the strawberry. Dust the cake and board with sifted caster sugar.

Chocolates Energy 4150kcal/17538kJ; Protein 46.5g; Carbohydrate 762.1g, of which sugars 641.6g; Fat 123g, of which saturates 46.5g; Cholesterol 388mg; Calcium 663mg; Fibre 6.7g; Sodium 2087mg.
Strawberry Energy 6810kcal/28566kJ; Protein 91.3g; Carbohydrate 931.7g, of which sugars 733.7g; Fat 327.4g, of which saturates 58.9g; Cholesterol 1007mg; Calcium 1054mg; Fibre 20.4g; Sodium 3073mg.

Sweetheart Cake

The heart-shaped run-outs can be made a week before the cake is made to ensure that they are completely dry.

Makes one 20cm/8in round cake
20cm/8in round sponge cake
115g/4oz/½ cup butter icing
45ml/3 tbsp apricot jam, warmed and served
450g/1lb marzipan

675g/1½lb/4½ cups sugarpaste icing
red food colouring
115g/4oz/¾ cup royal icing

Materials/equipment
25cm/10in round cake board
spoon with decorative handle
small baking parchment piping (icing) bag
no.1 writing nozzle
candles and holders
1.5m/1½yd x 2.5cm/1in wide ribbon

1 Split the cake and fill with butter icing. Place on the cake board and brush with apricot jam. Cover with a layer of marzipan. Tint the sugarpaste icing pale pink and cover the cake and board. Mark the edge of the icing with the decorative handle of a spoon.

2 Tint the royal icing dark pink. Make a heart-shaped template and draw round this several times on a sheet of baking parchment. Using a no.1 writing nozzle, pipe the outlines for the hearts in a continuous line. Then fill in until the hearts are rounded. You will need eight for the cake top. Make some extra in case of mistakes. Leave to dry for at least 2 days.

3 Arrange the hearts on top of the cake and place the candles in the centre. Tie the ribbon around the cake.

Cook's Tip
When using royal icing to create shapes such as these hearts, make sure that it is the correct consistency. If it is too thin the icing will overflow the edge of the shape; if it is too thick it will form a lumpy surface. Always make several more shapes than you need in case any are damaged when you transfer them from the paper to the cake.

Gift-wrapped Parcel

If you don't have a tiny flower cutter for the "wrapping paper" design, then press a small decorative button into the icing while still soft to create a pattern.

45ml/3 tbsp apricot jam, warmed and sieved
450g/1lb marzipan
350g/12oz/2¼ cups pale lemon yellow sugarpaste icing
red and green food colouring
30ml/2 tbsp royal icing

Makes one 15cm/6in square cake
15cm/6in square cake
50g/2oz/4 tbsp butter icing

Materials/equipment
20cm/8in square cake board
small flower cutter (optional)

1 Split the cake and fill with butter icing. Place on the cake board and brush with the warmed apricot jam. Cover with half the marzipan, then with the yellow sugarpaste icing, and mark with a small flower cutter.

2 To make the ribbons divide the remaining marzipan in half, and colour one half pink and the other pale green. Roll out the pink marzipan and cut into four 2.5 x 18cm/1 x 7in strips. Roll out the green marzipan and cut into four 1cm/½in strips the same length.

3 Centre the green strips on top of the pink strips and stick on to the cake with a little water. Cut two 5cm/2in strips from each colour and cut a "V" from the ends to form the ends of the ribbon. Stick in place and leave to dry overnight.

4 Cut the rest of the green into four 2.5 x 7.5cm/1 x 3in lengths and the pink into four 1 x 7.5cm/½ x 3in lengths. Centre the pink on top of the green, fold in half, stick the ends together and slip over the handle of a wooden spoon, dusted with cornflour. Leave to dry overnight.

5 Cut the ends into "V" shapes to fit neatly together on the cake. Cut two pieces for the join in the centre. Remove the bows from the spoon and stick in position with royal icing.

Parcel Energy 5031kcal/21295kJ; Protein 72.6g; Carbohydrate 992g, of which sugars 596g; Fat 116.3g, of which saturates 36g; Cholesterol 107mg; Calcium 442mg; Fibre 8.6g; Sodium 417mg.
Sweetheart Energy 7060kcal/29760kJ; Protein 64.8g; Carbohydrate 1224.6g, of which sugars 1092.6g; Fat 245g, of which saturates 55.1g; Cholesterol 735mg; Calcium 1013mg; Fibre 14g; Sodium 2274mg.

Rosette Cake

This impressive cake could be used for a Christening or anniversary cake.

Makes one 20cm/8in square cake
20cm/8in square sponge cake
450g/1lb/2 cups butter icing
60ml/4 tbsp apricot jam, warmed and sieved

mulberry-red food colouring
crystallized violets

Materials/equipment
25cm/10in square cake board
serrated scraper
piping (icing) bag
large star nozzle
candles and holders

1 Split the cake and fill with a little butter icing. Place in the centre of the cake board and brush with apricot jam. Tint the remaining butter icing dark pink using the mulberry-red food colouring. Spread the top and sides with butter icing.

2 Using the serrated scraper, hold it against the cake and move it from side to side across the top to make waves. Hold the scraper against the side of the cake, resting the flat edge on the board, and draw it along to give straight ridges along each side.

3 Put the rest of the butter icing into a piping bag fitted with a large star nozzle. Mark a 15cm/6in circle on the top of the cake and pipe stars around it and around the base of the cake. Place the candles and violets in the corners.

Cook's Tip
So that you have perfect little stars for your cake, practise piping icing on to a plate beforehand. Make sure there is no air in the icing by twisting the top of the bag and then squeezing a little icing out before you start. Hold the twist between the joint of the thumb and first finger and hold the bag in the palm of your hand. Hold the piping (icing) bag with the star nozzle directly over and close to the surface to be iced. Squeeze out some icing while gently pushing downwards and then move the icing bag upwards without squeezing to form a point.

Number 10 Cake

Ideal as a birthday or anniversary cake, this is a very simple cake to decorate. If you can't master the shell edge, pipe stars instead.

Makes one 20cm/8in tall round cake
20cm/8in and 15cm/6in round sponge cakes
450g/1lb/2 cups butter icing
75ml/5 tbsp apricot jam, warmed and sieved

coloured vermicelli
cream food colouring

Materials/equipment
25cm/10in round cake board
wooden cocktail stick (toothpick)
plastic "10" cake decoration
small baking parchment piping (icing) bag
thick shell and star nozzles
10 candles and holders

1 Split both cakes and fill with a little butter icing. Brush the sides with the warmed apricot jam.

2 When the jam is cold, spread a layer of butter icing over the sides and then roll in coloured vermicelli to cover evenly.

3 Tint the rest of the icing cream, and spread over the top of each cake. Place the small cake on top of the large cake. Using a cocktail stick, make a pattern in the icing on top of the cake.

4 Using the remaining icing, pipe around the base of the cakes and around the edge. Stick the "10" decoration in the centre of the top tier and two candles on either side. Arrange the other candles evenly around the base cake.

Cook's Tip
To pipe shells, hold the piping bag at an angle and close to the surface to be iced and gently squeeze out some of the icing while you move the bag gently slightly upwards and away from you then towards you to make a tiny loop. Let the icing touch the surface a fraction behind the loop and continue as before. Practise on a plate before you ice the cake.

Rosette Energy 5702kcal/23805kJ; Protein 46.7g; Carbohydrate 618.4g, of which sugars 464.4g; Fat 354.8g, of which saturates 144.8g; Cholesterol 1210mg; Calcium 632mg; Fibre 6.3g; Sodium 3523mg.
Number 10 Energy 7142kcal/29826kJ; Protein 65.7g; Carbohydrate 786g, of which sugars 566g; Fat 436.4g, of which saturates 162.2g; Cholesterol 1545mg; Calcium 841mg; Fibre 9g; Sodium 4506mg.

Mobile Phone Cake

Copy your phone to make the latest model.

**Makes one 23 x 13cm/
9 x 5in cake**

sponge cake, baked in a 23 x 13cm/
    9 x 5in loaf tin (pan)
30ml/2 tbsp apricot jam, warmed
    and sieved
375g/13oz/2¼ cups
    sugarpaste icing
black food colouring
10 small square sweets (candies)
2 striped liquorice sweets (candies)
30–45ml/2–3 tbsp icing
    (confectioners') sugar
2.5–5ml/½–1 tsp water

Materials/equipment

25 x 18cm/10 x 7in cake board
diamond-shaped cutter
small piece of foil
small baking parchment piping
    (icing) bag
small round nozzle

1 Turn the cake upside-down. Make a 2.5cm/1in diagonal cut 2.5cm/1in from one end. Cut down vertically to remove the wedge. Remove the middle of the cake to the wedge depth up to 4cm/1½in from the other end.

2 Place the cake on the board and brush with the warmed apricot jam. Tint 275g/10oz/1¾ cups of the sugarpaste icing black. Use to cover the cake, smoothing it over the carved shape with your hand. Reserve the trimmings.

3 Tint 75g/3oz/½ cup of the sugarpaste icing grey. Cut a piece to fit the hollowed centre, leaving a 1cm/½in border, and another piece 2.5cm/1in square. Stamp out the centre of the square with the diamond cutter. Secure all the pieces on the cake with water.

4 Position the sweets and the foil for the display pad. For the glacé icing, mix the icing sugar with the water and tint black.

5 With the small round nozzle, pipe border lines around the edges of the phone, including the grey pieces of sugarpaste. Pipe the numbers on the keys. Roll a sausage shape from the reserved black sugarpaste for the aerial. Indent one side of the top with a knife and secure the aerial with water.

Shirt & Tie Cake

**Makes one 19 x 26.5cm/
7½ x 10½in cake**

coffee sponge cake, baked in a
    19 x 26.5cm/ 7½ x 5in loaf tin
350g/12oz/1½ cups coffee-
    flavour butter icing
90ml/6 tbsp apricot jam, warmed
    and sieved
about 1kg/2¼lb/6¾ cups
    sugarpaste icing
blue food colouring
125g/4oz/1 cup icing
    (confectioners') sugar, sifted
45–60ml/3–4 tbsp water

Materials/equipment

30 x 39cm/12 x 15½in
    cake board
steel ruler
small baking parchment piping
    (icing) bag
small round nozzle
card (stock) collar template
"Happy Birthday" decoration
tissue paper (optional)

1 Cut the cake in half horizontally and sandwich together with the butter icing. Brush the cake with apricot jam. Colour 675g/1½lb/4½ cups sugarpaste icing light blue and roll out to about 5mm/¼in thick. Use to cover the whole cake. Trim away any excess icing. Place the cake on the cake board.

2 Using a steel ruler, make grooves down the length and sides of the cake, about 2.5cm/1in apart. Mix the icing sugar and water to make a glacé icing to pipe into the grooves.

3 To make the collar, roll out 225g/8oz/1½ cups sugarpaste icing to a 40.5 x 10cm/16½ x 4in rectangle. Lay the piece of card for the collar on top. Brush water around the edges, then carefully lift one edge over the card to encase it completely. Trim the two short ends to match the angles of the card. Lift the collar and gently bend it round, and position on the cake.

4 Colour 175g/6oz/1 cup sugarpaste icing dark blue. Cut off one-third and shape into a tie knot. Position the knot. Roll out the rest to about 5mm/½in thick. Cut out a tie piece to fit under the knot and long enough to hang over the edge of the cake. Position the tie piece, tucking it under the knot and securing in place with a little water. Finish the cake with the "Happy Birthday" decoration, and tissue paper, if you like.

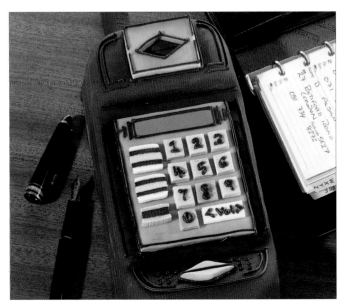

Shirt and Tie Energy 9078kcal/38128kJ; Protein 62.4g; Carbohydrate 1370.9g, of which sugars 1172.9g; Fat 409.2g, of which saturates 156.4g; Cholesterol 1434mg; Calcium 1092mg; Fibre 8.1g; Sodium 4220mg.
Mobile Phone Energy 5134kcal/21571kJ; Protein 54g; Carbohydrate 781.2g, of which sugars 597.2g; Fat 220.5g, of which saturates 48.4g; Cholesterol 895mg; Calcium 807mg; Fibre 8.3g; Sodium 2660mg.

Heart Cake

For Valentine's Day, an engagement or just to say "I love you".

Makes one 20cm/8in heart-shaped cake
3 egg whites
350g/12oz/1¾ cups caster (superfine) sugar
30ml/2 tbsp cold water
30ml/2 tbsp fresh lemon juice
1.5ml/¼ tsp cream of tartar

red food colouring
20cm/8in heart-shaped sponge cake
75–115g/3–4oz/¾–1 cup icing (confectioners') sugar

Materials/equipment
30cm/12in square cake board
small greaseproof piping (icing) bag
small nozzle

1 Make the icing by combining 2 of the egg whites, the caster sugar, water, lemon juice and cream of tartar in the top of a double boiler or in a bowl set over a pan of simmering water. With an electric mixer, beat until thick and holding soft peaks, about 7 minutes. Remove from the heat and continue beating until the mixture is thick enough to spread. Colour the icing pale pink.

2 Put the cake on the cake board and spread the icing evenly on the cake. Smooth the top and sides. Leave to set for 3–4 hours, or overnight.

3 Place 15ml/1 tbsp of the remaining egg white in a bowl and whisk until frothy. Gradually beat in enough icing sugar to make a stiff mixture suitable for piping.

4 Spoon the white icing into a piping bag and pipe the decorations on the top and sides of the cake as shown in the photograph above.

> **Cook's Tip**
> This simple and attractive frosting develops a thin sugar crust as it dries.

Bowl-of-Strawberries Cake

The strawberry theme of the painting is carried on into the moulded decorations on this summery birthday cake.

Makes one 20cm/8in petal-shaped cake
350g/12oz/1½ cups butter icing
red, yellow, green and claret food colouring
20cm/8in petal-shaped Madeira cake

45ml/3 tbsp apricot jam, warmed and sieved
675g/1½lb/4½ cups sugarpaste icing
yellow powder tint

Materials/equipment
25cm/10in petal-shaped cake board
paint palette or small saucers
fine paintbrushes
thin red and green ribbons

1 Tint the butter icing pink. Cut the cake horizontally into three. Sandwich together with the butter icing. Brush the cake with apricot jam.

2 Use 500g/1¼lb/3¾ cups of the sugarpaste icing to cover the cake. Place on the cake board and leave to dry overnight.

3 For the strawberries, tint three-quarters of the remaining sugarpaste icing red, and equal portions of the rest yellow and green. Make the strawberries by rolling small balls of red sugarpaste then making them slightly elongated. Roll out tiny dots of yellow sugarpaste and add as seeds to the strawberries.

4 Cut out a green star shape for a calyx and stick to the top, then add a green stalk. Secure with water if necessary. Leave the strawberries to dry on baking parchment.

5 Put the red, green, yellow and claret food colouring in a palette and water them down slightly. Paint the bowl and strawberries, using yellow powder tint to highlight the bowl.

6 Decorate the cake with the ribbons. Secure two of the strawberries to the top of the cake, and arrange the others around the base.

Heart Energy 3638kcal/15233kJ; Protein 53.2g; Carbohydrate 455.6g, of which sugars 301.6g; Fat 190.4g, of which saturates 40.6g; Cholesterol 783mg; Calcium 533mg; Fibre 6.3g; Sodium 2470mg.
Strawberries Energy 5837kcal/24534kJ; Protein 36.4g; Carbohydrate 905.1g, of which sugars 773.8g; Fat 255g, of which saturates 154.8g; Cholesterol 426mg; Calcium 558mg; Fibre 5.4g; Sodium 3535mg.

Tablecloth Cake

This draped "tablecloth" makes a most unusual effect for a cake.

Makes one 20cm/8in round cake
20cm/8in round sponge cake
115g/4oz/½ cup butter icing
45ml/3 tbsp apricot jam, warmed
 and sieved
450g/1lb marzipan
675g/1½lb/4½ cups
 sugarpaste icing
red food colouring

115g/4oz/¾ cup royal icing

Materials/equipment
25cm/10in round cake board
spoon with decorative handle
8 wooden cocktail
 sticks (toothpicks)
sharp needle
skewer
8 red ribbon bows
small baking parchment piping
 (icing) bags
very fine and fine plain nozzles

1 Split the cake and fill with butter icing. Place on the board and brush with apricot jam. Cover with a layer of marzipan.

2 Tint 450g/1lb/3 cups of the sugarpaste icing red and cover the cake and board. Roll the rest of the red sugarpaste into a thin rope long enough to go around the cake. Stick around the base of the cake with water. Mark with the decorative handle of a spoon. Leave to dry overnight.

3 Roll out the remaining icing to a 25cm/10in circle and trim. Lay this icing over the cake and drape the "cloth" over the wooden cocktail sticks set at equidistant points.

4 Mark a 10cm/4in circle in the centre of the cake. Make a template of the flower design and transfer to the cake with a needle. Use a skewer to make the flowers; the red colour should show through.

5 Remove the cocktail sticks and stick on the bows with royal icing. With a fine plain nozzle and white royal icing pipe around the circle in the centre. With a very fine plain nozzle, pipe small dots around the edge of the cloth. Colour some royal icing red and pipe a name in the centre.

Barley Twist Cake

This makes a lovely Christening cake.

Makes one 20cm/8in round cake
20cm/8in round sponge cake
115g/4oz/½ cup butter icing
45ml/3 tbsp apricot jam, warmed
 and sieved
450/1lb marzipan
450g/1lb/3 cups pale yellow
 sugarpaste icing
115g/4oz/¾ cup white
 sugarpaste icing

115g/4oz/¾ cup royal icing
blue food colouring
edible pink dusting powder

Materials/equipment
25cm/10in round cake board
wooden cocktail stick (toothpick)
fine paintbrush
very fine plain nozzle
small baking parchment piping
 (icing) bags
6 small blue bows

1 Split the cake and fill with butter icing. Place on the board and brush with jam. Cover with marzipan, then yellow sugarpaste icing, extending it over the board. Mark six equidistant points around the cake with a cocktail stick.

2 Colour 40g/1½oz/1 tbsp of the white sugarpaste icing pale blue and roll out thinly. Moisten a paintbrush with water and brush lightly over it. Roll out the same quantity of white icing, lay on top and press together. Roll out to a 20cm/8in square.

3 Cut 5mm/¼in strips, carefully twist each one, moisten the six marked points around the cake with water and drape each barley twist into place, pressing lightly to stick to the cake.

4 Cut out a jersey shape from white icing and stick on to the top of the cake with water. Roll some icing into a ball and colour a small amount dark blue. Roll into two tapering 7.5cm/3in long needles with a small ball at the end. Dry overnight. Stick the needles and ball in position. Using royal icing and the very fine nozzle, pipe the stitches and wool in position. Pipe a white border around the base of the cake. Stick small bows around the edge of the cake with a little royal icing and carefully brush the knitting with pink powder tint.

Barley Twist Energy 7304kcal/30793kJ; Protein 71g; Carbohydrate 1276.8g, of which sugars 1122.8g; Fat 247.6g, of which saturates 45.2g; Cholesterol 783mg; Calcium 1077mg; Fibre 14.9g; Sodium 2418mg.
Tablecloth Energy 7673kcal/32303kJ; Protein 73.7g; Carbohydrate 1258.6g, of which sugars 1104.6g; Fat 295g, of which saturates 71.8g; Cholesterol 890mg; Calcium 1092mg; Fibre 15.8g; Sodium 2728mg.

Pizza Cake

Quick and easy, this really is a definite winner for pizza fanatics everywhere.

Makes one 23cm/9in round cake
23cm/9in shallow sponge cake
350g/12oz/1½ cups butter icing
red and green food colouring
175g/6oz yellow marzipan

25g/1oz/4 tbsp sugarpaste icing
15ml/1 tbsp desiccated
(dry unsweetened
shredded) coconut

Materials/equipment
25cm/10in pizza plate
leaf cutter

1 Place the cake on the pizza plate. Tint the butter icing red and spread evenly over the cake, leaving a 1cm/½in border.

2 Knead the marzipan for a few minutes, to soften slightly, then grate it like cheese, and sprinkle all over the red butter icing.

3 Tint the sugarpaste icing green. Use the leaf cutter to cut out two leaf shapes to look like basil leaves.

4 Mark the veins with the back of a knife and place on the pizza cake.

5 For the chopped herbs, tint the desiccated coconut dark green. Then sprinkle over the pizza cake.

Variation
Go to town with the topping for this pizza, if you like. For a seafood lover you could make tiny prawns (shrimp) or clams out of sugarpaste or buy prawn-shaped sweets (candies) or chocolate shells. You could also make slices of ham, mushrooms, sausage, or red or green (bell) pepper, as well as whole black or green olives - all from coloured sugarpaste. Or you could cut up cubes of marzipan to look like cubes of cheese and sprinkle them over the top.

Flowerpot Cake

The perfect gift for a gardening enthusiast or plant lover.

Makes one round cake
Madeira cake, baked in a 1.2-litre/
   2-pint/5-cup pudding bowl
175g/6oz/generous ½ cup jam
175g/6oz/¾ cup butter icing
30ml/2 tbsp apricot jam, warmed
   and sieved

575g/1lb 6oz/4¼ cups
   sugarpaste icing
dark orange-red, red, silver,
   green, purple and yellow
   food colouring
125g/4oz/¾ cup royal icing
2 flaked chocolate bars,
   coarsely crushed

Materials/equipment
fine paintbrush

1 Slice the cake into three layers and stick together again with jam and butter icing. Cut out a shallow circle from the cake top, leaving a 1cm/½in rim.

2 Brush the outside of the cake and rim with apricot jam. Tint 400g/14oz/2¼ cups of the sugarpaste orange-red and cover the cake, moulding it over the rim. Reserve the trimmings. Leave to dry.

3 Use the trimmings to make decorations and handles for the flowerpot. Leave to dry on baking parchment. Sprinkle the chocolate flakes into the pot for soil.

4 Tint a small piece of sugarpaste very pale orange-red. Use to make a seed bag. When dry, paint on a pattern in food colouring. Tint two small pieces of icing red and silver. Make a trowel and dry over a wooden spoon handle.

5 Tint the remaining icing green, purple and a small piece yellow. Use to make the flowers and leaves, attaching together with royal icing. Score leaf veins with the back of a knife. Leave to dry on baking parchment.

6 Attach all the decorations to the flowerpot and arrange the plant, seed bag and trowel with soil, seeds and grass made from leftover tinted sugarpaste.

Pizza Energy 6488kcal/27075kJ; Protein 62.3g; Carbohydrate 670.3g, of which sugars 494.3g; Fat 413.5g, of which saturates 160.4g; Cholesterol 1322mg; Calcium 773mg; Fibre 12.6g; Sodium 3867mg.
Flowerpot Energy 6068kcal/25587kJ; Protein 47.3g; Carbohydrate 1079.5g, of which sugars 904.3g; Fat 203g, of which saturates 119.5g; Cholesterol 213mg; Calcium 617mg; Fibre 7.2g; Sodium 3732mg.

Glittering Star Cake

With a quick flick of a paintbrush you can give a sparkling effect to this glittering cake. Sparkle and glitter food colours make a cake very special.

Makes one 20cm/8in round cake

20cm/8in round rich fruit cake
40ml/2½ tbsp apricot jam, warmed and sieved

675g/1½lb/4½ cups marzipan
450g/1lb/3 cups sugarpaste icing
115g/4oz/¾ cup royal icing
silver, gold, lilac shimmer, red sparkle, glitter green and primrose sparkle food colouring and powder tints

Materials/equipment

paintbrush
25cm/10in round cake board

1 Brush the cake with the apricot jam. Use two-thirds of the marzipan to cover the cake. Leave to dry overnight.

2 Cover the cake with the sugarpaste icing. Leave to dry.

3 Place the cake on a large sheet of baking parchment. Dilute a little powdered silver food colouring and, using a loaded paintbrush, flick it all over the cake to give a spattered effect. Allow to dry.

4 Make templates of two different-size moon shapes and three irregular star shapes.

5 Divide the remaining marzipan into six pieces and tint them silver, gold, lilac, pink, green and yellow. Cut the coloured sugarpaste into stars and moons using the templates as a guide, cutting some of the stars in half.

6 Place the cut-outs on baking parchment and brush each with its own colour powder tint. Allow to dry.

7 Secure the cake on the board with royal icing. Arrange the marzipan stars and moons at different angles all over the cake, attaching with royal icing, and position the halved stars upright as though coming out of the cake. Allow to set.

Racing Ring Cake

Liquorice makes simple but effective tracks for brightly coloured cars.

Serves 12

ring mould sponge cake
350g/12oz/1½ cups butter icing
500g/1¼lb/3¾ cups sugarpaste icing
125g/4oz/¾ cup royal icing, for fixing
black, blue, yellow, green, orange, red, purple food colouring

selection of liquorice sweets (candies), dolly mixtures and teddy bears
113g/4½oz packet liquorice Catherine wheels

Materials/equipment

25cm/10in round cake board
wooden kebab skewer
fine paintbrush

1 Cut the cake in half horizontally and fill with some butter icing. Cover the outside with the remaining butter icing.

2 Use 350g/12oz/2¼ cups of sugarpaste icing to coat the top and inside of the cake. Use the trimmings to roll an oblong for the flag. Cut the skewer to 13cm/5in and fold one end of the flag around it, securing with water. Paint on the pattern with black food colouring. Colour a ball of icing black, and stick on top of the skewer. Make a few folds in the flag and leave to dry.

3 Colour the remaining sugarpaste icing blue, yellow, green, orange, red and a very small amount purple. Shape each car in two pieces, attaching in the centre with royal icing where the seat joins the body of the car. Add decorations and headlights and attach dolly mixture wheels with royal icing. Place a teddy bear in each car and leave to set.

4 Unwind the Catherine wheels and remove the centre sweets. Fix them to the top of the cake with royal icing. Secure one strip around the bottom. Cut some of the liquorice into small strips and attach around the middle of the outside of the cake with royal icing. Arrange small liquorice sweets around the bottom of the cake. Position the cars on top of the cake on the tracks and attach the flag to the outside with royal icing.

Star Energy 7800kcal/33013kJ; Protein 73.6g; Carbohydrate 1548.9g, of which sugars 1448.1g; Fat 159.5g, of which saturates 28.6g; Cholesterol 415mg; Calcium 1427mg; Fibre 26.3g; Sodium 1573mg.
Racing Ring Energy 622kcal/2603kJ; Protein 5.2g; Carbohydrate 77.8g, of which sugars 60.6g; Fat 34.3g, of which saturates 13.2g; Cholesterol 119mg; Calcium 80mg; Fibre 0.8g; Sodium 350mg.

Artist's Cake

Making cakes is an art in itself, and this cake proves it! Take your time to model the handle and catches for the box for the best effect.

Makes one 20cm/8in square cake

20cm/8in square rich fruit cake
45ml/3 tbsp apricot jam, warmed and sieved

450g/1lb marzipan
800g/1¾lb/5¼ cups sugarpaste icing
chestnut, yellow, blue, black, silver, paprika, green and mulberry food colouring
115g/4oz/¾ cup royal icing

Materials/equipment
25cm/10in square cake board
fine paintbrush

1 Brush the cake with the apricot jam. Cover in marzipan and leave to dry overnight.

2 Make a template of a painter's palette that will fit the cake top. Tint 175g/6oz/generous 1 cup of the sugarpaste very pale chestnut. Cut out the palette shape, place on baking parchment and leave to dry overnight.

3 Tint 450g/1lb/3 cups of the sugarpaste icing dark chestnut. Use to cover the cake. Secure the cake on the board with royal icing. Leave to dry.

4 Divide half the remaining sugarpaste icing into seven equal parts and tint yellow, blue, black, silver, paprika, green and mulberry.

5 Make all the decorative pieces for the box and palette, using the remaining white sugarpaste for the paint tubes.

6 Leave all the decorative pieces to dry on baking parchment.

7 Paint black markings on the paint tubes and chestnut wood markings on the box.

8 Position all the sugarpaste pieces on the cake and board using royal icing. Leave to dry.

"Liquorice" Cake

Scaled-up versions of favourite sweets (candies) make a great decoration for a cake.

Makes one 20cm/8in square cake

20cm/8in and 15cm/6in square Madeira cakes
675g/1½lb/3 cups butter icing
45ml/3 tbsp apricot jam, warmed and sieved

350g/12oz marzipan
800g/1¾lb/5¼ cups sugarpaste icing
egg-yellow, black, blue and mulberry food colouring

Materials/equipment
25cm/10in square cake board
4.5cm/1¾in round cutter

1 Cut both cakes horizontally into three. Fill with butter icing, reserving a little to coat the smaller cake. Wrap and set aside the smaller cake. Brush the larger cake with apricot jam. Cover with marzipan and secure on the cake board with butter icing. Leave to dry overnight.

2 Tint 350g/12oz/2¼ cups of the sugarpaste icing yellow. Take 115g/4oz/¾ cup of the remaining sugarpaste icing and tint half black and leave the other half white. Cover the top and one-third of the sides of the cake with yellow sugarpaste icing.

3 Use the white icing to cover the lower third of the sides of the cake. Use the black icing to fill the central third.

4 Cut the smaller cake into three equal strips. Divide two of the strips into three squares each. Cut out two circles from the third strip, using a cutter as a guide.

5 Tint 115g/4oz/¾ cup of the remaining sugarpaste black. Divide the rest into four equal portions; leave one white and tint the others blue, pink and yellow.

6 Coat the outsides of the cake cut-outs with the reserved butter icing. Use the tinted and white sugarpaste to cover the pieces to resemble liquorice sweets (candies). Make small rolls from the trimmings. Arrange on and around the cake.

Artist's Energy 7370kcal/31233kJ; Protein 58.8g; Carbohydrate 1546g, of which sugars 1456.3g; Fat 122.8g, of which saturates 23.8g; Cholesterol 369mg; Calcium 1305mg; Fibre 20.6g; Sodium 1385mg.
"Liquorice" Energy 9108kcal/38287kJ; Protein 61.9g; Carbohydrate 1409.7g, of which sugars 1256.4g; Fat 396.8g, of which saturates 218.9g; Cholesterol 640mg; Calcium 955mg; Fibre 12.9g; Sodium 4603mg.

Sun Cake

This smiling sun is very easy to make from two round cakes with a quickly piped icing design.

Makes one 20cm/8in star-shaped cake

2 sponge cakes, 20 x 5cm/
  8 x 2in each
25g/1oz/2 tbsp unsalted
  (sweet) butter
450g/1lb/4 cups sifted icing
  (confectioners') sugar
120ml/4fl oz/½ cup
  apricot jam
30ml/2 tbsp water
2 large (US extra large)
  egg whites
1–2 drops glycerine
juice of 1 lemon
yellow and orange
  food colouring

Materials/equipment
40cm/16in square
  cake board
fabric piping (icing) bag
small star nozzle

1 Cut one of the cakes into eight wedges. Trim the outsides to fit around the other cake.

2 To make the butter icing, combine the butter with 25g/1oz/ 2 tbsp of the icing sugar.

3 Place the whole cake on a 40cm/16in board and attach the sunbeams with the butter icing.

4 Warm the jam with the water in a small bowl set over a pan of simmering water. Brush the jam all over the cake.

5 For the icing, beat the egg whites until they are stiff. Gradually add the icing sugar, glycerine and lemon juice, and beat together for 1 minute.

6 Tint three-quarters of the icing yellow and spread it all over the cake.

7 Tint the remaining icing bright yellow and orange.

8 Pipe the details on to the cake with the small star nozzle .

Strawberry Basket Cake

For a summer birthday what could be nicer than a basket full of strawberries?

Makes one small rectangular cake

sponge cake baked in a 450g/
  1lb/3 cup loaf tin (pan)
45ml/3 tbsp apricot jam, warmed
  and sieved
675g/1½lb marzipan
350g/12oz/1½ cups chocolate-
  flavour butter icing
red food colouring
50g/2oz/¼ cup caster
  (superfine) sugar

Materials/equipment
small star nozzle
small baking parchment piping
  (icing) bag
10 plastic strawberry stalks
30 x 7.5cm/12 x 3in strip foil
30cm/12in thin red ribbon

1 Level the top of the cake and make it perfectly flat. Score a 5mm/¼in border around the edge and scoop out the inside to make a shallow hollow.

2 Brush the sides and border edges of the cake with apricot jam. Roll out 275g/10oz/scant 2 cups of the marzipan, cut into rectangles and use to cover the sides of the cake, overlapping the borders. Press the edges together to seal.

3 Using the star nozzle and the butter icing, pipe vertical lines 2.5cm/1in apart all around the sides of the cake. Pipe short horizontal lines of butter icing alternately crossing over and then stopping at the vertical lines to give a basketweave effect. Pipe a decorative line of icing around the top edge of the basket to finish.

4 Tint the remaining marzipan red and mould it into ten strawberry shapes. Roll in the caster sugar and press a plastic strawberry calyx into each top. Arrange in the "basket".

5 For the basket handle, fold the foil into a thin strip and wind the ribbon around it to cover. Bend up the ends and then bend into a curve. Push the ends into the sides of the cake. Decorate with bows made from the ribbon.

Sun Cake Energy 7899kcal/33176kJ; Protein 84.5g; Carbohydrate 1182g, of which sugars 918g; Fat 346.9g, of which saturates 82.6g; Cholesterol 1396mg; Calcium 1089mg; Fibre 10.8g; Sodium 4247mg.
Basket Energy 6807kcal/28601kJ; Protein 69.4g; Carbohydrate 1011.2g, of which sugars 901.2g; Fat 303.9g, of which saturates 88g; Cholesterol 773mg; Calcium 946mg; Fibre 17.3g; Sodium 2399mg.

Children's Party Cakes

A home-made cake adds the finishing touch to a table laden with delicious food for a children's party, and the response you will get will make your efforts worthwhile. Included in the chapter are cakes of all shapes and sizes that are suitable for every age, including Porcupine Cake, Bumble Bee Cake, Fire Engine Cake, Noah's Ark Cake, Kite Cake, Spider's Web Cake and even a Hotdog Cake.

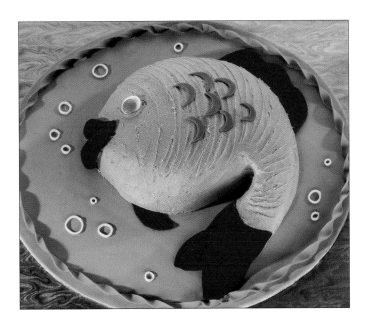

Pink Monkey Cake

This cheeky little monkey could be made in any colour icing you wish.

Makes one 20cm/8in cake
20cm/8in round sponge cake
115g/4oz/½ cup butter icing
45ml/3 tbsp apricot jam, warmed and sieved

450g/1lb marzipan
500g/1¼lb/3¾ cups sugarpaste icing
red, blue and black food colouring

Materials/equipment
25cm/10in round cake board
2 candles and holders

1 Trace the outline and paws of the monkey from the photograph. Using a photocopier or a computer enlarge to fit the cake and then cut out a template.

2 Split the cake and fill with butter icing. Place on the cake board and use the template to cut out the basic shape of the monkey. Use the trimmings to shape the nose and tummy. Brush with apricot jam and cover with a layer of marzipan.

3 Tint 450g/1lb/3 cups of the sugarpaste icing pale pink and use to cover the cake. Leave to dry overnight.

4 Mark the position of the face and paws. Tint a little of the sugarpaste icing blue and use for the eyes. Tint a little icing black and cut out the pupils and tie.

5 Tint the remaining sugarpaste icing dark pink and cut out the nose, mouth, ears and paws. Stick all the features in place with water. Roll the trimmings into balls and place on the board to hold the candles.

> **Variation**
> *You could adapt this circular cake to make a cat or an elephant, perhaps side on with his trunk curling upwards. Try some different shapes on paper then transfer your finished idea on to baking parchment to use as a template.*

Fish-shaped Cake

A very easy and colourful cake, this fun little fish is perfect for a small child's birthday party.

Makes one cake
450g/1lb/3 cups sugarpaste icing
blue, orange, red, mauve and green food colouring
sponge cake, baked in a 3.5 litre/6 pint/15 cup ovenproof mixing bowl

350g/12oz/1½ cups butter icing
1 blue sweet (candy)

Materials/equipment
large oval cake board
2.5cm/1in plain cutter
baking parchment piping (icing) bag

1 Tint two-thirds of the sugarpaste icing blue, roll out very thinly and use to cover the dampened cake board.

2 Make a template of a fish out of paper. Invert the cake, place the template on top and trim into the fish shape. Slope the sides. Place on the cake board.

3 Tint all but 15ml/1 tbsp of the butter icing orange. Use to cover the cake, smoothing with a metal spatula. Score curved lines for scales, starting from the tail end.

4 Tint half the remaining sugarpaste icing red. Shape and position two lips.

5 Cut out the tail and fins. Mark with lines using a knife and position on the fish. Make the eye from white sugarpaste and the blue sweet.

6 Tint a little sugarpaste mauve, cut out crescent-shaped scales using a biscuit cutter and place on the fish. Tint the remaining sugarpaste green and cut into long thin strips. Twist each strip and arrange around the board.

7 To make the bubbles around the fish, place the reserved butter icing in a piping bag, snip off the end and pipe small circles on to the board.

Fish Energy 5866kcal/24548kJ; Protein 41g; Carbohydrate 733.6g, of which sugars 601.6g; Fat 327.6g, of which saturates 139g; Cholesterol 1098mg; Calcium 662mg; Fibre 5.4g; Sodium 3192mg.
Monkey Energy 6888kcal/28960kJ; Protein 70.3g; Carbohydrate 1068.1g, of which sugars 914.1g; Fat 288.6g, of which saturates 71.3g; Cholesterol 890mg; Calcium 980mg; Fibre 14.9g; Sodium 2709mg.

Porcupine Cake

Melt-in-the-mouth pieces of flaked chocolate give this porcupine its spiky coating.

Serves 15–20
2 chocolate sponge cakes, baked in a 1.2 litre/2 pint/5 cup and a 600ml/1 pint/2½ cup pudding bowl
500g/1¼lb/2½ cups chocolate-flavour butter icing

cream, black, green, brown and red food colouring
5–6 flaked chocolate bars
50g/2oz/⅓ cup white marzipan

Materials/equipment
35cm/14in long rectangular cake board
wooden cocktail stick (toothpick)
fine paintbrush

1 Use the smaller cake for the head and shape a pointed nose at one end. Reserve the trimmed wedges.

2 Place the cakes side-by-side on the cake board, inverted, and use the trimmings to fill in the sides and top where they meet. Secure with butter icing.

3 Cover the cake with the remaining butter icing and mark the nose with a cocktail stick.

4 Make the spikes by breaking the flaked chocolate into thin strips and sticking them into the butter icing all over the body section of the porcupine.

5 Reserve a small portion of marzipan. Divide the remainder into three and tint cream, black and green.

6 Tint a tiny portion of the reserved marzipan brown.

7 Shape cream ears and feet, black-and-white eyes, and black claws and nose. Arrange all the features on the cake and press them into the buttercream.

8 Make green apples and highlight in red with a fine paintbrush. Make the stalks from the brown marzipan and push them in to the apples.

Mouse-in-bed Cake

This cake is suitable for both girls and boys. Make the mouse well in advance to give it time to dry.

Makes one 20 x 15cm/ 8 x 6in cake
20cm/8in square sponge cake
115g/4oz/½ cup butter icing
45ml/3 tbsp apricot jam, warmed and sieved

450g/1lb marzipan
675g/1½lb/4½ cups sugarpaste icing
blue and red food colouring

Materials/equipment
25cm/10in square cake board
flower cutter
blue and red food colouring pens

1 Cut 5cm/2in off one side of the cake. Split and fill the main cake with butter icing. Place on the cake board, brush with apricot jam and cover with a layer of marzipan.

2 With the cake off-cut, shape a pillow with a hollow for the mouse's head, and the torso and the legs of the mouse. Cover with marzipan and leave to dry overnight.

3 Cover the cake and pillow with white sugarpaste icing. Lightly frill the edge of the pillow with a fork. To make the valance, roll out 350g/12oz/2¼ cups of sugarpaste icing and cut into four 7.5cm/3in wide strips. Attach to the bed with water. Arrange the pillow and mouse body on the cake.

4 For the quilt, tint 75g/3oz/½ cup of sugarpaste icing blue and roll out to an 18cm/7in square. Mark with a diamond pattern and the flower cutter. Cover the mouse with the quilt.

5 Cut a 2.5 x 19cm/1 x 7½in white sugarpaste icing strip for the sheet, mark the edge and place over the quilt, tucking it under at the top edge.

6 Tint 25g/1oz/2 tbsp of marzipan pink and make the head and paws of the mouse. Put the head on the pillow, tucked under the sheet, and the paws over the edge of the sheet. Use food colouring pens to draw on the face of the mouse.

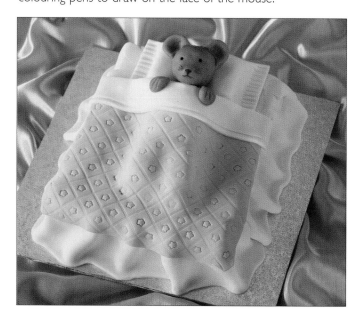

Porcupine Energy 364kcal/1523kJ; Protein 4.1g; Carbohydrate 39g, of which sugars 28.1g; Fat 22.4g, of which saturates 5.7g; Cholesterol 21mg; Calcium 47mg; Fibre 0.1g; Sodium 277mg.
Mouse Energy 7749kcal/32592kJ; Protein 77.1g; Carbohydrate 1225g, of which sugars 1049g; Fat 315.8g, of which saturates 77.1g; Cholesterol 1002mg; Calcium 1102mg; Fibre 15.8g; Sodium 3041mg.

Teddy's Birthday

After the sugarpaste pieces have been assembled and stuck into the cake, an icing smoother is useful to flatten the design.

Makes one 20cm/8in round cake

20cm/8in round cake
115g/4oz/½ cup butter icing
45ml/3 tbsp apricot jam, warmed and sieved
350g/12oz marzipan
450g/1lb/3 cups sugarpaste icing
brown, red, blue and black food colouring
115g/4oz/¾ cup royal icing
edible silver balls

Materials/equipment

25cm/10in round cake board
small baking parchment piping (icing) bags
medium shell and star nozzles
1.5m/1½yd red ribbon
2 candles and holders

1 Copy the teddy design on to a piece of paper that will fit the top of the cake.

2 Split the cake and fill with butter icing. Place on the cake board and brush with apricot jam. Cover with a layer of marzipan then a layer of sugarpaste icing.

3 Using the paper template, mark the design on top of the cake.

4 Colour one-third of the remaining sugarpaste icing pale brown. Colour a piece pink, a piece red, some blue and a tiny piece black. Using the template, cut out the pieces and place in position on the cake. Stick down by lifting the edges carefully and brushing the undersides with a little water.

5 Roll small ovals for the eyes and stick in place with the nose and eyebrows. Cut out a mouth and press flat.

6 Tie the ribbon around the cake. Colour the royal icing blue and pipe the border around the base of the cake with the shell nozzle. Pipe tiny stars around the small cake with the star nozzle. Insert silver balls on the piped stars. Put the candles on the cake.

Party Teddy Bear Cake

The cuddly teddy on this cake is built up with royal icing and coloured coconut and is a very simple effect to achieve.

Makes one 20cm/8in square cake

20cm/8in square sponge cake
115g/4oz/½ cup butter icing
45ml/3 tbsp apricot jam, warmed and sieved
450g/1lb marzipan
350g/12oz/2¼ cups white sugarpaste icing
25g/1oz/⅓ cup desiccated (dry unsweetened shredded) coconut
blue and black food colouring
115g/4oz/¾ cup royal icing

Materials/equipment

25cm/10in square cake board
2 small baking parchment piping (icing) bags
small red bow
no.7 shell nozzle
1.5m/1½yd red ribbon
6 candles and holders

1 Make a paper template of the teddy so that it will fit the top of the cake.

2 Cut the cake in half and sandwich together with butter icing. Place on the cake board and brush with apricot jam. Cover with a thin layer of marzipan and then white sugarpaste icing. Leave to dry overnight.

3 Using the template, carefully mark the position of the teddy on to the cake.

4 Put the coconut into a bowl and mix in a drop of blue colouring to colour it pale blue. Spread a thin layer of royal icing on to the cake within the outline of the teddy. Before the icing dries, sprinkle on some pale blue coconut and press it down lightly.

5 Roll out the sugarpaste trimmings and cut out a nose, ears and paws. Stick in place with a little royal icing. Tint some royal icing black and pipe on the eyes, nose and mouth. Use the red bow as a tie and attach in place with royal icing. Pipe a white royal icing border around the base of the cake, tie the ribbon around the cake and position the candles on top.

Teddy Energy 6210kcal/26127kJ; Protein 58.8g; Carbohydrate 995.4g, of which sugars 863.4g; Fat 248.8g, of which saturates 64.5g; Cholesterol 778mg; Calcium 879mg; Fibre 12.1g; Sodium 2355mg.
Party Teddy Energy 7900kcal/33215kJ; Protein 78.5g; Carbohydrate 1226.6g, of which sugars 1050.6g; Fat 331.4g, of which saturates 90.4g; Cholesterol 1002mg; Calcium 1108mg; Fibre 19.2g; Sodium 3048mg.

Fairy Castle Cake

If the icing on this cake dries too quickly, dip a metal spatula into hot water to help smooth the surface.

Makes one cake
20cm/8in round sponge cake
115g/4oz/1/2 cup butter icing
45ml/3 tbsp apricot jam, warmed and sieved
675g/11/2lb/41/2 cups marzipan
8 mini Swiss rolls (jelly rolls)
675g/11/2lb/41/2 cups royal icing

red, blue and green food colouring
jelly diamonds
4 ice cream cones
2 ice cream wafers
50g/2oz/2/3 cup desiccated (dry unsweetened shredded) coconut
8 marshmallows

Materials/equipment
30cm/12in square cake board
wooden cocktail stick (toothpick)

I Split the cake and fill with butter icing, place in the centre of the board and brush with apricot jam. Cover with a layer of marzipan.

2 Cover each of the Swiss rolls (jelly rolls) with marzipan. Stick four of them around the cake and cut the other four in half.

3 Tint two-thirds of the royal icing pale pink and cover the cake. Ice the extra pieces of Swiss roll and stick them around the top of the cake.

4 Use a cocktail stick to score the walls with a brick pattern. Make windows on the corner towers from jelly diamonds. Cut the ice cream cones to make the tower spires and stick them in place. Leave to dry overnight.

5 Tint half the remaining royal icing pale blue and cover the cones. Use a fork to pattern the icing. Shape the wafers for the gates, stick to the cake and cover with blue icing. Use the back of a knife to mark planks.

6 Tint the coconut with a few drops of green colouring. Spread the board with the remaining royal icing and sprinkle over the coconut. Stick on the marshmallows with a little royal icing to make the small turrets.

Iced Fancies

These cakes are ideal for a children's tea-party. Ready-made cake decorating products may be used instead, if you like.

Makes 16
115g/4oz/1/2 cup butter, at room temperature
225g/8oz/generous 1 cup caster (superfine) sugar
2 eggs, at room temperature
175g/6oz/11/2 cups plain (all-purpose) flour
1.5ml/1/4 tsp salt

7.5ml/11/2 tsp baking powder
120ml/4fl oz/1/2 cup milk
5ml/1 tsp vanilla extract

For the icing
2 large egg whites
400g/14oz/31/2 cups sifted icing (confectioners') sugar
1–2 drops glycerine
juice of 1 lemon
food colourings of your choice
coloured vermicelli, and crystallized lemon and orange slices, to decorate

I Preheat the oven to 190°C/375°F/Gas 5. Line a 16-cup bun tray with paper cases.

2 Cream the butter and sugar until light and fluffy. Add the eggs, one at a time, beating well after each addition.

3 Sift over and stir in the flour, salt and baking powder, alternating with the milk. Add the vanilla extract.

4 Half-fill the cups and bake for about 20 minutes, or until the tops spring back when touched. Stand in the tray to cool for 5 minutes, then unmould on to a wire rack.

5 To make the icing, beat the egg whites until stiff. Gradually add the sugar, glycerine and lemon juice, and beat for 1 minute.

6 Tint the icing with the different food colourings, and use to ice the tops of the cakes.

7 Decorate the cakes with coloured vermicelli and crystallized lemon and orange slices. You can also make freehand decorations such as animal faces using a paper piping (icing) bag.

Iced Fancies Energy 259kcal/1094kJ; Protein 2.7g; Carbohydrate 49.7g, of which sugars 41.4g; Fat 6.9g, of which saturates 4g; Cholesterol 40mg; Calcium 50mg; Fibre 0.3g; Sodium 66mg.
Castle Energy 9249kcal/38959kJ; Protein 91.7g; Carbohydrate 1545.3g, of which sugars 1358.7g; Fat 342.6g, of which saturates 82.4g; Cholesterol 1041mg; Calcium 1387mg; Fibre 19.1g; Sodium 3405mg.

Spider Cake

A delightfully spooky cake for any occasion, fancy dress or otherwise.

Makes one 900g/2lb cake
900g/2lb dome-shaped lemon
*   sponge cake*
225g/8oz/³⁄₄ cup lemon-flavour
*   glacé icing*
black and yellow food colouring

For the spiders
115g/4oz plain chocolate, broken
*   into pieces*
150ml/¹⁄₄ pint/²⁄₃ cup double
*   (heavy) cream*

45ml/3 tbsp ground almonds
unsweetened cocoa powder,
*   for dusting*
chocolate vermicelli
2–3 liquorice wheels, sweet
*   centres removed*
15g/¹⁄₂oz/2 tbsp sugarpaste icing

Materials/equipment
small baking parchment piping
*   (icing) bag*
wooden skewer
20cm/8in cake board

1 Place the cake on baking parchment. Tint 45ml/3 tbsp of the glacé icing black. Tint the rest yellow and pour it over the cake, letting it run down the side.

2 Fill a piping bag with the black icing and, starting at the centre top, drizzle it round the cake in an evenly-spaced spiral. Finish the web by drawing downwards through the icing with a skewer. When set, place on the cake board.

3 To make the spiders, gently melt the chocolate with the cream, stirring frequently. Transfer to a bowl, allow to cool, then beat the mixture for 10 minutes, or until thick and pale. Stir in the ground almonds, then chill until firm enough to handle. Dust your hands with a little cocoa, then make walnut-size balls with the mixture. Roll the balls in chocolate vermicelli.

4 For the legs, cut the liquorice into 4cm/1¹⁄₂in lengths. Make holes in the sides of the spiders and insert the legs. For the spiders' eyes, tint a piece of sugarpaste icing black and form into tiny balls. Make larger balls with white icing. Stick on using water. Arrange the spiders on and around the cake.

Sailing Boat

For chocoholics, make this cake using chocolate sponge.

Makes one cake
20cm/8in square sponge cake
225g/8oz/1 cup butter icing
15ml/1 tbsp unsweetened
*   cocoa powder*
4 large flaked chocolate bars
blue and red powder tints

115g/4oz/³⁄₄ cup royal icing
blue food colouring

Materials/equipment
25cm/10in square cake board
rice paper
paintbrush
plastic drinking straw
wooden cocktail stick (toothpick)
2 small cake ornaments

1 Split the cake and fill with half of the butter icing. Cut 7cm/2³⁄₄in from one side of the cake. Shape the larger piece to resemble the hull of a boat. Place diagonally across the cake board.

2 Mix the cocoa powder into the remaining butter icing and spread evenly over the top and sides of the boat.

3 Make the rudder and tiller from short lengths of flaked chocolate bars and place them at the stern of the boat. Split the rest of the flaked chocolate bars lengthways and press on to the sides of the boat, horizontally, to resemble planks of wood. Sprinkle the crumbs over the top.

4 Cut two rice paper rectangles, one 14 x 16cm/5³⁄₄ x 6¹⁄₂in and the other 15 x 7.5cm/6 x 3in. Cut the bigger one in a gentle curve to make the large sail and the smaller one into a triangle. Brush a circle of blue powder tint on to the large sail.

5 Wet the edges of the sails and stick on to the straw. Make a hole for the straw 7.5cm/3in from the bow of the boat and push into the cake.

6 Cut a rice paper flag and brush with red powder tint. Stick the flag on to a cocktail stick and insert into the top of the straw. Tint the royal icing blue and spread on the board in waves. Place the small ornaments on the boat.

Boat Energy 5147kcal/21498kJ; Protein 55.6g; Carbohydrate 568g, of which sugars 390.1g; Fat 310.1g, of which saturates 104.6g; Cholesterol 1110mg; Calcium 664mg; Fibre 9.6g; Sodium 3366mg.
Spider Energy 6266kcal/26208kJ; Protein 71g; Carbohydrate 734.2g, of which sugars 547.9g; Fat 358.4g, of which saturates 119.8g; Cholesterol 1108mg; Calcium 965mg; Fibre 14.5g; Sodium 2697mg.

Toy Telephone Cake

Very small children love to chat on the phone so this cake would be sure to appeal. The child's name could be piped in a contrasting colour of icing, if you wish.

Makes one cake
15cm/6in square sponge cake
50g/2oz/¼ cup butter icing
30ml/2 tbsp apricot jam, warmed and sieve
275g/10oz marzipan
350g/12oz/2¼ cups sugarpaste icing
yellow, blue, red and black
    food colouring
liquorice strips
115g/4oz/¾ cup royal icing

Materials/equipment
20cm/8in square cake board
piping nozzle
small baking parchment piping (icing) bag
very fine writing nozzle

1 Split the cake and fill with butter icing. Trim to the shape of a telephone. Round off the edges and cut a shallow groove where the receiver rests on the telephone. Place the cake on the cake board and brush with apricot jam.

2 Cover the cake with marzipan and then cover with the sugarpaste icing. Tint half the remaining sugarpaste icing yellow, a small piece blue and the rest of the icing red.

3 To make the dial, cut out an 8cm/3½in diameter circle in yellow and a 4cm/1½in diameter circle in blue. Stamp out 12 red discs for the numbers with the end of a piping nozzle and cut out a red receiver. Position on the cake with water.

4 Twist the liquorice around to form a curly cord and use royal icing to stick one end to the telephone and the other end to the receiver. Tint the royal icing black and pipe the numbers on the discs and the child's name on the telephone.

Variation
If you like, you could cut the cake into two rectangles and make a modern push-button phone with its receiver lying beside it.

Bumble Bee Cake

The edible sugar flowers that are used to decorate this cake were bought ready-made but you can make your own if you like.

Makes one cake
20cm/8in round sponge cake
115g/4oz/½ cup butter icing
45ml/3 tbsp apricot jam, warmed and sieved
350g/12oz marzipan
500g/1¼lb/3¾ cups sugarpaste icing
yellow, black, blue and red
    food colouring
115g/4oz/¾ cup royal icing
50g/2oz/⅔ cup desiccated (dry unsweetened shredded) coconut
6 sugarpaste daisies

Materials/equipment
25cm/10in square cake board
1 paper doily
adhesive tape
1 pipe cleaner

1 Split the cake and fill with butter icing. Cut in half to make semicircles, sandwich the halves together and stand upright on the cake board. Trim the ends to shape the head and tail.

2 Brush with apricot jam and cover with a layer of marzipan. Tint 350g/12oz/2¼ cups of the sugarpaste icing yellow and use to cover the cake.

3 Tint 115g/4oz/¾ cup of the sugarpaste icing black. Roll out and cut three stripes, each 2.5 × 25cm/1 × 10in. Space evenly on the cake and stick on with water.

4 Use the remaining icing to make the eyes and mouth, tinting the icing blue for the pupils and pink for the mouth. Stick on with water.

5 Tint the coconut with a drop of yellow colouring. Cover the cake board with royal icing then sprinkle with coconut. Place the daisies on the board.

6 To make the wings, cut the doily in half, wrap each half into a cone shape and stick together with adhesive tape. Cut the pipe cleaner in half and stick the pieces into the cake, just behind the head. Place the wings over the pipe cleaners.

Telephone Energy 6250kcal/26250kJ; Protein 66.8g; Carbohydrate 929g, of which sugars 753g; Fat 277.2g, of which saturates 64.9g; Cholesterol 959mg; Calcium 896mg; Fibre 12.4g; Sodium 2871mg.
Bee Energy 7859kcal/33037kJ; Protein 74.8g; Carbohydrate 1212.8g, of which sugars 1036.8g; Fat 334.1g, of which saturates 102.8g; Cholesterol 1002mg; Calcium 1074mg; Fibre 20.7g; Sodium 3038mg.

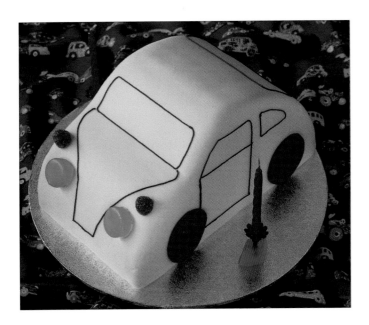

Toy Car Cake

You can add a personalized number plate with the child's name and age to the back of this bright yellow car, if you like.

Makes one car-shaped cake
20cm/8in round sponge cake
115g/4oz/¹/₂ cup butter icing
45ml/3 tbsp apricot jam, warmed and sieved
450g/1lb marzipan
500g/1¹/₄lb/3³/₄ cups sugarpaste icing

yellow, red and black food colouring
30ml/2 tbsp royal icing
red and green sweets (candies)

Materials/equipment
25cm/10in round cake board
wooden cocktail stick (toothpick)
cutters, 4cm/1¹/₂in and 2.5cm/1in
small baking parchment piping (icing) bag
very fine writing nozzle
candles and holders

1 Split the cake and fill with the butter icing. Cut in half and sandwich the halves together. Stand upright and slice off pieces to create the windscreen and bonnet. Place on the cake board and brush with apricot jam.

2 Cut a strip of marzipan to cover the top of the cake to level the joins. Then cover the cake all over with marzipan.

3 Tint 450g/1lb/3 cups of the sugarpaste icing yellow and use to cover the cake. Leave to dry overnight.

4 Mark the outlines of the doors and windows on to the car with a cocktail stick.

5 Tint the remaining sugarpaste icing red. Cut out four wheels with the larger cutter. Stick in place with water. Mark the hubs in the centre of each wheel with the smaller cutter.

6 Tint the royal icing black and pipe over the outline marks of the doors and windows.

7 Stick on sweets for headlights with royal icing. Press the candles into sweets and stick to the board with royal icing.

Fire Engine Cake

This bright and jolly fire engine is simplicity itself as the decorations are mainly bought sweets and novelties.

Makes one 20 x 10cm/ 8 x 4in cake
20cm/8in square sponge cake
115g/4oz/¹/₂ cup butter icing
45ml/3 tbsp apricot jam, warmed and sieved
350g/12oz marzipan
450g/1lb/3 cups sugarpaste icing

red, black and green food colouring
liquorice strips
115g/4oz/4 tbsp royal icing
sweets (candies)
50g/2oz/1²/₃ cup desiccated (dry unsweetened shredded) coconut

Materials/equipment
25cm/10in round cake board
small baking parchment piping (icing) bag
fine plain nozzle
2 silver bells
candles and holders

1 Split the cake and fill with the butter icing. Cut in half and sandwich one half on top of the other. Place on the cake board and brush with apricot jam.

2 Trim a thin wedge off the front edge to make a sloping windscreen. Cover with marzipan. Tint 350g/12oz/2¹/₄ cups of the sugarpaste icing red and use to cover the cake.

3 For the ladder, cut the liquorice into two strips and some short pieces for the rungs. Tint half the royal icing black and use some to stick the ladder to the top of the cake.

4 Roll out the remaining sugarpaste icing, cut out windows and stick them on to the cake with a little water.

5 Pipe around the windows in black royal icing using the fine plain nozzle. Stick sweets in place for headlights, lamps and wheels and stick the silver bells on the roof.

6 Tint the coconut green, spread a little royal icing over the cake board and sprinkle with the coconut so that it resembles grass. Stick sweets to the board with royal icing and press the candles into the sweets.

Toy Car Energy 7749kcal/32592kJ; Protein 77.1g; Carbohydrate 1225g, of which sugars 1049g; Fat 315.8g, of which saturates 77.1g; Cholesterol 1007mg; Calcium 1102mg; Fibre 15.8g; Sodium 3041mg.
Engine Energy 7662kcal/32196kJ; Protein 74.6g; Carbohydrate 1160.6g, of which sugars 984.6g; Fat 334.1g, of which saturates 102.8g; Cholesterol 1002mg; Calcium 1047mg; Fibre 20.7g; Sodium 3035mg.

Clown Face Cake

Children will love this clown whose bright, frilly collar is surprisingly simple to make.

Makes one 20cm/8in cake
20cm/8in round sponge cake
115g/4oz/½ cup butter icing
45ml/3 tbsp apricot jam, warmed and sieved
450g/1lb marzipan
450g/1lb/3 cups sugarpaste icing
115g/4oz/¾ cup royal icing

edible silver balls
red, green, blue and black food colouring

Materials/equipment
25cm/10in round cake board
small baking parchment piping (icing) bag
medium star nozzle
wooden cocktail stick (toothpick)
cotton wool (balls)
candles and holders

1 Split the cake and fill with butter icing. Place on the cake board and brush with apricot jam. Cover with a thin layer of marzipan then with white sugarpaste icing. Mark the position of the features. Using the star nozzle, pipe stars around the base of the cake with some royal icing, placing silver balls on some of the stars as you work, and leave to dry overnight.

2 Make a paper template for the face and features. Tint half the remaining sugarpaste icing pink and cut out the face base. Tint and cut out all the features, rolling a thin sausage to make the mouth. Cut thin strands for the hair. Stick all the features and hair in place with a little water.

3 Tint the remaining sugarpaste icing green. Cut three strips 4cm/1½in wide. Give each a scalloped edge and stretch by rolling a cocktail stick along it to make the frill. Stick the frills on with water and arrange, holding them in place with cotton wool (cotton balls) until dry. Put the candles at the top of the head.

Sandcastle Cake

Crushed digestive cookies (graham crackers) make realistic-looking sand when used to cover this cake.

Makes one 15cm/6in round cake
2 x 15cm/6in round sponge cakes
115g/4oz/½ cup butter icing
45ml/3 tbsp apricot jam, warmed and sieved

115g/4oz digestive cookies (graham crackers)
115g/4oz/¾ cup royal icing
blue food colouring
shrimp-shaped sweets (candies)

Materials/equipment
25cm/10in square cake board
rice paper
plastic drinking straw
4 candles and holders

1 Split both of the cakes, then sandwich all the layers together with the butter icing. Place in the centre of the cake board.

2 Cut 3cm/1¼in off the top just above the filling and set aside. Shape the rest of the cake with slightly sloping sides.

3 Cut four 3cm/1¼in cubes from the reserved piece of cake. Stick on the cubes for the turrets and brush with apricot jam.

4 Crush the digestive cookies and press through a sieve to make the "sand". Press some crushed cookies on to the cake, using a metal spatula to get a smooth finish.

5 Colour some royal icing blue and spread on the board around the sandcastle to make a moat.

6 Spread a little royal icing on to the board around the outside edge of the moat and sprinkle on some crushed cookie.

7 To make the flag, cut a small rectangle of rice paper and stick on to half a straw with water. Push the end of the straw into the cake.

8 Stick candles into each turret and arrange the shrimp-shaped sweets on the board.

> **Cook's Tip**
> For colouring sugarpaste always use paste colours, as liquid colours will make the sugarpaste too wet; this is especially important when you are making a strong or dark colour.

Sandcastle Energy 5154kcal/21569kJ; Protein 58.7g; Carbohydrate 633.9g, of which sugars 394.7g; Fat 282g, of which saturates 82.8g; Cholesterol 1049mg; Calcium 725mg; Fibre 9.7g; Sodium 3620mg.
Clown Energy 7422kcal/31187kJ; Protein 76.6g; Carbohydrate 1120.6g, of which sugars 944.6g; Fat 323.2g, of which saturates 81.8g; Cholesterol 1021mg; Calcium 1051mg; Fibre 15.8g; Sodium 3090mg.

Pinball Machine

Make this brightly coloured cake for the pinball wizard in your life.

Serves 8–10

25cm/10in square sponge cake
225g/8oz/1½ cups butter icing
45ml/3 tbsp apricot jam, warmed and sieved
450g/1lb marzipan
115g/4oz/¾ cup royal icing
450g/1lb/3 cups sugarpaste icing

yellow, blue, green and red food colouring
sweets (candies)
2 ice cream fan wafers

Materials/equipment

20cm/8in round cake tin (pan)
30cm/12in square cake board
small baking parchment piping (icing) bag
no.1 writing nozzle

1 Split the sponge cake and fill with butter icing. Cut off a 5cm/2in strip from one side and reserve. Cut a thin wedge off the top of the cake, diagonally along its length, to end just above the halfway mark. This will give a sloping table.

2 Using the round cake tin (pan) as a guide, cut the reserved strip of cake to make a rounded back for the pinball table. Brush the back and table with apricot jam, then cover separately with marzipan and place on the board. Stick them together with royal icing. Leave to dry overnight.

3 Cover with a layer of sugarpaste icing and leave to dry. Use a template to mark out the pinball design on the top of the cake. Colour the remaining sugarpaste icing yellow, blue, green and pink. Roll out the colours and cut to fit the design. Stick on the pieces with water and smooth the joins carefully.

4 Using royal icing, stick sweets on the cake as buffers, flippers, lights and knobs. Roll some blue sugarpaste icing into a long sausage and use to add an edge to the pinball table and divider.

5 Cut zigzags for the sides and a screen for the back. Stick on with water. Stick the ice cream fans at the back of the screen. Load the pinball sweets. Add the child's name on the screen with iced letters or piping.

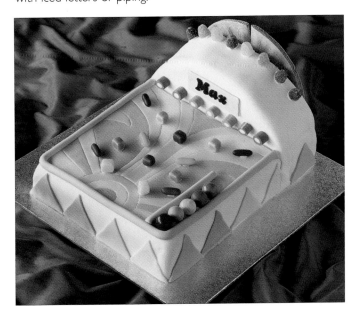

Pirate's Hat

If you prefer, buy ready-made black sugarpaste icing for the hat rather than tinting it yourself.

Serves 8–10

25cm/10in round sponge cake
225g/8oz/1 cup butter icing
45ml/3 tbsp apricot jam, warmed and sieved
450g/1lb marzipan

500g/1¼lb/3¾ cups sugarpaste icing
black and gold food colouring
chocolate money
jewel sweets (candies)

Materials/equipment

30cm/12in square cake board
fine paintbrush

1 Split the cake and fill with butter icing. Cut in half and sandwich the halves together. Stand upright diagonally across the cake board and cut shallow dips from each end to create the brim of the hat. Brush with apricot jam.

2 Cut a strip of marzipan to lay over the top of the cake. Then cover the whole of the cake with a layer of marzipan. Tint 450g/1lb/3 cups of the sugarpaste icing black. Use to cover the cake.

3 Roll out the remaining sugarpaste icing and cut some 1cm/½in strips. Stick the strips in place with a little water around the brim of the pirate's hat and mark with the prongs of a fork to make a braid.

4 Make a skull and crossbones template and mark on to the hat. Cut the shapes out of the white sugarpaste icing and stick in place with water. Paint the braid strip gold and arrange the chocolate money and jewel sweets on the board.

> **Variation**
> *To make a sandy board for your pirate's hat to rest on, simply cover the board with a thin layer of butter icing and sprinkle finely crushed cookies over.*

Pinball Energy 792kcal/3320kJ; Protein 6.5g; Carbohydrate 106.9g, of which sugars 93.7g; Fat 40.5g, of which saturates 15.7g; Cholesterol 115mg; Calcium 97mg; Fibre 1.4g; Sodium 345mg.
Hat Energy 699kcal/2938kJ; Protein 6.5g; Carbohydrate 106.8g, of which sugars 93.6g; Fat 30.3g, of which saturates 9.2g; Cholesterol 88mg; Calcium 95mg; Fibre 1.4g; Sodium 269mg.

Noah's Ark Cake

This charming cake is decorated with small animals, about 4cm/1½in high, available from cake decorating stores.

450g/1lb marzipan
450g/1lb/3 cups sugarpaste icing
brown, yellow and blue
food colouring
115g/4oz/¾ cup royal icing
chocolate mint stick

**Makes one 20 x 13cm/
8 x 5in cake**
20cm/8in square sponge cake
115g/4oz/½ cup butter icing
45ml/3 tbsp apricot jam, warmed
and sieved

Materials/equipment
25cm/10in square cake board
skewer
rice paper
small animal cake ornaments

I Split the cake and fill with butter icing. Cut off and set aside a 7.5cm/3in strip. Shape the remaining piece of cake to form the hull of the boat. Place diagonally on the cake board.

2 Use the set-aside piece of cake to cut a rectangle 10 x 6cm/ 4 x 2½in for the cabin and a triangular piece for the roof. Sandwich the roof and the cabin with butter icing or apricot jam.

3 Cover the three pieces with a layer of marzipan. Tint the sugarpaste icing brown and use most of it to cover the hull and cabin.

4 Use the remaining brown icing to make a long sausage. Stick around the edge of the hull with water. Mark planks with the back of a knife. Leave to dry overnight.

5 Tint one-third of the royal icing yellow and spread it over the cabin roof with a metal spatula. Roughen it with a skewer to create a thatch effect.

6 Tint the remaining royal icing blue and spread over the cake board, making rough waves. Cut a small triangle out of rice paper to make a flag. Stick the flag on to the chocolate mint stick and press on the back of the boat. Stick the small animals on to the boat with a dab of icing.

Balloons Cake

This is a simple yet effective cake design that can be adapted to suit any age.

red, blue, green and yellow
food colouring
115g/4oz/¾ cup royal icing

**Makes one 20cm/8in
round cake**
20cm/8in round cake
115g/4oz/½ cup butter icing
45ml/3 tbsp apricot jam, warmed
and sieved
450g/1lb marzipan
450g/1lb/3 cups sugarpaste icing

Materials/equipment
25cm/10in round cake board
2 small baking parchment piping
(icing) bags
fine plain and medium
star nozzles
1.5m/1½yd blue ribbon
candles and holders

I Split the cake and fill with butter icing. Place on the cake board and brush with apricot jam. Cover with a layer of marzipan then sugarpaste icing.

2 Divide the remaining sugarpaste icing into three pieces and tint pink, blue and green. Make a balloon template, roll out the coloured sugarpaste and cut out one balloon from each colour. Stick on to the cake with water and rub the edges gently to round them off.

3 Tint the royal icing yellow. With a plain nozzle, pipe on the balloon strings and then pipe a number on to each balloon. Using the star nozzle, pipe a border around the base of the cake.

4 Tie the ribbon around the cake and place the candles in their holders on top.

> **Cook's Tip**
> *If you are not a fan of marzipan, it is not necessary to cover any sponge cake with marzipan that you will be covering with sugarpaste. Simply spread a thin layer of butter icing over the cake first to stick the sugarpaste.*

Ark Energy 6888kcal/28960kJ; Protein 70.3g; Carbohydrate 1068.1g, of which sugars 914.1g; Fat 288.6g, of which saturates 71.3g; Cholesterol 890mg; Calcium 980mg; Fibre 14.9g; Sodium 2709mg.
Balloons Energy 6888kcal/28960kJ; Protein 70.3g; Carbohydrate 1068.1g, of which sugars 914.1g; Fat 288.6g, of which saturates 71.3g; Cholesterol 890mg; Calcium 980mg; Fibre 14.9g; Sodium 2709mg.

Horse Stencil Cake

Make this cake for a horse lover. You can find stencils at art stores or sugarcraft suppliers. Use a fairly dry brush when painting the design on this cake and allow each colour to dry before adding the next.

Makes one 20cm/8in round cake
20cm/8in round sponge cake
115g/4oz/½ cup butter icing
45ml/3 tbsp apricot jam, warmed and sieved
450g/1lb marzipan
450g/1lb/3 cups sugarpaste icing
yellow, brown, black, red, orange and blue food colouring

Materials/equipment
25cm/10in round cake board
fine paintbrush
spoon with decorative handle
horse and letter stencils
1.5m/1½yd blue ribbon
candles and holders

1 Split the cake and fill with butter icing. Place on the cake board and brush with apricot jam. Cover with a layer of marzipan.

2 Tint the sugarpaste icing yellow, roll out and use to cover the cake. Roll the trimmings into two thin ropes, long enough to go halfway round the cake. Brush water in a thin band around the base of the cake, lay on the ropes and press together. Pattern the border with the decorative spoon handle. Leave to dry overnight.

3 If you do not have a stencil, make one by tracing a simple design on to a piece of thin card (stock) and cutting out the shape with a craft (utility) knife.

4 Place the horse stencil in the centre of the cake. With a fairly dry brush, gently paint over the parts you want to colour first. Allow these to dry completely before adding another colour, otherwise the colours will run into each other. Clean the stencil between colours.

5 When the horse picture is finished carefully paint on the lettering. Tie the ribbon around the side of the cake and place the candles in their holders on top.

Dolls' House Cake

This is a very straightforward cake to make and is decorated with store-bought flowers, or you can make your own if you like.

Serves 8–10
25cm/10in square sponge cake
225g/8oz/1 cup butter icing
45ml/3 tbsp apricot jam, warmed and sieved
450g/1lb marzipan
450g/1lb/3 cups sugarpaste icing
red, yellow, blue, black, green and gold food colouring
115g/4oz/¾ cup royal icing

Materials/equipment
30cm/12in square cake board
pastry wheel
large and fine paintbrushes
wooden cocktail stick (toothpick)
small baking parchment piping (icing) bags
fine writing nozzle
flower decorations

1 Split the cake and fill with butter icing. Cut triangles off two corners and use the pieces to make a chimney. Place on the cake board and brush with apricot jam. Cover with a layer of marzipan then sugarpaste icing.

2 Mark the roof with a pastry wheel and the chimney with the back of a knife. Paint the chimney red and the roof yellow.

3 Tint 25g/1oz/2 tbsp of sugarpaste icing red and cut out a 7.5 x 12cm/3 x 4½in door. Tint enough sugarpaste icing blue to make a fanlight. Stick to the cake with water.

4 Mark windows, 6cm/2½in square, with a cocktail stick. Paint on curtains with blue food colouring. Tint half the royal icing black and pipe around the windows and the door.

5 Tint the remaining royal icing green. Pipe the flower stems and leaves under the windows with the fine writing nozzle and the climber up on to the roof. Stick the flowers in place with a little icing and pipe green flower centres.

6 Pipe the house number or child's age on the door and add a knocker and handle. Leave to dry for 1 hour, then paint with gold food colouring.

Horse Energy 6691kcal/28120kJ; Protein 70g; Carbohydrate 1015.9g, of which sugars 861.9g; Fat 288.6g, of which saturates 71.3g; Cholesterol 890mg; Calcium 953mg; Fibre 14.9g; Sodium 2706mg.
House Energy 832kcal/3496kJ; Protein 7.8g; Carbohydrate 127.8g, of which sugars 110.2g; Fat 35.7g, of which saturates 10.3g; Cholesterol 111mg; Calcium 114mg; Fibre 1.6g; Sodium 335mg.

Treasure Chest Cake

Allow yourself a few days before the party to make this cake as the lock and handles need to dry for 48 hours.

**Makes one 20 x 10cm/
8 x 4in cake**
20cm/8in square sponge cake
115g/4oz/½ cup butter icing
45ml/3 tbsp apricot jam, warmed
    and sieved
350g/12oz marzipan
400g/14oz/generous 2½ cups
    sugarpaste icing

brown and green food colouring
50g/2oz/⅔ cup desiccated
    (dry unsweetened
    shredded) coconut
115g/4oz/¾ cup royal icing
edible gold dusting powder
edible silver balls
chocolate money

Materials/equipment
30cm/12in round
    cake board
fine paintbrush

1 Split the cake and fill with butter icing. Cut the cake in half and sandwich the halves on top of each other with butter icing. Place on the cake board.

2 Shape the top of the cake into a rounded lid (you could make a paper template to use on the ends if you like) and brush with apricot jam. Cover with a layer of marzipan. Tint 350g/12oz/2¼ cups of the sugarpaste icing brown and use to cover the cake.

3 Use the brown sugarpaste trimmings to make strips. Stick on to the chest with water. Mark the lid with a sharp knife. Tint the coconut with a few drops of green colouring. Spread a little royal icing over the cake board and press the green coconut lightly into it to make the grass.

4 From the remaining sugarpaste icing, cut out the padlock and two handles. Cut a keyhole shape from the padlock and shape the handles over a small box. Leave to dry for 48 hours. Stick the padlock and handles in place with royal icing and paint them with the gold dusting powder. Stick silver balls on to look like nails. Arrange the chocolate money around the chest on the board.

Lion Cake

For an animal lover or a celebration cake for a Leo horoscope sign, this cake is ideal. The shaggy mane is simply made with grated marzipan.

**Makes one 28 x 23cm/
11 x 9in oval cake**
25 x 30cm/10 x 12in sponge cake
350g/12oz/1½ cups orange-
    flavour butter icing

orange and red food colouring
675g/1½lb yellow marzipan
50g/2oz/generous 4 tbsp
    sugarpaste icing
red and orange liquorice bootlaces
long and round marshmallows

Materials/equipment
30cm/12in square
    cake board
small heart-shaped cutter

1 With the flat side of the cake uppermost, cut it to make an oval shape with an uneven scallop design around the edge. Turn the cake over and trim the top level.

2 Place the cake on the cake board. Tint the butter icing orange and use it to cover the cake.

3 Roll 115g/4oz/¾ cup of marzipan to a 15cm/6in square. Place in the centre of the cake for the lion's face.

4 Grate the remaining marzipan and use to cover the sides and the top of the cake up to the face panel.

5 Tint the sugarpaste icing red. Use the heart-shaped cutter to stamp out the lion's nose and position on the cake with water.

6 Roll the remaining red icing into two thin, short strands to make the lion's mouth, and stick on with water.

7 Cut the liquorice into graduated lengths, and place on the cake for the whiskers.

8 Use two flattened round marshmallows for the eyes and two snipped long ones for the eyebrows and place in position on the cake.

Chest Energy 6600kcal/27758kJ; Protein 62.7g; Carbohydrate 1045.1g, of which sugars 891.1g; Fat 269.6g, of which saturates 69.7g; Cholesterol 890mg; Calcium 921mg; Fibre 12g; Sodium 2684mg.
Lion Energy 8108kcal/33970kJ; Protein 87.9g; Carbohydrate 1043.6g, of which sugars 867.6g; Fat 426.6g, of which saturates 131.5g; Cholesterol 1215mg; Calcium 1109mg; Fibre 20g; Sodium 3662mg.

Train Cake

This cake is made in a train-shaped tin, so all you need to do is decorate it.

Makes one train-shaped cake
train-shaped sponge cake, about 35cm/14in long
675g/1½lb/3 cups butter icing
yellow food colouring
red liquorice bootlaces

90–120ml/6–8 tbsp coloured vermicelli
4 liquorice wheels

Materials/equipment
25 x 38cm/10 x 15in cake board
2 fabric piping bags
fine round and small star nozzles
pink and white cotton wool (cotton balls)

1 Slice off the top surface of the cake to make it flat. Place diagonally on the cake board.

2 Tint the butter icing yellow. Use half of it to cover the cake.

3 Using a round piping nozzle and a quarter of the remaining butter icing, pipe a straight double border around the top edge of the cake.

4 Place the red liquorice bootlaces on the piped border. Snip the bootlaces around the curves on the train.

5 Using a small star nozzle and the remaining butter icing, pipe small stars over the top of the cake. Add extra liquorice and piping, if you like. Use a metal spatula to press on the coloured vermicelli all around the sides of the cake.

6 Pull a couple of balls of cotton wool apart for the steam and stick on to the cake board with butter icing. Press the liquorice wheels in place for the wheels.

> **Cook's Tip**
> *You can buy novelty cake tins (pans) in all kinds of shapes or hire them from specialist cake suppliers if you are not confident that you could shape your cake well.*

Number 7 Cake

Any combination of colours will work well for this cake with its marbled effect.

Makes one 30cm/12in long cake
23 x 30cm/9 x 12in sponge cake
350g/12oz/1½ cups orange-flavour butter icing
60ml/4 tbsp apricot jam, warmed and sieved

675g/1½lb/4½ cups sugarpaste icing
blue and green food colouring
rice paper sweets

Materials/equipment
25 x 33cm/10 x 13in cake board
small "7" cutter

1 Place the cake flat side up and cut out the number seven. Slice the cake horizontally, sandwich together with the butter icing and place on the board.

2 Brush the cake evenly with apricot jam. Divide the sugarpaste icing into three and tint one of the pieces blue and another green. Set aside 50g/2oz/scant ½ cup from each of the coloured icings. Knead together the large pieces of blue and green icing with the third piece of white icing to marble. Use to cover the cake.

3 Immediately after covering, use the "7" cutter to remove several sugarpaste shapes in a random pattern from the covered cake.

4 Roll out the reserved blue and green sugarpaste icing and stamp out shapes with the same cutter. Use these to fill the stamped-out shapes from the cake. Decorate the board with some rice paper sweets.

> **Cook's Tip**
> *You could make any number out of sponge cake using round and/or rectangular cakes (or you could hire a purpose-made tin (pan) instead). Use two cakes for numbers in their teens and over.*

Train Energy 8457kcal/35303kJ; Protein 72.7g; Carbohydrate 921.4g, of which sugars 654.2g; Fat 521.7g, of which saturates 216.3g; Cholesterol 1759mg; Calcium 1009mg; Fibre 10.1g; Sodium 5132mg.
Number 7 Energy 8883kcal/37220kJ; Protein 56.1g; Carbohydrate 1193.9g, of which sugars 1017.9g; Fat 464.2g, of which saturates 202.7g; Cholesterol 1535mg; Calcium 984mg; Fibre 7.2g; Sodium 4485mg.

Musical Cake

Creating a sheet of music requires delicate piping work, so it is best to practise first.

Makes one 20 x 25cm/ 8 x 10in cake
25cm/10in square sponge cake
225g/8oz/1 cup butter icing
45ml/3 tbsp apricot jam, warmed and sieved
450g/1lb marzipan
450g/1lb/3 cups sugarpaste icing

115g/4oz/³⁄₄ cup royal icing
black food colouring

Materials/equipment
25 x 30cm/10 x 12in cake board
wooden cocktail stick (toothpick)
2 small baking parchment piping (icing) bags
very fine writing and fine shell nozzles
1.5m/1¹⁄₂yd red ribbon

1 Split the cake and fill with a little butter icing. Cut a 5cm/2in strip off one side of the cake. Place the cake on the cake board and brush with apricot jam. Cover with a layer of marzipan then sugarpaste icing. Leave to dry overnight.

2 Make a template for the sheet of music and the child's name. Lay the template on the cake and trace over the music and name with a cocktail stick. Using white royal icing and a very fine writing nozzle, begin by piping the lines and bars. Leave to dry.

3 Tint the remaining icing black and pipe the clefs, name and notes. With the shell nozzle, pipe a royal icing border around the base of the cake. Finally, tie a ribbon around the side.

Cook's Tip
Find a sheet of simple music to copy for the cake – a beginner's piano book would be ideal. Practise writing the treble clef on paper first, and always start at the centre of the symbol: make a dot and then curl round to the right; curl to the left and then up and out to the right to make the loop at the top; finish with the downward line that ends with a curl to the left at the base of the symbol.

Magic Rabbit Cake

Delight a child with this cute rabbit bursting out of a hat.

Makes one 15cm/6in tall round cake
2 x 15cm/6in round cakes
225g/8oz/1 cup butter icing
115g/4oz/³⁄₄ cup royal icing
45ml/3 tbsp apricot jam, warmed and sieved
675g/1¹⁄₂lb marzipan

675g/1¹⁄₂lb/4¹⁄₂ cups sugarpaste icing
black and pink food colouring
edible silver balls

Materials/equipment
25cm/10in square cake board
2 small baking parchment piping (icing) bags
medium star nozzle
1.5m/1¹⁄₂yd pink ribbon

1 Split the cakes and fill with butter icing, then sandwich them one on top of the other. Stick on the centre of the cake board with a little royal icing. Brush with apricot jam. Use 450g/1lb/ 3 cups of the marzipan to cover the cake.

2 Tint the sugarpaste icing grey. Use about two-thirds of it to cover the cake. For the hat's brim roll out the remaining grey sugarpaste to a 20cm/8in round. Cut a 15cm/6in circle from its centre. Lower the brim over the cake. Shape the brim sides over wooden spoon handles until dry.

3 Cut a cross in the 15cm/6in grey circle and place on the hat. Curl the triangles over a wooden spoon handle to shape. Smooth the join at the top and sides of the hat using the warmth of your hand

4 Tint the remaining marzipan pink and make the rabbit's head, about 5cm/2in wide with a pointed face. Mark the position of the eyes, nose and mouth. Leave to dry overnight.

5 Stick the rabbit in the centre of the hat with a little royal icing. Pipe a border of royal icing around the top and base of the hat and decorate with silver balls while still wet. Tint the remaining royal icing black and pipe the rabbit's eyes and mouth. Tie the ribbon around the hat.

Musical Energy 7924kcal/33281kJ; Protein 77.1g; Carbohydrate 1173.1g, of which sugars 997g; Fat 356.9g, of which saturates 103.1g; Cholesterol 1108mg; Calcium 1084mg; Fibre 15.8g; Sodium 3341mg.
Rabbit Energy 10054kcal/42289kJ; Protein 96.3g; Carbohydrate 1586.6g, of which sugars 1388.6g; Fat 412.7g, of which saturates 111.2g; Cholesterol 1220mg; Calcium 1408mg; Fibre 20.9g; Sodium 3724mg.

Nurse's Kit Cake

The box is easy to make and is simply filled with toys from a nurse's or doctor's set. It's sure to delight any budding medical professionals.

Makes one 20 x 17cm/ 8 x 6½in cake
35 x 20cm/14 x 8in chocolate sponge cake

120ml/4fl oz/½ cup apricot jam, warmed and sieved
675g/1½lb/4½ cups sugarpaste icing
red food colouring

Materials/equipment
25cm/10in square cake board
selection of toy medical equipment

1 Place the cake dome-side down and cut in half widthways.

2 To make the base of the nurse's box, turn one cake half, dome-side up, and hollow out the centre to a depth of 1cm/½in, leaving a 1cm/½in border on the three uncut edges. Brush the tops and sides of both cake halves with jam.

3 Tint 150g/5oz/scant 1 cup sugarpaste icing deep pink. Use a little to make a small handle for the box. Wrap in clear film (plastic wrap) and set aside. Cover the cake board with the remainder of the pink icing. Tint 25g/1oz/2 tbsp of the sugarpaste icing red. Cover with clear film and set aside.

4 Tint the remaining icing light pink and divide into two portions, one slightly bigger than the other. Roll out the bigger portion and use to cover the base of the box, easing it into the hollow and along the edges. Trim, then position the base on the cake board.

5 Roll out the other portion and use to cover the lid of the box. Trim, then place on top of the base at a slight angle.

6 Stick the handle to the base of the box using water. Cut a small cross out of red icing and stick it on the lid. Place a few toy items of medical equipment under the lid, protruding slightly. Arrange some more items around the board and cake.

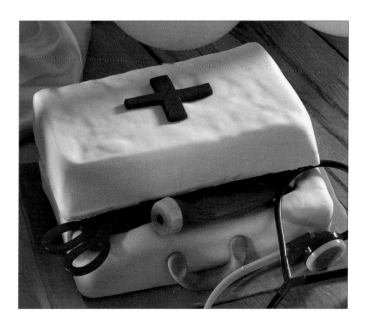

Ballerina Cake

Use flower cutters with ejectors to make the tiny flowers for this cake.

Makes one 20cm/8in round cake
20cm/8in round sponge cake
115g/4oz/½ cup butter icing
45ml/3 tbsp apricot jam, warmed and sieved
450g/1lb marzipan
450g/1lb/3 cups sugarpaste icing
pink, yellow, blue and green food colouring
115g/4oz/¾ cup royal icing

Materials/equipment
25cm/10in round cake board
small flower cutter
small circle cutter
wooden cocktail stick (toothpick)
cotton wool (cotton balls)
fine paintbrush
3 small baking parchment piping (icing) bags
fine shell nozzle
1.5m/1½yd pink ribbon

1 Split the cake and fill with butter icing. Place on the board and brush with apricot jam. Cover with marzipan then sugarpaste icing. Leave to dry overnight. Divide the rest of the sugarpaste into three. Tint flesh tone, light pink and dark pink. Stamp out 15 pale pink flowers. Leave to dry.

2 Make a template of the ballerina. Mark her position on the cake. Cut out a flesh-tone body and dark pink bodice. Stick on with water, rounding off the edges.

3 Cut two dark pink underskirts, a pale pink top skirt and a dark pink bodice extension to make the tutu. Stamp out hollow, fluted circles, divide the circles into four and frill the fluted edges with a cocktail stick. Stick the tutu in place, supported with cotton wool. Cut out and stick on pale pink shoes. Leave to dry overnight.

4 Paint the ballerina's face and hair. Position 12 hoop and three headdress flowers. Tint some royal icing green and dark pink to complete the flowers and ballet shoes. Pipe a border around the base with the shell nozzle. Tie the pink ribbon around the outside of the cake.

Nurse's Kit Energy 5993kcal/25233kJ; Protein 69.3g; Carbohydrate 954.4g, of which sugars 759.1g; Fat 237.6g, of which saturates 0g; Cholesterol 0mg; Calcium 901mg; Fibre 0g; Sodium 3929mg.
Ballerina Energy 6771kcal/28459kJ; Protein 70g; Carbohydrate 1037.1g, of which sugars 883g; Fat 288.6g, of which saturates 71.3g; Cholesterol 890mg; Calcium 975mg; Fibre 14.9g; Sodium 2696mg.

Monsters on the Moon

A great cake for little monsters! This cake is covered with a sugar frosting and is best eaten on the day of making.

Serves 12–15
1 quantity quick-mix sponge cake
500g/1¼lb/3¾ cups sugarpaste icing
black food colouring
225g/8oz marzipan

edible silver glitter powder (optional)
375g/12oz/1¾ cups caster (superfine) sugar
2 egg whites
60ml/4 tbsp water

Materials/equipment
ovenproof wok
various sizes of plain round and star cutters
30cm/12in round cake board
small monster toys

1 Preheat the oven to 180°C/350°F/Gas 4. Grease the wok and line with baking parchment. Spoon in the cake mixture and smooth the surface.

2 Bake in the centre of the oven for 35–40 minutes. Leave for 5 minutes, then turn out on to a rack and peel off the paper. Leave to cool completely.

3 With the cake dome-side up, use the round cutters to cut out craters. Press in the cutters to about 2.5cm/1in deep, then remove and cut the craters out of the cake with a knife.

4 Use 115g/4oz/¾ cup of the sugarpaste icing to cover the cake, pulling off small pieces and pressing them in uneven strips around the edges of the craters.

5 Tint the remaining sugarpaste icing black. Roll out and cover the board. Stamp out stars and replace with marzipan stars of the same size. Dust with glitter powder, if using, and place on the board.

6 Put the sugar, egg whites and water in a heatproof bowl over a pan of simmering water. Beat until thick and peaky. Spoon the icing over the cake, swirling it into the craters and peaking it unevenly. Sprinkle over the silver glitter powder, if using, then position the monsters on the cake.

Circus Cake

This colourful design is easy to achieve and is sure to delight young children.

Makes one 20cm/8in cake
20cm/8in round sponge cake
115g/4oz/½ cup butter icing
45ml/3 tbsp apricot jam, warmed and sieved
450g/1lb marzipan
450g/1lb/3 cups sugarpaste icing
red and blue food colouring

115g/4oz/¾ cup royal icing
edible silver balls
3 digestive cookies (graham crackers)

Materials/equipment
25cm/10in round cake board
small baking parchment piping (icing) bag
small star nozzle
5cm/2in plastic circus ornaments

1 Split the cake and fill with butter icing. Place on the cake board and brush with apricot jam. Cover with a layer of marzipan then sugarpaste icing.

2 Tint 115g/4oz/¾ cup sugarpaste icing pink, then roll into a rope and stick around the top edge of the cake with a little water.

3 Tint half the remaining sugarpaste icing red and half blue. Roll out each colour and cut into twelve 2.5cm/1in squares. Stick the squares alternately at an angle around the side of the cake with a little water. Using the star nozzle, pipe stars around the base of the cake with royal icing and stick in the edible silver balls.

4 Crush the digestive cookies by pressing through a sieve to make the "sand" for the circus ring. Sprinkle the "sand" over the top of the cake and place small circus ornaments on top.

Variation
Instead of a circus you could make the cake into an ice rink. Cover the top of the cake with very pale blue marbled sugarpaste (by colouring two or three balls of sugarpaste different shades of pale blue and then rolling them out with the white to get a marbled effect). Then buy some ice skaters to go on the top.

Monsters Energy 438kcal/1850kJ; Protein 3.9g; Carbohydrate 81.9g, of which sugars 73.1g; Fat 12.8g, of which saturates 2.5g; Cholesterol 45mg; Calcium 63mg; Fibre 0.6g; Sodium 144mg.
Circus Energy 6888kcal/28960kJ; Protein 70.3g; Carbohydrate 1068.1g, of which sugars 914.1g; Fat 288.6g, of which saturates 71.3g; Cholesterol 890mg; Calcium 980mg; Fibre 14.9g; Sodium 2709mg.

Frog Prince Cake

Our happy frog will bring a smile to any young child's face – and will probably even get a kiss!

Serves 8–10
20cm/8in round sponge cake
115g/4oz/½ cup butter icing
45ml/3 tbsp apricot jam, warmed
   and sieved
450g/1lb marzipan

cornflour (cornstarch), for dusting
500g/1¼lb/3¾ cups
   sugarpaste icing
115g/4oz/¾ cup royal icing
green, red, black and gold
   food colouring

Materials/equipment
25cm/10in square cake board
glass
fine paintbrush

1 Split the cake and fill with butter icing. Cut in half and sandwich the halves together with apricot jam. Stand upright diagonally across the cake board. Brush the cake with apricot jam and cover with marzipan.

2 Tint 450g/1lb/3 cups of the sugarpaste icing green and cover the cake. Roll the remaining green sugarpaste icing into 1cm/½in diameter sausages. You will need two folded 20cm/8in lengths for the back legs and 14 10cm/4in lengths for the front legs and feet. Stick in place with a little royal icing. Roll balls for the eyes and stick in place.

3 Roll out the reserved sugarpaste icing and cut a 5 x 19cm/2 x 7½in strip. Cut out triangles along one edge to make the crown shape. Wrap around a glass dusted with cornflour and moisten the edges to join. Leave to dry.

4 Cut a 10cm/4in circle for the white shirt. Stick in place and trim the base edge. Cut white circles and stick to the eyes.

5 Tint a little sugarpaste pink, roll into a sausage and stick on for the mouth. Tint the rest black and use for the pupils and the bow tie. Stick in place.

6 Paint the crown with gold food colouring, leave to dry, then stick into position with royal icing.

Ladybird Cake

Children will love this colourful and appealing ladybird, and it is very simple to make.

Serves 10–12
3-egg quantity quick-mix
   sponge cake
175g/6oz butter icing

60ml/4 tbsp lemon curd, warmed
icing (confectioners') sugar,
   for dusting
1kg/2¼lb/6¾ cups
   sugarpaste icing
red, black and green food colourings
5 marshmallows
50g/2oz marzipan
2 pipe cleaners

1 Preheat the oven to 180°C/350°F/Gas 4. Grease and line the base of a 1.2 litre/2 pint/5 cup ovenproof bowl. Spoon in the cake mixture and smooth the surface. Bake for 55–60 minutes, or until a skewer inserted into the centre comes out clean. Cool.

2 Cut the cake in half crossways and sandwich together with the butter icing. Cut vertically through the cake, about a third of the way in. Brush both pieces with the lemon curd.

3 Colour 450g/1lb/3 cups of the sugarpaste icing red. Dust a work surface with icing sugar and roll out the icing to about 5mm/¼in thick. Use to cover the larger piece of cake to make the body. Using a wooden skewer, make an indentation down the centre for the wings. Colour 350g/12oz of the sugarpaste icing black, roll out three-quarters and use to cover the smaller piece of cake for the head. Place both cakes on a cake board, press together.

4 Roll out 50g/2oz/4 tbsp icing and cut out two 5cm/2in circles for the eyes, stick to the head with water. Roll out the remaining black icing and cut out eight 4cm/1½in circles. Use two of these for the eyes and stick the others on to the body.

5 Colour some icing green and squeeze through a garlic press to make grass. Flatten the marshmallows and stick a marzipan round in the centre of each. Colour the pipe cleaners black and press a ball of black icing on to the end of each for the feelers. Arrange grass on the board, with the decorations.

Frog Energy 681kcal/2862kJ; Protein 7g; Carbohydrate 104.7g, of which sugars 89.3g; Fat 28.9g, of which saturates 7.1g; Cholesterol 89mg; Calcium 97mg; Fibre 1.5g; Sodium 271mg.
Ladybird Energy 539kcal/2270kJ; Protein 3.8g; Carbohydrate 92.7g, of which sugars 80.2g; Fat 19.5g, of which saturates 6.3g; Cholesterol 70mg; Calcium 69mg; Fibre 0.5g; Sodium 209mg.

Spaceship Cake

The perfect cake for all would-be astronauts.

Serves 10–12
25cm/10in square sponge cake
225g/8oz/1 cup butter icing
60ml/4 tbsp apricot jam, warmed and sieved

350g/12oz marzipan
450g/1lb/3 cups sugarpaste icing
blue, red and black food colouring

Materials/equipment
30cm/12in square cake board
silver candles and holders
gold paper stars

1 Split the sponge cake and fill with butter icing. Cut a 10cm/4in wide piece diagonally across the middle of the cake, about 25cm/10in long. Shape the nose end and straighten the other end.

2 From the off-cuts make three 7.5cm/3in triangles for the wings and top of the ship. Cut two smaller triangles for the booster jets.

3 Position the main body, wings and top of the cake diagonally across the cake board. Add extra pieces of cake in front of the triangle on top of the cake to shape it as shown in the picture.

4 Brush the cake and booster jets with apricot jam, then cover with a layer of marzipan and sugarpaste icing.

5 Divide the remaining sugarpaste icing into three. Tint blue, pink and black. Roll out the blue icing and cut it into 1cm/½in strips. Stick around the base of the cake with water and outline the boosters. Cut a 2.5cm/1in strip and stick down the centre of the spaceship.

6 Roll out the pink and black sugarpaste icing separately and cut shapes, numbers and the child's name to finish the design. When complete, position the boosters.

7 Make small cubes with the off-cuts of sugarpaste icing and use to stick the candles to the cake board. Decorate the board with gold stars.

Racing Track Cake

This simple cake will delight eight-year-old racing car enthusiasts.

Serves 10–12
2 x 15cm/6in round sponge cakes
115g/4oz/½ cup butter icing
60ml/4 tbsp apricot jam, warmed and sieved
450g/1lb marzipan
500g/1¼lb/3¾ cups sugarpaste icing

blue and red food colouring
115g/4oz/¾ cup royal icing

Materials/equipment
25 x 35cm/10 x 14in cake board
5cm/2in fluted cutter
2 small baking parchment piping (icing) bags
medium star and medium plain nozzles
8 candles and holders
2 small toy racing cars

1 Split the cakes and fill with a little butter icing. Cut off a 1cm/½in piece from the side of each cake and place the cakes on the cake board, cut edges together.

2 Brush the cake with apricot jam and cover with a layer of marzipan. Tint 450g/1lb/3 cups of the sugarpaste icing pale blue and use to cover the cake.

3 Mark a 5cm/2in circle in the centre of each cake. Roll out the remaining white sugarpaste icing, cut out two fluted 5cm/2in circles and stick them in the marked spaces.

4 Tint the royal icing red. Pipe a shell border around the base of the cake using the star nozzle.

5 Pipe a track for the cars using the plain nozzle and stick the candles into the two white circles. Place the cars on the track.

Variation
You can adapt this cake by changing the colours or decorating with other shapes, such as colouring the sugarpaste green and adding some toy horses; perhaps add some cut-out flowers to make it look like a meadow.

Spaceship Energy 320kcal/1350kJ; Protein 1.8g; Carbohydrate 58.1g, of which sugars 58.1g; Fat 10.6g, of which saturates 4.6g; Cholesterol 18mg; Calcium 39mg; Fibre 0.6g; Sodium 60mg.
Racing Track Energy 624kcal/2624kJ; Protein 6.5g; Carbohydrate 95.7g, of which sugars 81g; Fat 26.6g, of which saturates 6.4g; Cholesterol 83mg; Calcium 89mg; Fibre 1.4g; Sodium 254mg.

Floating Balloons Cake

Make brightly coloured balloons to float above the cake from eggshells covered in sugarpaste.

Makes one 20cm/8in round cake

20cm/8in round sponge or fruit cake, covered with 800g/1¾lb marzipan if you like
900g/2lb/6 cups sugarpaste icing
red, green and yellow food colouring
3 eggs
2 egg whites
450g/1lb/4 cups icing (confectioners') sugar

Materials/equipment
25cm/10in round cake board
3 bamboo skewers, 25cm/10in, 24cm/9½in and 23cm/9in long
small star cutter
baking parchment piping bags
fine writing nozzle
1m/1yd fine coloured ribbon
candles

1 Using a skewer, pierce the eggs and carefully empty the contents. Wash and dry the shells.

2 Place the cake on the board. Tint 50g/2oz/scant ½ cup of the sugarpaste icing red, 50g/2oz/scant ½ cup green and 115g/4oz/1 cup yellow. Cover the cake with the remaining icing. Use just under half the yellow icing to cover the board.

3 Cover the eggshells carefully with the tinted sugarpaste and insert a bamboo skewer in each. Use the trimmings to stamp out a star shape of each colour. Thread on to the skewers for the balloon knots.

4 Trace 16 balloon shapes on to baking paper. Beat the egg whites with the icing sugar until smooth, and divide between four bowls. Leave one white and tint the others red, green and yellow. With the fine writing nozzle and white icing, trace around the balloon shapes. Thin the tinted icings with water. Fill the balloon shapes using snipped piping bags. Dry overnight.

5 Stick the balloon shapes around the side of the cake with icing. Pipe white balloon strings. Push the large balloons into the centre and decorate with the ribbon. Push the candles into the icing around the edge.

Number 6 Cake

Boys and girls will love this delightful cake.

Serves 10–12

15cm/6in round and 15cm/6in square sponge cakes
115g/4oz/½ cup butter icing
60ml/4 tbsp apricot jam, warmed and sieved
450g/1lb marzipan
500g/1¼lb/3¾ cups sugarpaste icing
yellow and green food colouring
115g/4oz/¾ cup royal icing

Materials/equipment
25 x 35cm/10 x 14in cake board
2 small baking parchment piping (icing) bags
7.5cm/3in fluted cutter
fine plain and medium star nozzles
plastic train set and 6 candles

1 Split the cakes and fill with butter icing. Cut the square cake in half and cut, using the round cake tin as a guide, a rounded end from one rectangle to fit around the round cake. Trim the cakes to the same depth and assemble the number 6 on the cake board. Brush with apricot jam and cover with a thin layer of marzipan.

2 Tint 450g/1lb/3 cups of the sugarpaste icing yellow and the rest green. Cover the cake with the yellow icing.

3 With the cutter, mark a circle in the centre of the round cake. Cut out a green sugarpaste icing circle. Stick in place with water and leave to dry overnight.

4 Mark a track the width of the train on the top of the cake. Tint the royal icing yellow and pipe the track with the plain nozzle. Use the star nozzle to pipe a border around the base and top of the cake. Pipe the name on the green circle and attach the train and candles with royal icing.

Variation
You could add a dancer or fairy in the centre and decorate the cake with sugarpaste or commercially made flowers.

Balloons Energy 10835kcal/45729kJ; Protein 122.1g; Carbohydrate 1952.8g, of which sugars 1776.8g; Fat 335.8g, of which saturates 59.3g; Cholesterol 1466mg; Calcium 1672mg; Fibre 22.4g; Sodium 3157mg.
Number 6 Energy 667kcal/2801kJ; Protein 7g; Carbohydrate 100.9g, of which sugars 84.4g; Fat 28.9g, of which saturates 6.9g; Cholesterol 93mg; Calcium 96mg; Fibre 1.4g; Sodium 280mg.

Spider's Web Cake

Make the marzipan spider several days before you need the cake, to give it time to dry.

Makes one 20cm/8in round cake

20cm/8in round deep sponge cake
225g/8oz/1 cup butter icing
45ml/3 tbsp apricot jam, warmed and sieved
30ml/2 tbsp unsweetened cocoa powder
chocolate vermicelli

40g/1½oz marzipan
yellow, red, black and brown food colouring
225g/8oz/1½ cups icing (confectioners') sugar
15–30ml/1–2 tbsp water

Materials/equipment

25cm/10in round cake board
2 small baking parchment piping (icing) bags
wooden cocktail stick (toothpick)
medium star nozzle
candles and holders

1 Split the cake and fill with half the butter icing. Brush the sides with apricot jam, add the cocoa to the remaining butter icing then smooth a little over the sides of the cake. Roll the sides of the cake in chocolate vermicelli. Place on the board.

2 For the spider, tint the marzipan yellow. Roll half of it into two balls of equal size for the head and body. Tint a small piece of marzipan red and make a mouth, and three balls to stick on the spider's body. Tint a tiny piece of marzipan black for the eyes. Roll the rest of the yellow marzipan into eight legs and two smaller feelers. Stick together.

3 Gently heat the icing sugar and water over a pan of hot water. Use two-thirds of the glacé icing to cover the cake top.

4 Tint the remaining glacé icing brown and use it to pipe concentric circles on to the cake. Divide the web into eighths by drawing lines across with a cocktail stick. Leave to set.

5 Put the rest of the chocolate butter icing into a piping bag fitted with a star nozzle and pipe a border around the web. Put candles around the border and the spider in the centre.

Dart Board Cake

This cake is very striking.

Makes one 25cm/10in round cake

25cm/10in round sponge cake
175g/6oz/¾ cup butter icing
5ml/3 tbsp apricot jam, warmed and sieved
450g/1lb marzipan
450g/1lb/3 cups sugarpaste icing
black, red, yellow and silver food colouring

115g/4oz/¾ cup royal icing

Materials/equipment

30cm/12in round cake board
icing smoother
1cm/½in plain circle cutter
small baking parchment piping (icing) bag
fine writing nozzle
3 candles and holders

1 Split the cake and fill with butter icing and put on to the board. Brush with jam and cover with marzipan. Colour some of the sugarpaste icing black, a small piece red and the remainder yellow. Cover the cake with black sugarpaste icing. Cut a 20cm/8in circular template out of baking parchment. Fold it in quarters, then divide each quarter into fifths.

2 Using the template, mark the centre and wedges on the top of the cake with a sharp knife. Cut out ten wedges from the yellow sugarpaste, using the template as a guide. Lay alternate sections on the cake, but do not stick in place yet. Repeat the process with the black sugarpaste. Cut 3mm/⅛in strips off the end of each wedge and swap the colour. Mark a 13cm/5in circle in the centre of the board and cut out 3mm/⅛in strips from each colour to swap with adjoining colours. Stick in place and use an icing smoother to flatten.

3 Use the cutter to remove the centre for the bull's eye. Replace with a circle of red sugarpaste, cut with the same cutter. Surround it with a strip of black sugarpaste. Roll the remaining black sugarpaste into a long sausage to fit round the base of the cake and stick in place with a little water. Mark numbers on the board and pipe on with royal icing using the fine writing nozzle. Leave to dry then paint with silver food colouring. Stick candles in at an angle to resemble darts.

Web Energy 5660kcal/23728kJ; Protein 54.3g; Carbohydrate 768.6g, of which sugars 611.1g; Fat 284.2g, of which saturates 96.9g; Cholesterol 997mg; Calcium 744mg; Fibre 10.7g; Sodium 3214mg.
Dart Board Energy 8090kcal/34014kJ; Protein 77.4g; Carbohydrate 1256.5g, of which sugars 1080.5g; Fat 340.5g, of which saturates 92.7g; Cholesterol 1066mg; Calcium 1123mg; Fibre 15.8g; Sodium 3225mg.

Camping Tent Cake

Dream of the outdoor life with this fun cake.

**Makes one 20 x 10cm/
8 x 4in cake**
20cm/8in square sponge cake
115g/4oz/1/2 cup butter icing
45ml/3 tbsp apricot jam, warmed
    and sieved
450g/1lb marzipan
500g/1 1/4lb/3 3/4 cups
    sugarpaste icing
brown, orange, green, red and blue
    food colouring

50g/2oz/1/3 cup desiccated (dry
    unsweetened shredded) coconut
115g/4oz/3/4 cup royal icing
chocolate mint sticks

Materials/equipment
25cm/10in square cake board
wooden cocktail sticks (toothpicks)
fine paintbrush
4 small baking parchment piping
    (icing) bags
very fine basketweave and
    plain nozzles
toy ball

1 Split the cake and fill with butter icing. Cut the cake in half. Cut one half in two diagonally from the top right edge to the bottom left edge to form the roof of the tent. Stick the two wedges, back-to-back, on top of the rectangle with jam. Trim to 10cm/4in high and use the trimmings on the base. Place the cake diagonally on the board and brush with jam.

2 Cover the entire cake with marzipan, reserving some for modelling. Tint 50g/2oz/scant 1/2 cup of the sugarpaste icing brown and cover one end of the tent. Tint the rest orange and cover the rest of the cake. Cut a semicircle for the tent opening and a central 7.5cm/3in slit. Lay over the brown end. Secure the flaps with royal icing. Put halved cocktail sticks in the corners and ridge.

3 Tint the coconut green. Spread the board with a thin layer of royal icing and sprinkle with the coconut.

4 Tint the reserved marzipan flesh-colour and use to make a model of a child. Paint on a blue T-shirt and leave to dry. Tint some royal icing brown and pipe on the hair with a basketweave nozzle. Tint the icing and pipe on the mouth and eyes. Make a bonfire with broken chocolate mint sticks.

Army Tank Cake

Create an authentic camouflaged tank by combining green and brown sugarpaste icing.

**Makes one 25 x 15cm/
10 x 6in cake**
25cm/10in square sponge cake
225g/8oz/1 cup butter icing
45ml/3 tbsp apricot jam, warmed
    and sieved
450g/1lb marzipan

450g/1lb/3 cups sugarpaste icing
brown, green and black
    food colouring
1 flaked chocolate bar
liquorice strips
60ml/4 tbsp royal icing
round cookies (cookies)
sweets (candies)

Materials/equipment
25 x 35cm/10 x 14in cake board

1 Split the sponge cake and fill with butter icing. Cut off a 10cm/4in strip from one side of the cake. Use the off-cut to make a 15 x 7.5cm/6 x 3in rectangle, and stick on the top.

2 Shape the sloping top and cut a 2.5cm/1in piece from both ends to form the tracks. Shape the rounded ends for the wheels and tracks. Place on the cake board and brush with apricot jam. Cover with a layer of marzipan.

3 Tint a quarter of the sugarpaste icing brown and the rest green. Roll out the green to a 25cm/10in square. Break small pieces of brown icing and place all over the green. Flatten and roll out together to give a camouflage effect. Turn the icing over and repeat.

4 Continue to roll out until the icing is 3mm/1/8in thick. Lay it over the cake and gently press to fit. Using your hand smooth the sugarpaste around all the curves of the tank. Cut away the excess.

5 From the trimmings cut a piece into a 6cm/2 1/2in disc and stick on the top with a little water. Cut a small hole in the front of the tank for the gun and insert the flaked chocolate. Stick liquorice on for the tracks, using a little black royal icing. Stick on cookies for the wheels and sweets for the lights and portholes.

Tent Energy 5636kcal/23658kJ; Protein 49.5g; Carbohydrate 819.4g, of which sugars 665.4g; Fat 262.5g, of which saturates 93.3g; Cholesterol 890mg; Calcium 721mg; Fibre 13.1g; Sodium 2636mg.
Tank Energy 8226kcal/34566kJ; Protein 78.7g; Carbohydrate 1244.3g, of which sugars 1068.3g; Fat 360.1g, of which saturates 103.4g; Cholesterol 1108mg; Calcium 1128mg; Fibre 16.2g; Sodium 3350mg.

Computer Game Cake

Making a cake look like a computer is easier than you think. This cake is ideal for a computer-game fanatic.

Makes one 14 x 13cm/ 5½ x 5in cake
15cm/6in square sponge cake
115g/4oz/½ cup butter icing
45ml/3 tbsp apricot jam, warmed and sieved
225g/8oz marzipan

275g/10oz/scant 2 cups sugarpaste icing
black, blue, red and yellow food colouring
royal icing, to decorate

Materials/equipment
20cm/8in square cake board
wooden cocktail stick (toothpick)
fine paintbrush
small baking parchment piping (icing) bag

1 Split the cake and fill with a little butter icing. Cut 2.5cm/1in off one side of the cake and 1cm/½in off the other side. Round the corners slightly.

2 Place the cake on the cake board and brush with apricot jam. Roll out the marzipan into a thin layer and use to cover the cake.

3 Tint 225g/8oz/1½ cups of the sugarpaste black. Use to cover the cake. Reserve the trimmings. With a cocktail stick, mark the speaker holes and position of the screen and knobs.

4 Tint half the remaining sugarpaste pale blue, roll out and cut out a 6cm/2½in square for the screen. Stick in the centre of the game with a little water.

5 Tint a small piece of sugarpaste red and the rest yellow. Use to cut out the switch and controls. Stick in position with water.

6 Roll the reserved black sugarpaste icing into a long, thin sausage and edge the screen and base of the cake.

7 With a fine paintbrush, draw the game on to the screen with a little blue colouring (choose the child's favourite game, if you like). Pipe letters on to the buttons with royal icing.

Chessboard Cake

To make this cake look most effective, ensure that the squares have very sharp and clear edges.

Makes one 25cm/10in square cake
25cm/10in square sponge cake
225g/8oz/1 cup butter icing
60ml/4 tbsp apricot jam, warmed and sieved
800g/1¾lb marzipan

500g/1¼lb/3¾ cups sugarpaste icing
black and red food colouring
edible silver balls
115g/4oz/¾ cup royal icing

Materials/equipment
30cm/12in square cake board
small baking parchment piping (icing) bag
medium star nozzle

1 Split the cake and fill with butter icing. Place on the cake board and brush with jam.

2 Roll out 450g/1lb/3 cups marzipan and use to cover the cake.

3 Once the marzipan has dried, cover with 450g/1lb/3 cups of the sugarpaste icing. Leave to dry overnight.

4 Divide the remaining marzipan into two, and tint black and red. To shape the chess pieces, roll 50g/2oz/4 tbsp of each colour into a sausage and cut into eight equal pieces. Shape into pawns.

5 Divide 75g/3oz/generous 4 tbsp of each colour into six equal pieces and use to shape into two castles, two knights and two bishops. (When shaping the chess pieces have a chess set to refer to so that the shapes are correct.)

6 Divide 25g/1oz/2 tbsp of each colour marzipan in half and shape a queen and a king. Decorate with silver balls. Leave to dry overnight.

7 Cut 1cm/½in black strips of marzipan to edge the board and stick in place with water. Pipe a border around the base of the cake with royal icing. Place the chess pieces in position.

Computer Energy 4558kcal/19093kJ; Protein 53.2g; Carbohydrate 583.9g, of which sugars 451.9g; Fat 239.2g, of which saturates 63.7g; Cholesterol 778mg; Calcium 636mg; Fibre 10.6g; Sodium 2330mg.
Chessboard Energy 9755kcal/41011kJ; Protein 99.2g; Carbohydrate 1498.4g, of which sugars 1311.4g; Fat 415g, of which saturates 109.6g; Cholesterol 1164mg; Calcium 1378mg; Fibre 22.9g; Sodium 3581mg.

Kite Cake

The happy face on this cheerful kite is a great favourite with children of all ages.

Serves 10–12
25cm/10in square sponge cake
225g/8oz/1 cup butter icing
45ml/3 tbsp apricot jam, warmed and sieved
450g/1lb marzipan
675g/1½lb/4½ cups sugarpaste icing
yellow, red, green, blue and black food colouring
115g/4oz/¾ cup royal icing

Materials/equipment
30cm/12in square cake board
wooden cocktail stick (toothpick)
small baking parchment piping (icing) bag
medium star nozzle
candles and holders

1 Trim the cake into a kite shape, then split and fill with butter icing. Place diagonally on the cake board and brush with apricot jam. Cover with a layer of marzipan.

2 Tint 225g/8oz/1½ cups of the sugarpaste icing pale yellow and cover the cake.

3 Make a template of the face, tie and buttons from baking parchment, and mark on to the cake with a cocktail stick. Divide the remainder of the sugarpaste icing into four and tint red, green, blue and black. Cut out the features and stick on with water.

4 Pipe a royal icing border around the base of the cake.

5 For the ribbons on the kite's tail, roll out each colour separately and cut two 4 x 1cm/1½ x ½in lengths in blue, red and green. Pinch each length to shape into a bow.

6 Roll the yellow sugarpaste into a long rope and lay it on the board in a wavy line from the narrow end of the kite. Stick the bows in place with water. To make the candleholders, roll balls of yellow sugarpaste, stick on the board with a little royal icing and press in the candles.

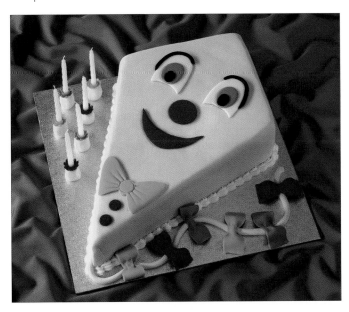

Hotdog Cake

This realistic hotdog cake is sure to be popular at a party.

Makes one 23cm/9in long cake
23 x 33cm/9 x 13in sponge roll
175g/6oz/¾ cup coffee flavour butter icing
90ml/6 tbsp apricot jam, warmed and sieved
450g/1lb/3 cups sugarpaste icing
brown and red food colouring
115g/4oz/¾ cup glacé icing
15–30ml/1–2 tbsp toasted sesame seeds

Filling
175g/6oz sponge cake pieces
50g/2oz/¼ cup soft dark brown sugar
45ml/3 tbsp orange juice
75ml/5 tbsp honey

Materials/equipment
fine paintbrush
2 small baking parchment piping (icing) bags
napkin, plate, knife and fork

1 Unroll the sponge roll, spread with butter icing, then roll up again. Slice the sponge roll along the centre lengthways, almost to the base, and ease the two halves apart.

2 Mix all the filling ingredients in a food processor or blender until smooth. Shape the mixture with your hands to a 23cm/9in sausage shape.

3 Tint all the sugarpaste icing brown. Set aside 50g/2oz/4 tbsp and use the rest to cover the cake.

4 Paint the top of the "bun" with diluted brown food colouring to give a toasted effect. Position the "sausage".

5 Divide the glacé icing in half. Tint one half brown and the other red. Pipe red icing along the sausage, then overlay with brown icing. Sprinkle the sesame seeds over the "bun".

6 Cut the reserved brown sugarpaste icing into thin strips. Place on the cake with the joins under the "sausage".

7 Place on a napkin on a serving plate, with a knife and fork.

Kite Energy 726kcal/3054kJ; Protein 6.5g; Carbohydrate 115.2g, of which sugars 100.5g; Fat 29.7g, of which saturates 8.6g; Cholesterol 92mg; Calcium 99mg; Fibre 1.3g; Sodium 279mg.
Hotdog Energy 4251kcal/18030kJ; Protein 45.9g; Carbohydrate 907.4g, of which sugars 810.9g; Fat 73.9g, of which saturates 11.4g; Cholesterol 196mg; Calcium 871mg; Fibre 6g; Sodium 1159mg.

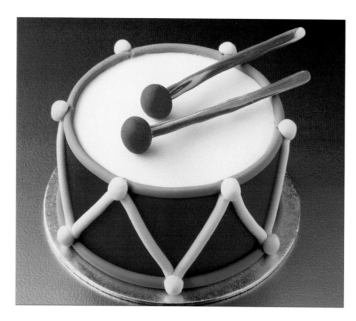

Drum Cake

This is a colourful cake for very young children. It even comes complete with bright drumsticks.

Makes one 15cm/6in round cake
15cm/6in round sponge cake
50g/2oz/4 tbsp butter icing

45ml/3 tbsp apricot jam, warmed and sieved
350g/12oz marzipan
450g/1lb/3 cups sugarpaste icing
red, blue and yellow food colouring
royal icing, for sticking

Materials/equipment
20cm/8in round cake board

1 Split the cake and fill with a little butter icing. Place on the cake board and brush with apricot jam. Cover with a layer of marzipan and leave to dry overnight.

2 Tint half of the sugarpaste icing red and roll it out to 25 × 30cm/10 × 12in. Cut in half and stick to the side of the cake with water.

3 Roll out a circle of white sugarpaste icing to fit the top of the cake and divide the remainder in half. Tint one half blue and the other yellow.

4 Divide the blue into four pieces and roll each into a sausage long enough to go halfway round the cake. Stick around the base and top of the cake with a little water.

5 To make the drum strings, mark the cake into six around the top and base. Roll the yellow sugarpaste icing into 12 strands long enough to cross diagonally from top to base to form the drum strings. Roll the rest of the yellow icing into 12 small balls and stick at the top and base of the zigzags where the strings join the drum.

6 Knead together the red and white sugarpaste icing until streaky, then roll two balls and sticks 15cm/6in long. Leave to dry thoroughly, ideally overnight in a warm, dry place such as an airing cupboard. Stick together with royal icing to make the drumsticks and place on top of the cake.

Ice Cream Cones

Individual cakes make a change for a party. Put a candle in the special person's one.

Makes 9
115g/4oz/¾ cup marzipan
9 ice cream cones
9 sponge fairy cakes
350g/12oz/1½ cups butter icing

red, green and brown food colouring
coloured and chocolate vermicelli, wafers and flaked chocolate bars
sweets (candies)

Materials/equipment
3 × 12-egg egg boxes
foil

1 Make the stands for the cakes by turning the egg boxes upside down and pressing three balls of marzipan into evenly spaced holes in each box. Wrap the boxes in foil.

2 Pierce the foil above the marzipan balls and insert the cones, being careful to press them in gently so that you do not crush the bottom of the cones.

3 Gently push a fairy cake into each cone. If the bases of the cakes are too large, trim them down with a small, sharp knife. The cakes should be quite secure in the cones.

4 Divide the butter icing between three bowls and tint them pale red, green and brown.

5 Using a small metal spatula, spread each cake with some of the pink icing, making sure that the finish on the icing is a little textured so that it looks like ice cream. Use the other coloured icings in the same way for all the ice cream cones.

6 To insert a wafer or chocolate stick into an ice cream, use a small, sharp knife to make a hole through the icing and into the cake, then insert the wafer or stick.

7 Add the finishing touches to the cakes by sprinkling over some coloured and chocolate vermicelli. Arrange sweets around the cones.

Drum Energy 5353kcal/22501kJ; Protein 57.9g; Carbohydrate 817.3g, of which sugars 685.3g; Fat 228.2g, of which saturates 51.4g; Cholesterol 725mg; Calcium 774mg; Fibre 12.1g; Sodium 2204mg.
Cones Energy 576kcal/2416kJ; Protein 5.6g; Carbohydrate 78.6g, of which sugars 56.8g; Fat 28.8g, of which saturates 10.5g; Cholesterol 86mg; Calcium 89mg; Fibre 1.1g; Sodium 326mg.

Royal Crown Cake

This bejewelled regal cake is sure to delight any prince or princess.

Serves 16–20

20cm/8in and 15cm/6in round sponge cake
175g/6oz/¾ cup butter icing
45ml/3 tbsp apricot jam, warmed and sieved
450g/1lb marzipan
500g/1¼lb/3¾ cups sugarpaste icing
red food colouring
450g/1lb/3 cups royal icing
small black jelly sweets (candies)
4 ice cream fan wafers
edible silver balls
jewel sweets (candies)

Materials/equipment

30cm/12in square cake board
wooden cocktail sticks (toothpicks)

1 Split the cakes and fill with butter icing. Sandwich one on top of the other and place on the cake board. Shape the top cake into a dome.

2 Brush the cake with apricot jam. Roll out the marzipan thinly and use to cover the cake. Set aside 115g/4oz/¾ cup of the sugarpaste icing and use the remainder to cover the cake.

3 Tint the reserved sugarpaste icing red, and use to cover the dome of the cake. Trim away the excess.

4 Spoon rough mounds of royal icing around the base of the cake and stick a black jelly sweet on each mound.

5 Cut the ice cream wafers diagonally in half. Spread both sides of the wafers with royal icing and stick to the cake to form the points of the crown, smoothing the icing level with the sides of the cake.

6 Use cocktail sticks to support the wafers until they are dry.

7 Position silver balls on top of each point and stick jewel sweets around the side of the crown using a little royal icing to stick them securely.

Treasure Map

Perhaps you could combine this map with a treasure hunt at the party.

Makes one 20 x 25cm/ 8 x 10in cake

25cm/10in square sponge cake
225g/8oz/1½ cups butter icing
45ml/3 tbsp apricot jam, warmed and sieved
450g/1lb/3 cups marzipan
675g/1½lb/4½ cups sugarpaste icing

yellow, brown, paprika, green, black and red food colouring
115g/4oz/¾ cup royal icing

Materials/equipment

25 x 35cm/10 x 14in cake board
fine paintbrush
kitchen paper
4 small baking parchment piping (icing) bags
medium shell and fine writing nozzles
candles and holders

1 Split the cake and fill with butter icing, cut it into a 20 x 25cm/8 x 10in rectangle and place on the cake board. Brush with apricot jam. Cover with a layer of marzipan then with 450g/1lb/3 cups sugarpaste icing.

2 Colour the remaining sugarpaste icing yellow and cut out with an uneven outline. Stick on to the cake with water and leave to dry overnight. Mark the island, river, lake, mountains and trees on the map.

3 With brown and paprika colours and a fine paintbrush, paint the edges of the map to look old, smudging the colours together with kitchen paper.

4 Paint the island pale green and the water around the island, the river and the lake pale blue. Dry overnight before painting on the other details, otherwise the colours will run.

5 Pipe a border of royal icing around the base of the cake with the shell nozzle. Colour a little royal icing red and pipe the path to the treasure, marked with an "X", with the writing nozzle.

6 Colour some icing green and pipe on grass and trees. Colour some icing black and pipe on a north sign with the writing nozzle.

Map Energy 8201kcal/34461kJ; Protein 77.3g; Carbohydrate 1246.5g, of which sugars 1070.5g; Fat 356.9g, of which saturates 103.1g; Cholesterol 1108mg; Calcium 1132mg; Fibre 15.8g; Sodium 3334mg.
Crown Energy 427kcal/1798kJ; Protein 3.6g; Carbohydrate 70.4g, of which sugars 62.7g; Fat 16.5g, of which saturates 4.9g; Cholesterol 50mg; Calcium 58mg; Fibre 0.7g; Sodium 152mg.

Cookies & Bars

Home-made cookies and bars are very moreish, and once you

have made some of the recipes in this chapter you will never

want to eat store-bought ones again. Cookies and bars range

from everyday snacks such as Ginger Cookies, Crunchy

Jumbles and Chocolate-chip Brownies to sweet treats

for special occasions, such as Christmas Cookies,

Brandy Snaps or Chocolate Amaretti.

Crunchy Oat Cookies

Home-made biscuits like these crunchy cookies are always a favourite, and the variations are endless.

Makes 14
175g/6oz/³/₄ cup butter or margarine, at room temperature
175g/6oz/generous ³/₄ cup caster (superfine) sugar
1 egg yolk
175g/6oz/1¹/₂ cups plain (all-purpose) flour
5ml/1 tsp bicarbonate of soda (baking soda)
2.5ml/¹/₂ tsp salt
50g/2oz/²/₃ cup rolled oats
50g/2oz/²/₃ cup small crunchy nugget cereal

1 Cream the butter or margarine and sugar together until light and fluffy. Mix in the egg yolk.

2 Sift over the flour, bicarbonate of soda and salt, then stir into the butter mixture. Add the oats and cereal, and stir to blend. Chill for at least 20 minutes.

3 Preheat the oven to 190°C/375°F/Gas 5. Grease a large baking sheet.

4 Roll the mixture into balls. Place them on the baking sheet and flatten with the base of a floured glass.

5 Bake until golden, about 10–12 minutes. Then, with a metal spatula, transfer to a wire rack to cool. Store the cookies in an airtight container.

Variations
• Add grated orange rind to the mixture to give a delicate citrus taste.
• You can substitute 50g/2oz/¹/₄ cup chopped walnuts or pecan nuts for the cereal to make nutty oatmeal cookies, or try chocolate chips, raisins or sultanas instead.
• Other dried fruits, such as papaya, also transform the cookies and can be substituted for all or part of the cereal.

Farmhouse Cookies

Delightfully wholesome, these melt-in-the-mouth farmhouse cookies are ideal to serve with morning coffee.

Makes 18
115g/4oz/¹/₂ cup butter or margarine, at room temperature
90g/3¹/₂oz/7 tbsp soft light brown sugar
65g/2¹/₂oz/5 tbsp crunchy peanut butter
1 egg
50g/2oz/¹/₂ cup plain (all-purpose) flour
2.5ml/¹/₂ tsp baking powder
2.5ml/¹/₂ tsp ground cinnamon
1.5ml/¹/₄ tsp salt
175g/6oz/1¹/₂ cups muesli
50g/2oz/¹/₂ cup raisins
50g/2oz/¹/₂ cup chopped walnuts

1 Preheat the oven to 180°C/350°F/Gas 4. Grease a large baking sheet.

2 Cream the butter or margarine and sugar until light and fluffy. Beat in the peanut butter and then beat in the egg.

3 Sift the flour, baking powder, cinnamon and salt over the peanut butter mixture and stir to blend. Stir in the muesli, raisins and walnuts. Taste the mixture to see if it needs more sugar, as the sugar content of muesli varies.

4 Drop rounded tablespoonfuls of the mixture on to the prepared baking sheet about 2.5cm/1in apart. Press gently with the back of a spoon to spread each mound into a circle.

5 Bake until lightly coloured, about 15 minutes. With a metal spatula, transfer to a wire rack to cool. Store the cookies in an airtight container.

Cook's Tip
Make these cookies extra wholesome by using a good-quality, rich-tasting peanut butter from your health-food store. You can also use luxury muesli with exotic fruits to make them even tastier.

Farmhouse Energy 165kcal/688kJ; Protein 2.9g; Carbohydrate 16.9g, of which sugars 10.1g; Fat 10g, of which saturates 4.1g; Cholesterol 24mg; Calcium 25mg; Fibre 1.1g; Sodium 94mg.
Crunchy Energy 220kcal/923kJ; Protein 2.3g; Carbohydrate 27.6g, of which sugars 14.3g; Fat 11.9g, of which saturates 6.8g; Cholesterol 41mg; Calcium 33mg; Fibre 0.8g; Sodium 81mg.

Nutty Nougat

Makes about 500g/1¼lb

225g/8oz/generous 1 cup
  granulated sugar
225g/8oz/²⁄₃ cup cup clear honey

1 large (US extra large) egg white
115g/4oz/1 cup flaked (sliced)
  almonds or chopped pistachio
  nuts, roasted

1 Line an 18cm/7in square cake tin (pan) with rice paper. Gently heat the sugar and honey with 60ml/4 tbsp water in a heavy pan, stirring until the sugar has completely dissolved.

2 Boil the syrup, without stirring, until soft crack stage (151°C/304°F on a sugar thermometer). Remove from the heat and cool slightly. Whisk the egg white until stiff, then drizzle over the syrup while still whisking. Stir in the nuts. Pour into the tin and leave to cool completely. Cut into squares before it hardens.

Oaty Coconut Cookies

The coconut gives these cookies a wonderful texture.

Makes 48

175g/6oz/generous 2 cups quick-
  cooking oats
75g/3oz/1 cup desiccated (dry
  unsweetened shredded) coconut
225g/8oz/1 cup butter
115g/4oz/generous ½ cup caster
  (superfine) sugar

50g/2oz/¼ cup soft dark
  brown sugar
2 eggs
60ml/4 tbsp milk
7.5ml/1½ tsp vanilla extract
115g/4oz/1 cup plain
  (all-purpose) flour, sifted
2.5ml/½ tsp bicarbonate of soda
  (baking soda)
2.5ml/½ tsp salt
5ml/1 tsp ground cinnamon

1 Preheat the oven to 200°C/400°F/Gas 6. Spread the oats and coconut on a baking sheet. Bake for 8–10 minutes.

2 Cream the butter and sugars. Beat in the eggs, milk and vanilla. Fold in the dry ingredients, and the oats and coconut. Drop spoonfuls of mixture on to two greased baking sheets, and bake for 8–10 minutes. Cool on a wire rack.

Crunchy Jumbles

For even crunchier cookies, add 50g/2oz/½ cup walnuts, coarsely chopped, with the cereal and chocolate chips.

Makes 36

115g/4oz/½ cup butter or
  margarine, at room temperature
225g/8oz/generous 1 cup caster
  (superfine) sugar

1 egg
5ml/1 tsp vanilla extract
150g/5oz/1¼ cups plain
  (all-purpose) flour, sifted
2.5ml/½ tsp bicarbonate of soda
  (baking soda)
1.5ml/¼ tsp salt
50g/2oz/2¼ cups crisped
  rice cereal
175g/6oz/1 cup chocolate chips

1 Preheat the oven to 180°C/350°F/Gas 4. Grease two baking sheets. Cream the butter or margarine and sugar until fluffy. Add the egg and vanilla extract. Add the flour, bicarbonate of soda and the salt, and fold in.

2 Add the cereal and chocolate chips and mix thoroughly. Drop spoonfuls 5cm/2in apart on to baking sheets and bake for 10–12 minutes. Transfer to a wire rack to cool.

Cinnamon Balls

Makes 126

175g/6oz/1½ ground almonds
75g/3oz/scant ½ cup caster
  (superfine) sugar

15ml/1 tbsp ground cinnamon
2 egg whites
icing (confectioners') sugar,
  for dredging

1 Preheat the oven to 180°C/350°F/Gas 4. Grease a large baking sheet. Mix the almonds, sugar and cinnamon in a bowl. Whisk the egg whites until stiff and fold into the almond mixture.

2 Roll small spoonfuls of the mixture into balls and place on the baking sheet. Bake for 15 minutes, then cool on a wire rack. Roll the cooled balls in some sifted icing sugar until completely covered.

Nougat Energy 2250kcal/9511kJ; Protein 4.1g; Carbohydrate 415g, of which sugars 263g; Fat 64.2g, of which saturates 5.1g; Cholesterol 21mg; Calcium 16mg; Fibre 8.5g; Sodium 42mg.
Coconut Energy 84kcal/352kJ; Protein 1.1g; Carbohydrate 8.3g, of which sugars 3.8g; Fat 5.4g, of which saturates 3.4g; Cholesterol 18mg; Calcium 11mg; Fibre 0.5g; Sodium 34mg.
Jumbles Energy 95kcal/398kJ; Protein 0.9g; Carbohydrate 14.2g, of which sugars 9.8g; Fat 4.2g, of which saturates 2.5g; Cholesterol 12mg; Calcium 18mg; Fibre 0.3g; Sodium 31mg.
Balls Energy 15kcal/63kJ; Protein 0.6g; Carbohydrate 1.8g, of which sugars 0.6g; Fat 0.8g, of which saturates 0.1g; Cholesterol 2mg; Calcium 3mg; Fibre 0.1g; Sodium 2mg.

Ginger Cookies

So much tastier than store-bought varieties, these ginger cookies will disappear quickly, so be sure to make a large batch!

Makes 60

275g/10oz/2½ cups plain
  (all-purpose) flour
5ml/1 tsp bicarbonate of soda
  (baking soda)
7.5ml/1½ tsp ground ginger
1.5ml/¼ tsp ground cinnamon
1.5ml/¼ tsp ground cloves
115g/4oz/½ cup butter
  or margarine, at
  room temperature
350g/12oz/1¾ cups caster
  (superfine) sugar
1 egg, beaten
60ml/4 tbsp treacle (molasses)
5ml/1 tsp fresh lemon juice

1 Preheat the oven to 160°C/325°F/Gas 3. Lightly grease three to four baking sheets.

2 Sift the flour, bicarbonate of soda and spices into a small bowl. Set aside.

3 Cream the butter or margarine and two-thirds of the sugar together. Stir in the egg, treacle and lemon juice. Add the flour mixture and mix in thoroughly with a wooden spoon to make a soft dough.

4 Shape the dough into 2cm/¾in balls. Roll the balls in the remaining sugar and place about 5cm/2in apart on the prepared baking sheets.

5 Bake until the cookies are just firm to the touch, about 12 minutes. With a metal spatula, transfer the cookies to a wire rack and leave to cool. The biscuits will firm up as they cool.

> **Variation**
> Coarsely chop 150g/5oz drained preserved stem ginger. Add 115g/4oz to the cookie mixture at the end of step 3, and press the remaining pieces into the top of each of the cookies at the end of step 4.

Cream Cheese Spirals

These spirals look so impressive and melt in the mouth, yet they are surprisingly easy to make.

Makes 32

225g/8oz/1 cup butter,
  at room temperature
225g/8oz/1 cup cream cheese
10ml/2 tsp caster (superfine) sugar
225g/8oz/2 cups plain
  (all-purpose) flour
1 egg white, beaten with
  15ml/1 tbsp water,
  for glazing
caster sugar,
  for sprinkling

For the filling
115g/4oz/1 cup finely
  chopped walnuts
115g/4oz/¾ cup soft light
  brown sugar
5ml/1 tsp ground cinnamon

1 Cream the butter, cream cheese and sugar until soft. Sift over the flour and mix until combined. Gather into a ball and divide in half. Flatten each half, wrap in baking parchment and chill for 30 minutes.

2 Meanwhile, make the filling. Mix the chopped walnuts with the light brown sugar and cinnamon, stirring well so that the nuts are well coated with the spices. Set aside.

3 Preheat the oven to 190°C/375°F/Gas 5. Grease two baking sheets. Working with one half of the dough at a time, roll out thinly into a 28cm/11in circle. Using a dinner plate as a guide, trim the edges with a knife.

4 Brush the surface with the egg-white glaze, and then sprinkle evenly with half the filling.

5 Cut the circle into 16 triangular segments. Starting from the base of a triangle, roll up the dough to form a spiral. Repeat with the remaining triangles.

6 Place the spirals on the prepared baking sheets and brush with the remaining egg and water glaze. Sprinkle with caster sugar. Bake until golden, about 15–20 minutes. Cool on a wire rack.

Ginger Energy 57kcal/239kJ; Protein 0.6g; Carbohydrate 10.3g, of which sugars 6.8g; Fat 1.7g, of which saturates 1g; Cholesterol 7mg; Calcium 16mg; Fibre 0.1g; Sodium 15mg.
Cream Cheese Energy 150kcal/621kJ; Protein 1.7g; Carbohydrate 9.7g, of which sugars 4.3g; Fat 11.8g, of which saturates 6g; Cholesterol 28mg; Calcium 24mg; Fibre 0.3g; Sodium 67mg.

Orange Cookies

These classic citrus-flavoured cookies are ideal for a tasty treat at any time of the day.

Makes 30
115g/4oz/generous ½ cup butter, at room temperature
200g/7oz/1 cup caster (superfine) sugar

2 egg yolks
15ml/1 tbsp fresh orange juice
grated rind of 1 large orange
200g/7oz/1¾ cups plain (all-purpose) flour
15ml/1 tbsp cornflour (cornstarch)
2.5ml/½ tsp salt
5ml/1 tsp baking powder

1 Cream the butter and sugar until light and fluffy. Add the yolks, orange juice and rind, and continue beating to blend.

2 In another bowl, sift together the flour, cornflour, salt and baking powder. Add to the butter mixture and stir until it forms a dough. Wrap the dough in baking parchment and chill for 2 hours.

3 Preheat the oven to 190°C/375°F/Gas 5. Grease two baking sheets. Roll spoonfuls of the dough into balls and place 2.5–5cm/1–2in apart on the baking sheets.

4 Press down with a fork to flatten. Bake until golden brown, about 8–10 minutes. Using a metal spatula, transfer to a wire rack to cool.

> **Variation**
> *These Orange Cookies are ideal for making into Orange Creams. Simply make a butter icing by creaming together 50g/2oz/ ¼ cup butter and 75g/3oz/¾ cup icing (confectioners') sugar until smooth. Add the grated rind of an orange and moisten to a spreadable consistency with a little freshly squeezed orange juice. Spread a little of the butter icing on to the flat side of a cookie and sandwich with another. Repeat with the remaining cookies. Chocolate butter icing would also go exceptionally well with the orange.*

Italian Almond Biscotti

Serve biscotti after a meal, for dunking in sweet white wine, such as an Italian Vin Santo or a French Muscat.

Makes 48
200g/7oz/1¼ cups whole unblanched almonds
215g/7½oz/scant 2 cups plain (all-purpose) flour

90g/3½oz/½ cup caster (superfine) sugar
a pinch of salt
a pinch of saffron powder
2.5ml/½ tsp bicarbonate of soda (baking soda)
2 eggs
1 egg white, lightly beaten

1 Preheat the oven to 190°C/375°F/Gas 5. Grease and flour two baking sheets.

2 Spread the almonds on an ungreased baking sheet and bake until lightly browned, about 15 minutes. When cool, grind 50g/2oz/½ cup of the almonds in a food processor, blender, or coffee grinder until pulverized.

3 Coarsely chop the remaining almonds into two or three pieces each. Set aside.

4 Combine the flour, sugar, salt, saffron powder, bicarbonate of soda and ground almonds in a bowl and mix to blend. Make a well in the centre and add the eggs. Stir to form a rough dough. Transfer to a floured surface and knead until well blended. Knead in the chopped almonds.

5 Divide the dough into three equal parts. Roll into logs about 2.5cm/1in in diameter. Place on one of the prepared baking sheets, brush with the egg white and bake for 20 minutes. Remove from the oven. Lower the oven temperature to 140°C/275°F/Gas 1.

6 With a very sharp knife, cut into each log at an angle making 1cm/½in slices. Return the slices on the baking sheets to the oven and bake for another 25 minutes. Transfer the biscotti to a wire rack to cool.

Biscotti Energy 51kcal/216kJ; Protein 1.6g; Carbohydrate 5.7g, of which sugars 2.2g; Fat 2.6g, of which saturates 0.3g; Cholesterol 8mg; Calcium 18mg; Fibre 0.4g; Sodium 5mg.
Orange Energy 83kcal/350kJ; Protein 0.9g; Carbohydrate 12.6g, of which sugars 7.1g; Fat 3.6g, of which saturates 2.1g; Cholesterol 22mg; Calcium 15mg; Fibre 0.2g; Sodium 25mg.

Raspberry Sandwich Cookies

These cookies may be stored in an airtight container with sheets of baking parchment between the layers.

Makes 32
175g/6oz/1 cup blanched almonds
175g/6oz/1½ cups plain (all-purpose) flour
175g/6oz/¾ cup butter, at room temperature
115g/4oz/generous ½ cup caster (superfine) sugar
grated rind of 1 lemon
5ml/1 tsp vanilla extract
1 egg white
1.5ml/¼ tsp salt
25g/1oz/¼ cup flaked (sliced) almonds
250ml/8fl oz/1 cup raspberry jam
15ml/1 tbsp lemon juice

1 Process the blanched almonds and 45ml/3 tbsp flour in a food processor or blender until finely ground. Cream the butter and sugar together until light and fluffy. Stir in the lemon rind and vanilla. Add the ground almonds and remaining flour, and mix well. Gather into a ball, wrap in baking parchment, and chill for 1 hour.

2 Preheat the oven to 160°C/325°F/Gas 3. Line two baking sheets with baking parchment. Divide the cookie mixture into four equal parts. Working with one section at a time, roll out to a thickness of 3mm/⅛in on a lightly floured surface.

3 With a 6cm/2½in fluted pastry (cookie) cutter, stamp out circles. Using a 2cm/¾in piping (icing) nozzle or pastry cutter, stamp out the centres from half the circles. Place the rings and circles 2.5cm/1in apart on the baking sheets.

4 Whisk the egg white with the salt until just frothy. Chop the flaked almonds. Brush the cookie rings with the egg white, then sprinkle over the almonds. Bake until lightly browned, about 12–15 minutes. Cool for a few minutes on the baking sheets then transfer to a wire rack.

5 In a pan, melt the jam with the lemon juice until it comes to a simmer. Brush the jam over the cookie circles and sandwich together with the rings.

Christmas Cookies

Decorate these delicious cookies with festive decorations or make them at any time of year.

Makes 30
175g/6oz/¾ cup unsalted (sweet) butter, at room temperature
275g/10oz/1½ cups caster (superfine) sugar
1 egg
1 egg yolk
5ml/1 tsp vanilla extract
grated rind of 1 lemon
1.5ml/¼ tsp salt
275g/10oz/2½ cups plain (all-purpose) flour

For decorating (optional)
175g/6oz/1½ cups icing (confectioners') sugar
food colouring
small decorations

1 Preheat the oven to 180°C/350°F/Gas 4. With an electric mixer, cream the butter until soft. Add the sugar gradually and continue beating until light and fluffy.

2 Using a wooden spoon, slowly mix in the whole egg and the egg yolk. Add the vanilla extract, lemon rind and salt. Stir to mix well. Add the flour and stir until blended.

3 Gather the mixture into a ball, wrap in baking parchment and chill for 30 minutes.

4 On a floured surface, roll out the mixture about 3mm/⅛in thick. Stamp out shapes or rounds with cookie cutters. Bake until lightly coloured, about 8 minutes. Transfer to a wire rack and leave to cool completely. The cookies can be left plain, or iced and decorated.

5 To ice the cookies, mix the icing sugar with enough water to make a thick icing consistency. Add a few drops of food colouring to create just one colour, or divide the mixture into small amounts and add different food colouring to each.

6 Fill a piping (icing) bag fitted with a fine nozzle with the icing and pipe dots, lines and patterns on to the cookies. Finish with small decorations such as edible silver balls.

Raspberry Energy 133kcal/554kJ; Protein 2g; Carbohydrate 13.9g, of which sugars 9.5g; Fat 8.1g, of which saturates 3.1g; Cholesterol 12mg; Calcium 27mg; Fibre 0.6g; Sodium 39mg.
Christmas Energy 118kcal/495kJ; Protein 1.3g; Carbohydrate 17.3g, of which sugars 10.1g; Fat 5.3g, of which saturates 3.2g; Cholesterol 26mg; Calcium 21mg; Fibre 0.3g; Sodium 39mg.

Apricot Specials

Walnuts complement the flavour of apricots perfectly in these fruity bars.

Makes 12
90g/3¹/₂oz/scant ¹/₂ cup soft light
    brown sugar
75g/3oz/²/₃ cup plain
    (all-purpose) flour
75g/3oz/6 tbsp cold unsalted
    (sweet) butter, cut in pieces

For the topping
150g/5oz/generous ¹/₂ cup
    ready-to-eat
    dried apricots
250ml/8fl oz/1 cup water
grated rind of 1 lemon
65g/2¹/₂oz/generous ¹/₄ cup
    caster (superfine) sugar
10ml/2 tsp cornflour (cornstarch)
50g/2oz/¹/₂ cup chopped walnuts

1 Preheat the oven to 180°C/350°F/Gas 4. In a mixing bowl, combine the brown sugar and flour. With a pastry blender, cut in the butter until the mixture resembles coarse breadcrumbs, or rub in with your fingertips.

2 Transfer to a 20cm/8in square baking tin (pan) and press level. Bake for 15 minutes. Remove from the oven but leave the oven on.

3 To make the topping, place the apricots and water in a pan and simmer until the fruit is soft; about 10 minutes. Strain the liquid and reserve. Chop the apricots.

4 Return the apricots to the pan and add the lemon rind, caster sugar, cornflour and 60ml/4 tbsp of the soaking liquid. Cook for 1 minute.

5 Cool slightly before spreading the topping over the base. Sprinkle over the walnuts and bake for 20 minutes more. Cool in the tin before cutting into bars.

> **Cook's Tip**
> *Vary the dried fruit for these bars depending on what you have in your cupboard. Prunes and dried peaches work especially well.*

Brandy Snaps

You could serve these brandy snaps with rich vanilla ice cream rather than the cream filling.

Makes 18
50g/2oz/¹/₄ cup butter,
    at room temperature
150g/5oz/³/₄ cup caster
    (superfine) sugar

20ml/1 rounded tbsp golden
    (light corn) syrup
40g/1¹/₂oz/¹/₃ cup plain
    (all-purpose) flour
2.5ml/¹/₂ tsp ground ginger

For the filling
250ml/8fl oz/1 cup
    whipping cream
30ml/2 tbsp brandy

1 Cream together the butter and sugar until light and fluffy, then beat in the golden syrup. Sift over the flour and ginger, and mix together. Transfer the mixture to a work surface and knead until smooth. Cover and chill for 30 minutes.

2 Preheat the oven to 190°C/375°F/Gas 5. Grease a baking sheet. Working in batches of four, shape the mixture into walnut-size balls. Place well apart on the baking sheet and flatten slightly. Bake until golden and bubbling, about 10 minutes.

3 Remove from the oven and leave to cool for a few moments. Working quickly, slide a metal spatula under each one, turn over, and wrap around the handle of a wooden spoon (have four spoons ready). If they firm up too quickly, reheat for a few seconds to soften. When firm, slide the brandy snaps off and place on a wire rack to cool.

4 When all the brandy snaps are cool, prepare the filling. Whip the cream and brandy until soft peaks form. Pipe into each end of the brandy snaps just before serving.

> **Cook's Tip**
> *Unfilled brandy snaps will keep well for up to 1 week if stored in an airtight container. However, you should eat filled brandy snaps as soon as they are made, as the cream softens them quite quickly.*

Apricot Energy 169kcal/711kJ; Protein 1.8g; Carbohydrate 23.9g, of which sugars 18.3g; Fat 8.1g, of which saturates 3.5g; Cholesterol 13mg; Calcium 30mg; Fibre 1.1g; Sodium 41mg.
Brandy Snaps Energy 121kcal/505kJ; Protein 0.6g; Carbohydrate 11.7g, of which sugars 10g; Fat 7.9g, of which saturates 5g; Cholesterol 21mg; Calcium 16mg; Fibre 0.1g; Sodium 24mg.

Chocolate Pretzels

Pretzels come in many different flavours – here is a delicious chocolate version that is guaranteed to please the tastebuds.

Makes 28
150g/5oz/1¼ cups plain (all-purpose) flour
1.5ml/¼ tsp salt
20g/¾oz/3 tbsp unsweetened cocoa powder
115g/4oz/½ cup butter, at room temperature
130g/4½oz/scant ¾ cup caster (superfine) sugar
1 egg
1 egg white, lightly beaten, for glazing
sugar crystals, for sprinkling

1 Sift together the flour, salt and cocoa powder. Set aside. Cream the butter until light. Add the sugar and continue beating until light and fluffy. Beat in the egg.

2 Add the dry ingredients and stir to blend thoroughly. Gather the dough into a ball, wrap it in clear film (plastic wrap) and chill for 1 hour.

3 Roll the dough into 28 small balls. Chill the balls until needed. Preheat the oven to 190°C/375°F/Gas 5. Lightly grease two baking sheets.

4 Roll each ball into a rope about 25cm/10in long. With each rope, form a loop with the two ends facing you. Twist the ends and fold them back on to the circle, pressing them in to make a pretzel shape. Place on the prepared baking sheets.

5 Brush each of the pretzels with the egg white. Sprinkle sugar crystals over the tops and bake in the oven until firm, about 10–12 minutes. Using a metal spatula, transfer to a wire rack to cool.

> **Variation**
> To make mocha-flavoured pretzels, replace 10ml/1 tsp of the unsweetened cocoa powder with instant coffee powder.

Iced Ginger Cookies

If your children enjoy cooking with you, mixing and rolling the dough, or cutting out different shapes, this is the ideal recipe to let them practise on.

Makes 16
115g/4oz/½ cup soft light brown sugar
115g/4oz/½ cup soft margarine
a pinch of salt
a few drops of vanilla extract
175g/6oz/1½ cups wholemeal flour
15g/½oz/2 tbsp unsweetened cocoa powder, sifted
10ml/2 tsp ground ginger
a little milk
glacé icing and glacé (candied) cherries, to decorate

1 Preheat the oven to 190°C/375°F/Gas 5. Grease two baking sheets. Cream the light brown sugar, margarine, salt and vanilla extract together until very soft and light.

2 Work in the flour, cocoa and ginger, adding a little milk, if necessary, to bind the mixture. Knead lightly on a floured surface until smooth.

3 Roll out the dough on a lightly floured surface to about 5mm/¼in thick. Stamp out shapes using cookie cutters and place on baking sheets.

4 Bake the cookies for 10–15 minutes, leave to cool on the baking sheets until firm, then transfer to a wire rack to cool completely. Decorate the cooled cookies with the glacé icing and glacé cherries.

> **Cook's Tip**
> This mixture is ideal for creating small gingerbread people, which children will love to make. Cut out the cookies using appropriate cutters and decorate with raisins for eyes and glacé (candied) cherries for a smiley mouth. Sesame seeds can be pressed into the mixture to make a pattern or the outline of clothing. Or pipe icing on to the finished cookies to make features, buttons, a bow tie or scarf and clothes.

Chocolate Energy 72kcal/303kJ; Protein 1g; Carbohydrate 9.1g, of which sugars 5g; Fat 3.8g, of which saturates 2.3g; Cholesterol 16mg; Calcium 13mg; Fibre 0.3g; Sodium 37mg.
Ginger Energy 119kcal/497kJ; Protein 1.6g; Carbohydrate 14.7g, of which sugars 7.8g; Fat 6.4g, of which saturates 3.9g; Cholesterol 15mg; Calcium 11mg; Fibre 1.1g; Sodium 53mg.

Chocolate Macaroons

Serve these delicious macaroons with coffee.

Makes 24

50g/2oz plain (semisweet) chocolate, melted

175g/6oz/1 cup blanched almonds

225g/8oz/generous 1 cup caster (superfine) sugar

3 egg whites

2.5ml/½ tsp vanilla extract

1.5ml/¼ tsp almond extract

icing (confectioners') sugar, for dusting

1 Preheat the oven to 160°C/325°F/Gas 3. Line two baking sheets with baking parchment and then grease them.

2 Grind the almonds in a food processor. Transfer to a bowl, then blend in the sugar, egg whites, vanilla and almond extracts.

3 Stir in the melted chocolate. The mixture should just hold its shape; if it is too soft, chill for 15 minutes.

4 Shape the mixture into walnut-size balls. Place on the baking sheets and flatten slightly. Brush with a little water and dust with icing sugar. Bake until just firm, 10–12 minutes. With a metal spatula, transfer to a wire rack to cool.

Big Macaroons

Makes 9

2 egg whites

5ml/1 tsp almond extract

115g/4oz/1 cup ground almonds

130g/4½oz/1 cup light muscovado (brown) sugar

1 Preheat the oven to 180°C/350°F/Gas 4. Line a large baking sheet with baking parchment. Whisk the egg whites until they form stiff peaks. Add the almond extract and whisk to combine. Fold the almonds and sugar into the mixture.

2 Place nine spoonfuls of the mixture on the baking sheet and flatten slightly. Bake for 15 minutes. Leave to cool on the sheet for 5 minutes before removing to a wire rack to cool completely.

Coconut Macaroons

Makes 24

40g/1½oz/⅓ cup plain (all-purpose) flour

1.5ml/1¼tsp salt

225g/8oz/4 cups desiccated (dry unsweetened shredded) coconut

170ml/5½fl oz/scant ¾ cup sweetened condensed milk

1 Preheat the oven to 180°C/350°F/Gas 4. Grease two baking sheets. Sift the flour and salt into a bowl and then stir in the coconut. Pour in the condensed milk and mix, stirring from the centre, to form a thick mixture.

2 Drop tablespoonfuls of the mixture 2.5cm/1in apart on the baking sheets. Bake until golden brown, about 20 minutes.

Chocolate Orange Sponge Drops

Light and crispy, with a zesty marmalade filling, these sponge drops are truly delightful.

Makes 14–15

2 eggs

50g/2oz/¼ cup caster (superfine) sugar

2.5ml/½ tsp grated orange rind

50g/2oz/½ cup plain (all-purpose) flour

60ml/4 tbsp fine-shred orange marmalade

40g/1½oz plain (semisweet) chocolate, melted

1 Preheat the oven to 200°C/400°F/Gas 6. Line three baking sheets with baking parchment.

2 Put the eggs and sugar in a bowl over a pan of simmering water. Whisk until thick and pale. Remove from the pan and whisk until cool. Whisk in the orange rind. Sift the flour over and fold it in gently.

3 Put 28–30 dessertspoonfuls of the mixture on the baking sheets. Bake for 8 minutes, until golden. Cool slightly, then transfer to a wire rack. Sandwich pairs together with marmalade. Melt the chocolate and drizzle over the drops.

Chocolate Energy 94kcal/393kJ; Protein 2.1g; Carbohydrate 11.6g, of which sugars 11.4g; Fat 4.7g, of which saturates 0.7g; Cholesterol 0mg; Calcium 23mg; Fibre 0.6g; Sodium 9mg.
Big Macaroons Energy 138kcal/577kJ; Protein 2.5g; Carbohydrate 16g, of which sugars 14.2g; Fat 7.1g, of which saturates 0.6g; Cholesterol 1mg; Calcium 31mg; Fibre 0.9g; Sodium 12mg.
Coconut Energy 86kcal/357kJ; Protein 1.8g; Carbohydrate 5.8g, of which sugars 9.8g; Fat 6.6g, of which saturates 5.5g; Cholesterol 0.5mg; Calcium 21mg; Fibre 1.3g; Sodium 8mg.
Sponge Drops Energy 58kcal/247kJ; Protein 1.3g; Carbohydrate 10.5g, of which sugars 8g; Fat 1.5g, of which saturates 0.7g; Cholesterol 26mg; Calcium 12mg; Fibre 0.2g; Sodium 12mg.

Peanut Butter Cookies

These moreish cookies must come close to the top of the list of America's favourites. They are quick and simple to make with ingredients that you will normally have in the store cupboard or pantry.

Makes 24

150g/5oz/1¼ cups plain (all-purpose) flour
2.5ml/½ tsp bicarbonate of soda (baking soda)
2.5ml/½ tsp salt
115g/4oz/½ cup butter, at room temperature
170g/5¾oz/generous ⅔ cup soft light brown sugar
1 egg
5ml/1 tsp vanilla extract
260g/9½oz/scant 1¼ cups crunchy peanut butter
icing (confectioner's) sugar, to dust

1 Sift together the flour, bicarbonate of soda and salt, and set aside. In another bowl, cream the butter and sugar together until light and fluffy.

2 In a third bowl, mix the egg and vanilla, then gradually beat into the butter mixture. Stir in the peanut butter and blend thoroughly. Stir in the dry ingredients. Chill for 30 minutes, or until firm.

3 Preheat the oven to 180°C/350°F/Gas 4. Grease two baking sheets. Spoon out rounded teaspoonfuls of the dough and roll into balls.

4 Place the balls on the baking sheets and shape into circles about 6cm/2½in in diameter.

5 Bake until lightly coloured, about 12–15 minutes. Using a spatula transfer to a wire rack to cool. Dust with icing sugar.

Variation
For extra crunch add 50g/2oz/½ cup chopped raw, skinned peanuts with the peanut butter at step 2. (Raw peanuts do not keep well so always buy in small quantities.)

Chocolate Chip Cookies

A perennial favourite with all the family, these cookies contain walnuts as well as chocolate chips.

Makes 24

115g/4oz/½ cup butter or margarine, at room temperature
45g/1¾ oz/scant ¼ cup caster (superfine) sugar
100g/3¾oz/scant ½ cup soft dark brown sugar
1 egg
2.5ml/½ tsp vanilla extract
175g/6oz/1½ cups plain (all-purpose) flour
2.5ml/½ tsp bicarbonate of soda (baking soda)
1.5ml/¼ tsp salt
175g/6oz/1 cup chocolate chips
50g/2oz/⅓ cup walnuts, chopped

1 Preheat the oven to 180°C/350°F/Gas 4. Lightly grease two large baking sheets. With an electric mixer, cream the butter or margarine and both the sugars together until light and fluffy.

2 In another bowl, mix the egg and the vanilla extract, then gradually beat into the butter mixture. Sift over the flour, bicarbonate of soda and salt and stir. Add the chocolate chips and walnuts, and mix to combine well.

3 Place heaped teaspoonfuls of the dough 5cm/2in apart on the baking sheets. Bake in the oven until lightly coloured, about 10–15 minutes. Transfer to a wire rack to cool.

Variations
All chocolate: substitute 15ml/1tbsp unsweetened cocoa powder for the same quantity of flour, and omit the vanilla.
Mocha: Use coffee essence instead of vanilla extract.
Macadamia nut or hazelnut: instead of the walnuts add whole or coarsely chopped macadamia nuts or hazelnuts.
Dried fruit: instead of the walnuts and chocolate chips add chopped dried fruit, such as rains, sultanas (golden raisins), glacé (candied) cherries, or tropical fruit.
Banana: substitute a ripe, mashed banana and 50g/2oz/¼ cup chopped banana chips for the walnuts and chocolate chips.

Peanut Energy 154kcal/641kJ; Protein 3.4g; Carbohydrate 13.7g, of which sugars 8.3g; Fat 9.9g, of which saturates 4g; Cholesterol 18mg; Calcium 19mg; Fibre 0.8g; Sodium 71mg.
Chocolate-chip Energy 139kcal/582kJ; Protein 1.7g; Carbohydrate 16.7g, of which sugars 11.1g; Fat 7.7g, of which saturates 3.9g; Cholesterol 19mg; Calcium 20mg; Fibre 0.5g; Sodium 33mg.

Almond Tile Cookies

Light and delicate as a
feather and truly delicious,
these cookies make the
perfect accompaniment to
a creamy dessert.

Makes about 24
65g/2½oz/scant ½ cup
  whole blanched almonds,
  lightly toasted

65g/2½oz/5 tbsp caster
  (superfine) sugar
40g/1½oz/3 tbsp unsalted
  (sweet) butter, softened
2 egg whites
2.5ml/½ tsp almond extract
40g/1½oz/⅓ cup plain
  (all-purpose) flour, sifted
50g/2oz/½ cup flaked
  (sliced) almonds

1 Preheat the oven to 200°C/400°F/Gas 6. Thoroughly grease
two baking sheets. Place the almonds and 30ml/2 tbsp of the
sugar in a blender or food processor and process until finely
ground, but not forming a paste.

2 Beat the butter until creamy, add the remaining sugar and
beat until light and fluffy.

3 Gradually beat in the egg whites until the mixture is well
blended, then beat in the almond extract.

4 Sift the flour over the butter mixture and fold in, then fold in
the almond mixture.

5 Drop tablespoonfuls of the mixture on to the baking sheets
15cm/6in apart. With the back of a wet spoon, spread each
mound into a paper-thin 7.5cm/3in circle. Sprinkle with the
flaked almonds.

6 Bake the cookies, one sheet at a time, for 5–6 minutes, or
until the edges are golden and the centres still pale.

7 Remove the baking sheet to a wire rack and, working quickly,
use a metal spatula to loosen the edges of a cookie. Lift the
cookie on the metal spatula and place over a rolling pin, then
press down the sides of the cookie to curve it. Repeat with
the remaining cookies, and leave to cool.

Brittany Butter Cookies

These little cookies are
similar to shortbread, but
they are richer in taste
and texture.

Makes 18–20
6 egg yolks, lightly beaten
15ml/1 tbsp milk

250g/9oz/2¼ cups plain
  (all-purpose) flour
175g/6oz/generous ¾ cup caster
  (superfine) sugar
200g/7oz/scant 1 cup lightly
  salted butter at room
  temperature, cut into
  small pieces

1 Preheat the oven to 180°C/350°F/Gas 4. Lightly butter a
large baking sheet. Mix 15ml/1 tbsp of the egg yolks with the
milk for a glaze. Set aside.

2 Sift the flour into a large bowl and make a central well. Add
the egg yolks, sugar and butter and, using your fingertips, work
them together until smooth and creamy. Gradually blend in the
flour to form a smooth but slightly sticky dough.

3 Using floured hands, pat out the dough to 8mm/⅓in thick
and cut out circles using a 7.5cm/3in cookie cutter.

4 Transfer the circles to the baking sheet, brush with egg glaze,
then score to create a lattice pattern.

5 Bake for 12–15 minutes, or until golden. Cool on the baking
sheet on a wire rack for 15 minutes, then transfer to the wire
rack to cool completely.

Variation
*To make a large Brittany Butter Cake, pat the dough with well-
floured hands into a greased 23cm/9in loose-based cake tin
(pan) or springform tin. Brush with the egg and milk glaze, and
score the lattice pattern on the top. Bake for 45–60 minutes,
or until firm to the touch and golden brown. Cool in the tin
for 15 minutes before carefully turning out on to a rack to
cool completely.*

Almond Energy 59kcal/246kJ; Protein 1.4g; Carbohydrate 4.5g, of which sugars 3.1g; Fat 4.1g, of which saturates 1.1g; Cholesterol 4mg; Calcium 16mg; Fibre 0.4g; Sodium 16mg.
Butter Energy 170kcal/711kJ; Protein 2.2g; Carbohydrate 19g, of which sugars 9.4g; Fat 10g, of which saturates 5.7g; Cholesterol 82mg; Calcium 32mg; Fibre 0.4g; Sodium 65mg.

Ginger Florentines

These colourful, chewy cookies are delicious served with vanilla or other flavoured ice cream.

Makes 30
50g/2oz/¼ cup butter
115g/4oz/generous ½ cup caster (superfine) sugar
50g/2oz/¼ cup mixed glacé (candied) cherries, chopped
25g/1oz/generous 1 tbsp candied orange peel, chopped
50g/2oz/½ cup flaked (sliced) almonds
50g/2oz/½ cup chopped walnuts
25g/1oz/1 tbsp glacé (candied) ginger, chopped
30ml/2 tbsp plain (all-purpose) flour
2.5ml/½ tsp ground ginger

To finish
50g/2oz plain (semisweet) chocolate, melted
50g/2oz white chocolate, melted

1 Preheat the oven to 180°C/350°F/Gas 4. Beat the butter and sugar together until light and fluffy.

2 Add the glacé cherries, candied orange peel, flaked almonds, chopped walnuts and glacé ginger to the mixture, and blend thoroughly. Sift the plain flour and ground ginger into the mixture and stir well to combine.

3 Line some baking sheets with non-stick baking paper. Put four small spoonfuls of the mixture on to each sheet, spacing them well apart to allow for spreading. Flatten the cookies and bake for 5 minutes.

4 Remove the cookies from the oven and flatten with a wet fork, shaping them into neat rounds.

5 Return to the oven for about 3–4 minutes, until they are golden brown. Work in batches if necessary.

6 Let them cool on the baking sheets for 2 minutes to firm up, and then transfer them to a wire rack. When they are cold and firm, spread plain chocolate on the undersides of half the cookies and white chocolate on the undersides of the rest. Allow the chocolate to set before serving.

Festive Cookies

Dainty, hand-painted cookies look delightful served at Christmas. These are great fun for children to make as presents, and any shape of cookie cutter can be used.

Makes about 12
75g/3oz/6 tbsp butter
50g/2oz/½ cup icing (confectioners') sugar
finely grated rind of 1 small lemon
1 egg yolk
175g/6oz/1½ cups plain (all-purpose) flour
a pinch of salt

To decorate
2 egg yolks
red and green food colouring

1 Beat the butter, icing sugar and lemon rind together until pale and fluffy. Beat in the egg yolk, and then sift in the flour and the salt. Knead together to form a smooth dough. Wrap and chill for 30 minutes.

2 Preheat the oven to 190°C/375°F/Gas 5 and lightly grease two baking sheets.

3 On a lightly floured surface, roll out the dough to 3mm/⅛in thick. Using a 6cm/2½in fluted cutter, stamp out as many cookies as you can, with the cutter dipped in flour to prevent it from sticking to the dough.

4 Transfer the cookies to the prepared baking sheets. Mark the tops lightly with a 2.5cm/1in holly leaf cutter and use a 5mm/¼in plain piping (icing) nozzle for the berries. Chill for 10 minutes, until firm.

5 Meanwhile, to make the decoration put each egg yolk into a small cup. Mix red food colouring into one and green food colouring into the other. Using a small, clean paintbrush, carefully paint the colours on to the cookies.

6 Bake for 10–12 minutes, or until they begin to colour around the edges. Let them cool slightly on the baking sheets, then transfer to a wire rack to cool completely.

Ginger Energy 71kcal/298kJ; Protein 0.9g; Carbohydrate 8.6g, of which sugars 7.8g; Fat 3.9g, of which saturates 1.3g; Cholesterol 2mg; Calcium 16mg; Fibre 0.3g; Sodium 11mg.
Festive Energy 118kcal/494kJ; Protein 1.7g; Carbohydrate 15.7g, of which sugars 4.6g; Fat 5.8g, of which saturates 3.4g; Cholesterol 30mg; Calcium 26mg; Fibre 0.5g; Sodium 39mg.

Traditional Sugar Cookies

These lovely old-fashioned cookies would be ideal to serve at an elegant tea party.

Makes 36
350g/12oz/3 cups plain
  (all-purpose) flour
5ml/1 tsp bicarbonate of soda
  (baking soda)
10ml/2 tsp baking powder
1.5ml/¼ tsp freshly
  grated nutmeg
115g/4oz/½ cup butter or
  margarine, at room temperature
225g/8oz/generous 1 cup caster
  (superfine) sugar
2.5ml/½ tsp vanilla extract
1 egg
120ml/4fl oz/½ cup milk
coloured or demerara (raw) sugar,
  for sprinkling

1 Sift the flour, bicarbonate of soda, baking powder and nutmeg into a small bowl. Set aside. Cream the butter or margarine, caster sugar and vanilla extract together until the mixture is light and fluffy. Add the egg and beat to mix well.

2 Add the flour mixture alternately with the milk, stirring with a wooden spoon to make a soft dough. Wrap the dough in clear film and chill for 30 minutes.

3 Preheat the oven to 180°C/350°F/Gas 4. Roll out the dough on a lightly floured surface to a 3mm/⅛in thickness. Cut into circles with a cookie cutter.

4 Transfer the cookies to ungreased baking sheets. Sprinkle each one with sugar. Bake until golden, 10–12 minutes. With a metal spatula, transfer the cookies to a wire rack to cool.

Variation
Transform these cookies into funky flower-power cookies for a children's party by omitting the final sprinkling of sugar and icing them when cold. Spoon a little icing on to the top of each cookie and spread into a circle, then top with a sugared flower. Choose wildly contrasting colours or dainty pastel shades for the icings and flowers.

Spicy Pepper Cookies

Don't be put off by their peppery name – try these warmly spiced cookies and you are sure to be pleasantly surprised by their fabulous flavour. They are also very quick and easy to make.

Makes 48
200g/7oz/1¾ cups plain
  (all-purpose) flour
50g/2oz/½ cup cornflour
  (cornstarch)
10ml/2 tsp baking powder
2.5ml/½ tsp ground cardamom
2.5ml/½ tsp ground cinnamon
2.5ml/½ tsp freshly
  grated nutmeg
2.5ml/½ tsp ground ginger
2.5ml/½ tsp ground allspice
2.5ml/½ tsp salt
2.5ml/½ tsp freshly ground
  black pepper
225g/8oz/1 cup butter
  or margarine, at
  room temperature
90g/3½oz/scant ½ cup soft
  light brown sugar
2.5ml/½ tsp vanilla extract
5ml/1 tsp finely grated
  lemon rind
50ml/2fl oz/¼ cup whipping cream
75g/3oz/¾ cup finely
  ground almonds
50ml/2 tbsp icing
  (confectioners') sugar

1 Preheat the oven to 180°C/350°F/Gas 4. Sift the flour, cornflour, baking powder, spices, salt and pepper into a bowl. Set aside.

2 Using an electric mixer, cream the butter or margarine and brown sugar until light and fluffy. Beat in the vanilla extract and lemon rind.

3 With the mixer on low speed, add the flour mixture alternately with the cream, beginning and ending with flour. Stir in the ground almonds.

4 Shape the dough into 2cm/¾in balls. Place them on ungreased baking sheets about 2.5cm/1in apart. Bake until golden brown underneath, about 15–20 minutes.

5 Leave to cool on the baking sheets for about 1 minute before transferring to a wire rack to cool completely. Before serving, sprinkle lightly with icing sugar.

Sugar Energy 85kcal/359kJ; Protein 1.2g; Carbohydrate 14.3g, of which sugars 6.9g; Fat 3g, of which saturates 1.8g; Cholesterol 12mg; Calcium 22mg; Fibre 0.3g; Sodium 23mg.
Pepper Energy 75kcal/314kJ; Protein 0.8g; Carbohydrate 6.8g, of which sugars 2.6g; Fat 5.2g, of which saturates 2.8g; Cholesterol 11mg; Calcium 12mg; Fibre 0.2g; Sodium 30mg.

Mexican Cinnamon Cookies

Pastelitos are traditional sweet shortbreads served at weddings in Mexico, dusted with icing sugar to match the bride's dress.

Makes 20
115g/4oz/½ cup butter
25g/1oz/2 tbsp caster (superfine) sugar
115g/4oz/1 cup plain (all-purpose) flour
50g/2oz/½ cup cornflour (cornstarch)
1.5ml/¼ tsp ground cinnamon
30ml/2 tbsp chopped mixed nuts
25g/1oz/¼ cup icing (confectioners') sugar, sifted

1 Preheat the oven to 160°C/325°F/Gas 3. Lightly grease a baking sheet. Place the butter and sugar in a bowl and beat until pale and creamy.

2 Sift the plain flour, cornflour and ground cinnamon into the butter and sugar mixture, and gradually work in with a wooden spoon until the mixture comes together. Knead the dough lightly until completely smooth.

3 Take tablespoonfuls of the mixture, roll into 20 small balls and arrange on the baking sheet. Press a few chopped nuts into the top of each one and then flatten slightly.

4 Bake the cookies for about 30–35 minutes, or until pale golden. Remove from the oven and, while they are still warm, toss them in the sifted icing sugar. Leave the cookies to cool on a wire rack before serving.

> **Cook's Tip**
> Choose two or three types of nut for this recipe. Cashew nuts, walnuts, raw skinned peanuts, almonds or hazelnuts all work well. Or choose from pecan nuts, pistachio nuts or macadamia nuts for a richer flavour. Make sure the nuts are chopped finely if small children are going to eat the cookies. You could even use some sesame seeds with the nuts if you like.

Sultana Cornmeal Cookies

These little yellow cookies come from the Veneto region of Italy, and contain Marsala wine, which gives them a rich flavour and enhances their regional appeal. Excellent served with a glass of wine.

Makes about 48
65g/2½oz/½ cup sultanas (golden raisins)
50g/2oz/½ cup finely ground yellow cornmeal
175g/6oz/1½ cups plain (all-purpose) flour
7.5ml/1½ tsp baking powder
a pinch of salt
225g/8oz/1 cup butter
200g/7oz/1 cup sugar
2 eggs
15ml/1 tbsp Marsala or
5ml/1 tsp vanilla extract

1 Soak the sultanas in a small bowl of warm water for about 15 minutes. Drain.

2 Preheat the oven to 180°C/350°F/Gas 4, and grease a baking sheet. Sift the cornmeal and flour, the baking powder and the salt together into a bowl.

3 Cream the butter and sugar together until light and fluffy. Beat in the eggs, one at a time. Beat in the Marsala or vanilla extract.

4 Add the dry ingredients to the batter, beating until well blended. Stir in the sultanas.

5 Drop heaped teaspoonfuls of batter on to the prepared baking sheet in rows about 5cm/2in apart. Bake for 7–8 minutes, or until the cookies are golden brown at the edges. Remove to a wire rack to cool.

> **Cook's Tip**
> Marsala is a fortified wine with an alcohol level of around 20 per cent. There are sweet and dry types; use the sweet wine to give this recipe an authentic flavour.

Sultana Energy 74kcal/311kJ; Protein 0.8g; Carbohydrate 8.9g, of which sugars 5.4g; Fat 4.2g, of which saturates 2.5g; Cholesterol 18mg; Calcium 10mg; Fibre 0.2g; Sodium 32mg.
Cinnamon Energy 91kcal/382kJ; Protein 0.8g; Carbohydrate 9.5g, of which sugars 2.8g; Fat 5.8g, of which saturates 3.1g; Cholesterol 12mg; Calcium 12mg; Fibre 0.2g; Sodium 37mg.

Meringues

You can make these classic meringues as large or small as you like.

Makes about 24 small meringues
4 egg whites
1.5ml/¼ tsp salt

275g/10oz/scant 1¼ cups caster (superfine) sugar
2.5ml/½ tsp vanilla or almond extract (optional)

To serve
250ml/8fl oz/1 cup whipping cream

1 Preheat the oven to 110°C/225°F/Gas ¼. Grease and flour two large baking sheets.

2 Beat the egg whites and salt in a metal bowl. When they start to form soft peaks, add half the sugar and continue beating until the mixture holds stiff peaks.

3 With a large metal spoon, fold in the remaining sugar and the vanilla or almond extract, if using.

4 Pipe or spoon the mixture on to the prepared baking sheets. Bake them for 2 hours, then turn off the oven. Loosen the meringues, invert, and set in another place on the baking sheets to prevent them from sticking.

5 Leave the meringues in the oven until they are cool. Whip the cream and use to sandwich the meringues together in pairs.

Variation
To make decorative Meringue Squiggles, line a baking sheet with parchment paper. Make half the amount of meringue mixture given above. Using a large plain nozzle, pipe squiggles about 13cm/5in long on to the baking sheet. Bake for 1 hour. Remove from the oven and leave to cool. Mix the icing sugar with a little water and brush over the meringues. Decorate with sugar sprinkles and serve on their own or with fruit salad and vanilla ice cream.

Toasted Oat Meringues

Try these oaty meringues for a lovely crunchy change.

Makes 12
50g/2oz/generous ½ cup rolled oats

2 egg whites
1.5ml/¼ tsp salt
7.5ml/1½ tsp cornflour (cornstarch)
175g/6oz/¾ cup caster (superfine) sugar

1 Preheat the oven to 140°C/275°F/Gas 1. Spread the oats on a baking sheet and toast in the oven until golden. Lower the heat to 120°C/250°F/Gas ½. Grease and flour a baking sheet.

2 Beat the egg whites and salt until they start to form soft peaks. Sift over the cornflour and continue beating until the whites hold stiff peaks. Add half the sugar; whisk until glossy. Add the remaining sugar and fold in carefully. Fold in the toasted oats.

3 Place tablespoonfuls of the mixture on to the baking sheet and bake for 2 hours, then turn off the oven. Turn over the meringues, and leave in the oven until completely cool.

Chewy Walnut Cookies

Makes 18
4 egg whites
275g/10oz/2½ cups icing (confectioners') sugar

5ml/1 tsp cooled strong coffee
115g/4oz/1 cup finely chopped walnuts

1 Preheat the oven to 180°C/350°F/Gas 4. Line two baking sheets with baking parchment and then grease the paper. Using an electric mixer beat the egg whites until frothy. Sift over the icing sugar and add the coffee.

2 Add 15ml/1 tbsp water; beat on low speed to blend, then on high until thick. Fold in the walnuts. Place spoonfuls of the mixture 2.5cm/1in apart on the sheets. Bake for 12–15 minutes. Transfer to a wire rack to cool.

Meringues Energy 78kcal/334kJ; Protein 1.1g; Carbohydrate 18.9g, of which sugars 15.2g; Fat 0.4g, of which saturates 0g; Cholesterol 0mg; Calcium 10mg; Fibre 0.3g; Sodium 13mg.
Oat Meringues Energy 87kcal/364kJ; Protein 0.7g; Carbohydrate 12.3g, of which sugars 12.3g; Fat 4.2g, of which saturates 2.6g; Cholesterol 11mg; Calcium 12mg; Fibre 0g; Sodium 13mg.
Walnut Cookies Energy 107kcal/449kJ; Protein 32.6g; Carbohydrate 16.2g, of which sugars 14.1g; Fat 4.4g, of which saturates 0.4g; Cholesterol 13mg; Calcium 15mg; Fibre 0.2g; Sodium 16mg.

Lavender Cookies

Makes about 30
150g/5oz/²/₃ cup butter
115g/4oz/generous ¹/₂ cup caster
  (superfine) sugar
1 egg, beaten

15ml/1 tbsp dried lavender flowers
175g/6oz/1¹/₂ cups self-raising
  (self-rising) flour
leaves and flowers,
  to decorate

1 Preheat the oven to 180°C/350°F/Gas 4. Grease two baking sheets. Cream the butter and sugar together, then stir in the egg. Mix in the lavender flowers and the flour.

2 Drop spoonfuls of the mixture on to the baking sheets. Bake for 15–20 minutes, or until the cookies are golden. Serve with some fresh leaves and flowers to decorate.

Amaretti

Makes 36
200g/7oz/1³/₄ cups
  blanched almonds
plain (all-purpose) flour for dusting
225g/8oz/generous 1 cup caster
  (superfine) sugar

2 egg whites
2.5ml/¹/₂ tsp almond extract
icing (confectioners') sugar,
  for dusting

1 Preheat the oven to 160°C/325°F/Gas 3. Spread the almonds on a baking sheet and dry them out in the oven, without browning, for 15 minutes. Turn the oven off.

2 Leave the almonds to cool, then dust with flour. Grind with half the sugar. Whisk the egg whites until soft peaks form. Gradually whisk in half the remaining sugar until stiff peaks form. Fold in the remaining sugar, the almonds and the extract.

3 Pipe in walnut-sized rounds on to a greased baking sheet. Sprinkle with icing sugar and leave to stand for 2 hours. Preheat the oven to 180°C/350°F/Gas 4 and bake for 15 minutes. Cool on a wire rack.

Chocolate Amaretti

Although it is always said that chocolate does not go with wine, enjoy these delightful cookies Italian-style with a glass of chilled champagne.

Makes 24
150g/5oz/scant 1 cup blanched,
  toasted whole almonds

115g/4oz/generous ¹/₂ cup caster
  (superfine) sugar
15ml/1 tbsp unsweetened
  cocoa powder
30ml/2 tbsp icing
  (confectioners') sugar
2 egg whites
a pinch of cream of tartar
5ml/1 tsp almond extract
flaked almonds, to decorate

1 Preheat the oven to 160°C/325°F/Gas 3. Line a large baking sheet with non-stick baking paper or foil. In a food processor fitted with a metal blade, process the toasted almonds with half the sugar until they are finely ground but not oily. Transfer to a bowl and sift in the cocoa and icing sugar; stir to blend. Set aside.

2 Beat the egg whites and cream of tartar until stiff peaks form. Sprinkle in the remaining sugar 15ml/1 tbsp at a time, beating well after each addition, and continue beating until the whites are glossy and stiff. Beat in the almond extract.

3 Sprinkle over the almond mixture and gently fold into the egg whites until just blended. Spoon the mixture into a large piping (icing) bag fitted with a plain 1cm/¹/₂in nozzle. Pipe 4cm/1¹/₂in rounds, 2.5cm/1in apart, on the baking sheet. Press a flaked almond into the centre of each.

4 Bake the cookies for 12–15 minutes, or until they appear crisp. Remove the baking sheet to a wire rack to cool for 10 minutes. With a metal spatula, remove the cookies to the wire rack to cool completely.

> **Variation**
> As an alternative decoration, lightly press a few coffee sugar crystals on top of each cookie before baking.

Lavender Energy 74kcal/310kJ; Protein 0.8g; Carbohydrate 8.4g, of which sugars 4.1g; Fat 4.4g, of which saturates 2.7g; Cholesterol 17mg; Calcium 24mg; Fibre 0.2g; Sodium 54mg.
Amaretti 59Kcal/249kJ; Protein 1.1g; Carbohydrate 6.9g, of which sugars 6.7g; Fat 3.1g, of which saturates 0.2g; Cholesterol 0mg; Calcium 14mg; Fibre 0.4g; Sodium 5mg.
Chocolate Energy 66kcal/278kJ; Protein 1.7g; Carbohydrate 7.2g, of which sugars 7g; Fat 3.6g, of which saturates 0.4g; Cholesterol 0mg; Calcium 19mg; Fibre 0.5g; Sodium 12mg.

Melting Moments

These cookies are very crisp and light – and they really do melt in your mouth.

Makes 16–20

40g/1½oz/3 tbsp butter
  or margarine
65g/2½oz/5 tbsp lard or
  white cooking fat

75g/3oz/scant ½ cup caster
  (superfine) sugar
½ egg, beaten
a few drops of vanilla or
  almond extract
150g/5oz/1¼ cups self-raising
  (self-rising) flour
rolled oats, for coating
4–5 glacé (candied) cherries,
  quartered, to decorate

1 Preheat the oven to 180°C/350°F/Gas 4, and grease two baking sheets.

2 Beat together the butter or margarine, lard and sugar, then gradually beat in the egg and vanilla or almond extract.

3 Stir the flour into the beaten mixture, with floured hands, then roll into 16–20 small balls. Spread the rolled oats on a sheet of baking parchment and toss the balls in them to coat evenly.

4 Place the balls, spaced slightly apart, on the baking sheets, place a piece of cherry on top of each and bake for about 15–20 minutes, or until lightly browned.

5 Allow the cookies to cool on the sheets for 5 minutes before transferring to a wire rack to cool completely.

> **Cook's Tips**
> • *The meltingly short texture for these cookies is achieved by using two different kinds of fat. Lard, made from processed pure pork fat, is often used to make light pastries; use a vegetarian white cooking fat (shortening) if you prefer. The butter adds richness and flavour.*
> • *To halve an egg, beat a whole egg in a measuring jug (cup) and then pour off half.*

Easter Cookies

Traditionally butter could not be eaten during the Lenten fast, so these cookies were a welcome Easter treat.

Makes 16–18

115g/4oz/½ cup butter
  or margarine
75g/3oz/scant ½ cup caster
  (superfine) sugar, plus extra
  for sprinkling

1 egg, separated
200g/7oz/1¾ cups plain
  (all-purpose) flour
2.5ml/½ tsp mixed (apple
  pie) spice
2.5ml/½ tsp ground cinnamon
50g/2oz/¼ cup currants
15ml/1 tbsp mixed chopped
  (candied) peel
15–30ml/1–2 tbsp milk

1 Preheat the oven to 200°C/400°F/Gas 6. Lightly grease two baking sheets. Cream together the butter or margarine and sugar until light and fluffy, then beat in the egg yolk.

2 Sift the flour, mixed spice and cinnamon over the egg mixture in the bowl, then fold in with the currants and chopped mixed peel, adding sufficient milk to make a fairly soft dough.

3 Turn the dough on to a floured surface, knead lightly until just smooth, then roll out using a floured rolling pin, to about a 5mm/¼in thickness. Cut the dough into circles using a 5cm/2in fluted cookie cutter. Transfer the circles to the baking sheets and bake for 10 minutes.

4 Beat the egg white, then brush over the cookies. Sprinkle with caster sugar and return to the oven for a further 10 minutes, until golden. Using a metal spatula transfer to a wire rack to cool.

> **Cook's Tip**
> *Cinnamon is one of the exceptions to the rule that you should, if possible, buy spices whole and grind them freshly when you need them. Although cinnamon sticks are widely available, they are difficult – almost impossible – to grind yourself.*

Melting Energy 88kcal/370kJ; Protein 0.7g; Carbohydrate 10.9g, of which sugars 5.4g; Fat 5g, of which saturates 2.4g; Cholesterol 7mg; Calcium 30mg; Fibre 0.3g; Sodium 40mg.
Easter Energy 116kcal/485kJ; Protein 1.5g; Carbohydrate 15.4g, of which sugars 7g; Fat 5.7g, of which saturates 3.4g; Cholesterol 24mg; Calcium 25mg; Fibre 0.4g; Sodium 46mg.

Shortbread

Once you have tasted this shortbread, you'll never buy a packet from a shop again.

Makes 8

150g/5oz/generous ½ cup unsalted (sweet) butter, at room temperature

115g/4oz/generous ½ cup caster (superfine) sugar

150g/5oz/1¼ cups plain (all-purpose) flour

65g/2½oz/generous ½ cup rice flour

1.5ml/¼ tsp baking powder

1.5ml/¼ tsp salt

1 Preheat the oven to 160°C/325°F/Gas 3. Lightly grease a 20cm/8in shallow round cake tin (pan) or an 18cm/7in square tin and set aside until needed.

2 Cream the butter and sugar together until light and fluffy. Sift over the flours, baking powder and salt, and mix well.

3 Press the mixture neatly into the prepared tin, smoothing the surface with the back of a spoon. Score into eight equal wedges or into fingers.

4 Bake until golden, about 40–45 minutes. Leave in the tin until cool enough to handle, then unmould and recut the wedges or fingers while still hot. Store in an airtight container.

> **Variation**
> To make a party sensation for children – Jewelled Shortbread Fingers – bake the shortbread in a greased 18cm/7in square tin (pan). Score the shortbread into fingers when warm and cut when cold. (Use a serrated knife and a sawing action to cut the shortbread neatly.) Make a fairly thin icing using 150g/5oz/ 1¼ cups icing (confectioners') sugar mixed with 10–15ml/ 2–3 tbsp lemon juice, and use to drizzle over the shortbread fingers in a random zigzag pattern. Crush some brightly coloured boiled sweets (hard candies) using a rolling pin and sprinkle them over the icing so that they stick. Add a few gold or silver edible balls to each decorated finger.

Flapjacks

For a spicier version, add 5ml/1 tsp ground ginger to the melted butter.

Makes 8

50g/2oz/¼ cup butter

20ml/1 rounded tbsp golden (light corn) syrup

65g/2½oz/scant ½ cup soft dark brown sugar

115g/4oz/⅔ cup rolled oats

1.5ml/¼ tsp salt

1 Preheat the oven to 180°C/350°F/Gas 4. Line and grease a 20cm/8in shallow round cake tin (pan) or an 18cm/7in square tin. Place the butter, golden syrup and sugar in a pan over a low heat. Cook, stirring, until melted and combined.

2 Remove from the heat and add the oats and salt. Stir the mixture to blend. Spoon the mixture into the prepared tin and smooth the surface. Place in the centre of the oven and bake until golden brown, 20–25 minutes.

3 Leave in the tin until cool enough to handle, then unmould and cut into wedges or fingers while still hot. Store in an airtight container.

> **Variations**
> Let your imagination go wild with variations on the flapjack theme.
> Apricot and Pecan: substitute maple syrup for the golden (light corn) syrup and add 50g/2oz/½ cup chopped pecan nuts and 50g/2oz/¼ cup chopped ready-to-eat dried apricots.
> Lemon: substitute Demerara (raw) sugar for the soft dark brown sugar and add the juice and grated rind of 1 lemon.
> Honey and seed: substitute honey for the golden (light corn) syrup and add 30ml/2 tbsp sesame or sunflower seeds.
> Fruit: add 50g/2oz/scant ½ cup raisins, sultanas (golden raisins) or dried tropical fruit.
> Chocolate: add 50g/2oz chocolate drops or chopped chocolate with some dried fruit as well, if you like.
> Apple: add a peeled and cored apple cut into small pieces for a softer flapjack.

Shortbread Energy 290kcal/1212kJ; Protein 2.5g; Carbohydrate 36.2g, of which sugars 15.4g; Fat 15.7g, of which saturates 9.8g; Cholesterol 40mg; Calcium 39mg; Fibre 0.8g; Sodium 116mg.
Flapjacks Energy 144kcal/604kJ; Protein 1.9g; Carbohydrate 21g, of which sugars 10.5g; Fat 6.4g, of which saturates 3.3g; Cholesterol 13mg; Calcium 14mg; Fibre 1g; Sodium 50mg.

Chocolate Delights

Simple and delicious, this method of making cookies ensures they are all of a uniform size.

Makes 50

25g/1oz plain (semisweet) chocolate
25g/1oz dark (bittersweet)
  cooking chocolate
225g/8oz/2 cups plain
  (all-purpose) flour

2.5ml/½ tsp salt
225g/8oz/1 cup unsalted
  (sweet) butter, at
  room temperature
225g/8oz/generous 1 cup caster
  (superfine) sugar
2 eggs
5ml/1 tsp vanilla extract
115g/4oz/1 cup finely
  chopped walnuts

1 Melt the chocolate in the top of a double boiler, or in a heatproof bowl set over a pan of gently simmering water. Set aside. In a bowl, sift together the flour and salt. Set aside.

2 Cream the butter until soft. Add the sugar and continue beating until the mixture is light and fluffy. Mix the eggs and vanilla extract, then gradually stir into the butter mixture. Stir in the chocolate, then the flour. Finally, stir in the nuts.

3 Divide the mixture into four equal parts, and roll each into a 5cm/2in diameter log. Wrap tightly in foil and chill or freeze until firm.

4 Preheat the oven to 190°C/375°F/Gas 5. Grease two baking sheets. With a sharp knife, cut the logs into 5mm/¼in slices. Place the circles on the baking sheets and bake until lightly coloured, about 10 minutes. Using a metal spatula, transfer to a wire rack to cool.

Variation
Try other nuts in this recipe, such as almonds, or use 50g/2oz/ scant ½ cup chopped ready-to-eat dried apricots, peaches or dates and halve the amount of nuts used. Almonds and apricots make a particularly pleasing combination, or try dates and pecan nuts.

Cinnamon Treats

Place these cookies in a heart-shaped basket, as here, and serve them up with love.

Makes 50

250g/9oz/2¼ cups plain
  (all-purpose) flour

2.5ml/½ tsp salt
10ml/2 tsp ground cinnamon
225g/8oz/1 cup unsalted (sweet)
  butter, at room temperature
225g/8oz/generous 1 cup caster
  (superfine) sugar
2 eggs
5ml/1 tsp vanilla extract

1 Sift the flour, salt and ground cinnamon together in a bowl. Set aside.

2 Cream the butter until soft. Add the sugar and continue beating until the mixture is light and fluffy. Beat the eggs and vanilla extract together, then gradually stir into the butter mixture. Stir in the dry ingredients.

3 Divide the mixture into four equal parts, then roll each into a 5cm/2in diameter log. Wrap the mixture tightly in foil and chill or freeze until it is firm.

4 Preheat the oven to 190°C/375°F/Gas 5. Grease two baking sheets. With a sharp knife, cut the logs into 5mm/¼in slices. Place the rounds on the baking sheets and bake until lightly coloured, about 10 minutes. Using a metal spatula, transfer to a wire rack to cool.

Variation
Transform these treats into sandwiched creams by making a chocolate orange butter icing. Cream together 50g/2oz/¼ cup butter and 75g/3oz/¾ cup icing (confectioner's) sugar until smooth. Add the grated rind of an orange. Blend 15ml/1 tbsp unsweetened cocoa powder with 15ml/1 tbsp water and add to the icing. Blend until smooth. Spread a little of the butter icing on to the flat side of a cookie and sandwich with another. Repeat with the remaining cookies.

Chocolate Energy 90kcal/377kJ; Protein 1.1g; Carbohydrate 8.9g, of which sugars 5.5g; Fat 5.8g, of which saturates 2.7g; Cholesterol 17mg; Calcium 13mg; Fibre 0.2g; Sodium 31mg.
Cinnamon Energy 71kcal/298kJ; Protein 0.8g; Carbohydrate 8.6g, of which sugars 4.8g; Fat 4g, of which saturates 2.4g; Cholesterol 17mg; Calcium 11mg; Fibre 0.2g; Sodium 31mg.

Chunky Chocolate Drops

Do not allow these cookies to cool completely on the baking sheet or they will break when you lift them.

Makes 18
175g/6oz plain (semisweet)
  chocolate
115g/4oz/½ cup unsalted
  (sweet) butter
2 eggs
90g/3½oz/½ cup caster
  (superfine) sugar
50g/2oz/¼ cup (packed) soft
  light brown sugar
40g/1½oz/⅓ cup plain
  (all-purpose) flour

25g/1oz/¼ cup unsweetened
  cocoa powder
5ml/1 tsp baking powder
10ml/2 tsp vanilla extract
pinch of salt
115g/4oz/⅔ cup pecan
  nuts, toasted and
  coarsely chopped
175g/6oz/1 cup plain (semisweet)
  chocolate chips
115g/4oz fine quality white
  chocolate, chopped into
  5mm/¼in pieces
115g/4oz fine quality milk
  chocolate, chopped into
  5mm/¼in pieces

1 Preheat the oven to 160°C/325°F/Gas 3. Grease two large baking sheets.

2 In a medium pan over a low heat, melt the plain chocolate and butter until smooth, stirring frequently. Remove from the heat to cool slightly.

3 Beat the eggs with the sugars until pale and creamy. Gradually beat in the melted chocolate mixture. Beat in the flour, cocoa, baking powder, vanilla extract and salt, until just blended. Add the nuts, chocolate chips and white chocolate pieces.

4 Drop 4–6 heaped tablespoonfuls of the mixture on to each baking sheet 10cm/4in apart and flatten each to a round about 7.5cm/3in. Bake for 8–10 minutes, or until the tops are shiny and cracked and the edges look crisp.

5 Cool the cookies on the baking sheets for about 2 minutes, or until they are just set, then remove them to a wire rack to cool completely.

Chocolate Crackle-tops

These dainty treats are always popular and are best eaten on the day they are baked, as they dry slightly on storage.

Makes 38
200g/7oz plain (semisweet)
  chocolate, chopped
90g/3½oz/7 tbsp unsalted
  (sweet) butter
115g/4oz/generous ½ cup caster
  (superfine) sugar

3 eggs
5ml/1 tsp vanilla extract
215g/7½oz/scant 2 cups plain
  (all-purpose) flour
25g/1oz/¼ cup unsweetened
  cocoa powder
2.5ml/½ tsp baking powder
a pinch of salt
175g/6oz/1½ cups icing
  (confectioners') sugar,
  for coating

1 Heat the chocolate and butter over a low heat until smooth, stirring frequently. Remove from the heat. Stir in the sugar, and continue stirring until dissolved. Add the eggs, one at a time, beating well after each addition; stir in the vanilla.

2 In a separate bowl, sift together the flour, cocoa, baking powder and salt. Gradually stir into the chocolate mixture until just blended. Cover and chill for at least 1 hour.

3 Preheat the oven to 160°C/325°F/Gas 3. Grease two or three large baking sheets. Place the icing sugar in a small, deep bowl. Using a teaspoon, scoop the dough into small balls and roll in your hands into 4cm/1½in balls.

4 Drop the balls, one at a time, into the icing sugar and roll until heavily coated. Remove each ball with a slotted spoon and tap against the bowl to remove any excess sugar. Place on the baking sheets 4cm/1½in apart.

5 Bake the cookies for 10–15 minutes, or until the tops feel slightly firm when touched with your fingertip.

6 Remove the baking sheets to a wire rack for 2–3 minutes, then remove the cookies to the wire rack to cool.

Drops Energy 301kcal/1256kJ; Protein 3.6g; Carbohydrate 28.4g, of which sugars 28g; Fat 20g, of which saturates 9.7g; Cholesterol 37mg; Calcium 52mg; Fibre 1g; Sodium 74mg.
Crackle-tops Energy 102kcal/428kJ; Protein 1.5g; Carbohydrate 15.8g, of which sugars 11.4g; Fat 4.1g, of which saturates 2.3g; Cholesterol 20mg; Calcium 17mg; Fibre 0.4g; Sodium 27mg.

Chocolate & Coconut Slices

These are easier to slice if they cool overnight.

Makes 24
175g/6oz/2 cups crushed digestive cookies (graham crackers)
50g/2oz/¼ cup caster (superfine) sugar
a pinch of salt
115g/4oz/½ cup butter or margarine, melted
75g/3oz/1 cup desiccated (dry unsweetened shredded) coconut
250g/9oz plain (semisweet) chocolate chips
250ml/8fl oz/1 cup sweetened condensed milk
115g/4oz/1 cup chopped walnuts

1 Preheat the oven to 180°C/350°F/Gas 4. In a bowl, combine the crushed digestive cookies, sugar, salt and butter or margarine. Press the mixture evenly over the base of an ungreased 33 x 23cm/13 x 9in baking dish.

2 Sprinkle the coconut over the cookie base, then scatter over the chocolate chips. Pour the condensed milk evenly over the chocolate. Sprinkle the walnuts on top. Bake in the oven for 30 minutes. Unmould and leave to cool before slicing.

Coconut Pyramids

Makes 15
225g/8oz/1 cup desiccated (dry unsweetened shredded) coconut
115g/4oz/generous ½ cup caster (superfine) sugar
2 egg whites

1 Preheat the oven to 190°C/375°F/Gas 5. Grease a baking sheet. Mix together the coconut and sugar. Lightly whisk the egg whites and fold enough into the coconut to make a firm mixture.

2 Form teaspoonfuls of the mixture into pyramids. Flatten the base and press the top into a point. Place on the baking sheet and bake for 12–15 minutes on a low shelf; the tips should be golden. Use a metal spatula to loosen them but let them cool on the baking sheet before transferring to a wire rack.

Chocolate Chip Oat Cookies

Oat cookies are given a delicious lift by the inclusion of chocolate chips. Try caramel chips for a change, if you like.

Makes 60
115g/4oz/1 cup plain (all-purpose) flour
2.5ml/½ tsp bicarbonate of soda (baking soda)
1.5ml/¼ tsp baking powder
1.5ml/¼ tsp salt
115g/4oz/½ cup butter or margarine, at room temperature
115g/4oz/generous ½ cup caster (superfine) sugar
90g/3½oz/scant ½ cup soft light brown sugar
1 egg
2.5ml/½ tsp vanilla extract
75g/3oz/scant 1 cup rolled oats
175g/6oz/1 cup plain (semisweet) chocolate chips

1 Preheat the oven to 180°C/350°F/Gas 4. Grease three or four baking sheets. Sift the flour, bicarbonate of soda, baking powder and salt into a mixing bowl. Set aside.

2 With an electric mixer, cream the butter or margarine and the sugars together. Add the egg and vanilla, and beat until light and fluffy.

3 Add the flour mixture to the egg and vanilla, and beat on low speed until thoroughly blended. Stir in the rolled oats and plain chocolate chips, mixing well with a wooden spoon. The dough should be crumbly.

4 Drop heaped teaspoonfuls on to the baking sheets, about 2.5cm/1in apart. Bake until just firm around the edges but still soft in the centres, about 15 minutes. With a metal spatula, transfer the cookies to a wire rack to cool.

Variation
For an elegant look suitable to accompany a chilled dessert, melt plain (semisweet) chocolate over a pan of hot, but not boiling water, stirring until smooth. Dip each baked cookie into the chocolate to cover one half of the cookie. Leave to set before serving.

Slices Energy 55kcal/233kJ; Protein 0.6g; Carbohydrate 7.8g, of which sugars 5.4g; Fat 2.6g, of which saturates 1.5g; Cholesterol 7mg; Calcium 7mg; Fibre 0.2g; Sodium 14mg.
Pyramids Energy 122kcal/509kJ; Protein 1.1g; Carbohydrate 9g, of which sugars 7.2g; Fat 9.3g, of which saturates 8g; Cholesterol 14mg; Calcium 22mg; Fibre 2.1g; Sodium 3mg.
Cookies Energy 217kcal/907kJ; Protein 2.8g; Carbohydrate 20g, of which sugars 15.8g; Fat 14.6g, of which saturates 7.5g; Cholesterol 18mg; Calcium 48mg; Fibre 1g; Sodium 89mg.

Nutty Lace Wafers

Serve these delicate cookies with smooth and creamy desserts.

Makes 18
65g/2½oz/scant ½ cup blanched almonds
50g/2oz/¼ cup butter
40g/1½oz/⅓ cup plain (all-purpose) flour
90g/3½oz/½ cup caster (superfine) sugar
30ml/2 tbsp double (heavy) cream
2.5ml/½ tsp vanilla extract

I Preheat the oven to 190°C/375°F/Gas 5. Lightly grease two baking sheets.

2 With a sharp knife, chop the almonds as finely as possible. Alternatively, use a food processor or blender to chop the nuts very finely.

3 Melt the butter in a pan over a low heat. Remove from the heat and stir in the flour, caster sugar, double cream and vanilla extract. Add the finely chopped almonds and mix well.

4 Drop teaspoonfuls 6cm/2½in apart on the prepared sheets. Bake until golden, about 5 minutes. Cool on the baking sheets briefly, just until the wafers are stiff enough to remove. With a metal spatula, transfer to a wire rack to cool.

Cook's Tip
Many cookies, like these ones here, are soft when cooked but crisp up as they cool. Don't allow them to overcook because you expect them to be firm when they come out of the oven.

Variation
Add 40g/1½oz/¼ cup finely chopped candied orange peel to the mixture at step 3.

Oat Lace Rounds

These nutty cookies are very quick and easy to make and they taste delicious.

Makes 36
165g/5½oz/⅔ cup butter or margarine
130g/4½oz/1¼ cups rolled oats
170g/5¾oz/generous ¾ cup soft dark brown sugar
155g/5¼oz/generous ¾ cup caster (superfine) sugar
40g/1½oz/⅓ cup plain (all-purpose) flour
1.5ml/¼ tsp salt
1 egg, lightly beaten
5ml/1 tsp vanilla extract
65g/2½oz/generous ⅓ cup pecan nuts or walnuts, finely chopped

I Preheat the oven to 180°C/350°F/Gas 4. Lightly grease two baking sheets. Melt the butter or margarine in a medium pan over a low heat. Set aside.

2 In a mixing bowl, combine the oats, brown sugar, caster sugar, flour and salt. Make a well in the centre and add the butter or margarine, egg and vanilla. Mix until blended, then stir in the chopped nuts.

3 Drop rounded teaspoonfuls of the mixture about 5cm/2in apart on the prepared baking sheets.

4 Bake in the oven until lightly browned on the edges and bubbling all over, about 5–8 minutes. Cool on the baking sheets for 2 minutes, then transfer to a wire rack to cool completely.

Cook's Tip
Rolled oats are also known as oatflakes and porridge oats. Fine oatmeal is also excellent for making cookies.

Variation
Substitute 5ml/1 tsp ground cinnamon for the vanilla extract for a tasty variation.

Wafers Energy 78kcal/327kJ; Protein 1g; Carbohydrate 7.2g, of which sugars 5.5g; Fat 5.2g, of which saturates 2.2g; Cholesterol 8mg; Calcium 16mg; Fibre 0.3g; Sodium 18mg.
Rounds Energy 103kcal/432kJ; Protein 1g; Carbohydrate 13.2g, of which sugars 9.7g; Fat 5.5g, of which saturates 2.5g; Cholesterol 15mg; Calcium 11mg; Fibre 0.4g; Sodium 32mg.

Nutty Chocolate Squares

These delicious squares are incredibly rich, so cut them smaller if you wish.

Makes 16
2 eggs
10ml/2 tsp vanilla extract
1.5ml/¼ tsp salt
175g/6oz/1 cup pecan nuts, coarsely chopped

50g/2oz/½ cup plain (all-purpose) flour
50g/2oz/¼ cup caster (superfine) sugar
120ml/4fl oz/½ cup golden (light corn) syrup
75g/3oz plain (semisweet) chocolate, finely chopped
40g/1½oz/3 tbsp butter
16 pecan nut halves, to decorate

1 Preheat the oven to 160°C/325°F/Gas 3. Line the base and sides of a 20cm/8in square baking tin (pan) with baking parchment and lightly grease the paper.

2 Whisk together the eggs, vanilla extract and salt. In another bowl, mix together the chopped pecan nuts and flour. Set both aside until needed.

3 In a pan, bring the sugar and golden syrup to the boil. Watch it carefully and remove from the heat as soon as it comes to the boil.

4 Stir in the chocolate and butter, and blend thoroughly with a wooden spoon. Mix in the beaten egg mixture, then fold in the pecan nut mixture.

5 Pour the mixture into the baking tin and bake until set, about 35 minutes. Cool in the tin for 10 minutes before unmoulding. Cut into 5cm/2in squares. Cool on a wire rack.

Variation
Toasted hazelnuts also taste great in place of the pecan nuts. Simply brown the hazelnuts under a hot grill (broiler), turning them every so often.. When toasted all over, leave to cool, then rub them in a clean dish towel until the skins are removed.

Raisin Brownies

Cover these divine fruity brownies with a light chocolate frosting for a truly decadent treat, if you like.

Makes 16
115g/4oz/½ cup butter or margarine
50g/2oz/½ cup unsweetened cocoa powder

2 eggs
225g/8oz/generous 1 cup caster (superfine) sugar
5ml/1 tsp vanilla extract
40g/1½oz/⅓ cup plain (all-purpose) flour
75g/3oz/¾ cup finely chopped walnuts
75g/3oz/generous ½ cup raisins

1 Preheat the oven to 180°C/350°F/Gas 4. Line the base and sides of a 20cm/8in square baking tin (pan) with baking parchment and grease the paper.

2 Gently melt the butter or margarine in a small pan. Remove from the heat and stir in the cocoa powder.

3 With an electric mixer, beat the eggs, caster sugar and vanilla extract together until light. Add the cocoa and butter mixture and stir to blend.

4 Sift the flour over the cocoa mixture and gently fold in. Do not overmix.

5 Add the walnuts and raisins, and scrape the mixture into the prepared baking tin.

6 Bake in the centre of the oven for 30 minutes. Leave in the tin to cool before cutting into 5cm/2in squares and removing from the tin. The brownies should be soft and moist.

Cook's Tip
Adding dried fruit makes brownies a little more substantial and adds to their delicious flavour. Try to find Californian or Spanish raisins for the best flavour and texture.

Squares Energy 172kcal/719kJ; Protein 2.4g; Carbohydrate 15.2g, of which sugars 12.7g; Fat 11.8g, of which saturates 2.9g; Cholesterol 29mg; Calcium 19mg; Fibre 0.7g; Sodium 45mg.
Brownies Energy 181kcal/759kJ; Protein 2.5g; Carbohydrate 20.4g, of which sugars 18.1g; Fat 10.5g, of which saturates 4.6g; Cholesterol 39mg; Calcium 26mg; Fibre 0.7g; Sodium 86mg.

Marbled Brownies

These fancy brownies have an impressive flavour as well as appearance.

Makes 24
225g/8oz plain (semisweet) chocolate
75g/3oz/6 tbsp butter
4 eggs
300g/11oz/1½ cups caster (superfine) sugar
150g/5oz/1¼ cups plain (all-purpose) flour
2.5ml/½ tsp salt
5ml/1 tsp baking powder
10ml/2 tsp vanilla extract
115g/4oz/1 cup chopped walnuts

For the plain mixture
50g/2oz/¼ cup butter, at room temperature
175g/6oz/¾ cup cream cheese
90g/3½oz/1½ cups caster (superfine) sugar
2 eggs
25g/1oz/¼ cup plain (all-purpose) flour
5ml/1 tsp vanilla extract

1 Preheat the oven to 180°C/350°F/Gas 4. Line a 33 x 23cm/ 13 x 9in baking tin (pan) with baking parchment and grease.

2 Melt the chocolate and butter in a small pan over a very low heat, stirring. Set aside to cool. Meanwhile, beat the eggs until light and fluffy. Gradually beat in the sugar. Sift over the flour, salt and baking powder, and fold to combine.

3 Stir in the cooled chocolate mixture. Add the vanilla extract and chopped walnuts. Measure and set aside 475ml/16fl oz/ 2 cups of the chocolate mixture.

4 For the plain mixture, cream the butter and cream cheese with an electric mixer. Add the sugar and continue beating until blended. Beat in the eggs, flour and vanilla extract.

5 Spread the unmeasured chocolate mixture in the tin. Pour over the plain mixture. Drop spoonfuls of the reserved chocolate mixture on top.

6 With a metal spatula, swirl the mixtures to marble them. Do not blend completely. Bake until just set, 35–40 minutes. Turn out when cool and cut into squares for serving.

Chocolate-chip Brownies

A double dose of chocolate is incorporated into these melt-in-the-mouth brownies.

Makes 24
115g/4oz plain (semisweet) chocolate
115g/4oz/½ cup butter
3 eggs
200g/7oz/1 cup caster (superfine) sugar
2.5ml/½ tsp vanilla extract
a pinch of salt
150g/5oz/1¼ cups plain (all-purpose) flour
175g/6oz/1 cup chocolate chips

1 Preheat the oven to 180°C/350°F/Gas 4. Then line a 33 x 23cm/13 x 9in baking tin (pan) with baking parchment and grease the paper.

2 Melt the chocolate and butter together in the top of a double boiler, or in a heatproof bowl set over a pan of gently simmering water.

3 Beat together the eggs, sugar, vanilla extract and salt. Stir in the chocolate mixture. Sift over the flour and fold in. Add the chocolate chips.

4 Pour the mixture into the baking tin and spread evenly. Bake until just set, about 30 minutes. The brownies should be slightly moist inside. Leave to cool in the tin.

5 To turn out, run a knife all around the edge and invert on to a baking sheet. Remove the paper. Place another sheet on top and invert again. Cut into bars for serving.

> **Variations**
> *Rich chocolate: use best quality chocolate (at least 70 per cent cocoa solids) cut into chunks to give the brownies a fantastic flavour.*
> *Chunky choc and nut: use 75g/3oz coarsely chopped white chocolate and 75g/3oz/¾ cup chopped walnuts.*
> *Almond: use almond extract, add 75g/3oz/¾ cup chopped almonds and reduce the chocolate chips to 75g/3oz/½ cup.*

Chocolate-chip Energy 161kcal/674kJ; Protein 2g; Carbohydrate 21.3g, of which sugars 16.4g; Fat 8.1g, of which saturates 4.7g; Cholesterol 35mg; Calcium 22mg; Fibre 0.5g; Sodium 39mg.
Marbled Energy 259kcal/1083kJ; Protein 3.8g; Carbohydrate 28.8g, of which sugars 23.1g; Fat 15.1g, of which saturates 7.1g; Cholesterol 66mg; Calcium 42mg; Fibre 0.6g; Sodium 73mg.

Oat & Date Brownies

These brownies are marvellous as a break-time treat. The secret of chewy, moist brownies is not to overcook them.

Makes 16
150g/5oz plain (semisweet) chocolate
50g/2oz/¼ cup butter
75g/3oz/scant 1 cup rolled oats
25g/1oz/3 tbsp wheatgerm
25g/1oz/⅓ cup milk powder
2.5ml/½ tsp baking powder
2.5ml/½ tsp salt
50g/2oz/½ cup chopped walnuts
50g/2oz/⅓ cup finely chopped dates
50g/2oz/¼ cup muscovado (molasses) sugar
5ml/1 tsp vanilla extract
2 eggs, beaten

1 Break the chocolate into a heatproof bowl and add the butter. Place over a pan of simmering water and stir until completely melted.

2 Cool the chocolate, stirring occasionally. Preheat the oven to 180°C/350°F/Gas 4. Grease and line a 20cm/8in square cake tin (pan).

3 Combine the oats, wheatgerm, milk powder and baking powder together in a bowl. Add the salt, walnuts, chopped dates and sugar, and mix well. Beat in the melted chocolate, vanilla and beaten eggs.

4 Pour the mixture into the cake tin, level the surface and bake in the oven for 20–25 minutes, or until firm around the edges yet still soft in the centre.

5 Cool the brownies in the tin, then chill in the fridge. When they are more solid, turn them out of the tin and cut into 16 squares.

Cook's Tip
When melting chocolate always make sure that the water in the pan does not touch the bowl, or it might bubble up the side of the bowl and splash into the chocolate, changing its texture.

Banana Chocolate Brownies

Nuts traditionally give brownies their chewy texture. Here oat bran is used instead, creating a wonderful alternative.

Makes 9
75ml/5 tbsp unsweetened cocoa powder
15ml/1 tbsp caster (superfine) sugar
75ml/5 tbsp milk
3 large bananas, mashed
215g/7½oz/scant 1 cup soft light brown sugar
5ml/1 tsp vanilla extract
5 egg whites
75g/3oz/⅔ cup self-raising (self-rising) flour
75g/3oz/⅔ cup oat bran
icing (confectioners') sugar, for dusting

1 Preheat the oven to 180°C/350°F/Gas 4. Line a 20cm/8in square cake tin (pan) with non-stick baking paper.

2 Blend the cocoa powder and caster sugar with the milk. Add the bananas, soft brown sugar and vanilla extract. Lightly beat the egg whites with a fork. Add the chocolate mixture and continue to beat well. Sift the flour over the mixture and fold in with the oat bran. Pour into the prepared tin.

3 Cook in the oven for 40 minutes, or until firm. Cool in the tin for 10 minutes, then turn out on to a wire rack. Cut into squares and lightly dust with icing sugar before serving.

Cook's Tips
Win a few brownie points by getting to know what makes them great.
• They should be moist and chewy with a sugary crust on the outside but squidgy on the inside.
• True versions contain a high proportion of sugar and fat and most contain nuts. Lighter versions often contain white chocolate and are often referred to as blondies.
• Brownies make superb individual cakes but the cooked slab can also be left whole and then served as a larger cake for dessert, decorated with cream and fruit.

Oat Energy 138kcal/577kJ; Protein 2.8g; Carbohydrate 13.3g, of which sugars 9.3g; Fat 8.6g, of which saturates 3.6g; Cholesterol 31mg; Calcium 32mg; Fibre 1g; Sodium 36mg.
Banana Energy 223kcal/947kJ; Protein 5.7g; Carbohydrate 46.4g, of which sugars 32.4g; Fat 2.9g, of which saturates 1.2g; Cholesterol 0mg; Calcium 70mg; Fibre 2.2g; Sodium 151mg.

Maple & Pecan Nut Brownies

This recipe provides a delicious adaptation of the classic American chocolate brownie.

Makes 12
115g/4oz/½ cup butter, melted
75g/3oz/scant ½ cup soft light brown sugar
90ml/6 tbsp maple syrup
2 eggs

115g/4oz/1 cup self-raising (self-rising) flour
75g/3oz/½ cup pecan nuts, chopped

For the topping
115g/4oz/⅔ cup plain (semisweet) chocolate chips
50g/2oz/¼ cup unsalted (sweet) butter
12 pecan nut halves, to decorate

1 Preheat the oven to 180°C/350°F/Gas 4. Line and grease a 25 x 18cm/10 x 7in cake tin (pan).

2 Beat together the melted butter, sugar, 60ml/4 tbsp of the maple syrup, the eggs and flour for 1 minute, or until smooth.

3 Stir in the nuts and transfer to the cake tin. Smooth the surface and bake for 30 minutes, or until risen and firm to the touch. Cool in the tin for 10 minutes, then transfer to a wire rack to cool completely.

4 Melt the chocolate chips, butter and remaining syrup over a low heat. Cool slightly, then spread over the cake. Press in the pecan nut halves, leave to set for about 5 minutes, then cut into squares or bars.

Cook's Tips
• Maple syrup is a sweet sugar syrup made from the sap of the sugar maple tree. It has a distinctive flavour which is delightful in a variety of sweet recipes as well as being added to ice creams and waffles.
• Buy a good quality maple syrup as blends are often disappointing.
• Store opened maple syrup in the refrigerator, as its delicate flavour will deteriorate once the bottle is opened.

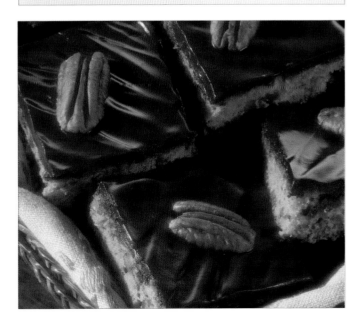

White Chocolate Brownies

If you wish, toasted and skinned hazelnuts can be substituted for the macadamia nuts in the topping.

Serves 12
150g/5oz/1¼ cups plain (all-purpose) flour
2.5ml/½ tsp baking powder
a pinch of salt
175g/6oz fine quality white chocolate, chopped
90g/3½oz/½ cup caster (superfine) sugar

115g/4oz/½ cup unsalted (sweet) butter, cut into pieces
2 eggs, lightly beaten
5ml/1 tsp vanilla extract
175g/6oz/1 cup plain (semisweet) chocolate chips

For the topping
200g/7oz milk chocolate, chopped
215g/7½oz/1⅓ cups unsalted macadamia nuts, chopped

1 Preheat the oven to 180°C/350°F/Gas 4. Grease a 23cm/9in springform tin (pan). Sift together the flour, baking powder and salt, and set aside.

2 In a medium pan over a medium heat, melt the white chocolate, sugar and butter until smooth, stirring frequently. Cool slightly, then beat in the eggs and vanilla. Stir in the chocolate chips. Spread evenly in the prepared tin, smoothing the top.

3 Bake for 20–25 minutes, or until a cocktail stick (toothpick) inserted 5cm/2in from the side of the tin comes out clean. Remove from the oven to a heatproof surface, sprinkle chopped milk chocolate over the surface (avoid touching the side of tin) and return to the oven for 1 minute.

4 Remove from the oven and, using the back of a spoon, gently spread out the softened chocolate. Sprinkle with the macadamia nuts and gently press into the chocolate. Cool on a wire rack for 30 minutes, and then chill for 1 hour.

5 Run a sharp knife around the side of the tin to loosen, then unclip and remove. Cut the brownies into thin wedges to serve.

Chocolate Energy 526kcal/2190kJ; Protein 6.3g; Carbohydrate 43.8g, of which sugars 34g; Fat 37.4g, of which saturates 16.1g; Cholesterol 64mg; Calcium 82mg; Fibre 2.1g; Sodium 154mg.
Maple Energy 285kcal/1189kJ; Protein 3.1g; Carbohydrate 26.2g, of which sugars 18.9g; Fat 19.4g, of which saturates 9.4g; Cholesterol 62mg; Calcium 52mg; Fibre 0.8g; Sodium 151mg.

American Chocolate Fudge Brownies

This is the classic American recipe, but omit the frosting if you find it too rich.

Makes 12

175g/6oz/³/₄ cup butter
40g/1¹/₂oz/¹/₃ cup unsweetened
   cocoa powder
2 eggs, lightly beaten
175g/6oz/1 cup soft light
   brown sugar
2.5ml/¹/₂ tsp vanilla extract
115g/4oz/1 cup chopped
   pecan nuts
50g/2oz/¹/₂ cup self-raising
   (self-rising) flour

For the frosting
115g/4oz plain
   (semisweet) chocolate
25g/1oz/2 tbsp butter
15ml/1 tbsp sour cream

1 Preheat the oven to 180°C/350°F/Gas 4. Grease a 20cm/8in square shallow cake tin (pan) and line with baking parchment. Melt the butter in a pan and stir in the unsweetened cocoa powder. Set aside to cool.

2 Beat together the eggs, sugar and vanilla extract in a bowl, then stir in the cooled cocoa mixture with the nuts. Sift over the flour and fold into the mixture with a metal spoon.

3 Pour the mixture into the cake tin and bake in the oven for 30–35 minutes, or until risen. Remove from the oven (the mixture will still be quite soft and wet, but it firms up further while cooling) and leave to cool in the tin.

4 To make the frosting, melt the chocolate and butter together in a pan and remove from the heat. Beat in the sour cream until smooth and glossy. Leave to cool slightly, and then spread over the top of the brownies. When set, cut into 12 pieces.

Cook's Tip
Brownies are firm family favourites and, once you find a favourite recipe, you will want to make them regularly. For brownie enthusiasts you can now buy a special pan with a slide-out base, which makes removing the cooked brownies so much easier.

Fudge-glazed Chocolate Brownies

These pecan nut-topped brownies are irresistible, so hide them from friends!

Makes 16
250g/9oz dark (bittersweet)
   chocolate, chopped
25g/1oz unsweetened
   chocolate, chopped
115g/4oz/¹/₂ cup unsalted
   (sweet) butter, cut
   into pieces
90g/3¹/₂oz/scant ¹/₂ cup soft light
   brown sugar
50g/2oz/¹/₄ cup caster
   (superfine) sugar
2 eggs
15ml/1 tbsp vanilla extract
65g/2¹/₂oz/9 tbsp plain
   (all-purpose) flour
115g/4oz/²/₃ cup pecan nuts or
   walnuts, toasted and chopped
150g/5oz white chocolate,
   chopped
pecan nut halves, to decorate
   (optional)

For the glaze
175g/6oz dark (bittersweet)
   chocolate, chopped
50g/2oz/¹/₄ cup unsalted (sweet)
   butter, cut into pieces
30ml/2 tbsp golden (light
   corn) syrup
10ml/2 tsp vanilla extract
5ml/1 tsp instant coffee

1 Preheat oven to 180°C/350°F/Gas 4. Line a 20cm/8in square baking tin (pan) with foil then grease the foil.

2 Melt the dark chocolates and butter in a pan over a low heat. Off the heat, add the sugars and stir for 2 minutes. Beat in the eggs and vanilla extract, and then blend in the flour.

3 Stir in the pecan nuts or walnuts and the chopped white chocolate.

4 Pour into the tin. Bake for 20–25 minutes. Cool in the tin for 30 minutes then lift, using the foil, on to a wire rack to cool for 2 hours.

5 To make the glaze, melt the chocolate in a pan with the butter, golden syrup, vanilla extract and instant coffee. Stir until smooth. Chill the glaze for 1 hour then spread over the brownies. Top with pecan nut halves, if you like. Chill until set then cut into bars.

American Energy 335kcal/1396kJ; Protein 3.6g; Carbohydrate 25.6g, of which sugars 21.9g; Fat 25.1g, of which saturates 11.7g; Cholesterol 69mg; Calcium 45mg; Fibre 1.2g; Sodium 161mg.
Fudge-glazed Energy 382kcal/1595kJ; Protein 4.1g; Carbohydrate 37.6g, of which sugars 34.1g; Fat 25g, of which saturates 12.4g; Cholesterol 47mg; Calcium 55mg; Fibre 1.2g; Sodium 89mg.

Chewy Fruit Muesli Slice

The apricots give these slices a wonderful chewy texture and the apple keeps them moist.

Makes 8

75g/3oz/scant ½ cup ready-to-eat dried apricots, chopped
1 eating apple, cored and grated
150g/5oz/1¼ cups Swiss-style muesli
150ml/¼ pint/⅔ cup apple juice
15g/½oz/1 tbsp sunflower margarine

1 Preheat the oven to 190°C/375°F/Gas 5. Grease a 20cm/8in round cake tin. Combine all the ingredients in a large bowl.

2 Press the mixture into the tin and bake for 35–40 minutes, or until lightly browned and firm. Mark the muesli slice into wedges and leave to cool in the tin.

Mincemeat Wedges

Makes 12

225g/8oz/2 cups self-raising (self-rising) wholemeal (whole-wheat) flour
75g/3oz/6 tbsp unsalted (sweet) butter, diced
75g/3oz/⅓ cup demerara (raw) sugar
1 egg, beaten
115g/4oz/⅓ cup good quality mincemeat
about 60ml/4 tbsp milk
crushed brown or white café (sugar) cubes or a mixture, for sprinkling

1 Preheat the oven to 200°C/400°F/Gas 6. Line the base of a 20cm/8in round sandwich tin (layer pan) and lightly grease the sides.

2 Rub the butter into the flour, using your fingertips or a pastry cutter. Stir in the sugar, egg and mincemeat. Add enough milk to make a soft dough. Spread evenly in the prepared tin and sprinkled over the crushed sugar. Bake for 20 minutes, or until firm. Cool in the tin then cut into wedges.

Chocolate Raspberry Macaroon Bars

Any seedless preserve, such as strawberry or apricot, can be substituted for the raspberry in this recipe.

Makes 16–18

115g/4oz/½ cup unsalted (sweet) butter, softened
50g/2oz/½ cup icing (confectioners') sugar
25g/1oz/¼ cup unsweetened cocoa powder
a pinch of salt
5ml/1 tsp almond extract
115g/4oz/1 cup plain (all-purpose) flour

For the topping

150g/5oz/½ cup seedless raspberry preserve
15ml/1 tbsp raspberry flavour liqueur
175g/6oz/1 cup milk chocolate chips
175g/6oz/1½ cups finely ground almonds
4 egg whites
a pinch of salt
200g/7oz/1 cup caster (superfine) sugar
2.5ml/½ tsp almond extract
50g/2oz/½ cup flaked (sliced) almonds

1 Preheat the oven to 160°C/325°F/Gas 3. Line a 23 × 33cm/9 × 13in baking tin (pan) with foil and then grease the foil. Beat together the butter, sugar, cocoa and salt until blended. Beat in the almond extract and flour to make a crumbly dough.

2 Turn the dough into the tin and smooth the surface. Prick all over with a fork. Bake for 20 minutes, or until just set. Remove the tin from the oven and increase the temperature to 190°C/375°F/Gas 5.

3 To make the topping, combine the raspberry preserve and liqueur. Spread over the cooked crust, then sprinkle with the chocolate chips.

4 In a food processor fitted with a metal blade, process the almonds, egg whites, salt, caster sugar and almond extract. Pour this mixture over the jam layer, spreading evenly. Sprinkle with almonds.

5 Bake for 20–25 minutes, or until the top is golden and puffed. Cool in the tin for 20 minutes. Carefully remove from the tin and cool completely. Peel off the foil and cut into bars.

Muesli Energy 266kcal/1115kJ; Protein 4.5g; Carbohydrate 32.1g, of which sugars 26.6g; Fat 14.1g, of which saturates 5.7g; Cholesterol 16mg; Calcium 66mg; Fibre 1.2g; Sodium 79mg.
Mincemeat Energy 168kcal/707kJ; Protein 2.5g; Carbohydrate 26.9g, of which sugars 13g; Fat 6.3g, of which saturates 3.5g; Cholesterol 30mg; Calcium 82mg; Fibre 0.7g; Sodium 116mg.
Macaroon Energy 107kcal/453kJ; Protein 2.3g; Carbohydrate 19.6g, of which sugars 11g; Fat 2.9g, of which saturates 1.1g; Cholesterol 4mg; Calcium 30mg; Fibre 1.9g; Sodium 85mg.

Blueberry Streusel Slice

If you are short of time, use ready-made pastry for this delightful summer streusel.

Makes 30
225g/8oz shortcrust pastry
50g/2oz/½ cup plain
  (all-purpose) flour
1.5ml/¼ tsp baking powder
40g/1½oz/3 tbsp butter
  or margarine
25g/1oz/2 tbsp fresh white
  breadcrumbs
50g/2oz/¼ cup soft light
  brown sugar
1.5ml/¼ tsp salt
50g/2oz/½ cup flaked (sliced) or
  chopped almonds
30ml/4 tbsp blackberry or
  bramble jelly
115g/4oz/1 cup blueberries,
  fresh or frozen

1 Preheat the oven to 180°C/350°F/Gas 4. Line an 18 x 28cm/ 7 x 11in Swiss roll tin (jelly roll pan) with baking parchment. Roll out the pastry on a lightly floured surface and place in the tin. Prick the base evenly with a fork.

2 Rub together the plain flour, baking powder, butter or margarine, breadcrumbs, sugar and salt until very crumbly, then mix in the almonds.

3 Spread the pastry with the jelly, sprinkle with the blueberries, then cover evenly with the streusel topping, pressing down lightly. Bake for 30–40 minutes, reducing the temperature after 20 minutes to 160°C/325°F/Gas 3.

4 Remove from the oven when golden on the top and the pastry is cooked through. Cut into slices while still hot, then allow to cool.

> **Variations**
> *Another summer fruit that would work well is the strawberry. If using strawberries, substitute a good strawberry conserve for the blackberry or bramble jelly. You could still enjoy this streusel slice in autumn with the season's blackberries, which will go perfectly with the bramble jelly.*

Sticky Date & Apple Bars

If possible allow these healthy and tempting bars to mature for 1–2 days before cutting – the mixture will get stickier and even more delicious!

Makes 16
115g/4oz/½ cup butter
  or margarine
50g/2oz/⅓ cup soft dark
  brown sugar
50g/2oz/4 tbsp golden (light
  corn) syrup
115g/4oz/⅔ cup chopped dates
115g/4oz/generous 1 cup
  rolled oats
115g/4oz/1 cup wholemeal self-
  raising (self-rising) flour
225g/8oz/2 eating apples, peeled,
  cored and grated
5–10ml/1–2 tsp lemon juice
20–25 walnut halves

1 Preheat the oven to 190°C/375°F/Gas 5. Line an 18–20cm/ 7–8in square or rectangular loose-based cake tin (pan) with baking parchment. In a large pan, heat the butter or margarine, sugar, syrup and dates, stirring until the dates soften completely.

2 Gradually work in the oats, flour, apples and lemon juice until well mixed. Spoon into the tin and spread out evenly. Top with the walnut halves.

3 Bake for 30 minutes, then reduce the temperature to 160°C/325°F/Gas 3 and bake for 10–20 minutes more, or until firm to the touch and golden.

4 Cut into squares or bars while still warm, or allow to cool uncut then wrap in foil when nearly cold and keep for 1–2 days before eating.

> **Variation**
> *Oranges and dates are also a favourite and tasty combination. To make Sticky Date and Orange Bars, finely chop half an orange, including the peel. Add to the pan at step 1 with the dates and syrup, and cook with the dates until soft. Continue with the recipe but omit the apple and lemon juice.*

Blueberry Energy 73kcal/304kJ; Protein 1.1g; Carbohydrate 8.2g, of which sugars 2.8g; Fat 4.2g, of which saturates 1.4g; Cholesterol 4mg; Calcium 17mg; Fibre 0.5g; Sodium 45mg.
Date Energy 195kcal/815kJ; Protein 2.8g; Carbohydrate 22.8g, of which sugars 12.2g; Fat 10.9g, of which saturates 0.4g; Cholesterol 0mg; Calcium 41mg; Fibre 1.4g; Sodium 96mg.

Spiced Fig Bars

Make sure you have napkins handy when you serve these deliciously sticky bars.

Makes 48

350g/12oz/2 cups dried figs
3 eggs
175g/6oz/scant 1 cup caster (superfine) sugar
75g/3oz/⅔ cup plain (all-purpose) flour
5ml/1 tsp baking powder
2.5ml/½ tsp ground cinnamon
1.5ml/¼ tsp ground cloves
1.5ml/¼ tsp freshly grated nutmeg
1.5ml/¼ tsp salt
75g/3oz/¾ cup finely chopped walnuts
30ml/2 tbsp brandy or cognac
icing (confectioners') sugar, for dusting

1 Preheat the oven to 160°C/325°F/Gas 3. Then line a 30 × 20 × 4cm/12 × 8 × 1½in baking tin (pan) with baking parchment and grease the paper.

2 With a sharp knife, chop the figs roughly. Set aside.

3 In a bowl, whisk the eggs and sugar until well blended. In another bowl, sift together the dry ingredients, then fold into the egg mixture in several batches.

4 Scrape the mixture into the baking tin and bake until the top is firm and brown, about 35–40 minutes. It should still be soft underneath.

5 Leave to cool in the tin for 5 minutes, then unmould and transfer to a sheet of baking parchment lightly sprinkled with icing sugar. Cut into bars.

Cook's Tip
Figs are healthy fruits containing calcium, iron and potassium. They also have antibacterial properties as well as being a laxative. Omit the brandy or cognac and these fig bars will make a good sweet to add to children's lunchboxes – but remember to add a paper napkin for those sticky fingers!

Lemon Bars

A surprising amount of lemon juice goes into these bars, but you will appreciate why when you taste them.

Makes 36

50g/2oz/½ cup icing (confectioners') sugar
175g/6oz/1½ cups plain (all-purpose) flour
2.5ml/½ tsp salt
175g/6oz/¾ cup butter, cut into small pieces

For the topping
4 eggs
350g/12oz/1¾ cups caster (superfine) sugar
grated rind of 1 lemon
120ml/4fl oz/½ cup fresh lemon juice
175ml/6fl oz/¾ cup whipping cream
icing (confectioners') sugar, for dusting

1 Preheat the oven to 160°C/325°F/Gas 3. Grease a 33 × 23cm/13 × 9in baking tin (pan).

2 Sift the sugar, flour and salt into a bowl. With a pastry blender, cut in the butter until the mixture resembles coarse breadcrumbs. Press the mixture into the base of the tin.

3 Bake until golden brown, about 20 minutes.

4 To make the topping, whisk the eggs and caster sugar together until well blended. Add the lemon rind and juice, and mix together well.

5 Lightly whip the cream and fold into the egg mixture. Pour over the still warm base, return to the oven, and bake until set, about 40 minutes. Cool completely before cutting into bars. Dust with icing sugar before serving.

Variation
Try orange in this recipe for a change. It will work just as well in the custard topping and will give the bars a delicately scented flavour.

Fig Bars Energy 53kcal/224kJ; Protein 1g; Carbohydrate 8.9g, of which sugars 7.7g; Fat 1.6g, of which saturates 0.2g; Cholesterol 12mg; Calcium 26mg; Fibre 0.7g; Sodium 9mg.
Lemon Bars Energy 124kcal/519kJ; Protein 1.3g; Carbohydrate 15.7g, of which sugars 12g; Fat 6.6g, of which saturates 3.9g; Cholesterol 37mg; Calcium 20mg; Fibre 0.2g; Sodium 39mg.

COOKIES & BARS

Spiced Raisin Bars

If you like raisins, these gloriously spicy bars are for you. Omit the walnuts if you prefer.

Makes 30
100g/3¾oz/scant 1 cup plain (all-purpose) flour
7.5ml/1½ tsp baking powder
5ml/1 tsp ground cinnamon
2.5ml/½ tsp freshly grated nutmeg
1.5ml/¼ tsp ground cloves
1.5ml/¼ tsp mixed (apple pie) spice
215g/7½oz/1½ cups raisins
115g/4oz/½ cup butter or margarine, at room temperature
90g/3½oz/½ cup caster (superfine) sugar
2 eggs
170g/5¾oz/scant ½ cup black treacle (molasses)
50g/2oz/½ cup chopped walnuts

1 Preheat the oven to 180°C/350°F/Gas 4. Line a 33 × 23cm / 13 × 9in baking tin (pan) with baking parchment and lightly grease the paper.

2 Sift together the flour, baking powder and spices. Place the raisins in another bowl and toss with a few tablespoons of the flour mixture.

3 With an electric mixer, cream the butter or margarine and caster sugar together until light and fluffy. Beat in the eggs, one at a time, and then add the black treacle. Stir in the flour mixture, raisins and chopped walnuts.

4 Spread evenly in the baking tin. Bake until just set, about 15–18 minutes. Cool in the tin before cutting into squares.

Cook's Tips
• If you are a real raisin fan, try to use Muscat raisins, as they have a rich and sweet quality.
• If you are making bars or cookies that contain nuts to serve to children always chop the nuts finely, as they can be a choking hazard. Although you can omit the nuts completely they are a good source of protein.

Toffee Meringue Bars

Two deliciously contrasting layers complement each other beautifully in these easy-to-make bars.

Makes 12
50g/2oz/¼ cup butter
215g/7½oz/scant 1¼ cups soft dark brown sugar
1 egg
2.5ml/½ tsp vanilla extract
65g/2½oz/9 tbsp plain (all-purpose) flour
2.5ml/½ tsp salt
1.5ml/¼ tsp freshly grated nutmeg

For the topping
1 egg white
1.5ml/¼ tsp salt
15ml/1 tbsp golden (light corn) syrup
90g/3½oz/½ cup caster (superfine) sugar
50g/2oz/½ cup finely chopped walnuts

1 Combine the butter and brown sugar in a pan and heat until bubbling. Set aside to cool.

2 Preheat the oven to 180°C/350°F/Gas 4. Line the base and sides of a 20cm/8in square cake tin (pan) with baking parchment and grease the paper.

3 Beat the egg and vanilla extract into the cooled sugar mixture. Sift over the flour, salt and nutmeg and fold in. Spread into the base of the cake tin.

4 To make the topping, beat the egg white with the salt until it holds soft peaks. Beat in the golden syrup, then the sugar, and continue beating until the mixture holds stiff peaks. Fold in the nuts and spread on top of the base. Bake for 30 minutes. Cut into bars when completely cool.

Cook's Tip
For this recipe, and any recipe that uses a traditional meringue, it is important to use a large grease-free bowl for whisking egg whites. Also, always check that the whisk or beaters are completely clean, as traces of grease will stop the whites from achieving stiff peaks.

Spiced Energy 102kcal/429kJ; Protein 1.2g; Carbohydrate 14.6g, of which sugars 12g; Fat 4.7g, of which saturates 2.2g; Cholesterol 21mg; Calcium 45mg; Fibre 0.3g; Sodium 43mg.
Toffee Energy 189kcal/797kJ; Protein 2g; Carbohydrate 31.9g, of which sugars 27.8g; Fat 6.8g, of which saturates 2.5g; Cholesterol 25mg; Calcium 28mg; Fibre 0.3g; Sodium 42mg.

Chocolate Walnut Bars

These delicious double-decker bars should be stored in the refrigerator in an airtight container.

Makes 24
50g/2oz/¹/₃ cup walnuts
55g/2¹/₄oz/generous ¹/₄ cup caster (superfine) sugar
100g/3³/₄oz/scant 1 cup plain (all-purpose) flour, sifted
90g/3¹/₂oz/7 tbsp cold unsalted (sweet) butter, cut into pieces

For the topping
25g/1oz/2 tbsp unsalted (sweet) butter
90ml/6 tbsp water
25g/1oz/¹/₄ cup unsweetened cocoa powder
90g/3¹/₂oz/¹/₂ cup caster (superfine) sugar
5ml/1 tsp vanilla extract
1.5ml/¹/₄ tsp salt
2 eggs
icing (confectioners') sugar, for dusting

1 Preheat the oven to 180°C/350°F/Gas 4. Grease the base and sides of a 20cm/8in square baking tin (pan).

2 Grind the walnuts with a few tablespoons of the caster sugar in a food processor or blender. In a bowl, combine the ground walnuts, remaining sugar and the flour.

3 Rub in the butter using your fingertips or a pastry cutter until the mixture resembles coarse breadcrumbs. Alternatively, use a food processor.

4 Pat the walnut mixture evenly into the base of the baking tin. Bake for 25 minutes.

5 To make the topping, melt the butter with the water. Whisk in the cocoa powder and sugar. Remove from the heat, stir in the vanilla extract and salt, then cool for 5 minutes.

6 Whisk in the eggs until blended. Pour the topping over the baked crust.

7 Return to the oven and bake until set, about 20 minutes. Set the tin on a wire rack to cool, then cut into bars and dust with icing sugar before serving.

Hazelnut Squares

These crunchy, nutty squares are made in a single bowl. What could be simpler?

Makes 9
50g/2oz plain (semisweet) chocolate
65g/2¹/₂oz/5 tbsp butter or margarine

225g/8oz/generous 1 cup caster (superfine) sugar
50g/2oz/¹/₂ cup plain (all-purpose) flour
2.5ml/¹/₂ tsp baking powder
2 eggs, beaten
2.5ml/¹/₂ tsp vanilla extract
115g/4oz/1 cup skinned hazelnuts, roughly chopped

1 Preheat the oven to 180°C/350°F/Gas 4. Grease a 20cm/8in square baking tin (pan).

2 In a heatproof bowl set over a pan of barely simmering water, melt the chocolate and butter or margarine. Remove the bowl from the heat.

3 Add the sugar, flour, baking powder, eggs, vanilla extract and half of the hazelnuts to the melted mixture and stir well with a wooden spoon.

4 Pour the mixture into the prepared tin. Bake in the oven for 10 minutes, then sprinkle the reserved hazelnuts over the top. Return to the oven and continue baking until firm to the touch, about 25 minutes.

5 Cool in the tin set on a wire rack for 10 minutes, then unmould on to the rack and cool completely. Cut into squares before serving.

Cook's Tip
To remove the skins from the hazelnuts put them on a foil-covered grill (broiling) pan and lightly toast them under the grill on a high heat until the skins loosen. Make sure that the hazelnuts do not brown too much or they will overcook when the Hazelnut Squares are baked in the oven.

Chocolate Energy 97kcal/407kJ; Protein 1.5g; Carbohydrate 9.8g, of which sugars 6.5g; Fat 6.1g, of which saturates 2.9g; Cholesterol 26mg; Calcium 16mg; Fibre 0.3g; Sodium 45mg.
Hazelnut Energy 299kcal/1252kJ; Protein 4.2g; Carbohydrate 34.8g, of which sugars 30.2g; Fat 16.9g, of which saturates 5.7g; Cholesterol 58mg; Calcium 48mg; Fibre 1.1g; Sodium 62mg.

Teabreads & Buns

Flavoursome and satisfying, teabreads, buns and muffins make a delicious mid-morning or afternoon snack, and they will be much appreciated by all the family. Choose from a selection of easy-to-make teabreads, including Apricot Nut Loaf, Mango Teabread, or Banana Bread. Or why not try making Raspberry Crumble Buns, Blueberry Muffins or Date Oven Scones for an extra-special teatime treat?

Date & Pecan Loaf

Walnuts may be used instead of pecan nuts to make this luxurious and moist teabread.

**Makes one 23 x 13cm/
9 x 5in loaf**
175g/6oz/1 cup chopped
  stoned (pitted) dates
175ml/6fl oz/³⁄₄ cup boiling water
50g/2oz/¹⁄₄ cup unsalted (sweet)
  butter, at room temperature
50g/2oz/¹⁄₄ cup soft dark
  brown sugar
50g/2oz/¹⁄₄ cup caster
  (superfine) sugar
1 egg, at room temperature
30ml/2 tbsp brandy
165g/5¹⁄₂oz/generous 1¹⁄₄ cups
  plain (all-purpose) flour
10ml/2 tsp baking powder
2.5ml/¹⁄₂ tsp salt
4ml/³⁄₄ tsp freshly
  grated nutmeg
75g/3oz/³⁄₄ cup coarsely
  chopped pecan nuts

1 Place the dates in a bowl and pour over the boiling water. Set aside to cool. Preheat the oven to 180°C/350°F/Gas 4. Line a 23 x 13cm/9 x 5in loaf tin (pan) with baking parchment and then grease the paper.

2 With an electric mixer, cream the butter and sugars until light and fluffy. Beat in the egg and brandy, then set aside.

3 Sift the flour, baking powder, salt and nutmeg together, at least three times. Fold the dry ingredients into the sugar mixture in three batches, alternating with the dates and water. Fold in the chopped pecan nuts.

4 Pour the mixture into the prepared tin and bake until a skewer inserted in the centre comes out clean, about 45–50 minutes. Leave the loaf to cool in the tin for 10 minutes before transferring it to a wire rack to cool completely.

Cook's Tip
Nutmeg is a particularly useful spice for sweet dishes and is used in small quantities in many dishes, as the spice is poisonous in larger quantities.

Fruity Teabread

Serve this bread thinly sliced, toasted or plain, with butter or cream cheese and home-made jam.

**Makes one 23 x 13cm/
9 x 5in loaf**
225g/8oz/2 cups plain
  (all-purpose) flour
115g/4oz/generous ¹⁄₂ cup caster
  (superfine) sugar
15ml/1 tbsp baking powder
2.5ml/¹⁄₂ tsp salt
grated rind of 1 large orange
160ml/5¹⁄₂fl oz/generous ²⁄₃ cup
  fresh orange juice
2 eggs, lightly beaten
75g/3oz/6 tbsp butter or
  margarine, melted
115g/4oz/1 cup fresh cranberries
  or bilberries
50g/2oz/¹⁄₂ cup chopped walnuts

1 Preheat the oven to 180°C/350°F/Gas 4. Then line a 23 x 13cm/9 x 5in loaf tin (pan) with baking parchment and grease the paper.

2 Sift the flour, sugar, baking powder and salt into a mixing bowl. Then stir in the orange rind.

3 Make a well in the centre and add the fresh orange juice, eggs and melted butter or margarine. Stir from the centre until the ingredients are blended; do not overmix. Add the berries and walnuts, and stir until blended.

4 Transfer the mixture to the prepared tin and bake until a skewer inserted in the centre of the loaf comes out clean, about 45–50 minutes. Leave to cool in the tin for 10 minutes before transferring to a wire rack to cool completely.

Cook's Tip
Margarine can be used instead of butter for most recipes except those with a high fat content such as shortbread. Margarine will not, however, produce the same flavour as butter but it is usually less expensive so can be useful. Block margarines are better for teabreads, buns and muffins than soft margarines.

Teabread Energy 2356kcal/9885kJ; Protein 43.9g; Carbohydrate 317g, of which sugars 145.2g; Fat 110.3g, of which saturates 45.4g; Cholesterol 540mg; Calcium 557mg; Fibre 12.4g; Sodium 630mg.
Loaf Energy 2458kcal/10331kJ; Protein 35.2g; Carbohydrate 356.4g, of which sugars 229.5g; Fat 101.7g, of which saturates 32.4g; Cholesterol 297mg; Calcium 446mg; Fibre 15.6g; Sodium 402mg.

Wholemeal Banana Nut Loaf

A hearty and filling loaf, this would be ideal as a winter tea-time treat.

**Makes one 23 x 13cm/
9 x 5in loaf**
115g/4oz/½ cup butter,
  at room temperature
115g/4oz/generous ½ cup caster
  (superfine) sugar
2 eggs, at room temperature

115g/4oz/1 cup plain
  (all-purpose) flour
5ml/1 tsp bicarbonate of soda
  (baking soda)
1.5ml/¼ tsp salt
5ml/1 tsp ground cinnamon
50g/2oz/½ cup wholemeal
  (whole-wheat) flour
3 large ripe bananas
5ml/1 tsp vanilla extract
50g/2oz/½ cup chopped walnuts

1 Preheat the oven to 180°C/350°F/Gas 4. Line the base and sides of a 23 x 13cm/9 x 5in loaf tin (pan) with baking parchment and grease the paper.

2 With an electric mixer, cream the butter and sugar together until light and fluffy. Add the eggs, one at a time, beating well after each addition.

3 Sift the plain flour, bicarbonate of soda, salt and cinnamon over the butter mixture, and stir to blend. Then stir in the wholemeal flour.

4 With a fork, mash the bananas to a purée, then stir into the mixture. Stir in the vanilla and nuts.

5 Pour the mixture into the prepared tin and spread level. Bake until a skewer inserted in the centre comes out clean, about 50–60 minutes. Leave to stand for 10 minutes before transferring to a wire rack to cool completely.

> **Cook's Tip**
> Wholemeal (whole-wheat) flour contains the wheat germ and bran, giving it a higher fibre, fat and nutritional content than white flour. Because of its fat content it is best stored in a cool larder.

Apricot Nut Loaf

Raisins and walnuts combine with apricots to make a lovely light teabread. Full of flavour, it is also ideal for a morning snack or children's lunchboxes.

**Makes one 23 x 13cm/
9 x 5in loaf**
115g/4oz/1 cup ready-to-eat
  dried apricots
1 large orange

75g/3oz/generous ½ cup raisins
150g/5oz/¾ cup caster
  (superfine) sugar
85ml/5½ tbsp/⅓ cup oil
2 eggs, lightly beaten
250g/9oz/2¼ cups plain
  (all-purpose) flour
10ml/2 tsp baking powder
2.5ml/½ tsp salt
5ml/1 tsp bicarbonate of soda
  (baking soda)
50g/2oz/½ cup chopped walnuts

1 Place the apricots in a bowl, cover with lukewarm water and leave to stand for 30 minutes. Preheat the oven to 180°C/ 350°F/Gas 4. Line a 23 x 13cm/9 x 5in loaf tin (pan) with baking parchment and grease the paper.

2 With a vegetable peeler, remove the orange rind, leaving the pith. Chop the strips finely.

3 Drain the softened apricots and chop them coarsely. Place in a bowl with the orange rind and raisins. Squeeze the peeled orange over a bowl. Measure the orange juice and add enough hot water to obtain 175ml/6fl oz/¾ cup liquid.

4 Add the orange juice mixture to the apricot mixture. Stir in the sugar, oil and eggs. Set aside.

5 In another bowl, sift together the flour, baking powder, salt and bicarbonate of soda. Fold the flour mixture into the apricot mixture in three batches, then stir in the walnuts.

6 Spoon the mixture into the prepared tin and bake until a skewer inserted in the centre of the loaf comes out clean, about 55–60 minutes. If the loaf browns too quickly, protect the top with a sheet of foil. Cool in the tin for 10 minutes, then transfer to a wire rack to cool completely.

Banana Energy 2632kcal/11017kJ; Protein 41.9g; Carbohydrate 313.4g, of which sugars 187.6g; Fat 143.4g, of which saturates 66.5g; Cholesterol 626mg; Calcium 384mg; Fibre 13.1g; Sodium 855mg.
Apricot Energy 2904kcal/12229kJ; Protein 51.6g; Carbohydrate 456.8g, of which sugars 265.9g; Fat 109.6g, of which saturates 13.6g; Cholesterol 381mg; Calcium 708mg; Fibre 20.3g; Sodium 227mg.

Bilberry Teabread

A lovely crumbly topping with a hint of cinnamon makes this teabread extra special.

Makes 8 pieces

50g/2oz/¼ cup butter or margarine, at room temperature
175g/6oz/scant 1 cup caster (superfine) sugar
1 egg, at room temperature
120ml/4fl oz/½ cup milk
225g/8oz/2 cups plain (all-purpose) flour
10ml/2 tsp baking powder
2.5ml/½ tsp salt
275g/10oz/2½ cups fresh bilberries or blueberries

For the topping

115g/4oz/generous ½ cup caster (superfine) sugar
40g/1½oz/⅓ cup plain (all-purpose) flour
2.5ml/½ tsp ground cinnamon
50g/2oz/¼ cup butter, cut into pieces

1 Preheat the oven to 190°C/375°F/Gas 5. Grease a 23cm/9in baking dish.

2 With an electric mixer, cream the butter or margarine with the caster sugar until light and fluffy. Add the egg and beat to combine, then mix in the milk until well blended.

3 Sift over the flour, baking powder and salt, and stir the mixture just enough to blend the ingredients. Add the bilberries and stir gently. Transfer the teabread mixture to the prepared baking dish.

4 To make the topping, place the caster sugar, flour, ground cinnamon and butter in a mixing bowl. Cut the butter into the dry ingredients using a pastry blender until the mixture resembles coarse breadcrumbs. Sprinkle the topping over the mixture in the baking dish. Bake until a skewer inserted in the centre comes out clean, about 45 minutes. Serve warm or cold.

> **Variation**
> In late summer and early autumn, when blackberries are plentiful, try to gather some to use instead of bilberries for this delicious teabread.

Dried Fruit Loaf

Use any combination of dried fruit you like in this delicious teabread. The fruit is soaked first making the loaf superbly moist.

Makes one 23 x 13cm/ 9 x 5in loaf

450g/1lb/2¾ cups mixed dried fruit, such as currants, raisins, chopped ready-to-eat dried apricots and dried cherries
300ml/½ pint/1¼ cups cold strong tea
200g/7oz/scant 1 cup soft dark brown sugar
grated rind and juice of 1 small orange
grated rind and juice of 1 lemon
1 egg, lightly beaten
200g/7oz/1¾ cups plain (all-purpose) flour
15ml/1 tbsp baking powder
1.5ml/¼ tsp salt

1 In a bowl, mix the dried fruit with the cold tea and leave to soak overnight.

2 Preheat the oven to 180°C/350°F/Gas 4. Line the base and sides of a 23 x 13cm/9 x 5in loaf tin (pan) with baking parchment and grease the paper.

3 Strain the soaked fruit, reserving the liquid. In a bowl, combine the dark brown sugar, orange and lemon rind, and strained fruit.

4 Pour the orange and lemon juice into a measuring jug (cup); if the quantity is less than 250ml/8fl oz/1 cup, then top up with the soaking liquid.

5 Stir the citrus juices and lightly beaten egg into the dried fruit mixture until combined.

6 Sift the flour, baking powder and salt together into another bowl. Stir the dry ingredients into the fruit mixture until well blended.

7 Transfer to the tin and bake until a skewer inserted in the centre comes out clean: about 1¼ hours. Leave in the tin for 10 minutes before unmoulding.

Teabread Energy 374kcal/1575kJ; Protein 5g; Carbohydrate 66.2g, of which sugars 40.9g; Fat 11.7g, of which saturates 6.9g; Cholesterol 51mg; Calcium 104mg; Fibre 2.1g; Sodium 95mg.
Loaf Energy 2763kcal/11770kJ; Protein 36.6g; Carbohydrate 673.9g, of which sugars 521.5g; Fat 10g, of which saturates 2g; Cholesterol 190mg; Calcium 838mg; Fibre 14.8g; Sodium 156mg.

Cardamom & Saffron Tea Loaf

An aromatic sweet bread ideal for afternoon tea, or lightly toasted for breakfast. The delicate spices of cardamom and saffron give it an unusual flavour.

Makes one 900g/2lb loaf
a generous pinch of saffron threads
750ml/1¼ pints/3 cups lukewarm milk
25g/1oz/2 tbsp butter

1kg/2¼lb/9 cups strong white bread flour
2 sachets easy-blend (rapid-rise) dried yeast
40g/1½oz/generous ¼ cup caster (superfine) sugar
6 cardamom pods, split open and seeds extracted
115g/4oz/scant ¾ cup raisins
30ml/2 tbsp clear honey, plus extra for glazing
1 egg, beaten

1 Crush the saffron straight into a cup containing a little of the warm milk and leave to infuse (steep) for 5 minutes.

2 Rub the butter into the flour using your fingertips or a pastry cutter, then mix in the yeast, sugar, cardamom seeds and raisins.

3 Beat the remaining milk with the honey and egg, then mix this into the flour, along with the saffron milk and threads, until the mixture forms a firm dough. Turn out the dough and knead it on a lightly floured surface for 5 minutes.

4 Return the dough to the mixing bowl, cover with oiled clear film (plastic wrap) and leave in a warm place until doubled in size.

5 Preheat the oven to 200°C/400°F/Gas 6. Grease a 900g/2lb loaf tin (pan). Turn the dough out on to a floured surface, knock back (punch down) and knead for 3 minutes.

6 Shape the dough into a fat roll and fit into the tin. Cover with a sheet of lightly oiled clear film and leave to stand in a warm place until the dough begins to rise again.

7 Bake the loaf for 25 minutes, or until golden brown and firm on top. Turn out on to a wire rack and as it cools brush the top with clear honey.

Sweet Sesame Loaf

Lemon and sesame seeds make a great partnership in this light teabread.

Makes one 23 x 13cm/ 9 x 5in loaf
75g/3oz/6 tbsp sesame seeds
275g/10oz/2½ cups plain (all-purpose) flour

12.5ml/2½ tsp baking powder
5ml/1 tsp salt
50g/2oz/¼ cup butter or margarine, at room temperature
130g/4½oz/scant ¾ cup caster (superfine) sugar
2 eggs, at room temperature
grated rind of 1 lemon
350ml/12fl oz/1½ cups milk

1 Preheat the oven to 180°C/350°F/Gas 4. Carefully line a 23 x 13cm/9 x 5in loaf tin (pan) with baking parchment and then grease the paper.

2 Reserve 25g/1oz/2 tbsp of the sesame seeds. Spread the rest on a baking sheet and bake in the oven until lightly toasted, about 10 minutes.

3 Sift the flour, baking powder and salt into a bowl. Stir in the toasted sesame seeds and set aside.

4 Cream the butter or margarine and sugar together until light and fluffy. Beat in the eggs, then stir in the lemon rind and milk. Pour the milk mixture over the dry ingredients and fold in with a large metal spoon until just blended.

5 Pour into the tin and sprinkle over the reserved sesame seeds. Bake until a skewer inserted in the centre comes out clean, about 1 hour. Cool in the tin for 10 minutes. Turn out on to a wire rack to cool completely.

Cook's Tip
Sesame seeds are nutty flavoured and slightly sweet. Their flavour is enhanced by light toasting in a dry pan. However, because of their high oil content they do not store well and so you should always buy them in small quantities.

Sesame Energy 2578kcal/10849kJ; Protein 64.8g; Carbohydrate 367g, of which sugars 157g; Fat 105.2g, of which saturates 39.7g; Cholesterol 508mg; Calcium 1443mg; Fibre 14.4g; Sodium 2590mg.
Cardamom Energy 4571kcal/19407kJ; Protein 128.6g; Carbohydrate 956.8g, of which sugars 194.8g; Fat 52.3g, of which saturates 24.6g; Cholesterol 288mg; Calcium 2409mg; Fibre 33.3g; Sodium 649mg.

Mango Teabread

This delicious teabread is baked with juicy ripe mango.

**Makes two 23 x 13cm/
9 x 5in loaves**

275g/10oz/2½ cups plain
  (all-purpose) flour
10ml/2 tsp bicarbonate of soda
  (baking soda)
10ml/2 tsp ground cinnamon
2.5ml/½ tsp salt
115g/4oz/½ cup margarine
3 eggs, at room temperature
285g/10½oz/1½ cups caster
  (superfine) sugar
120ml/4fl oz/½ cup vegetable oil
1 large ripe mango, peeled
  and chopped
85g/3¼oz/generous 1 cup
  desiccated (dry unsweetened
  shredded) coconut
65g/2½oz/½ cup raisins

1 Preheat the oven to 180°C/350°F/Gas 4. Line the base and sides of two 23 x 13cm/9 x 5in loaf tins (pans) with baking parchment and grease the paper.

2 Sift together the flour, bicarbonate of soda, cinnamon and salt.

3 Cream the margarine until soft. Beat in the eggs and sugar until light and fluffy. Beat in the oil.

4 Fold the dry ingredients into the creamed ingredients in three batches, then fold in the mango, two-thirds of the coconut and the raisins.

5 Spoon the batter into the tins. Sprinkle over the remaining coconut. Bake until a skewer inserted in the centre comes out clean, about 50–60 minutes. Leave to stand for 10 minutes before turning out on to a wire rack to cool completely.

> **Cook's Tip**
> *A simple way of dicing a mango is to take two thick slices from either side of the large flat stone without peeling the fruit. Make criss-cross cuts in the flesh on each slice and then turn inside out. The cubes of flesh will stand proud of the skin and can be easily cut off.*

Courgette Teabread

Like carrots, courgettes are a vegetable that works well in baking, adding moistness and lightness to the bread.

**Makes one 23 x 13cm/
9 x 5in loaf**

50g/2oz/¼ cup butter
3 eggs
250ml/8fl oz/1 cup vegetable oil
285g/10½oz/1½ cups caster
  (superfine) sugar
2 unpeeled courgettes
  (zucchini), grated
275g/10oz/2½ cups plain
  (all-purpose) flour
10ml/2 tsp bicarbonate of soda
  (baking soda)
5ml/1 tsp baking powder
5ml/1 tsp salt
5ml/1 tsp ground cinnamon
5ml/1 tsp freshly grated nutmeg
1.5ml/¼ tsp ground cloves
115g/4oz/1 cup chopped walnuts

1 Preheat the oven to 180°C/350°F/Gas 4. Line the base and sides of a 23 x 13cm/9 x 5in loaf tin (pan) with baking parchment and grease the paper.

2 In a pan, melt the butter over a low heat. Set aside.

3 With an electric mixer, beat the eggs and oil together until thick. Beat in the sugar, then stir in the melted butter and the grated courgettes. Set aside.

4 In another bowl, sift the flour with the bicarbonate of soda, baking powder, salt, ground cinnamon, grated nutmeg and ground cloves. Sift twice more and then carefully fold them into the courgette mixture. Fold in the chopped walnuts.

5 Pour into the tin and bake until a skewer inserted in the centre comes out clean, about 60–70 minutes. Leave to stand for 10 minutes before turning out on to a wire rack to cool.

> **Cook's Tip**
> *Sifting the flour and dry ingredients three times helps to make the teabread mixture light. Be careful to fold in the other ingredients gently so that the air that was incorporated is not lost.*

Courgette Energy 5135kcal/21437kJ; Protein 70.4g; Carbohydrate 522.8g, of which sugars 312g; Fat 321.5g, of which saturates 59.1g; Cholesterol 677mg; Calcium 839mg; Fibre 16.1g; Sodium 2515mg.
Mango Energy 2291kcal/9601kJ; Protein 26.7g; Carbohydrate 292.2g, of which sugars 187.2g; Fat 121.2g, of which saturates 29.8g; Cholesterol 285mg; Calcium 347mg; Fibre 12.7g; Sodium 611mg.

Sweet Potato & Raisin Bread

Serve buttered slices of this subtly spiced loaf at coffee or tea time.

Makes one 900g/2lb loaf
350g/12oz/3 cups plain
  (all-purpose) flour
10ml/2 tsp baking powder
2.5ml/½ tsp salt
5ml/1 tsp ground cinnamon
2.5ml/½ tsp freshly grated nutmeg
450g/1lb mashed cooked
  sweet potatoes
90g/3½oz/½ cup soft light
  brown sugar
115g/4oz/½ cup butter
  or margarine, melted
  and cooled
3 eggs, beaten
75g/3oz/generous ½ cup raisins

1 Preheat the oven to 180°C/350°F/Gas 4. Grease a 900g/2lb loaf dish or tin (pan).

2 Sift the flour, baking powder, salt, cinnamon, and nutmeg into a small bowl. Set aside.

3 With an electric mixer, beat the mashed sweet potatoes with the brown sugar, butter or margarine, and eggs until well mixed.

4 Add the flour mixture and the raisins. Stir with a wooden spoon until the flour is just mixed in.

5 Transfer the batter to the prepared dish or tin. Bake until a skewer inserted in the centre of the loaf comes out clean, about 1–1¼ hours.

6 Let the bread cool in the pan on a wire rack for 15 minutes, then unmould from the dish or tin on to the wire rack and leave to cool completely.

Cook's Tip
Soft light and dark brown sugars are both comprised of white sugar with added molasses, which gives them a moist and delicate flavour. Soft dark brown sugar has more molasses added to give it a richer colour and more intense flavour.

Lemon & Walnut Teabread

Beaten egg whites give this citrus-flavour loaf a lovely light and crumbly texture.

Makes one 23 x 13cm/
9 x 5in loaf
115g/4oz/½ cup butter or
  margarine, at room temperature
90g/3½oz/½ cup caster
  (superfine) sugar
2 eggs, at room temperature,
  separated
grated rind of 2 lemons
30ml/2 tbsp lemon juice
215g/7½oz/scant 2 cups plain
  (all-purpose) flour
10ml/2 tsp baking powder
120ml/4fl oz/½ cup milk
50g/2oz/½ cup chopped walnuts
1.5ml/¼ tsp salt

1 Preheat the oven to 180°C/350°F/Gas 4. Then line a 23 x 13cm/9 x 5in loaf tin (pan) with baking parchment and grease the paper.

2 Cream the butter or margarine with the sugar until light and fluffy. Beat in the egg yolks. Add the lemon rind and juice, and stir until blended. Set aside.

3 In another bowl, sift together the flour and baking powder three times. Fold into the butter mixture in three batches, alternating with the milk. Fold in the walnuts. Set aside.

4 Beat the egg whites and salt until stiff peaks form. Fold a large spoonful of the egg whites into the walnut mixture to lighten it. Fold in the remaining egg whites carefully until the mixture is just blended.

5 Pour the batter into the prepared tin and bake until a skewer inserted in the centre of the loaf comes out clean, about 45–50 minutes. Cool in the tin for 5 minutes before turning out on to a wire rack to cool completely.

Cook's Tip
Make sure that there is no egg yolk in the white or it will stop it from whisking up properly.

Date & Nut Maltloaf

Choose any type of nut you like to include in this deliciously rich and fruit-packed teabread.

Makes two 450g/1lb loaves

300g/11oz/2⅔ cups strong plain (all-purpose) flour
275g/10oz/2½ cups strong wholemeal (whole-wheat) bread flour
5ml/1 tsp salt
75g/3oz/⅓ cup soft light brown sugar
1 sachet easy-blend (rapid-rise) dried yeast
50g/2oz/¼ cup butter or margarine
15ml/1 tbsp black treacle (molasses)
60ml/4 tbsp malt extract
scant 250ml/8fl oz/1 cup lukewarm milk
115g/4oz/⅔ cup chopped dates
75g/3oz/½ cup sultanas (golden raisins)
50g/2oz/½ cup chopped nuts
75g/3oz/generous ½ cup raisins
30ml/2 tbsp clear honey, to glaze

1 Sift the flours and salt into a large bowl, then tip in the wheat flakes from the sieve. Stir in the sugar and yeast.

2 Put the butter or margarine in a small pan with the treacle and malt extract. Stir over a low heat until melted. Leave to cool, then combine with the milk.

3 Stir the milk mixture into the dry ingredients and knead thoroughly for 15 minutes, or until the dough is elastic.

4 Knead in the chopped dates, sultanas and chopped nuts. Transfer the dough to an oiled bowl, cover with clear film (plastic wrap) and leave in a warm place for about 1½ hours, or until the dough has doubled in size.

5 Grease two 450g/1lb loaf tins (pans). Knock back (punch down) the dough and knead lightly. Divide the dough in half, form into loaves and place in the tins. Cover and leave in a warm place for 30 minutes, or until risen. Meanwhile, preheat the oven to 190°C/375°F/Gas 5.

6 Bake for 35–40 minutes, or until well risen. Cool on a wire rack. Brush with honey while warm.

Orange Wheatloaf

Perfect just with butter as a breakfast teabread, and for banana sandwiches.

Makes one 450g/1lb loaf

275g/10oz/2½ cups plain (all-purpose) wholemeal (whole-wheat) flour
2.5ml/½ tsp salt
25g/1oz/2 tbsp butter
25g/1oz/2 tbsp soft light brown sugar
½ sachet easy-blend (rapid-rise) dried yeast
grated rind and juice of ½ orange

1 Lightly grease a 450g/1lb loaf tin (pan). Sift the flour into a large bowl and add any wheat flakes from the sieve to the flour. Add the salt and rub in the butter lightly with your fingertips or a pastry cutter.

2 Stir in the sugar, yeast and orange rind. Pour the orange juice into a measuring jug and use hot water to make up to 200ml/7fl oz/scant 1 cup (the liquid should not be more than hand hot).

3 Stir the liquid into the flour mixture and mix to a soft ball of dough. Knead gently on a lightly floured surface until quite smooth and elastic.

4 Place the dough in the tin and leave it in a warm place until nearly doubled in size. Preheat the oven to 220°C/425°F/Gas 7.

5 Bake the bread for 30–35 minutes, or until it sounds hollow when removed from the tin and tapped underneath. Tip out of the tin and cool on a wire rack.

> **Cook's Tip**
> *Easy-blend (rapid-rise) yeast is mixed directly with the dry ingredients and is the easiest yeast to use. Don't confuse this with active dried yeast, which needs to be mixed with liquid first and left to become frothy before it is mixed with the dry ingredients.*

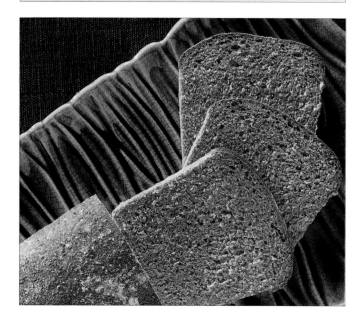

Date Energy 1939kcal/8200kJ; Protein 43.9g; Carbohydrate 361.7g, of which sugars 162.2g; Fat 45.2g, of which saturates 16.6g; Cholesterol 61mg; Calcium 693mg; Fibre 21.7g; Sodium 308mg.
Orange Energy 1146kcal/4848kJ; Protein 35.3g; Carbohydrate 204.2g, of which sugars 34.3g; Fat 26.6g, of which saturates 13.8g; Cholesterol 53mg; Calcium 125mg; Fibre 24.8g; Sodium 164mg.

Orange & Honey Teabread

Honey gives a special flavour to this teabread. Serve just with a scraping of butter.

**Makes one 23 x 13cm/
9 x 5in loaf**
385g/13½oz/scant 3½ cups
   plain (all-purpose) flour
12.5ml/2½ tsp baking powder
2.5ml/½ tsp bicarbonate of soda
   (baking soda)
2.5ml/½ tsp salt
25g/1oz/2 tbsp margarine
250ml/8fl oz/1 cup clear honey
1 egg, at room temperature,
   lightly beaten
25ml/1½ tbsp grated
   orange rind
175ml/6fl oz/¾ cup freshly
   squeezed orange juice
115g/4oz/1 cup chopped walnuts

1 Preheat the oven to 160°C/325°F/Gas 3. Line the base and sides of a 23 x 13cm/9 x 5in loaf tin (pan) with baking parchment and grease the paper.

2 Sift the flour, baking powder, bicarbonate of soda and salt together in a bowl.

3 Cream the margarine until soft. Stir in the honey until blended, then stir in the egg. Add the orange rind and combine well.

4 Fold the flour mixture into the honey mixture in three batches, alternating with the orange juice. Stir in the walnuts.

5 Pour into the prepared tin and bake in the oven until a skewer inserted in the centre comes out clean, about 60–70 minutes. Leave for 10 minutes before turning out on to a wire rack to cool completely.

> **Cook's Tip**
> *Although you can buy beautifully scented honey with the fragrance of wild flowers and herbs, the scents are usually destroyed in cooking, so for recipes such as this a less expensive honey will do perfectly well. Clear honey gradually becomes cloudy, but this can be rectified simply by gently heating it.*

Apple Loaf

The apple sauce in this loaf makes it beautifully moist – it tastes perfect simply sliced and spread with butter.

**Makes one 23 x 13cm/
9 x 5in loaf**
1 egg
250ml/8fl oz/1 cup bottled or
   home-made apple sauce
50g/2oz/¼ cup butter or
   margarine, melted
100g/3¾oz/scant ½ cup soft
   dark brown sugar
45g/1¾oz/scant ¼ cup caster
   (superfine) sugar
275g/10oz/2½ cups plain
   (all-purpose) flour
10ml/2 tsp baking powder
2.5ml/½ tsp bicarbonate of soda
   (baking soda)
2.5ml/½ tsp salt
5ml/1 tsp ground cinnamon
2.5ml/½ tsp freshly grated nutmeg
65g/2½oz/½ cup currants
   or raisins
50g/2oz/½ cup pecan nuts or
   walnuts, chopped

1 Preheat the oven to 180°C/350°F/Gas 4. Line the base and sides of a 23 x 13cm/9 x 5in loaf tin (pan) with baking parchment and grease the paper.

2 Break the egg into a bowl and beat lightly. Stir in the apple sauce, butter or margarine, and both sugars. Set aside.

3 In another bowl, sift together the flour, baking powder, bicarbonate of soda, salt, cinnamon and nutmeg. Fold the dry ingredients, including the currants or raisins and the nuts, into the apple sauce mixture in three batches.

4 Pour into the prepared tin and bake in the oven until a skewer inserted in the centre of the loaf comes out clean, about 1 hour. Leave to stand in the tin for 10 minutes, then turn out on to a wire rack to cool completely.

> **Variations**
> *Ring the changes with this moist loaf by using different nuts and dried fruit. Try ready-to-eat dried apricots with hazelnuts, for example.*

Orange Energy 3145kcal/13251kJ; Protein 61.3g; Carbohydrate 509.6g, of which sugars 215.4g; Fat 109.9g, of which saturates 8.8g; Cholesterol 190mg; Calcium 707mg; Fibre 16.1g; Sodium 335mg.
Apple Energy 2558kcal/10777kJ; Protein 42.6g; Carbohydrate 432.4g, of which sugars 222.5g; Fat 85g, of which saturates 30.9g; Cholesterol 297mg; Calcium 586mg; Fibre 15.3g; Sodium 442mg.

Glazed Banana Spiced Loaf

The lemony glaze perfectly sets off the warm flavours of nutmeg and cloves in this deliciously moist and light banana teabread.

Makes one 23 x 13cm/ 9 x 5in loaf
115g/4oz/¹/₂ cup butter, at room temperature
165g/5¹/₂oz/³/₄ cup caster (superfine) sugar
2 eggs, at room temperature
215g/7¹/₂oz/scant 2 cups plain (all-purpose) flour
5ml/1 tsp salt
5ml/1 tsp bicarbonate of soda (baking soda)
2.5ml/¹/₂ tsp freshly grated nutmeg
1.5ml/¹/₄ tsp mixed spice
1.5ml/¹/₄ tsp ground cloves
175ml/6fl oz/³/₄ cup sour cream
1 large ripe banana, mashed
5ml/1 tsp vanilla extract

For the glaze
115g/4oz/1 cup icing (confectioners') sugar
15–30ml/1–2 tbsp lemon juice

1 Preheat the oven to 180°C/350°F/Gas 4. Line a 23 x 13cm/ 9 x 5in loaf tin (pan) with baking parchment and grease the paper.

2 Cream the butter and sugar until light and fluffy. Add the eggs, one at a time, beating well after each addition.

3 Sift together the flour, salt, bicarbonate of soda, nutmeg, mixed spice and cloves. Add to the butter mixture and stir to combine well.

4 Add the sour cream, banana and vanilla extract, and mix to just blend. Pour this mixture into the prepared tin.

5 Bake until the top springs back when touched lightly, about 45–50 minutes. Cool in the tin for 10 minutes. Turn out on to a wire rack.

6 To make the glaze, combine the icing sugar and lemon juice until smooth, then stir until smooth. Place the cooled loaf on a rack set over a baking sheet. Pour the glaze over the loaf and allow to set.

Fruit & Brazil Nut Teabread

Mashed bananas are a classic ingredient in teabreads, and help to create a moist texture as well as adding a full flavour.

Makes one 23 x 13cm/ 9 x 5in loaf
225g/8oz/2 cups plain (all-purpose) flour
10ml/2 tsp baking powder
5ml/1 tsp mixed (apple pie) spice
115g/4oz/¹/₂ cup butter, diced
115g/4oz/¹/₂ cup light soft brown sugar
2 eggs, lightly beaten
30ml/2 tbsp milk
30ml/2 tbsp dark rum
2 bananas
115g/4oz/²/₃ cup dried figs, chopped
50g/2oz/¹/₃ cup brazil nuts, chopped

For the decoration
8 whole brazil nuts
4 whole dried figs, halved
30ml/2 tbsp apricot jam
5ml/1 tsp dark rum

1 Preheat the oven to 180°C/350°F/Gas 4. Grease and base-line a 23 x 13cm/9 x 5in loaf tin (pan). Sift the flour, baking powder and mixed spice into a bowl.

2 Rub in the butter using your fingertips or a pastry cutter until the mixture resembles fine breadcrumbs. Stir in the sugar.

3 Make a well in the centre and work in the eggs, milk and rum until combined. Peel and mash the bananas. Stir in the mashed bananas, chopped figs and brazil nuts and transfer to the prepared loaf tin.

4 To decorate the teabread press the whole brazil nuts and halved figs gently into the mixture, to form an attractive pattern. Bake for 1¹/₄ hours, or until a skewer inserted in the centre comes out clean. Cool in the tin for 10 minutes, then transfer to a wire rack.

5 Heat the jam and rum together in a small pan. Increase the heat and boil for 1 minute. Remove from the heat and pass through a fine sieve. Cool the glaze slightly, brush over the warm loaf, and leave to cool completely.

Teabread Energy 3095kcal/12984kJ; Protein 49.5g; Carbohydrate 405.9g, of which sugars 229.5g; Fat 145.6g, of which saturates 72.2g; Cholesterol 628mg; Calcium 874mg; Fibre 19.9g; Sodium 938mg.
Loaf Energy 3293kcal/13836kJ; Protein 41.1g; Carbohydrate 490.2g, of which sugars 324.1g; Fat 143.6g, of which saturates 85.4g; Cholesterol 731mg; Calcium 696mg; Fibre 7.8g; Sodium 933mg.

Banana Bread

For a change, add 50–75g/ 2–3oz/½–¾ cup chopped walnuts or pecan nuts with the dry ingredients.

Makes one 21 x 12cm/ 8½ x 4½in loaf
200g/7oz/1⅔ cups plain (all-purpose) flour
11.5ml/2¼ tsp baking powder
2.5ml/½ tsp salt

4ml/¾ tsp ground cinnamon (optional)
60ml/4 tbsp wheatgerm
65g/2½oz/5 tbsp butter, at room temperature
115g/4oz/generous ½ cup caster (superfine) sugar
4ml/¾ tsp grated lemon rind
3 ripe bananas, mashed
2 eggs, beaten

I Preheat the oven to 180°C/350°F/Gas 4. Grease and flour a 21 x 12cm/8½ x 4½in loaf tin (pan).

2 Sift the flour, baking powder, salt and cinnamon, if using, into a bowl. Stir in the wheatgerm.

3 In another bowl, combine the butter with the caster sugar and grated lemon rind. Beat thoroughly until the mixture is light and fluffy.

4 Add the mashed bananas and eggs, and mix well. Add the dry ingredients and blend quickly and evenly.

5 Spoon into the loaf tin. Bake for 50–60 minutes, or until a skewer inserted in the centre comes out clean.

6 Cool the bread in the tin for 5 minutes, then turn out on to a wire rack to cool completely.

> **Cook's Tip**
> *Wheatgerm is the heart of the wheat grain and contains many nutrients and important vitamins. It must be used fresh and should be stored in an airtight container. Do not store for long periods, as it will become bitter.*

Banana Orange Loaf

For the best banana flavour and a really good, moist texture, make sure that the bananas are perfectly ripe for this cake.

Makes one 23 x 13cm/ 9 x 5in loaf
90g/3½oz/¾ cup plain (all-purpose) wholemeal (whole-wheat) flour
90g/3½oz/¾ cup plain (all-purpose) flour
5ml/1 tsp baking powder

5ml/1 tsp mixed (apple pie) spice
45ml/3 tbsp flaked (sliced) hazelnuts, toasted
2 large ripe bananas
1 egg
30ml/2 tbsp sunflower oil
30ml/2 tbsp clear honey
finely grated rind and juice of 1 small orange
4 orange slices, halved
10ml/2 tsp icing (confectioners') sugar

I Preheat the oven to 180°C/350°F/Gas 4. Brush a 23 x 13cm/ 9 x 5in loaf tin (pan) with sunflower oil and line the base with baking parchment.

2 Sift the flours with the baking powder and spice into a large bowl, adding any bran that is caught in the sieve (strainer). Stir the hazelnuts into the dry ingredients.

3 Peel and mash the bananas in a large bowl. Add the egg, sunflower oil, honey, and the orange rind and juice to the mashed bananas and beat together.

4 Add the banana mixture to the dry ingredients and mix to combine thoroughly.

5 Spoon the mixture into the prepared tin and smooth the top. Bake in the oven for 40–45 minutes, or until the cake is firm and golden brown. Remove from the oven and turn out on to a wire rack to cool.

6 Meanwhile, sprinkle the orange slices with the icing sugar and place on a grill (broiling) rack. Grill until lightly golden. Arrange the glazed orange slices on the top of the loaf.

Bread Energy 2265kcal/9548kJ; Protein 51.9g; Carbohydrate 372.4g, of which sugars 195.9g; Fat 73.6g, of which saturates 38.4g; Cholesterol 519mg; Calcium 461mg; Fibre 18.9g; Sodium 553mg.
Loaf Energy 1483kcal/6238kJ; Protein 35.3g; Carbohydrate 214.3g, of which sugars 84.6g; Fat 59.9g, of which saturates 7g; Cholesterol 190mg; Calcium 276mg; Fibre 16.1g; Sodium 89mg.

Marmalade Teabread

If you prefer, leave the top of the loaf plain and serve sliced and lightly buttered instead.

Makes one 21 x 12cm/ 8½ x 4½in loaf

200g/7oz/1⅔ cups plain (all-purpose) flour
5ml/1 tsp baking powder
6.5ml/1¼ tsp ground cinnamon

90g/3½oz/7 tbsp butter or margarine
50g/2oz/¼ cup soft light brown sugar
60ml/4 tbsp chunky orange marmalade
1 egg, beaten
about 45ml/3 tbsp milk
60ml/4 tbsp glacé icing and shreds of orange and lemon rind, to decorate

1 Preheat the oven to 160°C/325°F/Gas 3. Lightly butter a 21 x 12cm/8½ x 4½in loaf tin (pan), then line the base with baking parchment and grease the paper.

2 Sift the flour, baking powder and cinnamon together, toss in the butter or margarine, then rub in using your fingertips or a pastry cutter until the mixture resembles coarse breadcrumbs. Stir in the sugar.

3 In a separate bowl, mix together the marmalade, egg and most of the milk, then stir into the flour mixture to make a soft dropping consistency, adding more milk if necessary.

4 Transfer the mixture to the tin and bake for 1¼ hours, or until firm to the touch. Leave the cake to cool in the tin for 5 minutes, then turn on to a wire rack, peel off the lining paper, and leave to cool completely.

5 Drizzle the glacé icing over the top of the cake and decorate with the orange and lemon rind.

Cook's Tip
To make citrus shreds, pare away strips of orange or lemon rind with a vegetable peeler, then cut into fine shreds with a knife.

Spiced Date & Walnut Cake

Nuts and dates are a classic flavour combination. Use pecan nuts instead of walnuts, if you wish.

Makes one 900g/2lb cake

300g/11oz/2⅔ cups self-raising (self-rising) wholemeal (whole-wheat) flour

10ml/2 tsp mixed (apple pie) spice
150g/5oz/¾ cup chopped dates
50g/2oz/½ cup chopped walnuts
60ml/4 tbsp sunflower oil
115g/4oz/½ cup dark muscovado (molasses) sugar
300ml/½ pint/1¼ cups milk
walnut halves, to decorate

1 Preheat the oven to 180°C/350°F/Gas 4. Line a 900g/2lb loaf tin (pan) with baking parchment and grease the paper.

2 Sift together the flour and spice, adding back any bran from the sieve. Stir in the dates and walnuts.

3 Mix the oil, sugar and milk in a separate bowl. Add the oil mixture to the dry ingredients and mix to combine thoroughly.

4 Spoon the cake mixture into the prepared loaf tin and arrange the walnut halves on top.

5 Bake the cake in the oven for about 45–50 minutes, or until it is golden brown and firm.

6 Turn out the cake, remove the lining paper, and leave to cool on a wire rack.

Cook's Tip
Dried fruits add natural sweetness as well as moisture to baking. Always chop dried fruits by hand, as a food processor will chop them too finely. Dates bought in a block are ideal for cooking as they have no stones and you can use a sharp knife to slice horizontally through the block in thin slices. The slices can then easily be broken up into small pieces and chopped smaller if you prefer.

Marmalade Energy 1725kcal/7238kJ; Protein 49.7g; Carbohydrate 209.3g, of which sugars 55.8g; Fat 82.5g, of which saturates 48.8g; Cholesterol 382mg; Calcium 408mg; Fibre 6.2g; Sodium 3324mg.
Spiced Energy 2666kcal/11243kJ; Protein 61.2g; Carbohydrate 429.6g, of which sugars 243.9g; Fat 90.2g, of which saturates 12.3g; Cholesterol 18mg; Calcium 649mg; Fibre 34.8g; Sodium 163mg.

Caraway Seed Buns

These fragrant buns are best served fresh from the oven.

Makes 12
350g/12oz/3 cups plain (all-purpose) flour
115g/4oz/⅔ cup ground rice or semolina
10ml/2 tsp baking powder
115g/4oz/½ cup butter
75g/3oz/⅓ cup caster (superfine) sugar, plus extra for sprinkling
30ml/2 tbsp caraway seeds
2 eggs
about 75ml/5 tbsp milk

1 Preheat the oven to 200°C/400°F/Gas 6. Line a baking sheet with baking parchment. Sift the flour, ground rice and baking powder together into a large mixing bowl.

2 Add the butter and, with your fingertips, rub it into the flour until the mixture resembles fine breadcrumbs. Stir the sugar and caraway seeds in to the flour mixture.

3 Lightly beat the eggs and stir them into the flour mixture, together with sufficient milk to enable you to gather the mixture into a ball of soft dough. Transfer the dough to a lightly floured surface.

4 Roll out to about 2.5cm/1in thick. Using a 5cm/2in biscuit (cookie) cutter, cut into rounds, gathering up the offcuts and re-rolling to make more.

5 Arrange the rounds on the lined baking sheet, setting them quite close together so they support each other as they rise.

6 Put into the hot oven and cook for 15–20 minutes until risen and golden brown. Transfer to a wire rack and dust with caster sugar. Leave to cool.

> **Cook's Tip**
> *Replace the caraway seeds with 50g/2oz dried fruit, such as raisins or finely chopped apricots.*

Prune & Peel Rock Buns

These fruity scones are delicious spread with butter.

Makes 12
225g/8oz/2 cups plain (all-purpose) flour
10ml/2 tsp baking powder
75g/3oz/scant ½ cup demerara (raw) sugar
50g/2oz/¼ cup chopped ready-to-eat dried prunes
50g/2oz/⅓ cup chopped mixed (candied) peel
finely grated rind of 1 lemon
50ml/2fl oz/¼ cup sunflower oil
75ml/5 tbsp skimmed milk

1 Preheat the oven to 200°C/400°F/Gas 6. Lightly oil a large baking sheet. Sift together the flour and baking powder, then stir in the sugar, prunes, peel and lemon rind.

2 Mix the oil and milk, then stir into the mixture, to make a dough which just binds together. Spoon into rocky heaps on the baking sheet and bake for 20 minutes, or until golden. Leave to cool on a wire rack.

Traditional Rock Buns

Makes 12
225g/8oz/2 cups plain (all-purpose) flour
10ml/2 tsp baking powder
115g/4oz/½ cup butter
115g/4oz/scant 1 cup mixed dried fruit
115g/4oz/1 cup demerara (raw) sugar
grated rind of half an orange
1 egg, beaten
30ml/2 tbsp milk

1 Preheat the oven to 200°C/400°F/Gas 6. Grease two baking sheets. Sift the dry ingredients into a bowl and rub in the fat using your fingertips or a pastry cutter.

2 Stir in the fruit, sugar and orange rind. Add the egg and enough milk to bind the dough. Place heaps of mixture on the baking sheets and bake for 15–20 minutes, or until golden. Cool on a rack.

Caraway Energy 244kcal/1026kJ; Protein 5.1g; Carbohydrate 36.9g, of which sugars 7.3g; Fat 9.5g, of which saturates 5.4g; Cholesterol 53mg; Calcium 60mg; Fibre 1.1g; Sodium 75mg
Prune Energy 132kcal/559kJ; Protein 2.1g; Carbohydrate 25.3g, of which sugars 11g; Fat 3.2g, of which saturates 0.4g; Cholesterol 0mg; Calcium 44mg; Fibre 1g; Sodium 16mg.
Traditional Energy 206Kcal/866kJ; Protein 2.1g; Carbohydrate 31.3g, of which sugars 13g; Fat 8.7g, of which saturates 5.2g; Cholesterol 0mg; Calcium 40mg; Fibre 0.8g; Sodium 20mg.

Raisin Bran Buns

Serve these buns warm or at room temperature, on their own, with butter, or with cream cheese.

Makes 15

50g/2oz/¼ cup butter
  or margarine
40g/1½oz/⅓ cup plain
  (all-purpose) flour
50g/2oz/½ cup plain wholemeal
  (whole-wheat) flour
7.5ml/1½ tsp bicarbonate of
  soda (baking soda)

1.5ml/¼ tsp salt
5ml/1 tsp ground cinnamon
25g/1oz/generous 1 cup bran
75g/3oz/generous ½ cup raisins
65g/2½oz/generous ¼ cup soft
  dark brown sugar
50g/2oz/¼ cup caster
  (superfine) sugar
1 egg
250ml/8fl oz/1 cup buttermilk
juice of ½ lemon

1 Preheat the oven to 200°C/400°F/Gas 6. Lightly grease 15 bun-tray cups. Put the butter or margarine in a pan and melt over a gentle heat. Set aside.

2 In a mixing bowl, sift together the flours, bicarbonate of soda, salt and cinnamon. Add the bran, raisins and sugars, and stir until well blended.

3 In another bowl, mix together the egg, buttermilk, lemon juice and melted butter. Add the buttermilk mixture to the dry ingredients and stir in lightly and quickly until just moistened. Do not mix until smooth.

4 Spoon the mixture into the prepared bun-tray cups, filling them almost to the top. Half-fill any empty cups with water. Bake until golden, about 15–20 minutes. Remove to a wire rack to cool slightly or serve immediately.

> **Cook's Tip**
> *When you use a bun tray if you half-fill any unused cups with water you will ensure that all the buns will cook evenly.*

Raspberry Crumble Buns

The crumble topping adds an unusual twist to these lovely fruit buns.

Makes 12

175g/6oz/1½ cups plain
  (all-purpose) flour
50g/2oz/¼ cup caster
  (superfine) sugar
45g/1¾oz/scant ¼ cup soft light
  brown sugar
10ml/2 tsp baking powder
1.5ml/¼ tsp salt
5ml/1 tsp ground cinnamon
115g/4oz/½ cup butter, melted

1 egg
120ml/4fl oz/½ cup milk
150g/5oz/¾ cup fresh raspberries
grated rind of 1 lemon

For the crumble topping

25g/1oz/¼ cup finely chopped
  pecan nuts or walnuts
50g/2oz/¼ cup soft dark
  brown sugar
45ml/3 tbsp plain
  (all-purpose) flour
5ml/1 tsp ground cinnamon
45ml/3 tbsp butter, melted

1 Preheat the oven to 180°C/350°F/Gas 4. Lightly grease 12 bun-tray cups or use 12 paper cases. Sift the flour into a bowl. Add the sugars, baking powder, salt and cinnamon, and stir to blend.

2 Make a well in the centre. Place the butter, egg and milk in the well and mix until just combined. Stir in the raspberries and lemon rind. Spoon the mixture into the prepared bun tray, filling the cups almost to the top.

3 To make the crumble topping, mix the nuts, dark brown sugar, flour and cinnamon in a bowl. Add the melted butter and stir to blend.

4 Spoon some of the crumble over each bun. Bake until browned, about 25 minutes. Transfer to a wire rack to cool slightly. Serve warm.

> **Variation**
> *Try strawberries or blackberries for a change.*

Raisin Energy 89kcal/373kJ; Protein 2g; Carbohydrate 13.4g, of which sugars 8.9g; Fat 3.4g, of which saturates 1.9g; Cholesterol 20mg; Calcium 34mg; Fibre 1.1g; Sodium 36mg.
Raspberry Energy 225kcal/940kJ; Protein 2.7g; Carbohydrate 25.2g, of which sugars 14.1g; Fat 13.3g, of which saturates 7.3g; Cholesterol 45mg; Calcium 48mg; Fibre 0.9g; Sodium 93mg.

Banana & Pecan Muffins

These satisfying muffins are quick and easy to make and contain the winning combination of banana and pecan nuts.

Makes 8
150g/5oz/1¼ cups plain (all-purpose) flour
7.5ml/1½ tsp baking powder
50g/2oz/¼ cup butter or margarine, at room temperature
150g/5oz/¾ cup caster (superfine) sugar
1 egg
5ml/1 tsp vanilla extract
3 bananas, mashed
50g/2oz/½ cup chopped pecan nuts
75ml/5tbsp milk

1 Preheat the oven to 190°C/375°F/Gas 5. Lightly grease eight deep muffin cups. Sift the flour and baking powder into a small bowl. Set aside.

2 With an electric mixer, cream the butter or margarine and sugar together. Add the egg and vanilla extract and beat until fluffy. Mix in the banana.

3 Add the pecan nuts. With the mixer on low speed, beat in the flour mixture alternately with the milk.

4 Spoon the mixture into the prepared muffin cups, filling them about two-thirds full. Bake the muffins until golden brown and a skewer inserted into the centre of a muffin comes out clean, about 20–25 minutes.

5 Let the muffins cool in the cups on a wire rack for about 10 minutes. To loosen, run a knife gently around each muffin and unmould on to the wire rack.

6 Leave to cool for another 10 minutes before serving.

> **Variation**
> Walnuts also taste good with bananas, so try these instead of pecan nuts for a change.

Blueberry & Cinnamon Muffins

These moist and "moreish" muffins have great appeal.

Makes 8
115g/4oz/1 cup plain (all-purpose) flour
15ml/1 tbsp baking powder
pinch of salt
65g/2½oz/generous ¼ cup soft light brown sugar
1 egg
175ml/6fl oz/¾ cup milk
45ml/3 tbsp vegetable oil
10ml/2 tsp ground cinnamon
115g/4oz/1 cup fresh or thawed frozen blueberries

1 Preheat the oven to 190°C/375°F/Gas 5. Lightly grease eight deep muffin cups.

2 Beat the first eight ingredients together until smooth. Fold in the blueberries. Spoon into the muffin cups, filling them two-thirds full. Bake for 25 minutes, or until lightly coloured. Leave in the cups for 5 minutes then transfer to a rack to cool.

Chocolate-chip Muffins

Makes 10
115g/4oz/½ cup butter or margarine, softened
75g/3oz/⅓ cup granulated sugar
30ml/2 tbsp soft dark brown sugar
2 eggs
175g/6oz/1½ cups plain (all-purpose) flour, sifted twice
5ml/1 tsp baking powder
120ml/4fl oz/½ cup milk
175g/6oz/1 cup plain (semisweet) chocolate chips

1 Preheat the oven to 190°C/375°F/Gas 5. Grease ten muffin cups. Cream the butter or margarine with both sugars until fluffy.

2 Add the eggs, one at a time, beating well after each addition. Fold in the flour, alternating with the milk. Divide half the mixture among the muffin cups. Sprinkle the chocolate chips on top, then cover with the remaining mixture.

3 Bake for 25 minutes. Leave in the tin (pan) for 5 minutes then transfer to a rack to cool.

Banana Energy 277kcal/1164kJ; Protein 4g; Carbohydrate 43.7g, of which sugars 28.5g; Fat 10.7g, of which saturates 4g; Cholesterol 38mg; Calcium 58mg; Fibre 1.3g; Sodium 53mg.
Blueberry Energy 141kcal/593kJ; Protein 3.1g; Carbohydrate 21.4g, of which sugars 10.5g; Fat 5.4g, of which saturates 0.9g; Cholesterol 25mg; Calcium 60mg; Fibre 0.9g; Sodium 19mg.
Chocolate Energy 296Kcal/1238kJ; Protein 7.2g; Carbohydrate 36.4g, of which sugars 17.2g; Fat 15.8g, of which saturates 3.4g; Cholesterol 85mg; Calcium 86mg; Fibre 1g; Sodium 38mg.

Dried Cherry Buns

Looking for something different? Then try these super little buns with their jewel-like cherries baked inside.

Makes 16
250ml/8fl oz/1 cup natural (plain) yogurt
175g/6oz/³⁄₄ cup dried cherries
115g/4oz/¹⁄₂ cup butter, at room temperature
175g/6oz/generous ³⁄₄ cup caster (superfine) sugar
2 eggs, at room temperature
5ml/1 tsp vanilla extract
200g/7oz/1³⁄₄ cups plain (all-purpose) flour
10ml/2 tsp baking powder
5ml/1 tsp bicarbonate of soda (baking soda)
1.5ml/¹⁄₄ tsp salt

1 In a mixing bowl, combine the yogurt and cherries. Cover and leave to stand for 30 minutes. Preheat the oven to 180°C/350°F/Gas 4. Grease 16 bun-tray cups or use paper cases.

2 With an electric mixer, cream the butter and sugar together until light and fluffy. Add the eggs, one at a time, beating well after each addition. Add the vanilla extract and the cherry mixture and stir to blend. Set aside.

3 In another bowl, sift together the flour, baking powder, bicarbonate of soda and salt. Fold into the cherry mixture in three batches.

4 Fill the prepared cups two-thirds full. For even baking, half-fill any empty cups with water. Bake until the tops spring back when touched lightly, about 20 minutes. Transfer to a wire rack to cool completely.

> **Cook's Tip**
> If you haven't tried dried cherries before, here is the recipe to begin enjoying their special flavour. They are quite unlike glacé (candied) cherries in that they have a wonderful tart taste. The best variety, Montmorency, has a sweet–sour flavour, perfect for this recipe. Dried cherries also make a healthy snack.

Carrot Buns

Using carrots gives these buns a lovely moist consistency, and a delightful taste too.

Makes 12
175g/6oz/³⁄₄ cup margarine, at room temperature
90g/3¹⁄₂oz/generous ¹⁄₂ cup soft dark brown sugar
1 egg, at room temperature
15ml/1 tbsp water
225g/8oz/1¹⁄₂ cups grated carrots
150g/5oz/1¹⁄₄ cups plain (all-purpose) flour
5ml/1 tsp baking powder
2.5ml/¹⁄₂ tsp bicarbonate of soda (baking soda)
5ml/1 tsp ground cinnamon
1.5ml/¹⁄₄ tsp freshly grated nutmeg
2.5ml/¹⁄₂ tsp salt

1 Preheat the oven to 180°C/350°F/Gas 4. Grease 12 bun-tray cups or use paper cases.

2 With an electric mixer, cream the margarine and sugar until light and fluffy. Beat in the egg and water, then stir in the grated carrots.

3 Sift over the flour, baking powder, bicarbonate of soda, cinnamon, nutmeg and salt. Stir to blend.

4 Spoon the mixture into the prepared bun tray, filling the cups almost to the top. Bake until the tops spring back when touched lightly, about 35 minutes.

5 Leave the buns to stand for about 10 minutes in the bun tray before transferring to a wire rack to cool completely.

> **Variation**
> These mini carrot cakes taste great with a traditional cream cheese topping. Beat 225g/8oz/2 cups icing (confectioners') sugar with 60g/2¹⁄₄oz/generous 4 tbsp cream cheese and 30g/1¹⁄₄oz/generous 2 tbsp softened butter. Add 5ml/1 tsp grated orange rind and blend well. Spread over the tops of the cooked and cooled buns.

Carrot Energy 193kcal/803kJ; Protein 1.9g; Carbohydrate 19.2g, of which sugars 9.6g; Fat 12.6g, of which saturates 0.2g; Cholesterol 16mg; Calcium 29mg; Fibre 0.8g; Sodium 128mg.
Cherry Energy 187kcal/787kJ; Protein 3.1g; Carbohydrate 29.9g, of which sugars 20.4g; Fat 7g, of which saturates 4g; Cholesterol 39mg; Calcium 63mg; Fibre 0.6g; Sodium 73mg.

Chelsea Buns

A traditional English recipe, not surprisingly Chelsea buns enjoy wide popularity elsewhere in the world.

Makes 12
225g/8oz/2 cups strong white
   bread flour
2.5ml/½ tsp salt
40g/1½oz/3 tbsp unsalted
   (sweet) butter

7.5ml/1½ tsp easy-blend
   (rapid-rise) dried yeast
120ml/4fl oz/½ cup milk
1 egg, beaten
75g/3oz/½ cup mixed
   dried fruit
25g/1oz/2½ tbsp chopped
   mixed (candied) peel
50g/2oz/¼ cup soft light
   brown sugar
clear honey, to glaze

1 Preheat the oven to 190°C/375°F/Gas 5. Grease a 20cm/8in round tin (pan). Sift together the flour and salt; rub in 25g/1oz/2 tbsp of the butter.

2 Stir in the yeast and make a central well. Slowly add the milk and egg, stirring, then beat until the dough leaves the sides of the bowl clean.

3 Knead the dough for several minutes until smooth. Place in an oiled bowl, cover with oiled clear film (plastic wrap) and set aside until doubled in size.

4 Transfer the dough to a floured surface, gently knock back (punch down) and roll it out to a rectangle 30 x 23cm/12 x 9in.

5 Mix together the dried fruit, peel and sugar in a bowl. Melt the remaining butter and brush over the dough. Sprinkle over the fruit mixture, leaving a 2.5cm/1in border. Roll up the dough from a long side. Seal the edges, then cut into 12 slices.

6 Place the slices, cut sides up, in the greased tin. Cover with clear film and set aside until doubled in size.

7 Bake for 30 minutes, or until a rich golden brown. Brush with honey and leave to cool slightly in the tin before turning out.

Sticky Nut Buns

These tasty buns will be extremely popular with adults and children alike, so save time by making double the quantity and freezing half for another occasion.

Makes 12
160ml/5½fl oz/generous ⅔ cup
   lukewarm milk
15ml/1 tbsp active dried yeast
30ml/2 tbsp caster
   (superfine) sugar
450g/1lb/4 cups strong white
   bread flour
5ml/1 tsp salt

115g/4oz/½ cup cold butter,
   cut into small pieces
2 eggs, lightly beaten
finely grated rind of 1 lemon

For the filling
275g/10oz/scant 1½ cups soft
   dark brown sugar
65g/2½oz/5 tbsp butter
120ml/4fl oz/½ cup water
75g/3oz/¾ cup chopped pecan
   nuts or walnuts
45ml/3 tbsp caster
   (superfine) sugar
10ml/2 tsp ground cinnamon
165g/5½oz/generous 1 cup raisins

1 Preheat the oven to 180°C/350°F/Gas 4. Mix the milk, yeast and sugar, and leave until frothy. Combine the flour and salt, and rub in the butter. Add the yeast mixture, eggs and lemon rind.

2 Stir to a rough dough. Knead until smooth, then return to the bowl, cover and leave until doubled in size.

3 To make the filling cook the brown sugar, butter and water in a heavy pan until syrupy, about 10 minutes. Place 15ml/1 tbsp syrup in the base of twelve 4cm/1½in muffin cups. Sprinkle a thin layer of nuts in each, reserving the remainder.

4 Knock back (punch down) the dough and roll out to a 45 x 30cm/18 x 12in rectangle. Combine the sugar, cinnamon, raisins and reserved nuts. Sprinkle over the dough. Roll up tightly from a long edge and cut into 2.5cm/1in rounds. Place in the muffin cups, cut sides up. Leave to rise for 30 minutes.

5 Bake until golden, about 25 minutes. Invert the tins on to a baking sheet, leave for 5 minutes, then remove the tins. Cool on a wire rack, sticky sides up.

Chelsea Buns Energy 138kcal/582kJ; Protein 2.8g; Carbohydrate 25g, of which sugars 10.7g; Fat 3.7g, of which saturates 2g; Cholesterol 24mg; Calcium 49mg; Fibre 0.8g; Sodium 41mg.
Nut Energy 439kcal/1844kJ; Protein 6.1g; Carbohydrate 66.3g, of which sugars 37.6g; Fat 18.4g, of which saturates 8.6g; Cholesterol 64mg; Calcium 100mg; Fibre 1.7g; Sodium 119mg.

Oatmeal Buttermilk Muffins

These easy-to-make muffins make a healthy treat for breakfast, or a snack at any time of the day.

Makes 12
75g/3oz/scant 1 cup rolled oats
250ml/8fl oz/1 cup buttermilk
115g/4oz/½ cup butter,
  at room temperature
75g/3oz/scant ½ cup soft dark
  brown sugar
1 egg, at room temperature
115g/4oz/1 cup plain
  (all-purpose) flour
5ml/1 tsp baking powder
1.5ml/¼ tsp bicarbonate of soda
  (baking soda)
1.5ml/¼ tsp salt
25g/1oz/¼ cup raisins

1 In a bowl, combine the oats and buttermilk, and leave to soak for 1 hour.

2 Grease 12 muffin cups or use paper cases.

3 Preheat the oven to 200°C/400°F/Gas 6. With an electric mixer, cream the butter and sugar until light and fluffy. Beat in the egg.

4 In another bowl, sift together the flour, baking powder, bicarbonate of soda, and salt. Stir into the butter mixture, alternating with the oat mixture. Fold in the raisins. Take care not to overmix.

5 Fill the prepared cups two-thirds full. Bake until a skewer inserted in the centre comes out clean, 20–25 minutes. Transfer to a rack to cool.

> **Cook's Tips**
> • For perfect muffins every time never overbeat the batter. Just mix enough to blend, but don't worry about there being a few lumps. An overbeaten batter will result in tough and rubbery muffins.
> • If you are not using a tray with muffin cups, use two paper cases for each muffin, to support the batter and stop the sides from collapsing.

Pumpkin Muffins

Molasses adds a delicious flavour to these spicy muffins. For a change, add chopped dried apricots instead of currants.

Makes 14
150g/5oz/10 tbsp butter or
  margarine, at room temperature
175g/6oz/¾ cup soft dark
  brown sugar
115g/4oz/⅓ cup molasses
1 egg, at room temperature, beaten
225g/8oz/1 cup cooked or
  canned pumpkin
200g/7oz/1¾ cups plain
  (all-purpose) flour
1.5ml/¼ tsp salt
5ml/1 tsp bicarbonate of soda
  (baking soda)
10ml/1 tsp ground cinnamon
5ml/1 tsp freshly grated nutmeg
50g/2oz/¼ cup currants
  or raisins

1 Preheat the oven to 200°C/400°F/Gas 6. Grease 14 muffin cups or use paper cases.

2 With an electric mixer, cream the butter or margarine. Add the sugar and molasses, and beat until light and fluffy.

3 Add the egg and pumpkin and stir until well blended.

4 Sift over the flour, salt, bicarbonate of soda, cinnamon, and nutmeg. Fold just enough to blend; do not overmix.

5 Fold in the currants or raisins.

6 Spoon the batter into the prepared muffin cups, filling them three-quarters full.

7 Bake for 12–15 minutes, or until the tops spring back when touched lightly. Serve warm or cold.

> **Cook's Tip**
> Strong-flavoured molasses, sometimes called black treacle, is the residue left when cane sugar is refined. Blackstrap molasses, especially, contains small amounts of minerals including iron.

Oatmeal Energy 172kcal/721kJ; Protein 3g; Carbohydrate 20.9g, of which sugars 9.1g; Fat 9.1g, of which saturates 5.2g; Cholesterol 37mg; Calcium 51mg; Fibre 0.8g; Sodium 77mg.
Pumpkin Energy 216kcal/906kJ; Protein 2.2g; Carbohydrate 32.5g, of which sugars 21.5g; Fat 9.4g, of which saturates 5.7g; Cholesterol 36mg; Calcium 84mg; Fibre 0.7g; Sodium 86mg.

Apple & Cranberry Muffins with Walnuts

Not too sweet but good and spicy, these muffins will be a favourite with family and friends.

Makes 12

50g/2oz/¼ cup butter
1 egg
90g/3½oz/½ cup caster (superfine) sugar
grated rind of 1 orange
120ml/4fl oz/½ cup fresh orange juice
150g/5oz/1¼ cups plain (all-purpose) flour
5ml/1 tsp baking powder
2.5ml/½ tsp bicarbonate of soda (baking soda)
5ml/1 tsp ground cinnamon
2.5ml/½ tsp freshly grated nutmeg
2.5ml/½ tsp mixed (apple pie) spice
1.5ml/¼ tsp ground ginger
1.5ml/¼ tsp salt
1 or 2 eating apples
175g/6oz/1½ cups cranberries
50g/2oz/½ cup chopped walnuts
icing (confectioners') sugar, for dusting (optional)

1 Preheat the oven to 180°C/350°F/Gas 4. Grease 12 muffin cups or use paper cases. Melt the butter over a gentle heat. Set aside to cool.

2 Place the egg in a mixing bowl and whisk lightly. Add the melted butter and whisk to combine, then add the sugar, orange rind and juice. Whisk to blend.

3 In a large bowl, sift together the flour, baking powder, bicarbonate of soda, spices and salt.

4 Quarter, core and peel the apples. Use a sharp knife to chop them coarsely.

5 Make a well in the dry ingredients and pour in the egg mixture. With a spoon, stir until just blended. Add the apples, cranberries and walnuts, and stir to blend.

6 Fill the cups three-quarters full and bake until the the tops spring back when touched lightly, about 25–30 minutes. Transfer to a wire rack to cool. Dust with icing sugar before serving, if you like.

Blueberry Muffins

Hot blueberry muffins with a hint of vanilla are an American favourite for breakfast, brunch or tea.

Makes 12

350g/12oz/3 cups plain (all-purpose) flour
10ml/2 tsp baking powder
1.5ml/¼ tsp salt
115g/4oz/½ cup caster (superfine) sugar
2 eggs, beaten
300ml/½ pint/1¼ cups milk
115g/4oz/½ cup butter, melted
5ml/1 tsp vanilla extract
175g/6oz/1½ cups fresh blueberries

1 Preheat the oven to 200°C/400°F/Gas 6. Grease 12 muffin cups or use paper cases.

2 Sift the flour, baking powder and salt into a large mixing bowl and stir in the sugar.

3 Place the eggs, milk, butter and vanilla extract in a separate bowl and whisk together well.

4 Fold the egg mixture into the dry ingredients with a metal spoon, then gently stir in the blueberries.

5 Spoon the mixture into the muffin cups, filling them to just below the top.

6 Place in the oven and bake for 20–25 minutes, or until the muffins are well risen and lightly browned.

7 Leave the muffins in the cups for about 5 minutes, and then turn them out on to a wire rack to cool. Serve warm or cold.

> **Variation**
> *Most fruit muffin recipes can be varied to use all kinds of different berries. Try blackcurrants or redcurrants instead of the blueberries here, if you like. Remember to stir the fruit in very gently so that the juice does not "bleed" into the batter.*

Blueberry Energy 236kcal/992kJ; Protein 4.9g; Carbohydrate 34.7g, of which sugars 12.4g; Fat 9.6g, of which saturates 5.6g; Cholesterol 54mg; Calcium 88mg; Fibre 1.4g; Sodium 82mg.
Apple Energy 149kcal/624kJ; Protein 2.5g; Carbohydrate 20.4g, of which sugars 10.8g; Fat 6.9g, of which saturates 2.6g; Cholesterol 25mg; Calcium 30mg; Fibre 0.9g; Sodium 34mg.

Yogurt & Honey Muffins

Here is just the recipe for a relaxed Sunday breakfast: fragrant honey muffins served warm – heaven!

Makes 12
50g/2oz/4 tbsp butter
75ml/5 tbsp clear honey
250ml/8fl oz/1 cup natural
   (plain) yogurt
1 large (US extra large) egg,
   at room temperature
grated rind of 1 lemon
50ml/2fl oz/¼ cup lemon juice
150g/5oz/1¼ cups plain
   (all-purpose) flour
175g/6oz/1½ cups wholemeal
   (whole-wheat) flour
7.5ml/1½ tsp bicarbonate of
   soda (baking soda)
1.5ml/¼ tsp freshly
   grated nutmeg

1 Preheat the oven to 190°C/375°F/Gas 5. Grease 12 muffin cups or use paper cases.

2 In a pan, melt the butter and honey. Remove from the heat and set aside to cool slightly.

3 In a bowl, whisk together the yogurt, egg, lemon rind and juice. Add the butter and honey mixture. Set aside.

4 In another bowl, sift together the plain and wholemeal flours with the bicarbonate of soda and nutmeg. Fold them into the yogurt mixture to blend.

5 Fill the prepared cups two-thirds full. Bake until the tops spring back when touched lightly, about 20–25 minutes.

6 Cool in the tin (pan) for 5 minutes before turning out. Serve warm or at room temperature.

> **Variation**
> You can make these fabulous muffins more substantial by adding 50g/2oz/½ cup chopped walnuts with the flour at step 4, if you like.

Prune Muffins

Prunes bring a delightful moisture to these tasty and wholesome muffins.

Makes 12
1 egg
250ml/8fl oz/1 cup milk
120ml/4fl oz/½ cup vegetable oil
45g/1¾oz/scant ¼ cup caster
   (superfine) sugar
25g/1oz/2 tbsp soft dark
   brown sugar
275g/10oz/2½ cups plain
   (all-purpose) flour
10ml/2 tsp baking powder
2.5ml/½ tsp salt
1.5ml/¼ tsp freshly
   grated nutmeg
115g/4oz/½ cup cooked pitted
   prunes, chopped

1 Preheat the oven to 200°C/400°F/Gas 6. Grease 12 muffin cups or use paper cases.

2 Break the egg into a mixing bowl and beat with a fork. Beat in the milk and oil. Stir in the sugars and set aside.

3 Sift the flour, baking powder, salt and nutmeg into a mixing bowl. Make a well in the centre, pour in the egg mixture and stir until moistened. Do not overmix; the batter should be slightly lumpy. Finally, fold in the prunes.

4 Fill the prepared cups two-thirds full. Bake until golden brown, about 20 minutes. Leave to stand for 10 minutes before turning out. Serve warm or at room temperature.

> **Cook's Tip**
> Soak the prunes for a few hours before cooking in water to cover. They will take about 20 minutes to cook. Remove the pits from the cooked fruit.

> **Variation**
> Try this recipe with dried peaches, soaked and cooked as for the prunes. You could use orange juice instead of water, if you like.

Yogurt Energy 155kcal/652kJ; Protein 4.7g; Carbohydrate 25.4g, of which sugars 6.9g; Fat 4.6g, of which saturates 2.5g; Cholesterol 25mg; Calcium 66mg; Fibre 1.7g; Sodium 50mg.
Prune Energy 190kcal/801kJ; Protein 3.7g; Carbohydrate 28.1g, of which sugars 10.7g; Fat 7.8g, of which saturates 1.2g; Cholesterol 17mg; Calcium 66mg; Fibre 1.3g; Sodium 17mg.

Honey & Spice Muffins

These light, fragrant muffins are great for tea.

Makes 18
250g/9oz/2 cups plain
  (all-purpose) flour, sifted
5ml/1 tsp ground cinnamon
5ml/1 tsp baking powder
125g/4½oz/½ cup butter, softened
125g/4½oz/½ cup soft brown
  sugar
1 large (US extra large) egg
125ml/4½oz clear honey
about 60ml/4 tbsp milk
caster (superfine) sugar, for
  sprinkling

1 Preheat the oven to 200°C/400°F/Gas 6. Butter the holes of a bun tin (pan) or, alternatively, line them with paper cases.

2 Sift the flour into a large mixing bowl with the cinnamon and the bicarbonate of soda.

3 Beat the butter with the sugar until light and fluffy. Beat in the egg yolk, then gradually add the honey.

4 With a large metal spoon and a cutting action, fold in the flour mixture plus sufficient milk to make a soft mixture that will just drop off the spoon.

5 In a separate bowl whisk the egg white until stiff peaks form. Using a large metal spoon, carefully fold the egg white into the cake mixture.

6 Divide the mixture among the paper cases or the holes in the tin. Put into the hot oven and cook for 15–20 minutes or until risen, firm to the touch and golden brown.

7 Sprinkle the tops lightly with caster sugar and leave to cool completely on a wire rack.

> **Cook's Tip**
> *Baking the muffins in paper cases enables them to rise higher, which makes the texture lighter.*

Raspberry Muffins

Adapt the traditional Cornish cream-tea tradition by serving these fabulous muffins barely warm, split and with a dollop of clotted cream.

Makes 12
50g/2oz/¼ cup butter, melted
115g/4oz/1 cup self-raising
  (self-rising) flour
115g/4oz/1 cup self-raising
  wholemeal (whole-wheat) flour
2.5ml/½ tsp salt
45ml/3 tbsp caster
  (superfine) sugar
2 eggs, beaten
200ml/7fl oz/scant 1 cup milk
175g/6oz/1 cup raspberries,
  fresh or frozen (defrosted for
  less than 30 minutes)

1 Melt the butter in a small pan over a low heat and then set it aside until required.

2 Preheat the oven to 190°C/375°F/Gas 5. Lightly grease 12 muffin cups, or use paper cases.

3 Sift the white and wholemeal flours with salt then tip in any wheat flakes left in the sieve. Add the caster sugar.

4 Beat the eggs, milk and melted butter together and stir into the dry ingredients to make a thick batter.

5 Stir the raspberries in gently. If you mix too much the raspberries begin to disintegrate and colour the dough. Spoon into the cups or paper cases.

6 Bake for 30 minutes, or until well risen and just firm to the touch. Leave to cool in the tin placed on a wire rack. Serve warm or cool.

> **Cook's Tips**
> *Frozen fruits, especially delicate ones like raspberries, are more likely to "bleed" into the batter than fresh soft fruits so just a quick stir will do. Frozen berries will also make the batter solidify so you need to add them and stir immediately.*

Honey Energy 152kcal/639kJ; Protein 1.9g; Carbohydrate 23.6g, of which sugars 13g; Fat 6.3g, of which saturates 3.8g; Cholesterol 26mg; Calcium 30mg; Fibre 0.4g; Sodium 49mg
Raspberry Energy 132kcal/555kJ; Protein 4g; Carbohydrate 19g, of which sugars 5.7g; Fat 5g, of which saturates 2.7g; Cholesterol 42mg; Calcium 48mg; Fibre 1.5g; Sodium 45mg.

Scones

Traditionally, scones should be served warm from the oven, with butter, clotted or whipped cream, and jam.

Makes 10–12

225g/8oz/2 cups plain (all-purpose) flour
15ml/1 tbsp baking powder
50g/2oz/4 tbsp cold butter, diced
1 egg, beaten
75ml/5 tbsp milk
1 beaten egg, to glaze

1 Preheat the oven to 220°C/425°F/Gas 7. Lightly butter a baking sheet. Sift the flour and baking powder together, then rub in the butter using your fingertips or a pastry cutter.

2 Make a well in the centre of the flour mixture, add the egg and milk and mix to a soft dough using a round-bladed knife.

3 Turn out the scone dough on to a floured surface, and knead very lightly until smooth.

4 Roll out the dough to about a 2cm/¾ in thickness and cut into ten or twelve circles using a 5cm/2in plain or fluted cutter dipped in flour.

5 Transfer to the baking sheet, brush with egg, then bake for about 8 minutes, or until risen and golden. Cool slightly on a wire rack before serving.

> **Cook's Tips**
> • For perfectly delicate scones every time, handle the dough as little as possible.
> • Always have the oven preheated so that once the dough is made and cut into rounds the scones can go straight into the oven.
> • As well as served warm from the oven, scones taste delicious when cool, and are even tasty the next day split and toasted under a preheated grill (broiler). Butter them while they are still hot.

Drop Scones

If you place the cooked scones in a folded dish towel they will stay soft and moist.

Makes 8–10

115g/4oz/1 cup plain (all-purpose) flour
5ml/1 tsp bicarbonate of soda (baking soda)
5ml/1 tsp cream of tartar
25g/1oz/2 tbsp cold butter, diced
1 egg, beaten
150ml/¼ pint/⅔ cup milk

1 Lightly grease a cast-iron griddle or heavy frying pan, then preheat it.

2 Sift the dry ingredients together, then rub in the butter until the mixture resembles breadcrumbs.

3 Make a well in the centre, then, using a wooden spoon, beat in the egg and sufficient milk to give the mixture the consistency of double (heavy) cream.

4 Drop spoonfuls of the mixture, spaced slightly apart, on to the griddle or frying pan. Cook over a steady heat for 2–3 minutes, until bubbles rise to the surface and burst.

5 Using a metal spatula, turn the scones over and cook for a further 2–3 minutes, or until golden underneath. Serve warm with butter and honey.

> **Cook's Tip**
> For best results always cook these traditional scones on a cast-iron griddle. The correct heat is important, as the crust of the drop scones will brown too quickly leaving the centre uncooked if the griddle is too hot. If the griddle is too cool, the scones will take too long to cook and will not be as light. To test the heat, preheat the griddle and then sprinkle a little flour over the surface. If it turns golden in about 3 minutes it is ready for the drop scones.

Scones Energy 104kcal/437kJ; Protein 2.5g; Carbohydrate 14.9g, of which sugars 0.6g; Fat 4.2g, of which saturates 2.4g; Cholesterol 25mg; Calcium 37mg; Fibre 0.6g; Sodium 34mg.
Drop Scones Energy 72kcal/303kJ; Protein 2.2g; Carbohydrate 9.7g, of which sugars 0.9g; Fat 3g, of which saturates 1.6g; Cholesterol 25mg; Calcium 37mg; Fibre 0.4g; Sodium 29mg.

Wholemeal Scones

Split these wholesome scones in two with a fork while still warm and spread with butter and home-made jam, if you wish.

Makes 16
175g/6oz/¾ cup cold butter
350g/12oz/3 cups plain
  (all-purpose) wholemeal
  (whole-wheat) flour

150g/5oz/1¼ cups plain
  (all-purpose) flour
30ml/2 tbsp caster
  (superfine) sugar
2.5ml/½ tsp salt
12.5ml/2½ tsp bicarbonate
  of soda (baking soda)
2 eggs
175ml/6fl oz/¾ cup buttermilk
35g/1¼oz/¼ cup raisins

1 Preheat the oven to 200°C/400°F/Gas 6. Grease and flour a large baking sheet.

2 Cut the butter into small pieces. Combine the wholemeal and plain flours with the sugar, salt and bicarbonate of soda in a bowl. Add the butter and rub in using your fingertips or a pastry cutter until the mixture resembles coarse breadcrumbs. Set aside.

3 In another bowl, whisk together the eggs and buttermilk. Set aside 30ml/2 tbsp for glazing, then stir the remaining egg mixture into the dry ingredients until it just holds together. Stir in the raisins.

4 Roll out the dough to about a 2cm/¾in thickness. Stamp out circles with a cookie cutter. Place on the baking sheet and brush with the reserved egg and buttermilk glaze.

5 Bake until golden, about 12–15 minutes. Allow to cool slightly before serving.

> **Variation**
> Raisin scones also go particularly well with cheese, so serve them for tea with a mature (sharp) Cheddar, a full-flavoured blue cheese or a creamy soft cheese such as Camembert or Brie.

Orange & Raisin Scones

As well as warm from the oven, these scones are also superb split when cool and toasted under a preheated grill. Butter them while still hot.

Makes 16
275g/10oz/2½ cups plain
  (all-purpose) flour

25ml/1½ tbsp baking powder
60g/2¼oz/generous ¼ cup caster
  (superfine) sugar
2.5ml/½ tsp salt
65g/2½oz/5 tbsp butter, diced
65g/2½oz/5 tbsp margarine, diced
grated rind of 1 large orange
50g/2oz/scant ½ cup raisins
120ml/4fl oz/½ cup buttermilk
milk, to glaze

1 Preheat the oven to 220°C/425°F/Gas 7. Grease and flour a large baking sheet.

2 Combine the flour with the baking powder, sugar and salt in a large bowl. Add the butter and margarine, and rub in using your fingertips or a pastry cutter until the mixture resembles coarse breadcrumbs.

3 Add the orange rind and raisins. Gradually stir in the buttermilk to form a soft dough.

4 Roll out the dough to about a 2cm/¾in thickness. Stamp out circles with a cookie cutter. Place on the baking sheet and brush the tops with milk.

5 Bake until golden, about 12–15 minutes. Serve hot or warm, with butter, or whipped or clotted cream and jam.

> **Cook's Tip**
> Try these scones the Cornish way (usually reserved for plain scones): split them and spread each half with a little home-made raspberry or strawberry jam (no butter); now add a dollop of real Cornish or Devon clotted cream. Enjoy with a cup of tea, and preferably choose a summer's afternoon so that you can eat them outdoors for the authentic experience.

Wholemeal Energy 207kcal/869kJ; Protein 4.9g; Carbohydrate 25.3g, of which sugars 4.6g; Fat 10.3g, of which saturates 6g; Cholesterol 48mg; Calcium 42mg; Fibre 2.3g; Sodium 82mg.
Orange Energy 145kcal/606kJ; Protein 2g; Carbohydrate 19.8g, of which sugars 6.7g; Fat 6.9g, of which saturates 2.2g; Cholesterol 9mg; Calcium 38mg; Fibre 0.6g; Sodium 63mg.

Cheese & Chive Scones

Feta cheese is used instead of butter in these delicious savoury scones, which make a tasty alternative to traditional scones.

Makes 9

115g/4oz/1 cup self-raising (self-rising) flour

150g/5oz/1 cup self-raising (self-rising) wholemeal (whole-wheat) flour

2.5ml/½ tsp salt

75g/3oz feta cheese

15ml/1 tbsp chopped fresh chives

150ml/¼ pint/⅔ cup milk, plus extra to glaze

1.5ml/¼ tsp cayenne pepper

1 Preheat the oven to 200°C/400°F/Gas 6. Sift the flours and salt into a large mixing bowl. Add any bran left in the sieve.

2 Crumble the feta cheese and rub it into the dry ingredients until the mixture resembles breadcrumbs. Stir in the chives, then add the milk and mix to a soft dough.

3 Turn the dough out on to a floured surface and lightly knead until smooth. Roll out to a 2cm/¾in thickness and stamp out scones with a 6cm/2½in cookie cutter.

4 Transfer the scones to a non-stick baking sheet. Brush with milk, then sprinkle with the cayenne pepper. Bake for 15 minutes, or until risen and golden. Cool slightly on a wire rack before serving.

Variation
For Cheddar cheese and mustard scones, add 2.5ml/½ tsp mustard powder to the flours. Dice 50g/2oz/½ cup cold butter, and rub it into the dry ingredients until the mixture resembles breadcrumbs. Stir 50g/2oz/½ cup grated mature (sharp) Cheddar cheese into the mixture, then pour in the milk. Stir gently to make a soft dough. Roll out on a lightly floured surface and cut into triangles. Place on a baking sheet, brush with milk and sprinkle with 25g/1oz/¼ cup cheese. Bake for 15 minutes, or until well risen.

Sunflower Sultana Scones

Sunflower seeds give these fruit scones an interesting flavour and texture.

Makes 10–12

225g/8oz/2 cups self-raising (self-rising) flour

5ml/1 tsp baking powder

25g/1oz/2 tbsp soft sunflower margarine

30ml/2 tbsp golden caster (superfine) sugar

50g/2oz/⅓ cup sultanas (golden raisins)

30ml/2 tbsp sunflower seeds

150g/5oz/scant ⅔ cup natural (plain) yogurt

about 30–45ml/ 2–3 tbsp skimmed milk

1 Preheat the oven to 230°C/450°F/Gas 8. Lightly oil a baking sheet. Sift the flour and baking powder into a bowl and rub in the margarine evenly.

2 Stir in the sugar, sultanas and half the sunflower seeds, then mix in the yogurt, with just enough milk to make a fairly soft, but not sticky, dough.

3 Roll out on a lightly floured surface to about a 2cm/¾in thickness. Cut into 6cm/2½in flower shapes or rounds with a cookie cutter and lift on to the baking sheet.

4 Brush with milk and sprinkle with the reserved sunflower seeds, then bake for 10–12 minutes, or until well risen and golden brown. Cool the scones on a wire rack. Serve split, spread with jam or low-fat spread.

Cook's Tip
Sunflower seeds are a wonder food, and a good and tasty way to add nutrients to the diet, especially selenium, which is often lacking. Don't buy too many at one time and source them from a store where they have a quick turnover so that the ones you buy are fresh. As sunflower seeds have a high fat content they don't store well for long periods. Buy small quantities at a time and put them in a sealed container in a cool place – even a refrigerator.

Cheese Energy 124kcal/524kJ; Protein 5.2g; Carbohydrate 21.5g, of which sugars 1.5g; Fat 2.5g, of which saturates 1.4g; Cholesterol 7mg; Calcium 74mg; Fibre 1.9g; Sodium 128mg.
Sunflower Energy 121kcal/513kJ; Protein 3g; Carbohydrate 21.2g, of which sugars 6.9g; Fat 3.3g, of which saturates 0.6g; Cholesterol 0mg; Calcium 99mg; Fibre 0.8g; Sodium 97mg.

Buttermilk Scones

If time is short, drop heaped
tablespoonfuls of the mixture
on to the baking sheet.

Makes 10
225g/8oz/2 cups plain
  (all-purpose) flour
5ml/1 tsp baking powder
2.5ml/½ tsp bicarbonate of soda
  (baking soda)
5ml/1 tsp salt
50g/2oz/¼ cup butter or
  margarine, chilled
175ml/6fl oz/¾ cup buttermilk

1 Preheat the oven to 220°C/425°F/Gas 7. Sift the dry
ingredients into a mixing bowl. Rub in the butter or margarine
until the mixture resembles coarse breadcrumbs.

2 Add the buttermilk and combine well to form a soft dough.
Turn on to a lightly floured surface and knead for 30 seconds.

3 Roll out to a 1cm/½in thickness. Cut rounds with a floured
6cm/2½in pastry (cookie) cutter. Transfer to a baking sheet and
bake for 10–12 minutes. Serve with butter and honey.

Lavender Scones

Makes 12
225g/8oz/2 cups plain
  (all-purpose) flour
15ml/1 tbsp baking powder
50g/2oz/¼ cup butter
40g/1½oz/3 tbsp caster
  (superfine) sugar
10ml/2 tsp fresh lavender
  florets, chopped
about 175ml/6fl oz/¾ cup milk

1 Preheat the oven to 220°C/425°F/Gas 7. Grease a baking
sheet. Sift the flour and baking powder into a bowl. Rub in the
butter until the mixture resembles breadcrumbs.

2 Stir in the sugar and most of the lavender, reserving a little to
decorate. Add enough milk to make a soft dough. Turn on to a
floured surface and roll out to 2.5cm/1in thick. Cut 12 rounds
with a floured cutter and place on the baking sheet. Brush the
tops with milk and sprinkle with lavender. Bake for 10–12 minutes.

Date Oven Scones

The rich taste of dates gives
these scones a full flavour but
you can adapt the recipe for
use with ready-to-eat dried
apricots or peaches as well.

Makes 12
225g/8oz/2 cups self-raising
  (self-rising) flour
a pinch of salt
50g/2oz/4 tbsp butter
50g/2oz/¼ cup caster
  (superfine) sugar
50g/2oz/⅓ cup finely
  chopped dates
150ml/¼ pint/⅔ cup milk
1 beaten egg, to glaze

1 Preheat the oven to 230°C/450°F/Gas 8. Sift the flour and
salt into a bowl and rub in the butter using your fingertips or
a pastry cutter until the mixture resembles fine breadcrumbs.

2 Add the sugar and chopped dates to the mixture, and stir
to blend.

3 Make a well in the centre of the dry ingredients and add the
milk. Stir with a fork until the mixture comes together into a
fairly soft dough.

4 Turn the dough out on to a lightly floured surface and knead
gently for 30 seconds. Roll it out to a 2cm/¾in thickness.

5 Cut out circles with a cookie cutter. Arrange them, not
touching, on an ungreased baking sheet, then glaze with
the beaten egg.

6 Bake in the oven for 8–10 minutes, or until well risen and
golden brown. Using a metal spatula, transfer the scones to a
wire rack to cool completely.

Cook's Tip
*For light and airy scones don't handle the dough too much and
be careful not the roll it out too thinly or the scones will not
rise sufficiently.*

Buttermilk Energy 120kcal/503kJ; Protein 2.7g; Carbohydrate 18.3g, of which sugars 1.1g; Fat 4.5g, of which saturates 2.7g; Cholesterol 11mg; Calcium 54mg; Fibre 0.7g; Sodium 235mg.
Lavender Energy 115kcal/484kJ; Protein 2.3g; Carbohydrate 18.8g, of which sugars 4.5g; Fat 3.9g, of which saturates 2.4g; Cholesterol 10mg; Calcium 46mg; Fibre 0.6g; Sodium 32mg.
Date Energy 128kcal/542kJ; Protein 2.4g; Carbohydrate 22.4g, of which sugars 8.1g; Fat 3.9g, of which saturates 2.4g; Cholesterol 10mg; Calcium 46mg; Fibre 0.8g; Sodium 32mg.

Cheese & Marjoram Scones

A great success for a hearty tea. With savoury toppings, these scones can make a good basis for a light lunch.

Makes 18

115g/4oz/1 cup plain (all-purpose) wholemeal (whole-wheat) flour
115g/4oz/1 cup self-raising (self-rising) flour
a pinch of salt
40g/1½oz/3 tbsp butter
1.5ml/¼ tsp dry mustard
10ml/2 tsp dried marjoram
50–75g/2–3oz/½–¾ cup finely grated Cheddar cheese
120ml/4fl oz/½ cup milk, or as required
50g/2oz/½ cup chopped pecan nuts or walnuts

1 Gently sift the two flours into a bowl and add the salt. Cut the butter into small pieces, and rub into the flour using your fingertips or a pastry cutter until the mixture resembles fine breadcrumbs.

2 Add the mustard, marjoram and grated cheese, and mix in sufficient milk to make a soft dough. Knead the dough lightly.

3 Preheat the oven to 220°C/425°F/Gas 7. Lightly grease two or three baking sheets.

4 Roll out the dough on a floured surface to about a 2cm/¾in thickness and cut it out with a 5cm/2in square cookie cutter. Place the scones, slightly apart, on the baking sheets.

5 Brush the scones with a little milk and then sprinkle the chopped pecan nuts or walnuts over the top. Bake for about 12 minutes. Serve warm, spread with butter.

Cook's Tip

English mustard has been a traditional ingredient in many cheese dishes, as it sharpens the flavour of the cheese making it more pronounced. Always use dry mustard for adding to recipes such as the scones here or to pep up cheese toasts made with grated cheese, and remember: a little goes a long way.

Dill & Potato Cakes

Adding dill to these potato cakes makes them irresistible.

Makes 10

225g/8oz/2 cups self-raising (self-rising) flour
40g/1½oz/3 tbsp butter, softened
a pinch of salt
15ml/1 tbsp chopped fresh dill
175g/6oz/2 cups mashed potato, freshly made
30–45ml/2–3 tbsp milk

1 Preheat the oven to 230°C/450°F/Gas 8. Grease a baking sheet. Sift the flour into a bowl and add the butter, salt and dill. Mix in the mashed potato and enough milk to make a soft, pliable dough.

2 Roll out the dough on a well-floured surface until fairly thin. Cut into circles with a 7.5cm/3in cookie)cutter. Place the potato cakes on the baking sheet and bake them for 20–25 minutes, or until risen and golden.

Savoury Cheese Whirls

Makes 20

250g/9oz frozen puff pastry, thawed
15ml/1 tbsp vegetable extract
1 egg, beaten
50g/2oz/½ cup grated Cheddar cheese

1 Preheat the oven to 220°C/425°F/Gas 7. Grease a large baking sheet. Roll out the pastry on a lightly floured surface to a large rectangle, measuring about 35 x 25cm/14 x 10in.

2 Spread the pastry with vegetable extract, leaving a 1cm/½in border. Brush the edges of the pastry with egg and sprinkle over the cheese. Roll the pastry up quite tightly, starting from a long edge. Brush the outside of the pastry with beaten egg. Cut the pastry roll into slices 4cm/1½in thick and place on the baking sheet. Bake for 12–15 minutes, until the pastry is well risen and golden. Arrange on a serving plate and serve warm or cold with carrot and cucumber sticks.

Cheese Energy 121kcal/504kJ; Protein 3g; Carbohydrate 9.8g, of which sugars 0.9g; Fat 8g, of which saturates 2.4g; Cholesterol 8mg; Calcium 44mg; Fibre 1.1g; Sodium 39mg.
Dill Energy 121kcal/508kJ; Protein 2.6g; Carbohydrate 20.6g, of which sugars 0.6g; Fat 3.7g, of which saturates 2.2g; Cholesterol 9mg; Calcium 37mg; Fibre 0.9g; Sodium 27mg.
Whirls Energy 62kcal/259kJ; Protein 2g; Carbohydrate 4.6g, of which sugars 0.2g; Fat 4.2g, of which saturates 0.6g; Cholesterol 12mg; Calcium 28mg; Fibre 0g; Sodium 94mg.

Low-fat Baking

Eating healthily does not necessarily mean that you have to deprive yourself of the occasional baked treat, and this chapter includes a range of recipes that are lower in fat than standard versions. Choose from light-as-air Lemon Sponge Fingers, Low-fat Drop Scones or Banana and Ginger Teabread, or for a special occasion, try Lemon Chiffon Cake or Strawberry Gateau.

Snowballs

These light and airy morsels make a crisp and sweet accompaniment to low-fat frozen yogurt.

Makes about 20
2 egg whites
115g/4oz/½ cup caster (superfine) sugar
15ml/1 tbsp cornflour (cornstarch), sifted
5ml/1 tsp white wine vinegar
1.5ml/¼ tsp vanilla extract

1 Preheat the oven to 150°C/300°F/Gas 2 and line two baking sheets with baking parchment.

2 Whisk the egg whites in a grease-free bowl, using a hand-held electric whisk, until very stiff.

3 Add the caster sugar, a little at a time, whisking after each addition until the meringue is very stiff and glossy. Whisk in the cornflour, vinegar and vanilla extract.

4 Using a teaspoon, mound the mixture into snowballs on the prepared baking sheets. Bake for 30 minutes.

5 Cool on the baking sheets, then remove the snowballs from the paper with a metal spatula.

> **Variation**
> Make Pineapple Snowballs by lightly folding about 50g/2oz/ ⅓ cup finely chopped semi-dried pineapple into the meringue.

> **Cook's Tip**
> These meringues contain the magic ingredients that give them a chewy centre rather than being crisp throughout. You can mix the cornflour, white wine vinegar and vanilla extract together in a small bowl and sprinkle it over the mixture before finally folding it in if you like.

Caramel Meringues

Muscovado sugar gives these almost fat-free meringues a lovely caramel flavour. Take care not to overcook them, so that they stay chewy in the middle.

Makes about 20
115g/4oz/½ cup light muscovado (brown) sugar
2 egg whites
5ml/1 tsp finely chopped walnuts (optional)

1 Preheat the oven to 160°C/325°F/Gas 3. Line two baking sheets with baking parchment.

2 Press the muscovado sugar through a metal sieve into a large bowl positioned below.

3 Whisk the egg whites in a separate, grease-free bowl until they are very stiff and dry.

4 Add the sieved brown sugar to the stiff egg white, about 15ml/1 tbsp at a time, whisking well between each addition, until the meringue is thick and glossy.

5 Spoon small mounds of the meringue mixture on to the prepared baking sheets.

6 Sprinkle each mound of meringue mixture with chopped walnuts, if you like.

7 Bake the meringues for 30 minutes, then leave them to cool for 5 minutes on the baking sheets.

8 Transfer the meringues to a wire rack to cool completely.

> **Cook's Tip**
> For an easy, sophisticated filling, mix 115g/4oz/½ cup low-fat soft cheese with 15ml/1 tbsp icing sugar. Chop 2 slices of fresh pineapple and add to the mixture. Sandwich the meringues together in pairs.

Snowballs Energy 26kcal/109kJ; Protein 0.3g; Carbohydrate 6.7g, of which sugars 6g; Fat 0g, of which saturates 0g; Cholesterol 0mg; Calcium 3mg; Fibre 0g; Sodium 7mg.
Caramel Meringues Energy 26kcal/109kJ; Protein 0.4g; Carbohydrate 6g, of which sugars 6g; Fat 0.2g, of which saturates 0g; Cholesterol 0mg; Calcium 3mg; Fibre 0g; Sodium 6mg.

Banana Gingerbread Slices

Bananas make this spicy bake delightfully moist and add a natural sweetness. The flavour develops on keeping, so store for a few days before cutting.

Makes 20 slices

275g/10oz/2½ cups plain (all-purpose) flour
20ml/4 tsp ground ginger
10ml/2 tsp mixed (apple pie) spice
5ml/1 tsp bicarbonate of soda (baking soda)
115g/4oz/½ cup soft light brown sugar
60ml/4 tbsp corn oil
30ml/2 tbsp molasses or black treacle
30ml/2 tbsp malt extract
2 eggs, beaten
60ml/4 tbsp orange juice
3 ripe bananas
115g/4oz/scant 1 cup raisins or sultanas (golden raisins)

1 Preheat the oven to 180°C/350°F/Gas 4. Line and grease a 28 x 18cm/11 x 7in baking tin (pan).

2 Sift the flour, ground ginger and mixed spice and the bicarbonate of soda into a mixing bowl. Spoon some of the mixture back into the sieve, add the brown sugar and sift the mixture back into the bowl.

3 Make a well in the centre of the dry ingredients and add the oil, molasses or treacle, malt extract, eggs, and orange juice. Gradually stir the dry ingredients into the liquid working from the centre outwards. Mix thoroughly.

4 Peel the bananas and mash them in a bowl. Add to the gingerbread mixture with the raisins or sultanas. Mix the ingredients thoroughly to combine well.

5 Scrape the mixture into the prepared tin. Bake for 35–40 minutes, or until the centre springs back when the surface of the cake is lightly pressed.

6 Leave the gingerbread in the tin to cool for 5 minutes, then turn on to a wire rack, remove the lining paper and leave to cool completely. Serve spread with butter, if you like.

Banana & Apricot Chelsea Buns

Old favourites get a new twist with a delectable fruity filling.

Serves 9

225g/8oz/2 cups strong plain (all-purpose) flour
10ml/2 tsp mixed (apple pie) spice
2.5ml/½ tsp salt
25g/1oz/2 tbsp soft margarine
7.5ml/1½ tsp easy-blend (rapid-rise) dried yeast
50g/2oz/¼ cup caster (superfine) sugar
90ml/6 tbsp hand-hot milk
1 egg, beaten

For the filling
1 large ripe banana
175g/6oz/1 cup ready-to-eat dried apricots
30ml/2 tbsp soft light brown sugar

For the glaze
30ml/2 tbsp caster (superfine) sugar
30ml/2 tbsp water

1 Grease an 18cm/7in square cake tin (pan). To prepare the filling, mash the banana in a bowl. Using kitchen scissors, cut up the apricots, and add to the bowl, then stir in the brown sugar. Mix together well.

2 Sift the flour, spice and salt into a large bowl. Rub in the margarine, then stir in the yeast and sugar. Make a well in the centre and pour in the milk and the egg. Mix to a soft dough, adding a little extra milk if necessary.

3 Turn the dough on to a floured surface and knead for 5 minutes until smooth and elastic. Roll out to a 30 x 23cm/12 x 9in rectangle. Spread the filling over the dough and roll up lengthways like a Swiss roll (jelly roll), with the join underneath. Cut into 9 pieces and place cut side downwards in the prepared tin. Cover and leave in a warm place until doubled in size, about 1½ hours.

4 Preheat the oven to 200°C/400°F/Gas 6. Bake the buns for 20–25 minutes, or until golden brown. Meanwhile make the glaze: mix the caster sugar and water in a small pan. Heat, stirring, until dissolved, then boil the mixture for 2 minutes. Brush the glaze over the buns while still hot, then remove from the tin and cool on a wire rack.

Slices Energy 132kcal/556kJ; Protein 2.3g; Carbohydrate 25.4g, of which sugars 14.6g; Fat 3g, of which saturates 0.5g; Cholesterol 19mg; Calcium 37mg; Fibre 0.7g; Sodium 14mg.
Buns Energy 193kcal/817kJ; Protein 4.3g; Carbohydrate 38.4g, of which sugars 19.1g; Fat 3.5g, of which saturates 0.3g; Cholesterol 22mg; Calcium 70mg; Fibre 2.1g; Sodium 148mg.

Lemon Sponge Fingers

These dainty sponge fingers are perfect for serving with fruit salads or light, low-fat creamy desserts.

Makes about 20
2 eggs
75g/3oz/6 tbsp caster (superfine) sugar
grated rind of 1 lemon
50g/2oz/ ¹/₂ cup plain (all-purpose) flour, sifted
caster (superfine) sugar, for sprinkling

1 Preheat the oven to 190°C/375°F/Gas 5. Line two baking sheets with baking parchment.

2 Whisk the eggs, sugar and lemon rind together with a hand-held electric whisk until thick and mousse-like: when the whisk is lifted, a trail should remain on the surface of the mixture for at least 30 seconds.

3 Carefully fold in the flour with a large metal spoon using a figure-of-eight action.

4 Place the mixture in a piping (pastry) bag fitted with a 1cm/½in plain nozzle. Pipe into finger lengths on the prepared baking sheets, leaving room for spreading.

5 Sprinkle the fingers with caster sugar. Bake for 6–8 minutes until golden brown, then remove to a wire rack to cool.

> **Variation**
> To make Hazelnut Fingers, omit the lemon rind and fold in 25g/1oz/ ¹/₄ cup toasted ground hazelnuts and 5ml/1 tsp mixed (apple pie) spice with the flour.

> **Cook's Tip**
> These delicate sponge fingers also make a good base for a rich sherry trifle if you are not watching your fat intake.

Apricot & Almond Fingers

These delicious high-fibre almond fingers will stay moist for several days, thanks to the addition of the apricots.

Makes 18
225g/8oz/2 cups self-raising (self-rising) flour
115g/4oz/ ¹/₂ cup soft light brown sugar
50g/2oz/ ¹/₂ cup semolina
175g/6oz/1 cup ready-to-eat dried apricots, chopped
30ml/2 tbsp clear honey
30ml/2 tbsp malt extract
2 eggs, beaten
60ml/4 tbsp skimmed milk
60ml/4 tbsp sunflower oil
a few drops of almond extract
30ml/2 tbsp flaked (sliced) almonds

1 Preheat the oven to 160°C/325°F/Gas 3. Grease and line a 28 x 18cm/11 x 7in baking tin (pan).

2 Sift the flour into a large bowl and stir in the sugar, semolina and apricots. Make a well in the centre and add the honey, malt extract, eggs, milk, oil and almond extract. Mix well until combined.

3 Turn the mixture into the prepared tin, spread to the edges and sprinkle with the flaked almonds.

4 Bake for 30–35 minutes, or until the centre springs back when lightly pressed. Invert the cake on a wire rack to cool. Remove the lining paper if necessary and cut into 18 slices with a sharp knife.

> **Cook's Tips**
> • If you cannot find ready-to-eat dried apricots, soak chopped dried apricots in boiling water for 1 hour, then drain them and add to the mixture. This works well with other dried fruit too. Try ready-to-eat dried pears or peaches for a change.
> • As well as going extremely well with coffee these fingers will also make a tasty low-fat dessert served with a low-fat ice cream or frozen yogurt.

Lemon Energy 31kcal/131kJ; Protein 0.9g; Carbohydrate 5.9g, of which sugars 4g; Fat 0.6g, of which saturates 0.2g; Cholesterol 19mg; Calcium 8mg; Fibre 0.1g; Sodium 7mg.
Apricot Energy 140kcal/589kJ; Protein 3.1g; Carbohydrate 23.6g, of which sugars 11.9g; Fat 4.3g, of which saturates 0.6g; Cholesterol 21mg; Calcium 40mg; Fibre 1.2g; Sodium 13mg.

Raspberry Muffins

Unlike English muffins, which are contain yeast and are cooked on a griddle, these American muffins are baked, giving them a deliciously light texture.

Makes 10–12
275g/10oz/2½ cups plain
    (all-purpose) flour
15ml/1 tbsp baking powder
115g/4oz/½ cup caster
    (superfine) sugar
1 egg
250ml/8fl oz/1 cup buttermilk
60ml/4 tbsp sunflower oil
150g/5oz/scant 1 cup
    fresh raspberries

1 Preheat the oven to 200°C/400°F/Gas 6. Arrange 12 paper cases in a deep muffin tin (pan). Sift the flour and baking powder into a mixing bowl, stir in the sugar, then make a well in the centre.

2 Mix the egg, buttermilk and oil together in a jug (pitcher), pour into the bowl and mix quickly until just combined.

3 Add the raspberries and lightly fold in with a metal spoon. Spoon into the paper cases to within a third of the top.

4 Bake the muffins for 20–25 minutes, or until golden brown and firm in the middle. Remove to a wire rack and serve while it is still warm.

Variation
Use blackberries, blueberries or blackcurrants instead of raspberries if you prefer.

Cook's Tips
• *To keep muffins as low fat as possible, paper cases are used for this recipe rather than greasing a muffin pan.*
• *This is a fairly moist batter which should only be lightly mixed. Over-mixing toughens the muffins and breaks up the fruit.*

Date & Apple Muffins

These healthy muffins are delicious with morning coffee or breakfast. You will only need one or two per person as they are very filling.

Makes 12
150g/5oz/1¼ cups self-raising
    (self-rising) wholemeal
    (whole-wheat) flour
150g/5oz/1¼ cups self-raising
    (self-rising) white flour
5ml/1 tsp ground cinnamon
5ml/1 tsp baking powder
25g/1oz/2 tbsp soft margarine
75g/3oz/6 tbsp soft light
    brown sugar
250ml/8fl oz/1 cup apple juice
30ml/2 tbsp pear and
    apple spread
1 egg, lightly beaten
1 eating apple
75g/3oz/½ cup chopped dates
15ml/1 tbsp chopped
    pecan nuts

1 Preheat the oven to 200°C/400°F/Gas 6. Arrange 12 paper cases in a deep muffin tin.

2 Put the wholemeal flour in a mixing bowl. Sift in the white flour with the cinnamon and baking powder.

3 Rub in the margarine until the mixture resembles breadcrumbs, then stir in the brown sugar.

4 In a bowl, stir a little of the apple juice with the pear and apple spread until smooth.

5 Add the remaining juice, mix well, then add to the rubbed-in mixture with the egg.

6 Peel and core the apple, chop the flesh finely and add it to the bowl with the dates. Mix quickly until just combined.

7 Divide the mixture between the muffin cases. Sprinkle with the chopped pecan nuts.

8 Bake the muffins for 20–25 minutes, or until golden brown and firm in the middle. Turn on to a wire rack and cool a little. Serve while still warm.

Raspberry Energy 165kcal/696kJ; Protein 3.6g; Carbohydrate 29.3g, of which sugars 11.9g; Fat 4.5g, of which saturates 0.7g; Cholesterol 17mg; Calcium 68mg; Fibre 1g; Sodium 17mg.
Date Energy 158kcal/670kJ; Protein 3.2g; Carbohydrate 30.7g, of which sugars 11.7g; Fat 3.4g, of which saturates 0.3g; Cholesterol 16mg; Calcium 45mg; Fibre 1g; Sodium 25mg.

Filo Scrunchies

Quick and easy to make, these fruit scrunchies are ideal to serve at teatime and contain little added sugar. They are best eaten warm.

Makes 6
5 apricots or plums

4 sheets of filo pastry, thawed
  if frozen
20ml/4 tsp soft margarine, melted
50g/2oz/¼ cup demerara
  (raw) sugar
30ml/2 tbsp flaked (sliced) almonds
icing (confectioners') sugar,
  for dusting

1 Preheat the oven to 190°C/375°F/Gas 5. Cut the apricots or plums in half, remove the stones (pits) and slice the fruit thinly.

2 Cut the filo pastry into 12 18cm/7in squares. Pile the squares on top of each other and cover with a clean, damp dish towel to prevent the pastry from drying out.

3 Remove one square and brush it with melted margarine. Lay a second filo square on top, then, using your fingers, mould the pastry into neat folds.

4 Lay the scrunched filo square on a baking sheet. Make five more scrunchies in the same way, working quickly so that the pastry does not dry out.

5 Arrange a few slices of fruit in the folds of each scrunchie, then sprinkle generously with demerara sugar and almonds.

6 Bake the scrunchies for 8–10 minutes, or until golden brown, then loosen from the baking sheet with a metal spatula. Place on a platter, dust with icing sugar and serve immediately.

> **Cook's Tip**
> *Filo pastry is the most healthy of all the pastries, as it contains very little fat. As long as you are sparing with the amount of fat you brush on to the layers, filo is a useful and tasty pastry to use in a variety of low-fat recipes, both sweet and savoury.*

Filo & Apricot Purses

Light filo pastry is very easy to use and is low in fat. Always keep a packet in the freezer ready for rustling up a speedy teatime treat.

Makes 12
115g/4oz/1 cup ready-to-eat
  dried apricots

45ml/3 tbsp apricot compôte
3 amaretti, crushed
3 sheets filo pastry, thawed
  if frozen
20ml/4 tsp soft
  margarine, melted
icing (confectioners') sugar,
  for dusting

1 Preheat the oven to 180°C/350°F/Gas 4, and grease two baking sheets.

2 Chop the apricots, put them in a bowl and stir in the apricot compôte. Mix in the amaretti.

3 Cut the filo pastry into 24 13cm/5in squares, pile the squares on top of each other and cover with a clean, damp dish towel to prevent the pastry from drying out.

4 Lay one pastry square on a flat surface, brush lightly with melted margarine and lay another square diagonally on top. Brush the top square with melted margarine.

5 Spoon a small mound of apricot mixture in the centre of the pastry, bring up the edges and pinch together in a money-bag shape. The margarine will help to make the pastry stick.

6 Repeat with the remaining filo squares and filling to make 12 purses in all. Arrange on the prepared baking sheets and bake for 5–8 minutes, or until golden brown. Dust with icing sugar and serve warm.

> **Cook's Tip**
> *The easiest way to crush the amaretti is to put them in a plastic bag and roll with a rolling pin.*

Purses Energy 62kcal/264kJ; Protein 0.9g; Carbohydrate 11.3g, of which sugars 7.1g; Fat 1.8g, of which saturates 0.2g; Cholesterol 0mg; Calcium 17mg; Fibre 0.8g; Sodium 24mg.
Scrunchies Energy 127kcal/534kJ; Protein 2.2g; Carbohydrate 18g, of which sugars 11.5g; Fat 5.7g, of which saturates 0.2g; Cholesterol 0mg; Calcium 33mg; Fibre 1.2g; Sodium 29mg.

Angel Cake

This heavenly cake contains virtually no fat and tastes simply divine! Serve in slices with fresh fruit for a delicious healthy dessert

Makes one 25cm/10in cake
130g/4½oz/generous 1 cup
  sifted plain (all-purpose) flour
30ml/2 tbsp cornflour (cornstarch)

285g/10½oz/1½ cups caster
  (superfine) sugar
10 egg whites
6.5ml/1¼ tsp cream of tartar
1.5ml/¼ tsp salt
5ml/1 tsp vanilla extract
1.5ml/¼ tsp almond extract
icing (confectioners') sugar,
  for dusting

1 Preheat the oven to 160°C/325°F/Gas 3. Sift the flours before measuring, then sift them four times together with 90g/3½oz/½ cup of the sugar.

2 Beat the egg whites until foamy. Sift over the cream of tartar and salt and beat until the egg whites form soft peaks.

3 Add the remaining sugar in three batches, beating well after each addition.

4 Stir in the vanilla and almond extracts. Fold in the flour mixture in two batches.

5 Transfer to an ungreased 25cm/10in cake tin (pan) and bake until just browned on top, about 1 hour.

6 Turn the tin upside-down on to a wire rack and cool for 1 hour. Then invert on to a serving plate. Lay a star-shaped template on top of the cake, sift over some icing sugar and remove the template.

> **Cook's Tip**
> For an exceptionally light sponge cake such as this one it is important to sift the dry ingredients several times to help incorporate air into the batter. Be careful to fold in the flour to the wet ingredients so that the air will not be lost.

Peach Roll

This is the perfect light cake for a summer afternoon tea in the garden.

Serves 6–8
3 eggs
115g/4oz/generous ½ cup caster
  (superfine) sugar

75g/3oz/⅔ cup plain
  (all-purpose) flour, sifted
15ml/1 tbsp boiling water
90ml/6 tbsp peach jam
icing (confectioners') sugar,
  for dusting (optional)

1 Preheat the oven to 200°C/400°F/Gas 6. Line and grease a 30 x 20cm/12 x 8in Swiss roll tin (jelly roll pan).

2 Combine the eggs and sugar in a bowl. Beat with a hand-held electric whisk until thick and mousse-like: when the whisk is lifted a trail should remain on the surface of the mixture for at least 30 seconds.

3 Carefully fold in the flour with a large metal spoon, then add the boiling water in the same way.

4 Spoon the mixture into the prepared tin, spread evenly to the edges and bake for 10–12 minutes, or until the cake springs back when lightly pressed.

5 Spread a sheet of baking parchment on a flat surface and sprinkle it with caster sugar. Carefully invert the cake on top and peel off the lining paper.

6 Make a neat cut two-thirds of the way through the cake, about 1cm/½in from the short edge nearest you – this will make it easier for you to roll the sponge cake. Trim the remaining edges to give a neat finish to the cake.

7 Spread the cake with the peach jam and roll up quickly from the partially cut end. Hold in position for a minute, making sure the join is underneath.

8 Cool on a wire rack. Dust with icing sugar, if you like.

Angel Cake Energy 131kcal/558kJ; Protein 4.1g; Carbohydrate 30.3g, of which sugars 23.6g; Fat 0.1g, of which saturates 0g; Cholesterol 0mg; Calcium 20mg; Fibre 0.1g; Sodium 80mg.
Peach Roll Energy 146kcal/618kJ; Protein 3.4g; Carbohydrate 30.1g, of which sugars 22.9g; Fat 2.2g, of which saturates 0.6g; Cholesterol 71mg; Calcium 33mg; Fibre 0.3g; Sodium 31mg.

Peach & Amaretto Cake

Try this delicious cake for dessert, with reduced-fat fromage frais, or serve it solo for afternoon tea.

Serves 8
3 eggs, separated
175g/6oz/³/4 cup caster
 (superfine) sugar
grated rind and juice of 1 lemon
50g/2oz/¹/2 cup semolina
40g/1¹/2oz/scant ¹/2 cup
 ground almonds

25g/1oz/¹/4 cup plain
 (all-purpose) flour

For the syrup
75g/3oz/6 tbsp caster
 (superfine) sugar
90ml/6 tbsp water
30ml/2 tbsp amaretto liqueur
2 peaches or nectarines, halved
 and stoned (pitted)
60ml/4 tbsp apricot jam, sieved,
 to glaze

1 Preheat the oven to 180°C/350°F/Gas 4. Grease a 20cm/8in round loose-based cake tin (pan). Whisk the egg yolks, caster sugar, lemon rind and juice in a bowl until thick, pale and creamy, then fold in the semolina, almonds and flour until the mixture is smooth.

2 Whisk the egg whites in a grease-free bowl until fairly stiff. Using a metal spoon, stir a generous spoonful of the whites into the semolina mixture to lighten it, then fold in the remaining egg whites. Spoon into the prepared cake tin.

3 Bake for 30–35 minutes, then remove the cake from the oven and carefully loosen the edges. Prick the top with a skewer and leave to cool slightly in the tin.

4 Meanwhile, make the syrup. Heat the sugar and water in a small pan, stirring until dissolved, then boil without stirring for 2 minutes. Add the amaretto liqueur and drizzle slowly over the cake. Leave to cool in the tin.

5 Remove the cake from the tin and transfer it to a serving plate. Slice the peaches or nectarines and arrange them in concentric circles over the top of the cake. Brush the fruit with the glaze.

Chestnut & Orange Roulade

A very moist roulade with a sweet and creamy filling – ideal to serve as an impressive low-fat dessert.

Serves 8
3 eggs, separated
115g/4oz/generous ¹/2 cup caster
 (superfine) sugar
¹/2 x 439g/15¹/2 oz can
 unsweetened chestnut purée

grated rind and juice of 1 orange
icing (confectioners') sugar,
 for dusting

For the filling
225g/8oz/1 cup low-fat
 soft cheese
15ml/1 tbsp clear honey
1 orange

1 Preheat the oven to 180°C/350°F/Gas 4. Line and grease a 30 x 20cm/12 x 8in Swiss roll tin (jelly roll pan).

2 Whisk the egg yolks and sugar in a bowl until thick. Put the chestnut purée into a separate bowl. Whisk the orange rind and juice into the purée, then whisk into the egg mixture.

3 Whisk the egg whites until fairly stiff. Stir a spoonful into the chestnut mixture, then fold in the remaining egg whites.

4 Spoon the mixture into the prepared tin and bake for 30 minutes, or until firm. Cool for 5 minutes in the tin, then cover with a clean damp dish towel and leave until completely cold.

5 Meanwhile, make the filling. Put the soft cheese in a bowl with the honey. Finely grate the orange rind and add to the bowl. Using a sharp knife, cut away all the peel and pith from the orange. Cut the fruit into segments, cutting either side of the membrane so that you have only the flesh. Chop roughly and set aside. Add any juice to the bowl, then beat until smooth. Mix in the orange segments.

6 Sprinkle a sheet of baking parchment with icing sugar. Turn the roulade out on to the paper; peel off the lining paper. Spread the filling over the roulade and roll up like a Swiss roll (jelly roll). Transfer to a plate and dust with icing sugar.

Peach Energy 244kcal/1034kJ; Protein 4.7g; Carbohydrate 46.7g, of which sugars 39.4g; Fat 5g, of which saturates 0.8g; Cholesterol 71mg; Calcium 47mg; Fibre 0.9g; Sodium 32mg.
Chestnut Energy 176kcal/741kJ; Protein 7.2g; Carbohydrate 28.1g, of which sugars 19.9g; Fat 5.1g, of which saturates 2.2g; Cholesterol 78mg; Calcium 64mg; Fibre 1.1g; Sodium 154mg.

Cinnamon & Apple Gateau

Make this lovely moist gateau as a guilt-free autumn teatime treat.

Serves 8
3 eggs
115g/4oz/½ cup caster
   (superfine) sugar
75g/3oz/¾ cup plain
   (all-purpose) flour
5ml/1 tsp ground cinnamon

For the filling and topping
4 large eating apples
15ml/1 tbsp water
60ml/4 tbsp clear honey
75g/3oz/½ cup sultanas
   (golden raisins)
2.5ml/½ tsp ground cinnamon
350g/12oz/1½ cups low-fat
   soft cheese
60ml/4 tbsp reduced-fat fromage
   frais or low-fat cream cheese
10ml/2 tsp lemon juice

1 Preheat the oven to 190°C/375°F/Gas 5. Line and grease a 23cm/9in shallow round cake tin (pan). Whisk the eggs and sugar until thick, then sift the flour and cinnamon over the surface and carefully fold in with a large metal spoon.

2 Pour into the prepared tin and bake for 25–30 minutes, or until the cake springs back when lightly pressed. Leave on a wire rack to cool completely.

3 To make the filling, peel, core and slice three of the apples and cook them in a covered pan with the water and half the honey until softened. Add the sultanas and cinnamon, stir well, replace the lid and leave to cool.

4 Put the soft cheese in a bowl with the fromage frais, the remaining honey and half the lemon juice; beat until smooth. Split the sponge cake in half, place the bottom half on a plate and drizzle over any liquid from the apples.

5 Spread with two-thirds of the cheese mixture, then top with the apple filling. Fit the top of the cake in place.

6 Swirl the remaining filling over the top of the sponge. Quarter, core and slice the remaining apple, dip the slices in the remaining lemon juice and use to decorate the edges.

Lemon Chiffon Cake

Tangy lemon mousse makes a delicious filling in this light cake, which is surprisingly low in saturated fat.

Serves 8
1 lemon sponge cake mix
lemon glacé icing
shreds of blanched lemon rind

For the filling
2 eggs, separated
75g/3oz/6 tbsp caster
   (superfine) sugar
grated rind and juice of
   1 small lemon
20ml/4 tsp water
10ml/2 tsp powdered gelatine
120ml/4fl oz/½ cup reduced-fat
   fromage frais or crème fraîche

1 Preheat the oven to 180°C/350°F/Gas 4. Line and grease a 20cm/8in loose-based cake tin (pan).

2 Add the sponge mixture and bake for 20–25 minutes, or until firm and golden. Cool on a wire rack, then split the cake in half. Return the lower half of the cake to the clean cake tin and set aside.

3 To make the filling, whisk the egg yolks, sugar, lemon rind and juice in a bowl until thick, pale and creamy. In a grease-free bowl, whisk the egg whites until they form soft peaks.

4 Sprinkle the gelatine over the water in a heatproof bowl. When the gelatine has become spongy, place the bowl over a pan of simmering water and dissolve the gelatine, stirring occasionally. Cool slightly, then whisk into the yolk mixture. Fold in the fromage frais.

5 When the mixture begins to set, fold in a generous spoonful of the egg whites to lighten it, then fold in the remaining whites.

6 Spoon the lemon mousse over the sponge in the cake tin. Set the second layer of sponge on top and chill until set.

7 Carefully transfer the cake to a serving plate. Pour the glacé icing over the cake and spread it evenly to the edges. Decorate with the lemon shreds.

Cinnamon Energy 239kcal/1010kJ; Protein 10.8g; Carbohydrate 39.9g, of which sugars 32.8g; Fat 5.8g, of which saturates 2.9g; Cholesterol 82mg; Calcium 97mg; Fibre 1.1g; Sodium 225mg.
Lemon Energy 356kcal/1491kJ; Protein 6.7g; Carbohydrate 43.6g, of which sugars 29.8g; Fat 18.4g, of which saturates 4g; Cholesterol 118mg; Calcium 68mg; Fibre 0.6g; Sodium 227mg.

Strawberry Gateau

It is difficult to believe that a cake that tastes so delicious can be low fat. It is the perfect way to enjoy the first locally grown strawberries of the season.

Serves 6

2 eggs
75g/3oz/6 tbsp caster
  (superfine) sugar
grated rind of ½ orange
50g/2oz/½ cup plain
  (all-purpose) flour

For the filling
275g/10oz/1¼ cups low-fat
  soft cheese
grated rind of ½ orange
30ml/2 tbsp caster
  (superfine) sugar
60ml/4 tbsp reduced-fat fromage
  frais or crème fraîche
225g/8oz/2 cups strawberries,
  halved and chopped
25g/1oz/¼ cup chopped
  almonds, toasted

1 Preheat the oven to 190°C/375°F/Gas 5. Line a 30 × 20cm/ 12 × 8in Swiss roll tin (jelly roll pan) with baking parchment.

2 In a bowl, whisk the eggs, sugar and orange rind until thick and mousse-like, then lightly fold in the flour.

3 Turn into the prepared tin. Bake for 15–20 minutes, or until the surface is firm to the touch and golden.

4 Turn the cake out on to on a wire rack to cool. When cold, remove the lining paper.

5 Meanwhile, make the filling. In a bowl, mix the soft cheese with the grated orange rind, sugar and fromage frais until smooth. Divide the mixture between two bowls.

6 Add half the strawberries to one bowl. Cut the sponge horizontally into three equal pieces and sandwich together with the strawberry filling. Place the gateau on a serving plate.

7 Spread the plain filling over the top and sides of the cake. Press the toasted almonds over the sides and decorate the top with the remaining strawberry halves.

Tia Maria Gateau

A feather-light coffee sponge with a creamy liqueur-flavoured filling spiked with preserved stem ginger.

Serves 8
75g/3oz/¾ cup plain
  (all-purpose) flour
30ml/2 tbsp instant
  coffee powder
3 eggs
115g/4oz/½ cup caster
  (superfine) sugar

For the filling
175g/6oz/generous ¾ cup low-fat
  soft cheese
15ml/1 tbsp clear honey
15ml/1 tbsp Tia Maria
50g/2oz/⅓ cup preserved stem
  ginger, chopped

For the icing
225g/8oz/2 cups icing
  (confectioners') sugar, sifted
10ml/2 tsp coffee extract
5ml/1 tsp fat-reduced cocoa
coffee beans (optional)

1 Preheat the oven to 190°C/375°F/Gas 5. Line and grease a 20cm/8in round cake tin (pan). Sift the flour and coffee powder together into a bowl.

2 Whisk the eggs and sugar in a bowl until thick and mousse-like, then fold in the flour mixture lightly. Turn the mixture into the prepared tin. Bake for 30–35 minutes, or until firm and golden. Leave to cool on a wire rack.

3 To make the filling, mix the soft cheese with the honey in a bowl. Beat until smooth, then stir in the Tia Maria and preserved stem ginger. Split the cake in half horizontally and sandwich together with the Tia Maria filling.

4 To make the icing, mix the icing sugar and coffee extract in a bowl with enough water to make an icing which will coat the back of a wooden spoon. Pour three-quarters of the icing over the cake.

5 Stir the cocoa into the remaining icing, spoon it into a piping (icing) bag fitted with a writing nozzle and drizzle the mocha icing over the coffee icing. Decorate with coffee beans, if you like.

Strawberry Energy 305kcal/1288kJ; Protein 25.6g; Carbohydrate 35.7g, of which sugars 22.4g; Fat 7.6g, of which saturates 1.1g; Cholesterol 64mg; Calcium 163mg; Fibre 7.2g; Sodium 37mg.
Tia Maria Energy 247kcal/1050kJ; Protein 4.9g; Carbohydrate 54.7g, of which sugars 47.4g; Fat 2.5g, of which saturates 1.5g; Cholesterol 12mg; Calcium 65mg; Fibre 0.5g; Sodium 120mg.

Chocolate Banana Cake

Fresh fruit is especially good for making a moist cake mixture. Here is a delicious sticky chocolate cake, moist enough to eat without the icing if you want to cut down on the calories.

Serves 8
225g/8oz/2 cups self-raising (self-rising) flour
45ml/3 tbsp reduced-fat unsweetened cocoa powder
115g/4oz/ ½ cup soft light brown sugar

30ml/2 tbsp malt extract
30ml/2 tbsp golden (light corn) syrup
2 eggs, beaten
60ml/4 tbsp skimmed milk
60ml/4 tbsp sunflower oil
2 large ripe bananas

For the icing
175g/6oz/1½ cups icing (confectioners') sugar, sifted
30ml/2 tbsp reduced-fat unsweetened cocoa powder, sifted
15–30ml/1–2 tbsp warm water

1 Preheat the oven to 160°C/325°F/Gas 3. Line and grease a deep 20cm/8in round cake tin (pan). Sift the flour into a mixing bowl with the cocoa powder. Stir in the sugar.

2 Make a well in the centre of the dry ingredients and add the malt extract, golden syrup, eggs, milk and oil. Mix well.

3 Mash the bananas thoroughly and stir them into the mixture until thoroughly combined.

4 Spoon the cake mixture into the prepared tin and bake for 1–1¼ hours, or until the centre of the cake springs back when lightly pressed.

5 Remove from the tin and turn on to a wire rack to cool.

6 To make the icing, put the icing sugar and cocoa in a mixing bowl and gradually add enough water to make a mixture thick enough to coat the back of a wooden spoon.

7 Pour over the top of the cake and ease to the edges, allowing the icing to dribble down the sides.

Spiced Apple Cake

As grated apple and dates give this cake a natural sweetness, it may not be necessary to add all the sugar.

Serves 8
225g/8oz/2 cups self-raising (self-rising) wholemeal (whole-wheat) flour
5ml/1 tsp baking powder
10ml/2 tsp ground cinnamon

175g/6oz/1 cup chopped dates
75g/3oz/ scant ½ cup soft light brown sugar
15ml/1 tbsp pear and apple spread
120ml/4fl oz/ ½ cup apple juice
2 eggs, beaten
90ml/6 tbsp sunflower oil
2 eating apples, cored and grated
15ml/1 tbsp chopped walnuts

1 Preheat the oven to 180°C/350°F/Gas 4. Line and grease a 20cm/8in deep round cake tin (pan).

2 Sift the flour, baking powder and cinnamon into a mixing bowl, then mix in the dates and make a well in the centre.

3 Mix some of the sugar with the pear and apple spread in a small bowl. Gradually stir in the apple juice.

4 Add to the dry ingredients with the eggs, oil and apples. Mix thoroughly. Taste and add the rest of the sugar if necessary.

5 Spoon into the prepared cake tin, sprinkle with the walnuts and bake for 60–65 minutes, or until a skewer inserted into the centre of the cake comes out clean.

6 Invert on a wire rack, remove the lining paper and leave to cool.

> **Cook's Tip**
> It is not necessary to peel the apples – the skin adds extra fibre and softens on cooking.

Chocolate Energy 352kcal/1487kJ; Protein 6.5g; Carbohydrate 64.4g, of which sugars 41.9g; Fat 9.4g, of which saturates 2.3g; Cholesterol 48mg; Calcium 145mg; Fibre 2.3g; Sodium 233mg.
Apple Energy 282kcal/1186kJ; Protein 4.9g; Carbohydrate 42.8g, of which sugars 21.3g; Fat 11.3g, of which saturates 1.5g; Cholesterol 48mg; Calcium 60mg; Fibre 1.6g; Sodium 22mg.

Irish Whiskey Cake

This moist rich fruit cake is drizzled with whiskey as soon as it comes out of the oven. It is high in fibre and full of flavour.

Serves 10

115g/4oz/³/4 cup sultanas (golden raisins)
115g/4oz/scant 1 cup raisins
115g/4oz/¹/2 cup currants
115g/4oz/¹/2 cup glacé (candied) cherries
175g/6oz/1¹/4 cups soft light brown sugar
300ml/¹/2 pint/1¹/4 cups cold tea
1 egg, beaten
300g/11oz/2²/3 cups self-raising (self-rising) flour, sifted
45ml/3 tbsp Irish whiskey

1 Mix the sultanas, raisins, currants, cherries, sugar and tea in a large bowl. Leave to soak overnight until the tea has been absorbed.

2 Preheat the oven to 180°C/350°F/Gas 4. Line and grease a 1kg/2¹/4lb loaf tin (pan).

3 Add the egg and flour to the fruit mixture and beat thoroughly until well mixed.

4 Pour into the prepared tin and bake for 1¹/2 hours or until a skewer inserted into the centre comes out clean.

5 Prick over the top of the cake with a skewer and drizzle over the whiskey while the cake is still hot.

6 Allow to stand for 5 minutes, then remove from the tin and cool completely on a wire rack.

> **Variation**
> For a tangy finish, drizzle with lemon icing. Mix the juice of 1 lemon with 225g/8oz/2 cup icing (confectioners') sugar and enough warm water for the icing to have a thin consistency. Drizzle the icing over the cooled cake and decorate with crystallized lemon slices, if you like.

Fruit & Nut Cake

A rich, fibrous fruit cake that matures with keeping. Omit the fruit and nut decoration from the top if you want to ice it for a Christmas cake.

Serves 12–14

175g/6oz/1¹/2 cups self-raising (self-rising) wholemeal (whole-wheat) flour
175g/6oz/1¹/2 cups self-raising (self-rising) white flour
10ml/2 tsp mixed (apple pie) spice
15ml/1 tbsp apple and apricot spread
45ml/3 tbsp clear honey
15ml/1 tbsp molasses
90ml/6 tbsp sunflower oil
175ml/6fl oz/³/4 cup orange juice
2 eggs, beaten
675g/1¹/2lb/4 cups luxury mixed dried fruit
115g/4oz/¹/2 cup glacé (candied) cherries, halved
45ml/3 tbsp split almonds

1 Preheat the oven to 160°C/325°F/Gas 3. Line and grease a deep 20cm/8in cake tin (pan). Tie a band of newspaper around the outside of the tin and stand it on a pad of newspaper on a baking sheet.

2 Combine the flours in a mixing bowl. Stir in the mixed spice and make a well in the centre.

3 Put the apple and apricot spread in a small bowl. Gradually stir in the honey and molasses. Add to the bowl with the oil, orange juice, eggs and mixed fruit. Stir with a wooden spoon to mix thoroughly.

4 Scrape the mixture into the prepared tin and smooth the surface. Arrange the cherries and almonds in a decorative pattern over the top. Bake for 2 hours, or until a skewer inserted into the centre of the cake comes out clean. Turn on to a wire rack to cool, then remove the lining paper.

> **Cook's Tip**
> For a less elaborate cake, omit the cherries, chop the almonds roughly and sprinkle them over the top.

Whiskey Energy 311kcal/1323kJ; Protein 4.4g; Carbohydrate 73g, of which sugars 50.1g; Fat 1.1g, of which saturates 0.2g; Cholesterol 19mg; Calcium 84mg; Fibre 1.7g; Sodium 23mg.
Fruit Energy 327kcal/1384kJ; Protein 5.2g; Carbohydrate 63g, of which sugars 43.8g; Fat 7.8g, of which saturates 1g; Cholesterol 27mg; Calcium 94mg; Fibre 2.2g; Sodium 40mg.

Pear & Sultana Teabread

This is an ideal teabread to make when pears are plentiful. There's no better use for autumn windfalls.

Serves 6 – 8

25g/1oz/3 cups rolled oats
50g/2oz/ ¼ cup soft light
  brown sugar
30ml/2 tbsp pear or apple juice
30ml/2 tbsp sunflower oil
1 large or 2 small ripe pears
115g/4oz/1 cup self-raising
  (self-rising) flour
115g/4oz/¾ cup sultanas
  (golden raisins)
2.5ml/ ½ tsp baking powder
10ml/2 tsp mixed (apple
  pie) spice
1 egg

1 Preheat the oven to 180°C/350°F/Gas 4. Line a 450g/1lb loaf tin (pan) with baking parchment.

2 Put the oats in a bowl with the sugar, and pour over the pear or apple juice and oil.

3 Mix the ingredients together well using a wooden spoon or electric whisk. Leave to stand for 15 minutes.

4 Quarter, core and grate the pear(s). Add to the bowl with the flour, sultanas, baking powder, spice and egg. Using a wooden spoon, mix thoroughly.

5 Spoon the tea bread mixture into the prepared loaf tin. Bake for 55–60 minutes, or until a skewer inserted into the centre comes out clean.

6 Invert the tea bread on a wire rack and remove the lining paper. Leave to cool.

> **Cook's Tips**
> • Health-food stores sell concentrated pear juice, ready for diluting as required.
> • You will also find some good-quality sultanas there and organic oats if you want to make a really healthy treat.

Banana & Ginger Teabread

The creaminess of the banana is given a delightful lift with chunks of stem ginger in this tasty teabread. If you like a strong ginger flavour add 5ml/1 tsp ground ginger with the flour.

Serves 6 – 8

175g/6oz/1 ½ cups self-raising
  (self-rising) flour
5ml/1 tsp baking powder
40g/1 ½oz/3 tbsp soft margarine
50g/2oz/ ¼ cup soft light
  brown sugar
50g/2oz/ ⅓ cup drained
  preserved stem ginger, chopped
60ml/4 tbsp skimmed milk
2 ripe bananas

1 Preheat the oven to 180°C/350°F/Gas 4. Line and grease a 450g/1lb loaf tin (pan).

2 Sift the flour and baking powder into a large bowl.

3 Using your fingertips or a pastry cutter rub the margarine into the dry ingredients until the mixture resembles breadcrumbs, then stir in the sugar.

4 Peel and mash the bananas in a separate bowl.

5 Add the preserved stem ginger, milk and mashed bananas to the mixture and mix to a soft dough. Spoon into the prepared tin and bake for 40–45 minutes.

6 Run a metal spatula around the edges of the cake to loosen them, then turn the teabread on to a wire rack and leave to cool completely.

> **Variation**
> To make Banana and Walnut Teabread, add 5ml/1 tsp mixed (apple pie) spice and omit the chopped stem ginger. Stir in 50g/2oz/ ½ cup chopped walnuts and add 50g/2oz/ ⅓ cup sultanas (golden raisins).

Pear Energy 184Kcal/780kJ; Protein 3.1g; Carbohydrate 36.3g, of which sugars 23.1g; Fat 4g, of which saturates 0.6g; Cholesterol 24mg; Calcium 43mg; Fibre 1.8g; Sodium 16mg.
Banana Energy 162Kcal/685kJ; Protein 2.7g; Carbohydrate 29.7g, of which sugars 12.5g; Fat 4.5g, of which saturates 0.1g; Cholesterol 0mg; Calcium 45mg; Fibre 1g; Sodium 45mg.

Low-fat Drop Scones

These little scones are quick easy to make and contain very little fat.

Makes 18
225g/8oz/2 cups self-raising (self-rising) flour
2.5ml/¹/₂ tsp salt
15ml/1 tbsp caster (superfine) sugar
1 egg, beaten
300ml/¹/₂ pint/1¹/₄ cups skimmed milk
oil, for brushing

1 Preheat a griddle, heavy frying pan or electric frying pan. Sift the flour and salt into a mixing bowl. Stir in the sugar and make a well in the centre.

2 Add the egg and half the milk. Stir from the centre to the outside, gradually incorporating the surrounding flour to make a smooth batter. Beat in the remaining milk.

3 Lightly grease the griddle or pan. Drop tablespoons of the batter on to the surface, making sure they are spaced well apart. Leave them to cook until they bubble and the bubbles begin to burst.

4 Turn the drop scones with a metal spatula and cook until the undersides are golden brown.

5 Keep the cooked drop scones warm and moist by wrapping them in a clean napkin while cooking successive batches. Serve with jam.

> **Variations**
> • *For Banana and Raisin Drop Scones mash two ripe bananas and add to the egg and half the milk before adding to the dry ingredients at step 2. Add 25g/1oz/¹/₄ cup of raisins to the banana mixture and then stir in from the centre as before.*
> • *For a savoury version of these tasty scones, add 2 chopped spring onions (scallions) and 15ml/1 tbsp freshly grated Parmesan cheese to the batter. Serve with cottage cheese.*

Pineapple & Spice Drop Scones

Making the batter with pineapple or orange juice instead of milk cuts down on fat and adds to the taste. Semi-dried pineapple has an intense flavour that makes it ideal to use in baking.

Makes 24
115g/4oz/1 cup self-raising (self-rising) wholemeal (whole-wheat) flour
115g/4oz/1 cup self-raising (self-rising) white flour
5ml/1 tsp ground cinnamon
15ml/1 tbsp caster (superfine) sugar
1 egg, beaten
300ml/¹/₂ pint/1¹/₄ cups pineapple juice
75g/3oz/¹/₂ cup semi-dried pineapple, chopped
oil, for brushing

1 Preheat a griddle, heavy frying pan or electric frying pan. Put the wholemeal flour in a mixing bowl. Sift in the white flour, ground cinnamon and sugar, and make a well in the centre of the dry ingredients.

2 Add the egg with half the pineapple juice. Stir from the centre to the outside, gradually incorporating the surrounding flour to make a smooth batter. Beat in the remaining juice with the chopped pineapple.

3 Lightly grease the griddle or pan. Drop tablespoons of the batter on to the surface, making sure they are spaced well apart. Leave them to cook until they bubble and the bubbles begin to burst.

4 Turn the drop scones with a metal spatula and cook until the underside is golden brown. Keep the cooked scones warm and moist by wrapping them in a clean napkin while cooking successive batches.

> **Cook's Tip**
> *Drop scones do not keep well – they are best eaten freshly cooked and taste especially good hot from the pan. These taste good with cottage cheese.*

Curry Crackers

These spicy, crisp little crackers are much lower in fat than other snacks.

Makes 12

50g/2oz/¹/₂ cup plain
(all-purpose) flour
5ml/1 tsp curry powder
1.5ml/¹/₄ tsp chilli powder
1.5ml/¹/₄ tsp salt
15ml/1 tbsp chopped
fresh coriander (cilantro)
30ml/2 tbsp water

1 Preheat the oven to 180°C/350°F/Gas 4. Sift the flour, curry powder, chilli powder and salt into a large bowl and make a well in the centre. Add the chopped coriander and water.

2 Stir from the centre outwards, gradually incorporating the flour and mixing to a fine dough.

3 Turn on to a lightly floured surface, and knead until smooth, then leave to rest for 5 minutes.

4 Cut the dough into 12 pieces and knead into small balls. Roll each ball out very thinly to a 10cm/4in round.

5 Arrange the rounds on two ungreased baking sheets. Bake for 15 minutes, turning over once during cooking.

Variations
These can be flavoured in many different ways. Omit the curry and chilli powders and add 15ml/1 tbsp caraway, fennel or mustard seeds. Any of the stronger spices such as nutmeg, cloves or ginger will give a good flavour but you will only need to add 5ml/1 tsp.

Cook's Tip
As this dough does not include yeast it only needs to be lightly kneaded; heavy handling is only suitable for yeast breads.

Oatcakes

Oatmeal not only tastes delicious, but it is also a good source of water-soluble fibre, is low in fat, and is thought to lower cholesterol levels. Try these delicious cakes spread with honey for a great start to the day.

Makes 8

175g/6oz/1¹/₂ cups medium
oatmeal, plus extra
for sprinkling
a pinch of bicarbonate of soda
(baking soda)
2.5ml/¹/₂ tsp salt
15g/¹/₂oz/1 tbsp butter
75ml/5 tbsp water

1 Preheat the oven to 150°C/300°F/Gas 2. Grease a baking sheet. Put the oatmeal, bicarbonate of soda and salt in a large bowl and mix well.

2 Melt the butter with the water in a small pan. Bring to the boil, then add to the oatmeal and mix to a moist dough.

3 Turn the dough on to a surface sprinkled with oatmeal and knead to a smooth ball. Turn a large baking sheet upside down, sprinkle it lightly with oatmeal and place the ball of dough on top. Dust the top of the ball with oatmeal, then roll out thinly to a 25cm/10in round.

4 Stamp out rounds with a 5cm/2in scone (cookie) cutter, or cut the round into eight sections, ease apart slightly and bake for 50–60 minutes, or until crisp. Leave to cool on the baking sheet, then remove the oatcakes with a metal spatula.

Cook's Tips
• To get a neat circle, place a 25cm/10in cake board or plate on top of the oatcake. Cut away any excess dough with a palette knife, then remove the board or plate.
• Oatmeal is ground from the whole kernel of the cereal and is graded according to how finely it is ground, with the coarsest type known as pinhead. Medium oatmeal is widely available but fine is also suitable for oatcakes.

Crackers Energy 14kcal/60kJ; Protein 0.4g; Carbohydrate 3.2g, of which sugars 0.1g; Fat 0.1g, of which saturates 0g; Cholesterol 0mg; Calcium 6mg; Fibre 0.1g; Sodium 49mg.
Oatcakes Energy 102kcal/429kJ; Protein 2.7g; Carbohydrate 15.9g, of which sugars 0g; Fat 3.5g, of which saturates 1g; Cholesterol 4mg; Calcium 12mg; Fibre 1.5g; Sodium 141mg.

Chive & Potato Scones

These little cakes should be fairly thin, soft and crisp. They are delicious served warm with cottage cheese as a filling yet low-fat snack at any time of the day.

Makes 20
450g/1lb potatoes
115g/4oz/1 cup plain
   (all-purpose) flour, sifted
30ml/2 tbsp olive oil
30ml/2 tbsp chopped chives
salt and ground black pepper
low-fat spread, for topping

1 Cook the potatoes in a pan of boiling salted water for 20 minutes, then drain thoroughly. Return the potatoes to the clean pan and mash them.

2 Preheat a griddle or heavy frying pan over low heat. Tip the hot mashed potatoes into a bowl. Add the flour, olive oil and chopped chives, with a little salt and ground black pepper. Mix to a soft dough.

3 Roll out the dough on a well-floured surface to a thickness of 5mm/¼in. Stamp out rounds with a 5cm/2in scone (cookie) cutter, re-rolling and cutting the trimmings, or cut into squares with a sharp floured knife.

4 Cook the scones, in batches, on the hot griddle or frying pan for about 10 minutes, or until they are golden brown. Keep the heat low and turn the scones once.

5 Remove from the griddle or pan, top with a little low-fat spread and serve immediately.

> **Cook's Tips**
> • Use floury potatoes such as King Edwards.
> • The potatoes must be freshly cooked and mashed and should not be allowed to cool before mixing.
> • Cook the scones over low heat so that the outside does not burn before the inside is cooked.

Ham & Tomato Scones

These make an ideal accompaniment for soup. If you have any left over the next day, halve them, toast under the grill (broiler) and top with low-fat spread.

Makes 12
225g/8oz/2 cups self-raising
   (self-rising) flour
5ml/1 tsp mustard powder
5ml/1 tsp paprika, plus extra
   for topping
2.5ml/½ tsp salt
25g/1oz/2 tbsp soft margarine
50g/2oz Black Forest
   ham, chopped
15ml/1 tbsp chopped
   fresh basil
50g/2oz/½ cup drained
   sun-dried tomatoes in
   oil, chopped
90–120ml/3–4fl oz/⅓–½ cup
   skimmed milk, plus extra
   for brushing

1 Preheat the oven to 200°C/400°F/Gas 6. Flour a large baking sheet.

2 Sift the flour, mustard, paprika and salt into a bowl. Rub in the margarine, using your fingertips or a pastry cutter until the mixture resembles breadcrumbs.

3 Stir in the ham, basil and sun-dried tomatoes; mix lightly. Pour in enough milk to mix to a soft dough.

4 Turn the dough on to a lightly floured surface, knead lightly and roll out to a 20 × 15cm (8 × 6in) rectangle.

5 Cut into 5cm/2in squares and arrange on the baking sheet.

6 Brush sparingly with milk, sprinkle with paprika and bake for 12–15 minutes. Transfer to a wire rack to cool.

> **Cook's Tip**
> Scone dough should be soft and moist and mixed for just long enough to bind the ingredients together. Too much kneading makes the scones tough.

Chive Energy 46kcal/193kJ; Protein 1g; Carbohydrate 8.1g, of which sugars 0.4g; Fat 1.3g, of which saturates 0.2g; Cholesterol 0mg; Calcium 12mg; Fibre 0.5g; Sodium 3mg.
Ham Energy 89kcal/378kJ; Protein 3g; Carbohydrate 15.6g, of which sugars 1.3g; Fat 2.1g, of which saturates 0.1g; Cholesterol 3mg; Calcium 37mg; Fibre 0.7g; Sodium 81mg.

Breads

There is nothing more appealing than the delicious aroma of
freshly baked bread, and this section reveals just how easy it
is to make your own. From everyday loaves, such as White
Bread, Multigrain Bread, or Corn Bread, to more unusual
ideas, such as Spiral Herb Bread, Pecan Nut Rye Bread
or Danish Wreath, there is a sweet or savoury
bread suitable for every requirement.

White Bread

There is nothing quite like the smell and taste of home-baked bread, eaten while still warm.

**Makes two 23 x 13cm/
9 x 5in loaves**
50ml/2fl oz/¼ cup
  lukewarm water
15ml/1 tbsp active dried yeast
30ml/2 tbsp caster
  (superfine) sugar
475ml/16fl oz/2 cups
  lukewarm milk
25g/1oz/2 tbsp butter or
  margarine, at room temperature
10ml/2 tsp salt
about 900g/2lb/8 cups strong
  white bread flour

1 Combine the water, yeast and 15ml/1 tbsp of the sugar in a measuring jug (cup) and leave for 15 minutes, or until frothy.

2 Pour the milk into a large bowl. Add the remaining sugar, the butter or margarine, and salt.

3 Stir in the yeast mixture, then stir in the flour, 150g/5oz/1¼ cups at a time, until a stiff dough is obtained.

4 Transfer the dough to a floured surface. Knead the dough until it is smooth and elastic, then place it in a large greased bowl, cover with clear film (plastic wrap), and leave to rise in a warm place until doubled in volume, about 2–3 hours.

5 Grease two 23 x 13cm/9 x 5in loaf tins (pans). Knock back (punch down) the dough and divide in half.

6 Form into loaf shapes and place in the tins, seam down. Cover and leave to rise again until almost doubled in volume, about 45 minutes. Meanwhile, preheat the oven to 190°C/375°F/Gas 5.

7 Bake the loaves until firm and brown, about 45–50 minutes. Turn out and tap the base of a loaf: if it sounds hollow the loaf is done. If necessary, return to the oven and bake for a few minutes longer. (Turn the loaf upside down in the tin if the top is done but the base is not.) Turn out and cool on a wire rack.

Braided Loaf

It doesn't take much effort to turn an ordinary dough mix into this work of art.

Makes one loaf
15ml/1 tbsp active dried yeast
5ml/1 tsp honey
250ml/8fl oz/1 cup
  lukewarm milk
50g/2oz/¼ cup butter, melted
425g/15oz/3⅔ cups strong
  white bread flour
5ml/1 tsp salt
1 egg, lightly beaten
1 egg yolk, beaten with
  5ml/1 tsp milk, to glaze

1 Combine the yeast, honey, milk and butter in a small bowl. Stir and leave for 15 minutes to dissolve and for the yeast to become frothy.

2 In a large bowl, mix together the flour and salt. Make a central well in the flour, and add the yeast mixture and egg. With a wooden spoon, stir from the centre, gradually incorporating the flour into the liquid, to obtain a rough dough.

3 Transfer the dough to a floured surface and knead until smooth and elastic. This will take about 10 minutes.

4 Place in a clean bowl, cover with clear film (plastic wrap) and leave to rise in a warm place until doubled in volume, about 1½ hours.

5 Grease a baking sheet. Punch down (knock back) the dough and divide into three equal pieces.

6 Roll each piece into a long thin strip. Begin braiding with the centre strip, tucking in the ends neatly when you reach the end of the braid. Cover loosely with clear film and leave to rise in a warm place for 30 minutes.

7 Meanwhile, preheat the oven to 190°C/375°F/Gas 5. Brush the bread with the egg and milk glaze and bake until it is golden, about 40–45 minutes. Turn the loaf out on to a wire rack to cool.

White Energy 1796Kcal/7623kJ; Protein 50.6g; Carbohydrate 376.6g, of which sugars 33.7g; Fat 20.2g, of which saturates 10g; Cholesterol 41mg; Calcium 925mg; Fibre 14g; Sodium 193mg.
Braided Energy 2033Kcal/8584kJ; Protein 55g; Carbohydrate 348.4g, of which sugars 24.5g; Fat 56.4g, of which saturates 31.1g; Cholesterol 312mg; Calcium 933mg; Fibre 13.2g; Sodium 494mg.

Wholemeal Bread

A simple wholesome bread to be enjoyed by the entire family at any time.

**Makes one 23 x 13cm/
9 x 5in loaf**
525g/1lb 5oz/5¼ cups strong
  wholemeal (whole-wheat)
  bread flour
10ml/2 tsp salt
20ml/4 tsp active dried yeast
450ml/¾ pint/scant 2 cups
  lukewarm water
30ml/2 tbsp honey
30ml/2 tbsp oil
40g/1½oz wheatgerm
milk, to glaze

1 Warm the flour and salt in a bowl in the oven at its lowest setting for 10 minutes.

2 Meanwhile, combine the yeast with half of the water in a bowl and leave to dissolve and for the yeast to become frothy.

3 Make a central well in the flour. Pour in the yeast mixture, the remaining water, honey, oil and wheatgerm. Stir in the flour from the centre, incorporating it as you go, until smooth.

4 Grease a 23 x 13cm/9 x 5in loaf tin (pan). Knead the dough just enough to shape into a loaf. Put it in the tin and cover with clear film (plastic wrap). Leave in a warm place until the dough is about 2.5cm/1in higher than the tin rim, about 1 hour.

5 Preheat the oven to 200°C/400°F/Gas 6. Brush the loaf with milk, and bake until the base sounds hollow when tapped, about 35–40 minutes. Cool on a wire rack.

Cook's Tip
For all yeast recipes use strong bread flours and not plain (all-purpose) or self-raising (self-rising) flours. Strong bread flours have a high gluten content, which is important to allow the yeast to rise well. Breads made with strong flours are light and have an airy crumb. Soda breads or any other breads not made with yeast do not use strong flours, however.

Multigrain Bread

Try different flours, such as rye, cornmeal, buckwheat or barley to replace the wheatgerm and the soya flour used here.

**Makes two 21 x 12cm/
8½ x 4½in loaves**
15ml/1 tbsp active dried yeast
50ml/2fl oz/¼ cup
  lukewarm water
65g/2½oz/¾ cup rolled oats
475ml/16fl oz/2 cups milk
10ml/2 tsp salt
50ml/2fl oz/¼ cup oil
50g/2oz/¼ cup soft light
  brown sugar
30ml/2 tbsp honey
2 eggs, lightly beaten
25g/1oz wheatgerm
175g/6oz/1½ cups soya flour
350g/12oz/3 cups strong
  wholemeal (whole-wheat) flour
about 450g/1lb/4 cups strong
  white bread flour

1 Combine the yeast and water in a small bowl, stir, and leave for about 15 minutes to dissolve and for the yeast to become frothy. Place the oats in a large bowl. Boil the milk, then pour over the rolled oats. Stir in the salt, oil, sugar and honey. Leave until lukewarm.

2 Stir in the yeast mixture, eggs, wheatgerm, soya and wholemeal flours. Gradually stir in enough strong white bread flour to obtain a rough dough.

3 Transfer the dough to a floured surface and knead, adding flour if necessary, until smooth and elastic. This will take about 10 minutes. Return to a clean bowl, cover with clear film (plastic wrap) and leave to rise in a warm place until doubled in volume, about 2½ hours.

4 Grease two 21 x 12cm/8½ x 4½in loaf tins (pans). Knock back (punch down) the risen dough and knead briefly. Then divide the dough into quarters. Roll each quarter into a cylinder 4cm/1½in thick. Twist together two cylinders and place in a tin; repeat for the remaining cylinders. Cover with clear film and leave to rise until doubled in volume again, about 1 hour. Meanwhile, preheat the oven to 190°C/375°F/Gas 5.

5 Bake until the bases sound hollow when tapped lightly, about 45–50 minutes. Turn out and cool on a wire rack.

Wholemeal Energy 1997Kcal/8459kJ; Protein 77.4g; Carbohydrate 361g, of which sugars 25.1g; Fat 37.2g, of which saturates 4.7g; Cholesterol 0mg; Calcium 222mg; Fibre 53.5g; Sodium 19mg.
Multigrain Energy 2266Kcal/9595kJ; Protein 104.9g; Carbohydrate 389.3g, of which sugars 69.5g; Fat 43.1g, of which saturates 8g; Cholesterol 204mg; Calcium 944mg; Fibre 38.7g; Sodium 211mg.

Country Bread

A filling bread made with a mixture of wholemeal and white flour.

Makes two loaves

350g/12oz/3 cups strong
   wholemeal (whole-wheat)
   bread flour
350g/12oz/3 cups plain
   (all-purpose) flour
150g/5oz/1¼ cups strong white
   bread flour
20ml/4 tsp salt

50g/2oz/¼ cup butter,
   at room temperature
475ml/16fl oz/2 cups
   lukewarm milk

For the starter

15ml/1 tbsp active dried yeast
250ml/8fl oz/1 cup
   lukewarm water
150g/5oz/1¼ cups plain
   (all-purpose) flour
1.5ml/¼ tsp caster
   (superfine) sugar

1 To make the starter, mix the yeast, water, plain flour and sugar in a bowl. Cover and leave in a warm place for 2–3 hours.

2 Place the flours, salt and butter in a food processor and process until just blended, about 1–2 minutes.

3 Stir together the milk and starter, then slowly pour into the processor, with the motor running, until the mixture forms a dough. Knead the dough until smooth. This will take about 10 minutes.

4 Place in an ungreased bowl, cover with clear film (plastic wrap), and leave to rise in a warm place until doubled in size, about 1½ hours. Knock back (punch down) and then return to the bowl and leave until tripled in size, about 1½ hours.

5 Grease a baking sheet. Divide the dough in half. Cut off one-third of the dough from each half and shape all the pieces into balls. Top each large ball with a small ball and press the centre with the handle of a wooden spoon to secure. Cover with oiled clear film, slash the top, and leave the dough to rise once again.

6 Preheat the oven to 200°C/400°F/Gas 6. Dust the loaves with flour and bake until browned and the bases sound hollow when tapped, 45–50 minutes. Cool on a wire rack.

Oatmeal Bread

A healthy, rustic-looking bread made with rolled oats as well as flour.

Makes two loaves

475ml/16fl oz/2 cups milk
25g/1oz/2 tbsp butter
50g/2oz/¼ cup cup soft dark
   brown sugar

10ml/2 tsp salt
15ml/1 tbsp active dried yeast
50ml/2fl oz/¼ cup
   lukewarm water
400g/14oz/4 cups rolled oats
675–900g/1½–2lb/6–8 cups
   strong white bread flour

1 Put the milk in a small pan and bring to boiling point. Quickly remove from the heat and stir in the butter, brown sugar and salt. Leave the mixture to cool until lukewarm.

2 Combine the yeast and warm water in a large bowl and leave for about 15 minutes until frothy.

3 Stir in the milk mixture. Add 275g/10oz/3 cups of the rolled oats and enough flour to obtain a soft dough.

4 Transfer the dough to a floured surface and knead until smooth and elastic.

5 Place in a greased bowl, cover with clear film (plastic wrap) and leave until doubled in volume, about 2–3 hours.

6 Grease a large baking sheet. Transfer the dough to a lightly floured surface and divide in half. Shape into rounds.

7 Place on the baking sheet, cover with a dish towel or oiled clear film and leave to rise until doubled in volume, about 1 hour.

8 Preheat the oven to 200°C/400°F/Gas 6. Score the tops of the loaves and sprinkle with the remaining oats.

9 Bake until the bases sound hollow when tapped, about 45–50 minutes. Turn out on to wire racks to cool.

Country Energy 1760Kcal/7482kJ; Protein 60.9g; Carbohydrate 375.5g, of which sugars 19.7g; Fat 12.1g, of which saturates 3.7g; Cholesterol 14mg; Calcium 807mg; Fibre 25.8g; Sodium 2082mg.
Oatmeal Energy 2254Kcal/9556kJ; Protein 64.8g; Carbohydrate 445.2g, of which sugars 42.4g; Fat 36.1g, of which saturates 9.8g; Cholesterol 41mg; Calcium 883mg; Fibre 24.1g; Sodium 256mg.

Rye Bread

Rye bread is popular in Northern Europe and makes an excellent base for open sandwiches.

Makes 2 loaves, each serving 10

350g/12oz/3 cups strong wholemeal (whole-wheat) flour
225g/8oz/2 cups rye flour
115g/4oz/1 cup strong white bread flour
7.5ml/1½ tsp salt
1 sachet easy-blend (rapid-rise) dried yeast
30ml/2 tbsp caraway seeds
475ml/16fl oz/2 cups hand-hot water
30ml/2 tbsp molasses
30ml/2 tbsp sunflower oil

1 Grease a baking sheet. Put the flours in a bowl with the salt and yeast. Set aside 5ml/1 tsp of the caraway seeds and add the remainder to the bowl. Mix well, then make a well in the centre.

2 Add the water to the bowl with the molasses and oil. Stir from the centre outwards, gradually incorporating the flour and mixing to a soft dough, and adding a little extra water if necessary.

3 Turn the dough on to a floured surface and knead for 5 minutes until smooth and elastic. Divide the dough in half and shape into two 23cm/9in long oval loaves.

4 Flatten the loaves slightly and place them on the prepared baking sheet. Brush them with water and sprinkle with the remaining caraway seeds. Cover and leave in a warm place until doubled in size, about 1½ hours. Meanwhile, preheat the oven to 220°C/425°F/Gas 7.

5 Bake the loaves for 30 minutes, or until they sound hollow when tapped underneath. Allow to cool on a wire rack.

Cook's Tip
Using warm rather than cold liquid helps the yeast to start working, as it is a living organism that thrives in warm and moist conditions.

Caraway Rye Bread

To bring out the flavour of the caraway seeds, toast them lightly in the oven first, if you like.

Makes one loaf

200g/7oz/scant 1¾ cups rye flour
475ml/16fl oz/2 cups boiling water
120ml/4fl oz/½ cup black treacle (molasses)
65g/2½oz/5 tbsp butter, cut into pieces
15ml/1 tbsp salt
30ml/2 tbsp caraway seeds
15ml/1 tbsp active dried yeast
120ml/4fl oz/½ cup lukewarm water
about 850g/1lb 14oz/7½ cups strong white bread flour
semolina or flour, for dusting

1 Mix the rye flour, boiling water, treacle, butter, salt and caraway seeds in a large bowl. Leave to cool.

2 In another bowl, mix the yeast and lukewarm water and leave to dissolve and for the yeast to become frothy.

3 Stir into the rye flour mixture. Stir in just enough strong white bread flour to obtain a stiff dough. If it becomes too stiff to mix with the spoon, stir with your hands. Transfer to a floured surface and knead until the dough is no longer sticky and is smooth and shiny. This will take about 10 minutes.

4 Place in a greased bowl, cover with clear film (plastic wrap), and leave in a warm place until doubled in volume, about 1½ hours.

5 Knock back (punch down) the dough, cover, and leave to rise again for 30 minutes.

6 Preheat the oven to 180°C/350°F/Gas 4. Dust a baking sheet with semolina or flour.

7 Shape the dough into a ball. Place on the sheet and score several times across the top. Bake until the base sounds hollow when tapped, about 40 minutes. Cool on a wire rack.

Rye Energy 127Kcal/540kJ; Protein 3.7g; Carbohydrate 25.7g, of which sugars 1.7g; Fat 1.8g, of which saturates 0.2g; Cholesterol 0mg; Calcium 19mg; Fibre 3.1g; Sodium 5mg.
Caraway Energy 4323Kcal/18332kJ; Protein 98.1g; Carbohydrate 893.3g, of which sugars 93.3g; Fat 64.4g, of which saturates 33.6g; Cholesterol 128mg; Calcium 1926mg; Fibre 49.8g; Sodium 6502mg.

Austrian Three-grain Bread

A mixture of grains gives this close-textured bread a delightful nutty flavour.

Makes 1 large loaf
225g/8oz/2 cups strong white
  bread flour
7.5ml/1½ tsp salt
225g/8oz/2 cups malted
  brown flour
225g/8oz/2 cups rye flour
75g/3oz/½ cup medium oatmeal
1 sachet easy-blend (rapid-rise)
  dried yeast
45ml/3 tbsp sunflower seeds
30ml/2 tbsp linseeds
475ml/16fl oz/2 cups
  hand-hot water
30ml/2 tbsp malt extract

1 Sift the plain flour and salt into a mixing bowl and add the remaining flours, oatmeal, yeast and sunflower seeds. Set aside 5ml/1 tsp of the linseeds and add the rest to the flour mixture. Make a well in the centre.

2 Add the water to the bowl with the malt extract. Gradually incorporate the flour and mix to a soft dough, adding extra water if necessary.

3 Flour a baking sheet. Turn the dough on to a floured surface and knead for 5 minutes, or until smooth and elastic.

4 Divide it in half. Roll each half into a sausage about 30cm/12in in length. Twist the two pieces together, dampen each end and press together firmly.

5 Lift the loaf on to the prepared baking sheet. Brush with water, sprinkle with the remaining linseeds and cover loosely with clear film (plastic wrap) (balloon it to trap the air inside). Leave in a warm place until doubled in size, about 1½ hours. Meanwhile, preheat the oven to 220°C/425°F/Gas 7.

6 Bake the bread for 10 minutes, then lower the oven temperature to 200°C/400°F/Gas 6 and cook for 20 minutes more, or until the loaf sounds hollow when tapped underneath.

7 Transfer the cooked loaf to a wire rack to cool completely.

Sesame Seed Bread

This delicious bread with its nutty flavour breaks into individual rolls. It is ideal for entertaining.

Makes one 23cm/9in loaf
10ml/2 tsp active dried yeast
300ml/½ pint/1¼ cups
  lukewarm water
200g/7oz/1¾ cups strong white
  bread flour
200g/7oz/scant 1¾ cups strong
  wholemeal (whole-wheat)
  bread flour
10ml/2 tsp salt
65g/2½oz/5 tbsp toasted
  sesame seeds
milk, to glaze
30ml/2 tbsp sesame seeds,
  for sprinkling

1 Combine the yeast and 75ml/5 tbsp of the water in a small bowl and leave to dissolve and for the yeast to become frothy.

2 Mix the flours and salt in a large bowl. Make a central well in the flour and pour in the yeast and water. Stir from the centre to obtain a rough dough.

3 Transfer to a floured surface and knead until smooth and elastic. This will take about 10 minutes. Return to the bowl and cover with clear film (plastic wrap). Leave in a warm place until the dough has doubled in size, about 1½–2 hours.

4 Grease a 23cm/9in round cake tin (pan). Knock back (punch down) the dough and knead in the sesame seeds.

5 Divide the dough into 16 balls and place in the tin. Cover with clear film (plastic wrap) and leave in a warm place until risen above the rim, about 1½ hours.

6 Preheat the oven to 220°C/425°F/Gas 7. Brush the loaf with milk and sprinkle with the sesame seeds. Bake for 15 minutes. Lower the heat to 190°C/375°F/Gas 5 and bake until the base sounds hollow when tapped, about 30 minutes. Turn the loaf out on a wire rack and leave to cool before breaking into individual rolls and serving.

Three-grain Energy 3076Kcal/13051kJ; Protein 92.2g; Carbohydrate 592g, of which sugars 32.2g; Fat 54.1g, of which saturates 5.2g; Cholesterol 0mg; Calcium 808mg; Fibre 57.3g; Sodium 126mg
Sesame Energy 1691Kcal/7142kJ; Protein 56g; Carbohydrate 283.8g, of which sugars 7.5g; Fat 44.7g, of which saturates 6.4g; Cholesterol 0mg; Calcium 793mg; Fibre 29.3g; Sodium 3955mg.

Malt Loaf

This is a rich and sticky loaf. If it lasts long enough to go stale, try toasting it for a delicious teatime treat.

Serves 8
350g/12oz/3 cups strong white bread flour
1.5ml/¼ tsp salt
5ml/1 tsp easy-blend (rapid-rise) dried yeast
a pinch of caster (superfine) sugar
30ml/2 tbsp soft light brown sugar
175g/6oz/1 cup sultanas (golden raisins)
150ml/¼ pint/⅔ cup hand-hot skimmed milk
15ml/1 tbsp sunflower oil
45ml/3 tbsp malt extract

To glaze
30ml/2 tbsp caster (superfine) sugar
30ml/2 tbsp water

1 Sift the flour and salt into a mixing bowl, and stir in the yeast, the pinch of sugar, brown sugar and sultanas.

2 Make a well in the centre of the dry ingredients. Add the hot milk with the oil and malt extract. Stir from the centre outwards, gradually incorporating the flour and mixing to a soft dough, and adding a little extra milk if necessary.

3 Turn on to a floured surface and knead for about 5 minutes until smooth and elastic. Lightly oil a 450g/1lb loaf tin (pan).

4 Shape the dough and place it in the prepared tin. Cover with a damp dish cloth or some oiled clear film (plastic wrap) and leave in a warm place until doubled in size, about 1½ hours. Meanwhile, preheat the oven to 190°C/375°F/Gas 5.

5 Bake the loaf for 30–35 minutes, or until it sounds hollow when tapped underneath.

6 While the loaf is baking, make the glaze by dissolving the sugar in the water in a small pan. Bring to the boil, stirring, then lower the heat and simmer for 1 minute.

7 Brush the loaf while hot, then transfer it to a wire rack to cool.

Prune Bread

Moist inside, with a crusty walnut topping.

Makes 1 loaf
225g/8oz/1 cup dried prunes
15ml/1 tbsp active dried yeast
75g/3oz/⅔ cup strong wholemeal (whole-wheat) bread flour
400–425g/14–15oz/3½–3⅔ cups strong white bread flour
2.5ml/½ tsp bicarbonate of soda (baking soda)
5ml/1 tsp salt
5ml/1 tsp pepper
25g/1oz/2 tbsp butter, at room temperature
175ml/6fl oz/¾ cup buttermilk
50g/2oz/½ cup walnuts, chopped
milk, for glazing

1 Simmer the prunes in water to cover until soft, about 20 minutes, or soak overnight. Drain, reserving 60ml/4 tbsp of the soaking liquid. Pit and chop the prunes.

2 Combine the yeast and the reserved prune liquid, stir and leave for 15 minutes to dissolve and so that the yeast becomes frothy.

3 In a large bowl, stir together the wholemeal and white flours, bicarbonate of soda, salt and pepper. Make a well in the centre. Add the prunes, butter and buttermilk. Pour in the yeast mixture. With a wooden spoon, stir from the centre, folding in more flour with each turn, to obtain a rough dough.

4 Transfer to a floured surface and knead until smooth and elastic. This will take about 10 minutes. Return to the bowl, cover with clear film (plastic wrap) and leave to rise in a warm place until doubled in volume, about 1½ hours. Grease a baking sheet.

5 Knock back (punch down) the dough with your fist, then knead in the walnuts. Shape the dough into a long, cylindrical loaf. Place on the baking sheet, cover loosely, and leave to rise in a warm place for 45 minutes. Preheat the oven to 220°C/425°F/Gas 7. With a sharp knife, score the top. Brush with milk and bake for 15 minutes. Lower to 190°C/375°F/Gas 5 and bake for 35 minutes more, or until the base sounds hollow. Cool.

Malt Energy 259Kcal/1101kJ; Protein 5.4g; Carbohydrate 58.4g, of which sugars 25g; Fat 2.1g, of which saturates 0.3g; Cholesterol 1mg; Calcium 101mg; Fibre 1.8g; Sodium 29mg.
Prune Energy 2520Kcal/10639kJ; Protein 65.6g; Carbohydrate 433.3g, of which sugars 93.2g; Fat 70.4g, of which saturates 19.9g; Cholesterol 70mg; Calcium 915mg; Fibre 33.4g; Sodium 2266mg.

Raisin Bread

Enjoy this with savoury or sweet dishes.

Makes 2 loaves

15ml/1 tbsp active dried yeast
450ml/¾ pint/1¾ cups
  lukewarm milk
150g/5oz/1 cup raisins
65g/2½oz/½ cup currants
15ml/1 tbsp sherry or brandy
2.5ml/½ tsp freshly grated nutmeg
grated rind of 1 large orange
60g/2¼oz/generous ¼ cup
  caster (superfine) sugar
15ml/1 tbsp salt
115g/4oz/½ cup butter, melted
700–850g/1lb 8oz–1lb 14oz/
  6–7½ cups strong white
  bread flour
1 egg beaten with 15ml/1 tbsp
  single (light) cream, to glaze

1 Stir the yeast with 120ml/4fl oz/½ cup of the milk and leave to stand for 15 minutes to dissolve. Mix the raisins, currants, sherry or brandy, nutmeg and orange rind together.

2 In another bowl, mix the remaining milk, sugar, salt and half the butter. Add the yeast mixture. With a wooden spoon, stir in half the flour, 150g/5oz at a time, until blended. Add the remaining flour as needed to form a stiff dough. Transfer to a floured surface and knead until smooth and elastic. This will take about 10 minutes. Place in a greased bowl, cover and leave to rise in a warm place until doubled in volume, about 2½ hours.

3 Knock back (punch down) the dough, return to the bowl, cover and leave to rise in a warm place for 30 minutes. Grease two 21 x 11cm/8½ x 4½in loaf tins (pans). Divide the dough in half and roll each half into a 50 x 18cm/20 x 7in rectangle.

4 Brush the rectangles with the remaining melted butter. Sprinkle over the raisin mixture, then roll up tightly, tucking in the ends slightly as you roll. Place in the prepared tins, cover, and leave to rise until almost doubled in volume, about 1 hour. Preheat the oven to 200°C/400°F/Gas 6. Brush the loaves with the egg glaze. Bake for 20 minutes. Lower to 180°C/350°F/Gas 4 and bake until golden, 25–30 minutes more. Cool on racks.

Coconut Bread

This bread is delicious served with a cup of hot chocolate or a glass of fruit punch.

Makes 1 loaf

175g/6oz/¾ cup butter
115g/4oz/½ cup demerara
  (raw) sugar
225g/8oz/2 cups self-raising
  (self-rising) flour
200g/7oz/1¾ cups plain
  (all-purpose) flour
115g/4oz/1⅓ cups desiccated
  (dry unsweetened
  shredded) coconut
5ml/1 tsp mixed (apple pie) spice
10ml/2 tsp vanilla extract
15ml/1 tbsp rum
2 eggs
about 150ml/¼ pint/⅔ cup milk
15ml/1 tbsp caster (superfine)
  sugar, blended with 30ml/
  2 tbsp water, to glaze

1 Preheat the oven to 180°C/350°F/Gas 4. Grease two 450g/1lb loaf tins (pans).

2 Place the butter and sugar in a large bowl and sift in the flour. Rub the ingredients together using your fingertips or a pastry cutter until the mixture resembles fine breadcrumbs.

3 Add the coconut, mixed spice, vanilla extract, rum, eggs and milk to the butter and sugar mixture, and mix together well with your hands. If you think that the mixture is too dry, moisten with milk. Turn out on to a floured board and knead until firm and pliable.

4 Halve the mixture and place in the prepared loaf tins. Glaze with sugared water and bake for 1 hour, or until the loaves are cooked. Test with a skewer; the loaves are ready when the skewer comes out clean.

> **Cook's Tips**
> This coconut bread is a cross between a teabread and a yeast bread. It is quick to make and needs no rising time. It is also delicious spread with butter or a fruit preserve.

Raisin Energy 2187Kcal/9239kJ; Protein 46.5g; Carbohydrate 388.3g, of which sugars 121.6g; Fat 58.9g, of which saturates 33.9g; Cholesterol 231mg; Calcium 866mg; Fibre 13g; Sodium 3490mg.
Coconut Energy 4148Kcal/17357kJ; Protein 65.6g; Carbohydrate 465.9g, of which sugars 142g; Fat 234.3g, of which saturates 158.1g; Cholesterol 763mg; Calcium 951mg; Fibre 28.9g; Sodium 1317mg.

Danish Wreath

This is a delicious sweet loaf for tea.

Serves 10–12
5ml/1 tsp active dried yeast
175ml/6fl oz/¾ cup milk
50g/2oz/½ cup caster
  (superfine) sugar
450g/1lb/4 cups strong white
  bread flour
2.5ml/½ tsp salt
2.5ml/½ tsp vanilla extract
1 egg, beaten

225g/8oz/1 cup unsalted
  (sweet) butter
1 egg yolk beaten with 10ml/
  2 tsp water
115g/4oz/1 cup icing
  (confectioners') sugar

For the filling
200g/7oz/scant 1 cup soft dark
  brown sugar
5ml/1 tsp ground cinnamon
50g/2oz/⅓ cup walnuts or
  pecans, plus extra to decorate

1 Mix the yeast, milk and 2.5ml/½ tsp of the sugar in a small bowl. Leave for 15 minutes to dissolve. Mix the flour, sugar and salt. Make a well and add the yeast, vanilla and egg to make a rough dough. Knead until smooth, wrap in clear film (plastic wrap) and chill. Roll the butter between sheets of baking parchment to form two 15 x 10cm/6 x 4in rectangles. Roll the dough to a 30 x 20cm/12 x 8in rectangle. Place one butter rectangle in the centre. Fold the bottom third of dough over and seal the edge. Place the other butter rectangle on top and cover with the top third of the dough.

2 Roll the dough into a 30 x 20cm/12 x 8in rectangle. Fold into thirds. Wrap and chill for 30 minutes. Repeat twice more. After the third fold, chill for 1–2 hours. Grease a baking sheet. Roll out the dough to a 62 x 15cm/25 x 6in strip. Mix the filling ingredients and spread over, leaving a 1cm/½in edge. Roll the dough into a cylinder, place on the baking sheet in a circle and seal the edges. Cover and leave to rise for 45 minutes.

3 Preheat the oven to 200°C/400°F/Gas 6. Slash the top every 5cm/2in, cutting 1cm/½in deep. Brush with the egg and milk. Bake for 35–40 minutes, or until golden. Cool. To serve, mix the icing sugar with a little water, then drizzle over the wreath. Sprinkle with some nuts.

Kugelhopf

A traditional round moulded bread from Germany, flavoured with Kirsch or brandy.

Makes one ring loaf
100g/3¾oz/¾ cup raisins
15ml/1 tbsp Kirsch or brandy
15ml/1 tbsp easy-blend
  (rapid-rise) dried yeast
120ml/4fl oz/½ cup lukewarm water
115g/4oz/½ cup unsalted (sweet)
  butter, at room temperature
90g/3½oz/½ cup caster
  (superfine) sugar

3 eggs, at room temperature
grated rind of 1 lemon
5ml/1 tsp salt
2.5ml/½ tsp vanilla extract
425g/15oz/3⅔ cups strong white
  bread flour
120ml/4fl oz/½ cup milk
25g/1oz/¼ cup flaked
  (sliced) almonds
80g/3¼oz/generous ½ cup whole
  blanched almonds, chopped
icing (confectioners') sugar,
  for dusting

1 In a bowl, combine the raisins and Kirsch or brandy. Combine the yeast and water, stir and leave for 15 minutes until the yeast becomes frothy.

2 Cream the butter and sugar until thick and fluffy. Beat in the eggs, one at a time. Add the lemon rind, salt and vanilla extract. Stir in the yeast mixture.

3 Add the flour, alternating with the milk, until well blended. Cover and leave to rise in a warm place until doubled in volume, about 2 hours.

4 Grease a 2.75 litre/4½ pint/11¼ cup kugelhopf mould, then sprinkle the flaked almonds evenly over the base. Work the raisins and chopped almonds into the dough, then spoon into the mould.

5 Cover with clear film (plastic wrap), and leave to rise in a warm place until the dough almost reaches the top of the tin, about 1 hour.

6 Preheat the oven to 180°C/350°F/Gas 4. Bake until golden brown, about 45 minutes. If the top browns too quickly, cover with foil. Cool in the tin for 15 minutes, then turn out on to a wire rack. Dust the top lightly with icing sugar.

Danish Energy 361Kcal/1520kJ; Protein 5.4g; Carbohydrate 61.8g, of which sugars 33.2g; Fat 11.9g, of which saturates 5.6g; Cholesterol 37mg; Calcium 94mg; Fibre 1.3g; Sodium 73mg.
Kugelhopf Energy 3828Kcal/16069kJ; Protein 84.1g; Carbohydrate 501.5g, of which sugars 174.8g; Fat 175.7g, of which saturates 70.1g; Cholesterol 816mg; Calcium 1047mg; Fibre 22.9g; Sodium 1000mg.

Individual Brioches

These buttery rolls with their distinctive topknots are delicious served with jam at coffee time.

Makes 8
15ml/1 tbsp active dried yeast
15ml/1 tbsp caster
  (superfine) sugar

30ml/2 tbsp warm milk
2 eggs
about 200g/7oz/1¾ cups strong
  white bread flour
2.5ml/½ tsp salt
75g/3oz/6 tbsp butter, cut into six
  pieces, at room temperature
1 egg yolk, beaten with 10ml/
  2 tsp water, to glaze

1 Butter eight individual brioche tins (pans) or muffin cups. Put the yeast and sugar in a small bowl, add the milk and stir until dissolved. Leave the yeast mixture to stand for 5 minutes so that the yeast begins to work, then beat in the eggs.

2 Put the flour and salt into a food processor, then, with the machine running, slowly pour in the yeast mixture. Scrape down the sides and process until the dough forms a ball.

3 Add the butter and pulse to blend. Alternatively, use your hand to incorporate the flour into the liquid.

4 Transfer the dough to a lightly buttered bowl and cover with a clean dish towel or clear film (plastic wrap). Leave to rise in a warm place for about 1 hour, then knock back (punch down) the dough.

5 Shape three-quarters of the dough into eight balls and place them into the prepared tins. Shape the last quarter into eight small balls, make a depression in the top of each large ball and set a small ball into it.

6 Leave the brioches to rise in a warm place for 30 minutes. Preheat the oven to 200°C/400°F/Gas 6.

7 Brush the brioches with the egg glaze. Bake for about 15–18 minutes, or until golden brown. Transfer to a wire rack and leave to cool completely.

Dinner Milk Rolls

Making bread especially for your dinner guests is not only a wonderful gesture, it is also quite easy to do.

Makes 12–16
750g/1lb 10oz/6½ cups strong
  white bread flour
10ml/2 tsp salt

25g/1oz/2 tbsp butter
1 sachet easy-blend (rapid-rise)
  dried yeast
450ml/¾ pint/1¾ cups
  lukewarm milk
cold milk, to glaze
poppy, sesame and sunflower
  seeds, or sea salt flakes,
  for sprinkling

1 Sift together the flour and salt into a large bowl. Rub in the butter, then stir in the yeast. Mix to a firm dough with the lukewarm milk (you may not need it all).

2 Knead the dough for 5 minutes on a lightly floured surface, then return it to the bowl, cover with a clean dish towel or clear film (plastic wrap), and leave to rise until doubled in volume, about 1½ hours.

3 Grease a baking sheet. Knock back (punch down) the dough and knead again, then divide into 12–16 pieces and form into shapes of your choice.

4 You can make mini-cottage loaves by setting a small ball on to a larger one and pressing a finger in the top; use three lengths of dough to make a braid; one long length can be made into a simple knot; or make three cuts in a round roll for an easier decoration.

5 Place the rolls or mini-cottage loaves on the baking sheet, glaze the tops with milk, and sprinkle over your chosen seeds or sea salt flakes.

6 Leave in a warm place to start rising again. Meanwhile, preheat the oven to 230°C/450°F/Gas 8. Bake the rolls for 12 minutes, or until golden brown and cooked. Turn out on to a wire rack. and leave to cool. (Eat the rolls the same day as they will not keep well.)

Brioches Energy 183Kcal/765kJ; Protein 4.1g; Carbohydrate 21.6g, of which sugars 2.6g; Fat 9.5g, of which saturates 5.4g; Cholesterol 68mg; Calcium 49mg; Fibre 0.8g; Sodium 77mg.
Rolls Energy 247Kcal/1047kJ; Protein 7.2g; Carbohydrate 50.4g, of which sugars 2.8g; Fat 3.2g, of which saturates 1.6g; Cholesterol 7mg; Calcium 136mg; Fibre 1.9g; Sodium 359mg.

Pleated Rolls

Fancy home-made rolls show that every care has been taken to ensure a welcoming dinner party.

Makes 48 rolls

15ml/1 tbsp active dried yeast
475ml/16fl oz/2 cups
  lukewarm milk
115g/4oz/½ cup margarine
50g/2oz/¼ cup caster
  (superfine) sugar
10ml/2 tsp salt
2 eggs
985g–1.2kg/2lb 3oz–2½lb/
  scant 7–8 cups strong white
  bread flour
50g/2oz/¼ cup butter

1 Combine the yeast and 120ml/4fl oz/½ cup milk in a large bowl. Stir and leave for 15 minutes. Scald the remaining milk, leave to cool for 5 minutes, then beat in the margarine, sugar, salt and eggs. Leave until lukewarm.

2 Pour the milk mixture into the yeast mixture. Stir in half the flour with a wooden spoon. Add the remaining flour, 150g/5oz/ 1¼ cups at a time, to obtain a rough dough.

3 Transfer the dough to a floured surface and knead until elastic. This will take about 10 minutes. Place in a clean bowl, cover with clear film (plastic wrap) and leave to rise in a warm place until doubled in volume. Melt the butter and set aside.

4 Lightly grease two baking sheets. Knock back (punch down) the dough and divide into four equal pieces. Roll each piece into a 30 x 20cm/12 x 8in rectangle, about 5mm/¼in thick. Cut each of the rectangles into four long strips, then cut each strip into three 10 x 5cm/4 x 2in rectangles.

5 Brush each rectangle with the melted butter, then fold the rectangles in half, so that the top extends about 1cm/½in over the bottom. Place the rectangles slightly overlapping on the baking sheet, with the longer sides facing up.

6 Cover and chill for 30 minutes. Preheat the oven to 180°C/ 350°F/Gas 4. Bake until golden, 18–20 minutes. Cool slightly before serving.

Clover Leaf Rolls

These rolls are delightful for a dinner party. For a witty touch, make one "lucky four-leaf clover" in the batch.

Makes 24

300ml/½ pint/1¼ cups milk
30ml/2 tbsp caster
  (superfine) sugar
50g/2oz/¼ cup butter,
  at room temperature
10ml/2 tsp active dried yeast
1 egg
10ml/2 tsp salt
450–500g/1–1¼lb/4–5 cups
  strong white bread flour
melted butter, to glaze

1 Heat the milk to lukewarm in a small pan, pour into a large bowl and stir in the sugar, butter and yeast. Leave for 15 minutes to dissolve and for the yeast to become frothy.

2 Stir the egg and salt into the yeast mixture. Gradually stir in 475g/1lb 2oz/4½ cups of the flour, and then add just enough extra flour to obtain a rough dough.

3 Knead the dough on a lightly floured surface until smooth. This will take about 10 minutes.

4 Place the dough in a greased bowl, cover with clear film (plastic wrap) and leave in a warm place until doubled in size, about 1½ hours.

5 Grease two 12-cup bun trays. Knock back (punch down) the dough, and divide to make 72 equal-size balls.

6 Place three balls, in one layer, in each bun cup. Cover the trays loosely with a clean dish towel and leave to rise in a warm place, until doubled in size, about 1½ hours.

7 Meanwhile, preheat the oven to 200°C/400°F/Gas 6. Brush the rolls with the melted butter glaze.

8 Bake the rolls for about 20 minutes, or until they are lightly browned. Carefully turn out on to a wire rack and allow to cool slightly before serving.

Wholemeal Rolls

To add interest, make these individual rolls into different shapes if you wish.

Makes 12
15ml/2 tbsp active dried yeast
50ml/2fl oz/¼ cup
  lukewarm water
5ml/1 tsp caster (superfine) sugar
175ml/6fl oz/¾ cup
  lukewarm buttermilk
1.5ml/¼ tsp bicarbonate of soda
  (baking soda)
5ml/1 tsp salt
40g/1½oz/3 tbsp butter,
  at room temperature
200g/7oz/scant 1¾ cups strong
  wholemeal (whole-wheat)
  bread flour
150g/5oz/1¼ cups plain
  (all-purpose) flour
1 beaten egg, to glaze

1 In a large bowl, combine the yeast, water and sugar. Stir, and leave for 15 minutes to dissolve and for the yeast to become frothy.

2 Add the buttermilk, bicarbonate of soda, salt and butter, and stir to blend. Stir in the strong wholemeal bread flour. Add just enough of the plain flour to obtain a rough dough.

3 Knead on a floured surface until smooth. This will take about 10 minutes. Divide into three equal parts. Roll each into a cylinder, then cut into four pieces.

4 Grease a baking sheet. Form the pieces into torpedo shapes, place on the baking sheet, cover with a clean dish towel and leave in a warm place until doubled in size, about 1 hour.

5 Preheat the oven to 200°C/400°F/Gas 6. Brush the rolls with egg. Bake until firm, about 15–20 minutes. Cool on a wire rack.

> **Cook's Tip**
> Kneading is the most important part of breadmaking, as it develops the dough and helps it to rise. You can be as rough as you like: make the dough into a ball and then press down and push it away from you with one hand, so that it stretches. Repeat until the dough is elastic.

Granary Baps

These baps make excellent picnic fare and are also good buns for hamburgers.

Makes 8
oil, for greasing
450g/1lb/4 cups malted
  brown flour
5ml/1 tsp salt
10ml/2 tsp easy-blend (rapid-rise)
  dried yeast
15ml/1 tbsp malt extract
300ml/½ pint/1¼ cups
  hand-hot water
15ml/1 tbsp rolled oats

1 Lightly oil a large baking sheet. Put the malted flour, salt and yeast in a large bowl and make a well in the centre. Dissolve the malt extract in the water and add it to the well.

2 Stir from the centre outwards, gradually incorporating the flour and mixing to a soft dough.

3 Turn the dough on to a floured surface and knead for 5 minutes, or until smooth and elastic. Divide the dough into eight pieces.

4 Shape into balls and flatten with the palm of your hand to make 10cm/4in rounds.

5 Place the rounds on the prepared baking sheet, cover loosely with oiled clear film (plastic wrap) (ballooning it to trap the air inside) and leave in a warm place until the baps have doubled in size. Preheat the oven to 220°C/425°F/Gas 7.

6 Brush the baps with water, sprinkle with the oats and bake for 20–25 minutes, or until they sound hollow when tapped underneath. Cool on a wire rack.

> **Variation**
> To make a large loaf, shape the dough into a round, flatten it slightly and bake for 30–40 minutes. Test by tapping the base of the loaf – if it sounds hollow, it is cooked.

Wholemeal Energy 127Kcal/538kJ; Protein 3.8g; Carbohydrate 21.5g, of which sugars 1.7g; Fat 3.5g, of which saturates 2g; Cholesterol 8mg; Calcium 42mg; Fibre 1.9g; Sodium 27mg.
Granary Energy 195Kcal/834kJ; Protein 7.3g; Carbohydrate 41.4g, of which sugars 2.4g; Fat 1.3g, of which saturates 0.2g; Cholesterol 0mg; Calcium 75mg; Fibre 3.7g; Sodium 254mg.

Wholemeal Herb Triangles

These make a good lunchtime snack when stuffed with ham and salad and also taste good when served with soup.

Makes 8

225g/8oz/2 cups strong wholemeal (whole-wheat) bread flour
115g/4oz/1 cup strong white bread flour
5ml/1 tsp salt
2.5ml/½ tsp bicarbonate of soda (baking soda)
5ml/1 tsp cream of tartar
2.5ml/½ tsp chilli powder
50g/2oz/¼ cup soft margarine
250ml/8fl oz/1 cup skimmed milk
60ml/4 tbsp chopped mixed fresh herbs
15ml/1 tbsp sesame seeds

1 Preheat the oven to 220°C/425°F/Gas 7. Lightly flour a baking sheet.

2 Put the wholemeal flour in a large bowl. Sift in the strong white bread flour, the salt, bicarbonate of soda, cream of tartar and the chilli powder, then rub in the margarine.

3 Add the milk and herbs and mix quickly to a soft dough. Turn on to a lightly floured surface. Knead only very briefly or the dough will become tough.

4 Roll out to a 23cm/9in circle and place on the prepared baking sheet. Brush lightly with water and sprinkle with the sesame seeds.

5 Cut the dough round into 8 wedges, separate slightly and bake for 15–20 minutes. Transfer the triangles to a wire rack to cool. Serve warm or cold.

> **Variation**
> Sun-dried Tomato Triangles: replace the mixed herbs with 30ml/2 tbsp chopped, drained sun-dried tomatoes in oil, and add 15ml/1 tbsp mild paprika, 15ml/1 tbsp chopped fresh parsley and 15ml/1 tbsp chopped fresh marjoram.

Poppy Seed Knots

The poppy seeds look attractive and add a slightly nutty flavour to these rolls.

Makes 12

300ml/½ pint/1¼ cups lukewarm milk
50g/2oz/¼ cup butter, at room temperature
5ml/1 tsp caster (superfine) sugar
10ml/2 tsp active dried yeast
1 egg yolk
10ml/2 tsp salt
500–575g/1¼lb–1lb 6oz/ 5–5½ cups strong white bread flour
1 egg beaten with 10ml/2 tsp water, to glaze
poppy seeds, for sprinkling

1 In a large bowl, stir together the milk, butter, sugar and yeast. Leave for 15 minutes to dissolve and for the yeast to become frothy.

2 Stir in the egg yolk, salt and 275g/10oz/2½ cups of the flour. Add half the remaining flour and stir to obtain a soft dough.

3 Transfer the dough to a floured surface and knead, adding flour if necessary, until smooth and elastic. This will take about 10 minutes.

4 Place in a bowl, cover with clear film (plastic wrap) and leave in a warm place until the dough doubles in volume, about 1½–2 hours.

5 Grease a baking sheet. Knock back (punch down) the dough with your fist and cut into 12 pieces the size of golf balls.

6 Roll each piece into a rope, twist to form a knot and place 2.5cm/1in apart on the prepared baking sheet. Cover loosely and leave to rise in a warm place until doubled in volume, about 1–1½ hours.

7 Meanwhile, preheat the oven to 180°C/350°F/Gas 4. Brush the knots with the egg glaze and sprinkle over the poppy seeds. Bake until the tops are lightly browned, about 30 minutes. Cool slightly on a wire rack before serving.

Triangles Energy 204Kcal/858kJ; Protein 6.3g; Carbohydrate 30.6g, of which sugars 2.3g; Fat 7.1g, of which saturates 0.3g; Cholesterol 1mg; Calcium 82mg; Fibre 3.1g; Sodium 65mg.
Knots Energy 191Kcal/807kJ; Protein 5g; Carbohydrate 33.9g, of which sugars 2.2g; Fat 4.9g, of which saturates 2.7g; Cholesterol 27mg; Calcium 91mg; Fibre 1.3g; Sodium 366mg.

Poppy Seed Rolls

Pile these soft rolls in a basket and serve them for breakfast or with dinner.

Makes 12
oil, for greasing
450g/1lb/4 cups strong white
 bread flour
5ml/1 tsp salt

5ml/1 tsp easy-blend (rapid-rise)
 dried yeast
300ml/½ pint/1¼ cups hand-hot
 skimmed milk
1 egg, beaten

For the topping
1 egg, beaten
poppy seeds

1 Lightly grease two baking sheets with oil. Sift the flour and salt into a mixing bowl.

2 Add the yeast. Make a well in the centre and pour in the milk and the egg. Stir from the centre outwards, gradually incorporating the flour and mixing to a soft dough.

3 Turn the dough on to a floured surface and knead for 5 minutes, or until smooth and elastic. Cut into 12 pieces and shape into rolls (make a variety of shapes or just simple round rolls if you prefer).

4 Place the rolls on the prepared baking sheets, cover loosely with clear film (plastic wrap), ballooning it to trap the air inside, and leave in a warm place until the rolls have doubled in size, about 1½ hours. Meanwhile, preheat the oven to 220°C/425°F/Gas 7.

5 Glaze the rolls with beaten egg, sprinkle with poppy seeds and bake for 12–15 minutes, or until golden brown. Transfer to a wire rack to cool completely.

> **Variations**
> Vary the toppings. Linseed, sesame and caraway seeds all look good; try adding caraway seeds to the dough, too, for extra crunch and flavour.

French Bread

For truly authentic bread you should use flour grown and milled in France.

Makes 2 loaves
15ml/1 tbsp active dried yeast
475ml/16fl oz/2 cups
 lukewarm water

15ml/1 tbsp salt
850–900g/1lb 14oz–2lb/
 7½–8 cups strong white
 bread flour
semolina or flour,
 for sprinkling

1 In a large bowl, combine the yeast and water, stir, and leave for 15 minutes for the yeast to dissolve and become frothy. Stir in the salt.

2 Add the flour, 150g/5oz/1¼ cups at a time, to obtain a smooth dough. Knead for 5 minutes.

3 Shape into a ball, place in a greased bowl and cover with clear film (plastic wrap). Leave to rise in a warm place until doubled in size, about 2–4 hours.

4 Knock back (punch down) the dough. On a lightly floured surface, shape the dough into two long loaves. Place on a baking sheet sprinkled with semolina or flour and leave to rise for 5 minutes.

5 Score the tops of the loaves diagonally with a sharp knife. Brush with water and place in a cold oven. Place an ovenproof pan of boiling water on the base of the oven and set the oven to 200°C/400°F/Gas 6. Bake the loaves until crusty and golden, about 40 minutes. Cool on a wire rack.

> **Cook's Tip**
> A pan of boiling water placed in the oven will ensure that you will get the traditional crusty top for your French bread. Bake the loaves at the top of the oven and use proper French bread tins (pans) if you can, as these keep the loaves in shape and are perforated to aid cooking.

Rolls Energy 142Kcal/603kJ; Protein 4.9g; Carbohydrate 30.2g, of which sugars 1.7g; Fat 1g, of which saturates 0.2g; Cholesterol 17mg; Calcium 85mg; Fibre 1.2g; Sodium 18mg.
Bread Energy 1559Kcal/6626kJ; Protein 48.1g; Carbohydrate 341.4g, of which sugars 17.6g; Fat 9.6g, of which saturates 3.4g; Cholesterol 14mg; Calcium 881mg; Fibre 13.2g; Sodium 3063mg.

Breadsticks

If you prefer, use other
seeds, such as poppy seeds,
in these sticks.

Makes 18–20
15ml/1 tbsp active dried yeast
300ml/½ pint/1¼ cups
   lukewarm water
425g/15oz/3⅔ cups strong white
   bread flour

10ml/2 tsp salt
5ml/1 tsp caster (superfine) sugar
30ml/2 tbsp olive oil
1 egg, beaten, to glaze
150g/5oz/10 tbsp sesame
   seeds, toasted
coarse salt, for sprinkling

1 Combine the yeast and water in a small bowl, stir and leave for
about 15 minutes for the yeast to dissolve and become frothy.

2 Place the flour, salt, sugar and olive oil in a food processor.
With the motor running, slowly pour in the yeast mixture and
process until the dough forms a ball. Alternatively, use your hand
to incorporate the liquid into the flour.

3 Knead until smooth. This will take about 10 minutes. Place in a
bowl, cover with clear film (plastic wrap) and leave to rise in a
warm place for 45 minutes. Grease two baking sheets.

4 Roll the dough into 18–20 30cm/12in sticks. Place on the
baking sheets, brush with the egg glaze then sprinkle with
toasted sesame seeds and coarse salt. Leave to rise, uncovered,
for 20 minutes.

5 Preheat the oven to 200°C/400°F/Gas 6. Bake until golden,
about 15 minutes. Turn off the heat but leave in the oven for
a further 5 minutes. Serve warm or cool.

Variation
*For Rye and Caraway Breadsticks, substitute 200g/7oz/scant
2 cups rye flour for 200g/7oz/scant 2 cups of the strong white
bread flour. Sprinkle with caraway seeds instead of sesame seeds.*

Caraway Bread Sticks

Ideal to nibble with drinks,
these can be made in a wide
variety of flavours, including
cumin seed, poppy seed and
celery seed, as well as the
coriander and sesame
variation given below.

Makes about 20
225g/8oz/2 cups plain
   (all-purpose) flour
2.5ml/½ tsp salt
2.5ml/½ tsp easy-blend
   (rapid-rise) dried yeast
10ml/2 tsp caraway seeds
150ml/¼ pint/⅔ cup
   hand-hot water
a pinch of sugar

1 Grease two baking sheets. Sift the flour, salt, yeast and sugar
into a large bowl, stir in the caraway seeds and make a well in
the centre.

2 Add the water and stir from the centre outwards, gradually
mixing the flour to make a soft dough, and adding a little extra
water if necessary.

3 Turn the dough on to a lightly floured surface and knead for
5 minutes until smooth and elastic.

4 Divide the mixture into 20 pieces and roll each one into a
30cm/12in stick.

5 Arrange the bread sticks on the baking sheets, leaving room
to allow for rising. Leave for 30 minutes, or until well risen.
Meanwhile, preheat the oven to 220°C/425°F/Gas 7.

6 Bake the bread sticks for 10–12 minutes, or until golden
brown. Cool on the baking sheets.

Variation
*To make Coriander and Sesame Sticks: replace the caraway seeds
with 15ml/1 tbsp crushed coriander seeds. Dampen the bread
sticks lightly and sprinkle them with sesame seeds before baking.*

Breadsticks Energy 128Kcal/538kJ; Protein 3.4g; Carbohydrate 16.8g, of which sugars 0.6g; Fat 5.7g, of which saturates 0.8g; Cholesterol 0mg; Calcium 80mg; Fibre 1.3g; Sodium 199mg.
Caraway Energy 41Kcal/176kJ; Protein 1.2g; Carbohydrate 8.7g, of which sugars 0.2g; Fat 0.4g, of which saturates 0.1g; Cholesterol 0mg; Calcium 19mg; Fibre 0.4g; Sodium 50mg.

Tomato Breadsticks

Once you've tried this exceptionally simple recipe you'll never buy manufactured breadsticks again.

Makes 16
225g/8oz/2 cups strong white
  bread flour
2.5ml/½ tsp salt
7.5ml/½ tbsp easy-blend
  (rapid-rise) dried yeast

5ml/1 tsp honey
5ml/1 tsp olive oil
150ml/¼ pint/⅔ cup
  warm water
6 halves sun-dried tomatoes in
  olive oil, drained and chopped
15ml/1 tbsp milk
10ml/2 tsp poppy seeds

1 Place the flour, salt and yeast in a food processor. Add the honey and olive oil and, with the machine running, gradually pour in the water until the dough starts to cling together (you may not need all the water).

2 Process for a further 1 minute. Alternatively, use your hand to incorporate the liquid into the flour.

3 Turn out the dough on to a floured surface and knead for 3–4 minutes, until springy and smooth. Knead in the sun-dried tomatoes.

4 Form the dough into a ball and place in a lightly oiled bowl. Cover with clear film (plastic wrap). Place in a warm position and leave to rise for 5 minutes.

5 Preheat the oven to 150°C/300°F/Gas 2. Lightly grease a baking sheet. Divide the dough into 16 pieces and roll each piece into a 28 × 1cm/11 × ½in stick.

6 Place on the lightly greased baking sheet and leave to rise in a warm place for 15 minutes.

7 Brush the breadsticks with milk and sprinkle with poppy seeds. Bake for 30 minutes. Leave the breadsticks to cool on a wire rack.

Croissants

Enjoy breakfast Continental-style with these melt-in-the-mouth croissants.

Makes 18
15ml/1 tbsp active dried yeast
325ml/11fl oz/1⅓ cups
  lukewarm milk

10ml/2 tsp caster (superfine) sugar
12.5ml/1½ tsp salt
450g/1lb/4 cups strong white
  bread flour
225g/8oz/1 cup cold unsalted
  (sweet) butter
1 egg, beaten with 10ml/2 tsp
  water, to glaze

1 In a large bowl, stir together the yeast and milk. Leave for about 15 minutes for the yeast to become frothy. Stir in the sugar and salt, and about 150g/5oz/1¼ cups of the flour.

2 Slowly add the remaining flour. Mix well until the dough pulls away from the sides of the bowl. Cover and leave to rise in a warm place until doubled in size, about 1½ hours.

3 Turn out on to a lightly floured surface and knead until smooth. Wrap in baking parchment and chill for 15 minutes.

4 Roll out the butter between two sheets of baking parchment to make two 15 × 10cm/6 × 4in rectangles. Roll out the dough to a 30 × 20cm/12 × 8in rectangle.

5 Interleave the butter with the dough. With a short side facing you, roll it out again to 30 × 20cm/12 × 8in. Fold in thirds again, wrap and chill for 30 minutes. Repeat this procedure twice, then chill for 2 hours.

6 Roll out the dough to a rectangle about 3mm/⅛in thick. Trim the sides, and then cut into 18 equal-size triangles. Roll up from the base to the point. Place point-down on baking sheets and curve to form crescents. Cover and leave to rise in a warm place until more than doubled in size, about 1–1½ hours.

7 Preheat the oven to 240°C/475°F/Gas 9. Brush with egg glaze. Bake for 2 minutes. Lower the heat to 190°C/375°F/Gas 5 and bake until golden, about 10–12 minutes. Serve warm.

Tomato Energy 53Kcal/227kJ; Protein 1.5g; Carbohydrate 11.7g, of which sugars 1g; Fat 0.4g, of which saturates 0.1g; Cholesterol 0mg; Calcium 22mg; Fibre 0.5g; Sodium 68mg.
Croissants Energy 189Kcal/789kJ; Protein 3g; Carbohydrate 20.9g, of which sugars 1.9g; Fat 10.9g, of which saturates 6.8g; Cholesterol 28mg; Calcium 59mg; Fibre 0.8g; Sodium 357mg.

Basic Recipes

In order to achieve the best possible results when making a
special occasion cake, you will need to be able to make
a variety of simple sponges, frostings, and decorations. This
chapter contains a range of easy-to-follow techniques and basic
recipes, including Sponge Roll, Rich Fruit Cake and Madeira
Cake as well Chocolate Curls, Sugar-frosting Flowers,
Royal Icing and Meringue Frosting.

Genoese Sponge Cake

This light sponge cake has a firm texture due to the addition of butter and is suitable for cutting into layers for gateaux.

Makes 1 x 20cm/8in round cake
4 eggs
115g/4oz/generous ½ cup caster (superfine) sugar
75g/3oz/6 tbsp unsalted (sweet) butter, melted and cooled slightly

75g/3oz/⅔ cup plain (all-purpose) flour

For the flavourings
Citrus: 10ml/2 tsp grated orange, lemon or lime rind
Chocolate: 50g/2oz plain (semisweet) chocolate, melted
Coffee: 10ml/2 tsp coffee granules, dissolved in 5ml/1 tsp boiling water

1 Preheat the oven to 180°C/350°F/Gas 4. Base line and grease a 20cm/8in round cake tin (pan).

2 Whisk the eggs and caster sugar together in a heatproof bowl until thoroughly blended.

3 Place the bowl over a pan of simmering water and continue to whisk the mixture until thick and pale.

4 Remove the bowl from the pan and continue to whisk until the mixture is cool and leaves a thick trail on the surface when the beaters are lifted.

5 Pour the butter carefully into the mixture, leaving any sediment behind.

6 Sift the flour over the surface and add your chosen flavouring, if using. Using a plastic spatula, carefully fold the flour, butter and any flavourings into the mixture until smooth and evenly blended.

7 Scrape the mixture into the prepared tin, tilt to level and bake for 30–40 minutes, until firm to the touch and golden. Cool on a wire rack and decorate as you like.

Quick-mix Sponge Cake

Choose either chocolate or lemon flavouring for this light and versatile sponge cake, or leave it plain.

Makes 1 x 20cm/8in round or ring cake
115g/4oz/1 cup self-raising (self-rising) flour
5ml/1 tsp baking powder
115g/4oz/½ cup soft margarine

115g/4oz/½ cup caster (superfine) sugar
2 eggs

For the flavourings
Chocolate: 15ml/1 tbsp unsweetened cocoa powder blended with 15ml/1 tbsp boiling water
Lemon: 10ml/2 tsp grated lemon rind

1 Preheat the oven to 160°C/325°F/Gas 3. Grease a 20cm/8in round cake tin (pan), line the base with baking parchment and grease the paper.

2 Sift the flour and baking powder into a bowl. Add the margarine, sugar and eggs with the chosen flavourings, if using.

3 Beat with a wooden spoon for 2–3 minutes. The mixture should be pale in colour and slightly glossy.

4 Spoon the mixture into the cake tin and smooth the surface. Bake in the centre of the oven for 30–40 minutes, or until a skewer inserted into the centre of the cake comes out clean. Turn out on to a wire rack, remove the lining paper and leave to cool completely.

Cook's Tips
• *This sponge cake is ideal for a celebration cake that will be simply iced, but do not use it for a cake that needs to be carved into an intricate shape. Madeira cake is best for that purpose.*
• *Always leave any cake to cool completely before decorating it. It is best to leave it overnight in a sealed, airtight container to settle if possible.*

Quick-mix Energy 1504kcal/6260kJ; Protein 28.2g; Carbohydrate 107.8g, of which sugars 3.2g; Fat 110g, of which saturates 5.3g; Cholesterol 381mg; Calcium 270mg; Fibre 6g; Sodium 1207mg.
Genoese Energy 1736kcal/7280kJ; Protein 34.5g; Carbohydrate 212.5g, of which sugars 163.3g; Fat 89.6g, of which saturates 48.1g; Cholesterol 900mg; Calcium 298mg; Fibre 3.2g; Sodium 680mg.

Madeira Cake

Enjoy this cake in the traditional way by serving it with a large glass of Madeira or sherry.

Serves 6–8
225g/8oz/2 cups plain (all-purpose) flour
5ml/1 tsp baking powder
225g/8oz/1 cup butter or margarine, at room temperature
225g/8oz/generous 1 cup caster (superfine) sugar
grated rind of 1 lemon
5ml/1 tsp vanilla extract
4 eggs

1 Preheat the oven to 160°C/325°F/Gas 3. Base line and grease a 20cm/8in cake tin (pan).

2 Sift the plain flour and baking powder into a bowl.

3 Cream the butter or margarine, adding the caster sugar about 30ml/2 tbsp at a time, until light and fluffy. Stir in the lemon rind and vanilla extract. Add the eggs one at a time, beating for 1 minute after each addition. Add the flour mixture and stir until just combined.

4 Pour the cake mixture into the prepared tin and tap lightly to level. Bake for about 1¼ hours, or until a metal skewer inserted in the centre comes out clean.

5 Cool in the tin on a wire rack for 10 minutes, then turn the cake out on to a wire rack and leave to cool completely.

Cook's Tips
• *Madeira cake is ideal for using as a celebration cake as it keeps better than a sponge cake and so will last for longer while you decorate it. It also has a firm texture that will be easy to ice with butter icing and sugarpaste.*
• *Level the domed top before icing the cake by putting a deep cake board inside the cake tin (pan) the cake was baked in and placing the cake on top. Cut the part of the cake that extends above the top of the tin using a sharp knife.*

Sponge Roll

Vary the flavour of the roll by adding a little grated orange, lime or lemon rind to the mixture, if you like.

Serves 6–8
4 eggs, separated
115g/4oz/½ cup caster (superfine) sugar, plus extra for sprinkling
115g/4oz/1 cup plain (all-purpose) flour
5ml/1 tsp baking powder

For a chocolate flavouring
Replace 25ml/1½ tbsp of the flour with 25ml/1½ tbsp unsweetened cocoa powder

1 Preheat the oven to 180°C/350°F/Gas 4. Base line and grease a 33 × 23cm/13 × 9in Swiss roll tin (jelly roll pan).

2 Whisk the egg whites until stiff peaks form and then beat in 30ml/2 tbsp of the caster sugar.

3 Beat the egg yolks with the remaining caster sugar and 15ml/1 tbsp water for about 2 minutes, or until the mixture is pale and leaves a thick ribbon trail.

4 Sift together the flour and baking powder into another bowl. Carefully fold the beaten egg yolks into the egg whites, then fold in the flour mixture.

5 Pour the mixture into the prepared tin and gently smooth the surface with a plastic spatula.

6 Bake in the centre of the oven for 12–15 minutes, or until the cake starts to come away from the edges of the tin.

7 Turn the cake out on to a piece of baking parchment lightly sprinkled with caster sugar. Peel off the lining paper and cut off any crisp edges.

8 Spread with jam, if you like, and roll up, using the baking parchment to help you.

9 Leave to cool on a wire rack, then dust with icing sugar.

Cake Energy 453kcal/1894kJ; Protein 6.1g; Carbohydrate 51.4g, of which sugars 30g; Fat 26.3g, of which saturates 15.5g; Cholesterol 155mg; Calcium 74mg; Fibre 0.9g; Sodium 208mg.
Roll Energy 142kcal/603kJ; Protein 4.6g; Carbohydrate 26.2g, of which sugars 15.2g; Fat 3g, of which saturates 0.8g; Cholesterol 95mg; Calcium 42mg; Fibre 0.5g; Sodium 36mg.

Rich Fruit Cake

This is an ideal recipe for a celebration cake. Make this cake a few weeks before icing, wrap and store in an airtight container to mature.

Makes 1 x 20cm/8in round or 18cm/7in square cake
375g/13oz/1½ cups currants
250g/9oz/1½ cups sultanas (golden raisins)
150g/5oz/1 cup raisins
90g/3½oz/scant ½ cup glacé (candied) cherries, halved
90g/3½oz/generous ½ cup almonds, chopped
65g/2½oz/scant ½ cup mixed (candied) peel
grated rind of 1 lemon
40ml/2½ tbsp brandy
250g/9oz/2¼ cups plain (all-purpose) flour, sifted
6.5ml/1¼ tsp mixed (apple pie) spice
2.5ml/½ tsp freshly grated nutmeg
65g/2½oz/generous ½ cup ground almonds
200g/7oz/scant 1 cup soft margarine or butter
225g/8oz/1¼ cups soft light brown sugar
15ml/1 tbsp black treacle (molasses)
5 eggs, beaten

1 Preheat the oven to 140°C/275°F/Gas 1. Grease a deep 20cm/8in round or 18cm/7in square cake tin (pan), line the base and sides with a double thickness of baking parchment and grease the paper.

2 Combine the ingredients in a large mixing bowl. Beat with a wooden spoon for 5 minutes, or until well mixed.

3 Spoon the mixture into the prepared cake tin. Make a slight depression in the centre.

4 Bake in the centre of the oven for 3–3½ hours. Test the cake after 3 hours. If it is ready it will feel firm and a skewer inserted into the centre will come out clean. Cover the top loosely with foil if it starts to brown too quickly.

5 Leave the cake to cool completely in the tin. Then turn out. The lining paper can be left on until you are ready to ice or serve, to help keep the cake moist.

Light Fruit Cake

This slightly less dense fruit cake is still ideal for marzipanning and icing.

Makes 1 x 20cm/8in round or 18cm/7in square cake
225g/8oz/1 cup soft margarine or butter
225g/8oz/generous 1 cup caster (superfine) sugar
grated rind of 1 orange
5 eggs, beaten
300g/11oz/2⅔ cups plain (all-purpose) flour
2.5ml/½ tsp baking powder
10ml/2 tsp mixed (apple pie) spice
175g/6oz/¾ cup currants
175g/6oz/generous 1 cup raisins
175g/6oz/1 cup sultanas (golden raisins)
50g/2oz/¼ cup dried, ready-to-eat apricots
115g/4oz/⅔ cup mixed (candied) peel

1 Preheat the oven to 150°C/300°F/Gas 2. Grease a deep 20cm/8in round or 18cm/7in square cake tin (pan), line the base and sides with a double thickness of baking parchment and grease the paper.

2 Beat the margarine and sugar together in a large bowl until soft. Add the orange rind and then the eggs, one at a time, beating after each addition and adding a spoonful of flour to stop them curdling. Sift the remaining flour with the baking powder and mixed spice. Stir in the currants, raisins and sultanas.

3 Cut up the apricots in strips, using kitchen scissors, and add to the mixture. Beat thoroughly with a wooden spoon for 3–4 minutes, until thoroughly mixed.

4 Spoon the mixture into the cake tin. Make a slight depression in the centre. Bake in the centre of the oven for 2½–3¼ hours. Test the cake after 2½ hours. If it is ready it will feel firm and a skewer inserted into the centre will come out clean. Test at intervals if necessary. Cover the top loosely with foil if it starts to brown too quickly.

5 Leave the cake to cool completely in the tin, then turn out. The lining paper can be left on until you are ready to ice or serve, to help keep the cake moist.

Rich Energy 7388kcal/31049kJ; Protein 123.7g; Carbohydrate 1047.9g, of which sugars 850.7g; Fat 320.2g, of which saturates 124.8g; Cholesterol 1378mg; Calcium 1781mg; Fibre 39.1g; Sodium 2041mg.
Light Energy 5719kcal/24077kJ; Protein 75.8g; Carbohydrate 918.1g, of which sugars 689.5g; Fat 218.7g, of which saturates 8.5g; Cholesterol 951mg; Calcium 1232mg; Fibre 28.3g; Sodium 2664mg.

Marzipan Roses

To decorate a cake, shape the roses in a variety of colours and sizes then arrange on top.

1 Form a small ball of coloured marzipan into a cone shape. This forms the central core which supports the petals.

2 Take a piece of marzipan about the size of a large pea, and make a petal shape that is thicker at the base.

3 Wrap the petal around the cone, pressing the petal to the cone to secure. Bend back the ends of the petal to curl. Repeat with more petals, each overlapping. Make some petals bigger until the required size is achieved.

Marzipan

Marzipan can be used on its own, under an icing or for modelling decorations.

Makes 450g/1lb/3 cups
225g/8oz/2 cups ground almonds
115g/4oz/generous 1/2 cup caster (superfine) sugar

115g/4oz/1 cup icing (confectioners') sugar, sifted
5ml/1 tsp lemon juice
a few drops of almond extract
1 egg or 1 egg white

1 Stir the ground almonds and sugars together in a bowl until evenly mixed. Make a well in the centre and add the lemon juice, almond extract and enough egg or egg white to mix to a soft but firm dough, using a wooden spoon.

2 Form the marzipan into a ball. Lightly dust a surface with icing sugar and knead the marzipan until smooth. Wrap in clear film (plastic wrap) or store in a plastic bag until needed. Tint with food colouring if required.

Sugarpaste Icing

Sugarpaste icing is wonderfully pliable and can be coloured, moulded and shaped in imaginative ways.

Makes 350g/12oz/2 1/4 cups
1 egg white
15ml/1 tbsp liquid glucose, warmed
350g/12oz/3 cups icing (confectioners') sugar, sifted

1 Put the egg white and glucose in a mixing bowl. Stir them together to break up the egg white.

2 Add the icing sugar and mix together with a metal spatula, using a chopping action, until well blended and the icing begins to bind together.

3 Knead the mixture with your fingers until it forms a ball.

4 Knead the sugarpaste on a work surface that has been lightly dusted with icing sugar for several minutes until it is smooth, soft and pliable.

5 If the icing is too soft, knead in some more sifted sugar until it reaches the right consistency.

Cook's Tips
• *Sugarpaste icing is sometimes known as rolled fondant and is available ready made in sugarcraft stores. It is easy to make yourself but if you are using a large quantity and are in a hurry you could purchase it ready made. It is available in a variety of colours.*
• *If you want to make the sugarpaste in advance wrap it up tightly in a plastic bag. The icing will keep for about three weeks.*
• *The paste is easy to colour with paste colours; add a little at a time using the tip of a knife.*
• *Roll out sugarpaste on a surface lightly sprinkled with icing (confectioners') sugar or a little white vegetable fat (shortening) to avoid the paste sticking.*

Marzipan Energy 2357kcal/9874kJ; Protein 54.9g; Carbohydrate 255.9g, of which sugars 249.8g; Fat 131.1g, of which saturates 11.5g; Cholesterol 190mg; Calcium 690mg; Fibre 16.6g; Sodium 115mg.
Sugarpaste Energy 1435kcal/6123kJ; Protein 4.7g; Carbohydrate 377.6g, of which sugars 377.6g; Fat 0g, of which saturates 0g; Cholesterol 0mg; Calcium 190mg; Fibre 0g; Sodium 122mg.

Royal Icing

Royal icing gives a professional finish. This recipe makes enough icing to cover the top and sides of an 18cm/7in cake.

Makes 675g/1½lb/4½ cups
3 egg whites
about 675g/1½lb/6 cups
   icing (confectioners')
   sugar, sifted
7.5ml/1½ tsp glycerine
a few drops of lemon juice
food colouring (optional)

1 Put the egg whites in a bowl and stir lightly with a fork to break them up.

2 Add the sifted icing sugar gradually, beating well with a wooden spoon after each addition.

3 Add enough icing sugar to make a smooth, shiny icing that has the consistency of very stiff meringue.

4 Beat in the glycerine, lemon juice and food colouring, if using.

5 Leave for 1 hour before using, covered with damp clear film (plastic wrap), then stir to burst any air bubbles.

Cook's Tips
• The icing will keep for up to three days in a refrigerator, stored in a plastic container with a tight-fitting lid.
• This recipe is for an "icing" consistency suitable for flat-icing a marzipanned rich fruit cake. When the spoon is lifted, the icing should form a sharp point, with a slight curve at the end, known as "soft peak". For piping, the icing needs to be slightly stiffer. It should form a fine sharp peak when the spoon is lifted.
• Royal icing is not appropriate for a sponge cake, as its stiff consistency would easily drag on the surface.
• Never use royal icing direct on to the cake's surface; a layer of marzipan will make a smooth surface for icing and stop cake crumbs mixing with the icing.

Butter Icing

The creamy rich flavour and silky smoothness of butter icing is popular with both children and adults.

Makes 350g/12oz/1½ cups
75g/3oz/6 tbsp soft margarine or
   butter, softened
225g/8oz/2 cups icing
   (confectioners') sugar, sifted
5ml/1 tsp vanilla extract
10–15ml/2–3 tsp milk

For the flavourings
Chocolate: blend 15ml/1 tbsp
   unsweetened cocoa powder with
   15ml/1 tbsp hot water. Cool
   before beating into the icing.

Coffee: blend 10ml/2 tsp coffee powder with 15ml/1 tbsp boiling water. Omit the milk. Cool before beating the mixture into the icing.

Lemon, orange or lime: substitute the vanilla extract and milk with lemon, orange or lime juice and 10ml/2 tsp of finely grated citrus rind. Omit the rind if using the icing for piping. Lightly tint the icing with food colouring, if you like.

1 Put the margarine or butter, icing sugar, vanilla extract and 5ml/1 tsp of the milk in a bowl.

2 Beat with a wooden spoon or an electric mixer, adding sufficient extra milk to give a light, smooth and fluffy consistency. For flavoured butter icing, follow the instructions above for the flavour of your choice.

Cook's Tips
• The icing will keep for up to three days in an airtight container stored in a refrigerator.
• Butter icing can be coloured with paste colours. Add a little at a time using a cocktail stick (toothpick) until you reach the desired shade.
• You can apply butter icing with a knife and make a smooth finish, or you can pipe the icing on to your cake using a plain or fluted nozzle, or use a serrated scraper for a ridged finish.

Royal Energy 2694kcal/11494kJ; Protein 12g; Carbohydrate 705.4g, of which sugars 705.4g; Fat 0g, of which saturates 0g; Cholesterol 0mg; Calcium 363mg; Fibre 0g; Sodium 223mg.
Butter Energy 1461kcal/6149kJ; Protein 2.8g; Carbohydrate 238g, of which sugars 238g; Fat 62g, of which saturates 0.5g; Cholesterol 3mg; Calcium 176mg; Fibre 0g; Sodium 633mg.

American Frosting

A light marshmallow icing which crisps on the outside when left to dry, this versatile frosting may be swirled or peaked into a soft coating.

Makes 350g/12oz/1½ cups
1 egg white
30ml/2 tbsp water
15ml/1 tbsp golden (light corn) syrup
5ml/1 tsp cream of tartar
175g/6oz/1½ cups icing (confectioners') sugar, sifted

1 Place the egg white with the water, golden syrup and cream of tartar in a heatproof bowl. Whisk together until blended.

2 Stir the icing sugar into the mixture and place the bowl over a pan of simmering water. Whisk until the mixture becomes thick and white.

3 Remove the bowl from the pan and continue to whisk the frosting until cool and thick, and the mixture stands up in soft peaks. Use immediately to fill or cover cakes.

Caramel Icing

A rich-tasting icing that makes a lovely cake topping.

Makes 450g/1lb/2 cups
75ml/5 tbsp creamy milk

75g/3oz/6 tbsp butter
30 ml/2 tbsp caster (superfine) sugar
350g/12oz/3 cups icing (confectioners') sugar

1 Warm the milk and butter in a pan. Heat the caster sugar in another pan over medium heat until it turns golden. Immediately remove from the heat before the caramel darkens.

2 Pour the milk mixture over the caramel and return the pan to a low heat. Heat the mixture until the caramel has dissolved, stirring occasionally. Sift in the icing sugar a little at a time, and beat with a wooden spoon until the icing is smooth. Use immediately.

Glacé Icing

An instant icing for quickly finishing the tops of large or small cakes.

Makes 350g/12oz/1½ cup
225g/8oz/2 cups icing (confectioners') sugar
30–45ml/2–3 tbsp hot water
food colouring (optional)

For the flavourings
Citrus: replace the water with orange, lemon or lime juice
Chocolate: sift 10ml/2 tsp unsweetened cocoa powder with the icing (confectioners') sugar
Coffee: replace the water with strong, liquid coffee

1 Sift the icing sugar into a bowl. Using a wooden spoon, gradually stir in enough of the hot water to obtain the consistency of thick cream.

2 Beat until white and smooth, and the icing thickly coats the back of the spoon. Tint with a few drops of food colouring, if you wish, or flavour the icing as suggested above. Use immediately to cover the top of the cake.

Simple Piped Flowers

Bouquets of iced blooms, such as roses, pansies and bright summer flowers, make colourful cake decorations.

Makes 350g/12oz/1½ cup
225g/8oz/2 cups icing (confectioners') sugar
30–45ml/2–3 tbsp hot water

1 For a rose, make a fairly firm icing. Colour the icing. Fit a petal nozzle into a paper piping (icing) bag, half-fill with icing and fold over the top to seal. Hold the piping bag so that the wider end is pointing at what will be the base of the rose and hold a cocktail stick (toothpick) in the other hand.

2 Pipe a small cone shape around the tip of the stick, pipe a petal halfway around the cone, lifting it so that it is at an angle and curling outwards, turning the stick at the same time. Repeat with more overlapping petals. Remove from the stick and leave to dry.

American Energy 746kcal/3181kJ; Protein 3.8g; Carbohydrate 194.7g, of which sugars 194.7g; Fat 0g, of which saturates 0g; Cholesterol 0mg; Calcium 97mg; Fibre 0g; Sodium 112mg.
Caramel Energy 2095kcal/8850kJ; Protein 4g; Carbohydrate 404.5g, of which sugars 404.5g; Fat 62.4g, of which saturates 39.5g; Cholesterol 163mg; Calcium 349mg; Fibre 0g; Sodium 523mg.
Glacé Energy 887kcal/3782kJ; Protein 1.1g; Carbohydrate 235.1g, of which sugars 235.1g; Fat 0g, of which saturates 0g; Cholesterol 0mg; Calcium 119mg; Fibre 0g; Sodium 14mg.
Flowers Energy 1888kcal/8044kJ; Protein 5.2g; Carbohydrate 478.3g, of which sugars 478.3g; Fat 8.2g, of which saturates 3.6g; Cholesterol 2mg; Calcium 242mg; Fibre 0g; Sodium 195mg.

Honey Icing

A simple and tasty topping for cakes.

Makes 275g/10oz/1¼ cups
75g/3oz/6 tbsp butter, softened

175g/6oz/1½ cups icing
(confectioners') sugar
15ml/1 tbsp clear honey
15ml/1 tbsp lemon juice

1 Put the softened butter into a bowl and gradually sift over the icing sugar, beating well after each addition.

2 Beat in the honey and lemon juice and combine well. Spread over the cake immediately.

Butterscotch Frosting

Soft light brown sugar and treacle make a rich and tempting frosting for cakes.

Makes 675g/1½lb/3 cups
75g/3oz/6 tbsp unsalted
(sweet) butter
45ml/3 tbsp milk
25g/1oz/2 tbsp soft light
brown sugar
15ml/1 tbsp black
treacle (molasses)
350g/12oz/3 cups icing
(confectioners') sugar, sifted

For the flavourings
Citrus: replace the treacle with
golden (light corn) syrup and
add 10ml/2 tsp finely grated
orange, lemon or lime rind
Chocolate: sift 15ml/1 tbsp
unsweetened cocoa
powder with the icing
(confectioners') sugar
Coffee: replace the treacle
(molasses) with 15ml/1 tbsp
coffee granules

1 Place the butter, milk, sugar and treacle in a bowl over a pan of simmering water. Stir until the butter melts and the sugar dissolves completely.

2 Remove from the heat and stir in the icing sugar. Beat until smooth. For different flavourings, follow the instructions above. Pour over the cake, or cool for a thicker consistency.

Chocolate Fudge Icing

A rich glossy icing which sets like chocolate fudge, this is versatile enough to smoothly coat, swirl or pipe, depending on the temperature of the icing when it is used.

Makes 450g/1lb/2 cups
115g/4oz plain (semisweet)
chocolate, in squares
50g/2oz/¼ cup unsalted
(sweet) butter
1 egg, beaten
175g/6oz/1½ cups icing
(confectioners')
sugar, sifted

1 Place the chocolate and butter in a heatproof bowl over a pan of hot water.

2 Stir the mixture occasionally with a wooden spoon until both the chocolate and butter are melted. Add the egg and beat well until thoroughly combined.

3 Remove the bowl from the pan and stir in the icing sugar, then beat until smooth and glossy.

4 Pour immediately over the cake for a smooth finish, or leave to cool for a thicker spreading or piping consistency.

Chocolate Curls

These tasty curls look spectacular on a gateau.

Makes around 20 curls
115g/4 oz plain (semisweet)
chocolate

1 Melt the chocolate, then pour on to a smooth surface, such as marble or plastic laminate. Spread evenly over the surface with a palette knife. Leave to cool slightly.

2 Hold a large, sharp knife at a 45° angle to the chocolate and push it along the chocolate in short sawing movements from right to left to make curls. Lift off with the knife and leave to cool.

Honey Energy 1876kcal/7879kJ; Protein 3g; Carbohydrate 289.3g, of which sugars 289.3g; Fat 62.4g, of which saturates 39.5g; Cholesterol 163mg; Calcium 163mg; Fibre 0g; Sodium 523mg.
Butterscotch Energy 2095kcal/8850kJ; Protein 4g; Carbohydrate 404.5g, of which sugars 404.5g; Fat 62.4g, of which saturates 39.5g; Cholesterol 163mg; Calcium 349mg; Fibre 0g; Sodium 523mg.
Icing Energy 1722kcal/7235kJ; Protein 13.2g; Carbohydrate 256.2g, of which sugars 255.2g; Fat 78.8g, of which saturates 46.9g; Cholesterol 304mg; Calcium 168mg; Fibre 2.9g; Sodium 390mg.
Curls Energy 285kcal/1193kJ; Protein 2.3g; Carbohydrate 35.1g, of which sugars 33.9g; Fat 15.1g, of which saturates 9.4g; Cholesterol 304mg; Calcium 168mg; Fibre 3.45g; Sodium 388mg.

Apricot Glaze

It is a good idea to make a large quantity of apricot glaze, especially when making celebration cakes.

Makes 450g/1lb/1½ cups
450g/1lb/generous 1½ cups apricot jam
45ml/3 tbsp water

1 Place the jam and water in a pan. Heat gently, stirring occasionally, until the jam has melted.

2 Boil the jam rapidly for 1 minute, then rub through a sieve, pressing the fruit against the sides of the sieve with the back of a wooden spoon.

3 Discard the skins left in the sieve.

4 Use the warmed glaze to brush cakes before applying marzipan, or use for glazing fruits on gateaux and cakes.

Pastillage

This paste sets very hard and is used for making firm decorative structures from icing sugar.

Makes 350g/12oz/1¼ cups
300g/11oz icing (confectioners') sugar
1 egg white
10ml/2 tsp gum tragacanth

1 In a large bowl, sift most of the icing sugar over the egg white, a little at a time, stirring continuously until the mixture sticks together.

2 Add the gum tragacanth and transfer the mixture to a work surface which has been dusted with icing sugar.

3 Knead the mixture well until the ingredients are thoroughly combined and the paste has a smooth texture.

4 Knead in the remaining icing sugar and mix until stiff.

Sugar-frosting Flowers

Choose edible flowers such as pansies, primroses, violets, roses, freesias, apple blossom, wild bergamot (monarda), borage, carnations, honeysuckle, jasmine and marigolds.

Makes 10–15 flowers, depending on their size
1 egg white
caster (superfine) sugar
10–15 edible flowers

1 Lightly beat an egg white in a small bowl and sprinkle some caster (superfine) sugar on a plate.

2 Wash the flowers then dry on kitchen paper. Evenly brush both sides of the petals with the egg white. Hold the flower by its stem over a plate lined with kitchen paper, sprinkle it evenly with the sugar, then shake off any excess. Place on a wire rack covered with kitchen paper and leave to dry in a warm place.

Glossy Chocolate Icing

A rich smooth glossy icing, this can be made with plain or milk chocolate.

Makes 350g/12oz/1¼ cups
175g/6oz plain (semisweet) chocolate
150ml/¼ pint/⅔ cup single (light) cream

1 Break up the chocolate into small pieces and place it in a pan with the cream.

2 Heat gently, stirring occasionally, until the chocolate has melted and the mixture is smooth.

3 Allow the icing to cool until it is thick enough to coat the back of a wooden spoon. Use it at this stage for a smooth glossy icing, or allow it to thicken to obtain an icing which can be swirled or patterned with a cake decorating scraper.

Apricot Energy 1175kcal/5022kJ; Protein 1.8g; Carbohydrate 311.9g, of which sugars 311.9g; Fat 0g, of which saturates 0g; Cholesterol 0mg; Calcium 45mg; Fibre 0g; Sodium 207mg.
Pastillage Energy 1258.6kcal/5286.4kJ; Protein 3.4g; Carbohydrate 318.8g, of which sugars 318.8g; Fat 5.5g, of which saturates 2.4g; Cholesterol 1.3mg; Calcium 161mg; Fibre 0g; Sodium 130mg.
Icing Energy 1182kcal/4937kJ; Protein 13.7g; Carbohydrate 114.4g, of which sugars 112.8g; Fat 77.7g, of which saturates 47.6g; Cholesterol 93mg; Calcium 191mg; Fibre 4.4g; Sodium 54mg.

Petal Paste

Makes 500g/1¼lb
10ml/2 tsp powdered gelatine
25ml/1½ tbsp cold water
10ml/2 tsp liquid glucose
10ml/2 tsp white vegetable
   fat (shortening)

450g/1lb/4 cups icing
   (confectioners') sugar, sifted
5ml/1 tsp gum tragacanth
1 egg white

1 Place the gelatine, water, liquid glucose and white fat in a heatproof bowl set over a pan of hot water until melted, stirring occasionally.

2 Remove the bowl from the heat.

3 Sift the icing sugar and gum tragacanth into a large bowl. Make a well in the centre and add the egg white and the gelatine mixture.

4 Thoroughly combine the ingredients to form a soft malleable white paste.

5 Knead the paste on a surface dusted with icing sugar until smooth, white and free from cracks.

6 Place in a plastic bag or wrap in clear film (plastic wrap), sealing well to exclude all the air.

7 Leave the paste for about two hours before using, then knead again and use small pieces at a time, leaving the remaining petal paste well sealed.

Piping Twisted Ropes

Fit nozzles nos 43 or 44, or a writing nozzle, into a baking parchment piping (icing) bag and half-fill with royal icing. Hold the bag at a slight angle and pipe in a continuous line with even pressure, twisting the bag as you pipe.

Marbling

Sugarpaste lends itself to tinting in all shades and marbling is a good way to colour the paste.

1 Using a cocktail stick (toothpick), add a little of the chosen edible food colour to some sugarpaste icing. Do not knead the food colouring fully into the icing.

2 When the sugarpaste is rolled out, the colour is dispersed in such a way that it gives a marbled appearance.

Meringue Frosting

This wonderfully light and delicate frosting needs to be used immediately.

Makes 450g/1lb/1½ cups
2 egg whites
115g/4oz/1 cup icing
   (confectioners') sugar, sifted
150g/5oz/⅔ cup unsalted
   (sweet) butter, softened

For the flavourings
Citrus: 10ml/2 tsp finely grated
   orange, lemon or lime rind.
Chocolate: 50g/2oz plain
   (semisweet) chocolate, melted
Coffee: 10ml/2 tsp coffee
   granules, blended with 5ml/
   1 tsp boiling water, cooled

1 Whisk the egg whites in a clean, heatproof bowl, add the icing sugar and gently whisk to mix well. Place the bowl over a pan of simmering water and whisk until thick and white. Remove the bowl from the pan and continue to whisk until cool when the meringue stands up in soft peaks.

2 Beat the butter in a separate bowl until light and fluffy. Add the meringue gradually, beating well after each addition, until thick and fluffy. Fold in the chosen flavouring, using a metal spatula, until evenly blended. Use immediately for coating, filling and piping on to cakes.

Petal Energy 1888kcal/8044kJ; Protein 5.2g; Carbohydrate 478.3g, of which sugars 478.3g; Fat 8.2g, of which saturates 3.6g; Cholesterol 2mg; Calcium 242mg; Fibre 0g; Sodium 195mg.
Meringue Energy 1592kcal/6620kJ; Protein 7.2g; Carbohydrate 121.1g, of which sugars 121.1g; Fat 123.3g, of which saturates 78.1g; Cholesterol 320mg; Calcium 91mg; Fibre 0g; Sodium 1038mg.

Index

Irish Soda Bread

Easy to make, this distinctive bread goes well with soup, cheese and traditional, rustic-style dishes.

Makes one loaf
275g/10oz/2½ cups plain (all-purpose) flour
150g/5oz/1¼ cups plain (all-purpose) wholemeal (whole-wheat) flour

5ml/1 tsp bicarbonate of soda (baking soda)
5ml/1 tsp salt
25g/1oz/2 tbsp butter or margarine, at room temperature
300ml/½ pint/1¼ cups buttermilk
15ml/1 tbsp plain (all-purpose) flour, for dusting

1 Preheat the oven to 200°C/400°F/Gas 6. Grease a baking sheet. Sift together the flours, bicarbonate of soda and salt.

2 Make a central well and add the butter or margarine and buttermilk. Working from the centre, stir to combine the ingredients until a soft dough is formed.

3 With floured hands, gather the dough into a ball. Knead for up to 3 minutes. Shape the dough into a large round.

4 Place on the baking sheet. Cut a cross in the top with a sharp knife and dust with the flour. Bake until brown, about 40–50 minutes. Transfer to a wire rack to cool.

Cook's Tips
• *It is the acid in buttermilk that acts with the bicarbonate of soda to make traditional soda bread rise. Because the bread does not include yeast it is not given any rising time. In fact, it is important to put the bread into the oven as soon as the liquid is added, as the gases start to form immediately and the loaf will be heavy if you don't put it straight in the oven.*
• *Soured cream or milk with 15ml/1 tbsp lemon juice can be used instead of buttermilk, but do not substitute plain milk for the buttermilk as this will not produce a successful loaf.*

Sage Soda Bread

This wonderful loaf, quite unlike bread made with yeast, has a velvety texture and a powerful sage aroma.

Makes one loaf
225g/8oz/2cups plain (all-purpose) wholemeal (whole-wheat) flour

115g/4oz/1 cup plain (all-purpose) flour
2.5ml/½ tsp salt
5ml/1 tsp bicarbonate of soda (baking soda)
30ml/2 tbsp shredded fresh sage
300–450ml/½–¾ pint/1¼–scant 2 cups buttermilk

1 Preheat the oven to 220°C/425°F/Gas 7. Lightly grease a baking sheet and set aside.

2 Sift the wholemeal and white flours with the salt and bicarbonate of soda into a large bowl.

3 Stir in the fresh sage and add enough buttermilk to make a soft dough. Do not overmix or the bread will be heavy.

4 Shape the dough into a round loaf and place on the lightly greased baking sheet.

5 Cut a cross in the top, cutting deep into the dough.

6 Bake in the oven for about 40 minutes, or until the loaf is well risen and sounds hollow when tapped on the base. Leave to cool on a wire rack.

Variations
• *Try this loaf made with all white flour rather than wholemeal (whole-wheat) and white for a finer and lighter texture.*
• *Fresh rosemary would also work well in place of the sage for this loaf.*
• *You could form the dough into two smaller loaves and bake them for 25–30 minutes.*
• *Fruit soda bread tastes great, too. In place of the sage add 150g/5oz/1 cup raisins.*

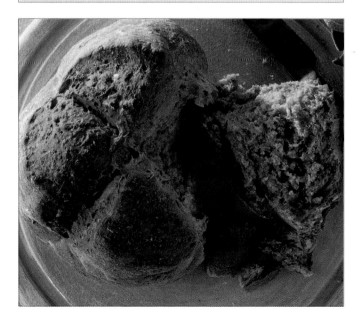

Sun-dried Tomato Plait

This makes a marvellous centrepiece for a summer buffet. If you only have dried tomatoes, soak them in a little boiling water for 15 minutes and add 15ml/ 1 tbsp oil to the mixture.

Serves 8 – 10

225g/8oz/2 cups strong wholemeal (whole-wheat) flour
225g/8oz/2 cups strong white bread flour
5ml/1 tsp salt
1.5ml/¹⁄₄ tsp ground black pepper
10ml/2 tsp easy-blend (rapid-rise) dried yeast
a pinch of sugar
300ml/¹⁄₂ pint/1¹⁄₄ cups hand-hot water
115g/4oz/2 cups drained sun-dried tomatoes in oil, chopped, plus 15ml/1 tbsp oil from the jar
25g/1oz/¹⁄₃ cup freshly grated Parmesan cheese
30ml/2 tbsp red pesto
2.5ml/¹⁄₂ tsp coarse sea salt

1 Oil a baking sheet. Put the wholemeal flour in a large bowl. Sift in the white flour, salt and pepper. Add the yeast and sugar.

2 Make a well in the centre and add the water, the sun-dried tomatoes, oil, Parmesan cheese and pesto. Gradually incorporate the flour and mix to a soft dough, adding a little extra water if necessary.

3 Turn the dough on to a floured surface and knead for 5 minutes until smooth and elastic. Shape into three 33cm/13in long sausages.

4 Dampen the ends of the three sausages. Press them together at one end, braid them loosely, then press them together at the other end. Transfer to the baking sheet, and cover and leave in a warm place until doubled in size, about 1½ hours. Meanwhile, preheat the oven to 220°C/425°F/Gas 7.

5 Sprinkle the braid with coarse sea salt. Bake for 10 minutes, then lower the oven temperature to 200°C/400°F/Gas 6 and bake for a further 15–20 minutes, or until the loaf sounds hollow when tapped underneath. Leave on a wire rack to cool completely.

Courgette Crown Bread

Adding grated courgettes and cheese to a loaf mixture will keep it tasting fresher for longer.

Serves 8

450g/1lb/2³⁄₄ cups coarsely grated courgettes (zucchini)
salt
500g/1¹⁄₄lb/5 cups strong white bread flour
2 sachets easy-blend (rapid-rise) dried yeast
60ml/4 tbsp freshly grated Parmesan cheese
ground black pepper
30ml/2 tbsp olive oil
lukewarm water, to mix
milk, to glaze
sesame seeds, to garnish

1 Spoon the courgettes into a colander, sprinkling them lightly with salt. Leave to drain for 30 minutes, then pat dry with kitchen paper.

2 Mix the flour, yeast and Parmesan cheese together and season with black pepper.

3 Stir in the oil and courgettes, and add enough lukewarm water to make a firm dough.

4 Knead the dough on a lightly floured surface until smooth. This will take about 10 minutes. Return to the mixing bowl, cover it with oiled clear film (plastic wrap) and leave it to rise in a warm place, until doubled in size, about 1½ hours.

5 Meanwhile, grease and line a 23cm/9in round cake tin (pan). Preheat the oven to 200°C/400°F/Gas 6.

6 Knock back (punch down) the dough, and knead it lightly. Break into eight balls, roll each one and arrange them, touching, in the tin. Brush the tops with the milk glaze and sprinkle over the sesame seeds.

7 Allow to rise again for 1 hour, then bake for 25 minutes, or until golden brown. Cool slightly in the tin, then turn out on to a wire rack to cool completely.

Tomato Energy 190Kcal/804kJ; Protein 7.7g; Carbohydrate 33.5g, of which sugars 2.4g; Fat 3.7g, of which saturates 1.4g; Cholesterol 6mg; Calcium 110mg; Fibre 3g; Sodium 89mg.
Courgette Energy 271Kcal/1144kJ; Protein 8.9g; Carbohydrate 49.6g, of which sugars 1.9g; Fat 5.4g, of which saturates 1.6g; Cholesterol 5mg; Calcium 162mg; Fibre 2.5g; Sodium 57mg.

Spinach & Bacon Bread

This bread is so tasty that it is a good idea to make double the quantity and freeze some of the loaves.

Makes 2 loaves

15ml/1 tbsp olive oil
1 onion, chopped
115g/4oz rindless smoked bacon
   rashers (strips), chopped
675g/1¹/₂lb/6 cups plain
   (all-purpose) flour
7.5ml/1¹/₂ tsp salt
2.5ml/¹/₂ tsp freshly grated
   nutmeg
1 sachet easy-blend (rapid-rise)
   dried yeast
475ml/16fl oz/2 cups
   hand-hot water
225g/8oz chopped spinach,
   thawed if frozen
25g/1oz/¹/₄ cup grated reduced-fat
   Cheddar cheese

1 Lightly oil two 23cm/9in cake tins (pans).

2 Heat the oil in a frying pan and fry the onion and bacon for 10 minutes, or until golden brown.

3 Sift the flour, salt and grated nutmeg into a mixing bowl, add the yeast and make a well in the centre. Add the water.

4 Tip in the fried bacon and onion, with the oil it was cooked in, then add the well-drained thawed spinach. Stir from the centre outwards, gradually incorporating the flour, and mix to a soft dough.

5 Turn the dough on to a floured surface and knead for 5 minutes until smooth and elastic. Divide the mixture in half. Shape each half into a ball, flatten slightly and place in a prepared tin, pressing the dough so that it extends to the edges.

6 Mark each loaf into six wedges and sprinkle with the cheese. Cover loosely with oiled clear film (plastic wrap) and leave in a warm place until each loaf has doubled in size, about 1½ hours. Meanwhile, preheat the oven to 200°C/400°F/Gas 6.

7 Bake the loaves for 25–30 minutes, or until they sound hollow when tapped underneath. Leave on a wire rack to cool completely.

Prosciutto & Parmesan Bread

This nourishing bread can be made very quickly, and makes a delicious meal when served with a tomato and feta cheese salad.

Serves 8

225g/8oz/2 cups self-raising
   (self-rising) wholemeal
   (whole-wheat) flour
225g/8oz/2 cups self-raising
   (self-rising) flour
5ml/1 tsp salt
5ml/1 tsp ground black pepper
75g/3oz prosciutto, chopped
30ml/2 tbsp chopped
   fresh parsley
25g/1oz/2 tbsp freshly grated
   Parmesan cheese
45ml/3 tbsp Meaux mustard
350ml/12fl oz/1¹/₂ cups
   buttermilk
skimmed milk, to glaze

1 Preheat the oven to 200°C/400°F/Gas 6 and lightly flour a baking sheet.

2 Put the wholemeal flour in a bowl and sift in the plain flour, salt and pepper. Stir in the ham and parsley. Set aside about half of the grated Parmesan cheese and add the rest to the flour mixture. Make a well in the centre.

3 Mix the mustard and buttermilk in a jug (pitcher), pour into the bowl and quickly mix to a soft dough.

4 Turn on to a well-floured surface and knead very briefly. Shape into an oval loaf and place on the baking sheet.

5 Brush the loaf with milk, sprinkle with the reserved Parmesan cheese and bake for 25–30 minutes, or until golden brown. Cool on a wire rack.

> **Cook's Tip**
> When chopping the ham, sprinkle it with flour so that it does not stick together. Do not knead the mixture as for a yeast dough, or it will become tough. It should be mixed quickly and kneaded very briefly before shaping.

Spinach Energy 160Kcal/680kJ; Protein 5.8g; Carbohydrate 32.6g, of which sugars 1.2g; Fat 1.6g, of which saturates 0.3g; Cholesterol 1mg; Calcium 98mg; Fibre 1.7g; Sodium 216mg.
Prosciutto Energy 229Kcal/972kJ; Protein 11.1g; Carbohydrate 42.4g, of which sugars 3.5g; Fat 2.9g, of which saturates 1g; Cholesterol 10mg; Calcium 146mg; Fibre 3.4g; Sodium 334mg.

Walnut Bread

This rich bread could be served at a dinner party with soup or the cheese course, or with a rustic ploughman's lunch.

Makes one loaf
420g/15oz/3⅔ cups strong wholemeal (whole-wheat) bread flour

150g/5oz/1¼ cups strong white bread flour
12.5ml/2½ tsp salt
550ml/18fl oz/2¼ cups lukewarm water
15ml/1 tbsp clear honey
15ml/1 tbsp active dried yeast
150g/5oz/1 cup walnut pieces, plus more to decorate
1 beaten egg, to glaze

1 Combine the wholemeal and white flours and salt in a large bowl. Make a well in the centre and add 250ml/8fl oz/1 cup of the water, the honey and the yeast. Set aside until the yeast dissolves and becomes frothy.

2 Add the remaining water. With a wooden spoon, stir from the centre, incorporating flour with each turn, to obtain a smooth dough. Add more flour if the dough is too sticky and use your hands if the dough becomes too stiff to stir.

3 Transfer to a floured board and knead, adding flour if necessary, until the dough is smooth and elastic. This will take about 10 minutes. Place in a greased bowl and roll the dough around in the bowl to coat thoroughly on all sides. Cover with clear film (plastic wrap) and leave in a warm place until doubled in volume, about 1½ hours. Knock back (punch down) the dough and knead in the walnuts evenly.

4 Grease a baking sheet. Shape the dough into a round loaf and place on the baking sheet. Press in walnut pieces to decorate the top. Cover loosely with a damp cloth or clear film and leave to rise in a warm place until doubled in size, 25–30 minutes.

5 Preheat the oven to 220°C/425°F/Gas 7. With a sharp knife, score the top of the loaf. Brush with the egg glaze. Bake for 15 minutes. Lower the heat to 190°C/375°F/Gas 5 and bake until the base sounds hollow when tapped, about 40 minutes.

Pecan Nut Rye Bread

A tasty homespun loaf that recalls the old folk-cooking of the United States.

**Makes two 21 x 11cm/
8½ x 4½in loaves**
25ml/1½ tbsp active dried yeast
700ml/22fl oz/2¾ cups lukewarm water

675g/1½lb/6 cups strong white bread flour
500g/1¼lb/5 cups rye flour
30ml/2 tbsp salt
15ml/1 tbsp clear honey
10ml/2 tsp caraway seeds, (optional)
115g/4oz/½ cup butter, at room temperature
225g/8oz pecan nuts, chopped

1 Combine the yeast and 120ml/4fl oz/½ cup of the water. Stir and leave for 15 minutes for the yeast to dissolve entirely and become frothy.

2 In the bowl of an electric mixer, combine the white and rye flours, salt, honey, caraway seeds and butter. With the dough hook, mix on low speed until well blended. Alternatively, use your hands to incorporate the liquid into the flour.

3 Add the yeast mixture and the remaining water and mix on medium speed, or use your hands, until the dough forms a ball. Transfer to a floured surface and knead in the chopped pecan nuts.

4 Return the dough to the bowl, cover with clear film (plastic wrap) and leave in a warm place until doubled, about 2 hours.

5 Grease two 21 x 11cm/8½ x 4½in loaf tins (pans). Knock back (punch down) the risen dough.

6 Divide the dough in half and form into two loaves. Place in the tins, seam sides down. Dust the tops with flour. Cover with oiled clear film and leave to rise in a warm place until doubled in volume, about 1 hour.

7 Preheat the oven to 190°C/375°F/Gas 5. Bake until the bases sound hollow when tapped, 45–50 minutes. Transfer to wire racks to cool completely.

Walnut Energy 2786Kcal/11722kJ; Protein 87.1g; Carbohydrate 393.2g, of which sugars 26g; Fat 107g, of which saturates 9.4g; Cholesterol 0mg; Calcium 489mg; Fibre 47g; Sodium 4941mg.
Pecan Energy 3213Kcal/13513kJ; Protein 63g; Carbohydrate 464.6g, of which sugars 16g; Fat 135.5g, of which saturates 37.8g; Cholesterol 123mg; Calcium 633mg; Fibre 45g; Sodium 4293mg.